Psychological Science

6TH EDITION

6TH EDITION

Psychological Science

MICHAEL S. GAZZANIGA
University of California, Santa Barbara

W. W. NORTON
NEW YORK • LONDON

W. W. NORTON & COMPANY has been independent since its founding in 1923, when William Warder Norton and Mary D. Herter Norton first published lectures delivered at the People's Institute, the adult education division of New York City's Cooper Union. The firm soon expanded its program beyond the Institute, publishing books by celebrated academics from America and abroad. By midcentury, the two major pillars of Norton's publishing program—trade books and college texts—were firmly established. In the 1950s, the Norton family transferred control of the company to its employees, and today—with a staff of four hundred and a comparable number of trade, college, and professional titles published each year—W. W. Norton & Company stands as the largest and oldest publishing house owned wholly by its employees.

Editor: Sheri L. Snavely
Developmental and Project Editor: Kurt Wildermuth
Editorial Assistant: Eve Sanoussi
Manuscript Editor: Ellen Lohman
Media Editor: Scott Sugarman
Associate Media Editor: Victoria Reuter
Digital Media Project Editor: Danielle Belfiore
Assistant Media Editor: Alex Trivilino
Ebook Production Manager: Mateus Manço Teixeira
Ebook Production Coordinator: Lizz Thabet
Marketing Manager: Ashley Sherwood
Production Manager: Sean Mintus
Design Director: Rubina Yeh
Designer: FaceOut Studio/Lissi Sigillo
Photo Editor: Patricia Marx
Permissions Manager: Megan Jackson
Permissions Clearer: Elizabeth Trammell
Composition: Jouve
Manufacturing: Transcontinental
Managing Editor, College: Marian Johnson
Managing Editor, College Digital Media: Kim Yi

ISBN 9780393624045 (hardcover)

W. W. Norton & Company, Inc., 500 Fifth Avenue, New York, N.Y. 10110
www.wwnorton.com
W. W. Norton & Company Ltd., 15 Carlisle Street, London W1D 3BS

1 2 3 4 5 6 7 8 9 0

InQuizitive: Your Tool for a Better Grade

InQuizitive is an online learning system in which you answer questions to learn and review course content.

Getting Started

How does it work?

- Use the registration code inside your copy of *Psychological Science* to register and go to the InQuizitive activity page.
- To complete each InQuizitive activity, you must answer a minimum number of questions.
- Your goal is to reach a designated target score, which varies for each activity.
- You can gain or lose up to 100 points for each question.

How are you graded?

- Once you reach the minimum number of questions, you'll get a grade for the activity based on the number of points you've earned.
- You can keep answering questions and accumulating points after you've finished the minimum number of questions.

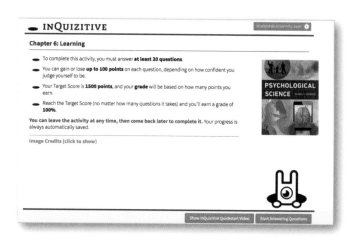

- As long as you make it to the target score, you'll get a perfect score, no matter how many questions it takes to get there.

Answering Questions

Many InQuizitive questions ask you to interact with each possible answer. For example, the question below asks you to place each label on the correct area of the diagram.

Interacting with each answer means you get feedback for all parts of the question. If you answer incorrectly, InQuizitive will take you to the relevant section of the ebook to review the material.

Gaming the System

Before you start answering each question, you can use the **Confidence Slider** to adjust how many points you want to risk. If you leave the slider on "I know I know it," you'll win 100 points if you get the question correct but lose 100 points if you get the question wrong. If you move the slider down to "I'm pretty sure," you'll lose fewer points if you're wrong.

Question Confidence

I'm pretty sure...

You can gain or lose up to 80 points on this question.

How Employable Are Psychology Majors?

With their unique and broad combination of skills, psychology majors can find employment in a wide range of settings. The figure below, from the U.S. Census Bureau (2014), shows how psychology majors apply their analytical skills and understanding of human behavior in a variety of careers from business, education, health care, and other occupations.

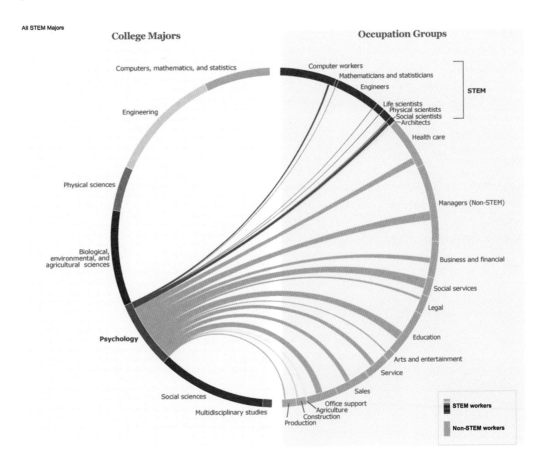

Putting Psychology to Work

NEW Putting Psychology to Work features in each chapter show students how the skills and knowledge they acquire in studying psychology can be directly applied in the workplace.

Ch. 1 How Employable Are Psychology Majors? (p. 27)

Ch. 2 How Useful Are Data Science Skills? (p. 67)

Ch. 3 What Are the Clinical and Consumer Applications of Neuroscience? (p. 119)

Ch. 4 How Is Psychology Related to Substance Abuse Prevention and Treatment? (p. 160)

Ch. 5 What Are the Employment Opportunities in Sensory Science? (p. 203)

Ch. 6 What Is the Business of Behavior Modification? (p. 247)

Ch. 7 What Are Sports Psychologists and Performance Psychologists? (p. 287)

Ch. 8 How Is the Psychology of Decision Making Used to Improve People's Lives? (p. 335)

Ch. 9 How Is a Psychology Degree Useful in Educational Settings? (p. 381)

Ch. 10 What Is Emotional Artificial Intelligence? (p. 425)

Ch. 11 What Are Health Psychologists? (p. 465)

Ch. 12 How Can Social Psychology Be Used in Politics? (p. 511)

Ch. 13 What Are I/O Psychologists? (p. 557)

Ch. 14 What Are Forensic Psychologists? (p. 611)

Ch. 15 Do you Want to Become a Clinical Psychologist? (p. 661)

Q: What's pictured on our front cover?

ANSWER: The images on the cover represent some of the ideas you'll encounter in *Psychological Science*. Clockwise from upper left: The white squiggles show the double helix, the structure of DNA. Within DNA are genes, the inherited material that makes up your genotype. The family picks up on this image, raising the issue of whether your behavior results from genes (nature), your environment (nurture), or both (hint: it's always both). The globe expands on that theme by asking how much of your behavior is influenced not just by your local environment but by your culture. The brain, of course, is involved in everything you think, feel, or do. Among the great psychological thinkers who helped put these ideas together is William James, shown as he appeared on a trip to Brazil in 1865.

This book is dedicated to Lilly, Emmy, Garth, Dante, Rebecca, and Leonardo

Brief Contents

Preface. ix

Chapter 1   The Science of Psychology 3

Chapter 2   Research Methodology 29

Chapter 3   Biology and Behavior 69

Chapter 4   Consciousness 121

Chapter 5   Sensation and Perception 163

Chapter 6   Learning 207

Chapter 7   Memory 249

Chapter 8   Thinking, Language, and Intelligence 289

Chapter 9   Human Development 337

Chapter 10   Emotion and Motivation 383

Chapter 11   Health and Well-Being 429

Chapter 12   Social Psychology 469

Chapter 13   Personality 515

Chapter 14   Psychological Disorders 561

Chapter 15   Treatment of Psychological Disorders 615

Glossary G-1
References R-1
Practice Tests PT-1
Permissions Acknowledgments PA-1
Name Index NI-1
Subject Index SI-1

Meet the Author

MICHAEL S. GAZZANIGA is Professor and Director of the Sage Center for the Study of the Mind at the University of California, Santa Barbara. He founded and presides over the Cognitive Neuroscience Institute and is founding editor-in-chief of the *Journal of Cognitive Neuroscience*. He is past president of the Association for Psychological Science and a member of the American Academy of Arts and Sciences, the National Academy of Medicine, and the National Academy of Sciences. He has held positions at the University of California, Santa Barbara; New York University; the State University of New York, Stony Brook; Cornell University Medical College; and the University of California, Davis. In his career, he has introduced thousands of students to psychology and cognitive neuroscience. He has written many notable books, including, most recently, *Tales from Both Sides of the Brain* and *The Consciousness Instinct*.

Preface

WELCOME TO THE SIXTH EDITION OF PSYCHOLOGICAL SCIENCE! Whether you are considering this book for the first time or have been using it since the beginning, you may find it helpful to hear about its approach to introductory psychology. The many instructors who have used previous editions have made countless helpful suggestions for improving the material in this book, and their continued support for the book's overall vision remains an inspiration. At the end of the preface, before the acknowledgments, there is a comprehensive, chapter-by-chapter table of changes to this edition. Here, the focus is on the book's major features.

A Contemporary Science Perspective

As reflected in the title, this book unabashedly embraces the science of psychology. From the beginning, the aim has been to show students how using the scientific method provides important insights about mind, brain, and behavior. This book was the first to integrate research on neuroscience throughout all the chapters.

In the 20 years since then, many things have changed. In the late 1990s, functional brain imaging was still in its infancy, we had not yet mapped out the human genome, and same-sex relationships were illegal in many U.S. states. Students did not have laptops or cell phones, and professors often used real slide or overhead projectors. Google had not yet revolutionized the internet. Our understanding of the mind, the brain, and behavior has also increased dramatically. For example, neuroscientists have developed several new techniques for studying the working brain. Awareness has grown that sports concussions can affect the developing brain. Concern has grown regarding the health and lifestyles of many Americans, some of whom are now dying earlier than in previous generations. Topics such as the effects of poverty on the developing brain and the circumstances surrounding the opioid epidemic have captured psychological scientific attention. Researchers have contributed to a greater understanding of memory reconsolidation, progress in understanding epigenetic consequences of different environmental conditions, new insights into disorders such as ADHD, and evidence for the success of new psychological treatments. They have also provided cautionary notes, such as the lack of progress in long-term prognosis for schizophrenia.

The Sixth Edition of *Psychological Science* keeps up with progress across the breadth of the field. This book documents with great admiration the advances across all subfields of psychology, from our better understanding of brain function to greater recognition of the variations in sexual orientation and identity. The citations refer to more than 250 new articles published in 2016 or 2017.

A Readable Book for All Your Students

Since the First Edition of *Psychological Science,* the primary goal has been to provide students with a readable book that both captures the excitement of contemporary research and respects the rich tradition of prior foundational studies. Newer findings cannot distract us from the general principles that guide human behavior. After all, a major function of this book is to help prepare students for the undergraduate major in psychology, one of the most popular majors at colleges and universities. In 2013, the American Psychological Association updated its guidelines for that major. The APA task force includes the content goal of establishing a firm knowledge base in the field, along with four skill-based goals that are valuable for psychology majors. This book provides a strong foundation for satisfying the guidelines.

Still, not every reader of this book will be a psychology major. The material must speak to students whose primary interest is not psychology, from fine arts majors to engineering majors to nursing majors. And a huge challenge for any instructor of undergraduates is presenting information at a level that is appropriate for students who are less prepared for college-level work, who may not have good study skills, and who may not be native speakers of English, while still challenging the top students in the course. To achieve these aims, this book emphasizes a multidisciplinary approach, includes information about how to study based on cognitive research, and emphasizes active learning. Students will come away from the course with an understanding of why psychology is a science, an appreciation for data and evidence-based arguments, a sense of the discipline's breadth and complexity, and an understanding that the scientific study of brain and mind and behavior relates to most aspects of life.

New Study Unit Format Facilitates Student Learning

No reader, however dedicated, can retain the details of every concept in psychology. Instead of an encyclopedic and homogenized compendium that dutifully covers worn themes and tired topics at the same level, this book presents key concepts in depth and discusses supporting concepts only as necessary. Students should be focusing on the concepts, not struggling to read the text. In this edition, unnecessary terms, examples, and digressions have been eliminated, shortening some chapters by as much as 10 percent. Thanks to the teamwork of advisors, writers, and editors, the Sixth Edition of *Psychological Science* is the most relevant, engaging, and accessible version yet.

Several changes to the chapter format will help students better understand and retain the material they read. Drawing on teaching and learning research, the Sixth Edition provides new tools to improve students' reading, focus, and self-assessment. More than 60 years ago, George Miller introduced the concept of chunking to explain how people are able to recall large amounts of information. Building on this classic idea, each chapter now consists of brief study units. To maximize reading comprehension, these study units create an organizational framework in which related material is presented in a coherent section focusing on a particular topic.

Each chapter has been subdivided into 16–18 study units. While instructors can choose which units to assign in a particular order, these units are not modules intended to stand alone. Background knowledge from earlier study units (e.g., neurotransmitters and synapse processes) is necessary to understand later ones (e.g., how drugs are used to alleviate psychological disorders). However, the units are designed so that students can master the material in one sitting. In this way, students can set goals to study a certain number of units in the amount of time they have available to study.

Based on research, such as the excellent work by Henry "Roddy" Roediger and Jeffrey Karpicke showing that frequent testing aids learning, each study unit ends with a red Q question that tests whether students understand a core concept within the unit. This feature enables students to quickly assess the success of their studying before they move on to the next study unit. Reviewers of this approach agree that breaking the material into meaningful chunks and immediately testing understanding will help students comprehend what they read and focus on key concepts and ideas.

In addition, multiple self-study questions—practice tests—are available at the end of the book and online.

Students Should Apply Their Learning

Even as it delivers new research and fundamentals, *Psychological Science* showcases applications of psychological findings. Throughout the book, the focus is on how psychological research is being used throughout society to improve lives.

PUTTING PSYCHOLOGY TO WORK   Many of us cringed when Jeb Bush proclaimed during the 2016 U.S. presidential primaries that he didn't think "people are getting jobs as psych majors." As professionals in the field who follow our graduates, we know Bush was flat-out wrong. For this edition, Ines Segert, at the University of Missouri, joined the team to remedy this misperception. Each chapter of *Psychology Science* features a new feature, "Putting Psychology to Work," coauthored by Ines. Each piece in this series explores how the knowledge and skills gained from the particular chapter can help prepare readers for their future careers. At the end of the final chapter, a summary of the series presents data from the U.S. Census Bureau study of STEM fields. These data document where those with psychology degrees work. As the evidence indicates, psychology is useful across a broad spectrum of occupations. Like other STEM fields, psychology serves as a strong foundation for career success. Thanks go out to Dana S. Dunn, at Moravian College, and Jane S. Halonen, at the University of West Florida, for their campaign to connect psychological concepts more fully to the workplace and graduate school. They provided important early advice regarding the "Putting Psychology to Work" feature and helpfully reviewed the finished manuscripts.

USING PSYCHOLOGY IN YOUR LIFE As engaged readers, students will learn more deeply, understand themselves and others more fully, and become better critical thinkers and decision makers. To help students apply what they learn in this course to their daily lives, the "Using Psychology in Your Life" features make clear how psychological concepts can have real-time usefulness.

Students Should Think Scientifically

This book has always emphasized a research-based approach to the discipline with the goal of helping students think critically and scientifically about psychology. Because so many findings in psychology are counterintuitive, students need to apply critical thinking skills to evaluate research claims they encounter in their everyday lives. Applying these principles also will help students better understand puzzling human thoughts and actions. Psychological science has studied the situations and contexts that tend to befuddle otherwise intelligent people and lead them to erroneous beliefs and faulty conclusions.

THINK LIKE A PSYCHOLOGIST Each chapter of *Psychological Science* includes a "Think like a Psychologist" feature, which describes research examining commonly held but misinformed beliefs. For example, Chapter 14 tackles the difficult topic of the claimed link between vaccines and autism. The feature walks students through the thought processes that lead people to perceive relationships that do not actually exist (such as between vaccines and autism) and then through the confirmation biases that sustain these false perceptions. The feature also discusses practical consequences of faulty psychological reasoning—for example, the global increase in infectious diseases, such as measles, due to the decline in vaccination rates.

Teaching students how to think like psychologists contributes an important weapon to their critical thinking and reasoning arsenal. This understanding builds on standard critical thinking skills, such as being skeptical, but it also provides practical rules for seeing when people are likely to believe things that simply are not true. They will help students recognize "fake news."

THE METHODS OF PSYCHOLOGY A new feature in each chapter, "The Methods of Psychology," presents examples of classic research studies. The layout of this feature is similar to that of an academic poster. Many of our students will conduct and present research (e.g., honors work), and this feature will familiarize them with the kind of material they will encounter at academic conferences.

The Content Reflects a Global, Multicultural Society

Psychological Science has always sought to represent the world in its diversity. The evidence indicates that this effort has succeeded. A research team led by Sheila Kennison, at Oklahoma State University, examined 31 major psychology textbooks for their coverage of diversity. The team's findings, presented at several meetings (including the 56th Meeting of the Southwestern Psychological Association; Tran, Curtis, Bradley, & Kennison, April 2010), made clear that *Psychological Science* had the greatest representation of diversity among all books. Indeed, this book had more than twice the average of the other 30 books. The Sixth Edition further increases coverage of many groups relatively neglected in psychological texts, including Latinos (Hispanic Americans), those who are transgendered, and those who face socioeconomic challenges, such as living in poverty.

Psychological Science also emphasizes the global nature of our field. Many psychology textbooks focus almost completely on research from North America, but a tremendous amount of exciting psychological research takes place around the world. Students should learn about the best psychological science, and this book presents the best psychological research, no matter where it originates. The Sixth Edition includes research from dozens of countries beyond North America, describing hundreds of global studies conducted during the past decade. Becoming aware of research from outside North America will not only help students learn more about psychology, it will also bring them new perspectives, encouraging a sense of themselves as global citizens.

The Book Will Prepare Students for the MCAT

Psychology has also become a popular major for premed students. Beginning in the 1980s, medical schools recognized that contemporary physicians need a holistic understanding of their patients, including their lifestyles, ways of thinking, and cultural values. As students will learn in the "Health and Well-Being" chapter, the vast majority of modern health problems are related to peoples' behavioral choices. Psychological factors influence how people think about and react to the world, and sociocultural influences influence behavior and behavioral change. In short, cognition and self-perception profoundly affect health.

In 2015, reflecting this new understanding, the Medical College Admissions Test (MCAT) began including a section that examines psychological, social, and biological foundations of behavior, along with a new section on critical analysis and reasoning skills. As a result of revisions that focus attention on psychology, psychological content now comprises nearly 25 percent of the MCAT score.

Available online is a comprehensive chart that links the specific MCAT material to be covered with the relevant page numbers in *Psychological Science.* As this chart illustrates, students using this textbook will be at a significant advantage for completing the section of the MCAT on critical analysis and reasoning skills.

Major Changes in the Sixth Edition

Chapter 1 THE SCIENCE OF PSYCHOLOGY	The new brief opener focuses on why studying psychology is relevant to students regardless of their chosen occupation.
	The discussion of how psychological science helps people understand biased or inaccurate thinking now focuses on four major examples: confirmation bias, seeing relations that do not exit, accepting after-the-fact explanations, and taking mental shortcuts.
	Humanistic psychology is now discussed as a school of thought. A new table lists the major schools of thought.
	Examples have been updated of the contributions of brain imaging to a wide range of psychological phenomena.
	A new figure showing employment settings for psychologists has been added.
	"Putting Psychology to Work" discusses the employability of psychology majors and the value of the degree.

Chapter 2 **RESEARCH METHODOLOGY**	The new brief opener describes the consequences of texting and driving.
	The figure showing the scientific method has been modified to better show what happens after research supports or fails to support a theory.
	The discussion of the scientific method has been reorganized to clarify the steps. Additional content addresses how to frame a good research question based on a theory and how to then develop a hypothesis to test the research question.
	A new figure shows students presenting posters at a poster session.
	The discussion of replication has been significantly expanded, including the need for critical thinking when designing replication studies. A new figure demonstrates the importance of considering context when designing a replication study.
	A new study unit covers the need to guard against bias for all descriptive studies.
	A new figure shows the relation between independent and dependent variables.
	"Putting Psychology to Work" discusses data science skills and their value in various industries.
Chapter 3 **BIOLOGY AND BEHAVIOR**	The new brief opener links brain activity to the enjoyment of eating (specifically a slice of pizza).
	The relation between epinephrine and norepinephrine has been clarified in terms of their effects in the brain and body.
	The section on the interpreter has been moved here from Chapter 4 to consolidate all the split-brain information in one location.
	A more detailed figure on the divisions of the nervous system has been added to the study unit on the peripheral nervous system.
	"Putting Psychology to Work" focuses on the clinical and consumer applications of neuroscience.
Chapter 4 **CONSCIOUSNESS**	The new brief opener encourages the reader to try a few moments of meditation.
	A major new section has been added on traumatic brain injuries and concussion. A new figure refers to the movie *Concussion*.
	A new "Think like a Psychologist" feature considers whether people are affected by subliminal messages.
	Avoidance of electronic devices (especially blue light) has been added as another good strategy for getting a good night's sleep.
	A brief discussion has been added of recent evidence that heavy marijuana use during adolescence may increase the likelihood of significant mental health problems.
	A major new section has been added on opioid abuse, including the scope of the epidemic (such as the dramatic increase in fatal overdoses) and why Narcan is useful in reversing opioid effects.
	A new figure shows the increase in overdose deaths compared to traffic accident deaths.
	A new figure depicts one standard drink for various beverages containing alcohol.
	A new model has been introduced showing that addiction appears to develop in stages and noting that this progression is due to changes in the brain that accompany drug use.
	"Putting Psychology to Work" discusses how psychology can be used for substance abuse counseling and prevention.
Chapter 5 **SENSATION AND PERCEPTION**	The new brief opener considers how sensation and perception work when expectations are violated.
	Information has been updated regarding the debate about whether ESP exists. A new figure shows the brain imaging methods that Moulton and Kosslyn used to test whether ESP exists.
	A new figure in the "Using Psychology in Your Life" feature shows a person using earbuds.
	"Putting Psychology to Work" considers how understanding sensation and perception is important for product design and marketing.

Chapter 6 **LEARNING**	The new brief opener describes using nonlethal doses of poison to condition wolves to not kill sheep for food. A new figure shows the adaptive value of stimulus generalization and discrimination. The structure of the section on expectancies and prediction has been changed to help students better understand prediction errors. A new figure shows Albert Barger, the likely Little Albert, as an adult. Information has been updated regarding the percentage of Americans who believe that spanking is sometimes necessary. In addition, new data are included from a recent meta-analysis of over 160,000 children showing that spanking is ineffective in improving child behavior. A new figure differentiates between wanting and liking. "Putting Psychology to Work" discusses using principles of behavioral modification in business settings.
Chapter 7 **MEMORY**	The new brief opener considers how we can misremember people who seem similar, such as the actors Matt Damon and Mark Wahlberg. The section on reconsolidation has been updated and a new figure added to show how memories might change over time. The description of long-term potentiation has been revised and expanded to help students more easily understand the role of the NMDA receptor. A new brief section presents recent work showing that brain training (such as training working memory) does not transfer to new domains. An expanded "Using Psychology in Your Life" feature describes the most recent research that will help students study for exams, such as the importance of attending class and spending time practicing retrieval. New examples have been provided of memory events that lead to posttraumatic stress disorder and methods for reducing unwanted and persistent memories. A discussion has been added of flashbulb memory effects and why people become more confident over time about memories that display typical rates of forgetting over time. "Putting Psychology to Work" discusses applying memory principles to enhance performance.
Chapter 8 **THINKING, LANGUAGE,** **AND INTELLIGENCE**	The new brief opener considers different ways of being intelligent. In the concepts section, a new paragraph discusses how concepts are represented in the brain and how researchers are using computational methods to recover those concepts. The discussion of the role of gender schemas regarding women and STEM has been increased. It now includes a figure about children drawing a female scientist. The coverage of hindsight bias has been increased with new examples from political outcomes. The discussion of creole languages has been modernized. The discussion of dyslexia and the role of phonemes has been increased. "Putting Psychology to Work" considers the use of decision science to improve people's lives.
Chapter 9 **HUMAN DEVELOPMENT**	The new brief opener encourages the reader to reflect on a younger self. A new section discusses the effects of the Zika virus as a teratogen. A new figure shows birth effects associated with prenatal exposure to Zika. Added material considers the epigenetic effects of stress across future generations. An added section considers intersexuality and its effects on gender identify. A new figure shows biological sex viewed along a continuum.

Chapter 9 HUMAN DEVELOPMENT (cont.)	A new major section discusses transgender, with a figure from the cover of *National Geographic*. A new major section considers bullying and its effects. A new figure shows the tragic effects of the bullying of Amanda Todd. A discussion has been added of the health behaviors of middle-aged adults, especially as they relate to excess body weight, alcohol use, and opioid abuse. The marriage section now includes a discussion of same-sex marriage. "Putting Psychology to Work" looks at using a psychology degree in educational settings.
Chapter 10 EMOTION AND MOTIVATION	The new brief opener describes the emotions involved in public speaking. Added information shows that there is specificity for bodily reactions related to different emotions. The discussion of cross-cultural universality of emotion has been expanded. A new figure shows the testing in Cambodia of the universality of emotions. A new figure shows that people differ in their optimal level of arousal. A new section covers grit and life outcomes. The discussion of how hormones influence eating behavior has been completely revised and updated, and a discussion has been added of the role of insulin in diabetes. A new figure shows the biological mechanisms that motivate eating. A major new section discusses the range of sexual orientations. A new figure shows that sexual orientation can be viewed as a continuum. "Putting Psychology to Work" discusses how detecting emotional expressions is important in emotional artificial intelligence.
Chapter 11 HEALTH AND WELL-BEING	The new brief opener discusses stress eating and its effect on health. The figure on life expectancy by race and sex has been updated with the most recent data. The figure showing trends in overweight, obesity, and extreme obesity has been updated with the most recent data. The discussion of the effects of overweight on health has been revised, noting that there have been several controversial and conflicting findings on this topic. The eating disorders section has been updated to include data about males. A major new section considers the health consequences of electronic cigarettes. The figure showing fears of terrorism has been updated with the most recent data. "Putting Psychology to Work" considers how health psychology can be employed in various settings.
Chapter 12 SOCIAL PSYCHOLOGY	The new brief opener provides an example of how people are affected by a social situation. The recent critiques of the Stanford prison study are now discussed. A new table summarizes the three ways of inducing compliance, with examples of each. A major new section considers various criticisms of the Milgram obedience studies, including ethical considerations as well as new perspectives on the factors other than obedience driving behavior among Milgram's participants. The section on the Implicit Association Test has been revised to better explain how the test works (including a new figure) and to discuss the recent concerns that the predictive power of the IAT has been exaggerated in the media and in public perception. A discussion has been added of new methods for combatting prejudice, including reframing and self-labeling.

Chapter 12 **SOCIAL PSYCHOLOGY** **(cont.)**	The section on modern prejudice has been revised to note that it is most people, not all people, who try not to express racist, sexist, or homophobic comments. "Putting Psychology to Work" discusses how understanding social psychology is important for political campaigns.
Chapter 13 **PERSONALITY**	The new brief opener considers how people can be very different in personality from their siblings. A new figure shows how psychologists can describe the personality of an individual. The "Methods of Psychology" feature focuses on inhibition and social anxiety. The discussion of social-cognitive theories of personality has been substantially revised. Reciprocal determinism is now included. A new figure illustrates reciprocal determinism. A new figure shows Rogers's person-centered approach to raising children. A new figure shows personality traits on a continuum. A major new section discusses the dark triad personality traits: narcissism, Machiavellianism, and psychopathy. A new figure shows an American psychopath (from the movie *American Psycho*). "Putting Psychology to Work" discusses industrial/organization psychology and how understanding personality traits is useful in the workplace.
Chapter 14 **PSYCHOLOGICAL** **DISORDERS**	The new brief opener considers bipolar disorder and celebrities who have the disorder. A new table shows NIMH Research Domain Criteria (RDoC). New information is included on the growing prevalence of anxiety disorders among college students. A new figure shows the differences between major depressive disorder and persistent depressive disorder. A revised and updated section considers the roles of culture and gender in depressive disorders. A new figure depicts disorganized behavior as a symptom of schizophrenia. New material discusses the genetic and environmental contributors to schizophrenia. A new section in the psychopathy section considers young people who have callous-unemotional traits. The section on attention-deficit/hyperactivity disorder has been significantly revised, including its growing prevalence among females and minorities. The section on the biological basis of ADHD has been updated. "Putting Psychology to Work" looks at forensic psychology.
Chapter 15 **TREATMENT OF** **PSYCHOLOGICAL** **DISORDERS**	The new brief opener speaks directly to readers about great progress in identifying successful treatments for many psychological disorders. Behavior therapy is now discussed separately from cognitive therapy. The use of exposure in behavioral treatment has been updated. The discussion of why the context of therapy matters has been expanded and now includes more information on group therapy. A discussion has been added of the debate regarding evidence-based treatments. A new figure shows the use of exposure and response prevention to treat obsessive-compulsive disorder. A new section considers novel use of antibiotics to enhance the effects of exposure therapy. The figure for the "Think like a Psychologist" feature on trusting drug companies has been revised to show the conflict between money and research.

Chapter 15 TREATMENT OF PSYCHOLOGICAL DISORDERS (cont.)	The section on the prognosis of schizophrenia has been revised to show that in spite of increasing scientific evidence regarding the causes of the disorder, treatment outcomes have not improved substantially over time.
	A new figure shows the process of treating borderline personality disorder using dialectical behavior therapy.
	New information has been added regarding the treatment of adolescent depression. A new figure shows treatment outcomes in the treatment for adolescents with depression (TADS) study.
	"Putting Psychology to Work" looks at clinical and counseling psychology.

Acknowledgments

Thanks go out to the many colleagues who supplied responses and advice. Some individuals deserve special recognition. Foremost is Ines Segert, who provided invaluable advice regarding the revision plan, brought her extensive knowledge and keen eye to each chapter, and coauthored the "Putting the Psychology to Work" features. Ines understands what psychology instructors care about most for their students. Rebecca Gazzaniga, M.D., reviewed all the chapters and aided the effort to speak directly to students. As a physician, she made sure the coverage of health-related issues was accurate, and she coauthored MCAT assessment questions for each chapter. Patrick Ewell, at the University of Alabama, provided counsel on educating students about how using electronic devices can interfere with sleep.

Students are now firmly digital natives. Dennis Miller, at the University of Missouri, provided expert feedback on seeing the text from a digital perspective. Dennis also suggested media that will engage students and improve their learning, and he made helpful observations that have improved the InQuizitive and Prospero platforms.

Debra Mashek has been an invaluable member of the team for several editions. For the Fourth Edition, Debra coauthored the "Using Psychology in Your Life" features. Because they were so well received, new or updated versions appeared in the Fifth Edition and have been revised as appropriate for this edition. Thanks in large part to Debra's engaging, insightful voice, students love applying the findings of psychological science to their own lives.

THE NORTON EDITORIAL TEAM In the modern publishing world, where most books are produced by large multinational corporations that focus primarily on the bottom line, W. W. Norton stands out as a beacon to academics and authors, both for remaining committed to the best-quality publications and for providing outstanding team members to help ensure that quality. Norton's employees own the company, and therefore every individual who worked on this book has a vested interest in its success; that personal connection shows in the great enthusiasm the team members brought to their work.

Sheri Snavely took over as editor during the Third Edition and played a central role in shaping each subsequent edition. Sheri brings this not only many years of expertise in science editing, but also a profound dedication to spreading the message about this book. There is not a more talented or insightful editor in psychology, and Sheri has lavished attention on this book even as she has built one of the best overall lists in psychology today. Thanks go to Roby Harrington, director of Norton's college division, for hiring Sheri and for his support of this book.

For the Sixth Edition, senior developmental editor and project editor Kurt Wildermuth continued to be wordsmith extraordinaire, making sure the writing was crisp and accessible. But Kurt does more and more in every edition. He really cares about this book, and it shows.

The innovative media and ancillaries team, led by media editor Scott Sugarman, was instrumental in producing a first-rate media and support package that provides instructors with the high quality support they need and helps students learn more effectively. Scott also moved mountains and more to develop a new Norton psychology videos program that helps students quickly master the most challenging concepts in each chapter. As every instructor knows, a well-conceived test bank is crucial to a successful course. Inadequate test banks with uneven or ambiguous items can frustrate students and instructors alike. Associate media editor Victoria Reuter worked tirelessly to create the best test bank available for introductory psychology (see p. xxiv for more details). Victoria also pulled together the coursepack material and quizzes, content that can easily be assigned within your own course management system. Assistant media editor Alex Trivilino skillfully managed the Interactive Instructors' Guide and a multitude of lecture presentation tools.

Many others also provided crucial support. Editorial assistant Eve Sanoussi helped by creating art manuscripts, recruiting reviewers, keeping track of pages, and keeping things organized as all the details came together. Photo editor Trish Marx did a wonderful job of researching and editing all the photos in the book and finding the captivating faces that begin each chapter. Production manager Sean Mintus made sure all the trains ran on time so the book and its ancillaries were ready for instructors to consider for their courses. Talented designers Rubina Yeh and Lissi Siglio worked with FaceOut to design the excellent new study unit format and new "Putting Psychology to Work" feature.

THE NORTON SALES AND MARKETING TEAM Thanks to the book's marketing manager, Ashley Sherwood, for rallying the troops, analyzing the market, and putting together a cutting-edge and informative marketing campaign. Ashley understands what instructors and students need to be successful and is doing a marvelous job of making sure the book's message reaches travelers and professors. A big thank you to the psychological science sales team—travelers, managers, science specialists, media specialists and institutional sales group. Indeed, the entire sales force, led by director of sales Michael Wright, has supported this book and is distinguished by their knowledge of psychology and consultative partnerships with instructors.

Finally, thanks go to the new president of Norton, Julia Reidhead, for inspiring a workforce that cares so deeply about publishing "books that live" and for having continued faith in this ongoing project.

PSYCHOLOGICAL SCIENCE, 6E, TEXT AND MEDIA REVIEWERS We thank the reviewers who have worked to further strengthen *Psychological Science*. Your excellent revisions, inspired ideas, and insightful guidance have shaped a book and resources that greatly benefit instructors and students alike.

Julie A. Alvarez, *Tulane University*

Cheryl Armstrong, *Fitchburg State University*

Matthew C. Bell, *Santa Clara University*

David Bilkey, *University of Otago*

Joseph L. Brooks, *University of Kent*

Natasha Buist, *Victoria University of Wellington*

Crystal Carlson, *Saint Mary's University of Minnesota*

Clarissa Chavez, *Auburn University*

Caroline Connolly, *University of Pennsylvania*

Marc Coutanche, *University of Pittsburgh*

Craig Cummings, *University of Alabama*

Dasa Zeithamova Demircan, *University of Oregon*

Dana S. Dunn, *Moravian College*

Patrick Ewell, *Kenyon College*

Sara Finley, *Pacific Lutheran University*

Adam E. Fox, *St. Lawrence University*

Jon Grahe, *Pacific Lutheran University*

Jane S. Halonen, *University of West Florida*

Nicholas Heck, *Marquette University*

Kurt Hoffman, *Virginia Polytechnic Institute and State University*

Lisa Kolbuss, *Lane Community College*

Emily Leskinen, *Carthage College*

Celia Lie, *University of Otago*

Christine Lomore, *St. Francis Xavier University*

Kate MacDuffie, *Duke University*

Howard Markowitz, *Hawaii Pacific University*

John McDowall, *Victoria University of Wellington*

Mary E. McNaughton-Cassill, *University of Texas at San Antonio*

Dennis Miller, *University of Missouri*

Michele M. Miller, *University of Illinois, Springfield*

Kristin Pauker, *University of Hawaii*

Cindy Miller-Perrin, *Pepperdine University*

Elizabeth Morgan, *Springfield College*

Ann Renken, *University of Southern California*

Wade C. Rowatt, *Baylor University*

Ines Segert, *University of Missouri*

Rachel Smallman, *Texas A&M University*

Jason Spiegelman, *Community College of Baltimore County*

Christopher Stanzione, *Georgia Institute of Technology*

Mary Hughes Stone, *San Francisco State University*

Benjamin C. Storm, *University of California, Santa Cruz*

Judith ter Vrugte, *University of Twente*

Anré Venter, *University of Notre Dame*

Fred Whitford, *Montana State University*

Karen Wilson, *St. Francis College*

Heather Cleland Woods, *University of Glasgow*

PSYCHOLOGICAL SCIENCE INTERNATIONAL REVIEWERS

George Alder, *Simon Fraser University*

Ron Apland, *Vancouver Island University*

Sunaina Assanand, *University of British Columbia, Vancouver*

Alan Baddelay, *University of York*

Lisa Best, *University of New Brunswick*

David Bilkey, *University of Otago*

Colin Blakemore, *Oxford University*

Karen Brebner, *St. Francis Xavier University*

Joseph L. Brooks, *University of Kent*

Natasha Buist, *Victoria University of Wellington*

Tara Callaghan, *St. Francis Xavier University*

Jennifer Campbell, *University of British Columbia*

Dennis Cogan, *Touro College, Israel*

Martin Conway, *City University London*

Michael Corballis, *University of Auckland*

Ian Deary, *University of Edinburgh*

James Enns, *University of British Columbia*

Raymond Fancher, *York University*

Margaret Forgie, *University of Lethbridge*

Laura Gonnerman, *McGill University*

Peter Graf, *University of British Columbia*

Pascal Haazebroek, *Leiden University*

John Hallonquist, *Thompson Rivers University*

Linda Hatt, *University of British Columbia Okanagan*

Steven Heine, *University of British Columbia*

Mark Holder, *University of British Columbia Okanagan*

Jacob Jolij, *University of Groningen*

Steve Joordens, *University of Toronto–Scarborough*

Gert Kruger, *University of Johannesburg*

Celia Lie, *University of Otago*

Christine Lomore, *St. Francis Xavier University*

Monicque M. Lorist, *University of Groningen*

Neil Macrae, *University of Aberdeen*

Karl Maier, *Salisbury University*

Doug McCann, *York University*

Peter McCormick, *St. Francis Xavier University*

John McDowall, *Victoria University of Wellington*

Patricia McMullen, *Dalhousie University*

Martijn Meeter, *VU University Amsterdam*

Heather Schellink, *Dalhousie University*

Enid Schutte, *University of the Witwatersrand*

Allison Sekuler, *McMaster University*

Andra Smith, *University of Ottawa*

Ashley Smyth, *South African College of Applied Psychology*

Rhiannon Turner, *Queen's University Belfast*

Judith ter Vrugte, *University of Twente*

Maxine Gallander Wintre, *York University*

Heather Cleland Woods, *University of Glasgow*

Stephanie Afful, *Fontbonne University*

Rahan Ali, *Pennsylvania State University*

Gordon A. Allen, *Miami University of Ohio*

Mary J. Allen, *California State University, Bakersfield*

Christopher Arra, *Northern Virginia Community College*

Lori Badura, *State University of New York, Buffalo*

Mahzarin Banaji, *Harvard University*

David H. Barlow, *Boston University*

Carolyn Barry, *Loyola University Maryland*

Scott Bates, *Utah State University*

Holly B. Beard, *Midlands Technical College*

Bernard C. Beins, *Ithaca College*

Joan Therese Bihun, *University of Colorado, Denver*

Joe Bilotta, *Western Kentucky University*

Andrew Blair, *Palm Beach State College*

Kathleen H. Briggs, *University of Minnesota*

John P. Broida, *University of Southern Maine*

Tom Brothen, *University of Minnesota*

Michele R. Brumley, *Idaho State University*

Dave Bucci, *Dartmouth College*

Joshua W. Buckholtz, *Harvard University*

Randy Buckner, *Harvard University*

William Buskist, *Auburn University*

Elisabeth Leslie Cameron, *Carthage College*

Katherine Cameron, *Coppin State University*

Timothy Cannon, *University of Scranton*

Tom Capo, *University of Maryland*

Stephanie Cardoos, *University of California, Berkeley*

Charles Carver, *University of Miami*

Michelle Caya, *Trident Technical College*

Christopher F. Chabris, *Union College*

Sarah P. Cerny, *Rutgers University, Camden*

Jonathan Cheek, *Wellesley College*

Stephen Clark, *Keene State College*

Brent F. Costleigh, *Brookdale Community College*

Graham Cousens, *Drew University*

Marc Coutanche, *Yale University*

Eric Currence, *The Ohio State University*

Dale Dagenbach, *Wake Forest University*

Haydn Davis, *Palomar College*

Suzanne Delaney, *University of Arizona*

Heidi L. Dempsey, *Jacksonville State University*

Joseph Dien, *Johns Hopkins University*

Michael Domjan, *University of Texas at Austin*

Wendy Domjan, *University of Texas at Austin*

Jack Dovidio, *Colgate University*

Dana S. Dunn, *Moravian College*

Howard Eichenbaum, *Boston University*

Naomi Eisenberger, *University of California, Los Angeles*

Sadie Leder Elder, *High Point University*

Clifford D. Evans, *Loyola University Maryland*

Valerie Farmer-Dougan, *Illinois State University*

Greg Feist, *San Jose State University*

Kimberly M. Fenn, *Michigan State University*

Fernanda Ferreira, *University of South Carolina*

Vic Ferreira, *University of California, San Diego*

Holly Filcheck, *Louisiana State University*

Joseph Fitzgerald, *Wayne State University*

Trisha Folds-Bennett, *College of Charleston*

Howard Friedman, *University of California, Riverside*

David C. Funder, *University of California, Riverside*

Christopher J. Gade, *University of California, Berkeley*

Christine Gancarz, *Southern Methodist University*

Wendi Gardner, *Northwestern University*

Preston E. Garraghty, *Indiana University*

Margaret Gatz, *University of Southern California*

Caroline Gee, *Saddleback College*

Peter Gerhardstein, *Binghamton University*

Katherine Gibbs, *University of California, Davis*

Bryan Gibson, *Central Michigan University*

Rick O. Gilmore, *Pennsylvania State University*

Jamie Goldenberg, *University of South Florida*

Leonard Green, *Washington University in St. Louis*

Raymond Green, *Texas A&M–Commerce*

Sarah Grison, *Parkland College*

James Gross, *Stanford University*

Tom Guilmette, *Providence College*

Meara Habashi, *University of Iowa*

Thomas Wayne Hancock, *University of Central Oklahoma*

Erin E. Hardin, *University of Tennessee, Knoxville*

Brad M. Hastings, *Mount Ida College*

Mikki Hebl, *Rice University*

John Henderson, *University of South Carolina*

Norman Henderson, *Oberlin College*

Mark Henn, *University of New Hampshire*

Justin Hepler, *University of Illinois at Urbana-Champaign*

Terence Hines, *Pace University*

Sara Hodges, *University of Oregon*

Cynthia Hoffman, *Indiana University*

Don Hoffman, *University of California, Irvine*

James Hoffman, *University of Delaware*

Tasha R. Howe, *Humboldt State University*

Howard C. Hughes, *Dartmouth College*

Jay Hull, *Dartmouth College*

Malgorzata Ilkowska, *Georgia Institute of Technology*

Jake Jacobs, *University of Arizona*

Alisha Janowsky, *University of Central Florida*

Jennifer Johnson, *Bloomsburg University of Pennsylvania*

Thomas Joiner, *Florida State University*

Linda Juang, *San Francisco State University*

William Kelley, *Dartmouth College*

Dacher Keltner, *University of California, Berkeley*

Lindsay A. Kennedy, *University of North Carolina at Chapel Hill*

Sheila M. Kennison, *Oklahoma State University–Stillwater*

Mike Kerchner, *Washington College*

Rondall Khoo, *Western Connecticut State University*

Stephen Kilianski, *Rutgers University*

Brian Kinghorn, *Brigham Young University, Hawaii*

Christopher Koch, *George Fox University*

Lisa Kolbuss, *Lane Community College*

William Knapp, *Eastern Oregon University*

Gabriel Kreiman, *Harvard University*

Caleb Lack, *University of Central Oklahoma*

Gerard A. Lamorte III, *Rutgers University*

Lori Lange, *University of North Florida*

Mark Laumakis, *San Diego State University*

Natalie Kerr Lawrence, *James Madison University*

Steven R. Lawyer, *Idaho State University*

Benjamin Le, *Haverford College*

Dianne Leader, *Georgia Institute of Technology*

Mark Leary, *Duke University*

Ting Lei, *Borough of Manhattan Community College*

Charles Leith, *Northern Michigan University*

Catherine Craver Lemley, *Elizabethtown College*

Gary W. Lewandowski Jr., *Monmouth University*

Stephanie Little, *Wittenberg University*

Christine Lofgren, *University of California, Irvine*

Liang Lou, *Grand Valley State University*

Jeff Love, *Pennsylvania State University*

Monica Luciana, *University of Minnesota*

Agnes Ly, *University of Delaware*

Margaret F. Lynch, *San Francisco State University*

Karl Maier, *Salisbury University*

Mike Mangan, *University of New Hampshire*

Gary Marcus, *New York University*

Leonard Mark, *Miami University (Ohio)*

Debra Mashek, *Harvey Mudd College*

Tim Maxwell, *Hendrix College*

Ashley Maynard, *University of Hawaii*

Dan McAdams, *Northwestern University*

David McDonald, *University of Missouri*

Bill McKeachie, *University of Michigan*

Corrine L. McNamara, *Kennesaw State University*

Matthias Mehl, *University of Arizona*

Paul Merritt, *Clemson University*

Peter Metzner, *Vance-Granville Community College*

Dennis Miller, *University of Missouri*

Hal Miller, *Brigham Young University*

Judi Miller, *Oberlin College*

Ronald Miller, *Saint Michael's College*

Vanessa Miller, *Texas Christian University*

Douglas G. Mook, *University of Virginia*

Kevin E. Moore, *DePauw University*

Beth Morling, *University of Delaware*

Heather Morris, *Trident Technical College*

Joe Morrisey, *State University of New York, Binghamton*

Todd Nelson, *California State University–Stanislaus*

Julie Norem, *Wellesley College*

Erica Kleinknecht O'Shea, *Pacific University*

Maria Minda Oriña, *St. Olaf College*

Dominic J. Parrott, *Georgia State University*

Lois C. Pasapane, *Palm Beach State College*

David Payne, *Wallace Community College*

James Pennebaker, *University of Texas at Austin*

Zehra Peynircioglu, *American University*

Brady Phelps, *South Dakota State University*

Elizabeth Phelps, *New York University*

Jackie Pope-Tarrance, *Western Kentucky University*

Steve Prentice-Dunn, *University of Alabama*

Gabriel Radvansky, *Notre Dame University*

Patty Randolph, *Western Kentucky University*

Catherine Reed, *Claremont McKenna College*

Lauretta Reeves, *University of Texas at Austin*

Heather Rice, *Washington University in St. Louis*

Jennifer Richeson, *Northwestern University*

Brent W. Roberts, *University of Illinois at Urbana-Champaign*

Alan C. Roberts, *Indiana University*

Caton Roberts, *University of Wisconsin–Madison*

William Rogers, *Grand Valley State University*

Alex Rothman, *University of Minnesota*

Paul Rozin, *University of Pennsylvania*

Sharleen Sakai, *Michigan State University*

Samuel Sakhai, *University of California, Berkeley*

Juan Salinas, *University of Texas at Austin*

Laura Saslow, *University of California, San Francisco*

Richard Schiffman, *Rutgers University*

Lynne Schmelter-Davis, *Brookdale Community College*

David A. Schroeder, *University of Arkansas*

Shannon Scott, *Texas Woman's University*

Constantine Sedikedes, *University of Southampton*

Ines Segert, *University of Missouri*

Margaret Sereno, *University of Oregon*

Andrew Shatté, *University of Arizona*

J. Nicole Shelton, *Princeton University*

Arthur Shimamura, *University of California, Berkeley*

Rebecca Shiner, *Colgate University*

Jennifer Siciliani-Pride, *University of Missouri–St. Louis*

Nancy Simpson, *Trident Technical College*

Scott Sinnett, *University of Hawaii*

Reid Skeel, *Central Michigan University*

John J. Skowronski, *Northern Illinois University*

Dennison Smith, *Oberlin College*

Kyle Smith, *Ohio Wesleyan University*

Mark Snyder, *University of Minnesota*

Sheldon Solomon, *Skidmore College*

Sue Spaulding, *University of North Carolina, Charlotte*

Faye Steuer, *College of Charleston*

Courtney Stevens, *Willamette University*

Dawn L. Strongin, *California State University–Stanislaus*

James R. Sullivan, *Florida State University*

Lorey Takahashi, *University of Hawaii*

George Taylor, *University of Missouri–St. Louis*

Lee Thompson, *Case Western Reserve University*

Dianne Tice, *Florida State University*

Rob Tigner, *Truman State College*

Boyd Timothy, *Brigham Young University, Hawaii*

Peter Tse, *Dartmouth College*

Lauren Usher, *University of Miami*

David Uttal, *Northwestern University*

Robin R. Vallacher, *Florida Atlantic University*

Instructor Resources

Psychological Science offers instructors a full set of both traditional and innovative tools designed to support a broad range of course needs and teaching styles. This support features:

Test Bank

To help you build exams, all 2,600+ questions in the Test Bank for *Psychological Science,* including 150 questions new to this edition, have been carefully crafted and thoroughly reviewed to ensure that they are as good as the textbook they support. Features of the Sixth Edition Test Bank include:

- extensive revisions to reflect the advice of subject-matter experts and star teachers for each chapter;
- higher question *quality* across all chapters;
- increased question *quantity,* with each chapter offering 170–200 multiple-choice questions, including 10-15 new questions per chapter;
- questions tagged by Bloom's taxonomy level, APA 2.0 learning goal, chapter, section, and difficulty.

Video Resources

Psychological Science offers instructors a variety of original videos as well as URLs to YouTube and other web-based videos depicting psychological concepts in everyday life and in popular culture. These URLs are usually accompanied by advice for using them in lecture, including discussion questions about the videos.

There are also two types of original videos—Demonstration Videos and Concept Videos:

- **Demonstration Videos** show students enacting 20+ important concepts in a classroom setting and are offered in two formats: *Student versions* are suitable for showing in class or online, whereas *instructor versions* show you how to re-create the demonstrations in your class.

"Classical Conditioning" Demonstration Video for Chapter 6.

- **Concept Videos** feature 20+ course concepts that students traditionally struggle to understand. The videos show scenarios to help students master these concepts as well as to see how they relate to their everyday lives.

PowerPoint® Sets

Create your lecture files to suit your specific course needs using this rich variety of PPT slides, which support each chapter of *Psychological Science:*

- **Art PPTs** provide every figure, photo, and table from the textbook, optimized for projection in lecture halls (in JPEGs as well as PPTs). **Supplemental Photo PPTs** feature art not found in the book.
- **Lecture PPTs** use outlines, key images from the text, and videos to thoroughly summarize the book's presentation.
- **Active Learning PPTs** provide you with examples and ideas for in-class participation activities, including clicker questions.

Interactive Instructor's Guide

Using our **Interactive Instructor's Guide** (IIG) website (iig.wwnorton.com/psysci6/full), you can easily find and quickly download hundreds of teaching tools created for *Psychological Science.* An invaluable tool for novice and veteran instructors alike, the IIG offers all of our Video Resources and PPT sets, as well as these resources for each chapter:

- chapter outlines and summaries;
- class activity ideas and handouts;
- lecture suggestions and discussion questions;
- ideas for using Norton's ZAPS online psychology labs in your course.

Coursepack Digital Content

Norton Coursepacks work with your existing Learning Management System to add rich, book-specific digital materials to your course—at no cost to you or your students. The *Psychological Science* expanded Coursepack includes:

- **Pre-Lecture Quizzes**, **Chapter Quizzes**, **Post-Study Quizzes**, and **NEW Learning Objective Quizzes**;
- **Guided Reading Activities** to help students focus on studying and reading the book;
- **Links to the Ebook, ZAPS Norton Psychology Labs,** and **InQuizitive**;
- **Chapter Outlines** and **Flashcards**.

Prospero

Norton's **NEW** online assignment platform makes it easier than ever to weave together Norton's book content, assessment, and interactive media with your own course materials and make it accessible to students all in one place.

InQuizitive and ZAPS Instructor Tools

Psychological Science offers two great student review tools: InQuizitive, Norton's new online formative, adaptive learning tool, and **ZAPS: The Norton Online Psychology Labs.** Both of these resources, fully described inside the front cover of this book, offer special capabilities that enable you to integrate them into your course. These resources can be accessed through the Digital Landing Page: digital.wwnorton.com/psychsci6.

 INQUIZITIVE

InQuizitive helps your students learn through a variety of question types, answer-specific feedback, and gamelike elements such as the ability to wager points. It is assignable and gradable, and—since all InQuizitive questions are assigned to the Big Questions in each chapter—gives you insights into the areas where your students need more help so you can adjust your lectures and class time accordingly. The Sixth Edition revision of InQuizitive for *Psychological Science* targeted questions and subjects that students struggled with most in the Fifth Edition, and also added APA goals to each question.

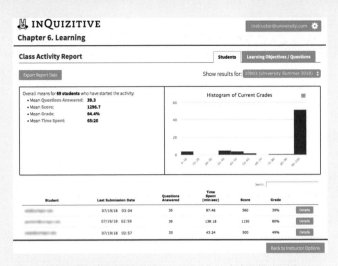

Class Activity Reports in InQuizitive allow you to quickly learn how well your students are doing.

ZAPS

The Norton Online Psychology Labs

With ZAPS labs, your students interactively explore key psychological concepts to gain a deeper understanding of the concepts as well as of the scientific process. You can choose from one to three ZAPS labs for each chapter in *Psychological Science*. You will receive summaries of your students' performance for each lab assigned, so credit can be given. You will also receive all the data your students generate in ZAPS, which you can share with the class to help them better understand the concepts. Instructor-only notes and activity ideas for each ZAPS lab are offered on the For Instructors tab of each ZAPS lab and through the *Psychological Science* Interactive Instructor's Guide.

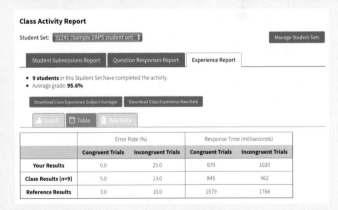

Class Activity Reports in ZAPS show data generated by your entire class and each student, as well as submitted answers to each question, for all labs.

Contents

Preface... ix

Acknowledgments... xviii

Instructor Resources... xxiv

1 The Science of Psychology 3

What Is Psychological Science? 4

  1.1 Psychological Science Is the Study of Mind, Brain, and Behavior 4

  1.2 Psychological Science Teaches Critical Thinking................................ 4

  1.3 Psychological Science Helps Us Understand Biased or Inaccurate Thinking 6

  1.4 **THINK LIKE A PSYCHOLOGIST**
    Why Are People Unaware of Their Weaknesses?................................ 8

What Are the Scientific Foundations of Psychology? 9

  1.5 Many Psychological Questions Have a Long History 10

  1.6 Experimental Psychology Initially Focused on the Structure, Not the Function, of Mental Activity 11

  1.7 Different Schools of Thought Reflected Different Perspectives on Mind, Brain, and Behavior.. 13

What Are the Latest Developments in Psychology? 17

  1.8 Biology Is Increasingly Emphasized in Explaining Psychological Phenomena 17

  1.9 Evolutionary Thinking Is Increasingly Influential............................... 18

  1.10 Culture Provides Adaptive Solutions.. 20

  1.11 Psychological Science Now Crosses Levels of Analysis 21

  1.12 Subfields in Psychology Focus on Different Levels of Analysis.................. 23

  1.13 **USING PSYCHOLOGY IN YOUR LIFE**
    Will Psychology Benefit You in Your Career?................................... 24

Your Chapter Review 26

2 Research Methodology 29

How Is the Scientific Method Used in Psychological Research? 30

  2.1 Science Has Four Primary Goals.. 30

  2.2 The Scientific Method Tests Hypotheses....................................... 32

  2.3 The Scientific Method Is Cyclical... 35

  2.4 Evaluating Scientific Findings Requires Critical Thinking....................... 36

What Types of Studies Are Used in Psychological Research? 38

2.5 Descriptive Research Consists of Case Studies, Observation, and
Self-Report Methods 39

2.6 Descriptive Studies Need to Guard Against Bias 41

2.7 Correlational Studies Describe and Predict How Variables Are Related 43

2.8 The Experimental Method Controls and Explains 46

2.9 Participants Need to Be Carefully Selected and Randomly
Assigned to Conditions 48

What Are the Ethics Governing Psychological Research? 51

2.10 There Are Ethical Issues to Consider in Research with Human Participants 51

2.11 There Are Ethical Issues to Consider in Research with Animals 53

2.12 **USING PSYCHOLOGY IN YOUR LIFE**
Should You Participate in Psychological Research? 54

How Are Data Analyzed and Evaluated? 55

2.13 Good Research Requires Valid, Reliable, and Accurate Data 55

2.14 Descriptive Statistics Provide a Summary of the Data 58

2.15 The Correlation Coefficient Summarizes the Relationships Between
Variables 60

2.16 Inferential Statistics Permit Generalizations 61

2.17 **THINK LIKE A PSYCHOLOGIST**
Should You Bet on a Hot Hand? 63

Your Chapter Review 65

3 Biology and Behavior 69

How Does the Nervous System Operate? 70

3.1 Neurons Are the Basic Units of the Nervous System 70

3.2 Action Potentials Produce Neural Communication 72

3.3 Neurotransmitters Influence Mental Activity and Behavior 75

What Are the Basic Brain Structures and Their Functions? 81

3.4 The Ability to Study Brain Function Has Improved Dramatically 81

3.5 The Brain Stem Houses the Basic Programs of Survival 84

3.6 Subcortical Structures Control Emotions and Appetitive Behaviors 85

3.7 The Cerebral Cortex Underlies Complex Mental Activity 87

3.8 Splitting the Brain Splits the Mind 92

3.9 **THINK LIKE A PSYCHOLOGIST**
Are There "Left Brain" and "Right Brain" Types of People? 96

How Does the Brain Communicate with the Body? 97

3.10 The Peripheral Nervous System Includes the Somatic and
Autonomic Systems 97

3.11 The Endocrine System Communicates Through Hormones 99

How Does the Brain Change? 101

3.12 The Brain Rewires Itself Throughout Life 101

3.13 The Brain Can Recover from Injury 104

3.14 **USING PSYCHOLOGY IN YOUR LIFE**
Will a Learning Disability Prevent You from Succeeding in College? 105

What Is the Genetic Basis of Psychological Science? 106

3.15 All of Human Development Has a Genetic Basis 106

3.16 Heredity Involves Passing Along Genes Through Reproduction 108

3.17 Genes Affect Behavior 111

3.18 Genetic Expression Can Be Modified 113

Your Chapter Review 117

4 Consciousness 121

What Is Consciousness? 122

4.1 Brain Activity Gives Rise to Consciousness 122

4.2 Consciousness Changes Following Brain Injury 124

4.3 Conscious Awareness Involves Attention 127

4.4 THINK LIKE A PSYCHOLOGIST
Are People Affected by Subliminal Messages? 131

What Is Sleep? 133

4.5 Sleep Is an Altered State of Consciousness 133

4.6 Sleep Disorders Interfere with Daily Life 135

4.7 Sleep Is an Adaptive Behavior 137

4.8 People Dream While Sleeping 139

4.9 USING PSYCHOLOGY IN YOUR LIFE
How Can You Get a Good Night's Sleep? 141

What Is Altered Consciousness? 143

4.10 Hypnosis Is Induced Through Suggestion 143

4.11 Meditation Produces Relaxation 145

4.12 People Can Lose Themselves in Activities 146

How Do Drugs Affect Consciousness? 147

4.13 Drugs Alter Brain Neurochemistry 148

4.14 People Use—and Abuse—Many Psychoactive Drugs 149

4.15 Alcohol Abuse Is Responsible for Many Societal Problems 154

4.16 Addiction Has Physical and Psychological Aspects 156

Your Chapter Review 159

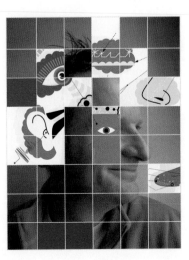

5 Sensation and Perception 163

How Does Perception Emerge from Sensation? 164

5.1 Sensory Information Is Translated into Meaningful Signals 164

5.2 Detection Requires a Certain Amount of the Stimulus 167

5.3 The Brain Constructs Stable Representations 170

5.4 THINK LIKE A PSYCHOLOGIST
Does ESP Exist? 171

How Are We Able to See? 172

5.5 Sensory Receptors in the Eye Transmit Visual Information to the Brain 172

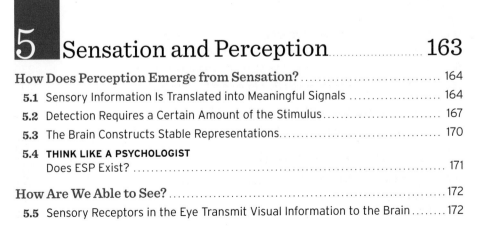

5.6 The Color of Light Is Determined by Its Wavelength............................176

5.7 Perceiving Objects Requires Organization of Visual Information 179

5.8 Perception Is Guided by Cues in the Environment 182

How Are We Able to Hear?..188

5.9 Audition Results from Changes in Air Pressure 188

5.10 Pitch Is Encoded by Frequency and Location......................................192

5.11 USING PSYCHOLOGY IN YOUR LIFE
Are Your Listening Habits Damaging Your Hearing? 193

How Are We Able to Taste?..194

5.12 There Are Five Basic Taste Sensations...194

How Are We Able to Smell?..196

5.13 Smell Detects Odorants 197

How Are We Able to Feel Touch and Pain?..199

5.14 The Skin Contains Sensory Receptors for Touch and Pain.....................200

Your Chapter Review..203

6 Learning 207

How Do We Learn?..208

6.1 Learning Results from Experience...208

6.2 Habituation and Sensitization Are Models of Nonassociative Learning........209

How Do We Learn Predictive Associations?...210

6.3 Behavioral Responses Are Conditioned...210

6.4 Learning Is Acquired and Persists Until Extinction 212

6.5 Learning Is Based on Evolutionary Significance 216

6.6 Learning Involves Expectancies and Prediction....................................218

6.7 Phobias and Addictions Have Learned Components 221

How Do Consequences of an Action Shape Behavior?.................................224

6.8 Operant Condition Involves Active Learning 224

6.9 THINK LIKE A PSYCHOLOGIST
How Do Superstitions Start?...227

6.10 There Are Many Types of Reinforcement 228

6.11 Operant Conditioning Is Influenced by Schedules of Reinforcement 230

6.12 Punishment Decreases Behavior 231

6.13 USING PSYCHOLOGY IN YOUR LIFE
How Can Behavior Modification Help You Get in Shape? 233

6.14 Biology and Cognition Influence Operant Conditioning 235

6.15 Dopamine Activity Underlies Reinforcement.......................................237

How Do We Learn from Watching Others?...238

6.16 Learning Can Occur Through Observation and Imitation 239

6.17 Watching Violence in Media May Encourage Aggression........................241

6.18 Fear Can Be Learned Through Observation 243

6.19 Mirror Neurons Are Activated by Watching Others...............................244

Your Chapter Review 245

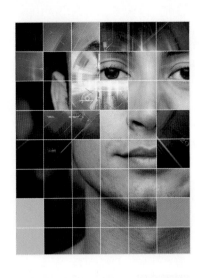

7 Memory 249

What Is Memory? 250

7.1 Memory Involves Processing Information 250

7.2 Memory Is the Result of Brain Activity 252

7.3 Memory Is Distributed Throughout the Brain 254

How Are Memories Maintained over Time? 256

7.4 Sensory Memory Is Brief 256

7.5 Working Memory Is Active 258

7.6 Long-Term Memory Is Relatively Permanent 260

How Is Information Organized in Long-Term Memory? 262

7.7 Long-Term Storage Is Based on Meaning 263

7.8 Information Is Stored in Association Networks 265

7.9 USING PSYCHOLOGY IN YOUR LIFE
Can You Ace Exams Without Cramming? 268

What Are the Different Long-Term Memory Systems? 270

7.10 Explicit Memory Involves Conscious Effort 271

7.11 Implicit Memory Occurs Without Deliberate Effort 272

How Is Memory Flawed? 273

7.12 Forgetting Is an Inability to Remember 274

7.13 Persistence Is Unwanted Remembering 277

7.14 People Reconstruct Events to Be Consistent 278

7.15 People Make Source Misattributions 280

7.16 Suggestibility Biases Memory 281

7.17 THINK LIKE A PSYCHOLOGIST
How Accurate Are Eyewitnesses? 284

Your Chapter Review 285

8 Thinking, Language, and Intelligence 289

What Is Thought? 290

8.1 Thinking Involves Two Types of Mental Representations 290

8.2 Concepts Are Symbolic Representations 291

8.3 Schemas Organize Useful Information About Environments 293

How Do We Make Decisions and Solve Problems? 296

8.4 Decision Making Often Involves Heuristics 297

8.5 Emotions Influence Decision Making 300

8.6 THINK LIKE A PSYCHOLOGIST
Why Is It Hard to Resist a Sale? 302

8.7 Problem Solving Achieves Goals 303

8.8 USING PSYCHOLOGY IN YOUR LIFE
How Can You Make Good Choices? 308

What Is Language? 310

  8.9 Language Is a System of Communication Using Sounds and Symbols 310

  8.10 Language Develops in an Orderly Way 313

  8.11 There Is an Inborn Capacity for Language 315

  8.12 Reading Needs to Be Learned 318

How Do We Understand Intelligence? 319

  8.13 Intelligence Is Measured with Standardized Tests 320

  8.14 General Intelligence Involves Multiple Components 322

  8.15 Intelligence Is Related to Cognitive Performance 324

  8.16 Genes and Environment Influence Intelligence 327

  8.17 Group Differences in Intelligence Have Multiple Determinants ... 330

Your Chapter Review 333

9 Human Development 337

What Factors Shape Infancy? 338

  9.1 Human Development Starts in the Womb 338

  9.2 Biology and Environment Influence Motor Development 341

  9.3 Infants Are Prepared to Learn 344

  9.4 THINK LIKE A PSYCHOLOGIST
     Does Mozart Make You Smarter? 346

  9.5 Infants Develop Attachments 347

How Do Children Learn About the World? 352

  9.6 Piaget Emphasized Stages of Cognitive Development 353

  9.7 Piaget Underestimated Children's Cognitive Abilities 356

  9.8 Children Learn from Interacting with Others 359

  9.9 Moral Development Begins in Childhood 361

What Changes During Adolescence? 363

  9.10 Puberty Causes Physical Changes 363

  9.11 A Sense of Identity Forms 365

  9.12 Peers and Parents Help Shape the Adolescent Self 369

What Brings Meaning in Adulthood? 371

  9.13 Adults Are Affected by Life Transitions 371

  9.14 USING PSYCHOLOGY IN YOUR LIFE
     Would Parenthood Make You Happy? 374

  9.15 The Transition to Old Age Can Be Satisfying 375

  9.16 Cognition Changes with Age 377

Your Chapter Review 379

10 Emotion and Motivation 383

What Are Emotions? 384
10.1 Emotions Vary in Valence and Arousal 384
10.2 Emotions Have a Physiological Component 385
10.3 THINK LIKE A PSYCHOLOGIST
Are Lie Detector Tests Valid? 389
10.4 There Are Three Major Theories of Emotion 390
10.5 USING PSYCHOLOGY IN YOUR LIFE
How Can You Control Your Emotions? 395

How Are Emotions Adaptive? 396
10.6 Facial Expressions Communicate Emotion 397
10.7 Emotions Strengthen Interpersonal Relations 400

How Are People Motivated? 402
10.8 Drives Motivate the Satisfaction of Needs 402
10.9 People Are Motivated by Incentives 405
10.10 People Set Goals to Achieve 408
10.11 People Have a Need to Belong 410

What Motivates Eating? 412
10.12 Many Physiological Factors Influence Eating 412
10.13 Eating Is Influenced by Time and Taste 414

What Motivates Sexual Behavior? 416
10.14 Biology Influences Sexual Behavior 416
10.15 Cultural Scripts and Cultural Rules Shape Sexual Interactions 419
10.16 People Differ in Sexual Orientations 421

Your Chapter Review 425

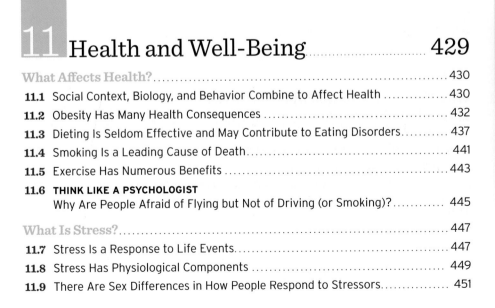

11 Health and Well-Being 429

What Affects Health? 430
11.1 Social Context, Biology, and Behavior Combine to Affect Health 430
11.2 Obesity Has Many Health Consequences 432
11.3 Dieting Is Seldom Effective and May Contribute to Eating Disorders 437
11.4 Smoking Is a Leading Cause of Death 441
11.5 Exercise Has Numerous Benefits 443
11.6 THINK LIKE A PSYCHOLOGIST
Why Are People Afraid of Flying but Not of Driving (or Smoking)? 445

What Is Stress? 447
11.7 Stress Is a Response to Life Events 447
11.8 Stress Has Physiological Components 449
11.9 There Are Sex Differences in How People Respond to Stressors 451

How Does Stress Affect Health? 452

11.10 Stress Disrupts the Immune System 452

11.11 Stress Increases the Risk of Heart Disease 454

11.12 Coping Reduces the Negative Health Effects of Stress 457

Can a Positive Attitude Keep People Healthy? 459

11.13 Being Positive Has Health Benefits 459

11.14 Social Support Is Associated with Good Health 461

11.15 USING PSYCHOLOGY IN YOUR LIFE
Can Psychology Improve Your Health? 463

Your Chapter Review 465

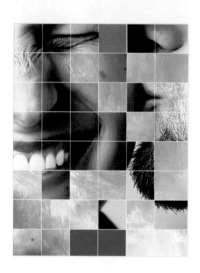

12 Social Psychology 469

How Does Group Membership Affect People? 470

12.1 People Favor Their Own Groups 470

12.2 Groups Influence Individual Behavior 473

12.3 People Conform to and Comply with Others 475

12.4 THINK LIKE A PSYCHOLOGIST
Can Social Norms Marketing Reduce Binge Drinking? 479

12.5 People Are Obedient to Authority 480

When Do People Harm or Help Others? 482

12.6 Many Factors Can Influence Aggression 482

12.7 Many Factors Can Influence Helping Behavior 485

12.8 Cooperation Can Reduce Outgroup Bias 488

How Do Attitudes Guide Behavior? 490

12.9 People Form Attitudes Through Experience and Socialization 490

12.10 Discrepancies Lead to Dissonance 493

12.11 Attitudes Can Be Changed Through Persuasion 494

How Do People Think About Others? 496

12.12 People Make Judgments About Others 496

12.13 Stereotypes Can Lead to Prejudice and Discrimination 498

12.14 Prejudice Can Be Reduced 502

What Determines the Quality of Relationships? 503

12.15 Situational and Personal Factors Influence Interpersonal
Attraction and Friendships 504

12.16 Love Is an Important Component of Romantic Relationships 507

12.17 USING PSYCHOLOGY IN YOUR LIFE
How Can Psychology Rekindle the Romance in Your Relationship? 509

Your Chapter Review 511

13 Personality   515

Where Does Personality Come From? 516
13.1 Genetic Factors Influence the Development of Personality 516
13.2 Temperaments Are Evident in Infancy 519

What Are the Theories of Personality? 521
13.3 Psychodynamic Theories Emphasize Unconscious and Dynamic
Processes 522
13.4 Personality Reflects Learning and Cognition 525
13.5 Humanistic Approaches Emphasize Integrated Personal Experience 526
13.6 Trait Approaches Describe Behavioral Dispositions 528
13.7 Traits Have a Biological Basis 529

How Stable Is Personality? 532
13.8 People Sometimes Are Inconsistent 532
13.9 Development and Life Events Alter Personality Traits 534
13.10 Culture Influences Personality 538

How Is Personality Assessed? 540
13.11 Researchers Use Multiple Methods to Assess Personality 540
13.12 Observers Show Accuracy in Trait Judgments 543
13.13 USING PSYCHOLOGY IN YOUR LIFE
What Personality Traits Should You Look for in a Roommate? 545

How Do We Know Our Own Personalities? 546
13.14 Our Self-Concepts Consist of Self-Knowledge 547
13.15 Perceived Social Regard Influences Self-Esteem 549
13.16 People Use Mental Strategies to Maintain a Positive Sense of Self 551
13.17 THINK LIKE A PSYCHOLOGIST
Are There Cultural Differences in the Self-Serving Bias? 554

Your Chapter Review 557

14 Psychological Disorders   561

How Are Psychological Disorders Conceptualized and Classified? 562
14.1 Views on Psychopathology Have Changed over Time 562
14.2 Psychological Disorders Are Classified into Categories 564
14.3 Psychological Disorders Have Many Causes 568
14.4 Psychological Disorders Vary by Sex and by Culture 570

Which Disorders Emphasize Emotional States? 573
14.5 Anxiety Disorders Make People Fearful and Tense 573
14.6 Unwanted and Intrusive Thoughts Increase Anxiety 577
14.7 Depressive Disorders Consist of Sad, Empty, or Irritable Moods 579
14.8 Bipolar Disorders Involve Depression and Mania 582
14.9 USING PSYCHOLOGY IN YOUR LIFE
You Think Your Friend Might Be Suicidal. What Should You Do? 584

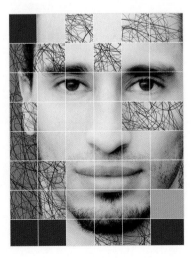

Which Disorders Emphasize Thought Disturbances?.......................586

14.10 Dissociative Disorders Are Disruptions in Memory,
Awareness, and Identity 586

14.11 Schizophrenia Involves a Disconnection from Reality 589

14.12 The Cause of Schizophrenia Involves Biological and
Environmental Factors 592

What Are Personality Disorders?.................................595

14.13 Personality Disorders Are Maladaptive Ways of Relating
to the World 596

14.14 Borderline Personality Disorder Is Associated with
Poor Self-Control 597

14.15 Antisocial Personality Disorder Is Associated with a Lack of
Empathy 599

Which Psychological Disorders Are Prominent in Childhood?...........601

14.16 Autistic Spectrum Disorder Involves Social Deficits and
Restricted Interests 603

14.17 **THINK LIKE A PSYCHOLOGIST**
Why Do People Believe Vaccinations Cause Autism?...........607

14.18 Attention-Deficit/Hyperactivity Disorder Is a Disruptive
Impulse Control Disorder 608

Your Chapter Review 611

15 Treatment of Psychological Disorders 615

How Are Psychological Disorders Treated? 616

15.1 Various Methods Have Been Used to Treat Psychopathology 616

15.2 Psychodynamic Therapy Seeks to Reduce Unconscious Conflicts 617

15.3 Behavioral and Cognitive Treatments Aim to Change Behavior,
Emotion, or Thought Directly 618

15.4 The Context of Therapy Matters 620

15.5 Medication Is Effective for Certain Disorders...................623

15.6 Alternative Biological Treatments Are Used in Extreme Cases.................625

15.7 Effectiveness of Treatment Is Determined by Empirical Evidence 628

15.8 Various Providers Can Assist in Treatment for Psychological Disorders 630

15.9 **USING PSYCHOLOGY IN YOUR LIFE**
How Do You Find a Therapist Who Can Help You?.............632

What Are the Most Effective Treatments? 633

15.10 Treatments That Focus on Behavior and on Cognition
Are Superior for Anxiety Disorders......................634

15.11 Both Antidepressants and CBT Are Effective for
Obsessive-Compulsive Disorder........................636

15.12 Many Effective Treatments Are Available for Depressive Disorders 638

15.13 **THINK LIKE A PSYCHOLOGIST**
Should You Trust Studies Sponsored by Drug Companies?...................644

15.14 Lithium and Atypical Antipsychotics Are Most Effective for
Bipolar Disorder 645

15.15 Antipsychotics Are Superior for Schizophrenia..................647

Can Personality Disorders Be Treated?............................... 650

15.16 Dialectical Behavior Therapy Is Most Successful for
Borderline Personality Disorder................................. 650

15.17 Antisocial Personality Disorder Is Extremely Difficult to Treat................. 651

How Should Childhood and Adolescent Disorders Be Treated?.......... 653

15.18 Children with ADHD Can Benefit from Various Approaches.................... 654

15.19 Children with Autism Spectrum Disorder Benefit from
Structured Behavioral Treatment............................... 656

15.20 The Use of Medication to Treat Adolescent Depressive Disorders Is
Controversial... 659

Your Chapter Review... 662

Glossary G-1

References R-1

Practice Tests PT-1

Permissions Acknowledgments.................................. PA-1

Name Index... NI-1

Subject Index... SI-1

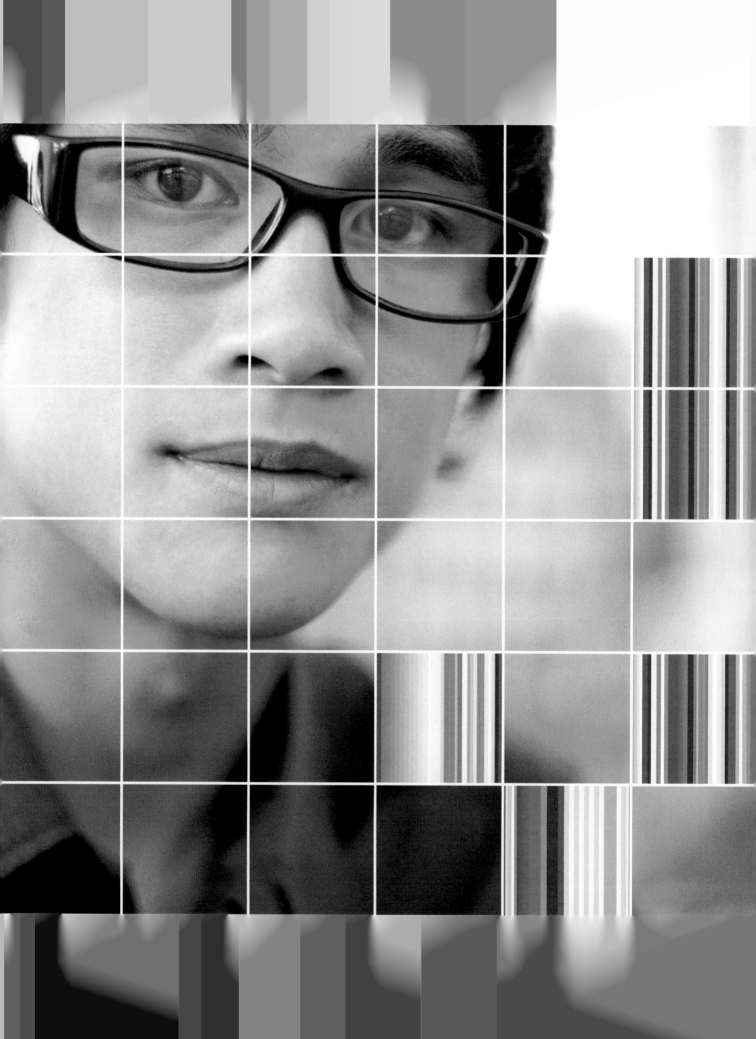

1

The Science of Psychology

Big Questions

- What Is Psychological Science? 4

- What Are the Scientific Foundations of Psychology? 9

- What Are the Latest Developments in Psychology? 17

WHY IS PSYCHOLOGY ONE OF THE MOST POPULAR MAJORS at many colleges? The simple answer is that people want to understand mental activity and behavior. The subject material of psychology is not just fascinating but personally relevant. It can help you understand your motives, your personality, even why you remember some things and forget others. In addition, psychology serves as excellent training for many professions. For instance, physicians need to know a lot more than anatomy and chemistry. They need to know how to relate to their patients, how the patients' behaviors are linked to health, and what motivates or discourages patients from seeking medical care or following treatment protocols. Much of the psychological research you read about in this book is being used today to make people's lives better.

Around the globe, psychological researchers are providing new insights into the nature of being human. Their findings will benefit you whether you're studying environmental science (e.g., how do you encourage people to recycle?), anthropology (e.g., how does culture shape behavior?), biology (e.g., how do animals learn?), or philosophy (e.g., do people have free will?). Whatever your major, this class will help you succeed in your academic work and your private life, now and in the future.

In this introductory chapter, the big questions about psychology are: What is psychological science? What are the scientific foundations of psychology? And what are the latest developments in psychology?

What Is Psychological Science?

Psychology involves the study of mental activity and behavior. The term *psychologist* is used broadly to describe someone whose career involves understanding mental life or predicting behavior. We humans are intuitive psychologists. That is, we try to understand and predict others' behavior. For example, defensive drivers rely on their intuitive sense of when other drivers are likely to make mistakes. People choose relationship partners they expect will best meet their emotional, sexual, and support needs. People try to predict whether others are kind, are trustworthy, will make good caretakers, will make good teachers, and so on. But people too often rely on apparent common sense or their gut feelings. They cannot intuitively know if many of the claims related to psychology are fact or fiction. For example, will taking certain herbs increase memory? Will playing music to newborns make them more intelligent?

1.1 Psychological Science Is the Study of Mind, Brain, and Behavior

The science of psychology is not simply about intuitions or common sense. **Psychological science** is the study, through research, of mind, brain, and behavior. But what exactly does each of these terms mean, and how are they all related?

Mind refers to mental activity. Examples of the mind in action include the perceptual experiences (sights, smells, tastes, sounds, and touches) we have while interacting with the world. The mind is also responsible for memories, thoughts, and feelings. Mental activity results from biological processes within the *brain*.

Behavior describes the totality of observable human (or animal) actions. These actions range from the subtle to the complex. Some occur exclusively in humans, such as debating philosophy or performing surgery. Others occur in all animals, such as eating, drinking, and mating. For many years, psychologists focused on behavior rather than on mental states. They did so largely because they had few objective techniques for assessing the mind. The advent of technology to observe the working brain in action has enabled psychologists to study mental states and has led to a fuller understanding of human behavior. Although psychologists make important contributions to understanding and treating mental disorders, most psychological science has little to do with therapeutic clichés such as couches and dreams. Instead, psychologists generally seek to understand mental activity (both normal and abnormal), the biological basis of that activity, how people change as they grow older, how people vary in response to social settings, and how people acquire healthy and unhealthy behaviors.

Q **What produces mental activity?**

ANSWER: biological activity in the brain

S. GROSS

"For God's sake, think! Why is he being so nice to you?"

1.2 Psychological Science Teaches Critical Thinking

 One of this textbook's most important goals is to provide a basic, state-of-the-art education about the methods of psychological science. Even if your only exposure to psychology is through the introductory course

---

Learning Objectives

- Define psychological science.
- Define critical thinking, and describe what it means to be a critical thinker.
- Identify major biases in thinking, and explain why these biases result in faulty thinking.

psychological science
The study, through research, of mind, brain, and behavior.

critical thinking
Systematically questioning and evaluating information using well-supported evidence.

---

for which *Psychological Science* is the textbook, you will become psychologically literate. With a good understanding of the field's major issues, theories, and controversies, you will also avoid common misunderstandings about psychology. You will learn how to separate the believable from the incredible. You will learn to spot poorly designed experiments, and you will develop the skills necessary to critically evaluate claims made in the popular media.

The media love a good story, and findings from psychological research are often provocative (**FIGURE 1.1**). Unfortunately, media reports can be distorted or even flat-out wrong. Throughout your life, as a consumer of psychological science, you will need to be skeptical of overblown media reports of "brand-new" findings obtained by "groundbreaking" research. With the rapid expansion of the Internet and thousands of new research findings available for searches on just about any topic, you need to be able to sort through and evaluate the information you find in order to gain a correct understanding of the phenomenon (observable thing) you are trying to investigate (**FIGURE 1.2**).

One of the hallmarks of a good scientist—or a savvy consumer of scientific research—is *amiable skepticism*. This trait combines openness and wariness. An amiable skeptic remains open to new ideas but is wary of new "scientific findings" when good evidence and sound reasoning do not seem to support them. An amiable skeptic develops the habit of carefully weighing the facts when deciding what to believe. The ability to think in this way—to systematically question and evaluate information using well-supported evidence—is called **critical thinking.**

Being a critical thinker involves looking for holes in evidence, using logic and reasoning to see whether the information makes sense, and considering alternative explanations. It also requires considering whether the information might be biased, such as by personal or political agendas. Critical thinking demands healthy questioning and keeping an open mind. Most people are quick to question information that does not fit with their beliefs. But as an educated person, you need to think critically about all information. Even when you "know" something, you need to keep refreshing that information in your mind. Ask yourself: Is my belief still true? What led me to believe it? What facts support it? Has science produced new findings that require us to reevaluate and update our beliefs? This exercise is important because you may be least motivated to think critically about information that verifies your preconceptions. In Chapter 2, you will learn much more about how critical thinking helps our scientific understanding of psychological phenomena.

Critical thinking is useful in every aspect of your life. It is also important in all fields of study throughout the humanities and the sciences. The integration of critical thinking in psychological science adds to our understanding of how people typically think when they encounter information. Many decades of psychological research have shown that people's intuitions are often wrong.

Daily Mail .com

Home | U.K. | News | Sports | U.S. Showbiz | Australia | Femail | **Health** | Science | Money

Latest Headlines | *Health* | Health Directory | Health Boards | Diets | Discounts

The quiz that makes over-60s better cooks: Computer brain games 'stave off mental decline'

- Computer brain games can help elderly perform better at everyday tasks
- Firms selling the gadgets and games consoles say they boost memory
- British research suggests brain exercises may delay onset of dementia

By BEN SPENCER, MEDICAL CORRESPONDENT FOR THE DAILY MAIL
PUBLISHED: 19:58 EST, 2 November 2015 | UPDATED: 03:06 EST, 3 November 2015

f Share · Twitter · P · g+ · ✉ · Share · **198** shares · ●**74** View comments

Computer brain games can help the elderly perform significantly better at everyday tasks, scientists have found.

Firms selling the handheld gadgets and games consoles say they boost memory and thinking power.

And the British research backs this claim, even suggesting that the brain exercises may delay the onset of dementia – although much more evidence would be needed to confirm this link.

FIGURE 1.1
Psychology in the News
Psychological research is often in the news because the findings are intriguing and relevant to people's lives.

Psychology Today ❝How do w

Home | Find a Therapist ▾ | Topic Streams ▾ | Get Help ▾ | Magazine ▾ | Tests | Psych Basics

Acacia Parks, Ph

The Motivated Brain
Understanding the Pursuit of Goals
by Elliot Berkman, Ph.D.

Does Brain-Training Work?
Don't believe the hype—there's a catch to mental skills training programs.
Published on December 31, 2013 by Dr. Elliot T. Berkman in The Motivated Brain

The recent proliferation of commercial online "brain-training" services that promise to enhance intelligence and other cognitive abilities is understandable: Who wouldn't want to be smarter and have greater working memory and inhibitory control? Seeing the potential for low-cost and reliable measurement of performance, some corporations have begun using similar tools to assess potential hires and evaluate employees ("people analytics"). No doubt there is some amount of benefit to be gained on both fronts. After all, people have an amazing capacity to develop expertise with practice in a huge range of skills (think video games, driving, or crosswords), and it is an open secret that qualitative interviews, the dominant tool currently used for evaluating new hires, are subject to bias and don't predict job performance in the first place.

Related Articles
- Brain Plasticity in Action: Getting smarter and happier
- Super Bowl: Battle of the Quarterback Brains
- A Simple Ritual That Will Make Your Goals "Stick"
- The Joy of Effort
- Is Your Brain Asleep on the Job?

Despite this potential, independent studies on brain-training services provide (at best) equivocal support for their effectiveness. This is true for a number of their claims, but particularly the implicit understanding that performance gains earned on the training tasks will generalize to untrained tasks (so-called "transfer effects"). It's one thing to get better at a particular task, but a more rigorous standard is whether users improve on other ones. Does practicing Tetris make you better at Pac-Man? The best work debunking studies claiming to produce training effects has been done by Randall Engel, Zach Shipstead, and their colleagues at Georgia Tech. They find that practice indeed improves skills at the trained tasks, but doesn't transfer to untrained tasks when adequate control groups are used. They also raise concerns about the durability of the training over longer periods of time used in the research (usually 3 or 6 months).

FIGURE 1.2
Critically Evaluating Research
Psychologists use critical thinking to evaluate provocative research questions. Here, Elliot Berkman cautions against believing the hype about brain training.

Intuitions also tend to be wrong in predictable ways. Indeed, human thought is often biased in ways that make critical thinking very difficult. Through scientific study, psychologists have discovered types of situations in which common sense fails and biases influence people's judgments.

 Q What is amiable skepticism?

1.3 Psychological Science Helps Us Understand Biased or Inaccurate Thinking

Psychologists have cataloged numerous ways that noncritical thinking can lead to erroneous conclusions (Gilovich, 1991; Hines, 2003; Kida, 2006; Stanovich, 2013). These errors and biases do not occur because we lack intelligence or motivation. Just the opposite is true. Most of these biases occur *because* we are motivated to use our intelligence. We want to make sense of events that involve us or happen around us. Our minds are constantly analyzing all the information we receive and trying to make sense of that information. These attempts generally result in relevant and correct conclusions.

Indeed, the human brain is highly efficient at finding patterns and noting connections between things. By using these abilities, we make new discoveries and advance society. But sometimes we get things wrong. Sometimes we see patterns that do not really exist (**FIGURE 1.3**). We look at the clouds and see images in them—clowns, faces, horses, what have you. We play recorded music backward and hear satanic messages. We believe that events, such as the deaths of celebrities, happen in threes. Often, we see what we expect to see and fail to notice things that do not fit with our expectations. For instance, as you will learn in Chapter 12, our stereotypes about people shape our expectations about them, and we interpret their behavior in ways that confirm these stereotypes.

Why is it important to care about errors and biases in thinking? The psychologist Thomas Gilovich answers this question insightfully in his book *How We Know What Isn't So: The Fallibility of Human Reason in Everyday Life* (1991). He points out that more Americans believe in extrasensory perception (ESP) than in evolution and that there are twenty times more astrologers than astronomers. Followers of ESP and astrology may base important life decisions on beliefs that are wrong. False beliefs can sometimes lead to dangerous actions. Some people hunt endangered animals because they believe the animals' body parts provide magical cures. Some people rely on fringe therapies to provide what they think is real medical or psychological treatment.

Knowing about biases in thinking will also help you do better in your classes, including this one. Before they have taken a psychology course, many students have false beliefs, or misconceptions, about psychological phenomena. The psychologists Patricia Kowalski and Annette Kujawski Taylor (2004) found that students who employ critical thinking skills complete an introductory course with a more accurate understanding of psychology than students who complete the same course but do not employ critical thinking skills. As you read this book, you will benefit from the critical thinking skills that are discussed. You

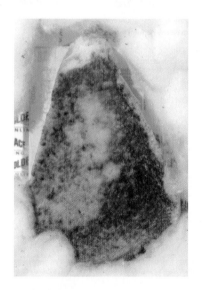

FIGURE 1.3

Patterns That Do Not Exist

People often think they see faces in objects. When the owner claimed to see the face of the Virgin Mary on this grilled cheese sandwich, the sandwich sold to a casino for $28,000 on eBay.

can apply these skills in your other classes, your workplace, and your everyday life.

Each chapter of the book draws your attention to at least one major example of biased or erroneous thinking and how psychological science has provided insights into them, in a feature called "Think like a Psychologist." Following are a few of the major biases you will encounter.

- *Ignoring evidence (confirmation bias)*. People show a strong tendency to place great importance on evidence that supports their beliefs. They tend to downplay evidence that does not match what they believe. When people hear about a study that is consistent with their beliefs, they generally believe the study has merit. When they hear about a study that contradicts those beliefs, they look for flaws or other problems.

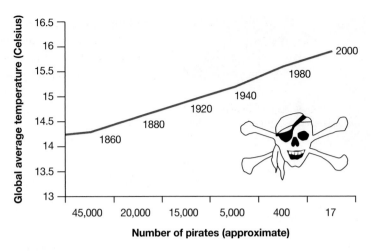

FIGURE 1.4
A Humorous Example
Sometimes things that appear related are not.

One factor that contributes to confirmation bias is the selective sampling of information. For instance, people with certain political beliefs may visit only Web sites that are consistent with those beliefs. However, if we restrict ourselves to evidence that supports our views, then of course we will believe we are right. Similarly, people show selective memory, tending to better remember information that supports their existing beliefs.

- *Seeing relationships that do not exist.* An extremely common reasoning error is the misperception that two events that happen at the same time must somehow be related. In our desire to find predictability in the world, we sometimes see order that does not exist. Believing that events are related when they are not can lead to superstitious behavior. For example, an athlete thinks she must eat a certain meal before a game in order to win, or a fan believes that wearing his favorite team's jersey helps the team win. But many times events that appear related are just coincidence. Consider a humorous example. Over the last 200 years, the mean global temperature has increased. During that same period, the number of pirates on the high seas has decreased. Would you argue that the demise of pirates has led to increased global warming (**FIGURE 1.4**)?

- *Accepting after-the-fact explanations.* Because people expect the world to make sense, they often come up with explanations for why events happen. They do so even when they have incomplete information. One form of this reasoning bias is known as *hindsight bias*. We are wonderful at explaining why things happened, but we are much less successful at predicting future events. Think about the woundings and fatal shootings in 2016 at the Pulse gay nightclub, in Orlando, Florida. In hindsight, we know that there were warning signs that the shooter, Omar Mateen, might become violent (**FIGURE 1.5**). Yet none of these warning signs prompted anyone to take action. People saw the signs but failed to predict the tragic outcome. More generally, once we know the outcome, we interpret and reinterpret old evidence to make sense of that outcome. Likewise, when political pundits predict an election outcome and get it wrong, they later come out with all sorts of explanations for the election result. If they had really seen those factors as important before the election, they should have made a different prediction. We need to be wary of after-the-fact explanations because they tend to distort the evidence.

- *Taking mental shortcuts.* People often follow simple rules, called heuristics, to make decisions. These mental shortcuts are valuable because they often produce

FIGURE 1.5
Orlando Pulse Shootings
In hindsight, there were warning signs that the shooter, Omar Mateen, was troubled. But it is very difficult to predict violent behavior in advance.

FIGURE 1.6
Judging a Performance
Judges react to an audition.

reasonably good decisions without too much effort (Kahneman, 2011). Unfortunately, many heuristics can lead to inaccurate judgments and biased outcomes. One example of this problem occurs when things that come most easily to mind guide our thinking. This shortcut is known as the availability heuristic. After hearing a series of news reports about child abductions, people overestimate how often such abductions happen. Parents become overly concerned that their children might be abducted. As a result, people may underestimate other dangers facing children, such as bicycle accidents, food poisoning, or drowning. Child abductions are much more likely to be reported in the news than these much more common dangers. The vivid nature of the abduction reports makes them easy to remember. Similar processes lead people to drive rather than fly even though the chances of injury or death from passenger vehicles are much greater than the chances of dying in a plane crash. In Chapter 8, we will consider a number of heuristic biases.

ANSWER: Once people know an outcome, they interpret and reinterpret old evidence to make sense of that outcome.

Q Why should you be suspicious of after-the-fact explanations?

1.4 Why Are People Unaware of Their Weaknesses?

Another bias in thinking is that people fail to see their own inadequacies. People are motivated to feel good about themselves, and this motivation affects how they think (Cai et al., 2016). For example, many people believe they are better than average on any number of dimensions. More than 90 percent of people think they are better-than-average drivers, but this percentage is illogical because only 50 percent can be above average on any dimension. People use various strategies to support their positive views, such as crediting personal strengths for their successes and blaming outside forces for their failures. In general, people interpret information in ways that support their positive beliefs about themselves. One factor that promotes overconfidence is that people often have difficulty recognizing their own weaknesses. Consider the following.

You are judging an audition for a musical, and the singer, while passionate, is just awful (**FIGURE 1.6**). Everyone in the room is laughing or holding back laughter out of politeness. When the judges react unenthusiastically and worse, the performer is crushed and cannot believe the verdict. "But everyone says I am a great singer," he argues. "Singing is my life!" You sit there thinking, *How does he not know how bad he is?*

Such moments make us cringe. We feel deeply uncomfortable about them, even as we tune in to watch them on television shows such as *America's Got Talent*. The German language has a word for how we feel, *Fremdschämen*. This term refers to times when we experience embarrassment for other people in

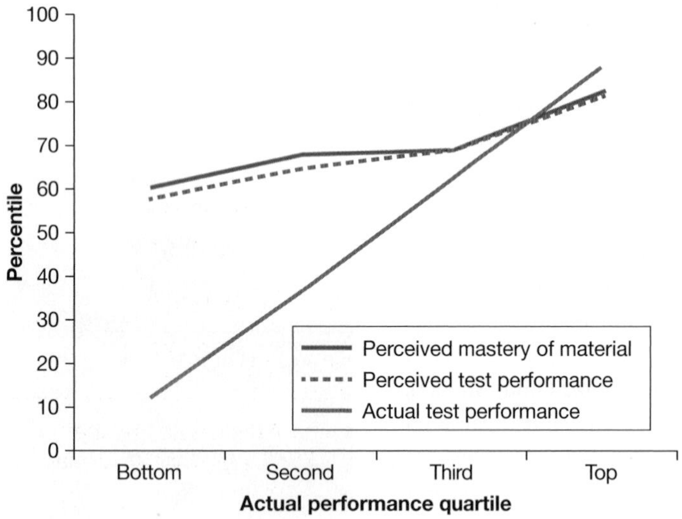

Legend:
Perceived mastery of material
Perceived test performance
Actual test performance

X-axis: Actual performance quartile (Bottom, Second, Third, Top)
Y-axis: Percentile (0–100)

FIGURE 1.7
Personal Ratings Versus Actual Performance
Students rated their mastery of course material and test performance. Points on the Y-axis reflect how the students perceived their percentile rankings (value on a scale of 100). Points on the X-axis reflect these students' actual performance rank (*quartile* here means that people are divided into four groups). The top students' predictions were close to their actual results. By contrast, the bottom students' predictions were far off.

part because they do not realize that they should be embarrassed for themselves. Comedies such as *The Office* owe much of their success to giving us this feeling of *Fremdschämen*.

How is it that people who are tone-deaf can believe their singing talents merit participating in singing competitions? The social psychologists David Dunning and Justin Kruger have an explanation: People are often blissfully unaware of their weaknesses because they cannot judge those weaknesses at all (Dunning et al., 2003; Kruger & Dunning, 1999). How does this limitation come about?

To judge whether someone is a good singer, you need to be able to tell the difference between good and bad singing. You need to know the difference even if you are judging your own singing. The same is true for most other activities. A lack of skill not only prevents people from producing good results, it also prevents those people from knowing what good results are. As noted by these researchers, "Thus, if people lack the skills to produce correct answers, they are also cursed with an inability to know when their answers, or anyone else's, are right or wrong" (Dunning et al., 2003, p. 85).

In studies of college students, Dunning and Kruger found that people with the lowest grades rate their mastery of academic skills much higher than is warranted by their performance (**FIGURE 1.7**). A student who receives a grade of C may protest to the instructor, "My work is as good as my roommate's, but she got an A." The protest may simply show that the student lacks the ability to evaluate performance in those areas where she is weakest. To make matters worse, people who are unaware of their weaknesses fail to make any efforts at self-improvements to overcome those weaknesses. They do not try to get better because they already believe they are performing well.

Kruger and Dunning (1999) have shown that teaching people specific skills helps them to be more accurate in judging their performance. This finding implies that people might need help in identifying their weaknesses before they can fix those weaknesses. But why are people so inaccurate in the first place? The likely answer is that they generally start with extremely positive views about their abilities. In Chapter 12, you will learn more about why most people believe they are better than average in many things. Such beliefs influence how people judge their talents and skills across multiple areas. Knowing about these beliefs helps us understand the driver who claims to be very skilled in spite of numerous car accidents and the singer who brags about an awesome vocal ability in spite of a train-wreck performance on national television. ■

FIGURE 1.8
Confucius
Ancient philosophers such as Confucius studied topics that remain important in contemporary psychology.

ANSWER: because people often fail to see their personal weaknesses

 Why should you be skeptical of people's descriptions of their personal strengths?

What Are the Scientific Foundations of Psychology?

Psychology originated in philosophy, as the great thinkers sought to understand human nature. For example, the ancient Chinese philosopher Confucius emphasized human development, education, and interpersonal relations, all of which remain contemporary topics in psychology around the world (Higgins & Zheng, 2002; **FIGURE 1.8**). As you will learn, in the 1800s psychologists began to use scientific methods to investigate mind, brain, and behavior.

Learning Objectives

- Trace the development of psychology since its formal inception in 1879.

- Define the nature/nurture debate and the mind/body problem.

- Identify the major schools of thought that have characterized the history of experimental psychology.

1.5 Many Psychological Questions Have a Long History

culture

The beliefs, values, rules, and customs that exist within a group of people who share a common language and environment.

nature/nurture debate

The arguments concerning whether psychological characteristics are biologically innate or acquired through education, experience, and culture.

mind/body problem

A fundamental psychological issue: Are mind and body separate and distinct, or is the mind simply the physical brain's subjective experience?

Since at least the times of ancient Greece, people have wondered why humans think and act in certain ways. Greek philosophers such as Aristotle and Plato debated whether an individual's psychology is attributable more to *nature* or to *nurture*. That is, are psychological characteristics biologically innate? Or are they acquired through education, experience, and **culture** (the beliefs, values, rules, norms, and customs existing within a group of people who share a common language and environment)?

The **nature/nurture debate** has taken one form or another throughout psychology's history. Psychologists now widely recognize that both nature and nurture dynamically interact in human psychological development. For example, psychologists study the ways that nature and nurture influence each other in shaping mind, brain, and behavior. Consider a college basketball player who is very tall (nature) and has an excellent coach (nurture). That player has a better chance of excelling enough to become a professional player than does an equally talented player who has only the height or the coach. In examples throughout this book, nature and nurture are so enmeshed that they cannot be separated.

The **mind/body problem** was perhaps the quintessential psychological issue: Are the mind and body separate and distinct, or is the mind simply the subjective experience of ongoing brain activity? Throughout history, the mind has been viewed as residing in many organs of the body, including the liver and the heart. The ancient Egyptians, for example, elaborately embalmed each dead person's heart, which was to be weighed in the afterlife to determine the person's fate. They simply threw away the brain. In the following centuries, especially among the Greeks and Romans,

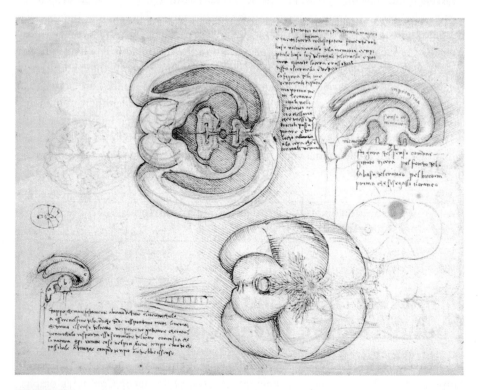

FIGURE 1.9
Da Vinci and the Brain
This drawing by Leonardo da Vinci dates from around 1506. Da Vinci used a wax cast to study the brain. He believed that sensory images arrived in the middle region of the brain. He called this region the *sensus communis*.

recognition grew that the brain was essential for normal mental functioning. Much of this change came from observing people with brain injuries. At least since the time of the Roman gladiators, it was clear that a blow to the head often produced disturbances in mental activity, such as unconsciousness or the loss of speech.

Nonetheless, scholars continued to believe that the mind was separate from and in control of the body. They held this belief partly because of the strong theological belief that a divine and immortal soul separates humans from nonhuman animals. Around 1500, the artist Leonardo da Vinci challenged this doctrine when he dissected human bodies to make his anatomical drawings more accurate. Da Vinci's dissections led him to many conclusions about the brain's workings. For example, da Vinci theorized that all sensory messages (vision, touch, smell, etc.) arrived at one location in the brain. He called that region the *sensus communis,* and he believed it to be the home of thought and judgment; its name may be the root of the modern term *common sense* (Blakemore, 1983). Da Vinci's specific conclusions about brain functions were not accurate, but his work represents an early and important attempt to link the brain's anatomy to psychological functions (**FIGURE 1.9**).

In the 1600s, the philosopher René Descartes promoted the influential theory of *dualism.* This term refers to the idea that the mind and the body are separate yet intertwined (**FIGURE 1.10**). In earlier views of dualism, mental functions had been considered the mind's sovereign domain, separate from body functions. Descartes proposed a somewhat different view. The body, he argued, was nothing more than an organic machine governed by "reflex." Many mental functions—such as memory and imagination—resulted from body functions. Deliberate action, however, was controlled by the rational mind. And in keeping with the prevailing religious beliefs, Descartes concluded that the rational mind was divine and separate from the body. Nowadays, psychologists reject dualism. In their view, the mind arises from brain activity. It does not exist separately.

FIGURE 1.10
René Descartes
According to Descartes, the mind and the body are separate yet intertwined. As discussed throughout this book, psychologists now reject such dualism.

Q Which is more important, nature or nurture?

ANSWER: Both are equally important.

1.6 Experimental Psychology Initially Focused on the Structure, Not the Function, of Mental Activity

In the mid-1800s in Europe, psychology arose as a field of study built on the experimental method. In *A System of Logic* (1843), the philosopher John Stuart Mill declared that psychology should leave the realms of philosophy and of speculation and become a science of observation and of experiment. Indeed, he defined psychology as "the science of the elementary laws of the mind" and argued that only through the methods of science would the processes of the mind be understood. As a result, throughout the 1800s, early psychologists increasingly studied mental activity through careful scientific observation.

In 1879, Wilhelm Wundt established the first psychology laboratory and institute (**FIGURE 1.11**). At this facility, in Leipzig, Germany, students could earn advanced academic degrees in psychology for the first time. Wundt trained many of the great early psychologists, a number of whom then established psychological laboratories throughout Europe, Canada, and the United States.

Wundt realized that psychological processes, the products of physiological actions in the brain, take time to occur. Therefore, he used a method developed earlier, called *reaction time,* to assess how quickly people can respond to events. Wundt presented

FIGURE 1.11
Wilhelm Wundt
Wundt founded modern experimental psychology.

introspection

A systematic examination of subjective mental experiences that requires people to inspect and report on the content of their thoughts.

structuralism

An approach to psychology based on the idea that conscious experience can be broken down into its basic underlying components.

stream of consciousness

A phrase coined by William James to describe each person's continuous series of ever-changing thoughts.

FIGURE 1.12
William James
In 1890, James published the first major overview of psychology. Many of his ideas have passed the test of time. In theorizing about how the mind works, he moved psychology beyond structuralism and into functionalism.

FIGURE 1.13
Mary Whiton Calkins
Calkins was an important early contributor to psychological science. In 1905, she became the first woman president of the American Psychological Association.

each research participant with a simple psychological task and a related but more complex one. He timed each task. He then performed a mathematical operation: subtracting the time a participant took to complete the simple task from the time the participant took to complete the more complex task. This method enabled Wundt to infer how much time a particular mental event took to occur. Researchers still widely use reaction time to study psychological processes, but their types of equipment are of course more sophisticated than Wundt's.

Wundt was not satisfied with simply studying mental reaction times. He wanted to measure conscious experiences. To do so, he developed the method of **introspection,** a systematic examination of mental experiences that requires people to inspect and report on the content of their thoughts. Introspection is a subjective process because it assesses how each individual personally experiences an event. Wundt asked people to use introspection in comparing their subjective experiences as they contemplated a series of objects—for example, by stating which object they found more pleasant.

STRUCTURALISM Edward Titchener, a student of Wundt's, used methods such as introspection to pioneer a school of thought that became known as **structuralism.** This school is based on the idea that conscious experience can be broken down into its basic underlying components, much as the periodic table breaks down chemical elements. Titchener believed that an understanding of the basic elements of conscious experience would provide the scientific basis for understanding the mind. He argued that one could take a stimulus such as a musical tone and, through introspection, analyze its "quality," "intensity," "duration," and "clarity." Wundt ultimately rejected such uses of introspection, but Titchener relied on the method throughout his career.

The general problem with introspection is that experience is subjective. Each person brings a unique perceptual system to introspection, and it is difficult for researchers to determine whether each participant in a study is employing introspection similarly. Additionally, the reporting of the experience changes the experience. Over time, psychologists largely abandoned introspection because it was not a reliable method for understanding psychological processes. Nonetheless, Wundt, Titchener, and other structuralists paved the way for developing a pure science of psychology with its own vocabulary and set of rules.

FUNCTIONALISM One critic of structuralism was William James, a brilliant scholar whose wide-ranging work has had an enormous, enduring impact on psychology (**FIGURE 1.12**). In 1873, James abandoned a career in medicine to teach physiology at Harvard University. He was among the first professors at Harvard to openly welcome questions from students rather than have them listen silently to lectures. James also was an early supporter of women trying to break into the male-dominated sciences. He trained Mary Whiton Calkins, who was the first woman to set up a psychological laboratory and was the first woman president of the American Psychological Association (**FIGURE 1.13**).

James's personal interests were more philosophical than physiological. He was captivated by the nature of conscious experience. In 1875, he gave his first lecture on psychology. He later quipped that it was also the first lecture on psychology he had ever heard. To this day, psychologists find rich delight in reading James's penetrating analysis of the human mind, *Principles of Psychology* (1890). It was the most influential book in the early history of psychology, and many of its central ideas have held up over time.

In criticizing structuralism's failure to capture the most important aspects of mental experience, James argued that the mind is much more complex than its elements and therefore cannot be broken down. For instance, he noted that the mind consists of an ever-changing, continuous series of thoughts. This **stream of consciousness** cannot be frozen in time, according to James, so the structuralists' techniques were sterile and artificial. Psychologists who used the structural approach, he said, were like people trying to understand a house by studying each of its bricks individually. More important to James was that the bricks together form a house and that a house has a particular function (i.e., a place where you can live). The mind's elements matter less than the mind's usefulness to people.

James argued that psychologists ought to examine the functions served by the mind—how the mind operates. According to his approach, which became known as **functionalism,** the mind came into existence over the course of human evolution. It works as it does because it is useful for preserving life and passing along genes to future generations. In other words, it helps humans *adapt* to environmental demands.

EVOLUTION, ADAPTATION, AND BEHAVIOR One of the major influences on functionalism was the work of the naturalist Charles Darwin (**FIGURE 1.14**). In 1859, Darwin published his revolutionary study *On the Origin of Species,* which introduced the world to **evolutionary theory.** By observing the variations in species and in individual members of species, Darwin reasoned that species change over time. Some of these changes—physical characteristics, skills, and abilities—increase individuals' chances of surviving and reproducing. Surviving and reproducing in turn ensure that these changes will be passed along to future generations. Changes passed along in this way are called **adaptations.**

Earlier philosophers and naturalists—including Darwin's grandfather, Erasmus Darwin—had discussed the possibility that species might evolve. But Charles Darwin first presented the mechanism of evolution. He called this mechanism **natural selection:** the process by which changes that are adaptive (i.e., that facilitate survival and reproduction) are passed along and those that are not adaptive (i.e., that hinder survival and reproduction) are not passed along. In other words, species struggle to survive. Those species that are better adapted to their environments will survive and reproduce, their offspring will survive and reproduce, and so on. This idea has come to be known as the *survival of the fittest.* In this sense, the term *fittest* has to do with reproductive success and survival and not merely strength.

Darwin's ideas have profoundly influenced science, philosophy, and society. Rather than being a specific area of scientific inquiry, evolutionary theory is a way of thinking that can be used to understand many aspects of mind and behavior (Buss, 2016).

FIGURE 1.14
Charles Darwin
Introduced in *On the Origin of Species,* Darwin's theory of evolution has had a huge impact on how psychologists think about the mind.

functionalism
An approach to psychology concerned with the adaptive purpose, or function, of mind and behavior.

evolutionary theory
A theory presented by the naturalist Charles Darwin; it views the history of a species in terms of the inherited, adaptive value of physical characteristics, of mental activity, and of behavior.

 Is the theory of natural selection related to structuralism or functionalism?

ANSWER: functionalism, because the theory focuses on the function of adaptive behavior—to increase survival and reproduction.

1.7 Different Schools of Thought Reflected Different Perspectives on Mind, Brain, and Behavior

As the discipline of psychology spread throughout the world and developed into a vital field of science and a vibrant profession, different ways of thinking about the content of psychology emerged. These ways of thinking are called *schools of thought.* As is true in every science, one school of thought would dominate the field for a while. There would be a backlash. Then a new school of thought would take over the field. In addition to structuralism and functionalism, five other major schools of thought have dominated the history of psychology (**TABLE 1.1**).

adaptations
In evolutionary theory, the physical characteristics, skills, or abilities that increase the chances of reproduction or survival and are therefore likely to be passed along to future generations.

natural selection
In evolutionary theory, the idea that those who inherit characteristics that help them adapt to their particular environments have a selective advantage over those who do not.

unconscious
The place where mental processes operate below the level of conscious awareness.

psychoanalysis
A method developed by Sigmund Freud that attempts to bring the contents of the unconscious into conscious awareness so that conflicts can be revealed.

Table 1.1 Major Schools of Thought in the History of Psychology

SCHOOL OF THOUGHT AND INFLUENTIAL SCIENTISTS	GOAL
Structuralism • Wilhelm Wundt • Edward Titchener	Identify basic parts, or structures, of the conscious mind
Functionalism • William James • Charles Darwin	Describe how the conscious mind aids adaptation to an environment
Psychoanalytic theory • Sigmund Freud	Understand how unconscious thoughts cause psychological disorders
Gestalt movement • Max Wertheimer • Wolfgang Köhler	Study subjective perceptions as a unified whole
Behaviorism • John B. Watson • B. F. Skinner	Describe behavior in response to environmental stimuli
Humanistic psychology • Abraham Maslow • Carl Rogers	Investigate how people become happier and more fulfilled; focus on the basic goodness of people
Cognitivism • George Miller • Ulric Neisser	Explore internal mental processes that influence behavior

PSYCHOANALYTIC APPROACH Twentieth-century psychology was profoundly influenced by one of its most famous thinkers, Sigmund Freud (**FIGURE 1.15**). Freud was trained in medicine, and he began his career working with people who appeared to have neurological disorders, such as paralysis of various body parts. He found that some of his patients had few medical reasons for their paralysis. Soon he came to believe their conditions were caused by psychological factors.

Psychology was in its infancy at the end of the nineteenth century, when Freud speculated that much of human behavior is determined by mental processes operating below the level of conscious awareness. This subconscious level is called the **unconscious.** Contrary to popular belief, Freud was not the first person to theorize the existence of an unconscious—Darwin's cousin Sir Francis Galton had earlier proposed the idea. However, Freud built on this basic idea. He believed that unconscious mental forces, often sexual and in conflict, produce psychological discomfort and in some cases even psychological disorders. According to Freudian thinking, many of these unconscious conflicts arise from troubling childhood experiences that the person is blocking from memory.

From his theories, Freud pioneered the clinical case study approach and developed **psychoanalysis.** In this therapeutic method, the therapist and the patient work together to bring the contents of the patient's unconscious into his or her conscious awareness. Once the patient's unconscious conflicts are revealed, the therapist helps the patient deal with them constructively. For example, Freud analyzed the apparent symbolic content in a patient's dreams in search of hidden conflicts. He also used *free*

FIGURE 1.15
Sigmund Freud
Freud was the father of psychoanalytic theory. His work hugely influenced psychology in the twentieth century.

association, in which a patient would talk about whatever he or she wanted to for as long as he or she wanted to. Freud believed that through free association, a person eventually revealed the unconscious conflicts that caused the psychological problems.

Freud's influence was considerable. His work and his image helped shape the public's view of psychology. However, many of his ideas, such as the meaning of dreams, are impossible to test using the methods of science. Contemporary psychologists no longer accept much of Freudian theory, but Galton's original idea that mental processes occur below the level of conscious awareness is now widely accepted.

BEHAVIORISM In 1913, the psychologist John B. Watson challenged, as inherently unscientific, psychology's focus on conscious and unconscious mental processes (**FIGURE 1.16**). Watson believed that if psychology was to be a science, it had to stop trying to study mental events that could not be observed directly. Scorning methods such as introspection and free association, he developed **behaviorism.** This approach emphasizes environmental effects on observable behavior.

The intellectual issue most central to Watson and his followers was the nature/nurture question. For Watson and other behaviorists, nurture was all. Heavily influenced by the work of the physiologist Ivan Pavlov (discussed further in Chapter 6, "Learning"), Watson believed that animals—including humans—acquire, or learn, all behaviors through environmental experience. Therefore, we need to study the environmental *stimuli,* or triggers, in particular situations. By understanding the stimuli, we can predict the animals' behavioral *responses* in those situations. Psychologists greeted Watson's approach with great enthusiasm. Many had grown dissatisfied with the ambiguous methods used by those studying mental processes. They believed that psychologists would not be taken seriously as scientists until they studied observable behaviors.

B. F. Skinner became the most famous and influential behaviorist. Like Watson, Skinner denied any special status for mental states. In his provocative book *Beyond Freedom and Dignity* (1971), Skinner argued that concepts about mental processes were of no scientific value in explaining behavior. He believed that mental states were simply another form of behavior, subject to the same behaviorist principles as publicly observable behavior. He wanted to understand how behaviors, whether occurring "inside the skin" or observable, are shaped or influenced by the events or consequences that follow them. For instance, an animal will learn to perform a behavior if doing so in the past led to a positive outcome, such as receiving food.

Behaviorism dominated psychological research well into the early 1960s. In many ways, these times were extremely productive for psychologists. Many of the basic principles established by behaviorists continue to be viewed as critical to understanding the mind, the brain, and behavior. At the same time, sufficient evidence has accumulated to show that thought processes influence outcomes. Few psychologists today describe themselves as strict behaviorists.

GESTALT MOVEMENT A school of thought that arose in opposition to structuralism was the *Gestalt* school. This way of thinking was founded by Max Wertheimer in 1912 and expanded by Wolfgang Köhler, among others. According to **Gestalt theory,** the whole of personal experience is not simply the sum of its constituent elements. In other words, *the whole is different from the sum of its parts.* So, for example, if a researcher shows people a triangle, they see a triangle—not three lines on a piece of paper, as would be the case for the introspective observations in one of Titchener's structural experiments. (When you look at **FIGURE 1.17,** do you

FIGURE 1.16
John B. Watson
Watson developed and promoted behaviorism. His views were amplified by thousands of psychologists, including B. F. Skinner.

behaviorism
A psychological approach that emphasizes the role of environmental forces in producing observable behavior.

Gestalt theory
A theory based on the idea that the whole of personal experience is different from the sum of its constituent elements.

FIGURE 1.17
What Do You See?
These fragments make up a picture of a dog sniffing the ground. The mind organizes the picture's elements automatically to produce the perception of the dog. The picture is processed and experienced as a unified whole. Once you perceive the dog, you cannot choose to not see it.

FIGURE 1.18
How Many Do You See?
This drawing by the psychologist Roger Shepard can be viewed as either a face behind a candlestick or two separate profiles. The mind organizes the scene into one or another perceptual whole, so the picture looks a specific way each time it is viewed. It is difficult to see both the single face and two profiles at the same time.

FIGURE 1.19
Carl Rogers
Carl Rogers was a founder of humanistic psychology. According to this school of thought, people are motivated to improve themselves and their lives.

humanistic psychology
This approach focuses on the basic goodness of people and how they become happier and more fulfilled.

cognitive neuroscience
The study of the neural mechanisms underlying thought, learning, perception, language, and memory.

see the parts or the whole?) In experimentally investigating subjective experience, the Gestalt psychologists did not rely on the reports of trained observers. They sought out ordinary people's observations.

The Gestalt movement reflected an important idea that was at the heart of criticisms of structuralism—namely, that the perception of objects is subjective and dependent on context. Two people can look at an object and see different things. Indeed, one person can look at an object and see it in completely different ways. (When you look at **FIGURE 1.18,** how many possible views do you see?) The Gestalt perspective has influenced many areas of psychology, including the study of vision and our understanding of human personality.

HUMANISTIC PSYCHOLOGY In the 1950s, most schools of thought viewed behavior as resulting from events outside of people's control. For Freud, behavior was determined by unconscious forces. For behaviorists, environmental factors were key. Rejecting these views, psychologists such as Abraham Maslow and Carl Rogers (**FIGURE 1.19**) focused on how people are free to choose activities that make them happy and bring them fulfillment. This more positive perspective became known as **humanistic psychology.** This approach emphasized the basic goodness of people. It focused on how people should accept themselves, work on personal goals, and try to live up to their full potential as human beings.

Building on these earlier ideas, the positive psychology movement was launched by the psychologist Martin Seligman (Seligman & Csikszentmihalyi, 2000). Seligman and others have encouraged the scientific study of qualities such as faith, values, creativity, courage, and hope. Positive psychology emphasizes the quality of relationships and taking enjoyment from life's accomplishments. You will learn in Chapter 11 that there are many benefits to being positive in your outlook.

COGNITIVISM During the first half of the twentieth century, psychology was largely focused on studying observable behavior. Evidence slowly emerged, however, that learning is not as simple as the behaviorists believed it to be. Perceptions of situations can influence behavior. Learning theorists were showing that animals could learn by observation. This finding made little sense according to behaviorist theory, because the animals were not being rewarded. The connections were all being made in their minds. Other research was being conducted on memory, language, and child development. These studies showed that the simple laws of behaviorism could not explain, for example, why culture influences how people remember a story, why grammar develops systematically, and why children interpret the world in different ways during different stages of development. All of these findings suggested that mental functions are important for understanding behavior—they demonstrated the limitations of a purely behavioral approach to psychology.

The psychologist George A. Miller began his career with a behavioristic bias. Shortly before 1957, he looked at the data concerning behavior and cognition. As a good scientist who used critical thinking, Miller changed his mind when the data did not support his theories. He and his colleagues launched the *cognitive revolution* in psychology (**FIGURE 1.20**). Ten years later, Ulric Neisser integrated a wide range of cognitive phenomena in his book *Cognitive Psychology.* This 1967 classic named and defined the field and fully embraced the mind, which Skinner had dismissed as the irrelevant "black box."

The rise of computers and artificial intelligence influenced many cognitive psychologists, who focused exclusively on the "software" and ignored the "hardware." That is, they studied the thought processes but had little interest in the specific brain mechanisms involved. However, some early cognitive psychologists recognized that the brain is important for cognition. In the early 1980s, cognitive psychologists joined forces with neuroscientists, computer scientists, and philosophers to develop an integrated view of mind and brain. During the next decade, **cognitive neuroscience** emerged. Researchers in this field study the neural mechanisms (mechanisms involving the brain, nerves, and nerve cells) that underlie thought, learning, perception, language, and memory. During the last decade, this approach has been used to study how people think about others, an approach known as *social neuroscience*.

 Which school of thought emphasized the freedom to choose activities that bring personal fulfillment?

ANSWER: humanism

What Are the Latest Developments in Psychology?

In the just over 135 years since psychology was founded, researchers have made significant progress in understanding mind, brain, and behavior. This understanding has progressed incrementally. New knowledge accumulates through the systematic study of questions generated by what is already known. During various periods in the history of the field, psychologists became especially excited about new approaches, such as when the behaviorists began studying observable phenomena, rejecting introspection and the search for unconscious processes. We do not know what approaches the future of psychology will bring, but this section outlines some of the developments that contemporary psychologists are most excited about.

1.8 Biology Is Increasingly Emphasized in Explaining Psychological Phenomena

The last four decades have seen remarkable growth in our understanding of the biological bases of mental activities (**FIGURE 1.21**). This section outlines three major advances that have helped further the scientific understanding of psychological phenomena: progress in understanding brain chemistry, developments in neuroscience, and advances in decoding the human genome.

BRAIN CHEMISTRY Tremendous progress has been made in understanding brain chemistry. It was long believed that only a handful of chemicals were involved in brain function, but in fact hundreds of substances play critical roles in mental activity and behavior. Why, for instance, do we have more-accurate memories for events that happened when we were aroused than for events that happened when we were calm? Brain chemistry is different when we are aroused than when we are calm, and those same chemicals influence the neural mechanisms involved in memory.

BRAIN IMAGING Since the late 1980s, researchers have been able to study the working brain as it performs its vital psychological functions. They are able to do so because of brain imaging methods, such as functional magnetic resonance imaging

FIGURE 1.20
George A. Miller
In 1957, Miller launched the cognitive revolution by establishing the Center for Cognitive Science at Harvard University.

Learning Objectives

- Identify recent developments in psychological science.

- Distinguish between subfields of psychology.

FIGURE 1.21
Biological Bases
How much are psychological phenomena, such as sensitivity to pain, influenced or even determined by our biology?

(fMRI). The progress in understanding the neural basis of mental life has been rapid and dramatic. Knowing where in the brain something happens does not by itself reveal much. However, when consistent patterns of brain activation are associated with specific mental tasks, the activation appears to be connected with the tasks. For over a century, scientists had disagreed about whether psychological processes are located in specific parts of the brain or are distributed throughout the brain. Research has made clear that there is some *localization* of function. That is, some areas are important for specific feelings, thoughts, and actions.

However, many brain regions have to work together to produce behavior and mental activity. One of the greatest contemporary scientific challenges is mapping out how various brain regions are connected and how they work together to produce mental activity. To achieve this mapping, the *Human Connectome Project* was launched in 2010 as a major international research effort involving collaborators at a number of universities. A greater understanding of brain connectivity may be especially useful for understanding how brain circuitry changes in psychological disorders.

Neuroscience approaches, such as fMRI, were originally used to study basic psychological processes, such as how people see or remember information. Today, such techniques are used to understand a wide range of phenomena, from how emotions change during adolescence (Silvers et al., 2016), to how people process information regarding social groups (Freeman & Johnson, 2016), to how thinking patterns contribute to depression (Hamilton et al., 2015).

THE HUMAN GENOME Scientists have made enormous progress in understanding the *human genome:* the basic *genetic code,* or blueprint, for the human body. For psychologists, this map represents the foundational knowledge for studying how specific genes—the basic units of hereditary transmission—affect thoughts, actions, feelings, and disorders. By identifying the genes involved in memory, for example, researchers soon may be able to develop treatments, based on genetic manipulation, that will assist people who have memory problems. Decades from now, at least some genetic defects might be corrected.

Meanwhile, the scientific study of genetic influences has made clear that very few single genes cause specific behaviors. Almost all biological and psychological activity is affected by the actions of multiple genes. Nonetheless, many physical and mental characteristics are inherited to some degree. In addition, scientists are beginning to understand the relationship between situations, genes, and behaviors. For example, the presence or absence of specific environmental factors can influence how genes are expressed. Gene expression, in turn, affects behavior.

What does brain imaging help psychologists study?

ANSWER: mental activity

1.9 Evolutionary Thinking Is Increasingly Influential

As William James and his fellow functionalists knew, the human mind has been shaped by evolution. Modern evolutionary theory has driven the field of biology for years, but it has only recently begun to inform psychology. From this perspective, the brain, its activity, and resulting behaviors have evolved over millions of years. The evolutionary changes in the brain have occurred in response to our ancestors' problems related to survival and reproduction. So some of our behaviors have their basis in the behaviors of our earliest ancestors, perhaps going back to the ancestor we share with nonhuman primates. Other human behaviors are unique to our species. Many human behaviors are universal, meaning that they are shared across cultures.

The field of evolutionary psychology attempts to explain mental traits as products of natural selection. In other words, functions such as memory, perception, and language are seen as adaptations. In addition, evidence is accumulating that the mind, the experience of the brain, also adapts. That is, while the brain adapts biologically, some of the contents of the mind adapt to cultural influences. In this way, the mind helps individuals overcome their particular challenges, but it also provides a strong framework for shared social understandings of how the world works. Some of those understandings, of course, vary from place to place and from culture to culture. For instance, all people prefer particular types of food, but the preferences are influenced by culture. Likewise, all cultures have inequalities in terms of individual members' prestige, but what is considered prestigious varies among cultures.

BEFORE THE WHEEL

Kanin

SOLVING ADAPTIVE PROBLEMS Evolutionary theory is especially useful for considering whether behaviors and physical mechanisms are adaptive—in other words, whether they affect survival and reproduction. Through evolution, specialized mechanisms and adaptive behaviors have been built into our bodies and brains. For instance, a mechanism that produces calluses has evolved, protecting the skin from the abuses of physical labor. Likewise, specialized circuits have evolved in the brain; these structures solve adaptive problems, such as dealing with other people (Cosmides & Tooby, 1997). For example, people who lie, cheat, or steal may drain group resources and thereby decrease the chances of survival and reproduction for other group members. Some evolutionary psychologists believe humans have "cheater detectors" on the lookout for this sort of behavior in others (Cosmides & Tooby, 2000).

OUR EVOLUTIONARY HERITAGE Knowledge of the challenges our early ancestors faced helps us understand our current behavior. Humans began evolving about 5 million years ago, but modern humans (*Homo sapiens*) can be traced back only about 100,000 years, to the Pleistocene era. If the human brain slowly adapted to accommodate the needs of Pleistocene hunter-gatherers, scientists should try to understand how the brain works within the context of the environmental pressures humans faced during the Pleistocene era (**FIGURE 1.22**).

For instance, today many people struggle to resist eating junk foods, which tend to contain lots of sugar, fat, and calories. In prehistoric times, such foods were rare, and eating them had great survival value. In other words, a preference for sweet, fatty foods was adaptive. Today, many societies have an abundance of foods, many of them high in sugar and fat. We still enjoy them and eat them, sometimes to excess, and this behavior may now be maladaptive. That is, eating foods high in sugar and fat can make us obese when we expend less energy than we consume. Nonetheless, our evolutionary heritage encourages us to eat foods that had survival value when food was relatively scarce. Many of our current behaviors, of course, do not reflect our evolutionary heritage. Driving cars, sitting at a desk all day, using computers, texting, and exercising to intentionally offset calorie intake are among the human behaviors that we have displayed only recently. (Further complexities in the evolutionary process are discussed in Chapter 3, "Biology and Behavior.")

FIGURE 1.22
Evolution in the Present
To understand who we are as individuals, we need to understand who we are as a species.

Q How does evolution lead to structural changes in the brain?

ANSWER: Over time, the brain changes in response to adaptive problems affecting survival and reproduction.

1.10 Culture Provides Adaptive Solutions

For humans, many of the most demanding adaptive challenges involve dealing with other humans. These challenges include selecting mates, cooperating in hunting and in gathering, forming alliances, competing for scarce resources, and even warring with neighboring groups. This dependency on group living is not unique to humans, but the nature of interactions among and between ingroup and outgroup members is especially complex in human societies. The complexity of living in groups gives rise to culture, and culture's various aspects are transmitted from one generation to the next through learning. For instance, musical preferences, some food preferences, subtle ways of expressing emotion, and tolerance of body odors are affected by the culture one is raised in. Many of a culture's "rules" reflect adaptive solutions worked out by previous generations.

Human cultural evolution has occurred much faster than human biological evolution. The most dramatic cultural changes have come in the last few thousand years. Although humans have changed only modestly in physical terms in that time, they have changed profoundly in regard to how they live together. Even within the last century, dramatic changes have occurred in how human societies interact. The flow of people, commodities, and financial instruments among all regions of the world, often referred to as *globalization,* has increased in velocity and scale over the past century in ways that were previously unimaginable. Even more recently, the Internet has created a worldwide network of humans, essentially a new form of culture with its own rules, values, and customs.

Over the past two decades, recognition has grown that culture plays a foundational role in shaping how people view and reason about the world around them—and that people from different cultures possess strikingly different minds (Heine, 2015). For example, the social psychologist Richard Nisbett and his colleagues (2001) have demonstrated that people from most European and North American countries are much more analytical than people from most Asian countries. Westerners break complex ideas into simpler components, categorize information, and use logic and rules to explain behavior. Easterners tend to be more holistic in their thinking, seeing everything in front of them as an inherently complicated whole, with all elements affecting all other elements (**FIGURE 1.23**).

The culture in which people live shapes many aspects of their daily lives. Pause for a moment and think about the following questions: How do people decide what is most important in their lives? How do people relate to family members? to friends? to colleagues at work? How should people spend their leisure time? How do they define themselves in relationship to their own culture—or across cultures? For instance, the increased participation of women in the workforce has changed the nature of contemporary Western culture in numerous ways, from a fundamental change in how women are viewed to more-practical changes, such as people marrying and having children later in life, a greater number of children in day care, and a greater reliance on convenient, fast foods.

Culture shapes beliefs and values, such as the extent to which people should emphasize their own interests versus the interests of the group. This effect is more apparent when we compare phenomena across cultures. Cultural rules are learned as *norms,* which specify how people ought to behave in different contexts. For example, norms tell us not to laugh uproariously at funerals and to keep quiet in libraries. Culture also has material aspects, such as media, technology, health care, and transportation. Many people find it hard to imagine life without computers, televisions, cell phones, and cars. We also recognize that each of these inventions has

(a)

(b)

FIGURE 1.23
Cultural Differences
(a) Westerners tend to be "independent" and autonomous, stressing their individuality.
(b) Easterners—such as this Cambodian family—tend to be more "interdependent," stressing their sense of being part of a collective.

changed the fundamental ways in which people interact. Psychologists have played a significant role in our understanding of the complex relationship between culture and behavior.

Q | What are cultural norms?

1.11 Psychological Science Now Crosses Levels of Analysis

Throughout the history of psychology, studying a phenomenon at one level of analysis has been the favored approach. Researchers have recently started to explain behavior at several levels of analysis. By crossing levels in this way, psychologists are able to provide a more complete picture of mental and behavioral processes.

Four broadly defined levels of analysis reflect the most common research methods for studying mind and behavior (**FIGURE 1.24**). The *biological level of analysis* deals with how the physical body contributes to mind and behavior (as through the chemical and genetic processes that occur in the body). The *individual level of analysis* focuses on individual differences in personality and in the mental processes that affect how people perceive and know the world. The *social level of analysis* involves how group contexts affect the ways in which people interact and influence each other. The *cultural level of analysis* explores how people's thoughts, feelings, and actions are similar or different across cultures. Differences between cultures highlight the role that cultural experiences play in shaping psychological processes, whereas similarities between cultures reveal evidence for universal phenomena that emerge regardless of cultural experiences.

To understand how research is conducted at the different levels, consider the many ways psychologists have studied listening to music (Hallam, Cross, & Thaut,

	LEVEL	FOCUS	WHAT IS STUDIED?
	Biological	Brain systems Neurochemistry Genetics	Neuroanatomy, animal research, brain imaging Neurotransmitters and hormones, animal studies, drug studies Gene mechanisms, heritability, twin and adoption studies
	Individual	Individual differences Perception and cognition Behavior	Personality, gender, developmental age groups, self-concept Thinking, decision making, language, memory, seeing, hearing Observable actions, responses, physical movements
	Social	Interpersonal behavior Social cognition	Groups, relationships, persuasion, influence, workplace Attitudes, stereotypes, perceptions
	Cultural	Thoughts, actions, behaviors—in different societies and cultural groups	Norms, beliefs, values, symbols, ethnicity

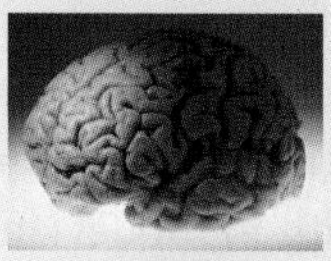

FIGURE 1.24
Levels of Analysis

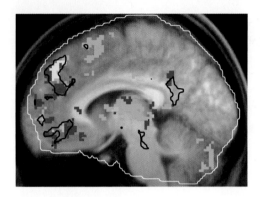

FIGURE 1.25
Your Brain on Music

The researcher Petr Janata played familiar and unfamiliar music to study participants. As shown here, many regions of the brain were activated by the music. Activity in green indicates familiarity with the music, activity in blue indicates emotional reactions to the music, and activity in red indicates memories from the past. The yellow section in the frontal lobe links together familiar music, emotions, and memories. This area is active, for example, if you have a fond memory of dancing to a particular song in junior high school.

2016). Why do you like some kinds of music and not others? Do you prefer some types of music when you are in a good mood and other types when you are in a bad mood? If you listen to music while you study, how does it affect how you learn? Music has many important effects on the mind, brain, and behavior, and psychologists examine these effects using the methods of science. They examine how musical preferences vary among individuals and across cultures, how music affects emotional states and thought processes, and even how the brain perceives sound as music rather than noise.

At the biological level of analysis, for instance, researchers have studied the effects of musical training. They have shown that training can change not only how the brain functions but also its anatomy, such as in changing brain structures associated with learning and memory (Herdener et al., 2010). Listening to pleasant music appears to increase the activation of brain regions associated with positive experiences (Koelsch, Offermanns, & Franzke, 2010). In other words, music does not affect the brain exactly the way other types of sounds, such as the spoken word, do. Instead, music recruits brain regions involved in a number of mental processes, such as those involved in mood and memory (Levitin & Menon, 2003; Peretz & Zatorre, 2005). Music appears to be treated by the brain as a special category of auditory information. For this reason, patients with certain types of brain injury become unable to perceive tones and melody but can understand speech and environmental sounds perfectly well.

In studies conducted at the individual level of analysis, researchers have used laboratory experiments to study music's effects on mood, memory, decision making, and various other mental states and processes (Levitin, 2006). In one study, music from participants' childhoods evoked specific memories from that period (Janata, 2009; **FIGURE 1.25**). Moreover, music affects emotions and thoughts. Listening to sad background music leads young children to interpret a story negatively, whereas listening to happy background music leads them to interpret the story much more positively (Ziv & Goshen, 2006). Our cognitive expectations also shape how we experience music (Collins, Tillmann, Barrett, Delbé, & Janata, 2014).

A study of music at the social level of analysis might compare the types of music people prefer when they are in groups with the types they prefer when alone. Psychologists have also sought to answer the question of whether certain types of music promote negative behaviors among listeners. For instance, researchers in Quebec found that certain types of rap music, but not hip-hop, were associated with more deviant behaviors, such as violence and drug use (Miranda & Claes, 2004). Of course, such associations do not mean that listening to music causes the behaviors studied. It could just as easily be that people practice the behaviors first and then develop these musical preferences. Listening to music with prosocial lyrics, however, led research participants to be more empathic and increased their helping behavior (Greitemeyer, 2009).

The cross-cultural study of music preferences has developed into a separate field, *ethnomusicology*. One finding from this field is that African music has rhythmic structures different from those in Western music (Agawu, 1995), and these differences in turn may reflect the important role of dancing and drumming in African culture. Because cultures prefer different types of music, some psychologists have noted that attitudes about outgroup members can color perceptions of their musical styles. For example, researchers from the United States and the United Kingdom found that the societal attitudes toward rap and hip-hop music revealed subtle prejudicial attitudes against blacks and a greater willingness to discriminate against them (Reyna, Brandt, & Viki, 2009).

As these examples show, research at different levels of analysis is creating a greater understanding of the psychology of music. Adding to that understanding is innovative research combining two or more levels of analysis. More and more, psychological science emphasizes examining behavior across multiple levels in an integrated fashion. Often psychologists collaborate with researchers from other scientific fields, such as biology, computer science, physics, anthropology, and sociology. Such collaborations are called *interdisciplinary*. For example, psychologists interested in understanding the hormonal basis of obesity might work with geneticists exploring the heritability of obesity as well as with social psychologists studying human beliefs about eating. Crossing the levels of analysis usually provides more insights than working within only one level. The Gestalt psychologists were right in asserting that the whole is different from the sum of its parts. Throughout this book, you will see how this multilevel approach has led to breakthroughs in understanding psychological activity.

 Suppose a research study explores people's memory for song lyrics. At what level of analysis are the researchers working?

1.12 Subfields in Psychology Focus on Different Levels of Analysis

Psychologists work in many different settings (**FIGURE 1.26**). The setting often depends on whether the psychologist's primary focus is on research, teaching, or applying scientific findings to improving the quality of daily living. Researchers who study the brain, the mind, and behavior may work in schools, businesses, universities, or clinics. There are also psychological practitioners, who apply the findings of psychological science to do things such as help people in need of psychological treatment, design safe and pleasant work environments, counsel people on career paths, or help teachers design better classroom curricula. The distinction between science and practice can be fuzzy, since many researchers are also practitioners. For example, many clinical psychologists both study people with psychological disorders and treat those people.

A scientist will choose to study at a particular level of analysis—or more than one level—based on his or her research interests, general theoretical approaches, and training. Because the subject matter of psychology is vast, most psychologists focus within relatively large subfields. Many of the subfields are represented by specific chapters of this book. **TABLE 1.2** lists some of the most popular subfields.

Psychologists also pursue many more specialties and research areas. For instance, *forensic psychologists* work in legal settings, perhaps helping choose juries or identifying dangerous offenders. *Sports psychologists* work with athletes to improve their performance, perhaps teaching athletes how to control their thoughts during pressure situations. Many psychologists follow an interdisciplinary approach that crosses these categories, such as those who use the methods of neuroscience to study topics traditionally examined by social psychologists. Another interdisciplinary approach is used by *health psychologists,* who study the factors that promote or interfere with physical health, such as how stress may cause disease.

A number of careers in psychology are predicted to grow substantially over the next decade. The growth areas include providing advice for programs that aim to tackle societal problems (e.g., the Bill

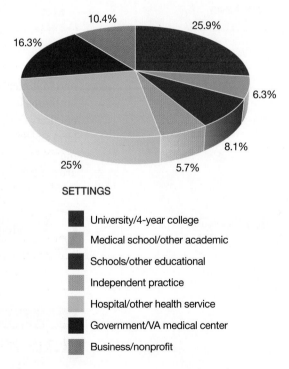

FIGURE 1.26
Employment Settings for Psychologists
This chart shows the type of settings where psychologists work, based on a survey of those obtaining their doctorates in psychology in 2009 (Michalski, Kohut, Wicherski, & Hart, 2011).

Table 1.2 Research-Related Subfields in Psychology

SUBFIELD	RESEARCH INTERESTS	SAMPLE RESEARCH QUESTIONS
Biological psychology	Study how biological systems give rise to mental activity.	• How do brain chemicals influence sexual behavior? • How do brain cells change during learning?
Cognitive psychology/ Neuroscience	Study attention, perception, memory, problem solving, and language, often based on brain processes.	• What makes some problems harder to solve than others? • How do cell phones distract people when they drive?
Developmental psychology	Study how people change from infancy through old age.	• How do children learn to speak? • How can older adults maintain mental abilities as they age?
Personality psychology	Study enduring characteristics that people display over time and across circumstances.	• Why are some people shy? • How do genes, circumstances, and culture shape personality?
Social psychology	Study how people are affected by others.	• When do people form impressions of others? • How do people form or dissolve intimate relationships?
Cultural psychology	Study how people are influenced by the societal rules that dictate behavior in their cultures.	• How does culture shape the sense of self? • Does culture create differences in perception?
Clinical psychology	Study the factors that cause psychological disorders and the best methods to treat them.	• What factors lead people to feel depressed? • How does the brain change as a result of therapy for depression?
Industrial/ organizational psychology	Study issues pertaining to industry and the workplace.	• How can building morale help motivate workers? • How can equipment be designed so workers can easily perform duties and avoid accidents?

and Melinda Gates Foundation); working with older adults, since they will make up an increasing proportion of the population; working with soldiers returning from conflicts in various parts of the world; working with the U.S. Department of Homeland Security to study terrorism; consulting with industry; and advising on legal matters based on courtroom expertise (DeAngelis, 2008). Because psychologists are concerned with nearly every aspect of human life, what they study is remarkably diverse, as you will soon discover in the following chapters.

 What do psychological practitioners do?

ANSWER: apply the findings of psychological science to help improve lives

USING PSYCHOLOGY IN YOUR LIFE

1.13 Will Psychology Benefit You in Your Career?

Some students take introductory psychology courses because of a long-standing interest in people and the desire to learn more about what makes people, including themselves, tick. Others enroll because they wish to fulfill a general education requirement or because the class is a prerequisite for another course they are eager to take.

Whatever *your* reason for being in this class, the things you will learn in this book will be highly relevant to multiple aspects of *your* life, including your chosen career.

Many careers involve interacting with coworkers, customers, clients, or patients (**FIGURE 1.27**). In these cases, understanding what motivates people, how to influence them, and how to support them is essential. For instance, a medical practitioner with interpersonal skills will create rapport with patients. That rapport may prompt the patients to be honest about their health behaviors, and the resulting disclosures may improve the practitioner's ability to accurately diagnose the patients' medical conditions. A rehabilitation nurse who understands the psychological challenges of complying with medical advice is better equipped to help patients respond to those challenges and thus improve. As noted in the chapter opener, given the many ways psychology is relevant to the medical field, it is not surprising that the Medical College Admission Test (MCAT), the standardized test required for admission to medical school, now includes an extensive 95-minute section on the psychological, social, and biological foundations of behavior.

Of course, many people use psychology every day. Teachers manage their students' behavior and foster their students' motivation to learn. Police officers gather eyewitness reports, elicit confessions, and control the behavior of both individuals and crowds. People in sales, marketing, and branding craft messages, create campaigns, and help manufacturers increase the appeal of their products. Anyone who works on a team benefits from knowing how to play nice, to engage in effective problem solving, and to focus on the task at hand.

Other workers shape information or technology that will be used by consumers or the public. For the information or technology to be accessible and effective, these workers need to understand how people make sense of information and the psychological barriers to modifying existing beliefs or adopting new technologies. For example, an engineer who designs cockpits for airplanes benefits from knowing how human attention shifts during an emergency. A statistician who understands how people process visual cues is well equipped to create graphs that will help consumers make accurate impressions of the data.

What about someone who works with animals? A solid grasp of psychological topics, such as the biological basis of behavior, can help in the training and retraining of nonhuman creatures. For example, an animal trainer could use behavior modification techniques (discussed in Chapter 6) to motivate an injured animal to engage in physical therapy.

Psychology is even relevant to traditionally solo enterprises. Fiction writers create compelling characters, convey personalities, indicate psychological depth, depict relatable struggles, and evoke emotions in readers.

In fact, is there a single career in which an understanding of psychology would not be at least a little bit helpful? Whatever your chosen field, understanding psychology will help you understand yourself and thus help you do your job. And if you are thinking about a career in psychology or a related field, there is good news. According to the U.S. Department of Labor (U.S. Bureau of Labor Statistics, 2015), opportunities for people with graduate degrees in psychology are expected to grow approximately 19 percent by 2024. This outlook is equally positive around the globe. ■

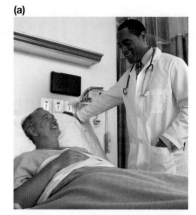
(a)

(b)

(c)

FIGURE 1.27

Studying Psychology Develops Interpersonal Skills

Dealing with other people is an important part of most careers. **(a)** Medical professionals need to gauge people's moods and their motivations to recover. **(b)** Teachers need to understand people's behavior and how people learn. **(c)** To convince people to buy products, salespeople need to understand the relationship between motivation and emotion.

Q Why might it be useful for a detective to study psychology?

ANSWER: Understanding people's motives for crime and knowing the limits of human memory are two of many possible reasons that psychology would be useful to a detective.

Your Chapter Review

Chapter Summary

What Is Psychological Science?

1.1 Psychological Science Is the Study of Mind, Brain, and Behavior

Mind refers to mental activity, which results from biological processes within the brain. *Behavior* describes the totality of observable human (or animal) actions. The term *psychologist* is used broadly to describe someone whose career involves understanding mental life or predicting behavior.

1.2 Psychological Science Teaches Critical Thinking

The use of critical thinking skills improves how people think. Amiable skepticism, an important element of science, requires a careful examination of how well evidence supports a conclusion. Using critical thinking skills and understanding the methods of psychological science are important for evaluating research reported in the popular media.

1.3 Psychological Science Helps Us Understand Biased or Inaccurate Thinking

People engage in common errors in thinking. These errors probably evolved along with the ability to quickly categorize information and make quick decisions. However, the errors often result in faulty conclusions. Some common errors in thinking include ignoring evidence (confirmation bias), seeing relationships that do not exist, accepting after-the-fact explanations, and taking mental shortcuts.

1.4 Think like a Psychologist: Why Are People Unaware of Their Weaknesses?

People often fail to see their own inadequacies. To tell the difference between good and bad performance, people need the expertise to recognize the differences between them. A lack of skill not only prevents people from producing good results, it also prevents those people from knowing what good results are.

What Are the Scientific Foundations of Psychology?

1.5 Many Psychological Questions Have a Long History

The nature/nurture debate contrasted whether psychological characteristics are biologically innate or are acquired through education, experience, and culture. Nature and nurture depend on each other. Their influences often cannot be separated. The mind/body problem was about whether the mind and body are separate and distinct or the mind is simply the subjective experience of ongoing brain activity. Dualist notions about the separation of the brain and mind have been replaced with the idea that the (physical) brain enables the mind.

1.6 Experimental Psychology Initially Focused on the Structure, Not the Function, of Mental Activity

Psychology started as a formal discipline in 1879, in Wilhelm Wundt's laboratory in Germany. Using the technique of introspection, scientists attempted to understand conscious experience. Structuralists used introspection to identify the basic underlying components of conscious experience. According to functionalists, however, the mind is best understood by examining its functions and purpose, not its structure.

1.7 Different Schools of Thought Reflected Different Perspectives on Mind, Brain, and Behavior

Freud advanced the psychoanalytic approach that unconscious processes are not readily available to awareness but nevertheless influence behavior. This understanding had an enormous impact on psychology. Gestalt psychologists asserted that the whole experience (the gestalt) is different from the sum of its parts. Discoveries that behavior is changed by its consequences caused behaviorism to dominate psychology until the 1960s. Humanism focused on how people are free to choose activities that make them happy and bring them fulfillment. Cognitivism and the computer analogy of the brain led to an emphasis on mental activity.

What Are the Latest Developments in Psychology?

1.8 Biology Is Increasingly Emphasized in Explaining Psychological Phenomena

Tremendous advances in neuroscience have revealed the working brain. Mapping of the human genome has furthered the role of genetics in analyzing behavior and disease. These advances are increasing our knowledge of mind, brain, and behavior.

1.9 Evolutionary Thinking Is Increasingly Influential

Evolution of the brain helped human ancestors solve problems related to survival and reproduction and helped them adapt to their environments. Many modern behaviors reflect adaptations to environmental pressures faced by our ancestors.

1.10 Culture Provides Adaptive Solutions

Cultural norms specify how people should behave in different contexts. They reflect solutions to adaptive problems that have been worked out by a group of individuals, and they are transmitted through learning.

1.11 Psychological Science Now Crosses Levels of Analysis

Psychologists examine behavior from various analytical levels: biological (brain systems, neurochemistry, genetics), individual (personality, perception, cognition), social (interpersonal behavior), and cultural (within a single culture, across several cultures).

1.12 Subfields in Psychology Focus on Different Levels of Analysis

Psychology is characterized by numerous subfields. Within each subfield, psychologists may focus on one or more levels of analysis. Psychologists work in many different settings.

1.13 Using Psychology in Your Life: Will Psychology Benefit You in Your Career?

The study of psychological science is highly relevant to multiple aspects of life, including a chosen career. There are growing opportunities for those with degrees in psychology.

Key Terms

adaptations, p. 13
behaviorism, p. 15
cognitive neuroscience, p. 17
critical thinking, p. 5
culture, p. 10
evolutionary theory, p. 13

functionalism, p. 13
Gestalt theory, p. 15
humanistic psychology, p. 16
introspection, p. 12
mind/body problem, p. 10
natural selection, p. 13

nature/nurture debate, p. 10
psychoanalysis, p. 14
psychological science, p. 4
stream of consciousness, p. 12
structuralism, p. 12
unconscious, p. 14

Putting Psychology to Work

How Employable Are Psychology Majors?

Suppose that after reading this chapter, you decide to become a psychology major. As you discuss your plans with your parents, however, they note their concern. Perhaps they worry because they believe that psychology majors have difficulty finding work after graduation, or they believe that you will need to pursue an advanced degree in order to be employable. They may also remind you of a family friend who was a psychology major and is currently unemployed. This perception about the employability of psychology majors was clearly voiced by presidential candidate Jeb Bush in a 2015 town hall meeting. After noting that  "the No. 1 degree program in the country is psychology," Bush went on to state, "I just don't think people are getting jobs as psych majors." Before you forgo your plans, however, you might decide to apply the "amiable skepticism" discussed earlier in this chapter: Are these claims true? Are the beliefs supported by evidence, or are they simply the result of preconceived ideas, confirmation bias, or other mental shortcuts?

The good news is that a careful examination of the data reveals that worries about employability are not well supported. Although 25 percent of undergraduate psychology majors go on to pursue graduate degrees, the majority of graduating psychology majors go directly to the workforce, with a projected median starting salary in 2016 of $45,000 (National Association of Colleges and Employers, 2016). According to 2014 data by the U.S. Census Bureau, baccalaureate-level majors are employed in a wide variety of settings and fields. The largest concentrations are in social services, management, education, and health care. Other fields include computer technology, statistics, finance, arts and entertainment, and sales.

If the job prospects are good, why might people mistakenly believe otherwise? Biased reasoning may be partially at fault. For example, few of the positions taken by recent graduates have "psychologist" in the title. This selective sampling of information may then result in the faulty conclusion that jobs either are not available or require advanced degrees. Similarly, news reports of Jeb Bush's comments, or of similar comments, may lead to overestimates by the public of the unemployment rate of psychology majors. Selective recall of the one family friend who is both a recent psychology major and unemployed may lead people to see relationships that don't exist.

The bottom line: While you may not always get a job labeled "psychologist," the skills you will develop as a psychology major are valued by employers. In subsequent chapters, we will highlight how specific psychological concepts are used in real-life work settings.

Want to earn a better grade on your test?
Go to **INQUIZITIVE** to learn and review this chapter's content, with personalized feedback along the way. Practice Tests and accompanying answer keys can be found at the back of the book on page PT-1.

2

Research Methodology

Big Questions

- How Is the Scientific Method Used in Psychological Research? 30

- What Types of Studies Are Used in Psychological Research? 38

- What Are the Ethics Governing Psychological Research? 51

- How Are Data Analyzed and Evaluated? 55

IN JANUARY 2010, 17-YEAR-OLD KELSEY RAFFAELE (**FIGURE 2.1**) was driving after school and decided to pass a slower vehicle in front of her. When she saw an oncoming vehicle in the passing lane, she misjudged the distance and crashed, fatally. Kelsey was talking to a friend on her cell phone while driving. Her last words were "Oh [no], I'm going to crash." The risky use of cell phones is common. Studies have found that 80 percent to 90 percent of college students admit talking or texting while driving on at least one occasion (Harrison, 2011). Many of these drivers think they will be safe doing so. Are they?

FIGURE 2.1
Phoning While Driving
Phoning while driving is extremely unsafe. Kelsey Raffaele lost her life because she engaged in this dangerous behavior.

How can we confirm (and convince people) that texting or using a smartphone in some other way while driving is dangerous? Indeed, how can we confirm (and convince people of) any claim that is made? This chapter will describe how evidence is gathered and verified in psychology. In this way, you will come to understand how psychologists study behavior and mental processes. By understanding these processes, you will learn how to interpret information that is being presented to you. And by understanding how to interpret information, you will become an educated consumer and presenter of information. In this chapter, the big questions about research methodology are: How is the scientific method used in psychological research? What types of studies are used in psychological research? What are the ethics governing psychological research? And how are data analyzed and evaluated?

How Is the Scientific Method Used in Psychological Research?

Psychology is a science. Because they are scientists, psychologists gain accurate knowledge about behavior and mental processes only by observing the world and measuring aspects of it. This approach is called *empiricism*. To be confident about the conclusions drawn from their observations, psychologists conduct empirical research. Such an approach requires carefully planned, systematic steps. Using the methods of science allows psychologists to be confident that empirical results provide a true understanding of mental activity and behavior.

2.1 Science Has Four Primary Goals

There are four primary goals of science: *description, prediction, control,* and *explanation.* Thus, the goals of psychological science are to describe *what* a phenomenon is, predict *when* it will occur, control *what causes* it to occur, and explain *why* it occurs. For example, consider the observation that texting interferes with driving. To understand how this interference happens, we need to address each of the four goals.

We begin by asking: How many people really text while driving? Answering this question can help us describe the phenomenon of texting while driving—as in noting how prevalent this unsafe behavior is. Now, under what circumstances are people likely to text while driving? Answering this question can help us predict when texting while driving may occur—as in which people tend to engage in the behavior.

Next, how can we know that texting is the source of the problematic driving? Answering this question can help us be sure that it is texting and not some other factor that is responsible for the observed effects. Ultimately, knowing the answers to each of these questions leads to the question of why texting interferes with driving. Is it because people use their hands to text, or that they take their eyes off the road, or that it interferes with their mental ability to focus on driving?

Careful scientific study also enables us to understand other aspects of texting and driving, such as why people do it in the first place. Understanding how texting interferes with driving skills and why people continue to text while driving, even when they know it is dangerous, will enable scientists, technology developers, and policymakers to develop strategies to reduce the behavior.

SCIENTIFIC METHOD Scientific evidence obtained through empirical research is considered the best possible evidence for supporting a claim. **Research** involves the careful collection, analysis, and interpretation of **data,** which are a collection of measurements gathered during the research process. In conducting research, scientists follow a systematic procedure called the **scientific method.** This procedure begins with the observation of a phenomenon and the question of why that phenomenon occurred.

research
A scientific process that involves the careful collection, analysis, and interpretation of data.

data
A collection of measurements gathered during the research process.

scientific method
A systematic and dynamic procedure of observing and measuring phenomena, used to achieve the goals of description, prediction, control, and explanation; it involves an interaction between research, theories, and hypotheses.

THE ROLE OF THEORY The scientific method is an interaction among research, theories, and hypotheses (**FIGURE 2.2**). A **theory** is an explanation or model of how a phenomenon works. Consisting of interconnected ideas or concepts, a theory is used to explain prior observations and to make predictions about future events. A **hypothesis** is a specific, testable prediction, narrower than the theory it is based on.

How can we know whether a theory is good? The best theories are those that produce a wide variety of testable hypotheses. An especially important feature of good theories is that they should be *falsifiable*. That is, it should be possible to test hypotheses that show the theory is wrong.

Moreover, a good theory is supported by the data. For instance, if our theory is that safe driving requires paying attention, then studies should show this. The more studies that show this, the better the support for the theory.

A classic example of a theory that is not falsifiable comes from Sigmund Freud. In his treatise *The Interpretation of Dreams* (1900), Freud outlined the theory that all dreams represent the fulfillment of an unconscious wish. From a scientific perspective, Freud's theory was not good, because it generated few testable hypotheses regarding the actual function of dreams. Since the theory lacked testable hypotheses, researchers were left with no way to evaluate whether the wish fulfillment theory was either reasonable or accurate. After all, unconscious wishes are, by definition, not known to anyone, including the person having the dreams. As a result, not only is there no way to prove that dreams do represent unconscious wishes, but there is no way to prove that dreams do not represent unconscious wishes. Thus, the theory is frequently criticized for not being falsifiable.

By contrast, the developmental psychologist Jean Piaget (1924) proposed a theory of infant and child development (see Chapter 9, "Human Development"). According to Piaget's theory, cognitive development occurs in a fixed series of "stages," from birth to adolescence. From a scientific standpoint, this theory was good because it led to a number of hypotheses. These hypotheses concerned the specific kinds of behaviors that should be observed at each stage of development. In the decades since its proposal, the theory has generated thousands of scientific papers. Our understanding of child development has been enhanced both by studies that supported Piaget's stage theory and by those that failed to support it.

Good theories also tend toward simplicity. This idea has historical roots in the writings of the fourteenth-century English philosopher William of Occam. Occam

theory
A model of interconnected ideas or concepts that explains what is observed and makes predictions about future events. Theories are based on empirical evidence.

hypothesis
A specific, testable prediction, narrower than the theory it is based on.

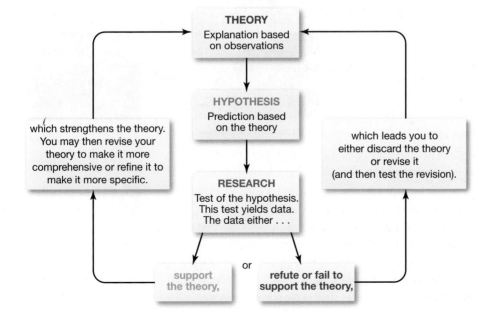

FIGURE 2.2
The Scientific Method
The scientific method reflects a cyclical process: A theory is formulated based on evidence from many observations and refined based on hypothesis tests (scientific studies). From the theory, scientists derive one or more testable hypotheses. Scientists then conduct research to test the hypotheses. Findings from the research might prompt scientists to reevaluate and adjust the theory. A good theory evolves over time, and the result is an increasingly accurate model of some phenomenon.

proposed that when two competing theories exist to explain the same phenomenon, the simpler of the two theories is generally preferred. This principle is known as *Occam's razor* or the *law of parsimony*. As long as a simple theory seems to describe the data, there is little need to develop more-complex theories.

 Why was Freud's theory of dreams not a good theory?

ANSWER: it did not yield testable hypotheses.

2.2 The Scientific Method Tests Hypotheses

The opening of this chapter considered cell phone use while driving. Let's say that, based on what you have read online, you develop the theory that safe driving requires paying attention. How can you determine if this theory is true? To do so, you need to conduct research. After an observation has been made and a theory has been formulated, the scientific method follows a series of seven steps (**FIGURE 2.3**):

Step 1: Frame a Research Question
A good theory leads to a wide variety of interesting research questions. For your theory that safe driving requires paying attention, the questions might include "Under

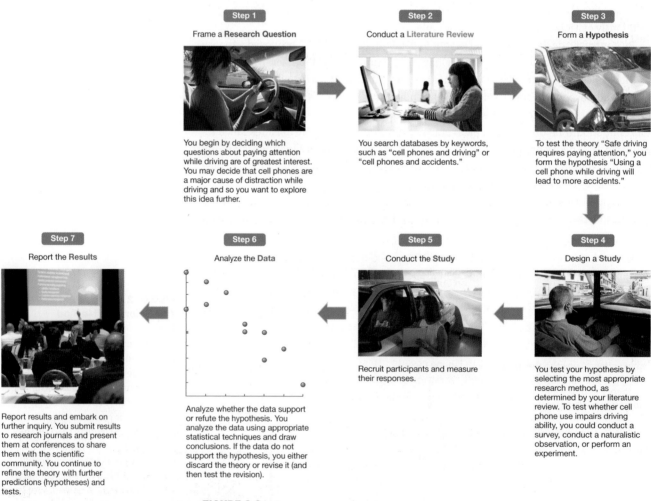

Step 1
Frame a **Research Question**

You begin by deciding which questions about paying attention while driving are of greatest interest. You may decide that cell phones are a major cause of distraction while driving and so you want to explore this idea further.

Step 2
Conduct a **Literature Review**

You search databases by keywords, such as "cell phones and driving" or "cell phones and accidents."

Step 3
Form a **Hypothesis**

To test the theory "Safe driving requires paying attention," you form the hypothesis "Using a cell phone while driving will lead to more accidents."

Step 7
Report the **Results**

Report results and embark on further inquiry. You submit results to research journals and present them at conferences to share them with the scientific community. You continue to refine the theory with further predictions (hypotheses) and tests.

Step 6
Analyze the **Data**

Analyze whether the data support or refute the hypothesis. You analyze the data using appropriate statistical techniques and draw conclusions. If the data do not support the hypothesis, you either discard the theory or revise it (and then test the revision).

Step 5
Conduct the **Study**

Recruit participants and measure their responses.

Step 4
Design a **Study**

You test your hypothesis by selecting the most appropriate research method, as determined by your literature review. To test whether cell phone use impairs driving ability, you could conduct a survey, conduct a naturalistic observation, or perform an experiment.

FIGURE 2.3
The Scientific Method in Action
This figure lays out the seven steps of the scientific method.

what circumstances do people not pay attention to their driving?" and "Does texting while driving interfere with attention?" Researchers can begin with any question, but typically they start with a basic question that directly tests the theory, such as "Does paying attention to texting interfere with driving ability?"

Step 2: Conduct a Literature Review

Once you have a research idea, you want to perform a literature review as soon as possible. A literature review is a review of the scientific literature related to your theory. There are many resources available to assist with literature reviews, including scientific research databases such as PsycINFO, Google Scholar, and PubMed. You can search these databases by keywords, such as "cell phones and driving" or "cell phones and accidents." The results of your searches will reveal if and how other scientists have been testing the same idea or similar ones. For example, different scientists may have approached this topic at different levels of analysis (discussed in Chapter 1). Their approaches may help guide the direction of your research.

Step 3: Form a Hypothesis

Based on what you learn in your literature review, you design tests—that is, specific research studies—aimed at examining the theory's predictions. These specific, testable research predictions are your hypotheses.

If your theory is true, then the tests should provide evidence that doing something distracting while driving is related to problems. One of your hypotheses therefore might be: "Using a cell phone while driving is associated with more accidents." To test this hypothesis, you might compare people who use a cell phone frequently while driving with people who do not use a cell phone frequently while driving. You would record how often the people in these groups have accidents. If these results do not differ, this finding raises questions about whether the theory is true.

Step 4: Design a Study

Designing a study refers to deciding which research method (and thus, level of analysis) you want to use to test your hypothesis. To test whether texting is related to more accidents, you could conduct a survey: Give people a questionnaire that asks how often they text while driving and how many accidents they have had. This method is used widely to gain initial insight into your hypothesis. In large surveys of high school students and college students, more than 40 percent reported texting while driving at least once in the previous 30 days (Olsen, Shults, & Eaton, 2013).

Instead of a survey, you could conduct a naturalistic observation: Watch a particular group of drivers over time and measure how often they text while driving or talk on a cell phone while driving. To establish how cell phone use affects driving, you could more intensively examine drivers by placing devices in their cars to measure aspects such as driving speed and acceleration. Or you could use video cameras to create an objective record of risky driving behaviors, such as running stop signs. One study of 151 drivers using such methods found that cell phone use, especially texting, was a strong predictor of crashes and near-crashes (Klauer et al., 2014).

Alternatively, you could perform an actual experiment, assigning one group of people to texting while driving and a second group of people to no texting, then comparing the number of accidents they have. Obviously, performing a test of this kind on public roads would be dangerous and unethical. Thus, for research like this, scientists use driving simulators that mimic real-world driving conditions (see the photo in Figure 2.3, Step 4). As you will see later when we discuss the different research methods available to test your hypothesis, there are advantages and disadvantages to each of these methods.

Step 5: Conduct the Study

Once you choose your research method, you have to conduct the study: Recruit participants and measure their responses. Many people call this step collecting data or gathering data. If you conduct a survey to see whether people who use cell phones while driving have more accidents, your data will include both the frequency with which people use cell phones while driving and how many accidents they have. All the research methods require you to clarify how you are defining "driving while texting" and "accidents." You must also take care in defining the appropriate size and type of sample of participants. These issues are addressed more completely later in this chapter, under the discussions of operational definitions and sampling.

Step 6: Analyze the Data

The next step is to analyze your data. There are two main ways to analyze data. First, you want to describe the data. What was the average score? How "typical" is that average? Suppose the average driver in your study has five years of driving experience. Does this statement mean five is the most common number of years of driving experience, or that five is the numerical average if you divide the total number of years driven by the total number of participants, or that about half of drivers have this many years of experience?

Second, you will want to know what conclusions you can draw from your data. You need to know whether your results are meaningful or whether they happened by chance. To determine the usefulness of your data, you analyze the data inferentially. That is, you ask whether you found a significant effect. Asking this question enables you to make inferences about your data—to infer whether your findings might be true for the general population. You accomplish data analyses by using descriptive and inferential statistics, which are described later in the chapter.

Step 7: Report the Results

Unreported results have no value, because no one can use any of the information. Instead, scientists make their findings public to benefit society, to support the scientific culture, and to permit other scientists to build on their work. Various forums are available for distributing the results of scientific research.

Brief reports can be presented at scientific conferences. The most popular formats for presenting data at conferences are talks and poster sessions. At the latter, people create large posters that display information about their study (**FIGURE 2.4A**). During these sessions, researchers stand by their posters and answer questions to those who stop by to read the poster (**FIGURE 2.4B**). Conference presentations are especially good for reporting preliminary data or for presenting exciting or cutting-edge results.

Full reports should be published in a peer-reviewed scientific journal. Full reports consist of the background and significance of the research, the full methodology for how the question was studied, the complete results of the descriptive and inferential statistical analyses, and a discussion of what the results mean in relation to the accumulated body of scientific evidence.

Sometimes the results of research are of interest to the general public. People in the media attend scientific conferences and read scientific journals so they can report on exciting findings. Eventually, interesting and important science will reach a general audience.

(a)

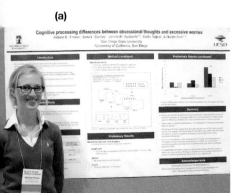

(b)

FIGURE 2.4
Poster Sessions
(a) A scientific poster presents information about the hypotheses, methods, results, and conclusions of a research study. **(b)** During a poster session, the researchers discuss their findings with interested observers.

Q In the scientific method, what do you call a specific, testable prediction?

ANSWER: hypothesis

2.3 The Scientific Method Is Cyclical

Good research reflects the cyclical process shown in Figure 2.2. Once the results of a research study are in, the researchers return to the original theory to evaluate the implications of the data. If the study was conducted competently (i.e., used appropriate methods and data analysis to test the hypothesis), the data either support and strengthen the theory or suggest that the theory be modified or discarded. Then the process starts all over again. Yes, the same sort of work needs to be performed repeatedly. No single study can provide a definitive answer about any phenomenon. No theory would be discarded on the basis of one set of data. Instead, we have more confidence in scientific findings when research outcomes are replicated.

REPLICATION Replication involves repeating a study to see if the results are the same (or similar). When the results from two or more studies are the same, or at least support the same conclusion, confidence increases in the findings. Ideally, researchers not affiliated with those who produced the original finding conduct replication studies. These independent replications provide more powerful support because they rule out the possibility that some feature of the original setting, such as the personality of the experimenter, may have contributed to the findings.

Replication has become an increasingly important topic in science. The last few decades have seen an explosion of research findings, particularly in medicine. Unfortunately, it seems that one week we hear about some finding and then the next week we hear about a conflicting finding. For example, does coffee give you cancer or help prevent it? It is hard for nonexperts to know what to believe about such phenomena. Recently, numerous scientists have called for new efforts to increase the likelihood that published studies are true (Ioannidis, 2014). Replication is an important method for increasing our confidence in scientific outcomes (Goodman, Fanelli, & Ioannidis, 2016).

The growing emphasis on replication has also been true within psychological science (Klein et al., 2014). In an initiative called the Reproducibility Project, a large group of psychologists sought to replicate findings that had been published during the year 2008 in three selected journals. Of the 100 studies they repeated, only 39 percent replicated (Open Science Collaboration, 2015). Their findings, published in the prestigious journal *Science*, provoked strong reactions from many psychologists.

Although all psychologists recognize the importance of replication, there is also a growing recognition that researchers need to think critically in conducting replication studies. For instance, some of the failed replications in the Reproducibility Project seem problematic. Consider an attempt to replicate a study conducted at Stanford University on race relations using a replication sample that consisted of nonnative English speakers in Amsterdam (Gilbert et al., 2016). Can you see how contextual factors, such as the research setting or time period, are likely to affect research findings? Imagine trying to replicate a study published in the 1950s on attitudes toward marriage equality (**FIGURE 2.5**). Attitudes and circumstances change. Study results also will differ depending on cultural norms. For instance, attitudes toward marriage equality vary substantially around the

replication
Repetition of a research study to confirm or contradict the results.

Do you think marriages between same-sex couples should or should not be recognized by the law as valid, with the same rights as traditional marriages?

■ % Should be valid   ▨ % Should not be valid

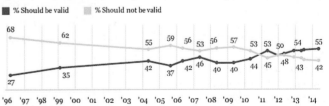

'96 '97 '98 '99 '00 '01 '02 '03 '04 '05 '06 '07 '08 '09 '10 '11 '12 '13 '14

Note: Trend shown for polls in which same-sex marriage question followed questions on gay/lesbian rights and relations
1996-2005 wording: "Do you think marriages between homosexuals ... "

GALLUP

FIGURE 2.5
The Importance of Context
The change in attitudes toward marriage equality makes it difficult to replicate studies on the topic conducted years ago.

globe. An analysis of the 100 studies in the Reproducibility Project found that those studies most influenced by contextual factors were the least likely to replicate (Van Bavel et al., 2016). Researchers need to be sensitive to contextual factors in designing replication studies.

Although contextual factors may explain some failures to replicate, other such failures can be explained by problematic research methods, such as poor design, not having enough research participants, or various experimenter biases. You will learn about many of these methodology problems in this chapter. You will also see how using good research methods strengthens what we learn through the scientific process.

THEORY REFINEMENT Often, more than one theory may apply to a particular aspect of human behavior. For instance, the theory that safe driving requires attention might be accurate, but suppose you want to know more about this phenomenon. How does failing to pay attention impair driving? You might develop new theories that take into account the skills needed to be a good driver.

You could theorize that distractions, such as using a cell phone, impair driving because they require taking your eyes off the road and so you do not notice road hazards. It is also possible that doing multiple things at once impairs your ability to think and therefore you make bad decisions while driving. If you have multiple theories, you can design *critical studies* that directly contrast the theories to see which theory best explains the data. Replication is another means of strengthening support for some theories, helping weed out weaker theories, and refining theories to make them more precise.

 Why is considering context important for replications?

ANSWER: People change over time and may differ across circumstances, such as different cultures. Such changes and differences may affect study results.

2.4 Evaluating Scientific Findings Requires Critical Thinking

As you learned in Chapter 1, one important goal of your education is to become a critical thinker. Critical thinking was defined in Chapter 1 as systematically questioning and evaluating information using well-supported evidence. As this definition makes clear, critical thinking is an *ability*—a skill. It is not something you can just memorize and learn, but something you have to practice and develop over time. Most of your courses should provide opportunities for you to practice being a critical thinker. Critical thinking is not just for scientists. It is essential for becoming an educated consumer of information.

The first step in critical thinking is to question information. What kind of information? To develop the skeptical mindset you need for critical thinking, you should question every kind of information. For any claim you see or hear, ask yourself, "What is the evidence in support of that claim?" For example, in the opening vignette of this chapter, we made the claim that texting while driving is dangerous. What kind of evidence did we present in support of this claim? Was the evidence based on direct, unbiased observation, or did it seem to be the result of rumor, hearsay, or intuition? In fact, think of your own beliefs and behavior. Do you believe that texting while driving is dangerous? If you do, what evidence led you to this belief? If you believe that texting while driving is dangerous, do you still text while driving? If so, why do you do it? Do you think the evidence you have seen or heard is not very good? If so, what makes the evidence not very good? Are you relying on so-called alternative facts to support your view? But how can facts be "alternative"? Facts are facts—pure information, not statements based on personal beliefs.

The Methods of Psychology
Cell Phone Versus Intoxication

HYPOTHESIS: Using a cell phone while driving is more dangerous than driving while intoxicated.

RESEARCH METHOD: Forty adults, ranging in age from 22 to 34, were recruited by a newspaper advertisement to participate in a research study on driving. In the study, the participants were asked to perform two separate tests in a driving simulator: (a) driving while having verbal conversations via a hand-held or handsfree device, and (b) driving after consuming enough alcohol to achieve a .08 percent blood-alcohol content (BAC), a level that is at or above the legal limit for intoxication in most states (see table). To establish their baseline driving performances, all the participants initially drove in the simulator without talking on the phone and without having consumed alcohol.

The tests occurred on two different days. Half of the participants talked on the phone while driving the first day and drank before driving on the second day. The other half drank before driving on the first day and talked on the phone while driving the second day.

RESULTS: Compared to the baseline driving performance, talking on the phone (with either a hand-held or hands-free device) caused a delayed response to objects in the driving scene, including brake lights on the car ahead, and a greater number of rear-end collisions. When they were intoxicated, the participants drove aggressively. They followed other cars more closely and hit the brake pedal much harder than they did in the baseline condition. Talking on a cell phone produced more collisions than driving while intoxicated.

CONCLUSION: Both talking on the cell phone and driving while intoxicated led to impaired driving compared to the baseline condition. Talking on the cell phone, whether holding the phone or not, led to more collisions than when the participants were intoxicated.

Blood Alcohol Content and Its Effects

In the United States, blood alcohol content is measured by taking a sample of a person's breath or blood and determining the amount of alcohol in that sample. The result is then converted to a percentage. For example, in many states the legal limit is .08 percent. To reach this level, a person's bloodstream needs to have 8 grams of alcohol for every 100 milliliters of blood.

Different blood alcohol levels produce different physical and mental effects. These effects also vary from person to person. This table shows typical effects.

BAC LEVEL	EFFECTS
.01-.06	Feeling of relaxation Sense of well-being Thought, judgment, and coordination are impaired.
.07-.10	Loss of inhibitions Extroversion Reflexes, depth perception, peripheral vision, and reasoning are impaired.
.11-.20	Emotional swings Sense of sadness or anger Reaction time and speech are impaired.
.21-.29	Stupor Blackouts Motor skills are impaired.
.30-.39	Severe depression Unconsciousness Breathing and heart rate are impaired.
>.40	Breathing and heart rate are impaired. Death is possible.

Source: Based on U.S. Department of Transportation, http://www-nrd.nhtsa.dot.gov/Pubs/811385.pdf

QUESTION: Did the results of the study support the original hypothesis?

ANSWER: Yes, because driving while talking on a cell phone led to more accidents than driving while intoxicated.

Source: Strayer, D. L., Drews, F. A., & Crouch, D. J. (2006). A comparison of the cell phone driver and the drunk driver. *Human Factors: The Journal of the Human Factors and Ergonomics Society, 48,* 381–391.

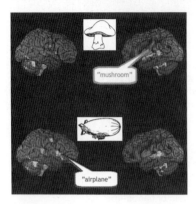

Journal of
Cognitive Neuroscience

Published by The MIT Press with the Cognitive Neuroscience Institute

FIGURE 2.6

Peer-Reviewed Journals

Research reports in peer-reviewed journals are the most trustworthy source for scientific evidence.

Another aspect of questioning when thinking critically is to ask for the definition of each part of the claim. For example, imagine you hear the claim that using a cell phone while driving is more dangerous than driving while intoxicated (see "The Methods of Psychology: Cell Phone Versus Intoxication," on p. 37). Upon hearing this claim, a critical thinker immediately asks for definitions. For example, what do they mean by "using a cell phone"? Do they mean talking or texting? Do they mean a handheld or a hands-free device? And what do they mean by "intoxicated"? Would achieving this state require only a little alcohol or a lot of alcohol? Could the person have used another drug?

Answering questions of this kind is the second step in critical thinking: the evaluation of information. To answer our questions, we need to go to the source of the claim.

To get to the source of any claim, you need to think about where you first saw or heard the claim. Did you hear the claim on TV or the radio? Did you read about it in a newspaper? Did you see it on the Internet? Was it from a Web site known for *fake news*, which is not news at all but stories without supporting evidence that are made up for personal reasons, advertising, or political purposes? Next, you need to think about the evidence offered by the source to support the claim.

Here is where the "well-supported evidence" comes in. Does the evidence at the source of the claim take the form of scientific evidence? Or does it take the form of intuition or simply someone in authority making the claim? Did the source retrieve this information from a newswire? Did it come from an interview with a scientist? Was it summarized from a scientific journal?

In science, well-supported evidence typically means research reports based on empirical data that are published in peer-reviewed journals (**FIGURE 2.6**). "Peer review" is a process by which other scientists with similar expertise evaluate and critique research reports before publication. Peer review ensures that published reports describe research studies that are well designed (using appropriate research and analysis methods, considering all factors that could explain the findings), that are conducted in an ethical manner, and that address an important question.

However, peer review does not mean that flawed studies are never published. Thus, critical thinkers must *always* stay vigilant—always be on the lookout for unreasonable claims and conclusions that may not be valid interpretations of the data. Hone your critical thinking skills by practicing them as often as possible.

ANSWER: it helps ensure that studies have been well designed, conducted in an ethical manner, and address an important question.

Q **Why is peer review important in the research cycle?**

Learning Objectives

- Distinguish between descriptive studies, correlational studies, and experiments.

- List the advantages and disadvantages of different research methods.

- Explain the difference between random sampling and random assignment, and explain when each might be important.

What Types of Studies Are Used in Psychological Research?

Once a researcher has defined a hypothesis, the next issue to be addressed is the type of research method to be used. There are three main types of research methods: *descriptive, correlational,* and *experimental.* These methods differ in the extent to which the researcher has control over the variables in the study. The amount of control over the variables in turn determines the type of conclusions the researcher can draw from the data.

All research involves variables. A **variable** is something in the world that can vary and that the researcher can manipulate (change), measure (evaluate), or both. In a study of texting and driving ability, some of the variables would be number of texts sent, number of texts received, familiarity with the texting device, how coordinated a person is, and driving ability and cell phone experience.

2.5 Descriptive Research Consists of Case Studies, Observation, and Self-Report Methods

Descriptive research involves observing behavior to *describe* that behavior objectively and systematically. Descriptive research helps scientists achieve the goals of describing what phenomena are and (sometimes) predicting when or with what other phenomena they may occur. However, by nature, descriptive research cannot achieve the goals of control and explanation (only the true experimental method, described later in this chapter, can do that).

Descriptive methods are widely used to assess many types of behavior. For example, an observer performing descriptive research might record the types of foods that people eat in cafeterias, count the number and types of mating behaviors that penguins engage in during their mating season, or tally the number of times poverty or mental illness is mentioned during a presidential debate (**FIGURE 2.7**). Each of these observations offers important information that can be used to describe current behavior and even predict future behavior. In no case does the investigator control the behavior being observed or explain why any particular behavior occurred.

There are three basic types of descriptive research methods: case studies, observations, and self-report methods and interviews.

CASE STUDIES A **case study** is the intensive examination of an unusual person or organization. By intensive examination, we mean observation, recording, and description. An individual might be selected for intensive study if he or she has a special or unique aspect, such as an exceptional memory, a rare disease, or a specific type of brain damage. An organization might be selected for intensive study because it is doing something very well (such as making a lot of money) or very poorly (such as losing a lot of money). The goal of a case study is to describe the events or experiences that lead up to or result from the exceptional aspect.

One famous case study in psychological science involves a young American man whose freak injury impaired his ability to remember new information (Squire, 1987). N.A. was born in 1938. After a brief stint in college, he joined the Air Force and was stationed in the Azores, where he was trained to be a radar technician. One night, he was assembling a model airplane in his room. His roommate was joking around with a miniature fencing foil, pretending to jab at the back of N.A.'s head. When N.A. turned around suddenly, his roommate accidentally stabbed N.A. through the nose and up into his brain (**FIGURE 2.8**).

Although N.A. seemed to recover from his injury in most ways, he developed extreme problems remembering events that happened to him during the day. He could remember events before his accident, and so he was able to live on his own, keeping his house tidy and regularly cutting his lawn. It was new information that he could not remember. He had trouble watching television because he forgot the storylines, and he had difficulty holding conversations because he forgot what others had just said. Subsequent studies of N.A.'s brain using imaging techniques revealed damage to specific regions not traditionally associated with memory difficulties (Squire, Amaral, Zola-Morgan, Kritchevsky, & Press, 1989). The case study of N.A. helped researchers develop new models of the brain mechanisms involved in memory.

However, not everyone who suffers damage to this brain region experiences the same types of problems as N.A. Such differences highlight the major problem with case studies. Because only one person or organization is the focus of a case study, scientists cannot tell from that study if the same thing would happen to other people

FIGURE 2.7
Descriptive Methods
Observational studies—such as this one, using a one-way mirror—are a method that researchers use to describe behavior objectively.

variable
Something in the world that can vary and that a researcher can manipulate (change), measure (evaluate), or both.

descriptive research
Research methods that involve observing behavior to describe that behavior objectively and systematically.

case study
A descriptive research method that involves the intensive examination of an unusual person or organization.

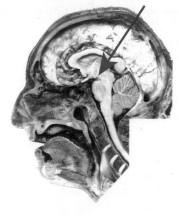

FIGURE 2.8
Case Study Data
In this image of Patient N.A., you can see where the miniature foil penetrated brain regions that had not traditionally been seen as involved in memory. This case study provided new insights into how the brain creates memories.

FIGURE 2.9
Participant Observation
The evolutionary psychologist and human behavioral ecologist Lawrence Sugiyama has conducted fieldwork in Ecuadorian Amazonia among the Shiwiar, Achuar, Shuar, and Zaparo peoples. Here, hunting with a bow and arrow, he is conducting a particularly active form of participant observation.

FIGURE 2.10
Naturalistic Observation
Using naturalistic observation, the primatologist Jane Goodall observes a family of chimpanzees. Animals are more likely to act naturally in their native habitats than in captivity.

or organizations who have the same experience(s). The findings from case studies do not necessarily *generalize,* or apply to the general population.

OBSERVATIONAL STUDIES   Two main types of observational techniques are used in research: participant observation and naturalistic observation. In **participant observation** (**FIGURE 2.9**), the researcher is involved in the situation. In **naturalistic observation** (**FIGURE 2.10**), the observer is passive, separated from the situation and making no attempt to change or alter ongoing behavior.

These observational techniques involve the systematic assessment and *coding* of overt behavior. Suppose you hear about a person who was texting while walking, stumbled off a curb, and was killed by an oncoming truck. You develop the hypothesis that using a cell phone while walking can cause problems with walking. How do you operationally define "problems with walking"? Once you have defined your terms, you need to code the forms of behavior you will observe. Your coding might involve written subjective assessments (e.g., "He almost got hit by a car when he walked into traffic"). Alternatively, your coding might use predefined categories (e.g., "1. Walked slowly," "2. Walked into traffic," "3. Stumbled"). Perhaps, after recording your data, you would create an index of impaired walking behavior by adding together the frequencies of each coded category. You might then compare the total number of coded behaviors when people were using a cell phone or not. Studies such as these have shown that cell phone use does impair walking ability (Schwebel et al., 2012; Stavrinos, Byington, & Schwebel, 2011). Pedestrian accidents—not all of them involving cell phones—kill more than 500 college-age students per year and injure more than 12,000 (National Highway Traffic Safety Administration, 2012b).

SELF-REPORTS AND INTERVIEWS   Ideally, observation is an unobtrusive approach for studying behavior. By contrast, asking people about themselves, their thoughts, their actions, and their feelings is a much more interactive way of collecting data. Methods of posing questions to participants include surveys, interviews, and questionnaires. The type of information sought ranges from demographic facts (e.g., ethnicity, age, religious affiliation) to past behaviors, personal attitudes, beliefs, and so on: "Have you ever used an illegal drug?" "Should people who drink and drive be jailed for a first offense?" "Are you comfortable sending food back to the kitchen in a restaurant when there is a problem?" Questions such as these require people to recall certain events from their lives or reflect on their mental or emotional states.

Self-report methods, such as surveys or questionnaires, can be used to gather data from a large number of people in a short time (**FIGURE 2.11**). Questions can be mailed out to a sample drawn from the population of interest or handed out in appropriate locations. They are easy to administer and cost-efficient.

Interviews, another type of interactive method, can be used successfully with groups that cannot be studied through surveys or questionnaires, such as young children. Interviews are also helpful in gaining a more in-depth view of a respondent's opinions, experiences, and attitudes. Thus, the answers from interviewees sometimes inspire avenues of inquiry that the researchers had not planned. (For a recap of the types of research methods, see **FIGURE 2.12**.)

 What is a major limitation of case studies?

ANSWER: Their findings might not generalize, or apply, to people beyond the particular case.

2.6 Descriptive Studies Need to Guard Against Bias

A problem common to all descriptive studies is that behavior may be affected by being studied. For instance, one problem in asking-based methods of data collection is that people often introduce biases into their answers. These biases make it difficult to discern an honest or true response. In particular, people may not reveal personal information that casts them in a negative light. We know we are not supposed to use cell phones while driving, and so we might be reluctant to admit regularly doing so. Researchers therefore have to consider the extent to which their questions produce *socially desirable responding,* or *faking good,* in which the person responds in a way that is most socially acceptable.

REACTIVITY When conducting observational research, scientists must consider the critical question of whether the observer should be visible. The concern here is that the presence of the observer might alter the behavior being observed. Such an alteration is called **reactivity.** People may feel compelled to make a positive impression on an observer, so they may act differently when they believe they are being observed. For example, drivers who know they are being observed might be less likely to use their cell phones.

Reactivity affected a now-famous series of studies on workplace conditions and productivity. Specifically, the researchers manipulated working conditions and then observed workers' behavior at the Hawthorne Works, a Western Electric manufacturing plant in Cicero, Illinois, between 1924 and 1933 (Olson, Hogan, & Santos, 2006; Roethlisberger & Dickson, 1939). The conditions included different levels of lighting, different pay incentives, and different break schedules. The main measured variable was how long the workers took to complete certain tasks.

Throughout the studies, the workers knew they were being observed. Because of this awareness, they responded to changes in their working conditions by increasing productivity. The workers did not speed up continuously throughout the various studies. Instead, they worked faster at the start of each new manipulation, regardless of the nature of the manipulation (longer break, shorter break, one of various changes to the pay system, and so on). The *Hawthorne effect* refers to changes in behavior that occur when people know that others are observing them (see "The Methods of Psychology: The Hawthorne Effect," on p. 42).

FIGURE 2.11
Self-Report Methods
Self-report methods, such as surveys or questionnaires, can be used to gather data from a large number of people. They are easy to administer, cost-efficient, and a relatively fast way to collect data.

participant observation
A type of descriptive study in which the researcher is involved in the situation.

naturalistic observation
A type of descriptive study in which the researcher is a passive observer, separated from the situation and making no attempt to change or alter ongoing behavior.

self-report methods
Methods of data collection in which people are asked to provide information about themselves, such as in surveys or questionnaires.

reactivity
The phenomenon that occurs when knowledge that one is being observed alters the behavior being observed.

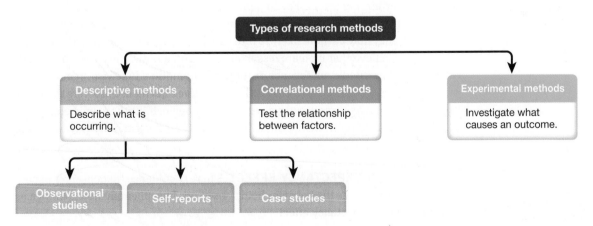

FIGURE 2.12
Types of Research Methods

The Methods of Psychology
The Hawthorne Effect

HYPOTHESIS: Being observed can lead participants to change their behavior.

RESEARCH METHOD (OBSERVATIONAL):

1 During studies of the effects of workplace conditions, the researchers manipulated several independent variables, such as the levels of lighting, pay incentives, and break schedules.

2 The researchers then measured the dependent variable, the speed at which workers did their jobs.

RESULTS: The workers' productivity increased when they were being observed, regardless of changes to their working conditions.

CONCLUSION: Being observed can lead participants to change their behavior.

QUESTION: Why do people change their behavior when they know they are being observed?

ANSWER: People like to make good impressions.

Source: Roethlisberger, F. J., & Dickson, W. J. (1939). *Management and the worker: An account of a research program conducted by the Western Electric Company, Hawthorne Works, Chicago*. Cambridge, MA: Harvard University Press.

OBSERVER BIAS In conducting observational research, scientists must guard against **observer bias**. This flaw consists of systematic errors in observation that occur because of an observer's expectations.

Observer bias can especially be a problem if cultural norms favor inhibiting or expressing certain behaviors. For instance, in many societies women are freer to express sadness than men are. If observers are coding men's and women's facial expressions, they may be more likely to rate female expressions as indicating sadness because they believe that men are less likely to show sadness. Men's expressions of sadness might be rated as annoyance or some other emotion. Likewise, in many societies women are generally expected to be less assertive than men. Observers therefore might rate women as more assertive when the women exhibit the same behavior as men. Cultural norms can affect both the participants' actions and the way observers perceive those actions.

EXPERIMENTER EXPECTANCY EFFECT There is evidence that observer expectations can even change the behavior being observed. This phenomenon is known as the **experimenter expectancy effect**.

In a classic study by the social psychologist Robert Rosenthal, college students trained rats to run a maze (Rosenthal & Fode, 1963). Half the students were told their

observer bias

Systematic errors in observation that occur because of an observer's expectations.

experimenter expectancy effect

Actual change in the behavior of the people or nonhuman animals being observed that is due to the expectations of the observer.

rats were bred to be very good at running mazes. The other half were told their rats were bred to be poor performers. In reality, there were no genetic differences between the groups of rats. Nonetheless, when students believed they were training rats that were bred to be fast maze learners, their rats learned the task more quickly! Thus, these students' expectations altered how they treated their rats. This treatment in turn influenced the speed at which the rats learned. The students were not aware of their biased treatment, but it existed. Perhaps they supplied extra food when the rats reached the goal box at the end of the maze. Or perhaps they gave the rats inadvertent cues as to which way to turn in the maze. They might simply have stroked the rats more often.

How do researchers protect against experimenter expectancy effects? It is best if the person running the study is *blind* to, or unaware of, the study's hypotheses. For example, the study just described seemed to be about rats' speed in learning to run through a maze. Instead, it was designed to study experimenter expectancy effects. The students believed they were "experimenters" in the study, but they were actually the participants. Their work with the rats was the subject of the study, not the method. Thus, the students were led to expect certain results so that the researchers could determine whether the students' expectations affected the results of the rats' training.

 Suppose that students who know they are in a study of race relations are careful to avoid saying anything offensive. What concern might you have about this study?

ANSWER: The study results—the participants' behaviors—are possibly being affected by reactivity.

correlational studies
A research method that describes and predicts how variables are naturally related in the real world, without any attempt by the researcher to alter them or assign causation between them.

scatterplot
A graphical depiction of the relationship between two variables.

positive correlation
A relationship between two variables in which both variables either increase or decrease together.

2.7 Correlational Studies Describe and Predict How Variables Are Related

Correlational studies examine how variables are naturally related in the real world, without any attempt by the researcher to alter them or assign causation between them (**FIGURE 2.13**). Correlational studies are used to describe and predict relationships between variables. They cannot be used to determine the causal relationship between the variables.

Consider an example. On your college application, you likely had to provide a score from a standardized test, such as the SAT or ACT. Colleges require these numbers because standardized test scores have been shown to *correlate* with college success. That is, generally, people who score higher on standardized tests tend to perform better in college. However, does this mean that scoring well on a standardized test will *cause* you to do better in college? Or that doing well in school will *cause* you to do better on standardized tests? Absolutely not. Many people score well on tests but do not perform well in school. Alternatively, many people score poorly on standardized tests but enjoy great success in college.

DIRECTION OF CORRELATION The first step in examining the correlation between two variables is to create a **scatterplot**. This type of graph provides a convenient picture of the data.

When higher or lower values on one variable predict higher or lower values on a second variable, we say there is a **positive correlation** between them. A positive correlation describes a situation where both variables either increase or decrease together—they "move" in the same direction (**FIGURE 2.14A**). For example, people with higher ACT scores generally have higher college GPAs. People with lower ACT

FIGURE 2.13
Correlational Studies
There may be a correlation between parents' body size and their children's body size. A correlational study cannot demonstrate the cause or causes of this relationship, which may include nature (biological propensities) and nurture (e.g., exercise and diet).

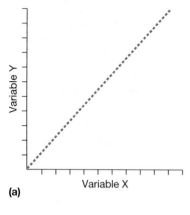

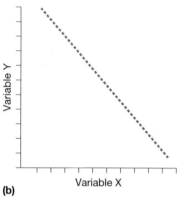

(a)

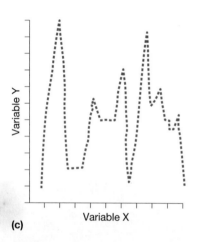

(b)

(c)

FIGURE 2.14
Scatterplots and Direction of Correlation

Each of these scatterplots illustrates a direction of correlation. **(a)** In a positive correlation, both variables "move" in the same direction. **(b)** In a negative correlation, the variables move in opposite directions. **(c)** In a zero correlation, one variable is not predictably related to a second variable.

scores generally have lower college GPAs. However, remember that correlation does not equal "cause and effect." Scoring higher or lower on the ACT will *not cause* you to earn a higher or lower GPA.

Remember, too, that *positive* in this case does *not* mean "good." For example, there is a very strong positive correlation between smoking and cancer. There is nothing good about this relationship. The correlation simply describes how the two variables are related: In general, people who smoke experience higher rates of cancer. The more they smoke, the higher their risk of getting cancer.

Some variables are negatively correlated. In a **negative correlation,** the variables move in opposite directions. An increase in one variable predicts a decrease in the other variable. A decrease in one variable predicts an increase in the other variable (**FIGURE 2.14B**). Here, *negative* does not mean "bad." Consider exercise and weight. In general, the more people exercise regularly, the less they are likely to weigh.

Some variables are just not related. In this case, we say there is a **zero correlation.** That is, one variable is not predictably related to a second variable (**FIGURE 2.14C**). For example, there is a zero correlation between height and intelligence. Tall people are neither smarter nor less smart than those who are shorter. You will learn more about correlations, and how to tell if they are statistically reliable, in Section 2.15.

THINKING CRITICALLY ABOUT CORRELATIONS Now that we have described the types of relationships that can exist, let's practice our critical thinking skills by interpreting what these relationships mean. Recall that there is generally a negative correlation between regular exercise and weight. For some people, however, there is a *positive* correlation between these variables. The more they exercise, the more weight they *gain*. Why? Because exercise builds muscle mass. Weight lifters might bulk up to help them lift even heavier weight. Sometimes, the same phenomena can exhibit a negative correlation or a positive correlation, depending on the specific circumstances.

Now consider the positive correlation between smoking and cancer. The more a person smokes, the greater that person's risk of cancer. Does that relationship mean smoking causes cancer? Not necessarily. Just because two things are related, even strongly related, does not mean that one is causing the other. Many genetic, behavioral, and environmental variables may contribute both to whether a person chooses to smoke and to whether the person gets cancer. Complications of this kind prevent researchers from drawing causal conclusions from correlational studies. Two such complications are the directionality problem and the third variable problem.

DIRECTIONALITY PROBLEM One problem with correlational studies is in knowing the direction of the relationship between variables. This sort of ambiguity is known as the **directionality problem.** For example, the more weight people gain, the less likely they might be to exercise, in part because exertion becomes more unpleasant. Consider another example. Suppose you survey a large group of people about their sleeping habits and their levels of stress. Those who report sleeping little also report having a higher level of stress. Does lack of sleep increase stress levels, or does increased stress lead to shorter and worse sleep? Both scenarios seem plausible:

> Sleep (A) and stress (B) are correlated.
>
> - Does less sleep lead to more stress? (A → B)
>   *or*
> - Does more stress lead to less sleep? (B → A)

THIRD VARIABLE PROBLEM Another drawback with all correlational studies is the **third variable problem.** Instead of variable A producing variable B, as a researcher might assume, it is possible that a third variable, C, is responsible for both A and B. Consider the relationship between texting while driving and dangerous driving. It is possible that people who are risk takers in their daily lives are more likely to text while driving. It is also possible that these people are likely to drive dangerously. Thus, the factor that leads to both texting while driving and dangerous driving is the third variable, risk-taking:

Texting while driving (A) is correlated with driving dangerously (B).

- Risk-taking (C) leads some people to text while driving. (C → A)
  and
- Risk-taking (C) leads some people to drive dangerously. (C → B)

Indeed, research has shown that those who text while driving are also likely to engage in a variety of other risky behaviors, such as not wearing seatbelts, riding with a driver who had been drinking, or even drinking alcohol and driving (Olsen, Shults, & Eaton, 2013). Thus, it is possible that both texting while driving and dangerous driving generally result from risk-taking, a third variable.

Sometimes the third variable is obvious. Suppose you were told that the more churches there are in a town, the greater the rate of crime. Would you conclude that churches cause crime? In looking for a third variable, you would realize that the population size of the town affects the number of churches and the frequency of crime. But sometimes third variables are not so obvious and may not even be identifiable. It turns out that even the relationship between smoking and cancer is plagued by the third variable problem. Evidence indicates that there is indeed a genetic predisposition—a built-in vulnerability to smoking—that can combine with environmental factors to increase the probability that some people will smoke *and* that they will develop lung cancer (Paz-Elizur et al., 2003; Thorgeirsson et al., 2008). Thus, it is impossible to conclude on the basis of correlational research that one of the variables is *causing* the other.

ETHICAL REASONS FOR USING CORRELATIONAL DESIGNS Despite such potentially serious problems, correlational studies are widely used in psychological science. Some research questions require correlational research designs for ethical reasons. For example, as mentioned earlier, it would be unethical to send drivers out into traffic and ask them to text as part of an experiment. Doing so would put the drivers and others at risk.

There are many important real-world experiences that we want to know about but would never expose people to as part of an experiment. Suppose you want to know if soldiers who experience severe trauma during combat have more difficulty learning new tasks after they return home than soldiers who have experienced less-severe trauma during combat. Even if you theorize that severely traumatic combat experiences *cause* later problems with learning, it would be unethical to induce trauma in some soldiers so that you could compare soldiers who had experienced different degrees of trauma. (Likewise, most research on psychopathology—psychological disorders—uses the correlational method, because it is unethical to induce disorders in people to study the effects.) For this research question, you would need to study the soldiers' ability to learn a new task after they had returned home. You might, for example, observe soldiers who were attempting to learn computer programming. The participants in your study would have to vary in how much they experienced trauma during combat. You would correlate the severity of the trauma they experienced with how well they learned computer programming.

negative correlation
A relationship between two variables in which one variable increases when the other decreases.

zero correlation
A relationship between two variables in which one variable is not predictably related to the other.

directionality problem
A problem encountered in correlational studies; the researchers find a relationship between two variables, but they cannot determine which variable may have caused changes in the other variable.

third variable problem
A problem that occurs when the researcher cannot directly manipulate variables; as a result, the researcher cannot be confident that another, unmeasured variable is not the actual cause of differences in the variables of interest.

FIGURE 2.15
Correlation or Causation?
According to the players on the 2013 Boston Red Sox baseball team, facial hair causes a person to play better baseball. After two newly bearded players made some game-saving plays, the rest of the team stopped shaving (Al-Khatib, 2013). Did their beards cause the Red Sox to win the World Series that year? The facial hair may have been correlated with winning, but it did not cause an increase in talent. The team won through ability, practice, and luck.

MAKING PREDICTIONS Correlational studies can be used to determine that two variables are associated with each other. In the example just discussed, the variables would be trauma during combat and learning difficulties later in life. By establishing such connections, researchers are able to make predictions. If you found the association you expected between severe trauma during combat and learning difficulties, you could predict that soldiers who experience severe trauma during combat will—again, on average—have more difficulty learning new tasks when they return than soldiers who do not experience severe trauma during combat. Because your study drew on but did not control the soldiers' wartime experiences, however, you have not established a causal connection (**FIGURE 2.15**).

By providing important information about the natural relationships between variables, researchers are able to make valuable predictions. For example, correlational research has identified a strong relationship between depression and suicide. For this reason, clinical psychologists often assess symptoms of depression to determine suicide risk. Typically, researchers who use the correlational method use other statistical procedures to rule out potential third variables and problems with the direction of the effect. Once they have shown that a relationship between two variables holds even when potential third variables are taken into account, researchers can be more confident that the relationship is meaningful.

> **Q** Suppose a study finds that hair length has a negative correlation with body weight: People with shorter hair weigh more. Should you grow your hair to lose weight?
>
> ANSWER: No, because correlation doesn't equal causation. Other variables could be affecting this relationship. For example, a person's sex is a third variable. Men typically have shorter hair and weigh more.

2.8 The Experimental Method Controls and Explains

Scientists ideally want to explain what causes a phenomenon. For this reason, researchers rely on the experimental method. In experimental research, the researcher has maximal control over the situation. Only the experimental method enables the researcher to control the conditions under which a phenomenon occurs and therefore to understand the cause of the phenomenon. In an **experiment,** the researcher manipulates one variable to measure the effect on a second variable.

FIGURE 2.16
Independent and Dependent Variables
The independent variable is under the control of the experimenter and is manipulated. It produces potential changes in the dependent variable, which is measured.

TYPES OF VARIABLES Scientists try to be as specific and as objective as possible when describing variables. Different terms are used to specify whether a variable is being manipulated or measured (**FIGURE 2.16**). An **independent variable** is the variable that gets manipulated. Researchers manipulate the variable by giving different levels of the variable to different participants. In a study, for example, one group of participants might be asked to text while driving in a simulator. Another group would be asked not to text while driving. Here, the independent variable is texting or not, which varies between the two groups.

A **dependent variable** is the variable that gets measured, which is why it is sometimes called the *dependent measure*. Another way to think of the dependent variable is as the outcome that gets measured after a manipulation occurs. That is, the value of the dependent variable *depends* on the changes produced in the independent variable. Thus, in a study you could measure how often people made driving mistakes. Here, the dependent variable is number of driving mistakes.

In addition to determining what variables will be studied, researchers must define these variables precisely and in ways that reflect the methods used to assess them. They do so by developing an **operational definition.** Operational definitions are important for research. They *qualify* (describe) and *quantify* (measure) variables so the variables can be understood objectively. The use of operational definitions enables other researchers to know precisely what variables were used, how they were manipulated, and how they were measured. These concrete details make it possible for other researchers to use identical methods in their attempts to replicate the findings.

For example, if you choose to study how driving performance is affected by cell phone use, how will you qualify cell phone use? Do you mean talking, texting, reading content, or some combination of these activities? How will you then quantify cell phone use? Will you count how many times a person uses the cell phone in an hour? Then, how will you quantify and qualify driving performance so you can judge whether it is affected by cell phone use? Will you record the number of accidents, the closeness to cars up ahead, the reaction time to red lights or road hazards, speeding? The operational definitions for your study need to spell out the details of your variables.

MANIPULATING VARIABLES In an experiment, the independent variable (IV) is what is manipulated. That is, the researchers choose what the study participants do or are exposed to.

In a study on the effects of using a cell phone while driving, the IV would be the type of cell phone use. While in a driving simulator, some participants might simply hold the phone, some might have to answer questions over the phone, and some might have to read and answer text messages.

An IV has "levels," meaning the different values that are manipulated by the researcher. All IVs must have at least two levels: a "treatment" level and a "comparison" level. In the study of cell phone use and driving ability, the people who actively used the cell phone received the "treatment." A group of study participants who receive the treatment is the **experimental group.** Since in this hypothetical study some participants talk on the cell phone and others text, there are actually two experimental groups.

In an experiment, you always want to compare your experimental group with at least one **control group.** A control group consists of similar (or identical) participants who receive everything the experimental group receives except for the treatment. In this example, the experimental group uses a cell phone to talk or text while driving. The control group simply holds a cell phone while driving. This use of a control group includes the possibility that simply the presence of a cell phone is disruptive. To test whether handling a cell phone is disruptive, the control group could be drivers not holding a cell phone.

So far, we have described research where different people are in the control and experimental groups. This is called a *between groups* design because different people receive different treatments. However, sometimes study participants serve as their own control group. In the *repeated measures* design (sometimes called within-subject design), the same people receive both treatments. For example, people would be tested driving once without a cell phone and then once with a cell phone. Differences in performance would be attributable to the different treatments. A disadvantage of

experiment
A research method that tests causal hypotheses by manipulating and measuring variables.

independent variable
The variable that gets manipulated in a research study.

dependent variable
The variable that gets measured in a research study.

operational definition
A definition that *qualifies* (describes) and *quantifies* (measures) a variable so the variable can be understood objectively.

experimental group
The participants in an experiment who receive the treatment.

control group
The participants in an experiment who receive no intervention or who receive an intervention that is unrelated to the independent variable being investigated.

FIGURE 2.17
Population
The population is the group researchers want to know about (e.g., U.S. college students). For the results of an experiment to be considered useful, the participants should be representative of the population.

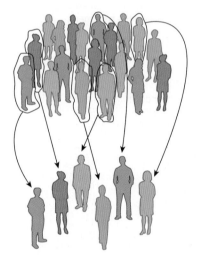

FIGURE 2.18
Random Sample
A random sample is taken at random from the population (e.g., selecting students from schools throughout the United States).

confound
Anything that affects a dependent variable and that may unintentionally vary between the experimental conditions of a study.

ANSWER: The independent variable is manipulated, and the dependent variable is measured.

population
Everyone in the group the experimenter is interested in.

sample
A subset of a population.

this method is that repeating the test means people have experience with the task the second time. This prior knowledge could influence performance.

The dependent variable (DV) is whatever behavioral effect is—or behavioral effects are—measured. For example, the researcher could measure how quickly the participants responded to red lights, how fast they drove, and the distance they maintained behind the car in front of them. The researcher would measure each of these DVs as a function of the IV, the type of cell phone use.

The benefit of an experiment is that the researcher can study the causal relationship between variables. If the IV (such as type of cell phone use) consistently influences the DV (such as driving performance), then the IV is assumed to cause the change in the DV.

ESTABLISHING CAUSALITY A properly performed experiment depends on rigorous control. Here, *control* means the steps taken by the researcher to minimize the possibility that anything other than the independent variable could be the cause of differences between the experimental and control groups.

A **confound** is anything that affects a dependent variable and that may unintentionally vary between the study's different experimental conditions. When conducting an experiment, a researcher needs to ensure that the only thing that varies is the independent variable. Control thus represents the foundation of the experimental approach, in that it allows the researcher to rule out alternative explanations for the observed data.

In the study of cell phone use and driving performance, what if a car with an automatic transmission is simulated to assess driving when participants are not using a cell phone, but a car with a manual transmission is simulated to assess performance when participants are texting? Given that manual transmissions require greater dexterity to operate than automatic transmissions, any apparent effect of texting on driving performance might actually be caused by the type of car and the fact that it requires greater use of the hands. In this example, the drivers' skills might be *confounded* with the type of transmission, making it impossible to determine the true effect of the texting.

Other potential confounds in research include changes in the sensitivity of the measuring instruments, such as a systematic change in a scale so that it weighs things more heavily in one condition than in another. Changes in the time of day or the season when the experiment is conducted can also confound the results. Suppose you conducted the texting and driving study so that the cell phone users were tested in snowy winter conditions and control participants were tested during dry, sunny weather. The road conditions associated with the season would be an obvious confound. The more confounds and thus alternative explanations that can be eliminated, the more confident a researcher can be that the change in the independent variable is causing the change (or effect) in the dependent variable. For this reason, researchers have to watch vigilantly for potential confounds. As consumers of research, we all need to think about confounds that could be causing particular results.

Q Which variable is manipulated, and which is measured?

2.9 Participants Need to Be Carefully Selected and Randomly Assigned to Conditions

An important issue for any research method is how to select participants for the study. Psychologists typically want to know that their findings generalize to people beyond the individuals in the study. In studying the effects of cell phone use on driving skills,

FIGURE 2.19
Larger Samples
Suppose researchers want to compare how many women go to the beach versus how many men do. Why might the results be more accurate if the researchers use a large sample (such as the big picture here) rather than a small sample (such as the detail)?

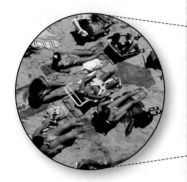

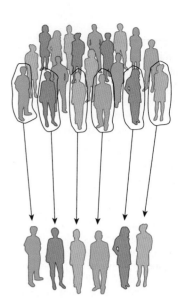

FIGURE 2.20
Convenience Sample
A convenience sample is taken from an available subgroup (e.g., students at a particular school) in the population (i.e., all students). Most of the time, circumstances force researchers to use a convenience sample.

you ultimately would not focus on the behavior of the specific participants. Instead, you would seek to discover general laws about human behavior. If your results generalized to all people, that would enable you, other psychologists, and the rest of humanity to predict, in general, how cell phone use would affect driving performance. Other results, depending on the nature of the study, might generalize to all college students, to students who belong to sororities and fraternities, to women, to men over the age of 45, and so on.

POPULATION AND SAMPLING The group you want to know about is the **population** (**FIGURE 2.17**). To learn about the population, you study a subset from it. That subset, the people you actually study, is the **sample.** *Sampling* is the process by which you select people from the population to be in the sample. In a case study, the sample size is one. The sample should represent the population, and the best method for making this happen is *random sampling* (**FIGURE 2.18**). This method gives each member of the population an equal chance of being chosen to participate. In addition, larger samples yield more-accurate results (**FIGURE 2.19**). However, sample size is often limited by resource constraints, such as time, money, and space in which to work.

Most of the time, a researcher will use a *convenience sample* (**FIGURE 2.20**). As the term implies, this sample consists of people who are conveniently available for the study. However, because a convenience sample does not use random sampling, the sample is likely to be biased. For instance, a sample of students at a small religious school may differ from a sample of students at a large state university. Researchers acknowledge the limitations of their samples when they present their findings.

RANDOM ASSIGNMENT Once researchers obtain a representative sample of the population, they use **random assignment** to assign participants to the experimental and control groups (**FIGURE 2.21**). Random assignment gives each potential research participant an equal chance of being assigned to any level of the independent variable.

For your study, there might be three levels: holding a cell phone, answering questions verbally over the phone, and answering questions by texting. First, you would gather participants by taking either a random sample or a convenience sample from

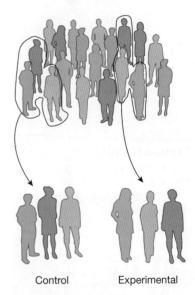

Control   Experimental

FIGURE 2.21
Random Assignment
In random assignment, participants are assigned at random to the control group or the experimental group. Random assignment is used when the experimenter wants to test a causal hypothesis.

random assignment
Placing research participants into the conditions of an experiment in such a way that each participant has an equal chance of being assigned to any level of the independent variable.

FIGURE 2.22
**The Experimental
Method in Action**

An experiment examines how one
variable changes as another is
manipulated by the researcher. The
results can demonstrate causal
relationships between the variables.

1 Researcher manipulates...	**2** Researcher randomly assigns participants to...	**3** Researcher measures...	**4** Researcher assesses result.	**5** Conclusion
independent variable	control group or experimental group	dependent variable	Are the results in the control group different from the results in the experimental group?	The explanation either supports or does not support the hypothesis. Are there confounds, which would lead to alternative explanations?

selection bias

In an experiment, unintended
differences between the participants
in different groups; it could be caused
by nonrandom assignment to groups.

culturally sensitive research

Studies that take into account the
role that culture plays in determining
thoughts, feelings, and actions.

(a)

(b)

FIGURE 2.23
Cross-Cultural Studies
(a) The living space and treasured
possessions of a family in Japan,
for example, differ from **(b)** those
of a family in Mali. Cross-cultural
researchers might study how either
family would react to crowding or to
the loss of its possessions.

the population. Then, to randomly assign those participants, you might have them
draw numbers from a hat to determine who is assigned to the control group (holding
the phone) and to each experimental group (one talking and the other texting).

Of course, individual differences are bound to exist among participants. For example, any of your groups might include some people with less experience with cell
phones and some people who talk or text a great deal, some people with excellent and
experienced driving skills and some people with comparably weaker skills. But these
differences will tend to average out when participants are assigned to either the control or experimental groups randomly, so that the groups are equivalent *on average*.
Random assignment tends to balance out known and unknown factors, given a large
enough sample size.

If random assignment to groups is not truly random, and groups are not equivalent because participants in different groups differ in unexpected ways, the condition
is known as **selection bias** (also known as *selection threat*). Suppose you have two of
the experimental conditions described earlier: a group assigned to hold the phone and
a group assigned to respond to text messages. What happens if the group assigned
to hold the phone includes many college students with lots of experience using cell
phones and the other group includes many older adults who have minimal experience
texting? How would you know if the people in the different conditions of the study are
equivalent? You could match each group for age, sex, cell phone use habits, and so on,
but you can never be sure that you have assessed all possible factors that may differ
between the groups. Not using random assignment can create confounds that limit
causal claims. (For a recap of the experimental method, see **FIGURE 2.22**.)

GENERALIZING ACROSS CULTURES It is important for researchers to assess
how well their results generalize to other samples, particularly in cross-cultural
research (Henrich, Heine, & Norenzayan, 2010). One difficulty in comparing people
from different cultures is that some ideas and practices do not translate easily across
cultures, just as some words do not translate easily into other languages. Apparent
differences between cultures may reflect such differences in language, or they may
reflect participants' relative willingness to report things about themselves publicly.
A central challenge for cross-cultural researchers is to refine their measurements to
rule out these kinds of alternative explanations (**FIGURE 2.23**).

Some psychological traits are the same across all cultures (e.g., care for the
young). Others differ widely across cultures (e.g., behaviors expected of adolescents).
Culturally sensitive research takes into account the significant role that culture plays
in how people think, feel, and act (Adair & Kagitcibasi, 1995; Zebian, Alamuddin,
Mallouf, & Chatila, 2007). Scientists use culturally sensitive practices so that their

research respects—and perhaps reflects—the "shared system of meaning" that each culture transmits from one generation to the next (Betancourt & Lopez, 1993, p. 630).

In cities with diverse populations, such as Toronto, London, and Los Angeles, cultural differences exist among different groups of people living in the same neighborhoods and having close daily contact. Researchers therefore need to be sensitive to cultural differences even when they are studying people in the same neighborhood or the same school. Researchers must also guard against applying a psychological concept from one culture to another without considering whether the concept is the same in both cultures. For example, Japanese children's attachment to their parents looks quite different from the attachment styles common among North American children (Miyake, 1993).

 How does random assignment help deal with existing differences between participants?

ANSWER: When participants are randomly assigned to study conditions, known and unknown differences between the participants tend to balance out.

What Are the Ethics Governing Psychological Research?

Psychologists want to know why and how we act, think, feel, and perceive the way we do. In other words, they want to understand the human condition. When conducting research, psychologists have a responsibility to carefully consider the ethics of their own actions. Will the study contribute to the betterment of humanity? What exactly will the participants be asked to do? Are the requests reasonable, or will they put the participants in danger of physical or emotional harm over the short term or the long term? If animals are involved, will they be treated humanely? Is their use justified?

Learning Objectives

- Identify ethical issues associated with conducting psychological research on human participants.

- Apply ethical principles to conducting research on animals, identifying the key issues regarding the humane treatment of animal subjects.

2.10 There Are Ethical Issues to Consider in Research with Human Participants

It makes sense for psychological studies to involve human participants. As in any science that studies human behavior, however, there are limits to how researchers can manipulate what people do in studies. For ethical and practical reasons, researchers cannot always use the experimental method.

Consider the question of whether smoking causes cancer. To explain why a phenomenon (e.g., cancer) occurs, experimenters must control the conditions under which that phenomenon occurs. And to establish that a cause-and-effect relationship exists between variables, experimenters need to use random assignment. So to determine causality between smoking and cancer, some study participants would have to be randomly "forced" to smoke a controlled number of cigarettes in a specific fashion for a controlled amount of time, while an equal number of different (but similar) participants would have to be randomly "prevented" from smoking for the same amount of time. However, ethics prevent researchers from randomly forcing people to smoke, so researchers cannot experimentally answer this question using human participants (FIGURE 2.24).

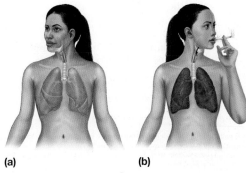

(a)   (b)

FIGURE 2.24
Research on Smoking and Cancer
Researchers can compare **(a)** a nonsmoker's lungs with **(b)** a smoker's lungs. They can compare the rates of cancer in nonsmokers with the rates of cancer in smokers. Ethically, however, they cannot perform an experiment that entails randomly forcing study participants to smoke, even though such experiments could help establish a link between smoking and cancer.

FIGURE 2.25
Informed Consent
The need for informed consent is illustrated by one of the most infamous unethical studies. Between 1932 and 1972, the U.S. Public Health Service and the Tuskegee Institute, in Alabama, studied the natural progression of untreated syphilis in rural African American men. Without their knowledge, 400 impoverished men with the venereal disease were randomly assigned to receive treatment or not. In 1987, the U.S. government publicly apologized to the participants and their families. Here, President Bill Clinton and Vice President Al Gore appear at a news conference with participant Herman Shaw.

institutional review boards (IRBs)
Groups of people responsible for reviewing proposed research to ensure that it meets the accepted standards of science and provides for the physical and emotional well-being of research participants.

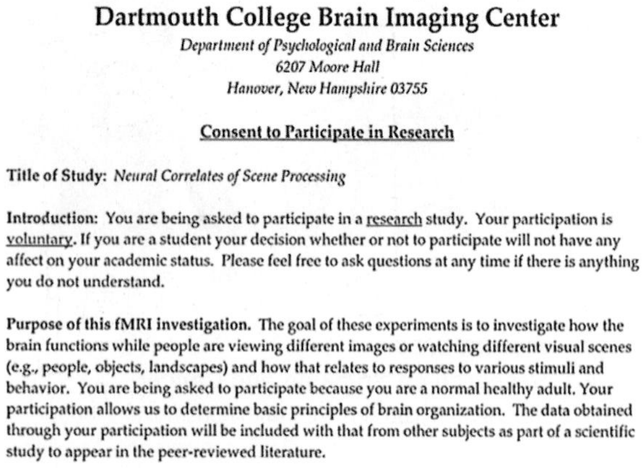

Dartmouth College Brain Imaging Center
Department of Psychological and Brain Sciences
6207 Moore Hall
Hanover, New Hampshire 03755

Consent to Participate in Research

Title of Study: *Neural Correlates of Scene Processing*

Introduction: You are being asked to participate in a research study. Your participation is voluntary. If you are a student your decision whether or not to participate will not have any affect on your academic status. Please feel free to ask questions at any time if there is anything you do not understand.

Purpose of this fMRI investigation. The goal of these experiments is to investigate how the brain functions while people are viewing different images or watching different visual scenes (e.g., people, objects, landscapes) and how that relates to responses to various stimuli and behavior. You are being asked to participate because you are a normal healthy adult. Your participation allows us to determine basic principles of brain organization. The data obtained through your participation will be included with that from other subjects as part of a scientific study to appear in the peer-reviewed literature.

FIGURE 2.26
Informed Consent Form
This portion of an approved form gives you a sense of how researchers typically obtain informed consent in writing.

INSTITUTIONAL REVIEW BOARDS (IRBs) To ensure the health and well-being of all study participants, strict guidelines exist regarding research. These guidelines are shared by all places where research is conducted, including colleges, universities, and research institutes. **Institutional review boards (IRBs)** are the guardians of the guidelines.

Convened at schools and other institutions where research is done, IRBs consist of administrators, legal advisers, trained scholars, and members of the community. At least one member of the IRB must not be a scientist. The purpose of the IRB is to review all proposed research to ensure that it meets scientific and ethical standards to protect the safety and welfare of participants. Most scientific journals today ask for proof of IRB approval before publishing research results. Three key issues are addressed in the IRB approval process: privacy, relative risks, and informed consent.

PRIVACY One major ethical concern about research is the expectation of privacy. Two main aspects of privacy must be considered. One aspect is *confidentiality*. This term means that personal, identifying information about participants absolutely cannot be shared with others. Research participants must be assured that any such information collected in a study will remain private. In some studies, *anonymity* is used. Although this term is often confused with confidentiality, anonymity means that the researchers do not collect personal, identifying information. Without such information, responses can never be traced to any individual. Anonymity helps make participants comfortable enough to respond honestly.

RELATIVE RISKS OF PARTICIPATION Another ethical issue is the relative risk to participants' mental or physical health. Researchers must always remain aware of what they are asking of participants. They cannot ask people to endure unreasonable amounts of pain or of discomfort, either from stimuli or from the manner in which data measurements are taken.

Fortunately, in the vast majority of studies being conducted, these types of concerns are not an issue. However, even though risk may be low, researchers still have to think carefully about the potential for risk. Therefore, the IRB will evaluate the relative trade-off between risk and benefit for any research study it approves. In some cases, the potential gains from the research may require asking participants to expose themselves to some risk to obtain important findings. The *risk/benefit ratio* is an analysis of whether the research is important enough to warrant placing participants at risk. If a study has any risk associated with it, then participants must be notified *before* they agree to participate. This process is known as *informed consent*.

INFORMED CONSENT Research involving human participants is a partnership based on mutual respect and trust. People who volunteer for psychological research have the right to know what will happen to them during the course of the study. Compensating people with either money or course credit for their participation in research does not alter this fundamental right. Ethical standards require giving people all relevant information that might affect their willingness to become participants (**FIGURE 2.25**).

Informed consent means that participants make a knowledgeable decision to participate. Typically, researchers obtain informed consent in writing (**FIGURE 2.26**). It is not always possible to inform participants fully about a study's details. If knowing the study's specific goals may alter the participants' behavior, thereby rendering the results meaningless, researchers may need to use deception. That is, they might mislead the participants about the study's goals or not fully reveal what will take place. Researchers use deception only when other methods are not appropriate and when the deception does not involve situations that would strongly affect people's willingness to participate. If deception is used, a careful *debriefing* must take place after the study's completion. Here, the researchers inform the participants of the study's goals. They also explain the need for deception, to eliminate or counteract any negative effects produced by the deception.

 What is the purpose of informed consent?

ANSWER: to inform potential research participants about the risks and benefits of participating in a particular study

2.11 There Are Ethical Issues to Consider in Research with Animals

Many people have ethical concerns about research with nonhuman animals. These concerns involve two questions: Does research threaten the health and well-being of the animals? And is it fair to the animals to study them to improve the human condition?

HEALTH AND WELL-BEING Research with animals must always be conducted with regard to the health and well-being of the animals. Federal mandates govern the care and use of animals in research, and these mandates are strictly enforced. An accounting and reporting system is in place for all institutions conducting animal research. Violators of the mandates are prevented from conducting further research.

All colleges, universities, and research institutions conducting research with vertebrate animals must have an Institutional Animal Care and Use Committee (IACUC). This committee is like an institutional review board (discussed earlier), but it evaluates animal research proposals. In addition to scientists and nonscientists, every IACUC includes a certified doctor of veterinary medicine, who must review each proposal to ensure that the research animals will be treated properly before, during, and after the study.

FAIRNESS Animals share similarities with humans that make them good "models" for particular human behaviors or conditions. For example, as you will learn more about in Chapters 3 and 7, the human brain has a region called the hippocampus, and people with damage to this region suffer from memory loss. It would be unethical for researchers to reproduce hippocampal damage in people in an effort to find treatments for their memory loss. However, many animals also have a hippocampus, and they display similar types of memory loss when this region is damaged. As a way to help humans, researchers thus may find it necessary to conduct animal research. For example, scientists can damage or temporarily "turn off" the hippocampus in rats or mice to test treatments that may help to reverse the resulting memory loss.

"WHAT IT COMES DOWN TO IS YOU HAVE TO FIND OUT WHAT REACTION THEY'RE LOOKING FOR, AND YOU GIVE THEM THAT REACTION."

FIGURE 2.27
Animal Research
Researchers observe the behaviors of transgenic mice to understand how certain genes affect behavior.

Another valuable animal model is the transgenic mouse. Transgenic mice have been produced by manipulating genes in developing mouse embryos—for example, by inserting strands of foreign DNA into the genes. Studying the behavior of mice with specific genetic changes enables scientists to discover the role that genes play in behavior and disease (**FIGURE 2.27**).

Are such treatments fair to the research animals? Scientists must balance their concern for individual animals' lives with their concern for humanity's future. The pursuit of scientific knowledge and medical advances is important for identifying causes and treatments for many disorders as well as better understanding the link between brain and behavior. At the same time, animals must be used respectfully in research. Such respect involves making sure that the research methods are sound and that the inclusion of animals is justified by the relative importance of the information that will be obtained by their use.

 Why are animals used in research?

2.12 Should You Participate in Psychological Research?

Someday, perhaps even this term, you will be invited to participate in a psychological research study (**FIGURE 2.28**). Because psychological researchers are a creative lot, they enjoy figuring out clever ways to study the human mind. As a result, participation in research can be a lot of fun. Even studies that simply involve answering self-report questions offer opportunities to reflect on your inner world and behaviors. However, some students in introductory psychology may worry that researchers will trick them into doing something they do not want to do. Others may feel anxious because they have no idea what to expect once they walk through the doors of a psychology laboratory. Understanding the ethical principles that guide psychological research arms potential research participants—like yourself—with insight about what to expect when participating in a study.

Psychologists in the United States conduct their studies according to a set of ethical principles, a few of which are described below.

First, no one can force you to participate in a study. Although many psychology departments "require" students to participate in research as part of their course work, they offer students alternatives for fulfilling this requirement. For example, in some departments, students can read and write about articles published in journals in lieu of participating in research. Even if you volunteer for a study, you have the right to discontinue your participation at any time, for any reason, and without penalty. And you can skip any questions you do not care to answer, perhaps because you find them intrusive or offensive. You are in the driver's seat when it comes to choosing if, and to what extent, you would like to participate in a study.

Second, you are legally and ethically entitled to know what you are getting into so you can make an informed decision about participating. Although the researchers will not be able to reveal their exact research questions and hypotheses, they will be able to tell you the general purpose of the study and the kinds of activities you will be asked to complete. You might be asked to answer questions, perform computer tasks, engage in moderate physical activity, navigate a real or imagined social scenario, rate the appeal of different consumer products, and so on. In addition, researchers must

FIGURE 2.28
Student Participation in Psychological Research
These students are enjoying the opportunity to contribute to scientific knowledge. Join them by participating in a study.

tell you about the risks and potential benefits faced by participants. For example, researchers studying ostracism would inform participants they might find the experimental tasks distressing. So even before a study begins, you will actually know a good deal about the research.

Third, after you complete the study, you can expect the researchers to debrief you. During the debriefing, the researchers will tell you if they used deception in the study. For example, if you participate in a study about cooperation, you might learn during the debriefing that the "person" you interacted with online was really a computer program.

Finally, you can expect that the data you provide will remain confidential. To protect confidentiality, the researchers will remove all identifying information, such as your name, from any data you submit. They will store consent forms separately from data, password-protect electronic files containing sensitive information, and keep all files in a secure location.

While researchers are governed by formal ethical guidelines (in addition to their own moral compasses), good study participants also engage the research process respectfully. When you sign up to participate in a study, record the researcher's contact information in case an emergency arises and you are unable to fulfill your commitment. Arrive at your session on time, and bring any paperwork your institution might require in order for you to receive class credit for your participation. During the study, minimize potential distractions, such as by turning off your cell phone. And, importantly, ask questions! One of the benefits of volunteering in research is learning firsthand about the research process. Getting answers to your questions helps you derive this benefit.

Study participants are essential to the research enterprise. The principles and procedures described here emerged out of concern for the well-being of participants. Understanding your rights and responsibilities prepares you to contribute meaningfully and confidently, without fear of trickery or unknown risks, to psychologists' efforts to understand and improve the human condition. On behalf of psychologists everywhere, thank you for joining us in this endeavor. ∎

 What is debriefing?

ANSWER: After a research study, the researchers explain to the participants the reason for the study and any deception involved.

How Are Data Analyzed and Evaluated?

So far, this chapter has presented the essential elements of scientific inquiry in psychology: thinking critically; asking an empirical question using theories, hypotheses, and research; deciding what type of study to run; considering the ethics of particular research; collecting and presenting data. This section focuses on the data. Specifically, it examines the characteristics that make for good data and the statistical procedures that researchers use to analyze data.

2.13 Good Research Requires Valid, Reliable, and Accurate Data

If you collect data to answer a research question, the data must be *valid*. That is, the data must be accurate measurements of the constructs (concepts) that you think they measure, accurately represent phenomena that occur outside of the laboratory, and accurately reveal effects due specifically and only to manipulation of the independent variable.

Learning Objectives

- Identify three characteristics that reflect the quality of data.

- Describe measures of central tendency and variability.

- Describe the correlation coefficient.

- Discuss the rationale for inferential statistics.

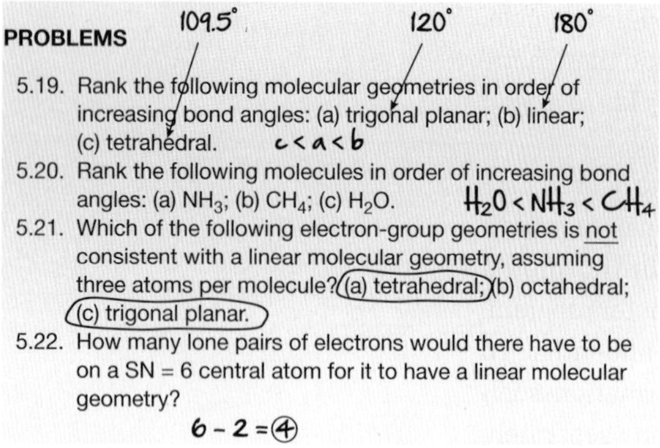

109.5°   120°   180°

5.19. Rank the following molecular geometries in order of increasing bond angles: (a) trigonal planar; (b) linear; (c) tetrahedral.   c < a < b

5.20. Rank the following molecules in order of increasing bond angles: (a) NH_3; (b) CH_4; (c) H_2O. $H_2O < NH_3 < CH_4$

5.21. Which of the following electron-group geometries is not consistent with a linear molecular geometry, assuming three atoms per molecule? (a) tetrahedral; (b) octahedral; (c) trigonal planar.

5.22. How many lone pairs of electrons would there have to be on a SN = 6 central atom for it to have a linear molecular geometry?   6 − 2 = 4

FIGURE 2.29
Construct Validity

Imagine having to answer questions like this on your psychology final. The results would lack construct validity because the course is about psychology, not chemistry.

Sample:

Students
(your sample is 50 college students taking introductory psychology)

Treatment (special tutoring)

= 82.5 percent on final

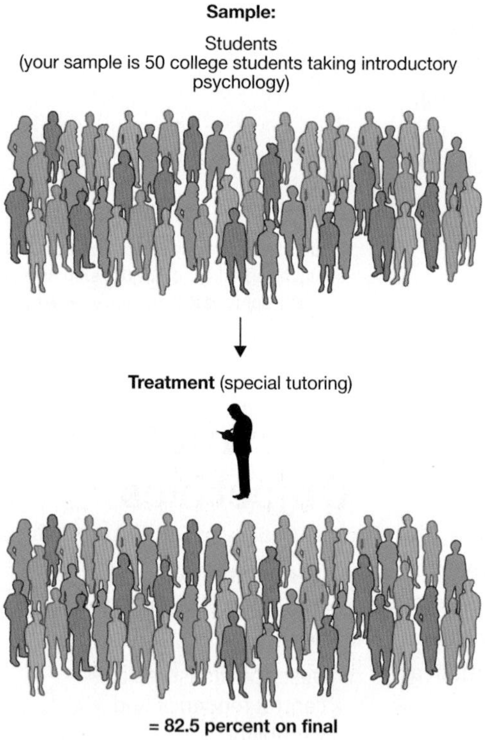

FIGURE 2.30
A Study Lacking Internal Validity

In this study, your entire sample is one experimental group, which receives the treatment of special tutoring. You determine the group's average score on the final exam, but you cannot compare that result with the result from a control group.

Construct validity is the extent to which variables measure what they are supposed to measure. For example, suppose at the end of the semester your psychology professor gives you a final examination that consists of chemistry problems. This kind of final examination would lack construct validity—it would not accurately measure your knowledge of psychology (**FIGURE 2.29**).

Now imagine you are a psychological researcher. You hypothesize that "A students" spend more time studying than "C students." To test your hypothesis, you assess the amount of time students spend studying. However, what if "C students" tended to do other things—such as sleeping, playing video games, or checking their Facebook status—while they claimed to be studying? If this were the case, the data would not accurately reflect studying and would therefore lack construct validity.

External validity is the degree to which the findings of a study can be generalized to other people, settings, or situations. A study is externally valid if (1) the participants accurately represent the intended population, and (2) the variables were manipulated and measured in ways similar to how they occur in the "real world."

Internal validity is the degree to which the effects observed in an experiment are due to the independent variable and not to confounds. For data to be internally valid, the experiment must be well designed and well controlled. That is, all the participants must be as similar as possible, and there must be a control group. Only by comparing experimental groups to control groups can you determine that any changes observed in the experimental groups are caused by the independent variable and not something else (for example, practice or the passage of time).

To understand internal validity, suppose you are conducting a study to see if special tutoring causes better grades. You randomly sample 50 students from introductory psychology classes at your university and give them special tutoring for 6 weeks. At the end of the 6 weeks, you find that the students earned an average score of 82.5 percent on the final exam (**FIGURE 2.30**). Can you conclude that the tutoring caused the grade? Wait a minute. How do you know if 82.5 is an improvement over scores typically received on the exam? Maybe all students in introductory psychology "mature" over the semester so that the average final exam grade is about 82, regardless of tutoring. Or perhaps having 6 weeks of practice taking other tests results in higher exam grades, even without tutoring. Only by having an equal comparison group—a control group of students that is otherwise identical to the experimental group except for the treatment—can you determine if your treatment caused the observed effect.

Indeed, a better way to conduct this study would be to sample 50 students from the class, randomly assign 25 of them the special tutoring for 6 weeks (the experimental group), and not give any special treatment to the other 25 (the control group). Say the 25 students in the experimental group average 82.5 percent on the final exam and the 25 students in the control group average 74.2 percent (**FIGURE 2.31**). The control group was similar in every way to the experimental group. As a result, you are fairly safe to conclude that the tutoring—not something else—led to higher exam grades. Thus, having a true control group can ensure that a study maintains internal validity.

Another important aspect of data is **reliability,** the stability and consistency of a measure over time. If the measurement is reliable, the data collected will not vary substantially over time. For instance, one option for measuring the duration of studying would be to have an observer use a stopwatch. There is likely to be some variability, however, in when the observer starts and stops the watch relative to when the

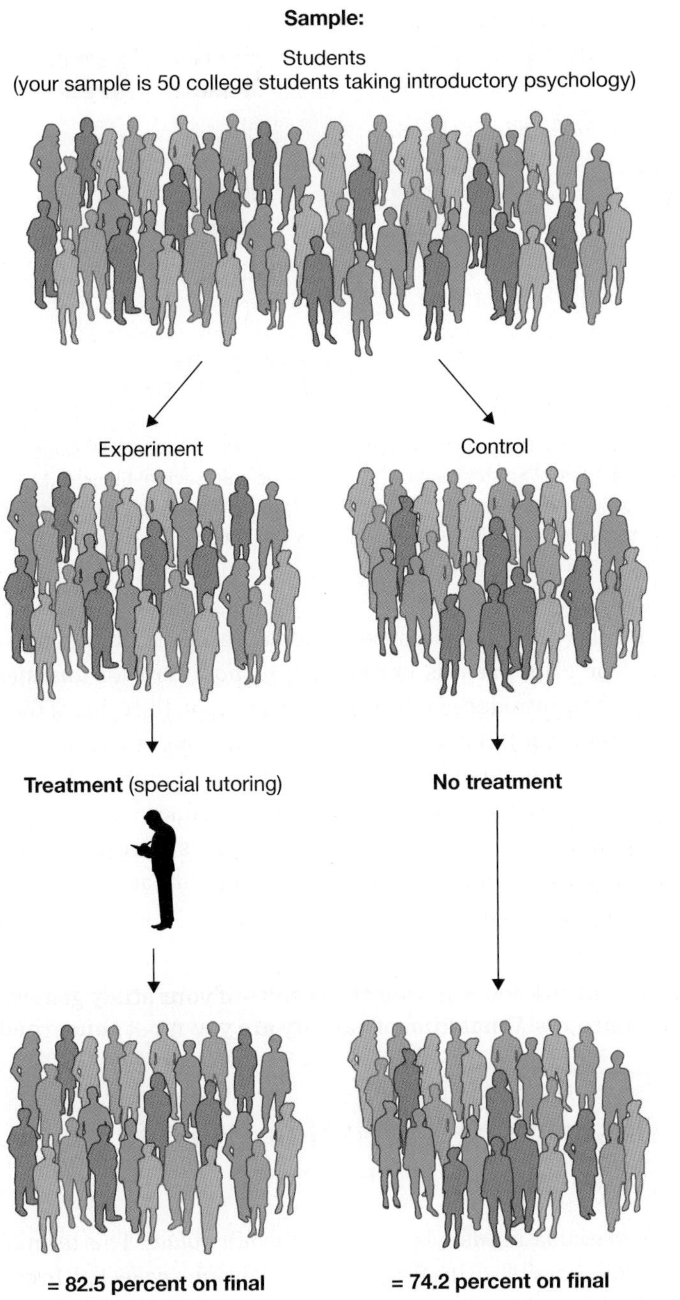

Sample:

Students
(your sample is 50 college students taking introductory psychology)

Experiment

Control

Treatment (special tutoring)

No treatment

= 82.5 percent on final

= 74.2 percent on final

FIGURE 2.31

A Study with Internal Validity

In this better study, you divide the sample into an experimental group and a control group. Only the experimental group receives the treatment. You can then compare the results with the results from the control group.

student actually starts studying. As a consequence, the data in this scenario would be less reliable than data collected by an online homework system that measured how much time students spent working on assignments.

The third and final characteristic of good data is **accuracy,** the degree to which the measure is error free. A measure may be reliable but still not be accurate. Psychologists think about this problem by turning it on its head and asking, How do errors creep into a measure?

Suppose you use a stopwatch to measure the duration of studying. The problem with this method is that each measurement will tend to overestimate or

construct validity

The extent to which variables measure what they are supposed to measure.

external validity

The degree to which the findings of a study can be generalized to other people, settings, or situations.

internal validity

The degree to which the effects observed in an experiment are due to the independent variable and not to confounds.

reliability

The degree to which a measure is stable and consistent over time.

accuracy

The degree to which an experimental measure is free from error.

1st recording   2nd recording   3rd recording

1st recording   2nd recording   3rd recording

Average time   **Actual time**
(rarely known)

Average time   **Actual time**
(rarely known)

FIGURE 2.32
Random Error
Data accuracy can be affected by random error. For example, say you time the same research participant several times. The stopwatch works accurately. But because your judgment of starting and stopping times differs each time, the degree of error varies each time.

FIGURE 2.33
Systematic Error
Data accuracy can be affected by systematic error. Here, you time the same research participant several times, but the stopwatch is off by 1 minute each time. The degree of error is constant.

underestimate the duration (because of human error or variability in recording times). This type of problem is known as a *random error* or *unsystematic error*. Although an error is introduced into each measurement, the value of the error differs each time (**FIGURE 2.32**). But suppose the stopwatch has a glitch, so that it always overstates the time measured by 1 minute. This type of problem is known as a *systematic error* or *bias*, because the amount of error introduced into each measurement is constant (**FIGURE 2.33**). Generally, systematic error is more problematic than random error because the latter tends to average out over time and therefore is less likely to produce inaccurate results.

 You want to know whether the results of your study generalize to other groups. What kind of validity are you most concerned about?

ANSWER: external validity

2.14 Descriptive Statistics Provide a Summary of the Data

The first step in evaluating data is to inspect the *raw values*. This term refers to data that are as close as possible to the form in which they were collected. In examining raw data, researchers look for errors in data recording. For instance, they assess whether any of the responses seem especially unlikely (e.g., studying for 72 hours or a 113-year-old participant). Once the researchers are satisfied that the data make sense, they summarize the basic patterns using **descriptive statistics.** These mathematical forms provide an overall summary of the study's results. For example, they might show how the participants, on average, performed in one condition compared with another.

The simplest descriptive statistics are measures of **central tendency.** This single value describes a typical response or the behavior of the group as a whole. The most intuitive measure of central tendency is the **mean,** the arithmetic average of a set of numbers. The class average on an exam is an example of a mean score. Consider our earlier hypothetical study of cell phone use and driving performance. A basic way to summarize the data would be to calculate the means for driving performances using number of seconds the participants took to travel once around a virtual racetrack in a driving simulator: You would calculate one mean for when participants were simply holding a cell phone and a second mean for when they were texting. If texting affects

descriptive statistics
Statistics that summarize the data collected in a study.

central tendency
A measure that represents the typical response or the behavior of a group as a whole.

mean
A measure of central tendency that is the arithmetic average of a set of numbers.

driving, you would expect to see a difference in the means between those holding cell phones and those using them.

A second measure of central tendency is the **median,** the value in a set of numbers that falls exactly halfway between the lowest and highest values. For instance, if you received the median score on a test, half the people who took the test scored lower than you and half the people scored higher.

Sometimes researchers will summarize data using a median instead of a mean because if one or two numbers in the set are dramatically larger or smaller than all the others, the mean will give either an inflated or a deflated summary of the average. This effect occurs in studies of average incomes. Perhaps approximately 50 percent of Americans make more than $52,000 per year, but a small percentage of people make so much more (multiple millions or billions for the richest) that the mean income is much higher (around $70,000) than the median and is not an accurate measure of what most people earn. The median provides a better estimate of how much money the average person makes.

A third measure of central tendency is the **mode,** the most frequent score or value in a set of numbers. For instance, the modal number of children in an American family is two, which means that more American families have two children than any other number of children. (For examples of how to calculate all three central tendency measures, see **FIGURE 2.34.**)

median
A measure of central tendency that is the value in a set of numbers that falls exactly halfway between the lowest and highest values.

mode
A measure of central tendency that is the most frequent score or value in a set of numbers.

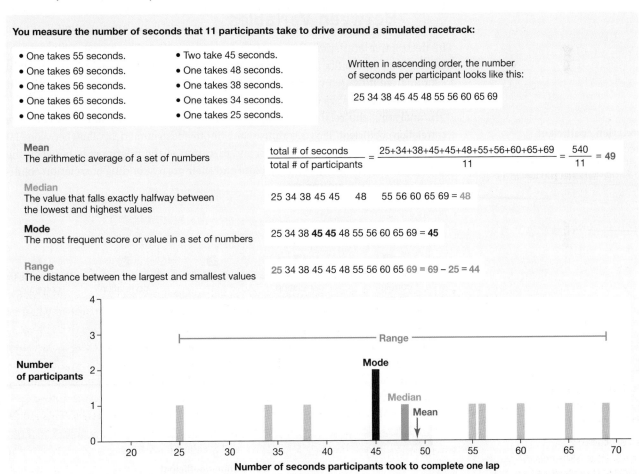

You measure the number of seconds that 11 participants take to drive around a simulated racetrack:

- One takes 55 seconds.
- One takes 69 seconds.
- One takes 56 seconds.
- One takes 65 seconds.
- One takes 60 seconds.

- Two take 45 seconds.
- One takes 48 seconds.
- One takes 38 seconds.
- One takes 34 seconds.
- One takes 25 seconds.

Written in ascending order, the number of seconds per participant looks like this:

25 34 38 45 45 48 55 56 60 65 69

Mean
The arithmetic average of a set of numbers

$$\frac{\text{total \# of seconds}}{\text{total \# of participants}} = \frac{25+34+38+45+45+48+55+56+60+65+69}{11} = \frac{540}{11} = 49$$

Median
The value that falls exactly halfway between the lowest and highest values

25 34 38 45 45   48   55 56 60 65 69 = 48

Mode
The most frequent score or value in a set of numbers

25 34 38 **45 45** 48 55 56 60 65 69 = **45**

Range
The distance between the largest and smallest values

25 34 38 45 45 48 55 56 60 65 69 = 69 − 25 = 44

FIGURE 2.34
Descriptive Statistics
Descriptive statistics are used to summarize a data set and to measure the central tendency and variability in a set of numbers. The mean, median, and mode are different measures of central tendency. The range is a measure of variability.

variability

In a set of numbers, how widely dispersed the values are from each other and from the mean.

standard deviation

A statistical measure of how far away each value is, on average, from the mean.

In addition to measures of central tendency, another important characteristic of data is the **variability** in a set of numbers. In many respects, the mean is meaningless without knowing the variability. Variability refers to how widely dispersed the values are from each other and from the mean. The most common measure of variability—how spread out the scores are—is the **standard deviation.** This measure reflects how far away each value is, on average, from the mean. For instance, if the mean score for an exam is 75 percent and the standard deviation is 5, most people scored between 70 percent and 80 percent. If the mean remains the same but the standard deviation becomes 15, most people scored between 60 and 90—a much larger spread.

Another measure of how spread out scores are is the *range*, the distance between the largest value and the smallest value. Often the range is not very useful, however, because it is based on only those two scores.

Q Why might you prefer the median to the mean?

ANSWER: Because the mean is an arithmetic average, it may be distorted by extreme values. By contrast, the median is simply the middle value, so it is less subject to distortion.

2.15 The Correlation Coefficient Summarizes the Relationships Between Variables

The descriptive statistics discussed so far are used for summarizing the central tendency and variability in a set of numbers. Descriptive statistics can also be used to summarize how two variables relate to each other. Recall from Section 2.7 that correlational designs are used to study how two variables relate to one another.

In analyzing the relationship between two variables, researchers can compute a **correlation coefficient.** This descriptive statistic provides a numerical value (between –1.0 and +1.0) that indicates the strength and direction of the relationship between the two variables. Some sample scatterplots and their corresponding correlation coefficients can be seen in **FIGURE 2.35.**

correlation coefficient

A descriptive statistic that indicates the strength and direction of the relationship between two variables.

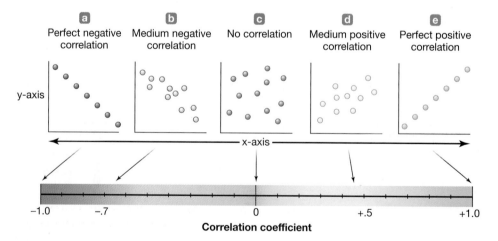

FIGURE 2.35
Correlation Coefficient
Correlations can have different values between -1.0 and +1.0. These values reveal the strength and direction of relationships between two variables. The greater the scatter of values, the lower the correlation. A perfect correlation occurs when all the values fall on a straight line.

Here, we are considering only one type of relationship: a linear relationship. In a linear relationship, an increase or decrease in one variable is associated with an increase or decrease in the other variable. When a linear relationship is strong, knowing how people measure on one variable enables you to predict how they will measure on the other variable. The two types of linear relationship, as discussed in Section 2.7, are positive correlations and negative correlations.

If two variables have a positive correlation, they increase or decrease together. For example, the more people study, the more likely they are to have a higher GPA. A perfect positive correlation is indicated by a value of +1.0 (see Figure 2.35e). If two variables have a *negative correlation*, as one increases in value, the other decreases in value. For example, as people spend more time multitasking, they become less able to study for their exams, so multitasking and GPA have a negative correlation. A perfect negative correlation is indicated by a value of –1.0 (see Figure 2.35a). If two variables show no apparent relationship, the value of the correlation will be a number close to zero (assuming a linear relationship for the purposes of this discussion; see Figure 2.35c).

"I think you should be more explicit here in step two."

Q | If two variables are completely unrelated to each other, what would be the correlation coefficient?

2.16 Inferential Statistics Permit Generalizations

Researchers use descriptive statistics to summarize data sets. They use **inferential statistics** to determine whether effects are probably due to chance or whether they reflect true differences in the groups being compared. For instance, suppose you find that the mean driving performance for drivers using cell phones is lower than the mean driving performance for those not using cell phones. How different do these means need to be for you to conclude that using a cell phone reduces people's ability to drive?

A review of 206 studies found that the skills necessary to drive a car can become impaired when people perform a second task (i.e., multitask; Ferdinand & Menachemi, 2014). Pretend for a moment, however, that cell phone use does not influence driving performance. If you measure the driving performances of those using cell phones and those not using them, just by chance there will be some variability in the mean performance of the two groups. The key is that if cell phone use does not affect driving performance, the probability of showing a large difference between the two means is relatively small. Researchers use statistical techniques to determine if the differences among the sample means are (probably) chance variations or if they reflect actual differences in the populations.

Consider **FIGURE 2.36.** This bar graph shows the means for a study that compared driving in a simulator while either texting or not texting. The mean is visibly higher for the texting group, but is this difference larger than would be expected by chance? The error bars for each group show the variability that was observed within each group during the study. The difference between the means is much larger than the observed variability within each group. Thus, this difference between the groups does not appear to have happened by chance. It appears to be a real difference.

inferential statistics

A set of procedures that enable researchers to decide whether differences between two or more groups are probably just chance variations or whether they reflect true differences in the populations being compared.

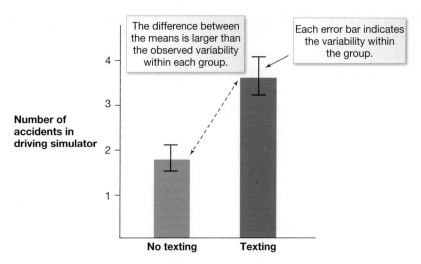

The difference between the means is larger than the observed variability within each group.

Each error bar indicates the variability within the group.

Number of accidents in driving simulator

No texting   Texting

FIGURE 2.36
Evaluating Differences in Research Results
In this hypothetical experiment comparing two groups in a driving simulator, the group assigned to the texting condition had significantly more accidents. That result is reflected in the difference between the means for the groups. Error bars have been added to show the variability of data within each condition.

When the results obtained from a study would be very unlikely to occur if there really were no differences between the groups of subjects, the researchers conclude that the results are *statistically significant*. According to generally accepted standards, researchers typically conclude there is a significant effect only if the obtained results would occur by chance less than 5 percent of the time.

meta-analysis

A "study of studies" that combines the findings of multiple studies to arrive at a conclusion.

META-ANALYSIS Meta-analysis is a type of study that, as its name implies, is an analysis of multiple analyses. In other words, it is a study of studies that have already been conducted. With meta-analysis, many studies that have addressed the same issue are combined and summarized in one "study of studies." The study we described that looked at 206 studies is an example of a meta-analysis.

Suppose that ten studies have been conducted on men's and women's effectiveness as leaders. Among these ten studies, five found no differences, two favored women, and three favored men. Researchers conducting a meta-analysis would not just count up the numbers of different findings from the research literature. Instead, they would weight more heavily those studies that had larger samples. Large samples are more likely to provide more accurate reflections of what is true in populations (see Figure 2.19). The researchers would also consider the size of each effect. That is, they would factor in whether each study found a large difference, a small difference, or no difference between the groups being compared—in this case, between women and men. (The researchers who conducted such a meta-analysis on men's and women's effectiveness found no overall differences; Eagly, Karau, & Makhijani, 1995.)

Because meta-analysis combines the results of separate studies, many researchers believe that meta-analysis provides stronger evidence than the results of any single study. As discussed earlier in this chapter, we can be more confident about results when the research findings are replicated. Meta-analysis has the concept of replication built into it.

ANSWER: The observed difference between groups is unlikely to have occurred by chance—something caused it. Statistical significance assumes that no other differences exist between the groups.

 What does it mean if an observed difference between groups is described as statistically significant?

2.17 Should You Bet on a Hot Hand?

In 2013, LeBron James, then playing for the Miami Heat, set a basketball record by scoring over 30 points, while making over 60 percent of his shots, for six straight games (**FIGURE 2.37**). In the seventh game, James's streak ended, when he scored on just under 60 percent of his shots.

Did James have a "hot hand" during this streak? Are there periods when particular athletes are relaxed, confident, and "in the zone" and play particularly well? Team members try to get the ball to a person who has made several shots in a row, because they think the person's hot hand will increase their chance of winning. Many sports journalists, coaches, athletes, and fans believe in some form of the phenomenon.

The psychologist Tom Gilovich and his colleagues (1985) conducted a series of studies on the hot hand, to assemble beliefs about the phenomenon and to scientifically examine whether it exists. Their first and crucial step was to turn the idea of the hot hand into a testable hypothesis: After a basketball shooter has made two or three shots in a row, that shooter will be more likely to make the next shot than after missing the last two or three shots. When the researchers asked 100 knowledgeable basketball fans, 91 agreed that this outcome was likely. If their belief were accurate, then an analysis of shooting records should show the increased probability of making a shot after previous successes than after previous failures.

To test whether the "hot hand" hypothesis is supported by evidence, Gilovich and colleagues examined the shooting records of the Philadelphia 76ers during the 1980–81 season. The 76ers kept records of the order that shots had been taken as well as the outcome of those shots. The data did not support the hot hand hypothesis. Players made on average 51 percent of their shots after making one previous shot, 50 percent after making two previous shots, and 46 percent after making three in a row. If anything, players were more likely to be successful after prior misses: 51 percent after one prior miss, 53 percent after two prior misses, and 56 percent after missing three in a row.

As a critical thinker, you might wonder whether the defensive team stops the streak by paying more attention to hot shooters and putting in more effort to defend against them. To test this alternative explanation, Gilovich and colleagues examined free throw shooting, where the defense does not matter and players get two free shots. Players made about the same number of second free throws whether they made the first one or not.

Upon hearing the results of this research, the famous coach Red Auerbach, of the Boston Celtics, exclaimed, "Who is this guy? So he makes a study. I couldn't care less" (Gilovich, 1991, p. 17). Should anyone care? After all, the results of any one study might be questionable until other scientists have replicated the findings. And as it turns out, the occasional study supports the idea of the hot hand for some sports, such as volleyball (Raab, Gula, & Gigerenzer, 2012) and baseball (Green & Zwiebel, 2017). Why there might be a hot hand in some sports but not others is open to speculation. However, a meta-analysis of 22 published articles on this phenomenon found no evidence that the hot hand exists (Avugos, Köppen, Czienskowski, Raab, & Bar-Eli, 2013). Some researchers have suggested that the very statistics used to assess the hot hand might be mistaken (Miller & Sanjurjo, 2016). There continues to be lively debate as to the best ways to measure streakiness in shooting and whether there is a hot hand. The psychologist Alan Reifman maintains an active blog on the topic at thehothand.blogspot.com.

Regardless of the scientific controversy, casual observers tend to overrate the occurrence of the hot hand. Why do people have such strong beliefs about shooting

FIGURE 2.37
LeBron James
Did a "hot hand" help James during his six-game streak in 2013, when he was playing for the Heat? Since then, James's excellent scoring percentage has helped lift his current team, the Cavaliers, to a championship.

streaks? The best answer is that people are bad at recognizing chance outcomes. If a fair coin is flipped, most people intuitively expect there to be a greater alternation of heads and tails than occurs by chance. But if you flip a coin 20 times in a row, there will be streaks of six heads or tails in a row 10 percent of the time, five in a row 25 percent of the time, and four in a row 50 percent of the time. Players do occasionally sink the shot six, seven, or eight times in a row, but these occurrences do not happen any more often than what we expect from chance, given the number of shots they take in a game. ■

 Why do people believe in shooting streaks?

ANSWER: People are bad at recognizing chance outcomes.

Your Chapter Review

Chapter Summary

How Is the Scientific Method Used in Psychological Research?

2.1 Science Has Four Primary Goals
The four primary goals of science are *description* (describing what a phenomenon is), *prediction* (predicting when a phenomenon might occur), *control* (controlling the conditions under which a phenomenon occurs), and *explanation* (explaining what causes a phenomenon to occur).

2.2 The Scientific Method Tests Hypotheses
Scientific inquiry relies on objective methods and empirical evidence to answer testable questions. The scientific method is based on the use of theories to generate hypotheses that can be tested by collecting objective data through research. After a theory has been formulated based on observing a phenomenon, the seven steps of the scientific method are framing research questions, reviewing the scientific literature to see if and/or how people are testing the theory, forming a hypothesis based on the theory, choosing a research method to test the hypothesis, conducting the research study, analyzing the data, and disseminating the results.

2.3 The Scientific Method Is Cyclical
The data from scientific studies either support and strengthen a theory or require reconsidering or revising the theory. Replication involves repeating a study to see if the same results occur. Replication is increasingly important in psychology. Researchers may refine theories to make them more precise.

2.4 Evaluating Scientific Findings Requires Critical Thinking
Critical thinking is a skill that helps people become educated consumers of information. Critical thinkers question claims, seek definitions for the parts of the claims, and evaluate the claims by looking for well-supported evidence.

What Types of Studies Are Used in Psychological Research?

2.5 Descriptive Research Consists of Case Studies, Observation, and Self-Report Methods
A case study, one kind of descriptive study, examines an unusual individual or an organization. However, the findings of a case study may not generalize. Researchers observe and describe naturally occurring behaviors to provide a systematic and objective analysis. Data collected by observation must be defined clearly and collected systematically. Surveys, questionnaires, and interviews can be used to directly ask people about their thoughts and behaviors.

2.6 Descriptive Studies Need to Guard Against Bias
Self-report data may be biased by the respondents' desire to present themselves in a particular way (e.g., smart, honest, or both). Bias may also occur in the data because the participants are aware that they are being observed or because of the observer's expectations.

2.7 Correlational Studies Describe and Predict How Variables Are Related
Correlational studies are used to examine how variables are naturally related in the real world. These studies cannot be used to establish causality or the direction of a relationship (i.e., which variable caused changes in the other variable).

2.8 The Experimental Method Controls and Explains
An experiment can demonstrate a causal relationship between variables. Experimenters manipulate one variable, the independent variable, to determine its effect on another, the dependent variable. Research participants are divided into experimental groups and control groups. The experimental groups experience the independent variable, and the control groups are used for comparison. In evaluating the data, researchers must look for confounds—elements, other than the variables, that may have affected the results.

2.9 Participants Need to Be Carefully Selected and Randomly Assigned to Conditions
Researchers sample participants from the population they want to study (e.g., drivers). They use random sampling when everyone in the population is equally likely to participate in the study, a condition that rarely occurs. To establish causality between an intervention and an outcome, random assignment must be used. When random assignment is used, all participants have an equal chance of being assigned to any level of the independent variable, and preexisting differences between the groups are controlled. Culturally sensitive research recognizes the differences among people from different cultural groups and from different language backgrounds.

What Are the Ethics Governing Psychological Research?

2.10 There Are Ethical Issues to Consider in Research with Human Participants
Ethical research is governed by principles that ensure fair, safe, and informed treatment of participants. Institutional review boards (IRBs) judge study proposals to make sure the studies will be ethically sound.

2.11 There Are Ethical Issues to Consider in Research with Animals
Research involving nonhuman animals provides useful, although simpler, models of behavior and of genetics. The purpose of such research may be to learn about animals' behavior or to make inferences about human behavior. Institutional Animal Care and Use Committee

(IACUC) judges study proposals to make sure the animals will be treated properly. Researchers must weigh their concerns for individual animals against their concerns for humanity's future.

2.12 Using Psychology in Your Life: Should You Participate in Psychological Research?

Study participants are essential to the research enterprise and must be treated ethically. Students often enjoy participating in psychological studies.

How Are Data Analyzed and Evaluated?

2.13 Good Research Requires Valid, Reliable, and Accurate Data

Data must be meaningful (valid) and their measurement reliable (i.e., consistent and stable) and accurate.

2.14 Descriptive Statistics Provide a Summary of the Data

Measures of central tendency (mean, median, and mode) and variability are used to describe data.

2.15 The Correlation Coefficient Summarizes the Relationships Between Variables

A correlation coefficient is a descriptive statistic that describes the strength and direction of the relationship between two variables. Correlations close to zero signify weak relationships. Correlations near +1.0 or –1.0 signify strong relationships.

2.16 Inferential Statistics Permit Generalizations

Inferential statistics enable us to decide whether differences between two or more groups are probably just chance variations (suggesting that the populations the groups were drawn from are the same) or whether they reflect true differences in the populations being compared. Meta-analysis combines the results of several studies to arrive at a conclusion.

2.17 Think Like a Psychologist: Should You Bet on a Hot Hand?

Although athletes have streaks of better than typical performance, such unusual patterns are not greater than would be expected by chance. People generally are bad at recognizing chance outcomes.

Key Terms

accuracy, p. 57
case study, p. 39
central tendency, p. 58
confound, p. 48
construct validity, p. 56
control group, p. 47
correlation coefficient, p. 60
correlational studies, p. 43
culturally sensitive research, p. 50
data, p. 30
dependent variable, p. 47
descriptive research, p. 39
descriptive statistics, p. 58
directionality problem, p. 44
experiment, p. 46
experimental group, p. 47
experimenter expectancy effect, p. 42

external validity, p. 56
hypothesis, p. 31
independent variable, p. 46
inferential statistics, p. 61
institutional review boards (IRBs), p. 52
internal validity, p. 56
mean, p. 58
median, p. 59
meta-analysis, p. 62
mode, p. 59
naturalistic observation, p. 40
negative correlation, p. 44
observer bias, p. 42
operational definition, p. 47
participant observation, p. 40
population, p. 49
positive correlation, p. 43

random assignment, p. 49
reactivity, p. 41
reliability, p. 56
replication, p. 35
research, p. 30
sample, p. 49
scatterplot, p. 43
scientific method, p. 30
selection bias, p. 50
self-report methods, p. 40
standard deviation, p. 60
theory, p. 31
third variable problem, p. 45
variability, p. 60
variable, p. 38
zero correlation, p. 44

How Useful Are Data Science Skills?

As you have likely come to appreciate, designing a study, conducting it, and analyzing the results are the essence of psychological research. These skills are routinely used by research psychologists to describe, predict, explain, and control human behavior. The example used in this chapter is of researchers seeking to determine the impact of cell phone use on driving. Another example is of researchers evaluating which treatments for psychological disorders are most effective (as will be discussed in Chapter 15). Of course, asking and answering questions about human behavior is not limited to psychology research. It is also extremely useful elsewhere, such as in the workplace.

Consider how online retailers, such as Amazon, accurately predict which movies, books, or other items you will like. Or think about how a particular ad targeted to your interests pops up in your browser. Amazon, Google, and other technology companies can gather enormous amounts of information from our online behavior. By carefully analyzing those data, these businesses can determine correlations between our previous purchases, activities, and browsing history and those of other customers. They use that information to suggest new products we are likely to purchase or activities we might pursue. Google can experimentally determine which ad is more effective by randomly presenting a particular ad to some customers and a different ad to others, then comparing "click" rates.

As technology generates more and more data about individual behavior, fluency in research design and data analysis will increasingly be in demand. A 2017 study commissioned by the Business—Higher Education Forum (BHEF) and PricewaterhouseCoopers estimates that by 2020, there will be 2.72 million new openings for jobs in "data science," which these organizations define as "the extraction of actionable knowledge directly from data through either a process of discovery, or hypothesis formulation and hypothesis testing."

In other words, the skills needed for work in data science overlap with those identified by the American Psychological Association (APA) learning goals for psychology majors. The APA refers to these skills as research design, data analysis, and interpretation. You have been introduced to those concepts in this chapter. Psychology majors study them in more depth through required courses in research methods and statistics.

The data science skills learned by psychology majors can be applied to a wide variety of jobs beyond the Web. Think of a human resource manager eager to improve work performance, a hospital administrator determined to reduce the spread of infections, or a teacher interested in identifying and improving ways of evaluating learning. All of these workplace settings require the accurate understanding and treatment of data.

The bottom line: As a psychology student, you can develop analytical skills by using and interpreting data. These skills are in great demand in the workplace. Taking additional courses in research methods and statistics will strengthen data science skills and employability.

Q **Want to earn a better grade on your test?**
Go to **INQUIZITIVE** to learn and review this chapter's content, with personalized feedback along the way.
Practice Tests and accompanying answer keys can be found at the back of the book on page PT-1.

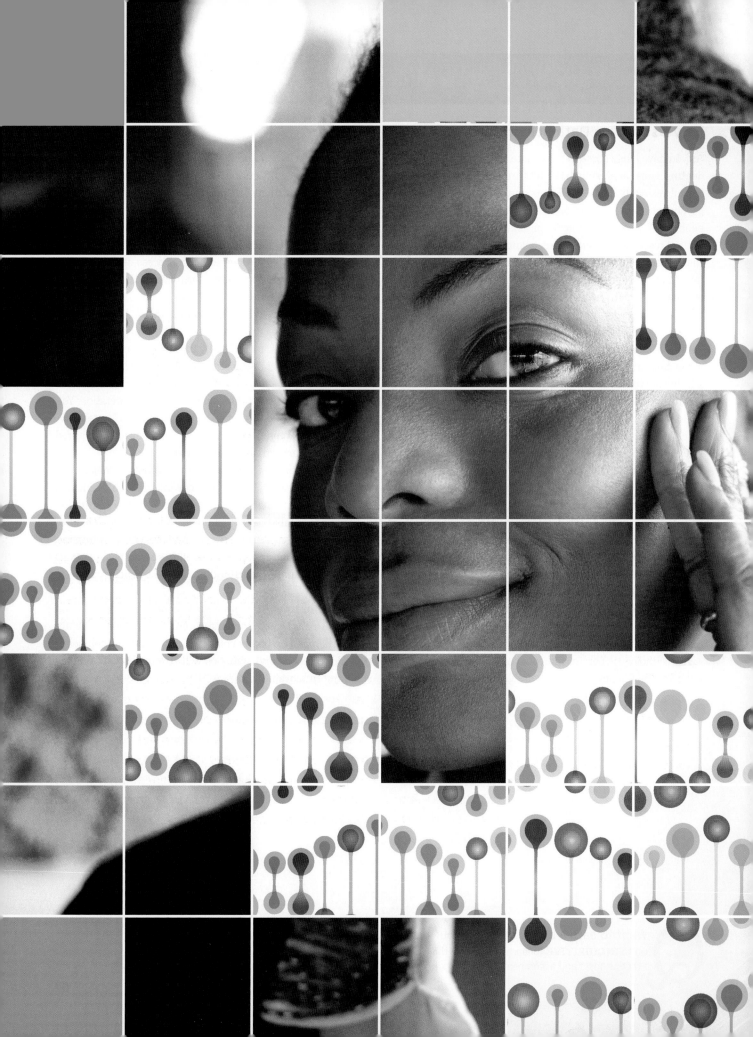

3

Biology and Behavior

Big Questions

- How Does the Nervous System Operate? 70

- What Are the Basic Brain Structures and Their Functions? 81

- How Does the Brain Communicate with the Body? 97

- How Does the Brain Change? 101

- What Is the Genetic Basis of Psychological Science? 106

PIZZA! THE BIG, CHEESY SLICES being sold by the sidewalk vendor look delicious. You feel a bit hungry, so you decide to splurge. The mouthwatering smell as you lift the slice to your mouth is matched by the textures and tastes. The result is that you feel happy and satisfied. All these rich experiences are produced by your nervous system, a network of billions of cells in your brain and body. From moving to sensing to choosing to determining your responses, you function because of your nerve cells.

To understand what makes us who we are, how we behave and why, we need to grasp how the nervous system works. Physiological processes—such as the activities of cells—are the basis of psychological processes. However, biology alone does not explain our behavior. Since aspects of our biology interact with our environments, we also need to consider how nature and nurture influence each other in shaping us. So for psychologists, the big questions about biology and behavior are: How does the nervous system operate? What are the basic brain structures and their functions? How does the brain communicate with the body? How does the brain change? And what is the genetic basis of psychological science?

Learning Objectives

- Distinguish between the two basic divisions of the nervous system.

- Distinguish between the functions of distinct types of neurons.

- Describe the structure of the neuron.

- Describe the electrical and chemical changes that occur when neurons communicate.

- Identify the major neurotransmitters and their primary functions.

central nervous system (CNS)
The brain and the spinal cord.

peripheral nervous system (PNS)
All nerve cells in the body that are not part of the central nervous system. The peripheral nervous system includes the somatic and autonomic nervous systems.

How Does the Nervous System Operate?

The nervous system's response to the world around us is responsible for everything we think, feel, or do. Essentially, each of us *is* a nervous system. The entire nervous system is divided into two basic units: the central nervous system and the peripheral nervous system. The **central nervous system (CNS)** consists of the brain and the spinal cord, both of which contain massive numbers of neurons (**FIGURE 3.1**). The **peripheral nervous system (PNS)** consists of all the other nerve cells in the rest of the body. The CNS and PNS are anatomically separate, but their functions are highly interdependent. The PNS sends a variety of information to the CNS. The CNS organizes and evaluates that information and then directs the PNS to perform specific behaviors or make bodily adjustments.

3.1 Neurons Are the Basic Units of the Nervous System

The basic units of this system are the nerve cells, called **neurons** (**FIGURE 3.2**). These cells receive, integrate, and transmit information in the nervous system. Complex networks of neurons sending and receiving signals are the functional basis of all psychological activity. Although the actions of single neurons are simple to describe, human complexity results from billions of neurons. Each neuron communicates with tens of thousands of other neurons. Neurons do not communicate randomly or arbitrarily, however. They communicate selectively with other neurons to form circuits, or *neural networks*. These networks develop through genetic influence, maturation and experience, and repeated firing. In other words, alliances form among groups of neurons.

As discussed more fully later in this chapter, the PNS includes the somatic and autonomic nervous systems. The somatic component of the PNS is involved in voluntary behavior, such as when you reach for an object to see how it feels. The autonomic component of the PNS is responsible for the less voluntary actions of your body, such as controlling heart rate and other bodily functions.

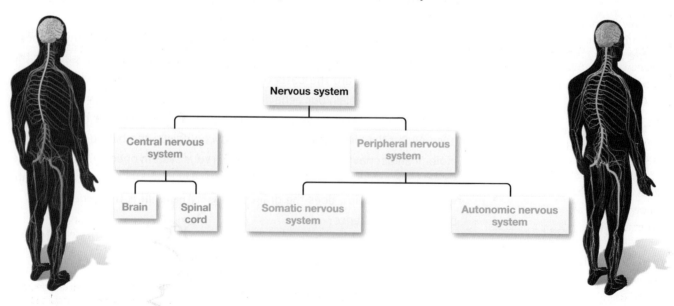

FIGURE 3.1
The Basic Divisions of the Nervous System

FUNCTIONS OF NEURONS Neurons are specialized for communication. That is, unlike other cells in the body, nerve cells are excitable: They are powered by electrical impulses and communicate with other nerve cells through chemical signals. During the reception phase, neurons take in the chemical signals from neighboring neurons. During integration, incoming signals are assessed. During transmission, neurons pass their own signals to yet other receiving neurons.

Some neurons (sensory neurons) detect information from the physical world and pass that information along to the brain, usually through the spinal cord. To get a sense of how fast that process can work, think of the last time you touched something hot or accidentally pricked yourself with a sharp object, such as a tack. Those signals triggered your body's nearly instantaneous response and sensory experience of the impact. The sensory nerves that provide information from the skin and muscles are called *somatosensory nerves.* (This term comes from the Greek for "body sense." It means sensations experienced from within the body.) Other neurons (motor neurons) direct muscles to contract or relax, thereby producing movement.

Sensory and motor neurons work together to control movement. For instance, if you are using a pen to take notes as you read these words, you are contracting and relaxing your hand muscles and finger muscles to adjust your fingers' pressure on the pen. When you want to use the pen, your brain sends a message via motor neurons to your finger muscles so they move in specific ways. Receptors in both your skin and your muscles send back messages through sensory neurons to help determine how much pressure is needed to hold the pen. This symphony of neural communication for a task as simple as using a pen is remarkable, yet most of us employ motor control so easily that we rarely think about it. In fact, our *reflexes*, automatic motor responses, occur before we even think about those responses. For each reflex action, a handful of neurons simply convert sensation into action.

NEURON STRUCTURE In addition to performing different functions, neurons have a wide assortment of shapes and sizes. A typical neuron has four structural regions that participate in communication functions: the dendrites, the cell body, the axon, and the terminal buttons (**FIGURE 3.3**). The **dendrites** are short, branchlike appendages that detect chemical signals from neighboring neurons. In the **cell body,** also known as the *soma* (Greek for "body"), the information received via the dendrites from thousands of other neurons is collected and integrated.

Once the incoming information from many other neurons has been integrated in the cell body, electrical impulses are transmitted along a long, narrow outgrowth known as the **axon.** Axons vary tremendously in length, from a few millimeters to more than a meter. The longest axons stretch from the spinal cord to the big toe. You may have heard the term *nerve* in reference to a "pinched nerve." In this context, a nerve is a bundle of axons that carry information between the brain and other

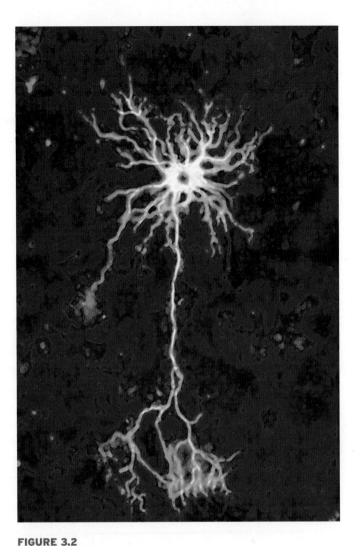

FIGURE 3.2
Human Neuron
Neurons like this one are the basic units of the human nervous system.

neurons

The basic units of the nervous system; cells that receive, integrate, and transmit information in the nervous system. They operate through electrical impulses, communicate with other neurons through chemical signals, and form neural networks.

dendrites

Branchlike extensions of the neuron that detect information from other neurons.

cell body

The site in the neuron where information from thousands of other neurons is collected and integrated.

axon

A long, narrow outgrowth of a neuron by which information is conducted from the cell body to the terminal buttons.

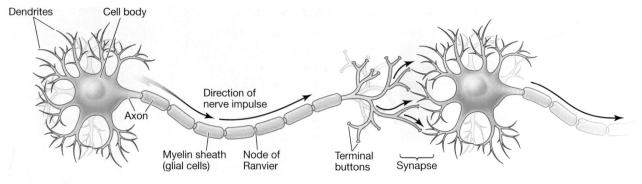

Dendrites　　Cell body

Direction of
nerve impulse

Axon

Myelin sheath　Node of　　　Terminal
(glial cells)　Ranvier　　　buttons　　Synapse

FIGURE 3.3
Neuron Structure
Messages are received by the dendrites, processed in the cell body, transmitted along the axon, and sent to other neurons via chemical substances released from the terminal buttons across the synapse. (The myelin sheath and the nodes of Ranvier are discussed on pp. 74-75.)

terminal buttons
At the ends of axons, small nodules that release chemical signals from the neuron into the synapse.

synapse
The gap between the terminal buttons of a "sending" neuron and the dendrites of a "receiving" neuron; the site at which chemical communication occurs between neurons.

specific locations in the body. At the end of the axon are knoblike structures called **terminal buttons.**

The site where chemical communication occurs between neurons is called the **synapse.** Since neurons do not touch one another, they communicate by sending chemicals into the synapse, a tiny gap between the terminal buttons of the "sending" neuron and the dendrites of the "receiving" neurons. Chemicals leave one neuron, cross the synapse, and pass signals along to the dendrites of other neurons.

The outer surface of a neuron is a *membrane*, a fatty barrier that does not dissolve in the watery environment inside and outside the neuron. The membrane is semipermeable. In other words, some substances move in or out of the membrane, and some do not. Located on the membrane are *ion channels*. These specialized pores allow *ions* to pass in and out of the cell when the neuron transmits signals down the axon. Ions are electrically charged molecules, some charged negatively and some charged positively. By controlling the movement of ions, the membrane plays an important role in communication between neurons: It regulates the concentration of electrically charged molecules that are the basis of the neuron's electrical activity.

ANSWER: After synapse, the order is dendrites, cell body, axon, terminal buttons, and then back to the synapse.

Q Place cell body, dendrites, terminal buttons, and axon in proper order, beginning and ending with the synapse.

action potential
The electrical signal that passes along the axon and subsequently causes the release of chemicals from the terminal buttons.

resting membrane potential
The electrical charge of a neuron when it is not active.

3.2 Action Potentials Produce Neural Communication

Neural communication depends on a neuron's ability to respond to incoming stimulation. The neuron responds by changing electrically and then passing along chemical signals to other neurons. An **action potential,** also called *neural firing*, is the electrical signal that passes along the axon. This signal causes the terminal buttons to release chemicals that transmit signals to other neurons. The following sections examine some factors that contribute to the firing of an action potential.

RESTING MEMBRANE POTENTIAL When a neuron is resting, not active, the electrical charge inside and outside the membrane is different. This difference is the **resting membrane potential.** The difference in the electrical charge occurs because the ratio of negative to positive ions is greater inside the neuron than outside it. Therefore, the electrical charge inside the neuron is slightly more negative than the electrical charge outside—typically –70 millivolts (about 1/20 the charge of a AA battery). When a neuron has more negative ions inside than outside, the neuron is described as being *polarized*. The polarized state of the resting neuron creates the electrical energy necessary to power the firing of the neuron.

Two types of ions that contribute to a neuron's resting membrane potential are *sodium ions* and *potassium ions*. Although other ions are involved in neural activity, sodium and potassium are most important for this discussion.

Ions pass through the neuron membrane at the ion channels (**FIGURE 3.4**). Each channel matches a specific type of ion: Sodium channels allow sodium ions but not potassium ions to pass through the membrane, and potassium channels allow passage of potassium ions but not sodium ions. The flow of ions through each channel is controlled by a gating mechanism. When a gate is open, ions flow in and out of the neuron through the cell membrane. A closed gate prevents their passage. Ion flow is also affected by the cell membrane's selective permeability. That is, much like a bouncer at an exclusive nightclub, the membrane allows some types of ions to cross more easily than others. Partially as a result of this selective permeability of the cell membrane, more potassium than sodium is inside the neuron.

Another mechanism in the membrane that contributes to polarization is the *sodium-potassium pump*. This pump increases potassium and decreases sodium inside the neuron, activity that helps maintain the resting membrane potential.

CHANGES IN ELECTRICAL POTENTIAL LEAD TO ACTION A neuron receives chemical signals from nearby neurons through its dendrites. By affecting polarization, these chemical signals tell the neuron whether to fire. The signals arrive at the dendrites by the thousands and are of two types: excitatory and inhibitory. *Excitatory signals* depolarize the cell membrane (i.e., decrease polarization by decreasing the negative charge inside the cell). Through depolarization, these signals increase the likelihood that the neuron will fire. *Inhibitory signals* hyperpolarize the cell (i.e., increase polarization by increasing the negative charge inside the cell). Through hyperpolarization, these signals decrease the likelihood that the neuron will fire. Excitatory and inhibitory signals received by the dendrites are combined within the neuron. If the total amount of excitatory input surpasses the neuron's firing threshold (–55 millivolts), an action potential is generated.

The action potential is an electrical ripple that travels down the axon. Because the neuron has been depolarized, ions can move freely. When a neuron fires, the sodium gates in the cell membrane open. The open gates allow sodium

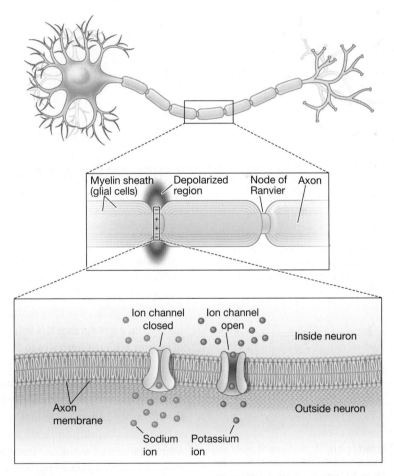

FIGURE 3.4
Resting Membrane Potential
A neuron at rest is polarized: It has a more negative electrical charge inside than outside. The passage of negative and positive ions inside and outside the neuron is regulated by ion channels in the membrane, such as those located at the nodes of Ranvier.

FIGURE 3.5
Action Potential

The electrical charge inside the neuron starts out slightly negative (resting membrane potential, -70 millivolts). As the neuron fires, it allows more positive ions inside the cell (depolarization). It then returns to its slightly negative resting state. This happens at each portion of the exposed axon as the action potential travels down the axon.

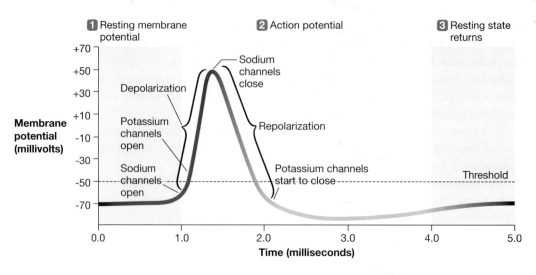

ions to rush into the neuron. This influx of sodium causes the inside of the neuron to become slightly more positively charged than the outside. A fraction of a second later, potassium channels open to allow the potassium ions inside the cell membrane to rush out. This change from a negative charge to a positive one inside the neuron is the basis of the action potential. As the sodium ion channels close, the sodium ions stop entering the cell. Similarly, as the potassium ion channels close, potassium ions stop exiting the cell. Thus, during the action potential, the electrical charge inside the cell starts out slightly negative in its initial resting state. As the cell fires and allows more positive ions inside, the charge becomes positive. Through natural restoration, including the activity of the sodium-potassium pump, the charge then returns to its slightly negative resting state (**FIGURE 3.5**).

ACTION POTENTIALS SPREAD ALONG THE AXON When the neuron fires, the cell membrane's depolarization moves along the axon like a wave. Sodium ions rush through their channels, causing adjacent sodium channels to open. Thus, like toppling dominoes, sodium ion channels open in a series. The action potential always moves down the axon away from the cell body to the terminal buttons. These electrical signals travel quickly down most axons because of the fatty **myelin sheath** that encases and insulates many axons like the plastic tubing around wires in an electrical cord (see Figure 3.3). Sensory and motor neurons must maintain their myelin to generate fast signals over long distances. Think of how fast you are able to remove your hand from a hot surface to avoid being burned. That speed of movement is the result of myelin, which allows you to feel the heat and reflexively remove your hand.

The myelin sheath is made up of *glial cells*, commonly called *glia* (Greek for "glue"). The sheath grows along an axon in short segments. Between these segments are small gaps of exposed axon called the **nodes of Ranvier** (after the researcher who first described them). Because of the insulation provided by the myelin sheath, the action potential skips quickly along the axon. It is recharged at each node along the axon. The action potential takes about 1/1000 of a second, permitting the fast and frequent adjustments required for coordinating motor activity. For those axons without myelin, sodium channels along each part of the membrane must open. The speed of conduction of the action potential is decreased greatly.

To understand the importance of neural insulation, consider the disease multiple sclerosis (MS), which affects more than 250,000 Americans (Goldenberg, 2012). The earliest symptoms can begin in young adulthood and often include

myelin sheath

A fatty material, made up of glial cells, that insulates some axons to allow for faster movement of electrical impulses along the axon.

nodes of Ranvier

Small gaps of exposed axon, between the segments of myelin sheath, where action potentials take place.

numbness in the limbs and blurry vision. This especially tragic neurological disorder is characterized by deterioration of the myelin sheath. Since the myelin insulation helps messages move quickly along axons, demyelination slows down neural impulses. The axons essentially short-circuit, and normal neural communication is interrupted. Motor actions become jerky, as those afflicted lose the ability to coordinate motor movements. Over time, movement, sensation, and coordination are severely impaired, and most people who have MS will need help walking. As the myelin sheath disintegrates, axons are exposed and may start to break down. The life expectancy of people with MS is five to 10 years less than that of people who are not afflicted.

ALL-OR-NONE PRINCIPLE Any one signal received by the neuron has little influence on whether the neuron fires. Normally, a neuron is barraged by thousands of excitatory and inhibitory signals, and its firing is determined by the number and frequency of those signals. If the sum of excitatory and inhibitory signals leads to a positive change in voltage that exceeds the neuron's firing threshold, an action potential is generated.

A neuron either fires or does not. It works like a light switch that is either on or off, not like a dimmer switch. The **all-or-none principle** dictates that a neuron fires with the same potency each time. In other words, it does not fire in a way that can be described as weak or strong. What is affected by the strength of the stimulation is how often the neuron fires: The stronger the stimulation, the more frequently the neuron fires action potentials.

For the sake of comparison, suppose you are playing a video game in which you fire missiles by pressing a button. Every time you press the button, a missile is launched at the same velocity as the previous one. It makes no difference how hard you press the button. If you keep your finger on the button, additional missiles fire in rapid succession. Likewise, if a neuron in the visual system, for example, receives information that a light is bright, it might respond by firing more rapidly and more often than when it receives information that the light is dim. Regardless of whether the light is bright or dim, the strength of the firing will be the same every time. Remember, it is all or none: A neuron either fires or does not.

Q **What happens when a neuron is depolarized past its firing threshold?**

ANSWER: An action potential occurs—i.e., the neuron fires.

3.3 Neurotransmitters Influence Mental Activity and Behavior

As noted earlier in this chapter, neurons do not touch one another. They are separated by a small space known as the synapse, the site of chemical communication between neurons. Action potentials cause neurons to release chemicals from their terminal buttons. These chemicals travel across the synapse and are received by other neurons' dendrites. The neuron that sends the signal is called the *presynaptic neuron*, and the one that receives the signal is called the *postsynaptic neuron*.

How do these chemical signals work (**FIGURE 3.6**)? Inside each terminal button are **neurotransmitters,** chemicals that are made in the axon and stored in vesicles (small, fluid-filled sacs). When released by the vesicles, the neurotransmitters convey signals across the synapse to postsynaptic cells.

FIGURE 3.6
How Neurotransmitters Work

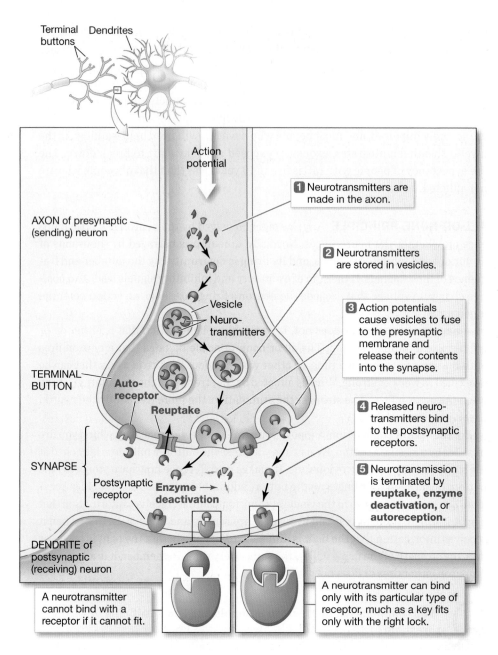

Terminal buttons Dendrites

Action potential

AXON of presynaptic (sending) neuron

1 Neurotransmitters are made in the axon.

2 Neurotransmitters are stored in vesicles.

Vesicle
Neuro-transmitters

3 Action potentials cause vesicles to fuse to the presynaptic membrane and release their contents into the synapse.

TERMINAL BUTTON

Auto-receptor

Reuptake

4 Released neuro-transmitters bind to the postsynaptic receptors.

SYNAPSE

Postsynaptic receptor **Enzyme deactivation**

5 Neurotransmission is terminated by **reuptake, enzyme deactivation,** or **autoreception.**

DENDRITE of postsynaptic (receiving) neuron

A neurotransmitter cannot bind with a receptor if it cannot fit.

A neurotransmitter can bind only with its particular type of receptor, much as a key fits only with the right lock.

receptors

In neurons, specialized protein molecules on the postsynaptic membrane; neurotransmitters bind to these molecules after passing across the synapse.

After an action potential travels to the terminal button, it causes the vesicles to attach to the presynaptic membrane and release their neurotransmitters into the synapse. These neurotransmitters then travel across the synapse and attach themselves, or *bind*, to receptors on the postsynaptic neuron. **Receptors** are specialized protein molecules located on the postsynaptic membrane that specifically respond to the chemical structure of the neurotransmitter available in the synapse. The binding of a neurotransmitter with a receptor can cause ion channels to open or close more tightly, producing an excitatory or an inhibitory signal in the postsynaptic neuron. An excitatory signal encourages the neuron to fire. An inhibitory signal discourages it from firing.

NEUROTRANSMITTERS BIND WITH SPECIFIC RECEPTORS More than 60 chemicals convey information in the nervous system. Different neurotransmitters influence emotion, thought, or behavior, depending on the type of receptor and the location within the brain. In addition, much the same way as a lock opens only with the correct key, each receptor can be influenced by only one type of neurotransmitter.

Once a neurotransmitter is released into the synapse, it continues to bind with receptors and continues to exert an inhibitory or excitatory effect. It also blocks new signals until its influence is terminated. The three major events that terminate the neurotransmitter's influence in the synapse are reuptake, enzyme deactivation, and autoreception. **Reuptake** occurs when the neurotransmitter is taken back into the presynaptic terminal buttons. An action potential prompts terminal buttons to release the neurotransmitter into the synapse and then take it back for recycling. The cycle of reuptake and release repeats continuously. *Enzyme deactivation* occurs when an enzyme destroys the neurotransmitter in the synapse. Different enzymes break down different neurotransmitters. Neurotransmitters can also bind with receptors on the presynaptic neuron. This process is called *autoreception*. Autoreceptors monitor how much neurotransmitter has been released into the synapse. When an excess is detected, the autoreceptors signal the presynaptic neuron to stop releasing the neurotransmitter.

All neurotransmitters have excitatory or inhibitory effects on action potentials. They do so by affecting the polarization of the postsynaptic cells. The effects are a function of the receptors that the neurotransmitters bind to. Recall the lock and key idea, in which a specific neurotransmitter binds only with certain receptors. The receptor always has a specific response, either excitatory or inhibitory. The same neurotransmitter can send excitatory or inhibitory postsynaptic signals, depending on the particular receptor's properties. In other words, the effects of a neurotransmitter are not a property of the chemical. Instead, the effects are a function of the receptor to which the neurotransmitter binds. Any neurotransmitter can be excitatory or inhibitory. Alternatively, it can produce radically different effects, depending on the properties of the receptor and on the receptor's location in the brain.

AGONISTS AND ANTAGONISTS Much of what we know about neurotransmitters has been learned through the systematic study of how drugs and toxins affect emotion, thought, and behavior. Drugs and toxins can alter a neurotransmitter's action in many ways. For example, they can alter how a neurotransmitter is synthesized. They can raise or lower the amount of a neurotransmitter released from the terminal buttons. Or, by blocking reuptake, they can change the way a neurotransmitter is deactivated in the synapse and therefore affect the concentration of the neurotransmitter.

Drugs and toxins that enhance the actions of neurotransmitters are known as *agonists*. Drugs and toxins that inhibit these actions are known as *antagonists*. Drugs and toxins can act as agonists by mimicking neurotransmitters and binding with their receptors as if they were the real thing (**FIGURE 3.7**). Addictive drugs such as heroin, for example, have their effects because they are chemically similar to naturally occurring neurotransmitters. The receptors cannot differentiate between the ingested drug and the real neurotransmitter released from a presynaptic neuron. That is, although a neurotransmitter fits a receptor the way a key fits a lock, the receptor/lock cannot tell a real neurotransmitter/key from a forgery—either will open it.

Researchers often inject agonists or antagonists into animals to assess how neurotransmitters affect behavior. The goal is to develop drug treatments for many psychological and medical disorders. For instance, researchers can test the hypothesis that a certain neurotransmitter in a specific brain region leads to increased eating. Injecting an agonist into that brain region should increase eating. Injecting an antagonist should decrease eating.

TYPES OF NEUROTRANSMITTERS There are many kinds of neurotransmitters. Seven of them are particularly important in understanding how we think, feel, and behave (**TABLE 3.1**).

reuptake
The process whereby a neurotransmitter is taken back into the presynaptic terminal buttons, thereby stopping its activity.

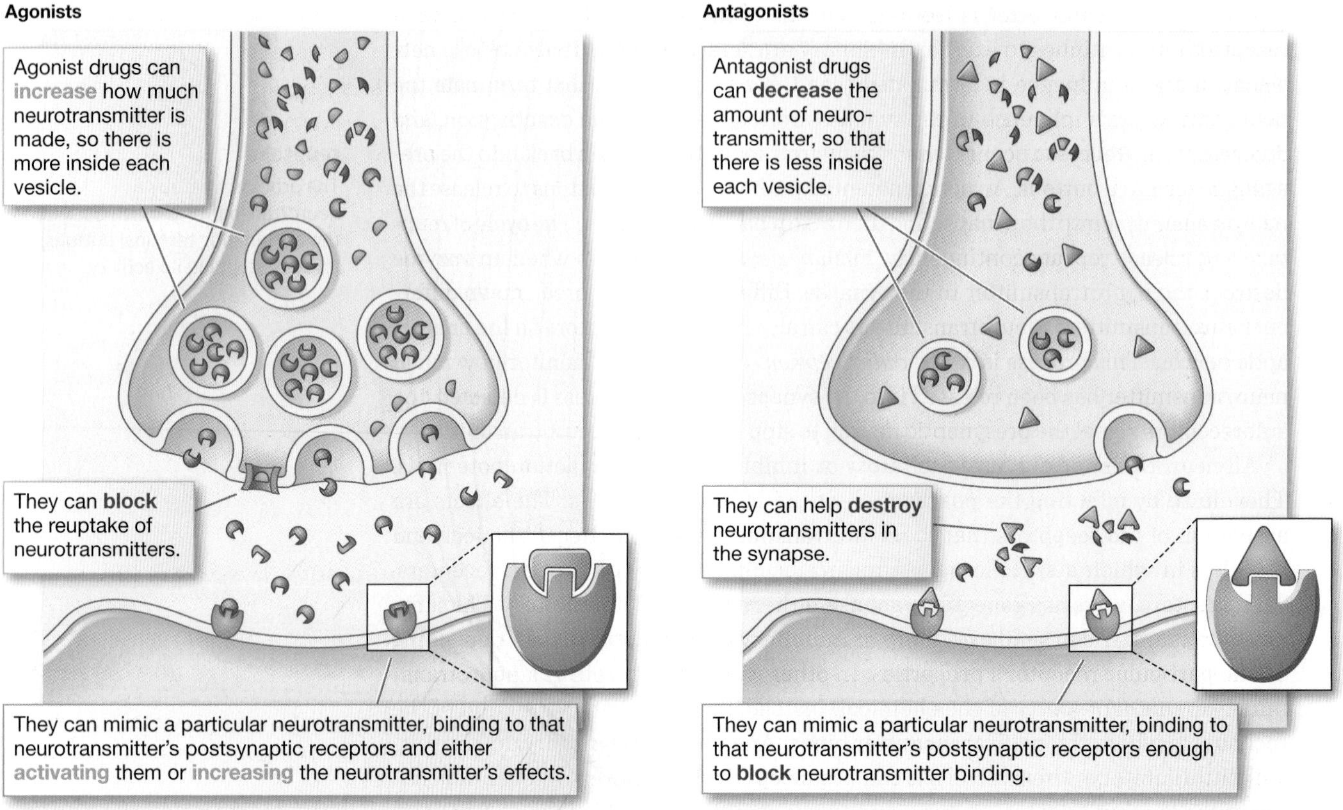

Agonist drugs can **increase** how much neurotransmitter is made, so there is more inside each vesicle.

They can **block** the reuptake of neurotransmitters.

They can mimic a particular neurotransmitter, binding to that neurotransmitter's postsynaptic receptors and either **activating** them or **increasing** the neurotransmitter's effects.

Antagonist drugs can **decrease** the amount of neurotransmitter, so that there is less inside each vesicle.

They can help **destroy** neurotransmitters in the synapse.

They can mimic a particular neurotransmitter, binding to that neurotransmitter's postsynaptic receptors enough to **block** neurotransmitter binding.

FIGURE 3.7
How Drugs Work

Table 3.1 Common Neurotransmitters and Their Major Functions

NEUROTRANSMITTER	PSYCHOLOGICAL FUNCTIONS
Acetylcholine	Motor control over muscles
	Learning, memory, sleeping, and dreaming
Norepinephrine	Arousal, vigilance, and attention
Serotonin	Emotional states and impulsiveness
	Dreaming
Dopamine	Reward and motivation
	Motor control over voluntary movement
GABA (gamma-aminobutyric acid)	Inhibition of action potentials
	Anxiety reduction
Glutamate	Enhancement of action potentials
	Learning and memory
Endorphins	Pain reduction
	Reward

acetylcholine (ACh)

The neurotransmitter responsible for motor control at the junction between nerves and muscles; it is also involved in mental processes such as learning, memory, sleeping, and dreaming.

The neurotransmitter **acetylcholine (ACh)** is responsible for motor control at the junctions between nerves and muscles. After moving across synapses, ACh (pronounced A-C-H) binds with receptors on muscle cells, making the muscles contract or relax. For instance, ACh excites skeletal muscles and inhibits heart muscle. As is true of all neurotransmitters, whether ACh's effects will be excitatory or inhibitory depends on the receptors.

Botulism, a form of food poisoning, is caused by Botulinum toxin. This neurotoxin inhibits the release of ACh. The resulting paralysis of muscles leads to difficulty in chewing, difficulty in breathing, and often death. Because of its ability to paralyze muscles, very small doses of Botulinum toxin are used for cosmetic surgery. Physicians inject the toxin, popularly known as Botox, into the eyebrow region, paralyzing muscles that produce certain wrinkles (**FIGURE 3.8**). Because the effects wear off over time, a new dose of Botox needs to be injected every two to four months. If too much Botox is injected, however, the result can be an expressionless face, because Botox paralyzes the facial muscles used to express emotions, as in smiling and frowning.

Acetylcholine is also involved in complex mental processes such as learning, memory, sleeping, and dreaming. Because ACh affects memory and attention, drugs that are ACh antagonists can cause temporary amnesia. In a similar way, Alzheimer's disease, a condition characterized primarily by severe memory deficits, is associated with diminished ACh functioning (Mesulam, 2013). Drugs that are ACh agonists may enhance memory and decrease other symptoms, but so far drug treatments for Alzheimer's have experienced only marginal success.

Three transmitters (norepinephrine, serotonin, and dopamine) are grouped together because each has the same basic molecular structure. Together they are called *monoamines*. Their major functions are to regulate arousal, regulate feelings, and motivate behavior.

The neurotransmitter **norepinephrine** is involved in states of arousal and attention. Very little norepinephrine is released during sleep. As norepinephrine increases, you become more alert. Norepinephrine helps you focus attention. It is especially important for vigilance, a heightened sensitivity to what is going on around you. A related substance produces an *adrenaline rush*, that sudden burst of energy that seems to take over your whole body. The adrenaline rush results from a release of *epinephrine* in the body. Epinephrine was originally called adrenaline. Epinephrine binds to receptors throughout the body. This energy boost is part of a system that prepares the body for dealing with threats from an environment (the fight-or-flight response, discussed in Chapter 11, "Health and Well-Being").

Serotonin is involved in a wide range of psychological activities. It is especially important for emotional states, impulse control, and dreaming. Low levels of serotonin are associated with sad and anxious moods, food cravings, and aggressive behavior. Some drugs block serotonin reuptake and thus leave more serotonin at the synapse to bind with the postsynaptic neurons. These drugs are used to treat a wide array of mental and behavioral disorders, including depression, obsessive-compulsive disorders, eating disorders, and obesity. One class of drugs that specifically target serotonin is prescribed widely to treat depression (Jakubovski, Varigonda, Freemantle, Taylor, & Bloch, 2016). These drugs, which include Prozac, are referred to as *selective serotonin reuptake inhibitors*, or *SSRIs*.

Dopamine serves many significant brain functions, especially those related to motivation and reward. Many theorists believe dopamine communicates which activities may be rewarding. For example, eating when hungry, drinking when thirsty, and having sex when aroused activate dopamine receptors and therefore are experienced as pleasurable. When we see food, dopamine activity motivates us to want to eat it. Dopamine activation is also involved in motor control and planning. It helps guide behavior toward things—objects and experiences—that will lead to additional reward. Dopamine's release makes behaviors more likely to occur in the future.

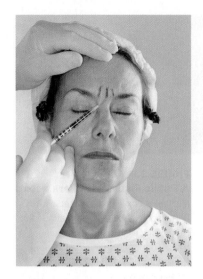

FIGURE 3.8
Acetylcholine and Botox
Acetylcholine (ACh) is responsible for motor control between nerves and muscles. Botox inhibits the release of ACh, paralyzing muscles. Here, a woman receives a Botox injection to remove wrinkles in her forehead.

norepinephrine
A monoamine neurotransmitter involved in states of arousal and attention.

serotonin
A monoamine neurotransmitter important for a wide range of psychological activity, including emotional states, impulse control, and dreaming.

dopamine
A monoamine neurotransmitter involved in motivation, reward, and motor control over voluntary movement.

"I'LL HAVE TO GET DR. KENDRICK TO REDUCE HIS DOSAGE OF PROZAC."

FIGURE 3.9

A Public Figure with Parkinson's

Michael J. Fox was diagnosed with Parkinson's disease in 1991, at age 30. He has since created the Michael J. Fox Foundation, which advocates for research toward finding a cure for Parkinson's.

GABA

Gamma-aminobutyric acid; the primary inhibitory transmitter in the nervous system.

glutamate

The primary excitatory transmitter in the nervous system.

endorphins

Neurotransmitters involved in natural pain reduction and reward.

FIGURE 3.10

Exercise and Endorphins

Endorphins are involved in both pain reduction and reward, and scientists think that endorphin production can be stimulated by strenuous exercise. An endurance event, such as a marathon or a speed skating competition, will yield an enormous endorphin rush. Here, Kayoko Fukushi of Japan crosses the finish line in the women's marathon at the Rio 2016 Olympics.

A lack of dopamine may be involved in problems with movement, and dopamine depletion is implicated in Parkinson's disease. Parkinson's is a degenerative and fatal neurological disorder marked by muscular rigidity, tremors, and difficulty initiating voluntary action. It affects about 1 in every 200 older adults and occurs in all known cultures. The actor Michael J. Fox is one of the many famous people who have developed this disease (**FIGURE 3.9**). Most people with Parkinson's do not experience symptoms until after age 50, but as Fox's case makes clear, the disease can occur earlier in life.

With Parkinson's disease, the dopamine-producing neurons slowly die off. In the later stages of the disorder, people suffer from cognitive and mood disturbances. Injections of one of the chief building blocks of dopamine, *L-DOPA*, help the surviving neurons produce more dopamine. When used to treat Parkinson's disease, L-DOPA often produces a remarkable, though temporary, recovery.

GABA (gamma-aminobutyric acid) is the primary inhibitory neurotransmitter in the nervous system. It is more widely distributed throughout the brain than most other neurotransmitters. Without the inhibitory effect of GABA, synaptic excitation might get out of control and spread through the brain chaotically. One cause of epileptic seizures may be low levels of GABA (Shetty & Upadhya, 2016). Drugs that are GABA agonists are widely used to treat anxiety disorders. For instance, benzodiazepines, which include drugs such as Valium and Xanax, help people relax. Ethyl alcohol—the type people drink—also facilitates GABA transmission, which is why alcohol is typically experienced as relaxing.

In contrast, **glutamate** is the primary excitatory transmitter in the nervous system and is involved in fast-acting neural transmission throughout the brain. Glutamate receptors aid learning and memory by strengthening synaptic connections. Excessive glutamate release can lead to overexcitement of the brain, which can produce seizures as well as destruction of neurons. Overexcitement caused by excess glutamate is linked to many diseases and types of brain damage. For example, much of the damage inflicted to the brain following a stroke or trauma to the brain is caused by the excessive release of glutamate that naturally occurs following brain injury (Cantu et al., 2015).

Endorphins are involved in both natural pain reduction and reward (**FIGURE 3.10**). In the early 1970s, researchers established that opiate drugs such as heroin and morphine bind to receptors in the brain, and this finding led to the discovery of naturally occurring substances in the body that bind to those sites (Pert & Snyder, 1973). Called *endorphins* (short for *endogenous morphine*), these substances are part of the body's natural defense against pain.

Pain is useful because it signals to animals, human and nonhuman, that they are hurt or in danger and therefore should try to escape or withdraw. Pain can also interfere with adaptive functioning, however. If pain prevents animals from engaging in behaviors such as eating, competing, and mating, the animals fail to reproduce. Endorphins' painkilling, or analgesic, effects help animals perform these behaviors even when they are in pain. Likewise, in humans, the administration of drugs, such as morphine, that bind with endorphin receptors reduces the subjective experience of pain. Apparently, morphine alters the way pain is experienced rather than blocking the nerves that transmit pain signals: People still feel pain, but they report detachment and do not care about the pain (Foley, 1993). Unfortunately, as you will learn in Chapter 4, there is currently an opiate abuse epidemic leading to many deaths from overdose. Administering the antagonist naloxone blocks the effect of opiates and thereby helps prevent overdose.

 How do agonists differ from antagonists?

ANSWER: Agonists enhance the effects of neurotransmitters, whereas antagonists inhibit effects.

What Are the Basic Brain Structures and Their Functions?

The brain is best viewed as a collection of interacting neural circuits. These circuits have accumulated and developed throughout human evolution. Just as our ancestors adapted to their environments, the brain has evolved specialized mechanisms to regulate breathing, food intake, body fluids, and sexual and social behavior. It has also developed sensory systems to aid in navigation and assist in recognizing friends and foes. Everything we are and do is orchestrated by the brain and, for more rudimentary actions, by the spinal cord (**FIGURE 3.11**). Early in life, overabundant connections form among the brain's neurons. Subsequently, life experiences help "prune" some of these connections to strengthen the rest, much as pruning weak or nonproductive branches will strengthen a fruit tree.

The brain's basic structures and their functions enable people to accomplish feats such as seeing, hearing, remembering, and interacting with others. Understanding these relationships also helps us understand psychological disorders.

3.4 The Ability to Study Brain Function Has Improved Dramatically

For most of human history, theorists and researchers have tried to understand how the brain works. By the beginning of the nineteenth century, anatomists understood the brain's basic structure reasonably well. But debates raged over how the brain produced mental activity. Did different parts do different things? Or were all areas of the brain equally important in cognitive activities such as problem solving and memory?

SPECIALIZED FUNCTIONS In the early nineteenth century, the neuroanatomist Franz Gall and his assistant, the physician Johann Spurzheim, hypothesized about the effects of mental activity on brain anatomy. Gall and Spurzheim proposed that if a person used a particular mental function more than other mental functions, the part of the brain where the emphasized function was performed would grow. This growth would produce a bump in the overlying skull. By carefully feeling the skull, one could describe the personality of the individual. This practice came to be known as *phrenology* (**FIGURE 3.12**).

Gall was a physician, not a scientist. He noted correlations, but he did not practice the scientific method and sought only to confirm, not disprove, his ideas. In any case, at the time, the technology was not available to test this theory scientifically. The pseudoscience of phrenology soon fell into the hands of frauds and quacks, but it helped spread the seemingly scientific principle that brain functions were localized.

The first strong scientific evidence that brain regions perform specialized functions came from the work of the nineteenth-century physician and anatomist Paul Broca (Finger, 1994). One of Broca's patients had lost the ability to say anything other than the word *tan*, though he could still understand language. After the patient died, in 1861, Broca performed an autopsy. At the time, an autopsy was the only way to link brain structure and function. When he examined the patient's brain, Broca found a large area of damage in a section of the front left side. This observation led him to conclude that this particular region was important for speech. Broca's theory has survived the test of time. This left frontal region, crucial for the production of language,

Learning Objectives

- Describe different methods for assessing brain function and activity.

- Identify the basic structures of the brain and their primary functions.

- Explain how the study of split brain contributes to understanding the functions of the cerebral hemispheres.

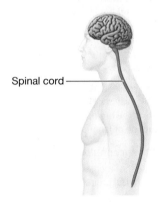

Spinal cord

FIGURE 3.11
The Brain and the Spinal Cord
This drawing illustrates the brain's exterior and its connection with the spinal cord. The view is from the left side of the body.

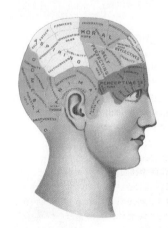

FIGURE 3.12
Phrenology
In a phrenological map, each region of the skull is associated with a feature. Each association is meant to reflect a process occurring in the brain under the skull.

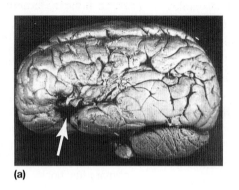

(a)

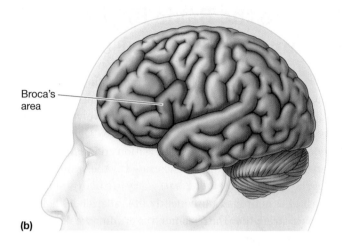

Broca's area

(b)

FIGURE 3.13
Broca's Area
(a) Paul Broca studied a patient's brain and identified the damaged area as crucial for speech production.
(b) This illustration shows the location of Broca's area.

Broca's area
A small portion of the left frontal region of the brain, crucial for the production of language.

electroencephalograph (EEG)
A device that measures electrical activity in the brain.

FIGURE 3.14
Polygraph
A polygraph (lie detector) measures changes in bodily functions (e.g., heart rate, perspiration rate, blood pressure) related to behaviors or mental states. These changes are *not* reliable measures of lying.

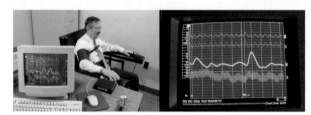

FIGURE 3.15
Electroencephalograph
An electroencephalograph (EEG) measures the brain's electrical activity.

became known as **Broca's area** (**FIGURE 3.13**). In Chapter 8, you will learn about other brain regions involved in language.

PSYCHOPHYSIOLOGICAL ASSESSMENT Psychologists collect data about the ways people's bodies respond to particular tasks or events. For instance, when people are frightened, their muscles become tense and their hearts beat faster. Other bodily systems influenced by mental states include blood pressure, blood temperature, perspiration rate, breathing rate, and pupil size. Measurements of these systems are examples of *psychophysiological assessment*. In this type of testing, researchers examine how bodily functions (physiology) change in association with behaviors or mental states (psychology).

Police investigators often use *polygraphs*, popularly known as "lie detectors," to assess some bodily states (**FIGURE 3.14**). The assumption behind these devices is that people who are lying experience more arousal and therefore are more likely to show physical signs of stress. This method is not precise, however, and so lie detectors do not accurately measure whether someone is lying. (The limitations of lie detectors are discussed further in the "Think like a Psychologist" section in Chapter 10.)

Electrophysiology is a data collection method that measures electrical activity in the brain. Small electrodes on the scalp act like small microphones that pick up the brain's electrical activity instead of sounds. The device that measures brain activity is an **electroencephalograph** (EEG; **FIGURE 3.15**). This measurement is useful because different behavioral states produce different and predictable EEG patterns. As a measure of specific cognitive states, however, the EEG is limited. Because the recordings (*electroencephalograms*) reflect all brain activity, they are too "noisy" or imprecise to isolate specific responses to particular stimuli. A more powerful way of examining how brain activity changes in response to a specific stimulus involves conducting many trials with a single individual and averaging across the trials. Because this method enables researchers to observe patterns associated with specific events, it is called *event-related potential (ERP)*. ERPs provide information about the speed at which the brain processes events but not about where in the brain those processes take place.

Until the 1980s, researchers did not have methods for localizing ongoing mental activity in the working brain. The invention of *brain imaging* methods changed that situation swiftly and dramatically. The new imaging techniques have advanced our understanding of the human brain the way the development of telescopes advanced our understanding of astronomy—and the brain's structures and functions may be as complex as distant galaxies.

The brain's electrical activity is associated with changes in the flow of blood carrying oxygen and nutrients to the active brain regions. Most brain imaging methods measure changes in the rate, or speed, of the flow of blood to different regions of the brain. By keeping track of these changes, researchers can monitor which brain areas are active when people perform particular tasks or experience particular events. Imaging is a powerful tool for uncovering where different systems reside in the brain and how different brain areas interact to process information.

- *Positron emission tomography (PET)* After the injection of a relatively harmless radioactive substance into the bloodstream, a **positron emission tomography (PET)** scan enables researchers to find the most active brain areas (**FIGURE 3.16**). The increased blood flow carrying the radioactive material leads these regions to emit more radiation. One downside of PET is the need to inject a radioactive substance into the body. For safety reasons, researchers limit the use of this technology.

- *Magnetic resonance imaging (MRI)* With **magnetic resonance imaging (MRI)**, a powerful magnetic field is used to momentarily disrupt the brain's magnetic forces (**FIGURE 3.17**). During this process, energy is released from brain tissue in a form that can be measured by detectors surrounding the head. Because different types of brain tissue release energy differently, the researchers can produce a high-resolution image of the brain. (The amount of energy released is very small, so having an MRI is not dangerous. Nor is there any danger in being exposed to the magnetic field at the levels used in research.) MRI is extremely valuable for providing information about the structure of the brain. For instance, it can be used to determine the location of brain damage or of a brain tumor.

- *Functional magnetic resonance imaging (fMRI)* **Functional magnetic resonance imaging (fMRI)** makes use of the brain's blood flow to map the working brain (**FIGURE 3.18**). Whereas PET measures blood flow directly by tracking a radioactive substance, fMRI measures blood flow indirectly by assessing changes in the blood's oxygen level. As with all brain imaging methods, the participant performs an experimental task that differs from a control task in only one way and that reflects the particular mental function of interest. The researchers then compare experimental and control images to examine differences in blood flow and therefore brain activity.

positron emission tomography (PET)

A method of brain imaging that assesses metabolic activity by using a radioactive substance injected into the bloodstream.

magnetic resonance imaging (MRI)

A method of brain imaging that uses a powerful magnetic field to produce high-quality images of the brain.

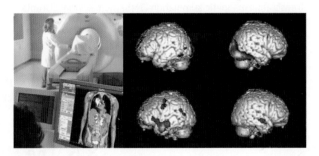

FIGURE 3.16
Positron Emission Tomography
Positron emission tomography (PET) scans the brain's metabolic activity.

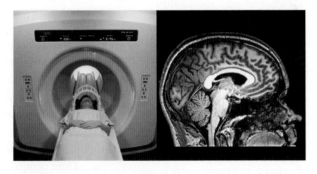

FIGURE 3.17
Magnetic Resonance Imaging
Magnetic resonance imaging (MRI) produces a high-resolution image of the brain.

FIGURE 3.18
Functional Magnetic Resonance Imaging
Functional magnetic resonance imaging (fMRI) maps mental activity by assessing the blood's oxygen level in the brain.

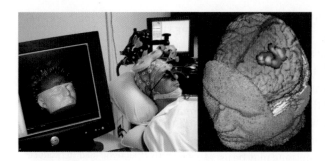

FIGURE 3.19
Transcranial Magnetic Stimulation
Transcranial magnetic stimulation (TMS) momentarily disrupts brain activity in a specific brain region.

ANSWER: EEG provides information on when a brain response occurs. By contrast, fMRI and PET provide information about where a response occurs.

One limitation of brain imaging is that the findings are necessarily correlational. We know that certain brain regions are active while a task is performed. We do not know whether each brain region is necessary for that particular task. To see whether a brain region is important for a task, researchers ideally want to compare performances when that area is working effectively and when it is not. **Transcranial magnetic stimulation (TMS)** uses a very fast but powerful magnetic field to disrupt brain activity momentarily in a specific brain region (**FIGURE 3.19**). This technique has its limitations, particularly that it can be used only for short durations to examine brain areas close to the scalp. When used along with imaging, however, it is a powerful method for examining which brain regions are necessary for specific psychological functions.

Q How do PET and fMRI differ from EEG in terms of the brain activity they measure?

3.5 The Brain Stem Houses the Basic Programs of Survival

The spinal cord is a rope of neural tissue. As shown in Figure 3.11, the cord runs inside the hollows of the vertebrae from just above the pelvis up into the base of the skull. One of its functions is the coordination of reflexes, such as the reflexive movement of your leg when a doctor taps your knee or the reflexive movement of your arm when you jerk your hand away from a flame. The cord's most important function is to carry sensory information up to the brain and carry motor signals from the brain to the body parts below to initiate action.

In cross section, the spinal cord is seen to be composed of two distinct tissue types: the *gray matter*, which is dominated by neurons' cell bodies, and the *white matter*, which consists mostly of axons and the fatty myelin sheaths that surround them. Gray matter and white matter are clearly distinguishable throughout the brain as well. In the brain, gray matter consists mostly of neuron bodies that have nonmyelinated axons and communicate only with nearby neurons. White matter consists mostly of myelinated axons that travel between brain regions.

In the base of the skull, the spinal cord thickens and becomes more complex as it transforms into the **brain stem** (**FIGURE 3.20**). The brain stem consists of the *medulla oblongata*, the *pons*, and the *midbrain*. It houses the nerves that control the most basic functions of survival, such as heart rate, breathing, swallowing, vomiting, urination, and orgasm. A significant blow to this region can cause death. As a continuous extension of the spinal cord, the brain stem also performs functions for the head similar to those that the spinal cord performs for the rest of the body. Many reflexes emerge from here, analogous to the spinal reflexes; gagging is one example.

The brain stem also contains a network of neurons known collectively as the *reticular formation*. The reticular formation projects up into the *cerebral cortex* (outer portion of the brain—discussed shortly) and affects general alertness. It is also involved in inducing and terminating the different stages of sleep (as discussed in Chapter 4, "Consciousness").

CEREBELLUM The **cerebellum** (Latin, "little brain") is a large protuberance connected to the back of the brain stem (**FIGURE 3.21**). Its size and convoluted surface

functional magnetic resonance imaging (fMRI)
An imaging technique used to examine changes in the activity of the working human brain by measuring changes in the blood's oxygen levels.

transcranial magnetic stimulation (TMS)
The use of strong magnets to briefly interrupt normal brain activity as a way to study brain regions.

brain stem
An extension of the spinal cord; it houses structures that control functions associated with survival, such as heart rate, breathing, swallowing, vomiting, urination, and orgasm.

cerebellum
A large, convoluted protuberance at the back of the brain stem; it is essential for coordinated movement and balance.

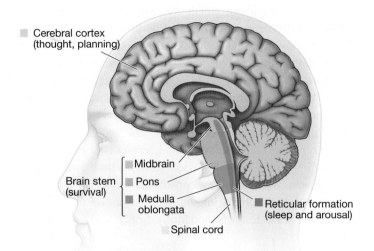

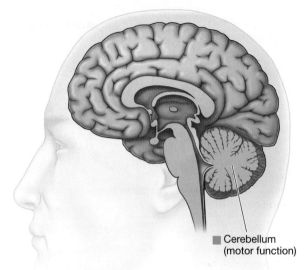

FIGURE 3.20
The Brain Stem
This drawing shows the brain stem and its parts, in relation to the cerebral cortex.

FIGURE 3.21
The Cerebellum
The cerebellum is located at the back of the brain: It is below the cerebral cortex and behind the brain stem.

make it look like an extra brain. The cerebellum is extremely important for proper motor function, and damage to its different parts produces very different effects. For example, damage to the little nodes at the very bottom causes head tilt, balance problems, and a loss of smooth compensation of eye position for head movement.

Try turning your head while looking at this book. Notice that your eyes remain focused on the material. Your eyes would not be able to do that if an injury affected the bottom of your cerebellum. Damage to the ridge that runs up the back of the cerebellum would affect your walking. Damage to the bulging lobes on either side would cause a loss of limb coordination, so you would not be able to perform tasks such as reaching smoothly to pick up a pen.

The cerebellum's most obvious role is in motor learning and motor memory. It seems to be "trained" by the rest of the nervous system and operates independently and unconsciously. For example, the cerebellum allows you to ride a bicycle effortlessly while planning your next meal. In fact, the cerebellum may be involved in cognitive processes such as making plans, remembering events, using language, and experiencing emotion.

 How does gray matter differ from white matter?

ANSWER: Gray matter consists mainly of neuronal cell bodies, whereas white matter consists of myelinated axons.

3.6 Subcortical Structures Control Emotions and Appetitive Behaviors

Above the brain stem and cerebellum is the *forebrain*, which consists of the two cerebral hemispheres (left and right; **FIGURE 3.22**). From the outside, the most noticeable feature of the forebrain is the cerebral cortex. Below the cerebral cortex are the

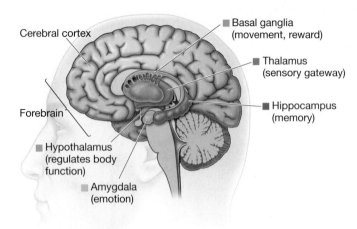

Cerebral cortex

Basal ganglia
(movement, reward)

Thalamus
(sensory gateway)

Forebrain

Hippocampus
(memory)

Hypothalamus
(regulates body
function)

Amygdala
(emotion)

FIGURE 3.22
The Forebrain and the Subcortical Regions
The subcortical regions are below the forebrain. They are
responsible for many aspects of emotion and motivation.

thalamus
The gateway to the brain; it receives
almost all incoming sensory
information before that information
reaches the cortex.

hypothalamus
A brain structure that is involved in
the regulation of bodily functions,
including body temperature, body
rhythms, blood pressure, and blood
glucose levels; it also influences our
basic motivated behaviors.

hippocampus
A brain structure that is associated
with the formation of memories.

amygdala
A brain structure that serves a vital
role in learning to associate things
with emotional responses and in
processing emotional information.

subcortical regions, which are so named because they lie
under the cortex. Subcortical structures that are important
for understanding psychological functions include the
hypothalamus, the thalamus, the hippocampus, the amygdala, and the basal ganglia. Some of these structures belong
to the *limbic system. Limbic* is the Latin word for "border,"
and this system serves as the border between the evolutionarily older parts of the brain (the brain stem and the
cerebellum) and the evolutionarily newer part (the cerebral cortex). The brain structures in the limbic system are
especially important for controlling appetitive behaviors,
such as eating and drinking, and emotions (as discussed in
Chapter 10, "Emotion and Motivation").

THALAMUS The **thalamus** is the gateway to the cortex:
It receives almost all incoming sensory information, organizes it, and relays it to the cortex. The only exception to
this rule is the sense of smell. The oldest and most fundamental sense, smell has a direct route to the cortex. During
sleep, the thalamus partially shuts the gate on incoming
sensations while the brain rests. (The thalamus is discussed further in Chapter 5,
"Sensation and Perception.")

HYPOTHALAMUS The **hypothalamus** is the brain's master regulatory structure.
It is indispensable to the organism's survival. Located just below the thalamus, it
receives input from almost everywhere in the body and brain, and it projects its influence to almost everywhere in the body and brain. It affects the functions of many
internal organs, regulating body temperature, body rhythms, blood pressure, and
blood glucose levels. It is also involved in many motivated behaviors, including thirst,
hunger, aggression, and lust.

HIPPOCAMPUS The **hippocampus** takes its name from the Greek for "sea horse,"
because of its sea horse shape. This structure plays an important role in the formation of new memories. It seems to do this by creating new interconnections within the
cerebral cortex with each new experience.

The hippocampus may be involved in how we remember the arrangements of
places and objects in space, such as how streets are laid out in a city or how furniture
is positioned in a room. An interesting study to support this theory focused on London
taxi drivers. Maguire and colleagues (2003) found that one region of the hippocampus was much larger in taxi drivers' brains than in most other London drivers' brains.
Moreover, the volume of gray matter in the hippocampal region was highly correlated
with the number of years of experience as a taxi driver. Is a person with a large hippocampus more likely to drive a taxi? Or does the hippocampus grow as the result of
navigational experience? Recall from Chapter 2 that correlation does not prove causation. The Maguire study did not *conclude* that the hippocampus changes with experience. However, there is evidence that the hippocampus is important for navigating
in our environments (Nadel et al., 2013).

AMYGDALA The **amygdala** takes its name from the Latin for "almond," because
it has an almond shape. This structure is located immediately in front of the hippocampus. The amygdala is involved in learning about biologically relevant stimuli,

such as those important for survival (Whalen et al., 2013). It plays a special role in responding to stimuli that elicit fear. The emotional processing of frightening stimuli in the amygdala is a hardwired circuit that has developed over the course of evolution to protect animals from danger. The amygdala is also involved in evaluating a facial expression's emotional significance (Adolphs et al., 2005). It appears to be part of a system that automatically directs visual attention to the eyes when evaluating facial expressions (Kennedy & Adolphs, 2010). Imaging studies have found that the amygdala activation is especially strong in response to a fearful face, especially to the large whites of the eyes that are seen in expressions of fear (Kim et al., 2016).

The amygdala also intensifies the function of memory during times of emotional arousal. For example, a frightening experience can be seared into your memory for life, although (as discussed further in Chapter 7, "Memory") your memory of the event may not be completely accurate. Research also shows that emotional arousal can influence what people attend to in their environments (Schmitz, De Rosa, & Anderson, 2009).

BASAL GANGLIA The **basal ganglia** are a system of subcortical structures crucial for planning and producing movement. These structures receive input from the entire cerebral cortex. They send that input to the motor centers of the brain stem. Via the thalamus, they also send the input back to the motor planning area of the cerebral cortex. Damage to the basal ganglia can produce symptoms that range from the tremors and rigidity of Parkinson's disease to the involuntary writhing movements of Huntington's disease. In addition, damage to the basal ganglia can impair the learning of movements and habits, such as automatically looking for cars before you cross the street.

One structure in the basal ganglia, the *nucleus accumbens*, is important for experiencing reward and motivating behavior. As discussed in Chapter 6, nearly every pleasurable experience—from eating food you like to looking at a person you find attractive—involves dopamine activity in the nucleus accumbens and makes you want the thing or person you are experiencing. The more desirable objects are, the more they activate basic reward circuitry in our brains.

basal ganglia

A system of subcortical structures that are important for the planning and production of movement.

 Which brain region is considered the gateway to the cortex?

ANSWER: the thalamus, because almost all sensory information goes first to the thalamus before being sent to relevant regions of the cortex

3.7 The Cerebral Cortex Underlies Complex Mental Activity

The **cerebral cortex** is the outer layer of the cerebral hemispheres and gives the brain its distinctive wrinkled appearance. (*Cortex* is Latin for "bark"—the kind on trees. The cerebral cortex does not feel like bark, however. It has the consistency of a soft-boiled egg.) Each hemisphere has its own cortex. In humans, the cortex is relatively enormous—the size of a large sheet of newspaper—and folded in against itself many times so as to fit within the skull. It is the site of all thoughts, detailed perceptions, and complex behaviors. It enables us to comprehend ourselves, other people, and the outside world. By extending our inner selves into the world, it is also the source of culture and communication. Each cerebral hemisphere has four "lobes": the occipital, parietal, temporal, and frontal lobes (**FIGURE 3.23**). The **corpus callosum**, a massive bridge of millions of axons, connects the hemispheres and allows information to flow between them (**FIGURE 3.24**).

cerebral cortex

The outer layer of brain tissue, which forms the convoluted surface of the brain; the site of all thoughts, perceptions, and complex behaviors.

corpus callosum

A massive bridge of millions of axons that connects the hemispheres and allows information to flow between them.

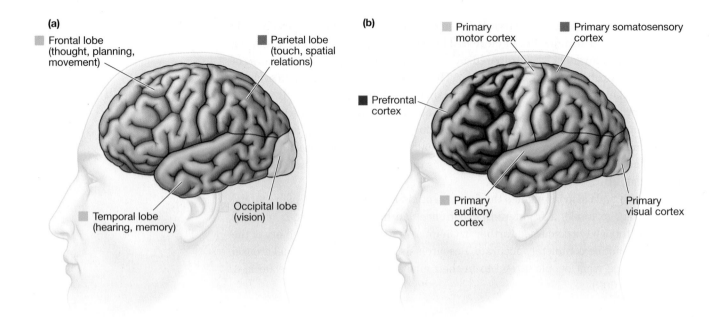

(a)

■ Frontal lobe
(thought, planning,
movement)

■ Parietal lobe
(touch, spatial
relations)

■ Temporal lobe
(hearing, memory)

Occipital lobe
(vision)

(b)

■ Primary
motor cortex

■ Primary somatosensory
cortex

■ Prefrontal
cortex

■ Primary
auditory
cortex

Primary
visual cortex

FIGURE 3.23
The Cerebral Cortex
(a) This diagram identifies the lobes of the cerebral cortex. **(b)** The colored areas mark important regions within those lobes.

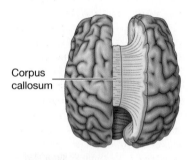

Corpus
callosum

FIGURE 3.24
The Corpus Callosum
In this top view of the brain, the right cerebral hemisphere has been pulled away to expose the corpus callosum. This fibrous structure connects the two hemispheres of the cerebral cortex.

occipital lobes
Regions of the cerebral cortex—at the back of the brain—important for vision.

parietal lobes
Regions of the cerebral cortex—in front of the occipital lobes and behind the frontal lobes—important for the sense of touch and for attention to the environment.

OCCIPITAL LOBES The **occipital lobes** are at the back portion of the head. Devoted almost exclusively to vision, they include many visual areas. By far, the largest of these areas is the *primary visual cortex*, the major destination for visual information. Visual information is typically organized for the cerebral cortex in a way that preserves spatial relationships. That is, the image relayed from the eye is "projected" more or less faithfully onto the primary visual cortex. As a result, two objects near one another in a visual image will activate neurons near one another in the primary visual cortex. Surrounding the primary visual cortex is a patchwork of secondary visual areas that process various attributes of the visual image, such as its colors, forms, and motions.

PARIETAL LOBES The **parietal lobes** are devoted partially to touch. Their labor is divided between the cerebral hemispheres. The left hemisphere receives touch information from the right side of the body, and the right hemisphere receives touch information from the left side of the body. In each parietal lobe, this information is directed to the *primary somatosensory cortex*, a strip in the front part of the lobe, running from the top of the brain down the sides. The primary somatosensory cortex groups nearby sensations: For example, sensations from the fingers are near sensations from the palm. The result, covering the primary somatosensory area, is a distorted representation of the entire body: the *somatosensory homunculus* (the latter term is Greek for "little man"). The homunculus is distorted because more cortical area is devoted to the body's more sensitive areas, such as the face and the fingers (**FIGURE 3.25A**).

This homunculus is based on brain mappings by the pioneering neurological researcher Wilder Penfield. Penfield created these mappings as he examined patients who were to undergo surgery for epilepsy (**FIGURE 3.25B**). The idea behind this work was to perform the surgery without damaging brain areas vital for functions such as speech. After a local anesthetic was applied to the scalp and while the patient was

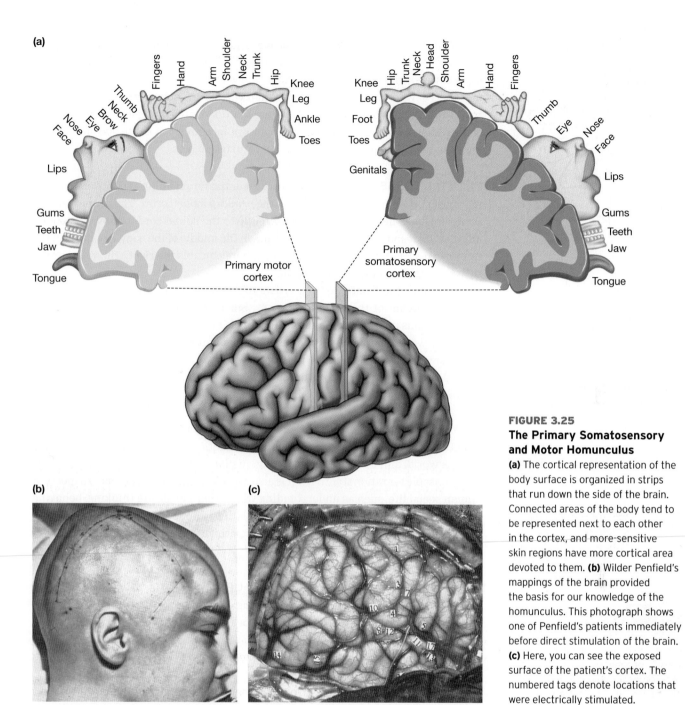

(a)

Fingers
Hand
Arm
Shoulder
Neck
Trunk
Hip
Thumb
Neck
Brow
Eye
Nose
Face
Lips
Gums
Teeth
Jaw
Tongue

Knee
Leg
Ankle
Toes

Hip
Trunk
Neck
Head
Shoulder
Arm
Hand
Fingers

Knee
Leg
Foot
Toes

Genitals

Thumb
Eye
Nose
Face
Lips
Gums
Teeth
Jaw
Tongue

Primary motor cortex

Primary somatosensory cortex

(b)

(c)

FIGURE 3.25

The Primary Somatosensory and Motor Homunculus

(a) The cortical representation of the body surface is organized in strips that run down the side of the brain. Connected areas of the body tend to be represented next to each other in the cortex, and more-sensitive skin regions have more cortical area devoted to them. **(b)** Wilder Penfield's mappings of the brain provided the basis for our knowledge of the homunculus. This photograph shows one of Penfield's patients immediately before direct stimulation of the brain. **(c)** Here, you can see the exposed surface of the patient's cortex. The numbered tags denote locations that were electrically stimulated.

awake, Penfield would electrically stimulate regions of the brain and ask the patient to report what he or she was experiencing (**FIGURE 3.25C**). Penfield's studies provided important evidence about the amount of brain tissue devoted to each sensory experience.

The parietal lobe is also involved in attention. A stroke or other damage to the right parietal region can result in the neurological disorder *hemineglect*. Patients with this syndrome fail to notice anything on their left side even though their eyes work perfectly well. Looking in a mirror, they will shave or put makeup on only the right side of their face. If two objects are held up before them, they will see only the one on the right. Asked to draw a simple object, they will draw only its right half (**FIGURE 3.26**).

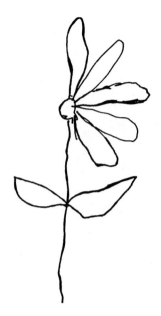

FIGURE 3.26
Hemineglect
This drawing, made by a hemineglect patient, omits much of the flower's left side.

temporal lobes
Regions of the cerebral cortex–below the parietal lobes and in front of the occipital lobes–important for processing auditory information, for memory, and for object and face perception.

frontal lobes
Regions of the cerebral cortex–at the front of the brain–important for movement and higher-level psychological processes associated with the prefrontal cortex.

prefrontal cortex
The frontmost portion of the frontal lobes, especially prominent in humans; important for attention, working memory, decision making, appropriate social behavior, and personality.

TEMPORAL LOBES The **temporal lobes** hold the *primary auditory cortex*, the brain region responsible for hearing. At the intersection of the temporal and occipital lobes is the *fusiform face area*. Its name comes from the fact that this area is much more active when people look at faces than when they look at other things. In contrast, other regions of the temporal lobe are more activated by objects, such as houses or cars, than by faces. Damage to the fusiform face area can cause specific impairments in recognizing people but not in recognizing objects.

FRONTAL LOBES The **frontal lobes** are essential for planning and movement. The rearmost portion of the frontal lobes is the *primary motor cortex*. The primary motor cortex includes neurons that project directly to the spinal cord to move the body's muscles. Its responsibilities are divided down the middle of the body, like those of the sensory areas: For example, the left hemisphere controls the right arm, whereas the right hemisphere controls the left arm.

The rest of the frontal lobes consists of the **prefrontal cortex,** which occupies about 30 percent of the brain in humans. Scientists have long thought that what makes humans unique in the animal kingdom is our extraordinarily large prefrontal cortex. However, there is evidence that what separates humans from other animals is not how much of the brain the prefrontal cortex occupies but rather the complexity and organization of prefrontal circuits—the way different regions within the prefrontal cortex are connected (Bush & Allman, 2004; Schoenemann, Sheehan, & Glotzer, 2005).

Parts of the prefrontal cortex are responsible for directing and maintaining attention, keeping ideas in mind while distractions bombard people from the outside world, and developing and acting on plans. The entire prefrontal cortex is indispensable for rational activity. It is also especially important for many aspects of human social life, such as understanding what other people are thinking, behaving according to cultural norms, and contemplating one's own existence. It provides both the sense of self and the capacity to empathize with others or feel guilty about harming them.

THE PREFRONTAL CORTEX IN CLOSE-UP Psychologists have learned a great deal of what they know about the functioning of different brain regions through the careful study of people whose brains have been damaged by disease or injury. Perhaps the most famous historical example of brain damage is the case of Phineas Gage. Gage's case provided the basis for the first modern theories of the prefrontal cortex's role in both personality and self-control.

In 1848, Gage was a 25-year-old foreman on the construction of Vermont's Rutland and Burlington Railroad. One day, he dropped a tool called a tamping iron, which was over a yard long and an inch in diameter. The iron rod hit a rock, igniting some blasting powder. The resulting explosion drove the rod into his cheek, through his frontal lobes, and clear out through the top of his head (**FIGURE 3.27**). Gage was still conscious as he was hurried back to town on a cart, and he was able to walk, with assistance, upstairs to his hotel bed. He wryly remarked to the awaiting physician, "Doctor, here is business enough for you." He said he expected to return to work in a few days. In fact, Gage lapsed into unconsciousness and remained unconscious for two weeks. Afterward, his condition steadily improved. Physically, he recovered remarkably well.

Unfortunately, Gage's accident led to major personality changes. Whereas the old Gage had been regarded by his employers as "the most efficient and capable" of workers, the new Gage was not. As one of his doctors later wrote, "The equilibrium or balance, so to speak, between his intellectual faculties and animal propensities

(a)

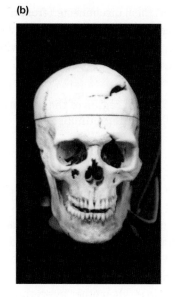
(b)

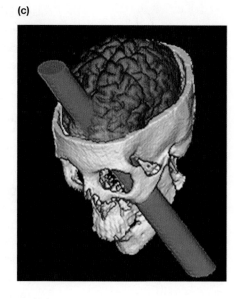
(c)

FIGURE 3.27
Phineas Gage
Analysis of Gage's damaged skull provided the basis for the first modern theories about the role of the prefrontal cortex in both personality and self-control. **(a)** This photo shows Gage holding the rod that passed through his skull. **(b)** Here, you can see the hole in the top of Gage's skull. **(c)** This computer-generated image reconstructs the rod's probable path through the skull.

seems to have been destroyed. He is fitful, irreverent, indulging at times in the grossest profanity . . . impatient of restraint or advice when it conflicts with his desires. . . . A child in his intellectual capacity and manifestations, he has the animal passions of a strong man" (Harlow, 1868, p. 340). In summary, Gage was "no longer Gage."

Unable to get his foreman's job back, Gage exhibited himself in various New England towns and at the New York Museum (owned by the circus showman P. T. Barnum). He worked at the stables of the Hanover Inn at Dartmouth College. In Chile, he drove coaches and tended horses. After a decade, his health began to decline, and in 1860 he started having epileptic seizures and died within a few months. Gage's recovery was initially used to argue that the entire brain works uniformly and that the healthy parts of Gage's brain had taken over the work of the damaged parts. However, the medical community eventually recognized that Gage's psychological impairments had been severe and that some areas of the brain in fact have specific functions.

Reconstruction of Gage's injury through examination of his skull has made it clear that the prefrontal cortex was the area most damaged by the tamping rod (Damasio, Grabowski, Frank, Galaburda, & Damasio, 1994). Recent studies of patients with injuries to this brain region reveal that it is particularly concerned with social phenomena, such as following social norms, understanding what other people are thinking, and feeling emotionally connected to others. People with damage to this region do not typically have problems with memory or general knowledge, but they often have profound disturbances in their ability to get along with others.

In the late 1930s, António Egas Moniz developed the *lobotomy*, a form of brain surgery that deliberately damaged the prefrontal cortex (**FIGURE 3.28**). Why would a surgeon want to perform this procedure? At the beginning of the 20th century, there was a significant increase in the number of patients living in mental institutions, and psychiatrists sought a physical means of treating these patients. The lobotomy generally left patients lethargic, emotionally flat, and therefore much easier to manage.

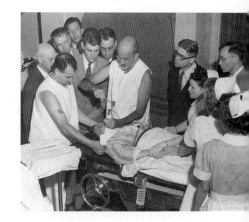

FIGURE 3.28
Lobotomy
This photo shows Dr. Walter Freeman performing a lobotomy in 1949. Freeman is inserting an ice pick-like instrument under the upper eyelid of his patient to cut the nerve connections in the front part of the brain.

It also left them disconnected from their social surroundings. Most lobotomies were performed in the late 1940s and early 1950s. In 1949, Egas Moniz received the Nobel Prize for developing the procedure, which was phased out with the arrival of drugs to treat psychological disorders.

 Q Which region of the cerebral cortex likely differs between humans and other animals?

ANSWER: The prefrontal cortex is organized differently in humans and also supports complex aspects of human social life, such as understanding other people and having a sense of self.

3.8 Splitting the Brain Splits the Mind

Studying people who have undergone brain surgery has given researchers a better understanding of the conscious mind. For example, on rare occasions when epilepsy does not respond to modern medications, surgeons may remove the part of the brain in which the seizures begin. Another strategy, pioneered in the 1940s and sometimes still practiced when other interventions have failed, is to cut connections within the brain to try to isolate the site where the seizures begin. After the procedure, a seizure that begins at that site is less likely to spread throughout the cortex.

The major connection between the hemispheres that may readily be cut without damaging the gray matter is the corpus callosum (see Figure 3.24). When this massive fiber bundle is severed, the brain's halves are almost completely isolated from each other. The resulting condition is called **split brain.** This surgical procedure has provided many important insights into the basic organization and specialized functions of each brain hemisphere (**FIGURE 3.29**).

What is it like to have your brain split in half? Perhaps the most surprising thing about split-brain patients after their operations is how normal they are. Unlike patients after other types of brain surgery, split-brain patients have no immediately apparent problems. In fact, some early investigations suggested the surgery had not affected the patients in any discernible way. They could walk normally, talk normally, think clearly, and interact socially. In the 1960s, this book's coauthor Michael Gazzaniga, working with the Nobel laureate Roger Sperry, conducted a series of tests on split-brain patients (Gazzaniga, 2015). The results were stunning: Just as the brain had been split in two, so had the mind!

The hemispheres normally work together. Images from the visual field's left side (left half of what you are looking at) go to the right hemisphere. Images from the

split brain

A condition that occurs when the corpus callosum is surgically cut and the two hemispheres of the brain do not receive information directly from each other.

FIGURE 3.29
Split Brain
(a) This image shows the brain of a normal person whose corpus callosum is intact. **(b)** This image shows the brain of a patient whose corpus callosum has been cut (area indicated by the red outline). With the corpus callosum severed, the two hemispheres of the brain are almost completely separated.

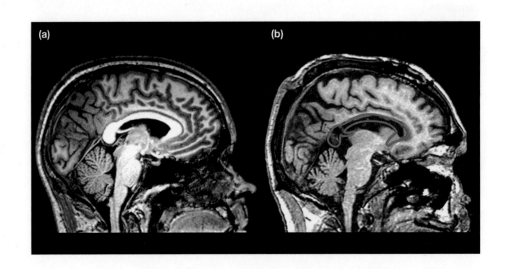

CHAPTER 3 **BIOLOGY AND BEHAVIOR**

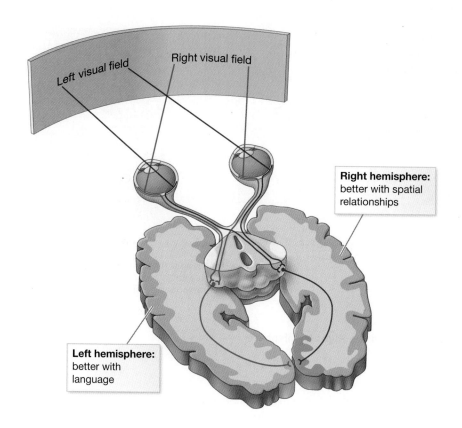

Left visual field

Right visual field

Right hemisphere:
better with spatial relationships

Left hemisphere:
better with language

visual field's right side go to the left hemisphere (**FIGURE 3.30**). The left hemisphere also controls the right hand, and the right hemisphere controls the left hand. In a healthy person, the corpus callosum allows the hemispheres to communicate so that the right brain knows what the left is doing. By contrast, in split-brain patients, the hemispheres are separated, so this communication cannot take place—the hemispheres function as completely independent entities. This division allows researchers to independently examine the function of each hemisphere without the influence of the other. The researchers can provide information to, and receive information from, a single hemisphere at a time.

Psychologists have long known that in most people the left hemisphere is dominant for language. If a split-brain patient sees two pictures flashed on a screen briefly and simultaneously—one to the visual field's right side and one to the left side—the patient will report that only the picture on the right was shown. Why is this? The left hemisphere (or "left brain"), with its control over speech, sees only the picture on the right side. It is the only picture a person with a split brain can talk about.

In many split-brain patients, the right hemisphere has no discernible language capacity. The mute right hemisphere (or "right brain"), having seen the picture on the left, is unable to articulate a response. However, the right brain can act on its perception: If the picture on the left was of a spoon, the right hemisphere can easily pick out an actual spoon from a selection of objects. It uses the left hand, which is controlled by the right hemisphere. Still, the left hemisphere does not know what the right one saw.

Splitting the brain, then, produces two half brains. Each half has its own perceptions, thoughts, and consciousness (**FIGURE 3.31**).

Normally, the competencies of each hemisphere complement each other. The left brain is generally hopeless at spatial relationships, whereas the right hemisphere is much more proficient. In one experiment (Bogen & Gazzaniga, 1965), a split-brain participant is given a pile of blocks and a drawing of a simple arrangement in which

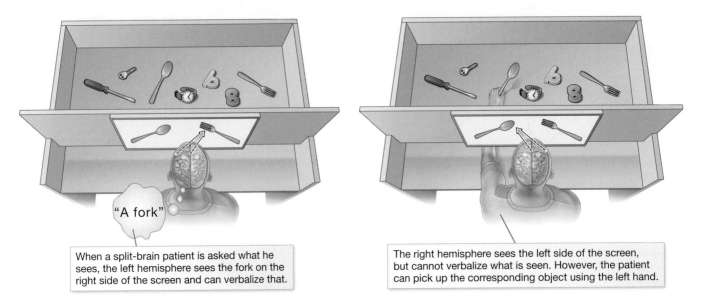

When a split-brain patient is asked what he sees, the left hemisphere sees the fork on the right side of the screen and can verbalize that.

"A fork"

The right hemisphere sees the left side of the screen, but cannot verbalize what is seen. However, the patient can pick up the corresponding object using the left hand.

FIGURE 3.31
Split-Brain Experiment: The Left Hemisphere Versus the Right Hemisphere

to put them. For example, the participant is asked to produce a square. When using the left hand, controlled by the right hemisphere, the participant arranges the blocks effortlessly. However, when using the right hand, controlled by the left brain, the participant produces only an incompetent, meandering attempt. During this dismal performance, the right brain presumably grows frustrated, because it makes the left hand try to slip in and help!

INTERPRETER Studies of split-brain patients have revealed an interesting relationship between the brain's hemispheres, which work together to construct coherent conscious experiences. This collaboration can be demonstrated by asking a split-brain patient to use his or her disconnected left hemisphere to explain behavior produced by the right hemisphere. Keep in mind that the left hemisphere does not know why the behavior was produced.

In one such experiment (Gazzaniga & LeDoux, 1978), the split-brain patient saw different images flash simultaneously on the left and right sides of a screen. Below those images was a row of other images. The patient was asked to point with each hand to a bottom image that was most related to the image flashed on that side of the screen above. In a particular trial, a picture of a chicken claw was flashed to the left hemisphere. A picture of a snow scene was flashed to the right hemisphere. In response, the left hemisphere pointed the right hand at a picture of a chicken head. The right hemisphere pointed the left hand at a picture of a snow shovel. The (speaking) left hemisphere could have no idea what the right hemisphere had seen or why the left hand pointed to the snow shovel. When the participant was asked why he pointed to those pictures, he (or, rather, his left hemisphere) calmly replied, "Oh, that's simple. The chicken claw goes with the chicken, and you need a shovel to clean out the chicken shed." The left hemisphere evidently had interpreted the left hand's response in a manner consistent with the left brain's knowledge, which was a chicken claw (**FIGURE 3.32**).

The left hemisphere's propensity to construct a world that makes sense is called the *interpreter*. This term means that the left hemisphere is interpreting what the

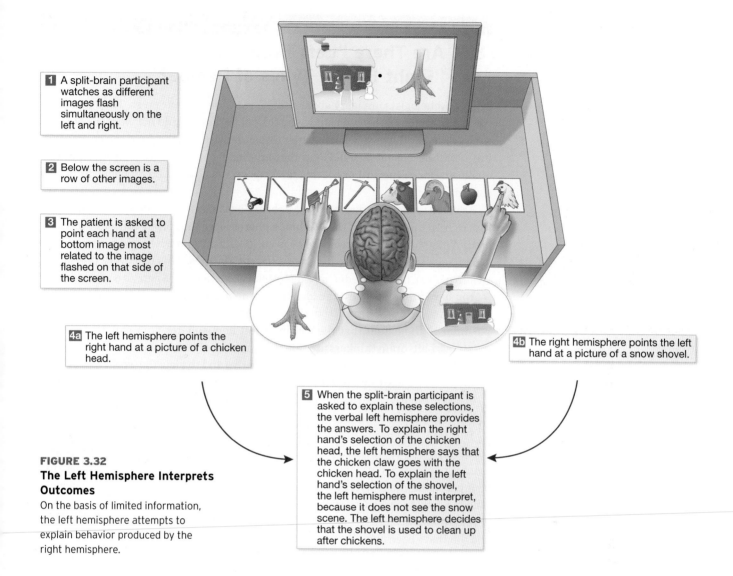

1 A split-brain participant watches as different images flash simultaneously on the left and right.

2 Below the screen is a row of other images.

3 The patient is asked to point each hand at a bottom image most related to the image flashed on that side of the screen.

4a The left hemisphere points the right hand at a picture of a chicken head.

4b The right hemisphere points the left hand at a picture of a snow shovel.

5 When the split-brain participant is asked to explain these selections, the verbal left hemisphere provides the answers. To explain the right hand's selection of the chicken head, the left hemisphere says that the chicken claw goes with the chicken head. To explain the left hand's selection of the shovel, the left hemisphere must interpret, because it does not see the snow scene. The left hemisphere decides that the shovel is used to clean up after chickens.

FIGURE 3.32
The Left Hemisphere Interprets Outcomes
On the basis of limited information, the left hemisphere attempts to explain behavior produced by the right hemisphere.

right hemisphere has done with only the information that is available to it (Gazzaniga, 2000). In this last example, the left hemisphere interpreter created a ready way to explain the left hand's action. Although the disconnected right hemisphere controlled the left hand, the left hemisphere's explanation was unrelated to the right hemisphere's real reason for commanding that action. Yet to the patient, the movement seemed perfectly plausible once the action had been interpreted.

To give another example: If the command *Stand up* is flashed to a split-brain patient's right hemisphere, the patient will stand up. But when asked why he or she has stood up, the patient will not reply, "You just told me to," because the command is not available to the (speaking) left hemisphere. Instead, unaware of the command, the patient will say something like, "I just felt like getting a soda." The left hemisphere is compelled to concoct a "makes sense" story that explains, or interprets, the patient's action after it has occurred.

Q What surgery creates the split brain?

ANSWER: cutting the corpus callosum so that the two hemispheres are separated

3.9 Are There "Left Brain" and "Right Brain" Types of People?

Many psychologists are leery about dealing with the popular press. They want psychological studies to become known by the public, but they do not want the findings to be garbled by the media. Seeing their research twisted in the press can be maddening in part because it overshadows the very findings the scientists have so proudly obtained. One of the authors of this textbook knows about such problems from personal experience.

As noted in the previous section, Michael Gazzaniga and Roger Sperry conducted research on the activity of the two hemispheres after the corpus callosum was severed. When the hemispheres have been surgically disconnected and are separately examined, each hemisphere displays different abilities. This discovery provided a wealth of data, but the media have distorted Gazzaniga and Sperry's early findings.

You have probably heard the idea that some people are "left brain" logical types and others are "right brain" artistic types. According to this popular notion, people differ to the extent that their right or left hemispheres dominate their thinking styles. Left-brain thinkers are said to be more analytical, rational, and objective. Right-brain thinkers are said to be more creative and to view the world more holistically and subjectively. Moreover, a dominant left brain supposedly suppresses right-brain creativity, so people could become more creative and passionate if their right hemisphere were released.

This false idea has permeated society (**FIGURE 3.33**). Multiple tests are available, particularly on the Internet, to determine whether you are left- or right-brain dominant. Countless pop psychology books give advice on living better by emphasizing your particular brain style or drawing on the other style. Teachers have been heavily influenced by the idea (Alferink & Farmer-Dougan, 2010). They have been urged to develop different classroom plans for left-brain thinkers than for right-brain thinkers, and they have been encouraged to liberate the "more creative" right brain. According to one study, nearly 90 percent of teachers in the United Kingdom and the Netherlands believe in the idea of left-brain versus right-brain thinking (Dekker et al., 2012).

As noted in Chapter 1, the media love a good story. To make scientific studies attention grabbing, journalists often oversimplify research findings and apply them in ways that go far beyond what can be concluded from the evidence. In this case, the evidence is overwhelming: People are not either left-brain or right-brain dominant (Hines, 1987).

The hemispheres *are* specialized for certain functions, such as language or spatial relationships. However, each hemisphere is capable of carrying out most cognitive processes, though sometimes in different ways. Most cognitive processes involve the coordinated efforts of both hemispheres. A recent study that examined brain activity in over 1,000 individuals ages 7 to 29 found no differences between people in the extent to which their right or left hemisphere was active (Nielsen et al., 2013). In contrast to the theory that a liberated right brain leads to better learning, some evidence suggests that people who perform best at math are those whose two hemispheres work most closely together (Prescott et al., 2010).

Of course, whenever you read media stories about psychological findings, you need to think about the source of your information. If you are really interested in the finding, consider looking up the original article to see if the journalist represented that article accurately. This advice is especially important if you plan to use the information in your life.

FIGURE 3.33
Left Brain Versus Right Brain
The media have helped promote the false ideas that individuals are dominant on one side of the brain or the other and that such different styles are important for classroom learning.

Findings from psychological science often have practical implications for daily living, but the value of research can be spoiled if the media outlet spreading the information gets it wrong. ∎

Q **Do people differ in the extent to which their hemispheres are dominant?**

How Does the Brain Communicate with the Body?

As discussed earlier in this chapter, the peripheral nervous system (PNS) transmits a variety of information to the central nervous system (CNS). It also responds to messages from the CNS to perform specific behaviors or make bodily adjustments. In the production of psychological activity, however, both of these systems interact with a different mode of communication within the body, the endocrine system.

3.10 The Peripheral Nervous System Includes the Somatic and Autonomic Systems

Recall that the PNS has two primary components: the somatic nervous system and the autonomic nervous system (**FIGURE 3.34**). The **somatic nervous system (SNS)** transmits sensory signals to the CNS via nerves. Specialized receptors in the skin, muscles, and joints send sensory information to the spinal cord, which relays it to

Learning Objectives

- Differentiate between the subdivisions of the nervous system.

- Identify the primary structures of the endocrine system.

- Explain how the nervous system and the endocrine system communicate to control thought, feeling, and behavior.

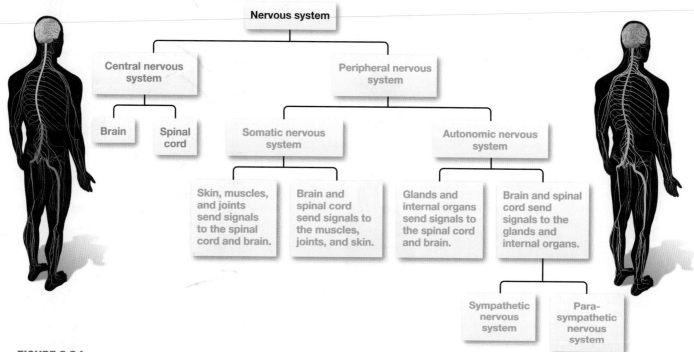

FIGURE 3.34
The Divisions of the Nervous System
This flowchart builds on Figure 3.1 by adding further information about the somatic and autonomic nervous systems.

the brain. In addition, the CNS sends signals through the SNS to muscles, joints, and skin to initiate, modulate, or inhibit movement.

The second major component of the PNS, the **autonomic nervous system (ANS),** regulates the body's internal environment by stimulating glands (such as sweat glands) and by maintaining internal organs (such as the heart). Nerves in the ANS also carry somatosensory signals from the glands and internal organs to the CNS. These signals provide information about, for example, the fullness of your stomach or how anxious you feel.

SYMPATHETIC AND PARASYMPATHETIC DIVISIONS Two types of signals, sympathetic and parasympathetic, travel from the central nervous system to organs and glands, controlling their activity (**FIGURE 3.35**). To understand these signals, imagine you hear a fire alarm. In the second after you hear the alarm, signals go out to parts of your body telling them to prepare for action. As a result, blood flows to skeletal muscles; epinephrine is released, increasing your heart rate and blood sugar; your lungs take in more oxygen; your digestive system suspends activity as a way of conserving energy; your pupils dilate to maximize visual sensitivity; and you perspire to keep cool.

These preparatory actions are prompted by the autonomic nervous system's **sympathetic division.** Should there be a fire, you will be physically prepared to flee. If the alarm turns out to be false, your heart will return to its normal steady beat, your breathing will slow, you will resume digesting food, and you will stop perspiring. This

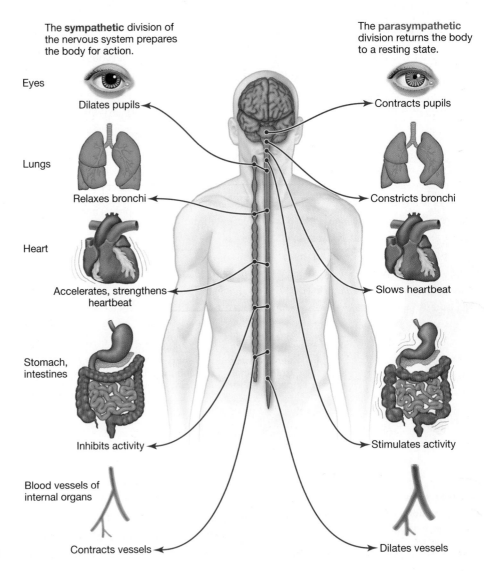

The **sympathetic** division of the nervous system prepares the body for action.

The **parasympathetic** division returns the body to a resting state.

Eyes — Dilates pupils / Contracts pupils

Lungs — Relaxes bronchi / Constricts bronchi

Heart — Accelerates, strengthens heartbeat / Slows heartbeat

Stomach, intestines — Inhibits activity / Stimulates activity

Blood vessels of internal organs — Contracts vessels / Dilates vessels

FIGURE 3.35

The Sympathetic and Parasympathetic Divisions of the Autonomic Nervous System

return to a normal state will be prompted by the ANS's **parasympathetic division.** Most of your internal organs are controlled by inputs from sympathetic and parasympathetic systems. The more aroused you are, the greater the sympathetic system's dominance.

It does not take a fire alarm to activate your sympathetic nervous system. For example, when you meet someone you find attractive, your heart beats quickly, you perspire, you might start breathing heavily, and your pupils widen. Such signs of sexual arousal provide nonverbal cues during social interaction. These signs occur because sexual arousal has activated the ANS's sympathetic division. The SNS is also activated by psychological states such as anxiety or unhappiness. Some people worry a great deal or do not cope well with stress. Their bodies are in a constant state of arousal. Important research in the 1930s and 1940s by Hans Selye demonstrated that chronic activation of the SNS is associated with medical problems that include heart disease and asthma. Selye's work is discussed further in Chapter 11, "Health and Well-Being."

Q Which division of the autonomic nervous system helps you calm down after taking a stressful exam?

3.11 The Endocrine System Communicates Through Hormones

Like the nervous system, the **endocrine system** is a communication network that influences thoughts, behaviors, and actions. Both systems work together to regulate psychological activity. For instance, from the nervous system the brain receives information about potential threats to the organism. The brain communicates with the endocrine system to prepare the organism to deal with those threats. (The threats could involve physical injury or be psychological, such as nervousness at having to talk in front of a group.) The main differences between the two systems are in their mode and speed of communication: Whereas the nervous system is fast and uses electrochemical signals, the endocrine system is slower and uses hormones.

Hormones are chemical substances released into the bloodstream by the ductless *endocrine glands*, such as the pancreas, thyroid, and testes or ovaries (**FIGURE 3.36**). Because they travel through the bloodstream, hormones can take from seconds to hours to exert their effects. Once hormones are in the bloodstream, their effects can last for a long time and affect multiple targets.

The endocrine system is primarily controlled by the hypothalamus (for the location of this structure, see Figure 3.36; for a more detailed look, see Figure 3.22). The hypothalamus controls the endocrine system via signals to the **pituitary gland,** which is located at the base of the hypothalamus. Neural activation causes the hypothalamus to secrete a particular one of its many *releasing factors*. The particular releasing factor causes the pituitary to release a hormone specific to that factor, and the hormone then travels through the bloodstream to endocrine sites throughout the body. Once the hormone reaches the target sites, it binds to receptor sites, which subsequently affects bodily reactions or behavior. The pituitary is often referred to as the "master gland" of the body: By releasing hormones into the bloodstream, it controls all other glands and governs major processes such as development, ovulation, and lactation.

GROWTH HORMONE The integration between the CNS and endocrine system can be finely tuned. Consider physical growth. *Growth hormone (GH)*, a hormone released from the pituitary gland, prompts bone, cartilage, and muscle tissue to grow or helps them regenerate after injury. Since the 1930s, many people have administered or self-administered GH to increase body size and strength. Many athletes have sought a

parasympathetic division
A division of the autonomic nervous system; it returns the body to its resting state.

endocrine system
A communication system that uses hormones to influence thoughts, behaviors, and actions.

hormones
Chemical substances, released from endocrine glands, that travel through the bloodstream to targeted tissues; the tissues are subsequently influenced by the hormones.

pituitary gland
A gland located at the base of the hypothalamus; it sends hormonal signals to other endocrine glands, controlling their release of hormones.

FIGURE 3.36
The Hypothalamus and the Major Endocrine Glands

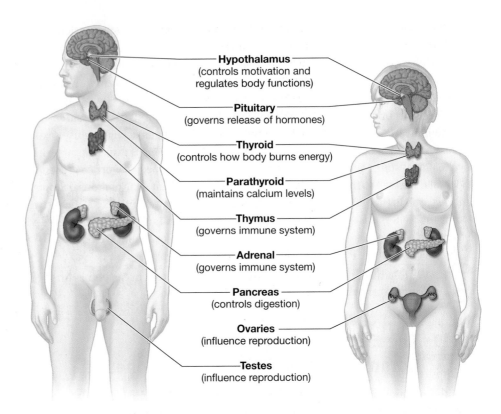

Hypothalamus
(controls motivation and
regulates body functions)

Pituitary
(governs release of hormones)

Thyroid
(controls how body burns energy)

Parathyroid
(maintains calcium levels)

Thymus
(governs immune system)

Adrenal
(governs immune system)

Pancreas
(controls digestion)

Ovaries
(influence reproduction)

Testes
(influence reproduction)

FIGURE 3.37
Growth Hormone and Cycling
In January 2013, Lance Armstrong appeared on *The Oprah Winfrey Show* to admit using doping techniques to enhance his cycling performance.

competitive advantage by using GH. For example, in early 2013, the legendary cyclist Lance Armstrong admitted to using GH and other hormones, including testosterone, to gain a competitive advantage. In an interview with Oprah Winfrey, Armstrong claimed that because doping was so pervasive in the sport, it was impossible for any cyclist to win a major championship without doping (**FIGURE 3.37**).

The releasing factor for GH stimulates the eating of protein by making it especially enjoyable (Dickson & Vaccarino, 1994). The area of the hypothalamus that stimulates release of GH is also involved in sleep/wake cycles. Thus, the bursts of GH, the need for protein, and the consumption of protein are controlled by the body's internal clock. All these connections illustrate how the CNS, the PNS, and the endocrine system work together to ensure the organism's survival: These systems prompt the behaviors that provide the body with the substances it needs when it needs them.

HORMONES' EFFECTS ON SEXUAL BEHAVIOR An example of hormonal influence is in sexual behavior. The main endocrine glands influencing sexual behavior are the **gonads:** the testes in males and the ovaries in females. Although many people talk about "male" and "female" hormones, the two major gonadal hormones are chemically the same in males and females. What differs is the quantity: *Androgens* such as testosterone are more prevalent in males, whereas *estrogens* such as estradiol and progesterone are more prevalent in females. Gonadal hormones influence the development of secondary sex characteristics (e.g., breast development in females, growth of facial hair in males). Gonadal hormones also influence adult sexual behavior.

For males, successful sexual behavior depends on having at least a minimum amount of testosterone. Prior to puberty, surgical removal of the testes, or *castration*, diminishes the capacity for developing an erection and lowers sexual interest. Yet a man castrated after puberty will be able to perform sexually if he receives an injection of testosterone. Testosterone injections do not increase sexual behavior in healthy men, however, and this finding suggests that a healthy man needs only a minimum amount of testosterone to perform sexually (Sherwin, 1988).

gonads
The main endocrine glands involved in sexual behavior: in males, the testes; in females, the ovaries.

In females, the influence of gonadal hormones is much more complex. Many nonhuman female animals experience a finite period, *estrus*, when the female is sexually receptive and fertile. During estrus, the female displays behaviors designed to attract the male. Surgical removal of the ovaries terminates estrus: No longer receptive, the female ends her sexual behavior. However, injections of estrogen reinstate estrus. Women's sexual behavior may have more to do with androgens than estrogens (Davis, Worsley, Miller, Parish, & Santoro, 2016). According to pioneering work by Barbara Sherwin (1994, 2008), women with higher blood levels of testosterone report greater interest in sex, and testosterone injections increase women's sexual interest after surgical removal of the uterus.

Women's sexual activity is not particularly linked to the menstrual cycle (Breedlove, Rosenzweig, & Watson, 2007). However, when they are ovulating, heterosexual women find men who look and act masculine more attractive (Gangestad, Simpson, Cousins, Garver-Apgar, & Christensen, 2004), and they show greater activity in brain regions associated with reward while viewing attractive male faces (Rupp et al., 2009). In addition, women report having lower self-esteem when ovulating, and their greater motivation to find a mate during that time may increase their efforts to appear attractive (Hill & Durante, 2009). Indeed, one study found that when their fertility was highest, women showed up for a laboratory study wearing more-revealing clothing than they normally wore (Durante, Li, & Haselton, 2008). Multiple recent studies are now providing evidence that using hormonal contraceptives might significantly alter both female and male mate choice by removing the hormone-related midcycle change in preferences (for a review: Alvergne & Lummaa [2010]).

"*You've been charged with driving under the influence of testosterone.*"

 Which gland releases hormones into the body?

ANSWER: the pituitary gland, which receives signals from the hypothalamus

How Does the Brain Change?

In terms of brain development, every experience is a learning experience. Throughout life, as we have experiences, our brains change. That is, the circuitry is reworked and updated. And as we mature, the brain normally develops according to a fairly predictable pattern. At specific points in life, particular brain structures progress and cognitive abilities increase.

Indeed, the brain is extremely adaptable, especially during childhood. This ability to change in response to experience or injury is known as **plasticity.** In general, such plasticity has *critical periods*. During these times, particular experiences must occur for development to proceed normally.

3.12 The Brain Rewires Itself Throughout Life

Connections form between brain structures when growing axons are directed by certain chemicals that tell them where to go and where not to go. The major connections are established by chemical messengers, but the detailed connections are governed by experience. Consider an extreme example, which came about through research on

plasticity

A property of the brain that allows it to change as a result of experience or injury.

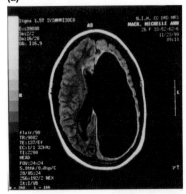

(a)

(b)

FIGURE 3.38

Michelle Mack and a Case of Extreme Plasticity

(a) While in her mother's womb, Michelle Mack suffered a stroke that obliterated her left hemisphere (black areas shown here, in a scan taken when she was an adult; note that hemispheres are reversed on this scan). **(b)** Over time, Mack's right hemisphere took over the duties of the left hemisphere—language production and moving the right side of the body—to a surprising extent. Mack's case shows the plasticity of the brain.

brain development. If a cat's eyes are sewn shut at birth, depriving the animal of visual input, the visual cortex fails to develop properly. If the sutures are removed weeks later, the cat is permanently blind, even though its eyes function normally. Adult cats that are similarly deprived do not lose their sight (Wiesel & Hubel, 1963). Thus, during brain development, ongoing activity in the visual pathways is necessary to refine the visual cortex enough for it to function.

The functions of portions of the cerebral cortex shift in response to their activity. Recall the somatosensory homunculus (see Figure 3.25a). As that representation makes clear, more cortical tissue is devoted to body parts that receive more sensation or are used more. Again, wiring in the brain is affected by amount of use.

To study the effects of experience on development, researchers reared rats in a number of different laboratory environments. For instance, one group was raised in deprived circumstances compared to that of normal laboratory rats, with minimal comfort and no opportunities for social interaction. Another group was raised in an enriched environment, with many companions, interesting things to look at, puzzles, obstacles, toys, running wheels, and even balance beams. The "luxury" items might simply have approximated rat life in the wild, but they enabled the luxury group to develop bigger, heavier brains than the deprived group (Rosenzweig, Bennett, & Diamond, 1972). Not only is experience important for normal development, but it may be even more so for superior development. Nowadays, as a result of these findings, most laboratory animals are kept in environments that provide enrichment (Simpson & Kelley, 2011). Some evidence suggests that the opportunity for physical exercise might have the most beneficial effects on brain development and learning (Mustroph et al., 2012).

The extent to which the brain can be reorganized is revealed in dramatic cases where an infant is born with only one hemisphere. Michelle Mack is one such person. When Mack was a youngster, her parents realized that she was different from other children because even simple tasks could give her problems. They could not explain these differences. When Mack was 27 years old, doctors discovered that she was missing the left hemisphere of her brain (**FIGURE 3.38**). This condition may have resulted from a stroke she experienced in the womb.

Without a left hemisphere, Mack should have shown severe deficits in skills processed in that half of the brain. For example, as discussed earlier in this chapter, the left hemisphere controls language, and it controls motor actions for the right side of the body. Losing a hemisphere as an adult would result in devastating loss of function. But Mack's speech is only minimally affected, and she can move the right side of her body with some difficulty. Mack is able to lead a surprisingly independent life. She graduated from high school, has a job, pays her bills, and does chores. Where did her capabilities come from? Somehow, her right hemisphere developed language processing capabilities as well as functions that ordinarily occur across both hemispheres.

Michelle Mack's case shows that nurture can influence nature. Over time, Mack interacted with the world. Her experiences enabled her brain to reorganize itself. Her right hemisphere took over processing for the missing left hemisphere.

PLASTICITY AND AGING Brain plasticity decreases with age. Even into very old age, however, the brain can grow new connections among neurons and even grow new neurons. The rewiring and growth within the brain represents the biological basis of learning. Until about 30 years ago, scientists believed that adult brains produced no new brain cells. There is now evidence that new neurons are produced in some brain regions (Eriksson et al., 1998). The production of new neurons is called *neurogenesis*. A fair amount of neurogenesis apparently occurs in the hippocampus (Christian, Song, & Ming, 2014). Recall from earlier in this chapter that the hippocampus is involved in the storage of new memories. These memories are eventually transferred to the cortex as the hippocampus is continuously overwritten. Perhaps, without disrupting memory, neurons in the hippocampus can be lost and replaced.

Elizabeth Gould and her colleagues have demonstrated that environmental conditions can play an important role in neurogenesis. For example, they have found that for rats, shrews, and marmosets, stressful experiences—such as being confronted by strange males in their home cages—interfere with neurogenesis during development and adulthood (Gould & Tanapat, 1999). When animals are housed together, they typically form dominance hierarchies that reflect social status. Dominant animals, those who possess the highest social status, show greater increases in new neurons than subordinate animals do (Kozorovitskiy & Gould, 2004). Thus, social environment can strongly affect brain plasticity, a dynamic process we are only beginning to understand (Opendak, Briones, & Gould, 2016). Neurogenesis may underlie neural plasticity. If so, further research might enable us, through neurogenesis, to reverse the brain's natural loss of neurons. Curbing neuron loss would probably slow age-based mental decline.

SEX DIFFERENCES Everything a person experiences alters his or her brain, and females and males differ in their life experiences. They also differ in their hormonal makeups. The differences between females' and males' brains reveal the intertwined influences of biology and environment. In general, males have larger brains than females, but for both sexes the sizes of brain structures are highly variable (Giedd et al., 1997). In any case, larger brains are not necessarily better, because longer distances between brain regions can translate into slower communication. Both in the womb and after birth, hormonal differences between the sexes affect brain development (Lombardo et al., 2012). As a result, hormonal difference might influence the way males and females differ on some cognitive tasks, such as the ease with which they mentally rotate objects or recall parts of a story (Kimura, 1999). But the different ways that men and women are treated in society may also contribute to these differences on cognitive tasks (Miller & Halpern, 2014).

As discussed earlier in the chapter, to some extent the brain's two hemispheres are lateralized: Each hemisphere is dominant for different cognitive functions. A considerable body of evidence indicates that females' brains are more bilaterally organized for language. In other words, the brain areas important in processing language are more likely to be found in both halves of females' brains. In males' brains the equivalent language areas are more likely to be in only one hemisphere, usually the left (Phillips et al., 2001; **FIGURE 3.39**).

One source of data that supports this distinction between male and female brains is people's experiences following strokes. Even when patients are matched on the location and severity of the brain damage caused by a stroke, women are less impaired in language use than men are (Jiang, Sheikh, & Bullock, 2006). A possible reason for women having better outcomes is that, because language is represented in both halves of their brain, damage to half of the brain will have less effect on a woman's ability to process language than it would if most of the language areas were in the damaged half of the brain.

While differences between females' brains and males' brains may be revealing, in fact their brains are mostly similar. A recent analysis of over 1,400 human brains revealed extensive overlap

(a)

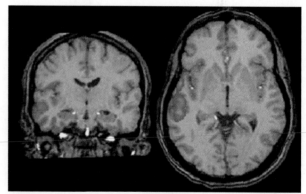

(b)

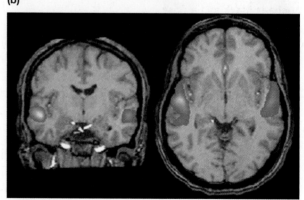

FIGURE 3.39

Males' Brains Versus Females' Brains

A considerable body of evidence indicates that female brains are more bilaterally organized for language than males' brains. For example, researchers studied men and women listening to someone reading aloud. As these fMRI images show, **(a)** the men listened with one side of their brains, whereas **(b)** the women tended to listen with both sides.

for males and females in gray matter, white matter, and the connections between brain regions (Joel et al., 2015). Ultimately, the interplay of biological and environmental effects on the brain is reflected in both the differences and the similarities between females' and males' brains.

Q What is neurogenesis?

3.13 The Brain Can Recover from Injury

Just as the brain reorganizes in response to amount of use, it also reorganizes in response to brain damage. Following an injury in the cortex, the surrounding gray matter assumes the function of the damaged area, like a local business scrambling to pick up the customers of a newly closed competitor. This remapping seems to begin immediately, and it continues for years. Such plasticity involves all levels of the central nervous system, from the cortex down to the spinal cord.

Reorganization is much more prevalent in children than in adults, in accord with the sensitive periods of normal development. Young children afflicted with severe and uncontrollable epilepsy that has paralyzed one or more limbs sometimes undergo a *radical hemispherectomy*. This surgical procedure removes an entire cerebral hemisphere. Just as in the case of Michelle Mack, the remaining hemisphere eventually takes on most of the lost hemisphere's functions. The children regain almost complete use of their limbs. However, adults cannot undergo radical hemispherectomy. If the procedure were performed on adults, the lack of neural reorganization in their brains would lead to permanent paralysis and loss of function.

Cortical reorganization can also have bizarre results. For example, an amputee can be afflicted with a *phantom limb*, the intense sensation that the amputated body part still exists. Some phantom limbs are experienced as moving normally, such as being used to gesture in conversation, whereas some are frozen in position. Moreover, a phantom limb is often accompanied by pain sensations, which may result from the misgrowth of the severed pain nerves at the stump. The cortex misinterprets the pain as coming from the amputated body part. This phenomenon suggests that the brain has not reorganized in response to the injury and that the missing limb's cortical representation remains intact.

The neurologist V. S. Ramachandran has discovered that an amputee who has lost a hand may, when his or her eyes are closed, perceive a touch on the cheek as if it were on the missing hand (Ramachandran & Hirstein, 1998). On the somatosensory homunculus, the hand is represented next to the face. The unused part of the amputee's cortex (the part that would have responded to the now-missing limb) assumes to some degree the function of the closest group, representing the face. Somehow, the rest of the brain has not kept pace with the somatosensory area enough to figure out these neurons' new job, so the neurons formerly activated by a touch on the hand are activated by a touch on the amputee's face. The brain still codes the input as coming from the hand, and thus the amputee experiences a "phantom hand" (**FIGURE 3.40**).

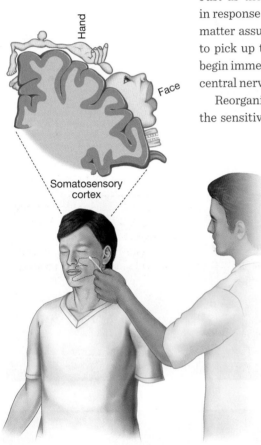

FIGURE 3.40
Cortical Remapping Following Amputation
The participant felt a cotton swab touching his cheek as touching his missing hand.

Q What do we call it when a person who has a limb amputated feels sensation in the missing limb?

3.14 Will a Learning Disability Prevent You from Succeeding in College?

Have you been diagnosed with a learning disability? Do you suspect you might have one?

According to the National Center for Learning Disabilities (2009), a learning disability is a "neurological disorder that affects the brain's ability to receive, process, store, and respond to information." One of the most common learning disabilities is dyslexia. This disability involves difficulties in acquiring and processing language, leading to problems with reading, spelling, or writing (**FIGURE 3.41**). Someone who has difficulty spelling or writing might, alternatively, have the learning disability dysgraphia, a disorder of written expression.

Learning disabilities may become apparent in childhood or later in life. Individuals might excel academically in high school, but the new academic and organizational challenges of college might help reveal a learning disability.

If you have a learning disability or suspect you have one, the earlier you seek help, the sooner you will have access to the resources available on your campus that will help you learn. Contact the disability support office or someone at Student Affairs, and they will be able to direct you. If your learning disability is verified, disability support office staff will work with you to determine the types of accommodations necessary to enable you to get the most of your academic experience.

Given your particular strengths and weaknesses in processing information, some types of accommodations will be helpful, whereas others will not. Disability support office staff will let your professors know you are entitled to a specific type of accommodation, but they will not tell your professors about the nature of your learning disability. For example, a disability support office staff member might send a note to your professors that reads, "[Your name will go here], a student in your introductory psychology course, has provided evidence of a condition that requires academic accommodation. As a result, please provide [him or her] with time and a half on exams and on in-class writing assignments."

Of course, you can also speak directly with individual professors about your learning disability and the kinds of resources likely to help you. Linda Tessler, a psychologist who works with persons with learning disabilities, writes:

> It must be clear that you are not asking for standards to be lowered. You are using tools to help you perform. To pass, you must perform the task that your classmates perform. You may, however, need to get there in a different way. Dyslexic students have to read the textbook just as nondyslexic students do. They may just do it differently through the use of books on tape. (Tessler, 1997, p. 2)

Will a learning disability prevent you from succeeding in college? Not if you can help it, and you can help it by advocating for yourself. Line up the resources you need to ensure that you are able to reap the rewards of college. ■

FIGURE 3.41
An Inspiring Example
The celebrity chef Jamie Oliver suffers from dyslexia. His disability has hardly kept him from achieving his career goals. Here, in June 2010, Oliver is announcing Home Cooking Skills, a new and inspirational program he has co-created to teach basic cooking skills to young people in England.

 What is a learning disability?

ANSWER: a neurological disorder that affects the brain's ability to receive, process, store, and respond to information

Learning Objectives

- Explain how genes are transmitted from parents to offspring.

- Discuss the goals and methods of behavioral genetics.

- Explain how environmental factors, including experience, influence genetic expression.

genes
The units of heredity that help determine the characteristics of an organism.

gene expression
Whether a particular gene is turned on or off.

chromosomes
Structures within the cell body that are made up of DNA, segments of which comprise individual genes.

What Is the Genetic Basis of Psychological Science?

So far, this chapter has presented the basic biological processes underlying psychological functions. The following section considers how **genes** and environment affect psychological functions. From the moment of conception, we receive the genes we will possess for the remainder of our lives, but to what extent do those genes determine our thoughts and behaviors? How do environmental influences, such as the families and cultures in which we are raised, alter how our brains develop and change?

Until the last few years, genetic research focused almost entirely on whether people possessed certain types of genes, such as genes for psychological disorders or for particular levels of intelligence. Although it is important to discover the effects of individual genes, this approach misses the critical role of environmental factors in shaping who we are. While the term *genetics* is typically used to describe how characteristics such as height, hair color, and eye color are passed along to offspring through inheritance, it also refers to the processes involved in turning genes "on" and "off." Research has shown that environmental factors can affect **gene expression.** This term refers to whether a particular gene is turned on or off. Environmental factors may also influence how a gene, once turned on, influences our thoughts, feelings, and behavior.

Genetic predispositions are often important in determining the environments people select for themselves. So, once again, biology and environment mutually influence each other. All the while, biology and environment—in other words, one's genes and every experience one ever has—influence the development of one's brain.

3.15 All of Human Development Has a Genetic Basis

Within nearly every cell in the body is the genome for making the entire organism. The *genome* is the master blueprint that provides detailed instructions for everything from how to grow a gallbladder to where the nose gets placed on a face. Whether a cell becomes part of a gallbladder or a nose is determined by which genes are turned on or off within that cell, and these actions are in turn determined by cues from both inside and outside the cell. The genome provides the options, and the environment determines which option is taken (Marcus, 2004).

Within each cell are **chromosomes.** These structures are made of *deoxyribonucleic acid (DNA)*, a substance that consists of two intertwined strands of molecules in a double helix shape. Segments of those strands are genes (**FIGURE 3.42**).

FIGURE 3.42
The Human Body Down to Its Genes
Each cell in the human body includes pairs of chromosomes, which consist of DNA strands. DNA has a double helix shape, and segments of it consist of individual genes.

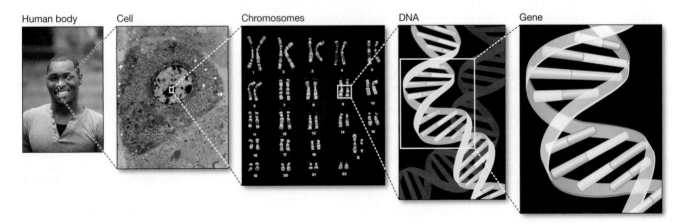

Human body   Cell   Chromosomes   DNA   Gene

(a)

(b)

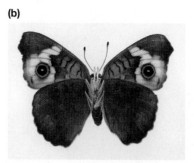

FIGURE 3.43

Gene Expression and Environment

The North American buckeye butterfly has seasonal forms that differ in the color patterns on their wings. **(a)** Generations that develop to adulthood in the summer—when temperatures are higher—take the "linea" form, with pale beige wings. **(b)** Generations that develop to adult in the autumn—when the days are shorter—take the "rosa" form, with dark reddish-brown wings.

In a typical human, nearly every cell contains 23 pairs of chromosomes. One member of each pair comes from the mother, the other from the father. In other words, each parent contributes half of a person's DNA, half of his or her genes.

Each gene—a particular sequence of molecules along a DNA strand—specifies an exact instruction to manufacture a distinct *polypeptide*. One or more polypeptides make up a protein. Proteins are the basic chemicals that make up the structure of cells and direct their activities. There are thousands of different types of proteins, and each type carries out a specific task. The environment determines which proteins are produced and when they are produced.

For example, a certain species of butterfly becomes colorful or drab, depending on the season in which the individual butterfly is born (Brakefield & French, 1999). The environment causes a gene to be expressed during the butterfly's development that is sensitive to temperature or day length (**FIGURE 3.43**). Similarly, although each cell in the human body contains the same DNA, cells become specialized, depending on which of their genes are expressed. As noted earlier, gene expression determines the body's basic physical makeup, but it also determines specific developments throughout life. It is involved in all psychological activity. Gene expression allows us to sense, to learn, to fall in love, and so on.

In February 2001, two groups of scientists published separate articles that detailed the results of the first phase of the *Human Genome Project*, an international research effort. This achievement represents the coordinated work of hundreds of scientists around the world to map the entire structure of human genetic material. The first step of the Human Genome Project was to map the entire sequence of DNA. In other words, the researchers set out to identify the precise order of molecules that make up each of the thousands of genes on each of the 23 pairs of human chromosomes (**FIGURE 3.44**). Since it was first launched, the Human Genome Project has led to many discoveries and encouraged scientists to work together to achieve grand goals (Green, Watson, & Collins, 2015).

One of the most striking findings from the Human Genome Project is that people have fewer than 30,000 genes. That number means humans have only about twice as many genes as a fly (13,000) or a worm (18,000), not much more than the number in some plants (26,000), and fewer than the number estimated to be in an ear of corn (50,000). Why are we so complex if we have so few genes? The number of genes might be less important than subtleties in how those genes are expressed and regulated (Baltimore, 2001).

 What is a gene?

ANSWER: a particular sequence of DNA

dominant gene

A gene that is expressed in the offspring whenever it is present.

recessive gene

A gene that is expressed only when it is matched with a similar gene from the other parent.

genotype

The genetic constitution of an organism, determined at the moment of conception.

phenotype

Observable physical characteristics, which result from both genetic and environmental influences.

(a)

(b)

FIGURE 3.45
Parent Plants Display Genetic Differences

Mendel studied pea plants. To observe the effects of cross-breeding, he started with **(a)** pea plants with purple flowers, and **(b)** pea plants with white flowers.

3.16 Heredity Involves Passing Along Genes Through Reproduction

The first clues to the mechanisms responsible for heredity were discovered by the monk Gregor Mendel around 1866. The monastery where Mendel lived had a long history of studying plants. For studying inheritance, Mendel developed an experimental technique, *selective breeding*, that strictly controlled which plants bred with which other plants.

In one simple study, Mendel selected pea plants that had either only purple flowers or only white flowers (**FIGURE 3.45**). He then cross-pollinated the two types to see which color of flowers the plants would produce. Mendel found that the first generation of pea offspring tended to be completely white or completely purple. If he had stopped there, he would never have discovered the basis of heredity. However, he then allowed each plant to self-pollinate into a second generation. This second generation revealed a different pattern: Of the hundreds of pea plants, about 75 percent had purple flowers and 25 percent had white flowers. This 3:1 ratio repeated itself in additional studies. It also held true for other characteristics, such as pod shape.

From this pattern, Mendel deduced that the plants contained separate units, now referred to as genes, that existed in different versions (e.g., white and purple). In determining an offspring's features, some of these versions would be dominant and others would be recessive. We now know that a **dominant gene** from either parent is expressed (becomes apparent or physically visible) whenever it is present. A **recessive gene** is expressed only when it is matched with a similar gene from the other parent. In pea plants, white flowers are recessive, so white flowers occur only when the gene for purple flowers is not present. All "white genes" and no purple ones was one of the four possible combinations of white and purple genes in Mendel's experiments.

GENOTYPE AND PHENOTYPE The existence of dominant and recessive genes means that not all genes are expressed. The **genotype** is an organism's genetic makeup. That genetic constitution is determined at the moment of conception and never changes. The **phenotype** is that organism's observable physical characteristics and is always changing.

Genetics, or nature, is one of the two influences on phenotype. So, for instance, in Mendel's experiments, two plants with purple flowers had the same phenotype but

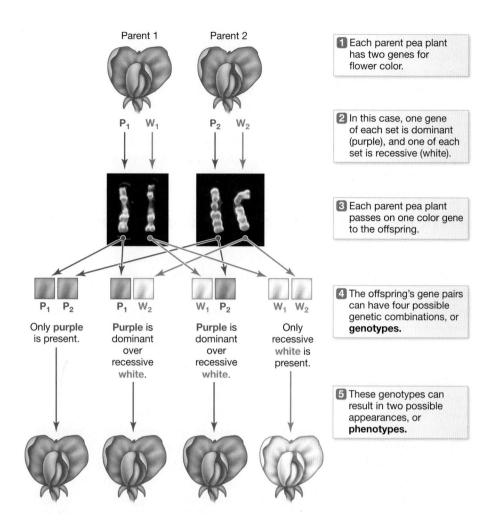

Parent 1   Parent 2

P₁ W₁   P₂ W₂

1 Each parent pea plant has two genes for flower color.

2 In this case, one gene of each set is dominant (purple), and one of each set is recessive (white).

3 Each parent pea plant passes on one color gene to the offspring.

P₁ P₂   P₁ W₂   W₁ P₂   W₁ W₂

Only **purple** is present.

Purple is dominant over recessive **white**.

Purple is dominant over recessive **white**.

Only recessive **white** is present.

4 The offspring's gene pairs can have four possible genetic combinations, or **genotypes.**

5 These genotypes can result in two possible appearances, or **phenotypes.**

FIGURE 3.46
Genotypes and Phenotypes
Mendel's experiments with cross-breeding pea plants resulted in purple flowers 75 percent of the time and white flowers 25 percent of the time.

might have differed in genotype. Either plant might have had two (dominant) genes for purple. Alternatively, either plant might have had one (dominant) purple gene and one (recessive) white gene (**FIGURE 3.46**). Environment, or nurture, is the second influence on phenotype. For instance, humans inherit their height and skin color. But good nutrition leads to increased size, and sunlight can change skin color.

POLYGENIC EFFECTS Mendel's flower experiments dealt with single-gene characteristics. Such traits appear to be determined by one gene each. When a population displays a range of variability for a certain characteristic, such as height or intelligence, the characteristic is *polygenic*. In other words, the trait is influenced by many genes (as well as by environment).

Consider human skin color. There are not just three or four separate skin colors. There is a spectrum of colors. The huge range of skin tones among Americans alone shows that human skin color is not inherited the same way as flower color was in Mendel's research. The rich variety of skin colors (phenotype) is not the end product of a single dominant/recessive gene pairing (genotype). Instead, the variety shows the effects of multiple genes.

SEXUAL REPRODUCTION Although they have the same parents, siblings may differ from each other in many ways, such as eye color, height, and personality. These differences occur because each person has a specific combination of genes. Most cells in the human body contain 23 pairs of chromosomes. These pairs include the sex chromosomes, which are denoted X and Y because of their shapes. Females have two X chromosomes. Males have one X chromosome and one Y (**FIGURE 3.47**).

(a)   (b)

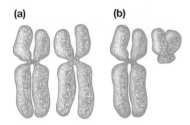

FIGURE 3.47
Sex Chromosomes
(a) In females, the 23rd pair of chromosomes consists of two X chromosomes. **(b)** In males, the 23rd pair consists of one X and one Y chromosome. The Y chromosome is much smaller than the X chromosome.

FIGURE 3.48
Industrial Melanism
These moths illustrate industrial melanism. As shown here, it is easier to spot light-colored insects against dark backgrounds. Because predators have an easier time catching insects they can spot, darker moths and darker butterflies are better able to survive in more-polluted areas. As a result, the lighter moths and lighter butterflies in those areas tend to die off, leaving more of the moths and butterflies with the selective advantage of darkness.

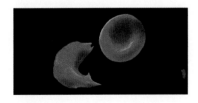

FIGURE 3.49
Sickle-Cell Disease
Sickle-cell disease occurs when people receive recessive genes for the trait from both parents. It causes red blood cells to assume the distinctive "sickle" shape seen here in the left cell. Sickle-cell disease is most common among African Americans.

ANSWER: The person is female.

After one sperm and one egg combine during fertilization, the resulting fertilized cell, known as a *zygote*, contains 23 pairs of chromosomes. Half of each pair of chromosomes comes from the mother, and the other half comes from the father. From any two parents, 8 million different combinations of the 23 chromosomes are possible. The net outcome is that a unique genotype is created at conception, accounting for the *genetic variation* of the human species.

The zygote grows through *cell division*. This process has two stages: First the chromosomes duplicate. Then the cell divides into two new cells with an identical chromosome structure. Cell division is the basis of the life cycle and is responsible for growth and development.

GENETIC MUTATIONS: ADVANTAGEOUS, DISADVANTAGEOUS, OR BOTH?
Errors sometimes occur during cell division, leading to *mutations*, or alterations in the DNA. Most mutations are benign and have little influence on the organism. Occasionally, a genetic mutation produces a selective advantage or disadvantage in terms of survival or reproduction. That is, mutations can be adaptive or maladaptive. The evolutionary significance of such a change in adaptiveness is complex. If a mutation produces an ability or a behavior that proves advantageous to the organism, that mutation may spread through the population. The mutation may spread because those who carry the gene are more likely to survive and reproduce.

Consider *industrial melanism*. This phenomenon accounts for the fact that in areas of the world with heavy soot or smog, moths and butterflies tend to be darker in color. What has created this dark coloration? Before industrialization, landscapes (trees, buildings, etc.) were lighter in color. Predators were more likely to spot darker insects against pale backgrounds, so any mutation that led to darker coloring in insects was disadvantageous and was eliminated quickly through natural selection. But with industrialization, pollution darkened the landscapes. Darker coloring in insects therefore became advantageous and more adaptive because the darker insects were harder to see against the darker backgrounds (**FIGURE 3.48**).

What about genetic mutations that are disadvantageous adaptively, such as by leading to disease? Genes that lead to diseases that do not develop until well beyond reproductive age do not have a reproductive disadvantage and are not removed from the population. The dominance or recessiveness of a gene also helps determine if it remains in the gene pool.

For instance, *sickle-cell disease* is a genetic disorder that alters the bloodstream's processing of oxygen. It can lead to pain, organ and bone damage, and anemia. The disease occurs mainly in African Americans: Approximately 8 percent of African Americans are estimated to have the (recessive) gene for it (Centers for Disease Control and Prevention, 2011b). Because the sickle-cell gene is recessive, only those African Americans who receive it from both parents will develop the disease. Those who receive a recessive gene from only one parent have what is called *sickle-cell trait*. They may exhibit symptoms under certain conditions (such as during exercise), but they will have a generally healthy phenotype in spite of a genotype that includes the trait (**FIGURE 3.49**).

Recessive genes do not interfere with most people's health. For this reason, the recessive genes for diseases such as sickle-cell anemia can survive in the gene pool. This particular gene also has some benefit in that it increases resistance to malaria, a parasitic disease prevalent in certain parts of Africa. People with only one sickle-cell gene enjoy this resistance without suffering from sickle-cell disease. In contrast to recessive gene disorders like this one, most dominant gene disorders are lethal for most of their carriers and therefore do not last in the gene pool.

 A person's 23rd pair of chromosomes is XX. What does this information tell you about the person?

3.17 Genes Affect Behavior

What determines the kind of person you are? What factors make you more or less bold, intelligent, or able to read a map? Your abilities and your psychological traits are influenced by the interaction of your genes and the environment in which you were raised or to which you are now exposed. The study of how genes and environment interact to influence psychological activity is known as *behavioral genetics*. Behavioral genetics has provided important information about the extent to which biology influences mind, brain, and behavior.

Any research suggesting that abilities to perform certain behaviors are biologically based is controversial. Most people do not want to be told that what they can achieve is limited or promoted by something beyond their control, such as their genes. It is easy to accept that genes control physical characteristics such as sex, race, eye color, and predisposition to diseases such as cancer and alcoholism. But can genes determine whether people will get divorced, how happy they are, or what careers they choose?

Increasingly, science indicates that genes lay the groundwork for many human traits. From this perspective, people are born essentially like undeveloped photographs: The image is already captured, but the way it eventually appears can vary based on the development process. Psychologists study the ways in which characteristics are influenced by nature, nurture, and their combination. In other words, who we are is determined by how our genes are expressed in distinct environments.

BEHAVIORAL GENETICS METHODS Most of us, at one time or another, have marveled at how different siblings can be, even those raised around the same time and in the same household. The differences are to be expected, because most siblings do not share identical genes or identical life experiences. Within the household and outside it, environments differ subtly and not so subtly. Siblings have different birth orders. Their mother may have consumed different foods and other substances during her pregnancies. They may have different friends and teachers. Their parents may treat them differently. Their parents are at different points in their own lives.

It is difficult to know what causes the similarities and differences between siblings, who always share some genes and often share much of their environments. Therefore, behavioral geneticists use two methods to assess the degree to which traits are inherited: twin studies and adoption studies.

Twin studies compare similarities between different types of twins to determine the genetic basis of specific traits. **Monozygotic twins,** or *identical twins*, result from one zygote (fertilized egg) dividing in two. Each new zygote, and therefore each twin, has the same chromosomes and the same genes on each chromosome (**FIGURE 3.50A**). However, monozygotic twins' DNA might not be as identical as long thought, due to subtle differences in how the mother's and father's genes are combined (Bruder et al., 2008). **Dizygotic twins,** sometimes called *fraternal* or *nonidentical twins*, result when two separately fertilized eggs develop in the mother's womb simultaneously. The resulting twins are no more similar genetically than any other pair of siblings (**FIGURE 3.50B**). To the extent that monozygotic twins are more similar than dizygotic twins, the increased similarity is considered most likely due to genetic influence.

Adoption studies compare the similarities between biological relatives and adoptive relatives. Nonbiological adopted siblings may share similar home environments, but they will have different genes. Therefore, the assumption is that similarities among nonbiological adopted siblings have more to do with environment than with genes.

How much influence would you say your home life has had on you? It turns out that growing up in the same home has relatively little influence on many traits, including personality traits. Indeed, after genetic similarity is controlled for, even biological

monozygotic twins
Also called *identical twins*; twin siblings that result from one zygote splitting in two and therefore share the same genes.

dizygotic twins
Also called *fraternal twins*; twin siblings that result from two separately fertilized eggs and therefore are no more similar genetically than nontwin siblings.

FIGURE 3.50
The Two Kinds of Twins

(a) Monozygotic (identical) twins result when one fertilized egg splits in two. **(b)** Dizygotic (fraternal) twins result when two separate eggs are fertilized at the same time.

(a) Monozygotic (identical) twins

One sperm fertilizes one egg…

and the zygote splits in two.

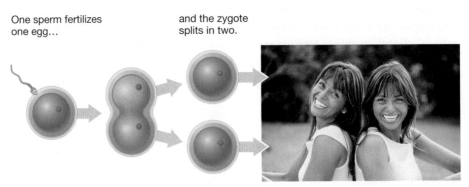

(b) Dizygotic (fraternal) twins

Two sperm fertilize two eggs…

which become two zygotes.

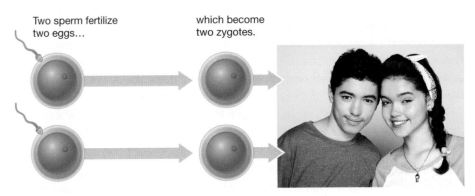

FIGURE 3.51
Identical Twins Raised Apart Are Also Similar

Identical twins Gerald Levey and Mark Newman, participants in Dr. Bouchard's study, were separated at birth. Reunited at age 31, they discovered they were both firefighters and had similar personality traits.

siblings raised in the same home are no more similar than two strangers plucked at random off the street. (This point is examined in greater detail in Chapter 9, "Human Development," and Chapter 13, "Personality.")

One way to conduct a behavioral genetic study is to compare monozygotic twins who have been *raised together* with ones who were *raised apart*. Thomas Bouchard and his colleagues at the University of Minnesota identified more than 100 pairs of identical and nonidentical twins, some raised together and some raised apart (1990). The researchers examined a variety of these twins' characteristics, including intelligence, personality, well-being, achievement, alienation, and aggression. The general finding from the Minnesota Twin Project was that identical twins, whether they were raised together or not, were likely to be similar (**FIGURE 3.51**).

Some critics have argued that most of the adopted twins in the Minnesota study were raised in relatively similar environments. This similarity came about, in part, because adoption agencies try to match the child to the adoptive home. However, this argument does not explain the identical twins Oskar Stohr and Jack Yufe, who were born in Trinidad in 1933 (Bouchard, Lykken, McGue, Segal, & Tellegen, 1990). Oskar was raised Catholic in Germany and eventually joined the Nazi Party. Jack was raised Jewish in Trinidad and lived for a while in Israel. Few twins have more-different backgrounds. Yet when they met, at an interview for the study, they were wearing similar clothes, exhibited similar mannerisms, and shared odd habits, such as flushing the toilet before using it, dipping toast in coffee, storing rubber bands on their wrists, and enjoying startling people by sneezing loudly in elevators.

Some critics feel that nothing more than coincidence is at work in these case studies. They argue that if a researcher randomly selected any two people of the same age, many surprising similarities would exist in those people and their lives, just by coincidence, even if the people and their lives differed in most other ways. But twins and other relatives share similarities beyond coincidental attributes and behavior quirks.

For instance, intelligence and personality traits such as shyness tend to run in families because of strong genetic components.

Moreover, there is some evidence that twins raised apart may be more similar than twins raised together. This phenomenon might occur if parents encouraged individuality in twins raised together by emphasizing different strengths and interests as a way of helping each twin develop as an individual. In effect, the parents would actively create a different environment for each twin.

UNDERSTANDING HERITABILITY **Heredity** is the transmission of characteristics from parents to offspring by means of genes. A term that is often confused with *heredity* but means something different is **heritability.** This term refers to the proportion of the variation in some specific trait in a population, not in an individual, that is due to genetics. That is, the trait cannot be due to environment or random chance.

Consider a specific trait, height, in a particular population, American women. The heritability for a trait depends on the *variation:* the measure of the overall difference among a group of people for that particular trait. To know the heritability of height, we need to know how much individual American women vary in that trait. Once we know the typical amount of variation within the population, we can see whether people who are related—sisters or a mother and daughter—show less variation than women chosen at random.

Say that within the population of American women, height has a heritability of .60. This figure means that 60 percent of the variation in height among American women is genetic. It does not mean that any individual necessarily gets 60 percent of her height from genetics and 40 percent from environment. Heritability estimates aid in identifying the causes of differences between individuals in a population.

For researchers to perform a heritability analysis, there must be variation in the population. For instance, almost everyone has two legs. There is very little variability in the population. More people lose legs through accidents than are born without them. Thus, the heritability value for having two legs is nearly zero, despite the obvious fact that the human genome includes instructions for growing two legs. The key lesson here is: Estimates of heritability are concerned only with the extent that people differ in terms of their genetic makeup within the group. So, the next time you hear that some trait or other is heritable, you need to appreciate that this refers to the distribution of that trait within a group, not to particular persons in that group.

 Q When studying trait similarity and genes, why do researchers compare monozygotic twins with dizygotic twins?

heredity
Transmission of characteristics from parents to offspring through genes.

heritability
A statistical estimate of the extent to which variation in a trait within a population is due to genetics.

ANSWER: Unlike dizygotic twins, monozygotic twins have the same genes. Therefore, if each pair of twins grew up in the same environment, then greater trait similarity in monozygotic twins than in dizygotic twins is likely due to genes, not environment.

3.18 Genetic Expression Can Be Modified

As noted at the beginning of this section, researchers focus more on how particular genes are expressed than whether they are possessed. During the past decade, there have been several exciting advances in understanding how environments influence gene expression as well as how researchers can manipulate that expression.

Consider how social and environmental contexts might shape gene expression during development. In a longitudinal study of criminality, Avshalom Caspi and his colleagues (2002) followed a group of more than 1,000 New Zealanders from their births in 1972–73 until adulthood. The group was made up of all the babies that were born in the town of Dunedin over the course of a year. Every few years, the researchers collected enormous amounts of information about the participants and their lives. When the participants were 26 years old, the investigators examined which factors predicted who became a violent criminal.

Prior research had demonstrated that children who are mistreated by their parents are more likely to become violent offenders. But not all mistreated children become violent, and these researchers wanted to know why not. They hypothesized that the enzyme monoamine oxidase (MAO) is important in determining susceptibility to the effects of mistreatment, because low levels of MAO have been implicated in aggressive behaviors (this connection is discussed further in Chapter 12, "Social Psychology").

The gene that controls MAO is called MAOA and comes in two forms. One form of the MAOA gene leads to higher levels of MAO, and the other form leads to lower levels. Caspi and colleagues found that boys with the low-MAOA gene appeared to be especially susceptible to the effects of early-childhood mistreatment. Those boys were also much more likely to be convicted of a violent crime than those with the high-MAOA gene. Only 1 in 8 boys was mistreated *and* had the low-MAOA gene. That minority, however, were responsible for nearly half of the violent crimes committed by the group (see "The Methods of Psychology: Caspi's Study of the Influence of Environment and Genes").

The New Zealand study is a good example of how nature and nurture together affect behavior—in this case, unfortunately, violent behavior. Nature and nurture are inextricably entwined. The Dunedin study has been crucial for providing evidence regarding gene effects. One of the impressive aspects of the study is that more than 95 percent of the participants still alive continue to participate (Poulton, Moffitt, & Silva, 2015).

EPIGENETICS An exciting new field of genetic study is *epigenetics* (Berger, Kouzarides, Shiekhattar, & Shilatifard, 2009; Holliday, 1987). This term literally means "on top of genetics." Here, environment is seen as layered over genetics. Epigenetics researchers are looking at the processes by which the environment affects genetic expression. They have found that various environmental exposures do not alter DNA, but they *do* alter DNA expression. That alteration makes it more or less likely that a gene will be expressed. For example, living under stress or consuming a poor diet makes some genes more active and some less active.

According to recent research, these changes in how DNA is expressed can be passed along to future generations (Daxinger & Whitelaw, 2012). For example, rats raised by stressed mothers are more likely to be stressed themselves (Zucchi et al., 2013). The biological mechanisms are too complex to consider here. A simple way to think about epigenetic processes is that a parent's experiences create tags on DNA that tell it when to express, and these tags are passed along with the DNA. They may then be passed along to future generations.

The potential implications of epigenetics for understanding health problems and health benefits are enormous. It is possible that smoking cigarettes or drinking alcohol, like chronic stress or bad nutrition, can create epigenetic tags (Pembrey et al., 2006). Further research will reveal how individuals' life circumstances might change how their genes operate and how such processes may affect future generations (Grossniklaus, Kelly, Ferguson-Smith, Pembrey, & Lindquist, 2013).

GENETIC MODIFICATIONS Researchers can employ various gene manipulation techniques to enhance or reduce the expression of a particular gene or even to insert a gene from one animal species into the embryo of another. The researchers can then compare the genetically modified animal with an unmodified one to test theories about the affected gene's function (**FIGURE 3.52**). Such techniques have dramatically increased our understanding of how gene expression influences thought, feeling, and behavior.

For instance, some of the transgenic mice discussed in Chapter 2 are called *knockouts*. Within these research mice, particular genes have been "knocked out," or rendered inactive by being removed from the genome or disrupted within the genome. If a gene is important for a specific function, knocking out that gene should interfere

FIGURE 3.52
Genetic Modifications
The two white mice and three brown mice in this photo are genetically normal. The sixth mouse is hairless because it has been genetically modified. Specifically, this mouse has received two *nu* genes, which cause the "nude" mutation. These genes also affect the immune system, so the mouse is a good laboratory subject for studies related to immune function.

The Methods of Psychology

Caspi's Study of the Influence of Environment and Genes

HYPOTHESIS: The MAOA gene regulates enzyme monoamine oxidase (MAO) and may be important in determining susceptibility to the effects of maltreatment, because low levels of MAO have been implicated in aggressive behaviors.

RESEARCH METHOD:

1 A group of more than 1,000 New Zealanders were followed from birth to adulthood.

2 Researchers measured which children were mistreated by their parents (**nurture**).

3 Researchers measured the presence of the MAOA gene, which comes in two forms. One form leads to higher levels of MAO, and the other form leads to lower levels (**nature**).

4 Researchers measured the tendency toward criminal behavior.

RESULTS: Those who had the MAOA gene for low MAO activity were much more likely than others to have been convicted of violent crimes if they had been maltreated as children. The effects of maltreatment had less influence on those with the high-MAOA gene.

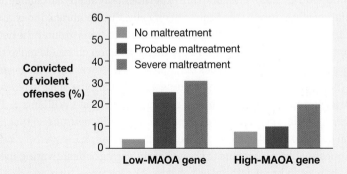

CONCLUSION: Nature and nurture can work together to affect human behavior.

QUESTION: Do this study's results indicate that child abuse does not affect some children?

ANSWER: No, mistreatment led to increased problems for all of the children studied. However, the relation was larger for those children with the low-MAOA gene.

Source: Caspi, A., McClay, J., Moffit, T. E., Mill, J., Martin, J., Craig, I. W., et al. (2002). Role of genotype in the cycle of violence in maltreated children. *Science, 29,* 851–854.

with the function. This experimental technique has revolutionized genetics, and in recognition the 2007 Nobel Prize was awarded to the three scientists who developed it: Mario Capecchi, Oliver Smithies, and Sir Martin Evans.

One remarkable finding from genetic manipulation is that changing even a single gene can dramatically change behavior. Through various gene manipulations, researchers have created anxious mice, hyperactive mice, mice that cannot learn or remember, mice that groom themselves to the point of baldness, mice that fail to take care of their offspring, and even mice that progressively increase alcohol intake when stressed (Marcus, 2004; Ridley, 2003).

In one study, a gene from the highly social prairie vole was inserted into the developing embryos of normally antisocial mice. The resulting transgenic mice exhibited social behavior more typical of prairie voles than of mice (Insel & Young, 2001). Another study found that knocking out specific genes led mice to forget other mice they had previously encountered. These "knockouts" also failed to investigate new mice placed in their cages, though normal mice would do so readily. In essence, knocking out one gene led to multiple impairments in social recognition (Choleris et al., 2003).

These findings do not indicate that mice have a specific gene for being social. It indicates that—in mice and in humans—changing one gene's expression leads to the expression or nonexpression of a series of other genes. This effect ultimately influences even complex behaviors. In other words, genes seldom work in isolation to influence mind and behavior. Rather, complex interaction among thousands of genes gives rise to the complexity of human experience.

OPTOGENETICS One problem with most studies of brain function is that they use correlational methods. Recall from Chapter 2 that correlational techniques do not allow us to show causality. For example, fMRI studies show which areas of the brain are most active while a person performs a task. These findings do not mean there is a causal relationship between the brain activity and the task.

To address this limitation, scientists have recently pioneered *optogenetics*. This research technique provides precise control over when a neuron fires. That control enables researchers to better understand the causal relationship between neural firing and behavior. Optogenetics combines the use of light (optics) with gene alterations (Boyden et al., 2005; **FIGURE 3.53**). The genes are experimentally altered to change a particular subpopulation of neurons in the brain. Specifically, the membrane ion channels are changed within the neurons—recall that ion channels allow ions to enter the neuron and trigger action potentials. The changes to the membrane ion channels make these specific neurons sensitive to different types of light (e.g., red, green, blue). By inserting fiberoptics into that region of the brain and shining a particular type of light, researchers are able to trigger action potentials in the neurons of interest (Williams & Deisseroth, 2013). Using similar techniques, researchers can modify neurons so that firing is inhibited when light is presented (Berndt, Lee, Ramakrishnan, & Deisseroth, 2014).

These techniques enable researchers to show that activating or deactivating specific neurons causes changes in brain activity or behavior. For instance, turning on one set of neurons led animals to act more anxiously (Tye et al., 2011). Turning off another set of neurons reduced cocaine use in animals addicted to that drug (Stefanik et al., 2013).

However, shining a light in a particular brain region enables researchers to better understand the causal relationships between brain activity and behavior. The development of optogenetics is an excellent example of how cutting-edge methods enable researchers to ask increasingly direct questions about biology and behavior.

FIGURE 3.53
Optogenetics
This mouse has been implanted with an optogenetic device.

ANSWER: the idea that the environment sometimes changes genetic expression in a way that might be passed along to offspring

 What is epigenetics?

Your Chapter Review

Chapter Summary

How Does the Nervous System Operate?

3.1 Neurons Are the Basic Units of the Nervous System

The human nervous system is divided into two basic units: the central nervous system (the brain and the spinal cord) and the peripheral nervous system (all the other nerve cells in the rest of the body). Nerve cells, or neurons, are the basic units of the nervous system. Neurons are linked as neural networks, and neural networks are linked together. Neurons receive and send electrical and chemical messages. All neurons have the same basic structure, but neurons vary by function and by location in the nervous system.

3.2 Action Potentials Produce Neural Communication

Changes in a neuron's electrical charge are the basis of an action potential, or neural firing. Firing is the means of communication within networks of neurons. A neuron at rest is polarized. That is, it has a greater negative electrical charge inside than outside. The passage of negative and positive ions inside and outside the neuron is regulated by ion channels, such as those located at the nodes of Ranvier.

3.3 Neurotransmitters Influence Mental Activity and Behavior

Neurons do not touch. They release chemicals (neurotransmitters) into the synapse, a small gap between the neurons. Neurotransmitters bind with the receptors of postsynaptic neurons, thus changing the charge in those neurons. Neurotransmitters' effects are halted by reuptake of the neurotransmitters into the presynaptic neurons, by enzyme deactivation, or by autoreception. Neurotransmitters have been identified that influence aspects of the mind and behavior in humans. For example, neurotransmitters influence emotions, motor skills, sleep, dreaming, learning and memory, arousal, pain control, and pain perception. Drugs and toxins can enhance or inhibit the activity of neurotransmitters by affecting their synthesis, their release, and the termination of their action in the synapse.

What Are the Basic Brain Structures and Their Functions?

3.4 The Ability to Study Brain Function Has Improved Dramatically

Through psychophysiological assessment, psychologists collect data about the ways people's bodies respond to particular tasks or events. For example, electrophysiology (often using an electroencephalograph, or EEG) measures the brain's electrical activity. Brain imaging is done using positron emission tomography (PET), magnetic resonance imaging (MRI), and functional magnetic resonance imaging (fMRI). Transcranial magnetic stimulation (TMS) disrupts normal brain activity, allowing researchers to infer the brain processing involved in particular thoughts, feelings, and behaviors.

3.5 The Brain Stem Houses the Basic Programs of Survival

The top of the spinal cord forms the brain stem, which is involved in basic functions such as breathing and swallowing. The brain stem includes the medulla, which controls heart rate, breathing, and other autonomic functions. The brain stem also includes the pons and the reticular formation, a network of neurons that influences general alertness and sleep. The cerebellum ("little brain") is the bulging structure connected to the back of the brain stem. This structure is essential for movement and controls balance.

3.6 Subcortical Structures Control Emotions and Appetitive Behaviors

The subcortical structures play a key part in psychological processes because they control relay of sensory information (the thalamus), vital functions (the hypothalamus), memories (the hippocampus), emotions (the amygdala), and the planning and production of movement (the basal ganglia).

3.7 The Cerebral Cortex Underlies Complex Mental Activity

The lobes of the cortex play specific roles in vision (occipital), touch (parietal), hearing (temporal), and movement, rational activity, social behavior, and personality (frontal).

3.8 Splitting the Brain Splits the Mind

Cutting the corpus callosum separates the brain's two hemispheres. Splitting the hemispheres from each other reveals their primary functions. The left hemisphere's propensity to construct a world that makes sense is called the interpreter.

3.9 Think like a Psychologist: Are There "Left Brain" and "Right Brain" Types of People?

The idea of "left brain" and "right brain" people is a myth. The hemispheres are specialized for certain functions, such as language or spatial relationships. However, each hemisphere is capable of carrying out most cognitive processes, though sometimes in different ways.

How Does the Brain Communicate with the Body?

3.10 The Peripheral Nervous System Includes the Somatic and Autonomic Systems

The somatic system transmits sensory signals and motor signals between the central nervous system and the skin, muscles, and joints. The autonomic system regulates the body's internal environment through the sympathetic division, which responds to alarm, and the parasympathetic division, which returns the body to its resting state.

3.11 The Endocrine System Communicates Through Hormones

Endocrine glands produce and release chemical substances. These substances travel to body tissues through the bloodstream and influence a variety of processes, including the stress response and sexual behavior. The endocrine system is largely controlled through the actions of the hypothalamus and the pituitary gland. The hypothalamus controls the release of hormones from the pituitary gland. The pituitary controls the release of hormones from other endocrine glands in the body.

How Does the Brain Change?

3.12 The Brain Rewires Itself Throughout Life

Plasticity is the brain's capacity to continually change in response to environment. Although brain plasticity decreases with age, the brain retains the ability to rewire itself throughout life. This ability is the biological basis of learning. Females' and males' brains are more similar than different.

3.13 The Brain Can Recover from Injury

The brain can reorganize its functions in response to brain damage. However, this capacity decreases with age. Perceptual irregularities, such as phantom limb syndrome, are attributed to the cross-wiring of connections in the brain during cortical reorganization.

3.14 Using Psychology in Your Life: Will a Learning Disability Prevent You from Succeeding in College?

Many resources are available to help people with learning disabilities succeed in college.

What Is the Genetic Basis of Psychological Science?

3.15 All of Human Development Has a Genetic Basis

Human behavior is influenced by genes. Through genes, people inherit both physical attributes and personality traits from their parents. Chromosomes are made of genes, and the Human Genome Project has mapped the genes that make up humans' 23 chromosomal pairs.

3.16 Heredity Involves Passing Along Genes Through Reproduction

Genes may be dominant or recessive. An organism's genetic constitution is referred to as its genotype. The organism's observable characteristics are referred to as its phenotype. Many characteristics are polygenic. An offspring receives half of its chromosomes from its mother and half of its chromosomes from its father. Because so many combinations of the 23 pairs of chromosomes are possible, there is tremendous genetic variation in the human species. Mutations resulting from errors in cell division also give rise to genetic variation.

3.17 Genes Affect Behavior

Behavioral geneticists examine how genes and environment interact to influence psychological activity. Twin studies and adoption studies provide insight into heritability.

3.18 Genetic Expression Can Be Modified

Genes and environmental contexts interact in ways that influence observable characteristics. Epigenetics is the idea that genetic expression may change due to experience. Genetic manipulation has been achieved in mammals such as mice. Animal studies using gene knockouts, which allow genes to be turned on and off, are valuable tools for understanding genetic influences on behavior and on health. Through optogenetics, researchers modify genes to trigger action potentials in neurons.

Key Terms

acetylcholine (ACh), p. 78
action potential, p. 72
all-or-none principle, p. 75
amygdala, p. 86
autonomic nervous system (ANS), p. 98
axon, p. 71
basal ganglia, p. 87

brain stem, p. 84
Broca's area, p. 82
cell body, p. 71
central nervous system (CNS), p. 70
cerebellum, p. 84
cerebral cortex, p. 87
chromosomes, p. 106

corpus callosum, p. 87
dendrites, p. 71
dizygotic twins, p. 111
dominant gene, p. 108
dopamine, p. 79
electroencephalograph (EEG), p. 82
endocrine system, p. 99

endorphins, p. 80

frontal lobes, p. 90

functional magnetic resonance imaging
    (fMRI), p. 84

GABA, p. 80

gene expression, p. 106

genes, p. 106

genotype, p. 108

glutamate, p. 80

gonads, p. 100

heredity, p. 113

heritability, p. 113

hippocampus, p. 86

hormones, p. 99

hypothalamus, p. 86

magnetic resonance imaging (MRI), p. 83

monozygotic twins, p. 111

myelin sheath, p. 74

neurons, p. 70

neurotransmitters, p. 75

nodes of Ranvier, p. 74

norepinephrine, p. 79

occipital lobes, p. 88

parasympathetic division, p. 99

parietal lobes, p. 88

peripheral nervous system (PNS), p. 70

phenotype, p. 108

pituitary gland, p. 99

plasticity, p. 101

positron emission tomography (PET), p. 83

prefrontal cortex, p. 90

receptors, p. 76

recessive gene, p. 108

resting membrane potential, p. 72

reuptake, p. 77

serotonin, p. 79

somatic nervous system (SNS), p. 97

split brain, p. 92

sympathetic division, p. 98

synapse, p. 72

temporal lobes, p. 90

terminal buttons, p. 72

thalamus, p. 86

transcranial magnetic stimulation
    (TMS), p. 84

Putting Psychology to Work

What Are the Clinical and Consumer Applications of Neuroscience?

As you have learned from this chapter, explaining how people think, feel, and behave requires knowledge about brain activity, physiology, and anatomy. Tools such as EEG recordings, fMRI brain imaging, and transcranial magnetic stimulation have contributed to a better understanding of how brain activity is translated into thought, feelings, and behavior.

Being able to interpret brain activity has clinical and consumer applications. Companies employ people with neuroscience experience in a range of settings: from using biometrics to measure responses (EEG technicians), to creating marketing materials, to developing brain/computer interfaces that help restore mobility and communication in paralyzed patients.

The second of these settings, neuromarketing, is the use of EEG and fMRI recordings to predict consumer behavior in response to particular ads and products. This approach has been somewhat successful, with fMRI activity of brain reward regions predicting actual consumer behavior (Venkatraman et al., 2015). However, early claims for neuromarketing went beyond what we are able to know about complex behavior based on brain activity. As neuromarketing methods improve, more companies will adopt its strategies, and this field will be a promising area of employment

for psychology graduates with neuroscience training (Ariely & Burns, 2010).

Individuals with advanced degrees in neuroscience are already using their skills in an exciting new area called neuroprosthetics. Braingate2, an ongoing collaborative project between university researchers and medical centers, employs neuroscientists, other scientists, and clinicians to develop technologies to help people with neurological disorders regain function. In neuroprosthetics, a computer "decodes" brain activity and uses that information to drive external devices. Results have made it possible for individuals with locked-in syndrome—the inability to talk or move due to brainstem damage or the neurodegenerative disease amyotrophic lateral sclerosis (ALS)—to control a cursor on a computer screen with just their thoughts. In addition, quadriplegic individuals have been able to regain control of their arms and hands.

The bottom line: Understanding how the brain translates neural activity into thought and behavior has vital clinical and consumer applications. Jobs such as EEG technician require only an undergraduate degree, with some laboratory experience; more-advanced degrees are required for jobs in neuroprosthetics research.

Want to earn a better grade on your test?

Go to **INQUIZITIVE** to learn and review this chapter's content, with personalized feedback along the way. Practice Tests and accompanying answer keys can be found at the back of the book on page PT-1.

4 Consciousness

Big Questions

- What Is Consciousness? 122

- What Is Sleep? 133

- What Is Altered Consciousness? 143

- How Do Drugs Affect Consciousness? 147

BEFORE YOU DIVE INTO THE SUBJECT OF CONSCIOUSNESS, why not take a few minutes to meditate? As this chapter will explain, there are different types of meditation. For this introductory exercise, focus your awareness on one specific aspect of your current experience: breathing. Breathe in and out slowly. Pay close attention to your breathing and nothing else. Then return to your reading in a few minutes. Ready? Begin.

You have just used meditation to alter your consciousness, which is your personal experience of the here and now. Perhaps while you tried to meditate you started daydreaming. That experience is also part of your consciousness, as are the dreams you have while sleeping.

This chapter looks at consciousness and its variations. All conscious experiences are associated with brain activity. To understand the relationship between the brain and consciousness, we need to consider how conscious experiences differ. As explored in this chapter, there are natural variations in consciousness (e.g., being awake or asleep or in coma). Moreover, people manipulate consciousness through natural methods (e.g., meditation) as well as artificial methods (e.g., drugs). In addition, because of the very nature of consciousness, conscious experiences differ from person to person. The big questions that psychologists consider in this area are: What is consciousness? What is sleep? What is altered consciousness? How do drugs affect consciousness?

- Define consciousness.
- Explain how brain activity gives rise to consciousness.
- Identify varied states of consciousness.
- Discuss how unconscious processes influence thought and behavior.

consciousness
One's subjective experience of the world, resulting from brain activity.

FIGURE 4.1
Seeing Red
One difficult question related to consciousness is whether people's subjective experiences of the world are similar. For instance, does red look the same to everyone who has normal color vision?

What Is Consciousness?

Consciousness consists of one's moment-by-moment, personal (i.e., subjective) experiences. Paying attention to your immediate surroundings is one such experience. Your current thoughts are another. You know you are conscious—that you have consciousness—because you are experiencing the outside world through your senses and because you know that you are thinking. Consciousness involves not just your sensations and thoughts but also your memories and anything else you are experiencing in the moment.

But what gives rise to your consciousness? Are you conscious simply because many neurons are firing in your brain? If so, how are the actions of these brain circuits related to your subjective experiences of the world? Your body includes many highly active biological systems, such as your immune system, that do not produce the sort of consciousness you are experiencing right now. At every minute, your brain is regulating your body temperature, controlling your breathing, calling up memories as necessary, and so on. You are not conscious of the brain operations that do these things. Why are you conscious only of certain experiences?

4.1 Brain Activity Gives Rise to Consciousness

The question of what it means to be conscious of something has been asked for centuries. As discussed in Chapter 1, the seventeenth-century philosopher René Descartes argued that the mind is physically distinct from the brain. This view, now discredited, is called *dualism*. Early pioneers in psychology attempted to understand consciousness through introspection, by having people interrogate their inner mental experiences. Psychologists largely abandoned this method because of its subjective nature. Conscious experiences exist, but their subjective nature makes them difficult to study empirically. Because each of us experiences consciousness personally, we cannot know if any two people experience the world in exactly the same way. What does the color red look like to you (**FIGURE 4.1**)? How does an apple taste?

Psychologists now examine, even measure, consciousness and other mental states that were previously viewed as too subjective to be studied. For example, in an early study Frank Tong and colleagues (1998) examined the relationship between consciousness and neural responses in the brain. Participants were shown images in which houses were superimposed on faces (**FIGURE 4.2**). The researchers used fMRI to measure neural responses in the participants' brains (imaging methods are discussed in Chapter 3, "Biology and Behavior"). When participants reported seeing a face, neural activity increased in brain regions associated with face recognition. When participants reported seeing a house, neural activity increased in brain regions associated with object recognition. This finding suggests that different types of sensory information are processed by different brain areas. The particular type of neural activity determines the particular type of awareness of the image.

Scientists cannot (yet) read all your thoughts by looking at your brain activity, but examining your patterns of brain activity can identify several aspects of your conscious experience. For example, brain activity patterns show whether you are looking at faces or bodies (Norman, Polyn, Detre, & Haxby, 2006; O'Toole et al., 2014), which emotions you are experiencing (Kragel & LeBar, 2016), or whether you are thinking of yourself or a close friend (Chavez, Heatherton, & Wagner, 2017). Some people have referred to these techniques as "mind reading," although that term implies a level of sophistication that researchers have not yet obtained. Nonetheless, people share common patterns of brain activity that provide insights into their conscious experiences (Haxby, Connolly, & Guntupalli, 2014).

Findings such as these have led most psychologists to reject dualism. Instead, they believe that the brain and the mind are inseparable. According to this view, the activity of neurons in the brain produces the contents of consciousness: the sight of a face, the smell of a rose. More specifically, for each type of content—each sight, each smell—there is an associated pattern of brain activity. The activation of this particular group of neurons in the brain somehow gives rise to conscious experience.

THE GLOBAL WORKSPACE MODEL Many different models for consciousness have been proposed. One, the *global workspace model*, posits that consciousness arises as a function of which brain circuits are active (Baars, 1988; Dehaene, Changeux, Naccache, Sackur, & Sergent, 2006). That is, you experience your brain regions' output as conscious awareness.

This idea is supported by studies of people with brain injuries, who are sometimes unaware of their deficits (that is, the consciousness-related problems that arise from their injuries). For instance, a person who has vision problems caused by an eye injury will know about those problems because the brain's visual areas will notice they are not getting input and that something is wrong. But if that same person then suffers damage to the brain's cortical visual areas so that they stop delivering output, the person may have no visual information to consider and thus will not be aware of vision problems. Of course, if the person suddenly becomes blind, that individual will know he cannot see. But someone who loses part of the visual field because of a brain injury tends not to notice the gap in visual experience. This tendency appears with hemineglect, for example (see Figure 3.26). A hemineglect patient is not aware that she is missing part of the visual world. In one patient's words, "I knew the word 'neglect' was a sort of medical term for whatever was wrong, but the word bothered me because you only neglect something that is actually there, don't you? If it's not there, how can you neglect it?" (Halligan & Marshall, 1998, p. 360). The hemineglect patients' unawareness of their visual deficits supports the idea that consciousness arises through the brain processes active at any point in time.

Most important, the global workspace model presents no single area of the brain as responsible for general "awareness." Rather, different areas of the brain deal with different types of information. Each of these systems in turn is responsible for conscious awareness of its type of information (**FIGURE 4.3**). From this

(a)

(b)

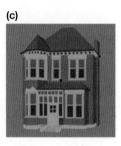
(c)

FIGURE 4.2
Consciousness and Neural Responses
(a) Research participants were shown images with houses superimposed on the faces. Then the participants were asked whether they saw **(b)** a face or **(c)** a house. When they reported seeing a face, activity increased in face-recognition areas of the brain. When they reported seeing a house, activity increased in object-recognition areas.

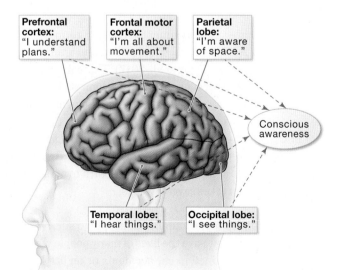

Prefrontal cortex: "I understand plans."

Frontal motor cortex: "I'm all about movement."

Parietal lobe: "I'm aware of space."

Conscious awareness

Temporal lobe: "I hear things."

Occipital lobe: "I see things."

FIGURE 4.3
Areas of Awareness
A central theme emerging from cognitive neuroscience is that awareness of different aspects of the world is associated with functioning in different parts of the brain. Activity in these various brain regions comes together to inform conscious awareness.

perspective, consciousness is the mechanism that makes people actively aware of information and that prioritizes what information they need or want to deal with at any moment.

Q What is the basic idea behind dualism? Is dualism the current model of consciousness?

ANSWER: The basic idea behind dualism is that the brain and the mind are separate. Most scientists reject dualism.

4.2 Consciousness Changes Following Brain Injury

At least since the time of the ancient Roman gladiators, people have understood that a head injury can produce disturbances in mental activity, such as unconsciousness or loss of speech. **Traumatic brain injury (TBI)** is impairment in mental functioning caused by a blow to or very sharp movement of the head, commonly caused by an accident or a sports injury. TBIs are responsible for about 30 percent of all injury deaths (Faul, Xu, Wald, & Coronado, 2010) and are also a substantial cause of disabilities that can last from days to decades. TBIs can impair thinking, memory, emotions, and personality. Recall the case of Phineas Gage, described in Chapter 3, who underwent substantial psychological changes after his brain injury.

TBIs can range from mild to severe. The greater the severity of the injury, the more likely the TBIs are to be permanent. A *concussion* is formally known as mild TBI. Despite the term *mild*, concussion is far from trivial, as the brain swelling and resulting brain damage can have long-lasting effects. Signs of concussion include mental confusion, dizziness, a dazed look, memory problems, and sometimes the temporary loss of consciousness. Most people will recover from concussion within one to two weeks (Baldwin, Breiding, & Sleet, 2016). However, concussions may have a cumulative effect with each new injury. That is, each concussion can lead to more-serious symptoms that are longer lasting (Baugh et al., 2012; Zetterberg, Smith, & Blennow, 2013).

There has been increased interest in the long-term effects of concussion, particularly as they affect professional athletes. In the 2015 movie *Concussion*, Will Smith plays the pathologist Bennet Omalu, who conducted an autopsy on the former NFL player Mike Webster (**FIGURE 4.4**). Webster had a history of homelessness and self-injury. Omalu found evidence of severe TBI, the type that results from repeated blows to the head. In the ensuing years, Omalu and his colleagues examined other NFL players and found that many had similar symptoms and evidence of TBIs (Omalu et al., 2005; Small et al., 2013). Numerous studies have since documented the long-term effects of sports concussions (Bailes et al., 2013). A recent study found evidence of brain damage in 99 percent of deceased former NFL players (Mez et al., 2017). These findings have led to guidelines for reducing the occurrence of such injuries (Harmon et al., 2013).

Concussions are a special concern for the developing brains of teen and college athletes. According to the Centers for Disease Control and Prevention (2011c), in 2009 nearly a quarter-million U.S. children (age 19 or younger) were diagnosed for concussion resulting from sports- and recreation-related injuries. According to the American Academy of Neurology (2013), an athlete should not return to action until all symptoms have cleared up, which often takes several weeks.

COMA Medical advances are enabling a greater number of people to survive traumatic brain injuries. For example, doctors now save the lives of many people who previously would have died from injuries sustained in car accidents or on battlefields. A good example is the remarkable survival of congresswoman Gabrielle Giffords, who

traumatic brain injury (TBI)
Impairments in mental functioning caused by a blow to or very sharp movement of the head.

FIGURE 4.4
Concussion
In *Concussion* (2015), Will Smith played Dr. Bennet Omalu. Omalu's pathology work was instrumental in revealing the relationship between concussions suffered by NFL players and severe TBIs.

was shot in the head by an assailant in 2011. Although Giffords remains partially paralyzed, her accomplishments since the shooting include hiking the Grand Canyon, sky diving, and continuing her governmental and political work (FIGURE 4.5).

Surviving is just the first step toward recovery, however, and many of those who sustain serious brain injuries fall into comas or, like Giffords, are induced into coma as part of medical treatment. The coma allows the brain to rest. Most people who regain consciousness after such injuries do so within a few days, but some people do not regain consciousness for weeks. In this state, they have sleep/wake cycles—they open their eyes and appear to be awake, close their eyes and appear to be asleep—but they do not seem to respond to their surroundings.

Because people in coma do not respond to external stimuli, it is hard to know whether they have consciousness. However, brain imaging may be used to identify those who are conscious but unable to respond. A 23-year-old woman in an apparent coma was asked to imagine playing tennis or walking through her house (Owen et al., 2006). This woman's pattern of brain activity became quite similar to the patterns of control subjects who also imagined playing tennis or walking through a house (FIGURE 4.6). The woman could not give outward signs of awareness, but researchers believe she was able to understand language and respond to the experimenters' requests.

The implications of this finding are extraordinary. Could the researchers' method be used to reach other people who are in coma, aware of their surroundings, but unable to communicate? Indeed, this research team has now evaluated 54 coma patients and found 5 who could willfully control brain activity to communicate (Monti et al., 2010). One 29-year-old man was able to answer five of six yes/no questions correctly by thinking of one type of image to answer yes and another type to answer no. The ability to communicate from a coma might allow some patients to express thoughts, ask for more medication, and increase the quality of their lives (Fernández-Espejo & Owen, 2013). These advances add up to one astonishing fact: Some people in comas are conscious! This situation is referred to as a *minimally conscious state*. In this state, people with brain injuries are able to make some deliberate movements, such as following an object with their eyes. They may try to communicate.

FIGURE 4.5
Gabrielle Giffords
Representative Gabrielle Giffords made a remarkable recovery from the traumatic brain injury she suffered after being shot in the head. Among her many accomplishments was delivering an energetic speech at the 2016 Democratic National Convention.

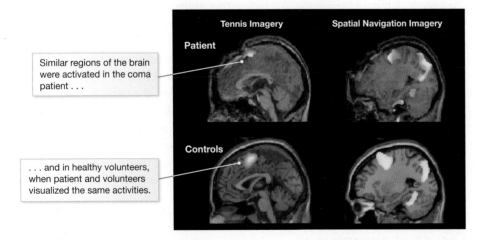

Similar regions of the brain were activated in the coma patient . . .

. . . and in healthy volunteers, when patient and volunteers visualized the same activities.

FIGURE 4.6
In a Coma but Aware
The brain images on the top are from the patient, a young woman in a coma who showed no outward signs of awareness. The images on the bottom are a composite from the control group, which consisted of healthy volunteers. Both the patient and the control group were told to visualize, first, playing tennis and, second, walking around a house. Right after the directions were given, the neural activity in the patient's brain appeared similar to the neural activity in the control group's brains.

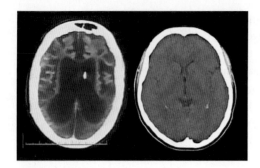

FIGURE 4.7
Unresponsive Wakefulness Syndrome
Terri Schiavo spent more than 15 years with unresponsive wakefulness syndrome before she was taken off life support. Her parents and their supporters believed she showed some awareness. A scan of Schiavo's brain (on the left) shows a loss of brain tissue in the dark regions, which were filled with only brain fluid. Various types of brain imaging can be used to determine if the patient is a good candidate for treatment.

When people appear to have emerged from coma (i.e., their eyes are open, and they have sleep/wake cycles) yet do not respond to external stimuli for more than a month, they are in a condition called an *unresponsive wakefulness syndrome* (Laureys et al., 2010). Until the last few years this condition was known as a vegetative state, a term that many clinicians and researchers felt uncomfortable using (people are not vegetables). This unresponsive state is not associated with consciousness. Normal brain activity does not occur when a person is in this state, in part because much of the person's brain may be damaged beyond recovery. The longer the unresponsive wakefulness state lasts, the less likely it is that the person will ever recover consciousness or show normal brain activity.

The prognosis for those in an unresponsive wakefulness state is much worse than for those in a minimally conscious state. Differentiating between states of consciousness by behavior alone is difficult, but brain imaging may prove useful for identifying the extent of a patient's brain injury and likelihood of recovery. Researchers have found that measuring brain metabolism via PET imaging can identify which patients in unresponsive states are likely to regain consciousness (Stender et al., 2016).

Terri Schiavo, a woman living in Florida, spent more than 15 years with unresponsive wakefulness syndrome. Eventually, her husband wanted to terminate her life support, but her parents wanted to continue it. Both sides waged a legal battle. A court ruled in the husband's favor, and life support was terminated. After Schiavo's death, an autopsy revealed substantial and irreversible damage throughout her brain and especially in cortical regions known to be important for consciousness (**FIGURE 4.7**).

FIGURE 4.8
Brain Death
Jahi McMath, depicted here on a necklace, was declared brain dead after complications from surgery.

BRAIN DEATH The imaging of brain activity can also be used to tell whether a person is brain dead. *Brain death* is the irreversible loss of brain function. Terri Schiavo had severe brain injury, but there was still activity in her brain stem. She was never declared brain dead.

With brain death, no activity is found in any region of the brain. As discussed in Chapter 3, the brain is essential for integrating brain activity that keeps the bodily organs, such as the heart and lungs, alive. When the brain no longer functions, the rest of the body quickly stops functioning. Under the right circumstances, machines may keep the organs functioning and make eventual organ donations possible.

Unfortunately, family members and others sometimes have difficulty accepting brain death and go to extraordinary lengths to try to keep the person's body "alive." Such was the case for 13-year-old Jahi McMath, who suffered brain death after routine tonsil surgery (**FIGURE 4.8**). McMath's family argued that she was still alive because her heart was still beating, although only because she was on artificial life support. They had her transferred from the hospital to a private facility that would continue her care. But when the brain is dead, the person is dead. The heart can beat only if it is artificially stimulated.

LOCKED-IN SYNDROME Imagine waking up in the hospital and the only thing you can move is your eyelids. You cannot talk or indicate that you are in pain. Finally, someone notices that you can voluntarily blink, and together you work out a system of communication. In 2000, when he was 16 years old, this situation happened to Erik Ramsey after his brain stem was damaged in a car accident. Since then, Ramsey has suffered from locked-in syndrome. In this rare condition, all or nearly all of a person's voluntary muscles are paralyzed. Even when Ramsey is awake and alert, he cannot communicate with those around him except by moving his eyes up and down (FIGURE 4.9).

As a psychological state, locked-in syndrome has been compared to being buried alive. You see all the sights around you and hear every noise, but you cannot respond physically to these sights and noises. You can feel every itch, but you cannot scratch yourself or move to gain relief. Hard as it is to imagine, Erik was lucky in that he was able to blink. Other such patients have no voluntary muscle movement. They have often been mistakenly thought to be in a coma for years, receiving no pain medication or socially appropriate communication.

Recent scientific advances have raised the possibility that Ramsey and patients like him will be able to communicate. That is, we might use the brain imaging methods described in the last section to "read" their thoughts by imaging brain activity in real time. Communication of this kind is the goal of researchers who, in 2004, planted electrodes in the speech region of Ramsey's left hemisphere. For the past decade or so, Ramsey has been listening to recordings of vowel sounds and mentally simulating those sounds. His simulation of each vowel sound should produce its own distinct pattern of brain activity. Ultimately, the researchers hope to use this brain activity to create a voice synthesizer that will translate Ramsey's neural patterns into understandable speech (Bartels et al., 2008). So far, researchers working with Ramsey have demonstrated that he can produce numerous specific vowel sounds, but he has not been able to produce more-complex sounds, such as words (Guenther et al., 2009).

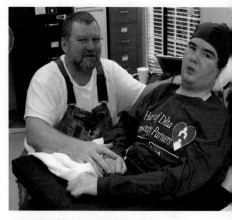

 How does unresponsive wakefulness syndrome differ from brain death?

ANSWER: Those in a state of unresponsive wakefulness may show some brain function, but they are unlikely to regain consciousness. Those who are brain dead have no brain function, so they cannot "live" without artificial means.

4.3 Conscious Awareness Involves Attention

Conscious experience is usually unified and coherent. In this view, the mind is a continuous stream, and thoughts float on that stream. There is a limit, however, to how many things the mind can be conscious of at the same time.

As you read this chapter, where are you directing your *attention,* or conscious awareness? Are you focused intently on the material? Is your mind wandering, occasionally or often? You cannot pay attention to reading while doing several other things, such as watching television or texting. As you focus on what is going on in the TV show, you might realize that you have no idea what you just read or what your friend just replied. Likewise, you can think about what you will do tomorrow, what kind of car you would like to own, and where you most recently went on vacation—but you cannot think about them all at the same time. Attention involves being able to focus selectively on some things and avoid focusing on others. Although they are not the same thing, attention and consciousness often go hand-in-hand.

In his book *Thinking, Fast and Slow* (2011), the Nobel laureate Daniel Kahneman differentiates between automatic and controlled processes. In general, all of us can execute routine or *automatic* tasks (such as driving, walking, or understanding the meanings of the words on this page) that are so well learned that we do them without much attention. Indeed, paying too much attention can interfere with these automatic behaviors. Try thinking of each step you take as you walk—it makes walking much more awkward. By contrast, difficult or unfamiliar tasks require people to pay attention. Such *controlled* processing is slower than automatic processing,

THE BIRTH OF SELF-CONSCIOUSNESS

HOLY SMOKE—I'M STANDING HERE!

(a)

(b)

(c)

FIGURE 4.10

Automatic Processing Versus Controlled Processing

(a) An experienced driver can rely on automatic processing while performing this task. **(b)** An inexperienced driver must use controlled processing. **(c)** During a rainstorm, an experienced driver must revert to controlled processing.

but it helps people perform in complex or novel situations. For example, if a rainstorm starts while you are driving, you will need to pay more attention to your driving and be very conscious of the road conditions (**FIGURE 4.10**). As noted in Chapter 2, behaviors such as reading, eating, talking on a cell phone, or texting are dangerous while driving because they distract the driver's attention. Hands-free cell phones do not solve the attention problem. Because drivers using hands-free phones still have to divide their attentional resources among multiple tasks, using a hands-free phone may be just as dangerous as talking while holding the phone (Ishigami & Klein, 2009).

In thinking about the power of distraction, consider the cocktail party phenomenon. In 1953, the psychologist E. C. Cherry described the process this way: You can focus on a single conversation in the midst of a chaotic cocktail party. However, a particularly pertinent stimulus—such as hearing your name mentioned in another conversation or hearing a juicy piece of gossip—can capture your attention. Because your attention is now divided, what you can understand of the new stimulus is less than if you had been giving it your full attention. If you really want to hear the other conversation or piece of gossip, you need to focus your attention on it. Of course, when you redirect your attention in this way, you probably will not be able to follow what the closer (and therefore probably louder) partygoer is saying. You will lose the thread of your original conversation.

Cherry developed selective-listening studies to examine what the mind does with unattended information when a person pays attention to one task. He used a technique called *shadowing*. In this procedure, a participant wears headphones that deliver one message to one ear and a different message to the other. The person is asked to attend to one of the two messages and "shadow" it by repeating it aloud. As a result, the person usually notices the unattended sound (the message given to the other ear) but will have little knowledge about the content of the unattended sound (**FIGURE 4.11**).

Imagine you are participating in an experiment about what happens to unattended messages. You are repeating whatever is spoken into one ear (shadowing) and ignoring the message spoken into the other ear. What would happen if your own name were spoken into the unattended ear? You would probably hear your own name but know nothing about the rest of the message. Some important information gets through the filter of attention. It has to be personally relevant information, such as your name or the name of someone close to you, or it has to be particularly loud or different in some obvious physical way.

SELECTIVE ATTENTION In 1958, the psychologist Donald Broadbent developed filter theory to explain the selective nature of attention. He assumed that people have a limited capacity for sensory information. They screen incoming information to let in only the most important material. In this model, attention is like a gate that opens for important information and closes for irrelevant information. But can we really close the gate to ignore some information? When and how do we close the gate?

Some stimuli demand attention and virtually shut off the ability to attend to anything else. Say you are focusing all your attention on reading this book, and suddenly you develop a muscle cramp. What will happen to your attention? The sharp jab of the cramp will demand your attention, and whatever you are reading will leave your consciousness until you attend to the muscle. Similarly, some stimuli, such as those that evoke emotions, may readily capture attention because they provide important information about potential threats in an environment (Phelps, Ling, & Carrasco, 2006). An object produces a stronger attentional response when it is viewed as socially relevant (e.g., an eye) than when it is viewed as nonsocial (e.g., an arrowhead; Tipper, Handy, Giesbrecht, & Kingstone, 2008).

Decisions about what to attend to are made early in the perceptual process. At the same time, however, unattended information is processed at least to some extent. Several selective-listening studies have found that even when participants cannot repeat an unattended message, they still have processed its contents. In one experiment, participants were told to attend to the message coming in one ear: "They threw stones at the bank yesterday." At the same time, the unattended ear was presented with one of two words: "river" or "money." Afterward, participants could not report the unattended words. However, those presented with "river" interpreted the sentence to mean someone had thrown stones at a riverbank. Those presented with "money" interpreted the sentence to mean someone had thrown stones at a financial institution (MacKay, 1973). Thus, the participants extracted meaning from the word even though they did not process the word consciously.

CHANGE BLINDNESS To understand just how inattentive we can be, consider the phenomenon known as **change blindness.** Because we cannot attend to everything in the vast array of visual information available, we are often "blind" to large changes in our environments. For example, would you notice if the person you were talking to suddenly changed into another person? In two studies, participants were on a college campus when a stranger approached them and asked for directions. Then the stranger was momentarily blocked by a large object and while out of view was replaced with another person of the same sex and race. Fifty percent of the people giving directions never noticed that they were talking to a different person. When giving directions to a stranger, we normally do not attend to the distinctive features of the stranger's face or clothing. If we are unable to recall those features later, it is not because we forgot them. More likely, it is because we never processed those features very much in the first place. After all, how often do we need to remember such information (Simons & Levin, 1998)? (See "The Methods of Psychology: Change Blindness Studies by Simons and Levin," on p. 130.)

In Simons and Levin's first study, older people were especially likely not to notice a change in the person asking them for directions. Younger people were pretty good at noticing the change. Are older people especially inattentive? Or do they tend to process a situation's broad outlines rather than its details? Perhaps the older people encoded the stranger as simply "a college student" and did not look for more-individual characteristics. To test this idea, Simons and Levin (1998) conducted an additional study. This time, the stranger was an easily recognizable type of person from a different social group. That is, the same experimenters dressed as construction workers and asked college students for directions. Sure enough, the college students failed to notice the replacement of one construction worker with another. This finding supports the idea that the students encoded the strangers as belonging to a broad category of "construction workers" without looking more closely at them. For these students, construction workers seemed pretty much all alike and interchangeable. Subsequent research has shown that people with a greater ability to maintain attention in the face of distracting information are less likely to experience a similar type of change blindness (Seegmiller, Watson, & Strayer, 2011).

As change blindness illustrates, we can attend to a limited amount of information. Large discrepancies exist between what most of us believe we see and what we actually see. Thus, our perceptions of the world are often inaccurate, and we have little awareness of our perceptual failures. We simply do not know how much information we miss in the world around us. This is why using cell phones while driving—or even walking—can be dangerous. We fail to notice important objects in the environment that might indicate threats to our safety. In one study (Hyman et al., 2010), students using cell phones while walking across campus failed to notice a brightly colored clown riding a unicycle who was heading toward their walking path. Students who were listening to music were much more likely to notice the clown.

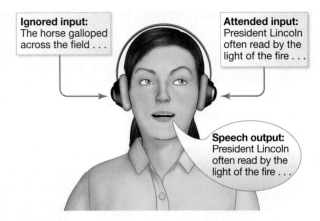

Ignored input: The horse galloped across the field . . .

Attended input: President Lincoln often read by the light of the fire . . .

Speech output: President Lincoln often read by the light of the fire . . .

FIGURE 4.11
Shadowing
In this procedure, the participant receives a different auditory message in each ear. The participant is required to repeat, or "shadow," only one of the messages.

change blindness
A failure to notice large changes in one's environment.

The Methods of Psychology
Change Blindness Studies by Simons and Levin

HYPOTHESIS: People can be "blind" to large changes around them.

RESEARCH METHOD:

1 A participant is approached by a stranger asking for directions.

2 The stranger is momentarily blocked by a larger object.

3 While being blocked, the original stranger is replaced by another person.

RESULTS: Half the participants giving directions never noticed they were talking to a different person (as long as the replacement was of the same race and sex as the original stranger).

CONCLUSION: Change blindness results from inattention to certain visual information.

QUESTION: What does change blindness tell us about how much attention we pay to strangers?

ANSWER: This phenomenon reveals that we attend to only a stranger's readily apparent characteristics, such as age, gender, and race.

Source: Photos from Simons, D. J., & Levin, D. T. (1998). Failure to detect changes to people during a real-world interaction. *Psychonomic Bulletin and Review, 5,* 644–649. © 1998 Psychonomic Society, Inc. Figure courtesy Daniel J. Simons.

FIGURE 4.12
Technology in the Classroom
Today's students use electronic devices in the classroom productively (as in taking notes) and nonproductively (as in texting).

LAPTOPS IN THE CLASSROOM It can be hard to pay complete attention for an entire class period even with the most engaging lecturers. For this reason, many of your instructors try to include active participation during class. The rise of laptop computers and smartphones in the classroom over the last decade has increased the difficulty for instructors to hold students' attention (**FIGURE 4.12**). Ideally, such technology enables students to take notes, access supplementary materials, or participate with classroom exercises. Unfortunately, students can also tune out lectures by checking Facebook or email, texting, or watching YouTube videos.

After reading the earlier sections of this chapter, you might not be surprised that attending to your computer or smartphone might lead you to miss important details going on around you, such as crucial information in the lecture. Overwhelming evidence shows that students who use Facebook, text, surf the Internet, and so on during class do more poorly in college courses (Gingerich & Lineweaver, 2014; Junco & Cotten, 2012). Poor performance can happen even if students do not multitask. According to one study, taking notes on a laptop rather than by hand leads to more-superficial processing and worse performance on tests of conceptual knowledge (Mueller & Oppenheimer, 2014). Even those who are simply sitting near someone playing around on the Internet score lower grades (Sana, Weston, & Cepeda, 2013). If you use your laptop or smartphone to look at irrelevant materials, you are hurting yourself and others.

Students often do not feel like they are missing anything when they multitask. The irony is that it takes attention to know what you are missing. If your attention is elsewhere and you miss something vital mentioned by your instructor, not only did you miss what she or he said, but you will not even know that you missed anything. Students have the illusion that they are paying attention because they have no awareness of events that happened when their attention was otherwise occupied.

UNCONSCIOUS INFLUENCE Just because people fail to attend to something in the environment does not mean that they are unaffected by it. As mentioned in Chapter 1, Sir Francis Galton (1879) first proposed the notion that mental activity below the level of conscious awareness can influence behavior. The influence of unconscious thoughts was also at the center of many of Freud's theories of human behavior. For example, the classic mistake called a *Freudian slip* occurs when an unconscious thought is suddenly expressed at an inappropriate time or in an inappropriate social context.

Many of the ways that Freud proposed that the unconscious works are difficult to test using scientific methods, and few psychologists today believe his interpretation of the unconscious is correct. However, psychologists agree that unconscious processes influence people's thoughts and actions as they go through their daily lives. Consider that smokers who watch a movie that has images of smoking, even if they are unaware of those images, report stronger cravings for cigarettes after they leave the theater (Sargent, Morgenstern, Isensee, & Hanewinkel, 2009). When smokers watch movies that show smoking, there is activation of brain regions involved in the handling of cigarettes, as if the viewers were sharing cigarettes with the on-screen characters (Wagner, Dal Cin, Sargent, Kelley, & Heatherton, 2011). Now consider a similar unconscious influence in many people's lives: the subtle smells of food in the mall. Might those aromas encourage a visit to the food court?

To study the power of unconscious influences, John Bargh and colleagues (1996) supplied participants with different groups of words. Some of the participants received words associated with the elderly, such as *old, Florida,* and *wrinkles.* The participants were asked to make sentences out of the supplied words. After they had made up a number of sentences, they were told the experiment was over. But the researchers continued observing the participants. They wanted to know whether the unconscious activation of beliefs about the elderly would influence the participants' behavior. Indeed, participants primed with stereotypes about old people walked much more slowly than did those who had been given words unrelated to the elderly. When questioned later, the slow-walking participants were not aware that the concept of "elderly" had been activated or that it had changed their behavior. Recently, these findings were called into question by a group of researchers from Belgium who were unable to replicate the effect among French speakers. However, findings such as these, where people are primed by the activation of unconscious beliefs, have been found many times in labs around the world (Stroebe & Strack, 2014). Such findings indicate that human behavior can occur without awareness or intention (Bargh, 2014; Dijksterhuis & Aarts, 2010).

When Trish was learning to knit, she had to pay attention to every stitch. Now she can knit while watching television. Why can she knit now without giving it full attention?

ANSWER: Learning a task requires controlled processing. Once you learn the task, it becomes automatic and no longer requires full attention.

THINK LIKE A PSYCHOLOGIST

4.4 Are People Affected by Subliminal Messages?

During the 2000 U.S. presidential election, a television advertisement critical of candidate Al Gore's Medicare plan contained a hidden word. Just before the phrase "BUREAUCRATS DECIDE" appeared, the word *RATS* stretched across the screen

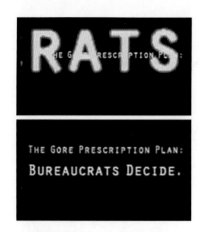

FIGURE 4.13
Subliminal Perception in Video
In this still image taken from a 2000 election ad criticizing Al Gore, the word *RATS* appears, perhaps in an attempt to subliminally persuade people not to vote for Gore.

subliminal perception
The processing of information by sensory systems without conscious awareness.

FIGURE 4.14
Subliminal Perception in Print
Do you see subliminal messages in this 1971 advertisement? Some viewers see suggestive imagery, such as the word *SEX* spelled out in the ice cubes.

for about one-thirtieth of a second (**FIGURE 4.13**). This ad aired in seventeen states, reaching over 30 million viewers (Stewart, 2008). The video is now widely available on the Internet. If you watch for *RATS*, you can see it, but most people would not notice the word if not looking for it. In 2000, an astute viewer in Seattle spotted the word and notified the local Democratic Party. Gore supporters expressed outrage about the apparent hidden message, but Gore's opponent, George W. Bush, stated that "the idea of putting subliminal messages into ads is ridiculous" (Bruni, 2000, A.19).

The idea that people can be influenced by hidden messages is referred to as subliminal perception. **Subliminal perception** occurs when stimuli get processed by sensory systems but, because of their short durations or subtle forms, do not reach consciousness. Urban legends concerning subliminal perception have long been a part of popular culture. According to these legends, movie theaters present brief statements suggesting that we buy a drink or some popcorn, musicians embed Satanic messages in their songs to encourage their listeners' malevolent impulses, and advertisers embed suggestive words in images (**FIGURE 4.14**). During the 1980s, marketers promoted programs that used subliminal messages for self-improvement. For example, hearing subliminal messages while sleeping was supposed to make you more confident or improve your memory. But can our behavior really be manipulated without our knowledge or awareness?

More than 8 out of 10 first-year college students believe that you can be influenced to purchase something through subliminal perception (Taylor & Kowalski, 2012). On the contrary, the evidence suggests that subliminal messages, if they work at all, have minimal effects on most behavior (Greenwald, 1992). In a classic study, Anthony Greenwald and colleagues (Pratkanis, Eskenazi, & Greenwald, 1994) assigned students to a subliminal program that was meant to improve their confidence or their memory. The researchers intentionally mislabeled some of the subliminal tapes, however. Half of the tapes labeled memory were actually about self-confidence and vice versa. This research indicated that people's beliefs about the tapes influenced the effects of the messages. People who thought they were hearing subliminal messages about memory reported improved memory. People who thought they were hearing subliminal messages about self-confidence reported improved self-confidence. However, reports of improvement happened even for those who listened to the mislabeled tapes.

There is evidence that material presented subliminally can influence how people think, even if it has little or no effect on complex actions (Kihlstrom, 2016a). (Buying something you did not intend to buy would count as a complex action.) In one study, participants exerted greater physical effort when large images of money were flashed at them, even though the flashes were so brief the participants did not report seeing the money (Pessiglione et al., 2007). The subliminal images of money also produced brain activity in areas of the limbic system, which is involved in emotion and motivation. Subliminal cues may be most powerful when they work on people's motivational states. For example, flashing the word *thirst* may prove more effective than flashing the explicit directive *Buy Coke*. Indeed, researchers found that subliminal presentation of the word *thirst* led participants to drink more Kool-Aid, especially when they were actually thirsty (Strahan, Spencer, & Zanna, 2002). Thus, many stimuli in the environment nudge us in one direction or another. Such a modest effect is very different from the notion that subliminal messages can improve our self-image or persuade us to buy things we do not want. ∎

ANSWER: No, but such messages did lead people to exert more effort and activated brain regions involved in emotion and motivation.

 Did subliminal flashes of money lead people to purchase products?

What Is Sleep?

At regular intervals, the brain does a strange thing: It goes to sleep. A common misconception is that the brain shuts itself down during sleep. Nothing could be further from the truth. Many brain regions are more active during sleep than during wakefulness. It is even possible that some complex thinking, such as working on difficult problems, occurs in the sleeping brain (Monaghan et al., 2015).

Sleep is part of the normal rhythm of life. Brain activity and other physiological processes are regulated into patterns known as **circadian rhythms.** (*Circadian* roughly translates to "about a day.") For example, body temperature, hormone levels, and sleep/wake cycles operate according to circadian rhythms. Regulated by a biological clock, circadian rhythms are influenced by the cycles of light and dark. Humans and nonhuman animals continue to show these rhythms, however, even when removed from light cues.

Learning Objectives

- Describe the stages of sleep.
- Identify common sleep disorders.
- Discuss the functions of sleeping and dreaming.

4.5 Sleep Is an Altered State of Consciousness

The average person sleeps around 8 hours per night, but individuals differ tremendously in the number of hours they sleep. Infants sleep much of the day. People tend to sleep less as they age. Some adults report needing 9 or 10 hours of sleep a night to feel rested, whereas others report needing only an hour or two a night. It might be that your genes influence the amount of sleep you need, as researchers have identified a gene that influences sleep (Koh et al., 2008). Called *SLEEPLESS*, this gene regulates a protein that, like many anesthetics, reduces action potentials in the brain (see Chapter 3 if you need a refresher on action potentials). Loss of this protein leads to an 80 percent reduction in sleep.

People's sleep habits can be quite extreme. When a 70-year-old retired nurse, Miss M., reported sleeping only an hour a night, researchers were skeptical. On her first two nights in a research laboratory, Miss M. was unable to sleep, apparently because of the excitement. But on her third night, she slept for only 99 minutes, then awoke refreshed, cheerful, and full of energy (Meddis, 1977). You might like the idea of sleeping so little and having all those extra hours of spare time, but most of us do not function well with a lack of sleep. And as discussed in later chapters, sufficient sleep is important for memory and good health and is often affected by psychological disorders, such as depression.

SLEEPING BRAIN Multiple brain regions are involved in producing and maintaining circadian rhythms and sleep. For instance, information about light detected by the eyes is sent to a small region of the hypothalamus called the *suprachiasmatic nucleus*. This region then sends signals to a tiny structure called the *pineal gland* (**FIGURE 4.15**). The pineal gland then secretes *melatonin*, a hormone that travels through the bloodstream and affects various receptors in the body, including the brain. Bright light suppresses the production of melatonin, whereas darkness triggers its release. Melatonin is necessary for circadian cycles that regulate sleep (Gandhi, Mosser, Oikonomou, & Prober, 2015). Researchers have noted that taking melatonin can help people cope with jet lag and shift work, both of which interfere with circadian rhythms (Crowley & Eastman, 2015). Taking melatonin also appears to help people fall asleep (Ferracioli-Oda, Qawasmi, & Bloch, 2013), although it is unclear why this happens.

circadian rhythms
Biological patterns that occur at regular intervals as a function of time of day.

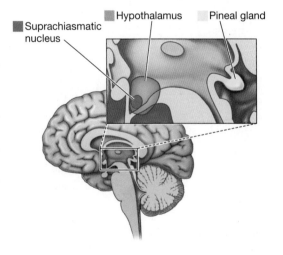

FIGURE 4.15
The Pineal Gland and the Sleep/Wake Cycle
Changes in light register in the suprachiasmatic nucleus of the hypothalamus. In response, this region signals the pineal gland when the time for sleep or the time for wakefulness has come.

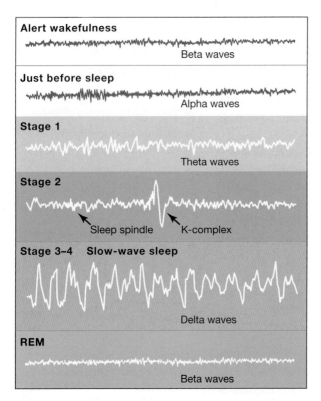

FIGURE 4.16

Brain Activity During Sleep

Using an EEG, researchers measured these examples of the patterns of electrical brain activity during different stages of normal sleep.

The difference between being awake and being asleep has as much to do with conscious experience as with biological processes. When you sleep, your conscious experience of the outside world is largely turned off. To some extent, however, you remain aware of your surroundings and your brain still processes information. Your mind is analyzing potential dangers, controlling body movements, and shifting body parts to maximize comfort. For this reason, people who sleep next to children or to pets tend not to roll over onto them. Nor do most people fall out of bed while sleeping—in this case, the brain is aware of at least the edges of the bed. (Because the ability to not fall out of bed when asleep is learned or perhaps develops with age, infant cribs have side rails and young children may need bed rails when they transition from crib to bed.)

Before the development of objective methods to assess brain activity, most people believed the brain went to sleep along with the rest of the body. In the 1920s, researchers invented the electroencephalograph, or EEG. As discussed in Chapter 3, this machine measures the brain's electrical activity. When people are awake, they have many different sources of sensory activity. As a result, the neurons in their brains are extremely active. The EEG shows this activity as short, frequent, irregular brain signals known as *beta waves* (shown in **FIGURE 4.16**). When people really focus their attention on something or when they close their eyes and relax, brain activity slows and becomes more regular. This pattern produces *alpha waves*.

STAGES OF SLEEP As evidenced by changes in EEG readings, sleep occurs in stages (see Figure 4.16). When you drift off to sleep, you enter stage 1. Here, the EEG shows short bursts of irregular waves called *theta waves*. You can easily be aroused from stage 1, and if awakened, you will probably deny that you were sleeping. In this light sleep, you might see fantastical images or geometric shapes. You might have the sensation of falling or that your limbs are jerking. As you progress to stage 2, your breathing becomes more regular, and you become less sensitive to external stimulation. You are now really asleep. Although the EEG continues to show theta waves, it also shows occasional bursts of activity called *sleep spindles* and large waves called *K-complexes*. Some researchers believe that these bursts are signals from brain mechanisms involved with shutting out the external world and keeping people asleep (Halász, 2016). Two findings indicate that the brain must work to maintain sleep. First, abrupt noises can trigger K-complexes. Second, as people age and sleep more lightly, their EEGs show fewer sleep spindles.

The progression to deep sleep occurs through stages 3 and 4, which nowadays are typically seen as one stage because their brain activity is nearly identical (Silber et al., 2007). This period is marked by large, regular brain patterns called *delta waves*, and it is often referred to as *slow-wave sleep*. People in slow-wave sleep are very hard to wake and are often very disoriented when they do wake up. People still process some information in slow-wave sleep, however, because the mind continues to evaluate the environment for potential danger. For example, parents in slow-wave sleep can be aroused by their children's cries. Yet they can blissfully ignore sounds, such as sirens or traffic noise, that are louder than the crying children but are not necessarily relevant.

REM SLEEP After about 90 minutes of sleep, the sleep cycle reverses, returning to stage 1. At this point, the EEG suddenly shows a flurry of beta wave activity that

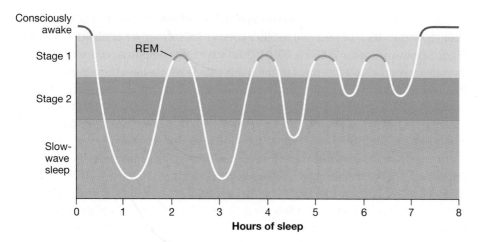

FIGURE 4.17
Stages of Sleep
This chart illustrates the normal stages of sleep over the course of the night.

usually represents an awake, alert mind. The eyes dart back and forth rapidly beneath closed eyelids. Because of these *rapid eye movements*, this stage is called **REM sleep.** It is sometimes called *paradoxical sleep* because of the paradox of a sleeping body with an active brain. Indeed, some neurons in the brain, especially in the occipital cortex and brain stem regions, are more active during REM sleep than during waking hours. But while the brain is active during REM episodes, most of the body's muscles are paralyzed. At the same time, the body shows signs of genital arousal: Most males of all ages develop erections, and most females of all ages experience clitoral engorgement.

REM sleep is psychologically significant because of its relation to dreaming. About 80 percent of the time when people are awakened during REM sleep, they report dreaming, compared with less than half of the time during non-REM sleep (Solms, 2000). As discussed later in this chapter, the dreams differ between these two types of sleep.

Over the course of a typical night's sleep, the cycle repeats about five times. The sleeper progresses from slow-wave sleep through to REM sleep, then back to slow-wave sleep and through to REM sleep (**FIGURE 4.17**). As morning approaches, the sleep cycle becomes shorter, and the sleeper spends relatively more time in REM sleep. People briefly awaken many times during the night, but they do not remember these awakenings in the morning. As people age, they sometimes have more difficulty going back to sleep after awakening.

 What hormone, released by the pineal gland, promotes sleep?

REM sleep
The stage of sleep marked by rapid eye movements, paralysis of motor systems, and dreaming.

ANSWER: melatonin

4.6 Sleep Disorders Interfere with Daily Life

Sleep problems are relatively common throughout life. Nearly everyone occasionally has trouble falling asleep, but for some people the inability to sleep causes significant problems in their daily lives. **Insomnia** is a sleep disorder in which people's mental health and ability to function in daily life are compromised by difficulty both falling asleep and staying asleep. Indeed, insomnia is associated with diminished psychological well-being, including feelings of depression (American Psychiatric Association, 2013; Bootzin & Epstein, 2011).

insomnia
A disorder characterized by an inability to sleep that causes significant problems in daily living.

FIGURE 4.18
Obstructive Sleep Apnea
This man suffers from obstructive sleep apnea. Throughout the night, a continuous positive airway pressure (CPAP) device blows air into his nose to keep his throat open.

obstructive sleep apnea
A disorder in which a person, while asleep, stops breathing because his or her throat closes; the condition results in frequent awakenings during the night.

narcolepsy
A sleep disorder in which people experience excessive sleepiness during normal waking hours, sometimes going limp and collapsing.

An estimated 12 percent to 20 percent of adults have insomnia; it is more common in women than in men and in older adults than in younger adults (Espie, 2002; Ram, Seirawan, Kumar, & Clark, 2010). One factor that complicates the estimation of how many people have insomnia is that many people who believe they are poor sleepers overestimate how long it takes them to fall asleep and often underestimate how much sleep they get on a typical night. For instance, some people experience *pseudoinsomnia*, in which they dream they are not sleeping. Their EEGs would indicate sleep. But if you roused them, they would claim to have been awake.

In an odd twist, a major cause of insomnia is worrying about sleep. When people experience this kind of insomnia, they may be tired enough to sleep. As they try to fall asleep, however, they worry about whether they will get to sleep and may even panic about how a lack of sleep will affect them. This anxiety leads to heightened arousal, which interferes with normal sleep patterns. To overcome these effects, many people take sleeping pills, which may work in the short run but can cause significant problems down the road. People may come to depend on the pills to help them sleep. Then if they try to stop taking the pills, they may lie awake wondering whether they can get to sleep on their own.

According to research, the most successful treatment for insomnia combines drug therapy with cognitive-behavioral therapy (CBT, discussed in Chapter 15, "Treatment of Psychological Disorders"). CBT helps people overcome their worries about sleep and relieves the need for the drugs, which should be discontinued before the end of therapy (Morin et al., 2009). Other factors that contribute to insomnia include poor sleeping habits. For ways to improve your sleeping habits, see Section 4.9, "Using Psychology in Your Life: How Can You Get a Good Night's Sleep?"

Another fairly common sleeping problem is **obstructive sleep apnea.** While asleep, a person with this disorder stops breathing for short periods. Basically, the sleeper's throat closes during these periods. In struggling to breathe, the person briefly awakens and gasps for air. Obstructive sleep apnea is most common among middle-aged men and is often associated with obesity, although it is unclear if obesity is the cause or consequence of apnea (Pack & Pien, 2011; Spurr, Graven, & Gilbert, 2008). People with apnea are often unaware of their condition, since the main symptom is loud snoring and they do not remember their frequent awakenings during the night. Yet chronic apnea causes people to have poor sleep, which is associated with daytime fatigue and even problems such as an inability to concentrate while driving. Moreover, apnea is associated with cardiovascular problems and stroke. For serious cases, physicians often prescribe a continuous positive airway pressure (CPAP) device. During sleep, this device blows air into the person's nose or nose and mouth (**FIGURE 4.18**).

A student who falls asleep during a lecture is likely sleep deprived, but a professor who falls asleep while lecturing is probably experiencing an episode of **narcolepsy.** In this rare disorder, excessive sleepiness that lasts from several seconds to minutes occurs during normal waking hours. During an episode of narcolepsy, a person may experience the muscle paralysis that accompanies REM sleep, perhaps causing him or her to go limp and collapse. Obviously, people with narcolepsy have to be very careful about the activities they engage in during the day, as unexpectedly falling asleep can be dangerous or fatal, depending on the situation. Evidence suggests that narcolepsy is a genetic condition that affects the neural transmission of a specific neurotransmitter in the hypothalamus (Chabas, Taheri, Renier, & Mignot, 2003; Nishino, 2007). The most widely used treatments for this condition are drugs that act as stimulants. Some researchers have found evidence, however, that narcolepsy may be an autoimmune disorder and that treating it as such (using appropriate medication) produces excellent results (Cvetkovic-Lopes et al., 2010; Mahlios, De la Herrán-Arita, & Mignot, 2013).

REM behavior disorder is roughly the opposite of narcolepsy. In this condition, the normal paralysis that accompanies REM sleep is disabled. Sufferers act out their dreams while sleeping, often striking their sleeping partners. No treatment exists for this rare sleep disorder. The condition is caused by a neurological deficit and is most often seen in elderly males.

By contrast, sleepwalking is most common among young children. Technically called *somnambulism*, this relatively common behavior occurs during slow-wave sleep, typically within the first hour or two after falling asleep. During an episode, the person is glassy-eyed and seems disconnected from other people and/or the surroundings. No harm is done if the sleepwalker wakes up during the episode. Being gently walked back to bed is safer for the sleepwalker than leaving the person to wander around and potentially get hurt.

 Q Suppose a person has trouble sleeping for a few weeks, but can function well enough in her daily life during this time. Does she have insomnia?

ANSWER: No. Insomnia is a condition that causes impairments in people's daily lives and affects their mental health.

4.7 Sleep Is an Adaptive Behavior

In terms of adaptiveness, sleep might seem illogical. Tuning out the external world during sleep can be dangerous and thus a threat to survival. Beyond that, humans might have advanced themselves in countless ways if they had used all their time productively rather than wasting it by sleeping. But we cannot override indefinitely the desire to sleep. Eventually, our bodies shut down and we sleep whether we want to or not.

Why do we sleep? Some animals, such as some frogs, never exhibit a state that can be considered sleep (Siegel, 2008). Most animals sleep, however, even if they have peculiar sleeping styles. (For example, some dolphin species have *unihemispherical sleep*, in which the cerebral hemispheres take turns sleeping.) Sleep must serve an important biological purpose. Research suggests sleep is adaptive for three functions: restoration, following of circadian rhythms, and facilitation of learning.

RESTORATION AND SLEEP DEPRIVATION According to the *restorative theory*, sleep allows the body, including the brain, to rest and repair itself. Various kinds of evidence support this theory: After people engage in vigorous physical activity, such as running a marathon, they generally sleep longer than usual. Growth hormone, released primarily during deep sleep, facilitates the repair of damaged tissue. Sleep apparently enables the brain to replenish energy stores and also strengthens the immune system (Hobson, 1999). More recently, researchers have demonstrated that sleep may help the brain clear out metabolic by-products of neural activity, just as a janitor takes out the trash (Xie et al., 2013). Neural activity creates by-products that can be toxic if they build up. These by-products are cleared away through the interstitial space—a small fluid-filled space between the cells of the brain. During sleep, a 60 percent increase in this space permits efficient removal of the debris that has accumulated while the person is awake.

Numerous laboratory studies have examined sleep deprivation's effects on physical and cognitive performance. Surprisingly, most studies find that two or three days of sleep deprivation have little effect on strength, athletic ability, or the performance of complex tasks. When deprived of sleep, however, people find it difficult to perform quiet tasks, such as reading. They find it nearly impossible to perform boring or mundane tasks.

FIGURE 4.19
Sleeping Predator
After a fresh kill, a lion may sleep for days.

A long period of sleep deprivation causes mood problems and decreases cognitive performance. People who suffer from chronic sleep deprivation may experience attention lapses and reduced short-term memory, perhaps in part because of the accumulation of metabolic by-products of neural activity (Kuchibhotla et al., 2008). Studies using rats have found that extended sleep deprivation compromises the immune system and leads to death. Sleep deprivation is also dangerous and potentially disastrous because it makes people prone to *microsleeps*, in which they fall asleep during the day for periods ranging from a few seconds to a minute (Coren, 1996).

Sleep deprivation might serve one very useful purpose: When people are suffering from depression, depriving them of sleep sometimes alleviates their depression. This effect appears to occur because sleep deprivation leads to increased activation of serotonin receptors, as do drugs used to treat depression (Wolf et al., 2016; the treatment of depression is discussed in Chapter 15, "Treatment of Psychological Disorders"). For people who are not suffering from depression, however, sleep deprivation is more likely to produce negative moods than positive ones.

CIRCADIAN RHYTHM AND SLEEP The *circadian rhythm theory* proposes that sleep has evolved to keep animals quiet and inactive during times of the day when there is greatest danger, usually when it is dark. According to this theory, animals need only a limited amount of time each day to accomplish the necessities of survival, and it is adaptive for them to spend the remainder of the time inactive, preferably hidden. Thus, an animal's typical amount of sleep depends on how much time that animal needs to obtain food, how easily it can hide, and how vulnerable it is to attack. Small animals tend to sleep a lot. Large animals vulnerable to attack, such as cows and deer, sleep little. Large predatory animals that are not vulnerable sleep a lot (**FIGURE 4.19**). We humans depend greatly on vision for survival. We are adapted to sleeping at night because our early ancestors were more at risk in the dark. That is, early humans who slept at night (and out of harm's way) were the ones who survived long enough to reproduce and thus became our ancestors.

FACILITATION OF LEARNING Scientists have found that neural connections made during the day, which serve as the basis of learning, are strengthened during sleep (Wilson & McNaughton, 1994). When research participants sleep after learning, their recall is better than in control conditions where participants remain awake (Mazza et al., 2016). Robert Stickgold and colleagues (2000) conducted a study in which participants had to learn a complex task. After finding that participants improved at the task only if they had slept for at least 6 hours following training, the researchers argued that learning the task required neural changes that normally occur only during sleep. Both slow-wave sleep and REM sleep appear to be important for learning to take place. People who dream about the task while sleeping may be especially likely to perform better. In one study, participants learned how to run a complex maze. Those who then slept for 90 minutes performed better on the maze than the sleepless competitors. Those who dreamed about the maze, however, performed the best (Wamsley, Tucker, Payne, Benavides, & Stickgold, 2010).

Indeed, there is some evidence that when students study more, such as during exam periods, they experience more REM sleep—that is, if they sleep and do not pull all-nighters—and during this sleep, a greater mental consolidation of information might be expected to take place (Smith & Lapp, 1991). The argument that sleep, especially REM sleep, promotes the development of brain circuits for learning is also supported by the changes in sleep patterns that occur over the life course. Infants and the very young, who learn an incredible amount in a few years, sleep the most and also spend the most time in REM sleep.

Findings linking sleep to learning should give caution to students whose main style of studying is the all-nighter. In one study, students who were sleep deprived for one night showed reduced activity the next day in the hippocampus, a brain area essential for memory (Yoo, Hu, Gujar, Jolesz, & Walker, 2007). These sleep-deprived students also showed poorer memory at subsequent testing. According to the investigators, there is substantial evidence that sleep does more than consolidate memories. Sleep also seems to prepare the brain for its memory needs for the next day (Oudiette & Paller, 2013). The best advice for preparing for exams is to study, sleep, and then study again (Mazza et al., 2016). To do well on exams, get your sleep!

"Look, don't try to weasel out of this. It was my dream, but you had the affair in it."

Q Suppose a person who runs a marathon sleeps a great deal the next night. Which theory of sleep does this behavior support?

ANSWER: the restorative theory

4.8 People Dream While Sleeping

Because **dreams** are the products of an altered state of consciousness, dreaming is one of life's great mysteries. Indeed, no one knows if dreaming serves any biological function. Why does the sleeper's mind conjure up images, fantasies, stories that make little sense, and scenes that ignore physical laws and rules of both time and space? Why does the mind then confuse these conjurings with reality? Why does it sometimes allow them to scare the dreamer awake? Usually, only when people wake up do they realize they have been dreaming. Of course, dreams sometimes incorporate external sounds or other sensory experiences, but this happens without the type of consciousness experienced during wakefulness.

Although some people report that they do not remember their dreams, everyone dreams unless a particular kind of brain injury or a particular kind of medication interferes. In fact, the average person spends six years of his or her life dreaming. If you want to remember your dreams better, you can teach yourself to do so: Keep a pen and paper or a voice recorder next to your bed so you can record your dreams as soon as you wake up. If you wait, you are likely to forget most of them.

dreams
Products of an altered state of consciousness in which images and fantasies are confused with reality.

REM DREAMS AND NON-REM DREAMS Dreams occur in REM and non-REM sleep, but the dreams' contents differ in the two types of sleep. REM dreams are more likely to be bizarre. They may involve intense emotions, visual and auditory hallucinations (but rarely taste, smell, or pain), and an uncritical acceptance of illogical events. Non-REM dreams are often very dull. They may concern mundane activities such as deciding what clothes to wear or taking notes in class.

The activation and deactivation of different brain regions during REM and non-REM sleep may be responsible for the different types of dreams. During non-REM sleep, there is general deactivation of many brain regions; during REM sleep, some areas of the brain show increased activity, whereas others show decreased activity (Hobson, 2009). The contents of REM dreams result from the activation of brain structures associated with motivation, emotion, and reward (e.g., the amygdala); the activation of visual association areas; and the deactivation of various parts of the

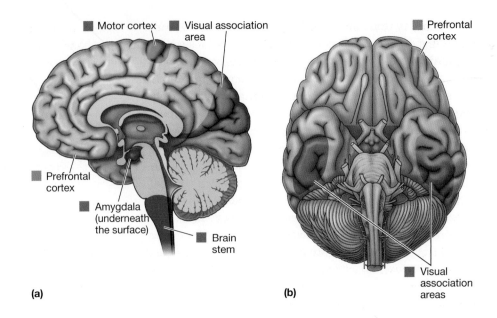

FIGURE 4.20

Brain Regions and REM Dreams

These two views of the brain show the regions that are activated (shown in red) and deactivated (shown in blue) during REM sleep. **(a)** As seen here from the side, the motor cortex, the brain stem, and visual association areas are activated, as are brain regions involved in motivation, emotion, and reward (e.g., the amygdala). A region of the prefrontal cortex is deactivated. **(b)** As shown here from below, other visual association areas are activated as well. (This view also reveals the full size of the prefrontal cortex.)

Labels in figure:
- Motor cortex
- Visual association area
- Prefrontal cortex
- Prefrontal cortex
- Amygdala (underneath the surface)
- Brain stem
- Visual association areas

(a)

(b)

prefrontal cortex (Schwartz & Maquet, 2002; **FIGURE 4.20**). As discussed in Chapter 3, the prefrontal cortex is indispensable for self-awareness, reflective thought, and conscious input from the external world. Because this brain region is deactivated during REM dreams, the brain's emotion centers and visual association areas interact without rational thought. Note, however, that REM and dreaming appear to be controlled by different brain mechanisms (Solms, 2000). In other words, REM does not produce the dream state. REM is simply linked with the contents of dreams.

WHAT DO DREAMS MEAN? Sleep researchers are still speculating about the meaning of dreams. Sigmund Freud published one of the first theories in his book *The Interpretation of Dreams* (1900). Freud speculated that dreams contain hidden content that represents unconscious conflicts within the mind of the dreamer. The *manifest content* is the dream the way the dreamer remembers it. The *latent content* is what the dream symbolizes; it is the material disguised to protect the dreamer from confronting a conflict directly. Virtually no support exists for Freud's ideas that dreams represent hidden conflicts and that objects in dreams have special symbolic meanings. Daily life experiences do, however, influence the content of dreams. For example, you may be especially likely to have dreams with anxious content while studying for exams.

Although most people think their dreams are uniquely their own, many common themes occur in dreams. Have you ever dreamed about showing up unprepared for an exam or finding that you are taking the wrong test? Many people in college have dreams like these. Even after you graduate and no longer take exams routinely, you probably will have similar dreams about being unprepared. Retired instructors sometimes dream about being unprepared to teach classes!

ACTIVATION-SYNTHESIS THEORY The sleep researchers John Alan Hobson and Robert McCarley (1977) proposed the **activation-synthesis theory,** which has dominated scientific thinking about dreaming. Hobson and McCarley theorized that random brain activity occurs during sleep and that this neural firing can activate mechanisms that normally interpret sensory input. The sleeping mind tries to make sense of the resulting sensory activity by synthesizing it with stored memories. From this perspective, dreams are the side effects of mental processes produced by random neural firing.

activation-synthesis theory

A theory of dreaming; this theory proposes that the brain tries to make sense of random brain activity that occurs during sleep by synthesizing the activity with stored memories.

In 2000, Hobson and his colleagues revised the activation-synthesis theory to take into account recent findings in cognitive neuroscience. For instance, they included activation of the limbic regions, associated with emotion and motivation, as the source of dreams' emotional content. They also proposed, as mentioned earlier in this chapter, that deactivation of the prefrontal cortex contributes to the delusional and illogical aspects of dreams.

Critics of Hobson's theory argue that dreams are seldom as chaotic as might be expected if they were based on random brain activity (Domhoff, 2003). Indeed, the conscious experience of most dreams is fairly similar to waking life, with some intriguing differences. The differences include a lack of self-awareness, reduced attention and voluntary control, increased emotionality, and poor memory (Nir & Tononi, 2010).

Meanwhile, the "mind-reading" methods described earlier in this chapter are being used to try to decode the content of dreams. Researchers had people sleep in the brain imaging machine, awakened them numerous times, and asked them what they were dreaming about (Horikawa, Tamaki, Miyawaki, & Kamitani, 2013). They then examined whether the brain activity that occurred just before the dream report was similar to how the brain responded when the participants were presented with various related images in a later imaging study. The researchers showed items that had appeared in many of the dream reports (e.g., person, house, car). They found that the brain activity associated with the content of the dream was similar to brain activity observed when people were looking at the related pictures. One day, it may be possible to know what people are dreaming about simply by recording their brain activity.

 Suppose a student dreams about folding and putting away laundry. Is this likely an REM dream or a non-REM dream?

ANSWER: a non-REM dream, as the content is dull and not bizarre

4.9 How Can You Get a Good Night's Sleep?

College students are incredibly busy. They juggle their academic work with extracurricular activities, jobs, volunteer positions, social calendars, and family commitments. Obligations seemingly expand beyond the available hours in a day. Not surprisingly, when it comes time to go to bed, racing thoughts can make it difficult to fall asleep. Over time, however, sleep deprivation poses risks to mind, body, and spirit. Thankfully, four simple "sleep hygiene" strategies can set you up for sleep success:

1. **Plan.** Create a weekly calendar. Use it to schedule your classes, study time, social time, exercise, down time, and so on. Honestly estimate the amount of time it will take you to complete tasks. Schedule sufficient time for each task in your calendar.

2. **Know your priorities.** There will be occasions when your schedule simply cannot accommodate all the to-dos. When you are so pressed for time, you will need to make decisions about what to cut. Knowing your priorities can help you make those decisions. If doing well on your biology exam is a top priority, consider skipping the party that weekend. Yes, your decision will have consequences (you might miss your friend's crazy antics), but knowing your priorities will make it easier to accept those consequences.

3. **Stick to the plan.** Procrastination can wreak havoc on your sleep. If you find yourself procrastinating on important tasks, consider working with a mental health practitioner to figure out why you procrastinate and how you might overcome this tendency.

FIGURE 4.21
One Strategy for Better Sleep
(a) When you cannot fall asleep, do not stay in bed. **(b)** Instead, get up and do something else, especially something relaxing, such as reading and drinking a cup of warm milk or (uncaffeinated) herbal tea.

4. Practice saying no. College is a great time to explore the activities available on your campus or in your community, but exploring all those options simultaneously is a recipe for disaster. Be selective.

Of course, sometimes sleep may elude you. Even when you long for sleep as you lie in bed, you may find yourself dog-tired but unable to doze off. In such cases, the strategies described below might help you develop better sleep:

1. **Establish a routine to help set your biological clock.** Every day (including weekends), go to bed at the same time and wake up at the same time. Changing the time you go to bed or wake up each day alters your regular nightly sleep cycle and can disrupt other physiological systems.

2. **Avoid alcohol and caffeine just before going to bed.** Alcohol might help you get to sleep more quickly, but it will interfere with your sleep cycle and may cause you to wake up early the next day. Caffeine is a stimulant: It interferes with a chemical (adenosine) that helps you sleep, so it will prevent you from falling asleep.

3. **Exercise regularly.** Regular exercise will help maintain your sleep cycle. Exercising creates arousal that interferes with sleep, however, so do not exercise right before going to bed. But a little stretching before bedtime can help your mind and body relax.

4. **Remember, your bed is for sleeping.** Most of us do not sleep in our kitchens, nor should we eat in our beds. Or watch TV. Or study. Your mind needs to associate your bed with sleeping. The best way to make that association is to use your bed exclusively for sleeping. And maybe a little cuddling.

5. **Relax.** Do not worry about the future (easier said than done, right?). Have a warm bath or listen to soothing music. Download a couple of meditation and relaxation podcasts. Use the techniques presented in them to help you deal with chronic stress and guide you to restfulness.

6. **Get up.** When you cannot fall asleep, get up and do something else. Do not lie there trying to force sleep (we all know how well that works, or rather does not work; **FIGURE 4.21**). If you start feeling sleepy a bit later, crawl back into bed and give sleep another try.

7. **Do not try to catch up on sleep.** When you have trouble falling asleep on a particular night, do not try to make up for the lost sleep by sleeping late the next morning or napping during the day. Those zzzz's are gone. You want to be sleepy when you go to bed the next night. Sleeping late, napping, or both will make the next night's sleep more difficult.

8. **Avoid electronic devices late at night.** Most electronic devices emit blue light, which can signal the brain to remain awake, making it more difficult to fall asleep. So if possible, you should put your phone, tablet, or both away early. You can also install programs on most devices that will cause the device to emit a red frequency rather than blue. Red light has the opposite effect of blue light and can signal the body to begin winding down.

The sleep attitudes and habits you establish during college will be with you for the rest of your life. Be good to yourself. Set yourself up for academic success, as well as physical and mental health, by prioritizing good sleep and taking charge of your sleep.

For additional resources, visit the National Sleep Foundation's Web site: https://sleepfoundation.org/ ∎

 What time should you go to bed if you want to establish good sleeping habits?

ANSWER: The specific time depends on you, but it should be the same time every night.

What Is Altered Consciousness?

A person's consciousness varies naturally over the course of the day. Often this variation is due to the person's actions. Watching television might encourage zoning out, whereas learning to play a piece on the piano might focus attention. The following sections discuss three ways of altering consciousness: hypnosis, meditation, and immersion in an action.

4.10 Hypnosis Is Induced Through Suggestion

"You are getting sleeeeeeepy. Your eyelids are drooping. . . . Your arms and legs feel very heavy." Your eyelids really are drooping. You are fully relaxed. You hear, "You want to bark like a dog," and the next thing you know, you are bow-wowing at the moon. In this way, stage performers or magicians sometimes hypnotize audience members and instruct them to perform silly behaviors. Has the hypnotist presented a real change in mental state or just good theater? Would you really sit up on stage and start bow-wowing on command? What exactly is hypnosis?

Hypnosis is a social interaction during which a person, responding to suggestions, experiences changes in memory, perception, and/or voluntary action (Kihlstrom, 2016b; Kihlstrom & Eich, 1994). Psychologists generally agree that hypnosis affects some people, but they do not agree on whether it produces a genuinely altered state of consciousness (Jamieson, 2007).

During a hypnotic induction, the hypnotist makes a series of suggestions to at least one person (**FIGURE 4.22**). As the listener falls more deeply into the hypnotic state, the hypnotist makes more suggestions. If everything goes according to plan, the listener follows all the suggestions as though they are true.

Sometimes the hypnotist suggests that, after the hypnosis session, the listener will experience a change in memory, perception, or voluntary action. Such a *posthypnotic suggestion* is usually accompanied by the instruction to not remember the suggestion. For example, a stage performer or magician serving as a hypnotist might suggest, much to the delight of the audience, "When I say the word *dog*, you will stand up and bark like a dog. You will not remember this suggestion." Therapists sometimes hypnotize patients and give them posthypnotic suggestions to help them diet or quit smoking, but evidence suggests that hypnosis has quite modest effects on these behaviors (Barnes et al., 2010; Wadden & Anderton, 1982). Evidence clearly indicates, however, that posthypnotic suggestions can at least subtly influence behaviors.

Consider a study of moral judgment conducted by Thalia Wheatley and Jonathan Haidt (2005). Participants in this study received a posthypnotic suggestion to feel a pang of disgust whenever they read a certain word. The word itself was neutral (e.g., the word *often*). Subsequently, participants made more-severe moral judgments when reading stories that included the word, even when the stories were innocuous. Like split-brain patients, discussed in Chapter 3, the participants were surprised by their reactions and sometimes made up justifications to explain their harsh ratings, such as saying that the lead character seemed "up to something." This result suggests that the left hemisphere interpreter might be involved in people's understanding their own behavior when that behavior results from posthypnotic suggestion or another unconscious influence.

Many people cannot be hypnotized. Hypnosis works primarily on those who score high on standardized tests for hypnotic suggestibility (Kallio & Revonsuo, 2003).

hypnosis
A social interaction during which a person, responding to suggestions, experiences changes in memory, perception, and/or voluntary action.

FIGURE 4.22
Hypnosis
Are hypnotized people merely playing a part suggested to them by the hypnotist?

Researchers have a hard time identifying the personality characteristics of the highly suggestible. Suggestibility seems related less to obvious traits such as intelligence and gullibility than to the tendencies to get absorbed in activities easily, to not be distracted easily, and to have a rich imagination (Balthazard & Woody, 1992; Crawford, Corby, & Kopell, 1996; Silva & Kirsch, 1992). Even with these tendencies, a person who dislikes the idea of being hypnotized or finds it frightening would likely not be hypnotized easily. To be hypnotized, a person must willingly go along with the hypnotist's suggestions. No evidence indicates that people will do things under hypnosis that they find immoral or otherwise objectionable.

THEORIES OF HYPNOSIS Some psychologists believe that a person under hypnosis essentially plays the role of a hypnotized person. That person is not faking hypnosis. Rather, he or she acts the part as if in a play, willing to perform actions called for by the "director," the hypnotist. According to this *sociocognitive theory of hypnosis*, hypnotized people behave as they expect hypnotized people to behave, even if those expectations are faulty (Kirsch & Lynn, 1995; Spanos & Coe, 1992). Alternatively, the *neodissociation theory of hypnosis* acknowledges the importance of social context to hypnosis, but it views the hypnotic state as an altered state (Hilgard, 1973). According to this theory, hypnosis is a trancelike state in which conscious awareness is separated, or dissociated, from other aspects of consciousness (Gruzelier, 2000).

It seems unlikely that a person could alter his or her brain activity to please a hypnotist, even if that hypnotist is a psychological researcher. Rather, numerous brain imaging studies have supported the dissociation theory of hypnosis (Rainville, Hofbauer, Bushnell, Duncan, & Price, 2002). In one of the earliest such studies, Stephen Kosslyn and colleagues (2000) demonstrated that when hypnotized participants were asked to imagine black-and-white objects as having color, they showed activity in visual cortex regions involved in color perception. Hypnotized participants asked to drain color from colored images showed diminished activity in those same brain regions. This activity pattern did not occur when participants were not hypnotized. These results suggest that the brain follows hypnotic suggestions.

FIGURE 4.23
Self-Hypnosis
This advertisement promotes one way that patients can learn self-hypnosis.

HYPNOSIS FOR PAIN One of the most powerful uses of hypnosis is *hypnotic analgesia*, a form of pain reduction. Laboratory research has demonstrated that this technique works reliably (Hilgard & Hilgard, 1975; Nash & Barnier, 2008). For instance, a person who plunges one of his or her arms into extremely cold water will feel great pain, and the pain will intensify over time. On average, a person can leave the arm in the water for only about 30 seconds, but a person given hypnotic analgesia can hold out longer. As you might expect, people high in suggestibility who are given hypnotic analgesia can tolerate the cold water the longest (Montgomery, DuHamel, & Redd, 2000).

There is overwhelming evidence that in clinical settings, hypnosis is effective in dealing with immediate pain (e.g., during surgery, undergoing dental work, recovering from burns) and chronic pain (e.g., from arthritis, cancer, diabetes; Patterson & Jensen, 2003). A patient can also be taught self-hypnosis to improve recovery from surgery (**FIGURE 4.23**). Hypnosis may work more by changing the patient's interpretation of pain than by diminishing pain. That is, the patient feels the sensations associated with pain but feels detached from those sensations (Price, Harkins, & Baker, 1987). An imaging study confirmed this pattern by showing that while hypnosis does not affect the sensory processing of pain, it reduces brain activity in regions that process the emotional aspects of pain (Rainville, Duncan, Price, Carrier, & Bushnell, 1997). Findings such as these provide considerable support for the dissociation theory of hypnosis. It seems implausible that either expectations about hypnosis or social pressure not to feel pain could explain how people given hypnotic analgesia are able to undergo painful surgery and not feel it. Nor does it seem likely that either expectations about hypnosis or social pressure not to feel pain could result in the changes in brain activity seen during hypnotic analgesia.

 Can anyone be hypnotized?

ANSWER: No. Hypnosis works only for certain people who are willing to go along with the experience.

meditation
A mental procedure that focuses attention on an external object or on a sense of awareness.

4.11 Meditation Produces Relaxation

Meditation is a mental procedure that focuses attention on an external object or on a sense of awareness. Through intense contemplation, the meditator develops a deep sense of tranquility. There are two general forms of meditation. In *concentrative meditation*, you focus attention on one thing, such as your breathing pattern, a mental image, or a specific phrase (sometimes called a *mantra*). In *mindfulness meditation*, you let your thoughts flow freely, paying attention to them but trying not to react to them. You hear the contents of your inner voice, but you allow them to flow from one topic to the next without examining their meaning or reacting to them in any way. At the start of this chapter, you tried a few minutes of concentrative meditation. Now, why not take a break from reading and try either that method or mindfulness meditation for at least 20 minutes (**FIGURE 4.24**)?

Different forms of meditation are popular in many Eastern religions, including Hinduism, Buddhism, and Sikhism. Religious forms of meditation are meant to bring enlightenment. Most forms of meditation popular in the West are meant to expand the mind, bring about feelings of inner peace, and help people deal with the tensions and stresses in their lives. These methods include *Zen, yoga,* and *transcendental meditation (TM)*, perhaps the best-known meditation procedure.

TM involves meditating with great concentration for 20 minutes twice a day. Many early studies found a number of benefits from TM, including lower blood pressure, fewer reports of stress, and changes in the hormonal responses underlying stress. These studies have been criticized, however, because they had small samples and lacked appropriate control groups. In a more rigorous recent study, a large number of heart patients were randomly assigned to TM or an educational program. After 16 weeks, the patients performing TM improved more than the control group on a number of health measures, including blood pressure and cholesterol level (Paul-Labrador et al., 2006). Unfortunately, this study does not show which aspects of TM produced the health benefits. Was it simply relaxing, or was it the altered state of consciousness? (As discussed in Chapter 11, reducing stress, no matter how it is done, yields substantial health benefits.)

Psychologists also study how meditation affects cognitive processing and brain function (Cahn & Polich, 2006). In one study, participants were assigned randomly to five days of either intensive meditation training or relaxation training. Those who underwent the meditation training showed greater stress reduction and more significant improvement in attention than did the group that underwent relaxation training (Tang et al., 2007). When participants in another study were made to feel sad, those

FIGURE 4.24
Meditation
To practice concentrative meditation, focus your attention on your breathing pattern, in and out. To practice mindfulness meditation, let your thoughts flow freely without reacting to them.

who had received meditation training felt less sad than those in a control group who did not receive meditation training (Farb et al., 2010; **FIGURE 4.25**). Some researchers argue that long-term meditation brings about structural changes in the brain that help maintain brain function over the life span. For instance, the volume of gray matter typically diminishes with age. One study found that this volume did not diminish in older adults who practiced Zen meditation (Pagnoni & Cekic, 2007). This finding suggests that Zen meditation might help preserve cognitive functioning as people age. As you know from reading Chapter 2, however, correlation is not causation. People who meditate may differ substantially from people who do not, especially in terms of lifestyle choices such as diet and a willingness to take care of their health. Careful empirical research using the methods of psychological science should contribute significantly to our understanding of meditation's effects.

> **Q** Suppose a person meditating focuses on thoughts of waves rolling onto a beautiful beach. Is the person practicing concentrative meditation or mindfulness meditation?
>
> **ANSWER:** concentrative, because the person is focusing on a specific image

4.12 People Can Lose Themselves in Activities

When a person performs an automatic task, such as riding a bicycle, that person's conscious thoughts might not include the process of riding. Instead, the rider's brain shifts to "autopilot" and automatically goes through the motor actions. During most of our daily activities, of course, we are consciously aware of only a small portion of both our thoughts and our behaviors.

EXERCISE, RELIGIOUS PRAYER, AND FLOW Why do many people listen to music while exercising? In offering a distraction from physical exertion, music can bring about an energizing shift in consciousness. Many people have had a similar but more extreme experience during exercise. One minute they are in pain and feeling fatigued, and the next minute they are euphoric and feeling a glorious release of energy. Commonly known as *runner's high*, this state is partially mediated by physiological processes (especially endorphin release, discussed in Chapter 3). It also occurs because of a shift in consciousness.

Shifts in consciousness that are similar to runner's high occur at other moments in our lives. Religious ceremonies often decrease awareness of the external world and create feelings of euphoria, or *religious ecstasy*. Indeed, such rituals often involve chanting, dancing, and/or other behaviors as a way for people to lose themselves. Like meditation, religious ecstasy directs attention away from the self. In this way, it allows a person to focus on his or her religious experience (**FIGURE 4.26**).

One psychological theory about such peak experiences is based on the concept of *flow*. Flow is "a particular kind of experience that is so engrossing and enjoyable [that it is] worth doing for its own sake even though it may have no consequence outside itself" (Csikszentmihalyi, 1999, p. 824). That is, a person might perform a particular task out of fascination with it rather than out of a desire for an external reward. Flow is an optimal experience in that the activity is completely absorbing and completely satisfying. The person experiencing flow loses track of time, forgets about his or her problems, and fails to notice other things going on (Csikszentmihalyi, 1990). The person's skills are well matched with the task's demands; the situation is less like bicycle riding, where much of the work happens automatically, than like rock climbing, where every thought is on the next step and is concrete, not deep and abstract (Leary, 2004). Flow experiences

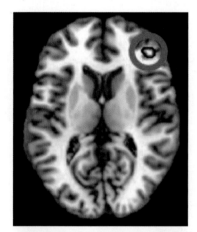

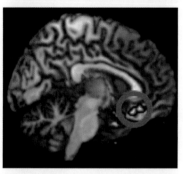

FIGURE 4.25
The Brain on Meditation
In these fMRI scans, the circles indicate brain areas that typically show less activity when people are sad. After control subjects watched sad clips from movies, these areas of their brains were less active, as expected. However, in the brains of participants who had received eight weeks of meditation training, these areas remained active, indicating that these participants felt less sadness.

have been reported during many activities, including playing music (O'Neil, 1999) or a moderately challenging version of the computer game *Tetris* (Keller & Bless, 2008), participating in sports (Jackson, Thomas, Marsh, & Smethurst, 2001), and simply doing satisfying jobs (Demerouti, 2006). In the view of the psychologist Mihaly Csikszentmihalyi (1999), flow experiences bring personal fulfillment and make life worth living.

ESCAPING THE SELF Conscious thoughts can be dominated by worries, frustrations, and feelings of personal failure. Sometimes people get tired of dealing with life's problems and try to make themselves feel better through escapist pursuits. Potential flow activities such as sports or work may help people escape thinking about their problems, but people engage in such activities mainly to feel personally fulfilled. The difference is between escaping and engaging. Sometimes people choose to escape the self rather than engage with life: To forget their troubles, they drink alcohol, take drugs, play video games, watch television, surf the Web, text, and so on. The selective appeal of escapist entertainment is that it distracts people from reflecting on their problems or their failures, thereby helping them avoid feeling bad about themselves.

Some escapist activities, such as running or reading, tend to have positive effects. Others tend to be relatively harmless distractions. Still others tend to come at great personal expense. For example, people obsessively playing online games such as *World of Warcraft* have lost their jobs and their marriages (**FIGURE 4.27**). They have even taken the lives of their offspring: In South Korea in 2010, Kim Jae-beom and his common-law wife, Kim Yun-jeong, neglected their 3-month-old daughter to the point that she died of starvation. The couple reportedly spent every night raising a virtual daughter as part of a role-playing game they engaged in at an Internet café.

Some ways of escaping the self can also be associated with self-destructive behaviors, such as binge eating, unsafe sex, and, at the extreme, suicide. According to the social psychologist Roy Baumeister (1991), people use such behaviors because, to escape their problems, they seek to reduce self-awareness. The state of being in lowered self-awareness may reduce long-term planning, reduce meaningful thinking, and help bring about uninhibited actions. Chapter 12 further discusses the connections between behavior and self-awareness. The next section of this chapter looks at a common way people try to escape their problems—namely, using drugs or alcohol to alter consciousness.

What is flow?

FIGURE 4.26
Religious Ecstasy
During a service at an evangelical church in Toronto, a man is overcome with religious ecstasy. According to the photographer, the man was speaking in tongues (a form of prayer that involves uttering unintelligible sounds).

FIGURE 4.27
Escapist Entertainment
Simple entertainment, such as playing video games, may have benefits. When such activity veers toward obsession, it may have negative effects.

ANSWER: the state of being deeply immersed in a completely enjoyable and satisfying experience that may have no consequences beyond itself

How Do Drugs Affect Consciousness?

Throughout history, people have discovered that ingesting certain substances can alter their mental states in various ways. Some of those altered states, however momentary, can be pleasant. Some, especially over the long term, can have negative consequences, including injury or death. According to the United Nations Office on Drugs and Crime (2013b), up to 317 million people around the globe age 15–64 use illicit drugs each year. Societal problems stemming from drug abuse are well known. Most people probably know and care about someone addicted to alcohol, to an illegal substance, or to a prescription medication. To investigate the biological, individual, and societal effects of drug use, psychologists ask questions such as: Why do people use drugs? Why do some people become addicted to drugs? Why do drug addicts continue to abuse drugs when doing so causes illness, turmoil, and suffering for themselves and people close to them?

Learning Objectives

- Describe the neurochemical, psychological, and behavioral effects of stimulants, depressants, opioids/narcotics, hallucinogens/psychedelics, and other commonly used drugs.

- Identify physiological and psychological factors associated with addiction.

4.13 Drugs Alter Brain Neurochemistry

Drugs are a mixed blessing. If they are the right ones, taken under the right circumstances, they can provide soothing relief from severe pain or a moderate headache. They can help people suffering from depression lead more satisfying lives. They can help children who have attention deficits or hyperactivity disorders settle down and learn better. But many of these same drugs can be used for "recreational" purposes: to alter physical sensations, levels of consciousness, thoughts, moods, and behaviors in ways that users believe are desirable. This recreational use can sometimes have negative consequences. **Addiction** is drug use that remains compulsive despite its negative consequences.

Psychoactive drugs are mind-altering substances that people typically take for recreational purposes. These drugs change the brain's neurochemistry by activating neurotransmitter systems: either by imitating the brain's natural neurotransmitters (e.g., marijuana, opiates) or changing the activity of particular neurotransmitter receptors (e.g., cocaine). The effect(s) of a particular drug depend(s) on which neurotransmitter system(s) it imitates or activates (**TABLE 4.1**).

Stimulants, for example, are drugs that increase behavioral and mental activity. They stimulate, or heighten, activity of the central nervous system. Stimulants also activate the sympathetic nervous system, increasing heart rate and blood pressure. They improve mood, but they also cause people to become restless, and they disrupt sleep. Amphetamines, methamphetamine, and cocaine are potent stimulants. Nicotine and caffeine are mild stimulants.

Some stimulants work by interfering with the normal reuptake of dopamine by the releasing neuron—allowing dopamine to remain in the synapse and thus prolonging its effects—whereas other stimulants also increase the release of dopamine (Fibiger, 1993). Activation of dopamine receptors seems to be involved in drug use in two ways. First, the increased dopamine is associated with greater reward, or increased liking (Volkow, Wang, & Baler, 2011). Second, the increased dopamine leads to a greater desire to take a drug, even if that drug does not produce pleasure. Thus, sometimes an addict *wants* a drug even if the addict does not *like* the drug when he or she uses it. Research indicates that endorphins also contribute to the liking aspect of addiction (Kringelbach & Berridge, 2009).

Depressants have the opposite effect of stimulants. They reduce behavioral and mental activity by depressing the central nervous system. Alcohol is the

addiction

Drug use that remains compulsive despite its negative consequences.

Table 4.1 Psychoactive Drugs

TYPE	PSYCHOLOGICAL EFFECT(S)	EXAMPLES	NEUROTRANSMITTER SYSTEM(S)
Stimulants	Increase behavioral and mental activity	Amphetamines, methamphetamine, cocaine, nicotine, caffeine	Dopamine, norepinephrine, acetylcholine (nicotine)
Depressants	Decrease behavioral and mental activity	Anti-anxiety drugs (barbiturates, benzodiazepines), alcohol	GABA
Opioids	Reduce the experience of pain, bring pleasure	Heroin, morphine, codeine	Endorphins
Hallucinogens/ psychedelics	Alter thoughts or perceptions	LSD, PCP, peyote, psilocybin, mushrooms	Serotonin (LSD, peyote, psilocybin), glutamate (PCP)
Combination	Mixed effects	Marijuana, MDMA	Cannabinoid (marijuana), serotonin, dopamine, norepinephrine (MDMA)

most widely used depressant—in fact, it is the most widely used and abused drug (**FIGURE 4.28**). Anti-anxiety drugs, such as benzodiazepines, commonly given to calm people and reduce worry, are also depressants. In sufficiently high doses, depressants can induce sleep, which is why they are sometimes referred to as sedatives. Chapter 15, "Psychological Treatments," discusses the clinical use of depressants.

Opioids, sometimes called narcotics, include heroin, morphine, and codeine. Recall from Chapter 3 that endorphins are the brain's natural mechanism for relieving pain. Various drugs derived from the opium poppy are able to bind with endorphin receptors and in doing so help relieve pain. Opioids also provide intense feelings of pleasure, relaxation, and euphoria. Activation of opioid receptors is involved in the experience of reward (Berridge & Kringelbach, 2013; Smith, Berridge, & Aldridge, 2011; this connection is discussed further in Chapter 6, "Learning").

Hallucinogens, sometimes called psychedelics, produce alterations in cognition, mood, and perception. These drugs change how users experience the world around them. The most common hallucinogen is *lysergic acid diethylamide (LSD)*. LSD was discovered in 1938 and is made from a chemical found in certain types of fungus that grows on rye and other wheats called ergot. It is usually taken orally, and the drug experience, informally referred to as a "trip," lasts for about 12 hours. LSD changes sensory experiences and can produce extreme hallucinations, pleasurable or unpleasurable. People using LSD have a distorted sense of time.

A naturally occurring form of LSD might have been responsible for the bizarre behavior that led to accusations of witchcraft in Salem, Massachusetts, in 1692. Some residents of Salem, especially teenagers and children, suffered from seizures, convulsions, hallucinations, blindness, prickling sensations, nausea, and other symptoms. Their behavior was taken as signaling demonic possession and witchery, and as punishment they were put to death by burning at the stake. It is possible, however, that ergot may have caused these symptoms. The "witches" of Salem may have inadvertently eaten LSD-tainted bread.

Many other substances, such as certain plants and fungi, have psychedelic properties. For example, eating the top part of the peyote cactus or certain types of mushrooms, such as *psilocybin mushrooms*, produces hallucinogenic effects. These psychedelic substances have been used in various religious rites throughout history.

Many commonly used drugs do not fit neatly into these major categories because they produce a range of psychological effects. For instance, marijuana acts as a depressant but also has a slight hallucinogenic effect, as you will see later in the chapter.

FIGURE 4.28
Alcohol
The open display and easy availability of alcohol make us forget that it is a widely abused depressant.

 Which type of drug heightens behavioral and mental activity?

ANSWER: stimulants, such as caffeine, nicotine, amphetamines, and cocaine

4.14 People Use—and Abuse—Many Psychoactive Drugs

This section considers a few common psychoactive drugs in more detail. Some of these drugs have legitimate medical uses, but all of them are frequently abused outside of medical use.

COCAINE Cocaine is a stimulant derived from the leaves of the coca bush, which grows primarily in South America. After inhaling (snorting) cocaine as a powder or smoking it in the form of crack cocaine, users experience a wave of confidence. They feel good, alert, energetic, sociable, and wide awake. Cocaine produces its

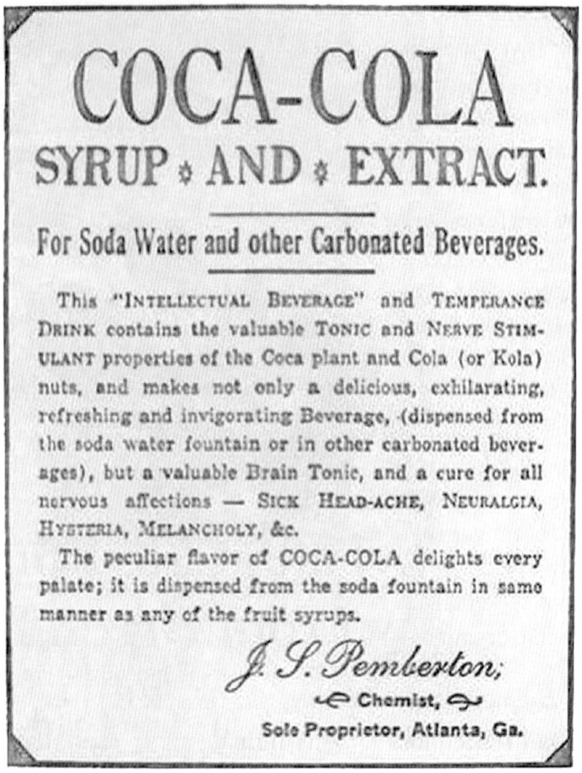

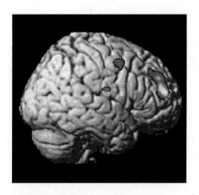

COCA-COLA

SYRUP ⁂ AND ⁂ EXTRACT.

For Soda Water and other Carbonated Beverages.

This "INTELLECTUAL BEVERAGE" and TEMPERANCE DRINK contains the valuable TONIC and NERVE STIMULANT properties of the Coca plant and Cola (or Kola) nuts, and makes not only a delicious, exhilarating, refreshing and invigorating Beverage, (dispensed from the soda water fountain or in other carbonated beverages), but a valuable Brain Tonic, and a cure for all nervous affections — SICK HEAD-ACHE, NEURALGIA, HYSTERIA, MELANCHOLY, &c.

The peculiar flavor of COCA-COLA delights every palate; it is dispensed from the soda fountain in same manner as any of the fruit syrups.

J. S. Pemberton;
⤳ Chemist, ↩
Sole Proprietor, Atlanta, Ga.

FIGURE 4.29
Early Coke Ad
This advertisement's claim that Coca-Cola is "a valuable Brain Tonic" may have been inspired by the incorporation of cocaine into the drink before 1906.

FIGURE 4.30
Methamphetamine's Effects on the Brain
This image is a composite of brain scans from 29 methamphetamine addicts. The red and yellow areas represent the brain damage that typically occurs in the frontal cortex as a result of methamphetamine abuse (Kim et al., 2006). Such damage may explain the cognitive problems associated with methamphetamine use.

stimulating effects by increasing the concentration of dopamine in synapses. These short-term effects are especially intense for crack cocaine users. In contrast, habitual use of cocaine in large quantities can lead to paranoia, psychotic behavior, and violence (Ottieger, Tressell, Inciardi, & Rosales, 1992).

Cocaine has a long history of use in America. John Pemberton, a pharmacist from Georgia, was so impressed with cocaine's effects that in 1886 he added the drug to soda water for easy ingestion, thus creating Coca-Cola. In 1906, the U.S. government outlawed cocaine, so it was removed from the drink. To this day, however, coca leaves from which the cocaine has been removed are used in the making of Coke (**FIGURE 4.29**).

AMPHETAMINES AND METHAMPHETAMINE Amphetamines are stimulants that increase dopamine in the synapse. Their primary effect is to reduce fatigue. Amphetamines have a long history of use for weight loss and for staying awake. However, their numerous negative side effects include insomnia, anxiety, and potential for addiction. Legitimate medical purposes include the treatment of narcolepsy and of attention-deficit/hyperactivity disorder (ADHD, discussed in greater detail in Chapter 15, "Treatment of Psychological Disorders"). The drug Adderall contains amphetamine and is prescribed to treat ADHD. It is also widely abused as a study aid on college campuses (Weyandt et al., 2013). Self-reports of nonmedical stimulant use by college students increased from 5 percent in 2003 to just under 10 percent in 2013 (McCabe, West, Teter, & Boyd, 2014).

Another widely used stimulant is methamphetamine, which breaks down into amphetamine in the body. Methamphetamine was first developed in the early twentieth century for use as a nasal decongestant, but its recreational use became popular in the 1980s. The National Survey of Drug Use and Health for 2012 estimates that over 4 percent of the U.S. population ages 12 and over have tried methamphetamine at some point in their lives (National Institute of Drug Abuse, 2014). The use of methamphetamine may have declined in recent years, however (Gonzales, Mooney, & Rawson, 2010). One factor that encourages the use of this drug and may explain its popularity over the past decade is that it is easy to make from common over-the-counter drugs, as depicted in the critically acclaimed television show *Breaking Bad*.

By blocking the reuptake of dopamine and increasing its release, methamphetamine produces very high levels of dopamine in the synapse. In addition, methamphetamine stays in the body and brain much longer than, say, cocaine, so its effects are prolonged. Over time, methamphetamine damages various brain structures, including the frontal lobes (**FIGURE 4.30**). Ultimately, it depletes dopamine levels. The drug's effects on the temporal lobes and the limbic system may explain the harm done to memory and emotion in long-term users (Kim et al., 2006; Thompson et al., 2004). Methamphetamine also causes considerable physical damage (**FIGURE 4.31**).

OPIOIDS Opioids are drugs that include prescription medications such as oxycodone and morphine as well as the illegal drug heroin. As noted in Chapter 3, opioids bind with receptors for naturally occurring endorphins, which blunt pain. Opioids have been used to relieve pain and suffering for hundreds of years. Indeed, before the twentieth century, heroin was widely available without prescription and was

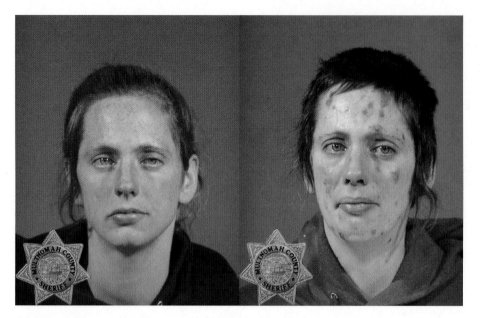

FIGURE 4.31
Methamphetamine's Effects on the Person
These before-and-after photos dramatically illustrate how the physical damage from methamphetamine can affect appearance. The photo on the left was taken in May 2000, and the photo on the right was taken six months later.

marketed by Bayer, the aspirin company (**FIGURE 4.32**). Opioids do not only block pain. They are experienced as extremely enjoyable if taken in larger doses. For instance, heroin provides a rush of intense pleasure that most addicts describe as similar to orgasm. This rush evolves into a pleasant, relaxed stupor. Opioids, however, may be highly addictive because they have dual physical effects: They increase pleasure by binding with opiate receptors and increase wanting of the drug by indirectly activating dopamine receptors (Kuhn, Swartzwelder, & Wilson, 2003).

During the past decade there has been an epidemic of opioid abuse. Most experts view the current epidemic as resulting from the greater use of prescription opiates for chronic pain (Compton, Jones, & Baldwin, 2016). Physicians had been encouraged to increase their prescription of opiates due to concerns that pain was not being treated aggressively enough. The greater availability of prescription drugs led to more recreational use as well as subsequent abuse and addiction. The effort to reduce prescription drug abuse by changing the drugs so that they produced less of a "high" and restricting access led those who were addicted to seek out cheaper and more powerful opioids, such as heroin. Heroin is often mixed with even-more-potent substances, such as the synthetic opioid fentanyl, to give users increased effects. Unfortunately, even small amounts of fentanyl can be deadly (Sutter et al., 2017). A version of fentanyl used to tranquilize elephants is 10,000 times more potent than morphine and so dangerous that even touching it can kill you.

One result of the increased use of potent mixes of opioids is a huge surge in the number of drug overdoses, many of them

FIGURE 4.32
Early Heroin Ad
Before 1904, Bayer advertised heroin as "the sedative for coughs."

fatal (Gladden, Martinez, & Seth, 2016; **FIGURE 4.33**). Indeed, more Americans are now killed by drug overdoses than by traffic accidents (**FIGURE 4.34**), and the majority of those overdoses are from opioids (Rudd, Aleshire, Zibbell, & Gladden, 2016). The group most affected by opiate overdoses is white middle-age males, who have the highest death rates by far (Hedegaard, Warner, & Miniño, 2017). Deaths from opioid overdose have risen similarly in Canada (Fischer et al., 2016). Many first responders now carry naloxone, an opioid antagonist, which can reverse opioid effects and help people survive an overdose. In 2015, the FDA approved Narcan, a nasal spray containing naloxone that is easy to administer. Narcan is now available without prescription in a growing number of states. The FDA is also establishing new guidelines for the safe and effective use of pain medications for the 9–12 million Americans who suffer chronic pain (Califf, Woodcock, & Ostroff, 2016).

MARIJUANA The most widely used illicit drug in the world is marijuana, the dried leaves and flower buds of the cannabis plant. Many drugs can easily be categorized as a stimulant, a depressant, or a hallucinogen, but marijuana can have the effects of all three types. The psychoactive ingredient in marijuana is *THC*, or tetrahydrocannabinol. This chemical produces a relaxed mental state, an uplifted or contented mood, and some perceptual and cognitive distortions. For some users, it impairs perception, whereas for others it makes perceptions more vivid, especially taste perceptions.

Like depressants, marijuana decreases reaction times, impairs motor coordination, impairs memory formation, and impairs the recall of recently learned information. As opposed to alcohol, which is metabolized and cleared in a few hours, THC and the by-products of its metabolism remain in the body for up to a month. With THC still in their system, frequent users of marijuana may get high with a lower dose than infrequent users. Most first-time users do not experience the "high" obtained by more experienced users. In this way, marijuana differs from most other drugs. Generally, the first time someone uses a drug, the effects are very strong, and over time the person has to use more of the drug to get the same effect. That progression is not the case with marijuana.

Although the brain mechanisms that marijuana affects remain somewhat mysterious, researchers have discovered a class of receptors that are activated by naturally occurring THC-like substances. Activation of these *cannabinoid receptors* appears to adjust mental activity and perhaps alter pain perception. The large concentration of these receptors in the hippocampus may partly explain why marijuana impairs memory (Ilan, Smith, & Gevins, 2004).

Heavy long-term use of marijuana is associated with a smaller hippocampus and amygdala, brain regions involved in processing memory and emotion (Yucel et al., 2008). Whether smoking marijuana causes long-term deficits in cognitive processes is more controversial. One study found that frequent marijuana use in childhood predicted cognitive problems in adulthood (Meier et al., 2012). But as you know, correlation does not prove causation. Other researchers who have looked at the same data argue that socioeconomic status is a confounding factor (Rogeberg, 2013). That is, children who grow up in impoverished circumstances are more likely to smoke marijuana *and* more likely to show

FIGURE 4.33
Public Overdose
In 2016, this photo went viral. Shown here are a child's grandmother and her friend passed out from heroin overdose while the child awaits help (the child's face is obscured in this version of the photo). Both the grandmother and her friend received prison terms for endangering the child.

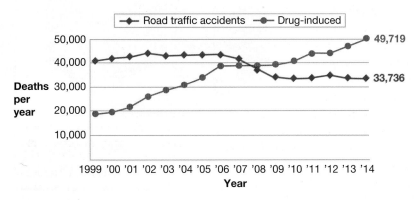

FIGURE 4.34
Fatal Overdoses
In the United States, the number of annual deaths due to drug use has increased dramatically since 1999.

cognitive deficits in adulthood. Recent evidence suggests, though, that marijuana may affect the developing brain to make adolescent heavy users more likely to eventually develop significant mental health problems (Bechtold, Hipwell, Lewis, Loeber, & Pardini, 2016; Ryan et al., 2017).

Marijuana is also used for its medicinal properties, and this use is legal in many countries and currently 20 American states (**FIGURE 4.35**). For instance, cancer patients undergoing chemotherapy report that marijuana is effective for overcoming nausea. Nearly 1 in 4 AIDS patients reports using marijuana to relieve nausea and pain (Prentiss, Power, Balmas, Tzuang, & Israelski, 2004). The medical use of marijuana is controversial because of the possibility that chronic use can cause health problems or lead to abuse of the drug. Some countries and American states have concluded that such risks are offset by a reduction in the problems created by criminal activity associated with illegal drug use. Moreover, although there was an increase in the percentage of adults who smoke marijuana in the United States from 2002 to 2014, the number of adult marijuana users who show signs of addiction has remained stable (Compton, Han, Jones, Blanco, & Hughes, 2016). The majority of states allow medical use of marijuana, and several states have legalized recreational use, including the populous state of California.

FIGURE 4.35
Medicinal Use of Marijuana
Employees assist customers at the River Rock Medical Marijuana Center in Denver, Colorado.

MDMA MDMA produces an energizing effect similar to that of stimulants, but it also causes slight hallucinations. The street version of MDMA is sold as pills named ecstasy or Molly, but these pills often contain other stimulants in addition to MDMA. According to the National Institute of Drug Abuse (2010), ecstasy use by high school students increased from 3.7 percent to 4.7 percent between 2009 and 2010. The drug first became popular in the 1990s among young adults in nightclubs and at all-night parties known as raves.

Compared with amphetamines, MDMA is associated with less dopamine activity and more serotonin activity. The serotonin release may explain ecstasy's hallucinogenic properties. Research on animals has shown that MDMA can cause damage to a number of brain regions, particularly the prefrontal cortex and the hippocampus (Halpin, Collins, & Yamamoto, 2014). Studies with humans show evidence of a range of impairments from long-term ecstasy use, especially memory problems and a diminished ability to perform complex tasks (Parrott, 2013). Of course, any drug can be toxic in large doses or taken for long periods. Currently, controversy exists over whether occasional recreational use of ecstasy by itself causes long-term damage. Some ecstasy users take very high doses or regularly use other drugs, such as methamphetamine, that are known to be neurotoxic (Gallagher et al., 2014). Growing evidence suggests that MDMA may have potential benefits for use in the treatment of posttraumatic stress disorder (Doblin et al., 2014; you will learn more about this disorder in Chapter 14). The drug promotes feelings of compassion and trust and reduces the negative emotions that people have about their traumatic experiences even after the drug wears off (Mithoefer et al., 2013). Recent evidence also suggests that MDMA may help those with autism cope with social anxiety (Milhoefer, Grob, & Brewerton, 2016). When used as part of treatment, MDMA does not have negative effects on health or cognition (White, 2014).

One concern is that many pills being sold as ecstasy or Molly contain other dangerous chemicals, such as drugs used to anesthetize animals. Even when they contain MDMA, the doses vary widely, increasing the likelihood of overdose (Morefield, Keane, Felgate, White, & Irvine, 2011; Wood, Stribley, Dargan, Davies, Holt, & Ramsey, 2011). Several northeastern college students attending concerts during the summer of 2013 died after consuming what they believed to be Molly (**FIGURE 4.36**).

FIGURE 4.36
Deaths from MDMA
Concertgoers are shown at Electric Zoo 2013, a Labor Day weekend of electronic dance music in New York City. Two attendees died after taking MDMA sold as Molly, and the festival was ended a day early.

 What type of drug is in Adderall, used to treat ADHD?

ANSWER: amphetamine

4.15 Alcohol Abuse Is Responsible for Many Societal Problems

Alcohol is a depressant that produces its effects by activating GABA receptors. Recall from Chapter 3 that GABA is the primary inhibitory neurotransmitter in the nervous system. Through its effects on GABA receptors, alcohol inhibits neural activity, which may be why alcohol is typically experienced as relaxing. GABA reception may also be the primary mechanism by which alcohol interferes with motor coordination and results in slowed reaction time and slurred speech. Drugs that block the effects of alcohol on GABA receptors also prevent alcohol intoxication. However, drugs that prevent the effects of alcohol are not used to treat alcoholics, because reducing the symptoms of being drunk could easily lead to even greater alcohol abuse.

Many societies have a love/hate relationship with alcohol. On the one hand, moderate drinking is an accepted aspect of social interaction and may even be good for one's health, although there is some controversy about its purported benefits (Stockwell et al., 2016). On the other hand, alcohol is a major contributor to many societal problems, such as spousal abuse and other forms of violence. Although the percentage of traffic fatalities due to alcohol is dropping, alcohol was still a factor in about one-third of fatal accidents in the United States in 2012 (National Highway Traffic Safety Administration, 2013). About 80,000 deaths each year in the United States are caused by alcohol, and the overall cost of problem drinking—from lost productivity due to employee absence, health care expenses, and so on—is estimated to be more than $223 billion annually (Sacks et al., 2013).

Although the legal age for drinking in the United States is 21, more than 70 percent of high school students (Johnston, O'Malley, Bachman, & Schulenberg, 2011) and 75 percent of college students (Barnes, Welte, Hoffman, & Tidwell, 2010) have consumed alcohol. A large percentage of drinking by college students is "binge drinking," or drinking more than five drinks in one sitting (FIGURE 4.37). Drinking to intoxication is associated with various negative outcomes for college students. Every year, more than 1,800

| 12 fl. oz. of regular beer | = | 8–9 fl. oz. of malt liquor (shown in a 12 oz. glass) | = | 5 fl. oz. of table wine | = | 1.5 fl. oz. shot of 80-proof distilled spirits (gin, rum, tequila, vodka, whiskey, etc.) |

about 5% alcohol   about 7% alcohol   about 12% alcohol   40% alcohol

The percent of "pure" alcohol, expressed here as alcohol by volume, varies by beverage.

Source: Based on http:www.niaaa.nih/gov/alcohol-health/overview-alcohol-consumption/what-standard-drink

FIGURE 4.37

One Standard Drink

It is important to remember that having more than five drinks in one sitting counts as binge drinking. But a drink of one kind may be much more powerful than a drink of another kind. How can you know just how much alcohol is in any one drink? These depictions show the standard drink for different types of alcohol. Note that each amount of liquid contains a different amount of alcohol by volume.

college students die as a result of excessive alcohol use (Hingson, Zha, & Weitzman, 2009; Thompson & Huynh, 2017). About one-third of college students reported having had sex during a drinking binge, and the heaviest drinkers were likely to have had sex with a new or casual partner (Leigh & Schafer, 1993), thus increasing their risk for exposure to AIDS and other sexually transmitted diseases. Date rape also often involves alcohol (White & Hingson, 2014).

In every region of the world, across a wide variety of measures—drinking versus abstinence, heavy drinking versus occasional drinking, alcohol-related disorders, and so on—men drink more than women (FIGURE 4.38). Men are twice as likely to report binge drinking, chronic drinking, and recent alcohol intoxication. Although gender differences in alcohol use are smaller for university students and adolescents (Swendsen et al., 2012), young males are much more likely to be binge drinkers (Patrick et al., 2013).

One possible explanation is that women do not metabolize alcohol as quickly as men do and generally have smaller body volumes, so they consume less alcohol than men to achieve the same effects. Another possible explanation is that women's drinking may be more hidden because it is less socially accepted than men's drinking. According to this view, women's alcohol consumption may be underreported, especially in cultures where it is frowned upon or forbidden. In some cultures, "real men" are expected to drink a lot and prove they can "hold" their liquor, whereas women who do the same are seen as abnormal.

Alan Marlatt (1999), a leading researcher on substance abuse, has noted that people view alcohol as the "magic elixir," capable of increasing social skills, sexual pleasure, confidence, and power. They anticipate that alcohol will have positive effects on their emotions and behavior. For example, people tend to think that alcohol reduces anxiety, so both light and heavy drinkers turn to alcohol after a difficult day. Alcohol *can* interfere with the cognitive processing of threat cues, so that anxiety-provoking events are less troubling when people are intoxicated. This effect occurs, however, only if people drink *before* the anxiety-provoking events. In fact, according to the research, drinking after a hard day can increase people's focus on and obsession with their problems (Sayette, 1993). In addition, while moderate doses of alcohol are associated with more-positive moods, larger doses are associated with more-negative moods.

Expectations about alcohol's effects are learned very early in life, through observation. Children may see that people who drink have a lot of fun and that drinking is an important aspect of many celebrations. Teenagers may view drinkers as sociable and grown up, two things they desperately want to be. Studies have shown that children who have very positive expectations about alcohol are more likely to start drinking and become heavy drinkers than children who do not share those expectations (Leigh & Stacy, 2004).

According to the social psychologists Jay Hull and Charles Bond (1986), expectations about alcohol profoundly affect behavior. They based this conclusion on studies in which researchers gave participants tonic water with or without alcohol. Regardless of the drinks' actual contents, some participants were told they were drinking just tonic water and some they were drinking tonic water with alcohol. This design allowed for a comparison of those who thought they were drinking tonic water but were actually drinking alcohol with those who thought they were drinking alcohol but were actually drinking tonic water. This research demonstrated that alcohol impairs motor processes, information processing, and mood, independent of whether the person thinks he or she has consumed it. In addition, thinking one has consumed alcohol—regardless of whether one has actually consumed it—leads to less inhibition about various social behaviors, such as aggression and sexual arousal. Thus, some behaviors generally associated with drunkenness are accounted for by learned beliefs about intoxication rather than by alcohol's pharmacological

FIGURE 4.38
Male Drinking
Across the globe, men drink the most alcohol.

properties. Sometimes the learned expectations and the pharmacology work in opposite ways. For instance, alcohol tends to increase sexual arousal, but it interferes with sexual performance.

 Through which neurotransmitter does alcohol have its effects?

4.16 Addiction Has Physical and Psychological Aspects

Drug addiction has physical and psychological factors. Physical dependence on a drug is a physiological state associated with *tolerance*, in which a person needs to consume more of a particular substance to achieve the same subjective effect. Failing to ingest the substance leads to symptoms of *withdrawal*, a physiological and psychological state characterized by feelings of anxiety, tension, and cravings for the addictive substance. The physical symptoms of withdrawal vary widely from drug to drug and from individual to individual, but they include nausea, chills, body aches, and tremors. A person can be psychologically dependent, however, without showing tolerance or withdrawal. This section focuses on addiction to substances that alter consciousness, but people can also become psychologically dependent on behaviors, such as shopping or gambling.

ADDICTION'S CAUSES About 8 to 10 percent of people age 12 or older are addicted to alcohol or other drugs (Volkow, Koob, & McLellan, 2016). How do people become addicted? One central factor appears to be dopamine activity in the limbic system, particularly the nucleus accumbens (a brain structure discussed in Chapter 3), because this activity underlies the *wanting* properties of taking drugs (Baler & Volkow, 2006). Other brain regions that are important for addiction include the prefrontal cortex, amygdala, thalamus, and hippocampus (Koob & Volkow, 2010).

A brain region called the insula also seems to be important for the craving component of addiction (Goldstein et al., 2009; **FIGURE 4.39**). Patients with insula damage report that immediately after being injured, they quit smoking easily. In fact, they no longer experience conscious urges to smoke. One patient who had a stroke to his left insula commented that he quit smoking because his "body forgot the urge to smoke" (Naqvi, Rudrauf, Damasio, & Bechara, 2007, p. 534).

Only about 5 percent to 10 percent of those who use drugs become addicted. Indeed, more than 90 million Americans have experimented with illicit drugs, yet most of them use drugs only occasionally or try them for a while and then give them up. In a longitudinal study, Jonathan Shedler and Jack Block (1990) found that those who had experimented with drugs as adolescents were better adjusted in adulthood than those who had never tried them. Complete abstainers and heavy drug users had adjustment problems compared with those who had experimented. This finding does not suggest, however, that everyone should try drugs or that parents should encourage drug experimentation. After all, no one can predict just who will become addicted or who is prepared to handle a drug's effects on behavior.

Addiction appears to develop in stages, and this progression is due to changes in the brain that accompany drug use (Volkow et al., 2016). For most people, initial drug use is associated with euphoria that the person looks forward to enjoying on some occasions. However, tolerance leads people to need to use more and more of the drug to achieve similar levels of pleasure. For some people, the drug starts to lose its ability to provide pleasure, while the person simultaneously starts desiring the drug more and

Insula

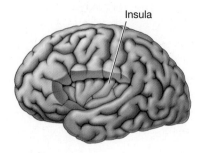

FIGURE 4.39
Insula
This brain region appears to play a role in craving.

more often. Eventually, these vulnerable individuals use drugs not to "get high," but to escape the negative feelings of withdrawal. When addicted, they become obsessed with planning to get the drug. Their desire for the drug becomes all-encompassing.

The loss of euphoria that comes from addiction occurs because the brain reward system becomes less sensitive, both to drug-related and non-drug-related rewards (Hyatt et al., 2012). As a consequence, addicts find drugs less pleasurable, and they fail to enjoy other activities they used to enjoy, such as spending time with others or working (Koob & Le Moal, 2005; Koob & Mason, 2016). Thus, addicts may neglect their friends and family members in their pursuit of satisfying their obsession with the drug to which they are addicted. Addicts often cannot understand why they continue to take the drug even though it causes them problems and is no longer as pleasurable as when they started (Volkow et al., 2016). Feeling bad about this situation, unfortunately, further compels them to use drugs. Although the drugs are not as enjoyable as before, at least they provide fleeting pleasure and escape from withdrawal and from feeling bad about their situation.

ADDICTION VULNERABILITY Some adolescents are especially likely to experiment with illegal drugs and to abuse alcohol. Adolescents high in sensation seeking (a personality trait that involves attraction to novelty and risk taking) are more likely to associate with deviant peer groups and to use alcohol, tobacco, and drugs (Patrick & Schulenberg, 2014; Wills, DuHamel, & Vaccaro, 1995). These adolescents and their parents tend to have poor relationships, which in turn promote the adolescent's association with deviant peer groups. Some theorists suggest that an inherited predisposition to sensation seeking may predict particular behaviors, such as affiliating with drug users. Such behaviors, in turn, may increase the possibility of substance abuse.

Some evidence points to genetic components of addiction, especially for alcoholism, but little direct evidence points to a *single* "alcoholism" or "addiction" gene. Rather, what people inherit is a cluster of characteristics (Volkow & Muenke, 2012). These inherited risk factors might include personality traits such as risk taking and impulsivity, a reduced concern about personal harm, a nervous system chronically low in arousal, or a predisposition to finding chemical substances pleasurable. In turn, such factors may make some people more likely to explore drugs and enjoy them.

Social learning theorists have sought to account for the initiation of drug or alcohol use among children or adolescents. They emphasize the roles of parents, the mass media, and peers, including self-identification with high-risk groups (e.g., "stoners" or "druggies"). Teenagers want to fit in somewhere, even with groups that society perceives as deviant. And as discussed further in Chapter 6, children imitate the behavior of role models, especially those they admire or with whom they identify. For children whose parents smoke, the modeling of the behavior may be continuous through early childhood and elementary school. When parents smoke, their children tend to have positive attitudes about smoking and to begin smoking early (Rowe, Chassin, Presson, & Sherman, 1996).

ADDICTION'S CONTEXT Some evidence suggests that context is important for understanding addiction. For example, in the late 1960s, drug abuse among U.S. soldiers, including the use of narcotics such as heroin and opium, appeared to be epidemic. The widespread drug use was not surprising. It was a time of youthful drug experimentation, soldiers in Vietnam had easy access to various drugs, and drugs helped the soldiers cope temporarily with fear, depression, homesickness, boredom, and the repressiveness of army regulations (**FIGURE 4.40**). The military commanders mostly ignored drug use among soldiers, viewing it as "blowing off steam."

(a)

(b)

FIGURE 4.40
The Sixties, Drugs, and Vietnam
(a) By the late 1960s, youth culture had taken many new forms in the United States and elsewhere. In exploring the boundaries of society and consciousness, many young people experimented with drugs. Here, two people share drugs at the Shiva Fellowship Church Earth Faire at Golden Gate Park, San Francisco, in April 1969. **(b)** Through those years and beyond, the United States played a leading role in the Vietnam War, a military conflict that took place in the "faraway lands" of Vietnam, Laos, and Cambodia. Perhaps inevitably, the changes and conflicts at home influenced the changes and conflicts away from home. For example, many U.S. soldiers abused drugs. Here, two soldiers exchange vials of heroin in Quang Tri Province, South Vietnam, July 1971.

Beginning in 1971, the military began mandatory drug testing of soldiers to identify and detoxify drug users before they returned to the United States. Amid speculation that a flood of addicted soldiers returning from Vietnam would swamp treatment facilities back home, the White House asked a team of behavioral scientists to study a group of returning soldiers and assess the extent of the addiction problem. Led by the behavioral epidemiologist Lee Robins, the research team examined a random sample of 898 soldiers who were leaving Vietnam in September 1971.

Robins and her colleagues found extremely high levels of drug use among the soldiers (Robins, Helzer, & Davis, 1975). Over 90 percent reported drinking alcohol, nearly three-quarters smoked marijuana, and nearly half used narcotics such as heroin, morphine, and opium. About half of the soldiers who used narcotics either had symptoms of addiction or reported believing they would be unable to give up their drug habits. The team's findings suggested that approximately 1 soldier in 5 returning from Vietnam was a drug addict. Given the prevailing view that addiction was a biological disorder with a low rate of recovery, these results indicated that tens of thousands of heroin addicts would soon be inundating the United States. But that did not happen.

Robins and her colleagues examined drug use among the soldiers after they returned to the United States. Of those who were apparently addicted to narcotics in Vietnam, only half sought out drugs when they returned to the States, and fewer still maintained their narcotic addictions. Approximately 95 percent of the addicts no longer used drugs within months of their return—an astonishing quit rate considering that the success rate of the best treatments is typically only 20 percent to 30 percent. A long-term follow-up study conducted in the early 1990s confirmed that only a handful of those who were addicts in Vietnam remained addicts.

Why did coming home help the addicts recover? In the United States, they likely did not have the same motivations or opportunities for taking the drugs as they did in Vietnam. No longer needing the drugs to escape combat's horrors, they focused on other needs and goals, such as careers and family obligations. An important lesson from this case study is that we cannot ignore environment when we try to understand addiction. Knowing drugs' physical actions in the brain may give us insights into addiction's biology, but that information fails to account for how these biological impulses can be overcome by other motivations.

 Is anyone who abuses drugs over a long period of time likely to become an addict?

ANSWER: No. Although people who abuse drugs may experience many negative consequences, only about 1 in 10 people who abuse drugs will become an addict.

Your Chapter Review

Chapter Summary

What Is Consciousness?

4.1 Brain Activity Gives Rise to Consciousness

Consciousness is our moment-by-moment subjective experiences. Consciousness is difficult to study because of its personal nature. Brain imaging research demonstrates that particular brain regions are activated by particular types of conscious experiences. According to the global workspace model, consciousness arises from activity in different cortical areas.

4.2 Consciousness Changes Following Brain Injury

A person in a minimally conscious state shows some awareness of external stimuli. A person with unresponsive wakefulness syndrome does not show consciousness. A person who is brain dead has no brain activity and is not alive; the person's body is being kept alive artificially.

4.3 Conscious Awareness Involves Attention

At any one time, each person can be conscious of a limited number of things. Change blindness illustrates how selective an individual's attention can be: We often do not notice large changes in an environment because we fail to pay attention. Thought and behavior can be influenced by stimuli that are not experienced at a conscious level.

4.4 Think like a Psychologist: Are People Affected by Subliminal Messages?

The idea that people can be influenced by hidden messages is known as subliminal perception. Although stimuli can have some effects on people without their awareness, there is currently no evidence that subliminal messages can compel people to perform complex actions against their will.

What Is Sleep?

4.5 Sleep Is an Altered State of Consciousness

Sleep is characterized by four stages that vary in brain activity. These stages range from short bursts of irregular waves (stages 1–2), to large, slow brain waves during deep, restful sleep (stages 3–4). REM sleep is marked by a return to short, fast brain waves and is accompanied by rapid eye movements, body paralysis, and dreaming.

4.6 Sleep Disorders Interfere with Daily Life

Insomnia is an inability to sleep that causes significant problems in daily living. Other sleep disorders include obstructive sleep apnea, narcolepsy, REM behavior disorder, and somnambulism (sleep walking).

4.7 Sleep Is an Adaptive Behavior

Three theories account for sleep: Sleep allows the body, including the brain, to rest and restore itself. Sleep protects animals from harm at times of the day when they are most susceptible to danger.

And sleep facilitates learning through the strengthening of neural connections.

4.8 People Dream While Sleeping

REM dreams and non-REM dreams activate and deactivate distinct brain regions. Sigmund Freud believed that dreams reveal unconscious conflicts. Evidence does not support this view. Activation-synthesis theory posits that dreams are the product of the mind's efforts to make sense of random brain activity during sleep.

4.9 Using Psychology in Your Life: How Can You Get a Good Night's Sleep?

Good sleep hygiene involves planning, setting priorities, sticking to a plan, and saying no to behaviors that might interfere with sleep. To sleep well, people should have a routine, avoid stimulants or alcohol before trying to sleep, exercise during the day, reserve the bed for sleep, relax at bedtime, get up for a while if they have trouble falling asleep, and not try to catch up on lost sleep.

What Is Altered Consciousness?

4.10 Hypnosis Is Induced Through Suggestion

Scientists debate whether hypnotized people merely play the role they are expected to play or truly experience an altered state of consciousness. Consistent with the latter view, brain imaging research has shown changes in brain activity among hypnotized participants.

4.11 Meditation Produces Relaxation

The goal of meditation, particularly as it is practiced in the West, is to bring about a state of deep relaxation. Studies suggest that meditation can have multiple benefits for people's physical and mental health.

4.12 People Can Lose Themselves in Activities

Exercise, religious practices, and other engaging activities can produce a state of altered consciousness called flow. In this state, people become completely absorbed in what they are doing. Flow is experienced as a positive state. In contrast to activities that generate flow, activities used to escape the self or reduce self-awareness can have harmful consequences.

How Do Drugs Affect Consciousness?

4.13 Drugs Alter Brain Neurochemistry

Psychoactive drugs are mind-altering substances. They can be divided into categories (stimulants, depressants, opioids, hallucinogens) based on their effects. Each drug has psychological effects that occur because the drugs affect specific neurotransmitters or multiple neurotransmitters. Some psychoactive drugs do not fit neatly into categories because they have various effects.

4.14 People Use—and Abuse—Many Psychoactive Drugs

Stimulants, including cocaine and amphetamines, increase behavioral and mental activity. Opioids, including morphine and heroin, produce a relaxed state, analgesia, and euphoria. During the past decade, there has been an epidemic of opioid abuse, especially of heroin addiction. THC (the active ingredient in marijuana) produces a relaxed state, an uplifted mood, and perceptual and cognitive distortions. MDMA, or ecstasy, produces energizing and hallucinogenic effects.

4.15 Alcohol Abuse Is Responsible for Many Societal Problems

Alcohol has its effects by activating GABA receptors. As a depressant, it decreases behavioral and mental activity. Throughout the world, men drink more than women. Alcohol's effects are influenced by the drinker's expectations.

4.16 Addiction Has Physical and Psychological Aspects

Physical dependence occurs when the body develops tolerance for a drug. Psychological dependence occurs when someone habitually and compulsively uses a drug or engages in a behavior, despite its negative consequences. Various brain regions are involved in addiction, particularly the nucleus accumbens. Addiction is influenced by personality factors, such as sensation seeking. Addiction is also influenced by the environment or context in which drug use occurs.

Key Terms

activation-synthesis theory, p. 140

addiction, p. 148

change blindness, p. 129

circadian rhythms, p. 133

consciousness, p. 122

dreams, p. 139

hypnosis, p. 143

insomnia, p. 135

meditation, p. 145

narcolepsy, p. 136

obstructive sleep apnea, p. 136

REM sleep, p. 135

subliminal perception, p. 132

traumatic brain injury (TBI), p. 124

How Is Psychology Related to Substance Abuse Prevention and Treatment?

The death of the musician Prince, in 2016, was a high-profile example of the increasing toll from opioid abuse, described in this chapter. While Prince reportedly used fentanyl and prescription medicine to relieve chronic pain, other individuals use and abuse drugs for various reasons: stimulants to increase attention and endurance, marijuana to alter mood or consciousness, or alcohol to relax in social settings.

Although most people who report using recreational drugs can avoid becoming addicted, more than 22 million people are estimated to require treatment for drug and alcohol abuse (Substance Abuse and Mental Health Services Administration [SAMHSA], 2013). Consistent with the increasing need, job prospects for occupations involved in treating and preventing substance abuse are projected to grow by 22 percent in 2014–24 (U.S. Bureau of Labor Statistics, 2015).

College graduates with a bachelor's degree in psychology and interest in how people use and abuse drugs to affect consciousness can find employment in many work settings, including mental health centers, schools, and prisons. Specific jobs include caseworkers in substance abuse treatment clinics or aides in community mental health centers. Social workers coordinate with community agencies to find housing, employment, and treatment options for individuals suffering from substance abuse. Psychiatric nurses and detox specialists work with patients to treat symptoms that accompany drug addiction and withdrawal, and they can guide patients through the process of weaning off drugs.

Graduates with a doctoral or master's degree in clinical or counseling psychology can provide therapy and treatment interventions for individuals who have substance abuse problems. Graduates in this field can work in hospital outpatient clinics or university counseling centers, or be self-employed in private practice settings. Many clinicians also conduct research in the development and treatment of addiction or track trends in the rate of drug abuse, and they are employed at universities and academic centers, such as SAMHSA or the Centers for Disease Control and Prevention (CDC).

The bottom line: Understanding how particular drugs affect consciousness, the reasons individuals seek out and use particular drugs, and the factors by which some people become addicted can lead to a wide range of careers in substance abuse counseling and prevention. Employment in this field is projected to grow at a much faster rate than average.

Want to earn a better grade on your test?
Go to **INQUIZITIVE** to learn and review this chapter's content, with personalized feedback along the way. Practice Tests and accompanying answer keys can be found at the back of the book on page PT-1.

5 Sensation and Perception

Big Questions

- How Does Perception Emerge from Sensation? 164

- How Are We Able to See? 172

- How Are We Able to Hear? 188

- How Are We Able to Taste? 194

- How Are We Able to Smell? 196

- How Are We Able to Feel Touch and Pain? 199

AT THE BEGINNING OF CHAPTER 3, YOU BOUGHT A SLICE OF PIZZA from a sidewalk vendor. The point there was that your entire nervous system was engaged in the experience. Now imagine that you order a cola to go with that slice. The vendor mistakenly hands you a root beer. You're busy eating the pizza, which is everything you hoped it would be, so you don't notice the problem with the soda. At your first taste of the beverage, you nearly spit it out. You do not mind root beer, but because you were expecting a different taste, this time it strikes you as horrible. The point here is that your experience of the world around you, brought to you through your senses, is influenced by your knowledge, expectations, and past experiences.

A number of brain regions work together to convert physical information from the environment into meaningful forms. In this way, light and sound waves, chemicals, air temperature, physical pressure, and so on become phenomena such as the smell of a spring day, the feeling of holding hands, and the sight of a person you love. For psychologists studying sensation and perception, the big questions are: How does perception emerge from sensation? How are we able to see? How are we able to hear? How are we able to taste? How are we able to smell? And how are we able to feel touch and pain?

Learning Objectives

- Distinguish between sensation and perception.

- Describe how sensory information is translated into meaningful signals.

- Explain the concept of threshold. Distinguish between absolute threshold and difference threshold.

- Explain how thresholds are related to signal detection and sensory adaptation.

How Does Perception Emerge from Sensation?

This chapter will discuss how various types of stimuli are detected, how the brain constructs useful information about the world on the basis of what has been detected, and how we use this constructed information to guide ourselves through the world around us. An important lesson in this chapter is that our sensation and perception of the world do not work like a camera or digital recorder, faithfully and passively capturing the physical properties of stimuli we encounter. Rather, our experience of the world (what we see, hear, taste, smell, or touch) results from brain processes that actively construct perceptual experiences from sensory information. This constant conversion of sensation to perception allows us to adapt to the details of our physical environments.

5.1 Sensory Information Is Translated into Meaningful Signals

Imagine that before you take a drink of root beer, you accidentally splash some of the soda on your face. What do your senses tell you? You smell a fragrance, you feel cool and tingly moisture on your skin, and you experience a sharp taste on your tongue. Your sensory systems have detected these features of the soda. This process is sensation.

Sensation is the detection of physical stimuli and transmission of that information to the brain. Physical stimuli can be light or sound waves, molecules of food or odor, or temperature and pressure changes. Sensation is the basic experience of those stimuli. It involves no interpretation of what we are experiencing.

Perception is the brain's further processing, organization, and interpretation of sensory information. Perception results in our conscious experience of the world. Whereas the essence of sensation is detection, the essence of perception is construction of useful and meaningful information about a particular sensation. For example, when you are splashed on the face, you associate the sensations (smell, moist and tingly feeling, and sharp taste) with the perception of root beer.

Say that you drive up to a traffic signal as the light turns green. The light is detected by specialized neurons in your eyes, and those neurons transmit signals to your brain. As a result of these steps, you have sensed the energy: light. When your brain processes the resulting neural signals, you experience the green light and register the meaning of that signal: go! As a result of these additional steps, you have perceived the light and the signal. (The basic movement from sensation to perception is depicted in **FIGURE 5.1.**)

Sensation and perception are integrated into experience. At the same time, experience guides sensation and perception. In other words, the processing of sensory information is a two-way street. **Bottom-up processing** is based on the physical features of the stimulus. As each sensory aspect of a stimulus is processed, the aspects build up into perception of that stimulus. You recognize a splash of root beer based on your experience of the scent, moisture, and taste. **Top-down processing** is how knowledge, expectations, or past experiences shape the interpretation of sensory information. That is, context affects perception: What we expect to see (higher level) influences what we perceive (lower level). We are unlikely to see a blue, apple-shaped object as a real apple because we know from past experience that apples are not blue.

sensation
The detection of external stimuli and the transmission of this information to the brain.

perception
The processing, organization, and interpretation of sensory signals.

bottom-up processing
Perception based on the physical features of the stimulus.

top-down processing
How knowledge, expectations, or past experiences shape the interpretation of sensory information.

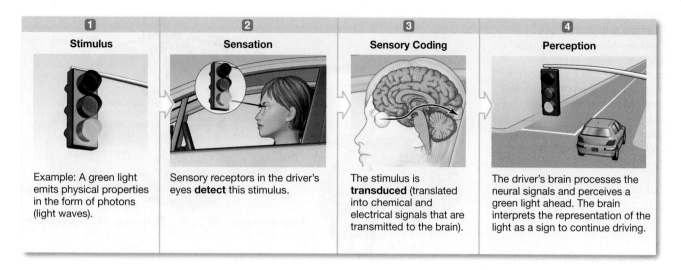

1	**2**	**3**	**4**
Stimulus	Sensation	Sensory Coding	Perception
Example: A green light emits physical properties in the form of photons (light waves).	Sensory receptors in the driver's eyes **detect** this stimulus.	The stimulus is **transduced** (translated into chemical and electrical signals that are transmitted to the brain).	The driver's brain processes the neural signals and perceives a green light ahead. The brain interprets the representation of the light as a sign to continue driving.

FIGURE 5.1
From Sensation to Perception

Consider the incomplete letters in **FIGURE 5.2.** The same shape appears in the center of each word, but you perceive (lower level) the shape first as "H" and then as "A." Your perception depends on which interpretation makes sense in the context of the particular word (higher level). Likewise, Y0U C4N R3AD TH15 PR377Y W3LL even though it is nonsensical. The ability to make sense of "incorrect" stimuli through top-down processing is why proofreading our own writing can be so difficult.

TRANSDUCTION Our sensory systems translate the physical properties of stimuli into patterns of neural impulses. This process is called *sensory coding*. The different features of the physical environment are coded by activity in different neurons. For example, a green stoplight will be coded by a particular neural response pattern in part of the eye before being read by areas of the brain involved in perceiving visual information.

When a hand touches a hot skillet, that information must be sent to the brain. The brain cannot process the physical stimuli directly, so the stimuli must be translated into signals the brain can interpret. The translation of stimuli is called **transduction.** This process involves specialized cells in the sense organs, called *sensory receptors*. The sensory receptors receive stimulation—physical stimulation in the case of vision, hearing, and touch, but chemical stimulation in the case of taste and smell. The sensory receptors then pass the resulting impulses to the brain in the form of neural impulses. With the exception of smell, most sensory information first goes to the thalamus, a structure in the middle of the brain (see Figure 3.22). With smell, sensory information bypasses the thalamus and goes directly to the cortex. Information from each sense other than smell is projected separately from the thalamus to a specific region of the cerebral cortex. In these primary sensory areas, the perceptual process begins in earnest (**FIGURE 5.3;** see also Figure 3.23).

Each sense organ contains different types of receptors designed to detect different types of stimuli. For example, receptors in the visual system respond only to light waves and can signal only visual information. (**TABLE 5.1** lists the stimuli, receptors, and pathways to the brain for each major sensory system.)

THE CAT

FIGURE 5.2
Context
Context plays an important role in object recognition.

transduction

The process by which sensory stimuli are converted to signals the brain can interpret.

FIGURE 5.3

Primary Sensory Areas

These are the primary brain regions where information about vision, hearing, taste, smell, and touch are projected. Visual information travels in separate "streams"—what you see and where it is—from the occipital lobe (visual cortex) to different parts of the brain for further processing.

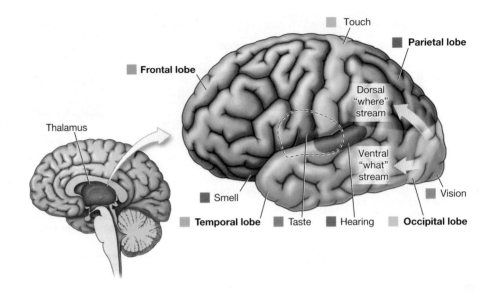

QUALITY VERSUS QUANTITY To function effectively, the brain needs *qualitative* and *quantitative* information about a stimulus. Qualitative information consists of the most basic qualities of a stimulus. For example, it is the difference between a tuba's honk and a flute's toot. It is the difference between a salty taste and a sweet one. Quantitative information consists of the degree, or magnitude, of those qualities: the loudness of the honk, the softness of the toot, the relative saltiness or sweetness. If you were approaching a traffic light, qualitative information might include whether the light was red or green. Regardless of the color, quantitative information would include the brightness of the light.

We can identify qualitative differences because different sensory receptors respond to qualitatively different stimuli. In contrast, quantitative differences in stimuli are coded by the rate of a particular neuron's firing. A more rapidly firing neuron is responding at a higher frequency to a more intense stimulus, such as a brighter light, a louder sound, or a heavier weight (**FIGURE 5.4**).

Table 5.1 The Stimuli, Receptors, and Pathways for Each Sense

SENSE	STIMULI	RECEPTORS	PATHWAYS TO THE BRAIN
Vision	Light waves	Light-sensitive rods and cones in retina of eye	Optic nerve
Hearing	Sound waves	Pressure-sensitive hair cells in cochlea of inner ear	Auditory nerve
Taste	Molecules dissolved in fluid on the tongue	Cells in taste buds on the tongue	Portions of facial, glossopharyngeal, and vagus nerves
Smell	Molecules dissolved in fluid on membranes in the nose	Sensitive ends of olfactory mucous neurons in the mucous membranes	Olfactory nerve
Touch	Pressure on the skin	Sensitive ends of touch neurons in skin	Cranial nerves for touch above the neck, spinal nerves for touch elsewhere

Qualitative information:
Sensory receptors respond to qualitative differences by firing in different combinations.

Quantitative information:
Sensory receptors respond to quantitative differences by firing at different rates.

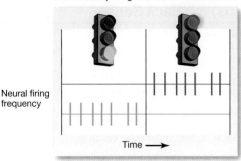
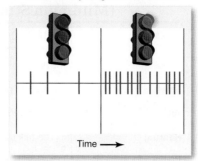

Neural firing frequency

Time ⟶

A green light is coded by different receptors than a red light.

Time ⟶

A bright light causes receptors to fire more rapidly (at a higher frequency) than a dim light.

FIGURE 5.4
Qualitative Versus Quantitative Sensory Information

Sensation and perception result from a symphony of sensory receptors and the neurons those receptors communicate with. The receptors and neurons fire in different combinations and at different rates. The sum of this activity is the huge range of perceptions that make up our experience of the world.

What is transduction?

ANSWER: the translation of physical stimuli received by sensory receptors into signals the brain can interpret

5.2 Detection Requires a Certain Amount of the Stimulus

We have long understood that perceptual experience is constructed from information detected by the sense organs. For more than a century, psychologists have tried to understand the relationship between the world's physical properties and how we sense and perceive them. *Psychophysics,* a subfield developed during the nineteenth century by the researchers Ernst Weber and Gustav Fechner, examines our psychological experiences of physical stimuli. For example, how much physical energy is required for our sense organs to detect a stimulus? How much change is required before we notice that change? To test such things, researchers present very subtle changes in stimuli and observe how participants respond. Perception researchers study the limits of humans' sensory systems.

absolute threshold
The minimum intensity of stimulation that must occur before you experience a sensation.

SENSORY THRESHOLDS Your sensory organs constantly acquire information from your environment. You do not notice much of this information. It has to surpass some level before you can detect it. The **absolute threshold** is the minimum intensity of stimulation that must occur before you experience a sensation. In other words, it is the stimulus intensity you would detect more often than by chance. The absolute threshold for hearing is the faintest sound a person can detect 50 percent of the time (**FIGURE 5.5**). For instance, how loudly must someone in the next room whisper for you to hear it? In this case, the absolute threshold for auditory stimuli would be

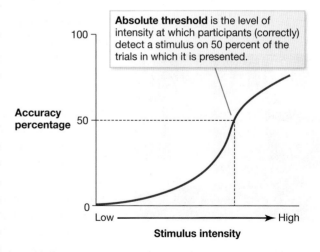

Absolute threshold is the level of intensity at which participants (correctly) detect a stimulus on 50 percent of the trials in which it is presented.

100

Accuracy percentage 50

0

Low ⟶ High

Stimulus intensity

FIGURE 5.5
Absolute Threshold
This graph shows the relation between the intensity of stimulus input and a person's ability to correctly detect the input.

Table 5.2 Approximate Absolute Sensory Threshold (Minimum Stimulus) for Each Sense

SENSE	MINIMUM STIMULUS
Taste	1 teaspoon of sugar in 2 gallons of water
Smell	1 drop of perfume diffused into the entire volume of six rooms
Touch	A fly's wing falling on your cheek from a distance of 0.04 inch
Hearing	The tick of a clock at 20 feet under quiet conditions
Vision	A candle flame seen at 30 miles on a dark, clear night

Source: Galanter (1962).

FIGURE 5.6
Difference Threshold
How much does the television volume need to change for you to notice? That amount of change is the difference threshold.

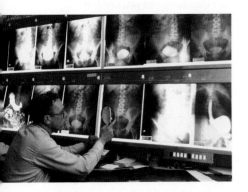

FIGURE 5.7
Signal Detection Theory
Radiology illustrates the subjective nature of detecting a stimulus.

the quietest whisper you could hear half the time. (**TABLE 5.2** lists some approximate minimum stimuli for each sense.)

A **difference threshold,** sometimes called a *just noticeable difference,* is the smallest difference between two stimuli that you can notice. In other words, it is the minimum amount of change required for a person to detect a difference. If your friend is watching a television show while you are reading and a commercial comes on that is louder than the show, you might look up, noticing that something has changed (**FIGURE 5.6**). The difference threshold is the minimum change in volume required for you to detect a difference.

The difference threshold increases as the stimulus becomes more intense. Pick up a 1-ounce letter and a 2-ounce letter, and you will easily detect the difference. But pick up a 5-pound package and a package that weighs 1 ounce more, and the difference will be harder, maybe impossible, to tell. The principle at work here is called *Weber's law.* This law states that the just noticeable difference between two stimuli is based on a proportion of the original stimulus rather than on a fixed amount of difference. That is, the more intense the stimulus, the bigger the change needed for you to notice.

SIGNAL DETECTION THEORY According to classical psychophysics, sensory thresholds were unambiguous. Either you detected something or you did not, depending on whether the intensity of the stimulus was above or below a particular level. As research progressed, it became clear that early psychophysicists had ignored the fact that people are bombarded by competing stimuli, from the "noise" produced by both internal stimuli (moods, emotions, memory, physical states such as nausea) and to other external stimuli (loud noises such as a baby crying, a bitterly cold wind, a cluttered room). The competing internal and external sources affect judgment and attention.

Imagine you are a participant in a study of sensory thresholds. You are sitting in a dark room, and an experimenter asks if you heard a sound. You didn't hear anything, but you might second-guess yourself since someone has asked about it. You might even convince yourself that you sensed a weak stimulus.

After realizing that their methods of testing absolute thresholds were flawed, researchers formulated **signal detection theory (SDT).** This theory states that detecting a stimulus is not an objective process. Detecting a stimulus is instead a subjective decision with two components: (1) sensitivity to the stimulus in the presence of distractions from other stimuli and (2) the criteria used to make the judgment from ambiguous information (Green & Swets, 1966).

Suppose that a radiologist is looking for the kind of faint shadow that, among other possibilities, might signal an early-stage cancer (**FIGURE 5.7**). The radiologist's judgment can be influenced by knowledge about the patient (e.g., age, sex, family medical history), medical training, experience, motivation, and attention. The radiologist's judgment can also be influenced by awareness of the consequences: Being wrong could mean missing a fatal cancer or, conversely, causing unnecessary and potentially dangerous treatment.

Any research study on signal detection involves a series of trials in which a stimulus is presented in only some trials. In each trial, the participant must state whether he or she sensed the stimulus. A trial of this kind, in which a participant judges whether an event occurs, can have one of four outcomes. If the signal is presented and the participant detects it, the outcome is a *hit*. If the participant fails to detect the signal, the outcome is a *miss*. If the participant "detects" a signal that was not presented, the outcome is a *false alarm*. If the signal is not presented and the participant does not detect it, the outcome is a *correct rejection* (**FIGURE 5.8**). The participant's sensitivity to the signal is usually computed by a formula comparing the hit rate with the false alarm rate. This comparison corrects for any bias the participant might bring to the testing situation.

Response bias is a participant's tendency to report detecting the signal in an ambiguous trial. The participant might be strongly biased against responding and need a great deal of evidence that the signal is present. Under other conditions, that same participant might need only a small amount of evidence.

SENSORY ADAPTATION Our sensory systems are tuned to detect changes in our surroundings. It is important for us to be able to detect such changes because they might require responses. It is less important to keep responding to unchanging stimuli. **Sensory adaptation** is a decrease in sensitivity to a constant level of stimulation (**FIGURE 5.9**).

Imagine you are studying and work begins at a nearby construction site. When the equipment starts up, the sound seems particularly loud and disturbing. After a few minutes, the noise seems to have faded into the background. Researchers have often noticed that if a stimulus is presented continuously, the responses of the sensory systems that detect it tend to diminish over time. Similarly, when a continuous stimulus stops, the sensory systems usually respond strongly as well. If the construction noise suddenly halted, you would likely notice the silence.

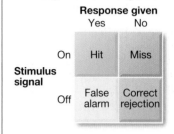

There are four possible outcomes when a participant is asked whether something occurred during a trial:

	Response given	
	Yes	No
Stimulus signal On	Hit	Miss
Off	False alarm	Correct rejection

Those who are biased toward reporting a signal tend to be "yea-sayers." They have many false alarms:

	Response given	
	Yes	No
Stimulus signal On	89%	11%
Off	41%	59%

Those who are biased toward denying that a signal occurred tend to be "nay-sayers." They have many misses:

	Response given	
	Yes	No
Stimulus signal On	45%	55%
Off	26%	74%

FIGURE 5.8
Payoff Matrices for Signal Detection Theory
The percentages in this figure were invented to show representative numbers. Actual percentages vary from question to question.

FIGURE 5.9
Sensory Adaptation
Because of sensory adaptation, people who live near constant noise eventually become less aware of the noise. Pictured here are homes near London's Heathrow Airport.

sensory adaptation
A decrease in sensitivity to a constant level of stimulation.

Q When watching for a friend, you mistakenly wave to someone who looks like your friend but is not. In signal detection terms, what type of outcome is this?

ANSWER: It is a false alarm, because you detected a signal that was not really present.

5.3 The Brain Constructs Stable Representations

Right this minute, your brain is making millions of calculations to produce a coherent experience of your environment. Despite the illusion that the objects and events you are experiencing exist in the space around you, your experience is a construction of your brain and resides inside your skull. Neurons inside your brain do not directly experience the outside world. Instead, they communicate with other neurons inside and outside your brain. Neurons talk to neurons in total darkness. Yet your conscious experience of the world emerges from this communication. This process happens in milliseconds.

If you lay this book flat and look at the pages as a whole, you will see one image. You will not see the thousands of images that dance across your eyes to create a constant, perhaps static view. What you perceive, then, is vastly different from the pattern of stimulation your eyes are taking in. If you were aware of what your brain was doing every moment, you would be paralyzed by information overload. Most of the computations the brain performs never reach your consciousness. Only important new outcomes do.

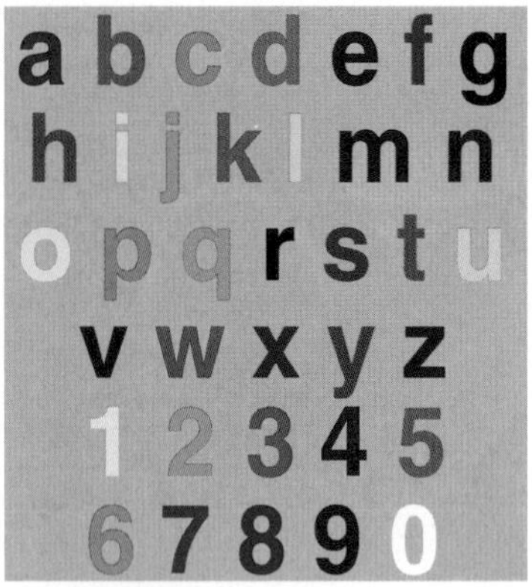

FIGURE 5.10
Synesthesia
This figure is an artistic rendering of the color/letter and color/number associations for one person with synesthesia.

SYNESTHESIA Although the brain creates stable representations, sometimes the resulting experience is quite unusual. Consider the case of Bill, who hates driving because the sight of road signs tastes like a mixture of pistachio ice cream and earwax (McNeil, 2006). This sort of experience—such as when a visual image has a taste—is called *synesthesia*. For another person with synesthesia, M.M., any personal name has a specific taste; for example, the name John tastes like corn bread (Simner et al., 2006). For others with synesthesia, colors evoke smells, sights evoke sounds, and numbers come in colors (e.g., 5 is always green, 2 is always orange; **FIGURE 5.10**). For each person, the associations do not vary—if road signs have a taste, for example, they always taste the same. Reports of people with synesthesia date as far back as ancient Greece (Ferry, 2002). Estimates of the percentage of the population that report these cross-sensory experiences range from 1 in 2,000 to 1 in 200. How can we understand such bizarre sensations?

The neurologist V. S. Ramachandran conducted a series of experiments to better understand what is happening when someone reports, for example, that a sound is lime green or that chicken tastes pointy (Ramachandran & Hubbard, 2001). Because the brain area involved in seeing colors is near the brain area involved in understanding numbers, he theorized that in people with color/number synesthesia, these two brain areas are somehow connected. In this situation, one area of the brain might have adopted another area's role. To test his hypothesis, Ramachandran examined brain scans taken of people with synesthesia when they looked at black numbers on a white background. He found evidence of neural activity in the brain area responsible for color vision. Control participants without synesthesia did not experience activity in this brain area when they looked at the same numbers. Although synesthesia is a rare condition, it shows that there is not a perfect correspondence between the physical world and our experience of it. Yes, our brains create stable representations based on the information our senses provide. Our senses often provide imperfect information, however, and our brains often interpret information imperfectly.

Q If a person heard the taste of food, what would this form of perception be called?

ANSWER: synesthesia

5.4 Does ESP Exist?

Do you believe in the so-called sixth sense, the "unexplainable" feeling that something is about to happen? Our many sensory systems provide information about the world, but they are sensitive to only a small range of the energy available in any environment. For instance, dogs can hear much higher frequencies than we can, and many insects can sense energy forms that we cannot detect. Is it possible that other frequencies or energy forms exist and scientists simply have not discovered them? If so, might these undiscovered energy forces allow people to read other people's minds or communicate with ghosts? In other words, could people be able to perceive information beyond ordinary sensory information through extrasensory perception (ESP)?

Many reports of ESP are supported only by anecdotes, not by valid evidence. In addition, many claims about people's ability to predict events can be explained through logic. For instance, if you see a couple fighting all the time, you might predict accurately that they will break up, but that does not make you a psychic. Finally, many instances of apparent ESP appear to be no more than coincidence.

Consider the day that the Nobel Prize–winning physicist Luis Alvarez found himself thinking of a long-lost friend from his college years. A few minutes later, he came across the friend's obituary in a newspaper. Might Alvarez have experienced some sort of premonition? As a scientist, he decided to calculate the probability of this coincidence. He developed reasonable estimates of how often people think about people from their pasts. He calculated that thinking about a person shortly before learning of that person's death likely happens around 3,000 times per year in the United States (Alvarez, 1965). Put another way: About 10 people in the United States in 2017 are likely to have this experience each day just by chance.

The social psychologist Daryl Bem and his collaborator Charles Honorton (1994) claimed to find some evidence of ESP. In their studies, a "sender" in a soundproof booth focused on a randomly generated image. A "receiver" in another room tried to sense the sender's imagery. The receiver was then asked to choose among four alternatives, one of which was correct. By chance, the receivers should have been correct 25 percent of the time. Across 11 studies, however, Bem and Honorton found that receivers were right about 33 percent of the time. Is this evidence of ESP? Many psychologists say that other factors in the experiments might have affected the results. A statistical review of many such studies found little support for ESP (Milton & Wiseman, 2001).

Samuel Moulton and Stephen Kosslyn (2008) conducted an fMRI study to examine brain-functioning evidence for the existence of ESP. Using a sender/receiver paradigm where the sender was in one room and the receiver was in the fMRI scanner, they looked for brain differences between responses to the image the sender was thinking about and another image that was not known to the sender (**FIGURE 5.11**).

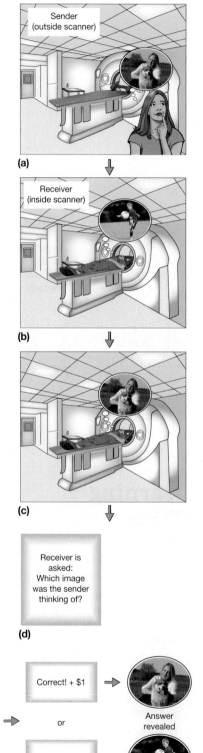

FIGURE 5.11

ESP Research

In Moulton and Kosslyn's 2008 laboratory study, **(a)** the "sender" participant was instructed to think about a particular picture in order to send that "message." **(b)** The "receiver" participant was in an fMRI scanner and was shown a picture unrelated to the one the sender was thinking about. **(c)** The receiver was also shown the picture the sender was thinking about. The fMRI was also recording the recipient's brain activity in response to both images. **(d)** The receiver was then asked to identify which of the two images the sender had in mind. **(e)** For a correct answer, the receiver earned a dollar—an incentive for trying to receive the sender's message.

To enhance the likelihood of effects, they included twins as sender/receiver pairs (since twins are supposed to be especially in tune with one another) and used emotional stimuli (which are supposed to enhance ESP effects). If ESP existed, the receivers' brains should have responded differently to the images the senders thought about than to the images the senders did not see. However, there were absolutely no differences in brain responses. Moulton and Kosslyn argue that since all experience and behavior result from brain activity, the absence of any such activity is strong evidence against the existence of ESP.

Yet in 2011, Bem published a paper that presented data from a series of studies that purported to show evidence of ESP. In an example of these studies, participants were asked to predict where erotic pictures would appear on a computer screen. On each trial, the participant would identify a location before a computer program would independently present the picture. At a rate better than chance, participants were able to predict where the computer would present the erotic images. These findings are highly controversial. Most of the positive results were quite small, and they may have been produced through an inappropriate use of statistical procedures. There has been lively debate since the publication of Bem's study, with Bem arguing that such effects are real (Bem et al., 2015) but most psychologists remaining extremely skeptical (Schwarzkopf, 2014). The only reasonable conclusion is that the evidence for ESP is currently weak or nonexistent and that only careful scientific study will provide conclusive answers (Franklin, Baumgart, & Schooler, 2014). ■

Q | **Does the available evidence support the existence of ESP?**

ANSWER: No. Although there is some debate among psychologists, the evidence is currently not strong enough to demonstrate that ESP is real.

How Are We Able to See?

If we acquire knowledge through our senses, then vision is by far our most important source of knowledge. Vision allows us to perceive information at a distance. Does a place look safe or dangerous? Does a person look friendly or hostile? Even our metaphors for knowledge and for understanding are often visual: "I see," "The answer is clear," "I'm fuzzy on that point." It is not surprising, then, that most of the scientific study of sensation and perception is concerned with vision. Indeed, much of the brain is involved in seeing. Some estimates suggest that up to half of the cerebral cortex may participate in visual perception in some way.

5.5 Sensory Receptors in the Eye Transmit Visual Information to the Brain

Sight seems so effortless, so automatic, that most of us take it for granted. Every time a person opens his or her eyes, that person's brain springs into action to make sense of the energy arriving in the eyes. Of course, the brain can do so only based on sensory signals from the eyes. If the eyes are damaged, the sensory system fails to process new information.

This section focuses on how energy is transduced in the visual system and then perceived, but what we commonly call *seeing* is much more than transducing energy. As the psychologist James Enns notes in his book *The Thinking Eye, the Seeing Brain* (2005), very little of what we call seeing takes place in the eyes. Rather, what

Learning Objectives

- Explain how light is processed by the eyes and the brain.

- Compare and contrast trichromatic and opponent-process theories of color vision.

- Identify the Gestalt principles of perceptual organization.

- Distinguish between binocular and monocular depth cues.

- Describe size perception, motion perception, and object constancies.

we see results from constructive processes that occur throughout much of the brain to produce our visual experiences. In fact, the eyes can be completely normal, but damage to the visual cortex will impair vision.

Some people describe the human eye as working like a crude camera, in that it focuses light to form an image. This analogy does not do justice to the intricate processes that take place in the eye, however. Light first passes through the *cornea*, the eye's thick, transparent outer layer. The cornea focuses the incoming light, which then enters the *lens*. There, the light is bent farther inward and focused to form an image on the **retina**, the thin inner surface of the back of the eyeball. If you shine a light in someone's eyes so that you can see the person's retina, you are in fact looking at the only part of the brain that is visible from outside the skull. In fact, the retina is the one part of the central nervous system that is located where we can see it. The retina contains the sensory receptors that transduce light into neural signals.

More light is focused at the cornea than at the lens. But the lens is adjustable, whereas the cornea is not. The *pupil*, the dark circle at the center of the eye, is a small opening in the front of the lens. By contracting (closing) or dilating (opening), the pupil determines how much light enters the eye. The *iris*, a circular muscle, determines the eye's color and controls the pupil's size. The pupil dilates in dim light but also when we see something we like, such as a beautiful painting or a cute baby (Lick, Cortland, & Johnson, 2016).

Behind the iris, muscles change the shape of the lens. They flatten it to focus on distant objects and thicken it to focus on closer objects. This process is called *accommodation*. The lens and cornea work together to collect and focus light rays reflected from an object. As people get older, the lens hardens and it becomes more difficult to focus on close images, a condition known as *presbyopia*. After age 40, many people require reading glasses when trying to focus on nearby objects.

RODS AND CONES The retina has two types of receptor cells: **rods** and **cones**. The name of each type comes from its distinctive shape. Rods respond at extremely low levels of light and are responsible primarily for night vision. They do not support color vision, and they are poor at fine detail. This is why, on a moonless night, objects appear in shades of gray. In contrast to rods, cones are less sensitive to low levels of light. They are responsible primarily for vision under brighter conditions and for seeing both color and detail. Within the rods and cones, light-sensitive chemicals initiate the transduction of light waves into electrical neural impulses.

Each retina holds approximately 120 million rods and 6 million cones. Near the retina's center, cones are densely packed in a small region called the **fovea.** Although cones are spread throughout the remainder of the retina (except in the blind spot, as you will see shortly), they become increasingly scarce near the outside edge. Conversely, rods are concentrated at the retina's edges. None are in the fovea. If you look directly at a very dim star on a moonless night, the star will appear to vanish. Its light will fall on the fovea, where there are no rods. If you look just to the side of the star, however, the star will be visible. Its light will fall just outside the fovea, where there are rods.

TRANSMISSION FROM THE EYE TO THE BRAIN The visual process begins with the generation of electrical signals by the sensory receptors in the retina. These receptors contain *photopigments*, protein molecules that become unstable and split apart when exposed to light. Rods and cones do not fire action potentials like other neurons. Instead, decomposition of the photopigments alters the membrane potential of the photoreceptors and triggers action potentials in downstream neurons. Immediately after light is transduced by the rods and cones, other cells in the middle layer of the

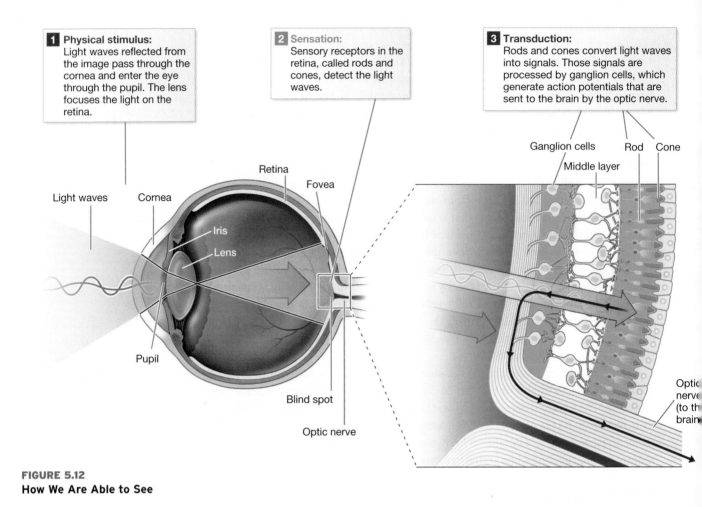

1 Physical stimulus:
Light waves reflected from the image pass through the cornea and enter the eye through the pupil. The lens focuses the light on the retina.

2 Sensation:
Sensory receptors in the retina, called rods and cones, detect the light waves.

3 Transduction:
Rods and cones convert light waves into signals. Those signals are processed by ganglion cells, which generate action potentials that are sent to the brain by the optic nerve.

Ganglion cells

Rod   Cone

Middle layer

Retina

Fovea

Light waves   Cornea

Iris

Lens

Pupil

Blind spot

Optic nerve

Optic nerve (to the brain)

FIGURE 5.12
How We Are Able to See

FIGURE 5.13
Find Your Blind Spot
To find your blind spot using your right eye, hold this book in front of you and look at the dot. Close your left eye. Move the book toward and away from your face until the rabbit's head disappears. You can repeat this exercise for your left eye by turning the book upside down.

retina perform a series of sophisticated computations. The outputs from these cells converge on the retinal *ganglion cells* (**FIGURE 5.12**). Ganglion cells are the first neurons in the visual pathway with axons. During the process of seeing, they are the first neurons to generate action potentials.

The ganglion cells send their signals along their axons from inside the eye to the thalamus. These axons are gathered into a bundle, the *optic nerve*, which exits the eye at the back of the retina. The point at which the optic nerve exits the retina has no rods or cones, producing a blind spot in each eye. If you stretch out one of your arms, make a fist, and look at your fist, the size that your fist appears to you is about the size of your blind spot. The brain normally fills in this gap automatically, so you assume the world continues and are not aware that a blind spot exists in the middle of your field of vision. However, you can find your blind spot by using the exercise in **FIGURE 5.13**.

At the *optic chiasm*, half of the axons in the optic nerves cross. (The axons that cross are the ones that start from the portion of the retina nearest the nose.) This arrangement causes all information from the left side of visual space (i.e., everything visible to the left of the point of gaze) to be projected to the right hemisphere of the brain, and vice versa. In each case, the information reaches the visual areas of the thalamus and then travels to the *primary visual cortex*, cortical areas in the occipital lobes at the back of the head. The pathway from the retina to this region carries all the information that we consciously experience as seeing.

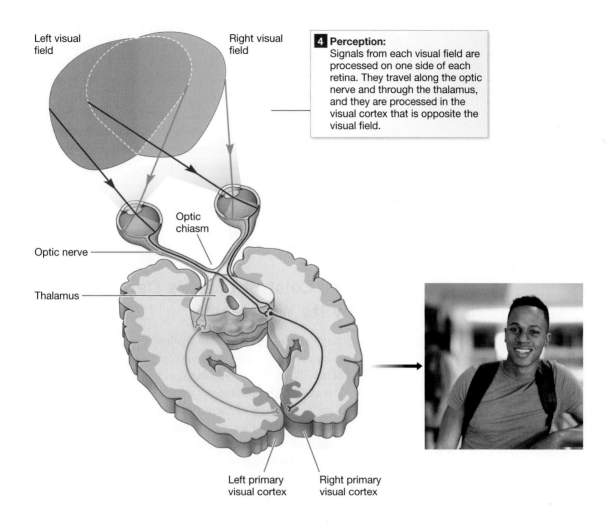

Left visual field

Right visual field

4 Perception:
Signals from each visual field are processed on one side of each retina. They travel along the optic nerve and through the thalamus, and they are processed in the visual cortex that is opposite the visual field.

Optic chiasm

Optic nerve

Thalamus

Left primary visual cortex

Right primary visual cortex

"WHAT" AND "WHERE" PATHWAYS One important theory proposes that visual areas beyond the primary visual cortex form two parallel processing streams, or pathways. The lower, *ventral stream* appears to be specialized for the perception and recognition of objects, such as determining their colors and shapes. The upper, *dorsal stream* seems to be specialized for spatial perception—determining where an object is and relating it to other objects in a scene. (Both streams are shown in Figure 5.3.) These two processing streams are therefore known as the *"what" stream* and the *"where" stream* (Ungerleider & Mishkin, 1982).

Damage to certain regions of the visual cortex provides evidence for distinguishing between these two streams of information. Consider the case of D.F. (Goodale & Milner, 1992). At age 34, she suffered carbon monoxide poisoning that damaged her visual system. Regions involved in the "what" pathway were particularly damaged. D.F. was no longer able to recognize the faces of her friends and family members, common objects, or even drawings of squares or of circles. She could recognize people by their voices, however, and objects if they were placed in her hands. Her condition—*object agnosia*, the inability to recognize objects—was striking in what she could and could not do. For example, if she were asked to draw an apple, she could do so from memory. But when shown a drawing of an apple, she could not identify or reproduce it.

Nonetheless, D.F. could use visual information about the size, shape, and orientation of the apple to control visually guided movements. She could reach around other objects and grab the apple. In performing this action, D.F. would put exactly the right distance between her fingers, even though she could not tell you what she was going to pick up or how large it was. Because D.F.'s conscious visual perception of objects—her "what" pathway—was impaired, she was not aware of taking in any visual information about objects she saw. Because her "where" pathway appeared to be intact, these regions of her visual cortex allowed her to use information about the size and location of objects despite her lack of awareness about those objects. As illustrated by D.F.'s case, different neurological systems operate independently to help us understand the world around us.

 Q **Does the fovea have more rods or cones?**

ANSWER: The fovea has only cones, no rods.

5.6 The Color of Light Is Determined by Its Wavelength

We can distinguish among millions of shades of color. An object appears to be a particular color, however, because of the wavelengths of light it reflects. The color is not a property of the object. It is a weird but true fact: Color does not exist in the physical world. Color is always a product of our visual system.

Visible light consists of electromagnetic waves ranging in length from about 400 to 700 nanometers (abbreviated *nm*; this length is about one billionth of a meter). In simplest terms, the color of light is determined by the wavelengths of the electromagnetic waves that reach the eye. In the center of the retina, the cone cells transduce light into neural impulses in downstream neurons. Different theories account for this transduction.

TRICHROMATIC THEORY According to the *trichromatic theory*, color vision results from activity in three different types of cones. These receptors are sensitive to different wavelengths. One type of cone is most sensitive to short wavelengths (blue–violet light), another type is most sensitive to medium wavelengths (yellow–green light), and the third type is most sensitive to long wavelengths (red–orange light; **FIGURE 5.14**). The three types of cones in the retina are therefore called "S," "M," and "L" cones because they respond maximally to short, medium, and long wavelengths, respectively. For example, yellow light looks yellow because it stimulates the L and M cones about equally and hardly stimulates the S cones. In fact, we can create yellow light by combining red light and green light because each type of light stimulates the corresponding cone population. As far as the brain can tell, there is no difference between yellow light and a combination of red light and green light!

There are two main types of color blindness, determined by the relative activity among the three types of cone receptors. The term *blindness* is somewhat misleading, because these people do see color. They just have partial blindness for certain colors. People may be missing the photopigment sensitive to either medium or long wavelengths, resulting in red–green color blindness. Alternatively, they may be missing the short-wavelength photopigment, resulting in blue–yellow

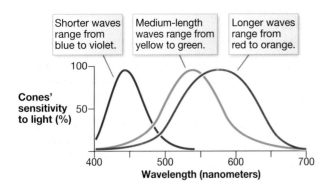

FIGURE 5.14

The Experience of Color

The color of light is determined by the wavelength of the electromagnetic wave that reaches the eye. This graph shows the percentage of light at different wavelengths that is absorbed by each kind of cone.

color blindness (**FIGURE 5.15**). These genetic disorders occur in about 8 percent of males but less than 1 percent of females.

OPPONENT-PROCESS THEORY Some aspects of color vision, however, cannot be explained by the responses of three types of cones in the retina. For example, why can some people with red–green color blindness see yellow? In addition, people have trouble visualizing certain color mixtures. It is easier to imagine reddish yellow or bluish green, say, than reddish green or bluish yellow. In addition, some colors seem to be "opposites."

An alternative to trichromatic theory is *opponent-process theory* (Hering, 1878/1964). According to this theory, red and green are opponent colors, as are blue and yellow. When we stare at a red image for some time, we see a green afterimage when we look away; when we stare at a green image, we see a red afterimage. In the former case, the receptors for red become fatigued when you stare at red. The green receptors are not fatigued and therefore the afterimage appears green (**FIGURE 5.16**).

Since colors are themselves optical effects, how do we account for what appear to be opponent colors? For this explanation, we must turn to the second stage in visual processing. This stage occurs in the ganglion cells—the cells that make up the optic nerve, which carries information to the brain. Different combinations of cones converge on the ganglion cells in the retina. One type of ganglion cell receives excitatory input from L cones (the ones that respond to long wavelengths, which are seen as red), but it is inhibited by M cones (medium wavelengths, which are seen as green). Cells of this type create the perception that red and green are opponents. Another type of ganglion cell is excited by input from S cones (short wavelengths, which are seen as blue), but it is inhibited by both L- and M-cone activity (when light includes long and medium wavelengths, the perception is of yellow). These different types of ganglion cells, working in opposing pairs, create the perception that blue and yellow are opponents.

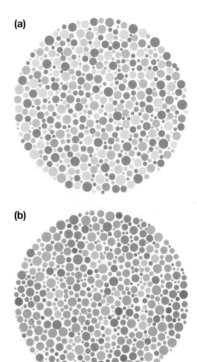

(a)

(b)

FIGURE 5.15
Red-Green Color Blindness
You should be able to see the number 45 in one of these circles. **(a)** If you are not red-green color-blind, you will see 45 here. **(b)** If you are red-green color-blind, you will see 45 here.

HUE, SATURATION, AND LIGHTNESS Ultimately, how the brain converts physical energy to the experience of color is quite complex and can be understood only by considering the response of the visual system to different wavelengths at the same time. In fact, when we see white light, our eyes are receiving the entire range of wavelengths in the visible spectrum (**FIGURE 5.17**).

Color is categorized along three dimensions: hue, saturation, and lightness. *Hue* consists of the distinctive characteristics that place a particular color in the spectrum—the color's greenness or orangeness, for example. These characteristics depend primarily on the light's dominant wavelength when it reaches the eye. *Saturation* is the purity of the color. Saturation varies according to the mixture of wavelengths in a stimulus. Basic colors of the spectrum (e.g., blue, green, red) have only one wavelength, whereas pastels (e.g., baby blue, lime green, and pink) have a mixture of many wavelengths, so they are less pure. *Lightness* is the color's perceived intensity. This characteristic is determined chiefly by the total amount of light reaching the eye. How light something seems also depends on the background, however, since the same color may be perceived differently depending on whether you are looking at it against a bright or dark background (**FIGURE 5.18**).

FIGURE 5.16
Afterimage
For at least 30 seconds, stare at this version of the Union Jack, flag of the United Kingdom. Then look at the blank space to the right. Because your receptors have adapted to the green and orange in the first image, the afterimage appears in the opponent colors red and blue. You can tell that afterimages are caused by events in the retina, because the afterimage moves with you as you move your eyes, as though it is "painted" on the retina.

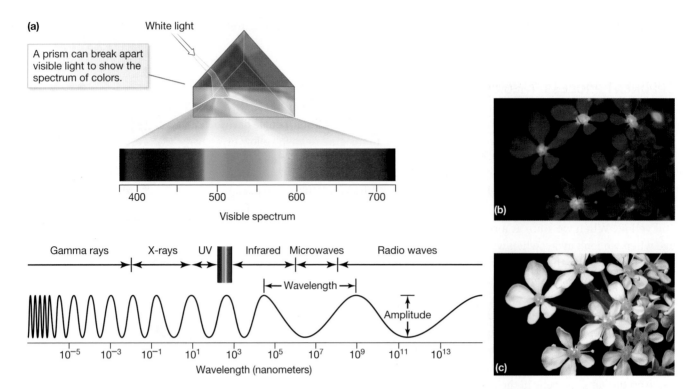

(a)

White light

A prism can break apart visible light to show the spectrum of colors.

400   500   600   700

Visible spectrum

Gamma rays   X-rays   UV   Infrared   Microwaves   Radio waves

←— Wavelength —→

Amplitude

10^{-5} 10^{-3} 10^{-1} 10^{1} 10^{3} 10^{5} 10^{7} 10^{9} 10^{11} 10^{13}

Wavelength (nanometers)

(b)

(c)

FIGURE 5.17
The Color Spectrum
(a) When white light shines through a prism, the spectrum of color that is visible to humans is revealed. As shown here, the visible color spectrum is only a small part of the electromagnetic spectrum: It consists of electromagnetic wavelengths from just under 400 nm (the color violet) to just over 700 nm (the color red). By using night-vision goggles, humans are able to see infrared waves (i.e., waves below red in terms of frequency). **(b)** Some insects can see ultraviolet light (i.e., light greater than violet in terms of frequency). This ability helps them find a flower's nectar glands, which can appear fluorescent in UV illumination. **(c)** When humans view the same flowers under visible light, they do not see the same nectar patterns that the insects see.

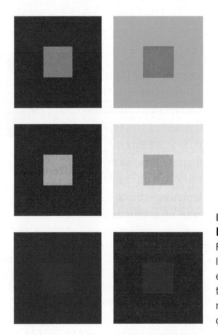

FIGURE 5.18
Lightness
For each pair, which central square is lighter? In fact, the central squares in each pair are identical. Most people see the gray square that is surrounded with red, for example, as lighter than the gray square surrounded with green.

ANSWER: Opponent-process theory best explains afterimages. According to this theory, staring at one color causes receptor fatigue. Looking elsewhere then leads unfatigued receptors for the "opposing" color to produce an afterimage.

Are afterimages best explained by trichromatic theory or opponent-process theory? How so?

5.7 Perceiving Objects Requires Organization of Visual Information

Within the brain, what exactly happens to the information the senses take in about an object's features? How does that information get organized? Optical illusions are among the tools psychologists have for understanding how the brain uses such information. Many perceptual psychologists believe that illusions reveal the mechanisms that help visual systems determine the sizes and distances of objects in the environment. In doing so, illusions illustrate how we form accurate representations of the three-dimensional world. Researchers rely on these tricks to reveal automatic perceptual systems that, in most circumstances, result in accurate perception (**FIGURE 5.19**).

GESTALT PRINCIPLES OF PERCEPTUAL ORGANIZATION *Gestalt* is a German word that means "shape" or "form." Gestalt psychologists theorized that perception is more than the result of accumulating sensory data. They postulated that the brain uses innate principles to organize sensory information into organized wholes. These principles explain why we perceive, say, "a car" as opposed to "metal, tires, glass, door handles, hubcaps, fenders," and so on. For us, an object exists as a unit, not as a collection of features. The Gestalt perceptual grouping rules include:

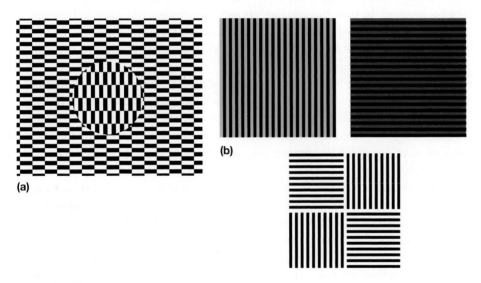

(a)

(b)

FIGURE 5.19
Optical Illusions
(a) The Ouchi illusion was named for the Japanese artist Hajime Ouchi, who invented it. This illusion shows how we separate a figure from its background. The circle is made of lines offset from the rest of the display. Scrolling the image horizontally or vertically gives a much stronger effect. Some people report seeing colors and movement. **(b)** The McCollough effect was named for the vision researcher Celeste McCollough, who first described it. Alternate your gaze from the green stimulus with vertical lines to the magenta stimulus with horizontal lines, changing from one to the other about every second for 40 seconds. Then look at the black-and-white stimulus with horizontal and vertical lines. You should see magenta vertical lines and green horizontal lines. Because the McCollough effect can last for hours or even a day, it cannot be explained by simple neural fatigue (where neurons reduce firing after repeated use). For this reason, the effect more likely occurs in higher brain regions, not in the eye. As noted in the text, the visual system is especially primed to process information about edges, and color-related edge perception may be involved.

FIGURE 5.20
Proximity
These 16 squares are not necessarily part of any group. Because of the Gestalt principle of proximity, they appear to be grouped as three objects.

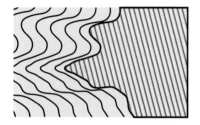

FIGURE 5.21
Similarity
Because of similarity, this rectangle appears to consist of two locked pieces.

FIGURE 5.22
Good Continuity
We tend to interpret intersecting lines as continuous. Here, as a result, the green bar appears to be completely behind the purple occluder.

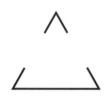

FIGURE 5.23
Closure
We find it difficult to see these forms as separate, not parts of a triangle.

- *Proximity:* The closer two figures are to each other, the more likely we are to group them and see them as part of the same object (**FIGURE 5.20**).
- *Similarity:* We tend to group figures according to how closely they resemble each other, whether in shape, color, or orientation (**FIGURE 5.21**).

In accordance with the principles of similarity and proximity, we tend to cluster elements of the visual scene. Clustering enables us to consider a scene as a whole rather than as individual parts. For example, we often perceive a flock of birds as a single entity because all the elements, the birds, are similar and in close proximity.

- *Continuity:* We tend to group together edges or contours that have the same orientation, known as "good continuation" to Gestalt psychologists. Good contour (boundary line) continuation appears to play a role in completing an object behind an occluder, which can be anything that hides a portion of an object or an entire object from view (**FIGURE 5.22**).
- *Closure:* We tend to complete figures that have gaps (**FIGURE 5.23**).
- *Illusory contours:* We sometimes perceive contours and cues to depth even when they do not exist (**FIGURE 5.24**).

FIGURE AND GROUND One of the visual perception system's most basic organizing principles is distinguishing between figure and ground. A classic illustration is the *reversible figure illusion.* Look back at Figure 1.18, where you can see either a full face or two faces looking at each other—but not both at the same time. In identifying either figure—indeed, *any* figure—the brain assigns the rest of the scene to the background. In this illusion, the "correct" assignment of figure and ground is ambiguous. The figures periodically reverse (switch back and forth) as the visual system strives to make sense of the stimulation. In ways like this, visual perception is dynamic and ongoing.

Richard Nisbett and colleagues (2001) have demonstrated cultural differences between Eastern people's perceptions and Western people's perceptions. Easterners focus on a scene holistically, whereas Westerners focus on single elements in the forefront. Thus, Easterners are more likely to be influenced by the (back)ground of a figure, and Westerners are more likely to extract the figure from its (back)ground.

Now look back at Figure 1.17. In this illusion, it is hard to see the Dalmatian standing among the many black spots scattered on the white background. This effect occurs because the part of the image corresponding to the dog lacks contours that define the dog's edges and because the dog's spotted coat resembles the background. Many observers find that they first recognize one part of the dog—say, the head. From that detail, they are able to discern the dog's shape. Once you perceive the dog, it becomes difficult to *not* see it the next time you look at the figure. Thus, experience can inform shape processing.

FACE PERCEPTION One special class of objects that the visual system is sensitive to is faces. Indeed, any pattern in the world that has face-like qualities will look like a face (**FIGURE 5.25**). As highly social animals, humans are well able to perceive and interpret facial expressions. Several studies support the idea that human faces reveal "special" information that is not available in any other way. For example, we can more readily discern information about a person's mood, attentiveness, sex, race, age, and so on by looking at that person's face than by listening to the person talk, watching the person walk, or studying his or her clothing (Bruce & Young, 1986).

People are better at recognizing members of their own race or ethnic group, however, than at recognizing members of other races or ethnic groups. There is some truth to the saying that others *all look alike*, but the saying applies to all groups. This effect may occur because people have more exposure to people of their own race or ethnicity (Gosselin & Larocque, 2000). In the United States, where whites greatly outnumber blacks, whites are much better at recognizing white faces than at recognizing black faces (Brigham & Malpass, 1985).

Some people have particular deficits in the ability to recognize faces—a condition known as *prosopagnosia*—but not in the ability to recognize other objects (Susilo & Duchaine, 2013). Patient D.F., also discussed earlier in this chapter, has prosopagnosia, so she cannot tell one face from another. Still, she is able to judge whether something is a face or not and whether that face is upside down or not. This ability implies that facial recognition differs from nonfacial object recognition (Steeves et al., 2006).

Faces are so important that certain brain regions appear to be dedicated solely to perceiving them (Haxby, Hoffman, & Gobbini, 2000). As part of the "what" stream discussed earlier, the *fusiform gyrus* in the right hemisphere is important for perceiving faces (Grill-Spector, Knouf, & Kanwisher, 2004; McCarthy, Puce, Gore, & Allison, 1997). Indeed, this brain area responds most strongly to upright faces, as we would perceive them in the normal environment (Kanwisher, Tong, & Nakayama, 1998).

People have a surprisingly hard time recognizing faces, especially unknown faces, that are upside down. We are much worse at this task than we are at recognizing other inverted objects. The inversion interferes with the way people perceive the relationships among facial features (Hayward et al., 2016). For instance, if the eyebrows are bushier than usual, this facial characteristic is obvious if the face is upright but not detectable when the face is inverted. One interesting example of the perceptual difficulties associated with inverted faces is evident in the Thatcher illusion (Thompson, 1980; **FIGURE 5.26**).

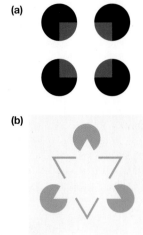

(a)

(b)

FIGURE 5.24
Illusory Contours
(a) Here, the contours are implied. **(b)** Here, the cues to depth are implied. The triangle is an illusion created by our visual system. It also appears brighter than the surrounding area, as would be expected if it were closer to us.

FIGURE 5.25
Face Perception
A face that appears to be crying can be seen in this dramatic photo of a Norwegian glacier.

FIGURE 5.26
The Thatcher Illusion
This effect got its name because it was first studied using photos of the former British prime minister Margaret Thatcher. Here, the two inverted pictures of Mila Kunis look normal. Turn your book upside down to reveal a different perspective. We tend to see the two faces as identical because the overall configuration is similar and we fail to notice the distortion. This effect implies that we pay most attention to the eyes and mouth. As long as those features are oriented correctly, the rest of the face appears normal even if it is not.

In a series of studies, researchers found that people more quickly and accurately recognize angry facial expressions than happy ones (Becker, Kenrick, Neuberg, Blackwell, & Smith, 2007). In addition, the researchers found that most people recognize anger more quickly on a man's face than on a woman's, and they found the reverse for happiness. The researchers think these results are due partly to people's beliefs that men express anger more often than women do and that women express happiness more often than men do (i.e., the beliefs would be contributing to top-down processing—we are more likely to "see" what we expect to see). They also think that female and male facial features drive the effect. For example, bushy eyebrows low on the face are more likely to be perceived as an expression of anger, and men typically have bushier and lower eyebrows than women.

According to evolutionary psychology, there is an adaptive advantage to the detection of angry faces. Given that men in every society commit most violent crimes, it is adaptive to be especially fast and accurate at recognizing angry male faces. Thus, facial recognition supports an idea emphasized throughout this book: The brain is adaptive.

Q How do the Gestalt principles of proximity and similarity help explain our visual perceptions of crowds?

ANSWER: According to the principle of proximity, we tend to group objects that are close together. According to similarity, we tend to group objects that share aspects. So when we look at large gatherings, we tend to group the people rather than see them as individuals.

5.8 Perception Is Guided by Cues in the Environment

When we look at an array of objects and a photograph of that array, both scenes create the exact same image on the retina. Despite this inherent ambiguity, we do not confuse the real, three-dimensional scene with the two-dimensional picture of it. Why not? Consider, too, that when an object moves past us, it may look completely different from the back than from the front, and its image grows smaller as the object moves away, yet we still know it is the same object. How do we do that? Such forms of perception result from environmental cues.

DEPTH PERCEPTION We are able to perceive depth in the two-dimensional patterns of photographs, movies, videos, and television images because the brain applies the same rules or mechanisms that it uses to work out the spatial relations between objects in the three-dimensional world. To do this, the brain draws on its existing knowledge about the appearance of the world. That is, the brain rapidly and automatically exploits certain prior assumptions it has about the relationship between two-dimensional image cues and the three-dimensional world. Among these assumptions are cues that help the visual system perceive depth. These depth cues can be divided into two types: **Binocular depth cues** are available from both eyes together and contribute to bottom-up processing. **Monocular depth cues** are available from each eye alone and provide organizational information for top-down processing.

One of the most important cues to depth perception is **binocular disparity** (or *retinal disparity*). This cue is caused by the distance between humans' two eyes. Because each eye has a slightly different view of the world, the brain has access to two different but overlapping retinal images. The brain uses the disparity between these two retinal images to compute distances to nearby objects

binocular depth cues
Cues of depth perception that arise from the fact that people have two eyes.

monocular depth cues
Cues of depth perception that are available to each eye alone.

binocular disparity
A depth cue; because of the distance between the two eyes, each eye receives a slightly different retinal image.

(**FIGURE 5.27**). The ability to determine an object's depth based on that object's projections to each eye is called *stereoscopic vision*.

A related binocular depth cue is **convergence.** This term refers to the way that the eye muscles turn the eyes inward when we view nearby objects. The brain knows how much the eyes are converging and uses this information to perceive distance (**FIGURE 5.28**).

Although binocular disparity is an important cue for depth perception, it is useful only for relatively close objects. Furthermore, we can perceive depth even with one eye closed, because of monocular depth cues. Artists routinely use these cues to create a sense of depth, so monocular depth cues are also called *pictorial depth cues*. The Renaissance painter, sculptor, architect, and engineer Leonardo da Vinci first identified many of these cues, which include:

- *Occlusion:* A near object occludes (blocks) an object that is farther away.
- *Relative size:* Far-off objects project a smaller retinal image than close objects do, if the far-off and close objects are the same physical size.
- *Familiar size:* Because we know how large familiar objects are, we can tell how far away they are by the size of their retinal images.
- *Linear perspective:* Seemingly parallel lines appear to converge in the distance.
- *Texture gradient:* As a uniformly textured surface recedes, its texture continuously becomes denser.

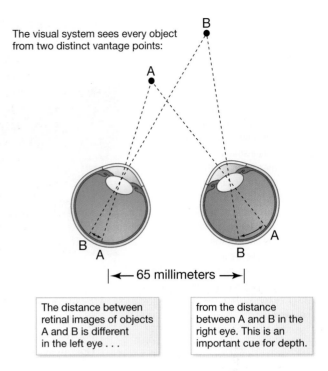

The visual system sees every object from two distinct vantage points:

|←— 65 millimeters —→|

| The distance between retinal images of objects A and B is different in the left eye . . . | from the distance between A and B in the right eye. This is an important cue for depth. |

FIGURE 5.27
Binocular Disparity
To demonstrate your own binocular disparity, hold one of your index fingers out in front of your face and close first one eye and then the other. Your finger appears to move because each eye, due to its position relative to the finger, has a unique retinal image.

convergence
A cue of binocular depth perception; when a person views a nearby object, the eye muscles turn the eyes inward.

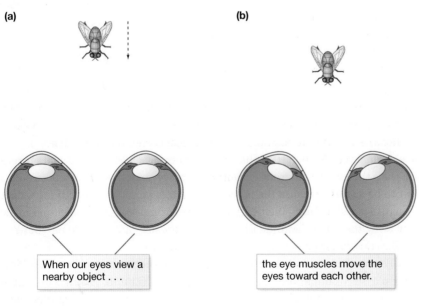

(a)

(b)

When our eyes view a nearby object . . .

the eye muscles move the eyes toward each other.

FIGURE 5.28
Convergence
(a) When viewing things at a distance, the eyes aim out on parallel lines. **(b)** As an object approaches, the eyes converge. To demonstrate such convergence, hold one of your index fingers out in front of your face, about a foot away. Slowly bring your finger toward your eyes. Do you notice your eyes converging?

FIGURE 5.29
Pictorial Depth Cues
In this photo, the cues to depth include **(a)** occlusion, because the woman's head is blocking the building; **(b)** position relative to the horizon, because the woman seems nearer than the people and objects on the sidewalk; **(c)** relative size, because this man projects a smaller retinal image than the men crossing the street; **(d)** familiar size, since our knowledge of car sizes lets us estimate how far away this car is by the size of its retinal image; **(e)** linear perspective, because the lines of the sidewalk appear to converge in the distance; and **(f)** texture gradient, because the pattern on the pavement becomes denser as the surface recedes from view.

▪ *Position relative to horizon:* All else being equal, objects below the horizon that appear higher in the visual field are perceived as being farther away. Objects above the horizon that appear lower in the visual field are perceived as being farther away (**FIGURE 5.29**).

SIZE PERCEPTION For size, distance matters. The size of an object's retinal image depends on that object's distance from the observer. The farther away the object is, the smaller its retinal image. So to determine an object's size, the visual system needs to know how far away the object is. Most of the time, enough depth information is available for the visual system to work out an object's distance and thus infer how large the object is. Size perception sometimes fails, however, and an object may look bigger or smaller than it really is (**FIGURE 5.30**).

This optical illusion arises when normal perceptual processes incorrectly represent the distance between the viewer and the stimuli. In other words, depth cues can fool us into seeing depth when it is not there. Alternatively, a lack of depth cues can fool us into *not* seeing depth when it *is* there. This section considers two phenomena related to both depth perception and distance perception: Ames boxes (also called Ames rooms) and the Ponzo illusion.

Ames boxes were crafted in the 1940s by Adelbert Ames, a painter turned scientist. These constructions present powerful depth illusions. Inside the Ames boxes, rooms play with linear perspective and other distance cues. One such room makes a far corner appear the same distance away as a near corner (**FIGURE 5.31**).

In a normal room and in this Ames box, the nearby child projects a larger retinal image than the child farther away. Normally, however, the nearby child would not appear to be a giant, because the perceptual system would take depth into account when assessing size. Here, the depth cues are wrong, so the nearby child appears farther away than he is, and the disproportionate size of his image on your retina makes him look huge.

The Ponzo illusion, first described by the psychologist Mario Ponzo in 1913, is another classic example of a size/distance illusion (**FIGURE 5.32**). The common explanation for this effect is that monocular depth cues make the two-dimensional figure seem three-dimensional (Rock, 1984). As noted earlier, seemingly parallel lines appear to converge in the distance. Here, the two lines drawn to look like railroad tracks receding in the distance trick your brain into thinking they are parallel. Therefore, you perceive the two parallel lines in the center as if they are at different distances and thus different in size when they actually are the same size.

FIGURE 5.30
Size Perception Depends on Distance
This picture, by Rebecca Robinson, captures what appears to be a tiny Sarah Heatherton standing on James Heatherton's head. This illusion occurs because the photo fails to present depth information: It does not convey the hill on which Sarah is standing.

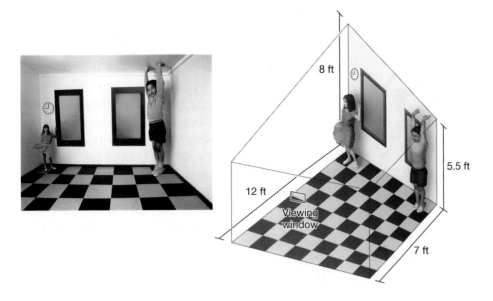

FIGURE 5.31
The Ames Box and Depth Perception
Ames played with depth cues to create size illusions. For example, he made a diagonally cut room appear rectangular by using crooked windows and floor tiles. When one child stands in a near corner and another (of similar height) stands in a far corner, the room creates the illusion that they are the same distance from the viewer. Therefore, the closer child looks like a giant compared with the child farther away.

This illusion shows how much we rely on depth perception to gauge size. The brain defaults to using depth cues even when depth is absent. Once again, the brain responds as efficiently as possible.

MOTION PERCEPTION We know how motion can cue depth perception, but how does the brain perceive motion? One answer is that we have neurons specialized for detecting movement. In other words, these neurons fire when movement occurs. But how does the brain know what is moving? If you look out a window and see a car driving past a house, how does your brain know the car is moving and not the house? Sometimes we can experience the illusion of movement when none is actually present (**FIGURE 5.33**).

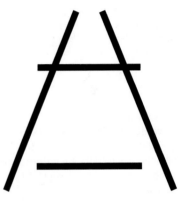

FIGURE 5.32
The Ponzo Illusion
The two horizontal lines appear to be different sizes but are actually the same length.

FIGURE 5.33
The Rotating Snakes Illusion
This illusion was created by the psychologist Akiyoshi Kitaoka, who has specialized in visual perception. Look at the scene for a few minutes. Do you notice some of the distant snakes revolving? The "snakes" are not moving. Their rotation is caused at least partly by your eye movements.

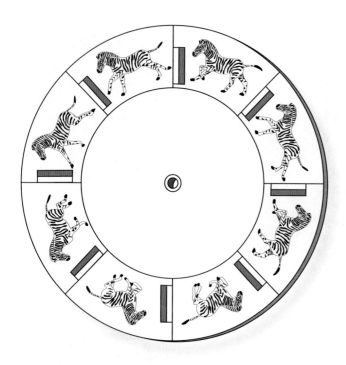

FIGURE 5.34

How Moving Pictures Work

This static series would appear transformed if you spun the wheel. With the slightly different images presented in rapid succession, the stroboscopic movement would tell your brain that you were watching a moving zebra.

Consider the dramatic case of M.P., a German woman. After receiving damage to secondary visual areas of her brain—areas critical for motion perception—M.P. saw the world as a series of snapshots rather than as a moving image (Zihl, von Cramon, & Mai, 1983). Pouring tea, she would see the liquid frozen in air and be surprised when her cup overflowed. Before crossing a street, she might spot a car far away. When she tried to cross, however, that car would be right in front of her. M.P. had a unique deficit: She could perceive objects and colors but not continuous movement.

There are two additional phenomena that offer insights into how the visual system perceives motion: motion aftereffects and stroboscopic motion perception. *Motion aftereffects* may occur when you gaze at a moving image for a long time and then look at a stationary scene. You experience a momentary impression that the new scene is moving in the opposite direction from the moving image. This illusion is also called the waterfall effect, because if you stare at a waterfall and then turn away, the scenery you are now looking at will seem to move upward for a moment.

Motion aftereffects are strong evidence that motion-sensitive neurons exist in the brain. According to the theory that explains this illusion, the visual cortex has neurons that respond to movement in a given direction. When you stare at a moving stimulus long enough, these direction-specific neurons begin to adapt to the motion. That is, they become fatigued and therefore less sensitive. If the stimulus is suddenly removed, the motion detectors that respond to all the other directions are more active than the fatigued motion detectors. Thus, you see the new scene moving in the other direction.

Movies are made up of still-frame images, presented one after the other to create the illusion of motion pictures. This phenomenon is based on *stroboscopic movement*, a perceptual illusion that occurs when two or more slightly different images are presented in rapid succession (**FIGURE 5.34**).

OBJECT CONSTANCY Illusions occur when the brain creates inaccurate representations of stimuli. In the opposite situation, **object constancy,** the brain correctly perceives objects as constant despite sensory data that could lead it to think otherwise. Consider your image in the mirror. What you see in the mirror might look like it is your actual size, but the image is much smaller than the parts of you being reflected. (If you doubt this claim, try tracing around the image of your face in a steamy bathroom mirror.) Similarly, how does the brain know that a person is 6 feet tall when the retinal image of that person changes size according to how near or far the person is? How does the brain know that snow is white and a tire is black, even when snow at night or a tire in bright light might send the same cues to the retina?

For the most part, changing an object's angle, distance, or illumination does not change our perception of that object's size, shape, color, or lightness. But to perceive any of these four constancies, we need to understand the relationship between the object and at least one other factor. For *size constancy*, we need to know how far away

object constancy

Correctly perceiving objects as constant in their shape, size, color, and lightness, despite raw sensory data that could mislead perception.

(a)　(b)

FIGURE 5.35
Size Constancy
When you look at each of these photos, your retinal image of the man in the blue shirt is the same. Why, then, does he appear larger in **(a)** than in **(b)**?

FIGURE 5.36
Object Constancy
The image on the retina is vastly different for these four drawings of a car. Since we know how large a car normally is, knowing how far away the car is from us enables us to maintain size constancy. Knowing the angles we are seeing the car from enables us to maintain shape constancy. The shadows help maintain color and lightness constancy because they suggest the angle of lighting and we know that light makes colors brighter.

the object is from us (**FIGURE 5.35**). For *shape constancy*, we need to know what angle or angles we are seeing the object from. For *color constancy*, we need to compare the wavelengths of light reflected from the object with those reflected from its background. Likewise, for *lightness constancy*, we need to know how much light is being reflected from the object and from its background (**FIGURE 5.36**). In each case, the brain computes the relative magnitude rather than relying on each sensation's absolute magnitude. The perceptual system's ability to make relative judgments allows it to maintain constancy across various perceptual contexts. Although their precise mechanisms are unknown, these constancies illustrate that perceptual systems do not just respond to sensory inputs. Perceptual systems are in fact tuned to detect changes from baseline conditions.

By studying how illusions work, many perceptual psychologists have come to believe that the brain has built-in assumptions that influence perceptions. The vast majority of visual illusions appear to be beyond our conscious control—we cannot make ourselves not see illusions, even when we know they are not true representations of objects or events (**FIGURE 5.37**). Thus, the visual system is a complex interplay of constancies. These constancies enable us to see both a stable world and perceptual illusions that we cannot control.

FIGURE 5.37
The Tabletop Illusion
Created by the psychologist Roger Shepard, this illusion demonstrates the brain's automatic perceptual processes. Even when we know the two tabletops are the same size and shape—even if we have traced one image and placed it on top of the other—perspective cues make us see them as different.

What sensory input in the eye usually determines our perception of an object's size?

ANSWER: The size of the retinal image. The larger the retinal image, the closer an object appears.

HOW ARE WE ABLE TO SEE?

Learning Objectives

- Describe how sound waves are transduced into neural activity in the ear.

- Discuss the advantages and disadvantages of cochlear implants.

- Explain the significance of temporal and place coding for auditory perception.

audition
Hearing; the sense of sound perception.

sound wave
A pattern of changes in air pressure during a period of time; it produces the percept of a sound.

How Are We Able to Hear?

For humans, hearing, or **audition,** is second to vision as a source of information about the world. It is a mechanism for determining what is happening in an environment, and it also provides a medium for spoken language.

The wonders of the auditory system are discussed by Daniel Levitin, a psychologist and former professional musician, in his best-selling book *This Is Your Brain on Music* (2006). Hearing music results from differences in brain activity, not from differentiated sound waves. For instance, when you hear guitars, drums, and singing, nothing in the sound waves themselves tells you which part of the music is which. Yet it is rather easy for most people to pick out the separate features in a piece of music. Through activity in different brain regions, the features all come together to create the experience of music.

5.9 Audition Results from Changes in Air Pressure

The process of hearing begins when the movements and vibrations of objects cause the displacement of air molecules. Displaced air molecules produce a change in air pressure, and that change travels through the air. The pattern of the changes in air pressure during a period of time is called a **sound wave** (FIGURE 5.38).

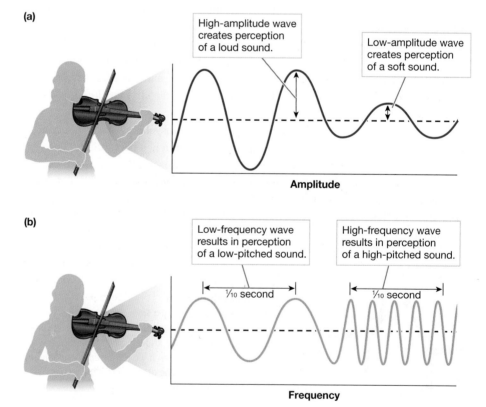

(a)

High-amplitude wave creates perception of a loud sound.

Low-amplitude wave creates perception of a soft sound.

Amplitude

(b)

Low-frequency wave results in perception of a low-pitched sound.

High-frequency wave results in perception of a high-pitched sound.

$\frac{1}{10}$ second $\frac{1}{10}$ second

Frequency

FIGURE 5.38
Sound Waves
The **(a)** amplitude and **(b)** frequency of sound waves are processed into the perceptual experiences of loudness and pitch.

A sound wave's *amplitude* determines its loudness: We hear a higher amplitude as a louder sound. The wave's *frequency* determines its pitch: We hear a higher frequency as a sound that is higher in pitch. The frequency of a sound is measured in vibrations per second, called *hertz* (abbreviated *Hz*). Most humans can detect sound waves with frequencies from about 20 Hz to about 20,000 Hz. Like all other sensory experiences, the sensory experience of hearing occurs within the brain, as the brain integrates the different signals provided by various sound waves.

The ability to hear is based on the intricate interactions of various regions of the ear. When changes in air pressure produce sound waves within a person's hearing distance, those sound waves arrive at the person's *outer ear* and travel down the auditory canal to the **eardrum.** This membrane, stretched tightly across the canal, marks the beginning of the *middle ear*. The sound waves make the eardrum vibrate. These vibrations are transferred to *ossicles*, three tiny bones commonly called the hammer, anvil, and stirrup. The ossicles transfer the eardrum's vibrations to the *oval window*. The oval window is actually a membrane located within the *cochlea*, in the *inner ear*. The cochlea is a fluid-filled tube that curls into a snail-like shape, with a membrane at the end called the *round window*. Running through the center of the cochlea is the thin *basilar membrane*. The oval window's vibrations create pressure waves in the cochlear fluid; these waves prompt the basilar membrane to oscillate. Movement of the basilar membrane stimulates *hair cells* to bend and to send information to the *auditory nerve*. These hair cells are the primary auditory receptors. Thus, sound waves, which are mechanical signals, hit the eardrum and are converted to neural signals that travel to the brain along the auditory nerve. This conversion of sound waves to brain activity produces the sensation of sound (**FIGURE 5.39**). Auditory neurons in the thalamus extend their axons to the *primary auditory cortex*, which is located in the temporal lobe.

"Great! O.K., this time I want you to sound taller, and let me hear a little more hair."

SOUND LOCALIZATION Locating the origin of a sound is an important part of auditory perception, but the sensory receptors cannot code where events occur. Instead, the brain integrates the different sensory information coming from each ear.

Much of our understanding of auditory localization has come from research with barn owls. These nocturnal birds have finely tuned hearing, which helps them locate their prey. In fact, in a dark laboratory, a barn owl can locate a mouse through hearing alone. The owl uses two cues to locate a sound: the time the sound arrives in each ear and the sound's intensity in each ear. Unless the sound comes from exactly in front or in back of the owl, the sound will reach one ear first. Whichever side it comes from, the sound will be softer on the other side because the owl's head acts as a barrier. These differences in timing and magnitude are minute, but they are not too small for the owl's brain to detect and act on. Although a human's ears are not as finely tuned to the locations of sounds as an owl's ears, the human brain uses information from the two ears similarly (**FIGURE 5.40**).

VESTIBULAR SYSTEM Another sensory system that relies on the ears helps us to maintain balance. The **vestibular sense** uses information from receptors in the semicircular canals of the inner ear. These canals contain a liquid that moves when

eardrum
A thin membrane that marks the beginning of the middle ear; sound waves cause it to vibrate.

vestibular sense
Perception of balance determined by receptors in the inner ear.

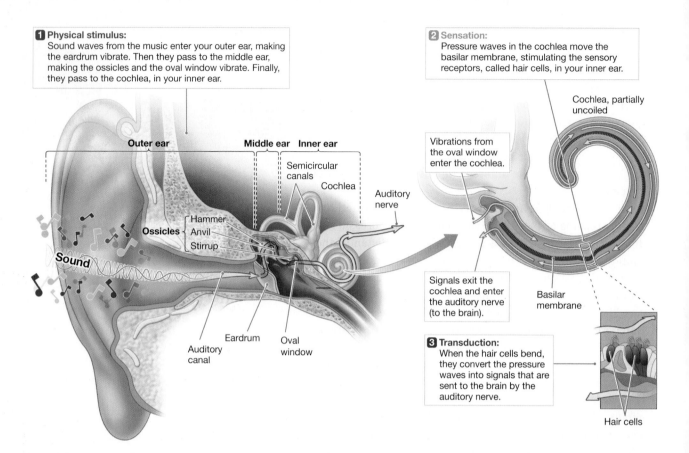

1 Physical stimulus:
Sound waves from the music enter your outer ear, making the eardrum vibrate. Then they pass to the middle ear, making the ossicles and the oval window vibrate. Finally, they pass to the cochlea, in your inner ear.

2 Sensation:
Pressure waves in the cochlea move the basilar membrane, stimulating the sensory receptors, called hair cells, in your inner ear.

Cochlea, partially uncoiled

Vibrations from the oval window enter the cochlea.

Outer ear   Middle ear   Inner ear

Semicircular canals

Cochlea

Auditory nerve

Ossicles — Hammer, Anvil, Stirrup

Sound

Signals exit the cochlea and enter the auditory nerve (to the brain).

Basilar membrane

Eardrum   Oval window

Auditory canal

3 Transduction:
When the hair cells bend, they convert the pressure waves into signals that are sent to the brain by the auditory nerve.

Hair cells

FIGURE 5.39
How We Are Able to Hear

the head moves, bending hair cells at the ends of the canal. The bending generates nerve impulses that inform us of the head's rotation. In this way, the vestibular sense is responsible for our sense of balance. It explains why inner-ear infections or standing up quickly can make us dizzy. The experience of being seasick or carsick results in part from conflicting signals arriving from the visual system and the vestibular system.

FIGURE 5.40
Auditory Localization
(a) Like barn owls, **(b)** humans draw on the intensity and timing of sounds to locate where the sounds are coming from.

(a)

(b)

3 Sound reaches left ear second, indicating the source is closer to the right ear.

2 Sound reaches right ear first.

1 Source of sound (here, a cell phone)

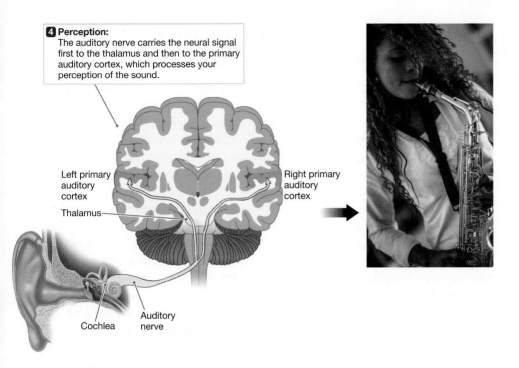

4 Perception:
The auditory nerve carries the neural signal first to the thalamus and then to the primary auditory cortex, which processes your perception of the sound.

Left primary auditory cortex

Right primary auditory cortex

Thalamus

Cochlea

Auditory nerve

COCHLEAR IMPLANTS A cochlear implant is a small electronic device that can help provide the sense of sound to a person who has a severe hearing impairment. The implant was the first neural implant used successfully in humans. Over 300,000 of these devices have been implanted worldwide since 1984, when the U.S. Food and Drug Administration (FDA) approved them for adults. In 1990, the FDA approved them for 2-year-olds. It has since approved them for 1-year-olds. Over 38,000 children in the United States have cochlear implants.

The cochlear implant has helped people with severe hearing problems due to the loss of hair cells in the inner ear. Unlike a hearing aid, the implant does not amplify sound. Rather, it directly stimulates the auditory nerve. The downside is that after the implant is put in place, the person who received it loses all residual normal hearing in that ear, because sound no longer travels along the ear canal and middle ear. Instead, sound is picked up by a tiny microphone behind the ear, sent through a computer processor, and then transmitted to the implant's electrodes inside the cochlea. If the devices are implanted at a young enough age in a congenitally deaf child (younger than 2 years being optimal), the child's hearing will be quite functional. He or she will learn to speak reasonably normally (**FIGURE 5.41**).

The benefits of cochlear implants might seem indisputable to many people with normal hearing. In the 1990s, however, deaf people who do not consider deafness a disability voiced concerns that the implants might adversely affect deaf culture. In fact, some deaf people believe that cochlear implants are a weapon being wielded by the medical community to wipe out deaf culture. They see this effort as being an extreme result of prejudice and discrimination against them, commonly known as *audism*. They argue that cochlear implants disrupt the deaf community's cohesiveness. While deaf people with cochlear implants can still use sign language, apparently they are not always welcome in the signing community (Chase, 2006). This attitude has slowly been changing, but is still held by many deaf signers.

FIGURE 5.41
Cochlear Implants
Cochlear implants, such as the one fitted on the side of this 10-year-old girl's head, consist of a microphone around the ear and a transmitter fitted to the scalp, linked to electrodes that directly stimulate the auditory nerve. When implanted at a young age, these devices can enable people with hearing loss to learn to hear and speak.

 Which are the primary auditory receptors?

ANSWER: the hair cells on the basilar membrane, which bend when auditory information is received

5.10 Pitch Is Encoded by Frequency and Location

How does the firing of auditory receptors signal different frequencies of sound, such as high notes and low notes? In other words, how is pitch coded by the auditory system? Two mechanisms for encoding the frequency of an auditory stimulus operate in parallel in the basilar membrane: temporal coding and place coding.

Temporal coding is used to encode relatively low frequencies, such as the sound of a tuba. The firing rates of cochlear hair cells match the frequency of the pressure wave, so that a 1,000 Hz tone causes hair cells to fire 1,000 times per second. Think of the boom, boom, boom of a bass drum. Physiological research has shown that this strict matching between the frequency of auditory stimulation and firing rate of the hair cells can occur only for relatively low frequencies—up to about 4,000 Hz. At higher frequencies, temporal coding can be maintained only if hair cells fire in volleys, in which different groups of cells take turns firing, so that the overall temporal pattern matches the sound frequency. Think of one group of soldiers firing their weapons together while another group reloads. Then that second group fires while another group reloads. Then that third group fires . . . and so on.

The second mechanism for encoding frequency is **place coding.** During the nineteenth century, the physiologist Hermann von Helmholtz proposed that different receptors in the basilar membrane respond to different frequencies. According to this idea, low frequencies would activate a different type of receptor than high frequencies would. Later, the perceptual psychologist Georg von Békésy discovered that Helmholtz's idea was theoretically correct but wrong in the details. Békésy (1957) discovered that different frequencies activate receptors at different locations on the basilar membrane. The receptors are similar but located in different places.

The basilar membrane responds to sound waves like a clarinet reed, vibrating in resonance with the sound. Because the membrane's stiffness decreases along its length, higher frequencies vibrate better at its base, while lower frequencies vibrate more toward its tip. Thus, hair cells at the base of the cochlea are activated by high-frequency sounds; hair cells at the tip are activated by low-frequency sounds (Culler, Coakley, Lowy, & Gross, 1943). The frequency of a sound wave, therefore, is encoded by the receptors on the area of the basilar membrane that vibrates the most (**FIGURE 5.42**).

temporal coding

A mechanism for encoding low-frequency auditory stimuli in which the firing rates of cochlear hair cells match the frequency of the sound wave.

place coding

A mechanism for encoding high-frequency auditory stimuli in which the frequency of the sound wave is encoded by the location of the hair cells along the basilar membrane.

FIGURE 5.42
Place Coding
In this "unrolled" cochlea, high-, medium-, and low-frequency sound waves activate different regions of the basilar membrane.

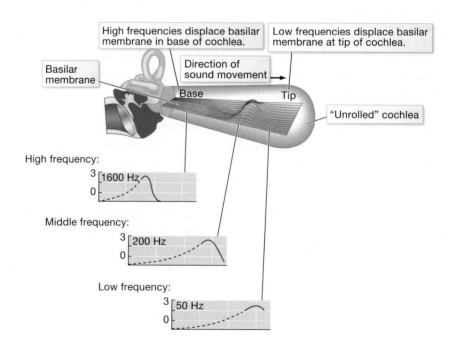

Both temporal coding and place coding are involved in the perception of pitch. Most of the sounds we hear—from conversations to concerts—are made up of many frequencies and activate a broad range of hair cells. Our perception of sound relies on the integrated activities of many neurons.

Q Which frequencies are best encoded by temporal coding, and which frequencies are best encoded by place coding?

5.11 Are Your Listening Habits Damaging Your Hearing?

Portable listening devices let us take our music wherever we go (**FIGURE 5.43**). State-of-the-art headphones and ear buds make the listening experience like being in the recording studio with our favorite artists. But blasting music through head-phones and ear buds is a known cause of hearing loss. According to the National Institutes of Health (2017), noise-induced hearing loss is caused by exposure to "sounds that are too loud or loud sounds that last a long time." Exposure to music typically occurs over long periods of time and thus falls into the second category of risk.

Loud noises—in headphones or ear buds, in the car, in a room, at a concert—can permanently damage the sensitive hair cells that line the ear canals and transmit signals to the nerves involved in sound perception. Once those hair cells are damaged, they cannot be repaired. Eventually, they die. If we do not protect those fragile structures, we will not be able to rely on them to hear music, lectures, the television, or any sounds at all.

Researchers based in New York City studied the noise exposure of college students who use personal listening devices, such as iPods (Levey, Levey, & Fligor, 2011). As students emerged from the subway adjacent to the urban campus, the researchers invited them to complete a short questionnaire to assess their music-listening habits and asked if they would put their headphones or ear buds on a special mannequin. This mannequin was equipped with a sound level meter that measured the intensity of the noise coming from the headset.

On average, the music was playing at 92.6 decibels (about the intensity of a power mower or a motorcycle roaring by). The research participants reported using their listening devices on average of 18.4 hours per week. The average intensity and duration of noise exposure certainly puts these students at risk for noise-induced hearing loss. To hear examples of other noises that can put your hearing at risk, check out the National Institutes of Health's "sound ruler": nidcd.nih.gov/health/hearing/pages/sound-ruler.aspx.

But how can we know if the energy waves we are pumping through our headphones need to be taken down a notch or two? The American Speech-Hearing-Language Association (2017) says that noise levels are dangerous if "you must raise your voice to be heard, you can't hear someone 3 feet away from you, speech around you sounds muffled or dull after you leave the noisy area, [or] you have pain or ringing in your ears (this is called 'tinnitus') after exposure to noise." According to the National Institutes of Health (2017), "If you wear headphones, the volume is too loud if a person standing near you can hear the music coming through the headphones."

Music is a part of who we are. But for those of us who have not already suffered hearing loss, so is our hearing. Enjoying music while protecting our hearing will help keep music part of us for the long haul. ■

FIGURE 5.43
Listening on the Go
Portable music is now a way of life, but it's important to listen smartly and safely—at a reasonable volume—to protect your hearing.

Q How do loud sounds lead to hearing loss?

How Are We Able to Taste?

Food provides us with the calories and nutrients necessary for survival. However, since we are not all dieticians, how do we know what to eat? The job of **gustation,** our sense of taste, is to keep poisons out of our digestive systems while allowing safe food in.

The stimuli for taste are chemical substances from food that dissolve in saliva. But the operations of these stimuli are still largely a mystery, and no simple explanation of taste could do justice to the importance of taste in our daily experience. Animals love tasty food, some flavors more than others. Humans in many cultures spend a substantial amount of time planning their meals to bring enjoyment. Beyond the basic chemistry of the sense and its importance for survival, how is the perception of taste determined?

5.12 There Are Five Basic Taste Sensations

The taste receptors are part of the **taste buds.** These sensory organs are mostly on the tongue (in the tiny, mushroom-shaped structures called *papillae*) but are also spread throughout the mouth and throat. Most individuals have approximately 8,000 to 10,000 taste buds. When food, fluid, or some other substance (e.g., dirt) stimulates the taste buds, they send signals to the thalamus. These signals are then routed to the frontal lobe, which produces the experience of taste (**FIGURE 5.44**).

In all the senses, a near-infinite variety of perceptual experiences arise from the activation of unique combinations of receptors. Scientists once believed that different regions of the tongue were more sensitive to certain tastes, but they now know that the different taste buds are spread relatively uniformly throughout the tongue and mouth (Lindemann, 2001).

Learning Objectives

- Discuss the five basic taste sensations.
- Describe how culture influences taste perception.

gustation
The sense of taste.

taste buds
Sensory organs in the mouth that contain the receptors for taste.

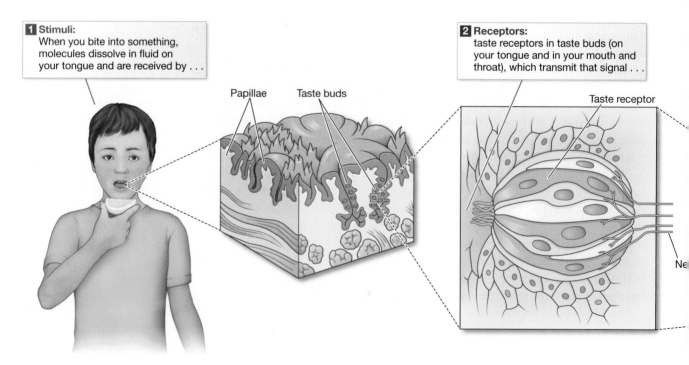

1 Stimuli:
When you bite into something, molecules dissolve in fluid on your tongue and are received by . . .

2 Receptors:
taste receptors in taste buds (on your tongue and in your mouth and throat), which transmit that signal . . .

Papillae   Taste buds

Taste receptor

Ne

FIGURE 5.44
How We Are Able to Taste

Every taste experience is composed of a mixture of five basic qualities: sweet, sour, salty, bitter, and *umami* (Japanese for "savory" or "yummy"). Only within the last decade have scientists recognized umami as the fifth taste sensation (Barretto et al., 2015). This delicious taste was perhaps first created intentionally in the late 1800s, when the French chef Auguste Escoffier invented a veal stock that did not taste primarily sweet, sour, salty, or bitter. Independently of Escoffier, in 1908, the Japanese cook and chemist Kikunae Ikeda identified the taste as arising from the detection of glutamate, a substance that occurs naturally in foods such as meat, some cheese, and mushrooms. Glutamate is the sodium salt in glutamic acid. As *monosodium glutamate*, or *MSG*, this salt can be added to various foods as a flavor enhancer. Soy sauce is full of the umami flavor.

Taste alone does not affect how much you like a certain type of food. As you might know from having had colds, food seems tasteless if your nasal passages are blocked. That is because taste relies heavily on the sense of smell. A food's texture also matters: Whether a food is soft or crunchy, creamy or granular, tender or tough affects the sensory experience. That experience is also affected if the food causes discomfort, as can happen with spicy chilies. The entire taste experience occurs not in your mouth but in your brain, which integrates these various sensory signals.

SUPERTASTERS Some people experience especially intense taste sensations, a trait largely determined by genetics. Linda Bartoshuk, the researcher who first studied these individuals, whom she called supertasters, found that they have more taste buds than normal tasters (Bartoshuk, Duffy, & Miller, 1994). Recent evidence, however, suggests that underlying genetics, rather than the number of taste buds, is the major determinant of whether a person is a supertaster (Garneau et al., 2014; **FIGURE 5.45**). First identified by their extreme dislike of bitter substances—such as grapefruit, broccoli, and coffee—supertasters are highly aware of flavors and textures and are more likely than others to feel pain when eating very spicy foods (Bartoshuk, 2000). They tend to be thin. Women are more likely than men to be supertasters. Taster status is

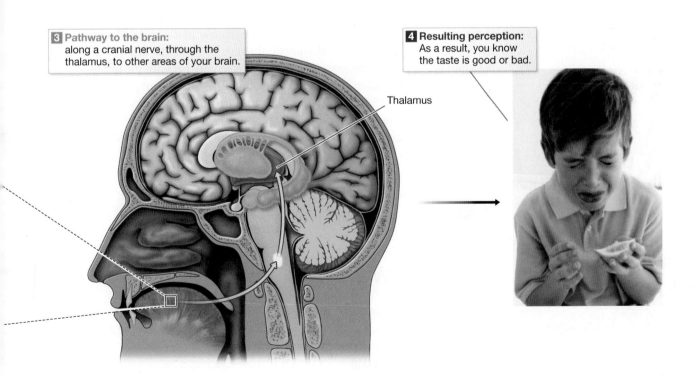

3 Pathway to the brain: along a cranial nerve, through the thalamus, to other areas of your brain.

4 Resulting perception: As a result, you know the taste is good or bad.

Thalamus

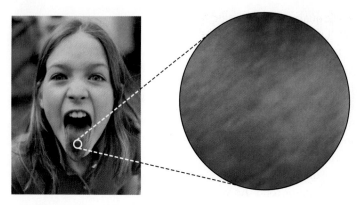

FIGURE 5.45
Are You a Supertaster?
The psychologist Linda Bartoshuk suggests the following test to determine whether you are a supertaster. (1) Punch a small hole (about 7 millimeters or .25 inches) into a small square of wax paper. (2) Swab some blue food coloring on the front of your tongue, then place the wax paper over it. (3) Use a magnifying glass to view the part of your tongue that shows through the small hole. (4) You will see pink dots, which are the papillae. They remain pink because they do not take up the blue dye. Count the number of pink dots you can see in the small hole. In general, fewer than 15 papillae means you have fewer taste buds than average, 15 to 35 is average, and above 35 means you may be among the 25 percent of the population who are supertasters.

also a function of age, because people lose half their taste receptors by age 20. Although it might sound enjoyable to experience intense tastes, many supertasters and young children are especially picky eaters because particular tastes can overwhelm them. When it comes to sensation, more is not necessarily better.

CULTURAL INFLUENCES Everyone has individual taste preferences. For example, some people hate anchovies, while others love them. Some people love sour foods, while others prefer sweet ones. These preferences come partly from differences in the number of taste receptors. The same food can actually taste different to different people, because the sensation associated with that food differs in different people's mouths. But cultural factors influence taste preferences as well. Some cultures like red hot peppers, others like salty fish, others rich sauces, and so on.

Cultural influences on food preferences begin in the womb. In a study of infant food preferences, pregnant women were assigned to four groups: Some drank carrot juice every day during the last two months of pregnancy, then drank carrot juice again every day during the first two months *after* childbirth; some drank a comparable amount of water every day during both of those periods; some drank carrot juice during the first period, then drank water during the second period; and some drank water during the first period, then drank carrot juice during the second period (Mennella, Jagnow, & Beauchamp, 2001). All the mothers breast-fed their babies, so the taste of what each mother ate was in the breast milk that constituted each newborn's sole food source during the first few months of life.

When the babies were several months old, they were all fed carrot juice (either alone or mixed with their cereal). The infants whose mothers drank carrot juice during the two months before childbirth, the first two months after childbirth, or both periods showed a preference for carrot juice compared with the infants whose mothers drank only water during those same months. Thus, through their own eating behaviors before and immediately following birth, mothers apparently pass their eating preferences on to their offspring. Once again, as noted throughout this book, nature and nurture are inextricably entwined (see "The Methods of Psychology: Infant Taste Preferences Affected by Mother's Diet").

ANSWER: sweet, sour, salty, bitter, and umami (savory)

Q What are the five basic taste qualities?

- Describe the neural pathway for smell.
- Explain the relationship between pheromones and smell.

How Are We Able to Smell?

The human sense of smell is vastly inferior to that of many animals. For example, dogs have 40 times more olfactory receptors than humans do and are 100,000 to 1 million times more sensitive to odors. Our less developed sense of smell comes from our ancestors' reliance on vision. Yet smell's importance in our daily lives is made clear, at least in Western cultures, by the vast sums of money spent on fragrances, deodorants, and mouthwash.

The Methods of Psychology
Infant Taste Preferences Affected by Mother's Diet

HYPOTHESIS: Taste preferences in newborns are influenced by their mothers' food preferences during the months immediately before and after birth.

RESEARCH METHOD:

Pregnant women were assigned at random to one of four groups instructed to drink a certain beverage every day for two months before the baby's birth and two months after the baby's birth:

	Before birth	After birth
Group 1:	carrot juice	water
Group 2:	carrot juice	carrot juice
Group 3:	water	carrot juice
Group 4:	water	water

RESULTS: Babies whose mothers were in Group 1, 2, or 3 preferred the taste of carrot juice more than did babies whose mothers were in Group 4 and did not drink carrot juice.

CONCLUSION: Babies become familiar with the taste of foods their mothers consume around the time of their birth, and they prefer familiar tastes.

QUESTION: How might the findings of this study account for cultural differences in food preferences?

ANSWER: What pregnant women eat influences their offspring develop in the womb. Cultural preferences shape what pregnant mothers eat. Therefore cultural preferences influence newborns' food preferences and presumably people's food preferences later in life.

Source: Mennella, J. A., Jagnow, C. P., & Beauchamp, G. K. (2001). Prenatal and postnatal flavor learning by human infants. *Pediatrics, 107,* e88.

5.13 Smell Detects Odorants

Of all the senses, smell, or **olfaction**, has the most direct route to the brain. It may, however, be the least understood sense. Like taste, it involves the sensing of chemicals that come from outside the body. We smell something when chemical particles, or *odorants*, pass into the nose and, when we sniff, into the nasal cavity's upper and back portions.

In the nose and the nasal cavity, a warm, moist environment helps the odorant molecules come into contact with the **olfactory epithelium.** This thin layer of tissue is embedded with thousands of smell receptors. Each receptor is responsive to different odorants. It remains unclear exactly how these receptors encode distinct smells. One possibility is that each type of receptor is uniquely associated with a specific odor. (For example, one type would encode only the scent of roses.) This explanation is unlikely, however, given the huge number of scents we can detect. (Moreover, the scent of a rose actually consists of a mixture of 275 chemical

olfaction
The sense of smell.

olfactory epithelium
A thin layer of tissue, within the nasal cavity, that contains the receptors for smell.

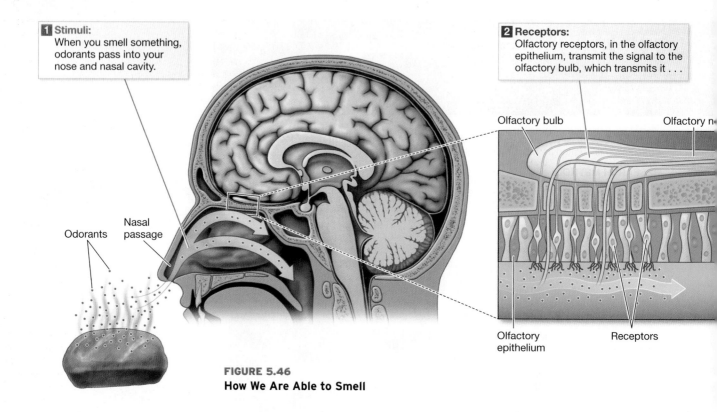

Olfactory bulb

Olfactory n

Odorants

Nasal passage

Olfactory epithelium

Receptors

FIGURE 5.46
How We Are Able to Smell

olfactory bulb
The brain center for smell, located below the frontal lobes.

components [Ohloff, 1994]. The combination of these odorants produces the smell that we recognize as a rose.) According to a recent estimate, humans can discriminate more than one trillion odorants (Bushdid, Magnasco, Vosshall, & Keller, 2014). Thus, a more likely possibility regarding encoding is that each odorant stimulates several types of receptors and the activation pattern across these receptors determines the olfactory perception (Lledo, Gheusi, & Vincent, 2005). As in all sensory systems, sensation and perception result from the specificity of receptors and the pattern of receptor responses.

Unlike other sensory information, smell signals bypass the thalamus, the early relay station. Instead, the smell receptors transmit information directly to the **olfactory bulb.** Located just below the frontal lobes, the olfactory bulb is the brain center for smell. From the olfactory bulb, smell information goes to other brain areas.

Information about whether a smell is pleasant or unpleasant is processed in the brain's prefrontal cortex, and people can readily make that distinction. However, although humans can discriminate over one trillion different odors, most people are pretty bad at identifying odors by name (Yeshurun & Sobel, 2010). Think about the smell of newly fallen rain. Even though it is familiar, it is hard to describe. If you test this claim by asking your friends or relatives to close their eyes and name familiar food items from the fridge, they will probably not be able to identify the smells at least half the time (de Wijk, Schab, & Cain, 1995). Women, though, are generally better than men at identifying odors (Bromley & Doty, 1995; Ohla & Lundström, 2013), perhaps because they have more cells in the olfactory bulb than men do (Oliveira-Pinto et al., 2014).

The intensity of a smell is processed in brain areas that are also involved in emotion and memory (Anderson, Christoff, et al., 2003). As a result, it is not surprising that olfactory stimuli can evoke feelings and memories (**FIGURE 5.46**). For example, many people find that the aromas of certain holiday foods cooking, the

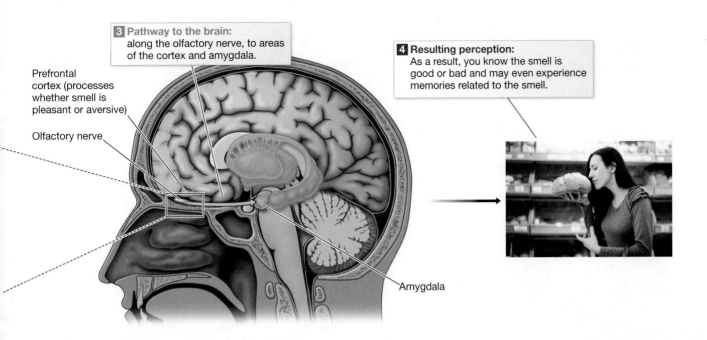

3 Pathway to the brain: along the olfactory nerve, to areas of the cortex and amygdala.

Prefrontal cortex (processes whether smell is pleasant or aversive)

Olfactory nerve

4 Resulting perception: As a result, you know the smell is good or bad and may even experience memories related to the smell.

Amygdala

smell of bread baking, and/or the fragrances of particular perfumes generate fond childhood memories.

PHEROMONES The sense of smell is also involved in an important mode of communication and involved in social behavior. *Pheromones* are chemicals released by animals, probably including humans, that trigger physiological or behavioral reactions in other animals and insects. These chemicals do not elicit "smells" that we are conscious of, but they are processed in a manner similar to the processing of olfactory stimuli. Specialized receptors in the nasal cavity respond to the presence of pheromones. Pheromones play a major role in sexual signaling in many animal species, and they may affect humans in similar ways (as discussed in Chapter 10, "Emotion and Motivation").

 How is the processing of olfactory information different from the other senses?

haptic sense
The sense of touch.

kinesthetic sense
Perception of the positions in space and movements of our bodies and our limbs.

ANSWER: Information about smell does not go through the thalamus. Instead, it goes directly to the olfactory bulb.

How Are We Able to Feel Touch and Pain?

Touch, the **haptic sense,** conveys sensations of temperature, of pressure, and of pain. It also delivers a sense of where our limbs are in space. A system related to touch is the **kinesthetic sense.** Kinesthetic sensations come from receptors in muscles, in tendons, and in joints. This information enables us to pinpoint the positions in space and the movements of our bodies and our limbs. Thus, it helps us coordinate voluntary movement and is invaluable in avoiding injury.

Learning Objectives

- Describe how the sense of touch is processed by the skin and the brain.
- Distinguish between the two types of pain.
- Discuss gate control theory and the control of pain.

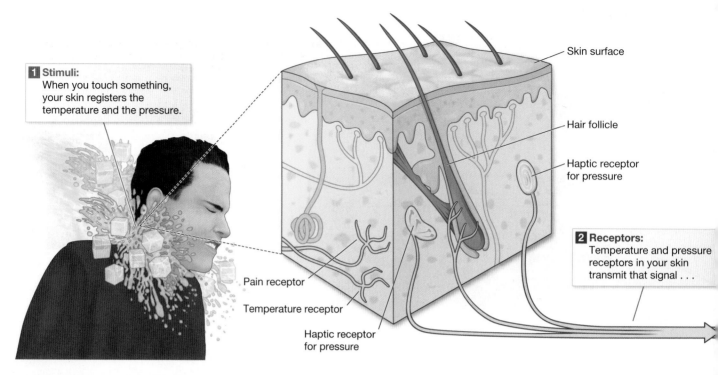

1 Stimuli:
When you touch something, your skin registers the temperature and the pressure.

Skin surface

Hair follicle

Haptic receptor for pressure

2 Receptors:
Temperature and pressure receptors in your skin transmit that signal . . .

Pain receptor

Temperature receptor

Haptic receptor for pressure

FIGURE 5.47
How We Are Able to Experience Touch: The Haptic Sense

5.14 The Skin Contains Sensory Receptors for Touch and Pain

Anything that makes contact with our skin provides *tactile stimulation*. This stimulation gives rise to the experience of touch. In fact, skin is the largest organ for sensory reception because of its large surface area. The haptic receptors for both temperature and pressure are sensory neurons that reach to the skin's outer layer. Their long axons enter the central nervous system by way of spinal or cranial nerves. (Simply put, spinal nerves travel from the rest of the body into the spinal cord and then to the brain. By contrast, cranial nerves connect directly to the brain.)

For sensing temperature, there appear to be receptors for warmth and receptors for cold. Intense stimuli can trigger both warmth and cold receptors, however. Such simultaneous activation can produce strange sensory experiences, such as a false feeling of wetness. Some receptors for pressure are nerve fibers at the bases of hair follicles that respond to movement of the hair. Four other types of pressure receptors are capsules in the skin. These receptors respond to: continued vibration; light, fast pressure; light, slow pressure; or stretching and steady pressure.

The integration of various signals and higher-level mental processes produces haptic experiences (**FIGURE 5.47**). For instance, stroking multiple pressure points can produce a tickling sensation, which can be pleasant or unpleasant, depending on the mental state of the person being tickled. By the way, imaging research has helped answer the question of why we cannot tickle ourselves: The brain areas involved in touch sensation respond less to self-produced tactile stimulation than to external tactile stimulation (Blakemore, Wolpert, & Frith, 1998).

Touch information travels to the thalamus. The thalamus sends it to the primary somatosensory cortex, in the parietal lobe. As discussed in Chapter 3, electrical stimulation of the primary somatosensory cortex can evoke the sensation of touch

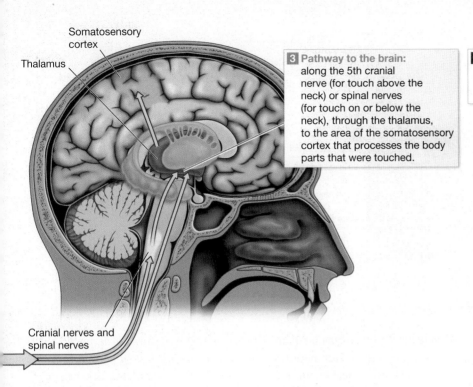

Somatosensory cortex

Thalamus

Cranial nerves and spinal nerves

3 Pathway to the brain: along the 5th cranial nerve (for touch above the neck) or spinal nerves (for touch on or below the neck), through the thalamus, to the area of the somatosensory cortex that processes the body parts that were touched.

4 Resulting perception: As a result, you perceive the shock of cold water on your neck and down the rest of your body.

in different regions of the body (see Figure 3.25a). Large amounts of cortical tissue are devoted to sensitive body parts, such as the fingers and the lips. Very little cortical tissue is devoted to other areas, such as the back and the calves. As a result, you can probably tell what something is if you feel it with your fingers, but you will not have equal sensitivity if the same thing touches your back.

TYPES OF PAIN Pain is part of a warning system that stops you from continuing activities that may harm you. For example, the message may be to remove your hand from a jagged surface or to stop running when you have damaged a tendon. Children born with a rare genetic disorder that leaves them insensitive to pain usually die young, no matter how carefully they are supervised. They simply do not know how to avoid activities that harm them or to report when they are feeling ill (Melzack & Wall, 1982).

Pain receptors exist throughout the body, not just in the skin. Like other sensory experiences, the actual experience of pain is created by the brain. For instance, a person whose limb has been amputated may sometimes feel phantom pain in the nonexistent limb (see Figure 3.40). The person really feels pain, but the pain occurs because of painful sensations *near* the site of the missing limb or even because of a nonpainful touch on the cheek. The brain simply misinterprets the resulting neural activity.

Most experiences of pain result when damage to the skin activates haptic receptors. The nerve fibers that convey pain information are thinner than those for temperature and for pressure and are found in all body tissues that sense pain: skin, muscles, membranes around both bones and joints, organs, and so on. Two kinds of nerve fibers have been identified for pain: *fast fibers* for sharp, immediate pain and *slow fibers* for chronic, dull, steady pain.

An important distinction between these fibers is the myelination or nonmyelination of their axons, which travel from the pain receptors to the spinal cord. As discussed in Chapter 3, myelination speeds up neural communication. Myelinated axons, like heavily insulated wire, can send information quickly. Nonmyelinated axons send information more slowly.

Think of a time when you touched a hot skillet. A sharp, fast, localized pain at the moment your skin touched the pan caused you to jerk your hand away. It was followed

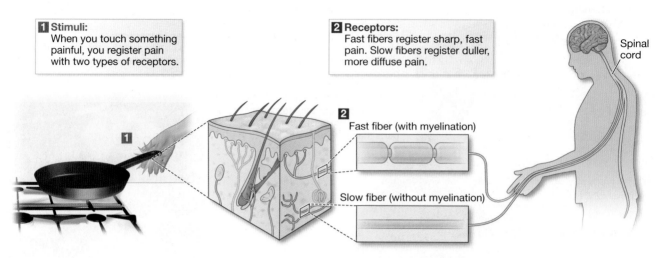

1 **Stimuli:**
When you touch something painful, you register pain with two types of receptors.

2 **Receptors:**
Fast fibers register sharp, fast pain. Slow fibers register duller, more diffuse pain.

Spinal cord

1

2

Fast fiber (with myelination)

Slow fiber (without myelination)

FIGURE 5.48
How We Experience Touch: The Sense of Pain

by a slow, dull, more diffuse burning pain. The fast-acting receptors are activated by strong physical pressure and temperature extremes, whereas the slow-acting receptors are activated by chemical changes in tissue when skin is damaged. In terms of adaptation, fast pain leads us to recoil from harmful objects and therefore is protective, whereas slow pain keeps us from using the affected body parts and therefore helps in recuperation (**FIGURE 5.48**).

GATE CONTROL THEORY The brain regulates the experience of pain, sometimes producing it, sometimes suppressing it. Pain is a complex experience that depends on biological, psychological, and cultural factors. The psychologist Ronald Melzack conducted pioneering research in this area. For example, he demonstrated that psychological factors, such as past experiences, are extremely important in determining how much pain a person feels.

With his collaborator Patrick Wall, Melzack formulated the *gate control theory of pain*. According to this theory, we experience pain when pain receptors are activated and a neural "gate" in the spinal cord allows the signals through to the brain (Melzack & Wall, 1965). These ideas were radical in that they conceptualized pain as a perceptual experience within the brain rather than simply a response to nerve stimulation. The theory states that pain signals are transmitted by small-diameter nerve fibers. These fibers can be blocked at the spinal cord (prevented from reaching the brain) by the firing of larger sensory nerve fibers. Thus, sensory nerve fibers can "close a gate" and prevent or reduce the perception of pain. This is why scratching an itch is so satisfying, why rubbing an aching muscle helps reduce the ache, and why vigorously rubbing the skin where an injection is about to be given reduces the needle's sting (**FIGURE 5.49**).

A number of cognitive states, such as distraction, can also close the gate. Athletes sometimes play through pain because of their intense focus on the game. Wounded soldiers sometimes continue to fight during combat, often failing to recognize a level of pain that would render them inactive at other times. An insect bite bothers us more when we are trying to sleep and have few distractions than when we are wide awake and active.

Conversely, some mental processes, such as worrying about or focusing on the painful stimulus, seem to open the pain gates wider. Research participants who are well rested rate the same level of a painful stimulus as less painful than do participants who are fearful, anxious, or depressed (Loggia, Mogil, & Bushnell, 2008; Sullivan et al., 2001). Likewise, positive moods help people cope with pain. In a systematic review of the literature, Swedish researchers found that listening to music was an

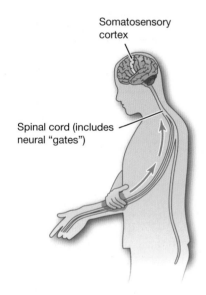

Somatosensory cortex

Spinal cord (includes neural "gates")

FIGURE 5.49
Gate Control Theory
According to the gate control theory of pain, neural "gates" in the spinal cord allow signals through. Those gates can be closed when information about touch is being transmitted (e.g., by rubbing a sore arm or by distraction).

extremely effective means of reducing postoperative pain, perhaps because it helps patients relax (Engwall & Duppils, 2009).

DeCharms and colleagues (2005) have pioneered techniques that offer hope for people who suffer from painful conditions. The researchers sought to teach people in pain—many of these people in chronic pain—to visualize their pain more positively. For example, participants were taught to think about a burning sensation as soothing, like the feeling of being in a sauna. As they tried to learn such techniques, they viewed fMRI images that showed which regions of their brains were active as they performed the tasks. Many participants learned techniques that altered their brain activity and reduced their pain.

Of course, there are more-traditional ways to control pain. Most of us have taken over-the-counter drugs, usually ibuprofen or acetaminophen, to reduce pain perception. If you have ever suffered from a severe toothache or needed surgery, you have probably experienced the benefits of pain medication. When a dentist administers Novocain to sensory neurons in the mouth, pain messages are not transmitted to the brain, so the mouth feels numb. General anesthesia slows down the firing of neurons throughout the nervous system, and the patient becomes unresponsive to stimulation (Perkins, 2007).

You can use your knowledge of pain perception anytime you need to reduce your own pain or to help others in pain. Distraction is usually the easiest way to reduce pain. If you are preparing for a painful procedure or suffering after one, watching an entertaining movie can help, especially if it is funny enough to elevate your mood. Music may help you relax, making it easier to deal with pain. Rapid rubbing can benefit a stubbed toe, for example, or a finger that was caught in a closing drawer. You will also feel less pain if you are rested, not fearful, and not anxious. Finally, try to visualize your pain as something more pleasant. Of course, severe pain is a warning that something in the body is seriously wrong. If you experience severe pain, you should be treated by a medical professional.

 Q Why do people often rub parts of their bodies that are injured?

ANSWER: Rubbing activates sensory receptors that can close the pain gate, reducing the experience of pain.

Your Chapter Review

Chapter Summary

How Does Perception Emerge from Sensation?

5.1 Sensory Information Is Translated into Meaningful Signals

Sensation is the detection of physical stimuli in the environment. Perception is our conscious experience of those stimuli. Bottom-up processing is based on features of a stimulus. Top-down processing is based on context and expectations. Transduction is the process of converting sensory stimuli into a pattern of neural activity. Transduction takes place at sensory receptors, specialized cells within each sense organ that respond to energy to activate neurons. Most sensory information goes to the thalamus and then specialized brain regions.

5.2 Detection Requires a Certain Amount of the Stimulus

Information from the environment needs to surpass some level before you can detect it. Absolute threshold is the minimum amount of stimulus intensity needed to activate a sensory receptor. Difference threshold is the amount of change required for detection by a sensory receptor. Signal detection theory is about the subjective nature of detecting a stimulus. Sensory adaptation occurs when sensory receptors stop responding to an unchanging stimulus.

5.3 The Brain Constructs Stable Representations

In perception, the brain integrates millions of diverse neural inputs to produce stable representations. This activity produces awareness, a conscious experience of the physical world. Sometimes those representations can produce unusual experiences, such as in synesthesia.

5.4 Think like a Psychologist: Does ESP Exist?

The ability to perceive information beyond ordinary sensory information is called extrasensory perception (ESP). Although psychologists continue to debate the existence of ESP, the available evidence is weak or nonexistent.

How Are We Able to See?

5.5 Sensory Receptors in the Eye Transmit Visual Information to the Brain

Light is focused by the lens onto the retina, which is at the back of the eye. The retina houses the photoreceptors: rods and cones. Rods and cones communicate with ganglion cells of the optic nerve. This nerve exits the eye at the blind spot and crosses into the brain at the optic chiasm. There, axons from each eye cross into opposite sides of the brain, so the left hemisphere processes information from the right visual field and vice versa. The information is processed in the thalamus and the primary visual cortex (in the occipital lobe). From the visual cortex, the ventral stream processes "what" information about objects, and the dorsal stream processes "where" information about locations.

5.6 The Color of Light Is Determined by Its Wavelength

The human eye detects electromagnetic radiation wavelengths of 400–700 nanometers. The retina contains three types of cones. Each type is responsive to a different wavelength (short, medium, or long), and this responsiveness enables us to perceive colors. Color blindness is caused by a malfunction in one or more of the cone types. Colors are differentiated by their hue, saturation, and lightness.

5.7 Perceiving Objects Requires Organization of Visual Information

Gestalt principles—such as proximity, similarity, continuity, and closure—account for the ways in which perceptual information is organized into wholes. Humans are especially good at recognizing faces. The fusiform gyrus is one of the brain regions most responsible for this ability.

5.8 Perception Is Guided by Cues in the Environment

Depth perception is critical for locating objects in space. To perceive depth using only a two-dimensional retinal image, the brain draws on binocular and monocular cues. Size perception depends on distance: Close objects produce large retinal images, whereas far objects produce small retinal images. Motion is detected by motion-sensitive neurons in the visual cortex. Object constancy refers to how the brain accurately perceives images even with minimal or changing stimulus cues. The four constancies are size, shape, color, and lightness.

How Are We Able to Hear?

5.9 Audition Results from Changes in Air Pressure

The amplitude and frequency of sound waves cause the perceptual experiences of loudness and pitch, respectively. Sound waves travel from the outer ear through the auditory canal to the eardrum. Vibrations from these waves stimulate the ossicles, bones of the inner ear. The vibrations of these bones stimulate the oval window, a membrane on the cochlea, a fluid-filled chamber in the inner ear. Pressure waves from the cochlear fluid stimulate the basilar membrane. This stimulation causes the ear's sensory receptors, the hair cells, to bend. The bending of the hair cells activates neurons in the auditory nerve. These neurons send messages through the thalamus and to the primary auditory cortex (in the temporal lobe). Cochlear implants can help with hearing loss by directly stimulating the auditory nerve, overcoming the lack of hair cells in the inner ear.

5.10 Pitch Is Encoded by Frequency and Location

Low-frequency sound waves are sensed through temporal coding, as cochlear hair cells fire at a rate equivalent to the frequency of the waves. High-frequency sound waves are sensed through place coding—that is, by hair cells at different locations in the cochlea. For high-frequency sound waves, groups of hair cells must take turns firing.

5.11 Using Psychology in Your Life: Are Your Listening Habits Damaging Your Hearing?

Loud noises can permanently damage the sensitive hair cells that line the ear canals and transmit signals to the nerves involved in sound perception. Once those hair cells are damaged, they cannot be repaired.

How Are We Able to Taste?

5.12 There Are Five Basic Taste Sensations

Gustation, the sense of taste, is produced by taste buds. The taste buds are located in the papillae, structures on the tongue. The five types of taste buds yield the taste sensations: sweet, sour, salty, bitter, and umami (savory). Cultural factors help determine taste preferences.

How Are We Able to Smell?

5.13 Smell Detects Odorants

Olfaction occurs when odorants stimulate smell receptors, which are located in the olfactory epithelium in the nose and nasal cavity. Smell receptors send messages to neurons in the olfactory bulb, located below the frontal lobes. The signals are sent directly to other brain areas, including those that regulate memory and emotion. Pheromones are chemicals that do not produce odor but are processed by the smell receptors. Pheromones can motivate sexual behavior in nonhuman animals and may function similarly in humans.

How Are We Able to Feel Touch and Pain?

5.14 The Skin Contains Sensory Receptors for Touch and Pain

Touch is known as the haptic sense. Tactile stimulation activates touch receptors in skin, which respond to temperature, pressure, and pain. Touch information travels to the thalamus, which sends it to the primary somatosensory cortex (in the parietal lobe). The perception of pain prompts organisms to protect themselves from damage. Fast, myelinated fibers process sharp sudden pain. Slow, nonmyelinated fibers process dull chronic pain. According to the gate control theory, pain perception requires both the activation of pain receptors and spinal cord processing of the signal. The gate can be closed or occupied if other stimuli are processed simultaneously. Activities such as rubbing an area around the painful one, distracting oneself, or thinking happy thoughts can decrease the perception of pain.

Key Terms

absolute threshold, p. 167
audition, p. 188
binocular depth cues, p. 182
binocular disparity, p. 182
bottom-up processing, p. 164
cones, p. 173
convergence, p. 183
difference threshold, p. 168
eardrum, p. 189
fovea, p. 173
gustation, p. 194

haptic sense, p. 199
kinesthetic sense, p. 199
monocular depth cues, p. 182
object constancy, p. 186
olfaction, p. 197
olfactory bulb, p. 198
olfactory epithelium, p. 197
perception, p. 164
place coding, p. 192
retina, p. 173
rods, p. 173

sensation, p. 164
sensory adaptation, p. 169
signal detection theory (SDT), p. 168
sound wave, p. 188
taste buds, p. 194
temporal coding, p. 192
top-down processing, p. 164
transduction, p. 165
vestibular sense, p. 189

Putting Psychology to Work

What Are the Employment Opportunities in Sensory Science?

Have you ever wondered how food companies come up with so many new flavors and products? Or how the colors and design of a package can enhance your gustatory experience? As you have seen in this chapter, our perception of stimuli is a psychological process. What we perceive as taste or color is actively constructed in our brains when physical stimuli such as food molecules or light waves reach sensory receptors. Understanding how perceptual experiences are determined and influenced by psychological factors has many applications in the workplace.

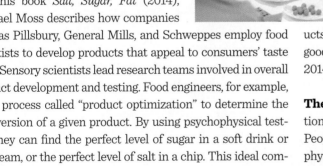

In his book *Salt, Sugar, Fat* (2014), Michael Moss describes how companies such as Pillsbury, General Mills, and Schweppes employ food scientists to develop products that appeal to consumers' taste buds. Sensory scientists lead research teams involved in overall product development and testing. Food engineers, for example, use a process called "product optimization" to determine the best version of a given product. By using psychophysical testing, they can find the perfect level of sugar in a soft drink or ice cream, or the perfect level of salt in a chip. This ideal combination of tastes is known as the "bliss point." Flavor analysts may work to develop formulations that are resistant to sensory adaptation, thus encouraging continued consumption.

Of course, our perception of taste is influenced by many factors, including our expectations and our other senses, as when we receive visual and olfactory cues. Accordingly, companies focus on choosing the appropriate colors and smells for food products. And their graphic designers draw on visual-system information, such as pictorial depth cues and Gestalt perceptual organization, to craft appealing containers.

Sensory scientists are employed not just by the food industry, but by many large consumer companies that test human sensation and perception processes to evaluate a wide range of products. The job outlook for food and other sensory scientists is good, with employment projected to increase by 5 percent from 2014 to 2024 (U.S. Bureau of Labor Statistics, 2017).

The bottom line: Understanding how sensation and perception operate can be useful in product design and marketing. People with knowledge in this area, experience with psychophysical testing, and knowledge of statistics and experimental design can pursue jobs in fields that draw on sensory sciences, such as the food industry.

Want to earn a better grade on your test?
Go to **INQUIZITIVE** to learn and review this chapter's content, with personalized feedback along the way. Practice Tests and accompanying answer keys can be found at the back of the book on page PT-1.

6 Learning

Big Questions

- How Do We Learn? 208

- How Do We Learn Predictive Associations? 210

- How Do Consequences of an Action Shape Behavior? 224

- How Do We Learn from Watching Others? 238

BY THE 1970S, ALL THE WOLVES IN YELLOWSTONE NATIONAL PARK had been killed as part of a predator control plan. In 1987, the U.S. Fish and Wildlife Service announced a recovery plan to reintroduce wolves to the park. Farmers and ranchers were skeptical, fearing that the wolves would prey on their sheep and cattle. Scientists came up with a solution. Nonlethal doses of poison were added to sheep carcasses, which were placed where wolves would find them. When the wolves ate the meat, they immediately vomited. The wolves soon learned to associate eating sheep with becoming ill, and they avoided preying on sheep. Using this procedure to help wolves learn to not eat sheep is an example of how psychological science can be put to work in "the real world."

The principles behind the wolves' learning are also the basis for how humans learn. This chapter examines how the process of learning takes place. This material represents some of psychology's central contributions to our understanding of behavior. Learning theories have been used to improve quality of life and to train humans as well as nonhuman animals to learn new tasks. To understand behavior, therefore, we need to know what learning is. For psychologists, the big questions about learning are: How do we learn? How do we learn predictive associations? How do consequences of an action shape behavior? And how do we learn from watching others?

Learning Objectives

- Define learning.
- Identify three types of learning processes.
- Describe the nonassociative learning processes: habituation and sensitization. Explain the significance of each.

learning
A relatively enduring change in behavior, resulting from experience.

FIGURE 6.1
Learning in Daily Life
Children whose parents encourage them to recycle may develop a positive attitude to the environment.

FIGURE 6.2
Learning Through Sensory Experiences
According to behaviorism, an infant learns through experience.

How Do We Learn?

The ability to learn is crucial for all animals. To survive, animals need to learn things such as which types of foods are dangerous, when it is safe to sleep, and which sounds signal potential dangers. Learning is central to almost all aspects of human existence. It makes possible our basic abilities (such as walking and speaking) and our complex ones (such as flying airplanes, performing surgery, or maintaining intimate relationships). Learning also shapes many aspects of daily life: clothing choices, musical tastes, cultural values about either exploiting or preserving the environment, and so on (**FIGURE 6.1**).

6.1 Learning Results from Experience

Psychologists define **learning** as a relatively enduring change in behavior, resulting from experience. Learning occurs when an animal benefits from experience so that its behavior is better adapted to the environment. In other words, the animal is more prepared to deal with the environment in the future. For example, the animal may be better able to predict when certain events are likely to happen.

Learning theory arose in the early twentieth century. Its development was partly a result of the dissatisfaction among some psychologists with the widespread use of introspection, such as that being used by the structuralists. Likewise, many psychologists were critical of Freud's psychodynamic approach. Freud and his followers used verbal report techniques, such as dream analysis and free association. They aimed to assess the unconscious mental processes that they believed were the primary determinants of behavior. John B. Watson (1924), however, argued that Freudian theory was unscientific and ultimately meaningless. He also rejected any psychological enterprise that focused on things that could not be observed directly, such as people's mental experiences. Although he acknowledged that thoughts and beliefs exist, he believed they could not be studied using scientific methods. According to Watson, observable behavior was the only valid indicator of psychological activity.

As discussed in Chapter 1, Watson founded behaviorism on such principles. This school of thought was based on the belief that humans and nonhuman animals are born with the potential to learn just about anything. In formulating his ideas, Watson was influenced by the seventeenth-century philosopher John Locke. An infant, according to Locke, is a *tabula rasa* (Latin for "blank slate"). Born knowing nothing, the infant acquires all of its knowledge through sensory experiences (**FIGURE 6.2**).

The essence of learning is that it enables us to gain knowledge about the world. We learn in three basic ways (**FIGURE 6.3**).

NONASSOCIATIVE LEARNING The simplest form of learning occurs after repeated exposure to a single stimulus, or event. For example, if you move to a new house by

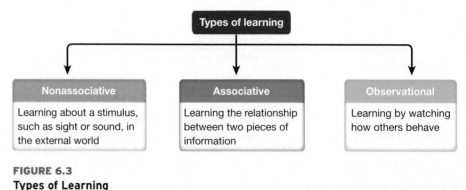

FIGURE 6.3
Types of Learning

Types of learning

Nonassociative	Associative	Observational
Learning about a stimulus, such as sight or sound, in the external world	Learning the relationship between two pieces of information	Learning by watching how others behave

some train tracks, the rumble of passing trains might disturb your sleep. After you live in the house for a while, you quit waking up to the sound of trains. This action, **nonassociative learning,** is a response to something in the environment. The change in response to the stimulus is a form of learning.

ASSOCIATIVE LEARNING The second type of learning is understanding how stimuli, or events, are related. For example, your dog runs for the door when you pick up the leash. You might associate working with getting paid. **Associative learning** is the linking of two events that, in general, take place one right after the other. Associations develop through *conditioning,* a process in which environmental stimuli and behavioral responses become connected.

OBSERVATIONAL LEARNING The third major type of learning occurs by watching others. **Observational learning** is acquiring or changing a behavior after exposure to another individual performing that behavior. For example, you might learn the steps to a new type of dance by watching a YouTube video. By watching others in person or in the media, people may learn what to appreciate or what to fear.

 You fear going to the dentist. What type of learning produced your fear?

6.2 Habituation and Sensitization Are Models of Nonassociative Learning

Nonassociative learning, the simplest form of learning, occurs when you gain new information after repeated exposure to a single stimulus, or event. The two most common forms of nonassociative learning are habituation and sensitization (**FIGURE 6.4**).

Habituation is a decrease in behavioral response after repeated exposure to a stimulus. We tend to notice new things around us. If something is neither rewarding nor harmful, habituation leads us to ignore it (**FIGURE 6.5**). Recall the discussion of sensory adaptation in Chapter 5. Habituation is unlike sensory adaptation in that you can still perceive the stimuli. You just do not respond to them because you have learned that they are not important.

We constantly habituate to meaningless events around us. If you have lived in or visited a major city, you were probably very reactive to sirens at first. When you heard one, you looked around to see if there was immediate danger. But soon you no longer reacted to sirens. In fact, you barely noticed them. It is not that you do not hear them. You just do not respond because you have habituated to them.

What happens if the background noise suddenly stops? You are likely to immediately notice the change. The increase in a response because of a change in something familiar is *dishabituation.* This process is important in the animal world. For instance, birds might stop singing when they detect a predator, such as a hawk. The absence of bird song alerts other animals, such as squirrels, to potential danger.

All animals show habituation and dishabituation. Indeed, we have learned a lot about how nonassociative learning works by studying simple invertebrates such as the aplysia, a small marine snail (**FIGURE 6.6**). Habituation can be demonstrated quite easily by repeatedly touching an aplysia. The first few touches cause it to withdraw its gills. After about 10 touches, it stops responding, and this lack of response lasts about 2 to 3 hours. Repeated habituation trials can lead to a state of habituation that lasts several weeks.

Sidebar glossary

nonassociative learning
Responding after repeated exposure to a single stimulus, or event.

associative learning
Linking two stimuli, or events, that occur together.

observational learning
Acquiring or changing a behavior after exposure to another individual performing that behavior.

habituation
A decrease in behavioral response after repeated exposure to a stimulus.

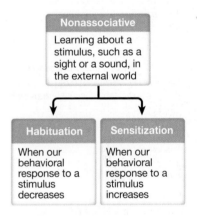

Nonassociative
Learning about a stimulus, such as a sight or a sound, in the external world

Habituation	Sensitization
When our behavioral response to a stimulus decreases	When our behavioral response to a stimulus increases

FIGURE 6.4
Types of Nonassociative Learning

FIGURE 6.5
Habituation
Suppose you live or work in a noisy environment. You learn to ignore the constant noise because you do not need to respond to it.

FIGURE 6.6
Simple Model of Learning
The aplysia, a marine invertebrate, is used to study the neurochemical basis of learning.

sensitization

An increase in behavioral response after exposure to a stimulus.

Sensitization is an increase in behavioral response after exposure to a stimulus (**FIGURE 6.7**). The stimuli that most often lead to sensitization are those that are threatening or painful. If you are studying and smell something burning, you probably will not habituate to this smell. In fact, you might focus even greater attention on your sense of smell to assess the possible threat of fire, and you will be highly vigilant for any indication of smoke or of flames. In general, sensitization leads to heightened responsiveness to other stimuli. Giving a strong electric shock to an aplysia's tail leads to sensitization. Following the shock, a mild touch anywhere on the body will cause the aplysia to withdraw its gills.

What activity at the synapse leads to nonassociative learning? The neurobiologist Eric Kandel and colleagues (Carew, Pinsker, & Kandel, 1972; Kandel, Dudai, & Mayford, 2014) have used the aplysia to study the neural basis of nonassociative learning. Their findings have shown that alterations in the functioning of the synapse lead to habituation and sensitization. For both types of simple learning, presynaptic neurons alter their neurotransmitter release. A reduction in neurotransmitter release leads to habituation. An increase in neurotransmitter release leads to sensitization. Knowing the neural basis of simple learning gives us the building blocks to understand more-complex learning processes in both human and nonhuman animals. For this research, Kandel received the Nobel Prize in 2000.

 What is the primary difference between habituation and sensitization?

Learning Objectives

- Define classical conditioning.
- Differentiate between the UR, US, CS, and CR.
- Describe acquisition, second-order conditioning, generalization, discrimination, extinction, and spontaneous recovery.
- Describe the Rescorla-Wagner model of classical conditioning, including the role of prediction error and dopamine in the strength of associations.

classical conditioning (Pavlovian conditioning)

A type of associative learning in which a neutral stimulus comes to elicit a response when it is associated with a stimulus that already produces that response.

How Do We Learn Predictive Associations?

Learning helps us solve adaptive challenges by being able to predict when things go together. Consider the need to find water. Over time, each person has learned to associate the sound of flowing liquid with drinking. If you were lost in the wilderness and desperately thirsty, you could listen for the sound of running water, hoping that by locating the sound you could find the source. The essence of learning is in understanding predictive associations, such as between the sound of water and being able to quench one's thirst.

6.3 Behavioral Responses Are Conditioned

We learn predictive associations through *conditioning*, the process that connects environmental stimuli to behavior (**FIGURE 6.8**).

In **classical conditioning**, also known as **Pavlovian conditioning**, a neutral stimulus elicits a response because it has become associated with a stimulus that already produces that response. In other words, you learn that one event predicts another. For example, you learn that certain music plays during scary scenes in a movie. Now you feel anxious when you hear that music.

The term *Pavlovian* is derived from the name of Ivan Pavlov. John B. Watson developed his ideas about behaviorism after reading the work of Pavlov, who had won a Nobel Prize in 1904 for his research on the digestive system. Pavlov was interested in the *salivary reflex*. This automatic, unlearned response occurs when a food stimulus is presented to a hungry animal, including a human. For his work on the digestive system, Pavlov created an apparatus that collected saliva from dogs. With this device, he measured the different amounts of saliva that resulted when he placed various types of food into a dog's mouth (**FIGURE 6.9**).

As with so many major scientific advances, Pavlov's contribution to psychology started with a simple observation. One day he was annoyed to realize that the laboratory dogs were salivating before they tasted their food. Indeed, the dogs started salivating the moment a lab technician walked into the room or whenever they saw the bowls that usually contained food. Pavlov's genius was in recognizing that this behavioral response was a window to the working mind. Unlike inborn reflexes, salivation at the sight of a bowl or of a person is not automatic. Therefore, that response must have been acquired through experience. This insight led Pavlov to devote the next 30 years of his life to studying the basic principles of learning.

Pavlov conducted the basic research on conditioning using the salivary reflex, such as happens when seeing a tasty cake causes your mouth to start watering. In these studies, a *neutral stimulus* unrelated to the salivary reflex, such as the clicking of a metronome, is presented along with a stimulus that reliably produces the reflex, such as food. The neutral stimulus can be anything that the animal can see or hear as long

FIGURE 6.7
Sensitization
Suppose you are sitting with your brother and he keeps annoying you. Finally, you react, perhaps by yelling. Your reaction (yelling) in response to your annoying brother (aversive stimulus) is an example of sensitization.

Associative
Learning the relationship between two pieces of information

Classical conditioning	Operant conditioning
When we learn that a stimulus predicts another stimulus	When we learn that a behavior leads to a certain outcome

FIGURE 6.8
Two Types of Associative Learning

(a)

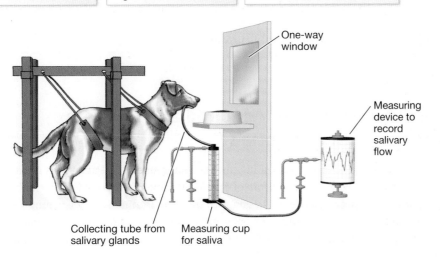

(b)

1 The dog is presented with a bowl that contains meat.

2 A tube carries the dog's saliva from the salivary glands to a container.

3 The container is connected to a device that measures the amount of saliva.

One-way window

Measuring device to record salivary flow

Collecting tube from salivary glands

Measuring cup for saliva

FIGURE 6.9
Pavlov's Apparatus and Classical Conditioning
(a) Ivan Pavlov, pictured here with his colleagues and one of his canine subjects, conducted groundbreaking work on classical conditioning.
(b) Pavlov's apparatus collected and measured a dog's saliva.

unconditioned response (UR)
A response that does not have to be learned, such as a reflex.

unconditioned stimulus (US)
A stimulus that elicits a response, such as a reflex, without any prior learning.

conditioned stimulus (CS)
A stimulus that elicits a response only after learning has taken place.

conditioned response (CR)
A response to a conditioned stimulus; a response that has been learned.

FIGURE 6.10
Classical Conditioning in a Thriller
Like many suspenseful or scary movies, *Jaws* uses a classical conditioning technique to make us feel afraid. The "duh-duh, duh-duh" soundtrack music plays just before each shark attack.

ANSWER: unconditioned stimulus

as it is not something that is usually associated with being fed. This pairing is called a *conditioning trial*. It is repeated a number of times. Then come the *test trials*. Here, the metronome sound is presented alone and the salivary reflex is measured. Pavlov found that under these conditions, the sound of the metronome on its own produced salivation. This type of learning is now referred to as classical conditioning, or Pavlovian conditioning.

Pavlov called the salivation elicited by food the **unconditioned response (UR)**. The response is "unconditioned" because it is unlearned. It occurs without prior training and is an automatic behavior, such as some simple reflexes. Similarly, the food is the **unconditioned stimulus (US)**. Normally, without any training, the food leads to salivation (UR). Thus, before learning takes place, the US produces the UR.

Because the clicking of the metronome produces salivation only after training, it is the **conditioned stimulus (CS)**. That is, before conditioning, the clicking of the metronome is unrelated to salivation. After learning takes place, the clicking serves as a "signal" that food is about to become available. The increased salivation that occurs when only the conditioned stimulus is presented is the **conditioned response (CR)**. It is the response that has been learned. In the case of Pavlov's dogs, both the CR and the UR were salivation. However, the CR and the UR are not always identical: The CR usually is weaker than the UR. Thus, the metronome sound produces less saliva than the food does. (The steps just described are outlined in "The Methods of Psychology: Pavlov's Classical Conditioning.")

Suppose you are watching a movie in which a character is attacked. As you watch the attack scene, you feel tense, anxious, and perhaps disgusted. In this scenario, the frightening scene and your feelings occur naturally. That is, the stimulus and your response to it are unconditioned. Now imagine a piece of music that does not initially have much effect on you but that you hear in the movie just before each frightening scene. (A good example is the musical theme from the classic 1975 movie *Jaws;* **FIGURE 6.10.**) Eventually, you will begin to feel tense and anxious as soon as you hear the music. You have learned that the music, the conditioned stimulus, predicts scary scenes. Because of this learning, you feel the tension and anxiety, the conditioned response. As in Pavlov's studies, the CS (music) produces a somewhat different emotional response than the US (the scary scene). The response may be weaker. It may be more a feeling of apprehension than one of fear or disgust. If you later hear this music in a different context, such as on the radio, you will again feel tense and anxious even though you are not watching the movie. You have been classically conditioned to be anxious when you hear the music. Because this association is learned, your anxious feeling from the music will typically be weaker than your response to the scary scene.

 What type of stimulus is food?

6.4 Learning Is Acquired and Persists Until Extinction

Like many other scientists (of his time and subsequently), Pavlov was greatly influenced by Darwin's *On the Origin of Species*. Pavlov believed that conditioning is the basis for how animals learn to adapt to their environments. By learning to predict what objects bring pleasure or pain, animals acquire new adaptive behaviors. For instance, when an animal learns that a metronome beat predicts the appearance of

The Methods of Psychology
Pavlov's Classical Conditioning

HYPOTHESIS: A dog can learn that a metronome predicts food.

RESEARCH METHOD:

1 Food (**unconditioned stimulus**) causes the dog to salivate (**unconditioned response**).

Before conditioning

US

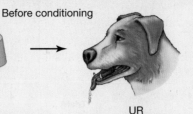

UR

The clicking metronome (**neutral stimulus**) does not cause the dog to salivate.

Neutral stimulus

No response

2 During conditioning trials, the clicking metronome is presented to a dog just before the food.

Neutral stimulus

Conditioning

+

US

3 During test trials, the clicking metronome (**conditioned stimulus**) is presented without the food, and the dog's response is measured.

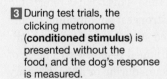

CS

After conditioning

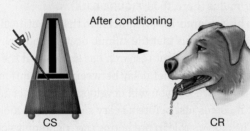

CR

RESULT: After conditioning, the metronome causes the dog to salivate (**conditioned response**).

CONCLUSION: The dog was conditioned to associate the metronome with food.

QUESTION: In this example, what is the unconditioned stimulus, and why is it considered unconditioned?

ANSWER: Food is the unconditioned stimulus because it causes salivation without learning.

Source: Pavlov, I. P. (1927). *Conditioned reflexes: An investigation of the physiological activity of the cerebral cortex*. (Translated and edited by G. V. Anrep). London: Oxford University Press; Humphrey Milford.

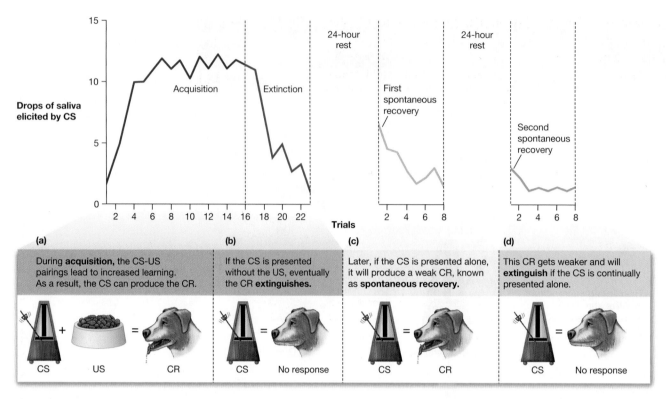

FIGURE 6.11
Acquisition, Extinction, and Spontaneous Recovery

Within the figure:

15 / 10 / 5 / 0 (y-axis)

Drops of saliva elicited by CS

Acquisition

Extinction

24-hour rest

First spontaneous recovery

24-hour rest

Second spontaneous recovery

2 4 6 8 10 12 14 16 18 20 22 (x-axis)

2 4 6 8

2 4 6 8

Trials

(a) During **acquisition**, the CS-US pairings lead to increased learning. As a result, the CS can produce the CR.

CS   US   CR

(b) If the CS is presented without the US, eventually the CR **extinguishes**.

CS   No response

(c) Later, if the CS is presented alone, it will produce a weak CR, known as **spontaneous recovery**.

CS   CR

(d) This CR gets weaker and will **extinguish** if the CS is continually presented alone.

CS   No response

---

acquisition

The gradual formation of an association between the conditioned and unconditioned stimuli.

food, this process of association is called **acquisition.** Acquisition is the formation of an association between a conditioned stimulus (here, a metronome) and an unconditioned stimulus (here, food; **FIGURE 6.11A**).

From his research, Pavlov concluded that the critical element in the acquisition of a learned association is that the stimuli occur together in time. This bond is referred to as *contiguity*. Subsequent research has shown that the strongest conditioning occurs when there is a very brief delay between the conditioned stimulus and the unconditioned stimulus. Thus you will develop a stronger conditioned response to a piece of music if it comes just before a scary scene than if it occurs during or after the scary scene: The music's role in predicting the frightening scene is an important part of the classical conditioning. The next time you watch a horror movie, pay attention to the way the music gets louder just before a scary part begins. And if you have not seen *Jaws* yet, now might be a good time, because you will really understand how that music works.

SECOND-ORDER CONDITIONING   Sometimes a conditioned stimulus does not become directly associated with an unconditioned stimulus. Instead, the conditioned stimulus becomes associated with other conditioned stimuli that are already associated with the unconditioned stimulus. Once an association between a CS and a US is well learned so that it consistently produces a CR, the CS itself can take on value. For example, we value money because of its associations, not because of its physical characteristics. Once the CS has value, other stimuli may become associated with the CS only and can also produce CRs. The CRs can be learned even without the learner ever associating the CS with the original US. This phenomenon is known as *second-order conditioning*.

In one of Pavlov's early studies, a CS-US bond was formed between a tone (CS) and meat (US) so that the tone (CS) led to salivation (CR). In a second training session, a black square was repeatedly presented just after the tone. There was no US (no presentation of the meat) during this phase of the study. After a few trials, the black square was presented alone. It too produced salivation.

Second-order conditioning helps account for the complexity of learned associations, especially in people. For instance, suppose a child has been conditioned to associate money with desirable objects, such as candy, which for most children is a US that produces happiness (UR). Once we learn that money can buy candy, money (CS) now produces happiness (CR). Now suppose that whenever the child's uncle visits, the uncle gives the child some money. Through second-order conditioning, the child will learn to associate the uncle (a new CS) with money (the old CS). This process can condition the child to feel happy (CR) when visiting the uncle (Domjan, 2014).

GENERALIZATION AND DISCRIMINATION   In any learning situation, hundreds of possible stimuli can be associated with the unconditioned stimulus to produce the conditioned response. How does the brain determine which stimulus is—or which stimuli are—relevant? For instance, suppose we classically condition a dog so that it salivates (CR) when it hears a 1,000-hertz (Hz) tone (CS). What does that tone sound like? If you have ever heard the "bleep" tone on television that covers up swearing, you know what a 1,000 Hz tone sounds like. After the dog is conditioned to the tone and the CR is established, tones similar to 1,000 Hz will also produce salivation. The farther the tones are from 1,000 Hz (i.e., the higher or lower the pitch), the less the dog will salivate. **Stimulus generalization** occurs when stimuli similar but not identical to the CS produce the CR (**FIGURE 6.12A**). Generalization is adaptive, because in nature the CS is seldom experienced repeatedly in an identical way. Slight differences in variables—such as background noise, temperature, and lighting—lead to slightly different perceptions of the CS. As a result of these different perceptions, animals learn to respond to variations in the CS.

Of course, generalization has limits. Sometimes it is important for animals to distinguish among similar stimuli. For instance, two plant species might look similar, but one might be poisonous. In **stimulus discrimination,** animals learn to differentiate between two similar stimuli if one is consistently associated with the unconditioned stimulus and the other is not. Pavlov and his students demonstrated that dogs can learn to make very fine distinctions between similar stimuli. For example, dogs can learn to detect subtle differences in tones of different frequencies (**FIGURE 6.12B**). The ability to generalize and discriminate among stimuli is important for many aspects of daily life, such as being able to detect poisonous plants (**FIGURE 6.13**).

EXTINCTION   Once a behavior is acquired, how long does it persist? For instance, what if the animal expects to receive food every time it hears the beat of the metronome, but food stops appearing and the metronome is still beating? Animals sometimes have to learn when associations are no longer meaningful. Normally, after standard Pavlovian conditioning, the metronome (CS) leads to salivation (CR) because the animal learns to associate the metronome with the food (US). If the metronome is presented many times and food does not arrive, the animal learns that the metronome is no longer a good predictor of food. Because of this new learning, the

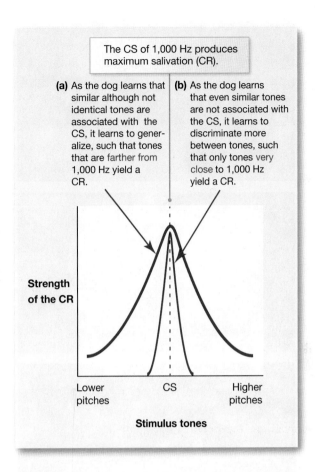

The CS of 1,000 Hz produces maximum salivation (CR).

(a) As the dog learns that similar although not identical tones are associated with the CS, it learns to generalize, such that tones that are farther from 1,000 Hz yield a CR.

(b) As the dog learns that even similar tones are not associated with the CS, it learns to discriminate more between tones, such that only tones very close to 1,000 Hz yield a CR.

Strength of the CR

Lower pitches

CS

Higher pitches

Stimulus tones

FIGURE 6.12
Stimulus Generalization and Stimulus Discrimination

stimulus generalization
Learning that occurs when stimuli that are similar but not identical to the conditioned stimulus produce the conditioned response.

stimulus discrimination
A differentiation between two similar stimuli when only one of them is consistently associated with the unconditioned stimulus.

(a)

(b)

(c)

FIGURE 6.13
The Adaptive Value of Stimulus Generalization and Stimulus Discrimination
Stimulus generalization and stimulus discrimination are important components of learning. These processes may take place even when a learned response has not been classically conditioned. **(a)** When people touch poison ivy and get an itchy rash, they learn to fear this three-leafed plant, and so they avoid it. **(b)** People may then experience stimulus generalization if they fear and avoid similar three-leafed plants—even nonpoisonous ones, such as fragrant sumac. By teaching people to avoid three-leafed plants, stimulus generalization therefore helps keep people safe. **(c)** People may also experience stimulus discrimination related to poison ivy. They do not fear and avoid dissimilar plants—such as Virginia creeper, which has five leaves and is nonpoisonous. If stimulus discrimination did not occur, fear of poison ivy would cause us to avoid activities near wooded areas, such as hiking and gardening.

animal's salivary response gradually disappears. This process is known as **extinction.** The conditioned response is *extinguished* when the conditioned stimulus no longer predicts the unconditioned stimulus (**FIGURE 6.11B**).

Now suppose, some time after extinction, the metronome is set in motion. Starting the metronome will once again produce the conditioned response of salivation. Through such **spontaneous recovery,** the extinguished CS again produces a CR (**FIGURE 6.11C**). This recovery is temporary, however. It will fade quickly unless the CS is again paired with the US. Even a single pairing of the CS with the US will reestablish the CR, which will then again diminish if CS-US pairings do not continue. Thus, extinction replaces the associative bond, but it does not eliminate that bond. Extinction is a form of learning that overwrites the previous association: The animal learns that the original association no longer holds true (e.g., the metronome no longer signals that it will be followed by meat; Bouton, 1994; Bouton, Trask, & Carranza-Jasso, 2016; **FIGURE 6.11D**).

 Which learning process helps you tell one of your friends from her identical twin?

ANSWER: stimulus discrimination

6.5 Learning Is Based on Evolutionary Significance

extinction
A process in which the conditioned response is weakened when the conditioned stimulus is repeated without the unconditioned stimulus.

spontaneous recovery
A process in which a previously extinguished conditioned response reemerges after the presentation of the conditioned stimulus.

Pavlov's original explanation for classical conditioning was that any two events presented in contiguity (i.e., together in time) would produce a learned association. Any object or phenomenon could be converted to a conditioned stimulus when associated with any unconditioned stimulus. Pavlov and his followers believed that the association's strength was determined by factors such as the intensity of the conditioned and unconditioned stimuli. For example, the more intense the stimuli were, the greater the learning would be. (A louder metronome or a larger piece of meat would produce stronger associations than a quieter metronome or a smaller piece of meat.)

In the mid-1960s, a number of challenges to Pavlov's theory suggested that some conditioned stimuli were more likely than others to produce learning. Contiguity was not sufficient to create CS-US associations.

CONDITIONED TASTE AVERSIONS   Research conducted by the psychologist John Garcia and colleagues showed that certain pairings of stimuli are more likely to become associated than others. For instance, when animals receive nonlethal amounts of poison in their food that make them ill, they quickly learn to avoid the tastes or smells associated with the food (Garcia & Koelling, 1966).

Likewise, many people can recall a time when they ate a particular food and later became ill with nausea, stomach upset, and vomiting. Whether or not the food caused the illness, most people respond to this sequence of events by demonstrating a *conditioned taste aversion*. This response occurs even if the illness clearly was caused by a virus or some other condition. Contrary to Pavlov's ideas, the association occurs even though the food and the sickness were not contiguous. It is especially likely to occur if the taste was not part of the person's usual diet (Lin, Arthurs, & Reilly, 2017). The association between a novel taste and getting sick, even when the illness occurs hours after eating, is so strong that a taste aversion can be formed in one trial (**FIGURE 6.14**). Some people cannot stand even the smell of a food they associate with a stomach-related illness.

Conditioned taste aversions are easy to produce with food, but they are very difficult to produce with light or sound. This difference is also contrary to what would be expected by Pavlovian theory. The difference makes sense, however, because smell and taste—not light or sound—are the main cues that guide an animal's eating behavior. From an evolutionary viewpoint, animals that quickly associate a certain taste with illness, and therefore avoid that taste, will be more successful. That is, they will be more likely to survive and pass along their genes.

The adaptive value of a response varies according to the evolutionary history of the particular species. For example, taste aversions are easy to condition in rats but difficult to condition in birds. This difference occurs because in selecting food, rats rely more on taste and birds rely more on vision. Accordingly, birds quickly learn to avoid a visual cue they associate with illness. Different types of stimuli cause different reactions even within a species. Rats freeze and startle if a CS is auditory, but they rise on their hind legs if the CS is visual (Holland, 1977).

BIOLOGICAL PREPAREDNESS Such differences in learned adaptive responses may reflect the survival value that different auditory and visual stimuli have for particular animals in particular environments. Those meanings are of course related to the potential dangers associated with the stimuli. For example, monkeys can more easily be conditioned to fear snakes than to fear objects such as flowers or rabbits (Cook & Mineka, 1989). The psychologist Martin Seligman (1970) has argued that animals are genetically programmed to fear specific objects. He refers to this programming as *biological preparedness*. Preparedness helps explain why animals tend to fear potentially dangerous things (e.g., snakes, fire, heights) rather than objects that pose little threat (e.g., flowers, shoes, babies; **FIGURE 6.15**).

The threats may also come from within an animal's own species. For example, when people participate in conditioning experiments in which aversive stimuli are paired with members of their own racial group or members of a different racial group, they more easily associate the negative stimuli with outgroup members (Olsson, Ebert, Banaji, & Phelps, 2005). This finding indicates that people are predisposed to wariness of outgroup members. Presumably, this tendency has come about because

(a)

(b)

FIGURE 6.14
Conditioned Taste Aversion
(a) After eating a poisonous mushroom, **(b)** this woman vomited and thus learned to be more careful when picking wild mushrooms.

(a)

(b)

FIGURE 6.15
Biological Preparedness
Animals have evolved to be able to detect threats. Thus, **(a)** we will quickly see the snake in this group of images, and **(b)** we will have a harder time detecting the flowers in this group. In both cases, the snakes grab our attention (Hayakawa, Kawai, & Masataka, 2011).

outgroup members have been more dangerous over the course of human evolution. The tendency has sometimes been exploited to create or enhance prejudice toward outgroups during wars and other intergroup conflicts.

 Q A friend who consumed too many Bloody Mary drinks no longer likes beverages that taste like tomato. Why?

ANSWER: Drinking excessive alcohol made the person ill and led to a conditioned taste aversion.

6.6 Learning Involves Expectancies and Prediction

Until the 1970s, most learning theorists were concerned only with observable stimuli and observable responses. Since then, learning theorists have placed a greater emphasis on trying to understand the mental processes that underlie conditioning. An important principle has emerged from this work: Classical conditioning is a way that animals come to *predict* the occurrence of events.

Consider rain. Dark clouds are usually present when it rains. Umbrellas are often present when it rains but not always. Sometimes there are dark clouds and rain but no umbrellas. Indeed, sometimes umbrellas are used on sunny days. We eventually learn that dark clouds are better signals of rain than umbrellas are (Schoenbaum, Esber, & Iordanova, 2013). When we see dark clouds, we tend to predict rain.

The psychologist Robert Rescorla (1966) conducted one of the first studies that highlighted the role of expectation and prediction in learning. He argued that for learning to take place, the conditioned stimulus must come before the unconditioned stimulus, thereby setting up an expectation for it. For instance, a stimulus that occurs *before* the US is more easily conditioned than one that comes *after* it. Even though the two are both contiguous presentations with the US (close to it in time), the first stimulus is more easily learned because it predicts the US.

Rescorla-Wagner model
A cognitive model of classical conditioning; it holds that learning is determined by the extent to which a US is unexpected or surprising.

The cognitive model of classical learning, published by Rescorla and his colleague Allan Wagner, profoundly changed our understanding of learning (Rescorla & Wagner, 1972). The **Rescorla-Wagner model** states that an animal learns an expectation that some predictors (potential CSs) are better than others. According to this model, learning is determined by the extent to which a US is unexpected or surprising. Learning theorists refer to the difference between the expected and actual outcomes as *prediction error*.

PREDICTION ERRORS Suppose that after a stimulus appears, something better than expected happens. This prediction error is considered positive. A *positive prediction error* strengthens the association between the CS and the US. Now suppose an expected event does not happen. The absence of the event leads to a negative prediction error. A *negative prediction error* weakens the CS-US association. Note here that positive and negative do not mean good and bad. Rather, positive means the presence of something unexpected, whereas negative refers to the absence of something expected. In both cases, the prediction error affects the association between the CS and the US.

Say you always use an electric can opener to open a can of dog food. Your dog associates the sound of the can opener (CS) with the appearance of food (US). That is, the dog has learned the sound signals the arrival of food. The dog wags its tail and runs around in circles when it hears that sound. It expects to be fed. Now say the electric can opener breaks and you replace it with a manual one. Without hearing the sound of the electric can opener, your dog receives food. This change will produce a large positive prediction error. In turn, the error will cause your dog to pay attention to events in the environment that might have produced the unexpected food. Over time, your dog will learn to associate being fed with your use of the new can opener (**FIGURE 6.16**).

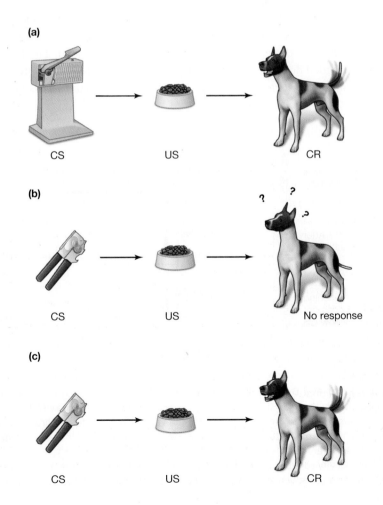

(a)

CS   US   CR

(b)

CS   US   No response

(c)

CS   US   CR

FIGURE 6.16
Rescorla-Wagner Model
The Rescorla-Wagner model of learning emphasizes prediction error. **(a)** Here, a dog associates the sound of an electric can opener with the arrival of food. **(b)** With the substitution of a manual can opener for the electric one, the dog is initially surprised. What happened to the reliable predictor of the dog's food? **(c)** This prediction error causes the dog to check the environment for a new stimulus. When the dog comes to associate the manual can opener with the arrival of food, the new stimulus has become the better predictor of the expected event: time to eat!

Eventually, learning will reach its maximum. At that point, no prediction errors will be generated because the food is fully predicted by the new can opener and no further updates to the association are needed. Of course, if the new can opener breaks, it will stop signaling the arrival of food. The dog will need to learn what new event signals the arrival of food.

ROLE OF DOPAMINE What biological mechanisms are in effect during such learning? To investigate the brain mechanisms involved in prediction error, Wolfram Schultz and his colleagues (1997) examined how dopamine neurons respond during conditioning. In their studies, monkeys were initially left thirsty. When those monkeys unexpectedly received fruit juice (US), they experienced a positive prediction error, and the reward regions in their brains showed a great deal of dopamine activity (**FIGURE 6.17A**). The monkeys were then conditioned to predict the arrival of juice (US) after the presentation of a light or tone (CS). In subsequent trials, after the monkeys had learned the association well, the reward regions of their brains showed a burst of dopamine activity in response to the CS but none for the US (**FIGURE 6.17B**). Why was the US no longer producing dopamine activity? Because the monkeys had learned that the light or tone predicted the juice, the juice was no longer a surprise. The less the prediction error, the less the dopamine activity.

Then, in additional trials, the juice (US) was no longer given. The monkeys experienced a negative prediction error—the expected result did not happen—and the reward regions showed a reduction in dopamine activity (**FIGURE 6.17C**).

These findings support the idea that prediction error signals alert us to important events in the environment (Schultz, 2016). For example, unexpected food alerts us that we need to learn how to predict the arrival of that food. We notice a cue associated with food, and the cue becomes a way to predict the food. Then, if the cue arrives but the food does not, we slowly learn that the cue no longer predicts anything important. Indeed, negative prediction errors now lead us to associate the cue

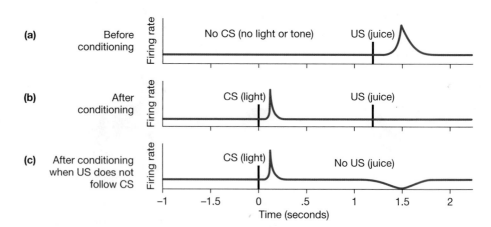

FIGURE 6.17

Prediction Error and Dopamine Activity

Dopamine activity in the brain signals the receipt of a reward. **(a)** The blue line clearly shows a spike in dopamine activity. This activity resulted from a positive prediction error after the unexpected arrival of the US. **(b)** Once the US was associated with the CS, the spike in dopamine activity occurred after the arrival of the CS but not after the arrival of the expected US. **(c)** Dopamine activity continued after the arrival of the CS. However, once the US no longer appeared, negative prediction error resulted in decreased dopamine activity.

with a *lack* of food. Thus, it appears that error prediction and its related dopamine activation play an important role in conditioning (Eshel, Tian, & Uchida, 2013; Glimcher, 2011; Smith, Berridge, & Aldridge, 2011).

 Q **What produces a prediction error?**

6.7 Phobias and Addictions Have Learned Components

Classical conditioning helps explain many behavioral phenomena, especially phobias and addiction.

PHOBIAS A **phobia** is an acquired fear that is out of proportion to the real threat of an object or of a situation. Common phobias include the fears of heights, of dogs, of insects, of snakes, and of the dark. According to classical-conditioning theory, phobias develop through the generalization of a fear experience, as when a person stung by a wasp develops a fear of all flying insects. (Phobias are discussed further in Chapter 14, "Psychological Disorders.")

Animals can be classically conditioned to fear neutral objects. This process is known as **fear conditioning** and can be observed in animals within the first weeks of life (Deal, Erickson, Shiers, & Burman, 2016). In a typical study of fear conditioning, a rat is classically conditioned to produce a fear response to an auditory tone: Electric shock follows the tone, and eventually the tone produces fear responses on its own. These responses include specific physiological and behavioral reactions. One interesting response is *freezing,* or keeping still. Humans are among the many species that respond to fear by freezing. Immediately keeping still might be a hardwired response that helps animals deal with predators, which often are attracted by movement (LeDoux, 2002; Tovote et al., 2016).

In 1919, John B. Watson became one of the first researchers to demonstrate the role of classical conditioning in the development of phobias. In this case study, Watson taught an infant named Albert B. to fear neutral objects. It is important to note Watson's motives for conditioning "Little Albert." At the time, the prominent theory of phobias was based on Freudian ideas about unconscious repressed sexual desires. Believing that Freudian ideas were unscientific and unnecessarily complex, Watson proposed that phobias could be explained by simple learning principles, such as classical conditioning.

To test his hypothesis, Watson devised a learning study. He asked a woman to let him use her son, Albert B., in the study. Because this child was emotionally stable, Watson believed the experiment would cause him little harm. When Albert was 9 months old, Watson and his lab assistant, Rosalie Rayner, presented him with various neutral objects, including a white rat, a rabbit, a dog, a monkey, costume masks, and a ball of white wool. Albert showed a natural curiosity about these items, but he displayed no overt emotional responses.

When Albert was 11 months old, Watson and Rayner (1920) began the conditioning trials (**FIGURE 6.18A**). This time, as they presented the white rat and Albert reached for it, Watson banged a hammer into an iron bar, producing a loud clanging sound. The sound scared the child, who immediately withdrew and hid his face. Watson did this a few more times at intervals of five days until Albert would whimper and cringe when the rat was presented alone. Thus, the US (smashing sound) led to a

phobia
An acquired fear that is out of proportion to the real threat of an object or of a situation.

fear conditioning
A type of classical conditioning that turns neutral stimuli into feared stimuli.

UR (fear response). Eventually, the pairing of the CS (rat) and US (smashing sound) led to the rat's producing a fear response (CR) on its own. The fear response generalized to other stimuli that Watson had presented along with the rat at the initial meeting (**FIGURE 6.18B**). Over time, Albert became frightened of them all, including the rabbit and the ball of wool. Even a Santa Claus mask with a white beard produced a fear response. Thus, classical conditioning was shown to be an effective method of inducing phobia.

Watson had planned to extinguish Little Albert's learned phobias. However, Albert's mother removed the child from the study before Watson could conduct the extinction trials. For many years, no one seemed to know what had become of Little Albert. His fate was one of psychology's great mysteries. Although Watson did not keep track of Albert, various researchers have sought to identify him over the years (Griggs, 2015). The available evidence suggests that he was William Albert Barger,

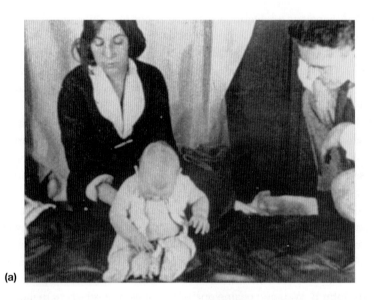

(a)

(b)

FIGURE 6.18
Case Study of "Little Albert"
(a) In Watson's experiment, Little Albert was presented with a neutral object—a white rat—that provoked a neutral response. Albert learned to associate the rat with a loud clanging sound that scared him. Eventually he showed the conditioned fear response when he saw the previously neutral rat. **(b)** The fear response generalized to other stimuli presented with the rat, such as costume masks.

who died in 2007 at age 87 (Powell, Digdon, Harris, & Smithson, 2014). Barger's relatives described him as easygoing, so he does not seem to have suffered long-term problems from being in the study (**FIGURE 6.19**). However, Barger reportedly disliked animals, especially dogs, throughout his life and covered his ears whenever he heard barking.

In his detailed plans for the reconditioning, Watson described a method of continually presenting the feared items to Albert paired with more pleasant things, such as candy. A colleague of Watson's used this method on a child who was afraid of rabbits and other furry objects. The behavioral pioneer Mary Cover Jones (1924) eliminated the fear of rabbits in a 3-year-old named Peter by bringing the rabbit closer as she provided Peter with a favorite food. Such classical-conditioning techniques have since proved valuable for developing very effective behavioral therapies to treat phobias. For instance, when a person is suffering from a phobia, a clinician might expose the patient to small doses of the feared stimulus while having the client engage in an enjoyable task. This technique, called *counterconditioning,* may help the client overcome the phobia. You will learn more about these kinds of behavioral treatments in Chapter 15.

DRUG ADDICTION   Classical conditioning also plays an important role in drug addiction (which is discussed in Chapter 4). Conditioned drug effects are common and demonstrate conditioning's power. For example, the smell of coffee can become a conditioned stimulus (CS). The smell alone can lead coffee drinkers to feel activated and aroused, as though they have actually consumed caffeine (Plassmann & Wager, 2014; **FIGURE 6.20**).

Likewise, for heroin addicts, the sight of the needle and the feeling when it is inserted into the skin become a CS. For this reason, addicts sometimes inject themselves with water to reduce their cravings when heroin is unavailable. Even the sight of a straight-edge razor blade, used as part of administering heroin, can briefly increase an addict's cravings (Siegel, 2005).

When former heroin addicts are exposed to environmental cues associated with their drug use, such as people and places, they often experience cravings. This effect occurs partly because the environmental cues have previously signaled ingestion of the drugs. If the resulting cravings are not satisfied, the addict may experience withdrawal (as discussed in Chapter 4, the unpleasant physiological and psychological state of tension and anxiety that occurs when addicts stop using drugs). Addicts who quit using drugs in treatment centers often relapse when they return to their old environments because they experience conditioned craving.

In laboratory settings, researchers have presented heroin addicts or cocaine addicts with cues associated with drug ingestion. These cues have led the addicts to experience cravings and various physiological responses associated with withdrawal, such as changes in heart rate and blood pressure. Brain imaging studies have found that such cues lead to activation of the prefrontal cortex and various regions of the limbic system, areas of the brain involved in the experience of reward (Kelley, Wagner, & Heatherton, 2015). When you are hungry, seeing a tantalizing food item activates these same brain regions. This effect occurs because seeing food usually signals that you will be eating it. Recall the earlier discussion where a burst of dopamine occurred for the CS (tone) rather than the US (juice). In the same way, the sight of drug cues produces an expectation that the drug high will follow. According to the psychologist Shepard Siegel (2005), it is therefore important that treatment for addiction include exposing addicts to drug cues. Such exposure helps extinguish responses to those cues. In this way, the cues are prevented from triggering cravings in the future.

FIGURE 6.19
Little Albert as an Adult
The best evidence indicates that Watson's study participant Little Albert was William Albert Barger, who lived to be 87.

FIGURE 6.20
Experiencing Coffee
For people who regularly drink coffee, just the smell of the beverage can produce some of the effects of caffeine.

Siegel and his colleagues have also conducted research into the relationship between drug tolerance and specific situations. As discussed in Chapter 4, tolerance is a process in which addicts need more and more of a drug to experience the same effects. Siegel's research has shown that tolerance is greatest when the drug is taken in the same physical location as that in which previous drug use occurred. Presumably, the body has learned to expect the drug in that location and then to compensate for the drug, such as by altering neurochemistry or physiology to metabolize it. For example, college students show greater tolerance to alcohol when it is provided with familiar cues (e.g., a drink that looks and tastes like beer) than when the same amount of alcohol is provided in a novel form (e.g., a blue, peppermint-flavored drink; Siegel, Baptista, Kim, McDonald, & Weise-Kelly, 2000). Tolerance can be so great that addicts regularly use drug doses that would be fatal for the inexperienced user. Conversely, Siegel's findings imply that if addicts take their usual large doses in novel settings, they are more likely to overdose. That is, because the addicts are taking drugs under different conditions, their bodies will not respond sufficiently to compensate for the drugs (Siegel, 1984; Siegel, Hinson, Krank, & McCully, 1982; Siegel, 2016).

Q Why might it be easier for addicts to abstain in a clinic than in their own neighborhood?

ANSWER: The clinic will most likely present the addicts with fewer learned drug cues.

operant conditioning (instrumental conditioning)

A learning process in which the consequences of an action determine the likelihood that it will be performed in the future.

How Do Consequences of an Action Shape Behavior?

Our behaviors often represent means to particular ends. We buy food to eat it, we study to get good grades, we work to receive money, and so on. We learn that behaving in certain ways leads to rewards, and we learn that not behaving in other ways keeps us from punishment. A particular behavior produces a particular outcome. How do the consequences of our actions shape learning?

6.8 Operant Conditioning Involves Active Learning

Classical conditioning is a relatively passive and automatic process. Through classical conditioning, an animal learns predictive associations between stimuli, regardless of the animal's behavior. This form of learning does not account for situations when an animal acts because it has received a reward for doing that action. Our behaviors often represent a way to achieve something (i.e., a reward) or avoid something (i.e., punishment). They are *instrumental*—done for a purpose.

This type of learning is called **operant conditioning,** or **instrumental conditioning.** B. F. Skinner, the psychologist most closely associated with this process, chose the term *operant* to express the idea that animals *operate* on their environments to produce effects (**FIGURE 6.21**).

Operant conditioning is the learning process in which an action's consequences determine the likelihood of that action being repeated. Thus, in operant conditioning, the human or animal makes associations between events that it can control. By contrast, in classical conditioning, the association is made between events that cannot be controlled.

LAW OF EFFECT The study of operant conditioning began in the late nineteenth century, in Cambridge, Massachusetts, at the home of the Harvard psychologist William James. A young graduate student working with James, Edward Thorndike, took inspiration from Charles Darwin's painstakingly precise observations of animal behavior. In James's basement, Thorndike performed the first reported carefully controlled experiments in comparative animal psychology. Specifically, he studied whether nonhuman animals showed signs of intelligence. As part of his research, Thorndike built a *puzzle box,* a small cage with a trapdoor (**FIGURE 6.22A**). The trapdoor would open if the animal inside performed a specific action, such as pulling a string. Thorndike placed food-deprived animals, initially chickens, inside the puzzle box to see if they could figure out how to escape.

When Thorndike moved to Columbia University to complete his Ph.D., he switched from using chickens to using cats in his studies. To motivate the cats, he would place food just outside the box. When a cat was first placed in the box, it usually attempted to escape through numerous behaviors that did not work. After 5 to 10 minutes of struggling, the cat would *accidentally* press a lever that pulled a string, and the door would open. Thorndike would then return the cat to the box and repeat the trial. On each subsequent trial, the cat would press the lever a bit more quickly, gradually getting faster and faster at escaping. Over the course of many trials, it would learn to escape from the puzzle box within seconds (**FIGURE 6.22B**).

From this line of research, Thorndike (1927) developed a general theory of learning. According to this **law of effect,** any behavior that leads to a "satisfying state of affairs" is likely to occur again. Any behavior that leads to an "annoying state of affairs" is less likely to occur again.

FIGURE 6.21
B. F. Skinner
B. F. Skinner studies an animal's operations on its laboratory environment.

law of effect
Thorndike's general theory of learning: Any behavior that leads to a "satisfying state of affairs" is likely to occur again, and any behavior that leads to an "annoying state of affairs" is less likely to occur again.

(a)

(b)

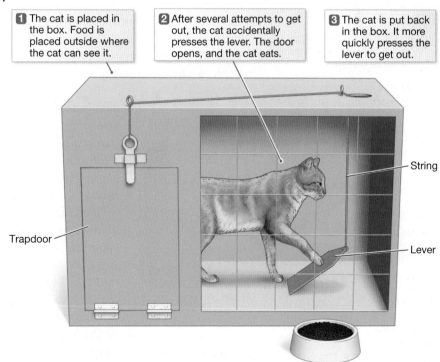

1 The cat is placed in the box. Food is placed outside where the cat can see it.

2 After several attempts to get out, the cat accidentally presses the lever. The door opens, and the cat eats.

3 The cat is put back in the box. It more quickly presses the lever to get out.

String

Lever

Trapdoor

FIGURE 6.22
Thorndike's Puzzle Box
(a) Thorndike used puzzle boxes, such as the one depicted here, **(b)** to assess learning in animals.

REINFORCEMENT INCREASES BEHAVIOR B. F. Skinner developed a formal learning theory based on the law of effect developed by Thorndike. As a young man, Skinner had wanted to be a novelist so that he could explore large questions about the human condition. Then he read two works of nonfiction that changed his life. The first was the 1924 book *Behaviorism,* by John B. Watson. The second was a 1927 article in the *New York Times Magazine,* in which the novelist H. G. Wells expressed admiration for the work of Ivan Pavlov. Increasingly, the behaviorists' perspective made sense to Skinner. He became convinced that psychology was his calling.

Skinner received his Ph.D. from Harvard University in 1931, but he differed with his professors about what psychologists should study. Many faculty members were concerned about his disregard for their efforts to analyze the mind through introspection, an approach then common at Harvard. As discussed in Chapter 1, introspection is the process of using verbal reports to assess mental states. After thinking about your own thoughts and feelings, you talk about them as a way of making them public and available for others to study. The main objection to using introspection as a research method is that it is not very reliable. As noted earlier in this chapter, behaviorists believed that to be scientists, psychologists had to instead study observable actions. In other words, psychologists needed to focus on the behaviors that people and nonhuman animals display.

Inspired by the work of Watson and of Pavlov, Skinner believed that he could dramatically change an animal's behavior by providing incentives to the animal for performing particular acts. For the next half century, he conducted systematic studies of animals, often pigeons or rats, to discover the basic rules of learning. His groundbreaking work led Skinner to form radical ideas about behaviorism, such as how it might be applied to entire communities to create a utopian way of life (Skinner, 1948b). In the process, he outlined many of the most important principles that shape the behavior of animals, including humans. These principles remain as relevant today as they were 70 years ago.

Skinner objected to the subjective aspects of Thorndike's law of effect. According to Skinner, states of "satisfaction" are not observable empirically. To describe an observable event that produces an observable learned response, Skinner coined the term *reinforcement.* A **reinforcer** is a stimulus that occurs after a response and increases the likelihood that the response will be repeated. Skinner believed that behavior—studying, eating, driving on the proper side of the road, and so on—occurs because it has been reinforced.

reinforcer
A stimulus that follows a response and increases the likelihood that the response will be repeated.

To assess operant conditioning, Skinner developed a simple device. It consists of a small chamber or cage. Inside, one lever or response key is connected to a food supply, and a second lever or response key is connected to a water supply. An animal, usually a rat or pigeon, is placed in the chamber or cage. The animal learns to press one lever or key to receive food, the other lever or key to receive water. In his earlier research, Skinner had used a maze. There, a rat had to make a specific turn to get access to the reinforcer, usually a small piece of food at the end of one arm of the maze. After the rat completed a trial, Skinner had to return the rat to the beginning of the maze. He developed the *operant chamber,* as he called it, basically because he grew tired of fetching rats. With the device—which came to be known as the *Skinner box,* although he never used that term—he could expose rats or pigeons to repeated conditioning trials without having to do anything but observe (**FIGURE 6.23**).

FIGURE 6.23
Operant Chamber
This diagram shows B. F. Skinner's operant chamber. Skinner is pictured with one in Figure 6.21.

Lever
Food tray

Skinner later built mechanical recording devices that allowed the experimenter to conduct trials without being present. Today's operant chambers interface with computers to enable researchers to record behavioral data.

SHAPING When performing operant conditioning, you cannot provide the reinforcer until the animal displays the appropriate response. An animal inside a Skinner box has so little to do that it typically presses the lever or key sooner rather than later. One major problem with operant conditioning outside the Skinner box is that the same animal might take a while to perform the action you are looking for. Rather than wait for the animal to spontaneously perform the action, you can use an operant-conditioning technique to teach the animal to do so. This powerful process is called **shaping.** It consists of reinforcing behaviors that are increasingly similar to the desired behavior.

Suppose you are trying to teach your dog to roll over. You initially reward any behavior that even slightly resembles rolling over, such as lying down. Once this behavior is established, you reinforce behaviors more selectively. Reinforcing *successive approximations* eventually produces the desired behavior. In other words, the animal learns to discriminate which behavior is being reinforced.

Shaping has been used to condition animals to perform amazing feats: pigeons playing table tennis, dogs playing the piano, pigs doing housework such as picking up clothes and vacuuming, and so on (**FIGURE 6.24**). Shaping has been used to teach appropriate social skills to people with psychological disorders; to teach language to children with autism; and to teach basic skills, such as dressing themselves, to individuals with intellectual disabilities. More generally, parents and educators often use shaping to encourage appropriate behavior in children. For example, they praise children for their initial—often illegible—attempts at handwriting.

 Studying an extra hour per day for the exam produced an impressive grade. What is the likely reinforcer?

ANSWER: receiving the grade

6.9 How Do Superstitions Start?

Do you have a lucky charm? Do you wear your "good luck" socks every time you take an exam? The list of people's superstitions is virtually endless (**FIGURE 6.25**). In North America and Europe, people avoid the number 13. In China, Japan, Korea, and Hawaii, they avoid the number 4. The basketball player Michael Jordan, a graduate of the University of North Carolina, always wore shorts with the North Carolina logo under his uniform for good luck. A recent beer commercial portrayed a hapless fan who wanted to watch the game, but because his team scored each time he went to the basement to get a cold one, he decided to stay in the basement. By missing the game, he was trying to help the team win.

Even pigeons might be superstitious. In one study, Skinner (1948a) placed hungry pigeons in a cage and delivered food every 15 seconds regardless of what the pigeons

FIGURE 6.24
Shaping
Shaping, an operant conditioning technique, consists of reinforcing behaviors that are increasingly similar to the desired behavior. This technique can be used to train animals to perform extraordinary behaviors. Here, a trained dog water-skis for a boat show.

shaping
A process of operant conditioning; it involves reinforcing behaviors that are increasingly similar to the desired behavior.

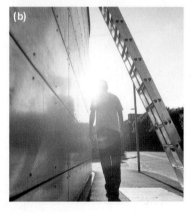

FIGURE 6.25
Superstitions
According to superstition, bad luck will come your way if **(a)** a black cat crosses your path or **(b)** you walk under a ladder.

were actually doing. He found that pigeons quickly learned to repeat behaviors they had been performing when the food was delivered. This repetition meant the pigeons were more likely to be performing those behaviors the next time food arrived. One pigeon was conditioned to turn counterclockwise, another to thrust its head into one corner of the cage. Yet another developed a pendulum motion of the head and body, in which the head was extended forward and swung from right to left with a sharp movement followed by a somewhat slower return.

Because these pigeons were performing particular actions when the reinforcers were given, their actions were accidentally reinforced. The tendency to associate events that occur together in time is incredibly strong because the brain is compelled to figure things out. When a chance reinforcer occurs close in time to some behavior, humans and nonhuman animals sometimes associate the reinforcement with the behavior. Whereas pigeons just develop behaviors that look like superstitions, people look for reasons to explain outcomes, and the observed association serves that purpose. Their resulting associations can lead people, at least, to cling to superstitions.

Most superstitions are harmless, but some can interfere with daily living when they get too extreme. As a critical thinker who understands psychological reasoning, you should be aware of the tendency to associate events with other events that occur at the same time. Ask yourself whether the timing was simply a coincidence—and then "risk" wearing different socks to your next exam! ■

Q In terms of learning, what is the main cause of superstitious behavior?

ANSWER: receiving chance reinforcement

6.10 There Are Many Types of Reinforcement

The most obvious stimuli that act as reinforcers are those necessary for survival, such as food or water. Because they satisfy biological needs, these stimuli are called *primary reinforcers*. From an evolutionary standpoint, the learning value of primary reinforcers makes a great deal of sense: Animals that repeatedly perform behaviors reinforced by food or water are more likely to survive and pass along their genes. But many apparent reinforcers do not directly satisfy biological needs. For example, a compliment, money, or an A on a paper can be reinforcing.

Stimuli that serve as reinforcers but do not satisfy biological needs are called *secondary reinforcers*. These reinforcers are established through classical conditioning, as described earlier in this chapter: We learn to associate a neutral stimulus, such as money (CS), with rewards such as food, security, and power (US). Money is really only pieces of metal or of paper, or electronic payment systems such as Bitcoin, but these and other neutral objects become meaningful through their associations with unconditioned stimuli.

Other aspects of reinforcers also follow principles similar to those found in classical conditioning. For

"Oh, not bad. The light comes on, I press the bar, they write me a check. How about you?"

instance, generalization and discrimination learning may occur with a reinforcing stimulus. And if an action previously reinforced no longer leads to reinforcement, that action will eventually extinguish. So a child who throws a tantrum to gain his father's attention will eventually stop misbehaving if that behavior is not reinforced.

REINFORCER POTENCY Some reinforcers are more powerful than others. The psychologist David Premack (1959; Holstein & Premack, 1965) theorized about how a reinforcer's value could be determined. The key is the amount of time a person, when free to do anything, willingly engages in a specific behavior associated with the reinforcer. For instance, most children would choose to spend more time eating ice cream than eating spinach. Ice cream is therefore more reinforcing for children than spinach is. One great advantage of Premack's theory is that it can account for differences in individuals' values. For people who prefer spinach to ice cream, spinach serves as a more potent reinforcer. Also, a reinforcer's value can vary with context. If you are hungry, ice cream will have a high value. If you are very full, its value will drop, and you might find something else—not necessarily a food—more reinforcing.

One logical application of Premack's theory is the *Premack principle*. According to this principle, a more-valued activity can be used to reinforce the performance of a less-valued activity. Parents use the Premack principle all the time. They tell their children, "Eat your spinach and then you'll get dessert," "Finish your homework and then you can go out," and so on.

POSITIVE AND NEGATIVE REINFORCEMENT Reinforcement always increases behavior. Through the administration of a stimulus after a behavior, **positive reinforcement** increases the probability of that behavior's being repeated (**FIGURE 6.26A**). Positive reinforcement is often called *reward*. "Positive" simply means that something is being added, not whether the reinforcement is good. Rewarded behaviors increase in frequency, as when people work harder in response to praise or increased pay.

In contrast, **negative reinforcement** increases behavior through the *removal* of an unpleasant stimulus (**FIGURE 6.26B**). For instance, when a rat is required to press a lever to turn off an electric shock, the pressing of the lever has been negatively reinforced. "Negative" simply means that something is being removed, not whether the reinforcement is bad.

Negative reinforcement is quite common in everyday life. You take a pill to get rid of a headache. You close the door to your room to shut out noise. You change the channel to avoid watching an awful program. You pick up a crying baby. In each case, you are engaging in a behavior to try to avoid or escape an unwanted stimulus. If the action you take successfully reduces the unwanted stimulus, then the next time you have a headache, hear noise in your room, see an awful program, or are with a crying baby, the more likely you are to repeat the behavior that reduced the stimulus. The behavior has been negatively reinforced.

Note, however, that while picking up the crying infant is negatively reinforcing for you, it positively reinforces the infant for crying! The infant learns that crying increases the likelihood of being picked up and comforted. Likewise, the parent who gives a child candy to stop a tantrum is negatively reinforced (the tantrum stops), but the child is positively reinforced to have more tantrums in the future.

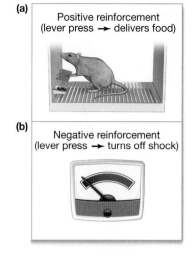

FIGURE 6.26
Positive Reinforcement and Negative Reinforcement
(a) In positive reinforcement, the response rate increases because responding causes the stimulus to be given. **(b)** In negative reinforcement, the response rate increases because responding causes the stimulus to be removed.

positive reinforcement
The administration of a stimulus to increase the probability of a behavior's being repeated.

negative reinforcement
The removal of an unpleasant stimulus to increase the probability of a behavior's being repeated.

 Q What is the basic difference between positive and negative reinforcements?

ANSWER: In positive reinforcement, something is added. In negative reinforcement, something is removed.

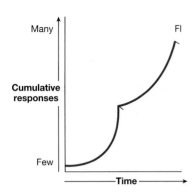

FIGURE 6.27
Fixed Interval Schedule
Imagine a cat learning to perform "feed me" behaviors right before the two feeding times each day. The reinforcer (slash mark) is the food.

continuous reinforcement
A type of learning in which behavior is reinforced each time it occurs.

partial reinforcement
A type of learning in which behavior is reinforced intermittently.

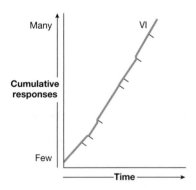

FIGURE 6.28
Variable Interval Schedule
Imagine yourself checking for texts and emails frequently throughout the day. The reinforcer (slash) is a message from a friend.

6.11 Operant Conditioning Is Influenced by Schedules of Reinforcement

How often should a reinforcer be given? For fast learning, behavior might be reinforced each time it occurs. This process is known as **continuous reinforcement**. In the real world, behavior is seldom reinforced continuously. People do not receive praise each time they behave acceptably. The intermittent reinforcement of behavior is more common. This process is known as **partial reinforcement**.

Partial reinforcement's effect on conditioning depends on the reinforcement schedule. Reinforcement can be scheduled in numerous ways. Most schedules vary in terms of the basis for providing reinforcement and the regularity with which reinforcement is provided. For instance, partial reinforcement can be administered according to either the number of behavioral responses or the passage of time, such as paying factory workers by the piece (behavioral responses) or by the hours spent working (passage of time).

A *ratio schedule* is based on the number of times the behavior occurs, as when a behavior is reinforced on every third or tenth occurrence. An *interval schedule* is based on a specific unit of time, as when a behavior is reinforced when it is performed every minute or hour. Partial reinforcement also can be given on a predictable *fixed schedule* or on a less predictable *variable schedule*. Crossing the basis for reinforcement with the regularity of reinforcement yields the four most common reinforcement schedules: fixed interval, variable interval, fixed ratio, and variable ratio.

- *Fixed Interval Schedule (FI)* A *fixed interval schedule* (*FI;* **FIGURE 6.27**) occurs when reinforcement is provided after a certain amount of time has passed. Imagine that you feed your cat twice a day. After some number of days, the cat will start to meow and rub against you at about the feeding times, especially if you are in the location where you typically put out the food. Your cat has not learned to read the clock. Rather, the cat has learned that after a certain amount of time has passed, feeding is likely. Once the cat is fed, it will probably go away and sleep. At the next mealtime, it will return and start meowing and rubbing again. Providing meals on this schedule reinforces the "feed me" behavior. Note the scalloping pattern in Figure 6.27, which indicates an increase in the behavior just before the opportunity for reinforcement and then a dropping off after reinforcement. Many students follow this kind of pattern when taking courses with regularly scheduled exams. They work extremely hard in the days before the exam and then slack off a bit immediately after the exam.
- *Variable Interval Schedule (VI)* A *variable interval schedule* (*VI;* **FIGURE 6.28**) occurs when reinforcement is provided after the passage of time, but the time is not regular. Although you know you will eventually be reinforced, you cannot predict when it will happen. For example, getting texts or emails from friends occurs on a variable interval schedule. You might check for messages throughout the day if you find receiving such messages reinforcing. Unlike the cat learning on an FI schedule, you never know when you will receive reinforcement, so you have to check back frequently. Professors who use pop quizzes do so because they encourage more regular studying by students. If you cannot predict when you will be quizzed, you have to keep up with your class work and always be prepared.
- *Fixed Ratio Schedule (FR)* A *fixed ratio schedule* (*FR;* **FIGURE 6.29**) occurs when reinforcement is provided after a certain number of responses have

been made. Factory workers who are paid based on the number of objects they make are a good example of the FR schedule. Teachers sometimes use this kind of schedule to reward children for cooperative classroom behavior. Students can earn a star for behaving well. After they collect a certain number of stars, they receive some kind of reinforcer, such as getting to select the next book the teacher will read. Likewise, your local pizzeria might give you a punch card that gives you a free pizza after you buy 10. In each case, the more you do, the more you get. Therefore, FR schedules typically produce high rates of responding.

- *Variable Ratio Schedule (VR)* A *variable ratio schedule* (*VR;* **FIGURE 6.30**) occurs when reinforcement is provided after an unpredictable number of responses. Games of chance provide an excellent example of a VR schedule. At a casino, you might drop a lot of money into a slot machine that rarely rewards you with a "win." Such behavior is not simply the result of an "addiction" to gambling. Rather, people put money in slot machines because the machines *sometimes* provide monetary rewards. VR schedules lead to high rates of responding that last over time because you know that eventually there will be a payoff for responding. You just do not know when it will happen—or even if you will still be the player on that machine at that time.

As mentioned earlier, continuous reinforcement leads to fast learning. But the behaviors do not last. The **partial-reinforcement extinction effect** refers to the greater persistence of behavior under partial reinforcement than under continuous reinforcement. During continuous reinforcement, the learner can easily detect when reinforcement has stopped. But when the behavior is reinforced only some of the time, the learner needs to repeat the behavior comparatively more times to detect the absence of reinforcement. Thus the less frequent the reinforcement during training, the greater the resistance to extinction. To condition a behavior so that it persists, you need to reinforce it continuously during early acquisition and then slowly change to partial reinforcement. Parents naturally follow this strategy in teaching behaviors to their children, as in toilet training.

 What type of partial reinforcement produces the most responses?

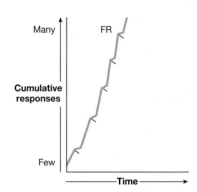

FIGURE 6.29
Fixed Ratio Schedule
Imagine factory workers who are paid based on making a certain number of objects. The reinforcer (slash mark) is payment.

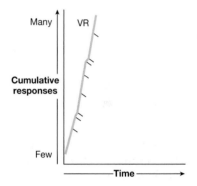

FIGURE 6.30
Variable Ratio Schedule
Imagine putting a lot of money into a slot machine in the hope that eventually you will win. The reinforcer (slash mark) is a payoff.

ANSWER: fixed ratio schedule

6.12 Punishment Decreases Behavior

Reinforcement and punishment have the opposite effects on behavior. Whereas reinforcement increases a behavior's probability, punishment decreases its probability. For example, giving your dog a treat each time she acts a certain way (reinforcement) will increase the likelihood she will act that way. Spraying water in her face and yelling "bad dog" each time she performs an action (punishment) will decrease the likelihood of her performing that action.

POSITIVE AND NEGATIVE PUNISHMENT Punishment reduces the probability that a behavior will recur. It can do so through positive or negative means. Again, "positive" or "negative" here means whether something is added or removed, not whether it is good or bad. **Positive punishment** decreases the behavior's probability through the administration of a stimulus. Usually the stimulus in positive punishment is unpleasant. Receiving a spray of water and being yelled at are forms of positive punishment. **Negative punishment** decreases the behavior's probability

partial-reinforcement extinction effect

The greater persistence of behavior under partial reinforcement than under continuous reinforcement.

positive punishment

The administration of a stimulus to decrease the probability of a behavior's recurring.

negative punishment

The removal of a stimulus to decrease the probability of a behavior's recurring.

HOW DO CONSEQUENCES OF AN ACTION SHAPE BEHAVIOR?

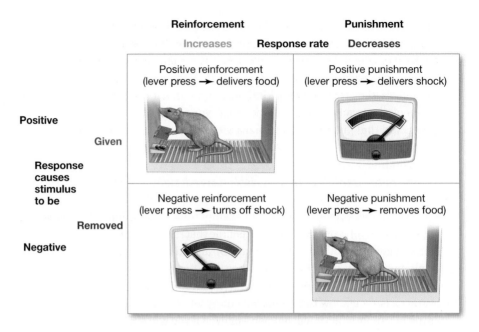

	Reinforcement	**Punishment**
	Increases **Response rate** Decreases	
Positive	Positive reinforcement (lever press → delivers food)	Positive punishment (lever press → delivers shock)
Given		
Response causes stimulus to be		
Removed		
Negative	Negative reinforcement (lever press → turns off shock)	Negative punishment (lever press → removes food)

FIGURE 6.31
Negative and Positive Reinforcement, Negative and Positive Punishment
Use this chart to help solidify your understanding of these very important terms.

through the removal of a usually pleasant stimulus. When a teenager loses driving privileges for speeding, he or she has received negative punishment. If that same teen has received a speeding ticket, the ticket serves as a positive punishment. Here, the negative and positive forms of punishment may produce the same result: The teen will be less likely to speed the next time he or she gets behind the wheel. For an overview of positive and negative kinds of both reinforcement and punishment, see **FIGURE 6.31.**

EFFECTIVENESS OF PARENTAL PUNISHMENT   To make their children behave, parents sometimes use punishment as a means of discipline. Many contemporary psychologists believe that punishment is often applied ineffectively, however, and that it may have unintended and unwanted consequences. Research has shown that for punishment to be effective, it must be reasonable, unpleasant, and applied immediately so that the relationship between the unwanted behavior and the punishment is clear. But considerable potential exists for confusion. For example, sometimes punishment is applied after a desired action. If a student is punished after admitting to cheating on an exam, the student may then associate the punishment with being honest rather than with the original offense. As a result, the student learns not to tell the truth. As Skinner once pointed out, one thing people learn from punishment is how to avoid it. Rather than learning how to behave appropriately, they may learn not to get caught.

Punishment can also lead to negative emotions, such as fear and anxiety. Through classical conditioning, these emotions may become associated with the person who administers the punishment. If a child thus learns to fear a parent or teacher, the long-term relationship between child and adult may be damaged (Gershoff, 2002). In addition, punishment often fails to offset the reinforcing aspects of the undesired behavior. In real life, any behavior can be reinforced in multiple ways. For instance, thumb sucking may be reinforced because it makes a child feel good, because it provides relief from negative emotions, and because it alleviates hunger. Punishment may not be sufficient to offset such rewards, but it may reinforce the child's secrecy about thumb sucking. For these and other reasons, most psychologists agree with Skinner's recommendation that reinforcement be used rather than punishment. A child complimented for being a good student is likely to perform better academically than one punished for doing poorly. After all, reinforcing good behavior tells the child what to do. Punishing the child for bad behavior does not tell the child how to improve.

One form of punishment that most psychologists believe is especially ineffective is physical punishment, such as spanking. Spanking is very common in the United States, however (**FIGURE 6.32A**). Although spanking has declined somewhat since the mid-1980s, 65 percent of women and 78 percent of men agreed or strongly agreed that it is sometimes necessary to give a child a "good, hard spanking" (Child Trends Databank, 2015). Beliefs about the appropriateness of spanking involve religious beliefs and cultural views, as well as legal issues. Many countries (e.g., Austria, Denmark, Israel, Sweden, and Italy) have banned corporal punishment in homes, schools, or both (**FIGURE 6.32B**). Even the United Nations has passed resolutions discouraging it.

A recent meta-analysis involving more than 160,000 children found that spanking was not effective in improving children's behavior (Gershoff & Grogan-Kaylor, 2016). Indeed, spanking was associated with many negative outcomes, including more aggression and antisocial behavior, more mental health problems, lower self-esteem, and negative relationships with parents. Importantly, the evidence indicates that other forms of punishment are more effective for decreasing unwanted behaviors (Kazdin & Benjet, 2003). Time-outs, small fines, and removal of privileges can effectively modify behavior. Yet many psychologists believe that any method of punishment is less effective than providing positive reinforcement for "better" behaviors. By rewarding the behaviors they wish to see, parents are able to increase those behaviors while building more positive bonds with their children.

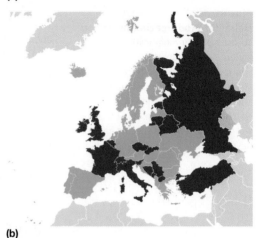

(a)

(b)

■ Spanking prohibited in schools and the home
■ Spanking prohibited in schools only
□ Spanking not prohibited

FIGURE 6.32
Legality of Spanking
These maps compare **(a)** the United States and **(b)** Europe in terms of the legality of spanking children.

 Q If you take away a child's toy because the child is banging it against the wall, what kind of punishment is this?

ANSWER: negative punishment

6.13 How Can Behavior Modification Help You Get in Shape?

Behavior modification is the use of operant-conditioning techniques to eliminate unwanted behaviors and replace them with desirable ones. The general rationale behind behavior modification is that most unwanted behaviors are learned and therefore can be unlearned. Parents, teachers, and animal trainers use conditioning strategies widely. People can be taught, for example, to be more productive at work, to save energy, and to drive more safely. Children with profound learning disabilities can be trained to communicate and to interact. As discussed in Chapter 15, operant techniques are also effective for treating many psychological conditions, such as depression and anxiety disorders.

behavior modification

The use of operant-conditioning techniques to eliminate unwanted behaviors and replace them with desirable ones.

FIGURE 6.33
Behavior Modification in Action
To see behavior modification in action, select a target behavior of your own that you wish to change. Maybe you feel that you should be studying more, exercising more, or watching less television. Any behavior will do, as long as it is specific and you have a realistic goal for changing it.

Another widespread behavior modification method draws on the principle of secondary reinforcement. People learn to perform tasks in exchange for tokens, which they can later trade for desirable objects or privileges. The tokens thus reinforce behavior, and people work as hard to obtain the tokens as they work to obtain food. Prisons, mental hospitals, schools, and classrooms often use *token economies,* in which people earn tokens for completing tasks and lose tokens for behaving badly. The people can later trade their tokens for objects or privileges. Here, the rewards not only reinforce good behavior but also give participants a sense of control over their environment. So, for instance, teachers can provide tokens to students for obeying class rules, turning in homework on time, and helping others. At some future point, the tokens can be exchanged for rewards, such as fun activities or extra recess time. In mental hospitals, token economies can encourage good grooming and appropriate social behavior and can discourage bizarre behavior.

The U.S. Department of Health and Human Services (2008) recommends that each adult engage in at least 150 minutes of moderate physical activity per week, but most of us fail to achieve this goal. Maybe you intend to exercise daily, then struggle to find the time to get to the gym. Or maybe you make working out a priority for a few weeks, then fall off the wagon. How can psychology help you stick with your exercise program (**FIGURE 6.33**)?

As you learned earlier in this chapter, experts regularly use the principles of operant conditioning to change the behaviors of animals, including humans. You do not have to be an expert, however, to condition yourself to perform healthful behaviors. Consider these steps:

1. **Identify a behavior you wish to change.** Before you begin a behavior modification program, you need to know which behavior you wish to modify. If your lack of physical activity is a concern, the behavior you need to target is being sedentary. In other words, you want to increase physical activity.

2. **Set goals.** Set goals that are realistic, specific, and measurable. If your current exercise program consists of a daily race to beat the closing elevator door, setting a goal to run 10 miles per day every day this month is not realistic. Likewise, a goal of "exercise more" will not do the trick, because it is too vague. Instead, you might set one of the following goals: Jog 1 mile on the treadmill at least four days this week, attend three yoga sessions this week, or walk at least 10,000 steps each day this week. Note that you can measure each of these goals objectively. You can use the treadmill's odometer to know whether you hit the 1-mile mark, or a calendar to indicate your performance of yoga, or the readout on a pedometer to track your daily steps.

   Note, too, that these goals sit on a relatively short time horizon. Setting goals you can meet in short order allows for more opportunities for reinforcement. If your ultimate goal is to run a marathon 12 months from now, you need to set small, incremental subgoals that you can reinforce along the way.

3. **Monitor your behavior.** Monitor your behavior for a week or more before you begin making changes. Simply noting the behavior will likely move you toward your goal, since you will be more conscious of it. Keeping careful track will also enable you to get a sense of your baseline. You will use this baseline as a point of comparison later to assess your progress. Record your observations. If you have a smartphone, you might download an app for recording physical activity. Register at an exercise-tracking Web site. Or just use a paper notebook.

4. **Select a positive reinforcer and decide on a reinforcement schedule.** When you choose a reinforcer, pick something attainable that you genuinely find enjoyable. For example, you could treat yourself to a movie each week that you meet your goal. Or you could give yourself one penny for every hundred steps you take each day.

Eventually, you could use the money to buy something you do not normally spend money on.

5. **Reinforce the desired behavior.** To cause the behavior change you want to see, you need to reinforce the desired behavior whenever it occurs. Be consistent. Suppose that if you work out at the gym three times this week, you treat yourself by watching the new episode of *Grey's Anatomy*. This is important: If you do not work out at the gym three times this week, do not watch *Grey's Anatomy*. If you're a *Grey's Anatomy* fan, it might be hard to resist streaming the newest episode (perhaps as you lounge on the couch instead of heading to the gym). But if you want the behavior modification to work, you have to resist. If you do not behave appropriately, you do not receive the reinforcer! Allow yourself no exceptions.

6. **Modify your goals, reinforcements, or reinforcement schedules, as needed.** Once you begin consistently hitting your stated goals, make the goals more challenging. Add more days per week, more miles per run, or more laps per workout. If you find yourself getting bored with a reinforcer, mix it up a bit. Just be sure to select reinforcers that are genuinely appealing. And change the reinforcement schedule so you have to work harder to get the reward. For example, rather than reinforcing your good behavior after each workout, use reinforcement after you complete two workouts or after you work out consistently for a week.

Of course, you can use these principles to address other behaviors, such as procrastinating on your studies, neglecting to call your family, spending too much time on Facebook, and so on. For now, just pick one behavior you want to modify and try implementing the steps outlined here. Once you get the hang of it, see if you can translate these steps to other areas of your life. Give it a try! ◼

Q What is it called when children earn points for good behavior that they can use to trade for items they want?

ANSWER: token economy

6.14 Biology and Cognition Influence Operant Conditioning

Behaviorists such as B. F. Skinner believed that all behavior could be explained by straightforward conditioning principles. In reality, however, reinforcement schedules explain only a certain amount of human behavior. Biology constrains learning, and reinforcement does not always have to be present for learning to take place.

BIOLOGICAL CONSTRAINTS   Behaviorists believed that any behavior could be shaped through reinforcement. We now know that animals have a hard time learning behaviors that run counter to their evolutionary adaptation. A good example of biological constraints was obtained by Marian and Keller Breland, a husband-and-wife team of psychologists who used operant-conditioning techniques to train animals for commercials (Breland & Breland, 1961). Many of their animals refused to perform certain tasks they had been taught. For instance, a raccoon learned to place coins in a piggy bank, but eventually it refused to perform this task. Instead, the raccoon stood over the bank and briskly rubbed the coins in its paws. This rubbing behavior was not reinforced. In fact, it delayed reinforcement. One explanation for the

FIGURE 6.34
Biological Constraints

Animals have a hard time learning behaviors that run counter to their evolutionary adaptation. For example, raccoons are hardwired to rub food between their paws, as this raccoon is doing. They have trouble learning *not* to rub objects.

cognitive map
A visual/spatial mental representation of an environment.

raccoon's behavior is that the task was incompatible with innate adaptive behaviors. The raccoon associated the coin with food and treated it the same way: Rubbing food between the paws is hardwired for raccoons (**FIGURE 6.34**).

Similarly, pigeons can be trained to peck at keys to obtain food or secondary reinforcers, but it is difficult to train them to peck at keys to avoid electric shock. They can learn to avoid shock by flapping their wings, because wing flapping is their natural means of escape. The psychologist Robert Bolles (1970) has argued that animals have built-in defense reactions to threatening stimuli. Conditioning is most effective when the association between the response and the reinforcement is similar to the animal's built-in predispositions.

ACQUISITION/PERFORMANCE DISTINCTION There is another challenge to the idea that reinforcement is responsible for all behavior. Namely, learning can take place without reinforcement. Edward Tolman, an early cognitive theorist, argued that reinforcement has more impact on performance than on learning. At the time, Tolman was conducting experiments in which rats had to learn to run through complex mazes to obtain food. Tolman believed that each rat developed a **cognitive map.** That is, during an experiment, each rat held in its brain a visual/spatial representation of the particular maze. The rat used this knowledge of the environment to help it find the food quickly.

To test his theory, Tolman and his students studied three groups of rats. The first group traveled through the maze but received no reinforcement: The rats reached the "goal box," found no food in the box, and simply wandered through the maze on each subsequent trial. The second group received reinforcement on every trial: Because the rats found food in the goal box, they learned to find the box quickly. The third group, critically, started receiving reinforcement only after the first 10 trials: At that point, the rats showed an amazingly fast learning curve and immediately caught up to the group that had been continuously reinforced (Tolman & Honzik, 1930; **FIGURE 6.35**).

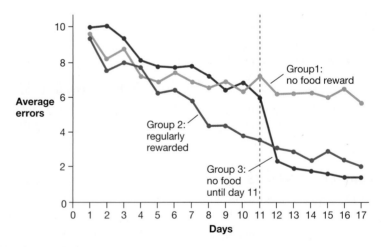

FIGURE 6.35
Tolman's Study of Latent Learning
Rats that were regularly reinforced for correctly running through a maze (Group 2) showed improved performance over time compared with rats that did not receive reinforcement (Group 1). Rats that were not reinforced for the first 1D trials but were reinforced thereafter showed an immediate change in performance (Group 3). Note that between days 11 and 12 Group 3's average number of errors decreased dramatically.

This result implies that the rats had learned a cognitive map of the maze and used it when the reinforcement began. Tolman's term **latent learning** refers to learning that takes place without reinforcement. For example, latent learning occurs when a person learns something simply by observing it. When most people drive for the first time, they do not need to be told that rotating the steering wheel turns the car. They already know that they need to rotate the steering wheel, even though they have never been reinforced for doing so. A great deal of learning takes place without people even realizing they are doing so (Reber, 2013).

Another form of learning that takes place without reinforcement is *insight learning*. In this form of problem solving, a solution suddenly emerges after either a period of inaction or contemplation of the problem. (Problem solving is discussed further in Chapter 8, "Thinking, Language, and Intelligence.") You probably have had this sort of experience, in which you mull over a problem for a while and then suddenly know the answer. The presence of reinforcement does not adequately explain insight learning, but it helps determine whether the behavior is subsequently repeated.

latent learning
Learning that takes place in the absence of reinforcement.

 Why does latent learning challenge traditional operant theories?

ANSWER: Latent learning takes place without reinforcement.

6.15 Dopamine Activity Underlies Reinforcement

As noted earlier, people often use the term *reward* as a synonym for positive reinforcement. By contrast, Skinner and other traditional behaviorists defined reinforcement strictly in terms of whether it increased behavior. They were relatively uninterested in *why* it increased behavior. For instance, they carefully avoided any speculation about whether subjective experiences had anything to do with behavior. After all, they believed that mental states were impossible to study empirically. Psychologists today are interested in mental states, such as liking and wanting, and the neural basis of those states.

One important component of the neural basis of reinforcement is the neurotransmitter dopamine. As discussed in Chapter 4, dopamine is involved in addictive behavior, especially in terms of increased wanting for the addictive substance. Research over the past 50 years has shown that dopamine plays an important role in reinforcement (Gershman & Daw, 2017; Schultz, 2016). In operant conditioning, dopamine release sets the value of a reinforcer. Drugs that block dopamine's effects disrupt operant conditioning.

Dopamine blockers are often given to individuals with Tourette's syndrome, a motor control disorder, to help them regulate their involuntary body movements. These individuals often have trouble staying on their drug regimens, however, because they feel the drugs prevent them from enjoying life. Conversely, as you might expect, drugs that enhance dopamine activation, such as cocaine and amphetamines, increase the reward value of stimuli.

When hungry rats are given food, they experience an increased dopamine release in the nucleus accumbens, a structure that is part of the limbic system: The greater the hunger, the greater the dopamine release (Rolls, Burton, & Mora, 1980). Food tastes better when you are hungry, and water is more rewarding when you are thirsty, because more dopamine is released under deprived conditions than under nondeprived conditions. Even looking at funny cartoons activates the nucleus accumbens (Mobbs, Greicius, Abdel-Azim, Menon, & Reiss, 2003). Have you ever experienced the chills while listening to a piece of music? This tingling sense feels like a shiver down

FIGURE 6.36
Enjoyment of Music
As music gives this listener pleasurable chills, dopamine activity is occurring in the listener's brain.

FIGURE 6.37
Wanting Versus Liking
Although this person wants a cigarette because he is addicted, he no longer enjoys the behavior of smoking.

the spine and might give you goosebumps (**FIGURE 6.36**). Using PET imaging and fMRI, researchers have shown that when people experience optimal pleasure while listening to music, there is dopamine activity in the nucleus accumbens (Salimpoor, Benovoy, Larcher, Dagher, & Zatorre, 2011).

Until recently, psychologists believed that rewards increase behavior primarily because of the pleasure those rewards produce and that dopamine was responsible for the subjective feelings associated with reward. But researchers have found that the relationship between dopamine and reward is a bit more nuanced. Robinson and Berridge (1993) introduced an important distinction between the *wanting* and *liking* aspects of reward. With drugs, for instance, wanting refers to the desire or the craving a user has for the substance. Liking refers to the subjective sense of pleasure the user receives from consuming the substance. Although wanting and liking often go together, there are circumstances under which wanting occurs without liking (Berridge, Ho, Richard, & DiFeliceantonio, 2010; Kringelbach & Berridge, 2009). For example, a smoker may desire a cigarette but then not particularly enjoy smoking it (**FIGURE 6.37**). As mentioned in Chapter 4, dopamine appears to be especially important for the wanting aspect of reward. Other neurotransmitters, such as endogenous opiates, may be more important for the liking aspect of reward (Berridge & Kringelbach, 2013).

What links dopamine activity to reinforcement? Recall the earlier discussion of prediction error. An important idea over the last decade is that the firing of dopamine neurons signals prediction error. When a behavior leads to an unexpected reward or a reward that is better than expected, a positive prediction error occurs. Dopamine activity in brain reward regions underlies this prediction error. If the same behavior did not produce a reward, this produces a negative prediction error. In that situation, dopamine activity in the brain would have decreased.

During the course of conditioning, we come to learn that certain cues signal rewards. Eventually, those cues themselves produce dopamine activity. Seeing a loved one, getting a good grade, or receiving a paycheck may be conditioned to produce dopamine activation. Money is an excellent example of a secondary reinforcer, as mentioned earlier, and anticipated monetary rewards have been found to activate dopamine systems (Knutson, Fong, Adams, Varner, & Hommer, 2001). Thus, things become reinforcing because they become associated with positive value. Through dopamine activity, these cues themselves become rewarding (Berridge, 2012).

 How does wanting something differ from liking it?

ANSWER: Wanting refers to the desire to do something, whereas liking refers to the subjective value associated with doing that something.

How Do We Learn from Watching Others?

Suppose you were teaching someone to fly an airplane. Obviously, just rewarding arbitrary correct behaviors would be a disastrous way to train an aspiring pilot. People learn many behaviors not by doing them but by watching others do them. For example, you learn social etiquette through observation. We often acquire attitudes about politics, religion, and the habits of celebrities from parents, peers, teachers, and the media. How much do we learn by observing others?

6.16 Learning Can Occur Through Observation and Imitation

As defined at the beginning of this chapter, observational learning is the acquisition or modification of a behavior after exposure to another individual performing that behavior. This kind of learning, sometimes called *social learning,* is a powerful adaptive tool for humans. For example, offspring can learn basic skills by watching adults perform those skills. They can learn which things are safe to eat by watching what adults eat (Wertz & Wynn, 2014). They can learn to fear dangerous objects and dangerous situations by watching adults avoid those objects and situations. Children even acquire beliefs through observation. Young children are sponges, absorbing everything that goes on around them. They learn by watching as much as by doing.

BANDURA'S OBSERVATIONAL STUDIES The most influential work on observational learning was conducted in the 1960s by the psychologist Albert Bandura. In a now-classic series of studies, Bandura divided preschool children into two groups. One group watched a film of an adult playing quietly with a large inflatable doll called Bobo. The other group watched a film of the adult attacking Bobo furiously: whacking the doll with a mallet, punching it in the nose, and kicking it around the room. When the children were later allowed to play with a number of toys, including the Bobo doll, those who had seen the more aggressive display were more than twice as likely to act aggressively toward the doll (Bandura, Ross, & Ross, 1961). These results suggest that exposing children to violence may encourage them to act aggressively (**FIGURE 6.38**).

MODELING (DEMONSTRATION AND IMITATION) Because humans can learn through observation, they can be taught many complex skills through demonstration. For instance, parents use slow and exaggerated motions to show their children how to tie their shoes. Indeed, YouTube is so popular in part because people can learn to do many things by watching instructional videos.

The imitation of observed behavior is called **modeling.** The term indicates that people are reproducing the behaviors of *models*—those being observed. Modeling in humans is influenced by numerous factors. Generally, we are more likely to imitate

Learning Objectives

- Define observational learning.

- Generate examples of observational learning, modeling, and vicarious learning.

- Discuss contemporary evidence regarding the role of mirror neurons in learning.

modeling
The imitation of observed behavior.

FIGURE 6.38
Bandura's Bobo Doll Studies
In Bandura's studies, two groups of preschool children were shown a film of an adult playing with a large inflatable doll called Bobo. One group saw the adult play quietly (not shown here), and the other group saw the adult attack the doll (shown in the top row here). When children were allowed to play with the doll later, those who had seen the aggressive display were more than twice as likely to act aggressively toward the doll.

FIGURE 6.39
Bend It Like Beckham?
Simply watching an athlete execute a move does not enable us to perform that move if it exceeds our physical ability.

the actions of models who are attractive, have high status, and are somewhat similar to ourselves. In addition, modeling is effective only if the observer is physically capable of imitating the behavior. Simply watching David Beckham launch a free kick does not mean we could bend it like Beckham (**FIGURE 6.39**).

The influence that models have on behavior often occurs implicitly, without people being aware that their behaviors are being altered. People might not want to admit that they have changed their ways of speaking or dressing to resemble those of people they admire, such as celebrities or the cool kids in the class. Overwhelming evidence says, however, that people imitate what they see in others. Adolescents whose favorite actors smoke in movies are much more likely to smoke (Tickle, Sargent, Dalton, Beach, & Heatherton, 2001). The more smoking that adolescents observe in movies, the more positive their attitudes about smoking become and the more likely they are to begin smoking (Sargent et al., 2005).

Surprisingly, these effects are strongest among children whose parents do not smoke. Why would this be so? Perhaps what such children learn about smoking comes completely through the media, which tends to glamorize the habit. For example, movies often present smokers as attractive, healthy, and wealthy, not like the typical smoker. Adolescents do not generally decide to smoke after watching one movie's glamorous depiction of smoking. Rather, images of smokers as mature, cool, sexy—things adolescents want to be—shape adolescents' attitudes about smoking and subsequently lead to imitation. As adolescent viewers learn to associate smoking with people they admire, they incorporate the general message that smoking is desirable.

In light of findings such as these, the movie industry has come under considerable pressure to reduce depictions of smoking. Indeed, since 1995 there has been a reduction in onscreen smoking and a related decline in adolescent smoking rates (Sargent & Heatherton, 2009; **FIGURE 6.40**). Of course, correlation is not proof of causation. There have been several public health efforts to reduce youth smoking, such as media campaigns and bans on marketing of tobacco products to children, and these other efforts might be responsible for the reductions of smoking as well as its reduced portrayals in the movies.

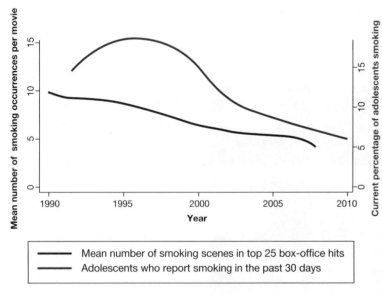

FIGURE 6.40
Movie Smoking and Adolescent Smoking
This double-Y-axis graph compares the declining rate of smoking in movies with the declining rate of adolescent smoking.

VICARIOUS LEARNING (REINFORCEMENT AND CONDITIONING) Another factor that determines whether observers imitate a model is whether the model is reinforced for performing the behavior. In one study, Bandura and colleagues showed children a film of an adult aggressively playing with a Bobo doll, but this time the film ended in one of three different ways (Bandura, Ross, & Ross, 1963). In the first version, a control condition, the adult experienced no consequences for the aggressive behavior. In the second version, the adult was rewarded for the behavior with candy and praise. In the third version, the adult was punished for the behavior by being both spanked and verbally reprimanded. When subsequently allowed to play with the Bobo doll, the children who observed the model being rewarded were much more likely to be aggressive toward the doll than were the children in the control group. In contrast, those who saw the model being punished were less likely to be aggressive than those in the control group. Through **vicarious learning,** people learn about an action's consequences by watching others being rewarded or punished for performing the action (**FIGURE 6.41**).

These findings do not mean that the children who did not show aggression did not learn the behavior. Later, all the children were offered small gifts to perform the model's actions, and all performed the actions reliably. As noted earlier, a key distinction in learning is between the *acquisition* of a behavior and its *performance*. Here, all the children acquired the behavior. But only those who saw the model being rewarded performed the behavior—at least until the children themselves were rewarded. Direct rewards prompted the children in the control group to reveal the behavior they had acquired.

6.17 Watching Violence in Media May Encourage Aggression

According to a study of over 2,000 American children and teens, television viewing has increased to nearly 4.5 hours per day in recent years (Ridout, Foehr, & Roberts, 2010). The study found that total media use—including music, computers, and video games—averages nearly 8 hours per day (**FIGURE 6.42**). The most popular media, including Saturday morning cartoons, contain considerable amounts of violence (Carnagey, Anderson, & Bartholow, 2007). Does watching so much violence on television encourage children to be aggressive? And what about violent video games? Might vicarious exposure to violence lead to violent actions, such as school shootings?

Media violence has been found to increase the likelihood of short-term and long-term aggressive and violent behavior (Anderson et al., 2003). In one study, after children played a violent video game for only 20 minutes, they were less physiologically

vicarious learning
Learning the consequences of an action by watching others being rewarded or punished for performing the action.

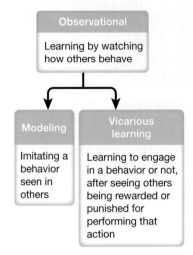

FIGURE 6.41
Two Types of Observational Learning

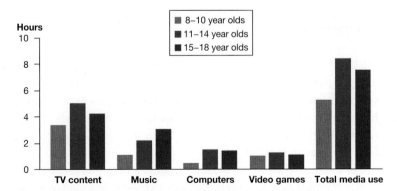

FIGURE 6.42
Media Use by Young Americans
This bar graph shows the results of a study sponsored by the Kaiser Family Foundation, which provides information about health issues. "Total media use" means total hours individuals spent using media. Sometimes these individuals used more than one category of media at once.

FIGURE 6.43
Media and Violent Behavior
Studies have shown that playing violent video games desensitizes children to violence.

aroused by scenes of real violence. In other words, they had become desensitized to violence, showing fewer helping behaviors and increased aggression (Carnagey, Anderson, & Bushman, 2007; **FIGURE 6.43**). In another study, Leonard Eron and colleagues found that TV viewing habits at age 8 predicted, for age 30, amounts of both violent behavior and criminal activity (Eron, 1987). A meta-analysis of studies involving the effects of media violence—taking into account laboratory experiments, field experiments, cross-sectional correlational studies, and longitudinal studies that assess the same people over time—showed that exposure to violent media increases the likelihood of aggression (Gentile, Saleem, & Anderson, 2007).

A number of problems exist, however, with the studies on this topic. The social psychologist Jonathan Freedman (1984) has noted that many of the so-called aggressive behaviors displayed by children could be interpreted as playful rather than aggressive. A more serious concern is whether the studies generalize to the real world. Viewing a violent film clip in a lab is not like watching TV in one's living room. The film clips used in studies are often brief and extremely violent, and the child watches them alone. In the real world, violent episodes are interspersed with nonviolent material, and children often watch them with others, who may buffer the effect. Another major problem is directionality. Recall from Chapter 2 that correlation does not equal causation. It could easily be that children prone to violence prefer to watch violent television programming (Alia-Klein et al., 2014; Gunter, 2016).

What about longitudinal studies, which follow participants over time in assessing childhood TV watching and later violent behavior? These studies fail to empirically support that TV caused the behavior. Additional variables—such as personality, poverty, or parental negligence—could have affected both TV viewing habits and violent tendencies. After all, not all of those who view violence on TV become aggressive later in life. Perhaps those who watch excessive amounts of TV, and therefore have fewer opportunities to develop social skills, act aggressively. Only through careful laboratory studies in which participants are randomly assigned to experimental conditions can we determine causality. Obviously, it is not practical to assign children randomly to experience different types of media, and it is ethically questionable to expose children to violence if it might make them more aggressive.

Despite the problems with specific studies, however, most research in this area shows a relationship between exposure to violence and aggressive behavior (Bushman & Anderson, 2015). Consider the contrast between adolescents who play video games that have mature themes and glorify violence and risky behavior, such as Grand Theft Auto III, and those who play video games that might contain some violence but do not glorify it in the same way, such as Spider-Man 2. Players of Grand Theft Auto III report many more deviant behaviors—such as early alcohol consumption, delinquency, and risky sex—than do players of Spider-Man 2 (Hull, Brunelle, Prescott, & Sargent, 2014). These individuals are also more likely to report risky driving, being pulled over by police, willingness to drink and drive, and more car accidents (Hull, Draghici, & Sargent, 2012). The take-home message from such studies is that the problem might not simply be violence. The problem might be how violence is portrayed, especially in how media misrepresent the prevalence of violence in real life.

Exposure to massive amounts of violence in media may lead children to believe that violence is common and inevitable. Because in movies few people are punished for acting violently, children may come to believe that such behaviors are justified (Bushman & Huesmann, 2001). That is, the portrayal of violence in movies teaches children questionable social scripts for solving personal problems (Gentile, Li, Khoo, Prot, & Anderson, 2014). By mentally rehearsing a violent scenario or observing the same violent scenario enacted many times and perhaps in different movies, a child might come to believe that engaging in brutality is an effective way to both solve problems and dispense with annoying people (Huesmann, 1998). Finally, simulating deviant lifestyles, such as occurs in risk-glorifying mature video games, may change how people view themselves. Practicing being the driver in Grand Theft Auto may influence a player into becoming that kind of person in real life (Hull et al., 2012, 2014).

Why is it difficult to conclude that there is a causal relationship between exposure to media violence and aggression in real life?

ANSWER: Outside the laboratory, researchers cannot randomly assign people to experience different kinds of media, and they cannot ethically risk increasing people's aggression.

6.18 Fear Can Be Learned Through Observation

The psychologist Susan Mineka noticed that monkeys raised in laboratories do not fear snakes, whereas monkeys raised in the wild fear snakes intensely. She set out to explore whether monkeys, by observing other monkeys reacting fearfully to snakes, could develop a phobia of snakes. Mineka and colleagues set up an experiment with two groups of rhesus monkeys. One group was reared in the laboratory, and one group was reared in the wild. To obtain food, the monkeys had to reach beyond a clear box that contained either a snake or a neutral object.

When a snake was in the box, the wild-reared monkeys did not touch the food. They also showed signs of distress, such as clinging to their cages and making threatening faces. The laboratory-raised monkeys reached past the box even if it contained a snake, and they showed no overt signs of fear. The researchers then showed the laboratory-raised monkeys the wild monkeys' fearful response, to see if it would affect the laboratory monkeys' reactions to the snake. The laboratory monkeys quickly developed a fear of the snakes, and this fear was maintained over a three-month period.

As mentioned earlier, it appears that monkeys are biologically prepared to fear certain objects, such as snakes. Subsequent research by Mineka and colleagues found that by watching other monkeys' reactions, monkeys could learn to fear snakes but not flowers (Cook & Mineka, 1990).

Humans, too, can learn to fear particular stimuli by observing others. For example, a person might become afraid of a specific neighborhood after watching news video of a person being assaulted there. In fact, people can learn to fear particular things simply by hearing that the things are dangerous. Thus social forces play an important role in the learning of fear (Olsson & Phelps, 2007).

This social learning of fear likely relies on the amygdala. In one imaging study, research participants watched another person experience and display distress when receiving an electric shock paired with a conditioned stimulus. The observing participants subsequently were presented with the CS. To ensure that all their learning was vicarious, however, they did not receive a shock. During the observation period and during the trials when the observers were presented with the CS, the investigators found heightened activity in the amygdala (Olsson, Nearing, & Phelps, 2007). This finding suggests that similar mechanisms are involved in conditioned and observational fear learning.

Why can monkeys learn to fear snakes but not flowers?

ANSWER: Because monkeys are biologically prepared to fear snakes but not flowers, they can learn to fear only snakes, not flowers, through observational learning.

FIGURE 6.44
Empathy in Observational Learning
We sometimes "feel the pain" when we watch someone experiencing an injury.

mirror neurons
Neurons in the brain that are activated when one observes another individual engage in an action and when one performs a similar action.

ANSWER: neurons that are activated by watching someone else perform an intentional action or performing the same action yourself

6.19 Mirror Neurons Are Activated by Watching Others

If you see someone handling a piece of paper and getting a paper cut, you might flinch as if you had received the cut (**FIGURE 6.44**). Why do you experience this empathy, the emotional response of feeling what someone else is experiencing?

During observational learning, such as when you watch someone reacting in pain, **mirror neurons** in your brain become activated (Iacoboni, 2009). Mirror neurons are especially likely to become activated when you observe someone making a movement that has some goal, such as reaching for a glass of water. Your mirror neurons are not activated when you see just a water glass or just a person sitting. But your mirror neurons, these same ones, are activated when *you* reach for a glass of water. Every time you watch another person engaging in an action, similar neural circuits are firing in that person's brain and in your brain.

Scientists are debating the function of mirror neurons (Hickok, 2009). This system may support observational learning (McGregor, Cashaback, & Gribble, 2016). However, the firing of mirror neurons in the observer's brain does not always lead that person to actually imitate the behavior being observed. Therefore, some theorists think that mirror neurons may help us explain and predict others' behavior. In other words, mirror neurons may enable us to step into the shoes of people we observe so we can better understand those people's actions (Gallese, 2013). Mirror neurons may therefore help us learn what other people are thinking. One theory is that mirror neurons are the neural basis for empathy (Braadbaart et al., 2014), such as flinching when someone else receives a paper cut.

 What are mirror neurons?

Your Chapter Review

Chapter Summary

How Do We Learn?

6.1 Learning Results from Experience

Learning is a relatively enduring change in behavior, resulting from experience. Learning enables animals to better adapt to the environment, and thus it facilitates survival. The three major types of learning are nonassociative, associative, and observational. Nonassociative learning is a change in behavior after repeated exposure to a single stimulus or event. Associative learning is the linking of two stimuli or events. Observational learning is acquiring or changing a behavior after exposure to another individual performing that behavior.

6.2 Habituation and Sensitization Are Models of Nonassociative Learning

Habituation is a decrease in behavioral response after repeated exposure to a stimulus. Habituation occurs when the stimulus stops providing new information. Sensitization is an increase in behavioral response after exposure to a repeated stimulus. Sensitization may occur in cases where increased attention to a stimulus may prove beneficial, such as in dangerous or exciting situations.

How Do We Learn Predictive Associations?

6.3 Behavioral Responses Are Conditioned

Pavlov established the principles of classical conditioning. Through classical conditioning, associations are made between two stimuli, such as the clicking of a metronome and the presence of food. What is learned is that one stimulus predicts another.

6.4 Learning Is Acquired and Persists Until Extinction

Acquisition, second-order conditioning, generalization, discrimination, extinction, and spontaneous recovery are processes associated with classical conditioning.

6.5 Learning Is Based on Evolutionary Significance

Not all stimuli are equally potent in producing conditioning. Animals are biologically prepared to make connections between stimuli that are potentially dangerous. This biological preparedness to fear specific objects helps animals avoid potential dangers, and thus it facilitates survival.

6.6 Learning Involves Expectancies and Prediction

The Rescorla-Wagner theory describes how the strength of association between two stimuli depends on how unexpected or surprising the unconditioned stimulus is. Positive prediction error results when an unexpected stimulus is presented. Positive prediction error strengthens the association between the CS and the US. Negative prediction error results when an expected stimulus is missing. Negative prediction error weakens the CS-US association.

The neurotransmitter dopamine provides one neurobiological basis for prediction error. Dopamine release increases after positive prediction error and decreases after negative prediction error.

6.7 Phobias and Addictions Have Learned Components

Phobias are learned fear associations. Addictions involve learned reward associations. Classical conditioning and second-order conditioning can explain not only how people learn to associate the fearful stimulus or drug itself with the fear or reward but also a host of other "neutral" stimuli as well. In the case of drug addiction, addicts often inadvertently associate environmental aspects of the purchase and use of the drug with the pleasurable feelings produced by the drug. These learned associations are major factors in relapse, as seemingly innocuous stimuli can trigger cravings even years after drug use is discontinued.

How Do Consequences of an Action Shape Behavior?

6.8 Operant Conditioning Involves Active Learning

Reinforcement (a stimulus following a response) makes behaviors more likely to occur. Shaping is a procedure in which successive approximations of a behavior are reinforced, leading to the desired behavior.

6.9 Think like a Psychologist: How Do Superstitions Start?

When a chance reinforcer occurs close in time to some behavior, humans and nonhuman animals sometimes associate the reinforcement with the behavior.

6.10 There Are Many Types of Reinforcement

Reinforcers may be primary (those that satisfy biological needs) or secondary (those that do not directly satisfy biological needs). Both positive and negative reinforcement increase the likelihood that a behavior will be repeated. In positive reinforcement, a pleasurable stimulus is delivered after a behavior (e.g., giving a dog a treat for sitting). In negative reinforcement, an aversive stimulus is removed after a behavior (e.g., letting a puppy out of its crate when it acts calmly).

6.11 Operant Conditioning Is Influenced by Schedules of Reinforcement

Learning occurs in response to continuous reinforcement and partial reinforcement. Partial reinforcement may be delivered on a ratio schedule or an interval schedule. Each type of schedule may be fixed or variable. Partial reinforcement administered on a variable-ratio schedule is particularly resistant to extinction.

6.12 Punishment Decreases Behavior

Punishment decreases the probability that a behavior will repeat. Positive punishment involves the administration of an aversive stimulus, such as a squirt of water in the face, to decrease behavior. Negative punishment involves the removal of an appetitive stimulus, such as money, to decrease behavior. Positive punishment has been shown to be generally ineffective for changing behavior, since it can produce fear, anxiety, and inappropriate imitation of the punishing behavior. Behavior modification involves the use of operant conditioning to eliminate unwanted behaviors and replace them with desirable behaviors. Behavior modification programs work by reinforcing appropriate behaviors and ignoring inappropriate behaviors. Punishment, especially positive punishment, is not used in behavior modification programs because it rarely stops undesirable behavior.

6.13 Using Psychology in Your Life: How Can Behavior Modification Help You Get in Shape?

Behavior modification is the use of operant conditioning techniques to eliminate unwanted behaviors and replace them with desirable ones. Token economies involve the use of secondary reinforcement, in which people earn tokens they can later use for objects or privileges.

6.14 Biology and Cognition Influence Operant Conditioning

An animal's biological makeup restricts the types of behaviors the animal can learn. Latent learning takes place without reinforcement. Latent learning may not influence behavior until a reinforcer is introduced.

6.15 Dopamine Activity Underlies Reinforcement

The brain has specialized centers that produce pleasure when stimulated. Behaviors that activate these centers are reinforced. The nucleus accumbens has dopamine receptors, which are activated by pleasurable behaviors. Through conditioning, secondary reinforcers can also activate dopamine receptors.

How Do We Learn from Watching Others?

6.16 Learning Can Occur Through Observation and Imitation

Observational learning is a powerful adaptive tool. Humans and other animals learn by watching the behavior of others. The imitation of observed behavior is referred to as modeling. Vicarious learning occurs when people learn about an action's consequences by observing others being reinforced or punished for their behavior.

6.17 Watching Violence in Media May Encourage Aggression

Media violence has been found to increase aggressive behavior, decrease prosocial behavior, and desensitize children to violence. However, laboratory research may not simulate real-life exposure to violence in the media, so further research is warranted.

6.18 Fear Can Be Learned Through Observation

Monkeys have learned to fear snakes (but not flowers) by watching other monkeys react fearfully. These findings suggest that monkeys can learn by observation if the behavior is biologically adaptive. People also learn fear by observation, such as in learning to avoid a neighborhood because of news reports about crime in the area. People observing other people receive a painful shock experience activation in the amygdala—a brain area important for processing emotional responses, including fear—even though they themselves did not receive any shocks.

6.19 Mirror Neurons Are Activated by Watching Others

Mirror neurons become activated when we observe others engaging in actions. In fact, the same neurons that become active when we observe another person engaging in a task become active when we perform the same task. Mirror neurons may be involved in learning about and predicting what others are thinking. They may also form the basis of empathy, the ability to understand the perspective of other people.

Key Terms

acquisition, p. 214

associative learning, p. 209

behavior modification, p. 233

classical conditioning (Pavlovian conditioning), p. 210

cognitive map, p. 236

conditioned response (CR), p. 212

conditioned stimulus (CS), p. 212

continuous reinforcement, p. 230

extinction, p. 216

fear conditioning, p. 221

habituation, p. 209

latent learning, p. 237

law of effect, p. 225

learning, p. 208

mirror neurons, p. 244

modeling, p. 239

negative punishment, p. 231

negative reinforcement, p. 229

nonassociative learning, p. 209

observational learning, p. 209

operant conditioning (instrumental conditioning), p. 224

partial reinforcement, p. 230

partial-reinforcement extinction effect, p. 231

phobia, p. 221

positive punishment, p. 231

positive reinforcement, p. 229

reinforcer, p. 226

Rescorla-Wagner model, p. 218

sensitization, p. 210

shaping, p. 227

spontaneous recovery, p. 216

stimulus discrimination, p. 215

stimulus generalization, p. 215

unconditioned response (UR), p. 212

unconditioned stimulus (US), p. 212

vicarious learning, p. 241

What Is the Business of Behavior Modification?

Have you ever stayed up much later than you had planned in order to get to the next level in your favorite video game? Or walked past the closest coffee stop to go to the one where you have a reward card? If so, you have experienced how powerfully our behavior is shaped by rewards and schedules of reinforcement. Understanding how to encourage certain behaviors has clear applications for the business world. Silicon Valley social engineers, as well as neighborhood office managers, are using behavior modification techniques to increase worker productivity and to shape consumer behavior.

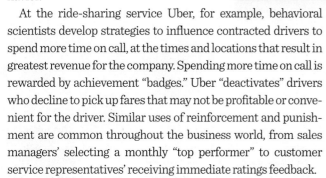

At the ride-sharing service Uber, for example, behavioral scientists develop strategies to influence contracted drivers to spend more time on call, at the times and locations that result in greatest revenue for the company. Spending more time on call is rewarded by achievement "badges." Uber "deactivates" drivers who decline to pick up fares that may not be profitable or convenient for the driver. Similar uses of reinforcement and punishment are common throughout the business world, from sales managers' selecting a monthly "top performer" to customer service representatives' receiving immediate ratings feedback.

Behavioral principles are also important in shaping consumer behavior. Video game designers incorporate just the right level of rewards and challenges in their games, at the optimal schedule, in order to keep players engaged. It is useful for Web developers and software engineers to understand what drives behaviors so as to increase the number of clicks generated on digital platforms, thereby increasing revenue. Advertising and marketing analysts can bolster customer loyalty, and increased spending, through reward programs.

As you may now appreciate, there are widespread employment opportunities in the business sector for people who are able to apply learning principles. According to the Bureau of Labor Statistics, the projected employment growth in 2014—24 for marketing analysts (19 percent) and Web and software developers (27 percent) is much stronger than average. Jobs for human resources managers are projected to grow 5 percent in the same period.

The bottom line: Understanding the ways in which customer or employee behavior can be shaped by learning principles is important for many business applications, from designing digital platforms to managing an office. Courses in software design, marketing, and human resources management augment psychology studies as a good foundation for entry-level positions.

Want to earn a better grade on your test?
Go to **INQUIZITIVE** to learn and review this chapter's content, with personalized feedback along the way.
Practice Tests and accompanying answer keys can be found at the back of the book on page PT-1.

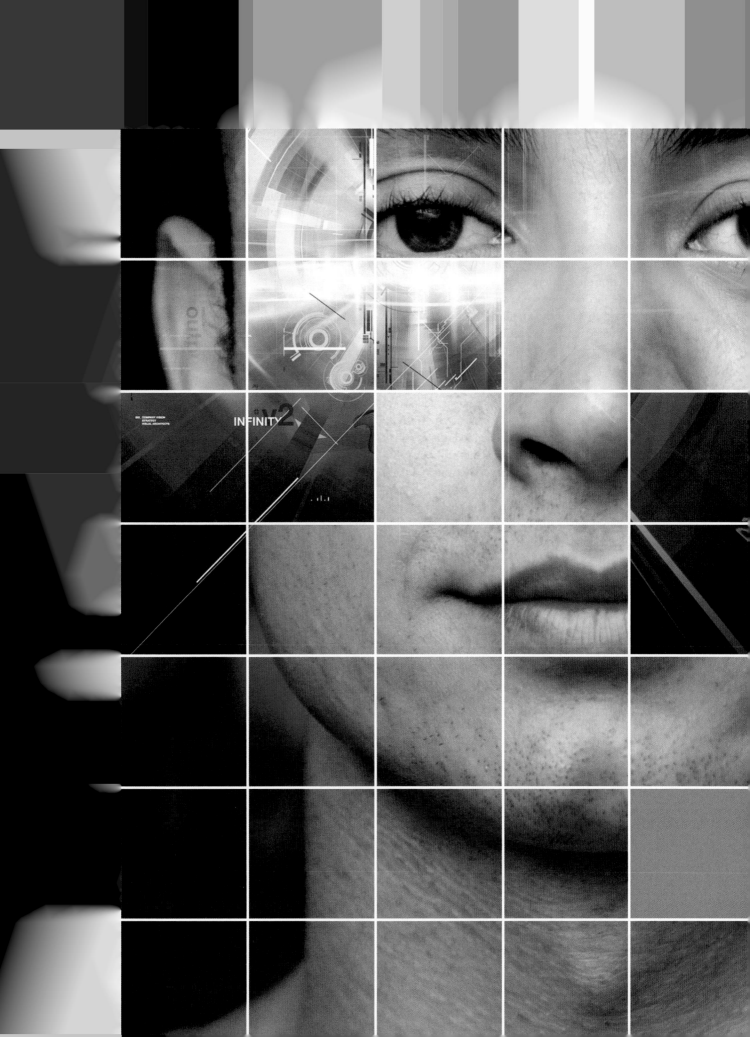

Memory

Big Questions

- What Is Memory? 250

- How Are Memories Maintained over Time? 256

- How Is Information Organized in Long-Term Memory? 262

- What Are the Different Long-Term Memory Systems? 270

- How Is Memory Flawed? 273

IMAGINE YOU ARE TALKING WITH A FRIEND about whether either of you would volunteer to go on a mission to Mars. Your friend says she would love to go to Mars, so she could learn to grow potatoes there as Mark Wahlberg did in the movie *The Martian*. "Wahlberg wasn't in *The Martian*," you correct her. "It was Matt Damon." Maybe your friend was confused because Damon plays an astronaut named Mark Watney, which kind of sounds like Mark Wahlberg. Or maybe she got the two actors mixed up, as Wahlberg and Damon say happens all the time (**FIGURE 7.1**). Suddenly you remember the time you confidently stated that Jonah Hill played Steve Wozniak in the movie *Steve Jobs* (it was Seth Rogan). As these slips illustrate, our memories are far from perfect.

Memory is crucial to every aspect of our everyday lives, and this chapter considers how we remember different types of information. Normally, each of us remembers millions of pieces of information. These memories range from the trivial to the vital. Each person's entire sense of self, or identity, is made up of what that person knows from memories, from his or her recollections of personal experiences and of things learned from others. The big questions that psychologists consider in this area are: What is memory? How are memories maintained over time? How is information organized in long-term memory? What are the different long-term memory systems? How is memory flawed?

Learning Objectives

- Define memory.
- Describe the three phases of memory.
- Describe the processes of consolidation and reconsolidation.
- Identify brain regions involved in learning and memory.

FIGURE 7.1
Appearances Can Be Deceiving
The physical similarities between people, such as the actors Mark Wahlberg **(bottom left)** and Matt Damon **(top right)**, can cause confusion and false memories related to the people.

memory
The nervous system's capacity to retain and retrieve skills and knowledge.

What Is Memory?

Memory is the nervous system's capacity to retain and retrieve skills and knowledge. This capacity enables organisms to take information from experiences and store it for later use. It is important to remember that memory does not work like a digital video camera that faithfully records and replays the events its operator experiences. Photographic memory does not exist. Instead, the information we store and the memories we retrieve are often incomplete, biased, and distorted. Two people's memories for the same event can differ vastly, because each person stores and retrieves memories of the event distinctively. In other words, memories are personal and unique stories.

In addition, all experiences are not equally likely to be remembered. Some life events pass swiftly, leaving no lasting memory. Others are remembered but later forgotten. Still others remain for a lifetime. We have multiple memory systems, and each memory system has its own "rules." For example, some brain processes underlie memory for information we will need to retrieve in 10 seconds. Those processes operate differently from the processes that underlie memory for information we will need to retrieve in 10 years.

7.1 Memory Involves Processing Information

Since the late 1960s, most psychologists have viewed memory as a form of information processing. In this model, the ways that memory works are roughly analogous to the ways computers process information. A computer receives information through the keyboard or modem, and software determines how the information is processed. The information may be stored in some altered format on the hard drive. Then the information may be retrieved when it is needed. Likewise, the multiple processes of memory can be thought of as operating over time in three phases: encoding, storage (including consolidation), and retrieval (**FIGURE 7.2**).

The **encoding** phase occurs at the time of learning, as information is transformed into a format that can be stored in memory. That is, the brain changes information into a neural code that it can use. Consider the process of reading this book. In the encoding phase, your brain converts the sensory stimuli on the page to meaningful neural codes.

The **storage** phase is the retention of the encoded representation. That is, a change in your nervous system registers what you just experienced, retaining it as a memorable event. So as you read this book, your brain is changed. Neural connections that support memory become stronger, and new synapses are constructed (Miller, 2005). This neural process is known as **consolidation.** Through consolidation, encoded information becomes stored in memory. Think of this phase as akin to keeping material you read in mind until test time or longer. There are at least three storage systems, which differ in how long they store information. Storage can last a fraction of a second or as long as a lifetime. These systems will be discussed in detail later in this chapter.

Retrieval is the third phase of memory. This stage consists of reaching into memory storage to find and bring to mind a previously encoded and stored memory when it is needed. Think of retrieval as drawing on the material in your brain for use on the midterm, on the final, or sometime long after graduation when someone asks you a question about psychology.

RECONSOLIDATION OF MEMORIES An exciting theory developed by Joseph LeDoux and colleagues proposes that once memories are activated, they need to be consolidated again to be stored back in memory (Alberini & LeDoux, 2013; LeDoux, 2002; Nader & Einarsson, 2010). These processes are known as **reconsolidation.** To

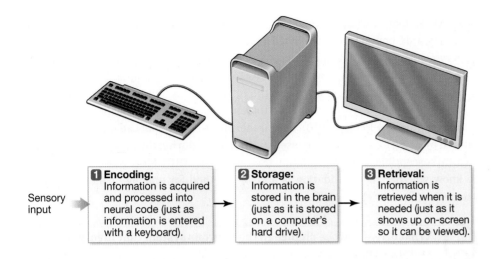

1 Encoding:
Information is acquired and processed into neural code (just as information is entered with a keyboard).

2 Storage:
Information is stored in the brain (just as it is stored on a computer's hard drive).

3 Retrieval:
Information is retrieved when it is needed (just as it shows up on-screen so it can be viewed).

Sensory input

understand how reconsolidation works, think of this image: A librarian returns a book to a shelf for storage so that it can be taken out again later.

When memories for past events are retrieved, those memories can be affected by current circumstances, so the newly reconsolidated memories may differ from their original versions (Nader, Schafe, & LeDoux, 2000). In other words, our memories begin as versions of what we have experienced. Then they actually might change when we use them, such as when they are changed by our mood, knowledge about the world, or beliefs. Say that last year you were dating a particular person. That relationship ended unhappily. When you recall a pleasant time you shared with your ex, you might reinterpret the memory in this new light. In the library book analogy, this change would be like tearing pages out of the book or adding new pages or notes before returning it. The book placed on the shelf differs from the one taken out. The information in the torn-out pages is no longer available for retrieval, and the new pages or notes that were inserted alter the memory the next time it is retrieved.

Reconsolidation happens each time a memory is activated and placed back in storage, and it may explain why our memories for events can change over time (**FIGURE 7.3**). For example, as we retell stories about past events, we embellish details that make the stories better, and we come to believe the embellished versions. So the

encoding
The processing of information so that it can be stored.

storage
The retention of encoded representations.

consolidation
The neural process by which encoded information becomes stored in memory.

retrieval
The act of recalling or remembering stored information when it is needed.

reconsolidation
Neural processes involved when memories are recalled and then stored again for retrieval.

(a)

Experience

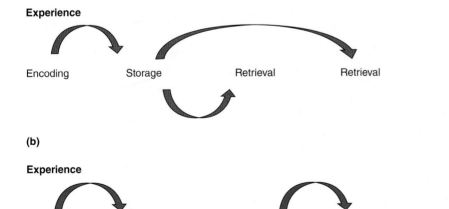

Encoding   Storage   Retrieval   Retrieval

(b)

Experience

Encoding   Storage   Retrieval   Storage   Retrieval

Source: Adapted from Alberini & LeDoux 2013.

FIGURE 7.3
Reconsolidation
(a) According to traditional views of memory, we gain information from experience. That information is encoded and then stored for retrieval. Each time it is retrieved, the information remains the same as it was during the original experience. **(b)** The idea of reconsolidation complicates these traditional views. According to this idea, memories can change each time they are retrieved. Each memory is of the previous retrieval, not the original experience.

six-inch fish that you caught when you were seven years old becomes, by the time you are thirty, a six-pound trout that tasted great in the mountain air.

As you might imagine, the idea of reconsolidation has received considerable attention. It has implications for what it means to remember something but also for the accuracy of that memory. It opens up the intriguing possibility that bad memories could be erased by activating them and then interfering with reconsolidation (Kroes, Schiller, LeDoux, & Phelps, 2016). Researchers have shown that bad memories can be altered by using extinction (discussed in Chapter 6) during the period when memories are susceptible to reconsolidation (Schiller et al., 2010). More research is needed to know whether reconsolidation is a viable method for erasing or modifying bad memories (Treavor et al., 2017).

Q What do we call the change in the nervous system that involves the storage of memories?

ANSWER: consolidation

7.2 Memory Is the Result of Brain Activity

What role does biology play in the processing of information? Researchers have made tremendous progress over the past two decades in understanding what happens in the brain when we store and retrieve memories.

In 1949, the psychologist Donald Hebb proposed that memory results from alterations in synaptic connections. In Hebb's model, memories are stored in multiple regions of the brain that are linked through memory circuits. When one neuron excites another, some change takes place that strengthens the connection between the two neurons. Subsequently, the firing of one neuron becomes increasingly likely to cause the firing of the other neuron. In other words, "cells that fire together wire together."

Recall from Chapter 6, "Learning," the work of Eric Kandel using the sea slug aplysia. Kandel showed that alterations in the functioning of the synapse lead to habituation and sensitization. His research also demonstrated that long-term storage of information results from the development of new synaptic connections between neurons (Kandel, 2001). This research supports the idea that memory results from physical changes in connections between neurons. In other words, Hebb was right: Memory involves the creation of neural circuits (Tonegawa, Liu, Ramirez, & Redondo, 2015).

long-term potentiation (LTP)
Strengthening of a synaptic connection, making the postsynaptic neurons more easily activated by presynaptic neurons.

LONG-TERM POTENTIATION In the 1970s, researchers discovered long-term potentiation, a process that is central to the neural basis of memory consolidation (Bliss & Lømo, 1973). The word *potentiate* means to strengthen, to make something more potent. **Long-term potentiation (LTP)** is strengthening of a synaptic connection, making the postsynaptic neurons more easily activated by presynaptic neurons. LTP serves as a model of how neural plasticity (discussed in Chapter 3) might underlie memory.

LTP also supports Hebb's contention that learning results from a strengthening of synaptic connections between neurons that fire together. As the synapse between two neurons strengthens during consolidation, the two neurons become better connected, as though a freeway had been built between them. To demonstrate this process in the lab, researchers first establish that stimulating one neuron with a single electrical pulse leads to a certain amount of firing in a second neuron. (Recall from Chapter 3 that neurons fire when they receive sufficient stimulation.) The researchers then provide intense electrical stimulation to the first neuron. For example, they might give it 100 pulses of electricity in 1 second. Finally, they administer a single electrical pulse to the first neuron and measure the second neuron's firing. If LTP has occurred, the

(a)

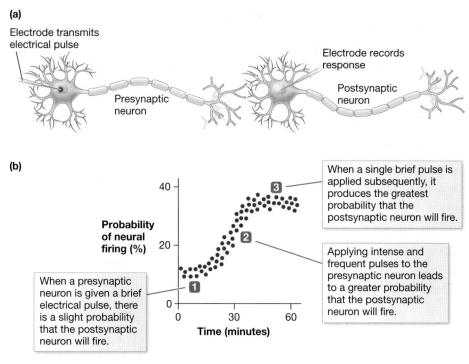

Electrode transmits electrical pulse

Electrode records response

Presynaptic neuron

Postsynaptic neuron

(b)

Probability of neural firing (%)

Time (minutes)

❸ When a single brief pulse is applied subsequently, it produces the greatest probability that the postsynaptic neuron will fire.

❶ When a presynaptic neuron is given a brief electrical pulse, there is a slight probability that the postsynaptic neuron will fire.

❷ Applying intense and frequent pulses to the presynaptic neuron leads to a greater probability that the postsynaptic neuron will fire.

FIGURE 7.4
Long-Term Potentiation (LTP)
(a) This diagram depicts the basic process used in testing for LTP between two neurons.
(b) This graph shows the steps involved in LTP.

intense electrical stimulation will have increased the likelihood that stimulating the first neuron produces firing in the second neuron (**FIGURE 7.4**). LTP changes the postsynaptic neuron so that it is more easily activated by the presynaptic neuron.

Over the last two decades, researchers have made considerable progress in understanding how LTP works (Herring & Nicoll, 2016). A critical player in LTP is the *NMDA receptor* on the postsynaptic neuron. This type of glutamate receptor responds only when large amounts of glutamate are available in the synapse and when the postsynaptic neuron is sufficiently depolarized. LTP leads to an increase in the number of glutamate receptors on the postsynaptic neuron, which increases its responsivity to glutamate released by the presynaptic neuron. It can also produce more synapses between neurons. So memory results from strengthening synaptic connections among networks of neurons. They fired together, they wired together.

The finding that the NMDA receptor is involved in LTP led researchers to examine genetic processes that might influence memory. For instance, the neuroscientist Joseph Tsien modified genes in mice to make the genes' NMDA receptors more efficient. When tested in standard memory tasks, these transgenic mice performed amazingly well, learning novel tasks more quickly and showing increased memory (Tsien, 2000). The mice were such great learners that Tsien named them "Doogie mice," after the 1990s television character Doogie Howser, a boy doctor (**FIGURE 7.5**).

EPIGENETICS OF MEMORY New research is showing that epigenetic mechanisms are important for memory (Schoch & Abel, 2014). Recall from Chapter 3 that epigenetic mechanisms control how DNA is expressed. One such epigenetic mechanism involves a class of enzymes called HDAC (histone deacetylases), which inhibit gene expression. There is emerging evidence that blocking HDAC leads to increased

FIGURE 7.5
Doogie Mice
Doogie mice (such as the one pictured here) and regular mice were given a test of learning and memory. In the first part, both kinds of mice had the chance to familiarize themselves with two objects. In the second part, the researchers replaced one of the objects with a novel object. The Doogie mice quickly recognized the change, but the normal mice did not recognize it.

memory (Gräff & Tsai, 2013). Likewise, drugs that block HDAC lead to increased LTP (Vecsey et al., 2007). The general idea is that HDAC serves as a molecular "brake," which has to be released for memory to occur (McQuown & Wood, 2011). Unless something critical happens in the environment, the molecular brake is on and nothing is stored in memory. Researchers are currently trying to understand how environmental events trigger release of these molecular brakes.

Might we be able to modify human gene expression, activate NMDA receptors, or both so that people learn more quickly and remember better? Some pharmaceutical companies are exploring drugs that might work in just such ways. If successful, these treatments could prove valuable for treating patients with diseases such as Alzheimer's, which primarily involves severe memory deficits. This especially active area of research is increasing our understanding of how genes, neurotransmitters, and the environment interact to produce learning (Poo et al., 2016).

Q How does LTP support Hebb's contention that neurons that fire together wire together?

ANSWER: LTP shows that memory results from a strengthening of synaptic connections.

7.3 Memory Is Distributed Throughout the Brain

Karl Lashley (1950) spent much of his career trying to figure out where in the brain memories are stored. Lashley's term *engram* refers to the physical site of memory storage—that is, the place where memory "lives." As part of his research, Lashley trained rats to run a maze, then removed different areas of their cortices. In testing how much of the maze learning the rats retained after the surgery, Lashley found that the size of the area removed was the most important factor in predicting retention. The location of the area was far less important. From these findings, he concluded that memory is distributed throughout the brain rather than confined to any specific location. This idea is known as *equipotentiality*. Lashley was right that memories are not stored in any one brain location. In many other ways, though, Lashley was wrong about how memories are stored.

Lashley's failure to find the brain regions critical for memory was due to at least two factors. First, the maze task he used to study memory involved multiple sensory systems, such as vision and smell. Thus, the rats could compensate for the loss of one sense by using other senses. Second, Lashley did not examine subcortical areas, which are now known to be important for memory retention.

Over the past three decades, researchers have identified many brain regions that contribute to memory (**FIGURE 7.6**). Much of this information was learned by studying individuals who had received brain injury.

THE CASE OF H.M. A great deal of what we know about human memory came about through studying Henry Molaison, known through most of his life by the initials H.M. to protect his privacy while he was alive. He was born in 1926 and died at a nursing home in 2008. In vital ways, though, his world stopped in 1953, when he was 27.

As a young man, Molaison suffered from severe epilepsy. Every day, he had several grand mal seizures, an affliction that

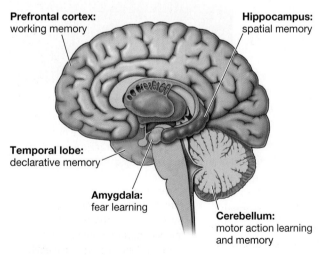

Prefrontal cortex: working memory

Hippocampus: spatial memory

Temporal lobe: declarative memory

Amygdala: fear learning

Cerebellum: motor action learning and memory

FIGURE 7.6
Brain Regions Associated with Memory

made it impossible for him to lead a normal life. Seizures are uncontrolled random firing of groups of neurons, and they can spread across the brain. Molaison's seizures originated in the temporal lobes of his brain and would spread from there.

Because the anticonvulsive drugs available at that time could not control Molaison's seizures, surgery was the only choice for treatment. The reasoning behind this surgery was that if the seizure-causing portion of his brain was removed, he would stop having seizures. In September 1953, Molaison's doctors removed parts of his medial temporal lobes, including the hippocampus (**FIGURE 7.7**). The surgery quieted his seizures, but it had an unexpected and very unfortunate side effect: Molaison lost the ability to remember new information for more than a few moments.

Until his death, the larger world did not know Molaison's real name or what he looked like (**FIGURE 7.8**). His privacy was guarded by the researchers who studied his memory. H.M. never remembered the day of the week, what year it was, or his own age. Still, he could talk about his childhood, explain the rules of baseball, and describe members of his family, things he knew at the time of the surgery. According to the psychologists who tested him, his IQ was slightly above average. His thinking abilities remained intact. He could hold a normal conversation as long as he was not distracted, but he forgot the conversation in a minute or less.

H.M.'s ability to hold a conversation showed that he was still able to remember things for short periods. After all, to grasp the meaning of spoken language, a person needs to remember the words recently spoken, such as the beginning and end of a sentence. But H.M. did not appear to remember any new information over time. People who worked with H.M.—such as the psychologist Brenda Milner (Milner, Corkin, & Teuber, 1968), who followed his case for over 40 years—had to introduce themselves to him every time they met. As H.M. put it, "Every day is alone in itself." Because of his profound memory loss, he remembered little from minute to minute. But he knew that he remembered nothing. How could this have been the case? What did it mean for H.M. to have memory at all?

H.M. learned some new things, although he did not know he had learned them. Most impressively, he learned new motor tasks. In one series of tests (Milner, 1962), he was required to trace the outline of a star while watching his hand in a mirror. Most people do poorly the first few times they try this difficult task. On each of three consecutive days, H.M. was asked to trace the star 10 times. His performance improved over the three days, and this result indicated that he had retained some information about the task. On each day, however, H.M. could not recall ever having performed the task before. His ability to learn new motor skills enabled him to get a job at a factory, where he mounted cigarette lighters on cardboard cases. But his condition left him unable to describe the job or the workplace.

REGIONS FOR MEMORY Although memory involves multiple regions of the brain, not all brain regions are equally involved. A great deal of neural specialization occurs. Because of this specialization, different brain regions are responsible for storing different aspects of information. Indeed, different memory systems use different brain regions.

Studies of H.M.'s strange condition contributed many clues to how memories are stored—normally and abnormally—in the brain. For instance, we know from studies of H.M. that regions within the temporal lobes, such as the hippocampus, are important for the ability to store new memories. The temporal lobes are important for being able to say what you remember, but they are less important for memory involving motor actions. The cerebellum is involved in memory for motor actions.

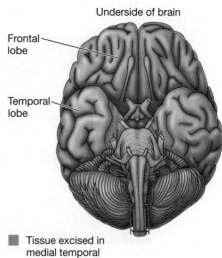

Underside of brain

Frontal lobe

Temporal lobe

■ Tissue excised in medial temporal lobotomy

FIGURE 7.7
A Drawing of H.M.'s Brain
The portions of the medial temporal lobe that were removed from H.M.'s brain are indicated by the shaded regions.

FIGURE 7.8
Henry Molaison (H.M.)
Known to the world only by his initials, Molaison became one of the most famous people in memory research by participating in countless experiments.

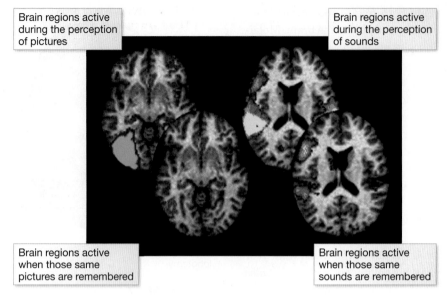

Brain regions active during the perception of pictures

Brain regions active during the perception of sounds

Brain regions active when those same pictures are remembered

Brain regions active when those same sounds are remembered

FIGURE 7.9

Brain Activation During Perception and Remembering

These four horizontally sliced brain images were acquired using magnetic resonance imaging. In each pair, the top image shows the brain areas that are activated during a particular sensory-specific perception. The bottom image shows the regions of the sensory cortex that are activated when that sensory-specific information is remembered. Notice that the perceptions and the memories involve similar cortical areas.

The take-home message here is that memory is distributed among different brain regions. Memory does not "live" in one part of the brain. If you lose a particular brain cell, you will not therefore lose a memory.

The middle section of the temporal lobes, called the *medial temporal lobes,* is responsible for the formation of new memories. The actual storage, however, occurs in the particular brain regions engaged during the perception, processing, and analysis of the material being learned. For instance, visual information is stored in the cortical areas involved in visual perception. Sound is stored in the areas involved in auditory perception. Thus, memory for sensory experiences, such as remembering something seen or heard, involves reactivating the cortical circuits involved in the initial seeing or hearing (**FIGURE 7.9**). The medial temporal lobes form links, or pointers, between the different storage sites, and they direct the gradual strengthening of the connections between these links (Squire, Stark, & Clark, 2004). Once the connections are strengthened sufficiently through consolidation, the medial temporal lobes become less important for memory.

 Where are memories stored?

ANSWER: in the specific brain regions engaged during the perception, processing, and analysis of the material being learned

How Are Memories Maintained over Time?

In 1968, the psychologists Richard Atkinson and Richard Shiffrin proposed a three-part model of memory. Their model consists of sensory memory, short-term memory, and long-term memory (**FIGURE 7.10**). Each of these systems determines the length of time that information is retained in memory. The following sections look at these systems in more detail.

7.4 Sensory Memory Is Brief

Sensory memory is a temporary memory system closely tied to the sensory systems. It is not what we usually think of when we think about memory, because it lasts only a fraction of a second. In fact, normally we are not aware that it is operating.

As discussed in Chapter 5, we obtain all our information about the world through our senses. Our sensory systems transduce, or change, that information into neural impulses. Everything we remember, therefore, is the result of neurons firing in the brain. For example, a memory of a sight or of a sound is created by intricate

Learning Objectives

- Distinguish between sensory memory, short-term memory, and long-term memory.

- Describe working memory and chunking.

- Review evidence that supports the distinction between working memory and long-term memory.

- Explain how information is transferred from working memory to long-term memory.

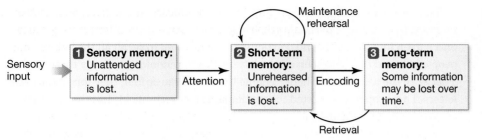

Maintenance rehearsal

Sensory input → **1 Sensory memory:** Unattended information is lost. →(Attention)→ **2 Short-term memory:** Unrehearsed information is lost. →(Encoding)→ **3 Long-term memory:** Some information may be lost over time.

Retrieval

FIGURE 7.10
Three Memory Systems
Atkinson and Shiffrin's model of three systems emphasizes that memory storage varies in duration.

patterns of neural activity in the brain. A sensory memory occurs when a light, a sound, an odor, a taste, or a tactile impression leaves a vanishing trace on the nervous system for a fraction of a second. When you look at something and quickly glance away, you can briefly picture the image and recall some of its details. When someone protests, "You're not paying attention to me," you often can repeat back the last few words the person spoke, even if you were thinking about something else. Visual sensory memory is called *iconic memory*. Auditory sensory memory is called *echoic memory*.

sensory memory
A memory system that very briefly stores sensory information in close to its original sensory form.

The Methods of Psychology
Sperling's Sensory Memory Experiment

HYPOTHESIS: Information in sensory memories is lost very quickly if it is not transferred for further processing.

RESEARCH METHOD:

1 Participants looked at a screen on which three rows of letters flashed for $\frac{1}{20}$ of a second.

2 When a high-pitched tone followed the letters, it meant the participants should recall the letters in the top row. When a medium-pitched tone followed the letters, it meant the participants should recall the middle row. And when a low-pitched tone followed the letters, it meant the participants should recall the bottom row.

3 The tones sounded at various intervals: 0.15, 0.30, 0.50, or 1 second after the display of the letters.

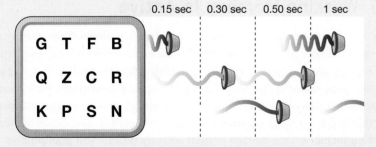

0.15 sec   0.30 sec   0.50 sec   1 sec

G T F B
Q Z C R
K P S N

RESULTS: When the tone sounded very shortly after the letters disappeared, participants remembered almost all the letters in the signaled row. The longer the delay between the disappearance of the letters and the tone, the worse the participants performed.

CONCLUSION: Sensory memory persists for about $\frac{1}{3}$ of a second and then progressively fades.

QUESTION: Why did people recall fewest letters on trials with long delays?

ANSWER: The sensory trace disappears after about $\frac{1}{3}$ of a second.

Source: Sperling, G. (1960). The information available in brief visual presentations. *Psychological Monographs, 74*, 1–29.

FIGURE 7.11
Sensory Storage
If you stood in front of this sparkler, you could see the word *LOVE* spelled by the sparkler because the visual input would be maintained briefly in sensory storage.

short-term memory
A memory storage system that briefly holds a limited amount of information in awareness.

working memory
An active processing system that keeps different types of information available for current use.

The psychologist George Sperling initially proposed the existence of sensory memory. In a classic experiment (Sperling, 1960), three rows of letters were flashed on a screen for $\frac{1}{20}$ of a second. Participants were asked to recall all the letters. Most people believed they had seen all the letters, but they could recall only three or four. That is, in the time it took them to name the first three or four, they forgot the other letters. These reports suggested the participants had very quickly lost their memories of exactly what they had seen.

An alternative hypothesis was that in the time given, the participants were able to encode only one line of letters. Sperling tested this hypothesis by showing all the letters exactly as he had done before but signaling with a high-, medium-, or low-pitched sound as soon as the letters disappeared. A high pitch meant the participants should recall the letters in the top row, a medium pitch meant they should recall the letters in the middle row, and a low pitch meant they should recall the letters in the bottom row. When the sound occurred very shortly after the letters disappeared, the participants correctly remembered almost all the letters in the signaled row. But the longer the delay between the letters' disappearance and the sound, the worse the participants performed. Sperling concluded that the visual memory persisted for about $\frac{1}{3}$ of a second. After that very brief period, the trace of the sensory memory faded progressively until it was no longer accessible (see "The Methods of Psychology: Sperling's Sensory Memory Experiment," on p. 257).

Our sensory memories enable us to experience the world as a continuous stream rather than in discrete sensations (**FIGURE 7.11**). Thanks to iconic memory, when you turn your head, the scene passes smoothly in front of you rather than in jerky bits. Your memory retains information just long enough for you to connect one image with the next in a smooth way that corresponds to the way objects move in the real world. In much the same way, a movie projector plays a series of still pictures that follow each other closely enough in time to look like continuous action (see Figure 5.34).

 How do iconic and echoic memory differ?

7.5 Working Memory Is Active

When we pay attention to something, the information passes from sensory stores to **short-term memory.** Researchers initially saw short-term memory as simply a buffer or holding place. There, verbal information was rehearsed until it was stored or forgotten. Subsequently, researchers learned that short-term memory is not a single storage system. Instead, it is an active processing unit that deals with multiple types of information. A more contemporary model of the short-term retention of information is **working memory.** This storage system actively retains and manipulates multiple pieces of temporary information from different sources (Baddeley, 2002; Baddeley & Hitch, 1974). For example, working memory includes sounds, images, and ideas.

Information remains in working memory for about 20 to 30 seconds. It then disappears unless you actively prevent that from happening. You retain the information by monitoring it—that is, thinking about or rehearsing it. As an example, try to remember some new information. Memorize a meaningless string of letters, the consonants X C J. As long as you keep repeating the string over and over, you will keep it in working memory. But if you stop rehearsing, you probably will soon forget the letters. After all, you are bombarded with other events that compete for your attention, and you may not be able to stay focused.

Try again to remember X C J. This time, count backward in threes from 309. Most people find it difficult to remember the meaningless consonants after a few seconds of backward counting, because the counting prevents rehearsal of the letter string. The longer people spend counting, the less able they are to remember the consonants. After only 18 seconds of counting, most people recall the consonants extremely poorly. This result indicates that working memory lasts less than half a minute without continuous rehearsing as a way to remember.

MEMORY SPAN AND CHUNKING Why do new items in working memory interfere with the recall of older items? Working memory can hold a limited amount of information. The cognitive psychologist George Miller (1956) noted that the limit is generally seven items (plus or minus two). This figure is referred to as *memory span*. More-recent research suggests that Miller's estimate may be too high and that working memory may be limited to as few as four items (Conway et al., 2005).

Memory span also varies among individuals. As a result, some intelligence tests use memory span as part of the measure of IQ. The capacity of working memory increases as children develop (Garon, Bryson, & Smith, 2008) and decreases with advanced aging (McCabe et al., 2010). Researchers have attempted to increase working memory through training exercises, with the hope that the exercises will boost intelligence (Klingberg, 2010; Morrison & Chein, 2011). Such training has increased working memory, but this learning has not transferred to other cognitive abilities involved in intelligence (Redick et al., 2013; Shipstead, Redick, & Engle, 2012). This type of limited learning is generally true of "brain training" apps or programs. That is, people get better at the task they practice, but do not improve in their general everyday cognition or memory (Simons et al., 2016).

Because working memory is limited, you might expect almost everyone to have great difficulty remembering a string of letters such as BCPHDNYUMAUCLABAMIT. These 19 letters would tax even the largest memory span. But what if we organized the information into smaller, meaningful units? For instance, BC PHD NYU MA UCLA BA MIT.

Here the letters are separated to produce acronyms for universities and academic degrees. This organization makes them much easier to recall, for two reasons. First, memory span is limited to as few as four items. The items can be letters or groups of letters, numbers or groups of numbers, words, or even concepts. Second, meaningful units are easier to remember than nonsense units. This process of breaking down information into meaningful units is known as **chunking.** The more efficiently you chunk information, the more you can remember.

Master chess players who glance at a scenario on a chessboard, even for a few seconds, later can reproduce the exact arrangement of pieces (Chase & Simon, 1973). They can do so because they instantly chunk the board into a number of meaningful subunits based on their past experiences with the game (**FIGURE 7.12**). If the pieces are arranged on the board in ways that make no sense in terms of chess, however, experts are no better than novices at reproducing the board. In general, the greater your expertise with the material, the more efficiently you can chunk information and therefore the more you can remember.

chunking
Organizing information into meaningful units to make it easier to remember.

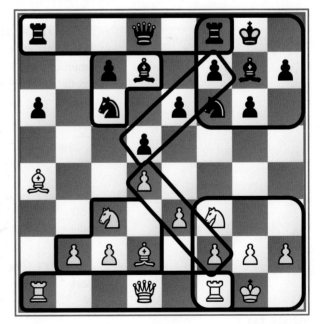

FIGURE 7.12
Chunking
Expert chess players chunk the game pieces into meaningful subunits.

Q Through what process is information maintained in working memory?

7.6 Long-Term Memory Is Relatively Permanent

long-term memory
The relatively permanent storage of information.

serial position effect
The idea that the ability to recall items from a list depends on the order of presentation, with items presented early or late in the list remembered better than those in the middle.

When people talk about memory, they are usually referring to the relatively permanent storage of information: **long-term memory.** In the computer analogy presented earlier in this chapter, long-term memory is like the storage of information on a hard drive. When you think about long-term memory's capacity, try to imagine counting everything you know and everything you are likely to know in your lifetime. It is hard to imagine what that number might be, because you can always learn more. Unlike computer storage, human long-term memory is nearly limitless. It enables you to remember nursery rhymes from childhood, the meanings and spellings of words you rarely use (such as *aardvark*), what you had for lunch yesterday, and so on.

DISTINGUISHING LONG-TERM MEMORY FROM WORKING MEMORY Long-term memory is distinct from working memory in two important ways: It has a longer duration, and it has a far greater capacity. A controversy exists, however, as to whether long-term memory represents a truly different type of memory storage from working memory.

Evidence suppoting the idea that long-term memory and working memory are separate systems came from research that required people to recall long lists of words. The ability to recall items from the list depended on the order of presentation. That is, items presented early or late in the list were remembered better than those in the middle. This phenomenon is known as the **serial position effect.** This effect actually consists of two separate effects: The *primacy effect* refers to the better memory that people have for items presented at the beginning of the list. The *recency effect* refers to the better memory that people have for the most recent items, the ones at the end of the list (**FIGURE 7.13**).

One explanation for the serial position effect relies on a distinction between working memory and long-term memory. When research participants study a long list of words, they rehearse the earliest items the most. As a result, that information is

FIGURE 7.13
The Serial Position Effect
This graph helps illustrate the primacy effect and the recency effect, which together make up the serial position effect. The serial position effect, in turn, helps illustrate the difference between long-term memory and working memory.

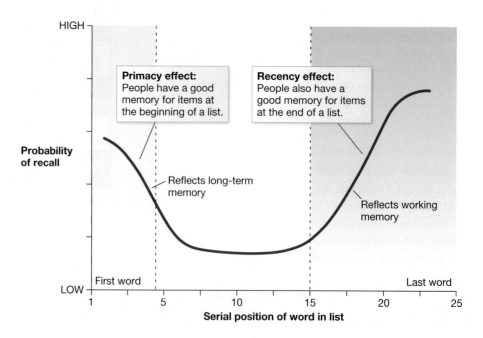

transferred into long-term memory. By contrast, the last few items are still in working memory when the participants have to recall the words immediately after reading them.

In some studies, there is a delay between the presentation of the list and the recall task. Such delays do not interfere with the primacy effect, but they do interfere with recency effect. You would expect this result if the primacy effect involves long-term memory and the recency effect involves working memory. The recency effect might not be entirely related to working memory, however. You probably remember your most recent class better than the classes you had earlier. If you had to recall the past presidents or past prime ministers of your country, you would probably recall the early ones and most recent ones best and have poorer recall for those in between. You most likely do not maintain the information about your classes or about world leaders in working memory.

Perhaps the best support for the distinction between working memory and long-term memory comes from case studies such as that of H.M., the patient described earlier in this chapter. His working memory system was perfectly normal, as shown by his ability to keep track of a conversation as long as he stayed actively involved in it. Much of his long-term memory system was intact, since he remembered events that occurred before his surgery. He was unable, however, to transfer new information from working memory into long-term memory.

In another case, a 28-year-old accident victim with damage to the left temporal lobe had extremely poor working memory, with a span of only one or two items. However, he had perfectly normal long-term memory: a fine memory for day-to-day happenings, and reasonable knowledge of events that occurred before his surgery (Shallice & Warrington, 1969). Somehow, despite the bottleneck in his working memory, he was relatively good at retrieving information from long-term memory.

These case studies demonstrate that working memory can be separated from long-term memory. Still, the two memory systems are highly interdependent, at least for most of us. For instance, to chunk information in working memory, people need to form meaningful connections based on information stored in long-term memory.

WHAT GETS INTO LONG-TERM MEMORY Paying attention is a way of storing information in sensory memory or working memory. To store information more permanently, we need to get that information into long-term memory. Normally, in the course of our daily lives, we engage in many activities and are bombarded with information. Some type of filtering system must constrain what goes into long-term memory. Researchers have provided several possible explanations for this process. One possibility is that information enters permanent storage through rehearsal.

To become proficient in any activity, you need to practice. The more times you repeat an action, the easier it is to perform that action. Motor skills—such as those used to play the piano, play golf, and drive—become easier with practice. Memories are strengthened with retrieval, so one way to make durable memories is to practice retrieval.

Recent research in classrooms has shown that repeated testing that includes practicing retrieval is a good way to strengthen memories (Carpenter, 2012; Putnam, Sungkhasettee, & Roediger, 2016). In fact, it is even better than spending the same amount of time reviewing information you have already read (Roediger & Karpicke, 2006). In a recent study, one group of students read a 276-word passage on sea otters and then practiced retrieving the information using free recall; a second group studied the information in four repeated 5-minute study periods; and a third group made concept maps to organize the information by linking together different ideas (Karpicke & Blunt, 2011). The time spent studying was the same for each group. One week later,

(a)

(b)

FIGURE 7.14

Details on Familiar Objects

(a) Abraham Lincoln appears on the penny, and **(b)** the first treasury secretary, Alexander Hamilton, is depicted on the 10-dollar bill. Which of the two versions shown is correct? (Answer: The left image is correct for the penny, and the bottom image is correct for the 10-dollar bill. The penny is the only regularly used U.S. coin on which the portrait faces right, and the 10-dollar bill is the only U.S. bill on which the portrait faces left.)

the students took a final test. Those who practiced retrieving the information had the best score on the final test.

Rehearsal is a way to get some information into long-term memory, but simply repeating something many times is not a good method for making information memorable. After all, sometimes we have extremely poor memory for objects that are highly familiar. Merely seeing something countless times does not necessarily enable us to recall its details. For example, ask a person in the United States to describe the details on the face of a penny or a 10-dollar bill (**FIGURE 7.14**). Even if people can name the people on the coins, they probably do not know if these people face left or right. This loss of information in memory really shows how well attention and memory function: We attend just enough for the task at hand and lose information that seems irrelevant. Did you know that the penny and the 10-dollar bill are unusual among U.S. currency?

Generally, information about an environment that helps us adapt to that environment is likely to be transformed into a long-term memory. Of the billions of sensory experiences and thoughts we have each day, we want to store only useful information so as to benefit from experience. Remembering that a 10-dollar bill is money and being able to recognize one when you see it are much more useful than being able to recall its specific features—unless you receive counterfeit bills and have to separate them from real ones.

Evolutionary theory helps explain how we decide in advance what information will be useful. Memory allows us to use information in ways that assist in reproduction and survival. For instance, animals that can use past experiences to increase their chances of survival have a selective advantage over animals that fail to learn from past experiences. Recognizing a predator and remembering an escape route will help an animal avoid being eaten. Accordingly, remembering which objects are edible, which people are friends and which are enemies, and how to get home is typically not challenging for people with intact memory systems, but it is critical for survival.

 What is the recency effect in memory?

ANSWER: Memory is better for the most recent items in a list—that is, the last items studied.

How Is Information Organized in Long-Term Memory?

Imagine if a library stored each of its books wherever there was empty space on a shelf. To find a particular book, a librarian would have to look through the inventory book by book. Just as this random storage would not work well for books, it would not work well for memories. When an event or some information is important enough, you want to remember it permanently. Thus, you need to store it in a way that enables you to retrieve it later. The following sections discuss the organizational principles of long-term memory.

7.7 Long-Term Storage Is Based on Meaning

As discussed in Chapter 5, perceptual experiences are transformed into representations in the brain. These representations are then stored in networks of neurons. For instance, when your visual system senses a shaggy, four-legged animal and your auditory system senses barking, you perceive a dog. The concept of "dog" is a *mental representation* for a category of animals that share certain features, such as barking and fur. You do not have a tiny picture of a dog stored in your head. Rather, you have a mental representation. The mental representation for "dog" differs from that for "cat," even though the two are similar in many ways. You also have mental representations for complex and abstract ideas, including beliefs and feelings (discussed in greater detail in Chapter 8).

Mental representations are stored by meaning. In the early 1970s, the psychologists Fergus Craik and Robert Lockhart developed an influential theory of memory based on depth of mental processing. According to their *levels of processing model,* the more deeply an item is encoded, the more meaning it has and the better it is remembered. Craik and Lockhart (1972) proposed that different types of rehearsal lead to different levels of encoding. *Maintenance rehearsal* is simply repeating the item over and over. *Elaborative rehearsal* encodes the information in more meaningful ways, such as thinking about the item conceptually or deciding whether it refers to oneself. In other words, in this type of rehearsal, we elaborate on basic information by linking it to knowledge from long-term memory.

How does the levels of processing model work? Suppose you show research participants a list of words and then ask them to do one of three things. You might ask them to make a *visual* judgment about what each word looks like. For example, "Is it printed in capital or lowercase letters?" You might ask them to make an *acoustic* judgment about the sound of each word. "Does it rhyme with *boat*?" Or you might ask them to make a *semantic* judgment about each word's meaning. "Does it fit in the sentence *They had to cross the ___ to reach the castle*?" Once participants have completed the task (that is, processed the information), you ask them to recall as many words as possible. You will find that words processed at the deepest level, based on meaning, are remembered the best (Craik & Tulving, 1975; **FIGURE 7.15**). Brain imaging studies have shown that semantic encoding activates more brain regions than shallow encoding and that this greater brain activity is associated with better memory (Cabeza & Moscovitch, 2013; Kapur et al., 1994).

SCHEMAS If people store memories by meaning, how do they determine the meanings of particular memories? Chunking, discussed earlier in this chapter, is a good way to encode groups of items for memorization. The more meaningful the chunks, the better they will be remembered. Decisions about how to chunk information depend on **schemas.** These are cognitive structures in long-term memory that help us perceive, organize, process, and use information. As we sort out incoming information, schemas guide our attention to an environment's relevant features. Thanks to schemas, we construct new memories by filling in holes within existing memories, overlooking inconsistent information, and interpreting meaning based on past experiences.

Learning Objectives

- Discuss the levels of processing model.
- Explain how schemas influence memory.
- Describe spreading activation models of memory.
- Identify retrieval cues.
- Define mnemonics.

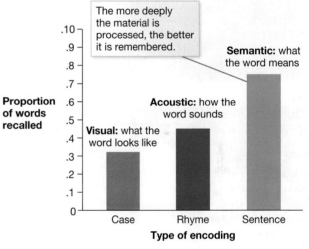

Source: Adapted from Craik & Tulving, 1975.

FIGURE 7.15
Encoding
This graph shows the results of a study of encoding. Participants were asked to consider a list of words according to how the words are printed (uppercase or lowercase), how they sound (whether they rhyme), or what they mean (whether they fit in a sentence). Later they are asked to recall the words.

schemas
Cognitive structures in long-term memory that help us perceive, organize, process, and use information.

"I CAN'T FIND THE BOOKS ON INFORMATION RETRIEVAL."

(a)

(b)

(c)

FIGURE 7.16
Cultural Influence on Schemas
Your schema for shopping in **(a)** a grocery store in the United States might not work so well in **(b)** a market in France or **(c)** a market in Morocco. As a result of the limitations in your schema, you might make mistakes when food shopping outside the U.S. Through learning from your mistakes, you will adjust your schema.

In Chapter 8, you will learn more about schemas and how they represent information. The basic idea is that they provide structures for understanding events in the world. For instance, you have a schema for grocery shopping at markets in the United States. That schema most likely includes shopping carts, abundant choices, and set prices. You may expect to choose your own fruit and vegetables in the produce section. You learned your grocery store schema from experience. It enables you to easily predict and navigate the grocery store experience.

Schemas can bias how information is encoded, however. This bias occurs in part because culture heavily influences schemas. Your grocery store schema will not be so useful when you go to the market in France, where you may not be allowed to touch the produce, or in Morocco, where you have to bargain for your prices. You may learn these differences the hard way: by making mistakes (**FIGURE 7.16**).

In a classic demonstration of biased encoding conducted in the early 1930s, the psychologist Frederic Bartlett (1932) asked British participants to listen to a Canadian First Nations folktale. The story involved supernatural experiences, and it was difficult to understand for those not familiar with such tales. Fifteen minutes later, Bartlett asked the participants to repeat the story exactly as they had heard it. The participants altered the story greatly. They also altered it consistently, so that it made sense from their own cultural standpoint. Sometimes they simply forgot the supernatural parts they could not comprehend.

To understand the influence of schemas on which information is stored in memory, consider a study in which students read a story about an unruly girl (Sulin & Dooling, 1974). Some participants were told that the subject of the story was Helen Keller, who was famous for having overcome her many disabilities as a child. Others were told it was Carol Harris, a made-up name. One week later, the participants who had been told the girl was Helen Keller were more likely to mistakenly report having read the sentence *She was deaf, mute, and blind* in the story than those who thought the story was about Carol Harris. The students' schema for Helen Keller included her disabilities. When they retrieved information about Keller from memory, they retrieved everything they knew about her along with the story they were trying to remember.

To see how schemas affect your ability to recall information, read the following paragraph carefully:

The procedure is actually quite simple. First arrange things into different bundles depending on makeup. Don't do too much at once. In the short run this may not seem important; however, complications easily arise. A mistake can be costly. Next, find facilities. Some people must go elsewhere for them. Manipulation of appropriate mechanisms should be self-explanatory. Remember to include all other necessary supplies. Initially the routine will overwhelm you, but soon it will become just another facet of life. Finally, rearrange everything into their initial groups. Return these to their usual places. Eventually they will be used again. Then the whole cycle will have to be repeated. (Bransford & Johnson, 1972, p. 722)

How easy did you find this paragraph to understand? Could you now recall specific sentences from it? It might surprise you to know that in a research setting, college students who read this paragraph found it easy to understand and relatively straightforward to recall. How is that possible? It was easy when the participants knew that the paragraph described washing clothes. Go back and reread the paragraph. Notice how your schema for doing laundry helps you understand and remember how the words and sentences are connected to one another. Schemas influence how we encode information in our daily lives.

 What model of memory suggests that thinking about the meaning of information will lead to greater memory than simply reading the information?

ANSWER: the levels of processing model

7.8 Information Is Stored in Association Networks

One highly influential set of theories about memory organization is based on *networks of associations*. In a network model proposed by the psychologists Allan Collins and Elizabeth Loftus (1975), an item's distinctive features are linked so as to identify the item. Each unit of information in the network is a *node*. Each node is connected to many other nodes. The resulting network is like the linked neurons in your brain, but nodes are simply bits of information. They are not physical realities. For example, when you look at a fire engine, all the nodes that represent a fire engine's features are activated. The resulting activation pattern gives rise to the knowledge that the object is a fire engine and not a car, a vacuum cleaner, a cat, and so on.

An important feature of network models is that activating one node increases the likelihood that closely associated nodes will also be activated. As shown in **FIGURE 7.17,** the closer the nodes are, the stronger the association between them. The stronger the association, the more likely that activating one node will activate the other. So seeing a fire engine activates nodes that indicate other vehicles. Once your fire engine nodes are activated, you will more quickly recognize other vehicles than, for instance, fruits or animals.

The main idea here is that activating one node increases the likelihood that associated nodes will become active. This idea is central to *spreading activation models* of memory. According to these models, stimuli in working memory activate specific

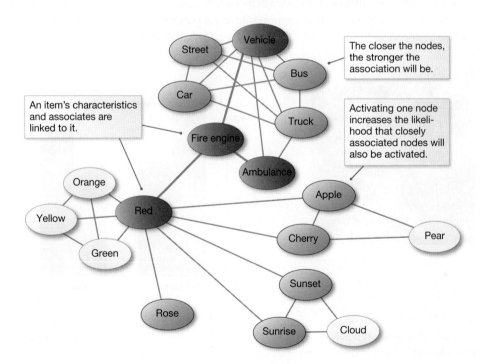

FIGURE 7.17
A Network of Associations
In this semantic network, similar concepts are connected through their associations.

nodes in long-term memory. This activation increases the ease of access to that material and thus makes retrieval easier. Indeed, one study showed that retrieval of some items led to enhanced memory for related items even when participants were told to forget those other items (Bäuml & Samenieh, 2010).

Given the vast amount of material in memory, it is amazing how quickly we can search for and obtain needed memories from storage. Each time we hear a sentence, we not only have to remember what all the words mean, we also have to recall all relevant information that helps us understand the sentence's overall meaning. For this process to occur, the information needs to be organized logically. Imagine trying to find a specific file on a full 600-gigabyte hard disk by opening one file at a time. Such a method would be hopelessly slow. Instead, most computer disks are organized into folders, within each folder are more-specialized folders, and so on. Associative networks in the brain work similarly.

retrieval cue

Any stimulus that increases memory recall.

encoding specificity principle

The idea that any stimulus that is encoded along with an experience can later trigger a memory of the experience.

RETRIEVAL CUES A **retrieval cue** can be anything that helps a person (or a nonhuman animal) recall a memory. Encountering stimuli—such as the fragrance of a roasting turkey, a favorite song from years past, a familiar building, and so on—can trigger unintended memories. In analyzing this phenomenon, the prominent memory researcher Endel Tulving proposed the **encoding specificity principle.** According to this principle, any stimulus encoded along with an experience can later trigger a memory of the experience (Tulving & Thomson, 1973).

In one study of encoding, participants studied 80 words in either of two rooms. The rooms differed in location, size, scent, and other aspects. The participants were then tested for recall in the room in which they studied or in the other room. When they were tested in the other room, participants recalled an average of 35 words correctly. When they were tested in the room where they studied, participants recalled an average of 49 words correctly (Smith, Glenberg, & Bjork, 1978). This kind of memory enhancement, when the recall situation is similar to the encoding situation, is known as *context-dependent memory.*

Context-dependent memory can be based on things such as physical location, odors, and background music, many of which produce a sense of familiarity (Hockley, 2008). In the most dramatic research demonstration of context-dependent memory, scuba divers who learned information underwater later recalled that information better underwater than on land (Godden & Baddeley, 1975; **FIGURE 7.18**).

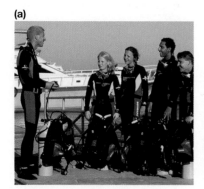

(a)   (b)   (c)

FIGURE 7.18
Context-Dependent Memory
A unique study showed that we encode the physical context of a memory along with the information, and the context can help retrieve the memory. **(a)** People learned lists of words either on land or **(b)** underwater. **(c)** When they had to recall the words later on, they remembered more words if they were tested in the same environment where they had learned the words.

Like physical context, internal cues can affect the recovery of information from long-term memory. Think about mood. When you are in a good mood, do you tend to recall good times? At the end of a bad day, do negative memories tend to surface? Memory can be enhanced when a person's internal states match during encoding and recall. This effect is known as *state-dependent memory*.

State-dependent memory also applies to internal states brought on by drugs or alcohol. You most likely will not remember much of anything you learn while intoxicated. Whatever you do learn, however, may be easier to recall when you are intoxicated than when you are sober—though do not count on it (Goodwin, Powell, Bremer, Hoine, & Stern, 1969).

PROSPECTIVE MEMORY "When you see Juan, tell him to call me, okay? And don't forget to buy milk." Unlike the other types of remembering discussed so far in this chapter, **prospective memory** is future oriented. It means that a person remembers to do something at some future time (Graf & Uttl, 2001).

In a study of prospective memory, participants had to learn a list of words (Cook, Marsh, Clark-Foos, & Meeks, 2007). In one condition, they also had to remember to do something, such as press a key when they saw a certain word. The group that had to remember to do something took longer to learn the list than the control group that learned the same list of words but did not have to remember to do something.

Retrieval cues can help prospective memory. For example, seeing Juan might automatically trigger your memory, so you effortlessly remember to give him the message. Sometimes particular environments do not have obvious retrieval cues for particular prospective memories. For example, you might not encounter a retrieval cue for remembering to buy milk. Remembering to buy milk might require some ongoing remembering as you head back to your room, even if you are not aware of that remembering. Prospective memory for events without retrieval cues is the reason sticky notes are so popular. In this case, you might stick a note that says "Buy milk" on your notebook or on the steering wheel of your car. By jogging your memory, the note helps you avoid the effort of remembering. For an even more urgent reminder, you might set your cell phone alarm or electronic calendar (**FIGURE 7.19**).

MNEMONICS Mnemonics are learning aids or strategies that use retrieval cues to improve recall. People often find mnemonics helpful for remembering items in long lists, for example. One of the oldest methods dates back to the lucky ancient Greek poet Simonides. While attending a banquet, he stepped out for a bit of air. Moments later, the ceiling collapsed on his dinner companions and killed them. By visualizing where people were seated at the banquet table, he could recall who was killed. Now referred to as the *method of loci* or the *memory palace,* this mnemonic consists of associating items you want to remember with physical locations.

Suppose you want to remember the names of classmates you just met. First, you might visualize items from various places on your typical route across campus, or you might visualize parts of the physical layout of some familiar location, such as your bedroom. Then you would associate your classmates' names with the items or parts you have visualized. You might picture Justin climbing on your dresser, Malia sitting on a chair, and Anthony hiding under the bed. When you later need to remember the names, you would visualize your room and retrieve the information associated with each piece of furniture.

The journalist Joshua Foer used this method when he competed in the U.S.A. Memory Championships in 2006 (Foer, 2011). During the contest, one of Foer's tasks was to memorize the order of two shuffled decks of playing cards. By imagining the cards in various locations in the house where he grew up, Foer was able to correctly remember the order of the cards in the two decks in just under 2 minutes. To keep

prospective memory
Remembering to do something at some future time.

FIGURE 7.19
Prospective Memory
Prospective memory involves remembering to do something in the future. When you use a device, such as a cell phone, to remember appointments and deadlines, you are assisting your prospective memory.

mnemonics
Learning aids or strategies that improve recall through the use of retrieval cues.

FIGURE 7.20
Memory Championships
Contestants in the Extreme Memory Tournament—as shown here at the 2015 meet, held at Dart NeuroScience in San Diego—memorize names, faces, and even decks of cards. Almost all participants in such memory contests use strategies involving chunking.

from being distracted, he wore headphones and dark glasses. Strategies such as these enable people to excel at memory contests. Such contest winners do not necessarily have better-functioning memories than most people. They are simply better able to use their memories to achieve such feats as becoming a Grand Master of Memory (**FIGURE 7.20**). To win this award, you must be able to memorize 1,000 digits in an hour, one randomly shuffled deck of cards in 2 minutes, and 10 randomly shuffled decks of cards (520 cards) in 1 hour.

 What is the main idea behind spreading activation models of memory?

7.9 Can You Ace Exams Without Cramming?

What tools does psychology offer to help you study more effectively for the many exams you will take during college? Many students read the text, highlight what they think is important, and then reread the highlighted material for hours the night before an exam. Despite the popularity of these methods, they are not associated with effective learning or good grades (Blasiman, Dunlosky, & Rawson, 2016). As mentioned throughout this chapter, researchers have identified a number of methods that will help you remember information more easily (Putnam et al., 2016). These methods include:

1. **Prepare for and attend class.** Many professors advise students on what to read before class. Do it! They are trying to maximize the likelihood you will learn the information. Read the material for comprehension, but take your time and try to understand the ideas as you read. Speed reading does not work, no matter how much you practice it. There is a trade-off between speed and accuracy (Rayner et al., 2016). Once you are prepared, be sure to attend class. You simply cannot get by with reading the text and looking at online lecture notes. Your instructor may tie together ideas across lectures, present new ways of thinking about the material, or mention information not found in the textbook. As mentioned in Chapter 4, unless otherwise instructed leave your laptop at home and take notes by hand. Writing by hand will encourage greater comprehension.

2. **Distribute your learning.** Cramming does not work. Instead, distribute your study sessions. Six sessions of 1 hour each are much better for learning than one 6-hour marathon. By spreading your studying over multiple sessions, you will retain the information for longer periods of time. During each session, you should

study each subject a little bit. Spacing out your study sessions requires you to begin earlier in the term rather than waiting until the night before exams, but distributing your time is perhaps the best way to learn the information and do well on exams.

3. **Elaborate the material.** Imagine you and two friends decide to engage in a little friendly competition. The challenge is to memorize a list of 20 words. Friend A simply reads the words. Friend B, after reading each word, copies the word's definition from a dictionary. You, after reading each word, think about how the word is relevant to you. For example, you see the word *rain* and think, "My car once broke down in the middle of a torrential rainstorm." Who is most likely to remember that list of words later? You are. The deeper your level of processing, the more likely you are to remember material, particularly if you make the material personally relevant.

When you are learning something new, do not just read the material or copy down textbook descriptions. Think about the meaning of the material and how the concepts are related to other concepts. Organize the material in a way that makes sense to you, putting the concepts in your own words. Making the material relevant to you is an especially good way to process material deeply and therefore to remember it easily.

4. **Practice retrieval.** To make your memories more durable, you need to practice retrieving the information you are trying to learn. In fact, repeated testing is a more effective memory-building strategy than spending the same amount of time reviewing information you have already read. Thus, to prepare for an exam, you should practice recalling the information over and over again. Sometimes the stress of taking an exam can interfere with memory. Practicing retrieval protects memories from the negative effects of stress (Smith, Floerke, & Thomas, 2016).

After reading a section in this or any other book, look back to the main section heading. If that heading is not already a question, rephrase it as a question. Test yourself by trying to answer the heading's question without looking at the text. Make use of in-chapter test questions by answering these questions as you encounter them. Then answer them again a couple of days later. For this book, be sure to take the practice test provided at the back. Take advantage of online test questions supplied by the textbook publisher. For this book, the online testing system is InQuizitive.

You can also develop your own practice materials. Write quiz questions. Make flash cards on pieces of card stock or on the computer (quizlet.com is a great Web site for creating and using flash cards). For example, on one side of the flash card, write a key term. On the other side, write the definition of that term. Then drill using the flash cards in both directions. Can you recall the term when you see the definition? Can you provide the definition when you see the term? A good way to drill is to study with another member of your class and take turns quizzing each other.

5. **Overlearn.** With material in front of us, we are often overly confident that we "know" the information and believe we will remember it later. But recognition is easier than recall. Thus, if you want to be able to recall information, you need to put in extra effort when encoding the material. Even after you *think* you have learned it, review it again. Test yourself by trying to recall the material a few hours (and a few days) after studying. Keep rehearsing until you can recall the material easily.

6. **Use verbal mnemonics for rote memory.** Sometimes people have to learn long lists of items, but understanding the items doesn't matter. In these cases, verbal mnemonics can help. People use many types of mnemonics. For example, how many days are there in September? In the Western world, at least, most people can readily answer this question thanks to the old saying that begins *Thirty days*

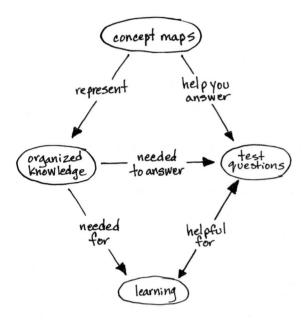

FIGURE 7.21

Concept Map as Memory Aid

This concept map presents some ideas about—you guessed it—concept maps. When you need to visualize the relationships between different ideas about any subject, you can adapt this model. The ovals represent main ideas. The arrows indicate connections between ideas. A concept map can become far more complex. In fact, it can become as complex as you need it to be. For example, you might use lots of branches to represent an especially complex idea or color-code ideas that originated from different sources.

hath September. Children also learn *i before e except after c* and, along with that saying, *"weird" is weird.* By memorizing such phrases, we more easily remember things that are difficult to remember. Advertisers, of course, often create slogans or jingles that rely on *verbal mnemonics* so that consumers cannot help but remember them.

Students have long used acronyms to remember information, such as HOMES to remember the great lakes (Huron, Ontario, Michigan, Erie, and Superior). In studying Chapter 13, the acronym OCEAN will help you remember the five major personality traits: openness to experience, conscientiousness, extraversion, agreeableness, and neuroticism. Even complex ideas can be understood through simple mnemonics. For example, the phrase *cells that fire together wire together* is a way to remember long-term potentiation, the brain mechanism responsible for learning (discussed in Section 7.2). Importantly, however, mnemonics are not useful for increasing understanding of the material, and ultimately having a greater conceptual understanding is important for learning and memory.

7. **Use visual imagery.** Creating a mental image of material may help you. Visual imagery strategies include doodling a sketch to help you link ideas to images, creating a flow chart to show how some process unfolds over time, or drawing a concept map that shows the relationships between ideas (**FIGURE 7.21**).

To use all of these strategies, you need to remember them. As a first step toward improving your study skills, create a mnemonic to remember these strategies! ■

 Which is more effective for studying, highlighting information and reading it very often or taking practice tests?

ANSWER: Taking practice tests allows for repeated retrieval of information, which leads to better memory.

Learning Objectives

- Explain implicit, explicit, declarative, episodic, semantic, and procedural memories.
- Generate examples of each of these types of memory.

What Are the Different Long-Term Memory Systems?

In the last few decades, most psychologists have come to view long-term memory as composed of several interacting systems. These systems share a common function: to retain and use information (Schacter & Tulving, 1994). However, they encode and store different types of information in different ways (**FIGURE 7.22**). For instance, several obvious differences exist between remembering how to ride a bicycle, recalling what you ate for dinner last night, and knowing that the capital of Canada is Ottawa. These are long-term memories, but they differ in how they were acquired (learned) and in how they are stored and retrieved.

Scientists do not agree on the number of human long-term memory systems. For instance, some researchers have distinguished between memory systems based on how information is stored in memory, such as whether the storage occurs with or without deliberate effort. Other researchers have focused on the types of information

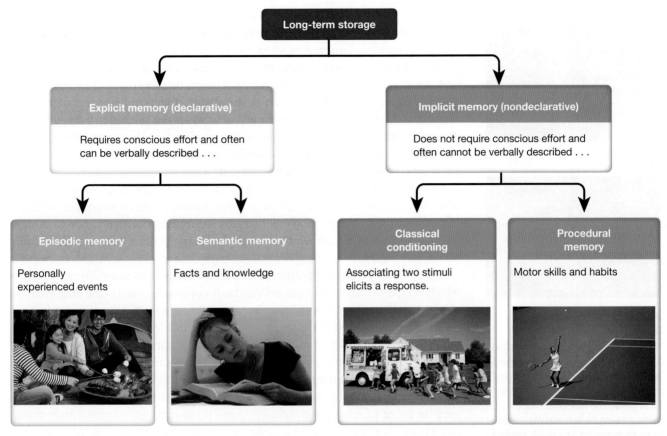

FIGURE 7.22
Different Types of Long-Term Memory
This graphic will help you remember the main types of long-term memory and the subtypes.

stored: words and meaning, particular muscle movements, information about a city's spatial layout, and so on. The following sections explore how the different long-term memory systems work.

7.10 Explicit Memory Involves Conscious Effort

The most basic distinction between memory systems is a division of memories: On one hand are memories we are consciously aware of. On the other hand are memories we acquire without conscious effort or intention—memories we do not know we know. Remember that H.M., the memory loss sufferer described earlier in this chapter, improved at mirror tracing (tracing a pattern when only its mirror image is visible). He must have learned this motor task even without knowing he had.

Peter Graf and Daniel Schacter (1985) referred to unconscious memory as **implicit memory.** They contrasted it with **explicit memory,** the processes we use to remember information we can say we know. The cognitive information retrieved from explicit memory is **declarative memory:** knowledge we can declare (consciously bring to mind).

For example, you use explicit memory when you recall what you had for dinner last night or what the word *aardvark* means. Declarative memories can involve words or concepts, visual images, or both. When you imagine Earth's orbit around the sun, you might also retrieve the images and names of the other planets. You could describe this knowledge in words, so it is declarative memory. Most of the examples presented in this chapter so far are of explicit memories. Most exams you have taken in school likely tested declarative memory.

implicit memory
The system underlying unconscious memories.

explicit memory
The system underlying conscious memories.

declarative memory
The cognitive information retrieved from explicit memory; knowledge that can be declared.

(a)

(b)

Who is
Leif Ericson?

FIGURE 7.23
Explicit Memory
Explicit memory involves information that individuals are aware of knowing. **(a)** When these World War II veterans assembled aboard the USS *Intrepid* to reminisce on Memorial Day, they were drawing on episodic memory, which is based on past experiences. **(b)** Game shows such as *Jeopardy!* test semantic memory: the memory of facts independent of personal experience. In 2004, Ken Jennings (pictured here) became the longest-defending champion on *Jeopardy!* when he won 74 games in a row.

 ANSWER: episodic, since it is a memory of an experience

episodic memory
Memory for one's personal past experiences.

semantic memory
Memory for knowledge of facts independent of personal experience.

procedural memory
A type of implicit memory that involves motor skills, habits, and other behaviors.

In 1972, Endel Tulving found that explicit memory can be divided into episodic memory and semantic memory. **Episodic memory** consists of a person's past experiences and includes information about the time and place the experiences occurred (**FIGURE 7.23A**). If you can remember aspects of your 16th birthday, for example, such as where you were and what you did there, this information is part of your episodic memory. **Semantic memory** is knowledge of facts independent of personal experience. You might not remember where or when you learned it, but you know it (**FIGURE 7.23B**). For instance, people know what Jell-O is, they know the capitals of countries they have never visited, and even people who have never played baseball know that three strikes mean the batter is out.

Scientists have learned a great deal about normal memory by studying people who have impaired memory (Jacoby & Witherspoon, 1982). Evidence that episodic and semantic systems of explicit memory are separate can be found in cases of brain injuries, such as H.M.'s, in which semantic memory is intact even though episodic memory is impaired.

Researchers found this pattern of abnormal memory in three British children who had experienced brain damage (Vargha-Khadem et al., 1997). One child suffered the damage during a difficult birth. The other two suffered it during early childhood (one had seizures at age 4; the other had an accidental drug overdose at age 9). Each of the three developed poor memory for episodic information. As children, they had trouble reporting what they had for lunch, what they had been watching on television 5 minutes earlier, what they did during summer vacation. Their parents reported that the children had to be constantly monitored to make sure they remembered things such as going to school. Remarkably, these three children attended mainstream schools and did reasonably well. Moreover, when tested as young adults, their IQs fell within the normal range. They learned to speak and read, and they could remember many facts. For instance, when asked "Who is Martin Luther King Jr.?" one of the children, tested at age 19, responded, "An American; fought for black rights, black rights leader in the 1970s [actually 1960s]; got assassinated [in 1968]." These three, then, were able to encode and retrieve semantic information even though they could not remember their own personal experiences.

> **Q** Let's say you are remembering what you had for breakfast yesterday. Is this a semantic memory or an episodic memory?

7.11 Implicit Memory Occurs Without Deliberate Effort

Implicit memory consists of memories you are not able to put into words. Classical conditioning (discussed in Chapter 6, "Learning") uses implicit memory. For example, if you always experience joy at hearing holiday music, you might have past associations between the holidays and having fun. These associations are implicit memories.

Implicit memories do not require conscious attention. They happen automatically, without deliberate effort. Suppose that while driving you realize you have been daydreaming and have no episodic memory of the past few minutes. During that time, you used implicit memories of how to drive and where you were going. Thus, you did not crash the car or go in the wrong direction. This type of implicit memory is called **procedural memory,** or *motor memory*. It involves motor skills, habits, and other behaviors used to achieve goals, such as coordinating muscle movements to ride a bicycle, ski, roller-skate, row a boat, or follow the rules of the road while driving (**FIGURE 7.24**). You remember to stop when you see a red light because you have learned to do so, and you might drive home on a specific route without even thinking about it.

Procedural memories are generally so unconscious that most people find that consciously thinking about automatic behaviors interferes with the smooth production of those behaviors. The next time you are riding a bicycle, try to think about each step involved in the process. What effects does thinking have? Thinking about automatic actions is why athletes sometimes choke under pressure while aiming a free throw, hovering over a short putt, or landing a triple axel. But procedural memories are very resistant to decay. Once you learn to ride a bike or ice skate, it is likely that, unless you suffer some brain damage, you will always be able to do so.

Implicit memory influences our lives in subtle ways, as when our attitudes are influenced by implicit learning. For example, you might like someone because he or she reminds you of another person you like, even if you are unaware of the connection. Advertisers rely on implicit memory to influence our purchasing decisions. Constant exposure to brand names makes us more likely to think of them when we buy products. If you find yourself wanting a particular brand of something, you might be "remembering" advertisements for that brand, even if you cannot recall the specifics.

Our implicit formation of attitudes can affect our beliefs about people, such as whether particular people are famous. Ask yourself: Is Richard Shiffrin famous? Try to think for a second how you know him. If you thought he was famous, you might have recalled that Shiffrin was one of the psychologists who introduced the model of sensory, short-term, and long-term memory (an accomplishment that might make him famous in some scientific circles). Alternatively, you might have remembered reading his name before, even if you could not remember where.

In studying what he called the *false fame effect,* the psychologist Larry Jacoby had research participants read aloud a list of made-up names (Jacoby, Kelley, Brown, & Jasechko, 1989). The participants were told that the research project was about pronunciation. The next day, Jacoby had the same people participate in an apparently unrelated study. This time, they were asked to read a list of names and decide whether each person was famous or not. The participants misjudged some of the made-up names from the previous day as being those of famous people. Because the participants knew they had heard the names before but probably could not remember where, implicit memory led them to assume the familiar names were those of famous people.

 Practicing a dance routine requires what type of implicit memory?

How Is Memory Flawed?

Most people believe that memories are permanently stored. Research has shown clearly, however, that human memory is flawed: biased, distorted, and prone to a great deal of forgetting. Memory is a constantly active process, involving consolidation and reconsolidation of information manipulated in working memory. It is not like burning a DVD and then rewatching the same burned DVD. For example, ten minutes after you see a movie, you probably remember plenty of its details, but the next day you might remember mostly the plot and the main characters. Years later, you might remember the gist of the story, or you might not remember having seen the movie at all. We forget far more than we remember. You might also have memories that are false, such as remembering a particular person was in a film when she wasn't

FIGURE 7.24
Implicit Memory
The innate muscle memory for knowing how to ride a bicycle is procedural, or motor, memory. It is also an example of implicit memory. Once you learn how to ride a bike, you can usually remember how to do it again, unconsciously, at any age.

ANSWER: procedural memory, which is also called motor memory

Learning Objectives

- Explain why people forget.
- Discuss methods to reduce persistence.
- Discuss flashbulb memories.
- Generate examples of source misattribution.
- Discuss susceptibility to false memories.
- Describe contemporary views on repressed memories.

or getting plot details wrong. In this section, you will learn how the human long-term memory systems provide less-than-accurate portrayals of past events.

7.12 Forgetting Is an Inability to Remember

Most people are unhappy about forgetting. They wish they could better remember the material for exams, their friends' birthdays, the geologic time periods, and so on. But imagine what life would be like if you could not forget. Imagine, for example, walking up to your locker and recalling not just its combination but the 10 or 20 combinations for all the locks you have ever used.

Consider the case of a Russian newspaper reporter who had nearly perfect memory. If someone read him a tremendously long list of items and he visualized the items for a few moments, he could recite the list, even many years later. But his memory was so cluttered with information that he had great difficulty functioning in society. Tortured by this condition, he was institutionalized (Luria, 1968). Not being able to forget is as maladaptive as not being able to remember. It is therefore not surprising

that we tend to best remember meaningful points. We remember the forest rather than the individual trees. Normal forgetting helps us retain and use important information.

The study of forgetting has a long history in psychological science. The late-nineteenth-century psychologist Hermann Ebbinghaus (1885/1964) used the so-called *methods of savings* to examine how long it took people to relearn lists of nonsense syllables (e.g., vut, bik, kuh). Ebbinghaus provided compelling evidence that forgetting occurs rapidly over the first few days but then levels off. Most of us do not need to memorize nonsense syllables, but Ebbinghaus's general findings apply to meaningful material as well. You may remember very little of the Spanish or calculus you took in high school, but relearning these subjects would take you less time and effort than it took to learn them the first time. The difference between the original learning and relearning is called *savings*. In other words, you save time and effort because of what you remember.

MEMORY DECAY Memory decay involves forgetting over time. Ebbinghaus observed this pattern in his studies of nonsense syllables. Many early theorists argued that such forgetting results from the memory trace's decay in a person's nervous system. Indeed, some evidence indicates that unused memories are forgotten. Research over the last few decades, however, has established that most forgetting occurs because of *interference* from other information. Additional information can lead to forgetting through *proactive* interference or *retroactive* interference. In both cases, competing information displaces the information we are trying to retrieve.

In **proactive interference,** old information inhibits the ability to remember new information. For instance, if you study for your psychology test, then switch to studying for your anthropology test, and then take the anthropology test, your performance on the test might be impaired by your knowledge about psychology (**FIGURE 7.25A**). In **retroactive interference,** new information inhibits the ability to remember old information. So when it comes time to take the psychology test, your performance might suffer because you recall the freshly reinforced anthropology material instead (**FIGURE 7.25B**).

BLOCKING Blocking occurs when a person is temporarily unable to remember something: You cannot recall the name of a favorite song, you forget the name of

proactive interference
Interference that occurs when prior information inhibits the ability to remember new information.

retroactive interference
Interference that occurs when new information inhibits the ability to remember old information.

blocking
The temporary inability to remember something.

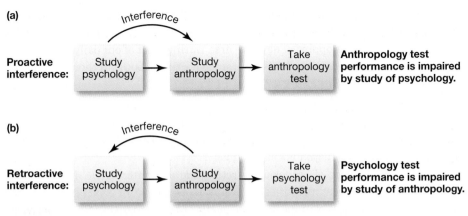

(a)

Interference

Proactive interference: Study psychology → Study anthropology → Take anthropology test | **Anthropology test performance is impaired by study of psychology.**

(b)

Interference

Retroactive interference: Study psychology → Study anthropology → Take psychology test | **Psychology test performance is impaired by study of anthropology.**

FIGURE 7.25
Proactive Interference Versus Retroactive Interference
(a) Proactive interference occurs when information already known (here, psychology material) interferes with the ability to remember new information (here, anthropology material).
(b) Retroactive interference occurs when new information (anthropology material) interferes with memory for old information (psychology material).

someone you are introducing, you "blank" on some lines when acting in a play, and so on. Such temporary blockages are common and frustrating.

Roger Brown and David McNeill (1966) described another good example of blocking: the *tip-of-the-tongue phenomenon,* in which people experience great frustration as they try to recall specific, somewhat obscure words. For instance, when asked to provide a word that means "patronage bestowed on a relative, in business or politics" or "an astronomical instrument for finding position," people often struggle (A. S. Brown, 1991). Sometimes they know which letter the word begins with, how many syllables it has, and possibly what it sounds like. Even with these partial retrieval cues, they cannot pull the precise word into working memory. (Did you know the words were *nepotism* and *sextant*?) Blocking often occurs because of interference from words that are similar in some way, such as in sound or meaning, and that recur. For example, you might repeatedly call an acquaintance Margaret although her name is Melanie. The tip-of-the-tongue phenomenon increases with age, perhaps because older people have more memories that might interfere.

ABSENTMINDESSNESS Absentmindedness is the shallow encoding of events. The major cause of absentmindedness is failing to pay attention. For instance, you absentmindedly forget where you left your keys because when you put them down, you were also reaching to answer your phone. You forget the name of a person you are talking with because when you met 5 minutes ago, you were paying attention to her face, not her name. You forget whether you took your vitamins this morning because you were distracted by an interesting question from your roommate (**FIGURE 7.26**).

Recall that when prospective memory fails, you fail to remember to do something. Often, this form of absentmindedness occurs because you are caught up in another activity. For instance, when you perform an automatic task, such as driving, your conscious thoughts might not include the driving experience. Your mind might wander to other ideas or memories.

This lack of attention can produce serious consequences. For example, in the United States over the past 15 years, more than 600 children, mostly infants, have died because they were left unattended in hot cars—39 in 2016 alone (Null, 2016). In many cases, the parent forgot to drop the child off at day care on his or her way to work. It is easy to imagine forgetting your lunch in the car, but your child? Fortunately, such incidents are rare, but they seem to be especially likely when the parent's typical

absentmindedness
The inattentive or shallow encoding of events.

FIGURE 7.26
Absentmindedness
The major cause of absentmindedness is failing to pay sufficient attention when encoding memories. The celebrated musician Yo-Yo Ma is pictured here with his $2.5 million eighteenth-century cello, which was returned to him after he absentmindedly left it in a cab.

routine does not include day care drop-off duty. While the parent is driving, his or her brain shifts to "autopilot" and automatically goes through the process of driving to the workplace instead of stopping at day care first. During most of our daily activities, of course, we are consciously aware of only a small portion of both our thoughts and our behaviors.

AMNESIA Sometimes people lose the ability to retrieve vast quantities of information from long-term memory. This condition is called **amnesia.** Amnesia results from disease, brain injury, or psychological trauma.

The two basic types of amnesia are retrograde and anterograde. In **retrograde amnesia,** people lose past memories for events, facts, people, or even personal information. Most portrayals of amnesia in the media are of retrograde amnesia, as when a character in a soap opera awakens from a coma and does not know who he or she is (**FIGURE 7.27A**). By contrast, in **anterograde amnesia,** people lose the ability to form new memories (**FIGURE 7.27B**).

As discussed earlier in this chapter, H.M. had a classic case of anterograde amnesia. He could remember old information about his past, but after his surgery he lost the ability to form new memories. However, H.M. may have acquired some new semantic knowledge about things that occurred after 1953. For instance, when given a list of people who became famous or infamous after 1953, H.M. was able to provide some information about them (O'Kane, Kensinger, & Corkin, 2004). This new learning may have occurred through his extensive repetition of materials over a long time. Given

amnesia

A deficit in long-term memory—resulting from disease, brain injury, or psychological trauma—in which the individual loses the ability to retrieve vast quantities of information.

retrograde amnesia

A condition in which people lose past memories, such as memories for events, facts, people, or even personal information.

anterograde amnesia

A condition in which people lose the ability to form new memories.

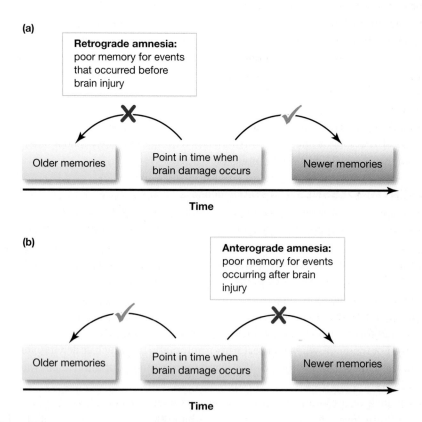

FIGURE 7.27

Retrograde Amnesia Versus Anterograde Amnesia

Amnesia can involve either of two forms of memory loss. **(a)** Retrograde amnesia is an inability to access memories that were created before the brain damage (see red X). **(b)** Anterograde amnesia is an inability to create new memories after the brain damage (see red X).

the name Lee Harvey Oswald, H.M. described him as the man who "assassinated the president." Oswald shot President John F. Kennedy in 1963. This happened long after H.M.'s surgery but long before researchers tested him. He somehow formed this new memory and retained that information over a long period of time.

 Your best friend growing up now likes to be called Kathleen rather than Katie, which is what you always called her. Now when you see her, you forget she likes to be called Kathleen. Why?

7.13 Persistence Is Unwanted Remembering

Sometimes you want to forget something but have difficulty doing so. **Persistence** occurs when unwanted memories are remembered in spite of the desire not to have them. Some unwanted memories are so traumatic that they destroy the life of the individual who suffers from them.

One prominent example of persistence occurs in posttraumatic stress disorder (PTSD; discussed further in Chapter 14, "Psychological Disorders"). PTSD is a serious mental health problem, with an estimated prevalence of 7 percent in the United States alone (Kessler et al., 2005b). The most common triggers of PTSD include events that threaten people or those close to them. For example, the unexpected death of a loved one, a physical or sexual assault, a car accident, a natural disaster, or the sight of someone badly injured or killed can be a source of PTSD. Emotional events are associated with amygdala activity, which might underlie the persistence of certain memories. Indeed, the release of hormones associated with emotional states strengthens memory consolidation and thereby enhances memories (McGaugh, 2015).

A problem with studying PTSD is that people often experience trauma in unique circumstances. It can be hard to compare memories across different types of traumatic events, such as being in a war or being in a car accident. One team of Canadian researchers examined survivors of a single life-threatening incident for which detailed information about the sequence of events was available. On August 24, 2001, a plane flying from Toronto to Portugal ran out of fuel while over the Atlantic Ocean. The nearly 300 passengers were told to prepare for the plane to ditch at sea. As you might expect, there was considerable panic as the aircraft lost power, cabin lights, and cabin pressure. Fortunately, the pilots located a remote military landing strip and were able to glide the large jet for 75 miles before coming to an extremely rough landing (**FIGURE 7.28**). Mercifully, those on board suffered only minor injuries, most caused from evacuating the plane. One passenger was the memory researcher Margaret McKinnon, who was able to study a sample of survivors, about half of whom had developed PTSD. Compared to their recollections of another highly negative event (the September 11, 2001, terrorist attacks), research participants showed enhanced memory for many details of their experience (McKinnon et al., 2015). Indeed, a brain imaging study showed heightened amygdala activity when survivors were remembering events from the doomed flight (Palombo et al., 2016). The heightened emotional experience and amygdala activity produced very powerful and vivid memories.

REDUCING PERSISTENCE Considerable research is under way to produce drugs that will erase unwanted memories. One drug, propranolol, blocks the postsynaptic receptors for the neurotransmitter norepinephrine. If propranolol is given before or right after a traumatic experience, the hormonally enhanced memories and fear

persistence
The continual recurrence of unwanted memories.

FIGURE 7.28
AirTransat Flight 236
The life-threatening landing of this aircraft left the survivors with powerful and vivid memories of their traumatic experience.

FIGURE 7.29
Altering Memories
In the 2004 movie *Eternal Sunshine of the Spotless Mind,* Joel Barish (played by Jim Carrey) undergoes a procedure that eliminates memories of his former girlfriend. Is it ethical to remove memories of our important life experiences and relationships?

ANSWER: Emotional states, such as being excited, are associated with stronger memory consolidation.

memory bias

The changing of memories over time so that they become consistent with current beliefs or attitudes.

response for that event are reduced, and the effect lasts for months (Cahill, Prins, Weber, & McGaugh, 1994; Pitman et al., 2002). Drugs such as propranolol might have side effects, however. Alternatively, as discussed earlier in this chapter, extinction can be used during reconsolidation to yield the same or similar results, potentially without side effects (Schiller et al., 2010).

Because propranolol has to be given close in time to the traumatic event and reconsolidation of the memory, it works only with relatively recent memories, not with well-established older memories (Costanzi, Cannus, Saraulli, Rossi-Arnaud, & Cestari, 2011). What about past traumas that persist? Researchers recently used HDAC inhibitors during reconsolidation of distant negative memories. Recall from earlier in this chapter that inhibiting HDAC removes the molecular brakes on memory. Could HDAC inhibition make reconsolidation powerful enough to wipe out the original memory and replace it with the new version? By inhibiting HDAC during the reconsolidation of a memory in a nonhuman animal, researchers were able to reduce an old conditioned fear response (Gräff & Tsai, 2013). This process is the equivalent of recalling a traumatic event from long ago and then having it erased. Although these methods have not been used yet with humans, HDAC inhibition shows promise in the treatment of enduring trauma (Yates, 2014).

But erasing memories leads to many ethical questions (**FIGURE 7.29**). If we can erase traumatic memories, should we remove only the memories of traumas that were beyond the sufferer's control? Or should a person be treated for suffering a guilty conscience after an intentional malicious act? Will reducing memories to take the emotional sting out of life make us less human?

 Why might you remember more information from an exciting speech than from a dull one?

7.14 People Reconstruct Events to Be Consistent

Memory bias is the changing of memories over time so that they become consistent with current beliefs or attitudes. As one of psychology's greatest thinkers, Leon Festinger (1987), put it: "I prefer to rely on my memory. I have lived with that memory a long time, I am used to it, and if I have rearranged or distorted anything, surely that was done for my own benefit" (p. 1).

Consider students who take courses in study skills. Students often fail to heed the advice they receive in such courses, and there is only modest evidence that the courses are beneficial. Yet most students who take them describe the courses as extremely helpful. How can something that generally produces unimpressive outcomes be endorsed so positively?

To understand this phenomenon, researchers randomly assigned students to either a genuine study skills course or a control group that received no special training. Students who took the real course showed few signs of improvement. In fact, their final-exam performances were slightly poorer than the control group's performances. Still, they considered the study skills program helpful. The experiment had one feature that helps explain why. At the beginning of the course, participants were asked to rate their studying skills. At the end of the course, they again rated themselves and were asked to recall how they had originally rated themselves. In describing their earlier ratings, students in the study skills course recalled themselves as having been significantly worse than they had rated themselves at the beginning.

In this way, the students were "getting what they want[ed] by revising what they had" (Conway & Ross, 1984).

People tend to recall their past beliefs and past attitudes as being consistent with their current ones. Often, they revise their memories when they change attitudes and beliefs. People also tend to remember events as casting them in prominent roles or favorable lights. As discussed further in Chapter 12, people also tend to exaggerate their contributions to group efforts, take credit for successes and blame failures on others, and remember their successes more than their failures. Societies, too, bias their recollections of past events. Groups' collective memories can seriously distort the past. Most societies' official histories tend to downplay their past behaviors that were unsavory, immoral, and even murderous. Perpetrators' memories are generally shorter than victims' memories.

FLASHBULB MEMORIES Some events cause people to experience what Roger Brown and James Kulik (1977) termed **flashbulb memories.** These vivid memories are of the circumstances in which people first learn of a surprising and consequential or emotionally arousing event. When in 1977 Brown and Kulik interviewed people about their memories of the assassination of President John F. Kennedy, they found that people described these 14-year-old memories in highly vivid terms. The details included whom they were with, what they were doing or thinking, who told them or how they found out, and what their emotional reactions were to the event. In other words, flashbulb memories are an example of episodic memory. They do not reflect the problem of persistence, however, in that they are not recurring unwanted memories. In addition, flashbulb memories are people's memories for public events that did not happen directly to them. By contrast, recall the enhanced memory of the life-threatening airplane episode discussed earlier. In that case, because they had the experience, the survivors were not experiencing flashbulb memories.

Do you remember where you were when you heard about the Boston Marathon bombings (**FIGURE 7.30A**)? An obvious problem affects research into the accuracy of flashbulb memories. Namely, researchers have to wait for a "flash" to go off and then immediately conduct their study.

Three years after the terrorist attacks on September 11, 2001, a study was conducted of more than 3,000 people in various cities across the United States (Hirst et al., 2009). Participants were initially surveyed one week after the attacks. Memories related to 9/11—such as where the person first heard about the attacks and what he was doing at the time and whom he was talking to—declined during the first year, but memory remained stable thereafter. As might be expected, people who were living in New York City on 9/11 had the most accurate memories of the objective details of the World Trade Center attacks, but they experienced the same level of forgetting for their personal memories of the day as did others across the country (**FIGURE 7.30B**). After ten years, people recalled the experience pretty much the same way they did after the first year, even though several aspects of those reports were inconsistent with their initial reports (Hirst et al., 2015). This pattern appears to be generally true of flashbulb memories. Although normal forgetting takes place, people tend to repeat the same story over time, and this repetition bolsters their confidence of their memory (Hirst & Phelps, 2016).

Although flashbulb memories are not perfectly accurate, they are at least as accurate as memory for ordinary events. As mentioned earlier in this chapter, to the extent that emotion is associated with an event, it tends to be better remembered. But even highly emotional memories can change over time. What does not seem to change is the extent to which people feel confident in their memories. Indeed, people are more confident about their flashbulb memories than they are about their ordinary memories

flashbulb memories
Vivid episodic memories for the circumstances in which people first learned of a surprising and consequential or emotionally arousing event.

(a)

(b)

FIGURE 7.30
Flashbulb Memories
Surprising and consequential or emotionally arousing events can produce flashbulb memories. Consider **(a)** the Boston Marathon bombings in 2013 and **(b)** the attack on the World Trade Center on September 11, 2001.

(Talarico & Rubin, 2003). Any event that produces a strong emotional response is likely to produce a vivid, although not necessarily accurate, memory (Christianson, 1992). Or a distinctive event might simply be recalled more easily than a trivial event, even if the resulting memory is inaccurate. This latter pattern is known as the *von Restorff effect,* named after the researcher who first described it in 1933.

 Why do inaccurate flashbulb memories stay consistent over time?

ANSWER: People keep repeating the inaccurate version and become confident in it.

7.15 People Make Source Misattributions

Source misattribution occurs when people misremember the time, place, person, or circumstances involved with a memory. A good example of this phenomenon is the false fame effect, discussed earlier in this chapter. Another example is the sleeper effect. Here, an argument initially is not very persuasive because it comes from a questionable source, but it becomes more persuasive over time.

Suppose you see an online ad for a way to learn French while you sleep. You probably will not believe the claims in the ad. Yet over time you might remember the promise but fail to remember the source. Because the promise occurs to you without the obvious reason for rejecting it, you might come to believe that people can learn French while sleeping, or you might at least wonder if it is possible.

SOURCE AMNESIA Source amnesia is a form of misattribution that occurs when a person has a memory for an event but cannot remember where he or she encountered the information. Consider your earliest childhood memory. How vivid is it? Are you actually recalling the event or some retelling of the event? How do you know you are not remembering either something you saw in a photograph or a story related to you by family members? Most people cannot remember specific episodic memories from before age 3. The absence of early episodic memories is called *childhood amnesia.* This type of memory loss may be due to the early lack of linguistic capacity as well as to immature frontal lobes.

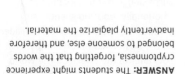

FIGURE 7.31
Cryptomnesia
The 2006 novel *How Opal Mehta Got Kissed, Got Wild, and Got a Life* became a possible case of cryptomnesia. The author, a student at Harvard University named Kaavya Viswanathan, admitted that several passages in the work were taken from books that she had read in high school. As a result, *How Opal Mehta Got Kissed* had to be recalled from bookstores. Perhaps Viswanathan, thinking she had come up with new material, had retrieved other people's writing from memory.

CRYPTOMNESIA An intriguing example of source misattribution is **cryptomnesia.** Here, a person thinks he or she has come up with a new idea. Instead, the person has retrieved an old idea from memory and failed to attribute the idea to its proper source (Macrae, Bodenhausen, & Calvini, 1999). For example, students who take verbatim notes while conducting library research sometimes experience the illusion that they have composed the sentences themselves (Ferro & Martins, 2016). This mistake can later lead to an accusation of plagiarism. (Be especially vigilant about indicating verbatim notes while you are taking them; see **FIGURE 7.31.**)

George Harrison, the late Beatle, was sued because his 1970 song "My Sweet Lord" is strikingly similar to the song "He's So Fine," recorded in 1962 by the Chiffons. Harrison acknowledged having known "He's So Fine," but he vigorously denied having plagiarized it. He argued that with a limited number of musical notes available to all musicians, and an even smaller number of chord sequences appropriate for rock and roll, some compositional overlap is inevitable. In a controversial verdict, the judge ruled against Harrison.

 Why should students doing library research be careful when taking verbatim notes?

ANSWER: The students might experience cryptomnesia, forgetting that the words belonged to someone else, and therefore inadvertently plagiarize the material.

7.16 Suggestibility Biases Memory

During the early 1970s, Elizabeth Loftus and her colleagues conducted important research on biased memories. The results demonstrated that people can develop biased memories when provided with misleading information, which is known as **suggestibility.**

These studies generally involved showing research participants an event and then asking them specific questions about it. The different wordings of the questions altered the participants' memories for the event. In one experiment, a group of participants viewed a videotape of a car—a red Datsun—approaching a stop sign (Loftus, Miller, & Burns, 1978). A second group viewed a videotape of that same scene but with a yield sign instead of a stop sign. Each group was then asked, "Did another car pass the red Datsun while it was stopped at the stop sign?" Some participants in the second group claimed to have seen the red Datsun stop at the stop sign, even though they had seen it approaching a yield sign (see "The Methods of Psychology: Loftus's Studies on Suggestibility").

In another experiment, Loftus and John Palmer (1974) showed participants a videotape of a car accident. When participants heard the word *smashed* applied to the tape, they estimated the cars to be traveling faster than when they heard *contacted, hit, bumped,* or *collided.* In a related study, participants saw a videotape of a car accident

source misattribution

Memory distortion that occurs when people misremember the time, place, person, or circumstances involved with a memory.

source amnesia

A type of misattribution that occurs when a person has a memory for an event but cannot remember where he or she encountered the information.

cryptomnesia

A type of misattribution that occurs when a person thinks he has come up with a new idea, yet has only retrieved a stored idea and failed to attribute the idea to its proper source.

suggestibility

The development of biased memories from misleading information.

The Methods of Psychology
Loftus's Studies on Suggestibility

HYPOTHESIS: People can develop biased memories when provided with misleading information.

RESEARCH METHOD:

1 One group of participants was shown a videotape of a red Datsun approaching a stop sign.

2 Another group of participants was shown a videotape of a red Datsun approaching a yield sign.

3 Immediately after viewing the tapes, the participants were asked, "Did another car pass the red Datsun while it was stopped at the stop sign?"

RESULTS: Some participants who had seen the yield sign responded to the question by claiming they had seen the car at the stop sign.

CONCLUSION: People can "remember" seeing nonexistent objects.

QUESTION: Why should police officers avoid leading questions when investigating crimes?

ANSWER: Leading questions might produce biased memories because of suggestibility.

Source: Loftus, E. F., Miller, D. G., & Burns, H. J. (1978). Semantic integration of verbal information into a visual memory. *Journal of Experimental Psychology: Human Learning and Memory, 4,* 19–31.

and then were asked about seeing the cars either *smash into* or *hit* each other. One week later, they were asked if they had seen broken glass on the ground in the video. No glass broke in the video, but nearly one-third of those who heard *smashed* falsely recalled having seen broken glass. Very few of those who heard *hit* recalled broken glass.

Are these sorts of laboratory analogues appropriate for studying eyewitness accuracy? After all, the sights and sounds of a traffic accident, for example, impress the event on the witness's awareness. Some evidence supports the idea that such memories are better in the real world than in the laboratory. One study examined the reports of witnesses to a fatal shooting (Yuille & Cutshall, 1986). All the witnesses had been interviewed by the police within two days of the incident. Months afterward, the researchers found the eyewitness reports, including the details, highly stable.

Given that emotional state affects memories, it makes sense for accounts from eyewitnesses to be more vivid than accounts from laboratory research participants. It remains unclear, however, how accurate those stable memories were in the first place. And by retelling their stories over and over again—to the police, to friends and relatives, to researchers, and so on—eyewitnesses might inadvertently develop stronger memories for inaccurate details. This alteration may occur because of reconsolidation.

FALSE MEMORIES How easily can people develop false memories? To consider this question, read aloud the following list: *sour, candy, sugar, bitter, good, taste, tooth, nice, honey, soda, chocolate, heart, cake, tart, pie.* Now put aside your book and write down as many of the words as you remember.

Researchers have devised tests such as this for investigating whether people can be misled into recalling or recognizing events that did not happen (Roediger & McDermott, 1995). For instance, without looking back at the list, answer this question: Which of the following words did you recall—*candy, honey, tooth, sweet, pie*?

If you recalled *sweet* or think you did, you have experienced a false memory, because *sweet* was not on the original list. All the words on that list are related to sweetness, though. This basic procedure produces false recollections reliably. It occurs because each word activates semantic knowledge of related words as explained by the spreading activation model, discussed earlier in this chapter. This semantic activation leads to potential confusion about which of the related words were actually read. A brain imaging study showed that related words produce overlapping patterns of brain activity in the very frontmost portion of the temporal lobe, where semantic information is processed (Chadwick et al., 2016). As a result, even though the memories are false, people are often extremely confident in saying they have seen or heard the words they recollect falsely.

Now think back to when you were 5. Do you remember getting lost in a mall and being found by a kind old man who returned you to your family? No? Well, what if your family told you about this incident, including how panicked your parents were when they could not find you? According to research by Elizabeth Loftus, you might then remember the incident, even if it did not happen.

In an initial study, a 14-year-old named Chris was told by his older brother Jim, who was part of the study, about the "lost in the mall" incident. The context was a game called "Remember When . . ." All the other incidents narrated by Jim were true. Two days later, when asked if he had ever been lost in a mall, Chris began reporting memories of how he felt during the mall episode. Within two weeks, he reported the following:

> I was with you guys for a second and I think I went over to look at the toy store, the Kay-bee toy and uh, we got lost and I was looking around and I thought, "Uh-oh. I'm in trouble now." You know. And then I . . . I thought I was never going to see my family again. I was really scared you know. And then this old man, I think he was wearing a blue flannel shirt,

came up to me. . . . [H]e was kind of old. He was kind of bald on top. . . . [H]e had like a ring of gray hair . . . and he had glasses. (Loftus, 1993, p. 532)

You might wonder if there was something special about Chris that made him susceptible to developing false memories. In a later study, however, Loftus and her colleagues used the same method to assess whether they could implant false memories in 24 participants. Seven of the participants falsely remembered events that had been implanted by family members who were part of the study. How could this be so?

When a person imagines an event happening, he or she forms a mental image of the event. The person might later confuse that mental image with a real memory. Essentially, the person has a problem monitoring the source of the image. To Chris, the memory of being lost in the mall became as real as other events in childhood. Children are particularly susceptible, and false memories—such as of getting fingers caught in mousetraps or having to be hospitalized—can easily be induced in them. It is unlikely, however, that false memories can be created for certain types of unusual events, such as receiving an enema (Pezdek & Hodge, 1999).

REPRESSED MEMORIES Over the past few decades, one of the most heated debates in psychological science has centered on repressed memories. On one side, some psychotherapists and patients claim that long-repressed memories for traumatic events can resurface during therapy. Recovered memories of sexual abuse are the most commonly reported repressed memories, and in the early 1990s there was a rash of reports about celebrities who had claimed to recover memories of such abuse. On the other side, memory researchers such as Elizabeth Loftus point out that little credible evidence indicates that recovered memories are genuine or at least sufficiently accurate to be believable. Part of the problem is best summarized by the memory researcher Daniel Schacter: "I am convinced that child abuse is a major problem in our society. I have no reason to question the memories of people who have always remembered their abuse, or who have spontaneously recalled previously forgotten abuse on their own. Yet I am deeply concerned by some of the suggestive techniques that have been recommended to recover repressed memories" (Schacter, 1996, p. 251).

Schacter alludes to the frightening possibility that false memories for traumatic events have been implanted by well-meaning but misguided therapists. Convincing evidence indicates that methods such as hypnosis, age regression, and guided recall can implant false memories. In a few infamous examples, adults have accused their parents of abuse based on memories that the accusers later realized were not reality but the products of therapy (**FIGURE 7.32**).

Consider the dramatic case of Diana Halbrook. Halbrook came to believe that she had been abused. She also believed that she had been involved in satanic ritualistic abuse that involved killing a baby. When she expressed doubts to her therapist and her "support" group about these events' veracity, they told her she was in denial and not listening to "the little girl" within. After all, the other members of the support group had recovered memories of being involved in satanic ritualistic abuse. After Halbrook left her therapy group, she came to believe she had not been abused and had not killed. Tellingly, "though thousands of patients have 'remembered' ritual acts, not a single such case has ever been documented in the United States despite extensive investigative efforts by state and federal law enforcement" (Schacter, 1996, p. 269).

Understandably, people on both sides of the debate about repressed memories hold strong and passionate beliefs. While research shows that some therapeutic techniques seem especially likely to foster false memories, it would be a mistake to dismiss all adult reports of early abuse. Some abuse certainly could have occurred and been forgotten until later, and we cannot ignore the memories of actual victims. In the

(a)

(b)

FIGURE 7.32
Fallibility of "Repressed Memory"
(a) Eileen Franklin **(center)** claimed to have recovered a previously repressed memory that her father had murdered a friend of hers two decades earlier. **(b)** George Franklin was found guilty and imprisoned based on his daughter's testimony. Evidence subsequently emerged proving his innocence, and he was released.

latter half of the 1990s, the incidence of recovered memories fell dramatically. However, we do not know whether this decline occurred because of less media attention to reports, because fewer people sought therapy to uncover their past memories, or because therapists stopped using these suggestive methods.

Q Which memory model can explain why people falsely believe they read a word when they read a series of semantically related words?

ANSWER: the spreading activation model, since reading a word activates words with similar semantic content

FIGURE 7.33
Eyewitness Accounts Can Be Unreliable
William Jackson (top) served five years in prison because he was wrongly convicted of a crime based on the testimony of two eyewitnesses. Note the similarities and differences between Jackson and the man on the bottom, the real perpetrator.

ANSWER: no, because confidence is unrelated to the accuracy of eyewitness memories

THINK LIKE A PSYCHOLOGIST

7.17 How Accurate Are Eyewitnesses?

In the criminal justice system, one of the most powerful forms of evidence is the eyewitness account. Research has demonstrated that very few jurors are willing to convict an accused individual on the basis of circumstantial evidence alone. But add one person who says, "That's the one!" and conviction becomes much more likely. This effect occurs even if it is shown that the witness had poor eyesight or some other condition that raises questions about the testimony's accuracy.

Gary Wells and his colleagues (1998) studied 40 cases in which DNA evidence indicated that a person had been falsely convicted of a crime. They found that in 36 of these cases the person had been misidentified by at least one eyewitness (**FIGURE 7.33**). Eyewitness testimony's power is troubling. If eyewitnesses are told that another witness chose the same person, their confidence increases, even when the identifications were false (Luus & Wells, 1994). Why is eyewitness testimony so prone to error?

One major problem with eyewitness testimony is that people tend to remember evidence that confirms their beliefs. For instance, they may believe that certain types of people are more likely to commit crimes and therefore might be more likely to identify people with those characteristics as the likely criminal. Confirmation biases might even affect what potential eyewitnesses notice in the world around them.

The way police interview eyewitnesses may also be influenced by confirmation bias (Wells & Seelau, 1995). For instance, police often ask witnesses to identify the culprit by showing them a lineup of potential suspects or a photospread of faces. The officers can unintentionally influence the identification, such as by asking more questions about their suspect than about the other potential culprits. Ideally, the person who conducts the lineup or presents the photos should not know the suspect's identity. That is, as noted in Chapter 2, the person running the "study" should be blind to the conditions of the study so as not to bias the results.

How good are observers, such as jurors, at judging eyewitnesses' accuracy? The general finding from a number of studies is that people cannot differentiate accurate eyewitnesses from inaccurate ones (Clark & Wells, 2008; Wells, 2008). The problem is that eyewitnesses who are wrong are just as confident as (or *more* confident than) eyewitnesses who are right. Eyewitnesses who vividly report trivial details of a scene are probably less credible than those with poor memories for trivial details. After all, eyewitnesses to real crimes tend to be focused on the weapons or on the action. They fail to pay attention to minor details. Thus, strong confidence for minor details may be a cue that the memory is likely to be inaccurate or even false. Some people are particularly confident, however, and jurors find them convincing. ■

Q Should we believe confident eyewitnesses more than ones who are not confident?

Your Chapter Review

Chapter Summary

What Is Memory?

7.1 Memory Involves Processing Information

Memory is the nervous system's capacity to retain and retrieve skills and knowledge. According to the information processing model, memory is formed through three phases: encoding, storage, and retrieval. Encoded information is consolidated for storage through changes in synaptic connections that can last briefly or endure permanently. Once stored, information has to be retrieved to be remembered. Reconsolidation theory suggests that during retrieval, events in the present can be incorporated to permanently alter past memories.

7.2 Memory Is the Result of Brain Activity

Memory involves the creation of neural circuits. Long-term potentiation (LTP) offers one model of how synaptic connections may be strengthened during learning. Emerging evidence suggests that epigenetic mechanisms play an important role in the formation of memory circuits.

7.3 Memory Is Distributed Throughout the Brain

Memory is distributed across many brain areas, including the hippocampus, medial temporal lobes, and sensory cortical areas. The study of patients such as H.M. has provided evidence regarding which brain regions are crucial for memory.

How Are Memories Maintained over Time?

7.4 Sensory Memory Is Brief

Sensory memory detects environmental information from each of the five senses and holds it for less than 1 second. Sensory memory enables the brain to experience the world as a continuous stream. Iconic memory is visual sensory memory. Echoic memory is auditory sensory memory.

7.5 Working Memory Is Active

Many memory researchers today describe short-term memory more accurately as working memory. This active processing system keeps a limited number of items available for use within 20 to 30 seconds. Working memory span can be increased by chunking, organizing information into meaningful units.

7.6 Long-Term Memory Is Relatively Permanent

Long-term memory is a relatively permanent, virtually limitless storage space. Information is more likely to enter long-term memory if it is repeatedly rehearsed, is deeply processed, or helps us adapt to an environment. Long-term memory is distinct from working memory, as evidenced by the serial position effect and case studies of individuals with certain types of brain damage.

How Is Information Organized in Long-Term Memory?

7.7 Long-Term Storage Is Based on Meaning

According to the levels of processing model, deep encoding enhances memory. Maintenance rehearsal—repeating an item over and over—leads to shallow encoding and poor recall. Elaborative rehearsal links new information with old, leading to deeper encoding and better recall. Schemas are cognitive structures that help us perceive, organize, process, and use information. Schemas can lead to biased encoding based on cultural expectations.

7.8 Information Is Stored in Association Networks

According to association network models, information in memory is stored in nodes, and nodes are connected via networks to many other nodes. Activating one node results in spreading activation of all associated nodes within the network. Retrieval cues aid memory recall. Prospective memory is remembering to do something at some future time. Mnemonics are learning strategies that can improve recall through the use of retrieval cues.

7.9 Using Psychology In Your Life: Can You Ace Exams Without Cramming?

Psychological research has identified several strategies for improving learning and exam performance. People should distribute learning, elaborate material, practice retrieval, and use strategies such as mnemonics or visual imagery.

What Are the Different Long-Term Memory Systems?

7.10 Explicit Memory Involves Conscious Effort

Long-term memory is divided into several systems. Explicit memory is a system that contains episodic memories for personal events and semantic memories for general knowledge of facts independent of personal experience. Explicit memories are often called declarative memories because they require conscious effort to declare them as knowledge. Episodic memory and semantic memory are believed to be distinct systems, based on evidence from some victims of brain damage who demonstrate recall of semantic but not episodic memories.

7.11 Implicit Memory Occurs Without Deliberate Effort

Implicit memories are automatic memories that are recalled without conscious attention. One type of implicit memory is procedural memory for how to perform a behavior. Other implicit memories can influence attitudes, by making things seem more familiar in the absence of memory for the source of the information.

How Is Memory Flawed?

7.12 Forgetting Is an Inability to Remember

Memory decay involves forgetting over time. This decay is likely caused by proactive and retroactive interference from older and newer memories. Blocking is a common retrieval failure that occurs when well-known information cannot be recalled, as in the tip-of-the-tongue phenomenon. Absentmindedness is forgetting caused by the shallow encoding of events. Inattention results in shallow encoding and absentmindedness. Amnesia is the inability to retrieve large amounts of information from long-term memory.

7.13 Persistence Is Unwanted Remembering

Persistence is the continued recurrence of unwanted memories. Highly stressful or traumatic events could cause significantly disruptive persistence, as in posttraumatic stress disorder (PTSD). Reconsolidation can reduce persistence but only for recent memories. HDAC inhibitors may help erase even remote persistent memories, but additional research is needed.

7.14 People Reconstruct Events to Be Consistent

Memory bias is the changing of memories so they become consistent with current beliefs or attitudes. Memory bias tends to cast memories in a favorable light and is common among individuals, groups, and societies. Flashbulb memories are vivid episodic memories of surprising, consequential, or emotionally arousing events. Flashbulb memories are no more accurate than other episodic memories, although people typically report them with more confidence.

7.15 People Make Source Misattributions

Source misattribution is memory distortion that occurs when people misremember the time, place, person, or circumstances involved with a memory. The false fame effect, the sleeper effect, source amnesia, and cryptomnesia are examples. Source amnesia is memory for an event without memory for the source. Cryptomnesia is the failure to remember the source of an idea, so the idea is remembered as original even though it may not be.

7.16 Suggestibility Biases Memory

Suggestibility is the development of biased memories due to misleading information. Suggestibility could play a role in eyewitness testimony, as research shows that eyewitnesses can develop biased memories based on leading questions. False memories are created as a result of the natural tendency to form mental representations of stories. Psychologists continue to debate the validity of repressed memories. Some therapeutic techniques are highly suggestive and may contribute to the occurrence of false repressed memories.

7.17 Think like a Psychologist: How Accurate Are Eyewitnesses?

One major problem with eyewitness testimony is that people tend to remember evidence that confirms their beliefs. The way police interview eyewitnesses may also be influenced by confirmation bias. In general, people cannot differentiate accurate eyewitnesses from inaccurate ones, in part because eyewitnesses are confident even when they are wrong.

Key Terms

absentmindedness, p. 275

amnesia, p. 276

anterograde amnesia, p. 276

blocking, p. 274

chunking, p. 259

consolidation, p. 250

cryptomnesia, p. 280

declarative memory, p. 271

encoding, p. 250

encoding specificity principle, p. 266

episodic memory, p. 272

explicit memory, p. 271

flashbulb memories, p. 279

implicit memory, p. 271

long-term memory, p. 260

long-term potentiation (LTP), p. 252

memory, p. 250

memory bias, p. 278

mnemonics, p. 267

persistence, p. 277

proactive interference, p. 274

procedural memory, p. 272

prospective memory, p. 267

reconsolidation, p. 250

retrieval, p. 250

retrieval cue, p. 266

retroactive interference, p. 274

retrograde amnesia, p. 276

schemas, p. 263

semantic memory, p. 272

sensory memory, p. 256

serial position effect, p. 260

short-term memory, p. 258

source amnesia, p. 280

source misattribution, p. 280

storage, p. 250

suggestibility, p. 281

working memory, p. 258

Putting Psychology to Work

What Are Sports Psychologists and Performance Psychologists?

As described in his 2017 memoir, *The Phenomenon: Pressure, the Yips, and the Pitch that Changed My Life,* Rick Ankiel ended an impressive rookie year (1999–2000) as a pitcher for the major league baseball team the St. Louis Cardinals. Then he choked in the first postseason game. After several more games of erratic pitching, Ankiel's once-promising career was put on hold, and he spent years fluctuating between the major, minor, and even rookie leagues. After working with a performance coach, he eventually returned full-time to the major league as both a pitcher and an outfielder, retiring in 2014.

What caused Ankiel to suddenly lose his ability to control the ball? As you learned in this chapter, procedural (motor) memories, such as pitching, are generally carried out automatically and without conscious effort. However, even well-practiced behaviors can be disrupted by the "yips"—pressure or anxiety—causing problems in performance. An understanding of memory formation and retrieval can help ease or prevent performance failures. In addition, such knowledge can lead to employment opportunities in sports psychology and performance psychology. One of the pioneers of sports psychology, Bob Rotella, has worked with professional athletes in baseball, basketball, hockey, and golf and with members of the U.S. Olympic ski and equestrian teams. Rotella helps athletes train their minds to focus on their goals and teaches them to deal with their doubts, worries, and frustrations.

Applied sports psychologists can work with individual athletes or with an entire team, to develop the cognitive factors that optimize athletic performance. They may, for example, incorporate visualization techniques and simulation techniques to mimic the real-world environment during practice. This technique can minimize context-dependent memory effects, increasing the likelihood that actions learned in practice will transfer to the competitive arena. Psychologists may also emphasize practicing beyond mastery so as to develop "overlearning," or teach "chunking" of game scenarios to increase working memory capacity.

Of course, choking under pressure is not limited to the athletic field. The same principles that improve a major league baseball pitcher's consistency can apply to clients in any occupation that requires top achievement under pressure. Candidates for such help include musicians, actors, dancers, military personnel, and CEOs.

How does one become a sports psychologist or performance psychologist? The American Psychological Association guidelines reserve these titles for individuals with postgraduate training. Generally, students complete a master's or doctoral program in psychology, with a specialization in sports, exercise, or performance psychology. Employment opportunities for sports psychologists range from professional sports teams, and many NCAA Division I college and university athletic departments, to health clubs and gyms. Performance psychologists work in human resources departments or military settings, or they may have personal consulting practices. Careers as sports consultants, mental coaches, or mental skills trainers are alternate routes that don't require graduate degrees.

The bottom line: There are numerous employment opportunities for psychology graduates interested in applying memory principles to enhance performance. Graduate degrees are needed in order to practice as a sports psychologist or performance psychologist, but sports coaches, consultants, and mental skills trainers need only undergraduate degrees.

Q **Want to earn a better grade on your test?**
Go to **INQUIZITIVE** to learn and review this chapter's content, with personalized feedback along the way.
Practice Tests and accompanying answer keys can be found at the back of the book on page PT-1.

8

Thinking, Language, and Intelligence

Big Questions

- What Is Thought? 290

- How Do We Make Decisions and Solve Problems? 296

- What Is Language? 310

- How Do We Understand Intelligence? 319

SOMETIMES YOU WONDER ABOUT YOUR FRIEND. She may be the smartest person you know. When the two of you play trivia games, she always knows the answers, even to the most obscure questions. She also has an amazing vocabulary. Yet that same person can act in ways that are anything but intelligent. She lets her emotions color her judgments, decides major life choices on a whim, and complains that her life is full of problems. As you watch her in action, you often find yourself wondering, "What was she thinking?" How can a person seem so smart most of the time but have such poor judgment in some situations? How do we explain different kinds of thinking and differences in intelligence?

This chapter is about thinking. Being able to think enables us to consider information. We come up with ideas, represent ideas in our minds, communicate ideas to others, and use ideas to solve problems and make decisions. Thinking is therefore tied to language. Complex thinking can occur without language, but language makes it possible to express our thoughts—ideas, problems, solutions, decisions, and so on. But in turn language shapes our thoughts. As a result, using language to explore the nature of thought can help us improve our thinking. The big questions that psychologists address in this area are: What is thought? How do we make decisions and solve problems? What is language? And how do we understand intelligence?

(a)　　　　(b)

Violin

FIGURE 8.1
Analogical Representations and Symbolic Representations
(a) Analogical representations, such as this picture of a violin, have some characteristics of the objects they represent. **(b)** Symbolic representations, such as the word *violin*, are abstract and do not have relationships to the physical qualities of objects.

What Is Thought?

In exploring the nature of thought, this chapter draws on the findings of cognitive psychology, which seeks to understand how the mind works. As defined in Chapter 1, cognitive psychology is the study of mental functions such as intelligence, thinking, language, memory, and decision making. In short, this branch of psychology studies **cognition.** Cognition can be broadly defined as the mental activity that includes thinking and the understandings that result from thinking.

8.1 Thinking Involves Two Types of Mental Representations

Cognitive psychology was originally based on two ideas about thinking: (1) Knowledge about the world is stored in the brain in representations, and (2) **thinking** is the mental manipulation of these representations.

In other words, we use representations to understand objects we encounter in our environments. Thinking allows us to take information, consider it, and use it to build models of the world, set goals, and plan our actions accordingly.

Representations are all around us. For example, a road map represents streets. A menu represents food options. A photograph represents part of the world. The challenge for cognitive psychologists is to understand the nature of our everyday mental representations. When are such representations similar to maps or pictures, but are purely in our minds? And when are they more abstract, like language?

In thinking, we use two basic types of mental representations: analogical and symbolic. Together, both types of representations form the basis of human thought, intelligence, and the ability to solve the complex problems of everyday life.

An analogy compares two things that are similar in some way: "This is to that as that is to . . ." Similarly, **analogical representations** have some characteristics of actual objects. These representations are usually images. For example, maps are analogical representations that correspond to geographical layouts. A clock corresponds to the passage of time. Family trees depict relationships between relatives. A realistic drawing of a violin is an attempt to show that musical instrument from a particular perspective (**FIGURE 8.1A**).

By contrast, **symbolic representations** are abstract. These representations are usually words, numbers, or ideas. They do not have relationships to physical qualities of objects in the world. For example, the word *violin* stands for a musical instrument (**FIGURE 8.1B**). There are no correspondences between what a violin looks like, what it sounds like, and the letters or sounds that make up the word *violin*.

In Chinese, the word for violin is

$$小提琴$$

In Mandarin, it is pronounced *xiǎotíqín,* or *shiaw ti chin.* Like the English word *violin,* it is a symbolic representation because it bears no systematic relationship to the object it names. The individual characters that make up the word stand for different parts of what makes a violin, but they are arbitrary. You cannot "see" any part of a violin in their shapes.

Mental maps rely on both analogical and symbolic representations. For example, most of us can pull up a visual image of Africa's contours even if we have never seen the actual contours with our own eyes. But to see the difference between these two types of mental representations, consider the following question about two U.S. cities: *Which is farther east, San Diego, California, or Reno, Nevada?*

If you are like most people (at least most Americans), you answered that Reno is farther east than San Diego. In fact, though, San Diego is farther east than Reno. Even if you formed an analogical representation of a map of the southwestern United States, your symbolic knowledge probably told you that a city on the Pacific Coast is always farther west than a city in a state that does not border the Pacific Ocean (**FIGURE 8.2**).

 When an architect produces a blueprint for a new house, is this representation analogical or symbolic?

8.2 Concepts Are Symbolic Representations

As the previous example shows, thinking also reflects a person's general knowledge about the world. Say that you are shown a drawing of a small, yellow, dimpled object and asked to identify it. Your brain forms a mental image (analogical representation) of a lemon and provides you with the word *lemon* (symbolic representation). So far, so good.

However, in the real world your information would be incomplete. Picturing a lemon and knowing its name does not tell you what to do with a lemon. But knowing that parts of a lemon are edible helps you decide how to use the fruit. For example, you could make lemonade. Because you know that the lemon juice will taste strong and sour, you might dilute it with water and add sugar. In short, how you think about a lemon influences what you do with it.

CATEGORIES One question of interest to cognitive psychologists is how we use knowledge about objects efficiently. As discussed in Chapter 7, our memory systems are organized so we can call up information quickly when we need it. The same principle holds true when we think about objects. For instance, if asked to say what a violin is, most people probably would begin by defining it broadly as a musical instrument.

Grouping things based on shared properties is called *categorization*. This mental activity reduces the amount of knowledge we must hold in memory and is therefore an efficient way of thinking. We can apply a category such as "musical instruments"—objects that produce music when played—automatically to all members of the category. Applying a category spares us the trouble of storing this same bit of knowledge over and over for each musical instrument. We have to store unique knowledge for each member of a category, however. A violin "has four strings"; a guitar "has six strings" (**FIGURE 8.3**).

CONCEPTS A **concept** is a category, or class, of related items (such as musical instruments or fruits). A concept consists of mental representations of those items. By enabling us to organize mental representations around a common theme, a concept ensures that we do not have to store every instance of an object individually. Instead, we store an abstract representation based on the properties particular items or particular ideas share.

Cognitive psychologists have described a number of ways that people form concepts, but there are two leading models. The **prototype model**, developed by Eleanor Rosch (1975), is based on a "best example." That is, when you think about a category, you tend to look for a best example, or prototype, for that category. Once you have the prototype, you categorize new objects based on how similar they are to the prototype.

FIGURE 8.2
Mental Maps and Symbolic Limitations
When you were asked whether San Diego or Reno is farther east, you probably formed a mental map—an analogical representation. However, your symbolic knowledge probably informed you that California is farther west than Nevada. Due to this knowledge, your mental map made you think that San Diego was west of Reno. You were not taking into account the way that northern Nevada juts west and Southern California juts east. But this real map, showing location relative to uniform lines of longitude, shows that symbolic knowledge was inadequate in this case.

concept
A category, or class, of related items; it consists of mental representations of those items.

prototype model
A way of thinking about concepts: Within each category, there is a best example—a prototype—for that category.

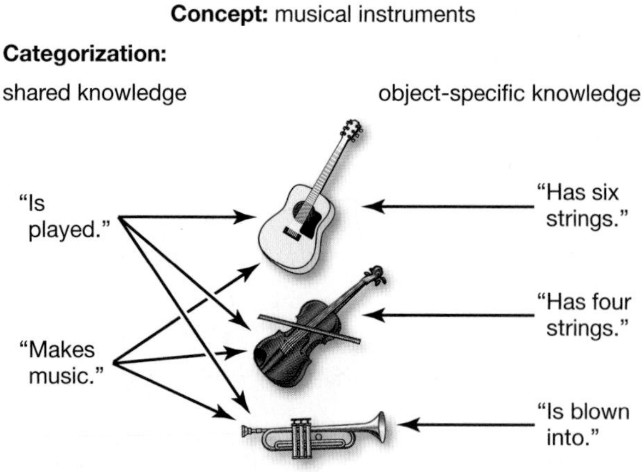

Concept: musical instruments

Categorization:

shared knowledge   object-specific knowledge

"Is played."   "Has six strings."

"Makes music."   "Has four strings."

                                    "Is blown into."

FIGURE 8.3
Categorization
We group objects into categories according to the objects' shared properties.

exemplar model

A way of thinking about concepts: All members of a category are examples (exemplars); together they form the concept and determine category membership.

In this model, each member of a category varies in how much it matches the prototype (**FIGURE 8.4**).

By contrast, the **exemplar model** proposes that any concept has no single best representation (Medin & Schaffer, 1978). Instead, all the examples, or exemplars, of category members that you have actually encountered form the concept. For instance, your representation of dogs is made up of all the dogs you have seen in your life. If you see an animal in your yard, you compare this animal with your memories of other animals you have encountered. If it most closely resembles the dogs you have encountered (as opposed to the cats, squirrels, rats, and other animals), you conclude it is a dog (**FIGURE 8.5**).

How would you explain the difference between a dog and a cat to someone who has never seen either? Most dogs bark, but a dog is still a dog if it does not bark. It is still a dog if it loses its tail or a leg. The exemplar model assumes that, through experience, people form a fuzzy representation of a concept because there is no single representation of any concept. And the exemplar model accounts for the observation that some category members are more prototypical than others: The prototypes are simply members a person has encountered more often. This model points to one way in which people's thoughts are unique and formed by personal experience.

CONCEPTS IN THE BRAIN Brain imaging methods have enabled researchers to study how knowledge is encoded in brain activity (Ghio, Vaghi, Perani, & Tettamanti, 2016; Haxby et al., 2014). As a result, we know that different types of knowledge are encoded differently. As mentioned in Chapter 4, patterns of brain activity can be used to identify aspects of conscious experience, such as whether people are looking at faces or objects, thinking about themselves or others, or feeling angry or happy. Imaging studies have shown that different categories of objects, such as animals or tools, are represented in different regions of the brain based on our perception of those objects (Martin, 2007). For instance, thinking about animals activates visual areas, indicating that simply what they look like allows us to categorize objects appropriately as animals. For tools, however, brain activity occurs in regions of the brain involved in movement as well as visual areas, suggesting that we categorize certain

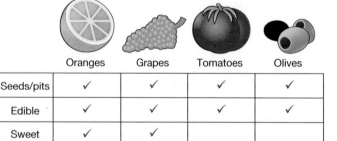

	Oranges	Grapes	Tomatoes	Olives
Seeds/pits	✓	✓	✓	✓
Edible	✓	✓	✓	✓
Sweet	✓	✓		

Characteristics

FIGURE 8.4
The Prototype Model of Concepts
According to the prototype model, some items within a group or class are prototypes. That is, they are more representative of that category than are other concepts in the category. For this reason, an orange seems to be the prototype of the category "fruit." By contrast, olives do not seem to be very representative of the category.

FIGURE 8.5
The Exemplar Model of Concepts
Quick—what animal are you looking at? Is it a dog or a sheep or a pig? How does it match your exemplar for these animals? It is actually a Mangalitsa pig.

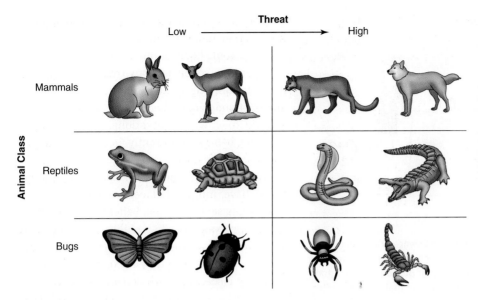

Threat
Low → High

Mammals

Reptiles

Bugs

Animal Class

FIGURE 8.6
Categorizing Animals as Dangerous or Not Dangerous
Patterns of brain activity enable us to distinguish between animals high or low in threat, even across different classes of animals.

objects as tools by how we use them in addition to what they look like (Martin, Wiggs, Ungerleider, & Haxby, 1996).

In addition, we categorize some objects in multiple ways. For instance, a recent imaging study found that patterns of brain activity could differentiate animals that pose threats to humans from those that do not, even across animal classes (Connolly et al., 2016). We most likely have this ability because categorizing animals as dangerous or not dangerous is adaptive, whether those animals are mammals, reptiles, or bugs (**FIGURE 8.6**). These different patterns of brain activity enable us to quickly and efficiently categorize important objects in the environment.

Q How does the prototype model of concepts differ from the exemplar model?

ANSWER: A prototype is the best example of the category, whereas exemplars are average examples of the category.

8.3 Schemas Organize Useful Information About Environments

The prototype and exemplar models explain how we classify objects we encounter and how we represent those objects in our minds. But how do we use such classifications and representations?

When we think about aspects of the world, our knowledge extends well beyond a simple list of facts about the specific items we encounter. Instead, a different class of knowledge enables us to interact with the complex realities of our environments. As we move through various real-world settings, we act appropriately by drawing on knowledge of what objects, behaviors, and events apply to each setting. Knowledge of how to behave in each setting relies on schemas. As discussed in Chapter 7, schemas help us perceive, organize, and process information. For example, at a casino blackjack table, it is appropriate to squeeze in between the people already sitting down. If a

Before | After

FIGURE 8.7

A Teen Draws a Scientist

A special program at the Virginia Institute of Marine Science brings real-life scientists—VIMS grad students—into classrooms at area middle schools and high schools. At the beginning of one semester, a student at Booker T. Washington Middle School drew the scientist on the left. At the end of that semester, after months of interacting with a marine researcher, the same student produced the drawing on the right.

stereotypes

Cognitive schemas that allow for easy, fast processing of information about people based on their membership in certain groups.

stranger tried to squeeze into a group of people dining together in a restaurant, however, the group's reaction would likely be quite negative.

We can use schemas for two reasons. First, common situations have consistent rules (e.g., libraries are quiet and contain books). Second, people have specific roles within situational contexts (e.g., a librarian behaves differently in a library than a reader does).

Unfortunately, schemas, like prototypes, sometimes have unintended consequences, such as reinforcing sexist or racist beliefs or other **stereotypes**. For example, when children and teens are asked to draw a scientist, very few draw women as scientists, because they unconsciously associate being a scientist with being male (Chambers, 1983; McCann & Marek, 2016; **FIGURE 8.7**). *Gender roles* are the prescribed behaviors for females and males. They represent a type of schema that operates at the unconscious level. In other words, we follow gender roles without consciously knowing we are doing so. One reason we need to become aware of the way schemas direct our thinking is that they may unconsciously cause us to think, for example, that women lack the intellectual abilities to become STEM scientists (O'Brien et al., 2017). Indeed, by age 6, girls are less likely to believe members of their gender are "really, really smart" and by this age also begin avoiding activities that are associated with being that smart (Bian, Leslie, & Cimpian, 2017).

Such gender role stereotypes can limit women's opportunities. In the past, orchestra conductors always chose men for principal positions because the conductors believed that women did not play as well as men. The schema of women as inferior musicians interfered with the conductors' ability to rate auditioners objectively when the conductors knew the names and sexes of the musicians. After recognizing this bias, the top North American orchestras began holding auditions with the musicians hidden behind screens and their names withheld from the conductors (**FIGURE 8.8**). Since these

(a)  **(b)**

FIGURE 8.8

Gender Roles Revised

(a) As shown in this photo of the New York Philharmonic in 1960, stereotypes about men's and women's abilities to play musical instruments often fueled the formation of all-male orchestras. **(b)** Changes in attitudes and in audition procedures have contributed to the diversification of talent in contemporary orchestras.

(a)

(b)

(c)

FIGURE 8.9
Script Theory of Schemas
According to this theory, we tend to follow general scripts of how to behave in particular settings. **(a)** At the movies, we expect to buy a ticket or print one if we bought it online. The cost of the ticket might depend on the moviegoer's age and the time of day. **(b)** Next, we might buy a snack before selecting a seat. Popcorn is a traditional snack at movie theaters. Caviar is not. **(c)** If we are part of a couple or group, we expect to sit with the other person in that couple or the people in the group. Although quiet talking might be appropriate before the movie, most of us expect talking to cease once the feature begins.

methods were instituted, the number of women in orchestras has increased considerably (Goldin & Rouse, 2000).

One common type of schema helps us understand the sequence of events in certain situations. Roger Schank and Robert Abelson (1977) have referred to these schemas about sequences as scripts. A **script** is a schema that directs behavior over time within a situation. For example, *going to the movies* is a script most of us are familiar with (**FIGURE 8.9**).

Scripts dictate appropriate behaviors and the sequence in which they are likely to occur. What is viewed as appropriate is shaped by culture. Like other schemas, scripts might limit behavior in undesirable ways. The script for a heterosexual date, perhaps "dating" back to the automobile's invention, traditionally has involved the male driving and paying for dinner. In the 1950s, before the civil rights movement, a black person's script for boarding a bus in the southern United States involved going to the back of the bus.

The schemas and scripts that children learn are likely to affect their behavior when they are older. In one study, children whose parents smoked or consumed alcohol were much more likely to choose cigarettes or alcohol in a simulated shopping experience (Dalton et al., 2005). When the children were asked about the items they chose, alcohol and cigarettes were clearly included in most children's scripts for adult social life. One 4-year-old girl who selected cigarettes explained, "I need this for my man. A man needs cigarettes" (see "The Methods of Psychology: Study of Preschoolers' Use of Cigarettes and Alcohol While Role Playing as Adults," on p. 296). These examples highlight the need for us to think critically about whether our automatic beliefs and actions reflect the values we wish to hold. (This subject is discussed in greater detail in Chapter 12, "Social Psychology.")

If schemas and scripts are potentially problematic, why do they persist? Their adaptive value is that, because they usually work well, these shortcuts minimize the amounts of attention required to navigate familiar environments. They also enable us to recognize and avoid unusual or dangerous situations. Mental representations in all forms assist us in using information about objects and events in adaptive ways.

script
A schema that directs behavior over time within a situation.

At fast-food restaurants we pay when we order, but at fine-dining restaurants we pay after eating. How do schemas help us behave appropriately in each place?

ANSWER: One type of schema is a script, which provides information about how to act within a specific situation.

Learning Objectives

- Explain how heuristics influence decision making and explore common heuristics.

- Discuss the role of emotions in decision making.

- Review strategies that facilitate problem solving and insight.

How Do We Make Decisions and Solve Problems?

The previous section discussed how we represent and organize knowledge of the world. But how do we use that knowledge to guide our daily actions? Throughout each day, we make decisions: what to eat for breakfast, which clothes to wear, which route to take to work or school, and so on. We scarcely notice making many of these decisions. Other decisions—such as which college to attend, whether to buy a house, and whom to marry—are much more consequential and require greater reflection. We also solve problems: how to get home if the car has broken down, how to earn extra

(a)

?   or   ?

(b)

?

decision making

Attempting to select the best alternative from among several options.

problem solving

Finding a way around an obstacle to reach a goal.

money for a vacation, how to break bad news, and so on. Thinking enables us to use information to make decisions and solve problems.

In **decision making,** we select among alternatives. Usually, we identify important criteria and determine how well each alternative satisfies these criteria. For example, if you can go to either Paris or Cancún for spring break, you need to choose between them. What criteria would you use in making this decision (**FIGURE 8.10A**)? In **problem solving,** we overcome obstacles to move from a present state to a desired goal state. For example, if you decide to go to Paris but do not have enough money for a plane ticket, you have a problem. In general, you have a problem when a barrier or a gap exists between where you are and where you want to be (**FIGURE 8.10B**).

8.4 Decision Making Often Involves Heuristics

Many, if not most, decisions are made under some degree of risk—that is, uncertainty about the possible outcomes. People's calculations of risk can lead to some questionable decisions. Why do people pay to insure themselves against low-risk occurrences (fire insurance) and then pay to take on high-risk actions (lottery tickets)? Why do people who want to lose weight sometimes choose to eat high-calorie junk food? Why do you go to a movie with your friend when you should be studying for a midterm? A rational observer, one who relies on logic, might conclude that people are puzzling decision makers.

For most of psychology's history, the prevailing theory was that people were rational; that they made decisions by considering possible alternatives and choosing the best one. In the 1970s, the researchers Daniel Kahneman and Amos Tversky (1979) shattered many intuitions and theories about how people make decisions. In doing so, Kahneman and Tversky helped us understand that people are far from calm and rational thinkers. Rather, decision makers are biased, use irrelevant criteria, and are unduly influenced by their emotions. These findings have had impacts on many fields, including economics, politics, and finance (**FIGURE 8.11**).

In examining how people make everyday decisions, Kahneman and Tversky identified several common mental shortcuts (rules of thumb, or informal guidelines). Known as **heuristics,** these shortcuts in thinking are fast and efficient strategies that people typically use to make decisions.

FIGURE 8.11
Groundbreaking Cognitive Research
Because of the importance of Daniel Kahneman and Amos Tversky's work, in 2002 Kahneman became the first psychologist to win the Nobel Prize, specifically the Nobel Prize in Economic Sciences. Here, he **(left)** is shown receiving the award. Tversky's influence was mentioned in the announcement. However, the Nobel Prize is awarded only to living scientists, and Tversky died in 1996.

"I'll be happy to give you innovative thinking. What are the guidelines?"

heuristics

Shortcuts (rules of thumb or informal guidelines) used to reduce the amount of thinking that is needed to make decisions.

anchoring

The tendency, in making judgments, to rely on the first piece of information encountered or information that comes most quickly to mind.

FIGURE 8.12
Anchoring
Which of these used cars would you choose? The cars themselves look identical. The words in the salesperson's descriptions are also identical. However, **(a)** the first description begins with "high mileage" and ends with "clean," whereas **(b)** the second description begins with "clean" and ends with "high mileage." Most people choose (b), where the initial emphasis is on a positive quality.

Heuristic thinking often occurs unconsciously: We are not aware of taking these mental shortcuts. Indeed, since the processing capacity of the conscious mind is limited, heuristic processing is useful partly because it requires minimal cognitive resources and allows us to focus our attention on other things. Heuristic thinking can be adaptive in that under some circumstances it is beneficial to make quick decisions rather than weigh all the evidence before deciding. Why do some people always want to buy the second-cheapest item, no matter what they are buying? They believe that by using this strategy, they save money but avoid purchasing the worst products. Other people want to buy only brand names. Such quick rules of thumb often provide reasonably good decisions, with outcomes that are acceptable for the individuals.

As Tversky and Kahneman have demonstrated, however, heuristics can also result in biases, and biases may lead to errors, faulty decisions, erroneous beliefs, and false predictions. In fact, as noted in Chapter 1, heuristic thinking is one of the principal sources of biases in reasoning. Consider the 2016 U.S. presidential election. Right until the results started arriving on election night, forecasters predicted a Hillary Clinton victory. Many of Clinton's supporters were overly optimistic because of *confirmation bias*, focusing attention only on information that supported their views. In addition, when events turned out contrary to their predictions, many people created after-the-fact explanations. This error in reasoning is known as *hindsight bias*. For instance, people who later claimed to have known that Donald Trump would defeat Clinton pointed to Clinton's defeat by Barack Obama in the 2008 Democratic primary and her narrow victory over Bernie Sanders in the 2016 primary. Other common heuristics that bias decision making are relative comparisons (anchoring and framing), availability, and representativeness. Let's look closer at these sometimes helpful, sometimes problematic strategies.

RELATIVE COMPARISONS (ANCHORING AND FRAMING) People often use comparisons to judge value. For example, you will feel much better with a score of 85 on an exam if you find out the class average was 75 than if you find out it was 95. In making relative comparisons, people are influenced by anchoring and framing.

An *anchor* serves as a reference point in decision making. **Anchoring** occurs when, in making judgments, people rely on the first piece of information they encounter or on information that comes most quickly to mind (Epley & Gilovich, 2001). For example, suppose people are asked to estimate how many residents Chicago has. Their answers depend on how the question is phrased. If they are asked if the population is more or less than 200,000, they provide a smaller number of residents than if they are asked if the population is more or less than 5 million (Jacowitz & Kahneman, 1995).

After making an initial judgment based on an anchor, people compare subsequent information to that anchor and adjust away from the anchor until they reach a point where the information seems reasonable. People often adjust insufficiently, leading to erroneous judgments (Asch, 1946). Suppose you are shopping for a used car. The salesperson describes one vehicle as having high mileage and being slightly rusty, dependable, fuel efficient, and clean. The same salesperson describes a second vehicle as being clean, fuel efficient, dependable, and slightly rusty and having high mileage. Which car would you choose (**FIGURE 8.12**)? Even though the descriptions are identical, people are influenced by the order of presentation and adjust their impressions based on the initial anchors. Anchoring effects can be found in many types of decisions.

The way information is presented can alter how people perceive their choices. Would you rather take a course where you have a 70 percent chance of passing or one where you have a 30 percent chance of failing? Even though the chances of passing (or failing) are identical, many students would choose the first course. This decision is an example of **framing.** This term refers to the tendency to emphasize the potential losses or potential gains from at least one alternative in decision making. Research on framing indicates that when people make choices, they may weigh losses and gains differently. They are generally much more concerned with costs than with benefits, an emphasis known as *loss aversion* (Kahneman, 2007; FIGURE 8.13).

AVAILABILITY HEURISTIC The **availability heuristic** is the general tendency to make a decision based on the answer that comes most easily to mind. In other words, when we think about events or make decisions, we tend to rely on information that is easy to retrieve. Recall the study on false fame discussed in Chapter 7, "Memory." Some participants read aloud a list of made-up names. The next day, those names were available in those participants' memories, even if the participants could not have said where they heard the names. Based on their familiarity with the names, the participants decided the people were famous.

Consider this question: In most industrialized countries, are there more farmers or more librarians? If you live in an agricultural area, you probably said farmers. If you do not live in an agricultural area, you probably said librarians. Most people who answer this question think of the librarians they know (or know about) and the farmers they know (or know about). If they can retrieve many more instances in one category, they assume it is the larger category. In fact, there are many more farmers than librarians in most industrialized countries. Because people who live in cities and suburbs tend not to meet many farmers, they are likely to believe there are more librarians. Information that is readily available biases decision making (FIGURE 8.14).

REPRESENTATIVENESS HEURISTIC The **representativeness heuristic** is the tendency to place a person or an object in a category if the person or object is similar to our prototype for that category. We use this heuristic when we base a decision on the extent to which each option reflects what we already believe about a situation. For example, say that Helena is intelligent, ambitious, and scientifically minded. She enjoys working on mathematical puzzles, talking with other people, reading, and gardening. Would you guess that she is a cognitive psychologist or a postal worker? Most people would use the representativeness heuristic: Because her characteristics seem more representative of psychologists than of postal workers, they would guess that Helena is a cognitive psychologist.

But the representativeness heuristic can lead to faulty thinking if we fail to take other information into account. One very important bit of information is the *base rate*. This term refers to how frequently an event occurs. People pay insufficient attention to base rates in reasoning. Instead, they focus on whether the information presented is representative of one conclusion or another. For example, there are many more postal workers than cognitive psychologists, so the base rate for postal workers is higher than that for cognitive psychologists. Therefore, any given person, including Helena, is much more likely to be a postal worker. Although Helena's traits may be

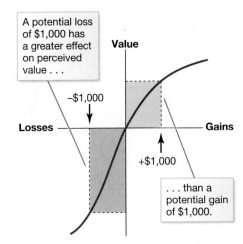

A potential loss of $1,000 has a greater effect on perceived value . . .

Value

−$1,000

Losses — Gains

+$1,000

. . . than a potential gain of $1,000.

FIGURE 8.13
Loss Aversion
Suppose you bought a stock. How bad would you feel if the value dropped and you sold the stock for a loss of $1,000 **(lower left)**? By contrast, how good would you feel if the value rose and you sold the stock for a profit of $1,000 **(upper right)**? For most people, potential losses affect decision making more than potential gains do.

framing
In decision making, the tendency to emphasize the potential losses or potential gains from at least one alternative.

availability heuristic
Making a decision based on the answer that most easily comes to mind.

representativeness heuristic
Placing a person or an object in a category if that person or object is similar to one's prototype for that category.

Is *r* more commonly the first letter in a word or the third letter?

r _ _ _ ?   _ _ *r* _ _ ?

How would you determine the answer?

FIGURE 8.14
The Availability Heuristic
If you are like most people, you thought of words with *r* as the first letter (such as *right* and *read*). Then you thought of words with *r* as the third letter (such as *care* and *sir*). Because words with *r* at the beginning came most easily to mind, you concluded that *r* is more often the first letter of a word. *R* is much more likely, however, to be the third letter in a word.

more representative of cognitive psychologists overall, they also likely apply to a large number of postal workers.

Q People sell stocks when the stock market goes down even though many finance experts advise investors to retain or increase their holdings at such times. How does loss aversion explain this behavior?

ANSWER: People are more concerned with not losing additional money if the stock market goes down than in making money if the stock market goes up.

8.5 Emotions Influence Decision Making

Kahneman and Tversky's work showed that people are not always rational in how they use information. This finding is particularly true in regard to how emotions affect people's judgments and decisions. For example, when people are in good moods, they tend to be persistent and to find creative, elaborate responses to challenging problems (Isen, 1993). When people are pursuing goals, positive feelings signal that they are making satisfactory progress and thereby encourage additional effort. As noted in Chapter 6, activation of dopamine systems in the brain play an important role in determining behaviors we want to perform. Brain imaging research shows that several brain regions are involved in how emotions affect judgment and decision making (Phelps, Lempert, & Sokol-Hessner, 2014). The specific brain regions depend on which affective experience is engaged. For instance, negative emotions such as fear activate the amygdala whereas rewarding responses activate the nucleus accumbens and regions of the prefrontal cortex.

Think about the effects of emotions on your own decision making. For example, would you prefer to go out dancing in a nightclub or to a poetry reading in a quiet cafe? In considering this question, did you think rationally about all the implications of either choice? Or did you flash on how you would feel in either situation? Emotions influence decision making in several different ways (Lerner, Valdesolo, & Kassam, 2015). For example, people anticipate future emotional states, which then serve as a source of information and a guide in decision making. In this way, individuals are able to make decisions more quickly and more efficiently. And in the face of complex, multifaceted situations, emotions serve as heuristic guides: They provide feedback for making quick decisions (Slovic, Finucane, Peters, & MacGregor, 2002). Risk judgments are strongly influenced by current feelings, and when emotions and cognitions are in conflict, emotions typically have the stronger impact on decisions (Loewenstein, Weber, Hsee, & Welch, 2001).

According to the *affect-as-information* theory, proposed by Norbert Schwarz and Gerald Clore (1983), people use current moods to make judgments and appraisals. They rely on their moods even if they are unaware of a mood's source. For instance, Schwarz and Clore asked people to rate their overall life satisfaction. To answer this question, people potentially must consider a multitude of factors, including situations, expectations, personal goals, and accomplishments. As the researchers noted, however, in arriving at their answers respondents did not labor through all these elements but instead seemed to rely on their current moods. People in good moods rated their lives as satisfactory, whereas people in bad moods gave lower overall ratings (FIGURE 8.15). Likewise, people's evaluations of plays, lectures, politicians, and even strangers are influenced by their moods. Moods, meanwhile, are influenced by the day of the week, the weather, health, and so on. If people are made aware of the sources of their moods (as when a researcher suggests that a good mood might be caused by the bright sunshine), their feelings have less influence over their judgments.

(a)

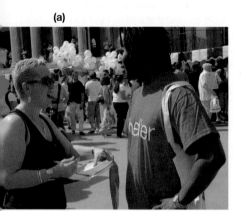

(b)

FIGURE 8.15
Moods and Life Satisfaction
Mood affects a person's satisfaction with life, and weather affects mood. As a result, people may report being more satisfied with their lives on **(a)** sunny days than on **(b)** rainy days.

SOMATIC MARKERS The neuroscientist Antonio Damasio has suggested that reasoning and decision making are guided by the emotional evaluation of an action's consequences. In his influential book *Descartes' Error* (1994), Damasio sets forth the *somatic marker theory*. According to this theory, most decisions are influenced by bodily reactions called **somatic markers.**

Have you ever had a queasy feeling in your stomach when you looked over the edge of a tall building? For Damasio, the term *gut feeling* can be taken almost literally. When you contemplate an action, you experience an emotional reaction based partly on your expectation of the action's outcome. Your expectation is influenced by your history of performing either that action or similar actions. For example, to the extent that driving fast has led to speeding tickets, which made you feel bad, you may choose to slow down when you see a speed limit sign. Hence, somatic markers may guide people to engage in adaptive behaviors.

Damasio has found that patients who have brain damage to the middle of the prefrontal region often are insensitive to somatic markers. When this region is damaged, people can still recall information, but the information has lost most of its affective meaning. They might be able to describe their current problems or talk about the death of a loved one, but they do so without experiencing any of the emotional pain that normally accompanies such thoughts. As a result, these people tend not to use past outcomes to regulate future behavior. For instance, in studies using a gambling task, patients who had damage to their frontal lobes continued to follow a risky strategy: They generally selected cards from a stack that had rare huge rewards but frequent bad losses rather than from a deck that had frequent small rewards and infrequent small losses (people without frontal injuries choose this safer strategy). Choosing cards from the high-risk deck had proved unsuccessful in previous trials, but as the patients contemplated selecting a card from the risky deck, they failed to show the more typical response of increased arousal (Bechara, Damasio, Tranel, & Damasio, 2005). That is, the somatic marker that would tell most people that something is a bad idea is absent among those with frontal lobe damage.

AFFECTIVE HEURISTIC People often decide to do things they believe will make them happy, whereas they avoid doing things they believe they will regret. Unfortunately, people are poor at **affective forecasting**—predicting how they will feel about things in the future (Gilbert & Wilson, 2007). Even more important, people generally do not realize how poor they are at predicting their future feelings.

People overestimate how happy they will be for positive events, such as getting married, having children, or having their candidate win an election or their team win a championship (Dolan & Metcalfe, 2010; **FIGURE 8.16**). Likewise, they overestimate the extent to which negative events—such as breaking up with a romantic partner, losing a job, or being diagnosed with a serious medical illness—will affect them in the future (Gilbert, Pinel, Wilson, Blumberg, & Wheatley, 1998; Wilson & Gilbert, 2003). It seems that when we think about getting married, we focus on the love we feel for our partner right now. When we think about the death of a loved one, we consider only the immediate, intense pain. Over time, however, life continues, with its daily joys and sorrows. The pleasure of the gain or the pain of the loss becomes less prominent against the backdrop of everyday events.

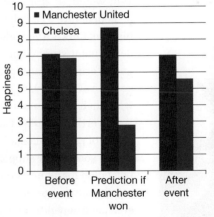

FIGURE 8.16
Faulty Affective Forecasting
In this study, diehard soccer fans were asked to predict their hap if Manchester won the contest between Manchester United and Chelsea for the 2008 UEFA Champions League Soccer Final. the match, there were no differences in happiness. Manches won fans expected to be much happier than Chelsea fans if Mar re the game. Seven days after Manchester won, however, the uch less happy than they expected to be, whereas Chelsea fa happier than they expected to be.

After a negative event, people engage in strategies that help them feel better (Gilbert & Wilson, 2007). For example, they rationalize why the event happened, and they minimize the event's importance. These strategies are generally adaptive in that they protect the sufferers' mental health. After all, making sense of an event helps reduce its negative emotional consequences. Even after suffering anguish because of a negative event, most people will adapt and return to their typical positive outlook.

People have an amazing capacity for manufacturing happiness. One study found that people who had been paralyzed were more optimistic about their futures than were people who had won lotteries (Brickman, Coates, & Janoff-Bulman, 1978). Generally, however, people seem unaware that they can find positive outcomes from tragic events. When asked to predict how they will feel following a tragic event, people overestimate their pain and underestimate how well they will cope with the event (Gilbert, Morewedge, Risen, & Wilson, 2004).

Q A person is asked to rate his overall life satisfaction. According to the affect-as-information theory, how would he respond to this question if his favorite sports team had recently lost the championship game?

ANSWER: A sad mood would lead him to report low overall life satisfaction.

8.6 Why Is It Hard to Resist a Sale?

Every weekend, the local department store seems to have a gigantic sale. Bold advertisements proclaim, "80% off!" That discount sounds like a great deal. When you shop around, however, you discover that the store's regular prices are substantially higher than the competition's. The sale simply lowers prices to match the going market rate. Why would the store use such an obvious tactic?

People love to think they are getting a bargain, so having high regular prices and big discounts is a very effective marketing strategy (Darke & Dahl, 2003). In 2012, the department store chain JCPenney tried to break this mold by ending weekly sales and offering "fair and square" everyday low prices for its merchandise. Shoppers quit going to JCPenney, and the executive who brought in the strategy was fired. Shoppers want their discounts. JCPenney is back to emphasizing weekly sales.

Advertisers exploit the tendency to view benefits and costs differently. Suppose a gallon of gasoline costs $4.05. You get a discount of $.10 a gallon if you pay with cash. Sound good? Now suppose gasoline is $3.95 a gallon and you pay a surcharge of $.10 per gallon for using a credit card. The cost is identical but fewer people are willing to pay the surcharge than to get the discount (**FIGURE 8.17**). Whether a deal is considered good depends on the type of comparison people are making. Aware of framing's powerful effects and borrowing from Kahneman and Tversky's work, advertisers usually frame the decision in terms of a discount (money gained) instead of a surcharge (money lost).

Framing influences many consumer decisions. In the grocery store, people are much more likely to purchase meat that is described as 75 percent lean than food described as 25 percent fat (Sanford, Fay, Stewart, & Moxey, 2002). Labels such as low-fat or low-carb are often used to hide the fact that products are respectively high in sugar or fat. Framing can also be used to promote healthy behavior. Beachgoers presented with information that frames sunscreen in terms of its benefits are more likely to request sunscreen than those who are told about the hazards of sunburn (Detweiler, Bedell, Salovey, Pronin, & Rothman, 1999). The point is that positively

FIGU
Bene
sus Costs
This pre
makes it n of the gas price
cash to ge active to pay in
instead, the ount. What if,
a credit card ed that if you use
would be an a the gas, there
cents per gallo.harge of five
view of the stat puld your
?

framed information is more influential in changing behavior than negatively framed information.

Anchoring also affects consumer decisions. The social psychologist Robert Cialdini (2008) describes a technique commonly used by real estate agents: When showing properties to prospective home buyers, real estate agents often start with an overpriced, run-down house they have little expectation of selling. With that "shack" as an anchor, buyers are more impressed with the houses they subsequently see and therefore become more likely to make offers. Car dealers often wait until the price of a new car has been agreed upon before suggesting additional options that seem small by comparison but might add up to several hundred more dollars. In other words, once a buyer agrees to pay $20,000 for a car, that price becomes the anchor against which the cost of options seems small. Why would a restaurant list at least one really expensive item on the menu? No one may order that item, but its price makes other prices look reasonable.

Anchoring and framing are among the major weapons that marketers use to increase sales. As a critical thinker aware of how psychological reasoning can be exploited, you should always consider the basis of comparisons when you are making purchases. ■

 One major online retailer charges high prices but gives free shipping whereas one of its competitors offers lower prices but charges for shipping. How might framing affect people's decisions about which site to use?

8.7 Problem Solving Achieves Goals

Problem solving is using available information to achieve a goal. Problems come in two forms. Some are easily defined, such as: How do you get into your car (goal) when you have locked the keys inside (problem)? How can you make enough money (problem) to spend your spring break somewhere nice (goal)? Other problems, perhaps more commonly, are less easily defined: What type of job should you aim for?

This section examines some of the best ways to solve problems. For the purposes of this discussion, a person has a problem when he or she has no simple and direct means of attaining a particular goal. To solve the problem, the person must make a plan to reach an attainable goal, devise strategies to overcome obstacles to carry out the plan, monitor progress to keep on track, and evaluate the results to see if the goal has been attained. How the person thinks about the problem can help or hinder the person's ability to find solutions.

ORGANIZATION OF SUBGOALS One approach to the study of problem solving is to identify people's steps in solving particular problems. Researchers examine how people proceed from one step to the next, the typical errors people make in negotiating tricky or unintuitive steps, and how people decide on more efficient (or, in some cases, less efficient) solutions. For example, in the classic Tower of Hanoi problem, participants are given a board that has a row of three pegs on it. The peg on one end has three disks stacked on it in order of size: small on top, medium in the middle, large on the bottom. The task is to move the disks, one at a time, to the peg

"Never, ever, think outside the box."

The task is to move the disks to the peg on the other end. You can move only one disk at a time. You cannot place a larger disk on top of a smaller disk.

The solution is presented below. Before you look at it, simulate the task by stacking three coins of unequal size. For example, if you have U.S. coins, use a penny, a nickel, and a quarter:

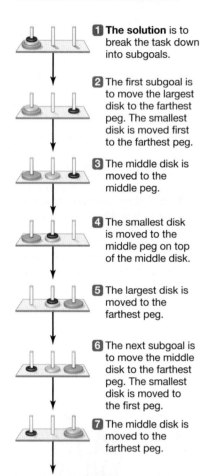

1 **The solution** is to break the task down into subgoals.

2 The first subgoal is to move the largest disk to the farthest peg. The smallest disk is moved first to the farthest peg.

3 The middle disk is moved to the middle peg.

4 The smallest disk is moved to the middle peg on top of the middle disk.

5 The largest disk is moved to the farthest peg.

6 The next subgoal is to move the middle disk to the farthest peg. The smallest disk is moved to the first peg.

7 The middle disk is moved to the farthest peg.

8 Finally, the smallest disk is moved to the farthest peg.

FIGURE 8.18
The Tower of Hanoi Problem

on the other end without putting a larger disk on a smaller disc. Solving the problem requires breaking the task into *subgoals*, which are shown in **FIGURE 8.18**.

Using subgoals is important for many problems. Suppose a high school senior has decided she would like to become a doctor. To achieve this goal, she first needs to attain the more immediate subgoal of being admitted to a good college. To get into a good college, she needs to earn good grades in high school. This additional subgoal would require developing good study skills and paying attention in class. When you are facing a complex problem and the next step is not obvious, identifying the appropriate steps or subgoals and their order can be challenging. How do you overcome obstacles to problem solving?

CHANGING REPRESENTATIONS TO OVERCOME OBSTACLES *Have you heard about the new restaurant that opened on the moon? It has great food but no atmosphere!* The premise of this joke is that *atmosphere* means one thing when interpreted in light of the restaurant schema but something else in the context of the moon. Humor often violates an expectation, so "getting" the joke means rethinking some common representation. In problem solving, too, we often need to revise a mental representation to overcome an obstacle. This skill is exactly what is needed to solve crossword puzzles.

One strategy that problem solvers commonly use to overcome obstacles is **restructuring** the problem. This technique consists of representing the problem in a novel way. Ideally, the new view reveals a solution that was not visible under the old problem structure. In one now-famous study, Scheerer (1963) gave each participant a sheet of paper that had a square of nine dots on it. The task was to connect all nine dots using at most four straight lines, without lifting the pencil off the page (**FIGURE 8.19**).

In trying to solve a problem, we commonly think back to how we have solved similar problems. We tend to persist with previous strategies, or **mental sets.** These established ways of thinking are often useful, but sometimes they make it difficult to find the best solution.

In 1942, the Gestalt psychologist Abraham Luchins demonstrated a classic example of a mental set. He asked participants to measure out specified amounts of water, such as 100 cups, using three jars of different sizes. Say that jar A held 21 cups, jar B held 127 cups, and jar C held 3 cups. The solution to this problem was to fill jar B, use jar A to remove 21 cups from jar B's 127 cups, then use jar C to remove 3 cups of water twice, leaving 100 cups in jar B. The structure to the solution is (B – A) – 2(C). Participants were given many of these problems. In each problem, the jar sizes and goal measurements differed, but the same formula applied.

Then participants were given another problem: They were given jar A, which held 23 cups; jar B, which held 49 cups; and jar C, which held 3 cups. They were asked to measure out 20 cups. Even though the simplest solution was to fill jar A and use jar C to remove 3 cups from jar A's 23, participants usually came up with a much more

restructuring
A new way of thinking about a problem that aids its solution.

mental sets
Problem-solving strategies that have worked in the past.

FIGURE 8.19
Scheerer's Nine-Dot Problem
Try to connect the dots by using at most four straight lines, without lifting your pencil off the page. Solutions appear in Figure 8.19B, on p. 306.

complicated solution that involved all three jars. Having developed a mental set of using three jars in combination to solve this type of problem, they had trouble settling on the simpler solution of using only two jars. Surprisingly, when given a problem with a simple solution for which the original formula did not work, many participants failed to solve the problem most efficiently (FIGURE 8.20).

One type of mental set results from having fixed ideas about the typical functions of objects. Such **functional fixedness** can also create difficulties in problem solving. The fictional television character MacGyver is famous for overcoming functional fixedness by performing amazing feats using every-day objects, such as his trusted Swiss Army knife. Perhaps you have used duct tape for a purpose not originally intended by its creators (FIGURE 8.21).

To overcome functional fixedness, the problem solver needs to reinter-pret an object's potential function. One research example involves the candle problem, developed by Karl Duncker (1945). Participants are in a room with a bulletin board on the wall. They are given a candle, a book of matches, a box of tacks, and the following challenge: *Using only these objects, attach the candle to the bulletin board in such a way that the candle can be lit and burn properly*. Most people have trouble coming up with an adequate solution (FIGURE 8.22A).

If people reinterpret the function of the box, however, a solution emerges. The side of the box can be tacked to the bulletin board so that it creates a stand. The candle is then placed on the box and lit (FIGURE 8.22B). In gen-eral, participants have difficulty viewing the box as a possible stand when it is being used as a container for the tacks. When participants are shown representations of this problem with an empty box and the tacks on the table next to it, they solve the problem somewhat more easily.

CONSCIOUS STRATEGIES Restructuring mental representations is a valuable way to develop insight into solving a problem. Still, we often find it difficult to enact this strategy consciously when we are stuck. Fortunately, we can always apply other strat-egies that may help lead to a solution.

One such strategy is using an *algorithm*. An algorithm is a guideline that if fol-lowed correctly will always yield the correct answer. If you wanted to know the area of a rectangle, for example, you could get the right answer by multiplying its length times its width. This formula is an algorithm because it will always work. Similarly, if

	Desired water	Jar A	Jar B	Jar C
Trial 1	100	21	127	3
Trial 2	8	18	48	11
Trial 3	62	10	80	4
Trial 4	31	20	59	4
Trial 5	29	20	57	4
Trial 6	20	23	49	3
Trial 7	25	28	76	3

FIGURE 8.20
Luchins's Mental Set

functional fixedness
In problem solving, having fixed ideas about the typical functions of objects.

(a)

(b)

FIGURE 8.21
Overcoming Functional Fixedness
(a) Some people may think of duct tape as something used only for mending ducts. **(b)** Thinking this way means missing out on the opportunity to use the material more creatively, such as making an outfit for the prom.

FIGURE 8.22A
Duncker's Candle Problem
Try to solve this problem: How would you attach the candle to the bulletin board on the wall so that it can be lit and burns properly?

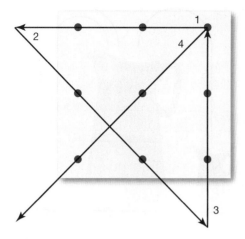

FIGURE 8.19B
Solutions to Scheerer's Nine-Dot Problem
Most participants consider only solutions that fit within the square formed by the dots. They tend to think that the problem includes that restriction. However, one solution is truly to think outside the box: to see that keeping the lines within the box is not a requirement. Another solution is to use one *very* fat line that covers all nine dots. Solving the problem requires restructuring the representation by eliminating assumed constraints.

FIGURE 8.22B
Solution to Duncker's Candle Problem
The box for the tacks can be used as a stand for the candle.

insight
The sudden realization of a solution to a problem.

you follow a recipe exactly, it should always yield pretty much the same outcome. Suppose, however, you substitute one ingredient for another: You use oil instead of the butter that the recipe calls for. Here, you are using a heuristic that one type of fat is equal to another. Your result will likely be fine, but there is no guarantee.

Another good conscious strategy for overcoming obstacles is *working backward*. When the appropriate steps for solving a problem are not clear, proceeding from the goal state to the initial state can help yield a solution. Consider the water lily problem (Fixx, 1978, p. 50):

> Water lilies double in area every 24 hours. On the first day of summer there is only one water lily on the lake. It takes 60 days for the lake to be completely covered in water lilies. How many days does it take for half of the lake to be covered in water lilies?

One way to solve this problem is to work from the initial state to the goal state: You figure that on day 1 there is one water lily, on day 2 there are two water lilies, on day 3 there are four water lilies, and so on, until you discover how many water lilies there are on day 60 and you see which day had half that many. But if you work backward, from the goal state to the initial state, you realize that if on day 60 the lake is covered in water lilies and that *water lilies double every 24 hours,* then on day 59 half of the lake must have been covered in water lilies.

A third good strategy for overcoming obstacles is *finding an appropriate analogy* (Reeves & Weisberg, 1994). This strategy is also known as analogical problem solving. Say that a surgeon needs to use a laser at high intensity to destroy a patient's tumor. The surgeon must aim that laser so as to avoid destroying the surrounding healthy tissue. She remembers reading a story about a general who wanted to capture a fortress. The general needed to move a large number of soldiers up to the fortress, but all the roads to the fortress were planted with mines. A large group of soldiers would have set off the mines, but a small group could travel safely. So the general divided the soldiers into small groups and had each group take a different road to the fortress, where the groups converged and attacked together. Because her problem has constraints *analogous* to the general's problem, the doctor gets the idea to aim several lasers at the tumor from different angles. By itself, each laser will be weak enough to avoid destroying the living tissue in its path. But the combined intensity of all the converging lasers will be enough to destroy the tumor.

To transfer a problem-solving strategy means using a strategy that works in one context to solve a problem that is structurally similar. To accomplish this kind of transfer, we must pay attention to the structure of each problem. For this reason, analogous problems may enhance our ability to solve each one. Some researchers have found that participants who solve two or more analogous problems develop a schema that helps them solve similar problems (Gick & Holyoak, 1983). Analogous solutions work, however, only if we recognize the similarities between the problem we face and those we have solved and the analogy is correct (Keane, 1987; Reeves & Weisberg, 1994).

SUDDEN INSIGHT Often, a problem is not identified as a problem until it seems unsolvable and the problem solver feels stuck. For example, it is only when you spot the keys in the ignition of your locked car that you know you have a problem. Sometimes, as you stand there pondering the problem, a solution will pop into your head—the "Aha" moment. **Insight** is the metaphorical mental lightbulb that goes on in your head when you suddenly realize the solution to a problem.

In 1925, the Gestalt psychologist Wolfgang Köhler conducted one of psychology's most famous examples of research on insight. Convinced that some nonhuman animals could behave intelligently, Köhler studied whether chimpanzees could solve problems. He would place a banana outside a chimp's cage, just beyond the chimp's reach, and provide several sticks that the chimp could use. Could the chimp figure out how to move the banana within grabbing distance?

In one situation, neither of two sticks was long enough to reach the banana. One chimpanzee, who sat looking at the sticks for some time, suddenly grabbed the sticks and joined them together by placing one stick inside an opening in the other stick. With this longer stick, the chimp obtained the banana. Köhler argued that, after pondering the problem, the chimp had the insight to join the sticks into a tool long enough to reach the banana. Having solved that problem, the chimp transferred this solution to similar problems and solved them quickly (**FIGURE 8.23**).

In another classic study of insight, Norman Maier (1931) brought participants, one at a time, into a room that had two strings hanging from the ceiling and a table in the corner. On the table were several random objects, including a pair of pliers. Each participant was asked to tie the strings together. However, it was impossible to grab both strings at once: If a participant was holding one string, the other string was too far away to grab (**FIGURE 8.24A**). The solution was to tie the pliers onto one string and use that string as a pendulum. The participant could then hold the other string and grab the pendulum string as it swung by (**FIGURE 8.24B**).

Although a few participants eventually figured out this solution on their own, most people were stumped by the problem. After letting these people ponder the problem for 10 minutes, Maier casually crossed the room and brushed up against the string, causing it to swing back and forth. Once the participants saw the brushed string swinging, most immediately solved the problem, as if they had experienced a new insight. These participants did not report that Maier had given them the solution, however. It is possible that they did not even notice Maier's actions consciously. They all believed they had come up with the solution independently.

FIGURE 8.23
Köhler's Study on Sudden Insight
Chimpanzees try to solve problems, such as reaching bananas that are too high. In one of Köhler's studies, a chimp seemed to suddenly realize a solution. It stacked several boxes on top of each other and stood on them to reach the bananas. This behavior suggested that the chimp solved the problem through insight.

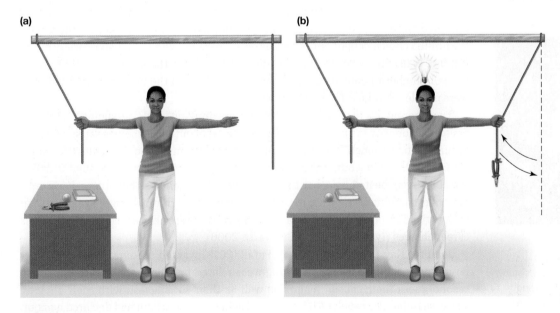

FIGURE 8.24
Maier's Study on Sudden Insight
(a) In this situation, how would you grab both strings so you could tie them together? **(b)** The solution is to weight one string with the pliers, then swing the weighted string as a pendulum that you can grab.

Maier's study also provides an example of how insight can be achieved when a problem initially seems unsolvable. In this case, most people had failed to see the pliers as a pendulum weight—they were suffering from functional fixedness. To solve the problem, these people needed to reconsider the possible functions of the pliers and string. As mentioned earlier, how we view or represent a problem can significantly affect how easily we solve it. Sometimes insight provides these new solutions for overcoming functional fixedness.

Q Your uncle uses a dial-up modem to connect to the Internet because it always works. How does the idea of a mental set explain why your uncle has not upgraded to more modern technology?

ANSWER: A mental set is a problem-solving strategy that has always worked in the past, so it seems reliable even though it might not be the best solution.

8.8 How Can You Make Good Choices?

Making your own decisions is one of the luxuries of adulthood. The flip side of this benefit is that making important life decisions can be stressful. What if you make the wrong decision? What if your decision has unanticipated consequences? Cognitive psychologists study how people make small and big decisions. Some cognitive researchers are particularly interested in college students' thinking about important academic decisions, such as choosing a major.

In modern society, many people believe that the more options they have, the better. But when too many options are available, especially when all of them are attractive, people experience conflict and indecision. Although some choice is better than none, some scholars note that too much choice can be frustrating, unsatisfying, and ultimately debilitating (Schwartz, 2004).

In a study by Sheena Iyengar and Mark Lepper (2000), shoppers at a grocery store were presented with a display of either 6 or 24 varieties of jam to sample. The shoppers also received a discount coupon for any variety of jam. The greater variety attracted more shoppers, but it failed to produce more sales: 30 percent of those with the limited choice bought jam, whereas only 3 percent with the greater variety did so (FIGURE 8.25). In a second study, the investigators found that people choosing among a small number of chocolates were more satisfied with the ones they selected than were people who chose from a wider variety.

Two approaches to decision making are "maximizing" and "satisficing." Maximizers seek to identify the perfect choice among a set of options, whereas satisficers seek to find a "good enough" choice that meets their minimum requirements (Schwartz et al., 2002). It turns out that maximizers, compared with satisficers, tend to select the objectively best choice, but those choices bring them less happiness. For example, college graduates who are maximizers land jobs with much higher salaries than their satisficing counterparts, but in the long run they are also less satisfied with their career choices (Iyengar, Wells, & Schwartz, 2006).

Jennifer Kay Leach and Erika A. Patall (2013) wanted to know if these two different approaches to decision making were related to college students' tendency to second-guess their chosen majors as well as their satisfaction with their choices. The researchers surveyed 378 juniors and seniors, all of whom had declared a major. Maximizers reported engaging in more upward counterfactual thinking than satisficers. This sort of thinking means considering how things might have turned out better if the choosers had made different decisions. For example, the maximizers in this study more strongly endorsed self-report items such as "I often consider how other

(a)

(b)

FIGURE 8.25
Too Much Choice
As part of Iyengar and Lepper's study, displays presented **(a)** 6 jams and **(b)** 24 jams. Bar-code labels on the jars indicated whether people bought more from one group of jams or the other. The results indicated that having many possibilities can make it difficult to choose one item.

1. No matter how satisfied I am with my job, it's only right for me to be on the lookout for better opportunities.

2. When I am in the car listening to the radio, I often check other stations to see if something better is playing, even if I am relatively satisfied with what I'm listening to.

3. When I watch TV, I channel surf, often scanning through the available options even while attempting to watch one program.

4. I treat relationships like clothing: I expect to try a lot on before finding the perfect fit.

5. I often find it difficult to shop for a gift for a friend.

6. Renting videos is really difficult. I'm always struggling to pick the best one.

7. When shopping, I have a hard time finding clothing that I really love.

8. I'm a big fan of lists that attempt to rank things (the best movies, the best singers, the best athletes, the best novels, etc.).

9. I find that writing is very difficult, even if it's just writing a letter to a friend, because it's so hard to word things just right. I often do several drafts of even simple things.

10. I never settle for second best.

11. Whenever I'm faced with a choice, I try to imagine what all the other possibilities are, even ones that aren't present at the moment.

12. I often fantasize about living in ways that are quite different from my actual life.

13. No matter what I do, I have the highest standards for myself.

FIGURE 8.26
Maximization Scale
For each item on this list, award yourself anywhere from 1 point (for "completely disagree") to 7 points (for "completely agree"). Then add up your points. People who get high scores on this scale are considered maximizers.

majors would have allowed me more career opportunities/options." Such thinking was related to lower satisfaction with the chosen major. Multiple studies point to the same general pattern: Maximizers go through a lot of effort to make good choices, but they are ultimately less than fully satisfied with the choices they make. To find out if you are a maximizer, complete the maximization scale in **FIGURE 8.26.**

If you are a maximizer, are you doomed to always second-guess your decisions? Will you always be dissatisfied? Not necessarily. Ultimately, you get to decide how you will feel about your decision making.

The psychologist Barry Schwartz leads a research team that has conducted many studies on maximizers. In his book *The Paradox of Choice* (2004), Schwartz offers advice we can all use to navigate choices. Here are some of his ideas applied to the decision of which major to select in college:

1. **Approach the decision with the mindset of a satisficer.** Try to articulate your minimum requirements for a good major. You might, for instance, seek a major that would both allow you to learn about people from different cultures and help you develop business skills. You do not need to find the one best major for achieving your goals. You need to choose a major that will set you on the right path.

2. **Promise yourself that you will stick with your decision.** Schwartz calls this promise "irreversibility." We tend to be less satisfied with our decisions if we know we can change them. Know that you picked your major for a good reason and accept that decision. Schwartz notes, "The only way to find happiness and stability in the presence of seemingly attractive and tempting options is to say, 'I'm simply not going there. I've made my decision. . . . I'm not in the market—end of story'" (p. 299).

3. **Have realistic expectations.** Sure, you will probably have to take some classes that you do not enjoy. A couple of your professors might even be boring. Tests and other requirements may challenge your limits. But such drawbacks will be true of all majors. As with any decision, you will experience dips in satisfaction.

4. **Practice an attitude of gratitude.** Schwartz finds that people who actively reflect on the good that has come from their decisions are more satisfied with those decisions than people who linger on the bad. Each semester, as you get ready to register for the next semester's classes, list 5–10 things you are grateful for related to your major: something surprising you learned, an eye-opening experience you had because of a class, a provocative conversation you had with an engaging professor, a new friend you met in class, and so on.

Finally, whether you are choosing a major or making another major decision, keep in mind that multiple perfectly fine options likely exist. Thinking carefully about your choices and making a "good enough" decision might help free your mind and give you time to engage in other, equally worthwhile pursuits. ■

Q When chef Gordon Ramsay tries to save a failing restaurant, he often reduces the number of items on the menu. Why might fewer options be better for maximizing customers?

ANSWER: When maximizers have too many options, they often find it difficult to choose, so they experience stress. Limiting the menu can make choosing and dining less stressful, especially for maximizers, and happier customers may be repeat customers.

Learning Objectives

- Discuss the roles of morphemes and phonemes in language.
- Identify the brain areas involved in language.
- Explain how language develops.
- Contrast the phonics and whole language approaches to the teaching of reading.
- Explain dyslexia.

language
A system of communication using sounds and symbols according to grammatical rules.

morphemes
The smallest language units that have meaning, including suffixes and prefixes.

What Is Language?

Language may be the most complex wonder of the human brain. While many species communicate, such as in birds' use of song, language represents a quantum leap beyond other forms of animal communication. It sets us apart from other species. In over 4,000 languages, humans can speak, write, and read, communicating everything from basic information to complex emotions and the subtle nuances of great literature. Language enables us to live in complex societies, because through language we learn the history, rules, and values of our culture or cultures.

How do we learn language? Some aspects can be taught formally, such as grammatical rules. Other aspects do not rely on formal teaching, such as when children who are exposed to several languages somehow learn all of them and keep them straight. They know that one set of words is English, one is Spanish, and another is French. Consider, too, that every fluent speaker of a language relies on extensive implicit knowledge of grammar even if he or she cannot explain the rules. Babies begin speaking without a great deal of formal teaching. What explains the human capacity for language?

8.9 Language Is a System of Communication Using Sounds and Symbols

Language is a system of communication using sounds and symbols according to grammatical rules. This system can be viewed as a hierarchical structure. That is, sentences can be broken down into smaller units, or *phrases*. Phrases can be broken down into words. Words can be broken down into sounds.

Each word consists of one or more **morphemes.** Morphemes are the smallest units that have meaning, including suffixes and prefixes. As an example, consider the words *frost,* de*frost,* and *defrost*er. The root word, *frost,* is a morpheme. The meaning of this morpheme is changed by adding the prefix *de,* which is also a morpheme. Adding a

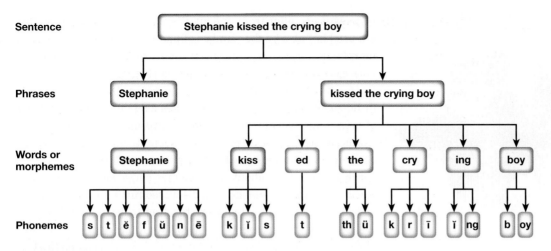

FIGURE 8.27
The Units of Language

third morpheme, the suffix *er,* changes the meaning once again (Gazzaniga, Ivry, & Mangun, 2014).

Each morpheme consists of one or more **phonemes.** Phonemes are the basic sounds of speech, the building blocks of language. For example, the word *kissed* has two morphemes ("kiss" and "ed") and four phonemes (the sounds you make when you say the word).

A language's *syntax* is the system of rules that govern how words are combined into phrases and how phrases are combined to make sentences. *Semantics* is the study of the system of meanings that underlie words, phrases, and sentences.

To clarify your understanding of all these terms, consider the sentence *Stephanie kissed the crying boy.* Semantics tells us why that sentence has a different meaning than *Crying, Stephanie kissed the boy.* Syntax dictates that the sentence cannot be *Kissed the crying boy Stephanie.* As shown in **FIGURE 8.27,** the sentence can be broken down into phrases, the phrases can be broken down into words or morphemes, and the words or morphemes can be broken down into phonemes.

phonemes
The basic sounds of speech, the building blocks of language.

THE SOUNDS OF LANGUAGE Every language is derived from a highly restricted set of phonemes. This fact is intriguing because the human vocal tract has the capacity to make many more sounds than any language uses. People speak by forcing air through the *vocal cords.* The vocal cords are folds of mucous membranes that are part of the larynx, an organ in the neck, often called the voice box (**FIGURE 8.28**). The air passes from the vocal cords to the oral cavity (part of the mouth behind the teeth and above the tongue). There, jaw, lip, and tongue movements change the shape of the mouth and the flow of the air, altering the sounds produced by the vocal cords. Some of those sounds are phonemes.

Phonemes signal meaningful differences between words. For example, the phonemes /p/ and /b/ carry no meanings in themselves, but they enable us to recognize *pat* and *bat* as having different meanings. Although both of these phonemes are consonants formed by closing and then opening the lips, the larynx vibrates to make /b/ but not to make /p/.

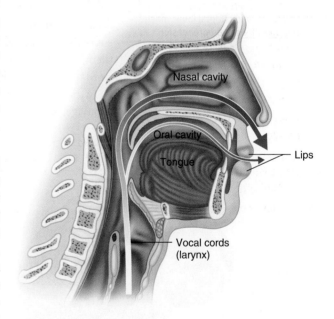

FIGURE 8.28
The Human Vocal Tract
Speech is produced by moving air through the vocal cords, part of the larynx, into the mouth. Lip and tongue movements then control the shape of the oral cavity and the flow of the air, resulting in particular sounds.

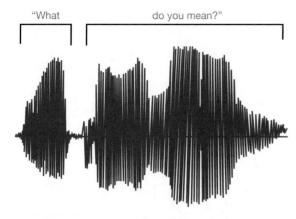

FIGURE 8.29
Speech Waveform
This is the waveform for the question "What do you mean?" There are no spaces between the words, yet the brain normally can segment the waveform so that the words can be understood.

aphasia
A language disorder that results in deficits in language comprehension and production.

Wernicke's area
An area of the left hemisphere where the temporal and parietal lobes meet, involved in speech comprehension.

Languages differ from one another not only by the words that are used but also by the number of phonemes and the patterns of morphemes. English consists of approximately 40 phonemes, whereas other languages use as few as 11 (the Rotokias language, from Papua New Guinea) or more than 110 (the !Xóõ language, used in Botswana and Namibia). Languages also differ in the patterns of morphemes within phrases. Such patterns help us separate the words we hear in conversation. The separate morphemes actually occur in a continuous stream, or waveform (**FIGURE 8.29**). People speak at the rate of about 15 phonemes per second, or about 180 words per minute. Somehow, as discussed further in the next section, different brain regions work together to separate out the relevant sounds into segments that allow for interpretation. Meaning plays an important role in this perception. When you listen to a language you are not fluent in, it can be difficult to separate the stream into segments.

LANGUAGE IN THE BRAIN Injuries in certain brain areas can lead to **aphasia.** This language disorder results in deficits in language comprehension and production. About 40 percent of all strokes produce some aphasia, which can be temporary or permanent (Pedersen et al., 1995). Most strokes that cause aphasia occur in the left hemisphere.

Recall from Chapter 3 that the physician and anatomist Paul Broca studied a patient who could say only the word *tan*. In examining the patient's brain, Broca found that this patient had a lesion in the left frontal lobe (see Figure 3.13). After studying other patients, Broca concluded that the area of the brain that produces speech, now called Broca's area, must be located in the left hemisphere. When Broca's area is damaged, patients develop *expressive aphasia* (also called *Broca's aphasia*), which interrupts their ability to speak. These individuals generally understand what is said to them, and they can move their lips and tongues, but they cannot form words or put one word together with another to form a phrase.

In the 1870s, the physician Carl Wernicke identified another brain area involved in language. Wernicke had two patients who, after each had suffered a stroke, had trouble understanding spoken language. These patients could speak fluently, but what they said was nonsensical. After these patients died, Wernicke autopsied them. He found damage in a region of the left hemisphere where the temporal and parietal lobes meet. This region is now known as **Wernicke's area** (**FIGURE 8.30**). When Wernicke's area is damaged, patients develop *receptive aphasia* (also called *Wernicke's aphasia*), in which they have trouble understanding the meaning of words. Those with receptive aphasia are often highly verbal, but what they say does not follow the rules of grammar or make sense.

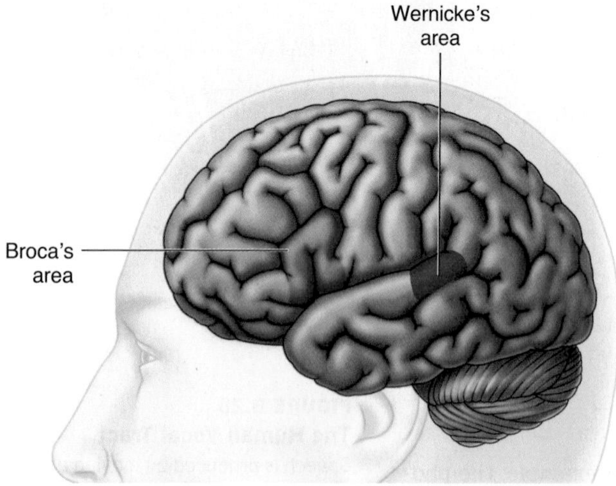

Since the work of Broca and Wernicke, researchers have shown that a network of brain regions work together to facilitate language (Gazzaniga, Ivry, & Mangun, 2014). For about 90 percent of people, the left hemisphere is most important for language. Extensive damage to the left hemisphere can cause *global aphasia*, where the person cannot produce or comprehend language. The right hemisphere also contributes to language in important ways, such as processing the

Wernicke's area

Broca's area

FIGURE 8.30
Left Hemisphere Regions Involved in Speech
Broca's area is important for speech production. Wernicke's area is important for speech comprehension.

rhythm of speech (Lindell, 2006) and interpreting what is said, especially understanding metaphors (Yang, 2014).

LANGUAGE AND THOUGHT What is the relationship between language and thought? Benjamin Whorf (1956) hypothesized that language reflects how people think. More specifically, culture determines language, which in turn determines how people form concepts and categorize objects and experiences. Whorf observed that the Inuit people, of the Arctic, use more words to describe variations in snow than English speakers do. According to Whorf, the greater number of words to describe snow was valuable to the Inuit people because subtleties in snow had practical and important implications for their daily living (**FIGURE 8.31**).

According to the **linguistic relativity theory,** language determines thought. That is, you can think only through language. However, this version of Whorf's hypothesis does not appear to be true (Gelman & Gallistel, 2004; Hunt & Agnoli, 1991). For instance, the theory means that those without language are incapable of thought. Considerable research shows that animals and prelinguistic infants are capable of complex thought (Keil, 2011; Newman, Keil, Kuhlmeier, & Wynn, 2010; Paulson, Chalmers, Kahneman, Santos, & Schiff, 2013).

Another version of the theory is that language influences rather than determines thought. This point remains controversial, but some research indicates that language influences thought in a number of domains, such as how people think about time, space, and quantities (Boroditsky, Fuhrman, & McCormick, 2011; Gordon, 2004; Levinson, 2003). Moreover, the use of sexist language can influence people's thoughts about males and females. Recall the earlier discussion that the schema for being a scientist is associated with males. Language with a masculine bias might reinforce beliefs about gender roles (Gastil, 1990).

(a)

(b)

FIGURE 8.31
Relative Importance of Snow
According to Whorf, **(a)** the Inuit may have developed many words for snow because different kinds of snow have played such important parts in their daily lives. **(b)** People in warmer climates do not need such an intricate snow-related vocabulary.

 Q What is aphasia, and damage to which hemisphere is most likely to cause it?

ANSWER: Aphasia is a deficit in language production or comprehension caused most often by injury to the left hemisphere.

8.10 Language Develops in an Orderly Way

As the brain develops, so does the ability to speak and form sentences. Thus, as children develop social skills, they also improve their language skills. There is some variation in the rate at which language develops, but overall the stages of language development are remarkably similar across individuals. According to Michael Tomasello (1999), the early social interactions between infant and caregiver are essential to understanding other people and being able to communicate with them through language. Research has demonstrated that infants and caregivers attend to objects in their environment together and that this joint attention promotes learning to speak (Baldwin, 1991; **FIGURE 8.32**). Children understand that speakers are usually thinking about what they are looking at (Bloom, 2002).

LEARNING PHONEMES Newborns are already well on their way to learning how to use language (Kuhl, 2004; Werker, Gilbert, Humphrey, & Tees, 1981). Janet Werker and colleagues (Byers-Heinlein, Burns, & Werker, 2010) found that the language or languages spoken by mothers during pregnancy influenced listening preferences in newborns. Canadian newborns whose mothers spoke only English during pregnancy showed a robust preference for sentences in English compared with sentences in Tagalog, a major language of the Philippines. Newborns of mothers who spoke

linguistic relativity theory
The claim that language determines thought.

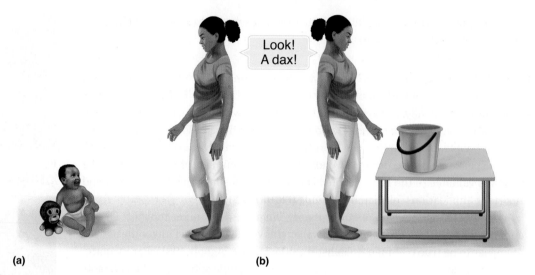

FIGURE 8.32
Joint Attention
Early interactions with caregivers lay the groundwork for children's acquisition of language.
(a) If the parent is looking at the toy when saying a new name, "dax," the child will assign the name "dax" to the toy. **(b)** If the parent is looking at something else when saying the new name, the child will not assign the name "dax" to the toy.

Tagalog and English during pregnancy paid attention to both languages. The latter finding implies that these newborns had sufficient bilingual exposure as fetuses to learn about each language before birth.

Patricia Kuhl and colleagues (Kuhl, 2006; Kuhl, Tsao, & Liu, 2003; Kuhl et al., 2006) found that up to six months of age, a baby can discriminate all the phonemes that occur in all languages, even if the sounds do not occur in the language spoken in the baby's home. For example, the distinction between the sounds /r/ and /l/ is important in English: *River* means something different from *liver*. The Japanese language does not distinguish those sounds, but it makes distinctions that English does not make. After several months of exposure to their own language, infants lose the ability to distinguish between sounds that do not matter in their language (Kuhl, 2004). Japanese infants eventually lose the ability to differentiate /r/ from /l/, which makes learning English as a second language challenging for them, as they need to learn to detect the differences in these phonemes (Bradlow, Pisoni, Akahane-Yamada, & Tohkura, 1997).

FROM 0 TO 60,000 From hearing differences between sounds immediately after birth and then learning the sounds of their own languages, young children go on to develop the ability to speak. Humans appear to go from babbling as babies to employing a full vocabulary of about 60,000 words as adults without working very hard at it.

Speech production follows a distinct path. During the first months of life, newborns' actions—crying, fussing, eating, and breathing—generate all their sounds. In other words, babies' first verbal sounds are cries, gurgles, grunts, and breaths. From three to five months, they begin to coo and laugh. From five to seven months, they begin babbling, using consonants and vowels. From seven to eight months, they babble in syllables (*ba-ba-ba, dee-dee-dee*). By the first year, infants around the world are saying their first words. These first words are typically labels of items in their environment (*kitty, cracker*), simple action words (*go, up, sit*), quantifiers (*all gone! more!*), qualities or adjectives (*hot*), socially interactive words (*bye, hello, yes, no*), and even internal states (*boo-boo* after being hurt; Pinker, 1984). Thus, even very young children use words to perform a wide range of communicative functions. They name, comment, request, and more.

By about 18 to 24 months, children begin to put words together. Their vocabularies start to grow rapidly. Rudimentary sentences of roughly two words emerge. Though they are missing words and grammatical markings, these mini-sentences have a logic, or syntax. Typically, the words' order indicates what has happened or should happen: for example, *Throw ball. All gone* translates as *I threw the ball, and now it's gone.* The psychologist Roger Brown, often referred to as the father of child language for his pioneering research, called these utterances **telegraphic speech.** The telegraph, discontinued in 2006, was a form of electronic communication that used coded signals. Telegraphic speech involves the use of rudimentary sentences that are missing words and grammatical markers but follow a logical syntax and convey a wealth of meaning. So when these children speak as if sending a telegram, they are putting together barebones words according to conventional rules (Brown, 1973).

OVERGENERALIZATIONS As children begin to use language in more-sophisticated ways, one relatively rare but telling error they make is to overapply new grammar rules they learn. Children may start to make mistakes at ages 3 to 5 with words they used correctly at age 2 or 3. For example, when they learn that adding *-ed* makes a verb past tense, they then add *-ed* to every verb, including irregular verbs that do not follow that rule. Thus they may say "runned" or "holded" even though they may have said "ran" or "held" at a younger age. Similarly, they may overapply the rule to add *–s* to form a plural, saying "mouses" and "mans," even if they said "mice" and "men" at a younger age.

Like many "immature" skills children exhibit as they develop, such overgeneralizations reflect an important aspect of language acquisition. Children are not simply repeating what they have heard others say. After all, they most likely have not heard anyone say "runned." Instead, these errors occur because children are able to use language effectively by perceiving patterns in spoken grammar and then applying rules to new sentences they have never heard before (Marcus, 1996). They make more errors with words used less frequently (such as *drank* and *knew*) because they have heard irregular forms of words less often. Adults tend to do the same thing, but they are more likely to make errors on the past tenses of words they do not use often, such as saying "treaded" for *trod* (Pinker, 1994).

Before 18 months of age, how does an infant typically speak?

telegraphic speech

The tendency for toddlers to speak using rudimentary sentences that are missing words and grammatical markings but follow a logical syntax and convey a wealth of meaning.

ANSWER: in single words. It is not until after this age that children begin to string words together.

8.11 There Is an Inborn Capacity for Language

Behaviorists such as B. F. Skinner (1957) proposed that children learn language the same way a rat learns to press a lever to obtain food: through a system of operant reinforcement. According to Skinner, children are reinforced for correctly repeating what their parents say. Speech that is not reinforced by parents is extinguished. Parents use learning principles such as shaping to help children refine their use of language.

But language acquisition does not work this way (Pinker & Bloom, 1990). Studies reveal that parents do not correct children's grammatical errors, nor do they constantly repeat words and phrases to their children. Parents correct young children if the content of what they say is wrong but not if the grammar is wrong (Brown & Hanlon, 1970; **FIGURE 8.33**). Furthermore, people do not need to see or hear language to learn it. For instance, deaf and blind children can still acquire language. Children also learn language much too quickly for behaviorist theories to make sense.

FIGURE 8.33
Teaching Language
Parents introduce young children to words and help them understand language, but they do not teach language using operant reinforcement.

The linguist Noam Chomsky (1959) transformed the field of linguistics when he hypothesized that language must be governed by *universal grammar*. In other words, according to Chomsky, all languages are based on humans' innate knowledge of a set of universal and specifically linguistic elements and relationships.

Until Chomsky came on the scene, linguists had focused on analyzing language and identifying basic components of grammar. All languages include similar elements, such as nouns and verbs, but how those elements are arranged varies considerably across languages. In his early work, Chomsky argued that how people combine these elements to form sentences and convey meaning is only a language's **surface structure**: the sound and order of words. He introduced the concept of **deep structure**: the implicit meanings of sentences. For instance, *The fat cat chased the rat* implies that there is a cat, it is fat, and it chased the rat. *The rat was chased by the fat cat* implies the same ideas even though on the surface it is a different sentence.

Chomsky believes people automatically and unconsciously transform surface structure to deep structure—the meaning being conveyed. In fact, people remember a sentence's underlying meaning, not its surface structure. For example, you may not remember the exact words of someone who insulted you, but you will certainly recall the deep structure behind that person's meaning. According to Chomsky, humans are born with a *language acquisition device,* which contains universal grammar. This hypothetical neurological structure in the brain enables all humans to come into the world prepared to learn any language. With exposure to a specific cultural context, the synaptic connections in the brain start to narrow toward a deep and rich understanding of that cultural context's dominant language over all other languages (Kuhl, 2000).

ACQUIRING LANGUAGE WITH THE HANDS Suppose that the perception and production of sound are key to language acquisition. In that case, babies exposed to signed languages should acquire these languages differently than babies who acquire spoken languages. Now suppose instead that language, signed or spoken, is a special form of communication because of its highly systematic patterns and the human brain's sensitivity to them. In that case, babies should acquire signed languages and spoken languages in highly similar ways.

To test this hypothesis, Laura-Ann Petitto and her students videotaped deaf babies of deaf parents in households using two entirely different signed languages: American Sign Language (ASL) and the signed language of Quebec, langue des signes québécoise (LSQ). They found that deaf babies exposed to signed languages from birth acquire these languages on an identical maturational timetable as hearing babies acquire spoken languages (Petitto, 2000; **FIGURE 8.34**). For example, deaf babies will "babble" with their hands. Just as hearing infants will repeat sounds such as *da da da,* which are not actually spoken words, deaf infants will repeat imitative hand movements that do not represent actual signs in signed languages.

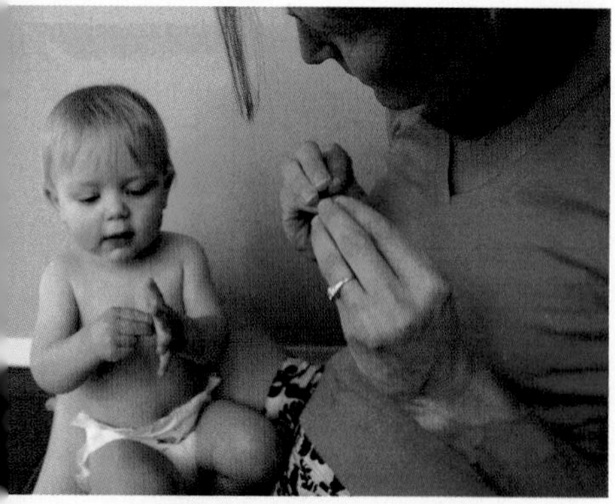

In demonstrating that speech does not drive all human language acquisition, this research shows that humans must possess a biologically endowed sensitivity to perceive and organize aspects of language patterns. This sensitivity launches a baby into the course of acquiring language.

SOCIAL AND CULTURAL INFLUENCES Of course, environment greatly influences a child's acquisition of language. Indeed, the fact that you speak English rather than (or in addition to) Swahili is determined entirely by your environment. Interaction across cultures also shapes language. The term *creole* describes a language that evolves over time from the mixing of existing languages (**FIGURE 8.35**). For example, a creole language may develop when a culture colonizes a place, as when the French established themselves in southern Louisiana and had to communicate with people

surface structure
In language, the sound and order of words.

deep structure
In language, the implicit meanings of sentences.

FIGURE 8.34
Acquiring Signed Language
Deaf infants have been shown to acquire signed languages at the same rates that hearing infants acquire spoken languages.

who did not speak French. The creole develops out of rudimentary communications, as populations that speak several languages attempt to understand each other. Often, the people mix words from each other's languages into a *pidgin,* an informal creole that lacks consistent grammatical rules.

The linguist Derek Bickerton (1998) has found that the children impose rules on their parents' pidgin, developing it into a creole. Bickerton argues that this is evidence for built-in, universal grammar. In other words, the brain changes a nonconforming language by applying the same basic rules to it. Bickerton has also found that creoles formed in different parts of the world, with different combinations of languages, are more similar to each other in grammatical structure than to long-lived languages.

ANIMAL LANGUAGE Nonhuman animals have ways of communicating with each other, but no other animal uses language the way humans do (Zuberbühler, 2015). Scientists have tried for years to teach language to chimpanzees, one of the species most closely related to humans. It was long believed that chimps lack the vocal ability to speak aloud, although recent evidence indicates that some nonhuman primates do have vocal tracts capable of producing speech (Fitch, de Boer, Mathur, & Ghazanfar, 2016). Researchers, however, have been unsuccessful in coaxing speech out of nonhuman primates, and therefore studies have used sign language or visual cues to determine whether they understand words or concepts such as causation.

Consider the work of the psychologists Herbert Terrace, Laura-Ann Petitto, and Tom Bever. To test Noam Chomsky's assertion that language is a uniquely human trait, these researchers attempted to teach American Sign Language to a chimpanzee. In honor of Chomsky, they named the chimp Neam Chimpsky. His nickname was Nim **(FIGURE 8.36)**.

After years of teaching Nim, the team admitted that Chomsky might be right. Like all other language-trained chimps, Nim consistently failed to master key components of human language syntax. While he was adept at communicating with a small set of basic signs ("eat," "play," "more"), he never acquired the ability to generate creative, rule-governed sentences. He was like a broken record, talking about the same thing over and over again in the same old way. As previously discussed, a young child can name, comment, request, and more with his or her first words. Nim and all the ASL-trained chimps used bits and pieces of language almost exclusively to make requests. They wanted things (food, more food) from their caretakers, but otherwise they were not able to express meanings, thoughts, and ideas by generating language (Petitto & Seidenberg, 1979).

Other research projects have found more support for the idea that nonhuman animals can learn and use language. For instance, there is some evidence that nonprimates such as orangutans can imitate humans by controlling their vocal cords (Lameira et al., 2016). Most of the evidence supporting nonhuman language, however, involves symbols to represent information. Kanzi, a bonobo ape, learned to use geometric shapes to represent words. He acquired several hundred words in this way and could use them in many different combinations. His spontaneous use of the symbols generally followed the rules of language. Kanzi was also quite good at following human verbal commands. Researchers gave him 660 commands, including novel ones such as "Hide the toy gorilla" and "Put on the monster mask and scare Linda." Kanzi successfully performed 72 percent of these requests (Savage-Rumbaugh, Shanker, & Taylor, 1998).

In separate research, a parrot named Alex displayed a relatively sophisticated use of human language (Pepperberg, 2010). Alex could use about 150 words, categorize and count objects, and describe the color of objects that were not physically present.

FIGURE 8.35
Creole Language
A creole language evolves from a mixing of languages. In Suriname, where this boy is reading a classroom blackboard, over 10 languages are spoken. The official language, Dutch, comes from the nation's colonial background. The other tongues include variants of Chinese, Hindi, Javanese, and half a dozen original creoles, among them Sranan Tongo (literally, "Suriname tongue").

FIGURE 8.36
Laura-Ann Petitto with Nim Chimpsky

He appeared able to express frustration, and he could indicate that he was bored by saying, "Wanna go back." Alex died in 2007, but Irene Pepperberg continues to study language and cognition with other parrots, such as in the recent demonstration that a parrot named Griffin has a sophisticated conceptual understanding of object shape (Pepperberg & Nakayama, 2016).

Many researchers remain enthusiastic about the possibility of using language to communicate with nonhuman animals. Still, learning to use symbols requires intensive training involving social interaction, and nonhuman animals seem unable to develop skills beyond those of human toddlers (Griebel, Pepperberg, & Oller, 2016).

Q In terms of surface structure and deep structure, how do the sentences *James yelled at John* and *John was yelled at by James* compare?

ANSWER: They differ in surface structure because they look different, but they are the same in deep structure because they mean the same thing—in both cases, the same person is yelling.

8.12 Reading Needs to Be Learned

Reading, like speaking, is nearly effortless for most adults. When we look at letters grouped into words, we automatically derive meaning from these groupings, even if they are misspelled. As noted in Chapter 5, Y0U C4N R3AD TH15 PR377Y W3LL even though it is nonsensical.

But what is the best method for teaching reading—that is, enabling readers to comprehend the words they process? And what happens when the cognitive processes involved in reading do not work properly?

In the English-speaking world, there are two major schools of thought regarding how to teach reading. Traditional methods use **phonics,** which teaches an association between letters and their phonemes. Children learn to make the appropriate sounds for the letters, then spell out words by how they sound (**FIGURE 8.37**). They learn a small number of simple words that teach the sounds of letters across most words of the English language. Because of the irregularities in English, children first learn the general rules and then learn to recognize exceptions to those rules. This approach emphasizes memorizing the mappings between letters and their sounds, rather than on building vocabulary or processing words' meanings.

Because of the complexity of the English language, in which the sounds of letters can vary across words, some educators have advocated **whole language** approaches. These approaches emphasize learning the meanings of words and understanding how words are connected in sentences. Whole language has dominated in most American schools for the past three decades. This popularity may be partly due to the philosophy behind the approach, which emphasizes student interest, enjoyment of reading, creativity, and thought.

The general idea behind whole language instruction is that children should learn to read the way they learn to talk. We do not process speech by breaking the sound stream into phonemes. Instead, we understand speech as a series of connected words that have meaning in the context of the entire sentence. Thus, according to whole language proponents, breaking words into sounds is unnatural, frustrating, and boring. Instead, students should learn to read naturally and unconsciously, by learning individual words and then stringing them together. But does whole language do a better job than phonics in helping children learn to read?

Classroom and laboratory research has consistently found that phonics is superior to whole language in creating proficient readers (Rayner,

phonics
A method of teaching reading in English that focuses on the association between letters and their phonemes.

whole language
A method of teaching reading in English that emphasizes learning the meanings of words and understanding how words are connected in sentences.

FIGURE 8.37
Using Phonics
In learning to read, these children are combining phonemes into morphemes.

Foorman, Perfetti, Pesetsky, & Seidenberg, 2001; Rayner, Pollatsek, Ashby, & Clifton, 2012). This result applies especially to children who are at risk of becoming poor readers, such as those whose parents do not read to them on a regular basis. Whole language motivates students to read, but phonics best teaches basic reading skills.

DYSLEXIA Although reading may happen automatically once you learn to do it, the process of learning to read is challenging for many people. These learners struggle to figure out which symbols are letters, which letters are clumped into words, and which words go together to make meaningful sentences. Sometimes this difficulty is the result of a reading disorder called *dyslexia*. People with dyslexia have trouble reading, spelling, and writing even though they have normal levels of intelligence. A recent meta-analysis of 21 studies found that children who develop dyslexia have more difficulty acquiring language as infants and toddlers, particularly with the ability to identify and use phonemes (Snowling & Melby-Lervåg, 2016). According to the overall evidence, the inability to hear, identify, and use phonemes is a central problem for those with dyslexia (Melby-Lervåg, Lyster, & Hulme, 2012).

What causes dyslexia? The condition may result from impaired sound and image processing, especially for words that rhyme (Temple et al., 2001). Dyslexia appears to run in families, so there may be a strong genetic component to it (Olson, 2011). However, rates of dyslexia tend to be higher in inner-city samples than in rural samples, so environment appears to be a factor, and factors such as parental education may play a role.

 How is the whole language approach to teaching reading better or worse than the phonics approach?

ANSWER: Whole language may be better at motivating students to read, but phonics reliably produces better reading.

How Do We Understand Intelligence?

So far, this chapter has considered how people use knowledge and language when they think. Now it is time to consider what it means to think *intelligently*.

Sometimes thought processes lead to great ideas and creative discoveries, but other times they lead to bad decisions and regret. Inevitably, some people seem to be better at using knowledge than others. When people are good at using knowledge, we say they are intelligent. Thus, **intelligence** is the ability to use knowledge to reason, make decisions, make sense of events, solve problems, understand complex ideas, learn quickly, and adapt to environmental challenges.

Think for a minute about that last skill: adapting to environmental challenges. Because environments differ, environmental challenges can differ. Someone considered intelligent in an industrialized nation may struggle to survive in the jungle, where being able to judge weather, identify local hazards, and find and prepare food are better indicators of intelligence. Do these differences mean that intelligence reflects environment? What exactly is intelligence? Psychologists have long struggled to define intelligence, and disagreement continues about what it means to be intelligent.

Psychological research generally focuses on two questions: How do knowledge and its applications in everyday life translate into intelligence? And how much is intelligence determined by genes and by environment (Neisser et al., 1996)?

intelligence
The ability to use knowledge to reason, make decisions, make sense of events, solve problems, understand complex ideas, learn quickly, and adapt to environmental challenges.

Learning Objectives

- Identify common measures of intelligence and discuss their validity.

- Review theories and research related to general intelligence, fluid intelligence, crystallized intelligence, and multiple intelligences.

- Discuss the relationship between intelligence and cognitive performance.

- Summarize research examining genetic and environmental influences on intelligence.

- Discuss sex and race differences in intelligence, and define stereotype threat.

8.13 Intelligence Is Measured with Standardized Tests

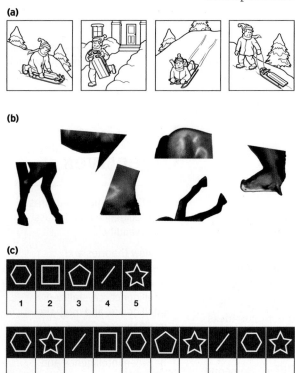

FIGURE 8.38
Alfred Binet
Binet launched the psychometric approach to assessing intelligence.

The *psychometric* approach to measuring intelligence focuses on how people perform on standardized tests that assess mental abilities. These tests examine what people know and how they solve problems. For much of the past century, the psychometric approach to intelligence has been dominant and influential. This approach has especially affected how we view intelligence in everyday life, at least within industrialized nations.

One type of standardized test focuses on achievement. The other type focuses on aptitude. *Achievement tests* assess people's current levels of skill and of knowledge. *Aptitude tests* seek to predict what tasks, and perhaps even what jobs, people will be good at in the future. For both kinds of tests, the stakes can be high. People's performances can hugely affect their lives.

The psychometric measurement of intelligence began just over a century ago. At the encouragement of the French government, the psychologist Alfred Binet developed a method of assessing intelligence (**FIGURE 8.38**). Binet's goal was to identify children in the French school system who needed extra attention and special instruction. He proposed that intelligence is best understood as a collection of high-level mental processes. Accordingly, with the help of his assistant Théodore Simon, Binet developed a test for measuring each child's vocabulary, memory, skill with numbers, and other mental abilities. The result was the Binet-Simon Intelligence Scale. One assumption underlying the test was that each child might do better on some components by chance, but how the child performed on average across the different components would indicate his or her overall level of intelligence. Indeed, Binet found that scores on his tests were consistent with teachers' beliefs about children's abilities *and* with the children's grades.

In 1919, the psychologist Lewis Terman, at Stanford University, modified the Binet-Simon test and established normative scores for American children (average scores for each age). This test—the Stanford Revision of the Binet-Simon Scale, known colloquially as the Stanford-Binet—remains the most widely used test for children in the United States. In 2003, it was revised for the fifth time.

In 1939, the psychologist David Wechsler developed an intelligence test for adults. Not only was the Stanford-Binet unsuitable for adults, but Wechsler was dissatisfied with various features of that scale, including its reliance on verbal information and its assessment of intelligence by a single score. The Wechsler Adult Intelligence Scale (WAIS)—the most current version being the WAIS-IV, released in 2008—has two parts. Each part consists of several tasks that provide separate scores. The verbal part measures aspects such as comprehension ("Why do people buy home insurance?"), vocabulary ("What does *corrupt* mean?"), and general knowledge ("What day of the year is Independence Day in the United States?"). It also includes tests of working memory, such as short-term memory capacity. The performance part involves nonverbal tasks, such as arranging pictures in proper order, assembling parts to make a whole object, identifying a picture's missing features, and measures of reaction time (**FIGURE 8.39**).

FIGURE 8.39
IQ Test Items Measuring Performance
The performance part of IQ tests includes nonverbal tasks. Here are some examples similar to items used in the WAIS III. **(a)** Picture arrangement: These pictures tell a story. Put them in the right order to tell the story. **(b)** Object assembly: If these pieces are put together correctly, they make something. Put them together as fast as you can. **(c)** Digit-symbol substitution: Using the code provided, fill in the missing information in the test picture.

INTELLIGENCE QUOTIENT Binet noticed that some children seem to think like children younger or older than themselves. To assess a child's intellectual standing compared with the standing of same-age peers, Binet introduced the important concept of **mental age.** This measure is determined by comparing the child's test score with the average score for children of each chronological age. For instance, an 8-year-old who is able to read Shakespeare and do calculus might score as well as an average 16-year-old. This 8-year-old would have a mental age of 16.

The **intelligence quotient (IQ),** developed by the psychologist Wilhelm Stern, is partly based on mental age. IQ is computed by dividing a child's estimated mental age by the child's chronological age and multiplying the result by 100. To calculate the IQ of the 8-year-old with a mental age of 16, we calculate $16/8 \times 100$. The result is 200, an extraordinarily high score.

The formula breaks down when used with adults, however, so the IQs of adults are measured differently. According to the standard formula, a 60-year-old would need to get twice as many test items correct as a 30-year-old to have the same IQ. Instead, IQ in the adult range is measured in comparison with the average adult and not with adults at different ages. Today, the average IQ is set at 100. Across large groups of people, the distribution of IQ scores forms a bell curve, or *normal distribution.* Most people are close to the average, and fewer and fewer people score at the tails of the distribution. A person's IQ is considered in terms of deviation from the average (**FIGURE 8.40**).

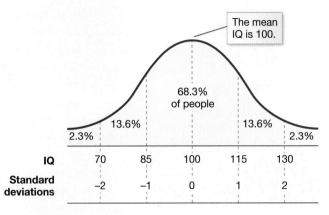

FIGURE 8.40
The Distribution of IQ Scores
IQ is a score on a normed test of intelligence. That is, one person's score is relative to the scores of the large number of people who already took the test. And as discussed in Chapter 2, the statistical concept of standard deviation indicates how far people are from an average. The standard deviation for most IQ tests is 15. The average, or mean, is 100. As shown in this bell-shaped curve, approximately 68 percent of people fall within 1 standard deviation of the mean (they score from 85 to 115). Just over 95 percent of people fall within 2 standard deviations (they score from 70 to 130).

VALIDITY OF TESTING Are intelligence tests reliable and valid? That is, are they stable over time, and do they really measure what they claim to measure? In terms of reliability, there is considerable evidence that a person's performance on an intelligence test at one time corresponds highly to the person's performance at another time (Matarazzo, Carmody, & Jacobs, 1980).

To evaluate the validity of tests, we need to consider what it means to be intelligent. If the word means doing well at school or at a complex career, intelligence tests perform reasonably well: The overall evidence indicates that IQ is a fairly good predictor of such life outcomes (Gottfredson, 2004b).

To explore the validity of intelligence tests, researchers analyzed data from 127 studies in which more than 20,000 participants took the Miller Analogy Test. This test is widely used for admissions decisions into graduate school as well as for hiring decisions in many work settings. It requires test takers to complete analogies such as "Fingers are to hands as toes are to ____." The researchers found that scores on the Miller Analogy Test predicted not only graduate students' academic performances but also individuals' productivity, creativity, and job performances in the workplace (Kuncel, Hezlett, & Ones, 2004). Similarly, people in professional careers—such as attorneys, accountants, and engineers—tend to have high IQs, while those who work as miners, farmers, lumberjacks, and barbers tend to have lower IQs (Jencks, 1979; Schmidt & Hunter, 2004). These statistics refer to averages, of course, not to individuals. Still, the data suggest modest correlations between IQ and work performance, IQ and income, and IQ and jobs requiring complex skills. Although higher IQ does not predict who will be a better truck driver, it predicts who will be a better computer programmer (Schmidt & Hunter, 2004).

mental age
An assessment of a child's intellectual standing compared with that of same-age peers; determined by comparing the child's test score with the average score for children of each chronological age.

intelligence quotient (IQ)
An index of intelligence computed by dividing a child's estimated mental age by the child's chronological age, then multiplying this number by 100.

When considering these findings, note that IQ scores typically predict only about 25 percent of the variation in performance at either school or work, so additional factors contribute to individuals' success (Neisser et al., 1996). In the late 1800s, the scientist Sir Francis Galton believed that to become eminent in a field—that is, to become an expert—required not only innate ability but also zeal and willingness to work long hours (see Ericsson, Krampe, & Tesch-Römer, 1993). One study found that children's self-control, assessed through teacher and parent reports as well as laboratory tasks, was much better than IQ in predicting final grades (Duckworth & Seligman, 2005).

People from privileged backgrounds tend to have higher IQs. They also tend to have other advantages. Family contacts, access to internships, and acceptance to schools that can cater to their needs may help determine their success. In other words, IQ may be important, but it is only one of the factors that contribute to success in the classroom, the workplace, and life generally. We will consider the importance of other environmental features in greater detail shortly.

Q Suppose a 2-year-old child is able to perform at a level of a 4-year-old on the Stanford-Binet. What is the 2-year-old's mental age and IQ score?

ANSWER: The mental age is 4, and the IQ is 200, because the formula for IQ is mental age (4) divided by chronological age (2) and multiplied by 100.

8.14 General Intelligence Involves Multiple Components

Binet viewed intelligence as a general ability. We all know people, however, who are especially talented in some areas but weak in others. For example, some people write brilliant poems but cannot solve difficult calculus problems—or at least they feel more confident doing one than doing the other. The question, then, is whether intelligence reflects one overall talent or many individual ones. An early line of research examined the correlations among intelligence test items using *factor analysis*. In this statistical technique, items similar to one another are clustered. The clusters are called factors.

Using this type of analysis, Charles Spearman (1904) found that most intelligence test items tended to cluster as one factor. People who scored highly on one type of item also tended to score highly on other types of items. In general, people who are very good at math are also good at writing, problem solving, and other mental challenges. Spearman viewed **general intelligence (g)** as a factor that contributes to performance on any intellectual task (**FIGURE 8.41**). In a sense, providing a single IQ score reflects the idea that one general factor underlies intelligence. At the same time, Spearman acknowledged that people could differ in the *specific skills (s)* that enabled them to perform better on some tasks than on others.

FLUID VERSUS CRYSTALLIZED INTELLIGENCE Raymond Cattell (1971) proposed that g consists of two types of intelligence. **Fluid intelligence** is being able to understand abstract relationships and think logically without prior knowledge. It involves information processing, especially in novel or complex circumstances, such as reasoning, drawing analogies, and thinking quickly and flexibly. In contrast, **crystallized intelligence** involves knowledge acquired through experience, such as vocabulary and cultural information, and the ability to use this knowledge to solve problems (Horn, 1968; Horn & McArdle, 2007).

Distinguishing between fluid intelligence and crystallized intelligence is somewhat analogous to distinguishing between working memory (which is more like fluid intelligence) and long-term memory (which is more like crystallized intelligence). As

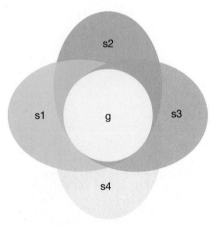

g = general intelligence

s1 = a specific ability (e.g., math)

s2 = a second specific ability (e.g., writing)

s3 = a third specific ability (e.g., problem solving)

s4 = a fourth specific ability (e.g., drawing)

FIGURE 8.41
General Intelligence as a Factor
As depicted in this cluster of overlapping ovals and circle, Spearman viewed g as a general factor in intelligence. This underlying factor influences an individual's specific abilities related to intelligence.

would be expected because both types of intelligence are components of g, people who score highly on one factor also tend to score highly on the other. This finding suggests that a strong crystallized intelligence is likely aided by a strong fluid intelligence. As you will see in Chapter 9, crystallized intelligence grows steadily throughout the adult years, while fluid intelligence declines steadily.

THE IMPORTANCE OF G Research has shown that g influences important life outcomes, such as by predicting performance in school and at work (Conway, Kane, & Engle, 2003; Deary, 2001; Garlick, 2002; Gray & Thompson, 2004; Haier, Jung, Yeo, Head, & Alkire, 2005). Low g is related to early death from causes including heart disease, diabetes, stroke, Alzheimer's disease, traffic accidents, and drownings (Gottfredson, 2004a; Gottfredson & Deary, 2004). One study followed Scottish people for 55 years, starting when they were schoolchildren, and examined the influence of intelligence and a personality variable related to emotional intelligence (emotional intelligence is described in the next section). Those who scored in the lower half on both measures were more than twice as likely to die over the next half century compared with those who scored in the top half on both measures (Deary, Batty, Pattie, & Gale, 2008).

These patterns might result from the different environmental forces at work on each of us. For example, people who do not perform well in academic settings may end up with dangerous jobs, people with less dangerous and/or better-paying jobs tend to have better access to health care, and so on. Indeed, it is possible that factors other than intelligence are responsible for early death. A study that followed people from age 10 until age 75 found that the more education people received, the longer they lived, independent of their IQ level (Lager, Bremberg, & Vågerö, 2009).

According to Linda Gottfredson (2004a), however, g may directly affect health. People who score higher on intelligence tests may generally be more literate about health issues: accumulating greater health knowledge, better able to follow medical advice, better able to understand the link between behavior and health. As medical knowledge rapidly advances and becomes more complex, trying to keep up with and process all this new information is a challenge, and people who are higher in g have an advantage in doing so. This provocative idea warrants further investigation. If it is true, it has a number of important implications for the medical system and the way doctors communicate medical advice.

MULTIPLE INTELLIGENCES Whereas Cattell argued that two types of intelligence contribute to g, other researchers have described various types of intelligence. For example, Howard Gardner (1983) proposed that people can be intelligent in any number of ways, such as being musically or athletically talented. According to Gardner, each person has a unique pattern of intelligences, and no one should be viewed as smarter than others—just differently talented. This view strikes some psychologists as a feel-good philosophy with little basis in fact. Yet standard intelligence tests can fail to capture the types of people who are extremely "book smart" but have trouble in the real world because they lack practical sense or social skills. A good example of the brilliant but clueless type is the television character Sheldon Cooper, played by Jim Parsons in the television series *The Big Bang Theory* (**FIGURE 8.42**). Moreover, people can have high IQs but lack curiosity or drive.

Robert Sternberg (1999) has theorized that there are three types of intelligence: analytical, creative, and practical. *Analytical intelligence* is similar to that measured by psychometric tests—being good at problem solving, completing analogies, figuring out puzzles, and other academic challenges. *Creative intelligence* involves the ability to gain insight and solve novel problems—to think in new and interesting ways.

general intelligence (g)
The idea that one general factor underlies intelligence.

fluid intelligence
Intelligence that reflects the ability to process information, understand relationships, and think logically, particularly in novel or complex circumstances.

crystallized intelligence
Intelligence that reflects both the knowledge acquired through experience and the ability to use that knowledge.

FIGURE 8.42
Brilliant but Clueless
On *The Big Bang Theory,* Sheldon Cooper is undeniably smart, yet he has trouble dealing with people. Perhaps part of Sheldon's problem is a lack of emotional intelligence (discussed below).

"I don't have to be smart, because someday I'll just hire lots of smart people to work for me."

Practical intelligence refers to dealing with everyday tasks, such as knowing whether a parking space is large enough for your vehicle, being a good judge of people, being an effective leader, and so on. Although this differentiation makes intuitive sense, some intelligence researchers have been critical, suggesting that the available evidence does not support Sternberg's model (Gottfredson, 2003).

The fictional Sheldon Cooper has great difficulty with social relations and understanding his friends' emotional expressions and gestures. In terms of the social domain, he would not be considered intelligent. **Emotional intelligence (EI)** consists of four abilities: managing one's emotions, using one's own emotions to guide thoughts and actions, recognizing other people's emotions, and understanding emotional language (Salovey & Grewel, 2005; Salovey & Mayer, 1990). People high in EI recognize emotional experiences in themselves and others, then respond to those emotions productively.

Emotional intelligence is correlated with the quality of social relationships (Reis et al., 2007). The idea of emotional intelligence has had a large impact in schools and industry, and programs have been designed to increase students' and workers' emotional intelligence. These efforts may be valuable, since emotional intelligence is a good predictor of high school grades (Hogan et al., 2010), and those high in emotional intelligence cope best with the challenges of college exams (Austin, Saklofske, & Mastoras, 2010). At the same time, some critics have questioned whether EI really is a type of intelligence or whether it stretches the definition of intelligence too far. A recent review found evidence that EI is correlated with more-traditional measures of intelligence, as well as academic performance among children and workplace performance among senior executives (Brackett, Rivers, & Salovey, 2011). The concept highlights the idea that many human qualities are important. Whether or not EI is a type of intelligence, it is advantageous for those who have it.

 Is the ability to do well at trivia contests related to fluid intelligence or crystallized intelligence?

ANSWER: crystallized intelligence, which involves learned knowledge—as opposed to fluid intelligence, which is the ability to think logically about abstract concepts without any previous knowledge

8.15 Intelligence Is Related to Cognitive Performance

Francis Galton led one of the earliest efforts to scientifically study intelligence. Galton believed that intelligence was related to the speed of neural responses and the sensitivity of the sensory/perceptual systems. The smartest people, Galton believed, had the quickest responses and the keenest perceptions. Galton also speculated that intelligent people have larger, more efficient brains. According to Galton, intelligence was related to the efficiency of the brain as well as to keen perceptual skills. Other psychologists believe intelligence is supported by low-level cognitive functions, such as mental processing, working memory, and attention. But can we equate these types of cognitive performance with intelligence? What brain processes are involved in producing intelligence?

emotional intelligence (EI)

A form of social intelligence that emphasizes the abilities to manage, recognize, and understand emotions and use emotions to guide appropriate thought and action.

SPEED OF MENTAL PROCESSING People who are not very intelligent are sometimes described as "a bit slow." That description might be accurate, because people who score higher on intelligence tests respond more quickly and consistently on reaction time tests than those who score lower on intelligence tests (Deary, 2000). A test of *simple reaction time* might require a person to press a computer key as quickly as possible whenever a stimulus appears on the screen—for example, "Press the X key every time you see an X." A more difficult test might require a person to choose, again as quickly as possible, the right response for the stimulus presented—for example, "Press the X key every time you see an X, press the A key every time you see an A, and so on." Scores on intelligence tests are related even more strongly to this *choice reaction time* (Jensen, 1998).

Further support for the relationship between general intelligence and speed of mental processing comes from *inspection time* tests. If a stimulus is presented and then covered up, how much viewing time does a particular person need to answer a question about the stimulus (**FIGURE 8.43**)? People who need very little time for this task tend to score higher on psychometric tests of intelligence (Deary, 2001). In addition, by measuring the electrical activity of brains in response to the presentation of stimuli, researchers have found that highly intelligent people's brains work faster than less intelligent people's brains.

The relationship between general intelligence and mental speed appears to be correlated with the greater longevity of people with high IQs. According to a longitudinal study led by Ian Deary, those higher in intelligence and those who had faster reaction times at age 56 were much less likely to die in the next 14 years (Deary & Der, 2005). This outcome was true even after factors such as smoking, social class, and education were controlled for. The relationship between reaction time and longevity was somewhat stronger than the relationship between scores on standardized intelligence tests and longevity. A recent 15-year follow-up study of over 5,000 Americans found that the relationship between slower reaction times and premature death was comparable in size to established health risk factors such as smoking (Hagger-Johnson, Deary, Davies, Weiss, & Batty, 2014).

WORKING MEMORY General intelligence scores are closely related to how people process information in working memory (Conway et al., 2003). The two are not identical, however (Ackerman, Beier, & Boyle, 2005). As discussed in Chapter 7, working memory is the active processing system that holds information for use in activities such as reasoning, comprehension, and problem solving. In that capacity, working memory might be related to intelligence (Kyllonen & Christal, 1990; Süß, Oberauer, Wittman, Wilhelm, & Schulze, 2002).

Many studies of the relationship between working memory and intelligence differentiate between simple tests of memory span and memory tests that require some form of secondary processing (**FIGURE 8.44**). Performance on a simpler test of memory, as in listening to a list of words and then repeating the list in the same order, is related weakly to general intelligence (Engle, Tuholski, Laughlin, & Conway, 1999). Memory tests that have dual components, however, show a strong relationship between working memory and general intelligence (Gray & Thompson, 2004; Kane, Hambrick, & Conway, 2005; Oberauer, Schulze, Wilhelm, & Süß, 2005).

The task is to determine whether side A or side B of the stimulus is longer. The stimulus is presented and then quickly followed by a mask.

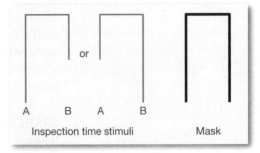

Judging the lengths is easy when you have enough time to view the stimulus but difficult when the mask decreases viewing time severely.

FIGURE 8.43
Inspection Time Tasks

For a simple *word span task,* a participant listens to a short list of words and then repeats the words in order.

For a more difficult *secondary processing task,* a participant has to solve simple mathematical operations at the same time the words are presented. Once again, the person has to repeat the words in the order they are presented (adapted from Conway et al., 2003).

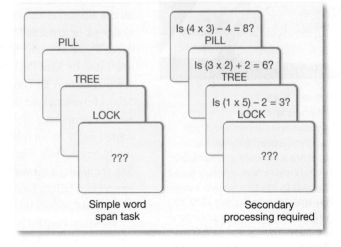

FIGURE 8.44
Memory Span Tasks

The link between working memory and general intelligence may be attention. In particular, being able to pay attention, especially while being bombarded with competing information or other distractions, allows a person to stick to a task until successfully completing it (Engle & Kane, 2004). The importance of staying focused makes great sense in light of the relationship, discussed earlier in this chapter, between general intelligence and the accomplishment of novel, complex tasks. The question, then, is whether brain regions that support working memory are involved in general intelligence. Let's consider the relationship between the brain and intelligence.

BRAIN STRUCTURE AND FUNCTION Intelligent people are sometimes called "brainy," but how are the brain and intelligence related? Many studies have documented a relationship between head circumference, which researchers use to estimate brain size, and scores on intelligence tests (Vernon, Wickett, Bazana, Stelmack, & Sternberg, 2000). Head circumference also predicts school performance, although the correlation is quite small (Ivanovic et al., 2004). Studies using brain imaging have found a small but significant correlation between the size of selected brain structures and scores on intelligence tests (Johnson, Jung, Colom, & Haier, 2008). These findings are correlations, however, so we cannot infer that brain size necessarily causes differences in intelligence.

Instead, the situation is more complicated. Different kinds of intelligence seem to be related to the sizes of certain brain regions (Basten, Hilgar, & Fiebach, 2015). These regions include ones associated with working memory, planning, reasoning, and problem solving. For example, studies have found that the volume of neuronal cell bodies (gray matter) in the frontal lobes and in other brain regions that support attentional control is related to fluid general intelligence (Frangou, Chitins, & Williams, 2004; Haier et al., 2005; Kamara et al., 2011; Wilke, Sohn, Byars, & Holland, 2003). Other studies have found no relationship between the volume of frontal gray matter and crystallized intelligence (Gong et al., 2005). These findings are consistent with evidence that injury to the frontal lobes causes impairments in fluid intelligence but not in crystallized intelligence (Duncan, Burgess, & Emslie, 1995). Because different regions of the brain support either fluid or crystallized intelligence, damage or abnormalities in a particular brain region may affect only some aspects of intelligence.

SAVANTS How would you like to be able to read a page of this textbook in 8 to 10 seconds? Perhaps less useful but even more impressive would be the ability to recite all the zip codes and area codes in the United States by the region to which they are assigned, or to name hundreds of classical music pieces just by hearing a few notes of each. These amazing abilities are just a few of the extraordinary memory feats demonstrated by Kim Peek (Treffert & Christensen, 2006). Peek, who died in 2008, was the inspiration for the character played by Dustin Hoffman in the 1988 movie *Rain Man*. He memorized the contents of over 9,000 books, but he could not button his own clothes or manage any of the usual chores of daily living, such as making change. He scored an 87 on an intelligence test, but this number did not adequately describe his intelligence. Peek was born, in 1951, with an enlarged head and many brain anomalies, including a missing corpus callosum, the thick band of nerves that connects the brain's two halves (see Figure 3.24). He also had abnormalities in several other parts of his brain, especially the left hemisphere.

We know very little about *savants* like Peek. Such people have minimal intellectual capacities in most domains, but at a very early age each savant shows an exceptional ability in some "intelligent" process. For example, a savant's exceptional ability may be related to math, music, or art. The combination of prodigious memory and the

FIGURE 8.45
Stephen Wiltshire
Despite having autism spectrum disorder, Stephen Wiltshire had published a book of his remarkably accurate, expressive, memory-based drawings by the time he was a young teenager. Here, in October 2010, he holds his drawing of an architectural site in London, England. Wiltshire observed the site briefly, then completed the picture largely from memory.

inability to learn seemingly basic tasks is a great mystery. Nonetheless, this rare combination adds a dimension to our understanding of intelligence.

Oliver Sacks (1995) recounts the story of Stephen Wiltshire, an artistic savant. Wiltshire has autism spectrum disorder (discussed further in Chapter 14, "Psychological Disorders"). In childhood, it took him the utmost effort to acquire language sufficient for simple verbal communication. Years after a single glance at a place, however, Wiltshire can draw a highly accurate picture of it (**FIGURE 8.45**).

What is the relation between IQ and speed of processing?

ANSWER: Those with high IQs tend to have quicker reaction times, especially on choice reaction time tests.

8.16 Genes and Environment Influence Intelligence

One of the most contentious battles in psychological science has been over the role of genes in determining intelligence. This battle exemplifies the nature/nurture debate. How much are individual differences in intelligence due to genes, and how much are they due to environment?

Nature and nurture are intertwined in the development of intelligence. For example, the capacity for having a large vocabulary is considerably heritable, but every word in a person's vocabulary is learned in an environment (Neisser et al., 1996). In addition, which words are learned is affected by the culture an individual is raised in, the amount of schooling she or he receives, and the general social context. So even if intelligence has a genetic component, the way intelligence becomes expressed is affected by various situational circumstances. Instead of seeking to demonstrate whether nature or nurture is the more important factor, psychologists try to identify how and in what way each of these crucial factors contributes to intelligence. Let's first look closely at genetics in relation to intelligence.

GENETIC FACTORS As discussed in Chapter 3, behavioral geneticists study the genetic basis of behaviors and traits such as intelligence. They use twin and adoption studies to estimate the extent to which particular traits are heritable. That is, they try to determine the portion of particular traits' variance that can be attributed to genes. Numerous behavioral genetics studies have made clear that genes help determine intelligence (Bouchard, 2014). For example, studies show that twins raised apart are highly similar in intelligence (**FIGURE 8.46**).

But are the genes people possess the whole story? Even when raised apart, twins who have inherited an advantage might receive some *social multiplier,* an environmental factor or an entire environment, that increases what might have started as a small advantage (Flynn, 2007). Suppose the twins have inherited a higher than average verbal ability. Adults who notice this ability might read to them more often and give them more books. The "intelligence gene" has eluded researchers, probably because thousands of genes contribute to intelligence and individually each has only a small effect (Plomin & Spinath, 2004). Indeed, one study that looked at a large number of gene differences across the genome concluded that about 40 percent of the variation in crystallized intelligence and 51 percent of the variation in fluid intelligence are due to genetic influence (Davies et al., 2011).

An additional possibility is that the expression of different genes is altered by environmental factors. As discussed in Chapter 3, epigenetics involves changes to gene expression rather than to DNA. The study of epigenetic processes may help

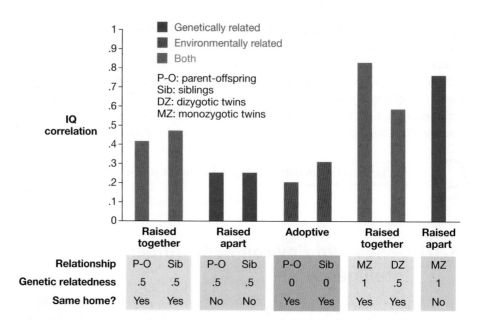

FIGURE 8.46
Genes and Intelligence
This graph represents average IQ correlations from family, adoption, and twin study designs. As shown by the red and blue bars on the left, siblings raised together show more similarity than siblings raised apart. As indicated by the relationships between parent and offspring (P-O) in the red and blue bars, a parent and child are more similar in IQ when the parent raises the child than when the child is raised by someone else. As shown by the red and blue bars on the right, the highest correlations are found among monozygotic twins, whether they are raised in the same household or not. Overall, the greater the degree of genetic relationship, the greater the correlation in intelligence.

(a)

(b)

FIGURE 8.47
Environmental Impacts
Within each of these planters, differences in the plants are likely due to genes. But note how different the plants are *as a whole* between one planter and the other. Those differences likely result from the environmental differences between the planters. **(a)** This planter has provided an impoverished environment. The poor conditions have negatively affected growth and development. **(b)** This planter has provided an enriched environment. The proper resources have contributed to robust growth and development.

researchers understand how factors such as diet might be related to intelligence through the alteration of gene expression (Haggarty et al., 2010). In the next section, we consider environmental factors that are potential triggers of epigenetic effects.

ENVIRONMENTAL FACTORS Richard Lewontin (1976) has provided an excellent example of the difficulties of contrasting groups of people who differ in their circumstances. Consider seeds planted in two separate containers (**FIGURE 8.47**). In one container, the soil is poor, and the seeds receive restricted water, few nutrients, and intermittent sunlight. In the other container, the soil is rich, and the seeds receive regular watering, all the necessary nutrients, and abundant sunlight. Within each planter, differences between individual plants' growth can be attributed to the seeds' genetic differences. After all, the environment is identical, so only genes can explain the differences. But in addition, as groups, the plants in one container will differ from those in the other container because of their different environments. The impoverished environment will stunt growth, whereas the enriched environment will help the seeds reach their potential.

Many environmental influences affect human intelligence. These influences consist of prenatal factors (e.g., parents' nutrition and intake of substances, including toxins) and postnatal factors (e.g., family, social class, education, nutrition, cultural beliefs about the value of education, and the person's intake of substances, including toxins). Each factor is likely to exert an independent influence during development. For instance, breast-feeding during infancy has been shown to enhance intellectual development (Mortensen, Michaelsen, Sanders, & Reinisch, 2002), and children who are breast-fed show higher IQ scores thirty years later (Victora et al., 2015). In an experimental study, more than 17,000 infants from 31 maternity hospitals in Belarus were randomly assigned to either a control group or a condition that encouraged prolonged and exclusive breast-feeding. After 6.5 years, the children in the group receiving the intervention had higher means on standardized measures of intelligence (Kramer et al., 2008). There is also an apparent relationship between birth weight and intelligence later in life (Shenkin, Starr, & Deary, 2004; **FIGURE 8.48**).

Another factor that is increasingly recognized as important for intellectual outcomes is family wealth, referred to as *socioeconomic status (SES)*. According to Richard Nisbett (2009), growing up in a wealthy family significantly increases IQ, by 12 to 18 points. Although the mechanism for this finding is not completely clear, there is growing evidence that SES is associated with differences in brain regions associated with cognitive functions (Lawson, Duda, Avants, Wu, & Farah, 2013). One possibility is that higher-SES families emphasize education and that the greater focus on education is associated with the development of more synaptic connections (Noble, Korgaonkar, Grieve, & Brickman, 2013).

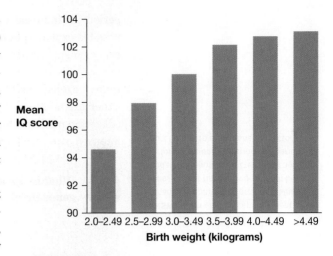

Birth weight (kilograms)

FIGURE 8.48
Birth Weight and Intelligence
Among children of normal birth weight, mean IQ scores increase with weight.

As noted in Chapter 3, rats raised in enriched environments show more synaptic connections than those raised in impoverished environments. Research from numerous laboratories has shown that enriched environments enhance cognitive processes as well (Lambert, Fernandez, & Frick, 2005; Tang, Wang, Feng, Kyin, & Tsien, 2001). The implication is that environment influences how genes involved in brain development are expressed.

In one study, genetically identical mice were split into groups. The groups were then exposed to different levels of an enriched environment—given toys, tunnels, and the like. Enrichment was associated with the activation of genes involved in a number of brain functions, including forming new synapses (Rampon et al., 2000). These results suggest that environment can affect properties associated with intelligence by influencing the expression of genes. Research has shown that humans as well as mice gain clear advantages from living in stimulating environments and that these environmental effects can be seen in the brain (May, 2011).

We do know that the intellectual opportunities a child receives affect intelligence. For instance, schooling makes an important contribution to intelligence and is associated with increased synaptic connections between brain regions involved in cognition (Noble et al., 2013). As Stephen Ceci (1999) notes, the longer children remain in school, the higher their IQs will be. In fact, students who start school early because of where their birth dates fall on the calendar have higher test scores than their same-age peers who start school a year later. Schooling not only builds knowledge but also teaches critical thinking skills, such as being able to think abstractly and learn strategies for solving problems (Neisser et al., 1996). Schooling encourages the development of children's brains and cognitive capacities and therefore fosters intelligence.

Taken together, the evidence is considerable that environmental factors contribute to intelligence. For example, IQ scores have risen dramatically during the last century of intelligence testing. This rise has been called the *Flynn effect* after James R. Flynn, the researcher who first described it (Flynn, 1981, 1987). (The various intelligence tests have been restandardized on numerous occasions over time so that the mean IQ score remains 100.) Because genes cannot have changed much during this period, the increase must be due to environmental factors or epigenetic effects. One possible explanation for the increase in IQ scores across generations is that, since every generation needs more education than the preceding one, and since work and leisure activities require more complex cognitive processing than they did in earlier times, cognitive abilities escalate within the span of one generation (Flynn, 2007). Other explanations include better nutrition, better health care, the refinement of education methods, longer school years, prosperity, and smaller families with more intensive parenting, as well as exposure to technology such as computers.

 What is the evidence that the environment influences how genes involved in cognitive development and IQ are expressed?

ANSWER: An enriched environment will enhance cognitive performance. Since genes cannot have changed much in modern humans, the increase in cognitive performance and IQ during this period must be due to environmental factors.

8.17 Group Differences in Intelligence Have Multiple Determinants

One of the most controversial aspects of intelligence testing over the last century has been whether there are differences between groups in level of intelligence and, if so, the basis of these differences. Here, we consider whether there are sex or racial differences in intelligence.

SEX A great deal of research has addressed the question of whether females or males are more intelligent. It might seem that the simplest way to answer the question is to determine whether females or males have the higher average IQ score. This solution does not work, however, because most of the commonly used intelligence tests were written in ways that would avoid creating an overall sex difference in IQ (Brody, 1992).

To study differences between males and females in intelligence, Arthur Jensen (1998) analyzed intelligence tests that "load heavily on g." Jensen used only tests that had not deliberately eliminated sex differences. As a result, he was more likely to find evidence for sex differences in intelligence, if those differences existed. Jensen concluded, "No evidence was found for sex differences in the mean level of g or in the variability of g. . . . Males, on average, excel on some factors; females on others" (pp. 531–532).

There are differences between females and males, on average, on some measures that presumably reflect intelligence. Females get better grades in school and tend to have the advantage on measures of writing and of language usage. By contrast, males tend to get higher scores on some standardized tests of math aptitude and of visuospatial processing (Halpern et al., 2007; Reilly, Neumann, & Andrews, 2015). Therefore, neither women nor men are "smarter."

RACE Multiple studies over the past 30 years have found that, on average, whites score about 10 to 15 points higher than African Americans on most measures of intelligence. The difference between groups exists. How much of the effect is genetic, and how much is environmental? At this time, there is no clear-cut basis for understanding why some racial groups may score lower on standardized tests of intelligence.

Early intelligence tests were criticized for being biased against minority test-takers. That is, doing well on intelligence tests often required knowing the language and practices of the mainstream, mostly white European cultures. Sometimes it is difficult to detect and quantify the bias in intelligence assessments. However, group differences emerge even for tests that are culturally neutral, such as the Raven Progressive Matrices Test (**FIGURE 8.49**).

In any case, it is not scientifically appropriate to conclude that genes cause differences between groups if there are any environmental differences between those groups. Recall the earlier discussion of plants grown in different environments. On average, compared with white Americans, African Americans make less money and are more likely to live in poverty, have fewer years of education, have lower-quality health care, and are more likely to face prejudice and discrimination. Around the world, minority groups that are the targets of discrimination—such as the Maori, in New Zealand; the burakumin, in Japan; and the Dalits, or "untouchables," in India— have lower intelligence scores on average.

John Ogbu (1994) has argued that poor treatment of minority-group members can make them pessimistic about their chances of success within their cultures, potentially making them less likely to believe that hard work will pay off for them. Such attitudes may lower their motivational levels and therefore their performances. Indeed, a lack of motivation is associated with poorer performance on IQ tests (Duckworth, Quinn, Lynam, Loeber, & Stouthamer-Loeber, 2011). This explanation is plausible, but it is not a clear-cut basis for understanding the differences in test scores between African Americans and white Americans (Neisser et al., 1996).

Another plausible explanation is **stereotype threat.** This effect is the apprehension or fear that some people might experience if they believe that their performances on tests might confirm negative stereotypes about their racial group (Spencer, Logel, & Davies, 2016; Steele and Aronson, 1995; **FIGURE 8.50**). Stereotype threat causes distraction and anxiety, interfering with performance by reducing the capacity of short-term memory and undermining confidence and motivation (Schmader, 2010). An fMRI study found that stereotype threat was associated with increased activity in brain regions involved in social and emotional processing (Krendl, Richeson, Kelley, & Heatherton, 2008). These results confirm the idea that anxiety about confirming stereotypes interferes with performance.

Stereotype threat applies to any member of a group who believes the group has a negative stereotype. For example, when women take standardized math tests, those who believe that men tend to do better on such tests tend to do worse than men. Women who do not hold this belief do not differ in their scores from men (Schmader, Johns, & Forbes, 2008; Spencer, Steele, & Quinn, 1999).

One study found an especially intriguing example of stereotype threat (Shih, Pittinsky, & Ambady, 1999). Asian American women did well on a math test when the "Asians are good at math" stereotype was primed by having them respond to questions about racial identity. They did poorly when the "women are bad at math" stereotype was primed by having them respond to questions about gender. In this same study, however, women from Vancouver showed a slightly different pattern. The stereotype that Asians perform at a superior level is less strong in Canada than in the United States. In other words, the researchers had a two-part hypothesis: They predicted that being primed as women would reduce these women's test scores on math items. They also predicted that being primed as Asians would not lead to increased performance.

The task is to identify the missing shape in this sequence.

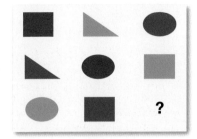

Choose from the eight shapes below to complete the sequence:

The solution is the first triangle in the bottom row.

FIGURE 8.49
Removing Bias from Tests
This nonverbal test requires test-takers to identify a missing element to complete a pattern. According to the creators of this test, the task is not culturally biased.

stereotype threat
Apprehension about confirming negative stereotypes related to one's own group.

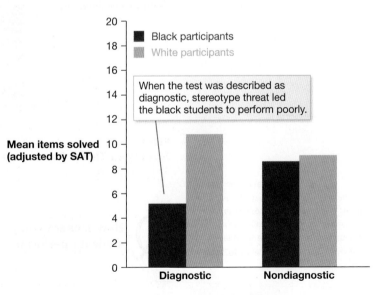

FIGURE 8.50
Stereotype Threat
Stereotype threat may lead black students to perform poorly on some standardized tests.

Their findings supported both parts of the hypothesis. As a result, they demonstrate the power of believing sociocultural stereotypes on individual performance.

A meta-analysis examined 39 independent laboratory studies on stereotype threat (Walton & Spencer, 2009). Together, these studies included 3,180 participants from five countries (Canada, France, Germany, Sweden, and the United States) and many stereotyped groups (e.g., blacks, Latinos, Turkish Germans, women). According to the meta-analysis, stereotyped groups perform worse than nonstereotyped groups when a test is presented as evaluative. However, this effect is reversed when the threat is reduced. For example, an exam can be presented as nonevaluative, such as giving questions in the form of games.

Interventions to reduce stereotype threat effects are often successful. For instance, informing people about the negative consequences of stereotype threat can inoculate them from the negative effects (Johns, Schmader, & Martens, 2005; **FIGURE 8.51**). Encouraging African American students to write about important personal values may protect them from stereotype threat, perhaps because it leads them to focus on positive aspects of their lives rather than on stereotypes about their group (Cohen, Garcia, Apfel, & Master, 2006). Other studies have found that bolstering peer relations and social connections can help prevent stereotype threat. Indeed, school environments that provide opportunities to develop social skills and create friendships are associated with better academic performance among Canadian aboriginal children (Baydala et al., 2009).

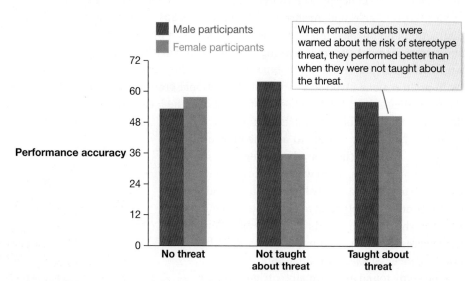

FIGURE 8.51
Stereotype Threat Counteracted
Stereotype threat can be counteracted when people are warned about it.

Q How does stereotype threat sometimes interfere with minority students' performance on intelligence tests?

ANSWER: When minority students focus on stereotypes about their groups, they may become anxious about confirming such stereotypes through their test results. This distraction makes them less likely to do well on the tests.

Your Chapter Review

Chapter Summary

What Is Thought?

8.1 Thinking Involves Two Types of Mental Representations

Cognition can be broadly defined as the mental activity that includes thinking and the understandings that result from thinking. Knowledge about the world is stored in the brain in representations. Analogical representations are images that contain characteristics of actual objects. Symbolic representations are abstract representations with no relationships to physical qualities of objects in the world. Mental maps rely on both analogical and symbolic representations.

8.2 Concepts Are Symbolic Representations

Concepts are mental representations that categorize items around commonalities. According to the prototype model, an individual forms a concept around a category and then chooses a prototype that best represents the concept. According to the exemplar model, the individual chooses a concept by combining representations of all the examples (exemplars) of a category ever encountered by the individual.

8.3 Schemas Organize Useful Information About Environments

Schemas are categories used to organize information. Schemas usually work because situations and appropriate behaviors follow consistent rules. Scripts are schemas that guide behavior over time in specific situations, such as going to the movies. A negative consequence of schemas and scripts is that they can reinforce stereotypes and biases. Schemas and scripts are adaptive because they minimize attentional requirements and help people recognize and avoid unusual or dangerous situations.

How Do We Make Decisions and Solve Problems?

8.4 Decision Making Often Involves Heuristics

Decision making is selecting among alternatives. People often use heuristics, or mental shortcuts, to make decisions. Common heuristics include relative comparisons (anchoring and framing), availability, and representativeness.

8.5 Emotions Influence Decision Making

Emotions influence decision making in many different ways, such as what people anticipate feeling in the future. Emotions also act as heuristic guides, allowing people to make quick decisions based on how they feel. People use their current moods as information to make judgments and appraisals. Somatic markers are bodily responses that reflect emotional reactions to different outcomes in decision making. People are typically bad at predicting their future feelings.

8.6 Think like a Psychologist: Why Is It Hard to Resist a Sale?

Whether a deal is considered good depends on the type of comparison people are making. Positively framed information is more influential in changing behavior than negatively framed information. Anchoring also affects consumer decisions, as when a low anchor influences the perception of other options. Anchoring and framing are among the major weapons that marketers use to increase sales.

8.7 Problem Solving Achieves Goals

Problem solving is using available information to achieve a goal. Problem solving can be improved by breaking the problem into subgoals or by restructuring the problem. Mental sets and functional fixedness inhibit problem solving. Two ways of countering these blockages are working backward from the goal and transferring an effective strategy from an analogous situation. Insight is the sudden realization of a solution to a problem and is often achieved by overcoming functional fixedness.

8.8 Using Psychology in Your Life: How Can You Make Good Choices?

Even though people prefer more choices, increasing the number of options decreases decision making and decreases satisfaction with decisions. When too many options are available, especially when all of them are attractive, people experience conflict and indecision. Two approaches to decision making are "maximizing" and "satisficing." Maximizers seek to identify the perfect choice among a set of options, whereas satisficers seek to find a "good enough" choice that meets their minimum requirements. Maximizers, compared with satisficers, tend to select the objectively best choice, but those choices bring them less happiness. There are several strategies available for helping people make good decisions that bring them happiness. One such strategy is having realistic expectations.

What Is Language?

8.9 Language Is a System of Communication Using Sounds and Symbols

Morphemes are the smallest units of language that have meaning. Phonemes are the basic sounds of speech, the building blocks of language. A network of left hemisphere brain regions—including Broca's area in the frontal lobe and Wernicke's area at the junction of the temporal and parietal lobes—govern speech production and comprehension. Language may influence thought, but thought does not depend on language.

8.10 Language Develops in an Orderly Way

Language production proceeds from babies' cooing to babbling to the use of single words to telegraphic speech to the use of full sentences to the eventual acquisition of some 60,000 words.

8.11 There Is an Inborn Capacity for Language

Behaviorists believed that language was learned through operant reinforcement. However, children acquire language even in the absence of reinforcement. Noam Chomsky proposed instead that humans are born with an innate capability for language, called the language acquisition device, which contains universal grammar rules.

8.12 Reading Needs to Be Learned

For most adults, reading is automatic and effortless, and we derive accurate meaning even from misspelled words. Phonics is a method for teaching reading by associating letters with phonemes. Whole language is a method for teaching reading by emphasizing the meanings of words and how words are connected in sentences. Whole language is a good way to encourage reading. Phonics is the best method for teaching basic reading skills, especially for children unfamiliar with reading. Dyslexia results from a lack of phoneme awareness.

How Do We Understand Intelligence?

8.13 Intelligence Is Measured with Standardized Tests

Intelligence is the ability to use knowledge to reason, make decisions, solve problems, understand complex ideas, learn quickly, and adapt to environmental challenges. The two types of standardized intelligence tests are achievement tests, which measure accumulated skill and knowledge, and aptitude tests, which assess ability and potential. Two commonly used intelligence tests are the Stanford-Binet test for children and the WAIS for adults. Intelligence quotient (IQ) is computed by dividing mental age by chronological age and then multiplying the result by 100. IQ tests have been shown to be valid measures of intelligence. Perseverance, zeal, and willingness to work long hours are also necessary for expertise.

8.14 General Intelligence Involves Multiple Components

General intelligence (g) is the idea that one general factor underlies intelligence. This factor may consist of two components: fluid intelligence (the ability to think logically about abstract concepts without prior knowledge) and crystallized intelligence (accumulated knowledge). Several theories have proposed multiple intelligences, such as emotional intelligence (how well people succeed in social situations). Additional research is needed to verify that multiple intelligences exist.

8.15 Intelligence Is Related to Cognitive Performance

High IQ is related to increased speed of mental processing, as measured by reaction time and inspection time tasks. Working memory may be related to intelligence for tasks that require attention. People who have higher levels of fluid intelligence have been found to have a greater density of neural cell bodies (gray matter) in the frontal lobes, an area of the brain that regulates working memory. Savants have minimal intellectual capacities in most domains, but at a very early age they show an exceptional ability in some "intelligent" process.

8.16 Genes and Environment Influence Intelligence

There is likely a complex genetic component to intelligence, but environment plays a large role in how intelligence is expressed. Epigenetics offers an explanation for how intelligence may develop, by describing how environmental influences such as enrichment and education can permit gene expression to promote synaptic connections and processing efficiency in the brain to increase intelligence.

8.17 Group Differences in Intelligence Have Multiple Determinants

There is no overall difference in intelligence between men and women, although women tend to score higher on tests of writing and language use and men tend to score higher on standardized tests of math ability and visuospatial processing. On standardized tests, white, European Americans tend to score 10–15 points higher than African Americans. There is no clear-cut basis for understanding this difference, but environmental factors likely play a large role. Stereotype threat is apprehension or fear that some test-takers might experience if they believe that their performance will confirm a negative stereotype about the test-taker's group. A few methods exist to counteract stereotype threat.

Key Terms

affective forecasting, p. 301

analogical representations, p. 290

anchoring, p. 298

aphasia, p. 312

availability heuristic, p. 299

cognition, p. 290

concept, p. 291

crystallized intelligence, p. 322

decision making, p. 297

deep structure, p. 316

emotional intelligence (EI), p. 324

exemplar model, p. 292

fluid intelligence, p. 322

framing, p. 299

functional fixedness, p. 305

general intelligence (g), p. 322

heuristics, p. 297

insight, p. 306

intelligence, p. 319

intelligence quotient (IQ), p. 321

language, p. 310

linguistic relativity theory, p. 313

mental age, p. 321

mental sets, p. 304

morphemes, p. 310

phonemes, p. 311

phonics, p. 318

problem solving, p. 297

prototype model, p. 291

representativeness heuristic, p. 299

restructuring, p. 304

script, p. 295

somatic markers, p. 301

stereotypes, p. 294

stereotype threat, p. 331

surface structure, p. 316

symbolic representations, p. 290

telegraphic speech, p. 315

thinking, p. 290

Wernicke's area, p. 312

whole language, p. 318

How Is the Psychology of Decision Making Used to Improve People's Lives?

For most people, each day involves many decisions. Simple choices, such as picking a movie to stream on Netflix, should be easy. Yet sometimes you might find it surprisingly difficult to settle on a movie. There are many genres and titles, and you get different results depending on where you start your search. To facilitate this task, you might settle for the movie that has the highest rating, or the one whose actors you just read about in the news. As you've seen in this chapter, decisions are influenced by numerous factors, such as the number of available options, or the order in which the options are presented, or information the decision maker has recently encountered. Often people rely on heuristics, automatic mental shortcuts, to help make decisions. Most of the time, heuristics—for example, using ratings to pick a movie—can lead to good decisions.

Now imagine making a more consequential decision, such as selecting a major, a medical procedure, or an investment option. As you have also learned in this chapter, heuristic thinking can lead to biases and errors. As decisions become more consequential, understanding how decision making is affected by heuristics becomes more important. The psychology research pioneered by Kahneman and Tversky, sometimes referred to as decision science or behavioral economics, has provided many insights that can be used to improve decision making in various employment sectors.

Physicians, for example, often have to make quick diagnostic decisions under conditions of uncertainty and incomplete information. These are exactly the kinds of situations in which heuristics are most used. Being aware of potential biases is therefore an essential part of physician training. Physicians are cautioned to be aware of the base rate in making decisions with the aphorism "When you hear hoofbeats, think of horses, not zebras" (i.e., first look for the most likely possibility). In addition, understanding how framing and risk aversion may influence a patient's choice of medical procedure is crucial in any discussion between patient and physician.

Public policy can also be influenced by behavioral economics research. Consider, for example, efforts to simplify the financial aid application process for federal loans. In 2015, President Obama signed an executive order, "Using Behavioral Science Insights to Better Serve the American People," that reflects the effort to use psychological insights to improve outcomes for citizens.

An undergraduate curriculum that includes courses in behavioral economics can be useful to students in many majors, not just medicine or public policy. For example, personal finance consultants can help clients better assess risk in choosing investment options, marketing analysts can improve consumer satisfaction by simplifying choices, and corporate managers can improve team decision making.

The bottom line: Understanding factors that influence judgment and choice can improve decision making by individuals and organizations. Accordingly, this information is increasingly important for many career paths, including medicine, public policy, finance, and management.

Want to earn a better grade on your test?
Go to **INQUIZITIVE** to learn and review this chapter's content, with personalized feedback along the way. Practice Tests and accompanying answer keys can be found at the back of the book on page PT-1.

9

Human Development

Big Questions

- What Factors Shape Infancy? 338

- How Do Children Learn About the World? 352

- What Changes During Adolescence? 363

- What Brings Meaning in Adulthood? 371

THINK BACK TO YOUR CHILDHOOD, or look at an old photo of yourself. Are you the same person now as you were at age 5 or 13? Will you be the same person when you are 50 or 80 or even older? Almost certainly, the answer to both questions is no. As virtually all people do, you have changed in many ways over the years and will continue to do so as you age. By changing, you are continually developing into a new version of yourself.

Throughout the history of psychology, theorists and scientists have vigorously debated the contributions of nature and nurture to human development. Nearly all psychologists now agree that nature and nurture are equally important, and current research focuses on how, exactly, genes and experiences interact to make us who we are. As discussed in Chapter 3, environment determines how specific genes are expressed. Some portion of who we are is hardwired in our genes, and some portion is the result of experience. This chapter examines the ways biological and social forces combine to shape the path of human development. For psychologists in this area, the big questions are: What factors shape infancy? How do children learn about the world? What changes during adolescence? And what brings meaning in adulthood?

What Factors Shape Infancy?

This chapter is concerned with changes, over the human life span, in physiology, cognition, emotion, and social behavior. In exploring these changes, the chapter presents the findings of **developmental psychology.** This subfield examines how genes interact with early experiences to make each of us different. Researchers in developmental psychology seek to understand how, while remaining individuals, people become members of society. In other words, each person grows and adapts within a particular culture or particular cultures.

For the most part, human physical development follows a predictable progression. Physically, each human matures at about the same periods in the life span: the prenatal period, which begins with conception and ends with birth; infancy, which begins at birth and lasts 18 to 24 months; childhood, which begins at the end of infancy and lasts until somewhere between ages 11 and 14; adolescence, which begins at the end of childhood and lasts until somewhere between 18 and 21 years; and adulthood, which begins at the end of adolescence and lasts until old age and death. The consistency of this pattern suggests that genes set the order and timing of development. The following sections focus on development within the first two periods: prenatal and infancy.

9.1 Human Development Starts in the Womb

From conception through birth approximately nine months later, remarkable developments occur (**FIGURE 9.1**). The process begins at the moment of conception, when the sperm from the male unites with the egg from the female to create the *zygote,* the first cell of a new life. At about 2 weeks after conception, the zygote is firmly implanted in the uterine wall, and the next stage of development begins. From about 2 weeks to 2 months, the developing human is known as an *embryo.* During this stage, the organs (such as the heart, lungs, liver, kidneys, and sex organs) and internal systems (such as the nervous system) begin to form. During this period, the embryo is especially vulnerable. Exposure to harm—such as toxins, drugs, extreme stress, or poor nutrition—can have lasting effects on developing organ systems.

After 2 months of prenatal development, all the organs are formed, the heart begins to beat, and the growing human is called a *fetus.* The body continues to grow into its infant form. The fetus grows larger, stronger, and fatter, as the body organs mature to a point where survival is possible outside the womb. With current medical technology helping out, many fetuses can now survive outside the womb after as little as 22 weeks of prenatal development (**FIGURE 9.2**). Most healthy full-term pregnancies, however, end with the birth of the baby at between 38 and 42 weeks.

(a)

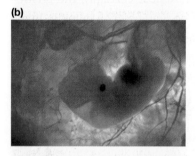

(b)

(c)

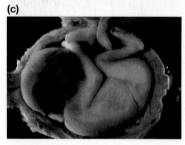

FIGURE 9.1
Development in the Womb
(a) The union of egg and sperm forms a zygote. **(b)** The zygote develops into an embryo. **(c)** The embryo becomes a fetus.

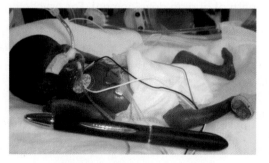

FIGURE 9.2
Extreme Prematurity
Amillia Sonja Taylor was born in 2006, after spending just 21 weeks and six days in the womb. At birth, she was a little longer than a ballpoint pen and weighed 10 ounces. Today, she is a healthy child.

BRAIN DEVELOPMENT Early brain growth has two important aspects. First, specific areas within the brain mature and become functional. Second, regions of the brain learn to communicate with one another through synaptic connections.

One important way that brain circuits mature is through myelination. This process begins on the spinal cord during the first trimester of pregnancy and on the neurons during the second trimester. As discussed in Chapter 3, myelination is the brain's way of insulating its "wires." Nerve fibers are wrapped with a fatty sheath, much like the plastic coating around electrical wire (see Figure 3.3). This wrapping increases the speed with which the fibers are able to transmit signals. The myelinated axons form synapses with other neurons. As you will learn, brain development continues into early adulthood.

Though most neurons are already formed at birth, the brain's physical development continues through the growth of neurons and the new connections they make. By age 4, the human brain has grown to about 80 percent of the adult size. This size increase is due to myelination and to new synaptic connections among neurons, particularly in the frontal lobes (Parades et al., 2016). Far more of these connections develop than the infant brain will ever use. Genetic instruction leads the brain to grow, but the organ is also highly "plastic." That is, the brain organizes itself in response to its environmental experiences, preserving connections it needs in order to function in a given context and pruning out others. In other words, "use it or lose it." When connections are used, they are preserved. When connections are not used, they decay and disappear. This process of **synaptic pruning** allows every brain to adapt well to any environment in which it may find itself. The brain continues to develop and mature through adolescence and beyond (Matsui et al., 2016).

Nutrition affects aspects of brain development, such as myelination, beginning in the womb and extending through childhood. Malnourished children might also lack the energy to interact with objects and people. This lack of stimulation would further undermine brain development. When a child's environment does not stimulate her brain, very few synaptic connections will be made. The brain will be less sophisticated and less able to process complex information, solve problems, or allow the child to develop advanced language skills (Perry, 2002; **FIGURE 9.3**). As discussed in Chapter 3, animals raised in enriched environments show increased generation of new neurons in the hippocampus, which may facilitate learning in complex environments (Garthe, Roeder, & Kempermann, 2016).

One factor that can diminish an environment is poverty. The living conditions that tend to come with poverty (e.g., stress, poor nutrition, exposure to toxins and violence) are bad for the development of human brains. These negative effects begin at a young age—probably before birth—and continue through life (Farah et al., 2008; Lawson, Duda, Avants, Wu, & Farah, 2013). One large study of nearly 400 children followed over two years found that living below the U.S. federal poverty level was associated with reductions in several brain areas linked to school readiness skills (Hair, Hanson, Wolfe, & Pollak, 2015). These children living in poverty went on to have lower scores on achievement tests. Other research shows that poor brain functioning associated with poverty at age 3 predicts several negative life outcomes 40 years later, including health problems, addiction, and greater criminal activity (Caspi et al., 2016). On a more positive front, a program designed to enhance parental support for those living in poverty reduced the effects of poverty on brain development (Brody et al., 2017). Thus, although genes provide instructions

developmental psychology
The study of changes, over the life span, in physiology, cognition, emotion, and social behavior.

synaptic pruning
The synaptic connections in the brain that are used are preserved, whereas those that are not used decay and disappear.

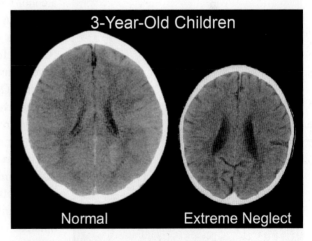

FIGURE 9.3
Environment and Synaptic Connections
These images illustrate the impact of neglect on the developing brain. The CT scan on the left is from a healthy 3-year-old child with an average head size. The CT scan on the right is from a 3-year-old child following severe sensory-deprivation neglect (e.g., minimal exposure to language, to touch, and to social interaction) during early childhood. This brain is significantly smaller than average, and its cortical, limbic, and midbrain structures are abnormally developed.

FIGURE 9.4
Zika as a Teratogen
Prenatal exposure to the Zika virus can produce major birth defects, such as microcephaly. This condition results in a significantly smaller head than expected, often due to abnormal brain development.

(a)

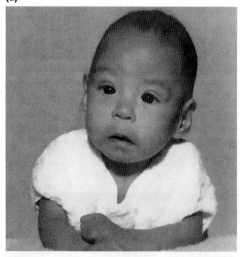

(b)   **(c)**

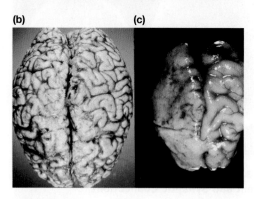

FIGURE 9.5
Fetal Alcohol Syndrome
(a) This is a typical child with FAS. The three most common features are small eye openings, an absence of the groove that normally appears between the nose and the lips, and a thin upper lip.
(b) Compare the brain of a normal 6-week-old baby with **(c)** the brain of a baby of the same age with FAS.

for the maturing brain, how the brain changes during infancy and early childhood is also very much affected by environment.

EXPOSURE TO TERATOGENS DURING PRENATAL DEVELOPMENT Teratogens are agents that harm the embryo or fetus. (The word *teratogens* comes from the Greek for "monster makers.") Specifically, these agents can impair development in the womb, sometimes with terrible consequences. Teratogens include drugs, alcohol, bacteria, viruses, and chemicals. In 2015, significant concerns were raised that the Zika virus was causing birth defects throughout the Americas. Zika, spread mainly by infected mosquitoes, can also be transmitted via sexual activity. A pregnant woman may pass the virus on to her fetus, which can produce serious birth defects such as brain abnormalities and microcephaly, an abnormally small head (Rasmussen, Jamieson, Honein, & Petersen, 2016). Such defects are usually quite rare, but 6 percent of infants exposed to Zika have virus-related defects, particularly if exposed during the first trimester (Honein et al., 2017; **FIGURE 9.4**).

The physical effects of exposure to certain teratogens may be obvious at birth, but disorders involving language, reasoning, social behavior, or emotional behavior may not become apparent until the child is older. The extent to which a teratogen causes damage depends on when the embryo or fetus is exposed to it, as well as the length and amount of exposure.

The most common teratogen is alcohol. Drinking alcohol during pregnancy can lead to *fetal alcohol syndrome (FAS)*. The symptoms of this disorder are low birth weight; face and head abnormalities; deficient brain growth; and evidence of impairment, as indicated by behavioral or cognitive problems or low IQ (Hoyme et al., 2016; **FIGURE 9.5**). FAS is most likely to occur among infants of women who drink heavily during pregnancy, especially if they binge drink. However, no minimal amount of alcohol has been determined to be safe for pregnant women and their developing babies. For this reason, many health workers recommend that women abstain from drinking alcohol when they are pregnant or trying to become pregnant (Mukherjee, Hollins, Abou-Saleh, & Turk, 2005). In the United States, the prevalence of FAS is estimated to be between 0.2 and 2.0 cases per 1,000 live births (Centers for Disease Control and Prevention, 2004), though recent studies have found higher numbers, with an estimated rate closer to 8 out of 1,000 children (May et al., 2014).

The use of recreational drugs—such as opiates, cocaine, or cannabis—during pregnancy can also affect a child's development. Premature birth and other complications have been associated with the use of all these drugs during pregnancy (Cain, Bornick, & Whiteman, 2013; Hayatbakhsh et al., 2011; Minnes, Lang, & Singer, 2011). Infants of women taking opiates, particularly methadone, have five to ten times greater risk for unexplained sudden death in infancy (Ali, Ahmed, & Greenough, 2012). Among infants exposed to opiates in the womb, 40–80 percent show symptoms of newborn withdrawal (Yazdy, Desai, & Brogly, 2015). These symptoms include irritability, high-pitched crying, tremors, vomiting, diarrhea, and rapid breathing. The recent opioid epidemic, discussed in Chapter 4, is associated with a nearly threefold increase in infants born with this condition (Volkow, 2016).

Historically, far less research has been done on the effects of paternal health and lifestyles on prenatal development. There is growing evidence, however, that paternal lifestyle factors, including diet, toxin exposure, and amount of stress experienced, can affect a child's health through epigenetic processes (Schagdarsurengin & Steger, 2016; Siklenka et al., 2015). Recall from Chapter 3 that epigenetic effects occur when parents' environments alter the way that genes are expressed in their offspring. The take-home message here is that life experiences and environmental circumstances can be passed along in sperm as epigenetic information (Chen, Yan, & Duan, 2016). These effects may then be passed along to subsequent generations.

An important point to remember is that some heavy substance users and many people exposed to toxins or stress have normal infants. Conversely, some people with only moderate exposure to teratogens have infants with serious developmental effects. Thus, we cannot say with certainty that any given baby born to a drug user or to a person who works around chemicals will be impaired. Likewise, we cannot be assured that light drinking or minimal teratogen exposure will allow for normal development. All potential parents face the responsibility of caring for their own mental and physical health to increase the odds of being able to parent a healthy and robust newborn.

Q | **Why is synaptic pruning valuable in the developing brain?**

teratogens
Agents that harm the embryo or fetus.

9.2 Biology and Environment Influence Motor Development

Although newborn infants cannot survive on their own, they are not completely helpless. Newborns have various motor reflexes that aid survival. Perhaps you have observed the *grasping reflex* when a baby held your finger (**FIGURE 9.6A**). This reflex is a survival mechanism that has persisted from our primate ancestors. Young apes grasp their mothers, and this reflex is adaptive because the offspring need to be carried from place to place. Also appearing at birth is the *rooting reflex,* the turning and sucking that infants automatically engage in when a nipple or similar object touches an area near their mouths (**FIGURE 9.6B**). If they find an object, they will show the *sucking reflex* (**FIGURE 9.6C**). These reflexes pave the way for learning more-complicated behavior patterns, such as feeding oneself or walking. Thus, at birth the brain is sufficiently developed to support basic reflexes, but further brain development is necessary for other development to occur.

No newborn talks immediately, nor does any baby walk before it can sit up. But most humans make eye contact quickly after they are born, display a first social smile at around 6 weeks, and learn to roll over, to sit up, to crawl, to stand, to walk, and to talk, in that order. Occasionally, a child skips one of these steps or reverses a couple of

(a)

(b)

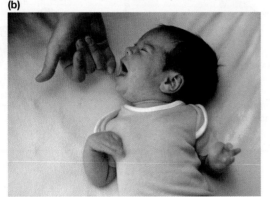

(c)

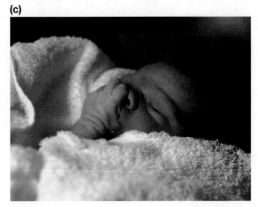

FIGURE 9.6
Infant Reflexes
Infants are born with innate abilities that help them survive, including the **(a)** grasping reflex, **(b)** rooting reflex, and **(c)** sucking reflex.

them, but generally each child follows these steps within a predictable range of ages (FIGURE 9.7).

Meanwhile, each person's environment influences what happens throughout that individual's development. For example, infants often achieve developmental milestones at different paces, depending on the cultures in which they are raised. Consider that healthy Baganda infants in Uganda were found to walk, on average, between 9 and 11 months of age, which was one month earlier than African American infants and about three months earlier than European American infants (Kilbride, Robbins, & Kilbride, 1970). Such differences are due in part to different patterns of infant care across cultures. For example, Western infants spend a lot more time in cribs and playpens than African infants do. African infants are often strapped to their mothers' backs all day, practicing holding their heads up virtually from birth.

Kipsigi mothers living in the Kohwet village culture in western Kenya were found to put their babies in shallow holes in the ground so the babies could practice sitting upright (Super, 1976). The mothers then marched their babies around while placing their own arms under the babies' underarms, so the children could practice walking. These infants walked about one to two months earlier than American and European infants. When middle-class Kipsigi families who had moved to a larger city were assessed in their Westernized homes, they still deliberately taught their infants motor skills. However, they also let their infants sleep in cribs and lie in playpens like their European counterparts. These urban infants walked two weeks later than the rural infants in Kohwet but one week earlier than infants in Boston, Massachusetts. These findings illustrate the importance of socialization experiences and parental goals in the development of infant motor skills.

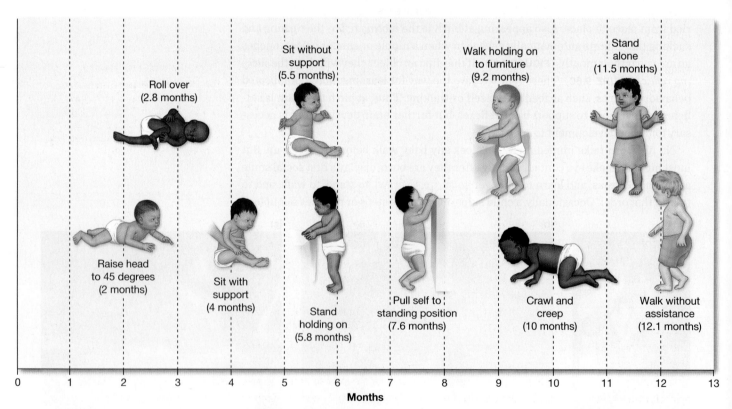

FIGURE 9.7
Learning to Walk
Usually, a human baby learns to walk without formal teaching, in a sequence characteristic of all humans. However, the numbers of months given here are averages. A child might deviate from this sequence or these times but still be developing normally.

The aim of these early studies was to find out whether the development of walking was genetically or environmentally determined. Contemporary research has moved beyond such questions because we now know that every new development is the result of complex and consistent interplays between biology and environment. Developmental psychologists now consider new forms of development (such as when an infant is able to walk two weeks after not being able to walk) to be part of a *dynamic system*. **Dynamic systems theory** views development as a self-organizing process, in which new forms of behavior emerge through consistent interactions between a biological being and cultural and environmental contexts (Smith & Thelen, 2003; **FIGURE 9.8**).

From this perspective, developmental advances in any domain (physiological, cognitive, emotional, or social) occur through both the person's active exploration of an environment and the constant feedback that environment provides. For example, an infant placed on a play mat may grow bored with the toys dangling above her on a mobile. She suddenly spies an attractive stuffed unicorn about 10 feet away, far from the play mat where her mother placed her. Her physical body is strong enough to get herself off the mat, but because she cannot crawl, she uses her own active strategizing in combination with feedback from the environment to figure out how to reach the toy. She rocks her body from side to side with her arm outstretched toward the toy. The environmental feedback tells her that after one more heavy roll, she will be on her stomach and possibly closer to the toy. She tries for over 10 minutes, and suddenly she rolls over. She continues to heave herself over and over until she has rolled 10 feet and can now grasp the unicorn. Her mother may walk into the room and think, "Wow, she just suddenly learned to roll around the room!" What her mother does not realize is that every new behavioral skill to emerge is the result of a complex and dynamic system of influences, including the child's motivation and personality, that respond to environmental cues.

dynamic systems theory
The view that development is a self-organizing process, in which new forms of behavior emerge through consistent interactions between a biological being and cultural and environmental contexts.

Why do children from some African cultures start to walk especially early?

9.3 Infants Are Prepared to Learn

Step into the nursery for newborns, bend over a bassinet, peer at the newborn inside, and stick your tongue out. The baby, less than one hour old, sticks her tongue out at you (FIGURE 9.9). Think about the remarkable activity going on in the baby's young brain. After seeing a face with a tongue sticking out, the baby somehow seems to know that she too has a face with a tongue. The brain finds the tongue in its long list of body parts, sends it a command to get a move on, and out it goes. How does the baby know a tongue is a tongue? How does the baby's brain know what neural system is in charge of the tongue? How does the baby know how to move the tongue? Why does the baby move her tongue? Obviously, this behavior was not learned by looking in a mirror, nor had it been taught. The ability to imitate must be innate.

Imitation is the baby's first social interaction, but babies are discerning. They will imitate the actions of other humans but not of objects. Babies are born categorizing, and newborns already understand they are in the people category, not the object category. The baby brain already has specific neural circuits for identifying biological motion and inanimate object motion, along with specific circuits to identify faces and facial movement (Lloyd-Fox, Blasi, Everdell, Elwell, & Johnson, 2011). What links him to you and you to him in the social world are his imitative actions. You purse your lips, and he purses his lips. He does not lie there like a lump of clay but responds in a way that you can relate to.

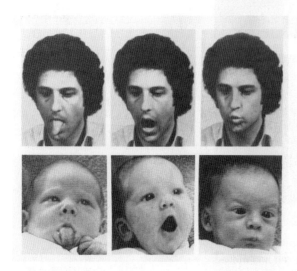

FIGURE 9.9
Infant Learning
Newborns have the ability to imitate adults' sticking out their tongues and other facial expressions (Meltzoff & Moore, 1977).

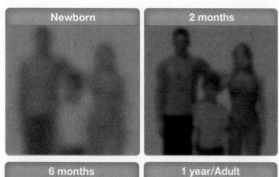
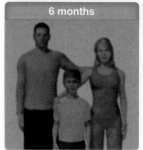

FIGURE 9.10
Infant Vision Improves over Time
Newborns have poor visual acuity and poor ability to see colors. These capacities improve rapidly over the first 6 months of life. By 1 year of age, children can see as well as adults.

PERCEPTION Newborns normally come into the world with fairly well-developed perceptual skills: smelling, hearing, tasting, and responding to touch. Although some of these skills are not fully developed at birth, the newborn is able to process a considerable range of sensory stimuli. For instance, 2-hour-old infants prefer sweet tastes to all other tastes (Mennella, Bobowski, & Reed, 2016). Young infants also have a reasonably acute sense of smell, at least for smells associated with feeding. In a number of studies, infants turned their heads toward a pad containing their own mother's milk but not toward pads containing milk from other breast-feeding mothers (e.g., Marin, Rapisardi, & Tani, 2015; Winberg & Porter, 1998).

The sense of hearing is also quite good shortly after birth: Infants are startled by loud sounds and often will turn their bodies toward the source of the sounds. When newborns are exposed to the crying of another infant, a distress response is induced, and the newborns will join in the crying. When they hear their own recorded cry played to them, or other random noises, a distress response is not induced, and they do not cry (Dondi, Simion, & Caltran, 1999). These responses suggest that newborns are able to distinguish between their own cry and other infants' cries and have some innate understanding of the difference between themselves and others (Martin & Clark, 1982). Infants' abilities to recognize sounds and locate those sounds in space improve continuously as the infants gain experience with objects and people and as the auditory cortex develops. By the age of 6 months, babies have a nearly adult level of auditory function (DeCasper & Spence, 1986).

The sense of vision develops more slowly than hearing. The ability to distinguish differences among shapes, patterns, and colors is known as *visual acuity*. Newborns' visual acuity for distant objects is poor, but it increases rapidly over the first six months (Teller, Morse, Borton, & Regal, 1974). Infants do not reach adult levels of acuity until they are about a year old (**FIGURE 9.10**). The increase in visual acuity is probably due to a combination of practice in looking at things in the world, the development of the visual cortex, and the development of the cones in the retina (as noted in Chapter 5, the cones are important for perceiving detail).

Infants respond more to objects with high-contrast patterns than to other stimuli. In the early 1960s, Robert Fantz (1963) and other developmental psychologists observed infants' reactions to patterns of black-and-white stripes as well as patches of gray (**FIGURE 9.11**). In these studies, the mother or another caregiver was asked to hold the infant in front of a display of the two images. The experimenter, not knowing which image was on which side, would observe through a peephole to see where the infant preferred to look. This research revealed that infants look at stripes with high contrast more readily than at gray images. The smaller the stripes are—that is, the less contrast between the images—the more difficult it becomes for infants to distinguish them from the gray patches. This type of research makes use of the *preferential-looking technique* (**FIGURE 9.12**). In using this technique, the researchers show an infant two things. If the infant looks longer at one of the things, the researchers know the infant can distinguish between the two and finds one more interesting.

MEMORY The development of memory helps children learn about the world around them. That is, children are able to use new information to build on what they already know. But how do researchers study memory in infants who cannot speak?

In a clever experiment (Rovee-Collier, 1999), a mobile hanging over a crib was attached to an infant's ankle with a ribbon (**FIGURE 9.13**). The infant learned that he could move the mobile by kicking his foot. When the infant was tested later, the ribbon was attached to the ankle but not to the mobile, so the kicks no longer moved the mobile. The rate at which the infant kicked when nothing was attached served

FIGURE 9.11
Vision in Infancy
Robert Fantz was the first scientist to determine that infants prefer patterns with high contrast. A more thorough understanding of infants' visual abilities has led parents to buy mobiles and toys that use some of Fantz's testing patterns.

A mother holds her infant in front of a display showing **(left)** a patch of gray and **(right)** a black-and-white pattern.

On the other side of the display, an experimenter looks through a peephole and notes whether the infant is looking left or right.

FIGURE 9.12
Preferential-Looking Technique
This research method is used to test visual acuity in infants.

(a)

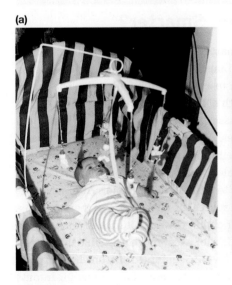

(b)

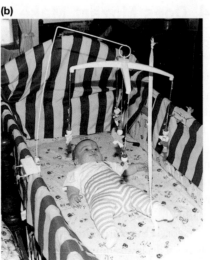

FIGURE 9.13
The Memory-Retention Test
(a) In this test, infants learn that kicking their feet moves a mobile because one foot is attached to the mobile by a ribbon around the ankle. **(b)** Then, after a delay, the infants are placed back under the mobile. If the infants soon kick their feet vigorously to get the mobile to move, they have shown that they remember moving the mobile during the learning phase.

as the baseline. If the baby recognized the mobile, presumably it would kick faster than the baseline rate to try to make the mobile move. Infants ranging in age from 2 months to 18 months were trained for two days on the mobile task and then tested after different lengths of time. The findings indicated that compared to younger infants, older infants could retain their memories regarding the connection between the ankle kicking and the mobile movement for longer periods of time. By 18 months, the infants could remember the event even if they were tested several weeks after they had learned the initial associations.

What is your earliest explicit memory? Most adults remember few events that occurred before they were 3 or 4 years old. Freud referred to this inability to remember events from early childhood as **infantile amnesia.** Researchers have offered various explanations for this phenomenon, including immature memory systems in the brain (Madsen & Kim, 2016). Some psychologists believe that children begin to retain explicit memories after developing the ability to create autobiographical memory based on personal experience. Other psychologists suggest that childhood memory develops with language acquisition because the ability to use words and concepts aids in memory retention. Still other psychologists theorize that children younger than 3 or 4 do not perceive contexts well enough to store memories accurately. They argue that improvements in children's abilities to encode new information, retain it for longer periods, and deliberately retrieve it underlie the decrease in infantile amnesia after the first 5 years of life (Hayne, 2004). There are cultural differences in earliest memory, with the native Māori of New Zealand recalling memories, on average, a few months before their third birthdays. Although Māori mothers do not elaborate events in greater detail, it appears they talk about events in a way that enables their children to understand the relative time when events happened (Hayne, Imuta, & Scarf, 2015).

infantile amnesia

The inability to remember events from early childhood.

ANSWER: Infants have poor color vision and low visual acuity, so they most easily perceive objects with stark contrasts, such as black against a white background.

Q | **Why are many toys for infants black-and-white?**

THINK LIKE A PSYCHOLOGIST

9.4 Does Mozart Make You Smarter?

Can playing music to infants make them smarter? In 1993, Rauscher, Shaw, and Ky reported in the prestigious journal *Nature* that listening to the music of Wolfgang Amadeus Mozart led to higher scores on a test related to intelligence. The media jumped onto the so-called Mozart effect with abandon. Web sites made bold claims about the power of Mozart, including wild assertions that listening to Mozart could cure neurological illness and other maladies. To this day, Amazon sells dozens of Mozart effect products claiming to boost intelligence or improve brain functioning.

Thanks to the media reports in the popular press, many parents played Mozart recordings to their young children and even to fetuses (**FIGURE 9.14**). After all, intellectual abilities are prized, and educational success is viewed as a cornerstone to a successful life. Parents are eager to give their children every possible advantage. The state of Georgia even provided free Mozart CDs for every newborn, while the state of Florida passed a law requiring state-funded day care centers to play one hour of classical music each day, both governments buying into the idea that serenading infants with Mozart and other composers would produce a smarter populace.

But what was the empirical basis of these claims? What is the true power of Mozart for the developing mind? To see the claims more clearly, we need to step back and critically evaluate the research underlying the Mozart effect. In the study, psychologists played the first 10 minutes of the Mozart Sonata for Two Pianos in D Major (K. 448)

FIGURE 9.14
The Mozart Effect?
In the early 1990s, a study on the cognitive benefits of listening to Mozart inspired people to increase infants' exposure to classical music. However, the research results were misrepresented.

to a group of college students (Rauscher, Shaw, & Ky, 1993). Compared with students who listened to relaxation instructions or who sat in silence, those who heard Mozart performed slightly better on a task that involved folding and cutting paper. This task was part of a larger overall measure of intelligence. The modest increase lasted for about 10–15 minutes.

However, subsequent research largely failed to get the same results, even when using a similar research design. Having carefully reviewed the studies testing the Mozart effect, Christopher Chabris (1999) concluded that listening to Mozart is unlikely to increase intelligence among listeners. According to Chabris, listening to Mozart appears to enhance only certain types of motor skills, not abilities more commonly associated with intelligence (such as increasing working memory or verbal ability). A more recent meta-analysis of nearly 40 studies failed to find any specific advantage for Mozart, but it did find a very small influence of music on tasks such as those used in the original study (Pietschnig, Voracek, & Formann, 2010).

An important question is whether it was the music or some other aspect of the situation that led to better performance on the folding and cutting task. A team of researchers has shown that the effect may occur simply because listening to music is more uplifting than sitting in silence or relaxing; that is, the increase in positive mood may be largely responsible for better performance (Schellenberg, 2012; Thompson, Schellenberg, & Husain, 2001).

Also note that all the studies to date have been conducted with college students as participants. Do you see the problem? All the publicity focused on whether listening to Mozart increases infants' intelligence! Of course, experiences during early life are important to later development. However, most of the claims about music go far beyond the data.

Why did the findings of one small study lead to such widespread media reporting, and why did those reports resonate so much with parents? Researchers who have examined the media response to the Mozart effect note that the original findings tapped into parental anxiety over early childhood education (Bangerter & Heath, 2004). Indeed, the two states that offered free classical music for infants were among states with the lowest teachers' salaries, national test scores, and per pupil spending. A second factor is that the media play on people's fascination with research on brain functioning, and news outlets quickly try to extend research findings into practical applications, such as early childhood education (Pasquinelli, 2012). Although we have learned an incredible amount from the past two decades of neuroscience research, the translation of those findings into everyday applications needs to be guided by careful evaluation and scientific procedure. As a consumer of scientific information, be skeptical of extravagant claims made by the media. It is always best to check the original research before you draw any conclusions. ■

 What are the reasons that the original "Mozart effect" study does not support playing music to children to increase their cognitive abilities?

ANSWER: There are a few reasons. In the original study, "intelligence" was tested in relation to a motor skill; the test results might have been influenced by the mood-enhancing qualities of the situation; and the participants were college students, so there was no way to know whether the results applied to infants.

9.5 Infants Develop Attachments

One fundamental need infants have is to bond emotionally with those who care for them. An **attachment** is a strong, intimate, emotional connection between people that persists over time and across circumstances. Such emotional bonds are the building blocks of a successful social life later on. The attachment process draws on humans' innate tendency to form bonds with others. This tendency to bond is, in

attachment
A strong, intimate, emotional connection between people that persists over time and across circumstances.

fact, an adaptive trait. Forming bonds with others provides protection for individuals, increases their chances of survival, and thus increases their chances of passing along their genes to future generations (Bowlby, 1982).

Like all young primates, human infants need nurturance and care from adults to survive. Unlike horses and deer, which can walk and find food within hours after birth, humans are born profoundly immature. At that early point, human infants cannot even hold up their own heads or roll over. But they are far from passive. Just minutes after birth, infants' cries cause psychological, physiological, and behavioral reactions in caregivers that compel the offering of food and comfort to the newborns. As discussed earlier, even a newborn can have a social life. Young infants quickly build highly interactive social relationships. For example, within 10 weeks after birth, infants are profoundly affected by their caregivers' facial expressions and may become very upset when their primary caregivers fail to display emotional reactions (Cohn & Tronick, 1983).

Caregivers shape much of an infant's early experience, from what the child eats to where the child sleeps to what social connections the child makes. These early interactions with people begin to shape the developing human. They are the first stages in which a person learns how to communicate with others, how to behave appropriately in various situations, and how to establish and maintain relationships. Ultimately, socialization also affects complex human characteristics such as gender roles, a sense of personal identity, and moral reasoning, each of which will be explored in this chapter.

Between 4 and 6 weeks of age, most infants display a first social smile. This expression of pleasure typically induces powerful feelings of love in caregivers. According to John Bowlby (1982), the architect of attachment theory, infants have innate attachment behaviors that motivate adult attention. For instance, they prefer to remain close to caregivers, act distressed when caregivers leave and rejoice when they return, and put out their arms to be lifted.

Likewise, adults generally seem predisposed to respond to infants, as in picking up and rocking a crying child. They also tend to respond to infants in ways that infants can understand, as in making exaggerated facial expressions and speaking in a higher-pitched voice (**FIGURE 9.15**). The next time you observe an adult talking to a baby, notice how even the gruffest men with deep voices change their voices to a higher pitch. Babies attend to high-pitched voices. In virtually every culture studied, men, women, and even children intuitively raise the pitch of their voices when talking to babies, and babies respond by maintaining eye contact (Fernald, 1989; Vallabha, McClelland, Pons, Werker, & Amano, 2007). Bowlby argued that these behaviors motivate infants and caregivers to stay in proximity. Because it heightens feelings of security, attachment is adaptive: It is a dynamic relationship that facilitates survival for the infant and parental investment for the caregivers.

FIGURE 9.15
Infant Attachment Behaviors
Newborns behave in ways, such as smiling, that make their caregivers want to nurture them.

ATTACHMENT IN OTHER SPECIES Attachment is important for survival in many other species as well. For instance, infant birds communicate hunger through crying chirps. In doing so, they prompt caregivers to find food for them. Some bird species seem to have a sensitive period in which fledgling chicks become strongly attached to a nearby adult, even one from another species. This pattern occurs for birds such as chickens, geese, and ducks. Because these birds can walk immediately after hatching, they are at risk of straying from their mothers. Therefore, within about 18 hours after hatching, the birds will attach themselves to an adult (usually to their mothers) and then follow the object of their attachment. The ethologist

Konrad Lorenz (1935) called such behavior *imprinting*. He noted that goslings that became imprinted on him did not go back to their biological mothers when later given access to them (**FIGURE 9.16**). Such birds preferentially imprint on a female of their species if one is available, however.

During the late 1950s, the psychologist Harry Harlow began conducting research that later allowed him to discover one of the most striking examples of nonhuman attachment. At that time, psychologists generally believed an infant needed its mother primarily as a food source. For example, Freud viewed the attachment bond as being primarily motivated by the goal of drive reduction. He felt that infants attached to their mothers through having their oral needs met through breast-feeding. Thus, the hunger drive was reduced. But Harlow saw explanations of attachment that were based on food as inadequate for explaining what he observed in infant monkeys. He recognized that the infants needed comfort and security in addition to food.

In a now-famous series of experiments, Harlow placed infant rhesus monkeys in a cage with two different "mothers" (Harlow & Harlow, 1966). One surrogate mother was made of bare wire and could give milk through an attached bottle. The second surrogate mother was made of soft terry cloth and could not give milk. Which of these two substitute mothers do you think the infant monkeys preferred—the wire one that provided milk or the soft and cuddly one that could not feed them?

The monkeys' responses were unmistakable: They clung to the cloth mother most of the day. They went to it for comfort in times of threat. The monkeys approached the wire mother only when they were hungry. Harlow tested the monkeys' attachment to these mothers in various ways. For example, he introduced a strange object, such as a menacing metal robot with flashing eyes and large teeth, into the cage. The infants always ran to the mother that provided comfort, never to the mother that fed them. Harlow repeatedly found that the infants were calmer, braver, and overall better adjusted when near the cloth mother. Once they clung to her, they would calm down and actually confront the feared object! Hence, the mother-as-food theory of mother/child attachment was debunked. Harlow's findings established the importance of contact comfort—the importance of physical touch and reassurance—in aiding social development (see "The Methods of Psychology: Harlow's Monkeys and Their 'Mothers,'" on p. 350).

FIGURE 9.16
Imprinting
Here, Konrad Lorenz walks the goslings that had imprinted themselves on him. The little geese followed Lorenz as if he were their mother.

ATTACHMENT STYLE If Bowlby and Harlow were correct in hypothesizing that attachment encourages proximity between infant and caregiver, then we might expect attachment responses to increase when children start moving away from caregivers. And indeed, just when infants begin to understand the difference between their attachment figures and strangers, and at the same time start to move away from strangers by crawling—at around 8–12 months—they typically display separation anxiety. That is, when the infants cannot see or are separated from their attachment figures or are left with babysitters, they may become very distressed. This pattern occurs in all human cultures.

To study attachment behaviors in humans, the developmental psychologist Mary D. Salter Ainsworth created the strange-situation test. The researchers observe the test through a one-way mirror in the laboratory. On the other side of the mirror is a playroom. There, the child, the caregiver, and a friendly but unfamiliar adult engage in a series of eight semi-structured episodes. The crux of the procedure is a standard sequence of separations and reunions between the child and each adult. Over the course of the eight episodes, the child experiences increasing distress and a greater need for caregiver proximity. The extent to which the child copes with distress and

The Methods of Psychology
Harlow's Monkeys and Their "Mothers"

HYPOTHESIS: Infant monkeys will form an attachment to a surrogate mother that provides comfort.

RESEARCH METHOD: Infant rhesus monkeys were put in a cage with two different "mothers":

1 One mother was made of cloth, but could not give milk.

2 The other was made of wire, but could give milk.

RESULTS: The monkeys clung to the cloth mother and went to it for comfort in times of threat. The monkeys approached the wire mother only when they were hungry.

CONCLUSION: Infant monkeys will prefer and form an attachment to a surrogate mother that provides comfort over a wire surrogate mother that provides milk.

NOTE: Photographs are not available from the original experiments. These images are from the CBS television show *Carousel*, which filmed Harlow simulating versions of his experiments in 1962. He deliberately manipulated the faces for another experiment.

QUESTION: Do these findings imply that children can become attached to their mothers even if they are regularly bottle-fed by others? Why or why not?

ANSWER: Yes, because the children can be comforted by contact with their mothers (and fathers) even if not fed by them.

Source: Harlow, H. F., & Harlow, M. (1966). Learning to love. *American Scientist, 54,* 244–272.

the strategies he uses to do so indicate the quality of the child's attachment to the caregiver. The researchers record the child's activity level and actions such as crying, playing, and paying attention to the mother and the stranger. Using the strange-situation test, Ainsworth identified infant/caregiver pairs that appeared secure as well as those that appeared insecure, or anxious (Ainsworth, Blehar, Waters, & Wall, 1978; **FIGURE 9.17**).

Secure attachment applies to approximately 60–65 percent of children. A secure child is happy to play alone and is friendly to the stranger as long as the attachment figure is present. When the attachment figure leaves the playroom, the child is distressed, whines or cries, and shows signs of looking for the attachment figure. When the attachment figure returns, the child usually reaches his arms up to be picked up and then is happy and quickly comforted by the caregiver. Then the child

secure attachment

The attachment style for a majority of infants; the infant is confident enough to play in an unfamiliar environment as long as the caregiver is present and is readily comforted by the caregiver during times of distress.

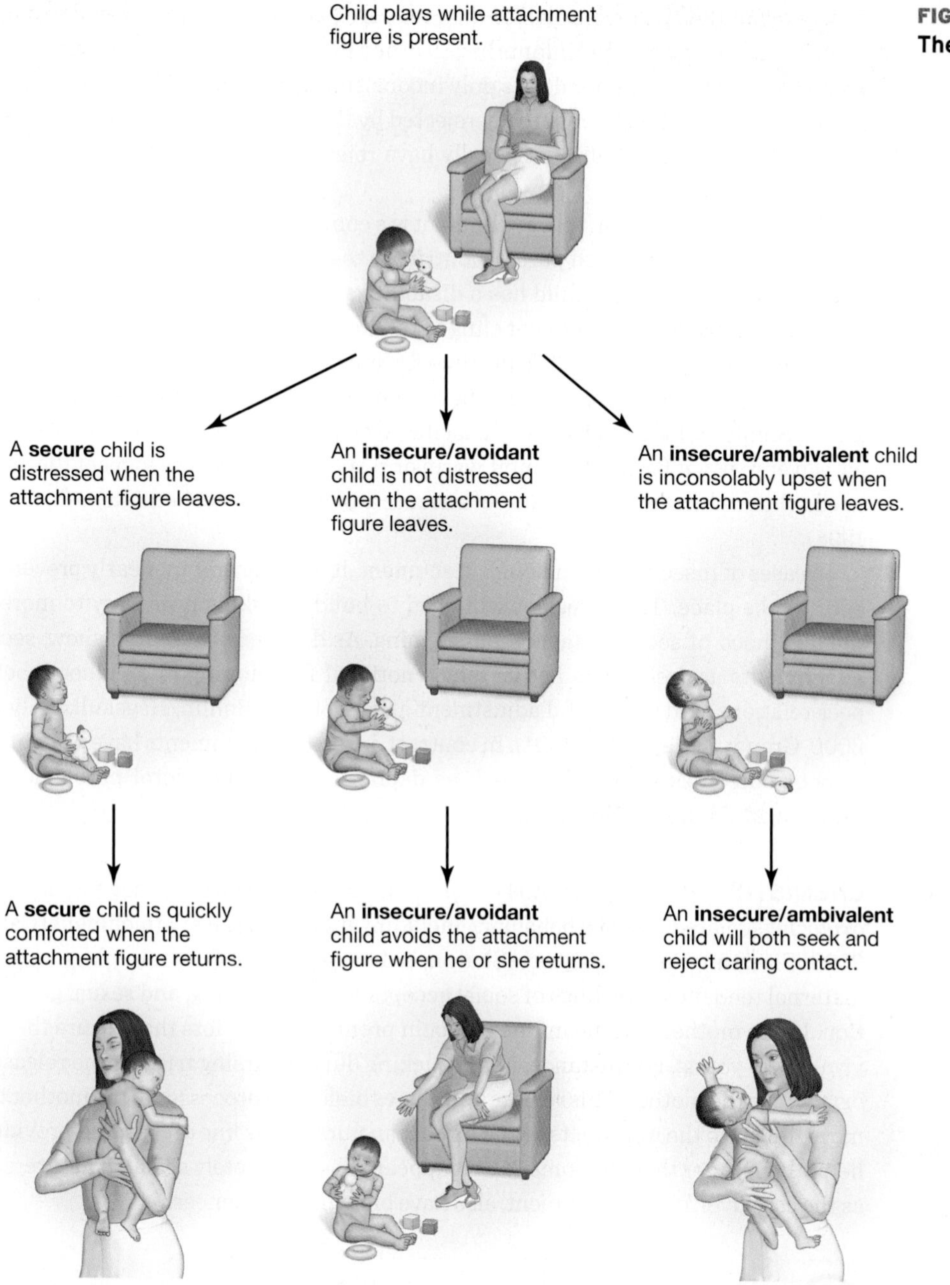

Child plays while attachment figure is present.

FIGURE 9.17
The Strange-Situation Test

A **secure** child is distressed when the attachment figure leaves.

An **insecure/avoidant** child is not distressed when the attachment figure leaves.

An **insecure/ambivalent** child is inconsolably upset when the attachment figure leaves.

A **secure** child is quickly comforted when the attachment figure returns.

An **insecure/avoidant** child avoids the attachment figure when he or she returns.

An **insecure/ambivalent** child will both seek and reject caring contact.

feels secure enough to return to playing. The key behavior to notice here, similar to what Harlow found with his monkeys, is the use of the caregiver as a source of security in times of distress. Just as a monkey would calm down when in contact with its cuddly cloth "mother," a securely attached human infant will be soothed immediately after a distressing separation when the caregiver picks up the infant.

Insecure attachment applies to the remaining 35–40 percent of children. Insecure attachments (sometimes referred to as *anxious* attachments) can take many forms, from an infant's completely avoiding contact with the caregiver during the strange-situation test to the infant's actively hitting or exhibiting angry facial expressions toward the caregiver (Ainsworth et al., 1978). Insecure attachments typically are of two types. Children with *avoidant* attachment do not get upset or cry at all when the caregiver leaves, and they may prefer to play with the stranger rather than the parent during their time in the playroom. Those with an *ambivalent* attachment style (sometimes called *anxious/resistant*) may cry a great deal when the caregiver leaves

insecure attachment
The attachment style for a minority of infants; the infant may exhibit insecure attachment through various behaviors, such as avoiding contact with the caregiver, or by alternating between approach and avoidance behaviors.

the room but then be inconsolable when the caregiver tries to calm them down upon return. Insecurely attached infants have learned that their caregiver is not available to soothe them when distressed or is only inconsistently available. These children may be emotionally neglected or actively rejected by their attachment figures. Caregivers of insecurely attached infants typically have rejecting or inconsistently responsive parenting styles.

Keep in mind, however, that attachment is a complex developmental phenomenon. As in all relationships, both parties contribute to the quality or success of the interactions. For example, if a child has a disability such as autism spectrum disorder—which may cause the infant to not cling to the caregiver or not make eye contact—the caregiver may have a more difficult time forming a secure emotional bond with the infant (Rutgers, Bakermans-Kranenburg, van Ijzendoorn, & van Berckelaer-Onnes, 2004). Similarly, if a caregiver is incapacitated by mental illness or extreme stress, the caregiver may not be able to exhibit warm or responsive behaviors to meet the baby's needs, thus reducing the likelihood of a secure attachment (Cicchetti, Rogosh, & Toth, 1998).

In cases of insecure (or anxious) attachment, it is important that early prevention efforts take place. The caregiver will need to build the skills necessary to increase the likelihood of secure attachments forming. As decades of research show, secure attachments are related to better socioemotional functioning in childhood, better peer relations, and successful adjustment at school (e.g., Bohlin, Hagekull, & Rydell, 2000; Granot & Mayseless, 2001). In contrast, insecure attachments have been linked to poor outcomes later in life, such as depression and behavioral problems (e.g., Munson, McMahon, & Spieker, 2001).

CHEMISTRY OF ATTACHMENT Researchers have discovered that the hormone *oxytocin* is related to social behaviors, including infant/caregiver attachment (Carter, 2003; Feldman, Weller, Zagoory-Sharon, & Levine, 2007). Oxytocin plays a role in maternal tendencies, feelings of social acceptance and bonding, and sexual gratification. In the mother and the infant, oxytocin promotes behaviors that ensure the survival of the young. For instance, infant sucking during nursing triggers the release of oxytocin in the mother. This release stimulates biological processes in the mother that move milk into the milk ducts so the infant can nurse. This line of research provides a helpful reminder that phenomena that appear to be completely social in nature, such as the caregiver/child attachment, also have biological influences.

ANSWER: Attachment motivates infants and caregivers to stay near each other, increasing the likelihood that the infants will survive and thrive.

 According to Bowlby, how is attachment adaptive?

How Do Children Learn About the World?

To learn, children need to obtain information from the world. They do so principally through their senses. As noted earlier, newborns have all their senses at birth, although some of the senses are not fully developed. The development of sensory capacities enables infants to observe and evaluate the objects and events around them. The infants then use the information gained from perception to try to make sense of how the world works. In other words, children think about things. How does cognition develop in childhood?

Learning Objectives

- List and describe the stages of development proposed by Piaget.

- Discuss challenges to Piaget's theory.

- Define theory of mind and explain its significance for prosocial behavior.

- Compare and contrast theories of moral reasoning and moral emotions.

9.6 Piaget Emphasized Stages of Cognitive Development

Ultimately, how do we account for the differences between children's ways of thinking and adults' ways of thinking? Are children merely inexperienced adults? Do they simply not have the skills and knowledge that adults normally have learned over time? Or do children's minds work in qualitatively different ways from those of adults?

Through careful observations of young children, Jean Piaget (1924) devised an influential theory about the development of thinking (**FIGURE 9.18**). Several of Piaget's ideas have been supported by subsequent research. For instance, Piaget viewed children as qualitatively different from adults, not simply as inexperienced adults. He also viewed children as actively trying to understand the world around them by interacting with objects and by observing the consequences of their actions. As you will see in the next section, however, researchers have challenged several of Piaget's other assertions.

One crucial aspect of Piaget's research is that he paid as much attention to how children make errors as to how they succeed on tasks. Children's mistakes, illogical by adult standards, provide insights into how young minds make sense of the world. By systematically analyzing children's thinking, Piaget developed the theory that children go through four *stages of development*, which reflect different ways of thinking about the world. These stages are called *sensorimotor, preoperational, concrete operational*, and *formal operational* (**FIGURE 9.19**).

FIGURE 9.18
Jean Piaget
Piaget introduced the idea that cognitive development occurs in stages.

Stage	Characterization
1 Sensorimotor (birth–2 years)	• Differentiates self from objects • Recognizes self as agent of action and begins to act intentionally; for example, pulls a string to set a mobile in motion or shakes a rattle to make a noise • Achieves object permanence: realizes that things continue to exist even when no longer present to the senses 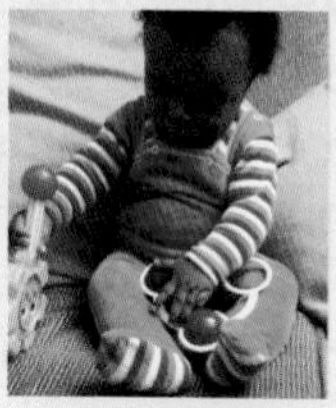
2 Preoperational (2–7 years)	• Learns to use language and to represent objects by images and words • Thinking is still egocentric: has difficulty taking the viewpoint of others • Classifies objects by a single feature; for example, groups together all the red blocks regardless of shape or all the square blocks regardless of color 
3 Concrete operational (7–12 years)	• Can think logically about objects and events • Achieves conservation of number (age 7), mass (age 7), and weight (age 9) • Classifies objects by several features and can order them in a series along a single dimension, such as size 
4 Formal operational (12 years and up)	• Can think logically about abstract propositions and test hypotheses systematically • Becomes concerned with the hypothetical, the future, and ideological problems 

FIGURE 9.19
Piaget's Stages of Cognitive Development

1 A young child believes that a tall 8 oz. glass contains more juice than a short 8 oz. glass.

2 Here, the child watches the juice being poured from the tall glass into a second short glass.

3 She is surprised to see that the short glass holds the same amount of juice as the tall glass.

FIGURE 9.20

The Preoperational Stage and the Law of Conservation of Quantity

In the preoperational stage, according to Piaget, children cannot yet understand the concept of conservation of quantity. They reason intuitively, not logically.

From Piaget's perspective, it is not that children know less than adults. Rather, children's views of how the world works are based on different sets of assumptions than those held by adults. Contemporary researchers argue that such developmental "immaturity" in early-stage thinking actually serves very important functions for children's mental abilities to grow (Bjorklund, 2007).

Piaget proposed that new schemes are formed during each stage of development. *Schemes* are ways of thinking based on personal experience. Piaget's idea of schemes is somewhat similar to the concept of schemas defined and discussed in Chapter 7. For Piaget, schemes were organized ways of making sense of experience, and they changed as the child learned new information about objects and events in the world. Piaget believed that each stage builds on the previous one through two learning processes: Through **assimilation,** a new experience is placed into an existing scheme. Through **accommodation** (not to be confused with the process of accommodation in the visual system, in Chapter 5), a new scheme is created or an existing one is dramatically altered to include new information that otherwise would not fit into the scheme.

For example, a 2-year-old sees a Great Dane and asks, "What's that?" The parent answers that it is a dog. But it does not look anything like the family Chihuahua. The toddler needs to assimilate the Great Dane into the existing dog scheme. The same 2-year-old might see a cow for the first time and shout, "Doggie!" After all, a cow has four legs and fur and is about the same size as a Great Dane. Thus, based on a dog scheme the child has developed, the label "doggie" can be considered logical. But the toddler's parent says, "No, honey, that's a cow! See, it doesn't say 'Arf!' It says 'Moo!' And it is much bigger than a dog." Because the child cannot easily fit this new information into the existing dog scheme using the process of assimilation, the child must now create a new scheme, cow, through the process of accommodation.

SENSORIMOTOR STAGE (BIRTH TO 2 YEARS) From birth until about age 2, according to Piaget, children are in the **sensorimotor stage.** During this period, children are firmly situated in the present and acquire information primarily through their senses and motor exploration. Thus, very young infants' understanding of objects occurs when they reflexively react to the sensory input from those objects. For example, they learn by sucking on a nipple, grasping a finger, or seeing a face—that is, through perception and observation of the results of their actions. They progress from being reflexive to being reflective. In other words, they become capable of mentally representing their world and experiences with increasingly complex schemes.

As infants begin to control their motor movements, they develop their first schemes. These conceptual models reflect the kinds of actions that can be performed on certain kinds of objects. For instance, the sucking reflex begins as a reaction to the sensory input from the nipple: Infants simply respond reflexively by sucking. Soon they realize they can suck on other things, such as a bottle, a finger, a toy, or a blanket. Piaget described sucking on other objects as an example of assimilation to the scheme of sucking. But sucking on a toy or a blanket does not result in the same experience as the reflexive sucking of a nipple. The difference between these experiences leads the child to alter the sucking scheme to include new experiences and information. In other words, the child must continually adjust her understandings of sucking. But you cannot suck something like a milk carton—so the child forms a scheme of things that provide liquid but cannot be sucked. The child creates this new scheme through accommodation.

According to Piaget, one important cognitive concept that develops in this stage is **object permanence.** This term refers to the understanding that an object continues to exist even when it is hidden from view. Piaget noted that until 9 months of age, most infants will not search for objects they have seen being hidden under a blanket.

At around 9 months, infants will look for the hidden object by picking up the blanket. Still, their search skills have limits. For instance, suppose during several trials an 8-month-old child watches an experimenter hide a toy under a blanket and the child then finds the toy. If the experimenter then hides the toy under a different blanket, in full view of the child, the child will still look for the toy in the first hiding place. Full comprehension of object permanence was, for Piaget, one key accomplishment of the sensorimotor period.

PREOPERATIONAL STAGE (2 TO 7 YEARS) In the **preoperational stage,** according to Piaget, children can begin to think about objects not in their immediate view. Having formed conceptual models of how the world works, children begin to think symbolically. For example, they can pretend that a stick is a sword or a wand. Piaget believed that what children cannot do at this stage is think "operationally." That is, they cannot imagine the logical outcomes of performing certain actions on certain objects. They do not base their reasoning on logic. Instead, they perform intuitive reasoning based on superficial appearances.

For instance, children at this stage have no understanding of the law of conservation of quantity. This law states that even if a substance's appearance changes, its quantity may remain unchanged. If you pour a short, fat glass of water into a tall, thin glass, you know the amount of water has not changed. However, if you ask children in the preoperational stage which glass contains more, they will pick the tall, thin glass because the water is at a higher level. The children will make this error even when they have seen someone pour the same amount of water into each glass or when they pour the liquid themselves. They are fooled by the appearance of a higher water line. They cannot think about how the thinner diameter of the taller glass compensates for the higher-appearing water level (**FIGURE 9.20**).

Piaget thought that another cognitive limitation characteristic of the preoperational period is *egocentrism.* This term refers to the tendency for preoperational thinkers to view the world through their own experiences. They can understand how others feel, and they have the capacity to care about others. They tend, however, to engage in thought processes that revolve around their own perspectives. For example, a 3-year-old may play hide-and-seek by crouching next to a large tree and facing it with her eyes closed (**FIGURE 9.21**). The child believes that if she cannot see other people, other people cannot see her. Instead of viewing this egocentric thinking as a limitation, modern scholars agree with Piaget that such "immature" skills prepare children to take special note of their immediate surroundings and learn as much as they can about how their own minds and bodies interact with the world. A clear egocentric focus prevents them from trying to expand their schemas too much before they understand all the complex information inside their own experience (Bjorklund, 2007).

CONCRETE OPERATIONAL STAGE (7 TO 12 YEARS) At about 7 years of age, according to Piaget, children enter the **concrete operational stage.** They remain in this stage until adolescence. Piaget believed that humans do not develop logic until they begin to perform mental operations. The first stage is performing mental operations on concrete objects in the world. That is, a preoperational child lacks logical thought, but a concrete operational child is able to think logically about actual objects. A classic *operation* is an action that can be undone, such as turning a light on and off. According to Piaget, the ability to understand that an action is reversible enables children to begin to understand concepts such as conservation of quantity. Children in this period are not fooled by superficial transformations in the liquid's appearance in conservation tasks. They can reason logically about the problem. And they begin to understand with much more depth how other people view the world and feel about things.

assimilation
The process by which new information is placed into an existing scheme.

accommodation
The process by which a new scheme is created or an existing scheme is drastically altered to include new information that otherwise would not fit into the scheme.

sensorimotor stage
The first stage in Piaget's theory of cognitive development; during this stage, infants acquire information about the world through their senses and motor skills. Reflexive responses develop into more deliberate actions through the development and refinement of schemes.

object permanence
The understanding that an object continues to exist even when it cannot be seen.

preoperational stage
The second stage in Piaget's theory of cognitive development; during this stage, children think symbolically about objects, but they reason based on intuition and superficial appearance rather than logic.

concrete operational stage
The third stage in Piaget's theory of cognitive development; during this stage, children begin to think about and understand logical operations, and they are no longer fooled by appearances.

FIGURE 9.21
Egocentrism
This little girl is "hiding" behind a tree by covering her own eyes. If she cannot see the searchers, she believes they cannot see her.

Although this development is the beginning of logical thinking, Piaget believed that children at this stage reason only about concrete things. They do not yet have the ability to reason abstractly, or hypothetically, about what might be possible.

FORMAL OPERATIONAL STAGE (12 YEARS TO ADULTHOOD) Piaget believed that after about age 12, individuals can reason in sophisticated, abstract ways. Thus, the **formal operational stage** is Piaget's final stage of cognitive development. Formal operations involve critical thinking. This kind of thinking is characterized by the ability to form a hypothesis about something and test the hypothesis through deductive logic. It also involves using information to systematically find answers to problems.

Piaget devised a way to study this ability. He gave teenagers and younger children four flasks of colorless liquid and one flask of colored liquid. He then explained that the colored liquid could be obtained by combining two of the colorless liquids. Adolescents, he found, can systematically try different combinations to obtain the correct result. Younger children just randomly combine liquids. Adolescents can form hypotheses and systematically test them. They are able to consider abstract notions and think about many viewpoints at once.

Q **According to Piaget, why might a child who is crying while trying to reach a toy stop crying when a caregiver places a towel over the toy?**

ANSWER: because the child does not have object permanence and so does not understand that the now-hidden toy still exists

9.7 Piaget Underestimated Children's Cognitive Abilities

Piaget revolutionized the understanding of cognitive development and was right about several things. For example, infants do learn about the world through sensorimotor exploration. Also, people do move from intuitive, illogical thinking to a more logical understanding of the world. Piaget also believed, however, that as children progress through each stage, they all use the same kind of logic to solve problems. His framework thus leaves little room for differing cognitive strategies or skills among individuals—or among cultures.

Work by Piaget's contemporary Lev Vygotsky emphasized social relations over objects in thinking about cognitive development. Vygotsky focused on the role of social and cultural context in the development of both cognition and language. According to Vygotsky, humans are unique because they use symbols and psychological tools—such as speech, writing, maps, art, and so on—through which they create culture. Culture, in turn, dictates what people need to learn and the sorts of skills they need to develop (**FIGURE 9.22**). For example, some cultures value science and rational thinking. Other cultures emphasize supernatural and mystical forces. These cultural values shape how people think about and relate to the world around them. Vygotsky distinguished between elementary mental functions (such as innate sensory experiences) and higher mental functions (such as language, perception, abstraction, and memory). As children develop, their elementary capacities are gradually transformed. Culture exerts the primary influence on these capacities (Vygotsky, 1978).

Central to Vygotsky's theories is the idea that social and cultural context influences language development. In turn, language development influences cognitive development. Children start by directing their speech toward specific communications with others, such as asking for food or for toys. As children develop, they begin directing speech toward themselves, as when they give themselves directions or talk

formal operational stage
The final stage in Piaget's theory of cognitive development; in this stage, people can think abstractly, and they can formulate and test hypotheses through deductive logic.

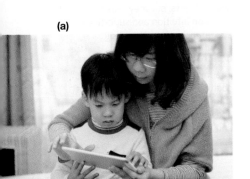

(a)

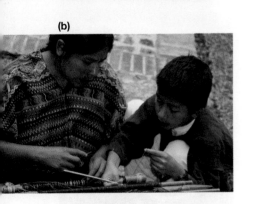

(b)

FIGURE 9.22
Culture and Learning
(a) People in Western, technology-driven cultures may learn different information or emphasize different skills than **(b)** people in non-Western, not fully technological cultures.

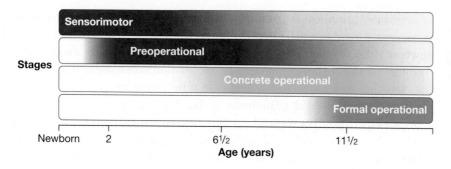

FIGURE 9.23
Trends in Cognitive Development

Modern interpretations view Piaget's theory in terms of trends, not rigid stages. Children shift gradually in their thinking over a wider range of ages than previously thought, and they can demonstrate thinking skills of more than one stage at a time.

to themselves while playing. Eventually, children internalize their words into inner speech: verbal thoughts that direct both behavior and cognition. From this perspective, your thoughts are based on the language you have acquired through your society and through your culture, and this ongoing inner speech reflects higher-order cognitive processes. In challenging Piaget's framework of universal developmental milestones, Vygotsky proposed the important interaction between self and environment.

Another challenge to Piaget's view is that many children move back and forth between stages if they are working on tasks that require varying skill levels. They may think in concrete operational ways on some tasks but revert to preoperational logic when faced with a novel task. Theorists believe that different areas in the brain are responsible for different skills and that development does not necessarily follow strict and uniform stages (Bidell & Fischer, 1995; Case, 1992; Fischer, 1980; **FIGURE 9.23**).

In addition, Piaget thought that all adults were formal operational thinkers. More-recent work has shown that without specific training or education in this type of thinking, many adults continue to reason in concrete operational ways, instead of using critical and analytical thinking skills. These adults may think abstractly regarding topics with which they are familiar but not on new and unfamiliar tasks (De Lisi & Staudt, 1980). A good example of this kind of thinking is the candle-and-tack problem illustrated in Figure 8.22a–b.

Moreover, Piaget underestimated the age at which certain skills develop. For example, contemporary researchers have found that object permanence develops in the first few months of life, instead of at 8 or 9 months of age, as Piaget thought. With new scientific methods that do not require infants to physically search for hidden objects, researchers have found object permanence abilities in infants as early as 3.5 months of age (Baillargeon, 1987).

Consider the apple/carrot test devised by the developmental psychologist Renée Baillargeon (1995). The researcher shows an apple to an infant who is sitting on his parent's lap. The researcher lowers a screen in front of the apple, then raises the screen to show the apple. Then the researcher performs the same actions, but this time raises the screen to show a carrot—a surprising, impossible event. If the infant looks longer at the carrot than he had looked at the apple, the researcher can assume that the infant expected to see the apple. By responding differently to such an impossible event than to possible ones, infants demonstrate some understanding that an object continues to exist when it is out of sight. Thus, in his various testing protocols, Piaget may have confused infants' physical capabilities with their cognitive abilities.

UNDERSTANDING THE LAWS OF NATURE: PHYSICS The tasks used by Piaget implied that infants and young children have a relatively poor understanding of physical forces, such as conservation of quantity. Numerous studies conducted by the developmental psychologist Elizabeth Spelke and colleagues have indicated that infants even have a primitive understanding of some of the basic laws of physics (Spelke, 2016). These researchers created cognitive tasks that do not rely on language

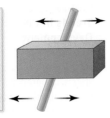

1 A 4-month-old is shown a rod that moves back and forth behind an occluding block. The infant becomes habituated to this stimulus.

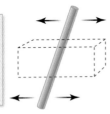

2 The infant is then shown one event: The block is removed to reveal a solid rod moving back and forth behind the block.

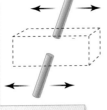

3 Finally, the infant is shown a second event: The block is removed to reveal two separate rods moving back and forth behind the block. The infant spends much more time looking at the second event (two moving rods) than at the first (one moving rod).

FIGURE 9.24
Perceptual Expectancies in Early Infancy
As shown by this rod-and-block test, infants are able to perceive that objects moving together are continuous. Understanding the relation between movement and physical properties requires cognitive skills beyond those that Piaget expected 4-month-old infants to have.

or physical capabilities. For example, humans are born with the ability to perceive movement. A newborn will follow a moving stimulus with her eyes and head, and a newborn will also prefer to look at a moving stimulus than to look at a stationary one. As infants get older, they use movement information to determine if an object is continuous—that is, if it is all one object, even if the infant cannot see the entire thing because it is partially hidden (Kellman, Spelke, & Short, 1986).

In one experiment, the researchers showed 4-month-old infants a rod moving back and forth behind a block. Once the infants had viewed the scene many times, they quit responding to it. That is, they had *habituated* to the stimulus (recall from Chapter 6 that habituation is decreased responding to an unchanging stimulus). The infants were then shown two scenes: In one scene, the block was removed and there was a single rod. In the other scene, the block was removed and there were two small rods. The infants looked longer at the two small rods (**FIGURE 9.24**). This response indicated that they expected the rod moving behind the block to be one continuous object rather than two small ones. Studies such as these rely on the *orienting reflex*. This term refers to humans' tendency to pay more attention to new stimuli than to stimuli to which they have become habituated (Fantz, 1966). Even from birth, an infant will look away more quickly from something familiar than from something unfamiliar or puzzling.

Understanding the relation between the movement and the physical properties of the rod requires various cognitive skills. It requires the ability to see the rod as an object separate from the block and to surmise that since the two ends are moving together, they must be part of the same whole rod, even though part of the rod is hidden. If the experiment is conducted with a stationary rod, however, the infants do not look longer at the two small rods. Therefore, infants appear to use movement to infer that objects moving together are continuous, whereas for infants two stationary objects may or may not be continuous.

UNDERSTANDING THE LAWS OF NATURE: MATHEMATICS How much do you think infants and toddlers know about counting and other mathematical operations? Piaget believed that young children do not understand numbers and therefore must learn counting and other number-related skills through memorization. For some of his experiments in this area, he showed two rows of marbles to children 4–5 years old. Both rows had the same number of marbles, but in one row the marbles were spread out. The children usually said the longer row had more marbles (**FIGURE 9.25**). Piaget concluded that children understand quantity—the concepts *more than* and *less than*—in terms of length. He felt that children do not understand quantity in terms of number.

Challenging Piaget's view, Jacques Mehler and Tom Bever (1967) argued that children younger than 3 years of age can understand *more than* and *less than*. To demonstrate their point, they cleverly repeated Piaget's experiment using M&M's candy. They showed the children two rows of four M&M's each and asked if the rows were the same. When the children said yes, the researchers then transformed the rows. For instance, they would add two candies to the second row, but compress that row so it was shorter than the row with fewer candies. Then they would tell the children to pick the row they wanted to eat. More than 80 percent picked the row with more M&M's, even though it was the visually shorter row (**FIGURE 9.26**). This research indicated that when children are properly motivated, they understand and can demonstrate their knowledge of *more than* and *less than*.

Despite Piaget's enormous contributions to the understanding of cognitive development, the growing evidence that infants have innate knowledge challenges his theory of distinct stages of cognitive development. Moreover, the available evidence

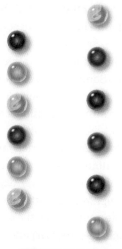

1 A 4-year-old is shown two rows of marbles. Each row has the same number of marbles, but one row is spread out.

2 When asked which row has more marbles, the 4-year-old says the longer row.

FIGURE 9.25
Piaget's Marble Test
This test led Piaget to conclude that very young children do not understand quantity in terms of number, that they understand it in terms of length.

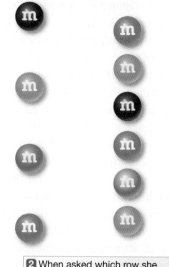

1 A 3-year-old is shown two rows of M&M's candies. One row has more candies, but is condensed.

2 When asked which row she wants to eat, the 3-year-old picks the row with more candies even though it is shorter.

FIGURE 9.26
The M&M's Version of Piaget's Marble Test
This test enabled Mehler and Bever to show that very young children can in fact understand quantity in terms of number.

indicates that within days after birth infants possess quite sophisticated thinking about spatial relations, time, and numbers (de Hevia, Izard, Coubart, Spelke, & Streri, 2014).

 How do research findings that infants understand some basic workings of physics and math challenge Piaget's theories?

ANSWER: Studies have shown that young infants possess cognitive abilities that Piaget believed did not develop until much later in childhood.

9.8 Children Learn from Interacting with Others

According to current thinking among developmental psychologists, early social interactions between infant and caregiver are essential for understanding other people and communicating with them through language. In turn, these skills enable individuals to live in society. To interact with other people successfully, individuals need to be aware of others' intentions, behave in ways that generally conform to others' expectations, develop moral codes that guide their actions, learn and follow rules, and so on. Consider a routine activity such as driving a car. To drive safely, a person needs to predict and respond to the actions of others: car drivers, truck drivers, motorcyclists, bicyclists, and pedestrians. Any of those people's actions can be erratic.

THEORY OF MIND Humans have an innate ability to understand that others have minds and that those minds have desires, intentions, beliefs, and mental states. People

theory of mind
The ability to understand that other people have mental states that influence their behavior.

are also able to form, with some degree of accuracy, theories about what those desires, intentions, beliefs, and mental states are. David Premack and Guy Woodruff (1978) coined the term **theory of mind** to describe this ability. In dealing with other people, we try to recognize each person's mental state. That is, we infer what the person is feeling or thinking. From that inference, we anticipate the other person's behavior. Predicting another person's behavior based on that person's mental state constitutes theory of mind.

Beginning in infancy, young children come to understand that other people perform actions for reasons (Gergely & Csibra, 2003; Sommerville & Woodward, 2005). The recognition that actions can be intentional reflects a capacity for theory of mind, and it allows people to understand, predict, and attempt to influence others' behavior (Baldwin & Baird, 2001).

In one study, an adult began handing a toy to an infant. On some trials, the adult became unwilling to hand over the toy (e.g., teasing the infant with the toy or playing with it himself). On other trials, the adult became unable to hand it over (e.g., "accidentally" dropping it or being distracted by a ringing telephone). Infants older than 9 months showed greater signs of impatience—for example, reaching for the toy—when the adult was unwilling than when the adult was unable (Behne, Carpenter, Call, & Tomasello, 2005). This research shows that very young children understand other peoples' intentions, capabilities, and reasoning behind their actions.

By the end of the second year, perhaps even by 13 to 15 months of age, children become very good at reading intentions (Baillargeon, Li, Ng, & Yuan, 2009). In other words, even though preschool-age children tend to behave in egocentric ways and view the world through their own perspectives, mounting evidence suggests that they have the cognitive abilities to understand others' perspectives (Baillargeon, Scott, & Bian, 2016). The understanding of complex mental states, such as that people can have false beliefs, develops later in childhood. A common test of false belief is shown in **FIGURE 9.27.**

Children's development of theory of mind appears to coincide with the maturation of the brain's frontal lobes. The importance of the frontal lobes for theory of mind is also supported by research with adults. In brain imaging studies, prefrontal brain regions become active when people are asked to think about other people's mental states (Mar, 2011; Schurz, Radua, Aichhorn, Richlan, & Perner, 2014). People with damage to this region have difficulty attributing mental states to characters in stories (Stone, Baron-Cohen, & Knight, 1998). Brain imaging studies of theory of mind conducted in Canada, the United States, England, France, Germany, Japan, and Sweden have found similar patterns of activity in prefrontal regions (Frank & Temple, 2009). These findings support the idea that the ability is universal and biologically based.

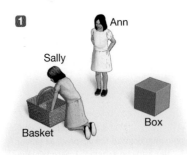

Sally puts her marble in the basket.

Sally goes away.

Ann moves the marble.

"Where will Sally look for her marble?"

FIGURE 9.27
A Classic Test for a Child's Theory of Mind
When a child acquires theory of mind, she is able to understand that different individuals have both different perspectives and knowledge based on their individual experiences.

UNDERSTANDING SOCIAL EMOTIONS Having insight into other minds enables us to predict how other people will feel in a given situation. Children learn to predict when their caregivers, siblings, and friends will be angry, sad, embarrassed, and so on. Research on children's social emotions has focused largely on empathy and sympathy. Empathy involves understanding another's emotional state and relies on theory of mind. Empathy involves feeling with the other person, as in wincing when you see another person injured. Recall the discussion of mirror neurons in Chapter 6. When people observe another person experiencing pain, such as a finger being cut, mirror neurons are active in the observer along with activity in brain regions that process pain (Decety & Howard, 2014; Lamm, Decety, & Singer, 2011). In contrast, sympathy arises from feelings of concern, pity, or sorrow for another (Eisenberg, 2000). Sympathy involves feeling for the other person. Sympathy may produce different emotions from those experienced by the other person, such as feeling pity for a person who recently lost his job.

Someone with the capacity for theory of mind might seek to comfort a person who is upset. Doing so is an example of *prosocial behavior*, which is any voluntary action performed with the specific intent of benefiting another person (Eisenberg, VanSchyndel, & Spinrad, 2016). Consider that young infants become distressed when they see other infants crying (Zahn-Waxler & Radke-Yarrow, 1990). Generally, children's early attempts to soothe other children are ineffective. For instance, they tend initially to comfort themselves rather than the other children. Still, this empathic response to other people's suffering suggests that prosocial behavior is hardwired in humans. Starting after 1 year of age, children become willing to help others, such as by picking up objects for someone who has dropped them (Warneken, 2015). A recent meta-analysis found that children with higher scores on theory of mind tests are more likely to behave prosocially (Imuta, Henry, Slaughter, Selcuk, & Ruffman, 2016).

Research has shown that parents' behaviors influence their children's level of both social emotions and prosocial behavior. When parents are high in sympathy, promote an understanding of and focus on others, do not express hostility in the home, allow their children to express negative emotions in ways that do not harm others, and help their children cope with negative emotions, they tend to have children who are high in sympathy (Eisenberg, 2002; **FIGURE 9.28**).

FIGURE 9.28
Parental Behavior Affects Children's Behavior
Parents who are high in sympathy, and who allow their children to express negative emotions without shame or hostility, tend to have children who are high in sympathy.

 What is the relationship between theory of mind and prosocial behavior?

ANSWER: Those who exhibit greater capacity for theory of mind are more likely to perform prosocial behavior.

9.9 Moral Development Begins in Childhood

Morality plays a central role in human life, influencing both trivial and consequential choices and actions. When is it okay to use or take someone else's possessions? When is it acceptable to perform an action that may harm others or that may break social contracts? The ability to consider questions about morality develops during childhood and continues into adulthood. Theorists typically divide morality into *moral reasoning*, which depends on cognitive processes, and *moral emotions*, which are linked to societal interests as a whole (Haidt, 2003). Moral emotions motivate people to do good things and avoid doing bad things. They include shame, guilt, disgust, embarrassment, pride, and gratitude.

Piaget suggested that children's developing cognitive skills allowed for increasingly sophisticated moral reasoning. In keeping with this cognitive perspective, psychologists who study moral behavior have focused largely on Lawrence Kohlberg's stage theory. Kohlberg (1984) tested moral-reasoning skills by asking people to respond to hypothetical situations in which a main character was faced with a moral dilemma. For example, the character had to steal a drug to save his dying wife because he could

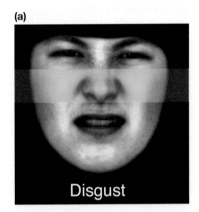

Disgust

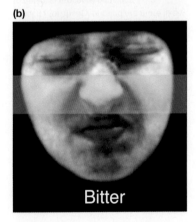

Bitter

FIGURE 9.29

Emotions, Judgments, and Facial Gestures

A person makes similar facial gestures, wrinkling the nose and raising the upper lip, when **(a)** disgusted by receiving unfair treatment and **(b)** tasting something unpleasant, such as a bitter taste.

not afford the drug. Kohlberg was most concerned with the reasons people provided for their answers, rather than the answers themselves. He devised a theory of moral judgment that involved three main levels of moral reasoning.

At the **preconventional level,** people classify answers in terms of self-interest or pleasurable outcomes. For example, a child at this level might say, "He should steal the drug because then he will have it." At the **conventional level,** people's responses conform to rules of law and order or focus on others' disapproval. For example, a person at this level might say, "He shouldn't take the drug. You are not supposed to steal, so everyone will think he is a bad person." At the **postconventional level,** the highest level of moral reasoning, people's responses center around complex reasoning about abstract principles and the value of all life. For example, a person at this level might say, "Sometimes people have to break the law if the law is unjust. In this case, it's wrong to steal, but it's more wrong to charge too much money for a drug that could save a person's life." Thus, Kohlberg considered advanced moral reasoning to include a consideration of the greater good for all people, with less thought given to personal wishes or fear of punishment.

There have been criticisms of Kohlberg's theory because the initial research examined only American males (Gilligan, 1977). At issue is whether the same stage theory applies to females or to those raised in different cultures (Snarey, 1985). Moral-reasoning theories have also been faulted for emphasizing the cognitive aspects of morality to the detriment of emotional issues that influence moral judgments. Of course, cognition and emotions are intertwined. If people lack adequate cognitive abilities, their moral emotions may not translate into moral behaviors (Tangney, Stuewig, & Mashek, 2007). Similarly, moral reasoning is enhanced by moral emotions (Moll & de Oliveira-Souza, 2007).

EMOTION AS THE BASIS OF MORALITY According to Jonathan Haidt's (2001) **social intuitionist model,** moral judgments reflect people's initial and automatic emotional responses. When most people are asked to consider sticking a pin in a child's hand or stealing money from a church they have automatic, intuitive negative emotional reactions. Subsequently, they might think about the actions using cognitive skills, but their thoughts are influenced by their emotional reactions. In other words, the emotions come first and thinking follows (Haidt, 2007).

Recall the study described in Chapter 4 in which a posthypnotic suggestion to feel disgust to an otherwise neutral word (e.g., the word *often*) led participants to make more-extreme moral judgments when reading innocuous stories that included the word. According to some researchers (Pizarro, Inbar, & Helion, 2011), emotions such as disgust may not produce moral responses as much as increase those responses. These researchers point out that some actions can be disgusting to think about (e.g., a person picking his nose in private) but would not be considered immoral. It is clear, however, that emotions bias moral judgments. In one study, people evaluated gay men more negatively when making judgments in a room that smelled disgusting than did those in a room that did not smell (Inbar, Pizarro, & Bloom, 2012). Immorality elicits the same physical disgust reaction as a bad taste. A person disgusted by receiving unfair treatment makes similar facial gestures as when tasting something unpleasant (Chapman, Kim, Susskind, & Anderson, 2009; **FIGURE 9.29**). Children's developing sense of morality is influenced by their emotional reactions to events.

BIOLOGICAL BASIS OF MORALITY Research using brain imaging has identified a number of brain regions involved in moral reasoning and during the experience of moral emotions. Many of the identified regions are similar to those that are active when people perform theory of mind tasks, such as the prefrontal cortex (Decety &

Porges, 2011). Researchers studied two people who had experienced prefrontal damage during infancy (Anderson, Bechara, Damasio, Tranel, & Damasio, 1999). This brain region was the one whose damage led to Phineas Gage's dramatic personality change (see Figure 3.27). Both individuals showed severe deficiencies in moral and social reasoning. When given Kohlberg's moral-dilemma task, both patients scored at the preconventional level. These patients also neglected social and emotional factors in their life decisions. Both failed to express empathy, remorse, or guilt for wrongdoing, and neither had particularly good parenting skills. One engaged in petty thievery, was verbally and physically threatening (once to the point of physical assault), and frequently lied for no apparent reason. There is consistent evidence that the prefrontal cortex supports the capacity for morality, likely by being involved in theory of mind abilities that enable people to consider how their actions affect others (Forbes & Grafman, 2010).

In addition to the prefrontal cortex, brain regions associated with emotional responses, including the insula and amygdala, are active during moral judgments (Greene, Sommerville, Nystrom, Darley, & Cohen, 2001; Shenhav & Greene, 2014). These regions are also active during the experience of moral emotions (Moll et al., 2002). The specific types of moral emotions are associated with activation of different brain regions. For example, people considering moral violations that elicit disgust show insula activity (Parkinson et al., 2011), whereas moral violations that cause injury produce amygdala activity (Shenhav & Greene, 2014). In short, the prefrontal cortex likely helps us judge the effects of our behavior on others, whereas the insula and amygdala produce the emotional responses that contribute to morality. As noted above, cognition and emotion interact to produce morality.

 Q According to the social intuitionist model, how might judges' emotional reactions to trials affect the sentences they give to those found guilty?

ANSWER: Emotions might color the judges' moral judgments. Therefore strong emotional reactions might lead to longer sentences, and weak emotional reactions might lead to shorter sentences.

What Changes During Adolescence?

Normal human development turns a child into an adolescent. An adolescent then develops into an adult. During these transitions, the person undergoes various changes. In addition to physical changes during and after puberty, social changes emerge as part of the renegotiation of relationships with caregivers and peers, cognitive changes arise as part of the emergence of critical and analytical thinking, and psychological changes accompany the formation of a gender identity and a cultural identity. Physical, social, cognitive, and psychological forces work together in the creation of a self.

9.10 Puberty Causes Physical Changes

Biologically, adolescence begins with **puberty,** the onset of sexual maturity and thus the ability to reproduce. Puberty typically begins around age 8 for females and age 10 for males (Ge, Natsuaki, Neiderhiser, & Reiss, 2007). Most girls complete pubertal development by the age of 16, with boys ending by the age of 18 (Lee, 1980; **FIGURE 9.30**). During puberty, hormone levels increase throughout the body. The increased hormones stimulate physical changes. For example, the clear dividing line between childhood and the start of puberty is the *adolescent growth spurt,* a rapid, hormonally driven increase in height and weight. Puberty also brings the development of the

- Understand how biology and environment interact to influence puberty.

- Explain key factors that influence gender identity development and gender-specific behaviors.

- Describe how peers, parents, and cultural forces shape the sense of self.

puberty
The beginning of adolescence, marked by the onset of sexual maturity and thus the ability to reproduce.

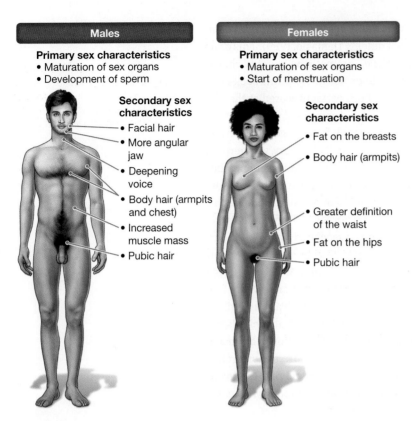

Males	Females
Primary sex characteristics	**Primary sex characteristics**
• Maturation of sex organs	• Maturation of sex organs
• Development of sperm	• Start of menstruation

Secondary sex characteristics (Males)
• Facial hair
• More angular jaw
• Deepening voice
• Body hair (armpits and chest)
• Increased muscle mass
• Pubic hair

Secondary sex characteristics (Females)
• Fat on the breasts
• Body hair (armpits)
• Greater definition of the waist
• Fat on the hips
• Pubic hair

FIGURE 9.30
Physical Development During Adolescence
These images show the major physical changes that occur as girls and boys mature into young adults.

primary sex characteristics: maturation of the male and female sex organs; in females, the beginning of menstruation; in males, the beginning of the capacity for ejaculation. Also developing at this time are the *secondary sexual characteristics,* including pubic hair, body hair, muscle mass increases for boys, and fat deposits on the hips and breasts for girls. Boys' voices deepen and their jaws become more angular. Girls lose baby fat on their bellies as their waists become more defined (Lee, 1980).

BIOLOGY AND ENVIRONMENT Puberty may appear to be a purely biological phenomenon. Like all aspects of human development, however, it is affected by a complex and dynamic interaction between biological systems and environmental experiences. For example, when girls live in homes with nongenetically related adult males (such as the mother's boyfriend or a stepfather), they tend to start puberty months earlier than girls who live in homes with only genetically related males. Also, girls who live in extremely stressful environments or have a history of insecure attachments to caregivers begin menstruating earlier than girls in peaceful or secure environments (Wierson, Long, & Forehand, 1993). These findings suggest that the body responds to cues of threat (in the form of stress or family changes). Evolutionarily speaking, these threat cues increase a female's need to reproduce sooner to increase her chances of continuing her gene pool. Thus, hormonal changes are triggered by environmental forces, which allow the girl to enter puberty (Belsky, Houts, & Fearon, 2010).

Because boys do not have an easily identifiable pubertal event like the initiation of menstruation in girls, we know less about environmental impacts on the timing and experience of puberty in boys. Boys and girls experience similar changes in their brain development during adolescence, however, so researchers are able to identify a few key characteristics of the "teenage brain." At the same time teenagers are experiencing pubertal changes, their brains are also in an important phase of reorganization, with synaptic connections being refined and gray matter increasing. The frontal cortex of the brain is not fully myelinated until the mid-20s (Mills, Lalonde, Clasen, Giedd, & Blakemore, 2014). Because a teenager's limbic system—the reward and emotional center of their brain—tends to mature more quickly than his frontal lobes, teenagers are likely to act on their impulses (Blakemore & Choudhury, 2006; Casey, Jones, & Somerville, 2011). The capacity to exert control is overwhelmed by strong temptations, which contribute to adolescent risk taking (Somerville, Hare, & Casey, 2011). The research on such physiological changes points to an important fact about adolescence: It is not necessarily a stressful period of life, full of turmoil. For those kids who already have stressful home lives, experience many family changes, or display attachment difficulties, adolescence may be difficult. But for most kids, pubertal and brain changes can be a bit annoying, but they do not necessarily lead to the high rates of depression or anger that many in the general public associate with teenagers. In fact, if adolescents receive warm, supportive parenting with the proper guidance and discipline, and if they are allowed to express themselves openly, adolescence can be a positive time of growth and change, solidifying the youth's sense of identity (Steinberg & Sheffield, 2001).

 What is the likely relationship between brain development and adolescent risk taking?

ANSWER: Because the limbic system matures faster than the frontal lobes, adolescents may experience reward-driven and emotional impulses stronger than their ability to exert control.

9.11 A Sense of Identity Forms

As a child develops and learns more about the world, she begins creating a sense of identity. That is, the child starts to establish who she is. Identity formation is an important part of social development, especially in Western cultures, where individuality is valued. After all, who a person is can enormously affect how that person interacts with others.

The psychologist Erik Erikson (1980) proposed a theory of human development that emphasized age-related, culture-neutral psychosocial challenges and their effects on social functioning across the life span. Erikson thought of identity development as composed of eight stages, which ranged from an infant's first year to old age (**TABLE 9.1**).

Table 9.1 Erikson's Eight Stages of Psychosocial Development

STAGE	AGE	MAJOR PSYCHOSOCIAL CRISIS	SUCCESSFUL RESOLUTION OF CRISIS
1. Infancy	0-1	Trust versus mistrust	Children learn that the world is safe and that people are loving and reliable.
2. Toddler	1-3	Autonomy versus shame and doubt	Encouraged to explore the environment, children gain feelings of independence and positive self-esteem.
3. Preschool	3-6	Initiative versus guilt	Children develop a sense of purpose by taking on responsibilities but also develop the capacity to feel guilty for misdeeds.
4. Childhood	6-12	Industry versus inferiority	By working successfully with others and assessing how others view them, children learn to feel competent.
5. Adolescence	12-18	Identity versus role confusion	By exploring different social roles, adolescents develop a sense of identity.
6. Young adulthood	18-29	Intimacy versus isolation	Young adults gain the ability to commit to long-term relationships.
7. Middle adulthood	30s to 50s	Generativity versus stagnation	Adults gain a sense that they are leaving behind a positive legacy and caring for future generations.
8. Old age	60s and beyond	Integrity versus despair	Older adults feel a sense of satisfaction that they have lived a good life and developed wisdom.

gender identity
One's sense of being male or female.

gender role
A behavior that is typically associated with being male or female.

Erikson further conceptualized each stage as having a major developmental "crisis," or development challenge to be confronted. Each of these crises is present throughout life, but each one takes on special importance at a particular stage. According to this theory, while each crisis provides an opportunity for psychological development, a lack of progress may impair further psychosocial development (Erikson, 1980).

The challenge at each stage provides skills and attitudes that the individual will need in order to face the next challenge successfully. Successful resolution of these challenges depends on the supportive nature of the person's environment as well as the person's active search for information about his own competence. According to Erikson's theory, adolescents face perhaps the most fundamental crisis: how to develop an adult identity. Erikson's theory has been influential but is lacking empirical support. There is little evidence that there are eight stages of psychosocial development, that psychosocial development is culture-neutral, and that human identity develops in this exact sequence. Nonetheless, Erickson's stages are helpful for considering the psychosocial challenges that people face at different times in their lives.

Given that adolescents are undergoing pubertal changes, brain development and the resultant emotional highs and lows, and myriad social role expectations, it is impressive that so many teenagers are able to negotiate a pathway to a stable identity. Part of this process includes breaking away from childhood beliefs by questioning and challenging parental and societal ideas (Erikson, 1968).

Three major changes generally cause adolescents to question who they are: Their physical appearance transforms, leading to shifts in self-image; their cognitive abilities grow more sophisticated, increasing the tendency for introspection; and they receive heightened societal pressure to prepare for the future (in particular, to make career choices), prompting exploration of real and hypothetical boundaries. In exploring boundaries, teenagers may investigate alternative belief systems and subcultures. They may wonder what they would be like if they were raised in other cultures, by other caregivers, or in other historical times. They may shift between various peer groups and try out different activities, hobbies, and musical styles. As teenagers move away from spending all their time with caregivers and toward a peer-oriented lifestyle, caregivers continue to shape adolescents' development, but peers also play an important role in identity development. Let's look more closely at some specific aspects of identity development.

DEVELOPMENT OF GENDER IDENTITY The terms used to discuss gender identity can be confusing, so we need to get them straight. Most psychologists use the term *sex* to refer to the biological status of being either male or female. That is, biological sex refers to the genes that differentiate males and females (i.e., XY versus XX chromosomes) and result in different physical characteristics (see Figure 9.30). They reserve the term *gender* for psychological differences between males and females. **Gender identity** is one's sense of being male or female. A **gender role** is a behavior that is typically associated with being male or female.

Most people believe that their sex and gender are major components of who they are. How different are females and males (**FIGURE 9.31**)? Certain physical differences are obvious, but how do females and males differ psychologically? According to evolutionary theory, gender differences ought to reflect different adaptive problems males and females have faced, and this notion is generally supported by research (Buss, 1995). Since males and females have faced similar adaptive problems, however, they are actually similar on most dimensions (Hyde, 2005).

The biological factors that influence gender come from many sources, such as brain chemistry. Gender identity begins very early in prenatal development. It results from a complex cascade of hormones, changes in brain structure and function, and intrauterine

(a)

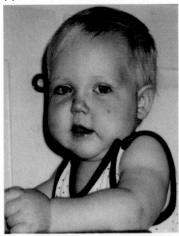

(b)

FIGURE 9.31
Girl or Boy?
Try to determine the sex of each infant. Consider the visual cues and cultural assumptions that inform your decisions. Are you surprised to learn that **(a)** is a girl and **(b)** is a boy?

environmental forces (Swaab, 2004). Recall from Chapter 3 that the gonads—testes in males and the ovaries in females—influence sexual behavior. They also influence the development of secondary sex characteristics (e.g., breast development in females, growth of facial hair in males). Androgens are more prevalent in males, and estrogens are more prevalent in females.

(a) Biological sex of male   **(c)** Intersexuality   **(b)** Biological sex of female

FIGURE 9.32

Biological Sex Can Be Viewed as a Continuum

Some people have biological traits of both sexes, and therefore it might be appropriate to view sex as a continuum of being more or less physically female or male. **(a)** Males have biological traits that are consistently male. **(b)** Females have biological traits that are consistently female. **(c)** People who experience intersexuality have aspects of biological sex that are both male and female.

For some people, the issue of being male or female is more complicated (Blackless et al., 2000). For these people, aspects of biological sex are either ambiguous or inconsistent with each other. This phenomenon is known as *intersexuality*. About 1 or 2 of every 100 people experience some ambiguity in their biological sex (Intersex Society of North America, 2008). The main causes of such ambiguity are abnormalities in the sex chromosomes or in hormones, both of which can affect how the genitals look (American Psychological Association, 2006). Given intersexuality, many people believe it is more accurate to view biological sex as not just male or female, but as including greater or lesser physical aspects of each sex (**FIGURE 9.32**). For example, in December 2016, New York City issued the first birth certificate in the United States listing "intersex" instead of "male" or "female" in the sex field. It was issued to 55-year-old Sara Keenan, who was born with male genes, female genitalia, and mixed internal reproductive organs.

Many of the differences between males and females have as much to do with socialization as with biology. This distinction is not always easy to make, because the biological and psychosocial aspects of being female or male are usually so entwined that we cannot separate them (Hyde, 2005). Each person is treated in certain ways based on his biological sex, and each person's behaviors reflect both biological components and social expectations. For example, as discussed in Chapter 3, researchers have identified some differences between the brains of men and of women. They have not determined whether these differences are the result of genetics, of the way girls and boys are treated during development, or, more likely, of genetics (nature) combined with treatment (nurture). Nor do we know how or if sex-related brain differences translate into thoughts and actions.

However it forms, your gender identity helps shape how you behave. Children as young as 2 years old can indicate whether they are boys or girls. Once children discover that they are boys or girls, they seek out activities that are culturally appropriate for their sex (Bem, 1981). Gender roles are culturally defined norms that differentiate behaviors, and attitudes, according to maleness and femaleness. In North American culture, for example, most parents and teachers discourage girls from playing too roughly and boys from crying. The separation of boys and girls into different play groups is also a powerful socializing force. Most boys and girls strive to fulfill the gender roles expected of them by their cultures.

Biology has a strong effect on whether people identify as female, male, or transgender. A *transgender* person was born as one biological sex but feels that her true gender identity is that of the other sex. One theory of why gender and biological sex differ for those who are transgender has to do with timing of hormonal events during pregnancy. Early in pregnancy, the presence or absence of testosterone leads to the formation of male or female sex organs, respectively. Later in pregnancy, hormones influence the sexual differentiation of the brain (Bao & Swaab, 2011). These developmental processes are independent and may produce different effects for those who are transgender. In keeping with this idea, various brain imaging studies have shown that brains of transgender people are more similar to those who share their gender identity than to those who share their biological sex (Nawata et al., 2010). Indeed, there is evidence that brain networks are wired differently for those who are transgender (Hahn et al., 2015).

"Do you know its sexual identity?"

FIGURE 9.33
Transgender
This special edition of *National Geographic* magazine reflects a new cultural focus on gender. The cover story illustrates the growing awareness of transgender.

Awareness has been growing about transgender over the last few years. For example, U.S. federal law now prohibits inappropriate treatment of people who are transgender and gender nonconforming. The increase in children reporting being transgender has led some to question whether the children are simply playing or pretending to be a different sex (**FIGURE 9.33**). A recent study looked at 32 transgender children 5–12 years old (Olson, Key, & Eaton, 2015). The research methods included self-reports and implicit measures of gender identity. The results indicated that the children thought of themselves in terms of their preferred gender identity, not their birth sex. In addition, the pattern of responses of the transgender children was similar to the pattern of responses from children who accepted their birth sex as their gender identity. In other words, transgender children are not confused or playacting. They are aware of their gender identity, which simply does not match their birth sex.

ETHNIC IDENTITY In addition to a gender identity, each adolescent establishes a racial and/or ethnic identity. The process of forming such an identity can be complicated. Because of prejudice and discrimination and the accompanying barriers to economic opportunities, children from underrepresented groups, such as people of color, often face challenges with regard to the development of their ethnic identities. Children entering middle childhood have acquired an awareness of their ethnic identities to the extent that they know the labels and attributes that the dominant culture applies to their ethnic groups. Many researchers believe that during middle childhood and adolescence, children in underrepresented groups often engage in additional processes aimed at ethnic identity formation (Phinney, 1990). The factors that influence these processes vary widely among individuals and groups.

Consider a child of Mexican immigrants to the United States. This child may struggle to live successfully in both a traditional Mexican household and an American neighborhood and school. The child may have to serve as a "cultural broker" for her family, perhaps translating materials sent home from school, calling insurance companies to ask about policies for her parents, and handling more adultlike responsibilities than other children the same age. In helping the family adjust to a stressful life as immigrants in a foreign country, the child may feel additional pressures but may also develop important skills in communication, negotiation, and caregiving (Cooper, Denner, & Lopez, 1999). Even for people of color born in the United States, it can be quite challenging to persevere in the face of racism and discrimination while also trying to succeed in the mainstream school system and work environment (Spencer, Fegley, & Harpalani, 2003).

When a minority child successfully forms a strong sense of identity related to both his own group and the majority culture, the child has developed a *bicultural identity*. That is, the child strongly identifies with two cultures and seamlessly combines a sense of identity with both groups (Vargas-Reighley, 2005). A bicultural individual who is able to develop a bicultural identity is likely to be happier, be better adjusted, and have fewer problems in adult social and economic roles than will an individual who identifies strongly with only one culture to the exclusion of recognizing the other aspects of who she is. Caregivers, teachers, and spiritual and community leaders play key roles in teaching young people the values of their specific cultures in order to help them formulate healthy ethnic identities.

 What is the difference between sex and gender?

ANSWER: Sex reflects a person's biological makeup—for example, genes and secondary sex characteristics. Gender refers to a person's psychological identification as male or female.

9.12 Peers and Parents Help Shape the Adolescent Self

The impact of parents versus peers on young people has become a controversial topic in developmental psychology. People often describe individuals as "coming from a good home" or as having "fallen in with the wrong crowd." These clichés reflect the importance of both peers and parents in influencing adolescent development.

THE IMPORTANCE OF PEERS Developmental psychologists increasingly recognize the importance of peers in shaping identity (**FIGURE 9.34**). Children, regardless of their cultures, tend to spend much of their time interacting with other children, usually playing in various ways. In developmental terms, attention to peers begins at the end of the first year of life, when infants begin to imitate other children, smile, and make vocalizations and other social signals to their peers (Brownell & Brown, 1992). Attention to peers may then continue throughout life. For example, people learn how to behave from their friends. When people behave appropriately, their friends provide social rewards. When people behave inappropriately, their friends provide social punishments.

In developing their identities, children and adolescents compare their strengths and weaknesses with those of their peers. For example, as part of the search for identity, teenagers form friendships with others whose values and worldviews are similar to their own. Adolescents use peer groups to help them feel a sense of belonging and acceptance. They also draw on peer groups as resources for social support and identity acceptance. Despite wide differences in the experiences of teenagers around the world, adolescent peer groups tend to be described by a fairly small set of stereotypical names: jocks, brains, loners, druggies, nerds, and other not-so-flattering designations.

Outside observers tend to quickly place teenagers who dress or act a certain way into groupings, called *cliques*. Members of cliques are thought to exhibit the same personality traits and be interested in the same activities. Individuals are seen as virtually interchangeable, and community members may respond to all youths from that group in similar ways (Urberg, Degirmencioglue, Tolson, & Halliday-Scher, 1995). The teenagers, however, may not see themselves as part of homogeneous groups of peers. In fact, they may see themselves as completely unique and individual, separate from anyone else, or they may see themselves as connected to a small subset of close friends (**FIGURE 9.35**).

Adolescent identity development is thus shaped by the perceptions of adults, the influences of peers, and the teen's own active exploration of the world. Keep in mind that even though peers become the primary concern for many teenagers, the importance of parental support and guidance does not wane with age.

BULLYING Bullying is a complex behavior with many contributing factors. However, experts tend to agree that bullies might not strongly feel the moral emotions of guilt and shame (Hymel, Rocke-Henderson, & Bonanno, 2005). Bullies also often show increased moral disengagement, such as indifference or pride, when explaining

FIGURE 9.34
Peers and Identity
Peers play an important role in each adolescent's development of a sense of identity.

FIGURE 9.35
Cliques and Individuality
Outside observers would tend to place these young men into a single clique, "punks," and would tend to react to them all in similar ways. Each adolescent, however, might view himself as individualistic.

FIGURE 9.36
The Bullying of Amanda Todd
Amanda Todd experienced repeated bullying and cyberbullying so extreme that she suffered from anxiety and depression. Despite attempts to treat Amanda's problems, she ended her life.

their behavior and more-positive attitudes about using bullying to respond to difficult social situations. This is especially true of bullies with high self-esteem, who tend to rationalize and justify their mistreatment of others (Menon et al., 2007). The advent of social networking sites produced the phenomenon of cyberbullying. Estimates of the prevalence of cyberbullying vary widely, with 3–72 percent of adolescents reporting being victims across separate studies (Selkie, Fales, & Moreno, 2016).

Whether in person or via the web, being bullied can have devastating effects. A study of over 1,400 participants found that being bullied during childhood is associated with psychological disorders such as anxiety disorders and depression (Copeland, Wolke, Angold, & Costello, 2013). Consider the case of 15-year-old Amanda Todd. In September 2012, Amanda posted a soundless YouTube video displaying a series of handwritten messages that described her years of being bullied (**FIGURE 9.36**). The bullying began in the seventh grade, when Amanda used video chat to meet people over the Internet. A man convinced Amanda to pose topless and then threatened to blackmail her unless she posted more-explicit sexual images of herself. Amanda informed her parents, who contacted the police. By this point, Amanda's pictures had been widely circulated over the Internet. Her fellow students started verbally abusing her. Amanda went into a tailspin, experiencing feelings of anxiety and depression. About a month after she posted her YouTube video, Amanda committed suicide. This tragic case shows the urgency of preventing bullying and of supporting people who are bullied.

THE IMPORTANCE OF PARENTS Much research has confirmed that parents have substantial influence throughout an individual's life. Significantly, researchers have emphasized that neither the peer group nor the family can be assigned the primary role in a child's social development. Instead, the two contexts play complementary roles. B. Bradford Brown and colleagues (1993) have argued that parents' influence can be direct or indirect. Parents contribute to specific individual behaviors, but they also affect social development indirectly by influencing the choices the child makes about what kind of clique to join. In observations of 695 young people from childhood through adolescence, Robert Cairns and Beverly Cairns (1994) found that parents and teachers played a major role in realigning social groups so they were consistent with family norms.

Important support for the significance of child-parent interaction comes from the New York Longitudinal Study, begun in 1956 by Stella Chess and Alexander Thomas. The study ran for six years, assessing 141 children from 85 middle- to upper-middle-class families. Chess and Thomas (1984) pinpointed the most important factor in determining a child's social development: the fit between the child's biologically based temperament or personality and the parents' behaviors.

For instance, most parents find it frustrating to raise a difficult child who tends to have negative moods and a hard time adapting to new situations. Parents who openly demonstrate their frustration with their child's behavior or who insist on exposing the child to conflict often unwittingly encourage negative behaviors. If the child is extremely uneasy about entering a new setting, pushing the child can lead to behavioral problems. If the child is very distractible, forcing her to concentrate for long periods may lead to emotional upset.

In this study and many others, parents who responded to a difficult child calmly, firmly, patiently, and consistently tended to have the most-positive outcomes. Such parents tended not to engage in self-blame for their child's negative behaviors, and they managed to cope with their own frustration with and disappointment in their child. Chess and Thomas also noted that overprotectiveness can encourage a child's anxiety in response to a new situation, thereby escalating the child's distress. Ultimately, then, the best style of parenting is dynamic and flexible, and it takes into account the parents' personalities, the child's temperament, and the particular situation (Steinberg, 2001).

Adolescence is a period of increased conflict between parents and their teenage children. For most families, however, this conflict leads to minor annoyances and not to feelings of hopelessness or doom. Research shows that such conflict actually helps adolescents develop many important skills, including negotiation, critical thinking, communication, and the development of empathy (Holmbeck, 1996). In fact, even though adolescents and their parents may argue and it may seem to parents that their children are not listening, across cultures parents have incredible influence over the development of their children's values and sense of autonomy (Feldman & Rosenthal, 1991).

Other research has shown that parents have multiple influences on their children's attitudes, values, and religious beliefs (Bao, Whitbeck, Hoyt, & Conger, 1999). Children learn about the world in part from the attitudes expressed by their parents, such as the belief in a higher power or even prejudices regarding certain groups of people. Parents who demonstrate the most warmth tend to raise children who experience more social emotions, such as appropriate guilt, perhaps because the parents encourage an empathic attitude toward others (Eisenberg & Valiente, 2002). Parents also help determine the neighborhoods in which their children live, the schools they attend, and the extracurricular activities that provide exercise and stimulation. All of these choices are likely to influence how adolescents develop.

 Why do bullies tend not to feel bad about their behavior?

ANSWER: Bullies might not feel the moral emotions of guilt and shame. In addition, bullies with high self-esteem tend to exhibit moral disengagement, such as indifference or pride, and to rationalize or justify their behavior.

What Brings Meaning in Adulthood?

For many years, developmental psychologists focused on childhood and adolescence, as if most important aspects of development occurred by age 20. In recent decades, researchers working in a wide range of fields have demonstrated that important changes occur physiologically, cognitively, and socioemotionally throughout adulthood and into old age. Therefore, many contemporary psychologists consider development from a life span perspective, trying to understand how mental activity and social relations change over the entire course of life. Such research shows that we should not equate growing old with despair. In fact, many positive things happen as people grow older. Although aging is associated with cognitive and physical decline, aging is an important part of life and can be very meaningful. Today, better health, better nutrition, and medical advances enable people to live longer than in previous generations. Understanding old age is becoming especially important, as most Western cultures are experiencing a boom in the aging population.

9.13 Adults Are Affected by Life Transitions

For many young people, college is a magical time of life. Meeting new friends, learning new ideas, and having a good time occur as adolescents emerge as adults. People in their 20s and 30s undergo significant changes as they pursue career goals and make long-term commitments in relationships, as in getting married and raising children. All of these developments correspond to Erikson's idea that individuals face challenges as they mature through adulthood. In essence, the major challenges of adulthood reflect the need to find meaning in one's life. Part of that search for meaning includes acknowledging, coping with, and playing an active role in the physiological, cognitive, and socioemotional changes of adulthood.

Learning Objectives

- Understand the physical changes that occur as we age.

- Explain key research findings on the benefits of a healthy marriage and how to keep a marriage healthy after the birth of a child.

- Understand why many older adults find life more satisfying than younger adults.

- Describe the cognitive changes that occur as we age.

THE SEVEN AGES OF MAN

SLEEPY   HAPPY   DOPEY

BASHFUL   DOC   SNEEZY   GRUMPY

PHYSICAL CHANGES FROM EARLY TO MIDDLE ADULT-HOOD Evolutionarily speaking, a 40-year-old is quite old. At the beginning of the twentieth century, the average life expectancy in the United States was 47 years! Human bodies remain on that timetable, ready to reproduce when individuals reach their teens and peaking in fitness during their 20s. Since 1900, through modern medicine and improvements in hygiene and food availability, the average life expectancy has increased by about 35 years. Still, between the ages of 20 and 40, people experience a steady decline in muscle mass, bone density, eyesight, and hearing (Shephard, 1997).

As people approach middle age, they start to notice that they can no longer drink as much alcohol, eat as much unhealthy food, or function on as little sleep as they could in their 20s. They find that the "middle-age spread," the accumulating fat around the belly, becomes harder and harder to work off. For these reasons, nutrition, exercise, and a healthy lifestyle are important in early adulthood. After middle age, it is much harder to get in shape, reduce fat in the arteries, or sharpen cognitive functioning. The better cognitive, physical, and psychological shape a person is in during early adulthood, the fewer significant declines she will experience with age.

As you will learn in the following sections, brain functioning and body health are "use it or lose it" phenomena: Oxygen and blood need to be kept flowing by caring for those systems through adequate sleep, proper diet, cognitive stimulation, and at least moderate daily exercise (Shephard, 1997). Unfortunately, as discussed extensively in Chapter 11, we are currently facing an obesity epidemic throughout the world, where today's generations may be the first to live shorter life spans than their parents' generations did. Life expectancy in the United States dropped in 2015 for the first time in decades (Xu, Murphy, Kochanek, & Arias, 2016). In the United Kingdom, 8 out of 10 people between 40 and 60 years of age are overweight, drink alcohol excessively, or do not exercise (Public Health England, 2016). Health researchers estimate that obesity-related factors will shorten the expected life span by two to five years if the trends in poor health are not reversed (Olshansky et al., 2005). One impetus to improving health can be life partners or children. The people we share our lives with sometimes motivate us to take care of ourselves.

MARRIAGE In adulthood, people devote a great deal of effort to achieving and maintaining satisfying relationships. Indeed, the vast majority of people around the world marry at some point in their lives or form some type of permanent bond with a relationship partner, although people today tend to marry later in life, and the percentage who marry is declining slowly in most industrialized countries.

Research shows that marriage tends to benefit the individuals involved. Overall, married people typically experience greater happiness and joy and are at less risk for mental illnesses such as depression when compared with unmarried people. Married people also live longer than people who were never married, are divorced, or are widowed (Frisch & Simonsen, 2013; Waite, 1995). Studies of traditional heterosexual marriages suggest that men may benefit from marriage because their wives make sure they smoke less, eat more healthily, and go to the doctor (Ross, Mirowsky, & Gold-steen, 1990). Women serve as the primary social support for their husbands. In fact, the benefits of marriage are more significant for men than for women (House, Landis, & Umberson, 1988; Umberson, 1992). Married men report higher sexual and relationship satisfaction than cohabiting and single men, while there is no difference across these same groups of women (Hughes & Waite, 2009). Married women report more

(a)

(b)

(c)

FIGURE 9.37
Marriage
Across cultures, marriage remains a building block of society. If the statistics hold true, **(a)** this Sami couple in Norway, **(b)** this Amhara couple in Ethiopia, and **(c)** this Hani couple in China will report being happy in their marriages.

emotional satisfaction, however, than cohabiting or single women (Christopher & Sprecher, 2000). In fact, like single adults, cohabiting adults are likely to be in worse health than married people (Robles & Kiecolt-Glaser, 2003).

Much of the research on marriage was conducted before same-sex marriage was legalized in many countries around the world, including the United States in 2015. The few studies conducted so far have found that marriage provides significant physical and mental health benefits for lesbian, gay, or bisexual individuals (Wight, LeBlanc, & Badgett, 2013). Still, the benefits of being in a relationship extend to cohabiting same-sex couples compared to those living on their own (Williams & Fredriksen-Goldsen, 2014).

All of these findings do not mean that marriage is a cure-all. For example, the benefits of marriage over cohabitation are stronger for European Americans than for African Americans (Liu & Reczek, 2012). In addition, unhappily married people are at greater risk for poor health and early death. Conflicts within marriage are associated with poor immune functioning. The risk is comparable to that experienced by smokers, those with high blood pressure, and those who are obese (Robles & Kiecolt-Glaser, 2003). In general, people who are in unhappy marriages, are separated, or are divorced have many physical and psychological struggles, from depression to physical illness to violent behavior (Carrère, Buehlman, Gottman, Coan, & Ruckstuhl, 2000). Note, though, that these studies are largely correlational. It could be that happy, well-adjusted people are more likely to get married and not that marriage causes good outcomes for people. Or perhaps unhappy, negative people have both health problems and strained marriages.

The good news is that according to national surveys, at any given time, the vast majority of married people report satisfaction with their marriages (**FIGURE 9.37**). Those reporting the most satisfaction tend to have sufficient economic resources, share decision making, and together hold the view that marriage should be a lifelong commitment (Amato, Johnson, Booth, & Rogers, 2003).

 Do heterosexual men or women benefit most from being married?

ANSWER: Husbands receive the most benefit from marriage, in part because their wives encourage healthy lifestyles and provide social support.

(a)

(b)

FIGURE 9.38
Having Children
When deciding whether to have children, it is important to consider both **(a)** the minuses, such as the stresses involved, and **(b)** the pluses, such as the rewarding feelings.

9.14 Will Parenthood Make You Happy?

For most couples, the birth of a first child is a profound event. In fact, this arrival changes their lives in almost every respect. Are these changes generally positive or negative?

Responding to an infant's cries and trying to figure out why the child is distressed often cause anxiety and frustration for first-time parents. Indeed, children can strain a marriage, especially when time and money are tight. Research consistently finds that couples with children, especially with adolescent children, report less marital satisfaction than those who are childless (Belsky, 1990; Cowan & Cowan, 1988; Hansen, 2012; **FIGURE 9.38A**).

But new parents also experience great joys. Seeing a baby's first social smile, watching the first few tentative steps, and hearing a child say "Mommy" or "Daddy" provide powerful reinforcement for parents. As a result of such rewards, parents often become immersed in their children's lives. They make sure their children have playmates, expose to new experiences, and seek ways to make them happy and healthy. Being a parent is central to the self-schemas of many adults. Having children can provide meaning in life and many moments of joy (Nelson, Kushlev, English, Dunn, & Lyubomirsky, 2013; **FIGURE 9.38B**).

This positive interpretation is complicated by the fact that people who have children, at least within wealthy nations, are more likely to be married, richer, better educated, more religious, and healthier (Deaton & Stone, 2014). All of these demographic factors are associated with well-being. Indeed, in their large study of more than 1.8 million Americans, Deaton and Stone (2014) found that once you take these factors into account, the presence of children has a reliably negative effect on life satisfaction, although the effect is small. Deaton and Stone also examined adults in 161 other nations. They found that having children has a much more negative impact on life satisfaction in less wealthy nations.

Contemporary researchers are trying to find ways to prepare couples for parenthood so the stress does not exert such a strain on the relationship. Much of the unhappiness may be the result of communication failure (Cowan & Cowan, 1988). For example, a husband who expresses great fondness toward his wife and is aware of her feelings and needs early in the marriage is less likely to report a dip in marital satisfaction after the baby arrives. Likewise, a wife who acknowledges and sympathizes with her husband's needs early on is likely to grow closer to her husband after the baby is born. Partners who report their early married life as chaotic or negative early on are more likely to find that having a baby does not bring them closer together or solve their problems, but in fact increases the existing strain. Thus, teaching newlyweds or young partners how to communicate and understand each other's needs may not only prevent divorce but also allow the couple to enjoy parenting when their children are young as well as when the parents grow older and the children leave home (Shapiro, Gottman, & Carrère, 2000).

Over the coming years, you may find yourself considering whether or not you would like to have children. After studying millions of people around the world, Deaton and Stone (2014) have concluded, "If parents choose to be parents, and nonparents choose to be nonparents, there is no reason to expect that one group will be better or worse off than the other one" (p. 1328). In other words, if you choose the parenting status that makes sense for you as an individual, the decision to have kids (or not) will not make or break your happiness. The important thing is to consider the consequences before you make your decision. ◼

ANSWER: learning to communicate effectively and understand their partners' problems

 What is the best way for parents to find happiness when raising children?

9.15 The Transition to Old Age Can Be Satisfying

In Western societies, people are living much longer, and the number of people over age 85 is growing dramatically. Indeed, it is becoming commonplace for people to live beyond 100. By 2030, more than one in five Americans will be over age 65, and these older people will be ethnically diverse, well educated, and physically fit. With this "graying" of the population in Western societies, much greater research attention has been paid to the lives of people over age 60.

The elderly contribute much to modern society. For instance, nearly 40 percent of U.S. federal judges are over 65, and they handle about 20 percent of the caseload (Markon, 2001). A 2010 survey found that 12 percent of federal justices are over 80 years old and 11 of the 1,200 judges are in their 90s (Goldstein, 2011). Many older adults work productively well past their 70s. Views of the elderly are likely to change a great deal as the baby boom generation ages. Consider music stars—such as Madonna, Stevie Wonder, and the Rolling Stones—who remain popular and vibrant well into their 50s, 60s, and beyond, certainly in defiance of common stereotypes of old people (FIGURE 9.39).

DETERIORATION The body and mind, however, start deteriorating slowly at about age 50. Trivial physical changes include the graying and whitening of hair and the wrinkling of skin. Some of the most serious changes affect the brain, whose frontal lobes shrink proportionally more than other brain regions (Cabeza & Dennis, 2012). Scientists once believed that cognitive problems such as confusion and memory loss were an inevitable, normal part of aging. They now recognize that most older adults, while remaining alert, do everything a bit more slowly as they grow older.

Older adults who experience a dramatic loss in mental ability often suffer from *dementia*. This brain condition causes thinking, memory, and behavior to deteriorate progressively. Dementia has many causes, including excessive alcohol intake and HIV. For older adults, the major causes are Alzheimer's disease and small strokes that affect

(a)   (b)   (c)

FIGURE 9.39
Changing Views of the Elderly
(a) Madonna is in her 50s and remains a cultural force. (b) Stevie Wonder, in his 60s, seems as timeless as his music. (c) The Rolling Stones, now in their 70s, are still rocking after five decades.

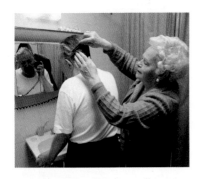

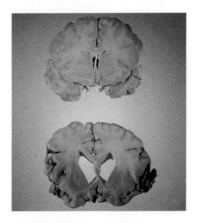

FIGURE 9.41
Damage from Alzheimer's Disease
The brain on the bottom shows the ravages of Alzheimer's disease in comparison to the normal brain on top. The holes (ventricles) in the middle of the brain are extremely large, and every section of gray and white matter has lost density.

socioemotional selectivity theory
As people grow older, they view time as limited and therefore shift their focus to meaningful events, experiences, and goals.

the brain's blood supply. After age 70, the risk of dementia increases with each year of life. Approximately 3–5 percent of people will develop Alzheimer's disease by age 70–75, and 6.5 percent will develop the disease after age 85 (Kawas, Gray, Brookmeyer, Fozard, & Zonderman, 2000). It takes about four years for people to progress from mild cognitive impairment to a diagnosis of Alzheimer's (Villemagne et al., 2013).

The initial symptoms of Alzheimer's are typically minor memory impairments, but the disease eventually progresses to more-serious difficulties, such as forgetting daily routines (**FIGURE 9.40**). Eventually, the person loses all mental capacities, including memory and language. Many people with Alzheimer's experience profound personality changes.

The exact cause of Alzheimer's is not known, but evidence suggests there is a genetic predisposition to its development. One gene involved in cholesterol functioning is predictive of Alzheimer's (Sala Frigerio & De Strooper, 2016). In addition, the memory-related neurotransmitter acetylcholine is very low in people who suffer from Alzheimer's, and this deficit results in abnormal protein accumulation in the brain (Knowles, Vendruscolo, & Dobson, 2014; **FIGURE 9.41**). Examining activity within brain networks can help predict which individuals are likely to progress from mild cognitive impairment to Alzheimer's (Spreng & Turner, 2013).

While some people may have a genetic predisposition to developing dementia of some kind, a predisposition is not a hopeless case. Decades of research show that when people challenge their brains by learning new tasks, working puzzles, reading, remaining socially active, and maintaining physical exercise at least three days per week, their risk of dementia declines significantly (Fratiglioni, Paillard-Borg, & Winblad, 2004; Larson et al., 2006). As you age, playing an active role in your own development can help make adulthood transitions rewarding experiences.

Despite the physical, social, and emotional challenges of aging, most older adults are surprisingly healthy and happy. Except for dementia, older adults have fewer mental health problems, including depression, than younger adults (Jorm, 2000). Indeed, some individuals thrive in old age, especially those with adequate financial resources and good health (Crosnoe & Elder, 2002). Most older adults report being just as satisfied with life, if not more so, as younger adults (Mroczek & Kolarz, 1998).

MEANING People of all ages are concerned with the meaning of life, but meaning often becomes a preoccupation for the elderly. According to Laura Carstensen's **socioemotional selectivity theory,** as people grow older they view time as limited and therefore shift their focus to emotionally meaningful events, experiences, and goals (Carstensen, 1995; Fung & Carstensen, 2004). For instance, they may choose to spend more time with a smaller group of close friends and avoid new people. They may spend an increasing amount of time reflecting on their lives and sharing memories with family members and friends. They are very selective in the ways they choose to spend their time (Sims, Hogan, & Carstensen, 2015). As they reminisce about their lives, older adults report more positive emotions than negative ones (Pasupathi & Carstensen, 2003). Indeed, they report shorter and fewer negative emotional experiences in their daily lives (Charles, Mogle, Urban, & Almeida, 2016). In essence, older adults want to savor their final years by putting their time and effort into meaningful and rewarding experiences. To the extent that they consider their time well spent, older adults are satisfied and can live their final years gracefully. This result is especially likely if throughout their lives they have worked hard to maintain their physical health, their social ties, and their cognitive capacities.

What is dementia?

ANSWER: a brain condition that over time leads to deterioration of thinking, memory, and behavior.

9.16 Cognition Changes with Age

Cognitive abilities eventually decline with age, but it is difficult to pinpoint exactly what causes the decline. We know that the frontal lobes, which play an important role in working memory and many other cognitive skills, typically shrink as people grow older. One of the most consistent and identifiable cognitive changes is a slowing of mental processing speed (Salthouse & Madden, 2013). Experiments that test the time it takes to process a sensory input and react with a motor response show an increase in response time as early as an individual's mid-20s (Era, Jokela, & Heikkinen, 1986). This increase in response time becomes larger as the individual ages. Sensory-perceptual changes occur with age and may account for some of the observed decline. For instance, as people age, their sensitivity to visual contrast decreases, so activities such as climbing stairs or driving at night may become more difficult and more dangerous. Sensitivity to sound also decreases with age, especially the ability to tune out background noise. This change may make older people seem confused or forgetful when they simply are not able to hear adequately. Let's look more closely at aging's effects on memory and intelligence.

MEMORY Older people have difficulty with memory tasks that require juggling multiple pieces of information at the same time. Tasks in which attention is divided, such as driving while listening to the radio, also prove difficult. Some scientists believe these deficits reflect a decreased ability to store multiple pieces of information simultaneously in working memory (Salthouse, 1992).

Generally speaking, long-term memory is less affected by aging than is working memory. Certain aspects of long-term memory appear to suffer in advanced age, however. For example, older people often need more time to learn new information (although once they learn it, they use it as efficiently as younger people do). The elderly also are better at recognition than at retrieval tasks (Fergus & McDowd, 1987). For example, if the word *cat* is shown to them, they have no trouble recognizing the word if they are asked, "Did you see the word *cat*?" But if they are simply asked what word they saw or whether they saw an animal name, they do not do as well. Consistent with the socioemotional selectivity theory is the finding that older people show better memory for positive than for negative information (Kennedy, Mather, & Carstensen, 2004). In other words, this finding might reflect a tendency to selectively ignore negative events in order to make one's later years feel more positive and meaningful (Mather & Carstensen, 2003).

As discussed in Chapter 7, the more deeply an item is encoded, the better it is remembered. Do older adults use less-efficient strategies for encoding information to be remembered? In an intriguing study, Jessica Logan and colleagues (2002) examined the memory processes of adults in their 20s and adults in their 70s and 80s. As expected, the older adults performed worse than the young adults. They showed less activation in left hemisphere brain areas known to support memory and greater activation in right hemisphere areas that do not aid memory. In a second study, the researchers sought to determine whether the memory deficit could be reduced if they gave the older participants a strategy to improve memorization. To produce deeper encoding, the older participants were asked to classify words as concrete or abstract. Undertaking this classification produced better memory and greater activation of the left frontal regions.

These findings suggest that one reason for the decline in memory observed with aging is that older adults tend not to use strategies that facilitate memory. In one study, providing specific and meaningful cues allowed older adults to remember just as many personal details about their lives as young adults did (Aizpurua & Koutstaal,

FIGURE 9.42
Maintaining Health and Happiness
By gathering to exercise, these women are taking positive steps to maintain their health and happiness.

2015). If it is the case that older adults do not use effective strategies for encoding or retrieving information, then cognitive training might be useful for postponing age-related memory deficits. Another potential reason for declines in working memory is age-related reductions in dopamine activity in the frontal lobes. When researchers blocked dopamine activity in younger adults, they found that performance on a working memory task was similar to that found for older adults (Fischer et al., 2010).

INTELLIGENCE Research has indicated consistently that intelligence, as measured on standard psychometric tests, declines with advanced age. As people age, do they really lose IQ points? Or do older people just have a shorter attention span or lack the motivation to complete such tests?

As discussed in Chapter 8, some researchers have distinguished between fluid intelligence and crystallized intelligence (Horn & Hofer, 1992). Fluid intelligence is the ability to process new general information that requires no specific prior knowledge. Many standardized tests measure this kind of intelligence, as when test takers need to recognize an analogy or arrange blocks to match a picture. Associated with the speed of mental processing, fluid intelligence tends to peak in early adulthood and decline steadily with age. Crystallized intelligence is based on specific knowledge— the kind that must be learned or memorized, such as vocabulary, specialized information, or reasoning strategies. This type of intelligence usually increases throughout life. It breaks down only when declines in other cognitive abilities prevent acquiring new information.

The Seattle Longitudinal Study addressed the question of aging's effects on intelligence (Schaie, 1990). The researchers recruited participants between the ages of 25 and 81, and they tracked them over seven years. By testing cognitive abilities such as verbal and mathematical skills, the researchers found that intellectual decline does not occur until people are in their 60s or 70s. Further, people who were healthy and remained mentally active demonstrated less decline. Although memory and the speed of processing may decline, the continued ability to learn new information may mitigate those losses in terms of daily functioning.

Because life expectancies generally have improved over time, much more research is likely to be devoted to understanding how people can maintain their cognitive capacities to get the most out of their final years. Moreover, research will continue to examine aging through a more nuanced lens, as contemporary work suggests there may be gender differences in both genetic susceptibility to the negative effects of aging and the level and severity of cognitive impairment late in life (Mortensen & Hogh, 2001).

Thus, this chapter ends where it began, with a reminder that all aspects of human development are caused by a complex cascade of influences. These influences include genes, neurotransmitters, family, social ties, culture, and each individual's motivations and actions (**FIGURE 9.42**). We all play active roles in our own development. We are not passive sponges absorbing our environments, nor are we slaves to our genes. How we experience each phase of the life span depends on our own perceptions, the social support we receive, and the choreographed dance that occurs between nature and nurture.

 How do fluid intelligence and crystallized intelligence change with aging?

ANSWER: Fluid intelligence decreases, but crystallized intelligence increases.

Your Chapter Review

Chapter Summary

What Factors Shape Infancy?

9.1 Human Development Starts in the Womb

The prenatal period is from conception (when sperm and egg unite to form a zygote) through birth (which occurs roughly 40 weeks after conception). From 2 weeks to 2 months prenatally, the developing cells are called an embryo and begin to form into organ systems. By 2 months prenatally, organ systems are formed, the heart begins to beat, and the developing human is called a fetus. Brain development begins early in fetal development. Myelination of the spinal cord occurs in the first trimester, and myelination of neurons occurs during the second trimester. Most neurons are formed at birth, but neural development via synaptic connections continues through early adulthood. Synaptic pruning is the reduction of synaptic connections due to nonuse. The embryo and the fetus are vulnerable to teratogens, environmental toxins that include drugs, viruses, and, chemicals.

9.2 Biology and Environment Influence Motor Development

Genetics and experiences influence motor development. Dynamic systems theory views development as a self-organizing process in which new forms of behavior emerge through the interaction of biology and environment.

9.3 Infants Are Prepared to Learn

Infants are capable of learning, although explicit long-term memories do not persist until about the age of 18 months. Virtually all humans experience infantile amnesia, the inability to remember events before the age of 3 or 4. Some psychologists suggest that infantile amnesia disappears with the development of language.

9.4 Think like a Psychologist: Does Mozart Make You Smarter?

According to a 1993 study, listening to Mozart can at least briefly enhance cognition. The popular press turned this study's results into the so-called Mozart effect, which inspired parents, educators, and politicians to increase infants' exposure to Mozart's music. However, the reporting and subsequent reactions misrepresented the original study, which showed only a motor skill improvement in college-age participants.

9.5 Infants Develop Attachments

An attachment is a strong emotional connection that can motivate care, protection, and social support. Research by Harry Harlow demonstrated that attachments form due to receiving comfort and warmth, not food. About 65 percent of infants display a secure attachment style, expressing confidence in unfamiliar environments as long as the caregiver is present. About 35 percent of infants display an insecure attachment style and may avoid contact with the caregiver, or they alternate between approach and avoidance behaviors. The hormone oxytocin plays a role in attachment.

How Do Children Learn About the World?

9.6 Piaget Emphasized Stages of Cognitive Development

Piaget believed that cognitive development occurs across four stages: sensorimotor (0–2 years), preoperational (2–7 years), concrete operational (7–12 years), and formal operational (12 years–adulthood). During each stage, babies develop schemes, cognitive categories used to organize information. Through assimilation and accommodation, individuals revise and adjust schemes so they remain useful throughout their lives.

9.7 Piaget Underestimated Children's Cognitive Abilities

While Piaget's theory correctly describes much of how cognitive abilities develop, it may underestimate early knowledge. Theories such as Vygotsky's emphasize that cognitive development is guided by cultural expectations and interactions with others. Young infants can use laws of physics and even demonstrate a basic understanding of addition and subtraction.

9.8 Children Learn from Interacting with Others

Theory of mind is the ability to understand that other people have mental states that will influence their behavior. Theory of mind develops by 15 months and is related to development of the frontal lobes.

9.9 Moral Development Begins in Childhood

According to Kohlberg's stage theory of moral reasoning, moral decisions are based on trying to avoid personal harm, trying to gain approval from others, or having true moral concern for the sanctity of life. Theories of moral reasoning have been criticized for being gender and culture biased and for ignoring emotional aspects of moral decisions. The social intuitionist model suggests that moral judgments reflect automatic emotional responses rather than conscious decisions based on moral rules. The prefrontal cortex, the insula, and the amygdala are three of the brain areas involved in moral thinking.

What Changes During Adolescence?

9.10 Puberty Causes Physical Changes

Adolescence begins with puberty, the onset of sexual maturity and thus the ability to reproduce. Biology and environment affect the timing of puberty. During puberty, changing hormone levels stimulate physical changes. Because the frontal lobes mature more slowly than brain reward systems, adolescents may tend to act impulsively and take risks. Yet adolescence is not characterized by as much emotional turmoil as is commonly believed.

9.11 A Sense of Identity Forms

Physical and cognitive changes, along with environmental and societal pressures to prepare for the future, prompt adolescents to establish their identities. Erikson proposed a theory of psychosocial development that describes a series of challenges individuals must overcome from birth through old age, and the challenge during adolescence is to develop an adult identity or risk role confusion. Gender identity, personal beliefs about whether one is male or female, develops during adolescence. Gender identity and gender roles are strongly influenced by biology and environment. Ethnic identity also develops during adolescence.

9.12 Peers and Parents Help Shape the Adolescent Self

Adolescents use peer groups to help them feel a sense of belonging and acceptance. Adolescents may come into conflict with attachment figures, peers, and community members, but they need support and guidance from people close to them. Parents influence peer group identification, values, and religious choices.

What Brings Meaning in Adulthood?

9.13 Adults Are Affected by Life Transitions

Adulthood requires people to meet certain challenges, such as physical and cognitive changes, getting married, and raising a family. In general, married people are healthier and happier than those who are single or cohabitating, and this advantage is more pronounced in men.

9.14 Using Psychology in Your Life: Will Parenthood Make You Happy?

According to the research, couples with children report less marital satisfaction than couples without children. However, raising children can be richly rewarding. Whether or not to become a parent is best considered a matter of individual choice.

9.15 The Transition to Old Age Can Be Satisfying

Although older adults are often characterized as feeble and senile, they are for the most part healthy, alert, and vital. Thoughtful planning and social support can make all phases of adult development rewarding. Older people are often more satisfied with their lives than younger adults are. People increasingly seek meaning in their lives as they age.

9.16 Cognition Changes with Age

Despite declines in memory and speed of mental processing, people generally maintain their intelligence into very old age. People who engage in social, physical, and mental activities tend to keep mental skills sharp into old age.

Key Terms

accommodation, p. 354

assimilation, p. 354

attachment, p. 347

concrete operational stage, p. 355

conventional level, p. 362

developmental psychology, p. 338

dynamic systems theory, p. 343

formal operational stage, p. 356

gender identity, p. 366

gender role, p. 366

infantile amnesia, p. 346

insecure attachment, p. 351

object permanence, p. 354

postconventional level, p. 362

preconventional level, p. 362

preoperational stage, p. 355

puberty, p. 363

secure attachment, p. 350

sensorimotor stage, p. 354

social intuitionist model, p. 362

socioemotional selectivity theory, p. 376

synaptic pruning, p. 339

teratogens, p. 340

theory of mind, p. 360

Putting Psychology to Work

How Is a Psychology Degree Useful in Educational Settings?

In April 2017, Mayor Bill de Blasio announced a plan to provide free, full-time preschool for all New York City three-year-olds. This program, known as 3-K for All, extends the early education programs already in place for four-year-olds and will be the largest program of its kind in the United States. As you have learned in this chapter, the preschool years are critical for the development of children's cognitive and social abilities. According to Piaget, children are learning about the world through sensorimotor activities and are gradually developing logical thinking. Social interactions, Vygotsky proposes, are essential for language development and higher-order cognitive processes. Even at this young age, children show some understanding of the laws of physics and mathematics. Finally, emotional processes are maturing, with the development of theory of mind, empathy, and sympathy.

Given the explosion of cognitive, social, and emotional growth in children between the ages of three and five, the potential benefits of quality preschool programs are significant, particularly for children in high-need groups. Not surprisingly, the number of preschool programs being implemented in school districts across the country is increasing dramatically. As the number of programs increases, so does the need for highly qualified teachers and school administrators.

What makes a preschool teacher "highly qualified"? The Institute of Medicine and National Research Council (2015, p. 328) recommends that early childhood teachers and directors hold at least a bachelor's degree, with expertise in "developmental science that underlies important domains of early learning and child development." This is, of course, good news for psychology graduates who are interested in working with children. Preschool teachers who are familiar with the cognitive, social, and emotional needs of very young children will be better able to design and implement age-appropriate programs, improving the likelihood of long-term benefits.

Employment opportunities are not limited, however, to preschool teachers, but can be found in a wide range of educational settings. Understanding developmental stages in older children and adolescents can help elementary and secondary school teachers better interact with, and design curricula for, those students. School administrators and leaders also benefit from knowing how to support student learning in a developmentally suitable fashion. School psychologists provide support to help students and families improve academic, mental, and behavioral outcomes.

The bottom line: An understanding of how cognitive, behavioral, and social skills develop in children has many applications in the educational job sector. Psychology majors with a baccalaureate degree, and who complete coursework for teacher certification, can be employed as teachers, whether in preschool, elementary, or secondary settings; a master's degree is required for school psychologist positions.

Want to earn a better grade on your test?
Go to **INQUIZITIVE** to learn and review this chapter's content, with personalized feedback along the way.
Practice Tests and accompanying answer keys can be found at the back of the book on page PT-1.

10 Emotion and Motivation

Big Questions

- What Are Emotions? 384

- How Are Emotions Adaptive? 396

- How Are People Motivated? 402

- What Motivates Eating? 412

- What Motivates Sexual Behavior? 416

YOU WANT TO DO A REALLY GOOD JOB ON YOUR CLASS PRESENTATION. You like the course and pride yourself on being a good public speaker. But when your professor starts taking notes during your talk, you become nervous. Your face feels warm, and you begin to sweat. You follow the sage advice of picturing your audience in their underwear, but that image makes you feel creepy. Finally, you pull yourself together, focus on the material, and do a great job. You walk out of the class feeling like you are floating on air.

Emotions permeate human life, for better and worse. For thousands of years, people have reflected on why we have emotions and what they do for us. An important and adaptive value of emotions is that they motivate certain actions. We seek out events, activities, and objects that make us feel good. We avoid events, activities, and objects that make us feel bad. But what does it mean to feel something? And why do those feelings influence our goals in life? This chapter examines how emotions and motivation are tied together. Research in this area considers: What are emotions? How are emotions adaptive? How are people motivated? What motivates eating? What motivates sexual behavior?

Learning Objectives

- Distinguish between primary and secondary emotions.

- Discuss the roles that the insula and the amygdala play in emotional experience.

- Compare and contrast the James-Lange, Cannon-Bard, and Schachter-Singer two-factor theories of emotion.

- Define misattribution of arousal and excitation transfer.

emotion
An immediate, specific negative or positive response to environmental events or internal thoughts.

What Are Emotions?

People have an intuitive sense of what *emotion* means. Still, the term is difficult to define precisely. The terms *emotion, feeling,* and *mood* are often used interchangeably in everyday language, but psychologists distinguish between them. An **emotion** is an immediate, specific negative or positive response to environmental events or internal thoughts. Emotions typically interrupt whatever is happening, or they trigger changes in thought and behavior. You are sitting at your desk and see a movement out of the corner of your eye and . . . eek, it is a rat! You are having a negative emotional response. For psychologists, emotion—sometimes called *affect*—has three components: a physiological process (e.g., heart beating fast, sweating), a behavioral response (e.g., eyes and mouth opening wide), and a feeling that is based on cognitive appraisal of the situation and interpretation of bodily states (e.g., I'm scared!). A *feeling* is the subjective experience of the emotion, such as feeling scared, but not the emotion itself.

By contrast, *moods* are diffuse, long-lasting emotional states that do not have an identifiable object or trigger. Rather than interrupting what is happening, they influence thought and behavior. Often people who are in good or bad moods have no idea why they feel the way they do. Thus, moods refer to people's vague senses that they feel certain ways. Think of the difference this way: Getting cut off in traffic can make a person angry (emotion), but for no apparent reason a person can be irritable (mood).

10.1 Emotions Vary in Valence and Arousal

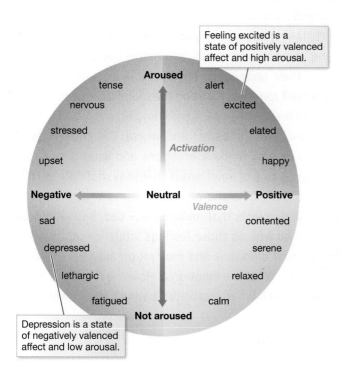

Feeling excited is a state of positively valenced affect and high arousal.

Depression is a state of negatively valenced affect and low arousal.

FIGURE 10.1
Circumplex Map of Emotion
Emotions can be categorized by valence (negative to positive) and by level of arousal (low to high).

Many emotion theorists distinguish between primary and secondary emotions. This approach is conceptually similar to viewing color as consisting of primary and secondary hues. Basic emotions, or **primary emotions,** are innate, evolutionarily adaptive, and universal (shared across cultures). These emotions include anger, fear, sadness, disgust, happiness, surprise, and contempt. **Secondary emotions** are blends of primary emotions. There are numerous secondary emotions, such as remorse, guilt, submission, shame, love, bitterness, and jealousy.

Emotions have also been classified along different dimensions. One such system is the *circumplex model.* In this model, emotions are plotted along two continuums: valence (how negative or positive they are) and arousal (how arousing they are; Kuppens, Tuerlinckx, Russell, & Barrett, 2013; Russell, 2003; **FIGURE 10.1**). *Arousal* is a generic term used to describe physiological activation (such as increased brain activity) or increased autonomic responses (such as quickened heart rate, increased sweating, or muscle tension).

To understand the difference between valence and arousal, imagine you discover that you have lost the $1 bill that was in your pants pocket. This experience will most likely make you unhappy, so you will judge it to have negative valence. It also might make you slightly aroused (increase your autonomic responses somewhat). Now imagine that

you find a lottery ticket that turns out to be worth a million dollars. This experience will most likely make you very, very happy, so you will judge it as on the positive side of the valence scale. Your arousal will probably be topping the chart.

Psychologists have debated the names for the emotion dimensions and even the whole idea of dimensions. However, circumplex models have proved useful as a basic taxonomy, or classification system, of mood states (Barrett, Mesquita, Ochsner, & Gross, 2007).

Some emotional states seem to contradict the circumplex approach of viewing emotions on a continuum from negative to positive. Consider the bittersweet feeling of being both happy and sad. For example, you might feel this way when remembering good times with someone who has died. In one study, research participants reported feeling happy and sad after moving out of their dormitories, after graduating from college, and after seeing the 1997 movie *Life Is Beautiful,* in which a good-natured father tries to protect his son in a Nazi prison camp (Larsen, McGraw, & Cacioppo, 2001). Neurochemical evidence supports the idea that positive affect and negative affect are independent (Watson, Wiese, Vaidya, & Tellegen, 1999). Positive activation states appear to be associated with an increase in dopamine, whereas negative activation states appear to be associated with an increase in norepinephrine (for explanations of neurochemistry, see Chapter 3, "Biology and Behavior").

Q Is jealousy a primary or secondary emotion?

ANSWER: It is a secondary emotion, as being jealous involves multiple primary emotions, such as anger, fear, and sadness.

10.2 Emotions Have a Physiological Component

While waiting for a job interview, you might find your heart racing. When someone tells you he loves you, you might feel warm all over. Even everyday language includes bodily descriptions to describe emotional experiences, such as getting "cold feet" when reconsidering a commitment, being "heartbroken" when extremely distressed, or having "knots in your stomach" when anxious. Emotions involve activation of the autonomic nervous system to prepare the body to meet environmental challenges (Levenson, 2003, 2014).

Controversy exists about such physiological responses. Does each emotion have a specific bodily response (Lench, Flores, & Bench, 2011)? Or do all emotions share core physical properties related to valence and arousal (Wilson-Mendenhall, Barrett, & Barselou, 2013), making them difficult to distinguish based on bodily response alone? Many of the autonomic responses to emotion overlap. However, the specific patterns across multiple autonomic responses (flushing or blanching, heart rate, sweating, pupil dilation, and goose bumps) suggest some level of specificity for each emotion (Comtesse & Stemmler, 2016; Eisenbarth, Chang, & Wager, 2016; Levenson, 2014). There is evidence from fMRI studies that patterns of brain activity differ among emotional experiences (Kragel & LaBar, 2016; Saarimäki, Gotsopoulos, Jääskeläinen, Lampinen, Vuilleumier, et al., 2016).

To study bodily responses and emotions, Finnish researchers asked people from various cultures to use a computer program to color which areas of the body were involved in feeling various emotions (Nummenmaa, Glerean, Hari, & Hietanen, 2014). Across five studies, emotions were generated in different ways (e.g., imagining the emotions, reading short stories, or watching movies). The reported activation of body parts by emotions overlapped somewhat, but specific emotions were characterized by

Emotions that are innate, evolutionarily adaptive, and universal (shared across cultures).

secondary emotions
Blends of primary emotions.

FIGURE 10.2
Body Maps of Emotion

These maps represent areas of the body that are more active (warm colors) or less active (cool colors) when people consider how various emotions make them feel. The color bar reflects the extent of increasing or decreasing activity.

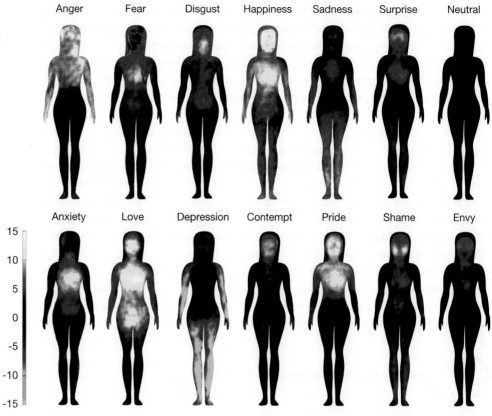

Anger   Fear   Disgust   Happiness   Sadness   Surprise   Neutral

Anxiety   Love   Depression   Contempt   Pride   Shame   Envy

15
10
5
0
-5
-10
-15

discrete patterns of activity in the body (**FIGURE 10.2**). According to the researchers, perception of these bodily sensations may play a role in how different emotions are experienced.

LIMBIC SYSTEM In 1937, the neuroanatomist James Papez proposed that many subcortical brain regions are involved in emotion. The physician and neuroscientist Paul MacLean (1952) expanded this list of regions and called it the limbic system. (As discussed in Chapter 3, the limbic system consists of brain structures that border the cerebral cortex.) We now know that many brain structures outside the limbic system are involved in emotion and that many limbic structures are not central to emotion per se. For instance, the hippocampus is important mostly for memory, and the hypothalamus is important mostly for motivation. Thus, the term *limbic system* is used mainly in a rough, descriptive way rather than as a means of directly linking brain areas to specific emotional functions. For understanding emotion, the most important limbic system structures are the insula (see Figure 4.39) and the amygdala (**FIGURE 10.3**) However, several other areas contribute to emotional processing. In addition, various regions of the prefrontal cortex are important for acting on emotions.

The insula receives and integrates somatosensory signals from the entire body. It is also involved in the subjective awareness of bodily states, such as sensing your heartbeat, feeling hungry, or needing to urinate. Given that emotions produce bodily responses, it is not surprising that the insula plays an important role in the experience of emotion (Craig, 2009; Zaki, Davis, & Ochsner, 2012). Imaging studies have found that the insula is particularly active when people experience disgust—such as when exposed to bad smells—or observe facial expressions of disgust in other people (Wicker et al., 2003). Damage to the insula interferes with the experience of disgust and also with recognizing disgust expressions in others (Calder, Keane, Manes,

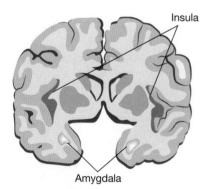

Insula

Amygdala

FIGURE 10.3
The Insula and the Amygdala

This figure shows the insula and the amygdala from the front and midway through the brain, indicating their relative locations. Figure 4.39 shows the insula from the side. Figure 10.4a shows the amygdala from the side.

Antoun, & Young, 2000). The insula is also activated in a variety of other emotions, including anger, guilt, and anxiety (Chang, Yarkoni, Khaw, & Sanfey, 2013).

The amygdala processes the emotional significance of stimuli, and it generates immediate emotional and behavioral reactions (Whalen & Phelps, 2009). According to the emotions theorist Joseph LeDoux (2007; 2015a), the processing of emotion in the amygdala involves a circuit that has developed over the course of evolution to protect animals from danger. LeDoux (2014) has established the amygdala as the brain structure most important for emotional learning, as in the development of classically conditioned fear responses (see Chapter 6, "Learning"). People with damage to the amygdala do not develop conditioned fear responses to objects associated with danger. Suppose that study participants receive an electric shock each time they see a picture of a blue square. Normally, such participants will develop a conditioned response—indicated by greater physiological arousal—when they see the blue square. But people with damage to the amygdala do not show classical conditioning of these fear associations (Anderson & Phelps, 2000).

Information reaches the amygdala along two separate pathways. The first path is a "quick and dirty" system that processes sensory information nearly instantaneously. Recall from Chapter 5 that with the exception of smell, all sensory information travels to the thalamus before going on to other brain structures and the related portions of the cortex (**FIGURE 10.4A**). Thus, along this fast path, sensory information travels quickly through the thalamus directly to the amygdala for priority processing (**FIGURE 10.4B, GREEN ARROW**).

The second path is somewhat slower, but it leads to more deliberate and more thorough evaluations. Along this slow path, sensory material travels from the thalamus to the cortex (the visual cortex or the auditory cortex), where the information is scrutinized in greater depth before it is passed along to the amygdala (see Figure 10.4b,

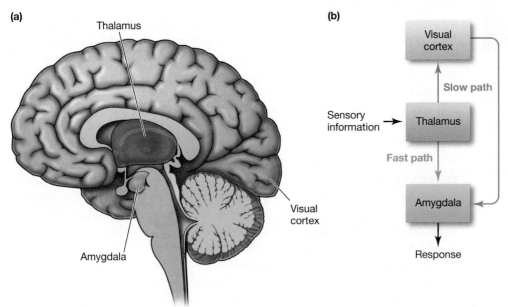

FIGURE 10.4
The Emotional Brain
(a) The amygdala is one of the most important brain structures for processing emotion. Before sensory information reaches the amygdala, it passes through the thalamus. From the thalamus, it may travel through the visual cortex (shown here) or auditory cortex (not shown). **(b)** When sensory information reaches the thalamus, it can take two paths. The fast path (from the thalamus to the amygdala) and the slow path (from the thalamus, through the visual cortex (shown here) or auditory cortex (not shown), to the amygdala) enable people to assess and respond to emotion-producing stimuli in different ways.

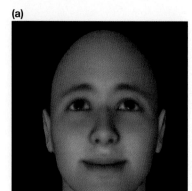

(a)

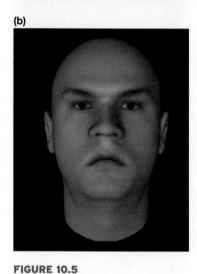

(b)

FIGURE 10.5
Evaluating Facial Expressions
Which of these people would you trust? Most people would say that **(a)** this person looks trustworthy and **(b)** this person looks untrustworthy. Viewing the untrustworthy face leads to greater amygdala activity. People with certain brain injuries cannot detect how trustworthy people are from facial expressions such as these.

ANSWER: Visual information is first sent via the fast path, from the thalamus to the amygdala. This "quick and dirty" signal allows for the spotting of danger and potentially quick action. Visual information also takes the slow path, from the thalamus to the visual cortex and on to the amygdala. This transmission allows for further evaluation of the threat.

orange arrows). Theorists believe that the fast system prepares animals to respond to a threat in case the slower pathway confirms the threat (LeDoux, 2000). You have experienced the two pathways if, for example, you have shied away from a blurry movement in the grass, only to realize it was the wind and not a snake.

AMYGDALA AND COGNITION As noted in Chapter 7, emotional events are especially likely to be stored in memory. The amygdala plays a role in this process. Brain imaging studies have shown that emotional events are likely to increase activity in the amygdala, and that increased activity is likely to improve long-term memory for the event (LaBar & Cabeza, 2006; Talmi, 2013). Researchers believe that the amygdala modifies how the hippocampus consolidates memory, especially memory for fearful events (Manns & Bass, 2016; Phelps, 2004, 2006). In short, thanks to the amygdala, emotions such as fear strengthen memories. This adaptive mechanism enables us to remember harmful situations and thus potentially avoid them.

The amygdala is also involved in the perception of social stimuli. It plays a role, for example, when we decipher the emotional meanings of other people's facial expressions, such as their trustworthiness (Freeman, Stolier, Ingbretsen, & Hehman, 2014; Todorov, Mende-Siedlecki, & Dotsch, 2013; **FIGURE 10.5**). Imaging studies demonstrate that the amygdala is especially sensitive to the intensity of fearful faces (Dolan, 2000). This effect occurs even if a face is flashed so quickly on a screen that participants do not know they have seen it (Whalen et al., 1998). Perhaps surprisingly, the amygdala reacts more when a person observes a face displaying fear than when the person observes a face displaying anger. On the surface, this difference makes little sense, because a person looking at you angrily is likely to be more dangerous. According to some researchers, the greater activity of the amygdala when a person looks at a frightened face is due to the ambiguity of the situation (Whalen et al., 2001). In other words, if a person is looking at you when she is angry, she is probably angry at you—no ambiguity there. But when the person shows fear and you are not doing anything to her, then she must be afraid of something else, such as a spider that is dangling behind you. The amygdala response to fear expressions in others warns of potential dangers to you. The amygdala also responds to other emotional expressions, even happiness. Generally, however, the effect is greatest for fear. One study showed that the amygdala can be activated even by neutral facial expressions, but this effect occurs only in people who are chronically anxious (Somerville, Kim, Johnstone, Alexander, & Whalen, 2004).

Given that the amygdala is involved in processing the emotional content of facial expressions, it is not surprising that social impairments result when the amygdala is damaged. Those with damage to the amygdala often have difficulty evaluating the intensity of fearful faces. They do not have difficulty, however, in judging the intensity of other facial expressions, such as happiness. One study suggests that those with damage to the amygdala can tell a smile from a frown but that they fail to use information within facial expressions to make accurate interpersonal judgments (Adolphs, Tranel, & Damasio, 1998). For instance, they have difficulty using photographs to assess people's trustworthiness—a task most people can do easily (Adolphs, Sears, & Piven, 2001; see Figure 10.5). They also tend to be unusually friendly with people they do not know. This extra friendliness might result from a lack of the normal mechanisms for caution around strangers and for the feeling that some people should be avoided.

Q You are swimming in the ocean. Up ahead you see a jellyfish, so you freeze. When it turns out to be a plastic bag, you relax and continue swimming. How are your responses related to the fast and slow paths for visual information?

10.3 Are Lie Detector Tests Valid?

One essential characteristic of human nature is that people occasionally lie to one another. As long as there have been lies, people have tried to develop methods for detecting such deception. Potential suspects in criminal investigations and applicants for certain types of jobs, such as those that involve classified documents, are often asked to take a polygraph test. This technique is known informally as a lie detector test. A *polygraph* is an electronic instrument that assesses the body's physiological response to questions (**FIGURE 10.6**). It records numerous aspects of arousal, such as breathing rate and heart rate.

The use of polygraphs is highly controversial. Most courts do not allow polygraph results as evidence, and they are banned in the private sector. Yet they continue to be used by criminal investigators and federal agencies, such as the FBI and CIA. How valid are polygraphs as lie detectors?

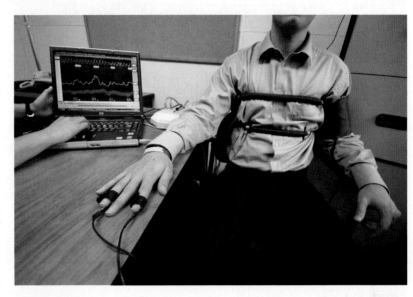

FIGURE 10.6
Polygraph
Here, a person is hooked up to a polygraph apparatus measuring heart rate, respiration, and skin conductance from sweating.

The goal of polygraphy is to determine a person's level of emotionality, as indicated by autonomic arousal, when confronted with certain information. For instance, criminals might be asked about specific illegal activities, job applicants might be asked about drug use, and potential Secret Service or CIA agents might be asked about sympathies for foreign countries. Lying is stressful for most people, so autonomic arousal should be higher when people are lying than when they are telling the truth. But some people become nervous simply because the whole procedure is new and scary, or they are upset that someone thinks they are guilty when they are innocent.

No absolute measure of autonomic arousal can indicate the presence or absence of a lie, because each person's level of autonomic arousal is different. Being highly aroused does not indicate guilt. Instead, to assess physiological arousal, polygraphers use a control-question technique in which they ask a variety of questions, some of which are relevant to the critical information and some of which are not. Control questions, such as "Is your hair brown?" and "Have you ever been to Canada?" are selected with the assumption that they should not produce a strong emotional response. Critical questions, such as "Did you steal the money?" or "Do you use drugs?" are those of specific interest to the investigators. The differences between the physiological responses to the control questions and physiological responses to the critical questions is the measure used to determine whether the person is lying (**FIGURE 10.7**). Sometimes the questions include information that only a guilty party would know, such as how a person was killed or where the body was found. Thus, simply having guilty knowledge should produce arousal and therefore be detected by the polygraph.

There are numerous problems with using polygraphs to uncover deception. One serious drawback is that innocent people are often falsely classified as being deceptive (Ben-Shakhar, Bar-Hillel, & Kremnitzer, 2002). Most people who fail the tests are actually telling the truth and are simply anxious about taking the test. The polygraph cannot tell whether a response is due to lying, nervousness, or anything else arousing. As a result, lie detector tests are pretty easy to pass if you use countermeasures, such

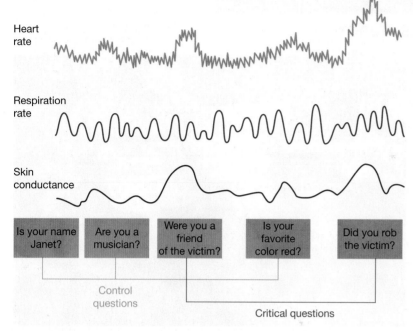

Heart rate

Respiration rate

Skin conductance

| Is your name Janet? | Are you a musician? | Were you a friend of the victim? | Is your favorite color red? | Did you rob the victim? |

Control questions

Critical questions

FIGURE 10.7
Lie Detection
A polygraph measures autonomic systems, such as heart rate, respiration, and skin conductance from sweating. Differences in autonomic reactions to critical questions, compared to control questions, indicate arousal. That arousal in turn may indicate nervousness as a result of lying. However, the arousal may instead be due to general nervousness and thus may falsely indicate that the person is lying.

as counting backward by sevens or pressing your feet to the floor during critical questions (Honts, Raskin, & Kircher, 1994). Anyone can easily learn to use these techniques.

Perhaps the most serious problem with lie detector tests is that the investigator has to make a subjective judgment as to whether the pattern of arousal indicates deception. This judgment is often influenced by the investigator's beliefs about whether the person is guilty. This type of confirmation bias has also been found in laboratory studies, especially when the polygraphy results are ambiguous (Elaad, Ginton, & Ben-Shakhar, 1994). Confirmation bias is a problem throughout forensic assessments, particularly when individuals develop "tunnel vision" and fixate on a particular suspect, ignoring or discounting evidence that is contrary (Kassin, Dror, & Kukucka, 2013).

As you might expect, researchers are seeking new strategies to uncover deception. For instance, numerous studies using EEG and fMRI have detected differences in brain activity between when people are lying and when they are telling the truth (Langleben & Moriarty, 2013). However, the deception tasks in these studies have been relatively trivial, and the participants probably did not feel anxious about being deceptive (after all, the experimenters asked them to lie). Whether the activation of various brain regions indicates genuine deception or simply reflects other cognitive processes is currently unknown. A thoughtful review of this research by a team of neuroscience experts highlighted several methodological problems with fMRI research to detect deception. These experts raised additional ethical issues, such as privacy, that need further consideration before fMRI is ready for the courtroom (Farah, Hutchinson, Phelps, & Wagner, 2014). ■

 Why can't a polygraphy test differentiate between telling a lie and feeling embarrassed?

ANSWER: Both actions produce arousal, which is all the test can measure.

10.4 There Are Three Major Theories of Emotion

James-Lange theory of emotion
People perceive specific patterns of bodily responses, and as a result of that perception they feel emotion.

Cannon-Bard theory of emotion
Information about emotional stimuli is sent simultaneously to the cortex and the body and results in emotional experience and bodily reactions, respectively.

Suppose you are in a rural area. You leave your house and notice your shed door is open. So you go to inspect it. Inside, a grizzly bear looks up at you from the bag of dog food it was eating. You might think that seeing the bear would make you scared. Your heart would start to race, and you would run back into the house. As this example illustrates, common sense suggests that experiences, such as seeing a bear, generate emotions, such as fear, which then lead to bodily responses and behavior. Three major theories have proposed different ways that these processes might work: the James-Lange theory, the Cannon-Bard theory, and the Schachter-Singer two-factor theory.

JAMES-LANGE THEORY Although common sense suggests that our bodies respond to emotions, William James (1884) made the counterintuitive argument that the situation is just the opposite. James asserted that a person's interpretation of physical changes leads that person to feel an emotion. As he put it, "We feel sorry because we cry, angry because we strike, afraid because we tremble[; it is] not that we cry, strike, or tremble because we are sorry, angry, or fearful" (p. 190).

James believed that physical changes occur in distinct patterns that translate directly into specific emotions. Around the same time, a similar theory was independently proposed by the physician and psychologist Carl Lange. According to what is called the **James-Lange theory of emotion,** we perceive specific patterns of bodily responses, and as a result of that perception we feel emotion (**FIGURE 10.8**). That is, seeing the bear causes your heart to race, and you perceive your racing heart as fear.

Some research supports the James-Lange theory. Studies using brain imaging have found that different primary emotions produce different patterns of brain activation (Kragel, Knodt, Hariri, & LaBar, 2016; Vytal & Hamann, 2010). These results suggest that different experiences that generate emotion are associated with different physiological reactions (Levenson, 2014).

One implication of the James-Lange theory is that if you mold your facial muscles to mimic an emotional state, you activate the associated emotion. In other words, facial expressions trigger the experience of emotions, not the other way around. In 1963, Silvan Tomkins proposed this idea as the *facial feedback hypothesis*. Researchers tested the idea by having people hold a pencil between their teeth or with their mouths in a way that produced a smile or a frown (**FIGURE 10.9**). When participants rated cartoons, those in a posed smile found the cartoons the funniest (Strack, Martin, & Stepper, 1988). Using slightly different methods, one team of researchers recently failed to replicate this effect (Wagenmakers et al., 2016). However, the general idea that changing facial expression changes emotional state has been demonstrated many times (Strack, 2016).

CANNON-BARD THEORY In 1927, James's former student Walter B. Cannon, a physiologist, offered some objections to James's theory. Cannon's student Philip Bard (1934) later expanded on Cannon's criticisms. Their alternative theory is now called the **Cannon-Bard theory of emotion.** Cannon and Bard thought that the autonomic nervous system was too slow to account for the subjective feelings of emotions. Experience happens quickly in the mind, but events in the body take much longer, at least a second or two to react. For instance, you may feel embarrassed before you blush.

Cannon and Bard also noted that many emotions produce similar bodily responses. The similarities make it too difficult for people to determine quickly which emotion they are experiencing. For instance, anger, excitement, and sexual interest all produce similar changes in heart rate and blood pressure. Exercise brings about these same

(a)

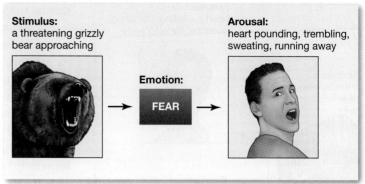

Stimulus: a threatening grizzly bear approaching

Emotion: **FEAR**

Arousal: heart pounding, trembling, sweating, running away

(b)

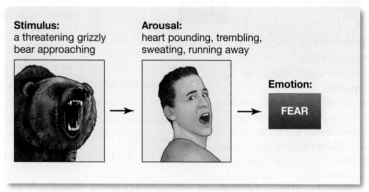

Stimulus: a threatening grizzly bear approaching

Arousal: heart pounding, trembling, sweating, running away

Emotion: **FEAR**

FIGURE 10.8
James-Lange Theory of Emotion
(a) According to the intuitive view of emotion, an experience—such as seeing a grizzly bear—may produce an emotion and then a bodily response. **(b)** According to the James-Lange theory, bodily perception comes before the feeling of emotion. For example, when a grizzly bear threatens you, you begin to sweat, experience a pounding heart, and run (if you can). These responses generate in you the emotion of fear.

FIGURE 10.9
Facial Feedback Hypothesis
According to this hypothesis, a person's facial expression triggers that person's experience of emotion. Even the forced alteration of a person's facial expression can change that person's experience of emotion.

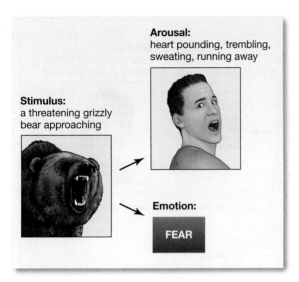

FIGURE 10.10

Cannon-Bard Theory of Emotion

According to this theory, emotion and physical reactions happen independently but at the same time. For example, when a grizzly bear threatens you, you simultaneously feel afraid, begin to sweat, experience a pounding heart, and run (if you can).

two-factor theory of emotion

A label applied to physiological arousal results in the experience of an emotion.

changes, and it may affect your emotional state, but it does not generate a specific emotion.

Cannon and Bard proposed that information about emotional stimuli is sent to the mind and body separately and simultaneously. As a result, mind and body experience emotions independently. According to the Cannon-Bard theory of emotion, the information from an emotion-producing stimulus is processed in subcortical structures (Cannon originally focused on the thalamus, but it is now known that many limbic system structures are involved in emotion). The subcortical structures then send information separately to the cortex and the body. As a result, people experience two separate things at roughly the same time: an emotion, produced in the cortex, and physical reactions, produced in the body (**FIGURE 10.10**). When you see the bear in the shed, separate signals cause your heart to race and you to feel scared.

Although the terms they use are different, Joseph LeDoux and Daniel Pine (2016) have proposed a similar model that separates behavior and bodily responses produced by subcortical systems from the felt emotions produced by the cortex. From this perspective, a person can be afraid even in the absence of a genuine threat. Indeed, just awareness of the potential for harm can lead a person to be afraid, such as if a person becomes afraid to go outside because of news reports that bears are raiding local sheds.

SCHACHTER-SINGER TWO-FACTOR THEORY The social psychologists Stanley Schachter and Jerome Singer (1962) saw some merit in both the James-Lange and the Cannon-Bard theories. Schachter and Singer thought that the James-Lange theory was right in equating the perception of the body's reaction with an emotion, but they agreed with Cannon-Bard that too many different emotions existed for there to be a unique autonomic pattern for each. Schachter and Singer proposed a **two-factor theory of emotion.** They proposed that the physiological response to all emotional stimuli was essentially the same, which they called undifferentiated physiological arousal. The arousal was just interpreted differently, depending upon the situation, and given a *label*.

According to this theory, when people experience arousal, they initiate a search for its source (**FIGURE 10.11**). The search for a cognitive explanation, or label, is often quick and straightforward, since a person generally recognizes the event that led to his or her emotional state. When seeing the bear in the shed, you experience arousal. Your knowledge that bears are dangerous leads you to attribute the arousal to the bear and label the arousal "fear."

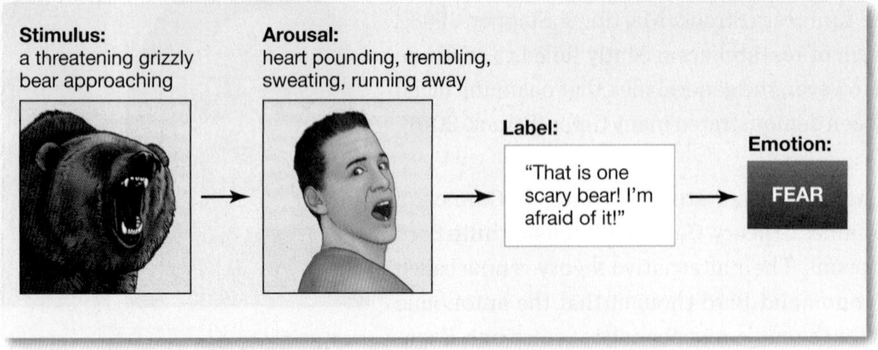

What happens when the situation is more ambiguous? According to the two-factor theory, whatever the person *believes* caused the emotion will determine how the person labels the emotion. A variety of evidence supports this aspect of the two-factor theory. An emotion

FIGURE 10.11

Schachter-Singer Two-Factor Theory

According to this theory, a person experiences physiological changes and applies a cognitive label to explain those changes. For example, when a grizzly bear threatens you, you begin to sweat, experience a pounding heart, and run (if you can). You then label those bodily actions as responses to the bear. As a result, you know you are experiencing fear.

involves physiological responses in brain and body that are influenced by how the person thinks about the situation (MacCormack & Lindquist, 2017; Satpute et al., 2016).

Schachter and Singer devised an ingenious experiment to test the two-factor theory. First, the participants, all of whom were male, were injected with either a stimulant or a placebo. The stimulant was adrenaline, which produced symptoms such as sweaty palms, increased heart rate, and shaking. Some of the participants who received adrenaline were told that the drug they took would make them feel aroused. The other participants were not told anything about the drug's effects. Finally, each participant was left to wait with a confederate of the experimenter. The confederate, also male, was working with the experimenter and behaved according to the research plan.

In the euphoric condition, each participant was exposed to a confederate who was in a great mood, played with a hula hoop, and made paper airplanes. In the angry condition, each participant was seated in a room with a confederate. Both the participant and the confederate were asked to fill out a long questionnaire that asked them very intimate, personal questions, such as "With how many men (other than your father) has your mother had extramarital relationships?" (To make the question even more insulting, the choices were 4 or fewer, 5 to 9, or 10 or more.) The confederate became increasingly angry as he filled out the questionnaire. Finally, he ripped it up and stormed out of the room.

When participants received adrenaline but were told how their bodies would respond to the drug, they had an easy explanation for their arousal. They attributed it to the adrenaline, not to the situation. In contrast, when participants received adrenaline but were not given information about its effects, they were just as aroused as the informed group, but they did not know why. They looked to the environment to explain or label their bodies' responses (sweating palms, increased heart rate, and shaking). Participants in the no-explanation group reported that they felt happy when they waited with the euphoric confederate and that they felt less happy when they waited with the angry confederate. While they attributed their feelings to what was happening in the environment, participants in the informed group did not (see "The Methods of Psychology: Testing the Schachter-Singer Two-Factor Theory," on p. 394). Those in the placebo condition responded in between the two adrenaline conditions, depending on how aroused they were by the confederate.

One interesting implication of the two-factor theory is that physical states caused by a situation can be attributed to the wrong emotion. When people misidentify the source of their arousal, it is called *misattribution of arousal*.

In one exploration of this phenomenon, researchers tried to see whether people could feel romantic attraction through misattribution (Dutton & Aron, 1974). Each participant, a heterosexual male, was asked to cross either of two bridges over the Capilano River, in British Columbia. One was a narrow suspension bridge with a low rail that swayed 230 feet above raging, rocky rapids. The other was a sturdy modern bridge just above the river. At the middle of the bridge, an attractive female research assistant approached the man and interviewed him. She gave him her phone number and offered to explain the results of the study at a later date if he was interested. According to the two-factor theory of emotion, the less stable bridge would produce arousal (sweaty palms, increased heart rate), which could be misattributed as attraction to the interviewer. Indeed, men interviewed on the less stable bridge were more likely to call the interviewer and ask her for a date (**FIGURE 10.12**).

Can you think of a possible confound affecting this study? What about initial differences between the men who chose to cross the less stable bridge and those who chose the safer bridge? Perhaps men who were more likely to take risks were more likely to choose a scary bridge *and* to call for a date. The general idea—that people can misattribute arousal for affection—has been supported in other studies, however.

FIGURE 10.12
Misattribution of Arousal
Men who walked across this narrow and scary bridge over the Capilano River displayed more attraction to the female experimenter on the bridge than did men who walked across a safer bridge.

The Methods of Psychology
Testing the Schachter-Singer Two-Factor Theory

HYPOTHESIS: Whatever a person believes caused an emotion will determine how the person experiences and labels the emotion.

1 Participants were injected with a stimulant (adrenaline) or a placebo.

2 Informed participants in the adrenaline condition were told the drug they were given might make them feel shaky, cause their hearts to beat faster, and make their faces feel flushed. All of these bodily activities are physical effects of taking adrenaline. Uninformed participants were not told anything about the drug's effects.

3 In the euphoric condition, each participant was exposed to a confederate who was in a great mood, played with a hula hoop, and made paper airplanes.

In the angry condition, each participant was seated with a confederate. Both the participant and the confederate were asked to fill out a questionnaire that asked very insulting questions, such as a question that implied their mothers had cheated on their fathers. The confederate became angry, tore up the questionnaire, and stormed out of the room.

4 The experimenters coded behavioral indicators of euphoria, such as joining in the fun. They also coded behavioral indicators of anger, such as agreeing with the angry confederate. In addition, participants were asked about their emotional states, such as whether they felt happy or angry.

Euphoric condition

Angry condition

RESULT: When participants received the adrenaline and were told how their bodies would respond to the drug, they had an easy explanation for their arousal. They attributed it to the adrenaline, not to the situation. In contrast, when participants received adrenaline but were not given information about its effects, they looked to the environment to explain or label their bodies' responses.

Euphoric condition

Behavioral euphoria

Informed participants   Uninformed participants

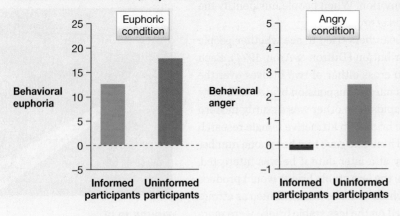

Angry condition

Behavioral anger

Informed participants   Uninformed participants

When uninformed participants waited with the euphoric confederates, they displayed behavioral indicators of euphoria (see left-side graph). They also reported feeling happy. When uninformed participants waited with the angry confederates, they displayed behavioral indicators of anger (see right-side graph). They also reported feeling angry. These results happened because the uninformed participants attributed their feelings to what was happening in the environment. Informed participants did not react in the same ways or make the same attributions. For example, in the angry condition, their behavioral indicators of anger decreased.

CONCLUSION: Feelings of arousal can be attributed to events in the environment, thereby shaping people's emotions.

QUESTION: Why did the actions of the confederate not affect the participants in the informed condition?

ANSWER: Those participants had an explanation for their arousal, so they did not attribute how they felt to the confederate.

Source: Schachter, S., & Singer, J. (1962). Cognitive, social, and physiological determinants of emotional state. *Psychological Review, 69,* 379–399.

Excitation transfer is a similar form of misattribution. Here, residual physiological arousal caused by one event is transferred to a new stimulus. For example, in the period after exercise, the body slowly returns to its baseline state. Residual arousal symptoms include an elevated heart rate. After a few minutes, most people will have caught their breath and may not realize their bodies are still aroused. During this interim period, they are likely to transfer the residual excitation from the exercise to any event that occurs. This response has a practical application: On your next date, you might suggest seeing a movie that you think will produce arousal, such as a tearjerker or an action film. Perhaps the person you are out with will misattribute residual arousal to you!

 According to the James-Lange theory, which comes first, the emotion or the bodily response?

ANSWER: the bodily response, which is then interpreted by the person as an emotion

10.5 How Can You Control Your Emotions?

Emotions can be disruptive and troublesome. Negative feelings can prevent people from behaving as they would like to, but so can positive feelings. Have you ever been so nervous that you found it hard to perform in front of an audience (**FIGURE 10.13A**)? Or have you ever felt so excited about an upcoming event that you were unable to concentrate on an exam (**FIGURE 10.13B**)? In our daily lives, circumstances often require us to control our emotions, but doing so is not easy. How do you mask your expression of disgust when you are obligated by politeness to eat something you dislike? How do you force yourself to be nice about losing a competition that really matters to you?

James Gross (1999; 2013) outlined various strategies people use to regulate their emotions. Some of these strategies help people prevent or prepare for events, and some of them help in dealing with events after they occur. Not all strategies for regulating emotional states are equally successful, however.

What not to do: Two common strategies, thought suppression and rumination, do not work. With *thought suppression,* people attempt to not feel or respond to the emotion at all. Daniel Wegner and colleagues (1990) have demonstrated that trying to suppress negative thoughts is extremely difficult. In fact, doing so often leads to a *rebound effect,* in which people think more about something after suppression than before. For example, people who are dieting and try to not think about tasty foods end up thinking about them more than if they had tried to engage in another activity as a way of not thinking about food.

Rumination involves thinking about, elaborating on, and focusing on undesired thoughts or feelings. This response prolongs the emotion, and it impedes successful emotion regulation strategies, such as distracting oneself or focusing on solutions for the problem (Lyubomirsky & Nolen-Hoeksema, 1995). So what can you do to regulate emotion? Research shows that the following strategies are more successful than thought suppression or rumination.

Control the location: If you want to feel romantic when proposing to your girlfriend, you are better off proposing in a quiet, intimate bistro than in a fast-food joint. If you want to avoid feeling jealous of your sister's athletic skill, you could choose not to attend her soccer, basketball, and softball games. By putting yourself in certain situations and avoiding other situations, you can influence the likelihood of experiencing certain emotions.

Change the meaning: It is also possible to directly alter emotional reactions to events by *reappraising* those events in more neutral terms. So if you get scared while watching a movie, you can remind yourself that the whole spectacle has been staged

(a)

(b)

FIGURE 10.13
Disruptive Emotions
Our actions can be disrupted by **(a)** negative feelings, such as nervousness, or **(b)** positive feelings, such as being distracted by looking forward to an exciting upcoming event.

and no one is actually being hurt. Brain imaging studies have found that engaging in reappraisal changes the activity of brain regions involved in the experience of emotion (Ochsner, Bunge, Gross, & Gabrieli, 2002; Ochsner, Silvers, & Buhle, 2012).

Find humor: Using humor has many mental and physical health benefits (Samson & Gross, 2012). Most obviously, humor increases positive affect. When you find something humorous, you smile, laugh, and enter a state of pleasurable, relaxed excitement. Research shows that laughter stimulates endocrine secretion, improves the immune system, and stimulates the release of hormones, dopamine, serotonin, and endorphins. When people laugh, they experience rises in circulation, blood pressure, skin temperature, and heart rate, along with a decrease in pain perception. All of these responses are similar to those resulting from physical exercise, and they are considered beneficial to short-term and long-term health.

People sometimes laugh in situations that do not seem very funny, such as at funerals or wakes. According to one theory, laughing in these situations helps people distance themselves from their negative emotions, and it strengthens their connections to other people. In one study on the topic, Dacher Keltner and George Bonanno (1997) interviewed 40 people who had recently lost a spouse. The researchers found that genuine laughter during the interview was associated with positive mental health and fewer negative feelings, such as grief. It was a way of coping with a difficult situation.

Distract yourself: Doing something other than the troubling activity or thinking about something other than the troubling thought is an especially good strategy for controlling emotion (Webb, Miles, & Sheeran, 2012). For example, if you are afraid of flying, you can distract yourself from your anxiety by helping the woman next to you entertain her restless toddler. By absorbing attention, distraction temporarily helps people stop focusing on their problems.

Some distractions backfire, however. People may change their thoughts but end up thinking about other problems. Or they may engage in maladaptive behaviors. For example, as noted in Chapter 4, people sometimes try to escape self-awareness by overeating or binge drinking. To temporarily escape your problems, you might try watching a movie that captures your attention. Choose a movie that will not remind you of your troubled situation. Otherwise, you might simply find yourself wallowing in self-pity. (For more suggestions on dealing with your day-to-day problems and stresses, see Chapter 11, "Health and Well-Being.") ■

 Is trying not to think about a problem a good way to control emotion? Why or why not?

ANSWER: no, because that effort can lead to a rebound effect, where you think about the problem even more

Learning Objectives

- Review research on the cross-cultural universality of emotional expressions.
- Define display rules.
- Discuss the interpersonal functions of guilt and embarrassment.

How Are Emotions Adaptive?

Over the course of human evolution, we have developed ways of responding to environmental challenges. In solving these adaptive problems, our minds have drawn on our emotions. Negative and positive experiences have guided our species to behaviors that increase the probability of our surviving and reproducing. In other words, emotions are adaptive because they prepare and guide successful behaviors, such as running when you are about to be attacked by a dangerous animal. But what are the precise connections between emotions and actions?

Emotions provide information about the importance of stimuli to personal goals, and then they prepare us for actions aimed at achieving those goals (Frijda, 1994). Emotions also guide us in learning social rules and are necessary in order to live cooperatively in groups. Indeed, we often regulate the emotional experiences of others

(Reeck, Ames, & Ochsner, 2016). For example, we calm other people down or cheer them up. Let's look more closely at how emotions have served cognitive and social functions that enable humans to adapt to their physical and social environments.

10.6 Facial Expressions Communicate Emotion

In his 1872 book *The Expression of the Emotions in Man and Animals,* Charles Darwin argued that expressive aspects of emotion are adaptive because they communicate feelings. People interpret facial expressions of emotion to predict other people's behavior. Facial expressions provide many clues about whether our behavior is pleasing to others or whether it is likely to make them reject, attack, or cheat us. Thus, facial expressions, like emotions themselves, provide adaptive information.

Both the eyes and the mouth convey emotional information. The eyes are extremely important in communicating emotion. For example, when people are afraid they open their eyes very wide so that more of their eye whites are showing. Simply showing people larger eye whites increases activity in the amygdala, even when the viewers are unaware that the whites are larger (Whalen et al., 2004). If people are presented with pictures of just eyes or just mouths and asked to identify the emotion expressed, they are more accurate when using the eyes (Baron-Cohen, Wheelwright, & Jolliffe, 1997).

The mouth, though, also influences perception of emotion. In a classic study, Knight Dunlap (1927) demonstrated that the mouth is a better indicator of positive or negative affect than the eyes are. A smile or a frown is so noticeable that it overrides any information provided by the eyes (Kontsevich & Tyler, 2004).

Much of the research on facial expression is conducted by showing people isolated faces. Yet in the real world faces appear in contexts that provide cues as to what emotion a person is experiencing. In an intriguing study, researchers showed identical facial expressions in different contexts and found that the context profoundly altered how people interpreted the emotion (Aviezer et al., 2008; **FIGURE 10.14**).

FACIAL EXPRESSIONS ACROSS CULTURES Darwin argued that the face innately communicates emotions to others and that these communications are understandable by all people, regardless of culture. His hypothesis was left untested for a century, until Paul Ekman set out to disprove it. Ekman believed that emotions vary on a scale from pleasant to unpleasant and that facial expression and what it signifies are learned socially. In other words, he proposed that the meaning of each facial expression varies from one culture to another. Ekman and his colleagues (1969) tested this hypothesis in Argentina, Brazil, Chile, Japan, and the United States. They found that Ekman's hypothesis was wrong and Darwin was right.

In each country, participants viewed photographs of posed emotional expressions and then were asked to identify the emotional responses. In all five countries, the participants recognized the expressions as anger, fear, disgust, happiness, sadness, and surprise. Because people in these countries had extensive exposure to each other's cultures, however, learning and not biology could have been responsible for the cross-cultural agreement. To control for that potential confound, the researchers then traveled to a remote area in New Guinea. The natives there had little exposure to outside cultures and received only minimal formal education. Nonetheless, the study participants were able to identify the emotions seen in the photos fairly well, although agreement was not quite as high as in other cultures. The researchers also asked participants in New Guinea to display certain facial expressions, and they found that evaluators from other countries identified the expressions at a level better than

(a)

(b)

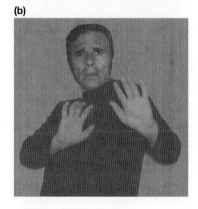

FIGURE 10.14
Contextual Effects on Categorizing Emotional Expression
Research participants were shown images such as these and asked to categorize them as depicting anger, fear, pride, sadness, disgust, surprise, or happiness. **(a)** This photo pairs a sad face with a sad posture. When the face appeared in this context, most participants categorized the expression as sad. **(b)** This photo pairs the same sad face with a fearful posture. When the face appeared in this context, most participants categorized the expression incorrectly, as fearful.

The Methods of Psychology
Ekman's Study of Facial Expressions Across Cultures

HYPOTHESIS: Ekman proposed that the meaning of facial expressions is socially learned. Therefore, the meaning of expressions should vary across cultures.

RESEARCH METHOD:

1 In this study, participants in New Guinea were photographed displaying certain facial expressions. For example, they were asked to look like they had come across a rotting pig or like one of their children had died.

 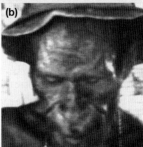

2 Participants from other countries were asked to identify the emotions being expressed by the New Guineans.

RESULTS: People across cultures largely agreed on the meaning of different facial expressions. The examples here are **(a)** happiness, **(b)** sadness, **(c)** anger, and **(d)** disgust.

CONCLUSION: Ekman's hypothesis was wrong. Recognition of facial expressions may be universal and therefore biologically based.

QUESTION: What does it mean when we say that recognition of facial expressions may be universal?

ANSWER: This statement means that across different cultures people are able to recognize similar emotions as expressed by faces. If this is the case, then such facial expressions are biologically based for all cultures.

Source: Ekman, P., & Friesen, W. V. (1971). Constants across cultures in the face and emotion. *Journal of Personality and Social Psychology, 17,* 124–129.

chance (Ekman & Friesen, 1971; see "The Methods of Psychology: Ekman's Study of Facial Expressions Across Cultures").

Subsequent research has found general support for cross-cultural agreement in identifying some facial expressions; support is strongest for happiness and weakest for fear and disgust (Elfenbein & Ambady, 2002). Some scholars believe that the results of these cross-cultural studies may be biased by cultural differences in the use of emotion words and by the way people are asked to identify emotions (Gendron, Roberson, van der Vyver, Marietta, & Barrett, 2014; Russell, 1994). Overall, the evidence indicates that some facial expressions are universal. Therefore, those expressions probably have a biological basis.

display rules
Rules learned through socialization that dictate which emotions are suitable in given situations.

UNIVERSALITY OF EMOTIONS Other evidence beyond facial expressions supports the idea that emotions are similar around the world. Creatively assessing the

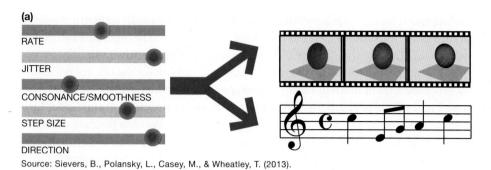

(a)
RATE
JITTER
CONSONANCE/SMOOTHNESS
STEP SIZE
DIRECTION

(b)

Source: Sievers, B., Polansky, L., Casey, M., & Wheatley, T. (2013).

FIGURE 10.15
Assessing the Universality of Emotion
(a) Research participants in the United States and in rural Cambodia manipulated five slider bars corresponding to five dynamic features to create either animations or musical clips that expressed different emotions. **(b)** The Cambodian participants were quickly able to use the program, and their results agreed considerably with those of American participants.

universality of emotion, researchers devised a computer program in which participants could use slider bars to adjust features of movement or music to indicate a particular emotion (**FIGURE 10.15A**; Sievers, Polansky, Casey, & Wheatley, 2013). For instance, bouncy movement and high notes indicated happiness, whereas fast and erratic movement or music indicated anger. The research team traveled to a rural and isolated village in Cambodia and taught the villagers to use the computerized slider system (**FIGURE 10.15B**). They found considerable agreement between American and Cambodian participants. That is, for example, the type of movement and music that represented sad was quite similar between the two groups.

Would you expect the physical expression of pride to be biologically based or culturally specific? Jessica Tracy has found that young children can recognize when a person feels pride and that isolated populations with minimal Western contact also accurately identify the physical signs, which include smiling face, raised arms, expanded chest, and torso pushed out (Tracy & Robins, 2008). Tracy and David Matsumoto (2008) examined pride responses among those competing in judo matches in the 2004 Olympic and Paralympic Games, in which sighted and blind athletes from 37 nations competed. After victory, the behaviors displayed by sighted and blind athletes were very similar. This finding suggests that pride responses are innate rather than learned by observing them in others (**FIGURE 10.16**).

DISPLAY RULES As we have seen, basic emotions, such as pride, seem to be expressed similarly across cultures. The situations in which people display emotions differ substantially, however. **Display rules** govern how and when people exhibit emotions. These rules are learned through socialization, and they dictate which emotions are suitable in given situations. Differences in display rules help explain cultural stereotypes, such as the loud and obnoxious Americans and Australians, the cold and bland English, and the warm and emotional Italians. Display rules also may explain why the identification of facial expressions is much better within cultures than between cultures (Elfenbein & Ambady, 2002).

From culture to culture, display rules tend to be different for women and men. In particular, the rules for smiling and crying differ between the sexes. It is generally believed that women display emotions more readily, frequently, easily, and intensely (Plant, Hyde, Keltner, & Devine, 2000). The evidence suggests that this belief is true—except perhaps for emotions related to dominance, such as anger (LaFrance & Banaji, 1992). Thus, men and women may vary in their emotional expressiveness for

(a)

(b)

FIGURE 10.16
Pride Expressions
In response to victory in separate judo matches, **(a)** a sighted athlete and **(b)** a congenitally blind athlete expressed their pride through similar behaviors. Because such similarities occur across cultures, the physical expression of pride appears to be biologically based.

HOW ARE EMOTIONS ADAPTIVE? **399**

evolutionary reasons: The emotions most closely associated with women are related to caregiving, nurturance, and interpersonal relationships. The emotions associated with men are related to dominance, defensiveness, and competitiveness.

While women may be more likely to display many emotions, they do not necessarily experience them more intensely. Although there is strong evidence that women report more-intense emotions, this finding might reflect societal norms about how women are supposed to feel (Grossman & Wood, 1993). Perhaps because of differences in upbringing in modern Western society, women tend to be better than men at articulating their emotions (Feldman Barrett, Lane, Sechrest, & Schwartz, 2000).

Ultimately, do sex differences in emotional expression reflect learned patterns of behaviors or biologically based differences? Nature and nurture work together here, so it is difficult—often impossible—to distinguish their effects.

 According to cultural stereotypes, Italians are very emotional, whereas the English are unemotional. How might display rules contribute to these impressions?

ANSWER: Display rules often differ from culture to culture. Thus, people in Italy might feel freer to express their emotions than people in England do.

10.7 Emotions Strengthen Interpersonal Relations

Because humans are social animals, many emotions involve interpersonal dynamics. People feel hurt when teased, angry when insulted, happy when loved, and proud when complimented. In interacting with others, people use emotional expressions as powerful nonverbal communications (**FIGURE 10.17**). Although English alone includes over 550 words that refer to emotions (Averill, 1980), people can communicate their emotions quite well without verbal language. For example, because infants cannot talk, they must communicate their needs largely through nonverbal actions and emotional expressions. Newborns are capable of expressing joy, interest, disgust, and pain. Nonverbal displays of emotions signal inner states, moods, and needs. It can even be argued that humans are a social species *because* emotions enable people to live together. As Steven Pinker (2011) notes, "We sympathize with, trust, and feel grateful to those who are likely to cooperate with us, rewarding them with our own cooperation. And we get angry at or ostracize those who are likely to cheat, withdrawing cooperation or meting out punishment" (p. 490).

For most of the twentieth century, however, psychologists paid little attention to interpersonal emotions. Guilt, embarrassment, and the like were associated with Freudian thinking and therefore not studied in mainstream psychological science. Theorists have since reconsidered interpersonal emotions in view of humans' evolutionary need to belong to social groups. Given that survival was enhanced for those who lived in groups, those who were expelled would have been less likely to survive and pass along their genes. According to this view, individuals were rejected primarily because they drained group resources or threatened group stability. The fundamental need to belong (as discussed more fully in Section 10.11) indicates that people will be sensitive to anything that might lead them to be kicked out of the group, and social emotions may reflect reactions to this possibility. Thus, social emotions may be important for maintaining social bonds.

GUILT STRENGTHENS SOCIAL BONDS Guilt is a negative emotional state associated with anxiety, tension, and agitation. The experience of guilt rarely makes sense outside the context of interpersonal interaction. For instance, the typical guilt

FIGURE 10.17
Emotion as Communication
Nonverbal expressions of emotion, such as these displays of love and joy, can communicate as powerfully as words.

experience occurs when someone feels responsible for another person's negative affective state. Thus, when we believe that something we did directly or indirectly harmed another person, we experience feelings of anxiety, tension, and remorse—feelings that can be labeled as guilt. Guilt occasionally can arise even when we are not personally responsible for others' negative situations. Consider, for example, survivor guilt, the guilt felt by people who survive incidents—accidents or catastrophes—in which others have died.

Although excessive feelings of guilt may have negative consequences, guilt is not entirely negative. One theoretical model of guilt outlines its benefits to close relationships. Roy Baumeister and colleagues (1994) contend that guilt protects and strengthens interpersonal relationships in three ways. First, feelings of guilt discourage people from doing things that would harm their relationships, such as cheating on their partners, and encourage behaviors that strengthen relationships, such as phoning their parents regularly. Second, displays of guilt demonstrate that people care about their relationship partners, thereby affirming social bonds. Third, guilt is a tactic that can be used to manipulate others. Guilt is especially effective when used against people who hold power over others. For instance, a person might try to make his boss feel guilty so he does not have to work overtime. Children may use guilt to get adults to buy them presents or grant them privileges.

There is evidence that socialization is more important than biology in determining specifically how children experience guilt. A longitudinal study involving identical and fraternal twins examined the impact of socialization on the development of various negative emotions (Zahn-Waxler & Robinson, 1995). The study found that all the negative emotions showed considerable genetic influence, but guilt was unique in being highly influenced by social environment. With age, the influence of a shared environment on guilt became stronger, whereas the evidence for genetic influences disappeared. Perhaps surprisingly, parental warmth is associated with greater guilt in children. This finding suggests that feelings of guilt arise in healthy and happy relationships. As children become citizens in a social world, they develop the capacity to empathize, and they subsequently experience feelings of guilt when they transgress against others.

EMBARRASSMENT AND BLUSHING ACKNOWLEDGE SOCIAL AWKWARDNESS A person is likely to feel embarrassed after violating a cultural norm, losing physical poise, being teased, or experiencing a threat to his self-image (Miller, 1996). Some theories of embarrassment suggest that it rectifies interpersonal awkwardness and restores social bonds. Embarrassment represents submission to and affiliation with the social group. It also represents recognition of the unintentional social error. Research supports these propositions in showing that individuals who look embarrassed after wrongdoing elicit more sympathy, more forgiveness, more amusement, and more laughter from onlookers (Cupach & Metts, 1990; **FIGURE 10.18**). Like guilt, embarrassment may reaffirm close relationships after wrongdoing.

The writer Mark Twain once said, "Man is the only animal that blushes. Or needs to." Darwin, in his 1872 book, called blushing the "most peculiar and the most human of all expressions," thereby separating it from emotional responses he deemed necessary for survival. Recent theory and research suggest that blushing occurs when people believe others view

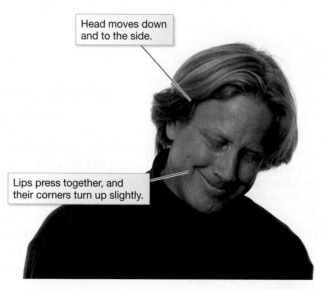

Head moves down and to the side.

Lips press together, and their corners turn up slightly.

FIGURE 10.18
Embarrassment
In this photo, the psychologist Dacher Keltner is demonstrating the classic facial signals of embarrassment.

them negatively and that blushing communicates a realization of interpersonal errors. This nonverbal apology is an appeasement that elicits forgiveness in others, thereby repairing and maintaining relationships (Keltner & Anderson, 2000).

Q Socialization has a bigger influence than genes on the capacity for feeling one particular negative emotion. What is that emotion?

How Are People Motivated?

What inspires you to get up in the morning? Why do you choose to eat certain foods? Does being in a sexual relationship interest you? Questions such as these are about why people do what they do. There is a close correspondence between emotion and motivation. Whereas emotion concerns how we feel, motivation concerns the forces that guide behavior. In fact, the words *emotion* and *motivation* come from the same Latin word: *movere,* "to move." When we encounter a snake, we experience alarm or even fear. We are motivated to avoid the potential threat and so we act, such as by walking around the snake. The feeling and the action are separate processes, but they both reflect adaptive processes that help the species survive (LeDoux, 2015b).

Most of the general theories of motivation emphasize four essential qualities of motivational states. First, motivational states are *energizing,* or stimulating. They activate behaviors—that is, they cause animals to do something. For instance, the desire for fitness might motivate you to get up and go for a run on a cold morning. Second, motivational states are *directive.* They guide behaviors toward satisfying specific goals or specific needs. Hunger motivates you to eat; thirst motivates you to drink; pride (or fear or another feeling) motivates you to study for exams. Third, motivational states help animals *persist* in their behavior until they achieve their goals or satisfy their needs. Hunger gnaws at you until you find something to eat; a desire to master the foul shot drives you to practice until you succeed. Fourth, most theories agree that motives differ in *strength,* depending on internal and external forces. Thus, for psychologists, **motivation** is a process that energizes, guides, and maintains behavior toward a goal. This section looks at a wide range of factors that, to different degrees, motivate people's behaviors.

10.8 Drives Motivate the Satisfaction of Needs

What do we really need to do to stay alive? For one, we have to satisfy our biological needs. We all *need* air, food, and water to survive. But satisfying our basic biological needs is not enough to live a fully satisfying life. We also have social needs, including the need for achievement and the need to be with others. People *need* other people, although preferences to be solitary or social vary. A **need,** then, is a state of deficiency, which can be either biological (e.g., water) or social (e.g., to be with other people). Either way, needs lead to goal-directed behaviors. Failure to satisfy a particular need leads to psychosocial or physical impairment.

MASLOW'S NEED HIERARCHY In the 1940s, Abraham Maslow proposed an influential "need theory" of motivation. Maslow believed that people are driven by many needs, which he arranged into a **need hierarchy** (FIGURE 10.19). He placed survival

Learning Objectives

- Distinguish between a need, a drive, and motivation.
- Describe Maslow's need hierarchy.
- Describe the Yerkes-Dodson law.
- Distinguish between extrinsic motivation and intrinsic motivation.
- Discuss the relationships between goal achievement, self-efficacy, the achievement motive, delayed gratification, and grit.
- Describe need to belong theory.

motivation
A process that energizes, guides, and maintains behavior toward a goal.

need
A state of biological or social deficiency.

need hierarchy
Maslow's arrangement of needs, in which basic survival needs must be met before people can satisfy higher needs.

self-actualization
A state that is achieved when one's personal dreams and aspirations have been attained.

drive
A psychological state that, by creating arousal, motivates an organism to satisfy a need.

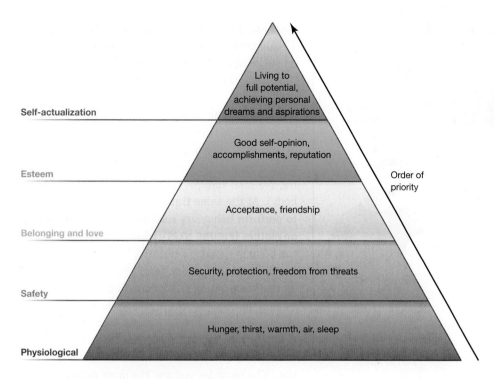

FIGURE 10.19
Need Hierarchy
According to Maslow's classification of needs, basic needs (such as for food and water) must be satisfied before people can address higher needs (such as for achievement).

needs (such as hunger and thirst) at the base of the hierarchy, believing they had to be satisfied first. He placed personal growth needs at the pinnacle. To experience personal growth, he believed, people must fulfill their biological needs, feel safe and secure, feel loved, and have a good opinion of themselves.

The pinnacle of Maslow's theory was **self-actualization.** This state occurs when a person achieves her personal dreams and aspirations. A self-actualized person is living up to her potential and therefore is truly happy. Maslow writes, "A musician must make music, an artist must paint, a poet must write, if he is ultimately to be at peace with himself. What a [hu]man *can* be, he *must* be" (Maslow, 1968, p. 46).

Maslow's need hierarchy has long been embraced in education and business, but it lacks empirical support. Self-actualization might or might not be a requirement for happiness, but the ranking of needs is not as simple as Maslow suggests. For instance, some people starve themselves in hunger strikes to demonstrate the importance of their personal beliefs. Others, who have satisfied their physiological and security needs, prefer to be left alone. Maslow's hierarchy, therefore, is more useful as a model of the relative priority of needs in average circumstances.

homeostasis
The tendency for bodily functions to maintain equilibrium.

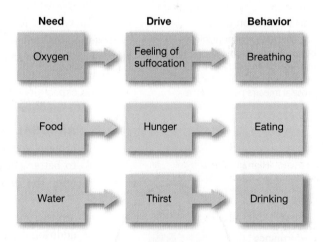

FIGURE 10.20
Needs, Drives, and Behaviors According to Drive Reduction
According to drive reduction, a need is a deficiency in some area that creates a drive—an internal psychological state. The drive motivates a person to behave in ways that satisfy a need. For example, if you hold your breath, you will start to feel a strong sense of urgency, even anxiety. This state of arousal is a drive. That drive will force you to breathe, satisfying your need for oxygen.

DRIVE REDUCTION AND HOMEOSTASIS What motivates people to satisfy their needs? A **drive** is a psychological state that, by creating arousal, motivates an organism to satisfy a need. A particular drive encourages behaviors that will satisfy a particular need. To experience one of your own needs and a drive in response to it, see **FIGURE 10.20.**

For biological states such as thirst or hunger, basic drives help animals maintain steadiness, or *equilibrium.* In the 1920s, Walter Cannon coined the term **homeostasis,** which means the tendency for bodily functions to maintain equilibrium. A good analogy is a home heating and cooling system controlled by a thermostat. The

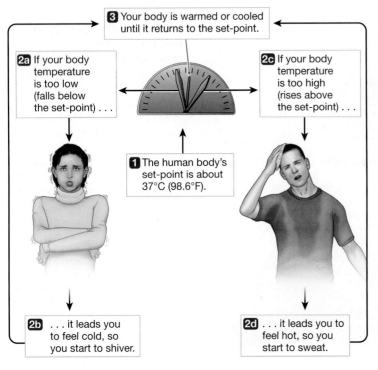

3 Your body is warmed or cooled until it returns to the set-point.

2a If your body temperature is too low (falls below the set-point) . . .

2c If your body temperature is too high (rises above the set-point) . . .

1 The human body's set-point is about 37°C (98.6°F).

2b . . . it leads you to feel cold, so you start to shiver.

2d . . . it leads you to feel hot, so you start to sweat.

FIGURE 10.21
A Negative-Feedback Model of Homeostasis

Yerkes-Dodson law

The psychological principle that performance on challenging tasks increases with arousal up to a moderate level. After that, additional arousal impairs performance.

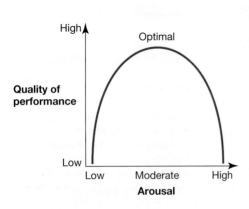

FIGURE 10.22
Graph of the Yerkes-Dodson Law
According to this law, performance on challenging tasks increases with arousal up to a moderate level. After that point, additional arousal interferes with performance.

thermostat is set to some optimal level, or *set-point*. That hypothetical state indicates homeostasis. If the actual temperature is different from the set-point, the furnace or air conditioner operates to adjust the temperature.

Similarly, the human body regulates a set-point of around 37°C (98.6°F). When people are too warm or too cold, brain mechanisms (particularly the hypothalamus) initiate responses such as sweating (to cool the body) or shivering (to warm the body). At the same time, people become motivated to perform behaviors such as taking off or putting on clothes (**FIGURE 10.21**). Models like this, in which the body responds to negative feedback, are useful for describing various basic biological processes, among them eating, fluid regulation, and sleep.

Building on Cannon's work, Clark Hull (1943) proposed that when an animal is deprived of some need (such as water, sleep, or sex), a drive increases in proportion to the amount of biological deprivation. The hungrier you are, the more driven you are to find food. The drive state creates arousal, which encourages you to do something to reduce the drive, such as having a late-night snack. Although the initial behaviors the animal engages in are arbitrary, any behavior that satisfies a need is reinforced and therefore is more likely to recur. Over time, if a behavior consistently reduces a drive, it becomes a *habit* and therefore the dominant response produced by arousal. The likelihood that a behavior will occur is due to drive and habit.

Suppose you feel the need to forget your troubles. To satisfy that need, you feel driven to distract yourself, so you go to YouTube and watch videos of cute animals. Watching those videos makes you forget your troubles, and that outcome reinforces further video viewing. Over time, you might develop the habit of watching cute animal videos, especially when you are stressed.

AROUSAL AND DRIVE Because drives motivate behavior by creating arousal, you might think that more arousal will lead to greater drive and thus to better performance. Consider, however, the **Yerkes-Dodson law** (named after the two researchers who formulated it, in 1908). This psychological principle dictates that performance on challenging tasks increases with arousal up to a moderate point. After that, performance is impaired by any additional arousal. A graph of this relationship is shaped like an inverted U (**FIGURE 10.22**). As the Yerkes-Dodson law predicts, students perform best on exams when feeling moderate anxiety. Too little anxiety can make them inattentive or unmotivated, while too much anxiety can interfere with their thinking ability. Likewise, athletes have to pump themselves up for their events, but they can fall apart under too much stress.

All people function better with some arousal. This goes against the idea that motivation always lowers tension and arousal. Instead, people are motivated to seek an optimal level of arousal—the level of arousal they most prefer. Too little, and they are bored; too much, and they are overwhelmed. People choose stimulating, exciting, or even frightening activities—those that arouse them and absorb their attention (**FIGURE 10.23**). As discussed further in Chapter 13,

(a)

(b)

however, people differ in how stimulating, exciting, frightening, or pleasurable they want those activities to be.

How are habits related to drives?

ANSWER: In response to a drive, such as the hunger drive, a person performs a behavior. If the behavior, such as late-night snacking, consistently reduces the drive, the behavior is reinforced. Over time, the reinforced behavior becomes a habit.

10.9 People Are Motivated by Incentives

Drive states push us to reduce arousal, but we are also pulled toward certain things in our environments. **Incentives** are external objects or external goals, rather than internal drives, that motivate behaviors. For example, getting a good grade on an exam is an incentive for studying hard. According to incentive theory, people do not always wait for deficient needs to drive behavior in daily life. Instead, people are motivated by their desires to achieve external goals.

Even forces outside of conscious awareness can provide incentives to behave in particular ways. For example, smokers sometimes develop cravings for cigarettes after watching people smoke on-screen. In some cases, the viewers have not even consciously registered that the on-screen figures are smoking (Wagner, Dal Cin, Sargent, Kelly, & Heatherton, 2011). As discussed in Chapter 4, subliminal cues influence behavior, even though they appear so quickly that people cannot report what they saw. Researchers from France and England found that study participants worked harder for a larger financial reward—in this case, a subliminally presented pound coin versus a real penny coin—even when they were unable to report how much money was at stake (Pessiglione et al., 2007).

EXTRINSIC AND INTRINSIC MOTIVATION Incentive theorists differentiate between two types of incentive motivation (**FIGURE 10.24**). **Extrinsic motivation** is directed toward an external goal, typically a reward. For example, most people work to earn paychecks. Many of the activities people find most satisfying, however—such as reading literature, solving crossword puzzles, or listening to music—seem to fulfill no obvious purpose other than enjoyment. Such activities are directed toward **intrinsic motivation**: value or pleasure associated with an activity, rather than for any external goal. Intrinsically motivated behaviors are performed for their own sake. They simply are enjoyable. Some students study to earn good grades (extrinsic motivation), whereas others study because they are curious and want to learn about the topic (intrinsic motivation). The incentives may differ, but the behaviors they bring about may be the same.

incentives
External objects or external goals, rather than internal drives, that motivate behaviors.

extrinsic motivation
Motivation to perform an activity because of the external goals toward which that activity is directed.

intrinsic motivation
Motivation to perform an activity because of the value or pleasure associated with that activity, rather than for an apparent external goal or purpose.

(a)

(b)

FIGURE 10.24
Extrinsic and Intrinsic Motivation
(a) Extrinsic motivation is an external factor that causes people to behave in a certain way. That factor is a reward. A major example is money. **(b)** Intrinsic motivation causes people to behave in a certain way simply because the activity, or the result of the activity, is enjoyable.

Some intrinsically motivated activities may satisfy natural curiosity and creativity. After playing with a new toy for a long time, children start to lose interest and will seek out something new. Playful exploration is characteristic of all mammals and especially primates. For example, as Harry Harlow and colleagues have shown, monkeys have a strong exploratory drive. They will work hard, without an external reward, to solve relatively complex puzzles (Harlow, Harlow, & Meyer, 1950). One function of play is that it helps people learn about the objects in an environment. This outcome clearly has survival value, since knowing how things work allows people to use those objects for more serious tasks.

Similarly, many of us are driven toward creative pursuits. Whether we are visiting an art museum or creating artwork ourselves, we may do so simply because we enjoy activities that allow us to express our creativity. Creativity is the tendency to generate ideas or alternatives that may be useful in solving problems, communicating, and entertaining ourselves and others (Franken, 2007). Although many creative pursuits are not adaptive solutions, creativity is an important factor in solving adaptive problems.

REWARDS CAN UNDERMINE INTRINSIC MOTIVES As discussed in Chapter 6, a basic principle of learning theory is that rewarded behaviors increase in frequency. You might expect that rewarding intrinsically motivated behaviors would reinforce them. Surprisingly, consistent evidence suggests that extrinsic rewards can undermine intrinsic motivation. In a classic study, Mark Lepper and colleagues allowed children to draw with colored marking pens (Lepper, Greene, & Nisbett, 1973). Most children find this activity intrinsically motivating. One group of children was extrinsically motivated to draw by being led to expect a "good player award." Another group of children was rewarded unexpectedly following the task. A third group was neither rewarded nor led to expect a reward. During a subsequent free-play period, children who were expecting an extrinsic reward spent much less time playing with the pens than did the children who were never rewarded or the children who received an unexpected reward. The first group of children responded as though it was their job to draw with the colored pens. In other words, why would they play with the pens for free when they were used to being "paid"? There are two theoretical explanations:

According to *self-determination theory,* people are motivated to satisfy needs for competence, relatedness to others, and autonomy, which is a sense of personal control. Self-determination theory argues that extrinsic rewards may reduce intrinsic value because such rewards undermine people's feeling that they are choosing to do something for themselves. In contrast, feelings of autonomy and competence make people feel good about themselves and inspire them to do their most creative work (Deci & Ryan, 1987).

According to *self-perception theory,* people are seldom aware of their specific motives. Instead, they draw inferences about their motives according to what seems to make the most sense (Bem, 1967). Suppose someone gives you a big glass of water. After drinking the whole thing, you exclaim, "Wow, I must have been thirsty!" You believe you were thirsty because you drank the whole glass, even though you were unaware of any physical sensations of thirst. When people cannot come up with obvious external explanations for their behaviors—such as that they acted with the expectation of being rewarded or to satisfy a biological drive—they conclude that they simply like the behaviors. Rewarding people for engaging in an intrinsic activity, however, gives them an alternative explanation for engaging in it. They performed the behavior not just for fun but because of the reward. Therefore, without the reward, they have no reason to engage in the behavior. The reward has replaced the goal of pure pleasure.

PLEASURE/PAIN AND APPROACH/AVOIDANCE MOTIVATION Sigmund Freud proposed that people act according to the *pleasure principle,* which encourages them to seek pleasure and avoid pain. This idea of seeking pleasure is central to incentive theories of motivation (Higgins, 1997). Originating with the ancient Greeks, the concept of *hedonism* refers to humans' desire for pleasantness. We do things that feel good. If something feels good, we do it again. Sexual activity is a good example of hedonism. Even though sex is crucial for the survival of the species, people engage in a variety of sexual behaviors even when they do not want to reproduce.

The idea that pleasure motivates behavior helps us understand a criticism of biological drive theories (such as Clark Hull's). If biological drives explain all behaviors, why do animals engage in behaviors that do not necessarily satisfy biological needs? These behaviors, such as eating dessert when you are not hungry, commonly occur because they are pleasurable (Cabanac, 1992). That is, the incentive to enjoy the taste motivates eating certain foods, regardless of your hunger state.

From an evolutionary perspective, positive and negative incentives are adaptive. We are motivated to approach certain things and avoid others. For instance, people experience *approach motivations* to seek out food, sex, and companionship because they are all typically associated with pleasure. By contrast, *avoidance motivation* encourages people to avoid negative outcomes, such as dangerous animals, because of the association with pain (Watson, Wiese, Vaidya, & Tellegen, 1999). A good example of this principle is the finding that most animals prefer to eat sweets. Infants given sweet solutions seem to find them pleasurable, as revealed by their facial expressions (Steiner, 1977; **FIGURE 10.25**). Sweetness usually indicates that food is safe to eat.

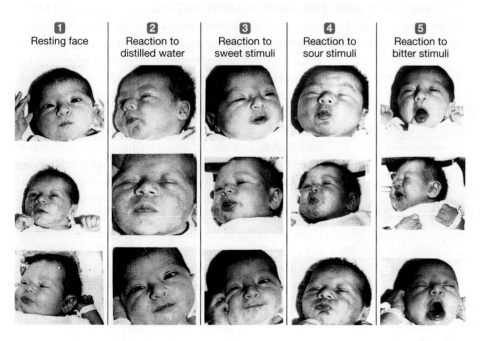

① Resting face **② Reaction to distilled water** **③ Reaction to sweet stimuli** **④ Reaction to sour stimuli** **⑤ Reaction to bitter stimuli**

FIGURE 10.25
Early Motivation
As these photos reveal, even newborns prefer sweet tastes to bitter ones.

In fact, as you will see later in this chapter, the inborn preference for sweets can lead to excessive consumption of sugar-added foods. By contrast, most poisons and toxins taste bitter, so it is not surprising that animals avoid bitter tastes.

 Parents sometimes pay their children for getting good grades in school. Will this reward increase the motivation for studying in children who enjoy schoolwork? Why or why not?

ANSWER: No, receiving a reward for this intrinsic behavior might decrease motivation and therefore reduce studying.

10.10 People Set Goals to Achieve

What would you like to be doing 10 years from now? What things about yourself would you change? So far, we have focused on motivation to fulfill short-term goals, such as satisfying our hunger or spending a pleasurable afternoon. But people have long-term aspirations as well. What motivates people to fulfill those goals?

In the 1930s, the personality psychologist Henry Murray proposed 27 basic *psychosocial needs,* including the needs for power, autonomy, achievement, and play. The study of psychosocial needs has yielded important insights into what motivates human behavior. A key insight is that people are especially motivated to achieve personal goals. *Self-regulation* of behavior is the process by which people change their behavior to attain personal goals.

Effective goals motivate people to work hard. But what is an effective goal? The organizational psychologists Edwin Locke and Gary Latham (1990) developed an influential theory. According to Locke and Latham, challenging and specific goals are the best, as long as they are not overly difficult. Challenging goals encourage effort, persistence, and concentration. In contrast, goals that are too easy or too hard can undermine motivation and therefore lead to failure. Dividing specific goals into concrete steps also leads to success. If you are interested in running the Boston Marathon, for instance, your first goal might be gaining the stamina to run 1 mile. When you can run a mile, you can set another goal and thus build up to running the 26-mile marathon. Focusing on concrete, short-term goals facilitates achieving long-term goals.

SELF-EFFICACY AND THE ACHIEVEMENT MOTIVE Albert Bandura (1977a) argued that people's personal expectations for success play an important role in motivation. For instance, if you believe studying hard will lead to a good grade on an exam, you will be motivated to study. *Self-efficacy* is the expectation that your efforts will lead to success. This expectation helps mobilize your energies. If you have low self-efficacy—that is, if you do not believe your efforts will pay off—you may be too discouraged even to study. People with high self-efficacy often set challenging goals that lead to success. Sometimes, however, people whose self-views are inflated set goals they cannot possibly achieve. Again, goals that are challenging but not overwhelming are usually most conducive to success.

People differ in how insistently they pursue challenging goals. The *achievement motive* is the desire to do well relative to standards of excellence. Compared with those low in achievement motivation, students high in achievement motivation sit closer to the front of classrooms, score higher on exams, and obtain better grades in courses

"What do you think . . . should we get started on that motivation research or not?"

relevant to their career goals (McClelland, 1987). Students with high achievement motivation are more realistic in their career aspirations than are students low in achievement motivation. Those high in achievement motivation set challenging but attainable personal goals, while those low in achievement motivation set extremely easy or impossibly high goals.

DELAYED GRATIFICATION One common challenge in self-regulation is postponing immediate gratification in the pursuit of long-term goals. For example, students who want to be accepted to graduate school often have to stay home and study while their friends are out having fun.

In a series of studies, the developmental psychologist Walter Mischel gave children the choice of waiting to receive a preferred toy or food item or having a less preferred toy or food item right away (Mischel, 1961). Mischel found that some children are better at delaying gratification than other children are. In addition, the ability to delay gratification is predictive of success in life. Children able to delay gratification at age 4 were rated 10 years later as being more socially competent and better able to handle frustration. The ability to delay gratification in childhood has been found to predict higher SAT scores and better school grades (Mischel, Shoda, & Rodriguez, 1989). A 40-year follow-up study found that the ability to delay gratification remained stable into adulthood (Casey et al., 2011). These researchers also conducted a brain imaging study in which participants had to inhibit responding to a rewarding stimulus. Those low in delay of gratification as children showed greater activity as adults in brain reward regions when they tried not to respond to the rewarding stimulus. These findings indicate that the inability to delay gratification and control behavior in childhood may have lifelong implications. Indeed, a study from New Zealand found that self-control in childhood predicted better physical health and personal finances, less substance abuse, and fewer criminal offenses at age 32 (Moffitt et al., 2011).

In Mischel's now-classic studies, how did some children manage to delay gratification? Given the choice between eating one marshmallow right away or two after several minutes, some children waited and engaged in strategies to help them not eat the marshmallow while they waited. One strategy was simply ignoring the tempting item rather than looking at it. Some of the children covered their eyes or looked away. Very young children tended to look directly at the item they were trying to resist, making the delay especially difficult. A related strategy was self-distraction, through singing, playing games, or pretending to sleep.

The most successful strategy involved what Mischel and his colleague Janet Metcalfe (1999) refer to as turning *hot cognitions* into *cold cognitions*. This strategy involves mentally transforming the desired object into something undesired. In one study, children reported imagining a tempting pretzel as a brown log or imagining marshmallows as clouds (**FIGURE 10.26**). Hot cognitions focus on the rewarding, pleasurable aspects of objects. Cold cognitions focus on conceptual or symbolic meanings.

Metcalfe and Mischel (1999) proposed that this hot/cold distinction is based on how the brain processes the information. As discussed in Chapter 3, subcortical brain regions such as the amygdala and the nucleus accumbens are important for motivating behavior. The prefrontal cortex performs cold-cognitive processes, such as the control of thought and of behavior.

GRIT One additional factor that is related to a person's ability to achieve long-term goals is *grit*. People with grit have a deep passion for their goals and a willingness to keep working toward them, even in spite of hardships and pitfalls (Duckworth, Peterson, Matthews, & Kelly, 2007). By contrast, people who have less grit get discouraged more easily, lose steam in the middle of pursuing their goals, or get sidetracked from

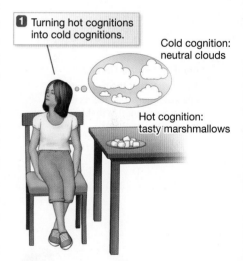

1 Turning hot cognitions into cold cognitions.

Cold cognition: neutral clouds

Hot cognition: tasty marshmallows

2 Ignoring

3 Self-distraction

FIGURE 10.26
Delaying Gratification
These three techniques help a person delay gratification.

their goals by new interests. There is evidence that grit is a better predictor than intelligence for achieving long-term goals in several areas, such as educational attainment, retention in the United States Military Academy at West Point, and ranking in a national spelling bee (Duckworth et al., 2007). In addition, grit has been shown to be a significant predictor for the grades of college students (Duckworth et al., 2007; Duckworth & Quinn, 2009), especially those of African American men (Strayhom, 2014). Research suggests that perseverance is the most important aspect of grit for predicting student outcomes (Muenks, Wigfield, Yang, & O'Neal, 2017; Wolters & Hussain, 2015).

According to research, what is the best strategy for delaying gratification?

ANSWER: mentally transforming the desired object into something undesirable

10.11 People Have a Need to Belong

Over the course of human evolution, our ancestors who lived with others were more likely to survive and pass along their genes. Children who stayed with adults (and resisted being left alone) were more likely to survive until their reproductive years because the adults would protect and nurture them. Similarly, adults capable of developing long-term, committed relationships were more likely to reproduce and to have offspring who survived to reproduce. Effective groups shared food, provided mates, and helped care for offspring, including orphans. Some survival tasks (such as hunting large mammals or looking out for predatory enemies) were best accomplished by group cooperation. It therefore makes great sense that, over the millennia, humans have committed to living in groups. Roy Baumeister and Mark Leary (1995) formulated the **need to belong theory,** which states that the need for interpersonal attachments is a fundamental motive that has evolved for adaptive purposes.

need to belong theory
The theory that the need for interpersonal attachments is a fundamental motive that has evolved for adaptive purposes.

MAKING AND KEEPING FRIENDS The need to belong theory explains how easily most people make friends (**FIGURE 10.27**). Societies differ in their types of groups, but all societies have some form of group membership (Brewer & Caporael, 1990).

Not belonging to a group increases a person's risk for various adverse consequences, such as illnesses and premature death (Cacioppo, Hughes, Waite, Hawkley, & Thisted, 2006). Such negative effects suggest that the need to belong is a basic motive driving behavior, just as hunger drives people to seek food and avoid dying from starvation.

If humans have a fundamental need to belong, they need to have some way of knowing whether they are included in particular groups (MacDonald & Leary, 2005). In other words, given the importance of being a group member, people need to be sensitive to signs that the group might kick them out. Indeed, evidence indicates that people feel anxious when facing exclusion from their social groups. Further, people who are shy and lonely tend to worry most about social evaluation and pay much more attention to social information (Gardner, Pickett, Jefferis, & Knowles, 2005). The take-home message is that just as a lack of food causes hunger, a lack of social contact causes emptiness and despair. In the movie *Cast Away,* Tom Hanks's character becomes stranded on a deserted island and has such

FIGURE 10.27
Making Friends
College provides many opportunities for making friends. First-year students often make lifelong friendships within days of arriving on campus.

a strong need for companionship that he begins carrying on a friendship with a volleyball he calls Wilson (named for the manufacturer, whose name is on the ball; **FIGURE 10.28**). As noted by the film reviewer Susan Stark (2000), this volleyball convinces us that "human company, as much as shelter, water, food and fire, is essential to life as most of us understand it."

ANXIETY AND AFFILIATION Do you like to be around other people when you are anxious, or do you prefer to avoid them? In a classic study, the social psychologist Stanley Schachter (1959) manipulated anxiety levels and then measured how much the participants, all female, preferred to be around others. The participants in these studies thought they were taking part in a routine psychological study. "Dr. Zilstein," a serious- and cold-looking man with a vaguely European accent, greeted them at the lab. After explaining that he was from the neurology and psychiatric school, the doctor said the study involved measuring "the physiological effects of electric shock." Zilstein told the participants he would hook them up to some electrical equipment and then administer electric current to their skin. Those in the low-anxiety condition were told the shocks would be painless—no more than a tickle. Those in the high-anxiety condition were told: "These shocks will hurt; they will be painful. As you can guess, if we're to learn anything that will really help humanity, it is necessary that our shocks be intense. These shocks will be quite painful, but, of course, they will do no permanent damage." As you might imagine, the participants who heard this speech were quite fearful and anxious.

FIGURE 10.28
Desperate for Friends
The need to belong is so strong that someone in extreme isolation might bond with an inanimate object. In this image from the movie *Cast Away*, the Hanks character is painting a face on a volleyball, "Wilson," which he then talks to for much of the movie.

Zilstein then said he needed time to set up his equipment, so there would be a 10-minute period before the shocks began. At that point, the participants were offered a choice: They could spend the waiting time alone or with others. This choice was the critical dependent measure. After the choice was made, the experiment was over. No one received a shock. Schachter found that increased anxiety led to increased affiliative motivations: Those in the high-anxiety condition were much more likely to want to wait with other people.

Thus, misery appears to love company. But does misery love just any company? A further study revealed that high-anxiety participants wanted to wait only with other high-anxiety participants, not with people who supposedly were waiting just to see their research supervisors. So misery loves miserable company, not just any company.

Why do people in a stressful situation prefer to be around other people in the same situation? According to Schachter, other people provide information that helps us evaluate whether we are acting appropriately. According to Leon Festinger's *social comparison theory* (1954), we are motivated to have accurate information about ourselves and others. We compare ourselves with those around us to test and validate personal beliefs and emotional responses. The effect occurs especially when the situation is ambiguous and we can compare ourselves with people relatively similar to us.

 If a person is anxious, would that person rather wait with a calm person or another anxious person?

Learning Objectives

- Identify neural structures associated with eating.
- Describe the glucostatic theory of eating.
- Discuss the role that hormones play in regulating eating behavior.
- Discuss the impact of time, taste, and cultural learning on eating behavior.

What Motivates Eating?

One of life's greatest pleasures is eating, and people tend to do a lot of it. Most people in industrialized countries consume between 80,000 and 90,000 meals during their lives—more than 40 tons of food! Everyone needs to eat to survive, but eating involves much more than simply survival. Around the globe, special occasions often involve elaborate feasts, and much of the social world revolves around eating.

Common sense assumes that most eating is strongly influenced by a biological hunger drive and *satiety*. That is, people eat when they feel hungry and stop eating when they are full. Some people, however, eat a lot even when they are not hungry or do not stop eating when they are sated. Others avoid eating even though they are not full. In other words, eating involves both drives and incentives. Hunger drives eating, but what people eat is often determined by what they like to eat. In other words, eating behavior is determined by complex interactions between biology, cultural influences, and cognition.

10.12 Many Physiological Factors Influence Eating

Animals need to eat to maintain vital body functions. Perhaps, then, it is not surprising that many different biological mechanisms encourage eating (Rogers & Brunstrom, 2016). The hypothalamus (see Figure 3.22) is the brain structure that most influences eating. Although it does not act alone, the hypothalamus integrates the various inhibitory and excitatory feeding messages and organizes behaviors involved in eating. In the first half of the twentieth century, research revealed that, depending on the specific area injured, damage to the hypothalamus dramatically changes eating behavior and body weight. One of the first observations occurred in 1939, when researchers discovered that patients with tumors of the hypothalamus became obese (Greene, 1939).

To examine whether obesity could be induced in animals of normal weight, researchers selectively damaged specific hypothalamic regions in rats (Graff & Stellar, 1962). When the middle, or *ventromedial,* region of the hypothalamus (*VMH*) is damaged, rats eat great quantities of food. This condition, *hyperphagia,* causes the rats with VMH damage to grow extremely obese. Sometimes damage to the VMH can cause obesity in humans (**FIGURE 10.29**).

In contrast, when the outer, or *lateral,* region of the hypothalamus (*LH*) is damaged, rats eat far less than normal. This condition, *aphagia,* leads to weight loss and eventual death unless the rat is force-fed. The idea that VMH signals fullness and LH signals hunger is too simplistic, however. Instead, the hypothalamus monitors various hormones and nutrients and operates to maintain a state of homeostasis.

In addition, brain structures other than the hypothalamus are involved in eating behavior. For instance, a region of the prefrontal cortex processes taste cues such as sweetness and saltiness (Rolls, 2007). Such cues indicate the potential reward value of particular foods. The craving triggered by seeing tasty food is associated with activity in the limbic system (Rapuano et al., 2017; Volkow, 2007). As discussed earlier in this chapter, the limbic system is the main brain region involved in emotion and reward (**FIGURE 10.30**).

Damage to the limbic system or the right frontal lobes sometimes produces *gourmand syndrome,* in which people become obsessed with the quality and variety of food and how food is prepared. One 48-year-old man who had suffered a stroke grew preoccupied with food and eventually left his job as a political correspondent to become a food critic (Regard & Landis, 1997). Despite their fascination with fine food and its preparation, those who have gourmand syndrome are not obsessed with eating. They

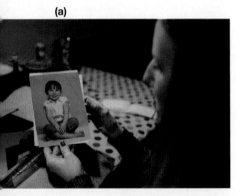

(a)

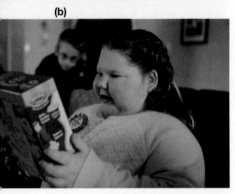

(b)

FIGURE 10.29
Hyperphagia in Humans
(a) In 2012, Alexis Shapiro underwent brain surgery that accidentally damaged her hypothalamus. **(b)** This damage caused her to feel extremely hungry all the time.

do not necessarily become overweight. Their obsession seems to center on the reward properties of food.

INTERNAL SENSATIONS For a long time, scientists recognized that eating is a classic homeostatic system. In other words, as discussed earlier, some sort of detector in the hypothalamus notices deviations from the set-point and signals that an animal should start or stop eating. But where do the hunger signals come from? The search for energy-depletion detectors has led scientists from the stomach to the bloodstream to the brain (**FIGURE 10.31**).

Contractions and distensions of the stomach can make the stomach growl. Over the past century, however, research has established that these movements are relatively minor determinants of hunger and eating. Indeed, people who have had their stomachs removed continue to report being hungry.

Other research has pointed to the existence of receptors in the bloodstream that monitor levels of vital nutrients. For instance, because glucose, also called blood sugar, is the primary fuel for metabolism and is especially crucial for neuronal activity, it makes sense for animals to become hungry when they are deficient in glucose. When people's glucose levels drop, they can feel tired or grouchy, and people often learn that eating, even just a snack, can reduce those feelings. Similarly, when people are deficient in sodium, brain systems are activated that elecit a craving for salty substances and increased reward when one ingests salty foods (Hurley & Johnson, 2015).

HORMONAL ACTIVITY Hunger signals are regulated by hormones (see Figure 10.31). As discussed in Chapter 3, hormones are chemicals that affect our thoughts and behaviors. Although dozens of hormones are involved in hunger and eating, the most important roles are played by three hormones: insulin, ghrelin, and leptin.

The hormone *insulin*, released from the pancreas, plays a vital role in hunger through its effects on blood glucose. As noted above, having low levels of glucose in the blood produces hunger. By contrast, when we have just eaten, our glucose levels are high so we are less motivated to eat. Insulin regulates glucose levels in the bloodstream and allows

FIGURE 10.30
The Reward Properties of Food
Do these "comfort foods" look tasty? How you respond to particular kinds of food is of course related to what kinds of food you are used to. It is also partly biological. If you are experiencing cravings at the sight of these items, your reaction is related to activity in your limbic system, the main brain region involved in reward.

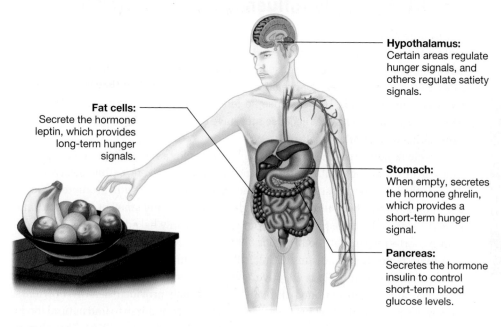

Hypothalamus: Certain areas regulate hunger signals, and others regulate satiety signals.

Fat cells: Secrete the hormone leptin, which provides long-term hunger signals.

Stomach: When empty, secretes the hormone ghrelin, which provides a short-term hunger signal.

Pancreas: Secretes the hormone insulin to control short-term blood glucose levels.

FIGURE 10.31
Biological Mechanisms That Motivate Eating
Several biological factors combine to influence our motivation to eat, including hormonal signals from fat cells, the stomach, and the pancreas. The hypothalamus regulates hunger and satiety signals.

the cells of the body to process the glucose so the body has energy to function. Insulin also directs fat cells to take in glucose, which is then converted to fat for storage for future energy needs. A deficiency in this process causes diabetes. Depending on the particular type of diabetes, the person's pancreas produces either little or no insulin (Type 1 diabetes), or the cells of the body do not process the insulin that is produced (Type 2 diabetes). In either case, the result is that the person's body cannot process high levels of glucose in the blood, which can ultimately lead to blindness, nerve damage, and liver damage.

The hormone *ghrelin* originates in the stomach. It surges before meals, then decreases after people eat, so it may play an important role in triggering eating (Abizaid, 2009; Higgins, Gueorguiev, & Korbonits, 2007). When people lose weight, an increase in ghrelin motivates additional eating in a homeostatic fashion (Zorrilla et al., 2006).

The hormone *leptin* (from the Greek word for thin) is involved in fat regulation. Leptin is released from fat cells as people eat and their bodies store fat. Leptin travels to the hypothalamus, where it acts to inhibit eating behavior. Some evidence indicates that leptin might affect the reward properties of food and make it less appetizing (Farooqi et al., 2007). Because leptin acts slowly, however, there is a significant delay after eating before leptin levels change in the body. Therefore, leptin may be more important for long-term body fat regulation than for short-term eating control. Animals lacking the gene necessary to produce leptin become extremely obese, and injecting leptin into these animals leads to a rapid loss of body fat (Friedman & Halaas, 1998).

How much any hormone contributes to human obesity is unclear. Considerable research is under way to find out whether manipulating hormones can help prevent or treat obesity. As you will learn in Chapter 11, many factors—from genes to culture to bad eating habits—contribute to obesity. You will also learn why most people who diet have trouble losing weight and keeping it off.

Which brain structure is most important for controlling eating?

ANSWER: the hypothalamus

10.13 Eating Is Influenced by Time and Taste

Eating is greatly affected by learning. Consider that most people eat lunch at approximately the same time—somewhere between noon and 2:00 PM. On a physiological level, this practice makes little sense because people differ greatly in their metabolic rates, the amounts they eat for breakfast, and the amounts of fat they have stored for long-term energy needs. However, people generally do not eat because they have deficient energy stores. They eat because they have been classically conditioned to associate eating with regular mealtimes.

The clock indicating mealtime is much like Pavlov's metronome. That is, mealtimes lead to various anticipatory responses that motivate eating behavior and prepare the body for digestion. For instance, an increase in insulin promotes glucose use and increases short-term hunger signals. The sight and smell of tasty foods can have the same effect. Just thinking about treats—freshly baked bread, pizza, a decadent dessert—may initiate bodily reactions that induce hunger.

A main factor that motivates eating is flavor. Humans have an inborn preference for sweetness, which likely is adaptive. Over the course of human evolution, sweetness was most often obtained through fruits, which provided healthy nutrients. However, a modern diet that includes added sugar leads children to find natural foods, such as fruits, not sweet enough (Mennella, Bobowski, & Reed, 2016). This change encourages the children to select diets high in added sugars (Foterek et al., 2016).

It is not just good-tasting food that promotes eating, but a variety of flavors. Animals, including humans, will stop eating relatively quickly if they have just one

FIGURE 10.32

The Impact of Variety on Eating Behavior

When people are presented with a variety of foods, they tend to eat more than when they are presented with only a few foods.

type of food to eat, but they will continue eating if presented with a different type of food. Thus, they tend to eat much more when various foods are available than when only one or two types of food are available (**FIGURE 10.32**).

One reason animals eat more when presented with a variety of foods is that they quickly grow tired of any one flavor. This phenomenon is called *sensory-specific satiety*. A region of the frontal lobes that is involved in assessing the reward value of food exhibits decreased activity when the same food is eaten over and over but shows increased activity when a new food is presented (Rolls, 2007). This increased activity, in encouraging people to continue eating, may explain people's behavior during celebration feasts or at buffets. For example, on Thanksgiving, Americans notoriously overstuff themselves. They cannot imagine eating another bite of turkey, yet when dessert comes around they can often find room for a piece—or two—of pumpkin or pecan pie to finish off the meal. From an evolutionary perspective, sensory-specific satiety may be advantageous because animals that eat many types of food are more likely to satisfy nutritional requirements and thus to survive than animals that rely on a small number of foods. In addition, eating large meals may have been adaptive when the food supply was scarce or unpredictable.

ROLE OF CULTURE What people will eat has little to do with logic and everything to do with what they believe is food. Nutritious foods such as fried termites are a favorite in Zaire and have more protein than beef, but North Americans find them disgusting. Spiders and other insects are nutritious and in many countries are eaten as tasty treats (**FIGURE 10.33**). Even when people are starving to death, they will refuse to eat perfectly nutritious substances. Infamous examples of this behavior occurred during famines in eighteenth-century Italy; nineteenth-century Ireland; and twentieth-century Bengal, where 3 million people died because they were unfamiliar with wheat as food.

What people will eat is determined by a combination of personal experience and cultural beliefs. As mentioned above, infants have an inborn preference for sweets, but they can learn to like just about anything. Generally, familiarity determines food preferences (**FIGURE 10.34**). The avoidance of unfamiliar foods makes great sense evolutionarily because unfamiliar foods may be dangerous or poisonous, so avoiding them is adaptive for survival (Galef & Whiskin, 2000). Getting children to like new foods often involves exposing them to small amounts at a time until they grow accustomed to the taste. Infants and toddlers also learn to try foods by observing their parents and siblings. Children are much more likely to eat a new food offered by their mothers than the same food offered by a friendly stranger. This behavior, too, makes great sense from an evolutionary standpoint. After all, if a parent eats something, it must be safe to eat.

Of course, what a parent prefers to eat is determined by her own upbringing and experiences. Therefore, families tend to like specific types of food. Ethnic differences in food preference often continue when a family moves to a new country. Although people often enjoy novel ethnic foods, in their regular diets most people prefer the foods of their own culture. As Paul Rozin (1996) points out, cultural rules govern which foods are appropriate in different contexts. For example, most people in North America like chocolate and french fries, but few people like them combined. Local norms for what to eat and how to prepare it—guidelines that Rozin calls *cuisine*—reinforce many food preferences. Moreover, religious and cultural values often tell people which foods to avoid. For example, those who follow

FIGURE 10.33
Tasty Treats
Crickets are a popular snack among Cambodians. What factors would influence you to eat or to refuse the fried cricket being offered by this vendor in Phnom Penh?

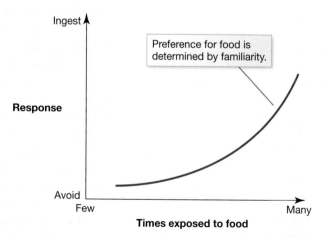

FIGURE 10.34
The Impact of Culture on Eating Behavior
As this graph illustrates, animals, including humans, tend to like the food they know. They tend to avoid unfamiliar food.

Jewish dietary law eat beef but not pork or shellfish. Some Hindus eat pork but not beef, and some Hindus are vegetarians. Taboos on certain types of food may have been adaptive in the past because those foods were likely to contain harmful bacteria. Many food taboos and preferences are idiosyncratic, however, and have nothing to do with avoiding harm. They simply reflect an evolved group preference for specific foods, prepared and eaten in certain ways.

How does sensory-specific satiety influence the amount people eat?

Learning Objectives

- Discuss the role that hormones play in sexual behavior.

- Identify the primary neurotransmitters involved in sexual behavior.

- Review the four stages of the human sexual response cycle.

- Discuss sex differences in sexual behavior and in mate preferences.

- Review contemporary theories of sexual orientation.

What Motivates Sexual Behavior?

Sexual desire has long been recognized as one of humanity's most durable and powerful motivators. Most human beings have a significant desire for sex, but sex drives vary substantially among individuals and across circumstances. Variation in sexual frequency can be explained by individual differences and by society's dominating influence over how and when individuals engage in sexual activity. This section examines what psychological science has learned about the motivation for sex.

10.14 Biology Influences Sexual Behavior

HORMONES As discussed in Chapter 3, hormones are involved in producing and terminating sexual behaviors. Hormones profoundly influence sexual activity in nonhuman animals. In many species, females are sexually receptive only when fertile, and estrogen is believed to control reproductive behaviors. Estrogen appears to play only a small role in human female sexuality, but hormones affect human sexual behavior in two ways. First, as discussed in Chapter 9, they influence physical development of the brain and body during puberty. Second, hormones influence sexual behavior through motivation. That is, they activate reproductive behavior (Schulz & Sisk, 2016).

Given the important role of the hypothalamus in controlling the release of hormones into the bloodstream, it is no surprise that the hypothalamus is the brain region considered most important for stimulating sexual behavior (**FIGURE 10.35**). Studies have shown that damaging the hypothalamus in rats interrupts sexual behavior (Clark, Pfeifle, & Edwards, 1981).

Sex hormones are released from the gonads (testes and ovaries), and females and males have some amount of all the sex hormones. But males have more androgen activity than females do, and females have more estrogens and progesterone activity. Androgens are apparently much more important for reproductive behavior than estrogens are, at least for humans. In men and women, testosterone—a type of androgen—is involved in sexual functioning (Sherwin, 2008). Males need a certain amount of testosterone to be able to engage in sex, but they do not perform better if they have more testosterone. The availability of testosterone, not large quantities of it, apparently drives male sexual behavior. The more testosterone women have, the more likely they are to have sexual thoughts and desires—although females typically have relatively low levels of testosterone (Meston & Frohlich, 2000). Adolescent females with higher than average testosterone levels for their age are more likely to engage in sexual intercourse (Halpern, Udry, & Suchindran, 1997).

Another important hormone in men and women is *oxytocin,* which is released during sexual arousal and orgasm. As discussed in Chapter 9, oxytocin promotes maternal tendencies and sexual gratification; it also seems to be involved in social behavior more generally (Bartels & Zeki, 2004; Carter, 2014).

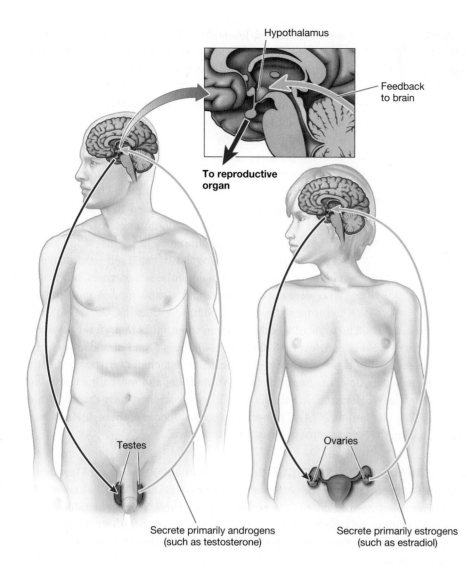

Hypothalamus

Feedback
to brain

To reproductive
organ

Testes

Ovaries

Secrete primarily androgens
(such as testosterone)

Secrete primarily estrogens
(such as estradiol)

FIGURE 10.35
Hypothalamus and Hormones Influence Sexual Behavior
The hypothalamus regulates sexual behavior by influencing production of the sex hormones, estrogens and androgens, in the reproductive organs.

NEUROTRANSMITTERS Neurotransmitters can affect various aspects of the sexual response. For instance, dopamine receptors in the limbic system are involved in the physical experience of pleasure, and dopamine receptors in the hypothalamus stimulate sexual activity (Pfaus, 2009). Serotonin also is implicated in sexual behavior. The most common pharmacological treatments for depression enhance serotonin function, but they seriously reduce sexual interest, especially for women. Small doses of drugs that enhance serotonin are also useful for treating premature ejaculation. Researchers currently do not know why these effects occur.

One chemical that acts as a neurotransmitter in the brain and is critical for sexual behavior is *nitric oxide*. Sexual stimulation leads to nitric oxide production. The increased nitric oxide promotes blood flow to the penis and the clitoris and subsequently plays an important role in sexual arousal, especially penile erections. When this system fails, males cannot maintain an erection. Various drugs that enhance this system, such as Viagra, have been developed to treat erectile disorders. It is not clear whether such drugs can be used to treat women's sexual disorders, but they appear to enhance the sexual experience for healthy women (Caruso, Intelisano, Farina, Di Mari, & Agnello, 2003).

THE MENSTRUAL CYCLE Women differ from men in how the hypothalamus controls the release of sex hormones. In men, hormones are released on a circadian cycle,

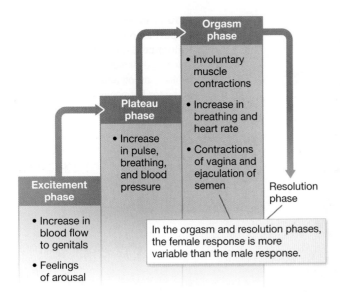

In the orgasm and resolution phases, the female response is more variable than the male response.

FIGURE 10.36
Diagram of the Sexual Response Cycle

sexual response cycle
A four-stage pattern of physical and psychological responses during sexual activity.

with testosterone levels highest in the morning. In women, the release of hormones varies according to a cycle that repeats approximately every 28 days: the menstrual cycle.

Research has found only minimal evidence that women's sexual behavior varies across the menstrual cycle. Recent evidence indicates, however, that women may process social information differently depending on whether they are in a fertile phase of the cycle. For instance, researchers used a computer program to alter masculinity and femininity in male faces (Penton-Voak et al., 1999). They found that, compared with preferences expressed in other phases of the menstrual cycle, during ovulation heterosexual women preferred the more masculine faces. In another study, heterosexual women who were ovulating rated self-assured men in videos as more desirable potential sex partners, but women who were not ovulating did not show a preference for self-assurance (Gangestad, Simpson, Cousins, Garver-Apgar, & Christensen, 2004). The topic of whether women show shifts in preferences across the menstrual cycle is controversial. One meta-analysis found abundant evidence that on high-fertility days of their cycle women prefer characteristics indicating desirable male genetic characteristics (e.g., symmetrical and masculine bodies and faces; Gildersleeve, Haselton, & Fales, 2014). Other researchers have disputed those findings (Wood & Carden, 2014). The everyday consequences of these differences on women, and on the men they interact with, are unknown.

THE SEXUAL RESPONSE CYCLE Beginning in the 1960s, William Masters and Virginia Johnson (1966) conducted laboratory studies of sexual behavior. This research enabled them to identify the **sexual response cycle.** This predictable pattern of physical and psychological responses consists of four stages (**FIGURE 10.36**).

The *excitement phase* occurs when people contemplate sexual activity or begin engaging in behaviors such as kissing and touching in a sensual manner. During this stage, blood flows to the genitals, and people report feelings of arousal. For men, the penis begins to become erect. For women, the clitoris becomes swollen, the vagina expands and secretes fluids, and the nipples enlarge.

As excitement continues into the *plateau phase,* pulse rate, breathing, and blood pressure increase, as do the various other signs of arousal. For many people, this stage is the frenzied phase of sexual activity. Inhibitions are lifted, and passion takes control.

The plateau phase leads into the *orgasm phase.* This stage consists of involuntary muscle contractions throughout the body, dramatic increases in breathing and heart rate, rhythmic contractions of the vagina for women, and ejaculation of semen for men. For healthy males, orgasm nearly always occurs. For females, orgasm is more variable. When it occurs, however, women and men report nearly identical pleasurable sensations.

Following orgasm, there is a dramatic release of sexual tension and a slow return to a normal state of arousal. In this stage, the *resolution phase,* the male enters a refractory period, during which he is temporarily unable to maintain an erection or have an orgasm. The female does not have such a refractory period and may experience multiple orgasms with short resolution phases between each one. Again, the female response is more variable than the male response.

 Are androgens or estrogens more important for sexual behavior in humans?

10.15 Cultural Scripts and Cultural Rules Shape Sexual Interactions

In the movies, sexual relationships often start when one person meets another by chance. They spend some exciting time together, an attraction develops, and sexual behavior ensues—often within a day or two. In real life, however, people generally do not fall into bed together as fast as they do in the movies. Most people know someone a long time before having sex. Nevertheless, the depiction of sexual behavior in movies and other media shapes beliefs and expectations about what sexual behaviors are appropriate and when they are appropriate.

Sexual scripts are cognitive beliefs about how a sexual episode should be enacted (for a discussion of scripts, see Chapter 8, "Thinking and Intelligence"). For instance, the sexual script indicates who should make the first move, whether the other person should resist, the sequence of sexual acts, and even how the partners should act afterward (**FIGURE 10.37**). In Westernized societies, the sexual script involves initial flirtation through nonverbal actions, the male initiating physical contact, the female controlling whether sexual activity takes place, and refusals typically being verbal and direct (Berscheid & Regan, 2005). The scripts differ in many places in the world, such as in countries where arranged marriages are common.

(a)

REGULATING SEXUAL BEHAVIOR The sexual revolution of the late twentieth century significantly changed sexual behaviors in many countries. Most of the changes in sexual behaviors must be attributed to changes in cultural pressures and cultural expectations. Although sexual customs and norms vary across cultures, all known cultures have some form of sexual morality. This universality indicates the importance to society of regulating sexual behavior. For example, one well-known pattern of regulating sexual behavior is the *double standard*. This unwritten law stipulates that certain activities (such as premarital or casual sex) are morally and socially acceptable for men but not for women. Cultures may seek to restrain and control sex for various reasons, including maintaining control over the birth rate, helping establish paternity, and reducing conflicts.

(b)

SEX DIFFERENCES IN SEXUAL BEHAVIOR A noticeable and consistent finding in nearly all measures of sexual desire is that men, on average, have a higher level of sexual motivation than women do. There are, of course, many individual exceptions. Research studies have found that, in general, men masturbate more frequently than women, want sex earlier in the relationship, think and fantasize about sex more often, spend more time and money (and other resources) in the effort to obtain sex, desire more different sexual activities, initiate sex more and refuse sex less, and rate their own sex drives as stronger than women's (Baumeister, Catanese, & Vohs, 2001).

(c)

In one study, researchers asked college-age men and women how many sex partners they ideally would like to have in their lives, if unconstrained by fears about disease, social pressures, and so on (Miller & Fishkin, 1997). Most women wanted one or two partners. Men's average answer was several dozen. A study of more than 16,000 people from 10 major regions around the world found that the greater male motivation for sexual activity and sexual variety occurs in all cultures (Schmitt et al., 2003).

The relative influence of nature and culture on sexual motivation may vary with gender. Roy Baumeister's (2000) term *erotic plasticity* refers to the extent that sex drive can be shaped by social, cultural, and situational factors. Evidence suggests that women have higher erotic plasticity than men. A woman's sexuality may evolve and change throughout her adult life, whereas a man's desires remain relatively constant (except for a gradual decline with age). Women's sexual desires and behaviors depend

FIGURE 10.37
Sexual Scripts
Sexual scripts influence behaviors such as **(a)** flirting, **(b)** pursuing romantic interest, and **(c)** dating.

sexual strategies theory

A theory that maintains that women and men have evolved distinct mating strategies because they faced different adaptive problems over the course of human history. The strategies used by each sex maximize the probability of passing along their genes to future generations.

significantly on social factors such as education and religion, whereas men's sexuality shows minimal relationships to such influences.

To account for these differences, the evolutionary psychologist David Buss has proposed the **sexual strategies theory** (Buss & Schmitt, 1993). From this perspective, throughout human history males and females have faced different adaptive problems. One result is that women differ from men in how they maximize passing along their genes to future generations. Women's basic strategy is to care for a relatively small number of infants. Their commitment is to nurture offspring rather than simply maximize production. Once a woman is pregnant, additional matings are of no reproductive use. Once she has a small child, an additional pregnancy can put her current offspring at risk. Thus, biological mechanisms ensure spacing between children. For example, frequent nursing typically makes ovulation less likely to occur. On purely reproductive grounds, men have no such sexual breaks. For them, all matings may have a reproductive payoff. They bear few of the personal costs of pregnancy, and their fertility is unaffected by getting a woman pregnant.

According to the sexual strategies theory, women are more likely to be more cautious about having sex because having offspring is a much more intensive commitment for them than it is for men. Indeed, there is evidence that women are much less willing than men to have sex with someone they do not know well. In one study of 96 university students, a stranger approached a person of the opposite sex and said, "I have been noticing you around campus. I find you attractive. Would you go to bed with me tonight?" (Clark & Hatfield, 1989). Each stranger was somewhere between mildly unattractive and moderately attractive. Not one woman said yes to the stranger's request, but three-quarters of the men agreed to the request (**FIGURE 10.38**). Indeed, the men were less likely to agree to go on a date with the stranger than they were to agree to have sex with her.

In another study, people were asked how long a couple should be together before it is acceptable for them to have sexual intercourse, given mutual desire. Women tend to think couples should be together for at least a month or more before sex is appropriate. Men tend to believe that even after relatively short periods of acquaintanceship, such as on the first or second date, sex is acceptable (Buss & Schmitt, 1993).

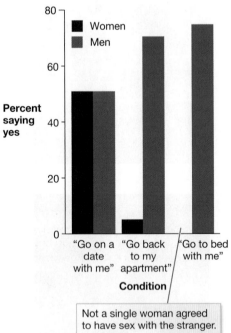

Not a single woman agreed to have sex with the stranger.

FIGURE 10.38

Sexual Behaviors and Responses

Men and women were propositioned by a stranger of the opposite sex. Both sexes were equally likely to accept a date. Men were much more willing than women to agree to go home with or to have sex with the stranger.

MATE PREFERENCES What do men and women want in their mates? It is perhaps easier to say what they do *not* want. In seeking mates, both sexes avoid certain characteristics, such as insensitivity, bad manners, loudness or shrillness, and the tendency to brag about sexual conquests (Cunningham, Barbee, & Druen, 1996).

According to sexual strategies theory, however, heterosexual men and women should differ in what they desire in mates. Both men and women should seek attractive partners, because relative youth and beauty imply potential fertility. Because women are limited in the number of offspring they can produce, they should be choosier in selecting mates. Therefore, women should seek men who can provide resources that will help them successfully nurture their children. In essence, men should care mainly about looks because looks imply fertility, whereas women should also be concerned about indications that their mates will be good fathers. Is there any scientific support for these ideas?

According to a study of 92 married couples in 37 cultures, women generally prefer men who are considerate, honest, dependable, kind, understanding, fond of children, well liked by others, good earners, ambitious, career oriented, from a good family, and fairly tall. By contrast, men tend to value good looks, cooking skills, and sexual faithfulness. Above all, women value a good financial prospect more than men do. In all 37 cultures, women tend to marry older men, who often are more settled and financially stable (Buss, 1989). In short, males and females differ in the relative emphases they place on social status and physical appearance, at least for long-term relationships.

In one study, men and women reported kindness and intelligence as necessary in their selection of mates, but their views of status and attractiveness differed. For the average woman seeking a long-term mate, status was a necessity and good looks were a luxury. In contrast, men viewed physical attractiveness as a necessity rather than a luxury in mate selection (Li, Bailey, Kenrick, & Linsenmeier, 2002).

This is not to say that women do not care about attractiveness. Women's preference for status over attractiveness depends on several factors. For example, is the relationship short term or long term? Looks are more important in the short term. Does the woman perceive herself as attractive? Women who view themselves as very attractive appear to want it all—status and good looks (Buss & Shackelford, 2008). In general, both men and women value physical attractiveness highly, but their relative emphases conform to evolutionary predictions.

The evolutionary account of human mating is controversial. Some researchers believe that behaviors shaped by evolution have little impact on contemporary relationships. We must consider two important factors. First, the modern era is a tiny fraction of human evolutionary history. The modern mind resides in a Stone Age brain, solving adaptive problems that have faced our species for thousands of years. Thus, remnants of behaviors that were adaptive in prehistoric times may linger even if they are not adaptive in contemporary society. Second, however, is that natural selection bestows biological urges as well as a strong sensitivity to cultural and group norms. In other words, instinctive behaviors are constrained by social context. The frontal lobes work to inhibit people from breaking social rules, which are determined largely by culture.

The current social context differs greatly from that of thousands of years ago, and human mating strategies are influenced by these contemporary norms. For example, from a biological view, it might seem advantageous for humans to reproduce as soon as they are able. But many contemporary cultures discourage sexual behavior until people are older and better able to care for their offspring. The critical point is that human behavior emerges to solve adaptive problems. To some degree, the modern era introduces new adaptive challenges based on societal standards of conduct. These standards shape the context in which men and women view sexual behavior as desirable and appropriate.

"I'm rich, you're thin. Together, we're perfect."

 According to the sexual strategies theory, why are women more cautious than men about having sex?

ANSWER: because of the risk of pregnancy, which is a much more intensive commitment for women than for men

10.16 People Differ in Sexual Orientations

Sexual orientation is a person's enduring sexual, emotional, and/or romantic attraction to people of the "opposite" sex, the same sex, or both sexes (Bailey et al., 2016). A person's sexual orientation may vary over time (Savin-Williams, 2016). To be clear: Sexual orientation is not about whom a person actually has sexual relations with. Rather, sexual orientation describes whom a person is sexually attracted to, emotionally close with, and/or establishes a romantic or committed relationship with. Much like biological sex and gender identity, sexual orientation is complex and multifaceted. The many different types of sexual orientation are completely normal variations in attraction.

Through history and across cultures, most people experience attraction to people of the opposite sex (Bullough, 1990). This sexual orientation is called *heterosexual*

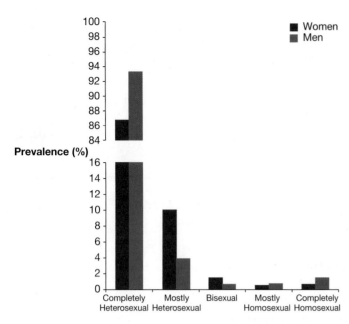

FIGURE 10.39
Range of Sexual Orientations
When given multiple categories to classify their sexual orientation, people vary from completely to mostly heterosexual or homosexual, while others view themselves as predominantly bisexual.

(from the Greek word *hetero*, meaning "other"). In everyday language, people with this sexual orientation are often called *straight*. By contrast, although it is hard to accurately determine, studies suggest that 2–5 percent of the population in the United States reports being exclusively attracted to people of the same sex (Bailey et al., 2016; Norris, Marcus, & Green, 2015). This sexual orientation is called *homosexual* (from the Greek word *homo*, meaning "same"). A male who is attracted to other males may call himself *gay*, whereas a female who is attracted to other females may call herself *lesbian* (American Psychological Association, 2008). In addition, estimates suggest that 1–2 percent of the population reports being attracted to both males and females. This sexual orientation is called *bisexual*. Bisexuality is more common in women than in men, perhaps because of women's higher erotic plasticity (Diamond, 2016). Finally, an unknown number of people report being *asexual*, that is, not having any sexual interest.

One difficulty in describing sexual orientation is that individuals vary, ranging from being exclusively attracted to the opposite sex to being somewhat attracted to both sexes to being exclusively attracted to the same sex (Savin-Williams, Cash, McCormack, & Rieger, 2017). Indeed, a number of individuals who see themselves predominantly as heterosexual report engaging in same-sex behavior at least occasionally. Likewise, individuals who are primarily gay or lesbian report sometimes having sex with the opposite sex (**FIGURE 10.39**; Savin-Williams & Vrangalova, 2013). As is the case with gender identity (discussed in Chapter 9), most psychologists view sexual orientation as reflecting a continuum (**FIGURE 10.40**).

SEXUAL ORIENTATION OVER TIME Homosexual behavior has been noted in various forms throughout recorded history. From an evolutionary perspective, homosexuality appears to make little sense. Exclusive homosexuality would not lead to reproduction and therefore would not survive in the gene pool. Many theories of sexual orientation have emerged, but none has received conclusive support. One evolutionary theory is that lesbians and gays often act as "spare" parents to their siblings' offspring. In this way, they might ensure the continuation of family genes. Of course, many gays and lesbians are parents, sometimes from earlier marriages and sometimes through artificial insemination or adoption.

In the nineteenth and much of the twentieth century, at least in Western cultures, homosexuality was regarded as deviant and abnormal, a psychological disorder. Until 1973, psychiatrists officially viewed homosexuality as a mental illness. Classic psychoanalytic theories of sexual orientation emphasized the importance of parenting practices. Families with a domineering mother and a submissive father were thought to cause the children to identify with the opposite-sex parent (e.g., a boy with his mother). Such identification translated into a sexual attraction toward the gender opposite of their identification—that is, a same-sex attraction. The overwhelming majority of studies, however, have found little or no evidence that how parents treat their children has anything to do with sexual orientation. Likewise, no other environmental factor has been found to account for homosexuality. The most common environmental finding is that attraction to the same sex, for both men and women, is associated with gender nonconformity in childhood, such as when boys dress like girls and play with dolls and when girls prefer rough play and competitive sports (Bailey et al., 2016). However, there is no evidence that environment determines whether children conform to traditional sex roles. So does biology determine sexual orientation?

BIOLOGICAL FACTORS Remember that when we ask whether something is biological, we really are talking about the relative contributions of biological factors compared with those of environmental factors. Every behavior results from biological processes, such as gene expression. Those processes are influenced by events in the person's environment.

One approach to examining the extent to which biological factors contribute to sexual orientation explores the effect of hormones. Early theorists speculated that lesbians had higher levels of testosterone and gay males had higher levels of estrogen, but those speculations were wrong. The levels of circulating hormones do not differ between straight and gay or lesbian individuals. Rather, the best available evidence suggests that exposure to hormones, especially androgens, in the prenatal environment might play some role in sexual orientation (Bailey et al., 2016; Mustanski, Chivers, & Bailey, 2002). For example, because of a mother's medical condition, some females are exposed to higher than normal levels of androgens during prenatal development. These females often have masculine characteristics at birth and throughout life. Later in life, they are more likely to report being lesbians.

An intriguing finding is that compared with straight males, gay males are more likely to have older male siblings. One explanation is that the mother's body develops an immune reaction during pregnancy with a male and that subsequent immune responses alter the level of hormones in the prenatal environment when the mother becomes pregnant with another male (Blanchard & Ellis, 2001; Bogaert, 2006). But most males with older brothers are not gay, so why would this response affect only some males?

A second approach to understanding the biological contribution to sexual orientation is through genetics. The idea that gene expression might be involved in sexual orientation is supported by a study using fruit flies. Researchers found that altering the expression of a single "master" gene reversed the sexual orientations of male and female flies (Demir & Dickson, 2005). But what about in humans? In 1993, the biologist Dean Hamer and colleagues reported finding a link between a marker on the X chromosome and sexual orientation in males (Hamer, Hu, Magnuson, Hu, & Pattatucci, 1993), and the media quickly dubbed the marker "the gay gene." Other researchers have failed to find any specific genes for sexual orientation.

Is sexual orientation inherited? Twin studies have provided some support for the idea of a genetic component to sexual orientation, particularly for males. As discussed in Chapter 3, identical twins are most similar in genetic makeup, but they also are likely to have had similar environments, and it is difficult to pull apart these two types of contributions. In a review of previous studies, Mustanski and colleagues (2002) report the heritability of sexual orientation as being greater for males than for females but with a significant genetic component for both. That is, there appears to be a genetic component to sexual orientation, but that is not the whole story. It remains unclear how human sexual orientation might be encoded in the genes or whether epigenetic processes play an important role (Bailey et al., 2016).

Some research suggests the hypothalamus may be related to sexual orientation. In postmortem examinations, the neuroscientist Simon LeVay (1991) found that an area of the hypothalamus that typically differs between men and women was only half as

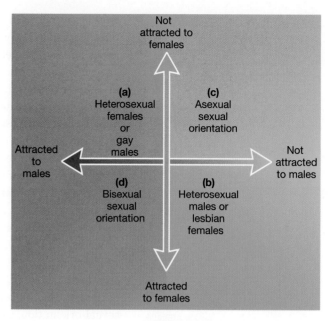

FIGURE 10.40
Sexual Orientation Can Be Viewed as a Continuum
It may be more accurate to view sexual orientation as a continuum. **(a)** Some people are attracted to males, not females. If they are female, their sexual orientation is heterosexual. If they are male, their sexual orientation is gay. **(b)** Some people are attracted to females, not males. If they are male, their sexual orientation is heterosexual. If they are female, their sexual orientation is lesbian. **(c)** Some people are not attracted to either males or females, in which case their sexual orientation is asexual. **(d)** People who are attracted to both males and females have a bisexual orientation.

large in gay men as in straight men. In fact, the size of this area in gay men was comparable to its size in straight women. Likewise, in a recent brain imaging study, straight males showed greater activation of the hypothalamus when they sniffed a female pheromone (a hormonal secretion that travels through the air; see the discussion in Chapter 5) than they did when they sniffed a male pheromone, whereas straight females showed greater activation when they sniffed a male pheromone rather than a female pheromone (Savic, Berglund, & Lindström, 2005). Gay men showed a pattern more similar to that of women than of straight men: greater activation of the hypothalamus in response to the male pheromone.

Of course, both of these studies can be criticized on the grounds that correlation does not equal causation. That is, a size difference or activation difference in any one part of the brain cannot establish whether this area determines sexual orientation, whether being straight or gay results in changes to brain structure or function, or whether a third variable is responsible for all these effects. For instance, some researchers believe that the size of the hypothalamus is determined by prenatal exposure to androgens. Thus, although these studies' findings are suggestive, evidence currently is insufficient to establish a causal connection between brain regions and sexual orientation. Considered together, the evidence is consistent that biological processes play some role in sexual orientation. The question is how and when biology contributes, and to what degree.

STABILITY OF SEXUAL ORIENTATION Even though there are Web reports of effective conversion for gays and lesbians, there is little empirical evidence that these programs do any more than suppress behavior. No good evidence exists that sexual orientation can be changed through therapy. Indeed, one prominent group that had been trying for nearly 40 years to convert gay people disbanded in 2013, its leader having concluded that sexual attraction cannot be changed (Lovett, 2013). Treatments that try to convert people also tend to emphasize that gay people are immoral, and therefore the inevitable treatment failures can lead to feelings of shame and of being morally flawed. Thus, so-called conversion therapy may inflict significant harm on mental health (Flentje, Heck, & Cochran, 2014). Several U.S. states and Canadian provinces have passed legislation banning the use of conversion therapy on minors (Drescher et al., 2016).

Contrary to some people's misconceptions, being with people whose sexual orientation differs from yours does not change your sexual orientation. In some cultures and subcultures, people may engage in same-sex behaviors for a period and then revert to heterosexual behaviors. In jail, for example, men and women often engage in same-sex relationships but do not consider themselves gay. For reasons such as these, few psychologists or physicians believe that sexual orientation—as opposed simply to sexual activity—is a choice or that it can be changed.

Modern society, too, is increasingly acknowledging gays' rights to express their sexuality: In the United States, the Supreme Court ruled in June 2015 that individual states must allow marriages between same-sex couples. Canada, Spain, Norway, Sweden, South Africa, Portugal, and an increasing number of other places around the world recognize same-sex relationships in varying ways. Attitudes toward same-sex sexual experiences have also become much more accepting in recent years (Twenge, Sherman, & Wells, 2016). The contemporary world is catching up with human history. Nonheterosexuals have always existed, whether or not they were free to be themselves (**FIGURE 10.41**).

FIGURE 10.41
Sexual Orientation
John Mace **(right)** and Richard Dorr became a couple in New York City in 1950. At the time, homosexuality was illegal in every state in the United States. In 2011, gay couples became legally allowed to marry in New York State, thanks to the advocacy work of people such as Mace and Dorr. The next year, Mace and Dorr were finally married, at ages 91 and 84 respectively. Dorr died in 2016; Mace, in 2017.

 How effective is conversion therapy for changing sexual orientation?

ANSWER: It is ineffective and may be harmful.

Your Chapter Review

Chapter Summary

What Are Emotions?

10.1 Emotions Vary in Valence and Arousal

Emotions are often classified as primary or secondary. Primary emotions are innate, evolutionarily adaptive, and universal (shared across cultures). These emotions include anger, fear, sadness, disgust, happiness, surprise, and contempt. Secondary emotions are blends of primary emotions. They include remorse, guilt, submission, shame, love, bitterness, and jealousy. Emotions have a valence (positive or negative) and a level of activation (arousal, from low to high).

10.2 Emotions Have a Physiological Component

The insula and amygdala play important roles in the experience of emotion. The insula receives and integrates somatosensory signals, helping us experience emotion, especially disgust, anger, guilt, and anxiety. The amygdala processes emotional significance of stimuli and generates immediate reactions. It is associated with emotional learning, memory of emotional events, and the interpretation of facial expressions of emotion.

10.3 Think like a Psychologist: Are Lie Detector Tests Valid?

Because the use of lie detectors is controversial, most courts do not allow their results as evidence. The goal of polygraphy is to use emotional reactivity to assess whether someone is being deceptive. However, no measure of autonomic arousal can definitively indicate the presence or absence of a lie. Measuring brain activity to detect deception also has methodological and ethical problems.

10.4 There Are Three Major Theories of Emotion

Three main theories of emotion differ in their relative emphases on subjective experience, physiological changes, and cognitive interpretation. The James-Lange theory states that specific patterns of physical changes give rise to the perception of associated emotions. The Cannon-Bard theory proposes that two separate pathways, physical changes and subjective experience, are activated at the same time. The Schachter-Singer two-factor theory emphasizes the combination of generalized physiological arousal and cognitive appraisals in determining specific emotions. Consistent with the Schachter-Singer two-factor theory, research has shown that we often misattribute the causes of our emotions, seeking environmental explanations for our feelings.

10.5 Using Psychology in Your Life: How Can You Control Your Emotions?

There are several strategies people can use to regulate their emotions. Some of these strategies help people prevent or prepare for events, and some of them help in dealing with events after they occur. Unsuccessful strategies include suppression and rumination. Successful strategies include location control, changing the meaning, finding humor, and distraction.

How Are Emotions Adaptive?

10.6 Facial Expressions Communicate Emotion

Facial expressions of emotion are adaptive because they communicate how we feel. Across cultures, some expressions of emotion are universally recognized, such as happiness, sadness, anger, and pride. Display rules are learned through socialization and dictate which emotions are suitable in given situations. Across cultures, display rules differ for females and males.

10.7 Emotions Strengthen Interpersonal Relations

Emotions facilitate the maintenance and repair of social bonds. Interpersonal emotions—for example, guilt and embarrassment—are particularly important for the maintenance and repair of close interpersonal relationships.

How Are People Motivated?

10.8 Drives Motivate the Satisfaction of Needs

Motivation energizes, directs, and sustains behavior. Needs arise from states of biological or social deficiency. Maslow described a hierarchy of needs. This model is not supported by data. Drives are psychological states that create arousal and motivate behaviors to satisfy needs. Drives help us maintain homeostasis—that is, equilibrium of bodily functions. The Yerkes-Dodson law suggests that if people are underaroused or overaroused, their performance will suffer.

10.9 People Are Motivated by Incentives

Incentives are external objects or goals. Some incentives are extrinsically motivating (directed toward an external reward). Other incentives are intrinsically motivating (directed toward an internal reward or simply enjoyable). Providing people with extrinsic rewards can undermine their intrinsic motivation.

10.10 People Set Goals to Achieve

According to research, the most successful motivation comes from goals that are challenging and specific but not overly difficult. People who are high in self-efficacy and have a high achievement motive are more likely to set challenging but attainable goals for themselves. People who are able to delay gratification are more likely to report successful outcomes later in life. Long-term perseverance, associated with grit, assists goal achievement.

10.11 People Have a Need to Belong

Need to belong theory suggests that people have a fundamental need for interpersonal attachments. Need to belong explains the ease with which people make friends, their sensitivity to social exclusion, the adverse feelings experienced in the absence of social contact, and efforts to affiliate with others when anxious.

What Motivates Eating?

10.12 Many Physiological Factors Influence Eating

A number of neural structures are associated with eating behavior, including the hypothalamus, prefrontal cortex, limbic system, and frontal lobes. Three hormones have been found to be of central importance to our eating behavior: insulin, ghrelin, and leptin. Insulin regulates glucose, or blood sugar, which regulates hunger. Ghrelin motivates eating behavior, whereas leptin is associated with long-term body fat regulation.

10.13 Eating Is Influenced by Time and Taste

Eating is strongly affected by learning. Through classical conditioning, people associate eating with regular mealtimes. Sensory-specific satiety is the phenomenon in which people quickly grow tired of any single flavor. This mechanism evolved in animals to encourage the consumption of foods that contain diverse nutrients. What people eat is greatly influenced by cultural rules regarding which foods are appropriate to eat in different contexts.

What Motivates Sexual Behavior?

10.14 Biology Influences Sexual Behavior

Hormones influence the development of secondary sex characteristics during puberty and motivate sexual behavior. The hypothalamus controls the release of hormones and stimulates sexual behavior. The hormones testosterone and oxytocin have been found to be particularly important determinants of sexual behavior. Neurotransmitters, including dopamine, serotonin, and nitric oxide, have also been found to influence sexual functioning. Masters and Johnson identified four stages in the human sexual response cycle that are very similar for men and women: excitement, plateau, orgasm, and resolution.

10.15 Cultural Scripts and Cultural Rules Shape Sexual Interactions

Sexual behavior is constrained by sexual scripts. These scripts are socially determined beliefs regarding the appropriate behaviors for men and women to engage in during sexual interactions. On average, men have a higher level of sexual motivation and engage in more sexual activity than women. Men and women look for similar qualities in potential partners, but men are more concerned about a potential partner's attractiveness, and women are more concerned with a potential partner's status. Sex differences in preference for partner qualities may be due to the different adaptive problems the sexes faced over the course of human evolutionary history.

10.16 People Differ in Sexual Orientations

Many theories have been proposed to explain sexual orientation. Researchers have suggested that prenatal hormone exposure, genes, and functional differences in the hypothalamus may influence sexual orientation. Although evidence has emerged to support each of these ideas, the data are correlational and cannot be used to make causal inferences. At this time we do not know what combination of genes and environment gives any particular person a heterosexual, homosexual, bisexual, or asexual orientation.

Key Terms

Cannon-Bard theory of emotion, p. 391

display rules, p. 399

drive, p. 403

emotion, p. 384

extrinsic motivation, p. 405

homeostasis, p. 403

incentives, p. 405

intrinsic motivation, p. 405

James-Lange theory of emotion, p. 391

motivation, p. 402

need, p. 402

need hierarchy, p. 402

need to belong theory, p. 410

primary emotions, p. 384

secondary emotions, p. 384

self-actualization, p. 403

sexual response cycle, p. 418

sexual strategies theory, p. 420

two-factor theory of emotion, p. 392

Yerkes-Dodson law, p. 404

Putting Psychology to Work

What Is Emotional Artificial Intelligence?

Imagine a future in which androids are virtually indistinguishable from humans. This is the premise of the 1982 science fiction movie *Blade Runner* and its 2017 sequel *Blade Runner 2049*. *Blade Runners* are special agents who track down androids, or "replicants," who have escaped off-Earth colonies, have returned to Earth, and are trying to pass for human.

But how can Blade Runners correctly identify these renegades? Enter the Voight-Kampff machine. It is an emotion detector, similar to a polygraph. Although replicants may look just like humans, they do not have emotions. So Blade Runners pose emotionally loaded questions and measure the listeners' bodily changes. Those listeners whose bodies respond appropriately are human. Those whose bodies don't respond are replicants.

After reading this chapter, you can appreciate why emotion may be the defining trait of humanness. The range of human experience includes feeling emotions and expressing them. Facial expressions of emotion convey important information that allows others to predict our thoughts and behavior. Emotions are necessary for normal interpersonal interactions and to strengthen social bonds.

Although the Voight-Kampff test is science fiction, devices that can accurately read emotional expressions are being developed and marketed. Many opportunities for employment now exist in the emerging field of emotional artificial intelligence (EAI).

Consider software apps. Companies such as Robbie AI and Affectiva develop apps that can read and analyze facial expressions from live video. Through these analyses, advertisers and market researchers can get immediate feedback from consumers. Alternatively, game developers can employ emotional recognition software so that their products recognize and respond to users' emotions. Educators can use apps to measure how students respond to online content and then apply that information in adapting the content to avoid boredom or confusion.

EAI can also be used in robotics. For example, Apple's Siri, Google's Alexa, and other voice interface systems use voices with appropriate emotional tones. Robots built for human companionship must recognize human emotions and adapt accordingly. However, creating and testing these products remain the jobs of humans, not robots.

Developers of EAI products generally work in teams. User experience (UX) designers and computational neuroscientists must have a psychology background. For software engineers, computer vision scientists, and industrial and electronic designers, knowledge of human emotional behavior is vital.

The bottom line: Understanding how to correctly detect and mimic human expressions of emotions has important applications in emotional artificial intelligence (EAI). Career paths in this field generally require courses in computer science and mathematics, in addition to psychology.

Want to earn a better grade on your test?
Go to **INQUIZITIVE** to learn and review this chapter's content, with personalized feedback along the way.
Practice Tests and accompanying answer keys can be found at the back of the book on page PT-1.

11

Health and Well-Being

Big Questions

- What Affects Health? 430

- What Is Stress? 447

- How Does Stress Affect Health? 452

- Can a Positive Attitude Keep People Healthy? 459

HAVE YOU EVER FOUND YOURSELF EATING A BOX OF COOKIES, a bag of potato chips, or a pint of ice cream in one sitting after something bad happened to you? If that's the case, then you have experienced stress eating. Stress eating is just what it sounds like: responding to stress by eating, usually overeating junk foods. Most people have experienced stress eating at one time or another. If this behavior is a person's consistent response to stress, however, it can lead to obesity and have other adverse effects on health. A healthier strategy than eating for dealing with stress is to distract yourself, such as by taking a walk, listening to music, reading a book, or watching a movie.

This chapter explores how health and well-being are intimately connected to psychological states. First it discusses common behaviors that place health at risk, and it examines the social, psychological, and biological factors that influence these outcomes. Then it looks at the physiological components of stress. Some bodily responses to stress can be beneficial in motivating people to action, but chronic exposure to stress can harm health in numerous ways. So in addition to considering how people cope with stress and suggesting methods for successful coping, this chapter examines the benefits of a positive attitude to health and well-being. The central questions for this subfield of psychology are: What affects health? What is stress? How does stress affect health? Can a positive attitude keep people healthy?

Learning Objectives

- Describe the biopsychosocial model of health.
- Discuss health disparities.
- Discuss the causes and consequences of obesity.
- Discuss the causes and consequences of smoking.
- Review the benefits of regular exercise.

What Affects Health?

People generally think about health and well-being in biological and medical terms. The traditional Western medical model defines health simply as the lack of disease. This approach focuses on disease states and the treatments to cure them. It views people as passive recipients of disease and of the medical treatments designed to return them to health after illness. The underlying assumption is that people's mental states have little effect on their physical states, in either health or disease.

Nearly four decades ago, psychologists, physicians, and other health professionals came to appreciate the importance of lifestyle factors to physical health. They launched the interdisciplinary field of **health psychology,** which integrates research on health and on psychology. Health psychologists rely on the research methods of psychology to understand the interrelationship between thoughts (health-related cognitions), actions, and physical and mental health. These researchers address issues such as ways to help people lead healthier lives. They study how behavior and social systems affect health and how ethnic and sex differences influence health outcomes. Health psychologists also study the inverse of these relationships: how health-related behaviors and health outcomes affect people's actions, thoughts, and emotions.

11.1 Social Context, Biology, and Behavior Combine to Affect Health

A central lesson in this chapter is that both mental states, such as outlook on life, and behaviors are critical in preventing illness, helping people regain health following illness, and helping achieve well-being. **Well-being** is a positive state that is sought by striving for optimal health and life satisfaction. To achieve optimal health, people need to actively participate in health-enhancing behaviors.

How do people's personalities, thoughts, or behaviors affect their health? To answer this question, you need to understand the **biopsychosocial model.** According to this model, health and illness result from a combination of factors, such as biological characteristics (e.g., genetic predisposition), behavioral factors (e.g., lifestyle, stress, and beliefs about health), and social conditions (e.g., cultural influences, family relationships, and social support). Research that integrates these levels of analysis helps to identify strategies that may prevent disease and promote health.

As shown in **FIGURE 11.1,** thoughts and actions affect people's choices of the environments they interact with. Those environments, in turn, affect the biological underpinnings of thoughts and actions. To understand how this continuous loop operates in real life, suppose a person is genetically predisposed to be anxious. He learns that one way to reduce his anxiety is to eat comfort foods such as potato chips, cookies, and ice cream. If he consumes these foods in excess, he may gain weight and eventually become overweight. Some people have genes that make becoming overweight more likely. Overweight people often find that exercise is not very pleasant.

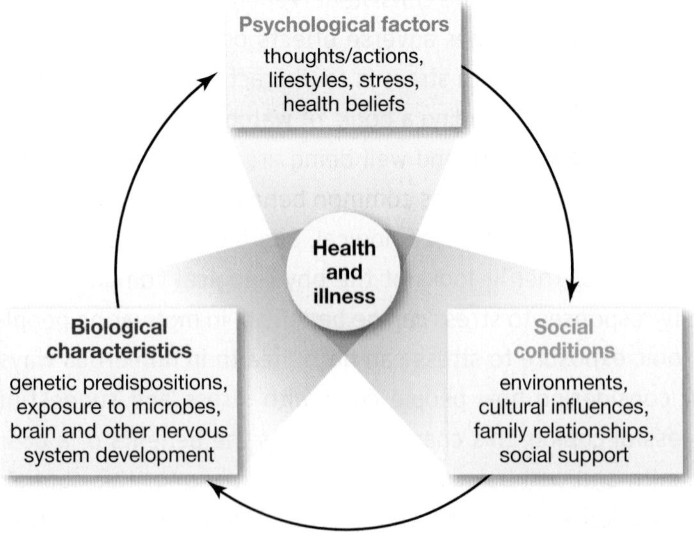

health psychology

A field that integrates research on health and on psychology; it involves the application of psychological principles to promote health and well-being.

well-being

A positive state that includes striving for optimal health and life satisfaction.

biopsychosocial model

A model of health that integrates the effects of biological, behavioral, and social factors on health and illness.

FIGURE 11.1
The Biopsychosocial Model
This model illustrates how health and illness result from a combination of factors.

If their extra weight makes even moderate exercise difficult, they may decrease their physical activity. That decrease might slow down their metabolism. The slower metabolism and decreased activity would likely cause them to gain weight. The circle would repeat. Additional examples of the interplay between biological, social, and psychological factors are presented throughout this chapter.

CAUSES OF MORTALITY Before the twentieth century, most people died from infections and from diseases transmitted person to person. Infections and communicable diseases remain the leading causes of mortality in some developing nations, but in most countries the causes have shifted dramatically. For example, in the United States people are now more likely to die from heart disease, cancer, strokes, lung disease, and accidents than from infectious diseases (Heron, 2016). All of these causes of death are at least partially outcomes of lifestyle. Daily habits such as poor nutrition, overeating, smoking, alcohol use, and lack of exercise contribute to nearly every major cause of death in developed nations (Smith, Orleans, & Jenkins, 2004). If being healthy means being physically active, not smoking, eating a healthy diet, and maintaining the recommended body fat level, then fewer than 3 percent of Americans meet all those criteria (Loprinzi, Branscum, Hanks, & Smit, 2016). Partially for this reason, life expectancy in the United States dropped in 2015, the first time this has happened in several decades (Xu, Murphy, Kochanek, & Arias, 2016). A dramatic rise in unintentional poisonings, mainly opioid overdoses, was the leading cause of higher death rates (the opioid epidemic is discussed in Chapter 4).

HEALTH DISPARITIES Worldwide, racial and ethnic groups have large disparities in health. For example, although life expectancies have increased in the United States over the last four decades (**FIGURE 11.2**), African Americans continue to have a lower

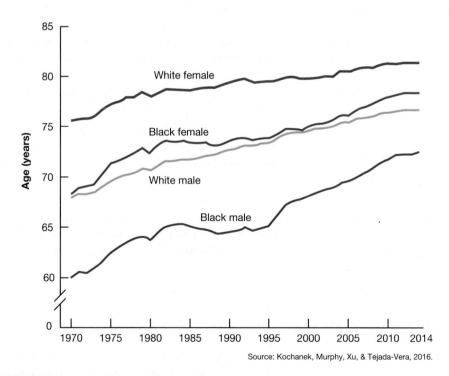

Source: Kochanek, Murphy, Xu, & Tejada-Vera, 2016.

FIGURE 11.2
Life Expectancy by Race and Sex
Although life expectancy has increased in the United States since 1970, African Americans continue to lag behind whites.

life expectancy than white Americans (Kochanek, Murphy, Xu, & Tejada-Vera, 2016). For children born in the United States in 2014, life expectancy varies as follows: 81.4 years for white females, 76.7 years for white males, 78.4 years for African American females, and 72.5 years for African American males (Centers for Disease Control and Prevention, 2016a). The reasons that racial and ethnic groups experience differences in their health include genetic variation in susceptibility to some diseases, access (or lack of access) to affordable health care, and cultural factors such as dietary and exercise habits (Cockerham, Bauldry, Hamby, Shikany, & Bae, 2017). African Americans are less likely to have cancer screenings. Moreover, they are less likely to receive recommended treatments, and perhaps as a result they have lower survival rates (DeSantis, Naishadham, & Jemal, 2013). Racial biases inherent in the U.S. medical system contribute to health disparities (Klonoff, 2014). The gap between black and white Americans has been closing over the past few years, but mainly because white Americans aged 25–54 are dying at higher rates (Kochanek, Arias, & Bastian, 2016). Lifestyle factors, such as alcohol and opioid abuse, have lowered life expectancy more for white, rural Americans than for other racial or ethnic groups (Case & Deaton, 2015; Keyes et al., 2014).

In impoverished countries, the resources may be lacking to provide adequate treatments for many health conditions, such as HIV, malaria, and rotavirus, an intestinal virus that kills over a half million children each year. The Bill and Melinda Gates Foundation has provided billions in grant funding to reduce infectious diseases in poor countries. Efforts such as these have lowered deaths from malaria by 42 percent globally and nearly 50 percent in Africa, where, on average, hundreds of children die each day from malaria (World Health Organization, 2014). Vaccines for rotavirus have led to dramatic reductions in childhood hospitalization and death around the globe, including in North America (Parashar et al., 2013).

Different lifestyles also contribute to health differences. Consider that in some countries, people most often walk or ride bicycles for transportation. In the United States and Canada, people often drive or use public transportation, so their physical activity comes not from daily activity but from purposeful exercise. These differences in health behaviors have long-term consequences for people's health and expected life spans (**FIGURE 11.3**). For example, the adoption of more Westernized lifestyles in countries like India and China, such as eating junk food and engaging in less physical activity, has led to dramatic increases in diseases related to obesity, such as diabetes (Zabetian, Sanchez, Narayan, Hwang, & Ali, 2014). Thus, researchers seek to understand how culture influences behaviors and how behaviors alter underlying biology. Each level of analysis provides a piece of the intricate puzzle that determines health and well-being.

Q Approximately what percent of Americans—3, 30, or 60—satisfy the following four health criteria: physically active, do not smoke, eat a healthy diet, and maintain the recommended body fat level?

ANSWER: Fewer than 3 percent of Americans satisfy all four criteria for being healthy.

11.2 Obesity Has Many Health Consequences

Obesity is a major health problem with physical consequences, such as heart disease, high blood pressure, diabetes, arthritis, and certain cancers (Berrington de Gonzalez et al., 2010). But do we know obesity when we see it? One widely used measure of obesity is **body mass index (BMI)**, a ratio of body weight to height. **FIGURE 11.4** shows how to determine BMI and how to interpret the value obtained. People with BMIs

FIGURE 11.3
The Longest-Living People
The Japanese tend to live very long lives. Their longevity is no doubt due to a combination of genetics and behavior. Pictured here are 99-year-old Matsu and 91-year-old Taido, both of Ogimi Village.

body mass index (BMI)
A ratio of body weight to height, used to measure obesity.

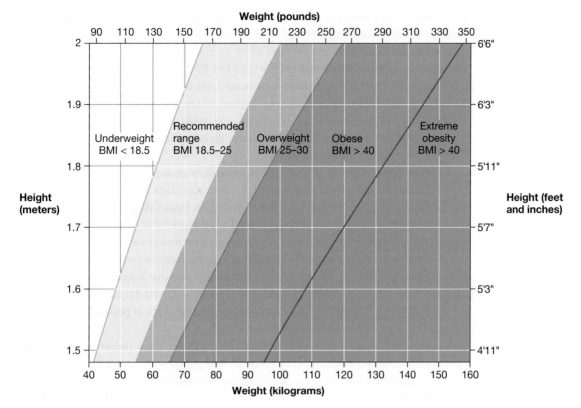

Weight (pounds)

Weight (kilograms)

Height (meters)

Height (feet and inches)

Underweight
BMI < 18.5

Recommended
range
BMI 18.5–25

Overweight
BMI 25–30

Obese
BMI > 40

Extreme
obesity
BMI > 40

FIGURE 11.4
Determining Body Mass Index
To determine your own BMI, find the point at which your weight and height meet on the graph.
According to the traditional view, beyond or below the recommended weight range of 18.5-25
means you are at greater risk for health problems.

over 25 are considered overweight, whereas those with BMIs over 30 are considered
obese.

There are at least two issues with the use of BMI to predict health. First, BMI does
not take age, sex, bone structure, or body fat distribution into account. Athletes or
those with significant amounts of muscle may have high BMIs despite being in excellent physical condition (Rothman, 2008). Perhaps because of these limitations, a
second issue is that a clear relationship between BMI and health outcomes does not
exist except for the very obese.

One recent approach has been to calculate *body shape index,* which considers the
amount of abdominal fat relative to BMI (Krakauer & Krakauer, 2012). In two large
studies in the United States and the United Kingdom, this method was found to
predict health outcomes better than BMI alone did (Krakauer & Krakauer, 2014).

BODY WEIGHT AND HEALTH OUTCOMES A meta-analysis (Flegal, Kit, Orpana, &
Graubard, 2013) looked at 97 studies that included nearly 3 million individuals, of
whom 270,000 had died during the various study periods. The researchers found that
people who were slightly overweight (BMIs 25–30) had a *lower* probability of dying
from any cause during the study periods than people with recommended BMIs of
less than 25. Moreover, slightly obese individuals (BMIs less than 35) did not have a
greater risk of death than those with BMIs under 25. Individuals with BMIs over 35,
however, were much more likely to die.

These findings are controversial. Some researchers have suggested that these findings underestimate the risk of obesity because those with poor nutrition, with chronic illnesses, or who smoke tend to be thin, and therefore these groups might artificially inflate the health risks of having a low BMI (Veronese et al., 2016). Indeed, individuals with low BMIs are also at increased risk for premature death (Aune et al., 2016), particularly if they are elderly (Hughes, 2013). A meta-analysis of 32 studies of nearly 200,000 people over age 65—living and dead—found that those whose BMIs were under 23 or over 34 were much more likely to have died (Winter, MacInnis, Wattanapenpaiboon, & Nowson, 2014).

Whether being slightly overweight is unhealthy or not is under debate. Meanwhile, it is increasingly clear that maladaptive eating habits, such as eating junk food, are likely responsible for much of the poor health associated with obesity. People who eat food high in both fat and sugar tend to store more body fat in the abdomen. These individuals are at increased risk for developing *metabolic syndrome,* a constellation of risk factors that includes high blood sugars, insulin resistance (in which the body produces but does not use insulin efficiently; see the discussion of insulin in Chapter 10), high blood levels of unhealthy cholesterol, and cardiovascular disease (Ford, Giles, & Dietz, 2002). Metabolic syndrome is the result of poor nutrition rather than body weight per se (Unger & Scherer, 2010).

The amount of body fat that people store might be more important for health outcomes than is body weight per se (Padwal, Leslie, Lix, & Majumdar, 2016). Storing fat in the abdomen may have more influence on health than the amount of fat that is stored in the body overall (Sahakyan et al., 2015). People with low BMIs but large amounts of abdominal fat are at higher risk for poor health, whereas people with high BMIs who have fat distributed throughout their bodies are at lower risk for health problems (Ahima & Lazar, 2013). The bottom line, however, is that many obese people store fat in the abdomen and therefore have symptoms of metabolic syndrome.

GLOBAL RISE IN OBESITY According to the World Health Organization (2016), obesity has doubled around the globe since 1980. Although developing nations have lower overall rates of obesity, their populations are becoming obese at a greater rate than developed nations (Ng et al., 2014). In the United States, the rate has jumped from less than 15 percent of the population in 1980 to 38 percent in 2014 (Flegal et al., 2016). Indeed, the numbers are even higher for racial and ethnic minorities, with more than half of African American women (56.7 percent) and nearly half of Hispanic

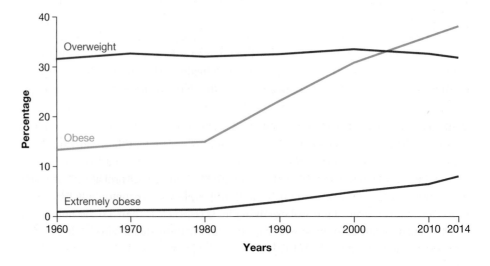

FIGURE 11.5
Trends in Overweight, Obesity, and Extreme Obesity
This graph shows the trends in overweight, obesity, and extreme obesity among adults over age 20 in the United States, 1960-2014.

women (43.3 percent) classified as obese. Extreme obesity (having a BMI over 40), which was almost unheard of in 1960, now characterizes nearly 1 in 12 Americans (Fryar, Carroll, & Ogden, 2016; **FIGURE 11.5**). Likewise, the percentage of obese children has quadrupled since the 1960s. About 1 in 6 children in the U.S. is obese, with African American and Hispanic children much more likely to be so (Ogden et al., 2016).

Given the health consequences associated with obesity, researchers have sought to understand why people are gaining weight and what might be done to reverse this trend. Understanding obesity requires a multilevel approach that examines behavior, underlying biology, cognition (how people think about food and obesity), and the societal context that makes cheap and tasty food readily available. In fact, obesity is an ideal example of the biopsychosocial model of health presented earlier in the chapter. As you read about obesity, keep in mind the linkages between genetic predispositions, thoughts, feelings, and behaviors as well as the continuous loop through which these variables cycle.

FOOD AVAILABILITY AND OVEREATING An increase in the variety of available food is another factor that contributes to maladaptive eating and therefore obesity. For instance, rats that normally maintain a steady body weight when eating one type of food eat huge amounts and become obese when presented with a variety of high-calorie foods, such as chocolate bars, crackers, and potato chips (Sclafani & Springer, 1976; **FIGURE 11.6**). Humans show the same effect, eating much more when various foods are available—as at a buffet—than when only one or two types of food are available (Epstein, Robinson, Roemmich, Marusewski, & Roba, 2010; Raynor & Epstein, 2001).

People also eat more when portions are larger (Rolls, Roe, & Meengs, 2007), and portion sizes have increased considerably in many restaurants. In addition, overweight people show more activity in reward regions of the brain when they see tasty-looking foods than do individuals who are not overweight (Rapuano et al., 2017). Together, these findings suggest that in industrialized nations, the increase in obesity and metabolic syndrome over the past few decades is partly explained by overeating. The overeating stems from three factors: the sheer variety of high-calorie foods, the large portions now served in many restaurants, and individual responses to food cues.

(a)

(b)

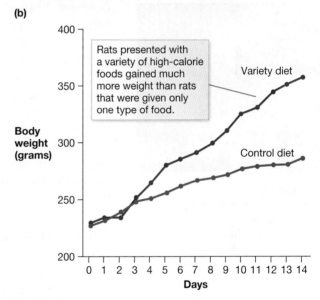

FIGURE 11.6

The Impact of Variety on Eating Behavior

(a) If you were presented with this table full of delicious foods, how many would you eat? Would you be tempted to try them all? **(b)** As shown in this graph, rats will become obese if given ample variety.

SOCIAL AND GENETIC INFLUENCES Body weight may be socially contagious. One study found that close friends of the same sex tend to be similar in body weight (Christakis & Fowler, 2007). This study also found that even when close friends live far apart from each other, if one friend is obese, the other one is likely to be obese as well. Studies of the social transmission of obesity suggest that it is not eating the same meals or cooking together that is critical. Instead, it is the implicit agreement on what body weight is acceptable or normal (**FIGURE 11.7**). If many of your close friends are obese, implicitly you learn that obesity is normal. Thus, subtle communications can affect how we think and act when we eat.

Obesity also tends to run in families. Family and adoption studies indicate that approximately half the variability in body weight is genetic (Klump & Culbert, 2007).

FIGURE 11.7
Body Weight Is Socially Contagious
Friends tend to influence one another's sense of what body weight is appropriate. Thus, friends often have similar body types.

The BMI of adopted children is more strongly related to the BMI of their biological parents than to the BMI of their adoptive parents (Sorensen, Holst, Stunkard, & Skovgaard, 1992). Studies of identical and fraternal twins provide even stronger evidence of the genetic control of body weight.

As discussed in Chapter 3, heritability refers to the proportion of variability, in a population, that can be attributed to genetic transmission of a trait from parents to their offspring. Estimates of the heritability of body weight range from 60 percent to 80 percent. Moreover, the similarity between the body weights of identical twins does not differ for twins raised together versus twins raised apart (Bouchard & Pérusse, 1993; Wardle, Carnell, Haworth, & Plomin, 2008). This finding suggests that genetics has far more effect on body weight than environment does.

If genes primarily determine body weight, why has the percentage of Americans who are obese doubled over the past few decades? Albert Stunkard, a leading researcher on human obesity, points out that genetics determines whether a person *can* become obese, but environment determines whether that person *will* become obese (Stunkard, 1996). In an important study conducted by the geneticist Claude Bouchard, identical twins were overfed by approximately 1,000 calories a day for 100 days (Bouchard, Tremblay, et al., 1990). Most of the twins gained some weight, but there was great variability among pairs in how much they gained (ranging from 4.3 kilograms to 13.3 kilograms, or 9.5 pounds to 29.3 pounds). Further, within the twin pairs there was a striking degree of similarity in how much weight they gained and in which parts of the body they stored the fat. Some of the twin pairs were especially likely to put on weight.

Thus, genetics determines sensitivity to environmental influences. Genes predispose some people to obesity in environments that promote overfeeding, such as contemporary industrialized societies. Many genes are involved in obesity, as might be expected for such a complex condition: More than 300 genetic markers or genes have been identified as playing some role (Snyder et al., 2004).

THE STIGMA OF OBESITY In most Western cultures, obese individuals are viewed as less attractive, less socially adept, less intelligent, and less productive than their normal-weight peers (DeJong & Kleck, 1986). Moreover, perceiving oneself as overweight is linked to depression, anxiety, and low self-esteem (Stice, 2002). Bear in mind, however, that researchers cannot randomly assign people to conditions related to weight, depression, anxiety, or self-esteem. Therefore, most of the obesity research with human participants is correlational. For example, we can note links between being overweight and having low self-esteem, but we cannot say that one factor causes the other. However, the unfortunate practice of fat shaming likely contributes to body dissatisfaction for those who perceive themselves to be overweight. Indeed, fat acceptance advocates argue that anti-fat stigma contributes to the health problems and emotional problems associated with obesity.

Not all cultures stigmatize obesity (Hebl & Heatherton, 1998). In some developing countries, such as many African nations, being obese is a sign of being upper class. Obesity may be desirable in developing countries because it helps prevent some infectious diseases and reduces the likelihood of starvation. It may also serve as a status symbol in developing countries. That is, obesity may indicate that one can afford to eat luxuriously. In Pacific Island countries such as Tonga and Fiji, being obese is a source of personal pride, and dieting is uncommon. In 2013, more than half of men and nearly two-thirds of women living in Tonga were obese (Ng et al., 2014; **FIGURE 11.8A**).

In most industrialized cultures, food is generally abundant. Indeed, in the United States fresh and nutritious foods are often more expensive than high-calorie fast food. Therefore, in the industrialized world, being overweight is associated with

(a)

(b)

lower socioeconomic status, especially for women. The relative affordability of fast food may contribute to overweight among those with limited finances.

The upper classes in Western cultures have a clear preference for very thin body types, as exemplified in fashion magazines (**FIGURE 11.8B**). The typical woman depicted by the fashion industry is 5 feet 11 inches tall and weighs approximately 110 pounds. In other words, the standard represented by models is 7 inches taller and 55 pounds lighter than the average woman in the United States. Such extreme thinness represents a body weight that is difficult, if not impossible, for most people to achieve. In fact, women report holding body weight ideals that are not only lower than average weight but also lower than what men find attractive (Fallon & Rozin, 1985).

 Is being thin always more healthy than being overweight?

ANSWER: No, because being very thin is associated with a shortened life span, just as being very heavy is. The problem with such thinness may be that smokers and people who are very sick tend to be very thin, so their health is at risk from factors beyond weight.

11.3 Dieting Is Seldom Effective and May Contribute to Eating Disorders

Obese people typically try multiple diets and other "cures" to lose weight, but dieting is a notoriously ineffective means of achieving permanent weight loss (Aronne, Wadden, Isoldi, & Woodworth, 2009). Most individuals who lose weight through dieting eventually regain the weight. Often, they gain back more than they lost. Most diets fail primarily because of the body's natural defense against weight loss (Kaplan, 2007). Body weight is regulated around a set-point determined primarily by genetic influence. Consider two examples.

In 1966, several inmates at a Vermont prison were challenged to increase their body weight by 25 percent (Sims et al., 1968). For six months, these inmates consumed more than 7,000 calories a day, nearly double their usual intake. If each inmate was eating about 3,500 extra calories a day (the equivalent of seven large cheeseburgers), simple math suggests that each should have gained approximately 170 pounds over the six months. In reality, few inmates gained more than 40 pounds, and most lost the weight when they went back to normal eating. Those who did not lose the weight had family histories of obesity.

At the other end of the spectrum, researchers have investigated the short-term and long-term effects of semi-starvation (Keys, Brozek, Henschel, Mickelsen, & Taylor, 1950). During World War II, more than 100 men volunteered to take part in this study as an alternative to military service. Over six months, the participants lost an average of 25 percent of their body weight (**FIGURE 11.9**). Most found this weight reduction very hard to accomplish, and some had great difficulty losing more than 10 pounds.

The men underwent dramatic changes in emotions, motivation, and attitudes toward food. They became anxious, depressed, and listless; they lost interest in sex

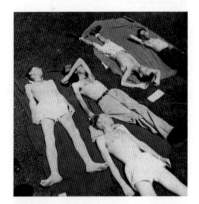

FIGURE 11.9
The Effects of Semi-starvation
These men took part in a study in which they attempted to drastically lose weight.

and other activities; and they became obsessed with eating. Many of these outcomes are similar to those experienced by people with eating disorders.

Although it is possible to alter body weight, the body responds to weight loss by slowing down metabolism and using less energy. Therefore, after the body has been deprived of food, it needs less food to maintain a given body weight. Likewise, weight gain occurs much faster in previously starved animals than would be expected by caloric intake alone. In addition, repeated alterations between caloric deprivation and overfeeding are maladaptive and have been shown to have cumulative metabolic effects. That is, each time an animal is placed on caloric deprivation, the animal's metabolic functioning and weight loss become slower than they were the previous time. When overfeeding resumes, the animal's weight gain occurs more rapidly (Brownell, Greenwood, Stellar, & Shrager, 1986). This pattern might explain why "yo-yo dieters" tend to become heavier over time.

RESTRAINED EATING Janet Polivy and Peter Herman (1985) characterize some chronic dieters as *restrained eaters*. According to Polivy and Herman, restrained eaters are prone to excessive eating in certain situations. These bouts of overeating may be occasional or not so occasional. For instance, if restrained eaters believe they have eaten high-calorie foods, they abandon their diets. Their mindset becomes, "I've blown my diet, so I might as well just keep eating." Many restrained eaters diet through the workweek. On the weekend, when they are faced with increased food temptations and at the same time are in less structured environments, they lose control. In one study, restrained eaters and unrestrained eaters each consumed a large milkshake (Demos, Kelley, & Heatherton, 2011). When the restrained eaters then viewed pictures of appetizing food, activity increased in the brain regions connected with reward. By contrast, when the unrestrained eaters viewed the same pictures, the reward activity in their brains was reduced. Presumably, the milkshake had satisfied the unrestrained eaters. Thus, the reward systems in the brains of restrained eaters seem to encourage additional eating after the eaters break their diets. Being under stress also leads restrained eaters to break their diets (Heatherton, Herman, & Polivy, 1991).

Binge eating by restrained eaters depends on their *perceptions* of whether they have broken their diets. Dieters can eat 1,000-calorie Caesar salads and believe their diets are fine. But if they eat 200-calorie chocolate bars, they feel their diets are ruined and they become disinhibited. Becoming disinhibited means that after first inhibiting their eating, they lose the inhibition. In short, the problem for restrained eaters is that they rely on cognitive control of food intake: Rather than eating according to internal states of hunger and satiety, restrained eaters eat according to rules, such as time of day, number of calories, and type of food. If they feel that food is healthy, whether it is or not, they eat more of it (Provencher, Polivy, & Herman, 2009). Such patterns are maladaptive and are likely to break down when dieters eat high-calorie foods or feel distressed. Getting restrained eaters back in touch with internal motivational states is one goal of sensible approaches to dieting.

DISORDERED EATING When dieters fail to lose weight, they often blame their lack of willpower. They may vow to redouble their efforts on the next diet. Repeated dietary failures may have harmful and permanent physiological and psychological consequences. In physiological terms, weight-loss and weight-gain cycles alter the dieter's metabolism and may make future weight loss more difficult. Psychologically, repeated failures diminish satisfaction with body image and damage self-esteem. Over time, chronic dieters tend to feel helpless and depressed. Some eventually engage in more extreme maladaptive behaviors to lose weight, such as taking drugs, fasting, exercising excessively, or purging. For a vulnerable individual, chronic dieting may promote the development of a clinical eating disorder. Although eating disorders

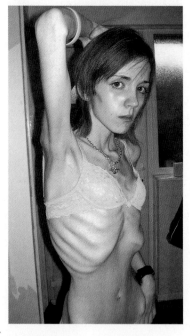

FIGURE 11.10
The Danger of Eating Disorders
When this photo was taken, the young woman was dying of anorexia. Her mother intervened to save her life.

affect both sexes, they are more common for women. It is possible that eating disorders are underestimated among males (Raevuori, Keski-Rahkonen, & Hoek, 2014). According to some research, being gay may increase the likelihood of eating disorders for men (Russell & Keel, 2002). The three most common eating disorders are anorexia nervosa, bulimia nervosa, and binge-eating disorder.

Individuals with **anorexia nervosa** have an excessive fear of becoming fat and severely restrict how much they eat (**FIGURE 11.10**). This reduction in energy intake leads to an unhealthy body weight. Anorexia most often begins in early adolescence. Although this disorder was once thought to mainly affect upper-middle-class and upper-class Caucasian girls, there is evidence that race and class are no longer defining characteristics of eating disorders (Polivy & Herman, 2002). This change might have come about because media images of a thin ideal have permeated all corners of contemporary society.

Although many adolescents strive to be thin, fewer than 1 in 100 meet the clinical criteria of anorexia nervosa as described by the most recent *Diagnostic and Statistical Manual of Mental Disorders* (*DSM-5*), which was released in 2013 (**TABLE 11.1**; *DSM-5*

anorexia nervosa
An eating disorder characterized by excessive fear of becoming fat and therefore restricting energy intake to obtain a significantly low body weight.

Table 11.1 *DSM-5* Diagnostic Criteria for Eating Disorders

CRITERIA FOR ANOREXIA NERVOSA	CRITERIA FOR BULIMIA NERVOSA	CRITERIA FOR BINGE-EATING DISORDER
A. Restriction of energy intake relative to requirements, leading to significantly low body weight in the context of age, sex, developmental trajectory, and physical health. *Significantly low weight* is defined as a weight that is less than minimally normal or, for children and adolescents, less than that minimally expected. B. Intense fear of gaining weight or of becoming fat, or persistent behavior that interferes with weight gain, even though at a significantly lower weight. C. Disturbances in the way in which one's body weight or shape is experienced, undue influence of body weight or shape on self-evaluation, or persistent lack of recognition of the seriousness of the current low body weight.	A. Recurrent episodes of binge eating. An episode of binge eating is characterized by both of the following: 1. Eating, in a discrete period of time (e.g., within any 2-hour period), an amount of food that is definitely larger than what most individuals would eat in a similar period of time under similar circumstances. 2. A sense of lack of control over eating during the episode (e.g., a feeling that one cannot stop eating or control what or how much one is eating). B. Recurrent inappropriate compensatory behaviors in order to prevent weight gain, such as self-induced vomiting; misuse of laxatives, diuretics, or other medications; fasting; or excessive exercise. C. The binge eating and inappropriate compensatory behaviors both occur, on average, at least once a week for 3 months. D. Self-evaluation is unduly influenced by body shape and weight. E. The disturbance does not occur exclusively during episodes of anorexia nervosa.	A. Recurrent episodes of binge eating. An episode of binge eating is characterized by both of the following: 1. Eating, in a discrete period of time (e.g., within any 2-hour period), an amount of food that is definitely larger than what most individuals would eat in a similar period of time under similar circumstances. 2. A sense of lack of control over eating during the episode (e.g., a feeling that one cannot stop eating or control what or how much one is eating). B. The binge-eating episodes are associated with three (or more) of the following: 1. Eating much more rapidly than normal. 2. Eating until feeling uncomfortably full. 3. Eating large amounts of food when not feeling physically hungry. 4. Eating alone because of feeling embarrassed by how much one is eating. 5. Feeling disgusted with oneself, depressed, or very guilty afterward. C. Marked distress regarding binge eating is present. D. The binge eating occurs, on average, at least once a week for 3 months. E. The binge eating is not associated with bulimia nervosa or anorexia nervosa.

Source: American Psychiatric Association (2013).

is discussed further in Chapter 14). There is evidence that adolescent boys and girls are equally likely to develop anorexia (Swanson et al., 2011). These criteria include both objective measures of thinness and psychological characteristics that indicate an abnormal obsession with food and body weight.

Those who have anorexia view themselves as fat even though they are at a significantly low weight, often with BMIs under 17. Issues of food and weight pervade their lives, controlling how they view themselves and how they view the world. Initially, the results of self-imposed starvation may draw favorable comments from others, such as "You look so thin you could be a fashion model." These comments might come from friends who are also influenced by social messages that being thin is an important part of being attractive. But as the anorexic approaches her emaciated ideal, family and friends usually become concerned. In many cases, medical attention is required to prevent death from starvation.

This dangerous disorder causes a number of serious health problems, in particular a loss of bone density, and about 15–20 percent of those with anorexia eventually die from the disorder—they literally starve themselves to death (American Psychiatric Association, 2000b).

bulimia nervosa
An eating disorder characterized by the alternation of dieting, binge eating, and purging (self-induced vomiting).

Individuals with **bulimia nervosa** alternate between dieting, binge eating, and purging (self-induced vomiting) or other inappropriate compensatory behaviors, such as abusing laxatives or excessive exercising. Bulimia often develops during late adolescence. Approximately 1–2 percent of women in high school and college meet the criteria for bulimia nervosa. These women tend to be of average weight or slightly overweight. Bulimia is much more common in females than in males (Klump, Culbert, & Sisk, 2017).

Bulimics are caught in a vicious cycle: In an effort to quell negative emotions, they eat large quantities of food in a short amount of time. This eating leads them to feel guilty that they may gain weight. They will then engage in one or more compensatory behaviors, such as self-induced vomiting, excessive exercise, or the abuse of laxatives. Whereas anorexics cannot easily hide their self-starvation, binge-eating behavior tends to occur secretly. Although bulimia is associated with serious health problems, such as dental and cardiac disorders, it is seldom fatal (Keel & Mitchell, 1997).

binge-eating disorder
An eating disorder characterized by binge eating that causes significant distress.

A disorder similar to bulimia is **binge-eating disorder.** The American Psychiatric Association officially recognized this condition as a disorder in 2013. People with the disorder engage in binge eating at least once a week, but they do not purge. These individuals often eat very quickly, even when they are not hungry. Those with binge-eating disorder often experience feelings of guilt and embarrassment, and they may binge eat alone to hide the behavior. Many people with binge-eating disorder are overweight or obese. Compared to bulimia, binge-eating disorder is more common among males and ethnic minorities (Wilfley, Bishop, Wilson, & Agras, 2007). Although bulimia and binge-eating disorder share many common features—differing most notably in that only bulimics purge—many researchers believe the two are distinct disorders (Striegel-Moore & Franko, 2008).

Eating disorders tend to run in families. Like obesity, these disorders are due partly to genetics. The incidence of eating disorders in the United States increased into the 1980s (Keel, Baxter, Heatherton, & Joiner, 2007). This increase suggests that when people have genetic predispositions for eating disorders, they will tend to develop the disorders if they live in societies with an abundance of food. Bulimia seems to be more culture bound, meaning that there are large cultural variations in its incidence. Anorexia is prevalent in all societies that have abundant food.

There are many effective treatments for eating disorders. Indeed, the outlook for those with eating disorders indicates reasons to be optimistic about outcome, with the majority symptom-free five years after diagnosis (Keel & Brown, 2010). Effective treatments focus on disordered thoughts, interpersonal relationships, and family dynamics (Peterson et al., 2016). You will learn more about these treatments in Chapter 15. Most college campuses have counseling centers with expertise in helping those with disorders.

Q How does bulimia nervosa differ from anorexia nervosa?

ANSWER: Those with bulimia alternate between dieting, binge eating, and purging (self-induced vomiting), whereas those with anorexia starve themselves to achieve extreme thinness.

11.4 Smoking Is a Leading Cause of Death

Despite overwhelming evidence that smoking cigarettes leads to premature death, millions around the globe continue to light up (Fiore, Schroeder, & Baker, 2014). According to the World Health Organization (2008), increasing numbers of people are smoking in low-income countries, and 5.4 million deaths are caused by tobacco every year. Thirty percent of all smokers worldwide are in China, 10 percent are in India, and an additional 25 percent come from Indonesia, Russia, the United States, Japan, Brazil, Bangladesh, Germany, and Turkey combined (**FIGURE 11.11**). According to the 2014 U.S. Surgeon General's Report, just under 1 in 5 American adults are current smokers (U.S. Department of Health and Human Services [USDHHS], 2014). Smoking is blamed for more than 480,000 deaths per year in the United States and decreases the typical smoker's life by more than 12 years (Jha et al., 2013).

Most smokers begin in childhood or early adolescence. This early start concerns health care providers because of how nicotine may affect the developing brain. Every day, approximately 3,200 Americans ages 11 to 17 smoke their first cigarette (USDHHS, 2014). About half of young smokers will likely continue smoking into adulthood, and if current smoking rates continue, 5.6 million American children alive today will die prematurely because of smoking (USDHHS, 2014). Fortunately, there has been a dramatic reduction in adolescent smoking over the last decade (Johnston, O'Malley, Bachman, & Schulenberg, 2011). Regular smoking dropped from approximately 13 percent to 6.6 percent, with a 33 percent drop in the number of adolescents who even try smoking (Centers for Disease Control and Prevention, 2010; USDHHS, 2014).

Smoking causes numerous health problems, including heart disease, respiratory ailments, and various cancers. Cigarette smoke also causes health problems for nonsmoking bystanders, a finding that has led to bans on smoking in many public and private places. Besides spending money on cigarettes, smokers pay significantly more for life insurance and health insurance. Why do they continue to smoke? Why does anyone start?

STARTING SMOKING It is hard to imagine any good reason to start smoking. First attempts at smoking often involve a great deal of coughing, watering eyes, a terrible taste in the mouth, and feelings of nausea. So why do kids persist? Most researchers point to powerful social influences as the leading cause of adolescent smoking (Chassin, Presson, & Sherman, 1990; **FIGURE 11.12**). Research has demonstrated that adolescents are more likely to smoke if their parents or friends smoke (Hansen et al., 1987). They often smoke their first cigarettes in the company of other smokers, or at least with the encouragement of their peers. Moreover, many adolescent smokers appear to show a false consensus effect: They overestimate the number of adolescent and adult smokers (Sherman, Presson, Chassin, Corty, & Olshavsky, 1983). Adolescents who incorrectly believe that smoking is common may take it up to fit in with the crowd.

Other studies have pointed to the potential meaning of "being a smoker" as having a powerful influence. For instance, research has shown that smokers are viewed as having positive qualities such as being tough, sociable, and good with members of the opposite sex. Children take up smoking partially to look "tough, cool, and independent of authority" (Leventhal & Cleary, 1980, p. 384). Thus, smoking may be one way for adolescents to enhance their self-images as well as their public images (Chassin et al.,

(a)

(b)

FIGURE 11.11
Smoking Is a Global Phenomenon
(a) These men are smoking in Tiananmen Square in Beijing, China. **(b)** These smokers belong to the Mentawi people, a seminomadic hunter-gatherer tribe in the coastal and rain forest regions of Indonesia.

FIGURE 11.12
Social Influence and Smoking
Adolescents are strongly affected by social situations. They are more likely to smoke if their friends or parents smoke.

FIGURE 11.13
Glamorous Portrayals of Smoking
In the AMC series *Preacher*, Dominic Cooper plays the preacher Jesse Custer. Cooper's pose here exemplifies the "cool" factor often seen in depictions of smoking.

1990). As discussed in Chapter 6, adolescents imitate models through observational learning. Smokers on television and in movies are often portrayed in glamorous ways that appeal to adolescents (**FIGURE 11.13**). Researchers in Germany found that the more German children ages 10 to 16 watched popular North American movies that depicted smoking, the more likely they were to try smoking (Hanewinkel & Sargent, 2008; compare with Figure 6.40, which illustrates how adolescent smoking rates decline when movie depictions of smoking decline).

By the 12th grade, 50–70 percent of adolescents in the United States have had some experience with tobacco products (Centers for Disease Control and Prevention, 2010; Mowery, Brick, & Farrelly, 2000). Of course, it is hard to look tough while gasping and retching; so while most adolescents try one or two cigarettes, most do not become regular smokers. Still, many young people who experiment go on to smoke on a regular basis (Baker, Brandon, & Chassin, 2004).

Over time, casual smokers become addicted. It is now widely acknowledged that the drug nicotine is of primary importance in motivating and maintaining smoking behavior (Fagerström & Schneider, 1989; USDHHS, 2004). Once the smoker becomes "hooked" on nicotine, going without cigarettes will lead to unpleasant withdrawal symptoms, including distress and heightened anxiety (Russell, 1990). Some people appear especially susceptible to nicotine addiction, perhaps because of genetics (Sabol et al., 1999). Nicotine may lead to increased activation of dopamine neurons, which can have a reinforcing effect. (The functions of dopamine neurons are discussed further in Chapter 3.)

ELECTRONIC CIGARETTES People continue to smoke in order to obtain nicotine. Within the past few years, a new way to get nicotine has become increasingly popular: e-cigarettes. According to the 2014 U.S. Surgeon General's report (USDHHS, 2014), approximately 6 percent of U.S. adults have at least tried e-cigarettes.

A positive aspect of e-cigarettes is that they do not contain tobacco or the thousands of chemicals, many of them cancer causing, that are in regular cigarettes. E-cigarettes also do not produce secondhand smoke, which can be harmful to nonsmokers. However, health officials do not yet know whether e-cigarettes are better or worse for individuals and society than traditional tobacco products (Glynn, 2014). Scientific data are lacking regarding the safety of e-cigarettes. We also do not know if they substitute for the look and feel of real cigarettes. Although there is some evidence that e-cigarettes are modestly helpful at helping smokers quit (Bullen et al., 2013), there is other evidence that e-cigarettes may hinder attempts to quit smoking (Al-Delaimy, Myers, Leas, Strong, & Hofstetter, 2015; Kalkhoran & Glantz, 2016).

Between 2011 and 2014, e-cigarette use by U.S. high school students increased dramatically. Of the 25 percent of high school students reporting any tobacco use, most use e-cigarettes rather than other tobacco products (Arrazola et al., 2015). Recent studies have found that adolescent nonsmokers who try e-cigarettes are more likely to become regular smokers—nicotine addicts—than those who do not (Primack, Soneji, Stoolmiller, Fine, & Sargent, 2015; Wills et al., 2017).

QUITTING SMOKING Many people who smoke worry about the health risks and consider quitting or do attempt to quit smoking. Numerous treatment options are available to assist smoking cessation efforts. One widely used method is *nicotine replacement therapy,* such as smoking e-cigarettes, chewing nicotine gum, or wearing a patch that delivers nicotine (**FIGURE 11.14**). As mentioned just above, the data suggest that e-cigarettes are not a very effective method for quitting smoking. Prescription medications may also play a part in efforts to quit. Chantix is a drug that acts as a partial agonist for nicotine receptors (recall from Chapter 3 that agonists can mimic the effects of drugs). This action reduces cravings and provides some of the desirable effects of

(a)  **(b)**  **(c)**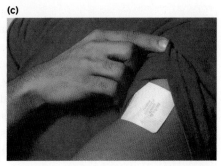

FIGURE 11.14
Nicotine Replacement Therapy
Three ways to quit smoking involve replacing the nicotine delivery system: **(a)** smoking e-cigarettes, **(b)** chewing nicotine gum, or **(c)** wearing the patch.

smoking. Wellbutrin is a drug used to treat depression (you will learn more about such drugs in Chapter 15). Wellbutrin also reduces tobacco cravings, although not as strongly as Chantix. A review paper that compared treatments found that Chantix is more effective than nicotine replacement or Wellbutrin (Wu, Wilson, Dimoulas, & Mills, 2006).

In addition, numerous behavioral treatments encourage people to quit, teach them effective alternative ways of dealing with stress, and help them try to prevent relapse (Baker et al., 2011). Unfortunately, most people who use these methods do relapse. Only 10–30 percent of people are able to quit smoking over the long term, even in the most effective treatment programs (Schlam & Baker, 2013).

In spite of these relatively unimpressive outcomes from treatment studies, millions of people have permanently given up smoking. How did they do it? Around 90 percent of people who successfully quit do so on their own, going "cold turkey" (Smith & Chapman, 2014). Often, some sort of critical event changes the way the smoker thinks about the addiction. The psychologist David Premack provides an example of a man who quit smoking one day because of something that happened when he was picking up his children from the city library: "A thunderstorm greeted him as he arrived there; and at the same time a search of his pockets disclosed a familiar problem: he was out of cigarettes. Glancing back at the library, he caught a glimpse of his children stepping out in the rain, but he continued around the corner, certain that he could find a parking space, rush in, buy the cigarettes and be back before the children got seriously wet" (Premack, 1970, p. 115).

For the smoker, it was a shocking revelation of himself "as a father who would actually leave the kids in the rain while he ran after cigarettes." The man quit smoking on the spot. Researchers have not yet identified the mechanisms that transform critical events into successful smoking cessation (Smith & Chapman, 2014). Because of the difficulty that many people have quitting smoking, much of current research on smoking examines ways to prevent people from smoking in the first place (USDHHS, 2014).

 What is the primary reason that smokers continue to smoke despite the health consequences?

ANSWER: addiction to nicotine

11.5 Exercise Has Numerous Benefits

In general, the more people exercise, the better their physical and mental health. Those with better fitness in middle age are likely to enjoy much longer lives (Ladenvall et al., 2016). They are less likely to have heart problems (Arem et al., 2015) and are at much lower risk for most types of cancer (Moore et al., 2016). Even weekend warrior types who exercise only once or twice a week show reductions in heart disease and cancer (O'Donovan, Lee, Hamer & Stamatakis, 2017). Scientists do not know exactly how exercise exerts all of its positive effects.

Unlike societies throughout most of human history, modern society allows and even encourages people to exert little physical energy. People drive to work, take elevators, spend hours watching remote-controlled television, spend even more hours online, use various labor-saving devices, and complain about not having time to exercise. Once people are out of shape, it is difficult for them to start exercising regularly. Because the modern world requires little physical activity, people need to purposefully exercise during their leisure time.

Research clearly shows the benefits of exercise on almost every aspect of our lives, including enhanced memory and enhanced cognition (Harburger, Nzerem, & Frick, 2007). Aerobic exercise—the kind that temporarily increases breathing and heart rate—promotes the growth of new neurons (Carmichael, 2007). The additional neurons created through exercise result in a larger brain, and the brain region that experiences the most growth is the hippocampus (Nokia et al., 2016). As discussed in Chapter 3, the hippocampus is important for memory and cognition.

Aerobic exercise is also especially good for cardiovascular health, because it lowers blood pressure and strengthens the heart and lungs (Lavie et al., 2015). A meta-analysis found that exercise is as effective as medications for preventing diabetes or heart disease or promoting recovery following heart attacks (Naci & Ioannidis, 2013). Although the different studies in the meta-analysis varied in the type of physical activity, as well as frequency, intensity, and duration, most included aerobic and muscle strengthening exercises. As little as 10 minutes of exercise can promote feelings of vigor and enhance mood, although at least 30 minutes of daily exercise is associated with the most positive mental state (Hansen, Stevens, & Coast, 2001). In fact, there is compelling evidence that exercise can contribute to positive outcomes for the clinical treatment of depression (Schuch et al., 2016a), as well as being beneficial in the treatment of addiction and alcoholism (Read & Brown, 2003). People who are not physically fit are also at greater risk of developing depression (Schuch et al., 2016b; you will learn more about depression in Chapter 14).

Fortunately, it is never too late to start exercising and receiving its positive benefits (**FIGURE 11.15**). In one study, sedentary adults between the ages of 60 and 79 were randomly assigned to either six months of aerobic training, such as running or fast dancing, or six months of a nonaerobic control group (Colcombe et al., 2006). Participants in aerobic training significantly increased their brain volume, including both white (myelinated) and gray matter. The nonaerobic control group experienced no comparable changes. In another study, older adults were assigned randomly to either three months of aerobic exercise or three months of a nonaerobic control group (Emery, Kiecolt-Glaser, Glaser, Malarkey, & Frid, 2005). All the participants agreed to have small cuts made on their bodies so the researchers could study whether aerobic exercise hastened the time it took for the wounds to heal. The wounds of the aerobic group took an average of 29.2 days to heal, whereas those of the nonaerobic group took an average of 38.9 days to heal. Besides faster healing time, the aerobic group had better cardiorespiratory (heart and lung) fitness.

In another study, older adults with memory problems were randomly assigned to an exercise group (3 hours a week for 2 weeks) or to a control group (Lautenschlager et al., 2008). The participants in the exercise group improved in their overall cognition, including memory. The control group showed no changes. The researchers concluded that exercise reduces cognitive decline in older adults with moderate memory problems.

FIGURE 11.15
Older Adults Exercising
People are never too old to enjoy the benefits of exercise.

ANSWER: No. Even exercising once or twice a week leads to benefits.

 Does a person have to exercise every day to see health benefits?

11.6 Why Are People Afraid of Flying but Not of Driving (or Smoking)?

Are you an anxious flyer? Like many people, you may be at least somewhat anxious about flying. A statistical expert explained the risk of death from flying this way: "It's once every 19,000 years—and that is only provided the person flew on an airplane once a day for 19,000 years!" ("Six most feared," 2005, p. 5). Other researchers have estimated that 1 in 13 million passengers dies in an airplane crash.

What about being the victim of terrorism—do you fear that? In the months following the September 11, 2001, terrorist attacks in the United States, many people avoided flying. Instead, they preferred what they believed to be the safety of driving. Yet after the attacks, the number of people who died in automobile accidents because they chose to drive instead of fly far exceeded the number of people who were killed in the attacks (Gigerenzer, 2004).

The more that the press reports crimes and acts of terrorism, the more that people feel they are likely to become the victims of crime or terrorism (Nellis & Savage, 2012). A 2015 Gallup poll found that 51 percent of Americans worry that they or a family member will be the victim of terrorism (**FIGURE 11.16**). The percentage varies considerably based on media accounts of terrorist incidents. For instance, there tend to be peak worries after well-publicized attacks, such as 9/11, the Boston Marathon bombings, and the Paris mass shootings. The 51 percent who worry are greatly overestimating the risk. According to a report from the U.S. Department of State (2012) for the year 2011, 17 American private citizens died as a result of terrorist actions. If we place this number in the context of the ways that people died in the United States during 2011 (Hoyert & Xu, 2012), the comparison means that people in the United

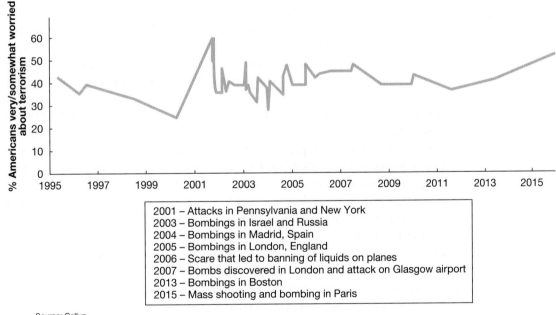

2001 – Attacks in Pennsylvania and New York
2003 – Bombings in Israel and Russia
2004 – Bombings in Madrid, Spain
2005 – Bombings in London, England
2006 – Scare that led to banning of liquids on planes
2007 – Bombs discovered in London and attack on Glasgow airport
2013 – Bombings in Boston
2015 – Mass shooting and bombing in Paris

Source: Gallup.

FIGURE 11.16

Fears of Terrorism

According to Gallup surveys over the past two decades, different percentages of Americans have worried that they or their family members will be victims of terrorism. Fear increases after terrorist events that are widely reported by the media.

stress

A type of response that typically involves an unpleasant state, such as anxiety or tension.

stressor

Something in the environment that is perceived as threatening or demanding and therefore produces stress.

coping response

Any attempt made to avoid, escape from, or minimize a stressor.

States are more than 35,000 times more likely to die from heart disease and 33,000 times more likely to die from cancer than from terrorism.

In terms of thinking about their health and well-being, people often fear the wrong things. They tend not to be worried at all about the things that are most likely to kill them. Rare causes of death—not just plane crashes or terrorism, but oddities such as "flesh-eating bacteria" or being murdered while vacationing in a foreign country—are often judged to occur much more frequently than they actually do, while common causes of death are underestimated (Lichtenstein, Slovic, Fischhoff, Layman, & Combs, 1978). People are most likely to die from causes that stem from their own behaviors, which they can learn to modify. For example, heart disease and cancer account for about half of all U.S. deaths (Hoyert & Xu, 2012). Those who suffer from heart disease or cancer are not always to blame for their conditions, but all of us can change our behaviors in ways that may reduce the likelihood of these illnesses (e.g., exercise, eat nutritiously, do not smoke). A report released by the Centers for Disease Control in 2014 indicated that over a quarter of a million early deaths could be prevented each year if people made better health choices (Yoon et al., 2014).

Why do people fear things that are unlikely to harm them but not worry about the things that are truly dangerous? Recall from Chapter 8 the availability heuristic, which refers to believing information that comes most easily to mind. People using this heuristic will judge an event as likely to occur if it is easy to imagine or recall (Slovic, Fischhoff, Lichtenstein, & Roe, 1981). The press widely and dramatically reports plane crashes, as when headlines blazed for weeks after the disappearance of Malaysian Airlines Flight 370 in March 2014. Press reports of other crashes often include vivid pictures or detailed accounts that can readily be recalled or easily imagined. The ease with which people recall this information biases their risk estimates.

By contrast, figuring out the risks associated with eating a hamburger and french fries is much more challenging. You would have to know how eating that food would affect your body, such as the likelihood that it would lead to weight gain. You would then need to compute the risk that your particular body weight places you at risk for disease. You would also have to include in your risk prediction your family history, your other risk behaviors, and other lifestyle factors that may be protective. These computations are difficult mental work! It is therefore difficult to look at a hamburger and fries and have the sense of dread that you might experience when you board an airplane.

Unless you are willing to hide in your house, you will have a very difficult time protecting yourself from a random act of terrorism. However, you can protect yourself from factors that are more likely to kill you as a student, such as excessive alcohol intoxication, an overdose of legal or illegal drugs, drinking and driving, or texting while driving. Because of optimism bias, young people also tend to feel invulnerable to many risky behaviors (Radcliffe & Klein, 2002). Yet each year many more college students die from these common behaviors than are killed by rare events such as plane crashes or terrorist activity.

The biopsychosocial model is central to understanding the difference between the traditional medical model and the approach taken by health psychologists. In the traditional model, the individual is passive. For health psychologists, the individual's thoughts, feelings, and behaviors are central to understanding and improving health. ∎

ANSWER: Press reports lead people to develop strong memories for unusual tragedies, and the availability heuristic means that those tragedies come easily to mind.

How might vivid media reports affect people's views of relative risks of dying?

What Is Stress?

Stress is a basic component of our daily lives. However, stress does not exist objectively, out in the world. Instead, it results directly from the ways we think about events in our lives. For example, some students experience final exams as extremely stressful and often get sick at exam time, whereas other students perceive the same finals as mere inconveniences or even as opportunities to demonstrate mastery of the material. When researchers study stress, then, what are they studying?

11.7 Stress Is a Response to Life Events

Stress is a type of response that typically involves an unpleasant state, such as anxiety or tension. A **stressor** is something in the environment that is perceived as threatening or demanding and therefore produces stress. One person's stressor, such as having to speak in front of a crowd, may be another person's cherished activity. Stress elicits a **coping response,** which is an attempt to avoid, escape from, or minimize the stressor. When too much is expected of us or when events are worrisome or scary, we perceive a discrepancy between the demands of the situation and our resources to cope with them. That discrepancy might be real, or we might be imagining it. In general, positive and negative life changes are stressful. Think about the stresses of going to college, getting a job, marrying, being fired, losing a parent, winning a major award, and so on. The greater the number of changes, the greater the stress, and the more likely the stress will affect physiological states.

Stress is often divided into two types: *Eustress* is the stress of positive events. For example, you might experience eustress when you are admitted to the college you really want to attend or when you are preparing for a party you are looking forward to. *Distress* is the stress of negative events. For example, you might experience distress when you are late for an important meeting and become trapped in traffic or when you are helping a loved one deal with a serious illness.

Most people use the term *stress* only in referring to negative events, but both distress and eustress put strains on the body. The number of stressful events a person experiences, whether they are negative or positive, predicts health outcomes. Some events are more stressful than others, of course (**FIGURE 11.17**).

One team of researchers assigned point values to 43 different life events. For instance, the death of a spouse was 100 points, pregnancy was 40 points, and a vacation was 13 points (Holmes & Rahe, 1967). A person's stress level could be determined by adding up the points for every event the person had experienced in the previous year. Someone who had been married, moved, started a new job, had a child, and had a change in sleeping pattern during the previous year would score very high on this scale and therefore be likely to suffer poor health as a result. A version of the scale for students can be found in **TABLE 11.2**.

Psychologists typically think of stressors as falling into two categories: major life stressors and daily hassles. *Major life stressors* are changes or disruptions that strain central areas of people's lives (Pillow, Zautra, & Sandler, 1996). Major life stressors include choices made by individuals, not just things that happen to them. For instance, some parents report that having their first child is one of the most joyful—but also one of the most taxing—experiences of their lives. Nonetheless, research has shown that unpredictable and uncontrollable catastrophic events—such as floods, earthquakes, or wars—are especially stressful (Kanno et al., 2013; Tang, 2007). To avoid serious health problems, combat soldiers and others in prolonged stressful situations often must use combinations of strategies to cope with the stress of their situations. Coping strategies are discussed in Section 11.12.

- Define stress.
- Describe the hypothalamic-pituitary-adrenal (HPA) axis.
- Describe the general adaptation syndrome.
- Discuss sex differences in responses to stressors.

FIGURE 11.17
Stress in Everyday Life
How do you cope with the stress in your life? What makes your strategies effective?

Table 11.2 Student Stress Scale

To determine the amount of stress in your life, select the events that have happened to you in the past 12 months.

EVENT	LIFE CHANGE UNITS	EVENT	LIFE CHANGE UNITS	EVENT	LIFE CHANGE UNITS
Death of close family member	100	Serious argument with close friend	40	Change in social activities	29
Death of close friend	73	Change in financial status	39	Serious argument with instructor	30
Divorce between parents	65	Change in major	39	Lower grades than expected	29
Jail term	63	Trouble with parents	39	Change in eating habits	28
Major personal injury or illness	63	New girlfriend or boyfriend	38	Chronic car trouble	26
Marriage	58	Increased workload at school	37	Change in number of family get-togethers	26
Being fired from job	50				
Failing important course	47	Outstanding personal achievement	36	Too many missed classes	25
Change in health of family member	45	First term in college	35	Change of college	24
				Dropping more than one class	23
Pregnancy	45	Change in living conditions	31		
Sex problems	44	Change in sleeping habits	29	Minor traffic violations	20

SCORING

Next to each event is a score that indicates how much a person has to adjust as a result of the change. Both positive events (outstanding personal achievement) and negative events (major personal injury or illness) can be stressful because they require one to make adjustments. Add together the life change unit scores to determine how likely you are to experience illness or mental health problems as a result of the stress of these events.

300 life change units or more: A person has a high risk for a serious health change.
150-299 life change units: About 1 of every 2 people is likely to have a serious health change.
149 life change units or less: About 1 of every 3 people is likely to have a serious health change.

Source: Adapted from Holmes & Rahe (1967).

Daily hassles are small, day-to-day irritations and annoyances, such as driving in heavy traffic, dealing with difficult people, or waiting in line. Daily hassles are stressful, and their combined effects can be comparable to the effects of major life changes (DeLongis, Folkman, & Lazarus, 1988). Because these low-level irritations are ubiquitous, they pose a threat to coping responses by slowly wearing down personal resources. Studies that ask people to keep diaries of their daily activities find consistently that the more intense and frequent the hassles, the poorer the physical and mental health of the participant (Almeida, 2005). People may habituate to some hassles but not to others. For example, conflicts with other people appear to have a cumulative detrimental effect on health and well-being. Living in poverty or in a crowded, noisy, or polluted place also can have cumulative detrimental effects on health and well-being (Santiago, Wadsworth, & Stump, 2011).

Q **Do only negative events cause stress?**

ANSWER: No, both negative and positive events can produce stress.

11.8 Stress Has Physiological Components

Researchers have a good understanding of the biological mechanisms that underlie the stress response. A stressor activates two systems: a fast-acting sympathetic nervous system response and a slower-acting response resulting from a complex system of biological events known as the **hypothalamic-pituitary-adrenal (HPA) axis.**

Stress begins in the brain with the perception of some stressful event. For our very distant ancestors, the event might have been the sight of a predator approaching rapidly. For us, it is more likely to be an approaching deadline, a stack of unpaid bills, a fight, an illness, and so on. The hypothalamus first activates the sympathetic nervous system, which activates the adrenal glands—located on top of the kidneys—to release epinephrine and norepinephrine, increasing heart rate, blood pressure, and respiration and making the body ready for action (see Chapter 3, "Biology and Behavior"). Meanwhile, in the HPA axis (**FIGURE 11.18**), the hypothalamus sends a chemical message to the pituitary gland, a major gland located at the base of the brain. In turn, the pituitary gland sends a hormone that travels through the bloodstream and eventually also reaches the adrenal glands (although a different region of the gland than the faster system). The adrenals then secrete *cortisol*. Cortisol circulates throughout the body and to various brain areas, especially the hypothalamus, hippocampus, and amygdala (De Kloet, Joëls, & Holsboer, 2005). In turn, cortisol increases the amount of glucose in the bloodstream. All of these actions help the body prepare to respond to the stressor. For example, the response might consist of fighting an attacker.

Because hormones have long-lasting effects, stress affects organs after the stressor has been removed. Studies of stress show that, in human and nonhuman animals, excessive stress disrupts working memory, an effect that is especially noticeable when the demands on working memory are high (Oei, Everaerd, Elzinga, Van Well, & Bermond, 2006; Otto, Raio, Chiang, Phelps, & Daw, 2013). Chronic stress has also been associated with long-term memory impairments (McEwen, 2016). Excessive cortisol damages neurons in brain areas such as the hippocampus, which is important for storing long-term memories (Sapolsky, 1994). Stress also interferes with the ability to retrieve information from long-term memory (Finsterwald & Alberini, 2014).

Early childhood stress is a risk factor for developing psychological disorders later in life (Heim, Newport, Mletzko, Miller, & Nemeroff, 2008). Emerging research suggests the possibility that stress experienced by mothers may be passed along to their offspring through epigenetics (genetic changes discussed in Chapter 3, "Biology and Behavior"). In one study, rats were exposed to unpredictable stress that led to physiological changes in their brains. These rats were mated 14 days later and subsequently had offspring. When those offspring became adults they showed abnormalities in fear learning and heightened physiological responses to stress (Zaidan, Leshem, & Gaisler-Salomon, 2013). Through epigenetics, the effect of stress on mothers also leads to altered social behaviors in their offspring (Franklin, Linder, Russig, Thöny, & Mansuy, 2011). Thus, highly stressful experience can affect behavior across generations (Bohacek, Gapp, Saab, & Mansuy, 2013; Turecki & Meaney, 2016).

hypothalamic-pituitary-adrenal (HPA) axis

A body system involved in stress responses.

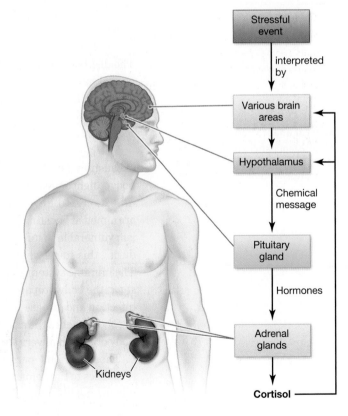

FIGURE 11.18
Hypothalamic-Pituitary-Adrenal (HPA) Axis
A stressful event will set off a complex chain of responses in the body.

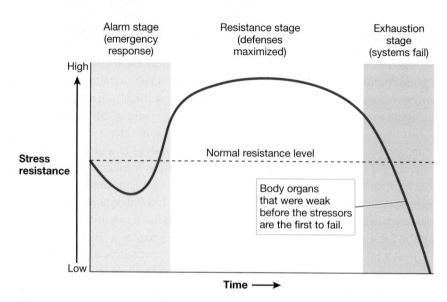

Alarm stage (emergency response) Resistance stage (defenses maximized) Exhaustion stage (systems fail)

High

Stress resistance

Normal resistance level

Body organs that were weak before the stressors are the first to fail.

Low

Time ⟶

FIGURE 11.19
The General Adaptation Syndrome
Selye described three stages of physiological response to stress. As shown here, the body may progress from alarm to resistance to exhaustion.

GENERAL ADAPTATION SYNDROME In the early 1930s, the endocrinologist Hans Selye began studying the physiological effects of sex hormones by injecting rats with hormones from other animals. The result was damage to a number of bodily systems. Surmising that the foreign hormones must have caused this damage, Selye conducted further tests. He tried different types of chemicals, and he even physically restrained the animals to create stressful situations. Selye found that each manipulation produced roughly the same pattern of physiological changes: enlarged adrenal glands, decreased levels of *lymphocytes*—specialized white blood cells—in the blood, and stomach ulcers. The decreased lymphocytes result from damage to part of the immune system (discussed more fully in Section 11.10). Together, the enlarged adrenal glands and damage to the immune system reduce the organism's potential ability to resist additional stressors. Selye concluded that these responses are the hallmarks of a *nonspecific stress response*. He called this pattern the **general adaptation syndrome** (Selye, 1932).

The general adaptation syndrome consists of three stages: alarm, resistance, and exhaustion (**FIGURE 11.19**). The *alarm stage* is an emergency reaction that prepares the body to fight or flee (it is identical to Walter Cannon's fight-or-flight response, discussed in Section 11.9). Physiological responses, such as the release of cortisol and epinephrine, are aimed at boosting physical abilities while reducing activities that make the organism vulnerable to infection after injury. There is a brief reduction in stress resistance during this stage, when the body is most likely to be exposed to infection and disease. The immune system kicks in, and the body begins fighting back. During the *resistance stage*, the body prepares for longer, sustained defense from the stressor. Immunity to infection and disease increases somewhat as the body maximizes its defenses. When the body reaches the *exhaustion stage*, various physiological and immune systems fail. Body organs that were already weak before the stress are the first to fail.

These various perspectives show that short-term stress produces adaptive responses to the demands of daily living. Prolonged or overwhelming stress, however, impairs health, which we consider in the next section.

general adaptation syndrome
A consistent pattern of responses to stress that consists of three stages: alarm, resistance, and exhaustion.

 Which hormone is released by the hypothalamic-pituitary-adrenal (HPA) axis in response to stress?

ANSWER: cortisol

11.9 There Are Sex Differences in How People Respond to Stressors

From an evolutionary perspective, the ability to deal effectively with stressors is important to survival and reproduction. The physiological and behavioral responses that accompany stress help mobilize resources to deal with danger. The physiologist Walter Cannon (1932) coined the term **fight-or-flight response** to describe the physiological preparation of animals to deal with an attack (**FIGURE 11.20**).

Within seconds, the sympathetic nervous system's response to a stressor enables the organism to direct all energy to dealing with the threat at hand. Our ancestors needed that energy for either outrunning a charging predator or standing their ground and fighting it. (Either response causes further stress.) The physical reaction includes increased heart rate, redistribution of the blood supply from skin and viscera (digestive organs) to muscles and brain, deepening of respiration, dilation of the pupils, inhibition of gastric secretions, and an increase in glucose released from the liver. Less critical autonomic activities such as food digestion, which can occur after the stressor is removed, are postponed. (The autonomic nervous system is described in more detail in Chapter 3.) At the same time, activation of the HPA axis helps prepare a prolonged response.

The generalizability of the fight-or-flight response has been questioned by Shelley Taylor and colleagues (Taylor, 2006; Taylor et al., 2002). They argue that because the vast majority of human and nonhuman animal research has been conducted using males (females represent fewer than 1 in 5 of the participants), the results have distorted the scientific understanding of responses to stress.

The exclusion of females from these early studies has many possible explanations. For example, researchers often use rats in heart disease studies that cannot be conducted with humans because the research might increase participants' risk of heart disease, and most rat studies use male rats to avoid complications that may be caused by female hormonal cycles. Similarly, most researchers have avoided using women in their studies of responses to stress because female menstrual patterns might make women more difficult to study. That is, women's responses could be mediated by (influenced by) fluctuations in circulating hormones that vary over the menstrual cycle. The result is a sex inequality in laboratory stress studies. This research bias can blind us to the fact that women and men often respond differently to stressors.

Taylor and colleagues argue that, in very general terms, females respond to stress by protecting and caring for their offspring, as well as by forming alliances with social groups to reduce risks to individuals, including themselves. They coined the phrase **tend-and-befriend response** to describe this pattern (**FIGURE 11.21**). Laboratory research supports the idea that stressed women are more attentive to infant distress than are stressed men (Probst et al., 2017).

Tend-and-befriend responses make sense from an evolutionary perspective. Females typically bear a greater responsibility for the care of offspring, and responses that protect their offspring as well as themselves would be maximally adaptive. When a threat appears, quieting the offspring and hiding may be more effective means of avoiding harm than trying to flee while pregnant or with a clinging infant. Furthermore, females who selectively affiliate with others, especially other females, might acquire additional protection and support.

FIGURE 11.20
Fight-or-Flight Response
This response is an organism's tendency to prepare for dealing with a stressor. Here, the man on the left appears to be the aggressor. If he strikes, the man on the right will need to respond, such as by fighting or fleeing.

fight-or-flight response
The physiological preparedness of animals to deal with danger by either fighting or fleeing.

tend-and-befriend response
Females' tendency to protect and care for their offspring and form social alliances rather than fight or flee in response to threat.

FIGURE 11.21
Tend-and-Befriend Response
This response is females' tendency to care for offspring and gather in social groups. Here, women guide a group of schoolchildren.

The tend-and-befriend stress response is an excellent example of how thinking about psychological mechanisms in view of their evolutionary significance may lead us to question long-standing assumptions about how the mind works. Females who respond to stress by nurturing and protecting their young and by forming alliances with other females apparently have a selective advantage over those who fight or flee, and thus these behaviors would pass to future generations.

Oxytocin, a hormone important for mothers in bonding to newborns (see Chapter 9's discussion of the chemistry of attachment), is produced in the hypothalamus and released into the bloodstream through the pituitary gland. Recent research has shown that oxytocin levels tend to be high for women—but not men—who are socially distressed. Although oxytocin exists naturally in men and women, it seems especially important in women's stress response. Thus, it provides a possible biological basis for the tend-and-befriend response to stress exhibited (mainly) by women (Taylor, 2006). A great deal of research is currently being conducted on the role of oxytocin during stress responses. According to one recent hypothesis, it is possible that the release of oxytocin during social stress encourages women to affiliate with, or befriend, others (Taylor, Saphire-Bernstein, & Seeman, 2010).

oxytocin

A hormone that is important for mothers in bonding to newborns and may encourage affiliation during social stress.

In terms of evolution, why might women be more likely to respond to stress with tend-and-befriend than fight-or-flight?

ANSWER: During the course of human evolution, our female ancestors bore more of the burden than males for child rearing and family maintenance.

How Does Stress Affect Health?

Although stress hormones are essential to normal health, over the long term they negatively affect health. Some stress is good for health, but too much is bad. People who have very stressful jobs—such as air traffic controllers, combat soldiers, and firefighters—tend to have many health problems that presumably are due partly to the effects of chronic stress. There is overwhelming evidence that chronic stress, especially psychosocial stress, is associated with the initiation and progression of a wide variety of diseases, from cancer to AIDS to cardiac disease (Cohen, Janicki-Deverts, & Miller, 2007; McEwen & Gianaros, 2011; Thoits, 2010). In addition, many people cope with stress by engaging in damaging behaviors. For instance, the number one reason that problem drinkers give for abusing alcohol is to cope with distress in their lives. When people are stressed, they drink, smoke cigarettes, eat junk food, use drugs, and so on (Baumeister, Heatherton, & Tice, 1994). As discussed in Section 11.1, most of the major health problems in industrialized societies are partly attributable to unhealthful behaviors, many of which occur when people feel stressed. Let's examine the specific effects of stress on health.

11.10 Stress Disrupts the Immune System

One of Selye's central points was that stress alters the functions of the immune system. The **immune system** is the body's mechanism for dealing with invading microorganisms, such as allergens, bacteria, and viruses. Normally, when these foreign substances enter the body, the immune system launches into action to destroy the invaders. Stress interferes with this natural process. At the time that Selye developed his theory, it was not known that a type of bacteria is the major cause of ulcers (Marshall & Warren, 1984). Although he thought another mechanism was at work, a less active immune system can account for the increased number of stomach ulcers. For

immune system

The body's mechanism for dealing with invading microorganisms, such as allergens, bacteria, and viruses.

example, bacteria can cause stomach ulcers when the immune system is less active due to stress (Levenstein, Ackerman, Kiecolt-Glaser, & Dubois, 1999). The field of psychoneuroimmunology studies the response of the body's immune system to psychological variables. More than 300 studies have demonstrated that short-term stress boosts the immune system, whereas chronic stress weakens it, leaving the body less able to deal with infection (Segerstrom & Miller, 2004).

The immune system is made up of three types of specialized white blood cells known as **lymphocytes:** *B cells, T cells,* and *natural killer cells.* B cells produce *antibodies,* protein molecules that attach themselves to foreign agents and mark them for destruction. Some types of B cells are able to remember specific invaders, making for easier identification in the future. For this reason, you have lifelong immunity to some diseases once you have been exposed to them naturally or through inoculation. The T cells are involved in attacking the intruders directly and also with increasing the strength of the immune response. Note that these so-called helper cells are incapacitated by infection with human immunodeficiency virus (HIV), which eventually leads to the immune disorder AIDS. Natural killer cells are especially potent in killing viruses and also help attack tumors. Brief stressors, including final exams, decrease the ability of white blood cells (Kiecolt-Glaser & Glaser, 1991) and natural killer cells (Kang, Coe, McCarthy, & Ershler, 1997) to fight off infection. The body heals more slowly when people are stressed than when not stressed (Kiecolt-Glaser, Page, Marucha, MacCullum, & Glaser, 1998). The detrimental effects of long-term stress on physical health are due partly to decreased lymphocyte production. This decrease renders the body less capable of warding off foreign substances.

Adding insult to injury, the immune systems of those who tend to be particularly anxious (Maes et al., 2002) or who are already juggling a bunch of other daily hassles (Marshall et al., 1998) tend to be especially vulnerable. Some of the behaviors that stressed-out college students may engage in—such as smoking cigarettes, drinking alcohol, and skipping sleep—further damage the immune system, making them vulnerable to illness or infection (Glaser & Kiecolt-Glaser, 2005).

In a particularly clear demonstration that stress affects the immune system, Sheldon Cohen and colleagues (1991) paid healthy volunteers to have cold viruses swabbed into their noses. Those who reported the highest levels of stress before being exposed to the cold viruses developed worse cold symptoms and higher viral counts than those who reported being less stressed (see "The Methods of Psychology: Cohen's Study of Stress and the Immune System"). (Surprisingly, behaviors such as smoking, maintaining a poor diet, and not exercising had very small effects on the incidence of colds.) Apparently, when the underlying physiological basis of the stress response is activated too often or too intensely, the functioning of the immune system is impaired, and the probability and severity of ill health increase (Herbert & Cohen, 1993; McEwen, 2008).

In a study that looked specifically at the effects of desirable and undesirable events on the immune system, participants kept daily diaries for up to 12 weeks (Stone et al., 1994). In the diaries, they recorded their moods and the events in their lives. They rated the events as desirable or undesirable. Each day, the participants took an antigen, a substance—in this case a protein from a rabbit—that their immune systems recognized as a threat and therefore formed antibodies against. Then the participants provided saliva samples so the researchers could examine their antibody responses. The more desirable events a participant reported, the greater the antibody production. Similarly, the more undesirable events reported, the weaker the antibody production. The effect of a desirable event on antibodies lasted for two days. These and subsequent findings provide substantial evidence that perceived stress influences the immune system. Although short-term stressors appear to boost immune

lymphocytes
Specialized white blood cells that make up the immune system; the three types are B cells, T cells, and natural killer cells.

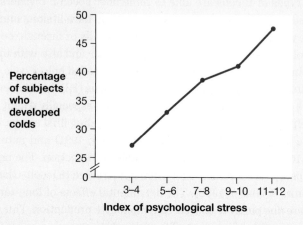
responses, chronic stress, especially when associated with changes in social roles or identity —such as becoming a refugee, losing a job, or getting divorced—has the greatest impact on the immune system (Segerstrom & Miller, 2004).

 How does stress affect the lymphocytes?

ANSWER: Stress reduces the ability of the lymphocytes to fight infection, in part by reducing their production.

11.11 Stress Increases the Risk of Heart Disease

Coronary heart disease is the leading cause of death for adults in the industrialized world. According to a World Health Organization report in 2011, each year more than 7 million people die from heart attacks (**FIGURE 11.22**). Even though the rate of heart disease is lower in women than in men, heart disease is the number one killer of women. Genetics is among the many factors that determine heart disease, but two extremely important determinants are health behaviors (such as bad eating habits, smoking, and lack of exercise) and a small number of personality traits related to the way people respond to stress.

TYPE A/B AND HEART DISEASE One of the earliest tests of the hypothesis that personality affects coronary heart disease was conducted by the Western Collaborative Group, in San Francisco (Rosenman et al., 1964). In 1960, this group of physicians began an 8½-year study. The participants were 3,500 men from northern California who were free of heart disease at the start of the study. The men were screened annually for established risk factors such as high blood pressure, accelerated heart rate, and high cholesterol. Their overall health practices were assessed. Personal details—such as education level, medical and family history, income, and personality traits—were also assessed.

The results indicated that a set of personality traits predicted heart disease. This set of traits is now known as the **Type A behavior pattern.** Type A describes people who are competitive, achievement oriented, aggressive, hostile, impatient, and time-pressed (feeling hurried, restless, unable to relax; **FIGURE 11.23**). Men who exhibited these traits were much more likely to develop coronary heart disease than were those who exhibited the **Type B behavior pattern.** Type B describes noncompetitive, relaxed, easygoing, accommodating people. In fact, this study found that a Type A personality was as strong a predictor of heart disease as was high blood pressure, high cholesterol, or smoking (Rosenman et al., 1975). Although the initial work was done only with men, subsequent research shows that these conclusions apply to women as well (Knox, Weidner, Adelman, Stoney, & Ellison, 2004; Krantz & McCeney, 2002).

FIGURE 11.22
Heart Disease Awareness
To increase people's awareness of this growing problem, countries, cities, and local agencies use public service campaigns such as this one.

HOSTILITY AND HEART DISEASE More recently, research has shown that only certain components of the Type A behavior pattern are related to heart disease. The most toxic factor on the list is hostility. Hot-tempered people who are frequently angry, cynical, and combative are much more likely to die at an early age from heart disease (Eaker, Sullivan, Kelly-Hayes, D'Agostino, & Benjamin, 2004). Indeed, having a high level of hostility while in college predicts greater risk for heart disease later in life (Siegler et al., 2003). There is also considerable evidence that negative emotional states not on the list, especially depression, predict heart disease (Carney & Freedland, 2017). Of course, having a heart condition might *make* people hostile and depressed. Still, having a hostile personality and being depressed also predicted the worsening of heart disease, so causes and effects might be connected in a vicious cycle.

Type A behavior pattern

A pattern of behavior characterized by competitiveness, achievement orientation, aggressiveness, hostility, restlessness, impatience with others, and inability to relax.

Type B behavior pattern

A pattern of behavior characterized by noncompetitive, relaxed, easygoing, and accommodating behavior.

(a)

(b)

(c)

FIGURE 11.23
Personality Traits Predict Heart Disease
(a) People with Type A behavior pattern are ambitious, aggressive, and impatient. They tend to respond more to stressors. Type As who are also hostile are more likely to develop heart disease. **(b)** People with Type B behavior pattern are noncompetitive, easygoing, and relaxed. They are less adversely affected by stressors and so are less likely to develop heart disease. **(c)** People with hostile personalities are hot-tempered, angry, and combative. They have strong physical responses to stressors and are more likely to experience heart disease.

TYPE Z BEHAVIOR

The evidence across multiple studies with different indices of disease and markers for the early development of disease is clear: Hostile, angry people are at greater risk for serious diseases and earlier death than are those with more optimistic and happier personalities. This conclusion appears to be universal. For example, a cross-cultural comparative study of college students replicated the association of anger and impatience with a wide range of health symptoms for students from all ethnic and cultural groups (Nakano & Kitamura, 2001).

In contrast, optimistic people tend to be at lower risk for heart disease (Maruta, Colligan, Malinchoc, & Offord, 2002). Learning to manage both stress and anger improves outcomes for those who have heart disease (Sirois & Burg, 2003). Later in this chapter, you will find many suggestions for managing stress.

PHYSIOLOGICAL EFFECTS OF STRESS ON THE HEART Being stressed or feeling negative emotions can cause heart problems in three ways. First, people often cope with these states through behaviors that are bad for health. Second, some personality traits, such as hostility and depression, have negative effects on people's social networks and on any support they may provide against stress (Jackson, Kubzansky, Cohen, Jacob, & Wright, 2007). Third, negative personality traits and stress can produce direct physiological effects on the heart.

The heart pumps nearly 2,000 gallons of blood each day, on average beating more than 100,000 times. A vast network of blood vessels carries oxygen and nutrients throughout the body. As people age, the arteries that supply the heart and those leading from the heart become narrow due to the buildup of fatty deposits, known as plaque, and become stiff. This narrowing raises the pressure against which the heart has to pump, making the heart work harder and eventually leading to coronary heart disease (**FIGURE 11.24**).

Like aging, stress decreases blood flow by making blood vessels less able to dilate. Even doing a simple stress test, in which the participants only have to push buttons quickly in response to particular colored lights, reduces by 50 percent the ability of blood vessels to expand, and this effect lasts for 45 minutes (Spieker et al., 2002). Blocking cortisol production prevents this dysfunction, suggesting a mechanism by which stress contributes to coronary heart disease and sudden cardiac death (Broadley et al., 2005).

Over time, stress causes wear and tear on the heart, making it more likely to fail. Chronic stress leads to overstimulation of the sympathetic nervous system, causing higher blood pressure, constriction of blood vessels, elevated levels of cortisol, increased release of fatty acids into the bloodstream, and greater buildup of plaque on arteries. In turn, each of these conditions contributes to heart disease. For these reasons, people who tend to be stressed out are more likely to have heart disease than are people who tend to be laid-back.

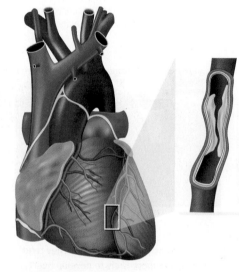

FIGURE 11.24
Heart Disease in Close-Up
Over time, plaque naturally builds up in the blood vessels around the heart, decreasing the heart's ability to function.

Think about a time when you were very angry with someone. How did it feel to be so angry? Your body responded by increasing your heart rate, shutting down digestion, moving more blood to your muscles. In short, your body acted as though you were preparing to fight or run away. You may have seen someone turn red with anger or start to shake. People with hostile personalities frequently experience such physiological responses, and these responses take a toll on the heart. Chronic hostility can lead to the same physical symptoms as chronic stress. Over time, then, being hostile or angry causes wear and tear on the heart, making the heart more likely to fail.

 What personality characteristics place people most at risk for developing heart disease?

11.12 Coping Reduces the Negative Health Effects of Stress

We all experience stressful events. To deal effectively with the stressors in our lives, we use cognitive appraisals that link feelings with thoughts. Cognitive appraisals enable us to think about and manage our feelings more objectively. Richard Lazarus (1993) conceptualized a two-part appraisal process: People use **primary appraisals** to decide whether stimuli are stressful, benign, or irrelevant. If the stimuli are determined to be stressful, people use **secondary appraisals** to evaluate response options and choose coping behaviors. Such cognitive appraisals also affect perceptions of potential stressors and reactions to stressors in the future. In other words, making cognitive appraisals can help people prepare for stressful events or downplay them. Coping that occurs before the onset of a future stressor is called *anticipatory coping*. For example, when parents are planning to divorce, they sometimes rehearse how they will tell their children.

TYPES OF COPING Susan Folkman and Richard Lazarus (1988) have grouped coping strategies into two general categories: emotion-focused coping and problem-focused coping. In **emotion-focused coping**, a person tries to prevent an emotional response to the stressor (**FIGURE 11.25A**). That is, the person adopts strategies, often passive, to numb the pain. Such strategies include avoidance, minimizing the problem, trying to distance oneself from the outcomes of the problem, or engaging in behaviors such as eating or drinking. For example, if you are having difficulty at school, you might avoid the problem by skipping class, minimize the problem by telling yourself school is not all that important, distance yourself from the outcome by saying you can always get a job if college does not work out, or overeat and drink alcohol to dull the pain of the problem. These strategies do not solve the problem or prevent it from recurring in the future.

By contrast, **problem-focused coping** involves taking direct steps to solve the problem: generating alternative solutions, weighing their costs and benefits, and choosing between them (**FIGURE 11.25B**). In this case, if you are having academic trouble, you might think about ways to alleviate the problem, such as arranging for a tutor or asking for an extension for a paper. Given these alternatives, you could consider how likely a tutor is to be helpful, discuss the problem with your professors, and so on. People adopt problem-focused behaviors when they perceive stressors as controllable and are experiencing only moderate levels of stress. Conversely, emotion-focused behaviors may enable people to continue functioning in the face of uncontrollable stressors or high levels of stress.

primary appraisals
Part of the coping process that involves making decisions about whether a stimulus is stressful, benign, or irrelevant.

secondary appraisals
Part of the coping process during which people evaluate their response options and choose coping behaviors.

emotion-focused coping
A type of coping in which people try to prevent having an emotional response to a stressor.

problem-focused coping
A type of coping in which people take direct steps to confront or minimize a stressor.

(a)

(b)

FIGURE 11.25
Emotion-Focused Coping and Problem-Focused Coping
(a) In emotion-focused coping, we avoid the stressor, minimize it, distance ourselves, or try to escape by eating or drinking. (b) In problem-focused coping, we try to address the stressor by solving problems.

The best way to cope with stress depends on personal resources and on the situation. Most people report using both emotion-focused coping and problem-focused coping. Usually, emotion-based strategies are effective only in the short run. For example, if your partner is in a bad mood and is giving you a hard time, just ignoring him or her until the mood passes can be the best option. In contrast, ignoring your partner's drinking problem will not make it go away, and eventually you will need a better coping strategy. Problem-focused coping strategies work, however, only if the person with the problem can do something about the situation.

POSITIVE REAPPRAISAL Susan Folkman and Judith Moskowitz (2000) have demonstrated that, in addition to problem-focused coping, three strategies can help people use positive thoughts to deal with stress. *Positive reappraisal* is a cognitive process in which a person focuses on possible good things in his or her current situation. That is, the person looks for the proverbial silver lining. Another strategy is to make a *downward comparison,* comparing oneself to those who are worse off. This kind of comparison has been shown to help people cope with serious illnesses. Finally, *creation of positive events* is a strategy of giving positive meaning to ordinary events.

If you were diagnosed with diabetes (discussed briefly in Chapter 10), you could use all three strategies. You could focus on how having diabetes will force you to eat a healthy diet and exercise regularly (positive reappraisal). You could recognize that diabetes is not as serious as heart disease (downward comparison). You could take joy in everyday activities (creation of positive events). For example, riding a bike, watching the sunset, or savoring a recent compliment might help you focus on the positive aspects of your life and deal with your negative stress.

INDIVIDUAL DIFFERENCES IN COPING People differ widely in their perceptions of how stressful life events are. Some people seem *stress resistant* because they are so capable of adapting to life changes by viewing events constructively. Suzanne Kobasa (1979) has named this personality trait *hardiness.* According to Kobasa, hardiness has three components: *commitment, challenge,* and *control.*

People high in hardiness are committed to their daily activities, view threats as challenges or as opportunities for growth, and see themselves as being in control of their lives. People low in hardiness typically are alienated, fear or resist change, and view events as being under external control. Numerous studies have found that people high in hardiness report fewer negative responses to stressful events (Maddi, 2013). In a laboratory experiment in which participants were given difficult cognitive tasks, people high in hardiness exhibited physiological changes that indicated active coping (Allred & Smith, 1989). Moreover, a questionnaire completed immediately after the tasks revealed that, in response to the stressor, participants high in hardiness increased the number of positive thoughts they had about themselves.

Generally, some people are more *resilient* than others, better able to cope in the face of adversity (Block & Kremen, 1996). When faced with hardships or difficult circumstances, resilient individuals bend without breaking, allowing them to bounce back quickly when bad things happen. Those who are highest in resilience are able to use their emotional resources flexibly to meet the demands of stressful situations (Bonanno, 2004).

In a study involving brain imaging, participants received one cue if they were about to see a threatening picture and a different cue if they were about to see a neutral picture (Waugh, Wager, Fredrickson, Noll, & Taylor, 2008). Sometimes, however, the threat cue was followed by a neutral picture rather than a threatening picture. In resilient individuals, activity increased in brain regions associated with anxiety only when threatening pictures appeared, regardless of the cue. In individuals low in resilience, heightened brain activity occurred following the cue whether the picture was threatening or not.

Michele Tugade and Barbara Fredrickson (2004) have found that people who are resilient experience positive emotions even when under stress. According to the *broaden-and-build theory,* positive emotions prompt people to consider novel solutions to their problems. Thus, resilient people tend to draw on their positive emotions in dealing with setbacks or negative life experiences (Fredrickson, 2001).

Can resilience be taught? Some researchers believe that people can become more resilient by following concrete steps (Algoe & Fredrickson, 2011). The steps in this process include coming to understand when particular emotions are adaptive, learning specific techniques for regulating both positive and negative emotions, and working to build healthy social and emotional relationships with others.

 Which is better for dealing with stress over the long term, emotion-focused coping or problem-focused coping?

ANSWER: Although emotion-focused coping can help in the short term, problem-focused coping is better for lasting results.

Can a Positive Attitude Keep People Healthy?

Psychologists from the humanist school of thought focused on what is positive in the human experience. Abraham Maslow, Carl Rogers, and Erik Erikson were among the early pioneers in the field of positive psychology, although it was not known by that title then. These early humanist psychologists enjoyed the greatest success in the decades from 1950 to 1970. Other schools of thought, especially cognitive perspectives, then took the leading roles in psychology. Since the 1990s, positive psychology has enjoyed a tremendous comeback as psychologists have begun to use the methods of science to study humanity's positive aspects.

Learning Objectives

- Discuss the goals of positive psychology.
- Describe the health benefits of positive affect, social support, trust, and spirituality.

11.13 Being Positive Has Health Benefits

The positive psychology movement was launched by the clinical psychologist Martin Seligman. He introduced the theme during his 1998 Presidential Address to the American Psychological Association. Seligman and others have encouraged scientific study of qualities such as faith, values, creativity, courage, and hope (Seligman & Csikszentmihalyi, 2000). The earliest emphasis in positive psychology was on understanding what makes people authentically happy. According to positive psychologists, happiness has three components: (1) positive emotion and pleasure, (2) engagement in life, and (3) a meaningful life (Seligman, Steen, Park, & Peterson, 2005). For example, outgoing college students high in authentic happiness might experience pleasure when interacting with other students (component 1), might be actively engaged in class discussions and course readings (component 2), and might find meaning in how the material influences their lives (component 3).

FIGURE 11.26
Well-Being in the United States

These 2009 data are from Gallup's Well-Being Index. Each day, 500 people in the United States were surveyed about their lives, emotional health, work environment, physical health, healthy behaviors, and access to food and shelter. The data reveal a general pattern of people's satisfaction with their lives.

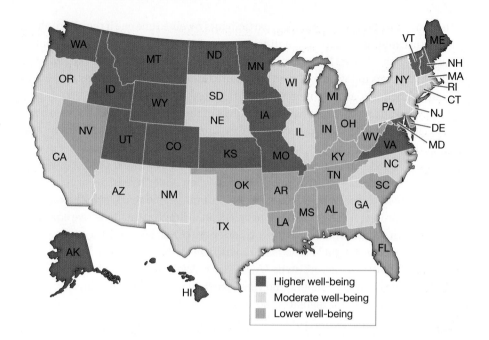

■ Higher well-being
■ Moderate well-being
■ Lower well-being

More recently, Seligman has promoted a shift away from focusing on happiness to a greater emphasis on overall well-being. In his book *Flourish* (2011), Seligman argues that a truly successful life involves not only happiness—that is, pleasure, engagement, and meaning—but also good relationships and a history of accomplishment.

The new positive psychology emphasizes the strengths and virtues that help people thrive. Its primary aim is an understanding of psychological well-being. One way to assess well-being is to ask people about various aspects of their lives, such as emotional health, quality of work environment, physical health, health behaviors, and access to food and shelter. Well-being varies across the United States (**FIGURE 11.26**). Ed Diener (2000) has also found that well-being varies across cultures. According to Diener, the wealthiest countries often have the highest levels of satisfaction. This finding fits well with Maslow's proposal that people need to satisfy basic needs such as food, shelter, and safety before they can address self-esteem needs.

Earlier in this chapter, you read about the health consequences of negative emotions, especially hostility and stress. You may have wondered about the flip side of this relationship: Are positive emotions and well-being associated with good health (**FIGURE 11.27**)?

To address this question, researchers asked more than 1,000 patients in a large medical practice to fill out questionnaires about their emotional traits (Richman et al., 2005). The questionnaires included scales that measured positive emotions (hope and curiosity) and negative emotions (anxiety and anger). Two years after receiving the questionnaires, the researchers used the patients' medical files to determine whether there was a relationship between these emotions and three broad types of diseases: high blood pressure, diabetes, and respiratory tract infections. Higher levels of hope were associated with reduced risk of these medical diseases, and higher levels of curiosity were associated with reduced risk of hypertension and diabetes. These findings support the suggestion that, in general, positive emotions are related to better health.

Of course, it is entirely plausible that poor health can cause both unhappiness and increased mortality. One large study from the United Kingdom found that once researchers controlled for people's initial self-rated health, positivity did not predict lower mortality (Liu et al., 2016). As mentioned earlier, it is possible that unhappy people, such as those who are stressed, engage in a variety of unhealthy behaviors, such as alcohol or drug use or overeating.

FIGURE 11.27
Positivity

Laughing clubs, such as this one in India, believe in laughter as therapy and a way to keep in shape.

A variety of research studies, though, show that having a positive affect, or being generally positive, predicts living longer (Lawrence, Rogers, & Wadsworth, 2015). It is possible that happy people live longer because they have stronger immune systems (Marsland, Pressman, & Cohen, 2007). People with a positive affect show enhanced immune system functioning and greater longevity than their less-positive peers (Dockray & Steptoe, 2010; Xu & Roberts, 2010). For example, they have fewer illnesses after exposure to cold and flu viruses (Cohen, Alper, Doyle, Treanor, & Turner, 2006). Thus, across multiple studies and types of measures, positive emotions are related to considerable health benefits.

 Does being happy cause better health? How do you know?

ANSWER: Not necessarily. Although happiness and living longer are related, correlation does not prove causation.

11.14 Social Support Is Associated with Good Health

Social interaction is beneficial for physical and mental health. People high in well-being tend to have strong social networks and are more socially integrated than those lower in well-being (Smith, Langa, Kabeto, & Ubel, 2005). People with larger social networks—more people they interact with regularly—are less likely to catch colds (Cohen, Doyle, Skoner, Rabin, & Gwaltney, 1997). Apparently, people who have more friends also live longer than those who have fewer friends.

A study that used a random sample of almost 7,000 adults found that people with smaller social networks were more likely to die during the nine-year period between assessments than were people with more friends (Berkman & Syme, 1979). Men with fewer friends were 2.3 times more likely to die than comparable men with more friends. Women with fewer friends were 2.8 times more likely to die than comparable women with more friends. Social support was independent of other factors, such as stated health at the time of the first contact, obesity, smoking, socioeconomic status, and physical activity. In addition, ill people who are socially isolated are likely to die sooner than ill people who are well connected to others (House, Landis, & Umberson, 1988). This effect may be related to the association between chronic loneliness and numerous psychological and health problems (Hawkley & Cacioppo, 2010). Indeed, accumulating evidence indicates that a lack of social connections predicts both physical illness and mortality. One recent meta-analysis concluded that the increased likelihood of death was 26 percent for subjective loneliness, 29 percent for lack of social contacts, and 32 percent for living alone (Holt-Lunstad, Smith, Baker, Harris, & Stephenson, 2015). Either being or feeling alone is associated with poor health outcomes.

Social support helps people cope and maintain good health in two basic ways. First, people with social support experience less stress overall. Consider single parents who have to juggle job and family demands. The lack of a partner places more demands on them, thus increasing their likelihood of feeling stressed. Therefore, social support can take tangible forms, such as providing material help or assisting with daily chores. To be most effective, however, social support needs to imply that people care about the recipient of the support. Knowing that other people care can lessen the negative effects of stress. The **buffering hypothesis** proposes that when others provide emotional support, the recipient is better able to cope with stressful events (Cohen & Wills, 1985). Examples of emotional support include expressions of caring and willingness to listen to another person's problems.

buffering hypothesis
The idea that other people can provide direct emotional support in helping individuals cope with stressful events.

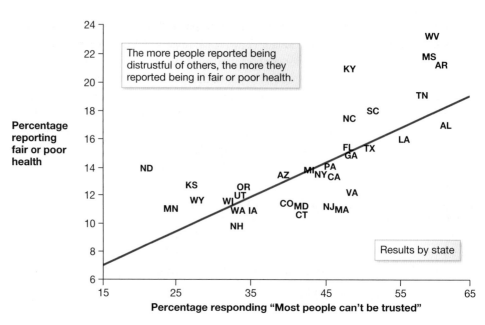

The more people reported being distrustful of others, the more they reported being in fair or poor health.

Percentage reporting fair or poor health

Results by state

Percentage responding "Most people can't be trusted"

FIGURE 11.28

Relationship Between Trust and Health

More than 160,000 people in the United States were asked if they agreed that most people cannot be trusted.

TRUSTING OTHERS IS ASSOCIATED WITH BETTER HEALTH An important feature of healthy relationships is that partners trust one another. Given that social relationships are critical for health, it should be clear that trust is essential for psychological and physical health. In fact, various sources of data suggest that trust is associated with better health and a longer life. This relationship was supported in a study of more than 160,000 people from every state in the United States. Each participant responded to the question *Most people can't be trusted. Do you agree or disagree with this statement?* In each state, as the percentage of respondents who believed most people cannot be trusted increased, so did the percentage who reported that their health was fair to poor (Kawachi, Kennedy, & Glass, 1999; **FIGURE 11.28**).

The hormone oxytocin appears to increase trust. In an experimental study on the relationship between oxytocin and trust, participants played a monetary exchange game (Uvnas-Moberg, 1998). In studies of this kind, participants are given money by the experimenter and then choose how much to give to another person. The experimenter then increases the amount of money received by the second person—say, by four or five times. The person who receives the money then chooses whether, or how much, to give back to the first person. Thus, to make the most money, the first person has to trust that the other person will share some of the larger pool of money.

In this study, oxytocin or a placebo was sprayed into the noses of the participants while they were playing. (Receptors for oxytocin exist throughout the brain but especially along the olfactory passages.) Players who had oxytocin sprayed in their noses gave the other players more money. In other words, they behaved as though they trusted the other players more than did players who had placebos sprayed in their noses. Oxytocin is also released when participants are engaged in trust relationships while playing monetary exchange games (Zak, Kurzban, & Matzner, 2005).

One way that oxytocin might increase both trust and well-being is by increasing social bonds. Recall from Section 11.9 that oxytocin has been implicated as critical to the tend-and-befriend response. This phenomenon describes people's tendency to respond to stress by attending to their social relationships. As discussed in Chapter 9,

FIGURE 11.29

Spirituality and Well-Being

A sense of spirituality can have positive effects on well-being. That sense does not have to be connected with a particular religion.

oxytocin is involved in attachments between mothers and their children. It is also released when people feel empathy toward others, and it is involved in feelings of love (Panksepp, 1992).

SPIRITUALITY In many studies, people who are religious report greater feelings of well-being than people who are not religious. According to David Myers (2000), religious people are better at coping with crises in their lives. Their religious beliefs serve as a buffer against hard knocks. This effect may occur because people achieve and maintain well-being through the social and physical support provided by faith communities. Many religions also support healthy behaviors, such as avoiding alcohol and tobacco.

From their faith, people also derive meaning and purpose in their lives. The positive effects are not associated with any single religion, however. The benefits come from a sense of spirituality that occurs across religions and the social support that comes from interacting with other people who hold similar beliefs (Nilsson, 2014; **FIGURE 11.29**). As Rabbi Harold Kushner notes, people need to feel they are "something more than just a momentary blip in the universe" (quoted in Myers, 2000, p. 64).

 What is the buffering hypothesis?

ANSWER: the idea that people with social support are better able to cope with stress

---

USING PSYCHOLOGY IN YOUR LIFE

11.15 Can Psychology Improve Your Health?

Over the last four decades, psychologists have learned much about the complex relationships among stress, behavior, and health. A hundred years ago, people did not know that smoking is so unhealthy, that junk foods high in both fat and sugar contribute to cardiovascular disease, or that being under prolonged stress can damage the body. We now know that to be healthy, people need to cope with stress, regulate their emotions, and control their daily habits. The following strategies will enhance your health and well-being. Are you willing to adopt them and take control of your life?

- **Eat natural foods.** Food fads come and go, but the basic rules never change: Eat a varied diet that emphasizes natural foods. Complex carbohydrates—such as whole grains, fruits, and vegetables—should be part of that diet, but various animal products, such as poultry or other meats, can also be part of it. Avoid processed foods and fast foods, especially those with added sugars. Avoid foods containing trans-fatty acids and other artificial types of fat that prolong shelf life.

- **Watch portion size.** Eat a varied diet in moderation, and eat only when you are hungry. Eating small snacks between meals may prevent you from becoming too hungry and overeating at your next meal. Remember that many prepared foods are sold in large portions, which encourages overeating. Over time, the extra calories from large portions may contribute to obesity.

- **Drink alcohol in moderation, if at all.** Some research indicates that one glass of wine per day, or similar quantities of other alcohol-containing drinks, may have cardiovascular benefits (Klatsky, 2009). But excessive alcohol consumption can cause serious health problems, including alcoholism, liver problems, some cancers, heart disease, and immune system deficiencies.

- **Keep active.** Exercise is an excellent daily strategy for keeping stress in check. Four times a week or more, engage in at least a half hour of moderate physical activity. Ignore the saying *no pain, no gain,* because discomfort may actually deter you from exercising over the long run. Start with moderate exercise that will not leave you breathless, and gradually increase the intensity. Look for other ways to be active, such as taking the stairs or walking to work or school.

- **Do not smoke.** This recommendation may seem obvious, yet every year many college students begin smoking. This habit eventually produces undesirable physical effects for all smokers, such as a hacking cough, unpleasant odor, bad breath, some cancers, and death at a younger age.

- **Practice safe sex.** Sexually transmitted diseases (STDs) affect millions of people worldwide—including college students. Many new HIV cases are occurring among those under age 25, who are infected through heterosexual or homosexual activity. Despite the devastating consequences of some STDs, many young adults engage in risky sexual practices, such as not using condoms, and they are especially likely to do so when using alcohol or other drugs. Ways to avoid STDs include condom use and abstinence.

- **Learn to relax or meditate.** Daily hassles and stress can cause many health problems. For example, conditions such as insomnia can interfere with the ability to function. By contrast, relaxation exercises can help soothe the body and mind. Seek help from trained counselors who can teach you these methods, such as using biofeedback to measure your physiological activity so you can learn to control it. You might also try a relaxing activity, such as yoga or meditation (for instructions on performing mindfulness meditation, see Figure 4.24).

- **Learn to cope.** Negative events are a part of life. Learn strategies for assessing them realistically and seeing what might be positive about them as well as accepting the difficulties they pose. You can learn strategies for dealing with stressors: seeking advice or assistance, attempting new solutions, distracting yourself with more pleasant thoughts or activities, reinterpreting situations humorously, and so on. Find out which strategies work best for you. The important thing is not to allow stress to consume your life.

- **Build a strong support network.** Friends and family can help you deal with much of life's stress, from daily frustrations to serious catastrophes. Avoid people who encourage you to act in unhealthy ways or are threatened by your efforts to be healthy. Instead, find people who share your values, who understand what you want from life, and who can listen and provide advice, assistance, or simply encouragement. Trusting others is a necessary part of social support, and it is associated with positive health outcomes.

- **Consider your spiritual life.** If you have spiritual beliefs, try incorporating them into your daily living. Benefits can accrue from living a meaningful life and from experiencing the support provided by faith communities.

- **Try some happiness exercises.** Each of the following exercises may enhance your happiness by helping you focus on positive events and more-positive explanations of troubling events (Lyubomirsky, King, & Diener, 2005).

1. In the next week, write a letter of gratitude and deliver it in person to someone who has been kind to you but whom you have never thanked.
2. Once a week, write down three things that went well that day and explain why they went well.
3. Tell a friend about a time when you did your very best, and then think about the strengths you displayed. Review this story every night for the next week.

COMPLEX CARBOHYDRATES

4. Imagine yourself 10 years in the future as your best possible self, as having achieved all your most important goals. Describe in writing what your life is like and how you got there.

5. Keep a journal in which you write about the positive aspects of your life. Reflect on your health, freedom, friends, and so on.

6. Act like a happy person. Sometimes just going through the motions of being happy will create happiness.

Activities such as these are called "shotgun interventions" because they are fast acting, cover a broad range of behaviors, have relatively large effects for such a small investment, and pose little risk. However, the long-term effects of the interventions are unknown. ∎

 Q Can writing thank you notes to other people increase your health?

ANSWER: Yes. Opportunities to express gratitude can produce positive emotions and therefore improve health.

Your Chapter Review

Chapter Summary

What Affects Health?

11.1 Social Context, Biology, and Behavior Combine to Affect Health
The leading causes of death in industrialized societies are influenced by lifestyle choices. Excessive eating, smoking, and lack of exercise contribute to most major causes of death in developed nations. Racial and ethnic groups exhibit health disparities, some of which can be attributed to differences in their health behaviors.

11.2 Obesity Has Many Health Consequences
Excessive eating is most likely to occur when a variety of high-calorie foods are available and larger portions are served. Although obesity is largely influenced by genetic makeup, social influences may also contribute to obesity, as in encouraging excessive intake of foods high in both fat and sugar. In addition to the adverse health consequences of obesity, individuals who are obese face a substantial social stigma.

11.3 Dieting Is Seldom Effective and May Contribute to Eating Disorders
Dieting is relatively ineffective in accomplishing weight loss because body weight is regulated at a set-point. Restrained eating tends to be ineffective because restrained eaters are prone to overeating when they believe they have broken their diets. In extreme cases, individuals may develop an eating disorder—for example, anorexia nervosa, bulimia nervosa, or binge-eating disorder—as a consequence of their efforts to control their weight and body shape.

11.4 Smoking Is a Leading Cause of Death
Smoking continues to be a major health concern. Individuals typically begin smoking in adolescence as a consequence of social influences

or in an effort to exhibit the positive qualities sometimes associated with smokers, such as being tough and independent. Methods for quitting smoking include nicotine replacement therapy (e-cigarettes, nicotine gum, or the patch,), prescription medications for use during therapy, and behavioral modification techniques. Even in the most effective programs, only 10–30 percent of smokers are able to quit long-term.

11.5 Exercise Has Numerous Benefits
Exercise is one of the best things people can do for their health. Regular physical activity improves memory and cognition, strengthens the heart and lungs, and enhances mental and emotional states.

11.6 Think like a Psychologist: Why Are People Afraid of Flying but Not of Driving (or Smoking)?
People generally fear the wrong things. They fear airplane crashes, being victims of terrorism, and catching rare diseases. The vast majority of deaths are due to cancer and heart disease, both of which are heavily influenced by lifestyle factors. Due to the availability heuristic, when people think about death, the thoughts that come most easily to mind are those most reported by media. However, these events tend to be so rare that they do not pose threats to most people.

What Is Stress?

11.7 Stress Is a Response to Life Events
Stress is a response that usually involves an unpleasant state. Stressors are situations that are perceived as threatening or demanding and therefore produce stress. They include major life changes as well as daily hassles.

11.8 Stress Has Physiological Components

The hypothalamic-pituitary-adrenal (HPA) axis is a complex series of biological events that responds to stress over longer periods. The sympathetic nervous system responds to stress by releasing epinephrine and norepinephrine into the bloodstream for immediate action. The hypothalamus sends a signal to the pituitary gland, which causes the adrenal gland to release cortisol. Hans Selye's general adaptation syndrome identifies three stages of physiological coping: alarm, resistance, and exhaustion.

11.9 There Are Sex Differences in How People Respond to Stressors

Research suggests that when confronted by a stressor, males are more likely to exhibit the fight-or-flight response, whereas females are more likely to exhibit the tend-and-befriend response.

How Does Stress Affect Health?

11.10 Stress Disrupts the Immune System

Stress alters the functions of the immune system. Specifically, stress decreases the production of lymphocytes: B cells, T cells, and natural killer cells. Fewer lymphocytes mean the body is less able to fight off infection and illness.

11.11 Stress Increases the Risk of Heart Disease

Individuals who are hostile, are depressed, or exhibit a Type A behavior pattern (competitive, achievement oriented, aggressive, and impatient) are more susceptible to heart disease than people who exhibit a Type B behavior pattern (easygoing and accommodating). Presumably, the personality factors increase the frequency of negative physiological responses that adversely affect the heart.

11.12 Coping Reduces the Negative Health Effects of Stress

Cognitive appraisals of potential stressors and the coping strategies that are used can alleviate the experience of stress or minimize its harmful effects. Emotion-focused coping strategies are attempts to prevent an emotional response by avoiding the stressor, minimizing the problem, or engaging in behaviors to try to forget, such as overeating or drinking. Problem-focused coping strategies involve taking direct steps to confront or minimize a stressor—for example, establishing alternatives and engaging in behaviors to solve the problem.

Can a Positive Attitude Keep People Healthy?

11.13 Being Positive Has Health Benefits

Positive psychology is concerned with the scientific study of the strengths and virtues that contribute to psychological well-being. A number of studies have shown that people who are positive are generally healthier and live longer than their more negative counterparts.

11.14 Social Support Is Associated with Good Health

Social support and being socially integrated in a group are also protective health factors, because concerned others provide material and emotional support. Trust is another factor associated with better health and longer life. The hormone oxytocin has been implicated in the experience of trust. Spirituality contributes to better health. Well-being is increased for spiritual people likely due to the support received from faith communities, the health behaviors that are promoted by religions, and the sense of meaning that can be derived from religious beliefs.

11.15 Using Psychology in Your Life: Can Psychology Improve Your Health?

People can follow many strategies for living a healthy life, primarily by avoiding things science has shown to be bad for us (e.g., high-sugar foods, excessive alcohol, smoking, unsafe sex) and engaging in behaviors known to benefit health (e.g., exercise, relaxing, meditating). Happiness exercises have been shown to help people cope with the stress in their lives.

Key Terms

anorexia nervosa, p. 439

binge-eating disorder, p. 440

biopsychosocial model, p. 430

body mass index (BMI), p. 432

buffering hypothesis, p. 461

bulimia nervosa, p. 440

coping response, p. 447

emotion-focused coping, p. 457

fight-or-flight response, p. 451

general adaptation syndrome, p. 450

health psychology, p. 430

hypothalamic-pituitary-adrenal (HPA) axis, p. 449

immune system, p. 452

lymphocytes, p. 453

oxytocin, p. 452

primary appraisals, p. 457

problem-focused coping, p. 457

secondary appraisals, p. 457

stress, p. 447

stressor, p. 447

tend-and-befriend response, p. 451

Type A behavior pattern, p. 455

Type B behavior pattern, p. 455

well-being, p. 430

What Are Health Psychologists?

What do you think was the most common New Year's resolution in 2017? As reported by NBC News, it was to get healthy. Perhaps at some time you too have pledged to exercise more, lose weight, or eat more healthfully. If you are like most people, however, your good intentions may not have been enough. Why are so few people able to change their bad habits in regard to health?

As you have learned in this chapter, a purely medical approach to health and disease can miss important social and psychological influences on health behaviors. Consider an initiative by the American Medical Association (AMA). In 2013, the AMA declared obesity a disease, emphasizing the biological aspects underlying weight gain. Framing obesity only in physiological terms, however, ignored the social and psychological factors behind obesity. It also missed the social and psychological *consequences* of that message. Individuals who received disease-based public health messages actually became less concerned about their weight, less likely to make healthy food choices, and less interested in dieting to control weight (Hoyt, Burnette, & Auster-Gussman, 2014). These results were, of course, the opposite of the intended goal.

So to help people improve their health and prevent disease, professionals need to promote an understanding of social and psychological factors that contribute to unhealthful behaviors. One group of such professionals is health psychologists.

Health psychologists may work independently or as part of multidisciplinary teams. For example, in private practice they may teach individuals effective ways to handle stress or to deal with a chronic health condition. Alternatively, in academic, clinical, or hospital settings, they may collaborate with physicians, nurses, and dieticians in encouraging patients to take prescribed medications or to follow diet recommendations.

Health psychologists can also address challenges to public health. Agencies employ individuals trained in health psychology to study health-related issues, such as obesity rates or outbreaks of contagious diseases. At colleges and universities, health psychologists conduct research and develop interventions to promote healthful behaviors.

Health psychologists typically complete a master's or doctoral program in psychology. Those interested in health psychology who don't pursue graduate degrees may work as health educators or research assistants, generally under the supervision of licensed psychologists.

The bottom line: Health psychologists work at the intersection of psychology and medicine. They are increasingly employed in a range of settings, including academic centers, hospitals and clinics, private practice, and public health organizations.

Want to earn a better grade on your test?
Go to **INQUIZITIVE** to learn and review this chapter's content, with personalized feedback along the way. Practice Tests and accompanying answer keys can be found at the back of the book on page PT-1.

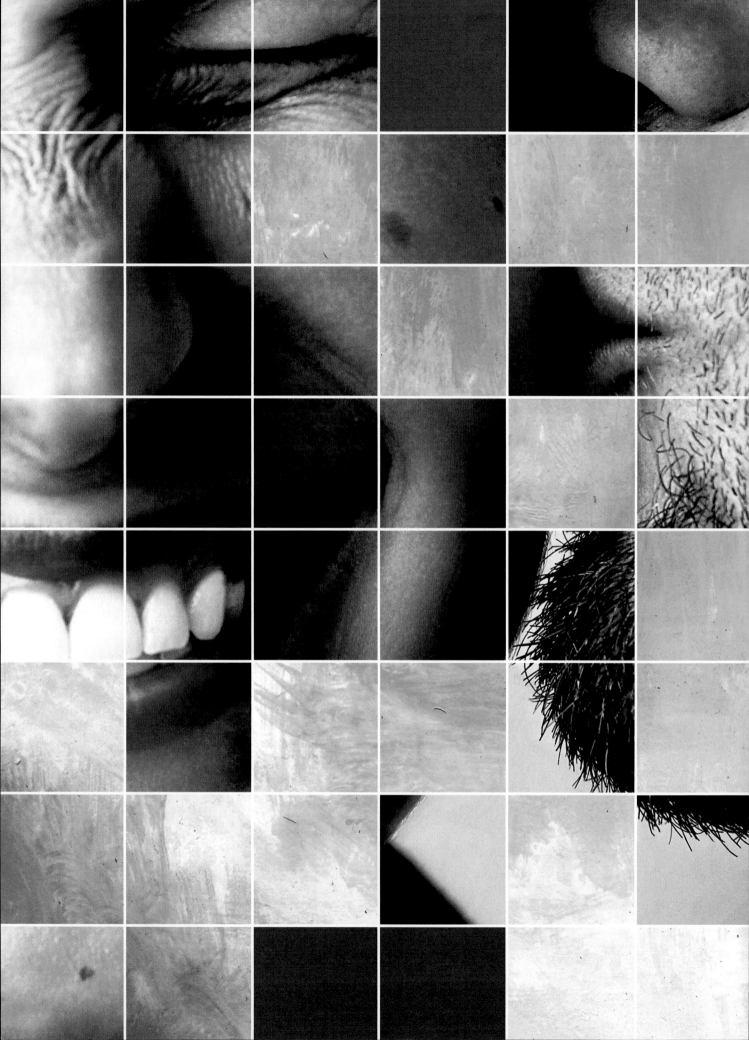

12 Social Psychology

Big Questions

- How Does Group Membership Affect People? 470

- When Do People Harm or Help Others? 482

- How Do Attitudes Guide Behavior? 490

- How Do People Think About Others? 496

- What Determines the Quality of Relationships? 503

ONE DAY WHILE WALKING DOWN THE STREET you notice two people looking up at the sky. Suddenly other people also start doing so. You wonder why and find yourself also looking up to see what has captured everyone's attention. Now there are many of you looking up at, well, apparently nothing. Why did everyone on the street feel compelled to look up? As a highly social species, humans are readily influenced by the actions of others.

The subfield of social psychology is concerned with how people influence other people's thoughts, feelings, and actions. Humans are social animals who live in a highly complex world. Because almost every human activity has a social dimension, research in social psychology covers expansive and varied territory: how people perceive and understand others, how people function in groups, why people hurt or help others, why people stigmatize and discriminate against certain others, why people fall in love. In this chapter, you will learn the basic principles of how people interact with each other. For social psychologists, the big questions are: How does group membership affect people? When do people harm or help others? How do attitudes guide behavior? How do people think about others? What determines the quality of relationships?

Learning Objectives

- Describe the advantages and disadvantages of groups.

- Explain factors that determine ingroup and outgroup formation.

- Describe the effects of group membership on social identity and on brain activity.

- Define social facilitation, deindividuation, group polarization, groupthink, and social loafing.

- Differentiate between conformity, compliance, and obedience.

outgroup homogeneity effect

The tendency to view outgroup members as less varied than ingroup members.

social identity theory

The idea that ingroups consist of individuals who perceive themselves to be members of the same social category and experience pride through their group membership.

ingroup favoritism

The tendency for people to evaluate favorably and privilege members of the ingroup more than members of the outgroup.

How Does Group Membership Affect People?

The genes of any species survive by being passed on from generation to generation. For that to happen, the animals that carry those genes must survive long enough to reproduce. To survive and reproduce, animals need food, water, shelter, and mates. These resources have been in limited supply throughout humans' evolutionary history. As a result, our ancestors competed for the limited resources. Those who won the competition passed on their genes. Contemporary humans have inherited the genes that are coded for the successful behaviors, and one of the successful strategies that humans evolved was to live in social groups. Since over the course of human evolution being kicked out of the group would have had dire consequences, people are motivated to maintain good relations with members of their groups.

But group membership brings many challenges, such as figuring out how to be a good group member. The *social brain hypothesis* (Dunbar, 1998; 2014) places such challenges in the context of brain size. The largest biological class that humans belong to is the order *primates,* which includes great apes and monkeys. According to this theory, primates have large brains—in particular, large prefrontal cortices—because they live in dynamic and complex social groups that change over time (**FIGURE 12.1**). Being a good group member requires the capacity to understand complex and subtle social rules, recognize when actions might offend others, and control desires to engage in behaviors that might violate group norms. Various brain regions involved in processing social information and controlling behavior work together to support human sociality (Heatherton, 2011).

12.1 People Favor Their Own Groups

Banding together in a group provides numerous advantages, such as security from predators and assistance in hunting and gathering food (Buss & Kenrick, 1998). Group living also provides mating opportunities. The downside of grouping is that other groups may compete for the same limited resources. Alternatively, other groups may be able to supply needed resources, as in trade, or cooperate in attaining the resources. Thus, over the course of human evolution it was critical for groups to identify other groups as friends (suppliers) or foes (competitors). Once such a categorization was made, it was equally critical to react accordingly, either by working together or by exhibiting aggression.

Social groups, or coalitions, are prevalent in some primate species, such as chimpanzees, and in other social mammals, such as dolphins. Humans automatically and pervasively form groups. Because human ancestors banded together for survival, people are powerfully connected to the groups they belong to: sororities and fraternities, sports teams, and so on. People cheer on their own groups, fight for them, and sometimes are even willing to die for them (Swann et al., 2014). Those groups to which particular people belong are *ingroups;* those to which they do not belong are *outgroups* (**FIGURE 12.2**). Beginning in infancy, humans readily differentiate between ingroups and outgroups (Guassi Moreira, Van Bavel, & Telzer, 2017).

FORMATION OF INGROUPS AND OUTGROUPS Two conditions appear to be critical for group formation: reciprocity and transitivity (Gray et al., 2014). *Reciprocity* means that if Person A helps (or harms) Person B, then Person B will help (or harm) Person A. In other words, if you scratch my back, I will scratch yours. *Transitivity* means that people generally share their friends' opinions of other people. If Person

A and Person B are friends, then if Person A likes Person C and dislikes Person D, then Person B will also tend to like Person C and dislike Person D.

Gray and colleagues (2014) developed a computer program in which simulated individuals interacted in a game that involved simple rules of reciprocity and transitivity. The rules were so simple that the program consisted of only 80 lines of code, whereas most programs include thousands or millions of lines. After 10,000 rounds of interaction, the simulated individuals formed into stable groups and showed many of the characteristics that are true of human groups. This research shows that ingroups and outgroups can be formed based on minimal rules of social interaction and thus may help explain the pervasive nature of groups throughout human history.

Once people categorize others as ingroup or outgroup members, they treat the others accordingly. For instance, due to the **outgroup homogeneity effect,** people tend to view outgroup members as less varied than ingroup members. University of Missouri students may think University of Kansas students are all alike, but when they think about Missouri students, they cannot help but notice the wide diversity of student types. Of course, for Kansas's students, the reverse is true about Missouri's students and themselves. Overall, people show a positivity bias for ingroup members, such as rating their smiles as indicating greater happiness than similar smiles by outgroup members (Lazerus, Stolier, Freeman, Ingbretsen, & Cikara, 2016).

SOCIAL IDENTITY THEORY Group memberships are an important part of social identities, and they contribute to each group member's overall sense of self-esteem (Hogg, 2012). According to **social identity theory** (Tajfel, 1982; Tajfel & Turner, 1979), ingroups consist of individuals who perceive themselves to be members of the same social category. Inherent in social identity theory is the idea that people value the groups with which they identify and in doing so also experience pride through their group membership. Whether it is pride in your school, your ethnicity, your country, and so on, defining yourself by that group status is part of your social identity.

As people define themselves as members of groups, they begin to conceive of themselves in terms of how other group members typically behave toward both ingroup and outgroup members (Hogg, 2016). One consequence of categorizing people as ingroup or outgroup members is **ingroup favoritism.** That is, people are more likely to distribute resources to ingroup members than to outgroup members. The simulated individuals in the study mentioned earlier showed this kind of behavior (Gray et al., 2014). In addition, people are more willing to do favors for ingroup members or to forgive their mistakes or errors. The power of group membership is so strong that people exhibit ingroup favoritism even if the groups are determined by arbitrary processes.

Henri Tajfel and John Turner (1979) randomly assigned volunteers to two groups, using meaningless criteria such as flipping a coin. This procedure is known as the *minimal group paradigm.* Participants were then given a task in which they divided up money. Not surprisingly, they gave more money to their ingroup members, but they also tried to prevent the outgroup members from receiving any money. These effects occurred even when the participants were told that the basis of group membership was arbitrary and that giving money to the outgroup would not affect how much money their own group obtained. Why do people favor members of their own groups? We can

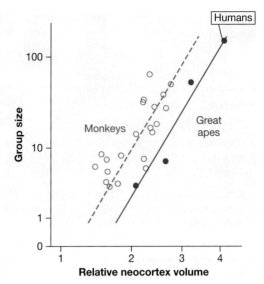

FIGURE 12.1
Social Brain Hypothesis
Most of the cerebral cortex consists of its outer layer, known as the neocortex. According to the social brain hypothesis, the size of a primate species' standard social group is related to the volume of that species' neocortex. Here, each open circle represents a species within the family monkeys, and each solid circle represents a species within the family great apes. In terms of neocortex size, great apes may lie on a separate line from monkeys because they need more cognitive resources to support group living. Humans are at the pinnacle of the great apes in terms of neocortex and average group size.

FIGURE 12.2
Ingroups and Outgroups
In this photo from the 2014 World Cup in soccer, it is easy to tell Brazilian supporters (in yellow) from Chilean supporters (in red).

FIGURE 12.3
Women and Ingroup Bias
Female friends tend to be comfortable expressing affection for each other.

speculate that those who work together to keep resources within their group and deny resources to outgroup members have a selective advantage over those who are willing to share with the outgroup. This advantage would become especially important when groups are competing for scarce resources.

In addition, women show a much greater automatic ingroup bias toward other women than men do toward other men (Rudman & Goodwin, 2004). Although men generally favor their ingroups, they fail to do so when the category is sex, at least within Western cultures. Rudman and Goodwin speculate that men and women depend on women for nurturing and that both are threatened by male violence. Moreover, women can freely express their affection for their female friends (**FIGURE 12.3**). Men may be less comfortable doing so for their male friends, perhaps because it might threaten their sexual identities (Morman & Floyd, 1998).

BRAIN ACTIVITY ASSOCIATED WITH GROUP MEMBERSHIP Being a good group member requires recognizing and following the group's social rules. When members violate these rules, they risk exclusion from the group. As noted in Chapter 10, group exclusion was likely a death sentence in the ancestral environment. People therefore need to be able to understand what other group members are thinking, especially how others are thinking about them. The middle region of the prefrontal cortex, called the medial prefrontal cortex, is especially important for thinking about other people—thinking about them generally or specifically, whether they are in ingroups or outgroups (Mitchell, Heatherton, & Macrae, 2002). Activity in this region is also associated with ingroup bias that emerges after assignment through the minimal group paradigm (Volz, Kessler, & von Cramon, 2009). However, when people observe others in pain, a different set of brain regions becomes activated (recall the idea of mirror neurons, from Chapter 6, which may enable people to empathize with others). These "pain regions" are more active when people see an ingroup member being harmed than when they see the same harm inflicted on an outgroup member (Xu, Zuo, Wang, & Han, 2009). Similarly, sports fans show activity in brain reward regions when a rival team performs poorly (Cikara, Botvinick, & Fiske, 2011). In general, various brain regions are differentially active when we consider ingroup versus outgroup members (Cikara & Van Bavel, 2014).

The medial prefrontal cortex is less active when people consider members of outgroups, at least members of extreme outgroups such as homeless persons or drug addicts (Harris & Fiske, 2006). One explanation for this reduction in activity is that people *dehumanize* some outgroups (Harris & Fiske, 2011). People more readily see human minds in ingroups than in outgroups (Hackel, Looser, & Van Bavel, 2014).

In developed nations, people tend to pass the homeless as if they were mere obstacles, and they generally do not feel much sympathy regarding people's plights in developing nations (Haslam & Loughnan, 2014). Indeed, such dehumanization of outgroups has been used as a propaganda tool to justify inhumane acts. In World War II-era Germany, the Nazis classified Jews as vermin. In Rwanda in 1994, the Hutu majority described the Tutsi minority as cockroaches. These descriptions were major factors in the subsequent genocides against the Jews and the Tutsi.

Q Although Tarika always agrees to help members of her sorority when asked, she seldom agrees to help those in other sororities. What is Tarika's behavior an example of?

ANSWER: ingroup favoritism

12.2 Groups Influence Individual Behavior

Given the importance of groups, it is not surprising that people's thoughts, emotions, and actions are strongly influenced by their desire to be good group members. One way people try to fit in is by presenting themselves positively. That is, they display their best behavior and try not to offend others.

Most people are easily influenced by others, conform to group norms, and obey commands made by authorities. In fact, the desire to fit in with the group and avoid being ostracized is so great that under some circumstances people willingly engage in behaviors they otherwise would condemn. As noted throughout this chapter, the power of the social situation is much greater than most people believe—and this truth is perhaps the single most important lesson from social psychology. Let's examine some of the ways that people are influenced by the presence of others.

SOCIAL FACILITATION The first social psychology experiment was conducted in 1897. Through that experiment, Norman Triplett showed that bicyclists pedal faster when they ride with other people than when they ride alone. They do so because of **social facilitation.** That is, the presence of others generally enhances performance. Social facilitation also occurs in other animals, including horses, dogs, rats, birds, fish, and even cockroaches.

Robert Zajonc (1965) proposed a model of social facilitation that involves three basic steps (**FIGURE 12.4**). According to Zajonc, all animals are genetically predisposed to become aroused by the presence of others of their own species. Why? Others are associated with most of life's rewards and punishments. Zajonc then invokes Clark Hull's well-known learning principle: Arousal leads animals to emit a dominant response—that is, the response most likely to be performed in the situation. In front of food, for example, the dominant response is to eat.

Zajonc's model predicts that social facilitation can either enhance or impair performance. The change depends on whether the response that is required in a situation is the individual's dominant response. If the required response is easy or well learned (such as an experienced cyclist riding a bike), so that the dominant response is good performance, the presence of others will enhance performance. If the required response is novel or less well learned (such as riding a unicycle for the first time), so that the dominant response is poor performance, the presence of others will further impair performance. These effects help explain why crowds of spectators distract professional golfers less than they distract novice golfers. The professionals practice so often that hitting a good shot is their dominant response. Therefore, the professionals may be even more likely to hit well in the presence of spectators. When you need to make a public presentation, try to practice your presentation repeatedly so that it becomes easy for you. You want your best work to be your dominant response, so that you do well even under pressure.

DEINDIVIDUATION In a classic study, the psychologists Philip Zimbardo and Chris Haney showed how quickly apparently normal students could be transformed into the social roles they were playing (Haney, Banks, & Zimbardo, 1973; **FIGURE 12.5A**). The researchers had male undergraduates at Stanford University play the roles of prisoners and guards in a mock prison. The students, who had all been screened and found to be psychologically stable, were randomly assigned to their roles. What the authors reported happening was unexpected and shocking.

Within days, some of the "guards" became brutal and sadistic. They constantly harassed the "prisoners," forcing them to engage in meaningless and tedious tasks and exercises. The prisoners became helpless to resist. Although the Stanford prison

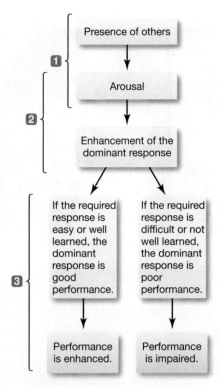

FIGURE 12.4
Zajonc's Model of Social Facilitation
According to this model, the mere presence of others leads to increased arousal. The arousal favors the dominant response (the response most likely to be performed in the situation). If the required response is easy or well learned, performance is enhanced. If the required response is novel or not well learned, performance suffers.

social facilitation
The idea that the presence of others generally enhances performance.

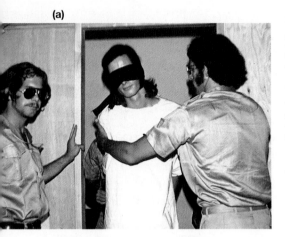

(a)

(b)

FIGURE 12.5

Effect of Groups in the Stanford Prison Study and at Abu Ghraib

(a) In the Stanford prison study, student-guards took on their roles with such vigor that the study was ended early because of the concerns for the well-being of the "guards" and the "prisoners." **(b)** Soldier-guards at Abu Ghraib harassed, threatened, and tortured prisoners.

deindividuation

A state of reduced individuality, reduced self-awareness, and reduced attention to personal standards; this phenomenon may occur when people are part of a group.

group polarization

The process by which initial attitudes of groups become more extreme over time.

study was scheduled to last two weeks, the researchers stopped it after only six days. The study lacked many of the features of a true experiment, and it is likely that the participants experienced reactivity for how they were supposed to behave (recall the Hawthorne effect from Chapter 2). Moreover, recent critiques of the Stanford prison study have noted that there was considerable variability in the behavior of the guards (Bartels, 2015; Bartels, Milovich, & Moussier, 2016). Nonetheless, the results demonstrate what some people are willing to do when put in a situation with defined social roles.

Because of a real-life situation that has been likened to the Stanford study, the Abu Ghraib prison in Iraq, now named the Baghdad Central Prison, will always be remembered as the site of horrible abuses of power. During 2003, the first year of the Iraq War, American soldiers brutalized Iraqi detainees at Abu Ghraib. The soldiers raped prisoners, threatened them with dogs, beat them, placed them in humiliating positions, and forced them to perform or simulate oral sex and masturbation (**FIGURE 12.5B**).

When the news media began to reveal the abuse at Abu Ghraib, U.S. military and government officials were quick to claim that these incidents were isolated and carried out by a small group of wayward soldiers. They emphasized that even amid the horrors of war, soldiers are expected to behave in a civilized and professional manner. The idea that only a few troubled individuals were responsible for the abuses is strangely comforting, but is it true?

The soldiers at Abu Ghraib, like the students in the Stanford study, were probably normal people who were caught up in overwhelming situations where being part of the group influenced their actions in extreme ways. Some people might be more prone to social influence than others, but most people can sometimes lose their individuality when they become part of a group. **Deindividuation** occurs when people are not self-aware and therefore are not paying attention to their personal standards. When self-awareness disappears, so do restraints. Deindividuated people often do things they would not do if they were alone or self-aware. A good example is crowd behavior. Most of us like to think we would try to help a person who was threatening suicide. But people in crowds often fail to intercede in such situations. Disturbingly, they also sometimes egg the person on, yelling "Jump! Jump!" to someone teetering on a ledge.

People are especially likely to become deindividuated when they are aroused and anonymous and when responsibility is diffused. Rioting by fans, looting following disasters, and other mob behaviors are the products of deindividuation. Not all deindividuated behavior is so serious, of course. Gamblers in crowded casinos, fans doing the wave, and people dancing the funky chicken while inebriated at a wedding are most likely in deindividuated states. Accordingly, in these situations, people act in ways they would avoid if they were self-aware (**FIGURE 12.6**).

GROUP DECISION MAKING Social psychologists have shown that being in a group influences decision making in complex ways. For instance, James Stoner (1963) found that groups often make riskier decisions than individuals do. Stoner identified this phenomenon as the *risky-shift effect*. It accounts for why teenagers in a group may try something dangerous that none of them would have tried alone. But sometimes groups become more cautious. Subsequent research has demonstrated that the initial attitudes of group members determine if the group becomes riskier or more cautious. If most of the group members are somewhat cautious, then the group becomes even more cautious. This process is known as **group polarization** (Myers & Lamm, 1976). For example, when a jury discusses a case, the discussion tends to make individual jurors believe more strongly in their initial opinions about a defendant's guilt or innocence.

When groups make decisions, they usually choose the course of action that was initially favored by the majority of individuals in the group. Through mutual persuasion, the decision-making individuals come to agreement.

Sometimes group members are particularly concerned with preserving the group and maintaining its cohesiveness. Therefore, for the sake of cordiality, the group may end up making a bad decision. In 1972, the social psychologist Irving Janis coined the term **groupthink** to describe this extreme form of group polarization. Consider some contemporary examples of groupthink: In 1998, when allegations arose of President Bill Clinton's affair with the White House intern Monica Lewinsky, Clinton and his advisers responded in devious ways that ultimately led to Clinton's impeachment. The second Bush administration went to war with Iraq in 2003 over weapons of mass destruction that turned out not to exist. The leadership of Penn State football tried to protect the reputation of a beloved coach, Joe Paterno, rather than protecting young children from sexual abuse by an assistant coach, Jerry Sandusky, whose crimes may have extended from the 1970s until his indictment in 2011.

Groupthink typically occurs when a group is under intense pressure, is facing external threats, and is biased in a particular direction. The group does not carefully process all the information available to it, dissent is discouraged, and group members assure each other they are doing the right thing. To prevent groupthink, leaders must refrain from expressing their opinions too strongly at the beginning of discussions. The group should be encouraged to consider alternative ideas, either by having someone play devil's advocate or by purposefully examining outside opinions. Carefully going through alternatives and weighing the pros and cons of each can help people avoid groupthink.

Of course, a group can make a bad decision even without falling victim to groupthink. Other factors, such as political values, can bias a group's decision making. The main point behind the concept of groupthink is that group members sometimes go along with bad decisions to protect group harmony.

SOCIAL LOAFING In some cases, people do not work as hard when in a group as when working alone. This effect is called **social loafing.** It occurs when people's efforts are pooled so that individuals do not feel personally responsible for the group's output. In a classic study, six blindfolded people wearing headphones were told to shout as loudly as they could. Some were told they were shouting alone. Others were told they were shouting with other people. Participants did not shout as loudly when they believed that others were shouting as well (Latané, Williams, & Harkins, 1979).

When people know that their individual efforts can be monitored, they do not engage in social loafing. Thus, if a group is working on a project, each person must feel personally responsible for some component of the project for everyone to exert maximum effort (Williams, Harkins, & Latané, 1981).

 How does social facilitation differ from social loafing?

FIGURE 12.6
Deindividuation
Here, deindividuated fans are doing the "wave" during a University of Oregon game.

groupthink

The tendency of a group to make a bad decision as a result of preserving the group and maintaining its cohesiveness; especially likely when the group is under intense pressure, is facing external threats, and is biased in a particular direction.

social loafing

The tendency for people to work less hard in a group than when working alone.

ANSWER: In social facilitation, the presence of others enhances performance. In social loafing, the presence of others leads to lower performance.

12.3 People Conform to and Comply with Others

Another powerful form of social influence is **conformity.** Why do people conform, altering their behaviors or opinions to match those of others or to match what is expected of them? Social psychologists have identified two primary reasons that

conformity

The altering of one's behaviors and opinions to match those of other people or to match other people's expectations.

FIGURE 12.7
Social Norms
One social norm in industrialized societies is to stand facing the elevator door and facing away from other passengers. Violating this norm may make the other passengers very uncomfortable.

people conform: **Normative influence** occurs when people go along with the crowd to fit in with the group and to avoid looking foolish. **Informational influence** occurs when people assume that the behavior of the crowd represents the correct way to respond. Suppose you are in a train station. You turn a corner and see a mass of people running for the exit. You might join them if you suspect they are exiting for a good reason. In situations such as this potential emergency, other people's actions provide information about the right thing to do.

Normative influence relies on the societal need for rules. For example, imagine the problems you would cause if you woke up one morning and decided that from then on you would drive on the wrong side of the road. Expected standards of conduct are called **social norms.** These norms influence behavior in multiple ways. For example, norms indicate which behavior is appropriate in a given situation and also how people will respond to those who violate norms. Standing in line is a social norm, and people who violate that norm by cutting in line are often reprimanded and directed to the back of the line. Normative influence works because people feel embarrassed when they violate social norms and they worry about what others think of them. The next time you enter an elevator, try standing with your back to the elevator door and facing people. You may find it quite difficult to defy this simple social norm (**FIGURE 12.7**).

Muzafer Sherif (1936) became one of the first researchers to demonstrate the power of conformity in social judgment. Sherif's studies relied on the *autokinetic effect*. Through this perceptual phenomenon, a stationary point of light appears to move when viewed in a totally dark environment. This effect occurs because people have no frame of reference and therefore cannot correct for small eye movements. Sherif asked participants who were alone in a room to estimate how far the light moved. Individual differences were considerable: Some saw the light move only an inch or two, whereas others saw it move 8 inches or more.

In the second part of the study, Sherif put two or more participants in the room and had them call out their estimates. Although there were initial differences, participants quickly revised their estimates until they agreed. They relied on the information provided by others to base their estimates. This result is an example of informational influence. In ambiguous situations, people often compare their reactions with the reactions of others to judge the correct course of action.

Solomon Asch (1955) speculated that Sherif's results probably occurred because the autokinetic effect is a subjective visual illusion. If perceptions were objective, Asch thought, participants would not conform. To test his hypothesis, Asch assembled male participants for a study of visual acuity. In the 18 trials, the participants looked at a reference line and three comparison lines. They decided which of the three comparison lines matched the reference line and said their answers aloud. Normally, people are able to perform this easy task with a high level of accuracy. But in these studies, Asch included a naive participant with a group of five confederates who pretended to be participants but were actually working for the experimenter. The real participant always went sixth, giving his answer after the five confederates gave theirs.

On 12 of the 18 trials, the confederates deliberately gave the same wrong answer. After hearing five wrong answers, the participant then had to state his answer. Because the answer was obvious, Asch speculated that the participant would give the correct answer. About one-third of the time, however, the participant went along with the confederates. More surprisingly, in repeated trials, three out of four people conformed to the incorrect response at least once. Why did most people conform? It was not because they knew others were providing the right answer. Instead, people conformed because they did not want to look foolish by going against the group (see

normative influence
The tendency for people to conform in order to fit in with the group.

informational influence
The tendency for people to conform when they assume that the behavior of others represents the correct way to respond.

social norms
Expected standards of conduct, which influence behavior.

The Methods of Psychology
Asch's Study on Conformity to Social Norms

HYPOTHESIS: Conformity would not take place if there were objective perceptions.

RESEARCH METHOD:

1 A naive participant joined a group of five other participants. The five others were confederates, secretly in league with the researcher. Each participant was asked to look at a reference line **(left)** and then say out loud which of three comparison lines matched it **(right)**.

Reference line   Comparison lines

2 On 12 of the 18 trials, the five confederates deliberately gave the wrong answer.

The real participant, in the middle, hears the answer given by the confederates.

He has a hard time believing their wrong answers.

But he starts to go along with the group's obviously wrong answer.

RESULTS: When confederates gave false answers first, ¾ of the real participants conformed by giving the wrong answer at least once.

CONCLUSION: People tend to conform to social norms, even when those norms are obviously wrong.

QUESTION: How do we know that the participants did not simply misperceive the line lengths, so that social rather than perceptual factors produced this effect?

ANSWER: Only the one line matched the reference line. The other two lines were obviously different from the reference line.

Source: Asch, S. E. (1955). Opinions and social pressure. *Scientific American, 193*, 31–35.

"The Methods of Psychology: Asch's Study on Conformity to Social Norms"). Thus, the findings of the Asch study were attributable to normative influence.

FACTORS AFFECTING CONFORMITY Research has consistently demonstrated that people tend to conform to social norms. This effect can be seen outside the laboratory as well: Adolescents conform to peer pressure to smoke; jury members go along with the group rather than state their own opinions; people stand in line to buy tickets. But when do people reject social norms? In a series of follow-up studies, Asch (1956) and others identified factors that decrease the chances of conformity. One factor is group size. When there are only one or two confederates, a naive participant usually does not conform. When the confederates number three or more, the participant is more likely to conform. Conformity seems to level off at a certain point, however. Subsequent research has found that even groups as large as 16 do not lead to greater conformity than groups of 7.

Asch found that lack of unanimity is another factor that diminishes conformity. If even one confederate gives the correct answer, conformity to the group norm decreases a great deal. Any dissent from majority opinion can diminish the influence of social norms. But dissenters are typically not treated well by groups. Stanley Schachter (1951) conducted a study in which a group of students debated the fate of a juvenile delinquent, Johnny Rocco. A confederate deviated from the group judgment of how Johnny should be treated. When it became clear that the confederate would not be persuaded by group sentiment, the group began to ostracize him. When group members subsequently were given the opportunity to reduce group size, they consistently rejected the "deviant" confederate.

The bottom line is that groups enforce conformity, and those who fail to go along are rejected. The need to belong, including the anxiety associated with the fear of social exclusion, gives a group powerful influence over its members. Indeed, a number of brain imaging studies have examined conformity to group standards. A review of these studies found that activity in the medial prefrontal cortex, the region mentioned earlier in terms of understanding group members, predicted people's conforming behaviors (Wu, Luo, & Feng, 2016).

COMPLIANCE People often influence others' behavior simply by asking them to do things. If someone does the requested thing, she is exhibiting **compliance.** A number of factors increase compliance. For instance, Joseph Forgas (1998) has demonstrated that a person in a good mood is especially likely to comply. This tendency may be the basis for "buttering up" others when we want things from them. In addition, according to Robert Cialdini (2008), people often comply with requests because they fail to pay attention. Wanting to avoid conflict, they follow a standard mental shortcut: They respond without fully considering their options. Thus, if you simply give people a reason for a request, they will be much more likely to comply, even if the reason makes little sense. Recall from Chapter 1 that heuristic processing is a form of psychological reasoning in which mental shortcuts can yield quick results, but noncritical thinking can also lead to poor conclusions or bad outcomes.

As shown in **TABLE 12.1,** people can use a number of powerful strategies to influence others to comply. Consider the *foot in the door* technique: If people agree to a small request, they become more likely to comply with a large and undesirable request. Jonathan Freedman and Scott Fraser (1966) asked homeowners to allow a large, unattractive "DRIVE CAREFULLY" sign to be placed on their front lawns. As you might imagine, fewer than 1 in 5 people agreed to do so. Other homeowners, however, were first asked to sign a petition that supported legislation intended to reduce traffic accidents. A few weeks later, these same people were approached about having the

compliance

The tendency to agree to do things requested by others.

Table 12.1 The Three Ways of Inducing Compliance

TECHNIQUE	INFLUENCE METHOD	EXAMPLE
Foot in the door	If you agree to a small request, you are more likely to comply with a large request.	You agree to help a friend move a couch. Now you are more likely to comply when she asks you to help her move all of her belongings to her new apartment.
Door in the face	If you refuse a large request, you are more likely to comply with a smaller request.	A marketer calls, and you refuse to answer a product questionnaire that takes 20 minutes. Now you are likely to agree to answer 5 questions about a product.
Low-balling	When you agree to buy a product for a certain price, you are likely to comply with a request to pay more for the product.	You agree to buy a used car for $4,750. When the salesman says he forgot to add some charges, you agree to buy the car for $5,275.

large sign placed on their lawns, and more than half agreed. Once people *commit* to a course of action, they behave in ways consistent with that commitment.

The opposite influence technique is the *door in the face:* People are more likely to agree to a small request after they have refused a large request (Cialdini et al., 1975). After all, the second request seems modest in comparison, and the people want to seem reasonable. The effectiveness of this strategy relies on reciprocity, in which the compliant person feels compelled to compromise because the requester has compromised. As you might have encountered, salespeople often use this technique.

Another favorite tactic among salespeople is *low-balling.* Here, a salesperson offers a product—for example, a car—for a very low price. Once the customer agrees, the salesperson may claim that the manager did not approve the price or that there will be additional charges. Whatever the reason, someone who has already agreed to buy a product will often agree to pay the increased cost. The big decision was whether to make a purchase at all. Once a person has committed to that option, then deciding to do so by spending a bit more money does not seem like such a big decision.

 A person does the wave because everyone else around her is doing so and she does not want to look foolish. Does this behavior represent normative or informational influence?

12.4 Can Social Norms Marketing Reduce Binge Drinking?

Can the power of social norms be harnessed to modify behavior in positive ways? As noted in Chapter 4, excessive drinking kills more than 1,800 college students each year, is often involved in unprotected sexual activity, and contributes to date rape. Across North America, universities have tried to use social norms marketing to reduce binge drinking on campus. The assumption of such programs is that students often overestimate how often and how much other students drink. Moreover, students use their beliefs about peer norms to judge their own behavior. Students who believe that most students drink heavily may do so themselves in order to fit in with their peer group. Social norms marketing tries to correct these false beliefs by giving factual normative comparisons for average students at a particular college (Miller & Prentice, 2016). Thus, to change norms, colleges put up posters with messages such as "Most students have fewer than four drinks when they party."

Some studies have found that social norms marketing reduces the level of binge drinking on college campuses (Mattern & Neighbors, 2004). Indeed, one large study of 18 college campuses, involving several thousand students, found that students attending schools that used social norms marketing had a lower risk of binge drinking than students at control schools (DeJong et al., 2006). One recent Australian study used Facebook to provide students with individualized feedback comparing their behavior with the actual behavior of students in their class (Ridout & Campbell, 2014). These students were selected because they reported excessive drinking on an initial survey. They were randomly assigned to an intervention or control group, and both groups reported their drinking in surveys they completed one and three months later. The researchers found considerable reductions in self-reported alcohol consumption for the intervention group (**FIGURE 12.8**). Because

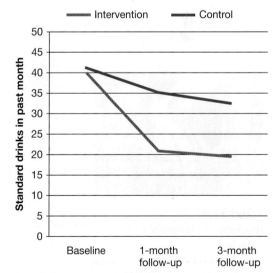

FIGURE 12.8

A Social Norms Study

This graph reports the results of using Facebook for social norms marketing at one college. The group that received intervention experienced a far greater decrease in drinking than the control group.

obedience

When a person follows the orders of a person of authority.

of findings such as these, the use of social norms marketing has become extremely popular, with most college campuses adopting some form of it.

Unfortunately, social norms marketing may inadvertently increase drinking among light drinkers, whose behavior is also susceptible to social norms (Russell, Clapp, & Dejong, 2005). Students who usually have only one drink might interpret the posters as suggesting that the norm is to have two or three drinks, and they might adjust their behavior accordingly. Indeed, one large study found that social norms marketing actually increased the drinking behavior and misperceived norms they set out to correct (Wechsler et al., 2003). One team of researchers demonstrated that simply providing descriptive norms (i.e., the frequency of behavior) can cause this sort of backfire effect. They found that adding a message that the behavior is undesirable might help prevent social norms marketing from increasing the behavior it is meant to reduce (Schultz, Nolan, Cialdini, Goldstein, & Griskevicius, 2007). These findings indicate that campuses that want to reduce student drinking need to do more than simply publicize drinking norms. They need to also convince students that there are numerous negative consequences associated with excessive drinking. Strategies that both change perceived norms and provide persuasive reasons to avoid binge drinking are most likely to be successful (Miller & Prentice, 2016). ∎

ANSWER: No. Light drinkers may drink more to match social norms.

FIGURE 12.9
Stanley Milgram
Milgram, pictured here with his infamous shock generator, demonstrated that average people will obey even hideous orders given by an authority figure.

 Q **Does social norms marketing to reduce binge drinking lead to lower drinking for all students?**

12.5 People Are Obedient to Authority

One of the most famous and most disturbing psychology experiments was conducted by Stanley Milgram (1963). Milgram wanted to understand why apparently normal German citizens willingly obeyed orders to injure or kill innocent people during World War II (**FIGURE 12.9**). Milgram was interested in the determinants of **obedience.** That is, he wanted to find out which factors influence people to follow orders given by an authority, such as a boss, parent, or police officer.

Imagine yourself as a participant in Milgram's experiment. You have agreed to take part in a study on learning. On arriving at the laboratory, you meet your fellow participant, a 60-year-old grandfatherly type. The experimenter describes the study as consisting of a teacher administering electric shocks to a learner engaged in a simple memory task that involves word pairs. Your role as the teacher is determined by an apparently random drawing of your name from a hat. On hearing that he may receive electric shocks, the learner reveals that he has a heart condition and expresses minor reservations. The experimenter says that although the shocks will be painful, they will not cause permanent tissue damage. You help the experimenter take the learner to a small room and hook him up to the electric shock machine (**FIGURE 12.10**). You then proceed to a nearby room and sit at a table in front of a large shock generator with switches that will deliver from 15 volts to 450 volts. Each voltage level carries a label, and the labels range from "slight" to "danger—severe shock" to, finally, an ominous "XXX."

FIGURE 12.10
Obedience in Milgram's Experiment
In this Milgram study, each participant (teacher) was instructed to "shock," from another room, a participant (learner). Here the teacher helps strap the learner to an electric shock machine. The teacher was unaware that the learner was secretly in league with the experimenter.

Each time the learner makes a mistake, your task as the teacher is to give him a shock. With each subsequent error, you increase the voltage. When you reach 75 volts, over the intercom you hear the man yelp in pain. At 150 volts, he screams, bangs on the wall, and demands that the experiment be stopped. At the experimenter's command, you apply additional, stronger shocks. The learner is clearly in agony. Each time you say you are quitting and try to stop the experiment, the experimenter replies, "The experiment requires that you continue," "It is essential that you go on," "There is no other choice;

you must go on!" So you do. At 300 volts, the learner refuses to answer any more questions. After 330 volts, the learner is silent. All along you have wanted to leave, and you severely regret participating in the study. You might have killed the man, for all you know.

Does this scenario sound crazy to you? If you really were the teacher, at what level would you stop administering the shocks? Would you quit as soon as the learner started to complain? Would you go up to 450 volts? Before conducting the experiment, Milgram asked various people for predictions. These people predicted that most participants would go no higher than 135 volts. They felt that fewer than one in a thousand participants would administer the highest level of shock. But that is not what happened. What did happen changed how people viewed the power of authority.

Almost all the participants tried to quit. Nearly two-thirds, however, completely obeyed all the experimenter's directives (**FIGURE 12.11**). The majority were willing to administer 450 volts to an older man with a heart condition (in reality a confederate not actually receiving shocks). These findings have been replicated by Milgram and others around the world. The conclusion of these studies is that ordinary people can be coerced into obedience by insistent authorities. This effect occurs even when what the people are coerced into doing goes against the way they usually would behave. At the same time, these results do not mean all people are equally obedient. Indeed, some aspects of personality seem related to being obedient, such as the extent to which people are concerned about how others view them (Blass, 1991). As discussed in Chapter 13, both situation and personality influence behavior.

Surprised by the results of his study, Milgram next studied ways to reduce obedience. He found that some situations produced less obedience. For instance, if the teacher could see or had to touch the learner, obedience decreased (**FIGURE 12.12**). When the experimenter gave the orders over the telephone and thus was more removed from the situation, obedience dropped dramatically. By contrast, a number of factors produce maximum obedience. Obedience is heightened when the shock level increases slowly and sequentially, when the victim starts protesting later in the study, when the orders help justify continuing with the study, and when the study is conducted at a high-status school, where the experimenters might be viewed as being more authoritative (Jetten & Mols, 2014).

Over the fifty years since the Milgram studies were conducted, a number of criticisms have emerged (Brannigan, Nicholson, & Cherry, 2015; Griggs, 2017). For instance, some participants received stronger encouragement than others to continue (Gibson, 2013). Moreover, some participants apparently did not fully believe that the victim was receiving a life-threatening shock (Hoffman, Myerberg, & Morawski, 2015). Some researchers have even questioned whether participants were truly obedient, or whether they were following the experimenter's directives because they believed in the value of the scientific enterprise and wanted to help the experimenter (Haslam, Reicher, Millard, & McDonald, 2014). Indeed, encouragements to continue for the sake of the experiment have greater impact on participants than telling them that they must obey because they have no choice (Burger, Girgis, & Manning, 2011). From this perspective, participants are willing to inflict harm because they identify with the goals of science and believe their actions are virtuous (Haslam, Reicher, & Birney, 2016). Still, people were willing to inflict significant pain on an innocent victim for the cause.

The earliest and most persistent critiques of Milgram's experiments revolved around the ethical treatment of the research participants (Baumrind, 1964). Even though Milgram claimed to be highly concerned with his participants' mental states,

The overall prediction was that fewer than 1/10 of a percent of participants in the Milgram experiments would obey completely and provide the maximum level of shock.

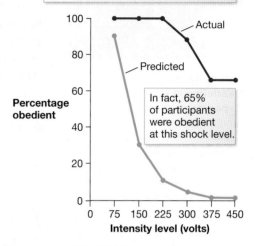

In fact, 65% of participants were obedient at this shock level.

FIGURE 12.11

Predicting the Results

Psychiatrists, college sophomores, middle-class adults, and both graduate students and professors in the behavioral sciences offered predictions about the results of Milgram's experiments. Their predictions were incorrect.

FIGURE 12.12

Personal Closeness Reduced Obedience in Milgram's Experiment

In another condition, each teacher was instructed to touch and "shock" a learner sitting next to the teacher. As in the first condition, the shocks were portrayed as increasingly intense and painful. When teachers had to force the learner's hand on the shock plate, only 30 percent completely obeyed the experimenters and administered the maximum voltage.

FIGURE 12.13

Debriefing in Milgram's Experiment

After the experiment, each teacher was introduced to the confederate learner and could see that the learner had not been harmed. However, not all of these debriefings happened quickly enough to be considered ethical today.

ANSWER: About two-thirds of people administered the shock in that study, although in other Milgram studies fewer participants obeyed.

aggression
Any behavior that involves the intention to harm another.

not all participants received timely debriefings in which they learned the true nature of the experiments (**FIGURE 12.13**; Nicholson, 2011; Perry, 2013). In an attempt to understand the long-term impact of taking part in the research, Milgram (1974) followed his participants over time and reported that most people were glad they had participated. They felt they had learned something about themselves and about human nature. Nowadays, as discussed in Chapter 2, researchers follow clear guidelines to protect the physical and mental health of research participants.

Despite the studies' flaws, Milgram's results document just how powerful situational influences can be. Most of us assume that only evil people would willingly inflict injury on others when ordered to do so. Milgram's research, and studies that followed up on it, demonstrated that ordinary people may do horrible things when ordered to do so by an authority. Although some people have speculated that these results would not be true today, a recent replication found that 70 percent of the participants were obedient up to the maximum voltage in the experiment (Burger, 2009).

 In the main Milgram study described in the text, approximately how many people administered the maximum, potentially dangerous shock to the elderly learner when ordered to do so?

When Do People Harm or Help Others?

Although obedience can lead people to commit horrible acts, the need to belong to a group can also lead to acts of altruism and of generosity. Events of the past decade have revealed the human capacities for harming and helping others. At points around the globe, we have seen terrorists, special forces, and militias killing civilians (**FIGURE 12.14A**). At the same time, we have also seen people being kind, compassionate, and giving in response to natural disasters. For example, members of the group Doctors Without Borders travel to dangerous regions to care for those in need (**FIGURE 12.14B**). This tension between our aggressive and altruistic sides is at the core of who we are as a species. Psychologists working at all levels of analysis have provided much insight into the roles that nature and nurture play in these fundamental human behaviors.

12.6 Many Factors Can Influence Aggression

Aggression can be expressed through countless behaviors. These behaviors all involve the intention to harm another. Among nonhuman animals, aggression often occurs in the context of fighting over a mate or defending territory from intruders. In the latter case, just the threat of aggressive action may be sufficient to dissuade. Among humans, physical aggression is common among young children but relatively rare in adults due to social norms discouraging it. Adults' aggressive acts more often involve words, or other symbols, meant to threaten, intimidate, or emotionally harm others.

Many situational factors have been associated with aggression. Recall from Chapter 6 that people can learn to be aggressive by observational learning and exposure to media violence. Aggression is also likely when people feel socially rejected. Throughout evolutionary history, rejection from the group has been akin to a death warrant, and therefore signs of rejection can activate defensive mechanisms that include lashing out at those who are perceived to be responsible for the rejection (MacDonald &

Leary, 2005). Feeling ostracized or rejected and the desire to retaliate have been identified as factors in many school shootings (Fox & DeLateur, 2014).

Another factor that influences aggression is heat (Van Lange, Rinderu, & Bushman, 2017). More crime occurs in the summer, and more violence occurs in hotter regions (Anderson, 1989; Anderson & DeLisi, 2011). Major league baseball pitchers are most likely to hit batters with pitches when the weather is hottest (Reifman, Larrick, & Fein, 1991), especially in hot weather when their own players have been hit by pitches (Larrick, Timmerman, Carton, & Abrevaya, 2011). A common thread through many of the situations that lead to aggression is that they involve negative emotions. Any situation that induces negative emotions—such as being insulted, afraid, frustrated, overly hot, or in pain—can trigger physical aggression (Berkowitz, 1990). This effect may occur because emotional states can disrupt the functioning of brain regions involved in controlling behavior (Heatherton & Wagner, 2011).

BIOLOGICAL FACTORS Genetic research has identified the role of the MAOA gene in aggression. The MAOA gene controls the amount of MAO (monoamine oxidase), an enzyme that regulates the activity of a number of neurotransmitters, including serotonin and norepinephrine. One study found an unusual MAOA gene mutation in an extended Dutch family in which several of the males had a history of impulsive aggression (Brunner, Nelen, Breakefield, Ropers, & Van Oost, 1993). Since the Dutch study, numerous other studies have shown that the MAOA gene is involved in aggressive violence (Buckholtz & Meyer-Lindenberg, 2008; Dorfman, Meyer-Lindenberg, & Buckholtz, 2014). Indeed, it is often referred to in the media as the "warrior gene."

MAOA is not a "violence gene" per se. Instead, a particular form of the gene appears to make individuals susceptible to environmental risk factors associated with antisocial behaviors. Recall the New Zealand study from Chapter 3, in which those who had one version of the MAOA gene and suffered childhood maltreatment were much more likely to become violent criminals (Caspi et al., 2002). In 2009, a man from Tennessee who brutally murdered his wife with a machete used the defense of possessing the warrior gene and having been abused as a child. The jury found him guilty of manslaughter rather than first-degree murder (Hagerty, 2010).

The MAOA gene regulates the neurotransmitter serotonin, and several lines of evidence suggest that serotonin is especially important in the control of aggressive behavior (Caramaschi, de Boer, & Koolhaus, 2007). Altered serotonin function has been associated with impulsive aggressiveness in adults and hostility and disruptive behavior in children (Carver & Miller, 2006). Alterations in serotonin activity increase the amygdala response to threat and interfere with the prefrontal cortex's control over aggressive impulses (Buckholtz & Meyer-Lindenberg, 2013). Disrupted serotonin systems may lead people to respond impulsively when provoked (Chester et al., 2015).

The hormone testosterone also appears to have a modest correlation with aggression. Males have more testosterone than females, and males carry out the vast majority of aggressive and violent acts. Boys play more roughly than girls at an early age. They become especially aggressive during early adolescence, a time when their levels of testosterone rise tenfold (Mazur & Booth, 1998). However, these increases in testosterone in boys coincide with other maturational changes that promote aggression, such as physical growth. Particularly aggressive men, such as violent criminals, and especially physical athletes, such as hockey players, have been found to have higher levels of testosterone than other males (Dabbs & Morris, 1990). This relationship is small, though, and it is unclear how testosterone is linked to greater aggressiveness. Testosterone may increase aggression because it reduces the activity of brain circuits that control impulses (Mehta & Beer, 2010).

(a)

(b)

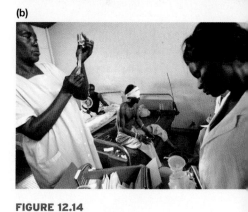

FIGURE 12.14
Harming Versus Helping
(a) Forces from the rebel group Séléka engage in military action in the Central African Republic in 2013.
(b) Members of Doctors Without Borders treat the wounded during the Central African Republic coup.

In addition, testosterone changes may be the result—rather than the cause—of aggressive behavior. That is, the situation may change testosterone levels. A number of studies have shown that testosterone rises just before athletic competition (Mazur & Booth, 1998). Testosterone remains high for the winners of competitive matches and drops lower for the losers (Booth, Shelley, Mazur, Tharp, & Kittok, 1989). Even those who simply watch a competition can be affected. Hockey players who watched a replay of a former victory by their team showed increased testosterone (Carré & Putnam, 2010). Fans are affected as well. Testosterone levels increased in Brazilian television viewers who watched Brazil beat Italy in the 1994 World Cup soccer tournament, but levels decreased in Italian television viewers (Bernhardt, Dabbs, Fielden, & Lutter, 1998). These results suggest that testosterone might not play a direct role in aggression, but rather may be related to social dominance, the result of having greater power and status (Mehta, Jones, & Josephs, 2008).

SOCIAL AND CULTURAL FACTORS Violence varies dramatically across cultures and even within cultures at different times. For example, over the course of 300 years, Sweden went from being one of the most violent nations on Earth to being one of the most peaceable. This cultural change did not correspond with a change in the gene pool or with other immediately apparent biological changes. Moreover, murder rates are far higher in some countries than in others (**FIGURE 12.15**). And analysis of crime statistics in the United States reveals that physical violence is much more prevalent in the South than in the North (UNODC, 2013a). Aggression may be part of human nature and influenced by situational factors, but society and culture influence people's tendencies to commit violent acts.

Some cultures may be violent because they subscribe to a *culture of honor*. In this belief system, men are primed to protect their reputations through physical aggression. Men in the southern United States, for example, traditionally were (and perhaps still are) raised to be ready to fight for their honor and to respond aggressively to personal threats. To determine whether southern males are more likely to be aggressive than

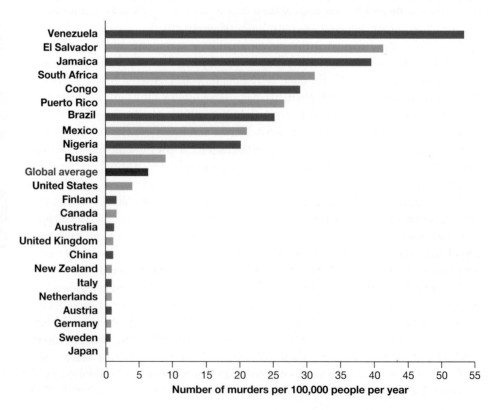

FIGURE 12.15
Aggression Varies Across Cultures
The numbers in this chart are the most recent available, from 2012. They come from the United Nations Office on Drugs and Crime (2013a).

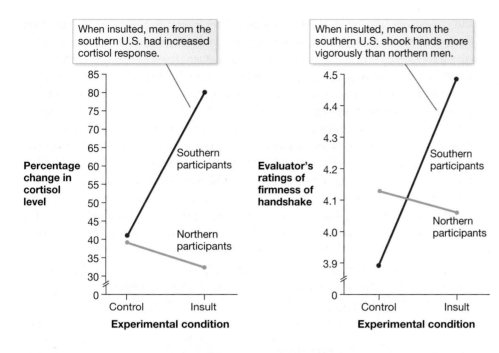

When insulted, men from the southern U.S. had increased cortisol response.

When insulted, men from the southern U.S. shook hands more vigorously than northern men.

Percentage change in cortisol level

Southern participants

Northern participants

Control   Insult
Experimental condition

Evaluator's ratings of firmness of handshake

Southern participants

Northern participants

Control   Insult
Experimental condition

FIGURE 12.16
Aggressive Responses to Insults
These graphs show differences in behavior between men from the South and those from the North in studies at the University of Michigan.

northern males, researchers at the University of Michigan conducted a series of studies (Cohen, Nisbett, Bowdle, & Schwarz, 1996). In each study, a male participant had to walk down a narrow hallway. The participant had to pass a filing cabinet, where a male confederate was blocking the hallway. As the participant tried to edge past the confederate, the confederate responded angrily and insulted the participant. Compared with participants raised in the North, those raised in the South became more upset and were more likely to feel personally challenged. Perhaps because of a need to express social dominance in this situation, the southern participants were more physiologically aroused (measured by cortisol and testosterone increases), more cognitively primed for aggression, and more likely to act in an aggressive and dominant manner for the rest of the experiment. For instance, in another part of the studies, participants raised in the South shook a new confederate's hand much more vigorously than the participants raised in the North did (**FIGURE 12.16**).

 Why is aggression more likely in hot climates than in cold ones?

ANSWER: Being overly hot can produce more of a negative emotion than being overly cold, and a negative emotion tends to bring out aggression.

12.7 Many Factors Can Influence Helping Behavior

People often act in ways that help others. **Prosocial behaviors** include doing favors, offering assistance, paying compliments, subjugating egocentric desires or needs, resisting the temptation to insult or hit another person, or simply being pleasant and cooperative. By providing benefits to others, prosocial behaviors promote positive interpersonal relationships. Living in groups, in which people necessarily engage in prosocial behaviors such as sharing and cooperating, may be a central human survival strategy. After all, a group that works well together is a strong group, and belonging to a strong group benefits the individual members.

Why are humans prosocial? Theoretical explanations range from selflessness to selfishness and from the biological to the philosophical. For instance, Daniel Batson

prosocial behaviors
Actions that tend to benefit others, such as doing favors or helping.

and colleagues (Batson et al., 1988; Batson, Turk, Shaw, & Klein, 1995) argue that prosocial behaviors are motivated by empathy, in which people share other people's emotions. Conversely, Robert Cialdini and colleagues (1987; also Maner et al., 2002) argue that most prosocial behaviors have selfish motives, such as wanting to manage one's public image or relieve one's negative mood. Other theorists have proposed that people have an inborn tendency to help others. Consider that young infants become distressed when they see other infants crying (Zahn-Waxler & Radke-Yarrow, 1990). Generally, children's early attempts to soothe other children are ineffective. For instance, they tend initially to comfort themselves rather than the other children. Still, this empathic response to other people's suffering suggests that prosocial behavior is hardwired in humans.

altruism
Providing help when it is needed, without any apparent reward for doing so.

Altruism is providing help when it is needed, without any apparent reward for doing so. The fact that people help others, and even risk personal safety to do so, may seem contrary to evolutionary principles. After all, those who protect themselves first would appear to have an advantage over those who risk their lives to help others. During the 1960s, the geneticist William Hamilton offered an answer to this riddle. Hamilton (1964) proposed that natural selection occurs at the genetic level rather than at the individual level.

EVOLUTIONARY EXPLANATIONS As discussed in Chapter 1, the "fittest" animals pass along the most genes to future generations. These animals increase the chances of passing along their genes by helping ensure that their offspring survive. Hamilton's concept of **inclusive fitness** describes the adaptive benefits of transmitting genes rather than focusing on individual survival. According to this model, people are altruistic toward those with whom they share genes. This phenomenon is known as *kin selection*. A good example of kin selection occurs among insects, such as ants and bees. In these species, workers feed and protect the egg-laying queen, but they never reproduce. By protecting the group's eggs, they maximize the number of their common genes that will survive into future generations (Dugatkin, 2004).

inclusive fitness
An explanation for altruism that focuses on the adaptive benefit of transmitting genes, such as through kin selection, rather than focusing on individual survival.

Of course, animals sometimes help nonrelatives. For example, dolphins and lions will look after orphans within their own species. Similarly, a person who jumps into a lake to save a drowning stranger is probably not acting for the sake of genetic transmission. To help explain altruism toward nonrelatives, Robert Trivers (1971) proposed the idea of *reciprocal helping*. According to Trivers, one animal helps another because the other may return the favor in the future. Consider grooming, in which primates take turns cleaning each other's fur: "You scratch my back, and I'll scratch yours."

For reciprocal helping to be adaptive, benefits must outweigh costs. Indeed, people are less likely to help others when the costs of doing so are high (Wagner & Wheeler, 1969). Reciprocal helping is also much more likely to occur among animals, such as humans, that live in social groups, because their species' survival depends on cooperation. Thus, as discussed earlier, people are more likely to help members of their ingroups than to help members of outgroups. From an evolutionary perspective, then, altruism confers benefits. When an animal acts altruistically, it may increase the chances that its genes will be transmitted. The altruistic animal may also increase the likelihood that other members of the social group will reciprocate when needed.

FIGURE 12.17
Kitty Genovese
News reports that 38 witnesses failed to help murder victim Kitty Genovese caused outrage.

BYSTANDER INTERVENTION In 1964, a young woman named Kitty Genovese was walking home from work in a relatively safe area of New York City. An assailant savagely attacked her for half an hour, eventually killing her. At the time, a newspaper reported that none of the 38 witnesses to the crime tried to help or called the police. As you might imagine, most people who followed the story were outraged that 38 people could sit by and watch a brutal murder (**FIGURE 12.17**). That story appears to have been wrong, however. Few of the witnesses were in a position to observe what was happening to Genovese (Manning, Levine, & Collins, 2007), and at least two people did call the police.

Yet the idea of 38 silent witnesses prompted researchers to undertake important research on how people react in emergencies. Shortly after the Genovese murder, the social psychologists Bibb Latané and John Darley examined situations that produce the **bystander intervention effect.** This term refers to the failure to offer help by those who observe someone in need. Common sense might suggest that the more people who are available to help, the more likely it is that a victim will be helped. Latané and Darley made the paradoxical claim, however, that a person is less likely to offer help if other bystanders are around.

To test their theory, Latané and Darley conducted studies in which people were placed in situations that indicated they should seek help. In one of the first situations, male college students were in a room, filling out questionnaires (Latané & Darley, 1968). Pungent smoke started puffing in through the heating vents. Some participants were alone. Some were with two other naive participants. Some were with two confederates, who noticed the smoke, shrugged, and continued filling out their questionnaires. When participants were on their own, most went for help. When three naive participants were together, however, few initially went for help. With the two calm confederates, only 10 percent of participants went for help in the first 6 minutes (**FIGURE 12.18**). The other 90 percent "coughed, rubbed their eyes, and opened the window—but they did not report the smoke" (p. 218).

In subsequent studies, people were confronted with mock crimes, apparent heart attack victims in subway cars, and people passed out in public places. The experimenters obtained similar results each time. The bystander intervention effect has been shown to occur in a wide variety of contexts. Even divinity students, while rushing to give a lecture on the Good Samaritan—a biblical figure who helps a severely injured traveler—failed to help a person in apparent need of medical attention (Darley & Batson, 1973).

Years of research have indicated four major reasons for the bystander intervention effect. First, a *diffusion of responsibility* occurs. In other words, bystanders expect other bystanders to help. Thus, the greater the number of people who witness someone in need of help, the less likely it is that any of them will step forward. Second, people fear making *social blunders* in ambiguous situations. All the laboratory situations had some degree of ambiguity, and people may have worried that they would look foolish if they sought help that was not needed. There is evidence that people feel less constrained from seeking help as the need for help becomes clearer (Fischer et al., 2011). In the Genovese murder case, some of the witnesses found the situation unclear and therefore might have been reluctant to call the police. Third, people are less likely to help when they are *anonymous* and can remain so. Therefore, if you need help, it is often wise to point to a specific person and request her help by saying something like, "You, in the red shirt, call an ambulance!" Fourth, people weigh two factors: How much harm do they risk to themselves by helping? What benefits might they have to forgo if they help? Imagine you are walking to a potentially dull class on a beautiful day. Right in front of you, someone falls down, twists an ankle, and needs transportation to the nearest clinic. You probably would be willing to help. Now imagine you are running to a final exam

bystander intervention effect
The failure to offer help by those who observe someone in need when other people are present.

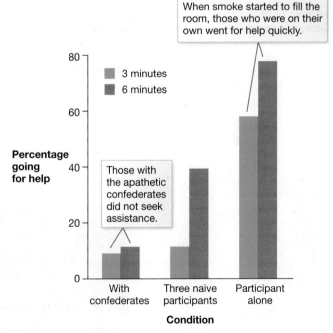

FIGURE 12.18
The Bystander Intervention Effect
In Latané and Darley's experiments, participants waited with two apathetic confederates, with two other naive participants, or alone. This chart records the participants' reactions to smoke filling the room.

that counts for 90 percent of your grade. In this case, you probably would be much less likely to offer assistance.

Q | **What is inclusive fitness?**

12.8 Cooperation Can Reduce Outgroup Bias

Can the findings of social psychology be used to encourage harmony between groups? Since the 1950s, social psychologists have worked with politicians, activists, and others in numerous attempts to alleviate the hostility and violence between factions. Beliefs about ethnic groups are embedded deeply in cultural and religious values, however, and it is extraordinarily difficult to change such beliefs. Around the world, groups clash over disputes that predate the births of most of the combatants. Sometimes people cannot even remember the original sources of particular conflicts. There have been success stories, however, such as the reconciliation between the Tutsi and Hutu 20 years after the genocide in Rwanda. There have also been examples of people banding together to help those outside their groups. Recall the earthquakes and tsunamis in Japan in 2011, when thousands of people were killed, or the devastating earthquake in Haiti in 2010, when hundreds of thousands of people were killed and millions were left homeless (**FIGURE 12.19**). The international responses to these tragedies show that people respond to outgroup members in need. In working together toward a greater purpose, people can overcome intergroup hostilities.

Social psychology may be able to suggest strategies for promoting intergroup harmony and producing greater tolerance for outgroups. The first study to suggest so was conducted in the 1950s by Muzafer Sherif and colleagues (1961). Sherif arranged for 22 well-adjusted and intelligent fifth-grade boys from Oklahoma City to attend a summer camp at a lake. The boys did not know each other. Before arriving at camp, they were divided into two groups that were essentially the same. During the first week, each group lived in a separate camp on a different side of the lake. Neither group knew that the other group existed.

The next week, over a four-day period, the groups competed in an athletic tournament. They played games such as tug-of-war, football, and softball, and the stakes

FIGURE 12.19
Global Cooperation
After the earthquake in Haiti in 2010, workers from around the world assisted efforts to rebuild the country. Dealing with a natural catastrophe can help people overcome their differences.

FIGURE 12.20
Phase 1 of Sherif's Study of Competition and Cooperation
During phase 1 of Sherif's study, boys from the two summer camps were pitted against one another and became hostile to each other.

FIGURE 12.21
Phase 2 of Sherif's Study
During phase 2, the two groups had to work together to achieve common goals. The shared goals led to cooperation and a reduction of hostility between the groups.

were high. The winning team would receive a trophy, individual medals, and appealing prizes. The losers would receive nothing. The groups named themselves the Rattlers and the Eagles. Group pride was extremely strong, and animosity between the groups quickly escalated. The Eagles burned the Rattlers' flag, and the Rattlers retaliated by trashing the Eagles' cabin. Eventually, confrontations and physical fights had to be broken up by the experimenters. All the typical signs of prejudice emerged, including the outgroup homogeneity effect and ingroup favoritism. (Prejudice and discrimination are defined and discussed in Sections 12.13–14.)

Phase 1 of the study was complete. Sherif had shown how easy it was to make people hate each other: Simply divide them into groups and have the groups compete, and prejudice and mistreatment will result (**FIGURE 12.20**). Phase 2 of the study then explored whether the hostility could be undone.

Sherif first tried what made sense at the time: simply having the groups come in contact with each other. This approach failed miserably. The hostilities were too strong, and skirmishes continued. Sherif reasoned that if competition led to hostility, then cooperation should reduce hostility. The experimenters created situations in which members of both groups had to cooperate to achieve necessary goals. For instance, the experimenters rigged a truck to break down. Getting the truck moving required all the boys to pull together. In an ironic twist, the boys had to use the same rope they used earlier in the tug-of-war. When they succeeded, a great cheer arose from the boys, with plenty of backslapping all around. After a series of tasks that required cooperation, the walls between the two sides broke down, and the boys became friends across the groups (**FIGURE 12.21**). Among strangers, competition and isolation created enemies. Among enemies, cooperation created friends.

Research over the past four decades has indicated that only certain types of contact between hostile groups is likely to reduce prejudice and discrimination. Shared *superordinate* goals—goals that require people to cooperate—reduce hostility between groups. People who work together to achieve a common goal often break down subgroup distinctions as they become one larger group (Dovidio et al., 2004). For example, athletes on multiethnic teams often develop positive feelings toward other ethnicities.

 What is the key to building cooperation between groups?

- Explain how attitudes are formed.

- Identify characteristics of attitudes that are predictive of behavior.

- Distinguish between explicit and implicit attitudes.

- Describe cognitive dissonance theory.

- Identify factors that influence the persuasiveness of messages.

- Describe the elaboration likelihood model.

attitudes
People's evaluations of objects, of events, or of ideas.

mere exposure effect
The idea that greater exposure to a stimulus leads to greater liking for it.

FIGURE 12.22
The Mere Exposure Effect
If he is like most people, Canadian prime minister Justin Trudeau will prefer **(right)** his mirror image to **(left)** his photographic image. There is nothing wrong with the photographic image. Trudeau will simply be more familiar with the mirror image.

How Do Attitudes Guide Behavior?

You probably have feelings, opinions, and beliefs about yourself, your friends, your favorite television program, and so on. These feelings, opinions, and beliefs are called **attitudes.** Such evaluations of objects, of events, or of ideas are central to social psychology. Attitudes are shaped by social context, and they play an important role in how we evaluate and interact with other people.

People have attitudes about all sorts of things. For example, people have opinions on trivial and mundane matters, such as which deodorant works best. They also form positions on grand issues, such as politics, morals, and religion—that is, the core beliefs and values that define who one is as a human being. Some attitudes are held consciously, while others remain below conscious awareness. This section considers how attitudes affect people's daily lives.

12.9 People Form Attitudes Through Experience and Socialization

Throughout life, people encounter new things. Those things can be objects, other people, or situations. When people hear about things, read about them, or experience them directly, they learn about them and perhaps explore them. Through this process, they gain information that shapes their attitudes. Generally, people develop negative attitudes about new things more quickly than they develop positive attitudes about them (Fazio, Eisner, & Shook, 2004). Throughout evolution, sensitivity to learning about danger would have been particularly adaptive. While missing out on something pleasurable may be a lost opportunity, it is unlikely that such a loss would produce a really bad outcome. Ignoring danger, however, might be deadly. In general, bad is always a stronger motivating force than good (Baumeister, Bratslavsky, Finkenauer, & Vohs, 2001).

People talk about acquiring a taste for foods that they did not like originally, such as bleu cheese or sushi. How do they come to like something that they could not stand the first time they were exposed to it? Typically, the more people are exposed to something, the more they tend to like it. In a classic set of studies, Robert Zajonc (1968, 2001) exposed people to unfamiliar items a few times or many times. Greater exposure to the item, and therefore greater familiarity with it, caused people to have more-positive attitudes about the item. This process is called the **mere exposure effect.**

For example, when people are presented with normal photographs of themselves and the same images reversed, they tend to prefer the reversed versions. Why would this be the case? The reversed images correspond to what people see when they look in the mirror (**FIGURE 12.22**). Their friends and family members prefer the true photographs, which correspond to how they view the person. You can try this yourself by taking a "selfie" and then flipping it. Which image do you prefer?

Because people's associations between things and their meanings can change, attitudes can be conditioned (for a full discussion of conditioning, see Chapter 6). Advertisers often use classical conditioning: When people see a celebrity paired with a product, they tend to develop more-positive attitudes about the product. After conditioning, a formerly neutral stimulus (e.g., a deodorant) triggers the same attitude response as the paired object (e.g., George Clooney if he were to endorse a deodorant). Operant conditioning also shapes attitudes: If you are rewarded with good grades each time you study, you will develop a more positive attitude toward studying.

Attitudes are also shaped through socialization (**FIGURE 12.23**). Caregivers, peers, teachers, religious leaders, politicians, and media figures guide people's attitudes about many things. For example, teenagers' attitudes about clothing styles and music, about behaviors such as smoking and drinking alcohol, and about the latest celebrities are heavily influenced by their peers' beliefs. Society instills many basic attitudes, including which things are edible. For instance, many Hindus do not eat beef, whereas many Jews do not eat pork.

ATTITUDE-BEHAVIOR CONSISTENCY In general, the stronger and more personally relevant the attitude, the more likely it is to predict behavior. The strong and personally relevant nature of the attitude will lead the person to act the same across situations related to that attitude. It will also lead the person to defend the attitude. For instance, someone who grew up in a strongly Democratic household, especially one where derogatory comments about Republicans were expressed frequently, is more likely to register as a Democrat and vote Democratic than someone who grew up in a more politically neutral environment.

Moreover, the more specific the attitude, the more predictive it is. For instance, your attitudes toward recycling are more predictive of whether you take your soda cans to a recycling bin than are your general environmental beliefs. Attitudes formed through direct experience also tend to predict behavior better. Consider parenthood. No matter what kind of parent you think you will be, by the time you have seen one child through toddlerhood, you will have formed very strong attitudes about child-rearing techniques. These attitudes will predict how you approach the early months and years of your second child.

Another factor predicting behavior is how quickly your attitude comes to mind. *Attitude accessibility* refers to the ease or difficulty that a person has in retrieving an attitude from memory. This accessibility predicts behavior consistent with the attitude. Russell Fazio (1995) has shown that easily activated attitudes are more stable, predictive of behavior, and resistant to change. Thus, the more quickly you recall that you like your psychology course, the more likely you are to attend lectures and read the textbook.

EXPLICIT AND IMPLICIT ATTITUDES How do you know your attitude about something? Recall from Chapter 4 that access to mental processes is limited and that unconscious processes can influence behavior. People's conscious awareness of their attitudes can be limited because of several factors, such as their desire to believe they hold positive attitudes about certain racial groups, but their actions can reveal their less positive attitudes (Nosek, Hawkins, & Frazier, 2011).

Over the last 20 years, researchers have demonstrated that attitudes can be explicit or implicit and that these different attitudes have different effects on behavior. **Explicit attitudes** are those you know about and can report to other people. If you say you like bowling, you are stating your explicit attitude toward it. Anthony Greenwald and Mahzarin Banaji (1995) have noted that people's many **implicit attitudes** influence their feelings and behaviors at an unconscious level. People access implicit attitudes from memory quickly, with little conscious effort or control. In this way, implicit attitudes function like implicit memories. As discussed in Chapter 7, implicit memories

FIGURE 12.23
Socialization Shapes Attitudes
This photo was taken in Gainesville, Georgia, in 1992. The child's attitudes about African Americans may have been socialized by his parents' involvement with a racist organization.

explicit attitudes
Attitudes that a person can report.

implicit attitudes
Attitudes that influence a person's feelings and behavior at an unconscious level.

FIGURE 12.24

Implicit Association Test
When a word appears on the screen, a person has to select whether it is bad or good or a male name or a female name. For example, in condition 1 the person presses the left button to indicate male or good, the right button to indicate female or bad. Which buttons to press changes in different conditions.

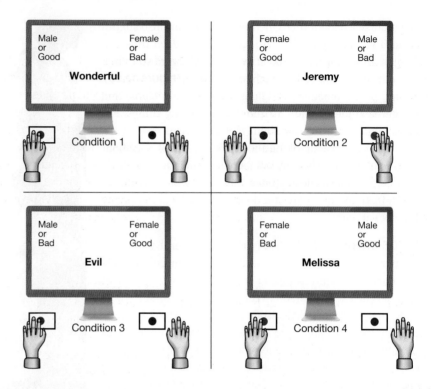

make it possible for people to perform actions, such as riding a bicycle, without thinking through all the required steps. Similarly, you might purchase a product endorsed by a celebrity even though you have no conscious memory of having seen the celebrity use the product. The product might simply look familiar to you. Some evidence suggests that implicit attitudes involve brain regions associated with implicit rather than explicit memory (Lieberman, 2000).

One method researchers use to assess implicit attitudes is a reaction time test called the Implicit Association Test (IAT; Greenwald, McGhee, & Schwartz, 1998). The IAT measures how quickly a person associates concepts or objects with positive or negative words. For example, according to the developers of the method, having to use the same button to indicate that a name is female or that a word is bad implies an association between female and bad (**FIGURE 12.24**). Responding more quickly when a button is used to indicate female or good (Figure 12.24, condition 2) than when the same button is used to indicate female or bad (Figure 12.24, condition 4) indicates a person's implicit attitude about females. A typical female will tend to respond more quickly when female is paired with good than when female is paired with bad. This difference in reaction time is proposed to indicate the degree of implicit bias.

Use of the IAT has become controversial. An early meta-analysis of more than 100 studies found that, in socially sensitive situations in which people might not want to admit their real attitudes, the IAT is a better predictor of behavior than explicit self-reports are (Greenwald, Poehlman, Uhlmann, & Banaji, 2009). However, more-recent evidence suggests that the IAT may not be an effective way to predict racial and ethnic discrimination (Oswald, Mitchell, Blanton, Jaccard, & Tetlock, 2013). Indeed, there is growing concern that the public perception of the IAT greatly exaggerates its ability to accurately identify racial bias or predict biased behavior. At this time, there is no reliable way to measure whether someone has unconscious bias.

Q **Suppose that the more times you taste an unfamiliar food, the more you like it. Why does this happen?**

ANSWER: According to the mere exposure effect, greater exposure leads to greater liking.

12.10 Discrepancies Lead to Dissonance

Generally, attitudes seem to guide behavior. Citizens vote for candidates they like, and people avoid foods they do not like. What happens when people hold conflicting attitudes? In 1957, the social psychologist Leon Festinger answered that question by proposing the theory of **cognitive dissonance** (FIGURE 12.25).

According to this theory, *dissonance*—a lack of agreement—occurs when there is a contradiction between two attitudes or between an attitude and a behavior. For example, people experience cognitive dissonance when they smoke even though they know that smoking might kill them. A basic assumption of cognitive dissonance theory is that dissonance causes anxiety and tension. Anxiety and tension cause displeasure. Displeasure motivates people to reduce dissonance. Generally, people reduce dissonance by changing their attitudes or behaviors. They sometimes also rationalize or trivialize the discrepancies.

INSUFFICIENT JUSTIFICATION In one of the original dissonance studies, each participant performed an extremely boring task for an hour (Festinger & Carlsmith, 1959). The experimenter then paid the participant $1 or $20 to lie and tell the next participant that the task was really interesting, educational, and worthwhile. Nearly all the participants subsequently provided the false information. Later, under the guise of a different survey, the same participants were asked how worthwhile and enjoyable the task had actually been. You might think that those paid $20 remembered the task as more enjoyable, but just the opposite happened. Participants who had been paid $1 rated the task much more favorably than those who had been paid $20.

According to the researchers, this effect occurred because those paid $1 had insufficient monetary justification for lying. Therefore, to justify why they went along with the lie, they changed their attitudes about performing the dull experimental task. Those paid $20 had plenty of justification for lying, since $20 was a large amount of money in 1959 (roughly equivalent to $150 today), so they did not experience dissonance and did not have to change their attitudes about the task (FIGURE 12.26). As this research shows, one way to get people to change their attitudes is to change their behaviors first, using as few incentives as possible.

POSTDECISIONAL DISSONANCE According to cognitive dissonance theory, dissonance can arise when a person holds positive attitudes about different options but has to choose one of the options. For example, a person might have trouble deciding which of many excellent colleges to attend. The person might narrow the choice to two or three alternatives and then have to choose. *Postdecisional dissonance* then motivates the person to focus on one school's—the chosen school's—positive aspects and the other schools' negative aspects. This effect occurs automatically, with minimal cognitive processing, and apparently without awareness. Indeed, even patients with long-term memory loss may show postdecisional effects for past choices, even if the patients do not consciously recall which items they chose (Lieberman, Ochsner, Gilbert, & Schacter, 2001).

JUSTIFYING EFFORT So far, the discussion of people's attitudes has focused on changes in individual behavior. What about group-related behavior? Consider the extreme group-related behaviors of initiation rites. On college campuses, administrators impose rules and penalties to discourage hazing, yet some fraternities and sororities continue to do it. The groups require new recruits to undergo embarrassing

FIGURE 12.25
Leon Festinger
Festinger's theory of cognitive dissonance was an important influence on research in experimental social psychology.

cognitive dissonance
An uncomfortable mental state resulting from a contradiction between two attitudes or between an attitude and a behavior.

Participants who were paid only $1 to mislead a fellow participant experienced cognitive dissonance. This dissonance led them to alter their attitudes about how pleasurable the task had been.

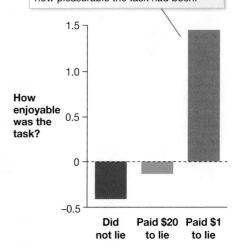

FIGURE 12.26
Cognitive Dissonance
In Festinger and Carlsmith's dissonance study, participants performed an extremely boring task and then reported to other participants how enjoyable it was. Some participants were paid $20 to lie, and some were paid $1.

FIGURE 12.27
The Aftermath of Hazing
Hazing can have dangerous effects and tragic consequences. Here, the family members of California State University Northridge student Armando Villa mourn Villa's death, which happened during a fraternity-hazing hike. Why do fraternity candidates submit to dangerous hazing activities?

ANSWER: Postdecisional dissonance makes her focus on the chosen car's positive features and the rejected car's negative features.

persuasion
The active and conscious effort to change an attitude through the transmission of a message.

or difficult rites of passage because these endurance tests make membership in the group seem much more valuable. The tests also make the group more cohesive.

To test these ideas, Eliot Aronson and Judson Mills (1959) required women to undergo a test to see if they qualified to take part in a research study. Some women had to read a list of obscene words and sexually explicit passages in front of the male experimenter. In the 1950s, this task was very difficult for many women and took considerable effort. A control group read a list of milder words, such as *prostitute*. Participants in both conditions then listened to a boring and technical presentation about mating rituals in lower animals. Women who had read the embarrassing words reported that the presentation was much more interesting, stimulating, and important than did the women who had read the milder words.

As this research shows, when people put themselves through pain, embarrassment, or discomfort to join a group, they experience a great deal of dissonance. After all, they typically would not choose to be in pain, embarrassed, or uncomfortable. Yet they made such a choice. They resolve the dissonance by inflating the importance of the group and their commitment to it. This justification of effort helps explain why people are willing to subject themselves to humiliating experiences such as hazing (**FIGURE 12.27**). More tragically, it may help explain why people who give up connections to families and friends to join cults or to follow enigmatic leaders are willing to die rather than leave the groups. If they have sacrificed so much to join a group, people believe the group must be extraordinarily important.

 Before buying a car, your aunt spent months choosing between two options. Once she decided, she claimed that the right choice was always obvious because the one car is so much better. Why might your aunt believe this?

12.11 Attitudes Can Be Changed Through Persuasion

A number of forces other than dissonance can conspire to change attitudes. People are bombarded by television advertisements; lectures from parents, teachers, and physicians; pressure from peers; public service announcements; politicians appealing for votes; and so on. **Persuasion** is the active and conscious effort to change an attitude through the transmission of a message. In the earliest scientific work on persuasion, Carl Hovland and colleagues (1953) emphasized that persuasion is most likely to occur when people pay attention to a message, understand it, and find it convincing. In addition, the message must be memorable, so its impact lasts over time.

Various factors affect the persuasiveness of a message (Petty & Wegener, 1998). These factors include the *source* (who delivers the message), the *content* (what the message says), and the *receiver* (who processes the message). Sources who are both attractive and credible are the most persuasive. Thus, television ads for medicines and medical services often feature very attractive people playing the roles of physicians. Even better, of course, is when a drug company ad uses a spokesperson who is both attractive *and* an actual doctor. Credibility and persuasiveness may also be heightened when the receiver perceives the source as similar to himself.

Of course, the arguments in the message are also important for persuasion (Greenwald, 1968). Strong arguments that appeal to emotions are the most persuasive. Advertisers also use the mere exposure effect, repeating the message over and over in the hope that multiple exposures will lead to increased persuasiveness. For this reason, politicians often make the same statements over and over during campaigns.

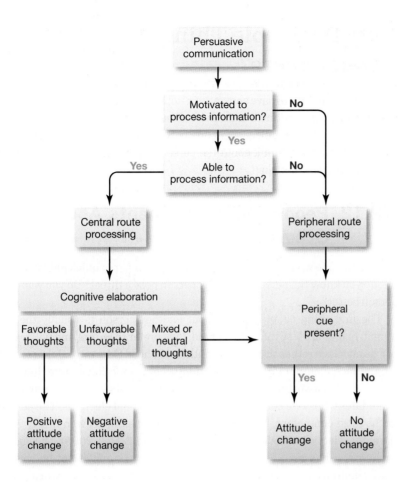

FIGURE 12.28
The Elaboration Likelihood Model
When people are motivated and able to consider information, they process it via the central route. As a result, their attitude changes reflect cognitive elaboration **(left)**. When people are either not motivated or not able to consider information, they process it via the peripheral route. As a result, their attitude changes reflect the presence or absence of shallow peripheral cues. For example, as a result of peripheral processing, people may be persuaded because the person making an argument is attractive or a celebrity **(right)**.

Those who want to persuade (including, of course, politicians) also have to decide whether to deliver one-sided arguments or to consider both sides of particular issues. One-sided arguments work best when the audience is on the speaker's side or is gullible. With a more skeptical crowd, speakers who acknowledge both sides but argue that one is superior tend to be more persuasive than those who completely ignore the opposing view.

According to the **elaboration likelihood model** (Petty & Cacioppo, 1986), persuasive communication leads to attitude change in two fundamental ways (**FIGURE 12.28**). When people are motivated to process information and are able to process that information, persuasion takes the *central route*. That is, people are paying attention to the arguments, considering all the information, and using rational cognitive processes. This route leads to strong attitudes that last over time and that people actively defend. When people are either not motivated to process information or are unable to process it, persuasion takes the *peripheral route*. That is, people minimally process the message. This route leads to more-impulsive action, as when a person decides to purchase a product because a celebrity has endorsed it or because of how an advertisement makes the person feel. Peripheral cues, such as the attractiveness or status of the person making the argument, influence what attitude is adopted. Attitudes developed through the peripheral route are weaker and more likely to change over time.

elaboration likelihood model
The idea that persuasive messages lead to attitude changes in either of two ways: via the central route or via the peripheral route.

 Q Describing both sides of a position before emphasizing the superiority of one side is particularly persuasive under what circumstance?

ANSWER: when the person being persuaded is skeptical about the speaker's position

Learning Objectives

- Discuss the roles of appearance and of nonverbal behavior in impression formation.

- Define the fundamental attribution error and the actor/observer discrepancy.

- Describe the functions of stereotypes.

- Distinguish between prejudice and discrimination.

- Define modern racism and discuss its impact on prejudice and discrimination.

- Discuss strategies to inhibit stereotypes and reduce prejudice.

How Do People Think About Others?

As social psychologists have shown, long-term evaluations of people are heavily influenced by first impressions. But the factors that affect first impressions can lead to perceptual biases. For instance, when one person's gender or skin color leads someone else to automatically think about the person in particular ways, those first impressions can often be mistaken.

12.12 People Make Judgments About Others

When someone walks toward you, you make a number of quick judgments. For example, do you know the person? Does the person pose a threat? Do you want to know the person better?

The first thing people notice about another person is usually the face. When human babies are less than an hour old, they prefer to look at and will track a picture of a human face rather than a blank outline of a head (Morton & Johnson, 1991). After all, the face communicates information such as emotional state, interest, competence, and trustworthiness. In one study, participants were shown pairs of faces of candidates who were competing in U.S. congressional elections. The people selected as the most competent, based solely on facial appearance, won nearly 70 percent of the actual elections (Todorov, Mandisodza, Goren, & Hall, 2005). Throughout human evolution, it has been crucial to identify others who might not be trustworthy. By age 7, children can make judgments about whether a face is trustworthy or not (using descriptors such as *nice* or *mean*) that match adult consensus judgments (Cogsdill, Todorov, Spelke, & Banaji, 2014). As mentioned in Chapter 10, the amygdala is particularly important for judging trustworthiness.

nonverbal behavior
The facial expressions, gestures, mannerisms, and movements by which one communicates with others.

NONVERBAL BEHAVIOR Facial expressions, gestures, mannerisms, and movements are all examples of **nonverbal behavior,** sometimes referred to as *body language* (**FIGURE 12.29**). How much can be learned from nonverbal behavior? Nalini Ambady and Robert Rosenthal (1993) have found that people can make accurate judgments based on only a few seconds of observation. Ambady and Rosenthal refer to such

FIGURE 12.29
Reading Nonverbal Behavior
(a) People's body language affects impressions of the people and their situations. **(b)** In one study, participants watched a 10-second silent video or figural outline of a real person walking or gesturing. The participants correctly guessed the person's sexual orientation at a better-than-chance rate (Ambady, Hallahan, & Conner, 1999).

(a)

(b)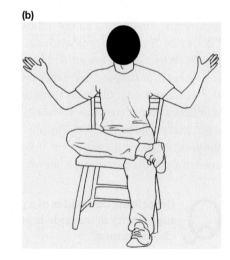

quick views as *thin slices of behavior*. Thin slices of behavior are powerful cues for impression formation. For instance, videotapes of judges giving instructions to juries reveal that a judge's nonverbal actions can predict whether a jury will find the defendant guilty or not guilty (Hart, 1995). Judges, perhaps unconsciously, may indicate their beliefs about guilt or innocence through facial expressions, tones of voice, and gestures. Another good example of thin slices is "gaydar," people's seeming ability to judge other people's sexual orientation from afar. There is substantial evidence that people are quite accurate in judging sexual orientation based on nonverbal behavior (Rule & Alaei, 2016).

ATTRIBUTIONAL DIMENSIONS People constantly try to explain other people's motives, traits, and preferences. **Attributions** are explanations for events or actions, including other people's behavior. People are motivated to draw inferences in part by a basic need for both order and predictability. The world can be a dangerous place in which many unexpected things happen. People prefer to think that things happen for reasons and that therefore they can anticipate future events. For instance, you might expect that if you study for an exam, you will do well on it.

In any situation, various plausible explanations may exist for specific outcomes. For example, doing well on a test could be due to brilliance, luck, intensive studying, the test's being unexpectedly easy, or a combination of factors. Fritz Heider (1944), the originator of attribution theory, drew an essential distinction between two types of attributions. **Personal attributions** are internal or dispositional attributions. These explanations refer to things within people, such as abilities, moods, or efforts. For instance, if you believe you did well on an exam because you worked hard and are smart, you are making a personal attribution. **Situational attributions** are external attributions. These explanations refer to outside events, such as luck, accidents, or the actions of other people. Thus, if you blame poor test performance on the quality of the exam items, then you are making a situational attribution.

Bernard Weiner (1974) noted that attributions can vary on other dimensions. For example, attributions can be stable over time (permanent) or unstable (temporary). They can be controllable or uncontrollable. Blaming your field hockey team's loss on the weather involves making situational, unstable, and uncontrollable attributions. Explaining that hard work produced your team's winning season reflects making personal, stable, and controllable attributions.

ATTRIBUTIONAL BIAS Social psychologists such as Fritz Heider and Harold Kelley have described people as intuitive scientists who try to draw inferences about others and make attributions about events. Unlike objective scientists, however, people tend to be systematically biased when they process social information. When explaining other people's behavior, people tend to overemphasize the importance of personality traits and underestimate the importance of situations. Edward Jones called it the *correspondence bias* to emphasize the expectancy that people's actions correspond with their beliefs and personalities (Jones & Davis, 1965). For example, someone who follows orders to inflict harm on another, as in the obedience study, is assumed to be an evil person. This tendency is so pervasive that it has been called the **fundamental attribution error** (Ross, 1977).

People generally fail to take into account that other people are influenced by social circumstances, such as the social pressures that lead to obedience to authority. Consider the host of *Jeopardy!,* Alex Trebek. Viewers exhibit the fundamental attribution error when they assume Trebek must be very smart because he knows so much information. Trebek may indeed be very smart. But when viewers develop this belief based on his performance on the show, they neglect to take into account that

attributions
People's explanations for why events or actions occur.

personal attributions
Explanations of people's behavior that refer to their internal characteristics, such as abilities, traits, moods, or efforts.

situational attributions
Explanations of people's behavior that refer to external events, such as the weather, luck, accidents, or other people's actions.

fundamental attribution error
In explaining other people's behavior, the tendency to overemphasize personality traits and underestimate situational factors.

FIGURE 12.30
Fundamental Attribution Error
Since 1984, Alex Trebek has hosted the enormously popular television game show *Jeopardy!* Here, Trebek converses with three contestants on the show. Can we judge from this interaction how smart Trebek is?

actor/observer discrepancy
People focus on situations to explain their own behavior while focusing on dispositions to explain other people's behavior.

ANSWER: You would attribute your lateness to situational factors, whereas you would attribute your classmate's lateness to her personality.

he knows the questions and the answers because writers have provided them on cards (**FIGURE 12.30**).

In contrast, when people make attributions about themselves, they tend to focus on situations rather than on their personal dispositions. In conjunction with the fundamental attribution error, this focus on personal situations leads to the **actor/observer discrepancy.** This term refers to two tendencies: When interpreting their own behavior, people tend to focus on situations. When interpreting other people's behavior, they tend to focus on dispositions. For instance, people tend to attribute their own lateness to external factors, such as traffic or competing demands. They tend to attribute other people's lateness to personal characteristics, such as laziness or lack of organization. According to a meta-analysis of 173 studies, the actor/observer effect is not large and happens mainly for negative events or when people explain the behavior of people they know well (Malle, 2006).

Is the fundamental attribution error really fundamental? That is, does it occur across cultures, or do attributional styles differ between Eastern cultures and Western cultures? As discussed in Chapter 1, people in Eastern cultures tend to be more holistic in how they perceive the world. They see the forest rather than individual trees. On average, people in Eastern cultures use much more information when making attributions than do people in Western cultures, and they are more likely to believe that human behavior is the outcome of both personal and situational factors (Choi, Dalal, Kim-Prieto, & Park, 2003; Miyamoto & Kitayama, 2002). Although Easterners are more likely than Westerners to take situational forces into account, however, they still tend to favor personal information over situational information when making attributions about others (Choi, Nisbett, & Norenzayan, 1999). Thus, in interpreting behavior, cultures tend not to differ in whether they emphasize personal factors. Instead, cultures differ in how much they emphasize the situation.

 What does the actor/observer discrepancy predict about how you would explain being late for class compared with another student's being late for class?

12.13 Stereotypes Can Lead to Prejudice and Discrimination

Do all Italians have fiery tempers? Do all Canadians like hockey? Can white women rap? People hold beliefs about groups because such beliefs make it possible to answer these sorts of questions quickly (**FIGURE 12.31**). As discussed in Chapter 8, such beliefs are stereotypes. That is, they are cognitive schemas that help in the organization of information about people on the basis of their membership in certain groups. Mental shortcuts are forms of heuristic thinking: They enable people to make quick decisions. Stereotypes are mental shortcuts that allow for easy, fast processing of social information. Stereotyping occurs automatically and, in most cases, outside of awareness (Devine, 1989).

In and of themselves, stereotypes are neutral. They simply reflect efficient cognitive processes. They can contain information that is negative or positive. Some stereotypes are based in truth: Men tend to be more violent than women, and women tend to be more nurturing than men. These statements are true on average. However, not all men are violent, nor are all women nurturing.

(a)

(b)

FIGURE 12.31
Stereotypes
(a) Would this photo, of fans at a 2010 Olympic Gold Medal Hockey game between Canada and the United States, lead you to think that all Canadians like hockey? **(b)** When you think of a rapper, do you picture a Caucasian woman? Probably not. But Iggy Azalea is one of the white female rappers establishing themselves in this traditionally male-dominated field.

People construct and use such categories for two basic reasons: to streamline the formation of impressions and to deal with the limitations inherent in mental processing (Macrae, Milne, & Bodenhausen, 1994). That is, because of limited mental resources, people cannot scrutinize every person they encounter. Rather than consider each person as unique and unpredictable, people categorize others as belonging to particular groups. They hold knowledge about the groups in long-term memory. For example, they might automatically categorize others on the basis of clothing or hairstyles. Once they have put others into particular categories, they will have beliefs about the others based on stereotypes about the particular categories. That is, stereotypes affect the formation of impressions, which can be positive or negative (Kunda & Spencer, 2003). Consider the stereotype that men are more likely than women to be famous. As a result of this stereotype, people are more likely to falsely remember a male name than a female name as that of a famous person (Banaji & Greenwald, 1995; this misremembering, the false fame effect, is discussed further in Chapter 7).

Once people form stereotypes, they maintain them by numerous processes. As schemas, stereotypes guide attention toward information that confirms the stereotypes and away from disconfirming evidence. Memories may also become biased to match stereotypes. As a result of directed attention and memory biases, people may see *illusory correlations*. Such correlations are an example of the psychological reasoning error (discussed in Chapter 1 and in Section 6.9, "Think like a Psychologist: How Do Superstitions Start?") of seeing relationships that do not exist. In this case, people believe false relationships because they notice only information that confirms their stereotypes. For example, one type of behavior might be perceived in different ways so it is consistent with a stereotype. A lawyer described as aggressive and a construction worker described as aggressive conjure up different images.

Moreover, when people encounter someone who does not fit a stereotype, they put that person in a special category rather than alter the stereotype. This latter process is known as *subtyping*. Thus, a racist who believes Latinos are lazy may categorize a superstar such as Salma Hayek or Jennifer Lopez as an exception to the rule rather than as evidence for the invalidity of the stereotype. Forming a subtype that includes successful Latinos allows the racist to maintain his or her stereotype that Latinos are lazy.

PREJUDICE AND DISCRIMINATION Stereotypes may be positive, neutral, or negative. When they are negative, stereotypes can lead to prejudice and discrimination. **Prejudice** involves negative feelings, opinions, and beliefs associated with a stereotype. **Discrimination** is the inappropriate and unjustified treatment of people as a result of prejudice. Prejudice and discrimination are responsible for much of the conflict and warfare around the world. Within nearly all cultures, some groups of people are treated negatively because of prejudice. Over the last half century, social psychologists have studied the causes and consequences of prejudice, and they have tried to find ways to reduce its destructive effects.

Why do stereotypes so often lead to prejudice and discrimination? Various researchers have theorized that only certain types of people are prejudiced, that people treat others as scapegoats to relieve the tensions of daily living, and that people discriminate against others to protect their own self-esteem. One overarching explanation, consistent with our discussion in Section 12.1, is that evolution has led to two processes that produce prejudice and discrimination: People tend to favor their own groups over other groups, and people tend to stigmatize those who pose threats to their groups. From the perspectives of competition between groups over scarce resources and of social identity theory, it is understandable that people can feel threatened by anything that favors the outgroup at the expense of the ingroup. People are hardwired to categorize people into groups and to defend the ingroups to which they belong and with which they identify.

STEREOTYPES AND PERCEPTION So far, the discussion of stereotypes has focused on beliefs and behavior. What does social psychology have to say about perception itself?

As mentioned earlier, stereotypes can affect attention. Indeed, research has shown that stereotypes can influence basic perceptual processes. In two experiments that demonstrated this influence, white participants looked at pictures of either tools or guns and were asked to classify them as quickly as possible (Payne, 2001). Immediately before seeing a picture, the participants were briefly shown a picture of a white face or a black face. They were told that the face was being shown to signal that either a gun or a tool would appear next. Being shown a black face led the participants to identify guns more quickly and to mistake tools for guns (**FIGURE 12.32**). Another study, in which over 90 percent of the participants were white, found that the reverse is also true: Priming people with pictures of weapons, such as guns and knives, may lead them to pay greater attention to pictures of black faces than to pictures of white faces (Eberhardt, Goff, Purdie, & Davies, 2004). In 2017, the Colgate University campus was locked down due to a report of an armed person in the student center. It turned out that a black student was holding a glue gun on his way to work on an art project. In a letter to the community, the Colgate president, Brian Casey, suggested that implicit bias might have played a role in both the reporting of the incident and the response of safety officers.

prejudice
Negative feelings, opinions, and beliefs associated with a stereotype.

discrimination
The inappropriate and unjustified treatment of people as a result of prejudice.

(a)

(b)

FIGURE 12.32
Stereotypes and Perception
(a) Participants were briefly shown a picture of a black or white face. **(b)** The participants were then immediately shown an object and asked to classify it as a gun or tool. Participants primed by seeing black faces identified guns more quickly and mistook tools for guns. The study revealed that stereotypes can influence basic perceptual processes.

Using a virtual reality simulation, Greenwald, Oakes, and Hoffman (2003) required each participant in a study to play the role of a police officer. On each trial, the participant had to respond, or not, as three things appeared: When a criminal was holding a gun, the participant needed to click a computer mouse to shoot the criminal; when a fellow police officer was holding a gun, the participant needed to press the space bar; when a civilian was holding a neutral object, the participant needed to do nothing. In some trials, the criminal holding a gun was a white male and the police officer holding a gun was a black male. In the other trials, these pairings were reversed. Whatever their assigned roles in the study, blacks were more likely to be incorrectly shot. These shootings occurred, in part, because the participants were more likely to identify as weapons the objects held by the blacks.

Fortunately, there is evidence that special computerized training—in which race is unrelated to the presence of a weapon—can help police officers avoid racial bias in deciding when to shoot (Plant & Peruche, 2005). Research compared police officers who received this training with community members who had not. In simulated decisions to shoot or not shoot blacks and whites, the police officers were much less likely to shoot unarmed people and were equally likely to shoot armed blacks and whites (Correll et al., 2007). The community members were more likely to shoot unarmed black targets. Thus, training seems to be able to override the effects of stereotypes.

MODERN PREJUDICE Even people who believe themselves to be egalitarian may hold negative implicit attitudes about certain groups of people. In 2014, when the Dallas Mavericks owner Mark Cuban said he would cross the street to avoid a black man in a hoodie or a white person looking like a skinhead, he was acknowledging his prejudices even as he condemned himself for having them. Although nowadays few people openly admit to being racist, and many explicitly reject racist attitudes, there remain more subtle forms of prejudice and discrimination. Social psychologists have introduced the idea of **modern racism,** which refers to subtle forms of prejudice that coexist with the rejection of racist beliefs. Modern racists tend to believe that discrimination is no longer a serious problem and that minority groups are demanding too much societal change, as in too many changes to traditional values (Henry & Sears, 2000). Modern racism often leaks out more through indifference to the concerns of minority group members than through overt negativity. For instance, people may condemn racist attitudes toward Latinos but be unwilling to help a Latino in need (Abad-Merino, Newheiser, Dovidio, Tabernero, & González, 2013).

Because most people are reluctant to acknowledge explicit racist attitudes, researchers use questionnaires, such as the Modern Racism Scale (McConahay, 1986), to measure subtle prejudices. For example, a version of this scale was used to assess subtle racism against Asians in Canada (Son Hing, Chung-Yan, Hamilton, & Zanna, 2008). Participants were asked to agree or disagree with statements such as "There are too many foreign students of Asian descent being allowed to attend university in Canada," "Discrimination against Asians is no longer a problem in Canada," and "It is too easy for Asians to illegally arrive in Canada and receive refugee status."

Modern racism arises in part because the equal treatment of minorities can challenge traditions associated with the majority. Other prejudices also have modern subtle forms, such as people who say that gay and lesbian people should not face discrimination but are reluctant to support same-sex marriage because it threatens the traditional definition of marriage as being between a man and a woman (**FIGURE 12.33**).

modern racism
Subtle forms of prejudice that coexist with the rejection of racist beliefs.

FIGURE 12.33
Controversy and Modern Prejudice
Gay rights issues can reveal subtle forms of prejudice. Many opponents of same-sex marriage, such as this protester in Utah, do not advocate discrimination against gay or lesbian people. They argue that same-sex marriage threatens traditional marriage.

Q What is the difference between prejudice and discrimination?

ANSWER: Prejudice involves negative attitudes associated with stereotypes, whereas discrimination is the inappropriate and unjustified treatment of people because of prejudice.

12.14 Prejudice Can Be Reduced

As noted in Section 12.8, having people work on superordinate goals can reduce outgroup bias. These methods also reduce prejudice. Even simply imagining positive social interactions with outgroup members can reduce prejudice and increase prosocial behaviors toward outgroup members (Miles & Crisp, 2014). In addition, other strategies have been shown to reduce prejudice. For example, bilingual instruction in schools lessens ingroup favoritism among elementary school children (Wright & Tropp, 2005). Prejudice can also be reduced through explicit efforts to train people about stereotypical associations. For example, participants who practice associating women and counter-stereotypical qualities—for example, strength and dominance—are more likely than a control group to choose to hire women (Kawakami, Dovidio, & van Kamp, 2005).

People who face discrimination can also take steps to combat prejudice. Strategies such as trying to hide or escape from a stigmatizing condition—think of a gay person "staying in the closet"—often leave prejudice intact, but two strategies that combat prejudice are *reframing* and *self-labeling* (Wang, Whitson, Anicich, Kray, & Galinksy, 2017). Reframing involves taking a negative stereotype and transforming it from a weakness into a strength. For instance, women are often stereotyped as being weak negotiators. However, if negotiation is reframed as requiring more stereotypically feminine traits, such as being a good listener and relying on intuition, then female negotiators outperform men. Self-labeling involves embracing the very slurs used against you (e.g., *queer*). Taking ownership of the slur can provide a sense of power to those who are stigmatized (Galinksy et al., 2013). Self-labeling with a slur can reduce its negative associations in the minds of observers.

INHIBITING STEREOTYPES Patricia Devine (1989) made the important point that people can override the stereotypes they hold and act in nondiscriminatory ways. For instance, most people in North America know some of the negative stereotypes associated with Muslim Americans. When a non-Muslim North American encounters a Muslim person, the information in the stereotypes becomes cognitively available. According to Devine, people who are motivated to be low in prejudice override this automatic activation and act in a nondiscriminatory fashion. Although some automatic stereotypes alter how people perceive and understand the behavior of those they stereotype, simply categorizing people does not necessarily lead to mistreating them.

Indeed, numerous studies have shown that people can consciously alter their automatic stereotyping (Blair, 2002). For instance, Dasgupta and Greenwald (2001) found that presenting positive examples of admired black individuals (e.g., Denzel Washington) produced more-favorable responses toward African Americans. In another study, training people to respond counter-stereotypically—as in having them press a "no" key when they saw an elderly person paired with a stereotype of the elderly—led to reduced automatic stereotyping in subsequent tasks (Kawakami, Dovidio, Moll, Hermsen, & Russin, 2000).

In everyday life, however, inhibiting stereotyped thinking is difficult and requires self-control (Monteith, Ashburn-Nardo, Voils, & Czopp, 2002). The challenge comes, in part, from the need for the frontal lobes to override the emotional responses associated with amygdala activity. As discussed throughout this book, the frontal lobes are important for controlling both thoughts and behavior, whereas the amygdala is involved in detecting potential threats. In one brain imaging study, the amygdala became activated when white participants were briefly shown pictures of black faces (Cunningham et al., 2004). In this context, the amygdala activity may indicate that the participants' immediate responses to black faces were negative. If the faces were presented longer, however, the frontal lobes became active and the amygdala response decreased. Thus, the frontal lobes appear to have overridden the immediate reaction.

PERSPECTIVE TAKING AND PERSPECTIVE GIVING The technique called *perspective taking* involves people actively contemplating the psychological experiences of other people. Such contemplation can reduce racial bias and help to smooth potentially awkward interracial interactions (Todd, Bodenhausen, Richeson, & Galinsky, 2011). Taking another group's perspective appears to reduce negative or positive stereotypes. In one study, participants who used perspective taking rated a typical construction worker to be smarter and more passionate and a typical doctor to be less intelligent and less passionate than did participants in the control condition who did not engage in perspective taking and used their stereotypes to rate a typical construction worker and doctor (Wang, Ku, Tai, & Galinksy, 2014). Taking the perspective of a transgender person markedly reduced prejudice in a sample of over 500 voters in Florida, an effect that persisted three months later (Broockman & Kalla, 2016).

The value of perspective taking for reducing prejudice may depend on whether the person is a member of the majority group or the minority group. In a study that included Palestinian and Israeli participants, perspective taking led the Israelis to the largest positive changes in attitude toward the Palestinians (Bruneau & Saxe, 2012). By contrast, *perspective giving,* in which people share their experiences of being targets of discrimination, led the Palestinians to the largest positive changes in attitude toward the Israelis. These results illustrate the critical roles, in reducing prejudice, of *being heard* for minority group members (e.g., the Palestinians) and *listening* for majority group members (i.e., the Israelis). Bruneau and Saxe (2012) found a similar pattern for Mexican immigrants and white Americans in Arizona (**FIGURE 12.34**). However, perspective taking by the Mexican group actually worsened their attitudes about white Americans. Disempowered groups may resent having to consider the perspectives of empowered groups (Bruneau & Saxe, 2010). Indeed, perspective taking can backfire whenever an individual feels threatened by the other group (Sassenrath, Hodges, & Pfattheicher, 2016). Social psychologists continue to conduct research to find the most useful ways to reduce intergroup hostility and reduce prejudice and discrimination (Oskamp, 2013).

 What is perspective giving?

What Determines the Quality of Relationships?

Involvements between people sometimes lead to relationships. Here, the term *relationships* refers to connections with friends and romantic partners. Researchers have made considerable progress in identifying the factors that lead people to form relationships (Berscheid & Regan, 2005). Many of these findings consider the adaptive value of forming lasting affiliative bonds with others. As discussed in Chapter 10, humans have a fundamental need to belong. This chapter has further explored that strong need for social contact and the various factors that influence how people select friends and mates. Now let's consider the quality of human relationships: how friendships develop, why people fall in love, why romantic relationships sometimes fail, and how people can work to sustain their romantic relationships. As you will see, many of the same principles are involved in choosing friends and choosing lovers.

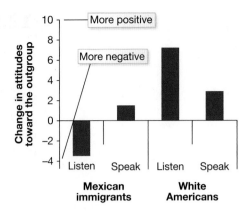

FIGURE 12.34
Groups and Communication
For the minority Mexican immigrants, being heard led to more-positive attitudes toward the outgroup. By contrast, perspective taking led to a worsening of attitudes. For the majority white Americans, being heard led to more-positive attitudes toward the outgroup, but listening produced even greater change.

ANSWER: an effective technique for reducing prejudice in majority group members, with whom minority group members share their experiences of discrimination

12.15 Situational and Personal Factors Influence Interpersonal Attraction and Friendships

What factors influence which people become friends, lovers, or even enemies? Social psychologists have discovered a number of factors that predict people becoming friends or romantically involved. Some of these factors are situational, such as the frequency with which people come into contact, whereas others depend on specific personal characteristics, such as whether a person is judged to be trustworthy. For romantic relationships, psychologists have also identified certain physical characteristics that are found to be more or less attractive in a potential partner.

PROXIMITY AND FAMILIARITY In an early study, Leon Festinger, Stanley Schachter, and Kurt Back (1950) examined friends in a college dorm. Because room assignments were random, the researchers were able to examine the effects of proximity on friendship. *Proximity* here simply means how often people come into contact with each other because they are physically nearby. The more people come into contact, the more likely they are to become friends. Indeed, friendships often form among people who belong to the same groups, clubs, and so on. In other words, people's social networks tend to form with individuals they regularly come into contact with (Rivera, Soderstrom, & Uzzi, 2010).

Proximity might have its effects because of familiarity: People like familiar things more than unfamiliar ones. In fact, humans generally fear anything novel. This phenomenon is known as *neophobia*. By contrast, as discussed earlier, when people are repeatedly exposed to something, they tend to like the thing more over time. This effect—the mere exposure effect—has been demonstrated in hundreds of studies that have used various objects, including faces, geometric shapes, Chinese characters, and nonsense words (Zajonc, 2001). Familiarity can sometimes breed contempt rather than liking. The more we get to know someone, the more aware we become of how different that person is from us (Norton, Frost, & Ariely, 2007). And we tend to prefer people who are similar to us.

FIGURE 12.35
Similarity in Attitudes and Attraction
Friends and romantic partners tend to be similar in personal characteristics, attitudes, beliefs, and attractiveness. A good example of this matching is Beyoncé and Jay-Z, both of whom are very attractive and successful musicians and entrepreneurs.

BIRDS OF A FEATHER Birds of a feather really do flock together (**FIGURE 12.35**). People similar in attitudes, values, interests, backgrounds, and personalities tend to like each other (Youyou, Schwartz, Stillwell, & Kosinski, 2017). In high school, people tend to be friends with those of the same sex, race or ethnicity, age, and year in school. College roommates who are most similar at the beginning of the school year are most likely to become good friends (Neimeyer & Mitchell, 1988). The most successful romantic couples also tend to be the most physically similar, a phenomenon called the *matching principle* (Bentler & Newcomb, 1978; Caspi & Herbener, 1990). Of course, people can and do become friends with, become romantic partners with, and marry people of other races, people who are much older or younger, and so on. Such friendships and relationships tend to be based on other important similarities, such as values, education, and socioeconomic status.

PERSONAL CHARACTERISTICS People tend to especially like those who have admirable personality characteristics and who are physically attractive. This tendency holds true whether people are choosing friends or lovers. In a now-classic study, Norman Anderson (1968) asked college students to rate 555 trait descriptions by how much they would like others who possessed those traits. As you might guess from the earlier discussion of who is rejected from social groups, people dislike cheaters and

Table 12.2 The Ten Most Positive and Most Negative
Personal Characteristics

MOST POSITIVE	MOST NEGATIVE
Sincere	Unkind
Honest	Untrustworthy
Understanding	Malicious
Loyal	Obnoxious
Truthful	Untruthful
Trustworthy	Dishonest
Intelligent	Cruel
Dependable	Mean
Open-Minded	Phony
Thoughtful	Liar

Source: Anderson (1968).

others who drain group resources. Indeed, as shown in **TABLE 12.2**, the least likable characteristics are related to dishonesty, insincerity, and lack of personal warmth. Conversely, people especially like those who are kind, dependable, and trustworthy. Generally, people like those who have personal characteristics valuable to the group. For example, people like those whom they perceive to be competent or reliable much more than those they perceive to be incompetent or unreliable. People who seem overly competent or too perfect make others feel uncomfortable or inadequate, however, and small mistakes can make a person seem more human and therefore more likable. In one study, a highly competent person who spilled a cup of coffee on himself was rated more favorably than an equally competent person who did not perform this clumsy act (Helmreich, Aronson, & LeFan, 1970). This "pratfall effect" helps to humanize people and make others like them more.

PHYSICAL ATTRACTIVENESS What determines physical attractiveness? Some standards of beauty, such as preferences for particular body types, appear to change over time and across cultures. Nevertheless, how people rate attractiveness is generally consistent across all cultures (Cunningham, Roberts, Barbee, Druen, & Wu, 1995). Indeed, brain imaging studies show activity in brain reward regions when both men and women see photographs of opposite-sex faces that have been rated as attractive by other people (Cloutier, Heatherton, Whalen, & Kelley, 2008).

As noted in Chapter 10, there is a general tendency in mate selection for men to seek physical attractiveness and for women to seek status. From an evolutionary point of view, men are attracted to signs of youth and fertility to maximize passing along their genes, whereas women are motivated to find partners who can provide resources for them and their offspring. If women truly are motivated in this way, we would expect them to show preferences for and be attracted to men displaying cues of dominance, strength, and earnings potential. Which physical characteristics might imply dominance in males? As noted earlier in this chapter, the hormone testosterone has been associated with ratings of dominance. One study found that men with the highest

Sample 1, lowest testosterone

Sample 1, highest testosterone

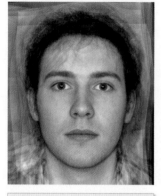

Sample 2, lowest testosterone

Sample 2, highest testosterone

FIGURE 12.36
Testosterone and Facial Width
This figure shows the average faces of twenty men with the **(left)** lowest and **(right)** highest testosterone levels in two different samples of men **(one sample on top, one sample on bottom).** The men with the highest testosterone levels have wider faces.

"what is beautiful is good" stereotype
The belief that attractive people are superior in most ways.

FIGURE 12.37
"Average" Is Attractive
The more faces that are averaged together, the more attractive people find the outcome. The face on the right, a combination of 32 faces, typically is rated most attractive.

level of testosterone had faces with a higher width-to-height ratio (Lefevre, Lewis, Perrett, & Penke, 2013; **FIGURE 12.36**). If higher width-to-height ratio is a sign of dominance, then heterosexual women might be expected to find men with such characteristics most attractive. Recently, researchers had participants meet many potential partners using speed dating. Width-to-height ratio in men was associated with their perceived dominance, physical attractiveness, and likelihood of being chosen for a second date (Valentine, Li, Penke, & Perrett, 2014).

At a more general level, most people find symmetrical faces more attractive than asymmetrical ones (Perrett et al., 1999). This preference may be adaptive, because a lack of symmetry could indicate poor health or a genetic defect. Indeed, one study found evidence that people with more-symmetrical faces reported using fewer antibiotics during the preceding three years, indicating they may be more disease resistant (Thornhill & Gangestad, 2006). There are no racial differences in the extent to which faces are symmetrical, but biracial people tend to have more-symmetrical facial features and correspondingly are rated as more attractive than those who are uniracial (Phelan, 2006). It does not seem to matter which two races are involved in the genetic makeup.

In a cleverly designed study of what people find attractive, Langlois and Roggman (1990) used a computer program to combine (or "average") various faces without regard to individual attractiveness. They found that as more faces were combined, participants rated the "averaged" faces as more attractive (**FIGURE 12.37**). People may view averaged faces as attractive because of the mere exposure effect. In other words, averaged faces may be more familiar than unusual faces. Other researchers contend that although averaged faces might be attractive, averaged *attractive* faces are rated more favorably than averaged *unattractive* faces (Perrett, May, & Yoshikawa, 1994).

Attractiveness can bring many important social benefits: Most people are drawn to those they find physically attractive (Langlois et al., 2000). Attractive people are less likely to be perceived as criminals; are given lighter sentences when convicted of crimes; are typically rated as happier, more intelligent, more sociable, more capable, more gifted, more successful, and less socially deviant; are paid more for doing the same work; and have greater career opportunities. These findings point to what Karen Dion and colleagues (1972) dubbed the **"what is beautiful is good" stereotype.**

Do attractive people actually possess characteristics consistent with the "what is beautiful is good" stereotype? The evidence on this issue is mixed. Attractive people tend to be more popular, more socially skilled, and healthier, but they are not necessarily smarter or happier (Feingold, 1992). Among studies of college students, the

2   4   8   16   32

⟶ Number of faces averaged together ⟶

correlation between objective ratings of attractiveness and other characteristics appears small. In one study, multiple judges objectively rated the attractiveness of the participants. The researchers did not find any relationship between appearance and grades, number of personal relationships, financial resources, or just about anything (Diener, Wolsic, & Fujita, 1995). In addition, attractive people are similar to less attractive people in intelligence, life satisfaction, and self-esteem. Why does having all the benefits of attractiveness not lead to greater happiness? Possibly, attractive people learn to distrust attention from others, especially romantic attention (Reis et al., 1982). They assume that people like them simply for their looks. Because they believe that good things happen to them primarily because they are good-looking, attractive people may come to feel insecure. After all, looks can change or fade with age.

 In terms of relationships, why don't opposites attract?

passionate love

A state of intense longing and desire.

companionate love

A strong commitment based on friendship, trust, respect, and intimacy.

12.16 Love Is an Important Component of Romantic Relationships

The pioneering work of Ellen Berscheid and Elaine (Walster) Hatfield (1969) has drawn an important distinction between passionate love and companionate love. **Passionate love** is a state of intense longing and sexual desire. This kind of love is often portrayed stereotypically in the arts and media. In passionate love, people fall head over heels for each other. They feel an overwhelming urge to be together. When they are together, they are continually aroused sexually (**FIGURE 12.38A**). Brain imaging studies show that passionate love is associated with activity in dopamine reward systems, the same systems involved in drug addiction (Fisher, Aron, & Brown, 2006; Ortigue, Bianchi-Demicheli, Hamilton, & Grafton, 2007).

People experience passionate love early in relationships. In most enduring relationships, passionate love evolves into companionate love (Sternberg, 1986). **Companionate love** is a strong commitment to care for and support a partner (Berscheid & Walster, 1969). This kind of love develops slowly over time because it is based on friendship, trust, respect, and intimacy (**FIGURE 12.38B**).

One theory of love is based on attachment theory. As discussed in Chapter 9, infants can form different levels of attachment with their parents. According to Cindy Hazan and Phillip Shaver (1987), adult relationships also vary in their attachment styles. Romantic relationships are especially likely to vary in terms of attachment. The attachment style a person has as an adult appears to be related to how the person's parents treated her or him as a child (Fraley & Shaver, 2000). People who believe their parents were warm, supportive, and responsive report having secure attachments in their relationships. They find it easy to get close to others and do not fear being abandoned. Just under 60 percent of adults report having this attachment style (Mickelson, Kessler, & Shaver, 1997). The remaining roughly 40 percent have insecure attachments. For example, people who believe their parents were cold and distant report having avoidant attachments. They find it hard to trust or depend on others, and they are wary of those who try to become close to them. Relationship partners make them uncomfortable. About 25 percent of adults report having this attachment style. People whose parents treated them inconsistently—sometimes warm and sometimes not—have ambivalent attachments. These people are best described as clingy. They worry that people do not really love them and are bound to leave them. About 11 percent of adults report having this attachment style.

These findings are based partly on people's recollections of how their parents treated them, however. It is possible that people's memories in this area are distorted.

(a)

(b)

FIGURE 12.38
Passionate Versus Companionate Love
(a) The arts tend to focus on passionate love. Consider this image from the 2016 movie *American Honey,* starring Sasha Lane and Shia LaBeouf. (b) Some romances, however, depict the development of companionate love. Contrast the *American Honey* shot with this image from the 2014 movie *The Fault in Our Stars,* starring Ansel Elgort and Shailene Woodley.

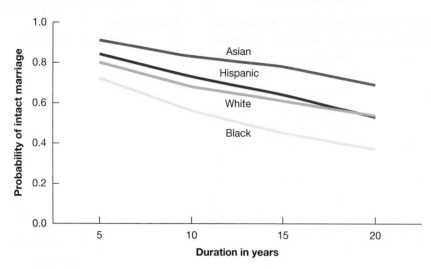

FIGURE 12.39
Success Rates for First Marriages
This graph shows the probability that first marriages in the United States will remain intact, without disruption.

Moreover, relationships can change people's attachment styles. People are likely to become secure in attachment style with a patient, understanding, and trustworthy partner. They may become insecure if paired with a "bad" partner.

PASSION FADES Passion typically fades over time. The long-term pattern of sexual activity within relationships shows a rise and then a decline. Typically, for a period of months or even years, the two people experience frequent, intense desire for one another. They have sex as often as they can arrange it. Past that peak, however, their interest in having sex with each other decreases. For example, from the first year of marriage to the second, frequency of sex declines by about half (James, 1983). After that, the frequency continues to decline, but it does so more gradually. In addition, people typically—and normally—experience less passion for their partners over time as they shift from passionate to companionate love. If people do not develop companionate forms of satisfaction in their romantic relationships—such as friendship, social support, and intimacy—the loss of passion leads to dissatisfaction and often to the eventual dissolution of the relationship (Berscheid & Regan, 2005).

Perhaps unsurprisingly, relatively few marriages meet the blissful ideals that newlyweds expect. Many contemporary Western marriages fail. In the United States, approximately half of all marriages end in divorce or separation. There are considerable racial differences in the probability of divorce, with Asians being the most likely to remain married after 20 years and African Americans the least likely (Copen, Daniels, Vespa, & Mosher, 2012; **FIGURE 12.39**).

DEALING WITH CONFLICT Even in the best relationships, some conflict is inevitable. Couples continually need to resolve strife. Confronting and discussing important problems is clearly an important aspect of any relationship. The way a couple deals with conflict often determines whether the relationship will last.

John Gottman (1995) describes four interpersonal styles that typically lead couples to discord and dissolution. These maladaptive strategies are *being overly critical, holding the partner in contempt* (i.e., having disdain, lacking respect), *being defensive,* and *mentally withdrawing from the relationship.* Gottman humorously uses the phrase *Four Horsemen of the Apocalypse* (a reference to the biblical Book of Revelation) to reflect the serious threats that these patterns pose to relationships. For example, when one partner voices a complaint, the other partner responds with his or her own complaint(s). The responder may raise the stakes by recalling all of the other person's failings. People use sarcasm and sometimes insult or demean their partners. Inevitably, any disagreement, no matter how small, escalates into a major fight over the core problems. Often, the core problems center on a lack of money, a lack of sex, or both.

When a couple is more satisfied with their relationship, the partners tend to express concern for each other even while they are disagreeing. They manage to stay relatively calm and try to see each other's point of view. They may also deliver criticism light-heartedly and playfully (Keltner, Young, Heerey, Oemig, & Monarch, 1998). In addition, optimistic people are more likely to use cooperative problem solving; as a result, optimism is linked to having satisfying and happy romantic relationships (Assad, Donnellan, & Conger, 2007; Srivastava, McGonigal, Richards, Butler, & Gross, 2006).

For additional suggestions about maintaining strong relationships, see Section 12.17, "Using Psychology in Your Life: How Can Psychology Rekindle the Romance in Your Relationship?"

ATTRIBUTIONAL STYLE AND ACCOMMODATION Happy couples also differ from unhappy couples in *attributional style,* or how one partner explains the other's behavior (Bradbury & Fincham, 1990). Happy couples make partner-enhancing attributions. That is, they overlook bad behavior or respond constructively, a process called *accommodation* (Rusbult & Van Lange, 1996). In contrast, unhappy couples make distress-maintaining attributions: They view each other in the most negative ways possible. Essentially, happy couples attribute good outcomes to each other, and they attribute bad outcomes to situations. Unhappy couples attribute *good* outcomes to situations, and they attribute *bad* outcomes to each other. For example, if a couple is happy and one partner brings home flowers as a gift, the other partner reflects on the gift-giver's generosity and sweetness. If a couple is unhappy and one of the partners brings home flowers as a gift, the other partner wonders what bad deed the first partner is making up for. Above all, then, viewing your partner in a positive light—even to the point of idealization—may be key to maintaining a loving relationship.

To investigate this hypothesis, Murray and colleagues (1996) investigated partners' perceptions of each other. Their study included couples who were dating and married couples. The results were consistent with their predictions. Those people who loved their partners the most also idealized their partners the most. That is, they viewed their partners in very positive terms compared with how they viewed other people and compared with how their partners viewed themselves. Those people with the most positively biased views of their partners were more likely to still be in the relationships with their partners several months later than were those people with more "realistic" views of their partners. These perceptions cannot be completely unfounded. It is about viewing your partner kindly, not unrealistically.

 Q How does companionate love differ from passionate love?

ANSWER: Companionate love is based on friendship, trust, and intimacy and builds over a long period. Passionate love happens quickly and is based on sexual desire.

|12.17 How Can Psychology Rekindle the Romance in Your Relationship?

Some couples seem loving and supportive. We look at them and think, "That's the kind of relationship I'd like to have someday!" Other couples seem downright mean to each other. We look at them and think, "That relationship seems so toxic! Why are they even together?" What factors help create these healthy and unhealthy relationships? How can their successes and failures help you create a healthy relationship that will thrive?

Over the past two decades, a number of psychologists have conducted research on healthy and unhealthy relationships. Among the foremost of these researchers is John Gottman. To understand what predicts marital outcomes, Gottman (1998) has studied thousands of married couples. In *Why Marriages Succeed or Fail . . . and How You Can Make Yours Last* (1995), Gottman outlines numerous differences between couples who are happy and those who are not.

Based on his research, Gottman believes that if a couple has about five positive interactions for every negative one, chances are good that the relationship will be stable. If the interactions fall below this level, the couple may be headed for a breakup. If there are as many negatives as positives in a relationship, the prognosis is pretty bleak.

(a)

(b)

FIGURE 12.40
Principles for a Committed Relationship
Positive interactions help keep a relationship stable. **(a)** A thoughtful gesture is one way to show your partner you care. **(b)** Doing activities you both enjoy is another way to spend quality time together.

Therefore, the task for any couple is to seek opportunities for positive feelings and interactions within the relationship. According to Gottman and others, the same principles apply to all long-term, committed relationships, heterosexual or homosexual:

1. **Show interest in your partner.** Listen to her describe the events of the day. Pay attention while she is speaking, and maintain eye contact. Try to be empathetic: Show you really understand and can feel what your partner is feeling. Such empathy and understanding cannot be faked. To convey that you understand your partner's feelings, say things like "That must have been really annoying." Ask follow-up questions to show you are engaged in what your partner is saying.

2. **Be affectionate.** You can show love in very quiet ways, such as simply touching the person once in a while. Reminisce about happy times together. Appreciate the benefits of the relationship. When a couple talks about the joys of their relationship, they tend to be happier with the relationship. Such conversation can include comparing the partnership favorably with the partnerships of other people.

3. **Show you care.** Try to do spontaneous things such as bringing your partner a special treat from the bakery or texting at an unexpected time just to see how he is doing (**FIGURE 12.40A**). Such actions let your partner know you think about him, even when you are not together. When people are dating, they flirt, give each other compliments, and display their best manners. Being in a committed relationship does not mean discarding these things. Be nice to your partner and show her that you value your mutual companionship. Praise your partner whenever possible. In turn, she will feel free to act in kind, which will help you feel good about yourself. Positivity begets positivity.

4. **Spend quality time together.** It is easy for a couple to drift apart and develop separate lives. Find time to explore joint interests, such as hobbies or other activities (**FIGURE 12.40B**). Partners should pursue independent interests, but having some activities and goals in common helps bring a couple closer. In fact, research shows that when a couple engages in novel and exciting activities, the couple's relationship satisfaction increases (Aron, Norman, Aron, McKenna, & Heyman, 2000). Having fun together is an important part of any relationship. Share private jokes, engage in playful teasing, be witty, have adventures. Enjoy each other.

5. **Maintain loyalty and fidelity.** Outside relationships can threaten an intimate partnership. Believing your partner is emotionally or physically involved with another person can pose harm to even the healthiest relationship, as can being distrustful or jealous for no reason. At their core, relationship partners have to trust each other. Anything that threatens that basic sense of trust will harm the relationship. When relationship partners dismiss attractive or threatening alternatives, the partners are better able to remain faithful (Rusbult & Buunk, 1993).

6. **Learn how to handle conflict.** Many people believe that conflict is a sign of a troubled relationship and that couples who never fight must be the happiest, but these ideas are not true. Fighting, especially when it allows grievances to be aired, is one of the healthiest things a couple can do for their relationship. Conflict is inevitable in any serious relationship, but resolving conflict positively is the key to happiness as a couple. Do not avoid conflict or pretend you have no serious issues. Rather, calm down, try to control your anger, and avoid name-calling, sarcasm, or excessive criticism. If you are unable to do so in the heat of the moment, call for a time-out. Return to the discussion when you both feel ready to engage respectfully. Validate your partner's feelings and beliefs even as you express your own feelings and beliefs. Look for areas of compromise.

Much of this advice may seem like common sense. However, many couples lose sight of how to express their love and commitment. Partners can get so caught up in

everything else in their lives, from work to stress about exams to worries about family, that it becomes easier to focus on what is wrong in a relationship than on what is right. When that happens, the relationship has taken a wrong turn. To make a relationship stronger, partners should put considerable effort into recognizing and celebrating all that is good about the relationship. Those affirming experiences might make relationships succeed. ■

 Q Why is conflict not necessarily bad for maintaining relationships?

ANSWER: Conflict is inevitable, and most healthy relationships have occasional conflict. Not dealing with conflict appropriately is what is bad for relationships.

Your Chapter Review

Chapter Summary

How Does Group Membership Affect People?

12.1 People Favor Their Own Groups

Social psychology is the study of how people influence others' thoughts, feelings, and actions. People readily identify ingroups, to which they belong, and outgroups, to which they do not belong. Ingroup and outgroup formation is affected by reciprocity (if Person A helps Person B, Person B will help Person A) and transitivity (friends having the same opinions toward other people). The outgroup homogeneity effect is the tendency to perceive outgroup members as stereotypically more similar than ingroup members are. People also tend to dehumanize members of outgroups. According to social identity theory, individual social identity is based on identification with an ingroup. Ingroup favoritism is pervasive and may reflect evolutionary pressure to protect the self and resources. The prefrontal cortex appears important for ingroup formation.

12.2 Groups Influence Individual Behavior

The presence of others can improve performance (social facilitation). Loss of individuality and self-awareness (deindividuation) can occur in groups. Group decisions can become extreme (group polarization), and poor decisions may be made to preserve group harmony (groupthink). Working in a group can result in decreased effort (social loafing) if group members think their individual efforts cannot be monitored.

12.3 People Conform to and Comply with Others

Conformity occurs when people alter their behaviors or opinions to match the behaviors, opinions, or expectations of others. Conformity results from normative influence (the attempt to fit in with the group and avoid looking foolish) and informational influence (the assumption that the behavior of others is the correct way to respond). People may reject social norms and not conform when group size is small or when the group includes at least one other dissenter. When group size is larger than six, conformity increases if the group demonstrates unanimity. Conformity likely results from a fear of social rejection. Compliance occurs when people agree to the requests of others. Compliance increases when people are in a good mood or are subjected to tactics such as the foot-in-the-door, door-in-the-face, and low-balling techniques.

12.4 Think like a Psychologist: Can Social Norms Marketing Reduce Binge Drinking?

Social norms marketing tries to correct false beliefs about drinking behavior by giving factual normative comparisons for average students. Although some programs have been successful, social norms marketing can backfire by increasing consumption of alcohol by light drinkers. The most successful programs include social norms marketing with persuasive arguments about the hazards of excessive alcohol consumption.

12.5 People Are Obedient to Authority

Obedience occurs when people follow the orders of an authority. As demonstrated by Milgram's famous study, people may inflict harm on others if ordered to do so by an authority. Individuals who are concerned about others' perceptions of them are more likely to be obedient. Obedience decreases with greater distance from the authority.

When Do People Harm or Help Others?

12.6 Many Factors Can Influence Aggression

Aggression is influenced by situational, biological, social, and cultural factors. Situational factors that lead to negative emotions—factors including social rejection, fear, heat, and pain—can influence aggression. A mutation in the MAOA gene and serotonin levels have been linked to aggressive behavior in some individuals. High levels of the hormone testosterone have also been associated with aggressive behavior. However, it is difficult to determine whether high testosterone levels motivate aggression, or whether threatening encounters produce high testosterone levels. It is also possible that testosterone is more important for dominance than for aggression. The effects of social and cultural factors on aggression can change over time. In societies that advocate a culture of honor, people are more likely to exhibit violence and aggression.

12.7 Many Factors Can Influence Helping Behavior

Prosocial behaviors promote positive interpersonal relationships. Altruism toward kin members increases the likelihood of passing on common genes. Altruism toward nonrelatives increases the likelihood that others

will reciprocate help when we need it. The bystander intervention effect is most likely to occur when people experience diffusion of responsibility, when a situation is unclear and people fear making social blunders, when people are anonymous, and when people perceive greater risk than benefit to helping others.

12.8 Cooperation Can Reduce Outgroup Bias

People can respond to outgroup members in need, as demonstrated by global response to natural disasters. Cooperation and working toward superordinate goals can increase harmony across groups.

How Do Attitudes Guide Behavior?

12.9 People Form Attitudes Through Experience and Socialization

Attitudes are evaluations of objects, of events, or of ideas. Attitudes are influenced by familiarity (the mere exposure effect) and may be shaped by conditioning and socialization. Attitudes that are strong, personally relevant, specific, formed through personal experience, and easily accessible are most likely to affect behavior. Explicit attitudes are attitudes that people are consciously aware of and can report. Implicit attitudes operate at an unconscious level. In some situations that are socially sensitive, implicit attitudes can predict behavior better than explicit attitudes.

12.10 Discrepancies Lead to Dissonance

A contradiction between attitudes or between an attitude and a behavior produces cognitive dissonance. This state is characterized by anxiety, tension, and displeasure. People reduce dissonance by changing their attitudes or behaviors; trivializing the discrepancies (such as through postdecisional dissonance); or rationalizing the discrepancies (such as through justifying effort).

12.11 Attitudes Can Be Changed Through Persuasion

Persuasion involves the use of a message to actively and consciously change an attitude. According to the elaboration likelihood model, persuasion through the central route (which involves careful thought about the message) produces stronger and more persistent attitude change than persuasion through the peripheral route (which relies on peripheral cues, such as the attractiveness of the person making the argument).

How Do People Think About Others?

12.12 People Make Judgments About Others

People are highly sensitive to nonverbal information (e.g., facial expression, eye contact), and they can develop accurate impressions of others on the basis of very thin slices of behavior. People use personal dispositions and situational factors to explain behavior. The fundamental attribution error occurs when people favor personal attributions over situational attributions in explaining other people's behavior. The actor/observer discrepancy is people's tendency to make personal attributions when explaining other people's behavior and situational attributions when explaining their own behavior.

12.13 Stereotypes Can Lead to Prejudice and Discrimination

Stereotypes are cognitive schemas that allow for fast, easy processing of social information. Illusory correlations cause people to see relationships that do not exist, and they result from confirmatory bias toward selecting information that supports stereotypes. Prejudice occurs when the feelings, opinions, and beliefs associated with a stereotype are negative. Prejudice can lead to discrimination, the inappropriate and unjustified treatment of others. Modern racism is a subtle form of prejudice that has developed as people have learned to inhibit the public expression of their prejudiced beliefs.

12.14 Prejudice Can Be Reduced

Sharing superordinate goals that require cooperation can lead to reduced prejudice and discrimination. Imagining positive social interactions with outgroup members, inhibiting stereotypes (for instance, by presenting people with positive examples of negatively stereotyped groups), perspective taking (actively contemplating the psychological experiences of other people), and perspective giving (describing personal experiences of discrimination) can also reduce prejudice and discrimination.

What Determines the Quality of Relationships?

12.15 Situational and Personal Factors Influence Interpersonal Attraction and Friendships

People are attracted to individuals they have frequent contact with, with whom they share similar attributes, who possess admirable characteristics, and who are physically attractive. Men are attracted by physical signs of youth and fertility. Women are attracted by signs of dominance, strength, and earnings potential, and these signs may include faces with a higher width-to-height ratio. People find "averaged" faces and symmetrical faces more attractive. Physically attractive people experience many social benefits, but they do not report greater happiness.

12.16 Love Is an Important Component of Romantic Relationships

Passionate love is characterized by intense longing and sexual desire. Companionate love is characterized by commitment and support. In successful romantic relationships, passionate love tends to evolve into companionate love. How a couple deals with conflict influences the stability of their relationship. Couples who attribute positive outcomes to each other and negative outcomes to situational factors and make partner-enhancing attributions report higher levels of marital happiness.

12.17 Using Psychology in Your Life: How Can Psychology Rekindle the Romance in Your Relationship?

In successful relationships, people express interest in their partners, are affectionate, show they care, spend quality time together, remain loyal to each other, and handle conflict appropriately. Putting effort into a relationship and engaging in these actions increase the likelihood of the relationship enduring over time.

Key Terms

actor/observer discrepancy, p. 498

aggression, p. 482

altruism, p. 486

attitudes, p. 490

attributions, p. 497

bystander intervention effect, p. 487

cognitive dissonance, p. 493

companionate love, p. 507

compliance, p. 478

conformity, p. 475

deindividuation, p. 474

discrimination, p. 500

elaboration likelihood model, p. 495

explicit attitudes, p. 491

fundamental attribution error, p. 497

group polarization, p. 474

groupthink, p. 475

implicit attitudes, p. 491

inclusive fitness, p. 486

informational influence, p. 476

ingroup favoritism, p. 471

mere exposure effect, p. 490

modern racism, p. 501

nonverbal behavior, p. 496

normative influence, p. 476

obedience, p. 480

outgroup homogeneity effect, p. 471

passionate love, p. 507

personal attributions, p. 497

persuasion, p. 494

prejudice, p. 500

prosocial behaviors, p. 485

situational attributions, p. 497

social facilitation, p. 473

social identity theory, p. 471

social loafing, p. 475

social norms, p. 476

"what is beautiful is good" stereotype, p. 506

Putting Psychology to Work

How Can Social Psychology Be Used in Politics?

What does it take to win an election? As you have learned in this chapter, social psychologists study the ways in which people can influence and change the thoughts and behavior of others. Persuading potential voters to choose one candidate over another, to take a position on an issue, or to vote at all can, of course, be quite useful in political campaigns.

Consider the persuasion techniques, studied in social psychology, that can be used to increase voter turnout. In an example of social norming, people may be informed that their neighbors are planning to vote. In foot-in-the-door appeals, potential voters may be asked to sign unofficial pledges to vote. Once people have complied with this small request, they will be much more likely to follow up with the promise on Election Day. Finally, attitude-behavior consistency may be primed by reminding potential voters that they have voted in past elections.

While social psychology research in persuasion and attitude formation has long been used in advertising and marketing, its application to the political realm has opened up many new employment opportunities. Lobbyists for advocacy organizations rely on persuasion techniques. Campaign managers, communication directors, voter outreach coordinators, and social media editors benefit from knowing how attitudes are formed and how they can be changed.

In addition, a subfield of psychology focuses on politics. Political psychology is an interdisciplinary area of research that examines politics, political parties, and the behavior of voters and politicians from a psychological perspective. Political psychologists have doctoral degrees and conduct research in academic centers or policy think tanks.

The bottom line: Even for those without college degrees, an understanding of social psychological concepts such as persuasion, attitude change, and social norms provides excellent training for jobs in the political sector. Those with baccalaureate degrees can work in campaign organizations or as lobbyists on Capitol Hill. Doctoral training is required for political psychologists.

Q **Want to earn a better grade on your test?**
Go to **INQUIZITIVE** to learn and review this chapter's content, with personalized feedback along the way. Practice Tests and accompanying answer keys can be found at the back of the book on page PT-1.

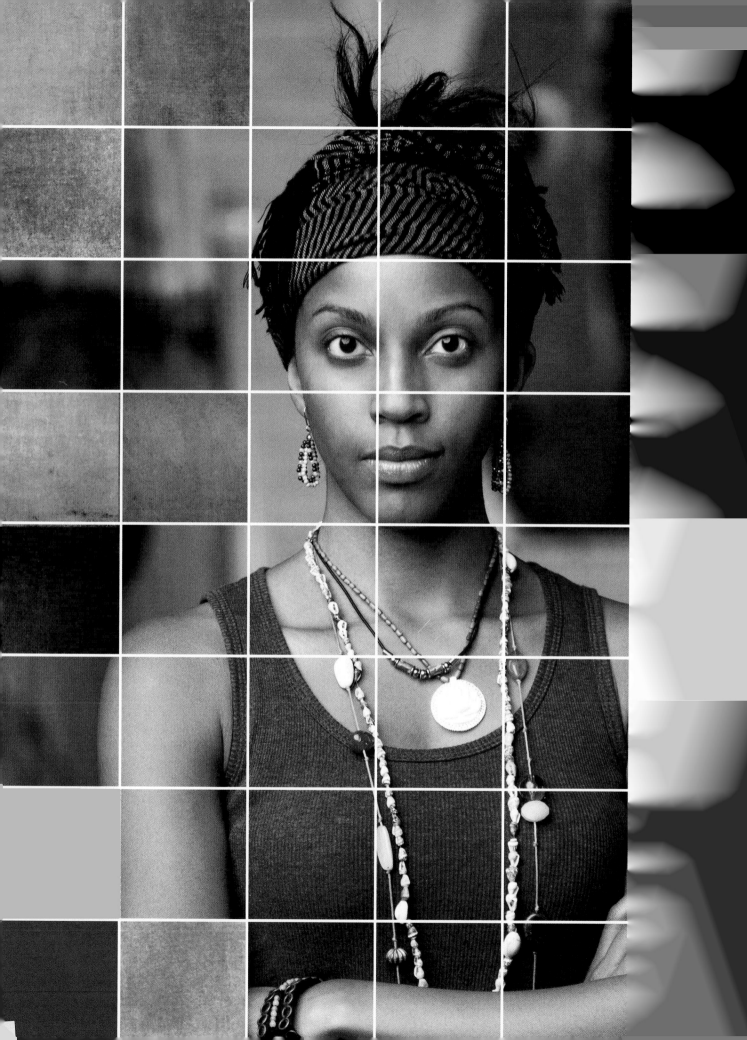

13 Personality

Big Questions

- Where Does Personality Come From? 516

- What Are the Theories of Personality? 521

- How Stable is Personality? 532

- How Is Personality Assessed? 540

- How Do We Know Our Own Personalities? 546

LIKE MANY PEOPLE, YOU SOMETIMES FEEL SHY IN NEW SITUATIONS. Most of the time, though, you are pretty relaxed and outgoing. By contrast, your brother is extremely shy in almost every situation outside the home. Unless he is at home and it is just family, he can barely speak or make eye contact. How is it that your brother, who grew up in the same house with the same parents, differs so much from you? How much of your personality is a product of your genes, and how much was affected by how you were raised? Where does personality come from?

People constantly try to figure out others—to understand why they behave in certain ways and to predict their behavior. In fact, many students take psychology courses partly because they want to know what makes other people tick. One challenge of figuring out people is that they may act differently in different situations. What does a person's behavior tell us about his or her personality? Imagine if everyone felt the same, thought the same, and acted the same. Life would be boring, because differences between individuals add zest to life. This chapter explores how people differ. The picture that emerges is a familiar one in psychology: Personality is a combination of people's genetics, forces in their environments, and the life choices they make. For personality psychologists, the big questions are: Where does personality come from? What are the theories of personality? How stable is personality? How is personality assessed? And how do we know our own personalities?

- Summarize the results of twin studies and adoption studies as those results pertain to personality.

- Understand how genes interact with environment to produce personality.

- Identify distinct temperaments.

FIGURE 13.1

Justin Bieber as an Individual
What kind of person is Justin Bieber? Personality psychologists try to understand individuals, and one characteristic of people like Bieber is how they deal with celebrity status.

FIGURE 13.2

Gordon Allport
In 1937, Allport published the first major textbook of personality psychology. His book defined the field. He also championed the study of individuals and established traits as a central concept in personality research.

Where Does Personality Come From?

For psychologists, **personality** consists of people's characteristic thoughts, emotional responses, and behaviors. Some personality psychologists are most interested in understanding *whole persons*. That is, they take one person, such as Justin Bieber, and try to understand as much as possible about him as an individual (**FIGURE 13.1**). Other personality psychologists study how particular characteristics, such as self-esteem or shyness, influence behavior. For instance, they want to know how people with low self-esteem differ from those with high self-esteem. Their interest is in how the particular characteristic influences behavior. Each characteristic is a **personality trait:** a pattern of thought, emotion, and behavior that is relatively consistent over time and across situations (Funder, 2012). Traits are dispositions to think, act, or feel in predictable ways in certain situations.

Personality is not just a list of traits, however. Gordon Allport, one of the founders of the field, gave a classic scientific definition of personality: "the dynamic organization within the individual of those psychophysical systems that determine [the individual's] characteristic behavior and thought" (1961, p. 28; **FIGURE 13.2**). This definition includes many of the concepts most important to a contemporary understanding of personality. The notion of *organization* indicates that personality is a coherent whole. This organized whole is *dynamic* in that it is goal seeking, sensitive to particular contexts, and adaptive to the person's environment. By emphasizing *psychophysical systems,* Allport brought together two ideas: He highlighted the mental nature of personality (i.e., the *psycho-* part of *psychophysical*), and he recognized that personality arises from basic biological processes (i.e., the *-physical* part). In addition, his definition stresses that personality causes people to have *characteristic* behaviors and thoughts (and feelings). In other words, people do and think and feel things relatively consistently over time.

13.1 Genetic Factors Influence the Development of Personality

Over the past few decades, evidence has emerged that biological factors—such as genes, brain structures, and neurochemistry—play an important role in determining personality. Of course, these factors are all affected by experience. As discussed in Chapter 3, every cell in the body contains the genome, or master recipe, that provides detailed instructions for physical processes. Gene expression—whether a gene is turned off or on—underlies all psychological activity. Ultimately, genes have their effects only if they are expressed. In terms of personality, genetic makeup may predispose certain traits or characteristics, but whether these genes are expressed depends on the unique circumstances that each person faces in life. For instance, as noted in Chapter 3, children with a certain gene variation were found to be more likely to become violent criminals as adults if they were abused during childhood. An important theme throughout this book is that nature and nurture work together to produce individuals, and this theme holds particularly true for personality.

There is overwhelming evidence that nearly all personality traits have a genetic component (Plomin, DeFries, Knopik, & Neiderhiser, 2016; Turkheimer, Pettersson, & Horn, 2014). One of the earliest studies to document the heritability of personality was conducted by James Loehlin and Robert Nichols (1976). The researchers examined similarities in personality in more than 800 pairs of twins. Across a wide variety of traits, identical twins proved much more similar than fraternal twins. This pattern reflects the actions of genes, since identical twins share nearly the same genes, whereas fraternal twins do not.

Numerous twin studies have subsequently found that genetic influence accounts for approximately half the variance (40–60 percent) between individuals for all personality traits, as well as in specific attitudes that reflect personality traits, such as attitudes toward the death penalty, abortion on demand, and how much they enjoy rollercoaster rides (Olson, Vernon, Harris, & Jang, 2001). Further, the genetic basis of the traits has been shown to be the same across cultures (Yamagata et al., 2006). These patterns persist whether the twins rate themselves or whether friends, family, or trained observers rate them (**FIGURE 13.3**).

ADOPTION STUDIES Further evidence for the genetic basis of personality comes from adoption studies. Say that two children who are not biologically related are raised in the same household as adopted siblings. Those two children tend to be no more alike in personality than any two strangers randomly plucked off the street (Plomin & Caspi, 1999). Moreover, the personalities of adopted children bear no significant relationship to those of the adoptive parents. Together these findings suggest that parenting style may have relatively little impact on personality.

In fact, current evidence suggests that parenting style has much less impact than has long been assumed (Turkheimer et al., 2014). For instance, studies typically find small correlations in personality between biological siblings or between children and their biological parents. These correlations are still larger than for adopted children. In other words, the similarities in personality between biological siblings and between children and their biological parents seem to have some genetic component.

"I could cry when I think of the years I wasted accumulating money, only to learn that my cheerful disposition is genetic."

personality
A person's characteristic thoughts, emotional responses, and behaviors.

personality trait
A pattern of thought, emotion, and behavior that is relatively consistent over time and across situations.

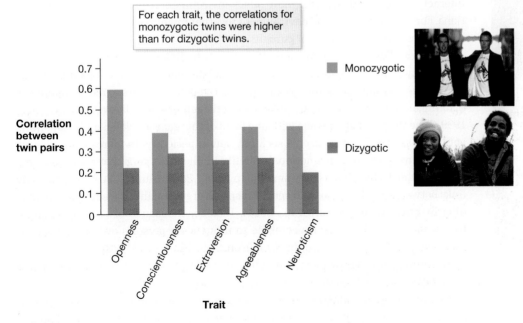

FIGURE 13.3
Correlations in Twins
Researchers examined correlations between 123 pairs of identical (monozygotic) twins and 127 pairs of fraternal (dizygotic) twins in Vancouver, Canada. This chart summarizes some of their findings (these traits, called the Big Five, are discussed in Section 13.6).

(a)

(b)

(c)

FIGURE 13.4
Three Types of Temperament
Temperaments are aspects of the personality that are more determined by biology. There are three temperaments, which are based on the degree of a child's **(a)** activity level, **(b)** emotionality, and **(c)** sociability.

Why, then, are children raised together in the same household—who are not identical twins—so different (Plomin & Daniels, 2011)? One explanation is that the lives of siblings diverge as they establish friendships outside the home (Rowe, Woulbroun, & Gulley, 2013). The types of peers that children have affect how they think, behave, and feel, and thoughts, behaviors, and feelings can all influence personality development (Harris, 1995; 2011). Even though the siblings are raised in the same household, their home environments differ as a function of age and the fact that they have younger or older sisters or brothers and their parents respond to each of them differently (Avinun & Knafo, 2014). Siblings' personalities slowly grow apart as their initial differences become magnified through their interactions with the world.

The small correlations in personality among siblings might imply that parenting style has little effect, but (as discussed in Chapter 9) parents play important roles in their children's development. Parents influence many aspects of their children's lives, such as by selecting where the family lives. The chosen neighborhood can have a major impact on the child's peer groups and other experiences that shape personality. By selecting neighborhoods with good schools and low crime rates, parents influence the likelihood that their children will fall in with good rather than bad crowds. By nurturing athletic or artistic talents, parents can increase the likelihood that their children will meet like-minded children or have experiences that foster future interests. Thus, parents help determine the environments that shape their children's personalities.

ARE THERE SPECIFIC GENES FOR PERSONALITY? Research has revealed genetic components for particular behaviors, such as television viewing habits or getting divorced, and even for specific attitudes, such as feelings about capital punishment or appreciation of jazz (Tesser, 1993). These findings do not mean, of course, that genes lurking in our DNA determine the amount or types of television we watch. Instead, genes predispose us to have certain personality traits. Those personality traits are associated with behavioral, cognitive, or emotional tendencies, referred to as dispositions. In most cases, researchers note the influence of multiple genes that interact independently with the individual's environment to produce general dispositions. For example, genes and environment together might result in a person's preferring indoor activities to outdoor pursuits.

Initial studies found evidence that genes can be linked with some specificity to personality traits. For instance, a gene that regulates one particular dopamine receptor has been associated with novelty seeking, the desire to pursue new experiences (Cloninger, Adolfsson, & Svrakic, 1996; Ekelund, Lichtermann, Jaervelin, & Peltonen, 1999). The theory is that people with one form of this gene are deficient in dopamine activity. As a result, these people seek out new experiences to increase the release of dopamine. Research on emotional stability implicates a gene that regulates serotonin, although the effect is very small (Jang et al., 2001; Munafò, 2012). In fact, any links between specific genes and specific aspects of personality appear to be extraordinarily small (Turkheimer et al., 2014). Instead, thousands of genes contribute to specific traits. These genes combine to influence a person's overall personality (Chabris, Lee, Cesarini, Benjamin, & Laibson, 2015; Plomin et al., 2016).

According to David Lykken and colleagues (1992), it may be that each chance aggregation of genes produces a unique individual. These researchers provide the analogy of a poker hand received by a child. Say that the child's mother has dealt the 10 and king of hearts and the child's father has dealt the jack, queen, and ace of hearts. Although neither parent alone has dealt a meaningful hand, together they have passed on a royal flush. Of course, some people receive winning hands and others receive difficult hands to play. The point is that each person's personality reflects the genetic hand dealt jointly by both parents.

Moreover, each person experiences different circumstances that may cause epigenetic changes and the selective expression of certain genes. Recall from Chapter 3 that epigenetic processes describe how environment affects genetic expression. Given the complexity of personality, the complexity of personality's underlying genetic basis is hardly surprising. Even though twin studies provide overwhelming evidence that genes account for about half the variance in personality, researchers may never identify the specific genes that produce these effects (Munafò & Flint, 2011). Adding in epigenetic changes that result from interactions with the environment makes it even more difficult to identify the influence of any specific gene (Zhang & Meaney, 2010).

On average, how similar are the personalities of adopted children to the personalities of the parents who adopt them and raise them?

ANSWER: There is little relation between the personalities of adopted children and the personalities of those who raise them.

13.2 Temperaments Are Evident in Infancy

Genes work by affecting biological processes. Since genes influence personality, it makes sense that genes help produce biological differences in personality. These differences are called **temperaments:** general tendencies to feel or act in certain ways. Temperaments are broader than personality traits. Life experiences may alter personality traits, as will be discussed later in this chapter, but temperaments represent the innate biological structures of personality and are more stable (Rothbart, 2011).

Arnold Buss and Robert Plomin (1984) have argued that three basic characteristics can be considered temperaments (**FIGURE 13.4**). *Activity level* is the overall amount of energy and of behavior a person exhibits. For example, some children race around the house, others are less vigorous, and still others are slow paced. *Emotionality* describes the intensity of emotional reactions. For example, children who cry often or easily become frightened, as well as adults who quickly anger, are likely to be high in emotionality. Finally, *sociability* refers to the general tendency to affiliate with others. People high in sociability prefer to be with others rather than to be alone.

These temperaments have been linked to people's propensities to move to new locations. A study of migration patterns in Finland found that people who scored high on sociability were more likely to migrate to urban areas and were more likely to migrate to places that were quite distant from their hometowns. Those people who had high activity levels were more likely, in general, to migrate to a new location, regardless of that location. Finally, those who were high in emotionality were likely to migrate to places that were close to their hometowns (Jokela, Elovainio, Kivimaki, & Keltikangas-Jarvinen, 2008). According to Buss and Plomin, these three temperamental styles are the main personality factors influenced by genes. Indeed, evidence from twin studies, adoption studies, and family studies indicates a powerful effect of heredity on these core temperaments. Researchers have also identified other temperaments, such as the extent to which children are able to control their behaviors and their emotions (Caspi, 2000).

Do temperament differences exist between girls and boys? A meta-analysis found robust gender differences in temperament in early childhood (Else-Quest, Hyde, Goldsmith, & Van

temperaments
Biologically based tendencies to feel or act in certain ways.

"Oh, he's cute, all right, but he's got the temperament of a car alarm."

B. Smaller

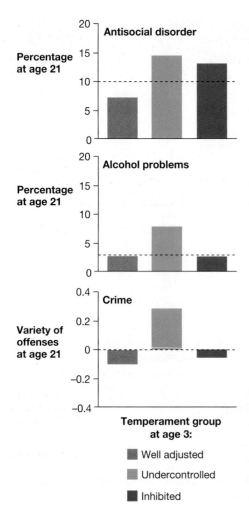

20

Antisocial disorder

Percentage
at age 21

15

10

5

0

20

Alcohol problems

Percentage
at age 21

15

10

5

0

0.4

Crime

Variety of
offenses
at age 21

0.2

0

−0.2

−0.4

**Temperament group
at age 3:**

■ Well adjusted

■ Undercontrolled

■ Inhibited

FIGURE 13.5
Predicting Behavior
Researchers investigated the personality development of more than 1,000 people. As shown in these graphs, the individuals judged undercontrolled at age 3 were later more likely to be antisocial, to have alcohol problems, and to be criminals than those judged either well adjusted or inhibited. In each graph, the dotted line indicates the average for the entire sample.

Hulle, 2006). Girls demonstrated stronger abilities to control their attention and resist their impulses. Boys were more physically active and experienced more high-intensity pleasure, such as in rough-and-tumble play. However, there were no temperamental differences in negative emotions, such as being angry or neurotic, during childhood. Later in this chapter, you will learn about how females and males differ in their adult personalities and how these differences vary across cultures.

LONG-TERM IMPLICATIONS OF TEMPERAMENTS Recent research has documented compelling evidence that early childhood temperaments significantly influence behavior and personality structure throughout a person's development (Caspi, 2000). As discussed in Chapter 3, researchers investigated the health, development, and personalities of more than 1,000 people born during a one-year period (Caspi et al., 2002). These individuals were examined approximately every two years. Most of them (95 percent) remained in the study through their 38th birthdays (Poulton, Moffitt, & Silva, 2015). At 3 years of age, they were classified into temperamental types based on examiners' ratings (the classification of temperament types differed from those identified by Buss and Plomin). The classification at age 3 predicted personality structure and various behaviors in adulthood. For instance, socially inhibited children were much more likely, as adults, to be anxious, to become depressed, to be unemployed, to have less social support, and to attempt suicide (Caspi, 2000; **FIGURE 13.5**). These findings suggest that early childhood temperaments may be good predictors of later behaviors (Slutske, Moffitt, Poulton, & Caspi, 2012).

The extent to which people are socially anxious in adolescence and adulthood has been linked to early differences in temperament. Research has shown that children as young as 6 weeks of age can be identified as likely to be shy (Kagan & Snidman, 1991). Approximately 15–20 percent of newborns react to new situations or strange objects by becoming startled and distressed, crying, and vigorously moving their arms and legs. The developmental psychologist Jerome Kagan refers to these children as *inhibited*, and he views this characteristic as biologically determined. Showing signs of inhibition at 2 months of age predicts later parental reports that the children are socially anxious at 4 years of age, and such children are likely to be shy well into their teenage years.

The biological evidence suggests that the amygdala—the brain region involved in emotional responses, especially fear—is involved in social anxiety. In one study, adults received brain scans while viewing pictures of familiar faces and of novel faces (Schwartz, Wright, Shin, Kagan, & Rauch, 2003). One group of these adults had been categorized as inhibited before age 2. The other group had been categorized as uninhibited before age 2. Compared with the uninhibited group, the inhibited group showed greater activation of the amygdala—a brain region involved when people are threatened—while viewing the novel faces. That is, after the passage of so many years, the inhibited group still seemed to show a threat response to novel faces (see "The Methods of Psychology: Inhibition and Social Anxiety"). In Chapter 14, you will learn that being shy and inhibited as a child may predispose some children to developing psychological disorders involving excessive anxiety in the absence of any real threat.

Although shyness has a biological component, it has a social component as well. Approximately one-quarter of behaviorally inhibited children are not shy later in childhood (Kagan, 2011). This development typically occurs when parents create supportive and calm environments in which children can deal with stress and novelty

HYPOTHESIS: People who had an inhibited temperamental style as children are more likely to show signs of social anxiety later in life.

RESEARCH METHOD:

1 Adults received brain scans while viewing pictures of familiar faces and of novel faces. One group of these adults had been categorized as inhibited before age 2. The other group had been categorized as uninhibited before age 2.

2 Two regions of the brain were more activated by novel faces. These areas were the amygdala (marked "Amy" in the brain scan below) and the occipito-temporal cortex (marked "OTC"). The amygdala is normally active when people are threatened. The occipitotemporal cortex is normally active when people see faces, whether the faces are novel or familiar.

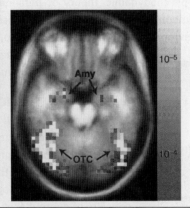

RESULTS: Compared with the uninhibited group, the inhibited group showed significantly greater activation of the amygdala while viewing novel faces. That activation indicated that, when seeing novel faces, the inhibited group showed greater brain activity associated with threat.

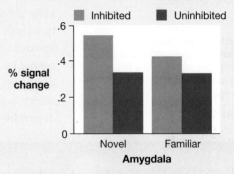

CONCLUSION: The results suggest that some aspects of childhood temperament are preserved in the adult brain. In particular, biological factors seem to play an important role in social anxiety.

QUESTION: Did inhibited children show increased amygdala activity to all faces?

ANSWER: No. They showed increased activity to only novel faces.

Source: Schwartz, C. E., Wright, C. I., Shin, L. M., Kagan, J., & Rauch, S. L. (2003, June 20). Inhibited and uninhibited infants "grown up": Adult amygdalar response to novelty. *Science, 300,* 1952–1953.

at their own paces. But these parents do not completely shelter their children from stress, so the children gradually learn to deal with their negative feelings in novel situations. This result points to the importance of gene-environment interactions.

 Which brain area is involved in social anxiety?

ANSWER: the amygdala, a brain region associated with responding to threat

What Are the Theories of Personality?

Understanding personality as both dynamic and consistent may be one of humankind's oldest quests. In fact, the word *personality* comes from the Latin word *persona,* meaning "mask." In ancient Greek and Roman plays, actors performed their roles wearing masks. Each mask represented a separate personality.

Since antiquity, many theories have been proposed to explain such basic differences between individuals. During the twentieth century, psychologists approached the study of personality from a number of theoretical perspectives. Psychologists' views on personality were based on their individual theoretical orientations. For example, psychodynamic theorists believed unconscious forces determined

Learning Objectives

- Describe the major approaches to the study of personality.

- Identify theorists associated with the major approaches to the study of personality.

psychodynamic theory

The Freudian theory that unconscious forces determine behavior.

id

In psychodynamic theory, the component of personality that is completely submerged in the unconscious and operates according to the pleasure principle.

superego

In psychodynamic theory, the internalization of societal and parental standards of conduct.

ego

In psychodynamic theory, the component of personality that tries to satisfy the wishes of the id while being responsive to the dictates of the superego.

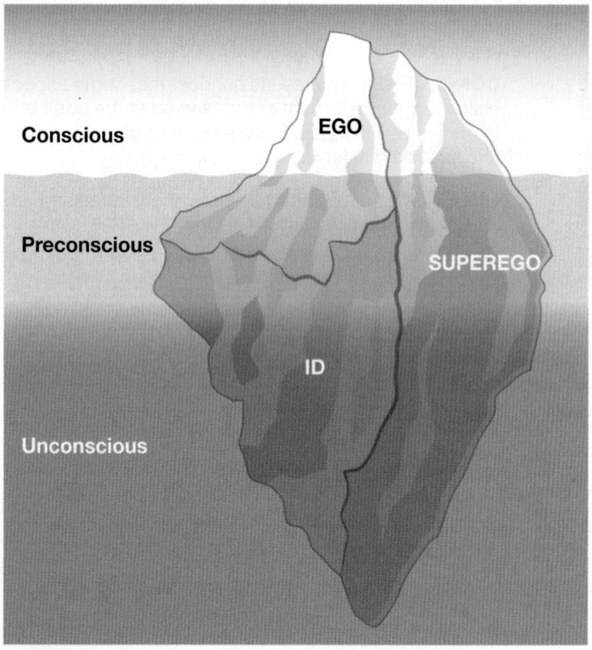

FIGURE 13.6
Levels of Consciousness
Sigmund Freud theorized that mental activity occurred at three levels. He believed that much of human behavior was influenced by unconscious processes, which can result in conflict between the three personality structures: the id, the ego, and the superego.

personality. Behaviorists believed that personality resulted from histories of reinforcement. Cognitively oriented psychologists focused on how thought processes affected personality. Humanistic psychologists emphasized personal growth and self-understanding. Contemporary psychologists are primarily interested in trait approaches and the biological basis of personality traits. The following sections consider these various theoretical perspectives.

13.3 Psychodynamic Theories Emphasize Unconscious and Dynamic Processes

As discussed in Chapter 1, Sigmund Freud was a physician who developed many ideas about personality by observing patients he was treating for psychological disturbances. For example, some of Freud's patients suffered from paralysis that had no apparent physical cause. Freud came to believe their problems were psychogenic—*caused* by psychological rather than physical factors. From his clinical work, Freud developed his **psychodynamic theory** of personality. The central premise of this theory is that unconscious forces—such as wishes, desires, and hidden memories—determine behavior. Many of Freud's ideas are controversial and not well supported by scientific research, but they had an enormous influence over psychological thinking for much of the early history of the field.

UNCONSCIOUS INFLUENCE Freud believed that conscious awareness was only a small fraction of mental activity. That is, conscious awareness represented the proverbial tip of the iceberg, with most mental processes buried under the surface (**FIGURE 13.6**). According to this model, the *conscious* level consists of the thoughts that people are aware of. The *preconscious* level consists of content that is not currently in awareness but that could be brought to awareness. This level is roughly analogous to long-term memory. The *unconscious* level contains material that the mind cannot easily retrieve, including hidden memories, wishes, desires, and motives.

For Freud, unconscious forces that drive behavior could produce conflict. In general, these conflicts are not accessible. Sometimes, however, this information leaks into consciousness. As discussed in Chapter 4, for example, people may accidentally reveal a hidden motive when uttering a *Freudian slip*. Think of someone introducing herself or himself to an attractive person by saying, "Excuse me, I don't think we've been properly seduced" instead of "properly introduced." For Freud, such slips were not accidents. Instead, they offered a glimpse into unconscious forces that indicate hidden, unconscious desires.

A STRUCTURAL MODEL OF PERSONALITY Freud (1923) also proposed a model of how personality is organized (see Figure 13.6). In this model, personality consists of three interacting structures, and these structures vary in their access to consciousness. The relative strengths of these structures are primarily responsible for an individual's personality.

The first structure, the **id,** exists at the most basic level: completely submerged in the unconscious. The id operates according to the *pleasure principle,* which directs the person to seek pleasure and to avoid pain. Freud called the force that drives the pleasure principle the *libido.* Although today the term *libido* has a sexual connotation, Freud used it to refer more generally to the energy that promotes pleasure seeking. In other words, the libido acts on impulses and desires. The id is like an infant, crying to be fed whenever hungry and to be held whenever anxious.

The second structure, the **superego,** acts as a brake on the id. Largely unconscious, the superego develops in childhood and is the internalization of parental and societal standards of conduct. It is a rigid structure of morality, or conscience.

The third structure, the **ego,** mediates between the id and the superego. That is, the ego tries to satisfy the wishes of the id while being responsive to the dictates of the superego. The ego operates according to the *reality principle,* which involves rational thought and problem solving. Some aspects of the ego's operations are open to conscious awareness. For example, the ego allows the person to delay gratification so that the wishes of the id can be realized while accommodating the rules of the superego. According to psychodynamic theory, unique interactions of the id, ego, and superego produce individual differences in personality.

Conflicts between the id and the superego lead to anxiety. The ego then copes with anxiety through various **defense mechanisms:** unconscious mental strategies that the mind uses to protect itself from distress. (Several common defense mechanisms are listed in **TABLE 13.1.**) For instance, people often *rationalize* their behavior by blaming situational factors over which they have little control. Perhaps you have told your parents or friends that you did not call them because you were too busy studying for an exam. Finding excuses like these keeps people from feeling bad and can also prevent others from feeling angry toward them.

Much of the theoretical work on defense mechanisms can be credited to Freud's daughter, Anna Freud (1936; **FIGURE 13.7**). Over the past 40 years, psychological research has provided considerable support for the existence of many of the defense mechanisms (Baumeister, Dale, & Sommers, 1998). According to contemporary researchers, however, these mechanisms do not relieve unconscious conflict over libidinal desires. Instead, defense mechanisms protect self-esteem.

PSYCHOSEXUAL DEVELOPMENT An important component of Freudian thinking is the idea that early childhood experiences have a major impact on the development of personality. Freud believed that children unconsciously aim to satisfy

defense mechanisms
Unconscious mental strategies that the mind uses to protect itself from anxiety.

FIGURE 13.7
Anna Freud
Anna Freud studied defense mechanisms and contributed to the understanding of children's development.

Table 13.1 Common Defense Mechanisms

MECHANISM	DEFINITION	EXAMPLE
Denial	Refusing to acknowledge source of anxiety	Ill person ignores medical advice.
Repression	Excluding source of anxiety from awareness	Person fails to remember an unpleasant event.
Projection	Attributing unacceptable qualities of the self to someone else	Competitive person describes others as supercompetitive.
Reaction formation	Warding off an uncomfortable thought by overemphasizing its opposite	Person with unacknowledged same-sex desires makes homophobic remarks.
Rationalization	Concocting a seemingly logical reason or excuse for behavior that might otherwise be shameful	Person cheats on taxes because "everyone does it."
Displacement	Shifting the attention of emotion from one object to another	Person yells at children after a bad day at work.
Sublimation	Channeling socially unacceptable impulses into constructive, even admirable, behavior	Sadist becomes a surgeon or dentist.

psychosexual stages
According to Freud, developmental stages that correspond to distinct libidinal urges; progression through these stages profoundly affects personality.

libidinal urges to experience pleasure. In their pursuit of these satisfactions, children go through developmental stages that correspond to the different urges. These developmental stages are called **psychosexual stages.**

In each psychosexual stage, libido is focused on one of the *erogenous zones:* the mouth, the anus, or the genitals. The *oral stage* lasts from birth to approximately 18 months. During this time, infants seek pleasure through the mouth. Because hungry infants experience relief when they breast-feed, they come to associate pleasure with sucking. When children are 2 to 3 years old, they enter the *anal stage.* During this time, toilet training—learning to control the bowels—leads them to focus on the anus. From age 3 to 5, children are in the *phallic stage.* That is, they direct their libidinal energies toward the genitals. Children often discover the pleasure of rubbing their genitals during this time, although they have no sexual intent per se. The phallic stage is followed by a brief *latency stage.* During this time, children suppress libidinal urges or channel them into doing schoolwork or building friendships. Finally, in the *genital stage,* adolescents and adults attain mature attitudes about sexuality and adulthood. They center their libidinal urges on the capacities to reproduce and to contribute to society.

One of the most controversial Freudian theories applies to children in the phallic stage. According to Freud, children desire an exclusive relationship with the opposite-sex parent. For this reason, children consider the same-sex parent a rival and develop hostility toward that parent. In boys, this phenomenon is known as the *Oedipus complex.* It is named after the Greek character Oedipus, who unknowingly killed his father and married his mother. Freud believed that children develop unconscious wishes to kill the one parent in order to claim the other parent. Children resolve this conflict by repressing their desires for the opposite-sex parent and identifying with the same-sex parent. That is, they take on many of that parent's values and beliefs. This theory was mostly applicable to boys. Freud's theory for girls was more complex and even less convincing. Few data support either theory.

According to Freud, progression through these psychosexual stages profoundly affects personality. For example, some people become *fixated* at a stage during which they receive excessive parental restriction or indulgence. For instance, those fixated at the oral stage develop *oral personalities.* They continue to seek pleasure through the mouth, such as by smoking. They are also excessively needy. Those fixated at the anal phase may have *anal-retentive personalities.* They are stubborn and highly regulating. Anal fixation may arise from overly strict toilet training or excessively rule-based childrearing. Again, evidence to support Freud's ideas is lacking.

PSYCHODYNAMIC THEORY SINCE FREUD Although Freud is the thinker most closely identified with psychodynamic theory, a number of influential scholars have modified his ideas in their own psychodynamic theories. While rejecting aspects of Freudian thinking, they have embraced the notion of unconscious conflict. These *neo-Freudians* include Carl Jung, Alfred Adler, and Karen Horney. For instance, Adler and Horney strongly criticized Freud's view of women, finding many of his ideas misogynistic. Consider that the phallic stage of development is named for the male sex organ, although Freud used this label for both female and male development. Many neo-Freudians rejected Freud's emphasis on sexual forces. Adler viewed the primary conflict as based on fears of inadequacy, which he called the *inferiority complex.* Horney focused on a fear of abandonment (i.e., basic insecurity). In her view, this fear resulted from the child's relationship with the mother.

Contemporary neo-Freudians focus on social interactions, especially children's emotional attachments to their parents or primary caregivers. This focus is embodied in *object relations theory.* According to this theory, a person's mind and sense of self develop in relation to others in the particular environment. "Objects" are real others in the world, and how the person relates to these others shapes her or his personality.

Psychological scientists have largely abandoned psychodynamic theories. After all, Freud's central premises cannot be examined through accepted scientific methods. Today, Freud has to be understood in the context of his time and the methods he had at his disposal. He was an astute observer of behavior and a creative theorist. His observations and ideas continue to affect personality psychology and have framed much of the research in personality over the last century (Hines, 2003; Westen, 1998). His terminology appears in many contexts, from literature and pop culture to most people's understanding—and misunderstanding—of psychology.

 Q According to Freud, which personality structure operates according to the reality principle?

ANSWER: the ego, which uses rational thought and problem solving to mediate between the id and superego

13.4 Personality Reflects Learning and Cognition

Behavioral psychologists such as B. F. Skinner rejected the idea that personality is the result of internal processes. Instead, behaviorists viewed personality mainly as learned responses to patterns of reinforcement. Over time, however, psychologists became dissatisfied with strict models of learning theory. They began to incorporate cognition into the understanding of personality. For instance, Julian Rotter (1954) introduced the idea that behavior is a function of two things: the person's *expectancies* for reinforcement and the *values* the person ascribes to particular reinforcers. Suppose you are deciding whether to study for an exam or go to a party. You will probably consider the likelihood that studying will lead to a good grade. You will consider how much that grade matters. Then you will weigh those two considerations against two others: the likelihood that the party will be fun and the extent to which you value having fun (**FIGURE 13.8**).

Rotter also proposed that people differ in how much they believe their efforts will lead to positive outcomes. **Locus of control** refers to how much control people believe they have over outcomes in their lives. People with an *internal locus of control* believe they bring about their own rewards. People with an *external locus of control* believe rewards—and therefore their personal fates—result from forces beyond their control. These generalized beliefs affect individuals' psychological adjustment.

The cognitive theorist George Kelly (1955) emphasized how individuals view and understand their circumstances. He referred to such views and understandings as *personal constructs:* personal theories of how the world works. Kelly believed that people view the world as if they are scientists—constantly testing their theories by observing ongoing events, then revising those theories based on what they observe. According to Kelly, personal constructs develop through experiences and represent each individual's interpretations and explanations for events in his or her social worlds.

In another influential social cognitive theory of personality, Albert Bandura (1977) argued that three factors influence how a person acts: The first factor is the person's environment. The second factor is multiple *person factors*, which include the person's characteristics, self-confidence, and expectations. The third factor is behavior itself. This approach to personality explains how each of these three factors affects the others to determine how personality is expressed through behavior. Because

FIGURE 13.8
Expectancies and Value
According to Julian Rotter, a student's expected value of events will determine whether she will decide to stay in and study or go out to a party.

locus of control
Personal beliefs about how much control people have over outcomes in their lives.

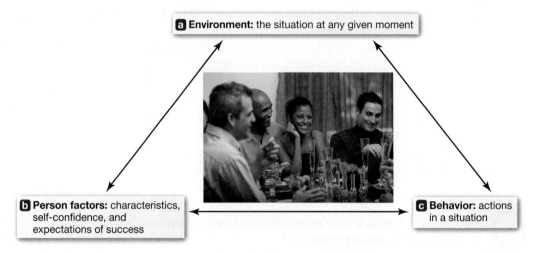

b **Person factors:** characteristics, self-confidence, and expectations of success

c **Behavior:** actions in a situation

FIGURE 13.9
Bandura's Reciprocal Determinism Theory of Personality
Bandura proposed that three factors interact with each other to influence personality: the environment, person factors, and behavior.

reciprocal determinism
The theory that how personality is expressed can be explained by the interaction of environment, person factors, and behavior itself.

personality is explained by the interaction of all three factors, the model is called **reciprocal determinism** (**FIGURE 13.9**).

Let's look at how these three factors affect the expression of someone's personality in a situation. For example, imagine that a new transfer student goes to a party. According to Bandura's model, the party is the environment. The specific features of the environment affect the transfer student's behavior. To judge the effects, we need to know the specifics. Therefore, let's specify that most of the people at the party are people the new student does not know (Figure 13.9a). In addition, the new student will have particular person factors. Let's say she is outgoing and sociable. These characteristics have probably been rewarded by her environment in the past. For example, people may have responded positively to her friendliness (Figure 13.9b). Lastly, the new student's behavior in this situation will reflect both the environment and her person factors. Specifically, at this party with many new faces, the new student most likely will be friendly and talkative (Figure 13.9c). In turn, her behavior will affect the environment. Because she is outgoing, the party becomes more fun for everyone.

Q In explaining why his date went badly, Joe blamed bad weather for forcing cancellation of the concert his date was excited to attend. Does Joe have an internal or external locus of control? Why?

ANSWER: an external locus of control because he believes that weather, which is beyond his control, was responsible for his date going badly

13.5 Humanistic Approaches Emphasize Integrated Personal Experience

By the early 1950s, most psychological theories of personality were heavily deterministic. That is, theorists viewed personality and behavioral characteristics as arising from forces beyond a person's control. For example, Freudians had believed that personality is determined by unconscious conflicts. Behaviorists such as B. F. Skinner argued that personality is based on response tendencies, which are determined by patterns of reinforcement (see Chapter 6, "Learning").

Against this backdrop, a new view of personality emerged: **Humanistic approaches** emphasize personal experience, belief systems, the uniqueness of the human condition,

humanistic approaches
Approaches to studying personality that emphasize how people seek to fulfill their potential through greater self-understanding.

FIGURE 13.10
Rogers's Person-Centered Approach to Personality
According to Rogers's theory, personality is influenced by how we understand ourselves and how others evaluate us, which leads to conditions of worth or unconditional positive regard.

and the inherent goodness of each person. They propose that people seek to fulfill their potential for personal growth through greater self-understanding. This process is referred to as *self-actualization*. Abraham Maslow's theory of motivation is an example. As discussed in Chapter 10, Maslow believed that the desire to become self-actualized is the ultimate human motive.

The most prominent humanistic psychologist was Carl Rogers. Rogers introduced a *person-centered approach* to understanding personality and human relationships. That is, he emphasized people's subjective understandings of their lives. In the therapeutic technique Rogers advocated, the therapist would create a supportive and accepting environment. The therapist and the client would deal with the client's problems and concerns as the client understood them.

Rogers's theory highlights the importance of how parents show affection for their children and how parental treatment affects personality development (**FIGURE 13.10**). Rogers speculated that most parents provide love and support that is conditional: The parents love their children as long as the children do what the parents want them to do. Parents who disapprove of their children's behavior may withhold their love. As a result, children quickly abandon their true feelings, dreams, and desires. They accept only those parts of themselves that elicit parental love and support. Thus, people lose touch with their true selves in their pursuit of positive regard from others.

To counteract this effect, Rogers encouraged parents to raise their children with *unconditional positive regard*. That is, parents should accept and prize their children no matter how the children behave. Parents might express disapproval of children's bad behavior, but at the same time they should express their love for the children. According to Rogers, a child raised with unconditional positive regard would develop a healthy sense of self-esteem and would become a *fully functioning person*.

Q When a parent says to a child, "I love you, but I am really angry that you were careless and broke the vase," is this likely to help or harm a child's self-esteem?

13.6 Trait Approaches Describe Behavioral Dispositions

Psychodynamic and humanistic approaches seek to explain the mental processes that shape personality. According to these theories, the same underlying processes occur in everyone, but individuals differ because they experience different conflicts, are treated differently by their parents, and so on. Other approaches to personality focus more on description than explanation. For example, in describing a friend, you probably would not delve into unconscious conflicts. Instead, you would describe your friend as a certain type. You might say, "Jessica is such an introvert" or "Jorge is a free spirit."

Most contemporary personality psychologists are concerned with traits. As discussed earlier, traits are patterns of thought, emotion, and behavior that are relatively consistent over time and across situations. Traits exist on a continuum, so that most people fall toward the middle and relatively few people fall at the extremes (**FIGURE 13.11**). Thus, for example, people range from being very introverted to very extraverted, but most are somewhere in the middle. The **trait approach** to personality focuses on how individuals differ in personality dispositions, such as sociability, cheerfulness, and aggressiveness (Funder, 2001).

How many traits are there? Early in his career, Gordon Allport, along with his colleague Henry Odbert, counted the dictionary words that could be used as personality traits (Allport & Odbert, 1936). They found nearly 18,000. Later, the researcher Raymond Cattell (1943) set out to ascertain the basic elements of personality. Cattell believed that statistical procedures would enable him to take the scientific study of personality to a higher level and perhaps uncover the basic structure of personality. He asked participants to fill out personality questionnaires that presented a number of trait items, which he had reduced from the larger set produced by Allport and Odbert. Cattell then performed *factor analysis,* grouping items according to their similarities. For instance, he grouped all the terms that referred to friendliness: *nice, pleasant, cooperative,* and so on. Through factor analysis, Cattell (1965) ultimately identified 16 basic dimensions of personality. These dimensions included intelligence, sensitivity, dominance, and self-reliance. Cattell gave many of the dimensions unusual names to avoid confusion with everyday language, but most personality psychologists no longer use these terms.

THE BIG FIVE In the last 30 years or so, many personality psychologists have embraced the **five-factor theory.** This theory identifies five basic personality traits (McCrae & Costa, 1999). These traits have emerged from factor analyses performed by personality researchers. The so-called *Big Five* are *openness to experience, conscientiousness, extraversion, agreeableness,* and *neuroticism* (**FIGURE 13.12**). For each factor, there is a continuum from low to high. In addition, each factor is a higher-order trait that is made up of interrelated lower-order traits. For instance, conscientiousness is determined by how careful and organized a person is. Agreeableness reflects the extent to which a person is trusting and helpful. A person high in openness to experience is imaginative and independent, whereas a person low in this basic trait is down-to-earth and conformist.

The Big Five emerge across cultures, among adults and children, even when vastly different questionnaires assess the factors. The same five factors appear

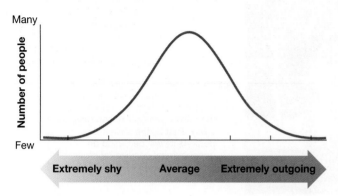

FIGURE 13.11
Personality Traits on a Continuum
Personality traits can be viewed on a continuum. For example, in shyness, people range from extremely shy to extremely outgoing. Most people are in the middle. Relatively few people are at the extremes of any personality trait.

trait approach
An approach to studying personality that focuses on how individuals differ in personality dispositions.

five-factor theory
The idea that personality can be described using five factors: openness to experience, conscientiousness, extraversion, agreeableness, and neuroticism.

whether people rate themselves or are rated by others. Furthermore, people's "scores" on the Big Five traits have been shown to predict a wide variety of different behaviors (Paunonen & Ashton, 2001). Their scores have also been shown to predict people's satisfaction with their jobs, their marriages, and life generally (Heller, Watson, & Ilies, 2004). Some cross-cultural differences emerge, however. For example, interpersonal relatedness, or harmony, is not an important trait in Western cultures, but personality studies conducted in China have shown that interpersonal relatedness is an important trait there (Cheung et al., 2001; Cheung, Cheung, & Leung, 2008). One possible explanation for this difference is that many Chinese live in densely populated areas. Therefore, getting along with others may be more essential in China than in societies where people live farther apart.

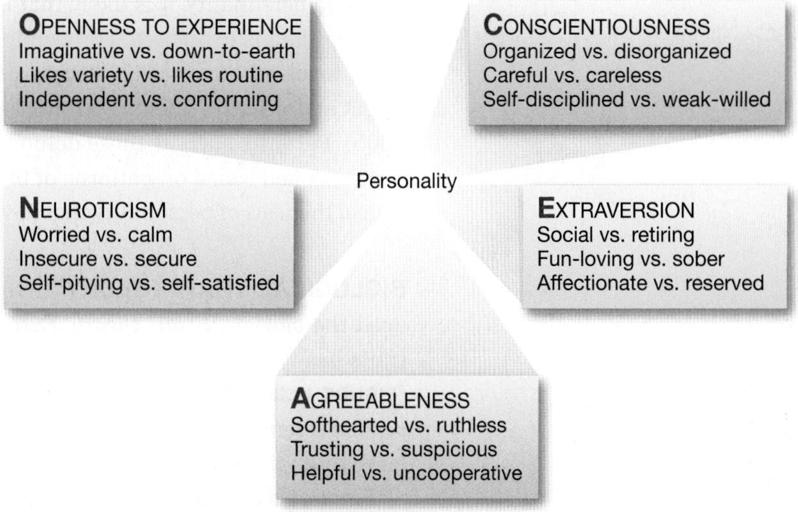

OPENNESS TO EXPERIENCE
Imaginative vs. down-to-earth
Likes variety vs. likes routine
Independent vs. conforming

CONSCIENTIOUSNESS
Organized vs. disorganized
Careful vs. careless
Self-disciplined vs. weak-willed

Personality

NEUROTICISM
Worried vs. calm
Insecure vs. secure
Self-pitying vs. self-satisfied

EXTRAVERSION
Social vs. retiring
Fun-loving vs. sober
Affectionate vs. reserved

AGREEABLENESS
Softhearted vs. ruthless
Trusting vs. suspicious
Helpful vs. uncooperative

FIGURE 13.12

The Big Five Personality Factors

The acronym *OCEAN* is a good way to remember these terms.

Some researchers have questioned whether the five-factor theory really clarifies personality. After all, the factor terms are descriptive rather than explanatory, and reducing all of human personality to five dimensions ignores individual subtleties. The theory is valuable, however, as an organizational structure for the vast number of traits that describe personality. By providing a common descriptive framework, the Big Five integrate and invigorate the trait approach (John & Srivastava, 1999). Today, the Big Five approach dominates much of the way that psychologists study personality.

Moreover, the factors uniquely predict certain outcomes. For instance, conscientiousness predicts grades in college but not scores on standardized tests, whereas openness to experience predicts scores on standardized tests but not grades (Noftle & Robins, 2007). These particular effects may occur because of connections between the traits and the results: Highly conscientious people tend to work very hard, and this characteristic matters for grades. People who are high in openness tend to use words very well, and this characteristic matters for achievement tests. Thus, factors exist at more than a descriptive level. Indeed, traits may reflect people's goals (McCabe & Fleeson, 2016). For instance, people who are extraverted have goals involving having fun and being the center of attention, whereas those high in conscientiousness have goals involving using time effectively and finishing tasks.

 Which of the following is not one of the Big Five traits: agreeableness, conscientiousness, openness to experience, dominance, neuroticism, and extraversion?

ANSWER: Dominance is not one of the Big Five traits.

13.7 Traits Have a Biological Basis

As with many areas of psychology, the recent advances in neuroimaging are starting to provide new insights into personality. In this area, specifically, the advances concern the biological basis of personality traits (DeYoung et al., 2010; Abram & DeYoung, 2017). However, much like the studies demonstrating thousands of small effects of genes on personality, it is likely that multiple brain areas influence how personality develops and is expressed. For example, extraversion is associated with many brain areas involved in reward, whereas neuroticism involves brain regions involved in threat and negative affect (DeYoung et al., 2010; Eisenberger, Lieberman, & Satpute, 2005). Patterns such as these demonstrate that the Big Five factors can be reliably distinguished based on patterns of brain activity. Let's consider two prominent biological theories of personality that have guided research within the field.

BIOLOGICAL TRAIT THEORY In the 1960s, the psychologist Hans Eysenck developed the *biological trait theory*. Eysenck (1967) initially proposed that personality traits had two major dimensions: introversion/extraversion and emotional stability (**FIGURE 13.13**). *Introversion* refers to how shy, reserved, and quiet a person is. *Extraversion* refers to how sociable, outgoing, and bold a person is. This dimension is similar to the extraversion trait in the Big Five theory.

Emotional stability refers to variability in a person's moods and emotions. *Stability* describes consistency in moods and emotions. This dimension is similar to the Big Five trait of neuroticism. A person who is more emotional may be considered *neurotic*. A neurotic person experiences frequent and dramatic mood swings, especially toward negative emotions, compared with a person who is more emotionally stable. In addition, a neurotic person often feels anxious, moody, and depressed and generally holds a very low opinion of himself.

Eysenck later proposed a third dimension of personality traits. *Psychoticism* reflects a mix of aggression, poor impulse control, self-centeredness, and a lack of empathy. The term *psychoticism* implies a level of psychological disorder that Eysenck did not intend. As a result, more-recent conceptions of this trait call it *constraint* (see Figure 13.13). According to this view of the trait, people range from generally controlling their impulses to generally not controlling them (Watson & Clark, 1997). This dimension is most similar to the Big Five trait of conscientiousness, or how careful and organized someone is.

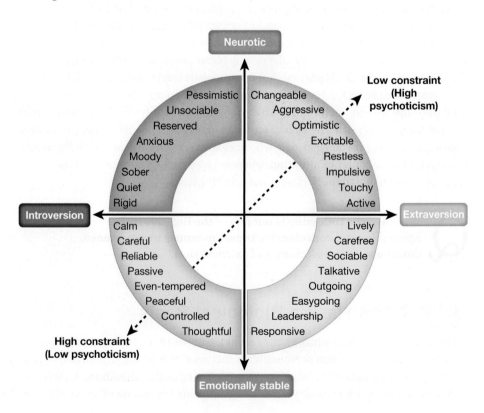

FIGURE 13.13

Eysenck's Biological Trait Theory of Personality

According to Eysenck, personality is composed of traits that occur in three dimensions: extraversion/introversion, emotionally stable/neurotic, and high constraint/low constraint (originally called psychoticism).

Eysenck proposed that personality traits are based on biological processes that produce behaviors, thoughts, and emotions. For instance, Eysenck believed that differences in arousal produce the behavioral differences between extraverts and introverts. Arousal, or alertness, is regulated by the *reticular activating system (RAS)*. The RAS affects alertness and is also involved in inducing and terminating the different stages of sleep. As discussed in Chapter 10, each person prefers to operate—and operates best—at some optimal level of arousal. Eysenck proposed that the resting levels of the RAS are higher for introverts than for extraverts (**FIGURE 13.14**). Extraverts typically are below their optimal levels. In other words, extraverts are chronically underaroused. To operate efficiently, they have to find arousal, so they impulsively seek out new situations and new emotional experiences. Introverts typically are above their optimal levels of arousal. Because they do not want any additional arousal, they prefer quiet solitude with few stimuli. If you are an introvert, a noisy environment will distract you. If you are an extravert, quiet places will bore you. Consistent with Eysenck's theory, research has demonstrated that extraverts perform better in noisy settings (Geen, 1984).

Generally, introverts appear to be more sensitive to stimuli at all levels of intensity. For example, they experience pain more intensely than extraverts do (Lynn & Eysenck, 1961). They also experience sourness more intensely: They salivate more when lemon juice is placed on their tongues than extraverts do (Eysenck & Eysenck, 1967). Evidence for baseline differences in arousal has been more difficult to produce. That is, the visible biological difference between introverts and extraverts appears to be their level of arousability, or how much they react to stimuli. As you might have guessed, introverts are more arousable (Geen, 1984).

BEHAVIORAL ACTIVATION AND INHIBITION SYSTEMS

A number of theorists have offered refinements to Eysenck's initial theory that reflect a more current understanding of how the brain functions. The various theories have some common features. For example, each theory differentiates between approach learning and avoidance learning. Jeffrey Gray (1982) incorporated this distinction in his approach/inhibition model of the relationships between learning and personality. Gray proposed that personality is rooted in two motivational functions: the *behavioral approach system* and the *behavioral inhibition system*. These functions have evolved to help organisms respond efficiently to reinforcement and punishment.

In Gray's model, the **behavioral approach system (BAS)** consists of the brain structures that lead organisms to approach stimuli in pursuit of rewards. This is the *"go"* system (**FIGURE 13.15A**). The *"stop"* system is known as the **behavioral inhibition system (BIS).** Because it is sensitive to punishment, the BIS inhibits behavior that might lead to danger or pain (**FIGURE 13.15B**). Gray's model has been revised to emphasize that the BIS is related more to anxiety than to fear (Gray & McNaughton, 2000) and to accommodate growing findings in neuroscience (Corr, DeYoung, & McNaughton, 2013).

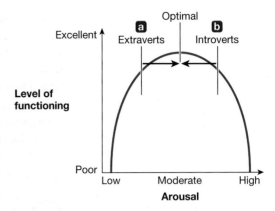

FIGURE 13.14

Optimal Arousal Influences Personality

(a) People who are extraverted have lower levels of arousal. To function optimally, they seek out exciting activities. **(b)** By contrast, people who are introverted have higher levels of arousal. To function optimally, they seek out calming activities.

behavioral approach system (BAS)

The brain system involved in the pursuit of incentives or rewards.

behavioral inhibition system (BIS)

The brain system that is sensitive to punishment and therefore inhibits behavior that might lead to danger or pain.

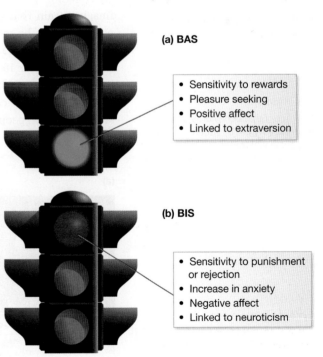

(a) BAS

- Sensitivity to rewards
- Pleasure seeking
- Positive affect
- Linked to extraversion

(b) BIS

- Sensitivity to punishment or rejection
- Increase in anxiety
- Negative affect
- Linked to neuroticism

FIGURE 13.15

Behavioral Approach System and Behavioral Inhibition System

(a) BAS signals "go." **(b)** BIS signals "stop."

The BAS is linked to extraversion. Extraverts are more influenced by rewards than by punishments and tend to act impulsively in the face of strong rewards, even following punishment (Patterson & Newman, 1993). The BIS is linked to neuroticism. People high in neuroticism become anxious in social situations in which they anticipate possible negative outcomes. Different brain regions involved in emotion and reward underlie BIS/BAS systems (DeYoung & Gray, 2009). Gray's model has been particularly useful for understanding personality differences in impulsivity and risk taking, such as when people act impulsively or take risks while drinking or using drugs (Franken, Muris, & Georgieva, 2006).

 Q Eve is an extravert. Would she prefer to study in a noisy café or a quiet library? Why?

ANSWER: Eve would choose the noisy café. Eve's extraversion leads her to select a setting that provides plenty of stimulation.

Learning Objectives

- Define situationism and interactionism.

- Distinguish between strong situations and weak situations.

- Describe how development and life events alter personality traits.

- Identify cultural influences on personality.

situationism
The theory that behavior is determined more by situations than by personality traits.

How Stable Is Personality?

If a person is shy as an adolescent, is she doomed to be shy all her life? There can be an unfortunate tendency for people to be fatalistic about personality, as if people are doomed to whatever personalities they currently possess. This section considers several issues related to the stability of personality. Is it stable across situations? What situational factors influence how personality is expressed? How much does personality change over time?

13.8 People Sometimes Are Inconsistent

Imagine again that you are shy. Are you shy in all situations? Probably not. Shy people tend to be most uncomfortable in new situations in which they are being evaluated (**FIGURE 13.16A**). They are not usually shy around family and close friends (**FIGURE 13.16B**). In 1968, Walter Mischel dropped a bombshell on the field of personality by proposing that behaviors are determined more by situations than by personality traits. This idea has come to be called **situationism.** For evidence, Mischel referred to studies in which people who were dishonest in one situation were completely honest

(a)   (b)

FIGURE 13.16
The Power of Situation
(a) A person might understandably be shy during a first date with someone he met online.
(b) That same person might be far from shy in a different situation.

in another. Suppose a student is not totally honest with a professor in explaining why a paper is late. That student probably is no more likely to steal or to cheat on taxes than is a student who admits to oversleeping.

Mischel's critique of personality traits caused considerable rifts between social psychologists, who emphasize situational forces, and personality psychologists, who focus on individual dispositions. After all, the most basic definition of personality holds that it is relatively stable across situations and circumstances. If Mischel was correct and there is relatively little stability, the whole concept of personality seems empty.

As you might expect, there was a vigorous response to Mischel's theory. The discussion has come to be called the *person/situation debate*. Personality researchers argued that how much a trait predicts behavior depends on three factors: the *centrality* of the trait, the *aggregation* of behaviors over time, and the *type* of trait being evaluated. People tend to be more consistent in their central traits than in their secondary traits, since the former are most relevant to them. In addition, if behaviors are averaged across many situations, personality traits are more predictive of behavior. Shy people may not be shy all the time, but on average they are shy more than people who are not shy. Some traits, such as honesty, are more likely to be consistent across situations. Other traits, such as shyness, might vary depending on the situation. Finally, some people may be more consistent than others. Consider the trait of self-monitoring, which involves being sensitive to cues of situational appropriateness. People high in *self-monitoring* alter their behavior to match the situation, so they exhibit low levels of consistency. By contrast, people low in self-monitoring are less able to alter their self-presentations to match situational demands, so they tend to be much more consistent across situations.

PERSON-SITUATION INTERACTION People are also highly sensitive to social context, and most people conform to situational norms. Few people would break the law in front of a police officer or drive on the wrong side of the road just because they felt like it. Situations such as these, where there are strong external influences, dictate behavior apart from personality.

Situational influences can be subtle. Consider your own behavior. You may reveal different aspects of your personality during your interactions with different people. Your goals for social interaction change. The potential consequences of your actions also change. For example, your family may be more tolerant of your bad moods than your friends are. Thus, you may feel freer to express your bad moods around your family.

Situations differ in how much they constrain the expression of personality (Kenrick & Funder, 1991). Suppose one person is highly extraverted, aggressive, and boisterous. A second person is shy, thoughtful, and restrained. At a funeral, these two people might display similar or even nearly identical behavior. At a party, the same two people would most likely act quite differently. Personality psychologists differentiate between *strong situations* and *weak situations*. Strong situations (e.g., elevators, religious services, job interviews) tend to mask differences in personality because of the power of the social environment. Weak situations—for example, parks, bars, one's house—tend to reveal differences in personality (**FIGURE 13.17**). Most trait theorists favor **interactionism.** That is, they believe that behavior is determined jointly by situations and underlying dispositions.

People also affect their social environments. First, people choose their situations (Sherman, Nave, & Funder, 2010). Introverts tend to avoid parties or other situations in which they might feel anxious, whereas extraverts seek out social opportunities. Once people are in situations, their behavior affects those around them. Some

FIGURE 13.17
Strong and Weak Situations
(a) A strong situation, such as a funeral, tends to discourage displays of personality. **(b)** A weak situation, such as hanging out with friends, tends to let people behave more freely.

interactionism
The theory that behavior is determined jointly by situations and underlying dispositions.

extraverts may draw people out and encourage them to have fun, whereas others might act aggressively and turn people off. Some introverts might create an intimate atmosphere that encourages people to open up and reveal personal concerns, whereas others might make people uncomfortable and anxious. A reciprocal interaction occurs between the person and the social environment so that they simultaneously influence each other. The important point is that personality reflects a person's underlying disposition, the activation of the person's goals in a particular situation, and the activation of the person's emotional responses in the pursuit of those goals.

Q Why might it be difficult to tell an introvert from an extravert at a funeral?

ANSWER: A funeral is a strong situation, in that the social norms for how one behaves at a funeral tend to mask individual differences in personality.

13.9 Development and Life Events Alter Personality Traits

The Jesuits have a maxim: *Give me a child until he is seven, and I will show you the man.* This proverbial saying is the thesis of Paul Almond and Michael Apted's *Up* series of documentary films. The series follows the development of a group of British people. Each participant has been interviewed at ages 7, 14, 21, 28, 35, 42, 49, and 56 (**FIGURE 13.18**). A striking aspect of these films is the apparent stability of personality over time. For example, the boy interested in the stars and science becomes a professor of physics. The boy who finds his childhood troubling and confusing appears to develop an odd and eccentric personality. The reserved, well-mannered, upper-class girl at age 7 grows into the reserved, well-mannered woman in her pastoral retreat at age 35.

FIGURE 13.18
The *Up* Series
Since 1964, this series of documentary films has traced the development of 14 British people from various socioeconomic backgrounds. New material has been collected every seven years, starting when the participants were 7 years old. Here, three participants—Jackie, Sue, and Lynn—are pictured from the film *49 Up*.

Are people really so stable? Childhood temperaments may predict behavioral outcomes in early adulthood, but what about change during adulthood? Clinical psychology is based on the belief that people can and do change important aspects of their lives. They exert considerable energy trying to change. They attend self-help groups, read self-help books, pay for therapy sessions, and struggle to make changes in their lives. But how much can people really change?

MOST TRAITS ARE STABLE The way we define the essential features of personality has tremendous implications for whether personality is fixed or changeable. Continuity over time and across situations is inherent in the definition of trait, and most research finds personality traits to be relatively stable over the adult life span (Heatherton & Weinberger, 1994). For instance, over many years the relative rankings of individuals on each of the Big Five personality traits remain stable (McCrae & Costa, 1990). A meta-analysis of 150 studies—through which a total of nearly 50,000 participants had been followed for at least one year—found strong evidence for stability in personality (Roberts & Friend-DelVecchio, 2000). The rank orderings of individuals on any personality trait were quite stable over long periods across all age ranges (**FIGURE 13.19**).

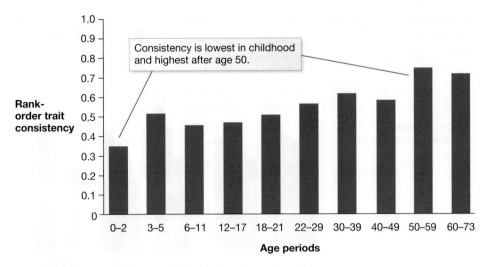

FIGURE 13.19
The Stability of Personality
This graph shows the rank ordering of the study participants' personalities. Participants ranged in age from newborn to 73.

In their research on potential change in personality, Robert McCrae and Paul Costa (1999) emphasize an important distinction. They separate basic tendencies of personality from characteristic adaptations. *Basic tendencies* are dispositional traits determined largely by biological processes. As such, they are very stable. *Characteristic adaptations* are adjustments to situational demands. Such adaptations tend to be somewhat consistent because they are based on skills, habits, roles, and so on. But changes in behavior produced by characteristic adaptations do not indicate changes in basic tendencies. Consider a highly extraverted woman. In her youth, she may go to parties frequently, be a thrill seeker, and have multiple sexual partners. In her old age, she will be less likely to do these things, but she may have many friends and enjoy traveling. Although the exact behaviors differ, they reflect the core basic tendency of extraversion.

Although traits show relative stability, they also change (Harris, Brett, Johnson, & Deary, 2016). According to this emerging perspective, traits reflect developmental constructs that change over the life course in response to life events (Roberts, 2009). When behaviors, thoughts, or emotions change, and do so repeatedly over time, people can come to see themselves in a new light. These stable shifts in behavior, thoughts, or feelings lead people to perceive themselves differently (Roberts, Wood, & Caspi, 2008). Traits change at typical points during the life course, but individual differences in the patterns of change reflect unique aspects of personality (Roberts & Mroczek, 2008).

AGING-RELATED CHANGE Individual personalities remain relatively stable over time, as when a person who is more shy than average as a child remains so as an adult. During the life course, however, most people's personalities reliably undergo certain changes. For instance, people generally develop increased self-control and emotional stability as they age (Caspi, Roberts, & Shiner, 2005). They become less neurotic, less extraverted, and less open to new experiences as they get older (Milojev & Sibley, 2016). They also tend to become more agreeable and more conscientious (Srivastava, John, Gosling, & Potter, 2003). Some aspects of personality, such as conscientiousness and emotional stability, change more in young adulthood (ages 20–40) than in

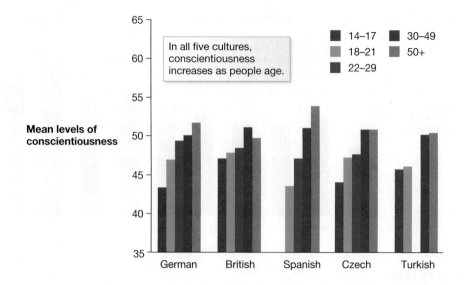

FIGURE 13.20

Conscientiousness at Different Ages in Five Cultures

Note that bars are missing from this graph because data were not available for the 14-17 age group in Spain and the 22-29 age group in Turkey.

In all five cultures, conscientiousness increases as people age.

14–17   30–49
18–21   50+
22–29

Mean levels of conscientiousness

German   British   Spanish   Czech   Turkish

any other part of the life course, including adolescence (Roberts, Walton, & Viechtbauer, 2006). As you will see shortly, this tendency may be due to the large number of life events that occur during young adulthood.

The pattern of personality changes across age holds in different cultures (McCrae et al., 2000; **FIGURE 13.20**). These findings suggest that age-related changes in personality occur independently of environmental influences and therefore that personality change itself may be based in human physiology. Indeed, the extent of personality change is more similar in monozygotic twins than in dizygotic twins, and this finding indicates that personality change has a genetic component (McGue, Bacon, & Lykken, 1993).

SITUATIONAL CAUSES OF PERSONALITY CHANGE Life's circumstances generally produce changes in personality, especially during the transition from adolescence to adulthood. Many of the changes observed as people go through adulthood may be due in part to the new duties and obligations that growing older typically involves, such as forming long-term relationships, having children, and building a career. Each of these life events typically leads to an altered lifestyle, in which behaviors, thoughts, and emotions change in predictable ways. For instance, a person's first job brings expectations that the person show up on time, work hard, and interact agreeably with coworkers and respectfully with bosses. Acting in these ways can instill new behaviors and help make the person more conscientious. Moreover, the tangible benefits of working, such as having more money and therefore an improved lifestyle, permit people to regularly engage in enjoyable behaviors. These connections may explain why greater job satisfaction can decrease neuroticism over time (Le, Donnellan, & Conger, 2014).

In general, personality changes occur as a consequence of the expectations and experiences associated with age-related roles, such as becoming a spouse, a parent, or an employee (Roberts et al., 2006). In colloquial terms, during the transition from adolescence to adulthood most people "grow up." Becoming involved in a committed relationship is associated with decreased neuroticism (Lehnart, Neyer, & Eccles, 2010). Life experiences, such as forming committed relationships, affect personality development (Roberts, Donnellan, & Hill, 2012). Even so, some people change more than others, perhaps because they experience these age-related events differently (Roberts & Mroczek, 2008). For example, in contrast to generally increasing emotional stability in adulthood, adolescents who face a lot of adversity sometimes become more neurotic as adults (Shiner, Allen, & Masten, 2017).

Even apparently trivial life events may have large effects on personality development. Consider that Charles Darwin's uncle generously offered to drive him 30 miles to take a voyage on the *Beagle*. In his autobiography, Darwin described the *Beagle* voyage as the most important event of his life, and it would not have happened except for his uncle's offer (Darwin, 1892). The discoveries he made on the trip profoundly shaped modern science, determined his career, and helped shape him as a person. Many life events are unpredictable, such as accidents and illnesses. These twists of fate can instigate behavioral, emotional, and cognitive patterns in ways that change personality. Indeed, apparently arbitrary events might help explain why even those who possess the same genes do not develop identical personalities (Plomin & Daniels, 1987; 2011).

One recent study examined personality change among people who were caregivers for a spouse with terminal cancer. They assessed personality before and approximately 7 months after the spouse's death. Compared with a control group, the bereaved caregivers became more agreeable, sociable (a component of extraversion), and conscientious (Hoerger et al., 2014; **FIGURE 13.21A**). Another study examined college students who traveled abroad compared with a group of control students who did not (Zimmermann & Neyer, 2013). Those who chose to travel were more extraverted and had higher scores on openness to experience at the beginning of the study, as you might imagine. However, one year later they showed reliable increases in openness and agreeableness (**FIGURE 13.21B**), along with a decrease in neuroticism (**FIGURE 13.21C**). These changes

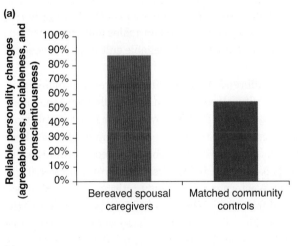

(a)

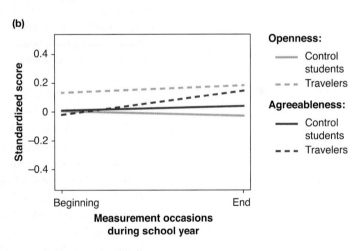

(b)

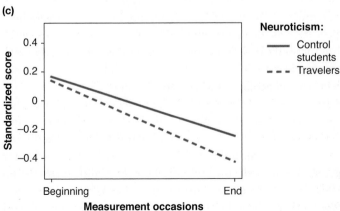

(c)

FIGURE 13.21

Life Experience and Personality Change

(a) As this graph illustrates, bereaved caregivers reliably experienced more positive personality changes than a control group did. **(b)** As this graph illustrates, college students who traveled abroad also reliably experienced more positive personality changes than a control group, and **(c)** they became less neurotic.

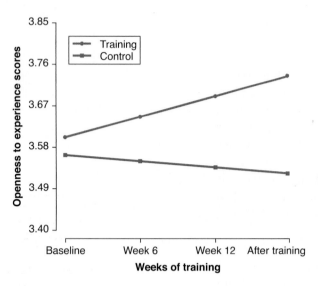

FIGURE 13.22
**Experimentally Produced
Personality Change**
Compared with a control group,
the experimental group showed an
increase in openness to experience.

typically occur as people get older (Roberts & Wood, 2006), suggesting that international travel is a life event that hastens increased maturation.

Researchers have even used experimental methods in an attempt to directly change personality. Jackson and colleagues (2012) had older adults practice cognitive tasks that included a challenging set of sudoku puzzles and training in problem solving. The participants enjoyed the experimental condition, spending an average of 11 hours per week on the puzzles for 16 weeks. Compared with a control group, the experimental group showed an increase in openness to experience (**FIGURE 13.22**). This finding is important because of the typical benefits of experimental design—alternative explanations for the change, such as baseline differences between groups, are ruled out. In other words, an experimental manipulation can cause changes in personality.

Q **If Sheri is highly extraverted in her 20s, how extraverted is she likely to be in her 50s?**

ANSWER: Sheri is likely to still be extraverted, but she will be less so as she ages.

13.10 Culture Influences Personality

How is personality affected by the culture in which one is raised? Cultural norms dictate appropriate behaviors and emotional reactions for males and females of different ages. Do different cultural norms translate into reliable cultural differences in personality?

Studying potential personality differences across cultures presents many challenges. As noted in Chapter 2, cross-cultural research can be difficult when language is a central component of what is being studied. Recall from Chapter 1 that people from Eastern cultures tend to think in terms of relations with other people, whereas those from Western cultures tend to think in terms of independence. People from Eastern cultures might therefore interpret a question about personality traits as referring to their family or group. People from Western cultures might interpret the same question as referring to them alone. Making comparisons across cultures also requires the use of standardized questionnaires that are reliably translated so that the questions clearly refer to the same personality trait in all cultures and all respondents interpret the questions in the same way. Another problem involves sampling: Often researchers use convenience samples, such as the college students who are taking the researchers' classes at the time of the study. In different countries, however, different types of people may go to college or university. Thus, apparent cultural differences may result from examining different types of people in the different cultures.

Recognizing these issues, one research team conducted a careful investigation of personality differences across 56 nations (Schmitt, Allik, McCrae, & Benet-Martinez, 2007). They found that the Big Five personality traits are valid across all the countries. This finding supports the argument that the Big Five are universal for humans. The investigators found modest differences in those traits across the 56 nations, however. People from East Asia (e.g., Japan, China, Korea) rated themselves comparatively lower than other respondents on extraversion, agreeableness, and conscientiousness, and they rated themselves comparatively higher on neuroticism

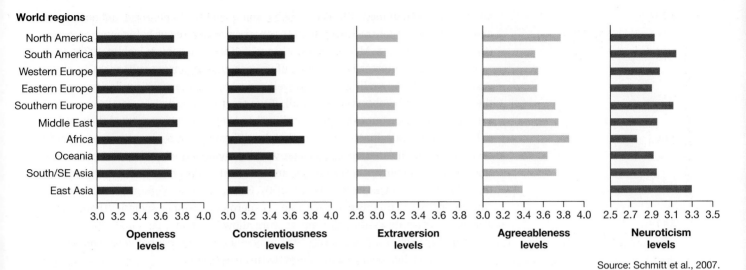

World regions

North America | South America | Western Europe | Eastern Europe | Southern Europe | Middle East | Africa | Oceania | South/SE Asia | East Asia

Openness levels 3.0 3.2 3.4 3.6 3.8 4.0

Conscientiousness levels 3.0 3.2 3.4 3.6 3.8 4.0

Extraversion levels 2.8 3.0 3.2 3.4 3.6 3.8

Agreeableness levels 3.0 3.2 3.4 3.6 3.8 4.0

Neuroticism levels 2.5 2.7 2.9 3.1 3.3 3.5

Source: Schmitt et al., 2007.

FIGURE 13.23

Cross-Cultural Research on Personality Traits

A team of more than 120 scientists investigated the Big Five personality traits around the world, from Argentina to Zimbabwe. This chart presents some of their findings.

(**FIGURE 13.23**). By contrast, respondents from countries in Africa rated themselves as more agreeable, more conscientious, and less neurotic than people from most other countries rated themselves. These ratings might have reflected differences, however, in cultural norms for saying good and bad things about oneself. People from East Asian countries might simply be the most modest.

Research findings have made clear that self-reports often do not match cultural stereotypes about the respondents. One team of researchers examined typical beliefs about the personality characteristics of people from 49 cultures (Terracciano et al., 2005). The researchers then compared those ratings with self-reports and observer reports of people from those cultures. There was little correspondence. For instance, Canadians were widely believed to be relatively low in neuroticism and high in agreeableness, yet self-reports by Canadians did not support this pattern. Canadians reported themselves to be just as neurotic and disagreeable as people from other cultures. Steven Heine and colleagues (2008) have argued that national reputations may be accurate and that self-reports might be biased by individuals' comparisons of themselves with their national reputations.

To understand this idea, imagine that everyone in Country X works extremely hard and is always on time. People in Country Y work only when the urge strikes them. Therefore, the people in Country X are high in conscientiousness compared with the people in Country Y. Meanwhile, an individual in Country X and an individual in Country Y may be equally conscientious. Compared with their fellow citizens in their respective countries, however, the person in Country X may feel average, whereas the person in Country Y may feel far above average. Thus, people can view the same behavior differently, depending on how they compare themselves with others. In other words, maybe Canadians really are especially agreeable, and it is simply hard to notice one person's agreeableness around all those other agreeable Canadians.

SEX DIFFERENCES What about differences related to sex? Earlier you learned that boys and girls show differences in temperament during childhood. Do they differ when grown up? Women and men are much more similar than different in terms of personality, but the differences between them largely support common stereotypes. That is, across various studies, women typically report and are rated as being more empathic and agreeable than men, but also as being somewhat more neurotic and concerned about feelings. By contrast, men tend to report and are rated as being more assertive (Costa, Terracciano, & McCrae, 2001; Feingold, 1994; Maccoby & Jacklin, 1974).

Of particular interest is how sex differences emerge across cultures. You might guess that the more egalitarian and developed a society, the more similarity between the sexes would be observed. After all, if we treat boys and girls equally, we might expect them to turn out to be more similar than they would if we treated them differently. Thus, it is puzzling to discover that sex differences in personality are largest in societies in North America and Europe, which provide more equal opportunities and treatment than many other societies, and smallest in Asian and African communities (Costa et al., 2001; Guimond et al., 2007; Schmitt, Realo, Voracek, & Allik, 2008). One theory to explain this pattern is that prosperous, developed societies that emphasize women's rights to education and to work allow for greater personal expression of individuality (Schmitt et al., 2008). Still, why might differences between females and males emerge when people can express themselves freely?

According to the social psychologist Serge Guimond (2008), people in individualist cultures—such as within Western Europe and North America—tend to compare themselves against other groups. As a result, women in such cultures describe themselves in ways that differentiate them from men, thereby creating gender differences in personality. From this perspective, the apparent cultural differences in the gender gap result from cultural differences in how people compare themselves rather than from any genuine cultural differences.

Q According to research, more people from East Asia report having neurotic personalities than people from Western cultures. Why might it not be reasonable to conclude that genuine personality differences exist?

ANSWER: People from East Asia may be more modest and therefore more likely to say negative things about themselves than those from Western cultures.

Learning Objectives

- Distinguish between idiographic and nomothetic approaches to the study of personality.

- Distinguish between projective and self-report measures of personality.

- Discuss the accuracy of observers' personality judgments.

How Is Personality Assessed?

What must we know to really understand someone's personality? The specific ways that psychologists try to answer this question vary greatly, often depending on their overall theoretical approaches. Some psychologists emphasize the biological and genetic factors that predispose behaviors. Others emphasize culture, patterns of reinforcement, or mental and unconscious processes.

To really understand people is to understand everything about them, from their biological makeups, to their early childhood experiences, to the way they think, to the cultures in which they were raised. All of these factors work together to shape a person. Thus, personality psychologists approach the study of personality on many levels. Psychologists measure personality by having people report on themselves, by asking people's friends or relatives to describe them, or by watching how people behave. Each method has strengths and limitations. This section considers how psychologists assess personality and how the different methods influence our understanding of individuals.

13.11 Researchers Use Multiple Methods to Assess Personality

Various methods have been used to assess personality. Assessment procedures include measures of unconscious processes; life history data; behavioral data; self-reports; and descriptions from people's friends, relatives, or both. The way researchers choose to measure personality depends to a great extent on their theoretical orientations. For instance, trait researchers rely on personality descriptions, whereas humanistic psychologists use more holistic approaches.

The assessment of personality follows two approaches: idiographic and nomothetic. **Idiographic approaches** are person-centered. They focus on individual lives and how various characteristics are integrated into unique persons. **Nomothetic approaches** focus on characteristics that are common among all people but that vary from person to person. In other words, idiographic approaches use a different metric for each person. Nomothetic approaches use the same metric to compare all people.

Idiographic approaches assume that each individual is unique. Suppose each person in your psychology class identified 10 personality traits that described himself. If your instructor compiled a list of everyone's traits, some of the traits would overlap. Other traits would probably apply to just one person in the class. After all, people like to be unique, so they tend to choose traits that distinguish themselves from other people. These *central traits* are especially important for how individuals define themselves. In contrast, people consider *secondary traits* less personally descriptive or not applicable. As you can imagine, certain traits are central for some people and secondary for others. You might define yourself in terms of how bold you are, but someone else might not consider boldness a very relevant part of her self-definition. In general, central traits are more predictive of behavior than secondary traits are.

Nomothetic approaches focus on common traits rather than individual uniqueness. Researchers in this tradition compare people by measuring traits such as agreeableness or extraversion. For example, they might give participants a questionnaire that lists 100 personality traits and have the participants rate themselves on each trait, using a scale of 1 to 10. From the nomothetic perspective, individuals are unique because of their unique combinations of common traits. The five-factor theory, discussed earlier, is an example of a nomothetic approach. That is, it looks at how all people vary on five basic personality traits.

PROJECTIVE MEASURES According to psychodynamic theory, personality is influenced by unconscious conflicts. **Projective measures** explore the unconscious by having people describe or tell stories about ambiguous stimulus items. The general idea is that people will project their mental contents onto the ambiguous items. Through these projections, according to the theory, people will reveal hidden aspects of personality such as motives, wishes, and unconscious conflicts. Several such procedures are used to assess psychopathology, but many of them have been criticized for being too subjective and insufficiently validated.

One of the best-known projective measures is the *Rorschach inkblot test*. In this procedure, a person looks at an apparently meaningless inkblot and describes what it appears to be (**FIGURE 13.24A**). How a person describes the inkblot is supposed to reveal unconscious conflicts and other problems. Unfortunately, raters often disagree with each other in how to interpret the descriptions. In addition, the Rorschach does a poor job of diagnosing specific psychological disorders, however, and it finds many normal adults and children to be psychologically disturbed (Wood, Garb, Lilienfeld, & Nezworski, 2002).

A classic projective measure used by personality psychologists is the *Thematic Apperception Test (TAT)*. In the 1930s, Henry Murray and Christiana Morgan developed the TAT to study various types of motivation. In this test, a person is shown an ambiguous picture and is asked to tell a story about it (**FIGURE 13.24B**). Scoring of the story is based on the motivational schemes that emerge, because the schemes are assumed to reflect the storyteller's personal motives. Indeed, the TAT has been

idiographic approaches
Person-centered approaches to assessing personality; they focus on individual lives and how various characteristics are integrated into unique persons.

nomothetic approaches
Approaches to assessing personality that focus on how common characteristics vary from person to person.

projective measures
Personality tests that examine unconscious processes by having people interpret ambiguous stimuli.

(a)

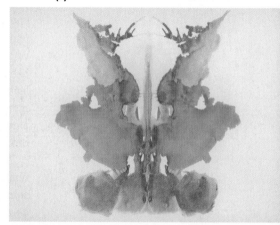

(b)

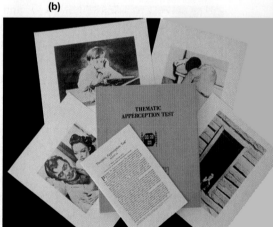

FIGURE 13.24
Projective Measures of Personality
Projective measures are meant to provide insight into a particular person's personality by allowing the person to project unconscious thoughts onto ambiguous images, as shown here in **(a)** a Rorschach inkblot test and **(b)** a Thematic Apperception Test (TAT).

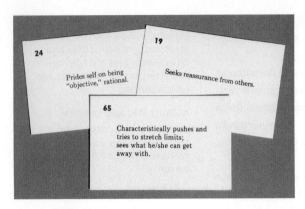

FIGURE 13.25
California Q-Sort
These are three of the cards a participant sorts when taking the Q-Sort assessment.

useful for measuring motivational traits—especially those related to achievement, power, and affiliation—and therefore it continues to be used in contemporary research (McClelland, Koestner, & Weinberger, 1989). If used properly, the TAT reliably predicts how interpersonally dependent people are (Bornstein, 1999). For example, this test predicts how likely people are to seek approval and support from others.

SELF-REPORTS Many assessments of personality involve self-report questionnaires. Measuring only what the person reports, they make no pretense of uncovering hidden conflicts or secret information. A questionnaire might target a specific trait, such as how much excitement a person seeks out of life. More often, questionnaires will include a large inventory of traits. For example, the *NEO Personality Inventory* consists of 240 items, which are designed to assess the Big Five personality factors (Costa & McCrae, 1992).

A widely used questionnaire for personality assessment is the *Minnesota Multiphasic Personality Inventory (MMPI)*. Developed during the 1930s, the *MMPI* was updated in the 1990s for language changes (Butcher & Williams, 2009). The latest full version (*MMPI-2*) consists of 567 true/false items that assess emotions, thoughts, and behaviors. The scale was originally designed to assess psychopathology (which you will learn more about in Chapter 14) but has also been widely used to assess personality more generally. The *MMPI* has 10 scales that measure psychological problems (e.g., paranoia, depression, mania, hysteria). Using these scales, the assessor generates a profile that indicates whether a person is likely to have a psychological disorder.

As discussed in Chapter 2, a common problem is shared by all self-report assessments, including the *MMPI*. Namely, to make favorable impressions, respondents sometimes distort the truth or lie outright. To avoid detection of psychological disorders, they may be evasive or defensive. People might also try to present themselves too positively by agreeing with a large number of items, such as "I always make my bed" and "I never tell lies." A high score on this category would indicate an attempt to present a perfectly positive image. Fabrications of this kind are known as faking good. By contrast, to look especially troubled, called faking bad, respondents may untruthfully lean toward negative items. To counter such response biases, the *MMPI-2* includes validity scales in addition to the clinical scales. The validity scales measure the probability that respondents are being less than truthful when taking the test.

One technique for assessing traits is the *California Q-Sort*. In this procedure, each participant is given 100 cards that have statements printed on them. The participant is asked to sort the cards into nine piles according to how accurately the statements describe the person. The piles represent categories that range from "not at all descriptive" to "extremely descriptive" (**FIGURE 13.25**). A participant may place only so many cards in each pile. Fewer cards are allowed at the extreme ends of the scale. Because the participant must pile most of the cards in the moderately descriptive categories, the Q-Sort has a built-in procedure for identifying those traits that people view as most central. The Q-Sort, like most objective measures, can also be used by observers. For example, parents, teachers, therapists, and friends can sort the cards to describe the person being evaluated.

FIGURE 13.26
Adolf Hitler
In his personality analysis of Hitler, Henry Murray (1943) stated that the German leader was impotent in heterosexual relations and had engaged in a same-sex relationship. Murray's report predicted Hitler's suicide.

LIFE HISTORY DATA Researchers who use idiographic approaches often examine case studies of individuals through interviews or biographical information. The personality psychologist Henry Murray pioneered this approach. For example, Murray was one of many scholars who tried to account for Adolf Hitler's behavior in Nazi Germany by studying Hitler's early childhood experiences, his physical stature, and his personal motivations (**FIGURE 13.26**). This type of study emphasizes the idea that personality unfolds over the life course as people react to their particular circumstances.

Another idiographic approach considers a human life as a narrative. To study personality, narrative psychologists pay attention to the stories people tell about themselves. According to Dan McAdams (1999, 2001), each person weaves a *life story*, which integrates self-knowledge into a coherent whole. In other words, the individual creates *personal myths* that bind together past events and future possibilities into one life story. These myths, whether true or not, help the individual make sense of the world and find meaning in life.

BEHAVIORAL DATA Researchers have also developed a number of objective measures that assess how personality emerges in daily life. For example, Matthias Mehl and James Pennebaker (Mehl, Pennebaker, Crow, Dabbs, & Price, 2001) created the electronically activated record (EAR). This device unobtrusively tracks a person's real-world moment-to-moment interactions. As the wearer goes about her or his daily life, the EAR picks up snippets of conversations and other auditory information. People quickly get used to wearing the EAR and have no idea when it is recording.

The EAR has been used to show that self-reports on the Big Five traits predict real-world behavior (Mehl, Gosling, & Pennebaker, 2006). According to this study, extraverts talk more and spend less time alone; agreeable people swear less often; conscientious people attend class more often; neurotic people spend more time arguing; and people open to experience spend more time in restaurants, bars, and coffee shops. Several ongoing studies are using smartphone sensors to provide information about how personality predicts behavior during daily life (Harari et al., 2016).

Other aspects of the environment can also be used to predict personality. Consider whether you keep your bedroom tidy or messy, warm or cold. In his book *Snoop*, Sam Gosling (2008) notes that each person's personality leaks out in many situations, such as through a Facebook profile (Back et al., 2010), a personal Web page (Vazire & Gosling, 2004), and the condition of a bedroom or office (Gosling, Ko, Mannarelli, & Morris, 2002; **FIGURE 13.27**). In each case, study participants who viewed public information about other people were able to form reasonably accurate impressions of how those people rated themselves on the Big Five personality traits.

FIGURE 13.27
Behavior and Personality
How a person maintains a home or office is just one area in which personality is on display.

 What is a major problem with the Rorschach test?

13.12 Observers Show Accuracy in Trait Judgments

People might be able to judge other people's personalities by looking at their bedrooms and Facebook profiles, but how well do the observers really know the other people? Imagine that you often feel shy in new situations, as many people do. Would others know that shyness is part of your personality? Some shy people force themselves to be outgoing to mask their feelings, so their friends might have no idea that they feel shy. Other people react to their own fear of social situations by remaining quiet and aloof, so observers might believe them to be cold, arrogant, and unfriendly. If you invite someone to a party because you expect her to be cheerful and sociable, and you are wrong, then the party might not be as pleasant as you hoped (Funder, 2012). In other words, judgments of personality are important because personality heavily influences behavior. Ultimately, how well do observers' personality judgments predict others' behavior?

An important study by David Funder (1995) found that a person's close acquaintances show a surprising degree of accuracy for trait judgments, at least in some

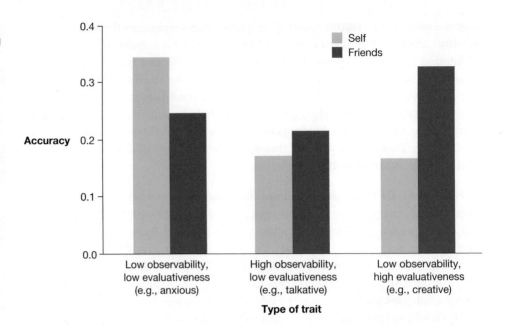

FIGURE 13.28

Self-Rating and Friends' Rating for Different Traits

In judgments of personality traits, how accurate are people's self-ratings versus their friends' ratings? This chart, based on the data from the Vazire (2010) study, shows the average accuracy scores for three types of traits. As shown on the left, self-ratings tend to be more accurate than friends' ratings for traits that are low in both observability and evaluativeness. As shown in the middle, friends' ratings tend to be more accurate than self-ratings for traits that are high in observability and low in evaluativeness. As shown on the right, friends' ratings tend to be especially accurate for traits that are low in observability and high in evaluativeness.

circumstances. In other studies, friends predicted assertiveness and other behaviors better than the person's own ratings did (Kolar, Funder, & Colvin, 1996; Vazire & Mehl, 2008). This effect may occur because our friends actually observe how we behave in situations. While we are in those situations, we may be preoccupied with evaluating other people and therefore fail to notice how we behave. Another possibility is that our subjective perceptions may diverge from our objective behaviors. In either case, these studies imply that there is a disconnect between how people view themselves and how they behave. Not surprisingly, evidence indicates that people come to know others better over time, as they witness others' behavior across different circumstances; thus we are more accurate in predicting a close friend's behavior than in predicting the behavior of a mere acquaintance (Biesanz, West, & Millevoi, 2007).

Simine Vazire (2010; Vazire & Carlson, 2011) has compared the accuracy of people's self-judgments with the accuracy of how their friends describe them. The comparative accuracy depends on whether the traits are observable and whether the people being rated are motivated to view themselves positively on the traits. Vazire argues that people have blind spots about aspects of their personalities because they want to feel good about themselves. This tendency is particularly true for highly evaluative traits, such as creativity.

On highly evaluative traits—traits that people care about—people are biased when judging themselves (biases in self-perception are discussed later in this chapter). Thus, people are more accurate in rating themselves for traits that are hard to observe and less prone to bias because they are neutral. For instance, a person might be accurate in knowing whether she is anxious or optimistic, because those traits are associated with feelings that can be ambiguous to observers. Friends might be more accurate in knowing whether the person is talkative or charming, because the behaviors associated with those traits are easy to observe. Vazire's key insight is that a trait easy to observe but also highly meaningful to people, such as creativity, is more likely to be judged accurately by friends than by the person with the trait (**FIGURE 13.28**).

Is Amara or her friend Jackson likely better at rating the extent to which Amara is extraverted?

ANSWER: Jackson is likely to be more accurate in rating Amara's extraversion, based on how talkative and social Amara is.

13.13 What Personality Traits Should You Look for in a Roommate?

If you live on campus, you may think of your residence hall as your home or at least your home away from home. You probably spend a good deal of time studying, sleeping, relaxing, and socializing in the comfy confines of your 200-square-foot space. And if you are like the majority of residential college students, you share your room with at least one roommate.

Positive roommate relationships can be a highlight of the college experience and can provide a foundation for lifelong friendships. Unfortunately, negative roommate relationships can add significant stress to the college experience and can even disrupt the mental health and academic performance of the students involved. How can you use a psychological understanding of personality to help ensure a positive roommate relationship? There are no guarantees in the realm of interpersonal relating, but the research on this topic points to some useful advice.

Carli and colleagues (1991) examined the association between personality similarity and relationship satisfaction among 30 college roommate pairs. The roommates had been randomly assigned to live together during the fall of their freshman year. After living together for six months, they completed self-report inventories. The researchers found that personality similarity between roommates was positively correlated with both relationship satisfaction and intent to live together the following year. That is, students liked their roommates when they were similar to those roommates.

Does this finding mean that personality similarity causes relationship satisfaction? Not necessarily. But two factors point to that possibility. First, personality tends to be stable over time. Second, these roommates had been randomly assigned to live together. Therefore, we cannot reject the results of this study as reflecting the possibility that people *choose* to live with people they like (and with whom they are alike).

What do the results of this study mean for you? When it comes time to select a roommate, look for someone who is similar to you, especially on the characteristics that are most important to you. If you really like routine, you might find it grating if your roommate insists on rearranging your furniture once a month or throws impromptu TV-viewing parties in the middle of the week. Likewise, if you are a trusting soul and do not mind sharing your belongings with your roommate, you might bristle at a suspicious roommate who runs a strip of masking tape down the center of the room to delineate your respective spaces.

Preference for—and comfort with—a tidy versus a messy living space is not a personality trait in the same way that openness or agreeableness is a personality trait. That said, this preference is certainly an individual difference worth paying attention to. Ogletree and colleagues (2005) found that a third of their college-age participants reported experiencing roommate conflict related to the cleanliness of their living space. Over a quarter of the students were dissatisfied with their roommates' housecleaning habits, and nearly half had talked with their roommates about these habits on multiple occasions. A fifth of the students had changed their living situations because of these sorts of concerns at some point during the preceding three years!

Thus, it is a good idea to ask potential roommates about their cleanliness preferences. You have at least three options for figuring out how a potential roommate compares with you on this and other valued dimensions. You can ask the potential roommate, you can ask her or his previous roommates, or you can rely on your own

Table 13.2 Level of Cleanliness Scale

How do you and your roommate's answers compare on these seven items from Ogletree and colleagues' level of cleanliness scale? Answer each item on a scale of 1 to 5, where 1 represents "very strongly disagree" and 5 represents "very strongly agree."

1. I don't mind having a messy apartment.
2. It is important to me that my house or apartment is nice and neat.
3. If my house is cluttered when guests drop by, I apologize for the mess.
4. Leaving a stack of dirty dishes in the sink overnight is disgusting.
5. An overflowing trashcan does not bother me.
6. It is important that anyone I live with share my cleanliness standards.
7. Leaving clothes that have been worn on a chair is an acceptable way of dealing with dirty clothes until doing laundry.

Source: Ogletree et al. (2005).

observations. **TABLE 13.2** offers some questions you might wish to ask of roommate candidates. In fact, many colleges and universities ask students to complete personality questionnaires before matching roommates in dorms. You might already have responded to questions like these as part of your application for residence. In that case, if the system has worked, you and your roommate might already be a good fit.

Understandably, you might feel a bit intrusive asking these sorts of questions of a potential roommate. You should, of course, be tactful in your approach. Remember, though, that you are doing yourself and your potential roommate a favor by addressing these issues before you commit to living together. In the long run, doing so can help create the very sort of relationship you tend to value. ■

 Q Are you likely to be more compatible with a roommate who is similar to you in personality or someone different so that you complement each other?

ANSWER: You are most likely to live successfully with someone who is similar to you.

How Do We Know Our Own Personalities?

In the previous sections, the subject was people's personalities generally. The central question was *What must we know to know a person well?* In considering our own personalities, we can rephrase that question as *What must we know to know ourselves well?* This section examines how we process information about ourselves and how that processing shapes our personalities.

Each of us has a notion of something we call the "self." Still, the self is difficult to define. We can say that each person's sense of self involves the person's mental representations of personal experiences. Those representations include both memories and perceptions of what is going on at any particular moment during the person's life. The self also encompasses the person's thought processes, physical body, and conscious awareness of being separate from others and unique. This sense of self is an integrated experience, continuous over time and space. For example, when you wake up in the morning, you do not have to figure out who you are (even if you sometimes have to figure out where you are, such as when you are on vacation).

13.14 Our Self-Concepts Consist of Self-Knowledge

Write down 20 answers to the question *Who am I?* The information in your answers is part of your *self-concept,* which is everything you know and believe about yourself. For example, answers commonly given by college students include gender, age, student status, interpersonal style (e.g., shy, friendly), personal characteristics (e.g., moody, optimistic), and body image. But how would thinking of yourself as shy or optimistic or overweight affect how you feel and function from day to day? What you believe about yourself guides your behavior, depending on the context. If you think of yourself as shy, you might avoid a raucous party. If you believe yourself to be optimistic, you might easily bounce back from a poor grade in organic chemistry. Look back at the 20 answers you provided earlier. Then think of some concrete examples of how those ideas about yourself have influenced your thoughts or behaviors.

SELF-SCHEMA Picture yourself at a loud, crowded party. You can barely hear yourself speak. When someone across the room mentions your name, however, you hear it clearly above the noise. As discussed in Chapter 4, psychologists refer to this as the cocktail party phenomenon. It occurs because each person processes information about himself deeply, thoroughly, and automatically. The information becomes part of the person's *self-schema.*

According to Hazel Markus (1977), the self-schema consists of an integrated set of memories, beliefs, and generalizations about the self. The set can be viewed as a network of interconnected knowledge about the self (**FIGURE 13.29**).

The self-schema helps each of us quickly perceive, organize, interpret, and use information about the self. It also helps each of us filter information so that we are likely to notice things that are self-relevant, such as our own names. Examples of our behavior, and aspects of our personalities, that are important to us become prominent in our self-schemas. For instance, being a good athlete or a good student may be a major component of your self-schema, whereas having few cavities probably is not. Thus, when asked if you are ambitious, you can answer without sorting through occasions in which you did or did not act ambitiously. Your self-schema summarizes the relevant past information.

Meanwhile, your self-schema may lead you to have enhanced memory for information that you process in reference to yourself. Tim Rogers and colleagues (1977) showed that when a person processes trait adjectives self-referentially, the person is likely to recall the words better than comparable words processed only for their general meanings. Suppose you are asked, "What does the word *honest* mean?" If you are later asked to recall the word you were asked about, you might or might not recall *honest.* Now suppose the initial question is, "Does the word *honest* describe you?" When asked later, you will be more likely to remember the word.

What brain activity is involved in this effect? Researchers typically find that when people process information about themselves, there is activity in the middle of the prefrontal cortex (Gillihan & Farah, 2005; Kelley et al., 2002; **FIGURE 13.30**). For example, this brain region is more active when we answer questions about ourselves (e.g., "Are you honest?") than when we answer questions about other people (e.g., "Is your mother honest?"). The greater the activation of this area during the self-referencing, the more likely the person is to remember the item later during a surprise memory task (Macrae, Moran, Heatherton, Banfield, & Kelley, 2004). Damage to the frontal lobes tends to alter how people see themselves. Thus, activation of the middle region

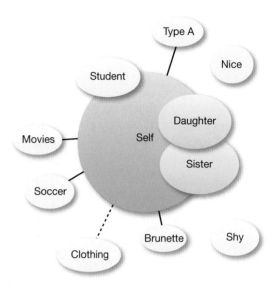

FIGURE 13.29
Self-Schema
As this example illustrates, the self-schema consists of interrelated knowledge about the self. Here, the concepts that overlap with the self—student, daughter, and sister—are most strongly related to the self. Concepts connected to self with a solid line—Type A, movies, soccer, and brunette—are not quite as strongly related to self-knowledge. Clothing, connected to self with a dotted line, is related more weakly. Concepts with no connecting lines do not relate to the self.

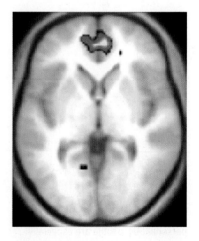

FIGURE 13.30
The Self and Prefrontal Cortex Activity
This brain scan comes from the 2002 study by Kelley and colleagues. The colored area is the brain region that was active when people made trait judgments about themselves.

of the prefrontal cortex clearly seems to be important for processing information about the self (Heatherton, 2011).

WORKING SELF-CONCEPT Psychologists refer to the immediate experience of the self as the *working self-concept*. This experience is limited to the amount of personal information that can be processed cognitively at any given time. Because the working self-concept includes only part of the vast array of self-knowledge, the sense of self varies from situation to situation. Suppose your self-concept includes the traits *fun-loving* and *intelligent*. At a party, you might think of yourself as fun-loving *rather than* intelligent. In other words, your self-descriptions vary. They depend on which memories you retrieve, which situation you are in, which people you are with, and your role in that situation.

When people consider who they are or think about different features of their personalities, they often emphasize characteristics that make them distinct from others. Think back to your 20 responses to the question *Who am I?* Which answers stressed your similarity to other people or membership in a group? Which ones stressed your differences from other people, or at least from the people immediately around you? A respondent is especially likely to mention features such as ethnicity, gender, or age if the person differs in these respects from others around him or her at the moment (**FIGURE 13.31**). For example, Canadians are more likely to note their nationality if they are in Boston than if they are in Toronto. Because the working self-concept guides behavior, this tendency implies that Canadians are also more likely to

FIGURE 13.31
Working Self-Concept
When considering themselves or their personalities, people are especially likely to mention characteristics that distinguish them from other people. For example, when working with a group of women, an African American man might be most aware of his maleness. When working with a group of Caucasians, he might emphasize his being African American.

feel and act like "Canadians" when in Boston than when in Toronto. Most people have optimal levels of distinctiveness, however, since generally they want to avoid standing out too much from the crowd.

 How is the self-schema useful?

13.15 Perceived Social Regard Influences Self-Esteem

North American culture has been obsessed with self-esteem since at least the 1980s. At a basic level, **self-esteem** is the evaluative aspect of the self-concept. In other words, self-esteem indicates a person's emotional response to contemplating personal characteristics: "Am I worthy or unworthy?" "Am I good or bad?" Although self-esteem is related to self-concept, people can objectively believe positive things about themselves without liking themselves very much. Conversely, people can like themselves very much, and therefore have high self-esteem, even when objective indicators do not support such positive self-views.

Many theories assume that people's self-esteem is based on how they believe others perceive them. This view is known as *reflected appraisal*. It suggests that when people internalize the values and beliefs expressed by important people in their lives, they adopt those attitudes (and related behaviors) as their own. Consequently, people come to respond to themselves in ways that are consistent with how others respond to them. From this perspective, when an important figure rejects, ignores, demeans, or devalues a person, the person is likely to experience low self-esteem.

Even though we might encourage children to have high self-esteem, there is a tendency for self-esteem to fall during adolescence and be at its lowest for people, especially young women, ages 18 to 22 (Robins, Trzesniewski, Tracy, Gosling, & Potter, 2002; **FIGURE 13.32**). Self-esteem then typically increases across adulthood, peaking when people are in their 60s and falling off toward the end of life. This pattern appears to be true in cultures around the world (Bleidorn et al., 2016). Studies typically find that females have lower self-esteem than males, particularly during adolescence. However, the gap between females and males appears to be decreasing (Zuckerman, Li, & Hall, 2016).

self-esteem
The evaluative aspect of the self-concept in which people feel worthy or unworthy.

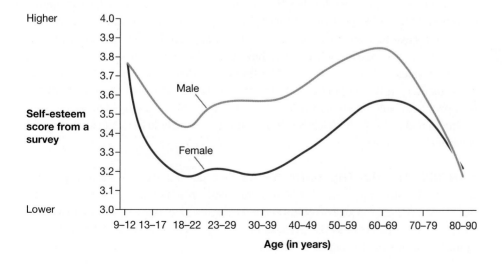

FIGURE 13.32
Self-Esteem Across the Life Span
Self-esteem varies across people's lives. It is very high in early childhood. Low points in self-esteem are seen in the late teens and early twenties, especially for females. Then low self-esteem is also experienced toward the end of people's lives. Self-esteem typically peaks when people are in their late sixties.

SOCIOMETER THEORY In an important account of self-esteem, Mark Leary and colleagues (1995) proposed that self-esteem is a mechanism for monitoring the likelihood of social exclusion. This theory assumes that, as discussed in Chapter 10, humans have a fundamental, adaptive need to belong. For most of human evolution, those who belonged to social groups have been more likely to survive and reproduce than those who were excluded and left to survive on their own. When people behave in ways that increase the likelihood that they will be rejected, they experience a reduction in self-esteem. Thus, self-esteem is a **sociometer,** an internal monitor of social acceptance or rejection (**FIGURE 13.33**).

When a person's sociometer indicates a low probability of rejection, the person will tend to experience high self-esteem. As long as the probability of rejection remains low, the person will probably not worry about how he or she is perceived by others. When a person's sociometer indicates the imminent possibility of rejection, the person will tend to experience low self-esteem. Therefore, the person will be highly motivated to manage his or her public image. Abundant evidence supports the sociometer theory, including the consistent finding that low self-esteem is highly correlated with social anxiety (Leary, 2004; Leary & MacDonald, 2003). Recall, though, that even high correlation does not prove causation.

SELF-ESTEEM AND LIFE OUTCOMES With such emphasis placed on self-esteem within Western culture, you might expect that having high self-esteem is the key to life success. The evidence from psychological science, however, indicates that self-esteem may be less important than is commonly believed. After reviewing several hundred studies, Roy Baumeister and colleagues (Baumeister, Campbell, Krueger, & Vohs, 2003, 2005) found that although people with high self-esteem report being much happier, self-esteem is weakly related to objective life outcomes. People with high self-esteem who consider themselves smarter, more attractive, and better liked do not necessarily have higher IQs and are not thought of more highly by others. That is, self-esteem has little to do with whether we like someone or not.

Many people with high self-esteem are successful in their careers, but so are many people with low self-esteem. While a small relationship exists between self-esteem and some outcomes, such as academic success, it is possible that success causes high self-esteem. That is, people might have higher self-esteem because they have done well in school.

In fact, there may even be some downsides to having very high self-esteem. Violent criminals commonly have very high self-esteem; indeed, some people become violent when they feel that others are not treating them with an appropriate level of respect (Baumeister, Smart, & Boden, 1996). School bullies also often have high self-esteem (Baumeister et al., 2003). When people with high self-esteem believe their abilities have been challenged, they may act in ways that cause other people to dislike them (Heatherton & Vohs, 2000; Vohs & Heatherton, 2004). For example, the sense of needing to prove their worth might lead people to become antagonistic or boastful. Ultimately, having high self-esteem seems to make people happier, but it does not necessarily lead to successful social relationships or life success.

NARCISSISM AND THE DARK TRIAD One personality trait associated with inflated self-esteem is *narcissism*. The term comes from Greek mythology, in which Narcissus rejected the love of others and fell in love with his own reflection in a pond. In the psychological sense of narcissism, self-centered people view themselves in grandiose terms, feel superior to others and entitled to special treatment, and are

sociometer
An internal monitor of social acceptance or rejection.

(a)

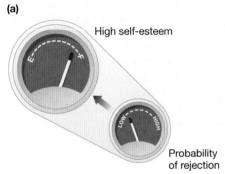

High self-esteem

Probability of rejection

(b)

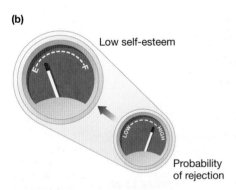

Low self-esteem

Probability of rejection

FIGURE 13.33
Sociometers
According to sociometer theory, self-esteem is the gauge that measures the extent to which a person believes he or she is being included in or excluded from a social group. **(a)** If the probability of rejection seems low, the person's self-esteem will tend to be high. **(b)** If the probability of rejection seems high, the person's self-esteem will tend to be low.

manipulative (Bosson et al., 2008). Because narcissists' greatest love is for the self, they tend to have poor relations with others (Campbell, Bush, Brunell, & Shelton, 2005). They become angry when challenged (Rhodewalt & Morf, 1998). They abuse people who do not share their lofty opinions of themselves (Bushman & Baumeister, 1998; Twenge & Campbell, 2003).

You might be interested to learn that a meta-analysis found an increase in narcissism among American college students between 1979 and 2006 (Twenge, Konrath, Foster, Campbell, & Bushman, 2008). The researchers point to a few possible contributing factors: programs aimed at increasing self-esteem among young schoolchildren (such as having them sing songs about how they are special), grade inflation that makes students feel more capable than they might really be, and a rise in the use of self-promotion Web sites such as Facebook and MySpace. A different team of researchers was unable to replicate the results of this meta-analysis, however, and there is controversy regarding what the findings mean (Trzesniewski, Donnellan, & Roberts, 2008).

Recently, personality psychologists have described three negative personality traits that make up a *dark triad*: narcissism, *psychopathy*, and *Machiavellianism* (Paulhus & Williams, 2002). Each of these traits is associated with tendencies toward self-promotion, emotional coldness, dishonesty, and aggression. Psychopathy revolves around a general lack of caring for the welfare of others. Those high in psychopathy are callous toward others and cunning in pursuing their personal goals. These individuals also tend to be impulsive and reckless, and they have low levels of fear. Machiavellianism is named after the Italian philosopher Niccolò Machiavelli, who in the 1500s cynically encouraged immoral behaviors, such as lying and cheating, as effective tools in politics. The personality trait named after him describes people who are especially manipulative of others for their own gain and lack concern with conventional morality. Uniting the dark triad are a lack of empathy, willingness to be dishonest, and a low level of the trait agreeableness (Furnham, Richards, & Paulhus, 2013).

Possession of the dark triad of traits is associated with career success, such as making more money, being in leadership positions, and winning political elections (Spain, Harms, & Lebreton, 2013; Spurk, Keller, & Hirschi, 2016; **FIGURE 13.34**). Moreover, there is some evidence that women initially view men who possess dark triad traits positively, perhaps because such men display confidence, dominance, and at least superficial charm (Carter, Campbell, & Muncer, 2014). Thus, although the dark triad traits are viewed negatively by society, they may provide benefits to those who possess them, at least in the short term (Paulhus, 2014).

It should be noted that some people's levels of either narcissism or psychopathy are so high that they are considered to have personality disorders. You will learn more about these conditions in Chapter 14.

 It is commonly said that we love people who love themselves. Are people with high self-esteem generally viewed as more likeable?

FIGURE 13.34
American Psychopath
In the 2000 movie *American Psycho*, Christian Bale plays Patrick Bateman, who appears to be a suave man-about-town, a successful professional, and a serial killer. The movie, like the Bret Easton Ellis novel it is based on, raises questions about the connections between a slick presentation of self, a knack for making and spending money, and psychopathy.

ANSWER: High self-esteem is not related to how much people are liked in most situations. However, people with high self-esteem may be disliked because of the negative ways they act when they feel their abilities have been challenged.

13.16 People Use Mental Strategies to Maintain a Positive Sense of Self

A consistent theme that emerges from research is that people show favoritism to anything associated with themselves. For example, people consistently prefer things they own to things they do not own (Beggan, 1992). People even prefer the letters of their

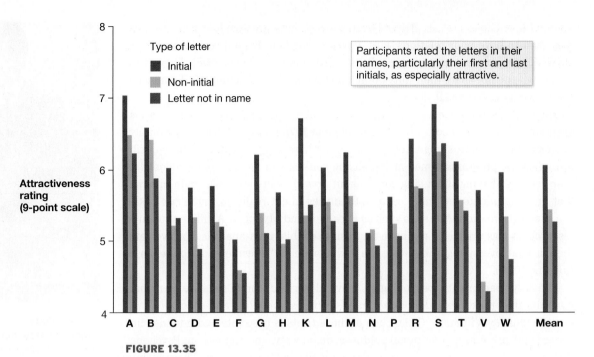

FIGURE 13.35
Favoritism
This graph shows the study participants' ratings of letters of the alphabet.

own names, especially their initials, to other letters (Koole, Dijksterhuis, & van Knippenberg, 2001; **FIGURE 13.35**).

Sometimes these positive views of the self seem inflated. For instance, 90 percent of adults claim they are better-than-average drivers, even if they have been hospitalized for injuries caused by car accidents in which they were one of the drivers involved (Guerin, 1994; Svenson, 1981). Similarly, when the College Entrance Examination Board surveyed more than 800,000 college-bound seniors, not a single senior rated herself or himself as below average, whereas a whopping 25 percent rated themselves in the top 1 percent (Gilovich, 1991). Most people describe themselves as above average in nearly every way; psychologists refer to this phenomenon as the *better-than-average effect* (Alicke, Klotz, Breitenbecher, Yurak, & Vredenburg, 1995). People with high self-esteem are especially likely to exhibit this effect, but even those with low self-esteem rate themselves as above average on many dimensions (Suls, Lemos, & Stewart, 2002).

According to Shelley Taylor and Jonathan Brown (1988), most people have *positive illusions*—overly favorable and unrealistic beliefs—in at least three domains. First, most people continually experience the better-than-average effect. Second, they unrealistically perceive their personal control over events. For example, some fans believe they help their favorite sports teams win if they attend games or wear their lucky jerseys. Third, most people are unrealistically optimistic about their personal futures. They believe they will probably be successful, marry happily, and live long lives. Positive illusions can be adaptive when they promote optimism in meeting life's challenges. Alternatively, positive illusions can lead to trouble when people overestimate their skills and underestimate their vulnerabilities. Recall from Chapter 1 that people often fail to recognize their incompetencies.

Life is filled with failure, rejection, and disappointment, yet most people feel pretty good about themselves. How do people maintain such positive views? Psychologists have cataloged a number of unconscious strategies that help people maintain a positive sense of self. Among the most common such strategies are *social comparisons* and *self-serving biases*. As you read the following discussions, bear in mind that psychologists do not necessarily endorse these strategies. Rather, this is what research has shown people do in these situations.

SOCIAL COMPARISONS Social comparison occurs when people evaluate their own actions, abilities, and beliefs by contrasting them with other people's. That is, people compare themselves with others to see where they stand. They are especially likely to perform such comparisons when they have no objective criteria, such as knowing how much money represents a good income. As discussed in Chapter 10, social comparisons are an important means of understanding people's actions and emotions. In general, people with high self-esteem make downward comparisons. That is, they contrast themselves with people inferior to them on relevant dimensions. People with low self-esteem tend to make upward comparisons. They contrast themselves with people superior to them. People also use a form of downward comparison when they recall their own pasts: They often view their current selves as better than their former selves (Wilson & Ross, 2001; **FIGURE 13.36**). These findings suggest that viewing ourselves as better than others or as better than we used to be makes us feel good about ourselves. But people who constantly compare themselves with others who do better may confirm their negative self-feelings.

social comparison
The tendency for people to evaluate their own actions, abilities, and beliefs by contrasting them with other people's.

SELF-SERVING BIASES People with high self-esteem tend to take credit for success but blame failure on external factors. Psychologists refer to this tendency as the **self-serving bias.** For instance, students who do extremely well on exams often explain their performance by referring to their skills or hard work. Those who do poorly might describe the test as an arbitrary examination of trivial details. People with high self-esteem also assume that criticism is motivated by envy or prejudice. Indeed, members of groups prone to discrimination (e.g., the disabled; those from underrepresented groups) tend to have high self-esteem. According to a theory proposed by Jennifer Crocker and Brenda Major (1989), members of these groups maintain

self-serving bias
The tendency for people to take personal credit for success but blame failure on external factors.

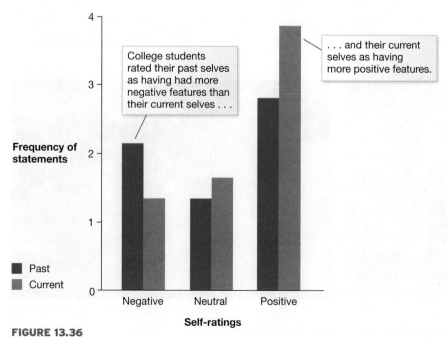

FIGURE 13.36
Rating the Self Across Time
This graph shows the results of Wilson and Ross's 2001 study.

positive self-esteem by taking credit for success and blaming negative feedback on prejudice. Thus, if they succeed, the success is due to personal strengths and occurs despite the odds. If they fail, the failure is due to external factors and unfair obstacles.

Over the last 40 years, psychologists have documented many ways that people show bias in thinking about themselves compared with how they think about others (Campbell & Sedikides, 1999). In thinking about our failures, for example, we compare ourselves with others who did worse, we diminish the importance of the challenge, we think about the things we are really good at, and we bask in the reflected glory of both family and friends. The overall picture suggests we are extremely well equipped to protect our positive beliefs about ourselves. Some researchers have even argued that self-serving biases reflect healthy psychological functioning (Mezulis, Abramson, Hyde, & Hankin, 2004; Taylor & Brown, 1988). Recall the earlier discussion of narcissism, however. This trait reflects more of a disorder of personality than healthy functioning.

 How common is it for people to think that they are better than average at most things?

ANSWER: Most people rate themselves better than average.

THINK LIKE A PSYCHOLOGIST

13.17 Are There Cultural Differences in the Self-Serving Bias?

Psychologists have generally viewed the self-serving bias as a universal human trait (Sedikides & Gregg, 2008). In other words, self-enhancement may be as much a part of human nature as eating. Although people suffering from depression might fail to show the effect, the assumption is that most healthy, functioning individuals show robust self-enhancement. Steven Heine and colleagues (1999) have argued, however, that the self-serving bias may be more common in Western cultures than in Eastern cultures (FIGURE 13.37). Consider some of the evidence.

An important way in which people differ in self-concept is whether they view themselves as fundamentally separate from or connected to other people. For example, as

(a)

(b)

FIGURE 13.37
Individualist Versus Collectivist Cultures
(a) Western cultures tend to highlight individual success. (b) Eastern cultures tend to value those who fall in line with the masses.

noted in Chapter 1, Westerners tend to be independent and autonomous, stressing their individuality. Easterners tend to be more interdependent, stressing their sense of being part of a collective. Harry Triandis (1989) notes that some cultures (e.g., in Japan, Pakistan, China, and some regions of Africa) emphasize the collective self more than the personal self. Collectivist cultures emphasize connections to family, to social groups, and to ethnic groups; conformity to societal norms; and group cohesiveness. Individualist cultures (e.g., in northern and western Europe, Australia, Canada, New Zealand, and the United States) emphasize rights and freedoms, self-expression, and diversity. For example, in the United States, people dress differently from one another, cultivate personal interests, and often enjoy standing out from the crowd. In Japan, people tend to dress more similarly and respect situational norms.

In addition, Hazel Markus and Shinobu Kitayama (1991) have noted that people in collectivist cultures tend to have interdependent self-construals. In other words, their self-concepts are determined to a large extent by their social roles and personal relationships (FIGURE 13.38). As children, they are raised to follow group norms and be obedient to parents, teachers, and other people in authority. They are expected to find their proper place in society and not to challenge or complain about their status. By contrast, people in individualist cultures tend to have independent self-construals. Parents and teachers encourage children to be self-reliant and to pursue personal success, even at the expense of interpersonal relationships. Thus, a child's sense of self is based on her feelings of being distinct from others. (Note, however, that within these broad patterns there is variability. Some people in individualist cultures have interdependent self-construals, and some people in collectivist cultures have independent self-construals.)

Given these findings, doesn't it make sense that self-enhancement and self-bias are more common in Western than Eastern cultures? After all, Western cultures emphasize individuality. Believing that someone is especially talented presupposes that some people are better than others. Such an attitude is less acceptable in Eastern, collectivistic cultures. There, the group is special, not the individual. Thus, self-enhancement and self-serving bias may be culturally determined, not universal. What is the evidence? In one study (Endo & Meijer, 2004), American and Japanese students were asked to list as many of their own successes and failures as they could. The Americans showed a bias for listing successes. The Japanese students listed failures and successes equally. In addition, the Americans used outside forces to explain failure, but the Japanese students used outside forces to explain success. Indeed, Markus and Kitayama (1991) have argued that in Asian cultures, self-criticism is more the social norm than self-promotion is. The overall evidence supports the view that people in individualist cultures are more concerned with self-enhancement than those in collectivist, particularly Asian, cultures (Heine, 2003). For example, in a

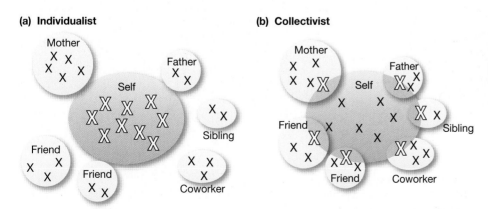

(a) Individualist

Mother
Father
Self
Sibling
Friend
Friend
Coworker

(b) Collectivist

Mother
Father
Self
Sibling
Friend
Friend
Coworker

FIGURE 13.38
Cultural Differences in Self-Construals
Self-construals differ across cultures. **(a)** In individualist cultures, the most important elements of a person's self-construal tend to reside within the person. **(b)** In collectivist cultures, the most important elements of a person's self-construal tend to reside in areas where the person's sense of self is connected with others.

meta-analysis involving more than 500 studies, people in Western cultures showed a much larger self-serving bias than those in Eastern cultures (Mezulis et al., 2004).

Might these differences reflect cultural rules about publicly admitting positive self-views? Perhaps people in the East engage in strategic self-enhancement, but they are just more modest in public. In studies using anonymous reporting, however—where presumably there is less call for modesty—Easterners continue to show a low level of self-serving bias (Heine, 2003). At the same time, indirect evidence using an implicit measure indicates that people from China and Japan show a positivity bias—a tendency to see themselves as better than others—equivalent to that of Americans (Yamaguchi et al., 2007). As discussed in Chapter 12, implicit attitude assessment is useful for situations in which people are hesitant to make explicit reports. In this case, the research finding suggests that although Easterners value themselves just as much as Westerners, they are hesitant to admit it.

According to another perspective, self-enhancement is universal, but the traits people focus on to achieve it vary across cultures (Brown & Kobayashi, 2002; Sedikides, Gaertner, & Toguchi, 2003). Thus, when the culture emphasizes personal achievement, people self-enhance as individuals. When the culture emphasizes group achievement, people self-enhance as group members. In yet another complication, however, some research reveals a pattern that contradicts these findings. Namely, people in Eastern cultures are more critical of their groups compared with people in Western cultures (Heine & Lehman, 1999). East Asians often are especially self-critical in aspects of life that are important to them (Heine, Kitayama, & Hamamura, 2007).

The debate goes on, but why? The universality issue matters, in part, because it relates to how culture shapes the sense of self (Heine, 2005; Sedikides et al., 2003). Does a particular culture say it is more important to be respected by others or to feel good about oneself no matter what others think? Might people in Eastern cultures feel better about themselves when they demonstrate that they are modest and self-effacing, whereas Westerners feel better when they can show they are successful? Perhaps what really matters is whether a person feels good about her or his behavior. In this way, all people might be self-serving. ■

 Do people in Eastern or Western cultures more often show self-serving biases?

ANSWER: In most studies, people from Western cultures more often show self-serving biases.

Your Chapter Review

Chapter Summary

Where Does Personality Come From?

13.1 Genetic Factors Influence the Development of Personality

The results of twin studies and adoption studies suggest that 40–60 percent of personality variation is the product of genetic variation. Parents play an important role in selecting the environments that shape their children's personalities. Personality characteristics are influenced by multiple genes, which interact with the environment to produce general dispositions. It is difficult to identify the influence of specific genes on personality, although some traits, such as novelty seeking, have been linked to a gene associated with dopamine activity, and emotional stability has been linked to a gene associated with serotonin levels.

13.2 Temperaments Are Evident in Infancy

Temperaments are biologically based personality tendencies. They are evident in early childhood and have long-term implications for adult behavior. Researchers have identified activity level, emotionality, and sociability as temperaments. Sex differences exist in temperament: Girls are more able to control attention and impulses, and boys are more active and gain more pleasure from physical activity. Childhood temperaments can predict adult personality. Shyness can be predicted as early as 2 months of age and involves the amygdala. Parental support and calm environments can help children overcome shyness.

What Are the Theories of Personality?

13.3 Psychodynamic Theories Emphasize Unconscious and Dynamic Processes

Freud believed that unconscious forces determine behavior. He theorized that personality consists of three structures: the id, the superego, and the ego. The ego mediates between the id and the superego, using defense mechanisms to reduce anxiety due to conflicts between the id and the superego. Freud proposed that people pass through five stages of psychosexual development and that these stages shape their personalities. In contrast to Freud, neo-Freudians have focused on relationships— in particular, children's emotional attachments to their parents.

13.4 Personality Reflects Learning and Cognition

According to learning theories, people learn patterns of responding that are guided by their expectancies, values, and personal constructs. Locus of control, the extent to which people feel they have control over outcome in their lives, is an important determinant of behavior. Reciprocal determinism indicates that how personality is expressed can be explained by the interaction of environment, person factors, and behavior itself.

13.5 Humanistic Approaches Emphasize Integrated Personal Experience

Humanistic approaches emphasize experiences, beliefs, the uniqueness of the human condition, and inherent goodness. According to these approaches, people strive to realize their full potential. According to Rogers's person-centered approach, unconditional positive regard in childhood enables people to become fully functioning.

13.6 Trait Approaches Describe Behavioral Dispositions

Trait theorists assume that personality is a collection of traits or behavioral dispositions. Five-factor theory maintains that there are five higher-order personality traits: openness to experience, conscientiousness, extraversion, agreeableness, and neuroticism. Research supports five-factor theory in a number of ways.

13.7 Traits Have a Biological Basis

Brain imaging research has distinguished activity in different brain regions based on traits. According to Eysenck's model of personality, there are three biologically based higher-order dimensions of personality traits: introversion/extraversion, emotional stability, and psychoticism or constraint.

How Stable Is Personality?

13.8 People Sometimes Are Inconsistent

According to Mischel's notion of situationism, situations are more important than traits in predicting behavior. The person/situation debate revolves around whether personality traits or situations are more important in predicting behavior. Research suggests that when evaluated over time, personality traits do predict behavior. According to interactionism, behavior is determined by both situations and dispositions. Strong situations mask differences in personality, whereas weak situations reveal differences in personality. Most trait theorists favor interactionism.

13.9 Development and Life Events Alter Personality Traits

A variety of research shows personality traits to be stable over the life span. Although traits are stable, they undergo developmental change. Developmental changes in personality traits are caused by changes in self-perception generated by life experiences. Common developmental changes in the Big Five personality factors include decreased neuroticism, extraversion, and openness and increased agreeableness and conscientiousness. Most changes to personality occur between the ages of 20 and 40, likely due to the large number of life experiences that occur during this period.

13.10 Culture Influences Personality

Cross-cultural research suggests that the Big Five personality factors are universal among humans. Sex differences in personality are consistent with common sex stereotypes, although cultural influences may explain these differences. For example, individualistic societies may highlight individual differences, while collectivist societies may minimize them.

How Is Personality Assessed?

13.11 Researchers Use Multiple Methods to Assess Personality

Idiographic approaches to the assessment of personality are person-centered. They focus on individual lives and each person's unique characteristics. Nomothetic approaches assess individual variation in characteristics that are common among all people. Personality can be assessed via several measures. Projective measures, such as the Rorschach inkblot test and the Thematic Apperception Test, assess unconscious processes by having people interpret ambiguous stimuli. Self-report measures, such as the *MMPI* and the California Q-Sort, are relatively direct measures of personality, typically involving the use of questionnaires. Life history data and behavioral data can also reveal personality traits.

13.12 Observers Show Accuracy in Trait Judgments

Personality traits can be accurately judged by others. Close acquaintances may better predict a person's behavior than the person can. This effect may be due to failure to pay attention to one's own behavior or due to biases in self-perception. Acquaintances are particularly accurate when judging traits that are readily observable.

13.13 Using Psychology in Your Life: What Personality Traits Should You Look for in a Roommate?

Roommates who are similar in personality tend to get along better than those who do not match. For this reason, many schools use surveys to try to match students. One important factor is the extent to which people are concerned about cleanliness.

How Do We Know Our Own Personalities?

13.14 Our Self-Concepts Consist of Self-Knowledge

The self-concept consists of everything people know or believe about themselves. The self-schema is the integrated set of memories, beliefs, and generalizations about the self. The self-schema allows the individual to remember self-referential information better, and it appears to rely on activation of the frontal lobes. The working self-concept is the immediate experience of the self at any given time. The working self-concept does not include the vast array of self-knowledge and therefore focuses on traits relevant only to the current situation.

13.15 Perceived Social Regard Influences Self-Esteem

Self-esteem is the evaluative aspect of the self-concept. Self-esteem usually decreases in adolescence and early 20s, especially for women, and again late in life. Self-esteem peaks in early childhood and then again in the 60s. According to sociometer theory, the need to belong influences self-esteem. Self-esteem is associated with happiness but is only weakly correlated with objective life outcomes.

13.16 People Use Mental Strategies to Maintain a Positive Sense of Self

Positive illusions of self are common. People use numerous unconscious strategies to maintain positive views of ourselves, including downward social comparisons and self-serving biases.

13.17 Think like a Psychologist: Are There Cultural Differences in the Self-Serving Bias?

People from collectivist cultures (e.g., Eastern cultures, such as Asian and African countries) tend to have interdependent self-concepts. People from individualist cultures (e.g., Western cultures, such as Australia, Canada, New Zealand, and the United States) tend to have independent self-concepts. Those from Western cultures are more likely to show self-serving biases, perhaps in part because people from Eastern cultures are more modest in their self-reports.

Key Terms

behavioral approach system (BAS), p. 531

behavioral inhibition system (BIS), p. 531

defense mechanisms, p. 523

ego, p. 523

five-factor theory, p. 528

humanistic approaches, p. 526

id, p. 522

idiographic approaches, p. 541

interactionism, p. 533

locus of control, p. 525

nomothetic approaches, p. 541

personality, p. 516

personality trait, p. 516

projective measures, p. 541

psychodynamic theory, p. 522

psychosexual stages, p. 524

reciprocal determinism, p. 526

self-esteem, p. 549

self-serving bias, p. 553

situationism, p. 532

social comparison, p. 553

sociometer, p. 550

superego, p. 523

temperaments, p. 519

trait approach, p. 528

What Are I/O Psychologists?

Are you a Gryffindor or a Slytherin? If you're familiar with *Harry Potter* lore, perhaps you have occasionally wished that a real-life Sorting Hat could assess your skills and preferences and assign you to the perfect graduate school or job. As you have learned in this chapter, individuals may not be the best judges of their own personality traits, skills, and preferences. Accordingly, using the judgment of others or of evidence-based personality measures may result in more-accurate assessments. In turn, knowing how to best use one's traits, skills, and preferences can have important implications for job and life satisfaction. This knowledge can also lead to employment opportunities in industrial/organizational (I/O) psychology.

I/O psychologists apply psychological research to improve workplace efficiency. They may be involved in selecting, recruiting, and training employees. They may apply personality tests, such as the Big Five, to optimize the fit between an employee's traits and a particular job requirement. They may observe how employees work in a team and make suggestions to improve productivity or to minimize interpersonal conflicts. NASA, for example, is using research produced by I/O psychologists to study and improve interactions among the team of astronauts traveling together for six months on a scheduled 2030 journey to Mars.

I/O psychologists can work in various settings. Some conduct research as university faculty in psychology or business departments. Others are hired by corporations as human resource specialists or as training and development managers, working directly with employees. Finally, I/O psychologists can work as independent consultants who are contracted by organizations to help with particular problems.

How do you become an I/O psychologist? The path starts with an undergraduate degree in psychology, perhaps combined with a business minor. It is possible to find employment in this area—for example, as a human resources specialist—with only a baccalaureate degree, but I/O jobs are more plentiful, and provide higher salaries, for those with advanced degrees. Those with master's degrees can find entry-level positions in management or consulting. Those with doctoral degrees have the most opportunities, whether in the academic sector or in the business world. According to the U.S. Bureau of Labor Statistics (2016), the median salary for I/O psychologists is $82,760 per year; those in the top 10 percent can earn over $184,000 annually.

The bottom line: Assessing and applying personality traits can be valuable in the workplace, from improving worker efficiency and satisfaction to improving team cohesiveness. An undergraduate degree in psychology, along with courses in business, can lead to entry-level positions. Advanced degrees open up more employment opportunities and lead to higher starting salaries.

Want to earn a better grade on your test?
Go to **INQUIZITIVE** to learn and review this chapter's content, with personalized feedback along the way. Practice Tests and accompanying answer keys can be found at the back of the book on page PT-1.

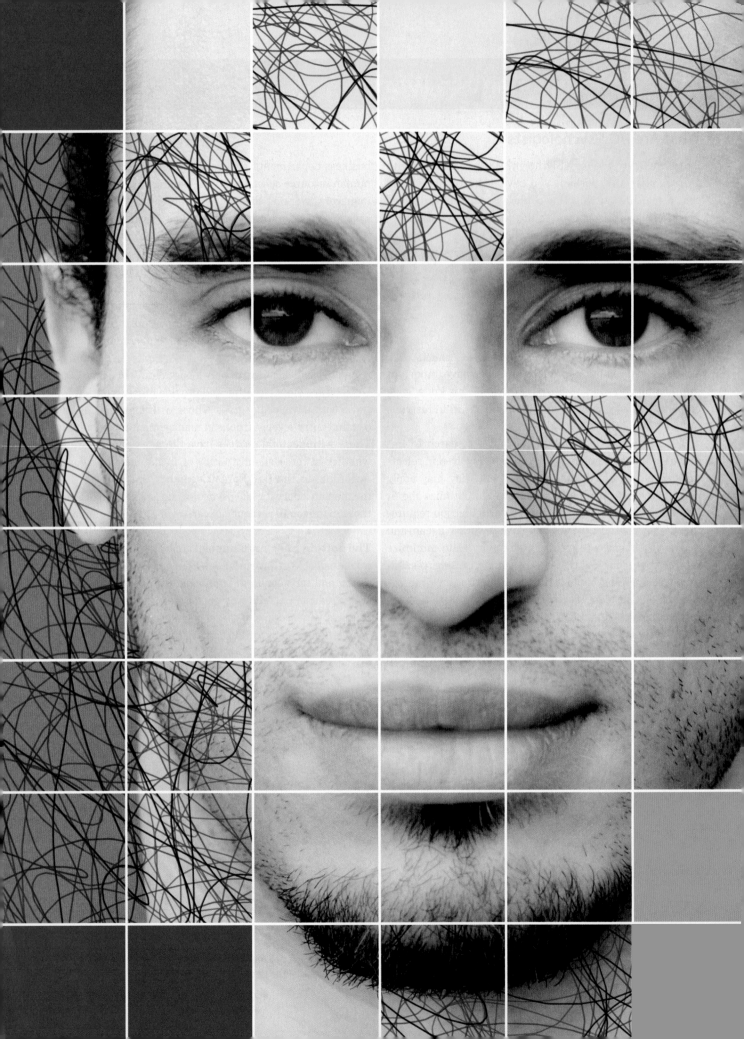

Big Questions

- How Are Psychological Disorders Conceptualized and Classified? 562

- Which Disorders Emphasize Emotional States? 573

- Which Disorders Emphasize Thought Disturbances? 586

- What Are Personality Disorders? 595

- Which Psychological Disorders Are Prominent in Childhood? 601

SOMETIMES YOU FEEL HAPPY, AND SOMETIMES YOU FEEL SAD. Like everyone, you experience life's ups and downs. For some people, however, mood swings and energy swings are much more intense, quickly changing from episodes of extreme listlessness and sadness to excited states of extraordinary joyfulness. This condition is known as bipolar disorder. A number of celebrities have been diagnosed with bipolar disorder, including Britney Spears, Demi Lovato, Russell Brand, and Catherine Zeta-Jones.

Many of us have friends or relatives who have been diagnosed with a psychological disorder. Perhaps you have been diagnosed with one. They are extremely common. A key question considered throughout this chapter is what determines when a psychological state is considered to be a disorder. When does being frequently sad turn into the psychological disorder depression? This chapter examines the most common psychological disorders, including what causes them, how to diagnose them, and how they affect people's lives. For psychologists, the big questions in this area are: How are psychological disorders conceptualized and classified? Which disorders emphasize emotional states? Which disorders emphasize thought disturbances? What are personality disorders? And which psychological disorders are prominent in childhood?

Learning Objectives

- Understand what is meant by the terms *psychopathology* and *psychological disorder*.
- Explain how psychological disorders are classified.
- Identify assessment methods for psychological disorders.
- Describe the diathesis-stress model.
- Identify biological, situational, and cognitive-behavioral causes of psychological disorders.
- Discuss sex differences and cultural differences in psychological disorders.

psychopathology

Sickness or disorder of the mind; psychological disorder.

etiology

Factors that contribute to the development of a disorder.

FIGURE 14.1
Historical View of Psychological Disorders
Throughout history, people believed that the gods, witches, or evil spirits caused psychological disorders.

How Are Psychological Disorders Conceptualized and Classified?

Those who have psychological disorders display symptoms of **psychopathology.** This term means sickness or disorder of the mind. From the writings of Aristotle to those of Freud, accounts exist of people suffering from various forms of psychopathology. Although considerable progress has been made over the last century, we are still struggling to determine the causes of psychopathology. To understand any disorder, psychologists investigate its **etiology:** the factors that contribute to its development. For example, they investigate commonalities among people such as Britney Spears and Demi Lovato to identify factors that might explain why they (and others) developed bipolar disorders.

14.1 Views on Psychopathology Have Changed over Time

The earliest views of psychopathology explained apparent "madness" as resulting from possession by demons or evil spirits (**FIGURE 14.1**). The ancient Babylonians believed a demon called Idta caused madness. Similar examples of demonology can be found among the ancient Chinese, Egyptians, and Greeks. This view of psychopathology continued into the Middle Ages. At that time, there was greater emphasis on possession as having resulted from the wrath of God for some sinful moral transgression. During any of these periods, people we now know to have bipolar disorder might have been persecuted and subjected to an array of methods to cast out their demons. Such "treatments" included exorcism, bloodletting, and the forced ingestion of magical potions.

In the latter half of the Middle Ages and into the Renaissance, people with psychopathology were removed from society so they would not bother others. In the 1700s, those with disorders likely would have been left in an understaffed, overcrowded mental institution called an asylum. Even there, the small staff would have made little attempt to understand people's disorders and even less of an attempt to treat the people. Indeed, those housed in asylums were often chained up and lived in incredibly filthy conditions, dealt with more like nonhuman animals than humans. "Treatments" included starvation, beatings, bloodletting, and isolation.

In 1793, Philippe Pinel, a French physician who believed that medical treatments should be based on empirical observations, became the head physician at Bicêtre Hospital, in Paris. At that time, among the hospital's 4,000 patients were about 200 with psychopathology being cared for by a former patient, Jean-Baptiste Pussin. Pussin treated his patients with kindness and care rather than violence. Impressed by the positive therapeutic results, Pinel removed patients from their chains and banished physical punishment. He instituted what came to be known as *moral treatment,* a therapy that involved close contact with and careful observation of patients. Pinel's benevolent treatment gained a foothold in Europe, and later—through the efforts of a Massachusetts schoolteacher, Dorothea Dix—in America.

As far back as ancient Greece, some people had a sense that there was a physical basis to psychopathology. Hippocrates (c. 460–377 BCE), often credited as the founder of modern medicine, classified psychopathologies into *mania, melancholia,* and *phrenitis,* the latter characterized by mental confusion. Hippocrates believed that such disorders resulted from the relative amount of "humors," or bodily fluids, a person possessed (Maher & Maher, 1994). For instance, having too much black bile led to melancholia, or extreme sadness and depression. From this term, we get the word *melancholy,* which we often use to describe people who are sad. The idea that bodily fluids cause mental illness was abandoned long ago, however. Increasingly throughout the nineteenth and twentieth centuries, psychopathology was viewed more as a medical condition than as a demonic curse caused by sin. The medical model viewed psychopathology as resulting from disease. During the last 200 years, recognition has grown that psychopathology reflects dysfunction of the body, particularly of the brain.

At various points in recent history, researchers and clinicians would have focused solely on environmental factors that contributed to a person's psychological disorder. For example, was she abused as a child? Although environmental factors are important, we now understand that biology plays a critical role in many psychological disorders, especially disorders such as bipolar disorder or schizophrenia. Indeed, an important lesson in this chapter is that environment and biology interact to produce psychological disorders. As noted throughout the book, it is meaningless to state that a condition is caused by just biology or just environment. Both factors affect all psychological disorders to some extent.

PSYCHOLOGICAL DISORDERS AS MALADAPTIVE How do you know if someone has a psychological disorder? It can be challenging to decide if a given behavior is caused by psychopathology. Keep in mind that behavior, especially unusual behavior, must always be reviewed in the context of the situation. A woman running through the streets screaming, sobbing, and grabbing and hugging people might have some form of psychological disorder—or she might be celebrating because she just won the lottery. Many behaviors considered normal in one setting may be considered deviant in other settings. Some Native American and East Asian cultures consider it a great honor to hear the voices of spirits. In urban America, hearing spirits would be seen as evidence of auditory hallucinations.

In determining whether behavior represents psychopathology, it is important to consider certain criteria: (1) Does the person act in a way that deviates from cultural norms for acceptable behavior? (2) Is the behavior maladaptive? That is, does the behavior interfere with the person's ability to respond appropriately in different situations? For example, a person who is afraid to leave the house may avoid feeling anxious by staying inside, and that behavior might prevent the person from working, having a social life, or both. (3) Is the behavior self-destructive, does it cause the individual personal distress, or does it threaten other people in the community? (4) Does the behavior cause discomfort and concern to others, thus impairing a person's social relationships?

It may be hard to draw the line between normal and abnormal. As a result, psychopathology is increasingly defined in terms of *maladaptiveness*. That is, a person with psychopathology exhibits thoughts, feelings, and behaviors that are maladaptive rather than deviant. For example, people concerned about germs may wash their hands more than average and therefore be deviant, but that behavior may be beneficial in many ways and therefore adaptive—after all, it is the best way of avoiding contagious disease. The same behavior, however, can be maladaptive when people cannot stop until they have washed their hands raw. Indeed, the diagnostic criteria for all the major disorder categories stipulate that the symptoms of the disorder must interfere with at least one aspect of the person's life, such as work, social relations, or self-care. This component is critical in determining whether given thoughts, emotions, or behaviors represent psychopathology or are simply unusual.

PSYCHOPATHOLOGY IS COMMON IN CONTEMPORARY SOCIETY Psychological disorders are common around the globe, in all countries and all societies (Patel et al., 2016). These disorders account for the greatest proportion of disability in developed countries, surpassing even cancer and heart disease (Centers for Disease Control and Prevention, 2011a; World Health Organization, 2017a). Indeed, about 1 in 4 Americans over age 18 has a diagnosable psychological disorder in a given year (Kessler, Chiu, Demler, & Walters, 2005a). About 1 in 5 American adults receives treatment over any two-year period (Kessler et al., 2005b). Nearly half of Americans will have some form of psychological disorder at some point in life, most commonly a depressive disorder, an attention-deficit/hyperactivity disorder, an anxiety disorder, or a substance-related and addictive disorder (Kessler & Wang, 2008). Of course, psychological disorders range in severity. Only about 7 percent of the U.S. population is severely affected, and this group also tends to suffer from multiple disorders (Kessler et al., 2005a).

As you read this chapter, you may realize that you have experienced some of the symptoms of many psychological disorders. Even if particular symptoms seem to describe you (or anyone you know) perfectly, resist the urge to make a diagnosis. Just like medical students who worry they have every disease they learn about, you need to guard against overanalyzing yourself and others. At the same time, what you learn in this chapter and the next one may help you understand the mental health problems you or others might experience.

 Why is the maladaptiveness of a condition considered more important than its abnormality in deciding whether a person has a psychopathology?

ANSWER: Whether a condition is maladaptive is considered most important in defining psychopathology because it is hard to define what is normal or abnormal.

14.2 Psychological Disorders Are Classified into Categories

In the late 1800s, the psychiatrist Emil Kraepelin recognized that not all patients with psychological disorders suffer from the same disorder (**FIGURE 14.2**). Kraepelin separated disorders into categories based on what he could observe: groups of symptoms that occur together. For instance, he separated disorders of mood (emotions) from disorders of cognition. He called the latter disorder *dementia praecox*. It is now better known as *schizophrenia* and is discussed fully in this chapter and Chapter 15.

The idea of categorizing psychological disorders systematically was not officially adopted until 1952, when the American Psychiatric Association published the first edition of the *Diagnostic and Statistical Manual of Mental Disorders (DSM)*. Since then, the *DSM* has undergone several revisions. It remains the standard in psychology and psychiatry. The guiding principle of the *DSM* is that if disorders can be grouped based on similar etiologies and symptoms, then figuring out how to treat those disorders should be easier.

In the current edition, *DSM-5* (released in 2013), disorders are described in terms of observable symptoms. A client must meet specific criteria to receive a particular diagnosis. The *DSM-5* consists of three sections: (1) an introduction with instructions for using the manual; (2) diagnostic criteria for all of the disorders, which are grouped so that similar categories of disorders are located near each other (**TABLE 14.1**); and (3) a guide for future psychopathology research, which also includes conditions not yet officially recognized as disorders, such as excessive Internet gaming and misuse of caffeine.

FIGURE 14.2
Emil Kraepelin
Kraepelin was one of the first researchers to propose a classification system for psychological disorders.

DIMENSIONAL NATURE OF PSYCHOPATHOLOGY One problem with the *DSM* approach is that it implies that a person either has a psychological disorder or does

Table 14.1 *DSM-5* Disorders

CATEGORY	EXAMPLES
Neurodevelopmental disorders	Autism spectrum disorder
Schizophrenia spectrum and other psychotic disorders	Schizophrenia
Bipolar and related disorders	Bipolar I disorder
Depressive disorders	Major depressive disorder
Anxiety disorders	Panic disorder
Obsessive-compulsive and related disorders	Body dysmorphic disorder
Trauma- and stressor-related disorders	Posttraumatic stress disorder
Dissociative disorders	Dissociative amnesia
Somatic symptom and related disorders	Conversion disorder
Feeding and eating disorders	Anorexia nervosa
Elimination disorders	Enuresis (bed wetting)
Sleep-wake disorders	Narcolepsy
Sexual dysfunctions	Erectile disorder
Gender dysphoria	Gender dysphoria
Disruptive, impulse-control, and conduct disorders	Pyromania
Substance-related and addictive disorders	Alcohol use disorder
Neurocognitive disorders	Delirium
Personality disorders	Borderline personality disorder
Paraphilic disorders	Exhibitionist disorder

Source: Based on American Psychiatric Association (2013).

not, which is known as a *categorical approach* (Bernstein, 2011). That is, the diagnosis is categorical, and a person is either in the category or not. This approach fails to capture differences in the severity of a disorder. Moreover, it allows for the possibility of a low threshold for diagnosis, which means that more people may receive diagnoses than is appropriate (Wakefield, 2016).

An alternative type of evaluation, called a *dimensional approach,* is to consider psychological disorders along a continuum in which people vary in degree rather than in kind (**FIGURE 14.3**). With categorization, the approach can be compared to a simple switch that turns a light on or off. By contrast, the dimensional approach is like a dimmer switch, which can provide light in varying amounts. A dimensional approach recognizes that many psychological disorders are extreme versions of normal feelings. We are all a little sad at times, and sometimes we feel more sad than usual. But no specific amount of sadness passes a threshold for depressive disorders.

In the third section of *DSM-5,* researchers are encouraged to examine whether a dimensional approach might

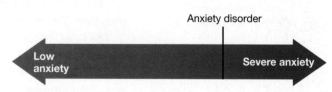

FIGURE 14.3

Dimensional Nature of Psychopathology
Symptoms of psychological disorders occur along continuums. They are not absolute states. A person who falls below the cutoff level may not meet the diagnostic criteria but may still experience symptoms that interfere with his or her life and will therefore benefit from treatment.

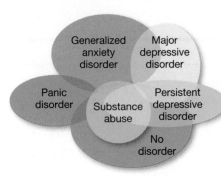

FIGURE 14.4
Comorbidity
Psychological disorders commonly overlap. For instance, substance abuse is common across psychological disorders, and people with depression (or a milder form known as persistent depressive disorder) often also have anxiety disorders (such as panic disorder or generalized anxiety disorder).

Research Domain Criteria (RDoC)
A method that defines basic aspects of functioning and considers them across multiple levels of analysis, from genes to brain systems to behavior.

be helpful for understanding many psychological disorders, particularly personality disorders. Indeed, research indicates that personality disorders can be viewed as maladaptive extremes of other personality traits. Consider the dark triad discussed in Chapter 13. The dark triad refers to personality traits (psychopathy, Machiavellianism, and narcissism) in which people show disregard for the feelings of others and a willingness to manipulate others to get their way. Not everyone who displays all three of these traits has a personality disorder. Only those whose selfish and uncaring behaviors cause significant problems for themselves or others might be considered to have a personality disorder.

COMORBIDITY Another problem with the *DSM* approach is that people seldom fit neatly into the precise categories provided. Indeed, many psychological disorders occur together even though the *DSM-5* treats them as separate disorders—for example, depression and anxiety, or depression and substance abuse. This state is known as *comorbidity* (**FIGURE 14.4**). Accordingly, people who are found to be depressed should also be examined for comorbid conditions. Though people may be diagnosed with two or more disorders, a dual diagnosis offers no advantages in terms of treatment because both conditions will usually respond to the same treatment.

It is possible that psychological disorders are comorbid because of common underlying factors. Although the *DSM-5* separates disorders involving anxiety from those involving depression, both types involve the trait *neuroticism,* the tendency to experience frequent and intense negative emotions (Barlow, Sauer-Zavala, Carl, Bullis, & Ellard, 2014). In fact, it has recently been proposed that psychopathology reflects a common general factor, analogous to general intelligence (or g, discussed in Chapter 8). Avshalom Caspi and colleagues (2014) examined symptoms of psychopathology in a large sample of individuals who were studied for more than 30 years, from childhood to middle adulthood. Using the statistical procedure factor analysis (see Section 8.14), they found that one underlying factor, which they called the *p factor,* was involved in all types of psychological disorders. Higher scores on the p factor were associated with more life impairment, such as suicide attempts, psychiatric hospitalizations, and criminal behaviors. High p scores also predicted a worsening of impairments over time. Just as the g dimension of intelligence reflects low to high cognitive abilities, the p dimension reflects low to high psychopathology severity. Low or high, an individual's p score is likely to remain stable over time (Snyder, Young, & Hankin, 2016).

RESEARCH DOMAIN CRITERIA (RDoC) The U.S. National Institute of Mental Health (NIMH) has proposed an entirely new way of classifying and understanding psychological disorders (Insel et al., 2010). Whereas the *DSM* approach classifies disorders by observable symptoms, the **Research Domain Criteria (RDoC)** method defines basic *domains* of functioning (such as attention, social communication, anxiety) and considers them across multiple levels of analysis, from genes to brain systems to behavior (**TABLE 14.2**). For example, researchers might study attention problems for people with anxiety disorders, depression, schizophrenia, and posttraumatic stress disorder.

The RDoC initiative is initially meant to guide research rather than classify disorders for treatment. The goal of the initiative is to understand the processes that give rise to disordered thoughts, emotions, and behaviors. Identifying the cause of these symptoms ultimately may provide insight into treating them.

The RDoC approach capitalizes on recent advances in genetics, neuroscience, and psychology in understanding adaptive behavior, as well as how functioning can be disrupted by various disorders (National Institute of Mental Health, 2011). For example, as you will learn later in this chapter, the same genetic mutation may be involved in a number of apparently different psychological disorders. This mutation may affect

Table 14.2 NIMH Research Domain Criteria (RDoC)

DOMAINS OF HUMAN BEHAVIOR AND FUNCTIONING

Negative Valence Systems (i.e., fear, anxiety, threat, loss)	Positive Valence Systems (i.e., decision making, reward, habit, prediction error)	Cognitive Systems (i.e., attention, memory, perception, cognitive control)	Social Processes (i.e., social communication, self-knowledge, theory of mind)	Arousal and Regulatory Systems (i.e., arousal, sleep, circadian rhythms)

UNITS OF ANALYSIS

Genes   Molecules   Cells   Circuits   Physiology   Behaviors   Self-reports   Paradigms

Source: nimh.nih.gov/research-priorities/rdoc/constructs/rdoc-matrix.shtml

how neurotransmitters function and cause similar impairments in thought processes across those disorders. In other instances, people diagnosed with the same *DSM* disorder can show radically different behaviors or responses, which might indicate that two different disorders share the same *DSM* diagnosis. Because of such problems, RDoC examines psychopathology without regard to *DSM* diagnoses. The ultimate aim of the RDoC initiative is for the classification and treatment of psychological disorders to be based on the underlying biological and psychosocial causes (Insel, 2014).

Some critics of RDoC argue that it is moving too quickly and that an abrupt shift in diagnostic criteria is no guarantee of better treatment results (Marder, 2014). Others worry that this initiative is focused on neuroscience at the expense of understanding personal experience (Parnas, 2014). At least within the United States, however, because the NIMH funds the majority of research, RDoC will be a driving force for research on psychopathology. Many researchers are optimistic that the RDoC approach will bring new insights into how to classify psychological disorders (Lilienfeld & Treadway, 2016).

assessment
In psychology, examination of a person's cognitive, behavioral, or emotional functioning to diagnose possible psychological disorders.

ASSESSMENT Physical disorders can generally be detected by medical tests, such as blood tests or biopsies. Determining whether a person has a mental disorder is not as straightforward. Examining a person's mental functions and psychological condition to diagnose a psychological disorder is known as **assessment.** This process often includes self-reports, psychological testing, observations, and interviews. It may also involve neuropsychological testing.

In the neuropsychological method, the client performs actions such as copying a picture; drawing a design from memory; sorting cards that show various stimuli into categories based on size, shape, or color; placing blocks into slots on a board while blindfolded; and tapping fingers rapidly (**FIGURE 14.5**). Each task requires an ability such as planning, coordinating, or remembering. By highlighting actions that the client performs poorly, the assessment might indicate problems with a particular brain region. For instance, people who have difficulty switching from one rule to another for categorizing objects, as in sorting by shape rather than by color, may have impairments in the frontal lobes. Subsequent assessment with MRI or PET (brain imaging techniques discussed in Chapter 3, "Biology and Behavior") might indicate brain damage caused by a tumor or by an injury. Often a medical evaluation

FIGURE 14.5
Neuropsychological Testing
The assessment depicted here uses a neuropsychological test to examine mental function. In this timed test, a researcher watches a client fit wooden blocks into a corresponding template to test for signs of Alzheimer's disease.

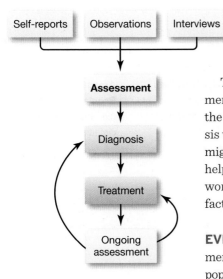

FIGURE 14.6
Assessing a Client
Clinical psychologists examine a person's mental functions and psychological health to diagnose a psychological disorder and determine an appropriate treatment. This flowchart shows the factors that lead to treatment.

diathesis-stress model
A diagnostic model that proposes that a disorder may develop when an underlying vulnerability is coupled with a precipitating event.

is indicated. For instance, the symptoms of depression or anxiety disorder can be similar to those of hypothyroidism, an endocrine disorder that should be ruled out before the psychological disorder is treated (Giynas Ayhan, Uguz, Askin, & Gonen, 2014).

The primary goal of assessment is to make a diagnosis so that appropriate treatment can be provided. The course and probable outcome, or *prognosis,* will depend on the particular psychological disorder that is diagnosed. Therefore, a correct diagnosis will help the client—and perhaps the client's family—understand what the future might bring. Assessment does not stop with diagnosis, however. Ongoing assessment helps mental health workers understand whether specific situations might cause a worsening of the disorder, whether progress is being made in treatment, and other factors that might help in understanding unique aspects of a given case (**FIGURE 14.6**).

EVIDENCE-BASED ASSESSMENT A key question is whether psychological assessments provide information that is useful for treating psychological disorders. Many popular methods of assessment, such as projective measures (discussed in Chapter 13), have not been shown to be helpful in predicting the kinds of treatments that are useful. Moreover, individual clinicians often choose assessment procedures based on their subjective beliefs and training rather than on scientific studies. For instance, when making diagnoses, some clinicians use their clinical judgment rather than a formal method—such as a structured interview that consists of standardized questions, derived from *DSM* criteria, in the same order each time.

Evidence-based assessment is an approach to clinical evaluation in which research guides the evaluation of psychopathology, the selection of appropriate psychological tests and neuropsychological methods, and the use of critical thinking in making a diagnosis (Hunsley & Mash, 2007; Joiner, Walker, Pettit, Perez, & Cukrowicz, 2005). Consider that, as noted earlier, scientific research indicates that many disorders are comorbid. Research also indicates that people who are depressed often have substance abuse disorders. Therefore, an evidence-based assessment approach would indicate that people found to be depressed should also be assessed for comorbid conditions, such as substance abuse.

 What does it mean to say that psychological disorders are dimensional?

14.3 Psychological Disorders Have Many Causes

Psychologists do not completely agree about the causes of most psychopathology. Still, some factors are thought to play important developmental roles. Because both nature and nurture matter, it is futile to try to identify biology or environment as solely responsible for a given disorder. The **diathesis-stress model** (presented as a flowchart in **FIGURE 14.7**) provides one way of thinking about the onset of psychopathology (Riboni & Belzung, 2017; Walder, Faraone, Glatt, Tsuang, & Seidman, 2014).

In this model, an individual can have an underlying vulnerability (known as *diathesis*) to a psychological disorder. This diathesis can be biological, such as a genetic predisposition to a specific disorder, or it can be environmental, such as childhood trauma. The vulnerability may not be sufficient to trigger a disorder, but the addition of stressful circumstances can tip the scales. If the stress level exceeds an individual's ability to cope, the symptoms of psychological disorder will occur. In this view, a family history of psychopathology suggests vulnerability rather than destiny.

BIOLOGICAL FACTORS The biological perspective focuses on how physiological factors, such as genetics, contribute to psychological disorders (Gatt, Burton, Williams, & Schofield, 2015). Chapter 3 describes how comparing the rates of psychological disorders between identical and fraternal twins and studying individuals who have been adopted have revealed the importance of genetic factors (Kendler, Prescott, Myers, & Neale, 2003; Krueger, 1999). Genetic factors can affect the production and levels of neurotransmitters and their receptor sites. Research has provided insights on the role of neurotransmitters in psychopathology. In some cases, based on what is known about the neurochemistry of psychological disorders, medications have been developed. In other cases, the unexpected effects of medications have led to discoveries about the neurotransmitters involved in psychological disorders.

Genetic factors can also affect the size of brain structures and their level of connectivity. Structural imaging and postmortem studies have revealed differences in brain anatomy, perhaps due to genetics, between those with psychological disorders and those without. Functional neuroimaging is currently at the forefront of research into the neurological components of mental disorders: PET and fMRI have revealed brain regions that may function differently in individuals with mental disorders (**FIGURE 14.8**). There is growing evidence that neuroimaging might be able to identify biomarkers associated with psychopathology that predict treatment outcomes (Gabrieli, Ghosh, & Whitfield-Gabrieli, 2015).

Environmental effects on the body also influence the development and course of psychological disorders. The fetus is particularly vulnerable to other biological factors—such as malnutrition, exposure to toxins (such as drugs and alcohol), and maternal illness—that because of their effects on the central nervous system may contribute to psychological disorders (Salum, Polanczyk, Miguel, & Rohde, 2010). Similarly, during childhood and adolescence, environmental toxins and malnutrition can put an individual at risk for psychological disorders. Epigenetic processes (discussed in Chapter 3) might also contribute to brain abnormalities. That is, environmental stress might change gene expression to cause lasting brain changes that render individuals susceptible to developing psychological disorders (Nestler, Peña, Kundakovic, Mitchell, & Akbarian, 2016). Again, biological factors often reflect the vulnerabilities that occur in individuals. As the diathesis-stress model reminds us, single explanations (nature *or* nurture, rather than nature *and* nurture) are seldom sufficient for understanding psychological disorders (Halldorsdottir & Binder, 2017).

SITUATIONAL FACTORS The first edition of the *DSM* was influenced heavily by Freudian psychoanalytic theory. Freud believed that psychopathology was mostly due to unconscious conflicts, often sexual in nature, dating back to childhood. Consistently with this perspective, the first edition of the *DSM* described many disorders as reactions to environmental conditions or as involving various defense mechanisms. Although Freud made important historical contributions in shaping psychology, most of his theories—particularly his theories on the causes of psychopathology—have not stood the test of time. Situational factors clearly play an important role, however, in the expression and treatment of psychological disorders.

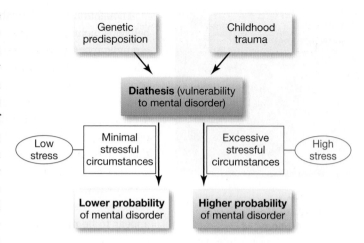

FIGURE 14.7
Diathesis-Stress Model
The onset of psychological disorders can be seen as resulting from the interactions of a diathesis and stress. The diathesis may be biological (e.g., genetic predisposition), environmental (e.g., childhood trauma), or both.

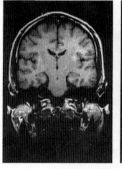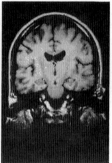

FIGURE 14.8
Biological Factors in Psychopathology
These brain MRIs are from twins. The twin on the right has schizophrenia, and the one on the left does not. In the MRI of the twin with schizophrenia, note the larger ventricles (these fluid-filled cavities appear dark in the image). This same pattern has emerged in the study of other twin pairs in which one has schizophrenia and the other does not. Thus, the brain may be deteriorating over time for those with schizophrenia, and this finding tells us that biological factors may be important for understanding schizophrenia.

FIGURE 14.9
Sociocultural Model of Psychopathology
According to the sociocultural model, psychopathology results from the interaction between individuals and their cultures. This woman's eccentric behavior might signal that she has a psychological disorder. However, eccentric behavior by the wealthy is often tolerated.

family systems model
A diagnostic model that considers problems within an individual as indicating problems within the family.

sociocultural model
A diagnostic model that views psychopathology as the result of the interaction between individuals and their cultures.

cognitive-behavioral approach
A diagnostic model that views psychopathology as the result of learned, maladaptive thoughts and beliefs.

ANSWER: an underlying vulnerability, because of genes or the environment, to developing a psychological disorder

Thoughts and emotions shaped by a particular environment can profoundly influence behavior, including disordered behavior. Not only traumatic events but also less extreme circumstances, such as constantly being belittled by a parent, can have long-lasting effects. The **family systems model** proposes that an individual's behavior must be considered within a social context, particularly within the family (Kazak, Simms, & Rourke, 2002). According to this model, problems that arise within an individual are manifestations of problems within the family (Goodman & Gotlib, 1999). Thus, developing a profile of an individual's family interactions can be important for understanding the factors that may be contributing to the disorder. A profile can also be important for determining whether the family is likely to be helpful or detrimental to the client's progress in therapy.

Similarly, the **sociocultural model** views psychopathology as the result of the interaction between individuals and their cultures. For example, disorders such as schizophrenia appear to be more common among those in lower socioeconomic classes. From the sociocultural perspective, these differences in occurrence are due to differences in lifestyles, in expectations, and in opportunities among classes. There may be biases in people's willingness to ascribe disorders to different social classes, however. Eccentric behavior among the wealthy elite might be tolerated or viewed as amusing (**FIGURE 14.9**). The same behaviors observed among those living in poverty might be taken as evidence of psychopathology. Moreover, people who develop schizophrenia may have trouble finding work, and so their lower socioeconomic status may be a result of their disorder.

COGNITIVE-BEHAVIORAL FACTORS The central principle of the **cognitive-behavioral approach** is that abnormal behavior is learned (Butler, Chapman, Forman, & Beck, 2006). As discussed in Chapter 6, through classical conditioning an unconditioned stimulus produces an unconditioned response. For example, a loud noise produces a startled response. A neutral stimulus paired with this unconditioned stimulus can eventually by itself produce a similar response. As was the case with Little Albert, if a child is playing with a fluffy white rat and is frightened by a loud noise, the white rat alone can later cause fear in the child. In fact, this process is how John B. Watson, the founder of behaviorism, demonstrated that many fears are learned rather than innate.

According to the cognitive-behavioral perspective, thoughts and beliefs are learned and therefore can be unlearned through treatment. The premise of this approach is that thoughts can become distorted and produce maladaptive behaviors and maladaptive emotions. In contrast to the psychologists who subscribe to the psychoanalytic perspective, cognitive-behavioral psychologists believe that thought processes are available to the conscious mind. Individuals are aware of, or easily can be made aware of, the thought processes that give rise to maladaptive emotions and behaviors.

 What is a diathesis?

14.4 Psychological Disorders Vary by Sex and by Culture

Some disorders, such as schizophrenia and bipolar disorder, are equally likely in both sexes (**FIGURE 14.10**). Rates of other disorders vary between the sexes. For example, dependence on alcohol is much more likely in males, whereas anorexia nervosa is much more likely in females. The reasons for these differences are both biological and environmental.

One way of categorizing psychological disorders is to divide them into two major groups: *Internalizing disorders* are characterized by negative emotions, and they

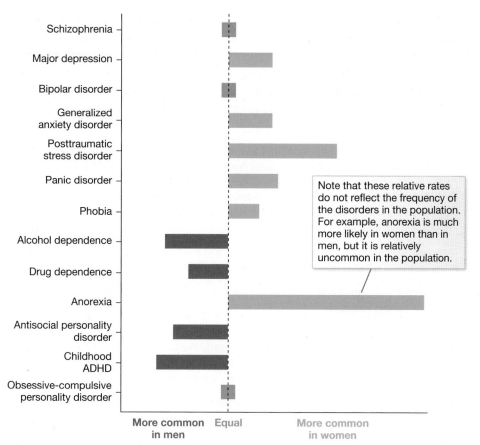

Note that these relative rates do not reflect the frequency of the disorders in the population. For example, anorexia is much more likely in women than in men, but it is relatively uncommon in the population.

More common in men   Equal   More common in women

FIGURE 14.10

Sex Differences in Psychological Disorders

The bars in this graph represent how common particular psychological disorders are for men and for women.

can be grouped into categories that reflect the emotions of distress and fear. These disorders include major depressive disorder, generalized anxiety disorder, and panic disorder. *Externalizing disorders* are characterized by disinhibition. These disorders include alcoholism, conduct disorders, and antisocial personality disorder (**FIGURE 14.11**). In general, the disorders associated with internalizing are more prevalent in females, and those associated with externalizing are more prevalent in males (Krueger & Markon, 2006).

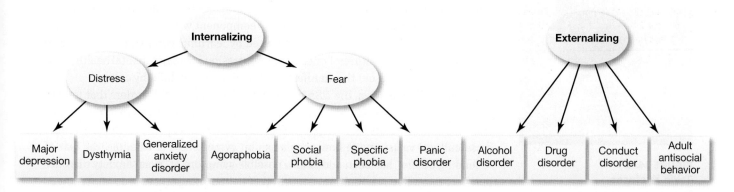

Source: Krueger & Markon, 2006.

FIGURE 14.11

Internalizing and Externalizing Model of Psychological Disorders

This diagram divides disorders into two basic categories, internalizing and externalizing. It also divides internalizing disorders into those related to fear and those related to distress.

Table 14.3 Cultural Syndromes

NAME	DEFINITION AND LOCATION
Ataque de nervios	Uncontrollable shouting and/or crying; verbal and physical aggression; heat in chest rising to head; feeling of losing control; occasional amnesia for experience (Caribbean and South American Latinos).
Dhat syndrome	Anxiety, fatigue, weakness, weight loss, and other bodily complaints; typically observed in young males who believe their symptoms are due to loss of semen (South Asia).
Khyâl cap	Belief that a "windlike" substance may rise in the body and cause serious effects; acute panic, autonomic arousal, anxiety; catastrophic cognitions (Cambodians in the United States and Cambodia).
Kufungisisa	Belief that thinking too much can damage the mind and body; an explanation for anxiety, depression, and somatic problems indicating distress (Zimbabwe).
Maladi moun	A cultural explanation that sickness has been sent by people to harm their enemies; visible success makes one vulnerable to attack; causes various illnesses, including psychosis, depression, and social failure (Haiti).
Nervios	A phrase used to refer to a general state of vulnerability to stressful life experience; common symptoms include headaches and "brain aches" as well as irritability and nervousness (Latinos in the United States and Latin America).
Shenjing shuairuo	A weakness in the nervous system; mental fatigue, negative emotions, excitement, nervous pain, and sleep disturbances; caused by stress, embarrassment, or acute sense of failure (China).
Susto	An illness attributed to a frightening event that causes the soul to leave the body; sadness, somatic complaints, lack of motivation, and difficulty functioning in daily living (Latinos in the United States and Latin America).
Taijin kyofusho	Intense fear of interpersonal relations; belief that parts of the body give off offensive odors or displease others (Japan).

Source: Based on American Psychiatric Association (2013).

FIGURE 14.12
Taijin Kyofusho
This Japanese woman may be exhibiting symptoms of a psychological syndrome unique to her culture. See Table 14.3 for an explanation of the syndrome.

CULTURAL SYNDROMES Increasingly, psychologists and other mental health professionals are recognizing the importance of culture in many aspects of our lives. Most psychological disorders show both universal and culture-specific symptoms. That is, the disorders may be very similar around the world, but they still reflect cultural differences. A disorder with a strong biological component will tend to be more similar across cultures. A disorder heavily influenced by learning, context, or both is more likely to differ across cultures. For example, depression is a major mental health problem around the world, but the manifestations of depression differ by culture.

Since the 1994 edition, the *DSM* has included a number of disorders that tend to occur within specific cultural settings. The *DSM-5* incorporates a greater consideration of cultural factors for each psychological disorder and updates criteria to reflect cross-cultural variations in how people exhibit symptoms. For example, the fear of "offending others" has been added as a possible symptom of social anxiety disorder to reflect the collectivist cultural concept that not harming others is as important as not harming the self. *DSM-5* also provides more details about cultural concepts of distress, such as encouraging clinicians to consider the specific words and phrases used by different cultural groups to describe their distress, as well as the cultural explanations for the cause of psychopathology. Finally, *DSM-5* provides examples of *cultural syndromes,* disorders that include a cluster of symptoms that are found in specific cultural groups or regions. (**TABLE 14.3** presents examples of common cultural syndromes, and **FIGURE 14.12** illustrates one of them.)

Clinicians and researchers need to be sensitive to cultural issues to avoid making mistakes in their diagnoses and treatments (Marsella & Yamada, 2007). Cultural factors can be critical in determining how a disorder is expressed and how an individual will respond to different types of therapies.

 Q What is the difference between internalizing disorders and externalizing disorders?

ANSWER: Internalizing disorders, more prevalent in women, involve negative emotions. Externalizing disorders, more prevalent in men, involve disinhibition.

Which Disorders Emphasize Emotional States?

People often feel emotional—down, anxious, and so on. Such feelings can be useful. They can prepare people for dealing with future events, motivating them to learn new ways of coping with challenges. For example, being anxious about tests reminds people to keep up with their homework and study. Being slightly anxious when meeting strangers helps people avoid doing bizarre things and making bad impressions. For some people, however, feelings such as sadness or anxiety can become debilitating and interfere with every aspect of life. Indeed, people diagnosed with anxiety or depressive disorders die about 8 years earlier than those without the disorders (Pratt, Druss, Manderscheid, & Walker, 2016).

Mental health problems associated with anxiety and depression are highly prevalent on college campuses. The recent American College Health Association (2014) National College Health Assessment II survey of over 94,000 students found that 34.9 percent of female and 27.8 percent of male participants report that they "felt so depressed it was difficult to function" some time within the last 12 months. More than half of the respondents reported overwhelming anxiety within the last 12 months. According to one recent meta-analysis, the prevalence of depression among college students is 30.6 percent, a higher rate than that found in the general population (Ibrahim, Kelly, Adams, & Glazebrook, 2013).

When emotions or moods go from being a normal part of daily living to being extreme enough to disrupt people's ability to work, learn, and play, these states are considered symptoms of psychological disorders. Of course, maladaptive thoughts contribute to many emotional disorders. In fact, most forms of psychopathology influence how people think as well as how they feel. However, thought disturbances are more central to some disorders, and emotional experiences are more central to others. In this section, we consider the most common disorders involving emotional states. In the next section, we will consider disorders involving thought disturbances.

14.5 Anxiety Disorders Make People Fearful and Tense

Imagine that you are about to make your first parachute jump out of an airplane. If you are like most people, your heart will be racing, and you will be sweating. You might feel queasy. While under these circumstances you may find such sensations thrilling, people who have an anxiety disorder experience these feelings all the time and are unhappy about them.

Learning Objectives

- Differentiate the various anxiety disorders.

- Understand the various causes of obsessive-compulsive disorder.

- Understand the role of trauma in posttraumatic stress disorders.

- Discuss cultural and gender differences in depressive disorders.

- Distinguish between bipolar I and bipolar II disorder.

Anxiety disorders are characterized by excessive fear and anxiety in the absence of true danger. Those with anxiety disorders feel tense and apprehensive. They are often irritable because they cannot see any solution to their anxiety. Constant worry can make falling asleep and staying asleep difficult, and attention span and concentration can be impaired. By continually arousing the autonomic nervous system, chronic anxiety also causes bodily symptoms such as sweating, dry mouth, rapid pulse, shallow breathing, increased blood pressure, and increased muscular tension. Chronic arousal can also result in hypertension, headaches, and other health problems. More than 1 in 4 Americans will have some type of anxiety disorder during their lifetimes (Kessler & Wang, 2008).

Because of their high levels of autonomic arousal, people who have anxiety disorders also exhibit restless and pointless motor behaviors. Exaggerated startle response is typical, and behaviors such as toe tapping and excessive fidgeting are common. Problem solving and judgment may suffer as well. Research has shown that chronic stress can produce atrophy in the hippocampus, a brain structure involved in learning and memory (McEwen, 2008). Because chronic stress can damage the body, including the brain, it is very important to identify and effectively treat disorders that involve chronic anxiety. The various anxiety disorders share some emotional, cognitive, somatic, and motor symptoms, even though the behavioral manifestations of these disorders are quite different (Barlow, 2002; Brown & Barlow, 2009). These disorders include specific phobia, social anxiety disorder, generalized anxiety disorder, panic disorder, and agoraphobia (**TABLE 14.4**).

SPECIFIC PHOBIA As discussed in Chapter 6, a phobia is a fear of a specific object or situation. Of course, some fear can be a good thing. As an adaptive force, fear can

Table 14.4 Five Types of Anxiety Disorders

CATEGORY	DESCRIPTION	EXAMPLE
Specific phobia	Fear of something that is disproportionate to the threat	Rachel is so afraid of snakes that if she sees even a picture of a snake, her heart begins to pound and she feels the need to run away.
Social anxiety disorder	Fear of being negatively evaluated by others in a social setting	Linda worries inensely that she will say or do the wrong thing around other people and they will think badly of her. So she prefers to be by herself and avoids being around lots of people.
Generalized anxiety disorder	Nearly constant anxiety not associated with a specific thing	Reginald is feeling very worried and has been for months, but he can't figure out why. It seems as through he is anxious about everything.
Panic disorder	Sudden attacks of overwhelming terror	Jennifer has had several panic attacks and worries she will have another one. This brings on more panic attacks, where she feels extreme fear and her heart pounds in her chest.
Agoraphobia	Fear of being in a situation from which one cannot escape	Rashad works for a company located in a skyscraper, but he is so terrified of not being able to get out of the building that he has begun to have panic attacks at work.

Source: Based on American Psychiatric Association (2013).

Table 14.5 Some Unusual Specific Phobias

- **Arachibutyrophobia:** fear of peanut butter sticking to the roof of one's mouth
- **Automatonophobia:** fear of ventriloquists' dummies
- **Barophobia:** fear of gravity
- **Dextrophobia:** fear of objects at the right side of the body
- **Geliophobia:** fear of laughter
- **Gnomophobia:** fear of garden gnomes
- **Hippopotomonstrosesquipedaliophobia:** fear of long words
- **Ochophobia:** fear of being in a moving automobile
- **Panophobia:** fear of everything
- **Pentheraphobia:** fear of mothers-in-law
- **Triskaidekaphobia:** fear of the number 13

help people avoid potential dangers, such as venomous snakes and rickety bridges. In phobias, however, the fear is exaggerated and out of proportion to the actual danger.

In *DSM-5*, people are diagnosed with *specific phobia* based on the object of the fear. Specific phobias, which affect about 1 in 8 people around the globe (Wardenaar et al., 2017), involve particular objects and situations. Common specific phobias include fear of snakes (ophidiophobia), fear of enclosed spaces (claustrophobia), and fear of heights (acrophobia). (**TABLE 14.5** lists some unusual specific phobias.) Another common specific phobia is fear of flying. Even though the odds of dying in a plane crash, compared with a car crash, are extraordinarily small, some people find flying terrifying (see Section 11.6, "Using Psychology to Understand: Why Are People Afraid of Flying but Not of Driving [or Smoking]?"). For those who need to travel frequently for their jobs, a fear of flying can cause significant impairment in daily living.

SOCIAL ANXIETY DISORDER *Social anxiety disorder,* formerly sometimes called *social phobia,* is a fear of being negatively evaluated by others. It includes fears of public speaking, speaking up in class, meeting new people, and eating in front of others. About 1 in 8 people will experience social anxiety disorder at some point in their lifetime, and around 7 percent are experiencing social anxiety disorder at any given time (Ruscio et al., 2008). It is one of the earliest forms of anxiety disorder to develop, often beginning at around age 13. The more social fears a person has, the more likely he is to develop other disorders, particularly depression and substance abuse problems. Indeed, assessment must consider the overlap between social anxiety disorder and related disorders to make an informed diagnosis (Stein & Stein, 2008; **FIGURE 14.13**).

GENERALIZED ANXIETY DISORDER The anxiety in specific phobia has a focus. By contrast, the anxiety in **generalized anxiety disorder (GAD)** is diffuse and always present. People with this disorder are constantly anxious and worry incessantly about even minor matters (Newman, Llera, Erickson, Przeworski, & Castonguay, 2013). They even worry about being worried! Because the anxiety is not focused, it can occur in response to almost anything, so the sufferer is constantly on the alert for problems. This hypervigilance results in distractibility, fatigue, irritability, and sleep problems, as well as headaches, restlessness, light-headedness, and muscle pain. Just

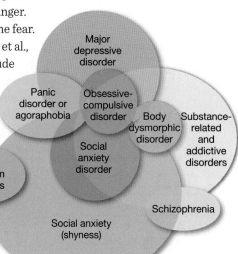

FIGURE 14.13
Comorbidity of Social Anxiety Disorder

As this diagram illustrates, social anxiety disorder is comorbid with many other psychological disorders. If a client has social anxiety disorder, all of these disorders need to be considered to make an accurate and complete diagnosis.

generalized anxiety disorder (GAD)

A diffuse state of constant anxiety not associated with any specific object or event.

under 6 percent of the United States population is affected by this disorder at some point in their lives, though women are diagnosed more often than men (Kessler et al., 1994; Kessler & Wang, 2008).

panic disorder
An anxiety disorder that consists of sudden, overwhelming attacks of terror.

PANIC DISORDER Panic disorder consists of sudden, overwhelming attacks of terror and worry about having additional panic attacks. The attacks seemingly come out of nowhere, or they are cued by external stimuli or internal thought processes. Panic attacks typically last for several minutes, during which the person may begin to sweat and tremble; feels her heart racing; feels short of breath; feels chest pain; and may feel dizzy and light-headed, with numbness and tingling in the hands and feet. People experiencing panic attacks often believe that they are going crazy or that they are dying, and those who suffer from persistent panic attacks attempt suicide much more often than those in the general population (Fawcett, 1992; Korn et al., 1992; Noyes, 1991). People who experience panic attacks during adolescence are especially likely to develop other anxiety disorders—such as generalized anxiety disorder—in adulthood (Goodwin et al., 2004). Panic disorder affects an estimated 3 percent of the population in a given year, and women are twice as likely to be diagnosed as men (Kessler & Wang, 2008).

agoraphobia
An anxiety disorder marked by fear of being in situations in which escape may be difficult or impossible.

AGORAPHOBIA A disorder related to panic disorder is **agoraphobia.** People with this disorder are afraid of being in situations in which escape is difficult or impossible. For example, they may fear being in a crowded shopping mall or using public transportation. Their fear is so strong that being in such situations causes panic attacks. As a result, people who suffer from agoraphobia avoid going into open spaces or to places where there might be crowds. In extreme cases, sufferers may feel unable to leave their homes. In addition to fearing the particular situations, they fear having a panic attack in public:

> Ms. Watson began to dread going out of the house alone. She feared that while out she would have an attack and would be stranded and helpless. She stopped riding the subway to work out of fear she might be trapped in a car between stops when an attack struck, preferring instead to walk the 20 blocks between her home and work. She also severely curtailed her social and recreational activities—previously frequent and enjoyed—because an attack might occur, necessitating an abrupt and embarrassing flight from the scene. (Spitzer, Skodol, Gibbon, & Williams, 1983)

This description demonstrates the clear links between panic attacks and agoraphobia. Indeed, agoraphobia without panic is quite rare (Kessler & Wang, 2008).

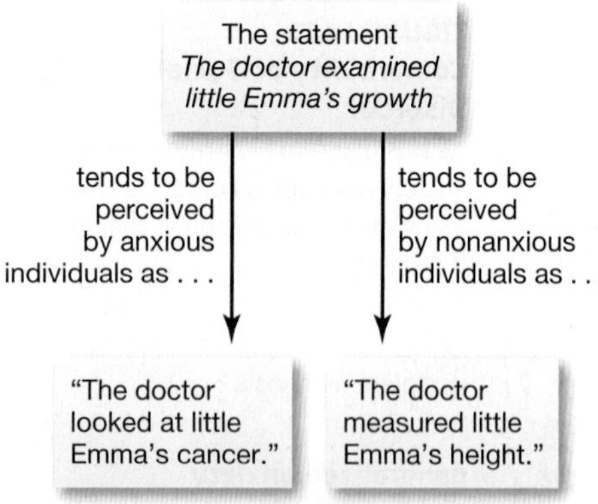

The statement
The doctor examined little Emma's growth

tends to be perceived by anxious individuals as . . .

tends to be perceived by nonanxious individuals as . . .

"The doctor looked at little Emma's cancer."

"The doctor measured little Emma's height."

FIGURE 14.14
Anxiety Disorders
As this example illustrates, anxious individuals tend to perceive ambiguous situations as threatening.

DEVELOPMENT OF ANXIETY DISORDERS The behavioral manifestations of anxiety disorders can be quite different, but all share some causal factors (Barlow, 2002). The first factor is biased thinking. When presented with ambiguous or neutral situations, anxious individuals tend to perceive them as threatening, whereas nonanxious individuals assume they are nonthreatening (Mathews, 2012; Mogg & Bradley, 2016; **FIGURE 14.14**). Anxious individuals also focus excessive attention on perceived threats (Klein et al., 2017; MacLeod & Mathews, 2012). They thus recall threatening events more easily than nonthreatening ones, exaggerating the events' perceived magnitude and frequency.

A second factor is learning (Lissek et al., 2014). As discussed in Chapter 6, monkeys develop a fear of snakes if they observe other monkeys responding to snakes fearfully.

Similarly, a person could develop a fear of flying by observing another person's fearful reaction to the closing of cabin doors. Such a fear might then generalize to other enclosed spaces, resulting in claustrophobia.

There is also a biological factor. As noted in Chapter 13, children who have an inhibited temperamental style are usually shy and tend to avoid unfamiliar people and novel objects. These inhibited children are more likely to develop anxiety disorders later in life (Buss & McDoniel, 2016; Fox, Henderson, Marshall, Nichols, & Ghera, 2005). They are especially at risk for developing social anxiety disorder (Chronis-Tuscano et al., 2009).

How does specific phobia differ from generalized anxiety disorder?

ANSWER: With specific phobia, a particular object is associated with fear. Generalized anxiety disorder is diffuse, with no specific threat.

FIGURE 14.15
Howie Mandel
The comedian Howie Mandel has been diagnosed with obsessive-compulsive disorder. Like many people with OCD, Mandel suffers from mysophobia, or the fear of germs. His trademark shaved head helps him with this problem, as it makes him feel cleaner. Mandel even built a second, sterile house, to which he can retreat if he feels he might be contaminated by anyone around him. Here, Mandel promotes his autobiography, *Here's the Deal: Don't Touch Me* (2009), in which he "comes clean" about suffering from OCD and other disorders.

14.6 Unwanted and Intrusive Thoughts Increase Anxiety

As noted above, many psychological disorders involve both cognitive and emotional impairments. In some cases, having unwanted thoughts leads to emotional distress and anxiety. *DSM-5* categorizes a number of disorders together that involve experiencing unwanted thoughts or the desire to engage in maladaptive behaviors. The commonality is an obsession with an idea or thought or the compulsion to repeatedly act in a certain way (see Table 14.1). These compulsive actions temporarily reduce anxiety. Related disorders in this category include people chronically pulling at their hair or picking at their skin, people being obsessed with deficiencies in their physical appearance, and *hoarding disorder,* in which people have persistent difficulty parting with their possessions and end up accumulating clutter and garbage that can make their living conditions seem like disaster zones.

OBSESSIVE-COMPULSIVE DISORDER The most common disorder in this *DSM-5* category is **obsessive-compulsive disorder (OCD)**, which involves frequent intrusive thoughts and compulsive actions (Kessler & Wang, 2008). Affecting 1–2 percent of the population, OCD is more common in women than men, and it generally begins in early adulthood (Robins & Regier, 1991; Weissman et al., 1994). *Obsessions* are recurrent, intrusive, and unwanted thoughts or ideas or mental images that increase anxiety. They often include fear of contamination, of accidents, or of one's own aggression. The individual typically attempts to ignore or suppress such thoughts but sometimes engages in particular behaviors to neutralize his or her obsessions (**FIGURE 14.15**).

Compulsions are particular acts that the OCD patient feels driven to perform over and over that reduce anxiety. The most common compulsive behaviors are cleaning, checking, and counting. For instance, a person might continually check to make sure a door is locked, because of an obsession that his home might be invaded, or a person might engage in superstitious counting to

obsessive-compulsive disorder (OCD)
A disorder characterized by frequent intrusive thoughts and compulsive actions.

"Is the Itsy Bitsy Spider obsessive-compulsive?"

protect against accidents, such as counting the number of telephone poles while driving. The compulsive behavior or mental act, such as counting, is aimed at preventing or reducing anxiety or preventing something dreadful from happening.

Those with OCD anticipate catastrophe and loss of control. However, as opposed to those who suffer from anxiety disorders—who fear what might happen to them—those with OCD fear what they might do or might have done. Checking is one way to calm the anxiety:

> While in reality no one is on the road, I'm intruded with the heinous thought that I *might* have hit someone . . . a human being! God knows where such a fantasy comes from. . . . I try to make reality chase away this fantasy. I reason, "Well, if I hit someone while driving, I would have *felt* it." This brief trip into reality helps the pain dissipate . . . but only for a second. . . . I start ruminating, "Maybe I did hit someone and didn't realize it. . . . Oh my God! I might have killed somebody! I have to go back and check." (Rapoport, 1990, pp. 22–27)

CAUSES OF OBSESSIVE-COMPULSIVE DISORDER A paradoxical aspect of OCD is that people are aware that their obsessions and compulsions are irrational, yet they are unable to stop them. One explanation is that the disorder results from conditioning. In the person with OCD, anxiety is somehow paired to a specific event, probably through classical conditioning. As a result, the person engages in behavior that reduces anxiety and therefore is reinforced through operant conditioning. This reduction of anxiety is reinforcing and increases the person's chance of engaging in that behavior again.

Suppose you are forced to shake hands with a man who has a bad cold. You have just seen him wiping his nose with his right hand. Shaking that hand might cause you to be anxious or uncomfortable because you do not want to get sick. As soon as the pleasantries are over, you run to the bathroom and wash your hands. You feel relieved. You have now paired handwashing with a reduction in anxiety, thus increasing the chances of handwashing in the future (**FIGURE 14.16**). If you develop OCD, however, the compulsive behavior will reduce your anxiety only temporarily, so you will need to perform the behavior over and over.

There is also good evidence that the etiology of OCD is in part genetic (Crowe, 2000). Indeed, various behavioral genetics methods, such as twin studies, have shown that OCD runs in families. The specific mechanism has not been identified, but the OCD-related genes appear to control the neurotransmitter glutamate (Pauls, 2008). As noted in Chapter 3, glutamate is the major excitatory transmitter in the brain, causing increased neural firing.

There is also growing evidence that OCD can be triggered by environmental factors. In particular, a streptococcal infection apparently can cause a severe form of OCD in some young children. Originally identified in 1998 by Susan Swedo and her colleagues at the National Institute of Mental Health, this syndrome strikes virtually overnight. The affected children suddenly display odd symptoms of OCD, such as engaging in repetitive behaviors, developing irrational fears and obsessions, and having facial tics. Researchers have speculated that an autoimmune response damages the caudate, thereby producing the symptoms of OCD (Snider & Swedo, 2004). Treatments that enhance the immune system have been found to diminish the symptoms of OCD in children with this syndrome. Why some children are susceptible to this autoimmune response is unknown.

POSTTRAUMATIC STRESS DISORDER OCD disorders are not the only type of psychopathology that can produce unwanted and intrusive thoughts. Such cognitive problems can also be caused by disorders that result from either experiencing or

FIGURE 14.16
OCD Cycle
This flowchart illustrates the operations of conditioning for the example given in the text. Classical conditioning (step 1) and operant conditioning (steps 2 and 3) reinforce behavior. Continued reinforcement may contribute to a person's developing OCD (step 4).

witnessing sexual violations or life-threatening events. The *DSM-5* category *trauma-and stressor-related disorders* (see Table 14.1) describes disorders where a person has trouble overcoming exposure to a highly stressful event. For example, a person who cries continually, has difficulty studying, and avoids social settings six months after a romantic breakup may have an *adjustment disorder*. This person is having difficulty adjusting to the stressor.

When people experience severe stress or emotional trauma—such as having a serious accident, being raped, fighting in active combat, or surviving a natural disaster—they often have negative reactions long after the danger has passed. In severe cases, people develop **posttraumatic stress disorder (PTSD)**, a psychological disorder that involves frequent and recurring unwanted thoughts related to the trauma, including nightmares, intrusive thoughts, and flashbacks. People with PTSD often try to avoid situations or stimuli that remind them of their trauma. The lifetime prevalence of PTSD is around 7 percent, with women being more likely to develop the disorder (Kessler et al., 2005b).

posttraumatic stress disorder (PTSD)
A disorder that involves frequent nightmares, intrusive thoughts, and flashbacks related to an earlier trauma.

An opportunity to study susceptibility to PTSD came about because of a tragedy at Northern Illinois University in 2008. On the campus, in front of many observers, a lone gunman killed 5 people and wounded 21. Among a sample of female students, those with certain genetic markers related to serotonin functioning were much more likely to show PTSD symptoms in the weeks after the shooting (Mercer et al., 2011). This finding suggests that some individuals may be more at risk than others for developing PTSD after exposure to a stressful event.

Those with PTSD often have chronic tension, anxiety, and health problems, and they may experience memory and attention problems in their daily lives. PTSD involves an unusual problem in memory: the inability to forget. PTSD is associated with an attentional bias, such that people with PTSD are hypervigilant to stimuli associated with their traumatic events. For instance, soldiers with combat-induced PTSD show increased physiological responsiveness to pictures of troops, sounds of gunfire, and even words associated with combat. Exposure to stimuli associated with past trauma leads to activation of the amygdala (Shin, Rauch, & Pitman, 2006). It is as if the severe emotional event is "overconsolidated," burned into memory (see Chapter 7 for a discussion of consolidation of memory). PTSD results in abnormalities in the various brain processes that normally lead to extinction in fear learning (Marin et al., 2016).

 How do obsessions and compulsions affect anxiety?

ANSWER: Obsessive thoughts increase anxiety, whereas compulsive actions temporarily reduce anxiety.

14.7 Depressive Disorders Consist of Sad, Empty, or Irritable Moods

When we feel down or sad about something, we often say we are depressed. Although this experience is relatively common, it often does not last very long. For some people, however, the negative feelings persist and turn into a psychological disorder. The *DSM-5* categorizes a number of disorders as *depressive disorders*. The common feature of all depressive disorders is the presence of sad, empty, or irritable mood along with bodily symptoms and cognitive problems that interfere with daily life.

MAJOR DEPRESSIVE DISORDER The classic disorder in this category is major depressive disorder. According to *DSM-5* criteria, to be diagnosed with **major depressive disorder**, a person must experience a *major depressive episode*, during

major depressive disorder
A disorder characterized by severe negative moods or a lack of interest in normally pleasurable activities.

which he or she experiences a depressed mood or a loss of interest in pleasurable activities every day for at least two weeks. In addition, the person must have other symptoms, such as appetite and weight changes, sleep disturbances, loss of energy, difficulty concentrating, feelings of self-reproach or guilt, and frequent thoughts of death, perhaps by suicide. The following excerpt is from a case study of a 56-year-old woman diagnosed with depression:

> She described herself as overwhelmed with feelings of guilt, worthlessness, and hopelessness. She twisted her hands almost continuously and played nervously with her hair. She stated that her family would be better off without her and that she had considered taking her life by hanging herself. She felt that after death she would go to hell, where she would experience eternal torment, but that this would be a just punishment. (Andreasen, 1984, p. 39)

Feelings of depression are relatively common, but only long-lasting episodes that impair a person's life are diagnosed as depressive disorders. Major depression affects about 7–8 percent of Americans at any one time (Pratt & Brody, 2014), whereas approximately 16 percent of Americans will experience major depression at some point in their lives (Kessler & Wang, 2008). Although major depressive disorder varies in severity, those who receive a diagnosis are highly impaired by the condition, and it tends to persist over several months, often lasting for years (Otte et al., 2016).

Depression is the leading risk factor for suicide, which claims approximately 788,000 lives annually around the world (World Health Organization, 2017b) and is among the top three causes of death for people between ages 15 and 35 (Insel & Charney, 2003). The suicide of the comedian and actor Robin Williams shocked many, but Williams reportedly had long battled depression and substance abuse (**FIGURE 14.17**). You will learn more about suicide, specifically about interventions to help prevent it, in Section 14.9.

FIGURE 14.17
Robin Williams
In 2014, the actor and comedian Robin Williams hanged himself. Although he built his career on making people laugh, Williams appears to have struggled for years with depression, along with drug and alcohol problems.

persistent depressive disorder
A form of depression that is not severe enough to be diagnosed as major depressive disorder.

PERSISTENT DEPRESSIVE DISORDER Unlike major depressive disorder, **persistent depressive disorder,** sometimes called *dysthymia,* is of mild to moderate severity (**FIGURE 14.18**). Most individuals with this disorder describe their mood as "down in the dumps." People with persistent depressive disorder have many of the same symptoms as people with major depressive disorder, but those symptoms are less intense. People diagnosed with this disorder—approximately 2–3 percent of the population—must have a depressed mood most of the day, more days than not, for at least 2 years. Periods of depressed mood last 2–20 or more years, although the typical duration is about 5–10 years. Because the depressed mood is so long-lasting, some psychologists consider it a personality disorder rather than a mood disorder.

The distinctions between a depressive personality, persistent depressive disorder, and major depressive disorder are unclear. In keeping with a dimensional view of psychological disorders, these states may be points along a continuum rather than distinct disorders (Lewinsohn, Allen, Seeley, & Gotlib, 1999; Lewinsohn, Rodhe, Seeley, & Hops, 1991).

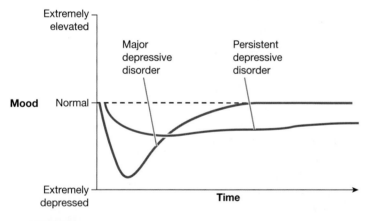

FIGURE 14.18
Depressed Mood in Depressive Disorders
This graphic provides a general way to understand the two main types of depressive disorders in relation to "normal mood." People with major depressive disorder tend to experience extremely depressed moods but for short periods. By contrast, people with persistent depressive disorder experience mildly or moderately depressed moods but for longer periods.

THE ROLES OF CULTURE AND GENDER IN DEPRESSIVE DISORDERS

Depression is so prevalent that it is sometimes called the common cold of psychological disorders. In its most severe form, depression is the leading cause of disability worldwide (World Health Organization, 2017b). Major depressive disorder affects about 41 million people in India and 49 million people in China (Baxter et al., 2016). Unfortunately, both countries have large gaps between mental health disorders and available resources to treat those disorders (Patel et al., 2017). The stigma associated with depressive disorder has especially dire consequences in developing countries, where people do not take advantage of the treatment options because they do not want to admit to being depressed (Andrade et al., 2014). One way to combat the stigma of psychological disorders is to focus attention on their high incidence and to educate more people about effective treatments (**FIGURE 14.19**). Promising efforts to reduce the stigma of mental health disorders are underway around the globe, but progress has been minimal in developing nations (Thornicroft et al., 2016).

Gender also plays a role in the incidence of depression. Across multiple countries and contexts, about twice as many women as men suffer from depressive disorders (Kessler et al., 2003; Pratt & Brody, 2014). Why are the rates of depressive disorders so much higher for women than for men? Some researchers have theorized that women's multiple roles in most societies—as wage earners and family caregivers—cause stress that results in increased incidence of depression, but other researchers have pointed out the health benefits of having multiple roles, such as wife, mother, and employee (Barnett & Hyde, 2001). Thus, it is not multiple roles per se but more likely overwork and lack of support that contribute to the high rate of depression in women.

CAUSES OF DEPRESSION Because of depression's profound effects, particularly the danger of suicide, much research has focused on understanding the causes of depression and treating it. Studies of twins, families, and adoptions support the notion that depression has a genetic component. Although there is some variability among studies, concordance rates—that is, the percentage who share the same disorder—for identical twins are generally around two to three times higher than rates for fraternal twins (Levinson, 2006). The genetic contribution to depression is somewhat weaker than the genetic contribution to schizophrenia or to bipolar disorder (Belmaker & Agam, 2008).

The existence of a genetic component implies that biological factors are involved in depression. In fact, there is evidence that major depressive disorder may involve one or more monoamines. (As discussed in Chapter 3, monoamines are neurotransmitters that regulate emotion and arousal and motivate behavior.) For instance, medications that increase the availability of norepinephrine, a monoamine, may help alleviate depression. Medications that decrease levels of this neurotransmitter can cause symptoms of depression. Medications such as Prozac are known as *selective serotonin reuptake inhibitors (SSRIs)*. SSRIs selectively increase another monoamine, serotonin, and are often used to treat depression (Barton et al., 2008; SSRIs and other medications are discussed in Chapter 15). Yet depression is not simply due to a lack of norepinephrine or serotonin. For example, research has found that medications that reduce serotonin can also alleviate depression (Nickel et al., 2003). At this time, there is not a clear understanding of the role of neurotransmitters in the development of depressive disorders.

Situational factors also play a role in depression. A number of studies have implicated life stressors in many cases of depression (Hammen, 2005). Particularly relevant for depression is interpersonal loss, such as the death of a loved one or a divorce (Paykel, 2003). Depression is especially likely in the face of multiple negative events (Brown & Harris, 1978), and patients with depression have often experienced negative life events during the year before the onset of their depression (Dohrenwend, Shrout, Link, Skodol, & Martin, 1986).

FIGURE 14.19
Informing the Public
Public-service ads may help "normalize" the treatment of psychological disorders. The more people hear about talking to doctors about problems, the more inclined they may be to visit doctors when problems arise.

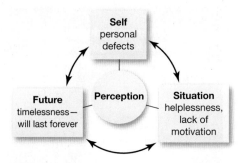

FIGURE 14.20
Cognitive Triad
According to Beck, people suffering from depression perceive themselves, their situations, and the future negatively. These perceptions influence each other and contribute to the disorder.

learned helplessness
A cognitive model of depression in which people feel unable to control events in their lives.

How an individual reacts to stress, however, can be influenced by interpersonal relationships, which play an extremely important role in depression (Joiner, Coyne, & Blalock, 1999). Regardless of any other factors, relationships contribute to the development of depression, alter people's experiences when depressed, and ultimately may be damaged by the constant needs of the person with depression. Many people report negative reactions to people with depression, perhaps because of their frequent complaining. Over time, people may avoid interactions with those suffering from depression, thus initiating a downward spiral by making the sufferers even more depressed (Dykman, Horowitz, Abramson, & Usher, 1991). By contrast, a person who has a close friend or group of friends is less likely to become depressed when faced with stress. This protective factor is not related to the number of friends. It is related to the quality of the friendships. One good friend is more protective than a large number of casual acquaintances.

Finally, cognitive processes play a role in depressive disorders. The psychologist Aaron Beck has hypothesized that people with depression think negatively about themselves ("I am worthless"; "I am a failure"; "I am ugly"), about their situations ("Everybody hates me"; "the world is unfair"), and about the future ("Things are hopeless"; "I can't change"). Beck refers to these negative thoughts about self, situation, and the future as the *cognitive triad* (Beck, 1967, 1976; Beck, Brown, Seer, Eidelson, & Riskind, 1987; Beck, Rush, Shaw, & Emery, 1979; **FIGURE 14.20**).

People with depression blame misfortunes on personal defects while seeing positive occurrences as the result of luck. People who are not suffering from depression do the opposite. Beck also notes that people with depression make errors in logic. For example, they overgeneralize based on single events, magnify the seriousness of bad events, think in extremes (such as believing they should either be perfect or not try), and take responsibility for bad events that actually have little to do with them.

A second cognitive model of depression is based on **learned helplessness** (Seligman, 1974, 1975). This term means that people come to see themselves as unable to have any effect on events in their lives. The psychologist Martin Seligman based this model on years of animal research. When animals are placed in aversive situations they cannot escape (such as receiving unescapable shock), the animals eventually become passive and unresponsive. They end up lacking the motivation to try new methods of escape when given the opportunity. Similarly, people suffering from learned helplessness come to expect that bad things will happen to them and believe they are powerless to avoid negative events. The *attributions,* or explanations, they make for negative events refer to personal factors that are stable and global, rather than to situational factors that are temporary and specific. This attributional pattern leads people to feel hopeless about making positive changes in their lives (Abramson, Metalsky, & Alloy, 1989). According to the scientific evidence, dysfunctional cognitive patterns are a cause rather than a consequence of depression.

 Which cognitive cause of depression involves people seeing themselves as unable to have any impact on events in their lives?

ANSWER: learned helplessness

14.8 Bipolar Disorders Involve Depression and Mania

As noted at the beginning of this chapter, we all experience variations in mood. Our normal fluctuations from sadness to exuberance seem minuscule, however, compared with the extremes experienced by people with *bipolar disorders. Mania* refers to an elevated mood that feels like being "on the top of the world." This positive mood can vary in degree and is accompanied by major shifts in energy level and physical activity (**FIGURE 14.21**). For some people, mania involves a sense of agitation and restlessness rather than positivity (Garriga et al., 2016).

True *manic episodes* last at least one week and are characterized by abnormally and persistently elevated mood, increased activity, diminished need for sleep, grandiose ideas, racing thoughts, and extreme distractibility. During episodes of mania, heightened levels of activity and extreme happiness often result in excessive involvement in pleasurable but foolish activities. People may engage in sexual indiscretions, buying sprees, risky business ventures, and similar "out of character" behaviors that they regret once the mania has subsided. They might also have severe thought disturbances and hallucinations. This form of the condition is known as **bipolar I disorder.** Bipolar I disorder is based more on the manic episodes than on depression. Although those with bipolar I disorder often have depressive episodes, these episodes are not necessary for a *DSM-5* diagnosis. The manic episodes in bipolar I disorder cause significant impairment in daily living and can often result in hospitalization.

Whereas people with bipolar I disorder experience true manic episodes, those with **bipolar II disorder** may experience less extreme mood elevations called *hypomania* (Phillips & Kupfer, 2013). These episodes are often characterized by heightened creativity and productivity, and they can be extremely pleasurable and rewarding. Although these less extreme positive moods may be somewhat disruptive to a person's life, they do not cause significant impairment in daily living or require hospitalization. However, the bipolar II diagnosis does require at least one major depressive episode, and therefore the depression might cause significant impairments. Thus, the impairments to daily living for bipolar I disorder are the manic episodes, but the impairments for bipolar II disorder are the major depressive episodes.

Bipolar disorders are much less common than depression. The lifetime prevalence for any type is estimated at around 3–4 percent (Kessler & Wang, 2008). In addition, whereas depression is more common in women, bipolar disorders are equally prevalent in women and men. Bipolar disorders emerge most commonly during late adolescence or early adulthood, with bipolar I disorder typically first diagnosed at a younger age than bipolar II disorder.

CAUSE OF BIPOLAR DISORDERS

A family history of a bipolar disorder is the strongest and most consistent risk factor for bipolar disorders (Craddock & Sklar, 2013). The concordance rate for bipolar disorders in identical twins is more than 70 percent, versus only 20 percent for fraternal, or dizygotic, twins (Nurnberger, Goldin, & Gershon, 1994).

In the 1980s, the Amish community was involved in a genetic research study. The Amish were an ideal population for this sort of research because they keep good genealogical records and few outsiders marry into the community. In addition, substance abuse is virtually nonexistent among Amish adults, so psychological disorders are

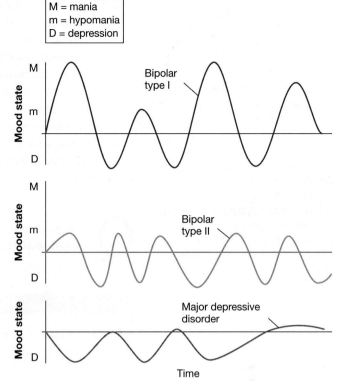

FIGURE 14.21
Bipolar I, Bipolar II, and Major Depressive Disorders
These graphs compare the mood changes over time for three disorders that involve mood states.

bipolar I disorder
A disorder characterized by extremely elevated moods during manic episodes and, frequently, depressive episodes as well.

bipolar II disorder
A disorder characterized by alternating periods of extremely depressed and mildly elevated moods.

easier to detect. The research results revealed that bipolar disorders ran in a limited number of families and that all of those afflicted had a similar genetic defect (Egeland et al., 1987).

Genetic research suggests, however, that the hereditary nature of bipolar disorders is complex and not linked to just one gene. Current research focuses on identifying several genes that may be involved (Wray, Byrne, Stinger, & Mowry, 2014). In addition, it appears that in families with bipolar disorders, successive generations have more-severe disorders and younger ages of onset (Petronis & Kennedy, 1995; Post et al., 2013). Research on this pattern of transmission may help reveal the genetics of the disorder, but the specific nature of the heritability of bipolar disorders remains to be discovered.

 Is depression or manic episodes the main cause of impairment for people with bipolar II disorder?

ANSWER: For those with bipolar II disorder, depressive episodes cause the most impairment. Instead of the manic episodes associated with bipolar I disorder, these individuals experience less extreme positive mood states in the form of hypomania.

14.9 You Think Your Friend Might Be Suicidal. What Should You Do?

Many people contemplate suicide at some point in their lives. Tragically, in 2014 suicide was the second leading cause of death among Americans ages 10 to 24 (Centers for Disease Control, 2016b). As a result of such prevalence, many college students will be or have been touched by suicide. Perhaps you know someone who died by suicide. Perhaps a friend of yours talks about wanting to die. Or maybe you have considered taking your own life. Understanding the risk factors associated with suicide is an important step toward preventing suicide. Knowing where and how to find support can save lives.

A major development in understanding suicide are theories that separate suicide ideation—that is, thinking about suicide—from suicide attempts (Klonsky, May, & Saffer, 2016). For example, in his book *Why People Die by Suicide* (2005), the clinical psychologist Thomas Joiner considers two key questions about suicide: Who *wants* to commit suicide? And who *can* commit suicide? In answering the first question, Joiner argues that "people desire death when two fundamental needs are frustrated to the point of extinction" (p. 47). The first of these fundamental needs is the need to belong, to feel connected with others (discussed in Chapter 10). We all want to have positive interactions with others who care about us. If we do not perceive those things in our lives, our need to belong is thwarted. The second of these fundamental needs is the need for competence. We all want to be capable agents in the world. If we do not perceive ourselves as able to do the things we think we should be able to do, our need for competence is thwarted. Joiner says that when the need to belong and the need for competence are frustrated, we desire death.

But as Joiner points out, just because a person wants to commit suicide does not mean she will be able to do so. Evolution has hardwired us with a tremendously strong self-preservation instinct. What makes a person able to endure the tremendous physical pain or overwhelming psychological fear many of us would experience if we tried to kill ourselves? Joiner presents a straightforward answer: practice. He writes that "those prone to serious suicidal behavior have reached that status through a process of exposure to self-injury and other provocative experiences" (pp. 85–86) and "when people get used to dangerous behavior . . . the groundwork for catastrophe is laid" (p. 48). For example, a person who drives recklessly, engages in self-cutting, and/or experiments with drugs is more practiced at self-harm than someone who does not engage in any of these behaviors. Thus, the person who engages in dangerous behavior is more likely to have the capacity to carry out lethal self-injury.

In **FIGURE 14.22,** the larger oval represents the people in the world who desire suicide. These individuals perceive themselves to be burdens on others and do not perceive themselves as having frequent and positive interactions with others who care about them. In other words, these are the people who may want to commit suicide. The smaller oval represents the people who, over time, have developed the ability to lethally injure themselves. The overlap between the ovals represents the small fraction of people who want to commit suicide and are able to do so. It also represents, conversely, the small fraction of people who are well practiced at endangering themselves and want to die. Again, Joiner posits that the individuals who are *most* at risk of dying by suicide both want to do so and are able to do so.

Of course, like so many other topics you have learned about in this book, suicide is a very complex psychological phenomenon. For instance, people show a variety of emotional responses before attempting suicide, so that it is difficult to use emotional state as a warning sign (Bagge, Littlefield, & Glenn, 2017). Perhaps you have heard that suicide tends to run in families or that everyone who commits suicide has a psychological disorder. Indeed, the data support a genetic risk factor for suicide (Roy, 1992), and the majority of people who commit suicide seem to suffer from psychological disorders (Cavanagh, Carson, Sharpe, & Lawrie, 2003). How do these factors figure into Joiner's model? He points out: "Genes, neurobiology, impulsivity, childhood adversity, and mental disorders are interconnected strands that converge and influence whether people acquire the ability for lethal self-injury, feel a burden on others, and fail to feel they belong" (Joiner, 2005, p. 202). In other words, many factors might lead someone to want to commit suicide. In addition, many factors might prompt someone to arm himself with the ability to endure self-harm.

With such risk factors in mind, we can now turn to the important question of what to do if you think a friend might be suicidal. First and foremost, take suicidal threats seriously. If you are concerned that a friend might be suicidal, do not be afraid to ask him directly. It will not put the thought in his head. Second, get help. Someone who is considering suicide should be screened by a trained professional. Contact a counselor at your school, ask a religious leader for help, or speak to someone at the National Suicide Prevention Lifeline: 1-800-273-TALK (8255). These individuals can help you get your friend the support he needs. Third, let your friend know you care.

Remember, suicide risk is particularly high when people do not feel a sense of connection with others and when they feel a lack of competence. You can remind the suicidal person that you value your relationship, that you care about his well-being, that you would be devastated if that person were no longer in your life. These forms of support can challenge the suicidal person's sense that he lacks belongingness. To challenge the person's perceived incompetence, you can remind your friend about the reasons you admire him, or you can ask for help on a project or issue you are genuinely struggling with.

And remember, suicide is forever. The problems that prompt a person to feel suicidal, however, are often temporary. If you ever find yourself or a friend feeling that suicide offers the best way out of an overwhelming or hopeless situation, know

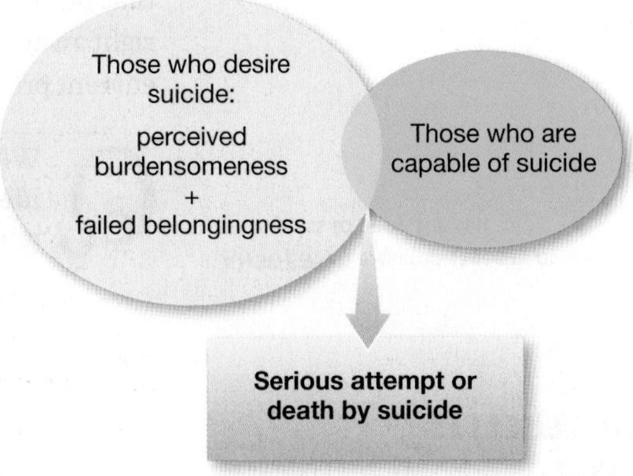

FIGURE 14.22
The Risk of Suicide: Desire + Capability = Attempt? According to Joiner, the individuals who are *most* at risk of dying by suicide both want to do so and are able to do so.

that other options exist. You or your friend might not be able to see those options right away. Reach out to someone who can help you or your friend see the ways out of current problems and into the future. ■

Q
What is the likely difference between someone with suicidal ideation who attempts suicide and someone with suicidal ideation who does not?

ANSWER: an acquired capacity or willingness to harm the self

Learning Objectives

- Describe dissociative amnesia, dissociative fugue, and dissociative identity disorder.

- Discuss the controversy regarding dissociative identity disorder.

- Describe the five symptoms of schizophrenia.

- Distinguish between negative and positive symptoms of schizophrenia.

- Identify biological and environmental factors that contribute to schizophrenia.

dissociative disorders
Disorders that involve disruptions of identity, of memory, or of conscious awareness.

Which Disorders Emphasize Thought Disturbances?

As discussed in the previous section, many psychological disorders include emotional impairments that influence how people think. For example, those with depression can have distorted thoughts about themselves or their futures. By contrast, disorders that revolve around thinking involve disruptions in the connection between thoughts and experiences, such as people losing their sense of identity or feeling that external forces are controlling their thoughts. Many disorders of thought involve *psychosis*, which is a break from reality in which the person has difficulty distinguishing her real perceptions from imaginary ones. People experiencing this disorder have extreme difficulty functioning in everyday life.

14.10 Dissociative Disorders Are Disruptions in Memory, Awareness, and Identity

As noted in Chapter 5, we sometimes get lost in our thoughts or daydreams, even to the point of losing track of what is going on around us. Many of us have had the experience of forgetting what we are doing while in the middle of an action ("Why was I headed to the kitchen?"). When we wake up in an unfamiliar location, we may momentarily be disoriented and not know where we are. In other words, our thoughts and experiences can become dissociated, or split, from the external world.

Dissociative disorders are extreme versions of this phenomenon. These disorders involve disruptions of identity, of memory, or of conscious awareness (Spiegel et al., 2013). The commonality among dissociative disorders is the splitting off of some parts of memory from conscious awareness. Dissociative disorders are believed to result from extreme stress. That is, the person with a dissociative disorder has split off a traumatic event in order to protect the self. Some researchers believe that people prone to dissociative disorders are also prone to PTSD (Cardeña & Carlson, 2011).

DISSOCIATIVE AMNESIA In *dissociative amnesia,* a person forgets that an event happened or loses awareness of a substantial block of time. For example, the person with this disorder may suddenly lose memory for personal facts, including his or her identity and place of residence. These memory failures cannot be accounted for by ordinary forgetting (such as momentarily forgetting where you parked your car) or by the effects of drugs or alcohol.

Consider the case of Dorothy Joudrie, from Calgary, Canada. In 1995, after suffering years of physical abuse from her husband, Joudrie shot her husband six times. Her husband survived, and he described her behavior during the shooting as very calm, as if she were detached from what she was doing. When the police arrived, however, Joudrie was extremely distraught. She had no memory of the shooting and told the police that she simply found her husband shot and lying on the garage floor, at which time she called for help. Joudrie was found not criminally responsible for her actions because of her dissociative state (Butcher, Mineka, & Hooley, 2007).

DISSOCIATIVE FUGUE The rarest and most extreme form of dissociative amnesia is *dissociative fugue*. The disorder involves a loss of identity. In addition, it involves travel to another location (the French word *fugue* means "flight") and sometimes the assumption of a new identity. The fugue state often ends suddenly, with the person unsure how she ended up in unfamiliar surroundings. Typically, the person does not remember events that occurred during the fugue state.

Consider the case of Jeff Ingram, who developed retrograde amnesia, a form of dissociative amnesia (**FIGURE 14.23**). After Ingram found himself in Denver not knowing who he was, his fiancée brought him home to Washington State. Ingram did not recognize his fiancée's face, but she felt familiar to him, as did his home.

DISSOCIATIVE IDENTITY DISORDER According to *DSM-5*, **dissociative identity disorder (DID)** consists of the occurrence of two or more distinct identities in the same individual, along with memory gaps in which the person does not recall everyday events. It used to be known as *multiple personality disorder*. Consider the strange case of Billy Milligan, who in 1978 was found innocent of robbery and rape charges on the grounds that he had dissociative identity disorder. Milligan clearly committed the robberies and rapes, but his lawyers successfully argued that he had multiple personalities and that different ones committed the crimes. Therefore, Billy could not be held responsible.

In his book *The Minds of Billy Milligan* (1981), Daniel Keyes describes the 24 separate personalities sharing the body of 26-year-old Billy Milligan. One is Arthur, who at age 22 speaks with a British accent and is self-taught in physics and biology. He reads and writes fluent Arabic. Eight-year-old David is the keeper of the pain. Anytime something physically painful happens, David experiences it. Christene is a 3-year-old dyslexic girl who likes to draw flowers and butterflies. Regan is 23 and Yugoslavian, speaks with a marked Slavic accent, and reads, writes, and speaks Serbo-Croatian. He is the protector of the "family" and acknowledges robbing his victims, but he denies raping them. Adalana, a 19-year-old lesbian who writes poetry, cooks, and keeps house for the others, later admitted to committing the rapes.

After his acquittal, Milligan spent close to a decade in various mental hospitals. In 1988, psychiatrists declared that Milligan's 24 personalities had merged into one and that he was no longer a danger to society. Milligan was released and reportedly has lived quietly since then. Many people respond to reports such as this with astonishment and incredulity, believing that people such as Milligan must be faking. To judge the facts, we need to examine what is known about this condition and how it is diagnosed.

Most people diagnosed with DID are women who report being severely abused as children. According to the most common theory of DID, children cope with abuse by pretending it is happening to someone else. They enter a trancelike state in which they dissociate their mental states from their physical bodies. Over time, this dissociated state takes on its own identity. Different identities develop to deal with different traumas. Often the identities have periods of amnesia, and sometimes only one identity is aware of the others. Indeed, diagnosis often occurs only when a person has difficulty accounting for large chunks of his or her day. The separate identities usually differ substantially, such as in gender identity, sexual orientation, age, language

FIGURE 14.23
Dissociative Fugue
Jeff Ingram, pictured here, experienced an episode of dissociative fugue when he developed retrograde amnesia after leaving his home, in Washington State. When he arrived in Denver, Colorado, four days later, he had no memory of his previous life. He was recognized two months later, when he appeared on the news pleading for help from anyone who knew who he was. Though he did not remember his three-year relationship with his fiancée (here, seated next to him), the two eventually married.

dissociative identity disorder (DID)
The occurrence of two or more distinct identities in the same individual.

spoken, interests, physiological profiles, and patterns of brain activation (Reinders et al., 2003). Even their handwritings can differ (**FIGURE 14.24**).

Despite this evidence, many researchers remain skeptical about whether DID is a genuine psychological disorder or whether it exists at all (Kihlstrom, 2005). Moreover, some people may have ulterior motives for claiming DID. A diagnosis of DID often occurs after someone has been accused of committing a crime. This timing raises the possibility that people are pretending to have multiple identities to avoid conviction.

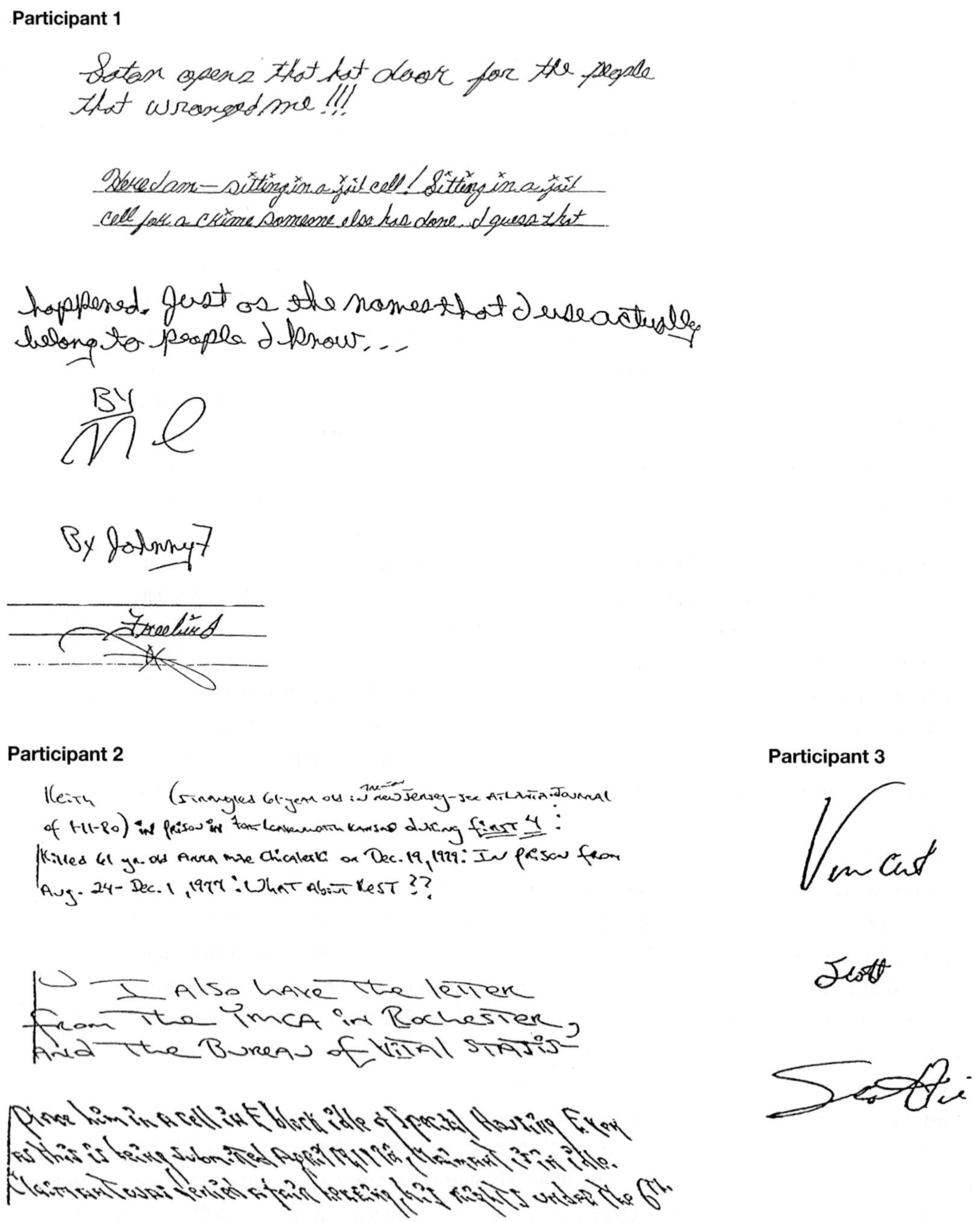

Participant 1

Participant 2

Participant 3

FIGURE 14.24

Handwriting Samples of Three People Diagnosed with Dissociative Identity Disorder

When researchers studied 12 murderers diagnosed with DID, writing samples from 10 of the participants revealed markedly different handwriting in each of their identities. Here, handwriting samples from three of the participants show different identities expressing themselves.

Ultimately, how can we know whether a diagnosis of DID is valid? As mentioned earlier, most often there is no objective, definitive test for diagnosing a psychological disorder. It can be difficult to tell if a person is faking, has come to believe what a therapist said, or has a genuine psychological disorder. Individuals who fake DID tend to report well-publicized symptoms of the disorder but neglect to mention the more subtle symptoms that are extremely common, such as major depressive episodes or PTSD (American Psychiatric Association, 2013; Boyson & VanBergen, 2014). Those faking it seem indifferent or even proud of the disorder. Those truly afflicted are ashamed of or overwhelmed by their symptoms.

Q **What is the difference between dissociative amnesia and dissociative fugue?**

ANSWER: Dissociative amnesia is the loss of memory for a specific event or for a period of time. Dissociative fugue involves a complete loss of identity and travel to a new location.

14.11 Schizophrenia Involves a Disconnection from Reality

The term *schizophrenia* literally means "splitting of the mind." In popular culture, schizophrenia is often confused with dissociative identity disorder, or split personality, but the two disorders are unrelated. With DID, the "self" is split. **Schizophrenia** is characterized by alterations in thought, in perceptions, or in consciousness (**FIGURE 14.25**). The essence of schizophrenia is a split or disconnection from reality, known as psychosis.

According to published estimates, around 1 of every 200 persons has schizophrenia (Simeone, Ward, Rotella, Collins, & Winisch, 2015). A meta-analysis of 188 studies from 46 countries found similar rates for men and women, roughly 4–7 per 1,000 people (Saha, Chant, Welham, & McGrath, 2006). These researchers also found that the rate of schizophrenia was slightly lower in developing nations. In addition, the prognosis is better in developing than in developed cultures (Kulhara & Chakrabarti, 2001). Perhaps in developing countries there is more tolerance for symptoms or greater sympathy for unusual or different people (Waxler, 1979). It is also possible that methods of defining and assessing recovery vary across countries, thereby exaggerating recovery in developing nations (Jääskeläinen et al., 2013).

Schizophrenia is arguably the most devastating disorder for the people who have it and the relatives and friends who support them. It is characterized by a combination of motor, cognitive, behavioral, and perceptual abnormalities. These abnormalities result in impaired social, personal, or vocational functioning. According to *DSM-5*, to be diagnosed with schizophrenia a person has to have shown continuous signs of disturbances for at least six months. There are five major *DSM-5* symptoms for schizophrenia, and a diagnosis requires a person to show two or more of the symptoms. At least one of those symptoms has to be among the first three listed in criterion A of **TABLE 14.6** (i.e., delusions, hallucinations, and disorganized speech). By tradition, researchers tend to group symptoms into two categories: positive and negative. *Positive symptoms* are excesses. They are not positive in the sense of being good or desirable, but in the sense of adding abnormal behaviors. The first four *DSM-5* criteria in Table 14.6 are considered positive symptoms.

As you will see, *negative symptoms* are deficits in functioning, such as apathy, lack of emotion, and slowed speech and movement.

schizophrenia
A psychological disorder characterized by alterations in thoughts, in perceptions, or in consciousness, resulting in psychosis.

FIGURE 14.25
Schizophrenia
In the 2001 film *A Beautiful Mind*, Russell Crowe plays the real-life Princeton mathematics professor and Nobel laureate John Forbes Nash, who fought his schizophrenia by intellectually rejecting his delusional thinking. Nash died in 2015.

Table 14.6 *DSM-5* Diagnostic Criteria for Schizophrenia

A. Two (or more) of the following, present for a significant portion of time during a 1-month period. At least one of these must be (1), (2), or (3).

    1. Delusions

    2. Hallucinations

    3. Disorganized speech (e.g., frequent incoherence)

    4. Grossly disorganized or catatonic behavior

    5. Negative symptoms (i.e., diminished emotional response or lack of motivation)

B. For a significant portion of time since the onset of the disturbance, level of functioning in one or more major areas, such as work, interpersonal relations, or self-care, is markedly below the level achieved prior to the onset.

C. Continuous signs of the disturbance persist for at least 6 months. This 6-month period must include at least 1 month of symptoms that meet criteria A (i.e., active phase symptoms) and may include periods where the symptoms are less extreme.

D. Other disorders and conditions have been ruled out (e.g., bipolar disorder, reactions to drugs, or other medical condition).

Source: Based on American Psychiatric Association (2013).

delusions

False beliefs based on incorrect inferences about reality.

DELUSIONS One of the positive (i.e., excessive) symptoms most commonly associated with schizophrenia is **delusions.** Delusions are false beliefs based on incorrect inferences about reality. (Common types of delusions are listed in **TABLE 14.7.**) Delusional people persist in their beliefs despite evidence that contradicts those beliefs.

Delusions are characteristic of schizophrenia regardless of the culture, but the type of delusion can be influenced by cultural factors (Tateyama et al., 1993). When the delusions of German and Japanese patients with schizophrenia were compared, the two groups had similar rates of grandiose delusions, believing themselves much more powerful and important than they really were. The two groups differed significantly, however, for other types of delusions. The German patients had delusions that involved guilt and sin, particularly as these concepts related to religion. By contrast, the Japanese patients had delusions of harassment, such as the belief that they were being slandered by others. The types of delusions that people with schizophrenia have can also be affected by current events:

> In summer, 1994, mass media in the U.S. reported that North Korea was developing nuclear weapons. At that time, in New York, a middle-age woman with schizophrenia told me that she feared a Korean invasion. In fall, 1995, during a psychiatric interview a young woman with psychotic disorder told me that she had secret connections with the United Nations, the Pope, and O. J. Simpson, and they were helping her. The celebration of the 50th

Table 14.7 Delusions and Associated Beliefs

Persecutory	Belief that others are persecuting, spying on, or trying to harm one
Referential	Belief that objects, events, or other people have particular significance to one
Grandiose	Belief that one has great power, knowledge, or talent
Identity	Belief that one is someone else, such as Jesus Christ or the president of the United States
Guilt	Belief that one has committed a terrible sin
Control	Belief that one's thoughts and behaviors are being controlled by external forces

Anniversary of the United Nations, the visit of the Pope to the U.S., and the O. J. Simpson criminal trial were the highly publicized events in the United States at that time. (Sher, 2000, p. 507)

HALLUCINATIONS Another positive symptom commonly associated with schizophrenia is **hallucinations.** Hallucinations are false sensory perceptions that are experienced without an external source. They are vivid and clear, and they seem real to the person experiencing them. Frequently auditory, they can also be visual, olfactory, or somatosensory:

> I was afraid to go outside and when I looked out of the window, it seemed that everyone outside was yelling, "Kill her, kill her.". . . Things continued to get worse. I imagined that I had a foul body odor and I sometimes took up to six showers a day. I recall going to the grocery store one day, and I imagined that the people in the store were saying "Get saved, Jesus is the answer." (O'Neal, 1984, pp. 109–110)

Auditory hallucinations are often accusatory voices. These voices may tell the person with schizophrenia that he is evil or inept, or they may command the person to do dangerous things. Sometimes the person hears a cacophony of sounds with voices intermingled.

The cause of hallucinations remains unclear. Neuroimaging studies suggest, however, that hallucinations are associated with activation in areas of the cortex that process external sensory stimuli. For example, auditory hallucinations accompany increased activation in brain areas that are normally activated when people engage in inner speech (Kühn & Gallinat, 2012). This finding has led to speculation that auditory hallucinations might be caused by a difficulty in distinguishing normal inner speech (i.e., the type we all engage in) from external sounds. People with schizophrenia need to learn to ignore the voices in their heads, but doing so is extremely difficult and sometimes impossible. Recent research indicates that those with schizophrenia may be likely to have structural abnormalities in the auditory cortex (Mørch-Johnsen et al., 2017).

DISORGANIZED SPEECH Another key positive symptom of schizophrenia is **disorganized speech.** It is disorganized in the sense that it is incoherent, failing to follow a normal conversational structure. A person with schizophrenia may respond to questions with tangential or irrelevant information. It is very difficult to follow what those with schizophrenia are talking about because they frequently change topics, which is known as a *loosening of associations*. These shifts make it difficult or impossible for a listener to follow the speaker's train of thought:

> They're destroying too many cattle and oil just to make soap. If we need soap when you can jump into a pool of water, and then when you go to buy your gasoline, my folks always thought they could get pop, but the best thing to get is motor oil, and money. May as well go there and trade in some pop caps and, uh, tires, and tractors to car garages, so they can pull cars away from wrecks, is what I believed in. (Andreasen, 1984, p. 115)

In more extreme cases, speech is so disorganized that it is totally incomprehensible, which is described by clinicians as *word salad*. This jumbling can also involve *clang associations:* the stringing together of words that rhyme but have no other apparent link. Those with schizophrenia might also display strange and inappropriate emotions while talking. Such strange speaking patterns make it very difficult for people with schizophrenia to communicate (Docherty, 2005).

hallucinations
False sensory perceptions that are experienced without an external source.

disorganized speech
Speaking in an incoherent fashion that involves frequently changing topics and saying strange or inappropriate things.

FIGURE 14.26
Disorganized Behavior
Inappropriately wearing multiple layers of clothing may be a symptom of schizophrenia.

disorganized behavior
Acting in strange or unusual ways, including strange movement of limbs, bizarre speech, and inappropriate self-care, such as failing to dress properly or bathe.

negative symptoms
Symptoms of schizophrenia that are marked by deficits in functioning, such as apathy, lack of emotion, and slowed speech and movement.

DISORGANIZED BEHAVIOR Another common symptom of schizophrenia is **disorganized behavior.** People with schizophrenia often act strangely, such as displaying unpredictable agitation or childish silliness. People exhibiting this symptom might wear multiple layers of clothing even on hot summer days, walk along muttering to themselves, alternate between anger and laughter, or pace and wring their hands as if extremely worried (**FIGURE 14.26**). They also have poor hygiene, failing to bathe or change clothes regularly. They have problems performing many activities, which interferes with daily living.

Sometimes those with schizophrenia may display *catatonic behavior,* where they show a decrease in responsiveness to the environment. For example, they might remain immobilized in one position for hours. Some have speculated that catatonic behavior may be an extreme fear response, akin to how animals respond to sudden dangers—the person is literally "scared stiff" (Moskowitz, 2004). Catatonic features can also include a rigid, masklike facial expression with eyes staring into the distance. In addition, people exhibiting catatonic behavior might mindlessly repeat words they hear, which is called *echolalia.*

NEGATIVE SYMPTOMS A number of behavioral deficits, called **negative symptoms,** associated with schizophrenia result in patients' becoming isolated and withdrawn (Fusar-Poli et al., 2015). Those with negative symptoms, about 15–25 percent of all schizophrenia patients (Üçok & Ergül, 2014), often avoid eye contact and seem apathetic. They do not express emotion even when discussing emotional subjects. Their speech is slowed, they say less than normal, and they use a monotonous tone of voice. Their speech may be characterized by long pauses before answering, failure to respond to a question, or inability to complete an utterance after initiating it. There is often a similar reduction in overt behavior: Patients' movements may be slowed and their overall amount of movement reduced, with little initiation of behavior and no interest in social participation. These symptoms, though less dramatic than delusions and hallucinations, can be equally serious. Negative symptoms are more common in men than in women (Mendrek & Mancini-Marïe, 2016). They are associated with a poorer prognosis.

Although the positive symptoms of schizophrenia (i.e., delusions, hallucinations, and disorganized speech and behavior) can be dramatically reduced or eliminated with antipsychotic medications, the negative symptoms often persist. Because negative symptoms are more resistant to medications, researchers have speculated that positive and negative symptoms have different biological causes. The apparent differences in biological causality lead some researchers to believe that schizophrenia with negative symptoms is in fact a separate disorder from schizophrenia with positive symptoms (Mucci, Meriotti, Üçok, Aleman, & Galderisi, 2017).

 Is disorganized behavior a positive or negative symptom of schizophrenia?

ANSWER: It is a positive symptom because it is the presence, not the absence, of strange behaviors.

14.12 The Cause of Schizophrenia Involves Biological and Environmental Factors

The etiology of schizophrenia is complex and not well understood. Schizophrenia runs in families, however, and it is clear that genetics plays a role in the development of the disorder (**FIGURE 14.27**). If one twin develops schizophrenia, the

FIGURE 14.27
Genetics and Schizophrenia

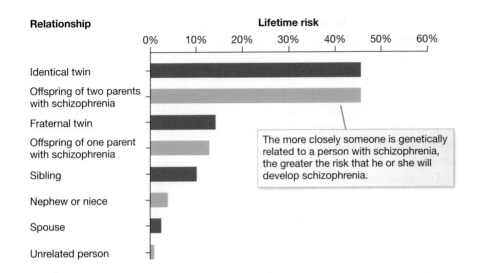

Relationship

Lifetime risk

The more closely someone is genetically related to a person with schizophrenia, the greater the risk that he or she will develop schizophrenia.

- Identical twin
- Offspring of two parents with schizophrenia
- Fraternal twin
- Offspring of one parent with schizophrenia
- Sibling
- Nephew or niece
- Spouse
- Unrelated person

likelihood of the other twin's developing it is almost 50 percent if the twins are identical but only 7–14 percent if the twins are fraternal. If one parent has schizophrenia, the risk of a child's developing the disease is 13 percent. If, however, both parents have schizophrenia, the risk jumps to 40–50 percent (Gottesman, 1991; Wray & Gottesman, 2012).

People with schizophrenia have rare mutations of their DNA about three to four times more often than healthy individuals do, especially in genes related to brain development and to neurological function (Fromer et al., 2014; Walsh et al., 2008). These mutations may result in abnormal brain development, which might lead to schizophrenia. No single gene causes schizophrenia. Instead, it is likely that multiple genes or gene mutations contribute in subtle ways to the expression of the disorder (Purcell et al., 2014). More than 100 candidate genes might modestly influence the development of schizophrenia (Schizophrenia Working Group of the Psychiatric Genomics Consortium, 2014).

BRAIN DISORDER Schizophrenia is primarily a brain disorder (Walker, Kestler, Bollini, & Hochman, 2004). As seen in imaging that shows the structure of the brain, the ventricles are enlarged in people with schizophrenia (see Figure 14.8). In other words, actual brain tissue is reduced. Moreover, greater reductions in brain tissue are associated with more-negative outcomes (Mitelman, Shihabuddin, Brickman, Hazlett, & Buchsbaum, 2005). Longitudinal studies show continued reductions over time (Ho et al., 2003; van Haren et al., 2011) that might become progressively worse after middle age (Cropley et al., 2017). This reduction of tissue occurs in many regions of the brain, especially the frontal lobes and medial temporal lobes. In addition, as seen in imaging that shows the functioning of the brain, activity is typically reduced in the frontal and temporal regions in people with schizophrenia (Barch, Sheline, Csernansky, & Snyder, 2003). Given that abnormalities occur throughout many brain regions in people with schizophrenia, some researchers have speculated that schizophrenia is more likely a problem of connection between brain regions than the result of diminished or changed functions of any particular brain region (Walker et al., 2004).

One possibility is that schizophrenia results from abnormality in neurotransmitters. Since the 1950s, scientists have believed that dopamine may play an important role. Drugs that block dopamine activity decrease symptoms, whereas drugs that increase the activity of dopamine neurons increase symptoms. There is now also evidence that a number of other neurotransmitter systems are involved.

If schizophrenia is a brain disorder, when do these brain abnormalities emerge? Because schizophrenia is most often diagnosed when people are in their 20s or 30s, it is hard to assess whether brain impairments occur earlier in life. There is evidence that some neurological signs of schizophrenia can be observed long before the disorder is diagnosed. Elaine Walker and colleagues (2004) have analyzed home movies taken by parents whose children later developed schizophrenia. Compared with their siblings, those who developed the disorder displayed unusual social behaviors, more-severe negative emotions, and motor disturbances. All of these differences often went unnoticed during the children's early years.

One study followed a group of children at risk for developing psychopathology because their parents suffered from a psychological disorder (Amminger et al., 1999). Adults who developed schizophrenia were much more likely to have displayed behavioral problems as children—such as fighting or not getting along with others—than those who developed mood disorders or drug abuse problems or did not develop any disorders in adulthood. Children at risk for schizophrenia display increasingly abnormal motor movements, such as strange facial expressions, as they progress through adolescence (Mittal, Neumann, Saczawa, & Walker, 2008).

In another study, Walker and colleagues followed a group of children, ages 11–13, with a high genetic risk of schizophrenia (Schiffman et al., 2004). These children were videotaped eating lunch in 1972. Those who later developed schizophrenia showed greater impairments in social behavior and motor functioning than those who developed other psychological disorders or those who developed no problems. Another team of researchers followed 291 high-risk youths (average age 16) over 2.5 years (Cannon et al., 2008). These psychologists determined that five factors predicted the onset of psychotic disorders: a family history of schizophrenia, greater social impairment, higher levels of suspicion/paranoia, a history of substance abuse, and higher levels of unusual thoughts. When youths had two or three of the first three factors, nearly 80 percent of them developed full-blown psychosis. Studies such as these suggest that schizophrenia develops over the life course but that obvious symptoms often emerge by late adolescence. Hints of future problems may even be evident in young children.

ENVIRONMENTAL FACTORS Since genetics does not account fully for the onset and severity of schizophrenia, other factors must also be at work. In those at risk for schizophrenia, environmental stress seems to contribute to its development (Walker et al., 2004). One study looked at adopted children whose biological mothers were diagnosed with schizophrenia (Tienari et al., 1990, 1994). If the adoptive families were psychologically healthy, none of the children became psychotic. If the adoptive families were severely disturbed, 11 percent of the children became psychotic and 41 percent had severe psychological disorders. More generally, growing up in a dysfunctional family may increase the risk of developing schizophrenia for those who are genetically at risk (Tienari et al., 2004; Walder, Faraone, Glatt, Tsuang, & Seidman, 2014; **FIGURE 14.28**).

For those with genetic vulnerability, a large number of factors have been identified that might increase the likelihood of developing schizophrenia (Davis et al., 2016). For instance, there is a wide variety of evidence that heavy cannabis use during adolescence produces a greater risk of developing psychosis (Manrique-Garcia et al., 2012). Some researchers have theorized that the increased stress of urban environments can trigger the onset of the disorder, since being born or raised in an urban area approximately doubles the risk of developing schizophrenia later in life (Torrey, 1999). Others have speculated that some kind of *schizovirus* exists. If so, the close quarters of a big city increase the likelihood of the virus spreading. In support of the virus hypothesis,

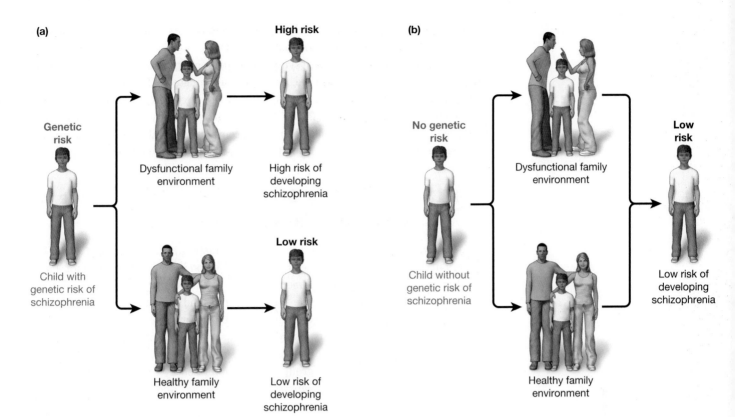

(a)
High risk

Genetic risk

Child with genetic risk of schizophrenia

Dysfunctional family environment

High risk of developing schizophrenia

Low risk

Healthy family environment

Low risk of developing schizophrenia

(b)
No genetic risk

Child without genetic risk of schizophrenia

Dysfunctional family environment

Low risk

Low risk of developing schizophrenia

Healthy family environment

FIGURE 14.28

Effects of Biology and Environment on Schizophrenia

(a) If a child has a genetic risk for schizophrenia and is raised in a dysfunctional family environment, he will have a high risk of developing schizophrenia. **(b)** By contrast, if a child has no genetic risk for schizophrenia, the child will have a low risk of developing the disorder whether raised in a dysfunctional family environment or a healthy family environment.

some researchers have reported finding antibodies in the blood of people with schizophrenia that are not found in those without the disorder (Waltrip et al., 1997). Moreover, people with schizophrenia are more likely to have been born during late winter and early spring (Mednick, Huttunen, & Machon, 1994; Torrey, Torrey, & Peterson, 1977). Consider that mothers of children born in late winter and early spring were in their second trimester of pregnancy during flu season. Indeed, there is now strong evidence that maternal inflammation, such as occurs from a virus, plays a significant role in schizophrenia (Brown & Derkits, 2009; Canetta et al., 2014). During the second trimester, a great deal of fetal brain development occurs. At that time, trauma or pathogens can interfere with the organization of brain regions.

 How does the brain change physically with schizophrenia?

ANSWER: Brain tissue is reduced, a condition that progressively becomes worse as people age.

What Are Personality Disorders?

As discussed in Chapter 13, personality reflects each person's unique response to her environment. Although individuals change somewhat over time, the ways they interact with the world and cope with events are fairly fixed by the end of adolescence. For example, some people interact with the world in maladaptive and inflexible ways.

Learning Objectives

- Distinguish between the clusters of personality disorders.

- Understand controversies related to defining personality disorders.

- Identify the symptoms and possible causes of borderline personality disorder and antisocial personality disorder.

When this style of interaction is long-lasting and causes problems in work and in social situations, it becomes a *personality disorder*.

Most people are likely to exhibit symptoms of personality disorders. At times, anyone might be indecisive, self-absorbed, or emotionally unstable. In fact, true personality disorders are relatively common, affecting just under 1 in 10 people (Lenzenweger, Lane, Loranger, & Kessler, 2007). People with personality disorders consistently behave in maladaptive ways, show a more extreme level of maladaptive behavior, and experience more personal distress and more problems as a result of their behavior.

14.13 Personality Disorders Are Maladaptive Ways of Relating to the World

DSM-5 divides personality disorders into three clusters, as listed in **TABLE 14.8**. Disorders in the Cluster A group are characterized by odd or eccentric behavior. Paranoid, schizoid, and schizotypal personality disorders make up this group. People with these disorders are often reclusive and suspicious, and they have difficulty forming personal relationships because of their strange behavior and aloofness. As you might expect, people with personality disorders in this category show some similarities to people with schizophrenia, but their symptoms are far less severe.

Disorders in the Cluster B group are characterized by dramatic, emotional, or erratic behaviors. *Histrionic, narcissistic, borderline,* and *antisocial* personality

Table 14.8 Personality Disorders and Associated Characteristics

CLUSTER A: ODD OR ECCENTRIC BEHAVIOR	
Paranoid	Tense, guarded, suspicious; holds grudges
Schizoid	Socially isolated, with restricted emotional expression
Schizotypal	Peculiarities of thought, appearance, and behavior that are disconcerting to others; emotionally detached and isolated
CLUSTER B: DRAMATIC, EMOTIONAL, OR ERRATIC BEHAVIOR	
Histrionic	Seductive behavior; needs immediate gratification and constant reassurance; rapidly changing moods; shallow emotions
Narcissistic	Self-absorbed; expects special treatment and adulation; envious of attention to others
Borderline	Cannot stand to be alone; intense, unstable moods and personal relationships; chronic anger; drug and alcohol abuse
Antisocial	Manipulative, exploitative; dishonest; disloyal; lacking in guilt; habitually breaks social rules; childhood history of such behavior; often in trouble with the law
CLUSTER C: ANXIOUS OR FEARFUL BEHAVIOR	
Avoidant	Easily hurt and embarrassed; few close friends; sticks to routines to avoid new and possibly stressful experiences
Dependent	Wants others to make decisions; needs constant advice and reassurance; fears being abandoned
Obsessive-compulsive	Perfectionistic; overconscientious; indecisive; preoccupied with details; stiff; unable to express affection

Source: Adapted from American Psychiatric Association (2013).

disorders make up this group. Borderline and antisocial personality disorders have been the focus of much research, and they are considered in more detail in the following sections.

Disorders in the Cluster C group are characterized by anxious or fearful behavior. *Avoidant, dependent,* and *obsessive-compulsive* personality disorders make up this group. These disorders share some characteristics of anxiety disorders such as social anxiety disorder or generalized anxiety disorder. However, the personality disorders in this group are different from anxiety disorders in that they refer more to general ways of interacting with others and of responding to events. For instance, a person with an obsessive-compulsive personality disorder may be excessively neat and orderly. The person might always eat the same food at precisely the same time or perhaps read a newspaper in a particular order each time. This pattern becomes problematic only when it interferes with the person's life, as in making it impossible to travel or to maintain relationships.

In modern clinical practice, personality disorders are controversial for several reasons. First, personality disorders appear to be extreme versions of normal personality traits, demonstrating the continuum between what is considered normal versus abnormal (Clark & Ro, 2014; Widiger, 2011). For example, indecisiveness is characteristic of obsessive-compulsive personality disorder, but the *DSM* does not define the degree to which someone must be indecisive to be diagnosed as obsessive-compulsive. Second, there is overlap among the traits listed as characteristic of different personality disorders, so the majority of people diagnosed with one personality disorder also meet the criteria for another (Clark, 2007). This overlap suggests that the categories may not be mutually exclusive and that fewer types of personality disorders may exist than are listed in the *DSM*. Indeed, there is evidence that personality disorders can be conceptualized and organized as extreme versions of the various personality traits, described in Chapter 13.

Acknowledging this weakness, but wanting to preserve continuity in current clinical practice, *DSM-5* describes an alternative model for personality disorders in Section III that aims to address many of the shortcomings of the traditional *DSM* approach. In this alternative model, personality disorders are viewed as impairments in personality functioning and the existence of pathological personality traits. That is, the person with the disorder shows extreme personality traits that interfere with successful functioning in society.

Personality disorders may not seem to affect daily life as much as do some of the other disorders discussed in this chapter, such as schizophrenia or bipolar disorders. Although people with personality disorders do not hallucinate or experience radical mood swings, their ways of interacting with the world can have serious consequences. The following in-depth considerations of borderline personality disorder and antisocial personality disorder illustrate the devastating effect of these disorders on the individual, family and friends, and society.

How are personality disorders related to personality traits?

ANSWER: They are extreme versions of normal personality traits.

14.14 Borderline Personality Disorder Is Associated with Poor Self-Control

Borderline personality disorder is characterized by disturbances in identity, in affect, and in impulse control. This disorder was officially recognized as a diagnosis in 1980. The term *borderline* was initially used because these patients were considered on the

borderline personality disorder
A personality disorder characterized by disturbances in identity, in affect, and in impulse control.

Table 14.9 *DSM-5* Diagnostic Criteria of Borderline Personality Disorder

A pervasive pattern of instability of interpersonal relations, self-image, and affects, along with marked impulsivity, beginning by early adulthood and present in a variety of contexts, as indicated by five (or more) of the following:

1. Frantic efforts to avoid real or imagined abandonment

2. A pattern of unstable and intense interpersonal relationships

3. Identity disturbance: markedly and persistently unstable self-image or sense of self

4. Impulsiveness in at least two areas that are potentially self-damaging (e.g., spending, sex, substance abuse, reckless driving, binge eating)

5. Recurrent suicidal behavior, gestures, or threats, or self-mutilating behavior

6. Affective instability due to a marked reactivity of mood, with periods of extreme depression, irritability, or anxiety usually lasting a few hours and only rarely more than a few days

7. Chronic feelings of emptiness

8. Inappropriate intense anger or difficulty controlling anger (e.g., displays of temper, constant anger, recurrent physical fights)

9. Transient, stress-related paranoid thoughts or severe dissociative symptoms

Source: Based on American Psychiatric Association (2013).

border between normal and psychotic (Knight, 1953). As presented in **TABLE 14.9,** the wide variety of clinical features of this disorder reflects its complexity. Approximately 1–2 percent of adults meet the criteria for borderline personality disorder, and the disorder is more than twice as common in women as in men (Lenzenweger et al., 2007; Swartz, Blazer, George, & Winfield, 1990; Torgerson, Kringlen, & Cramer, 2001).

People with borderline personality disorder seem to lack a strong sense of self. They cannot tolerate being alone and have an intense fear of abandonment. Because they desperately need an exclusive and dependent relationship with another person, they can be very manipulative in their attempts to control relationships, as shown in the following example:

> A borderline patient periodically rented a motel room and, with a stockpile of pills nearby, would call her therapist's home with an urgent message. He would respond by engaging in long conversations in which he "talked her down." Even as he told her that she could not count on his always being available, he became more wary of going out evenings without detailed instructions about how he could be reached. One night the patient couldn't reach him due to a bad phone connection. She fatally overdosed from what was probably a miscalculated manipulation. (Gunderson, 1984, p. 93)

In addition to problems with identity, borderline individuals have affective disturbances (Hazlett, 2016). Emotional instability is paramount. Episodes of depression, anxiety, anger, irritability, or some combination of these states can last from a few hours to a few days. Shifts from one mood to another usually occur with no obvious precipitating cause. Consider the therapist Molly Layton's description of her patient Vicki:

> She had chronic and debilitating feelings of emptiness and paralyzing numbness, during which she could only crawl under the covers of her bed and hide. On these days, she was sometimes driven to mutilate her thighs with scissors. Although highly accomplished as a medical student and researcher, who had garnered many grants and fellowships, she would sometimes panic and shut down in the middle of a project, creating unbearable pressures

on herself to finish the work. While she longed for intimacy and friendship, she was disablingly shy around men. (Layton, 1995, p. 36)

The third hallmark of borderline personality disorder is impulsivity, which may explain the much higher rate of the disorder in prison populations (Conn et al., 2010). This characteristic can include sexual promiscuity, physical fighting, and binge eating and purging. As was the case with Vicki, however, self-mutilation is also commonly associated with this disorder. Cutting and burning of the skin are typical, as well as a high risk for suicide. Some evidence indicates that those with borderline personality disorder have diminished capacity in the frontal lobes, which normally help control behavior (Salvador et al., 2016; Silbersweig et al., 2007).

Borderline personality disorder may also have an environmental component, as a strong relationship exists between the disorder and trauma or abuse (Lieb, Zanarini, Schmahl, Linehan, & Bohus, 2004). Some studies have reported that 70–80 percent of those with borderline personality disorder have experienced physical or sexual abuse or observed some kind of extreme violence. Other theories implicate early interactions with caretakers. Clients with borderline personality disorder may have had caretakers who did not accept them or who were unreliable or unavailable. The constant rejection and criticism made it difficult for the individuals to learn to regulate emotions and understand emotional reactions to events (Linehan, 1987). An alternative theory is that caregivers encouraged dependence, preventing the individuals in their charge from adequately developing a sense of self. As a result, the individuals became overly sensitive to others' reactions: If rejected by others, they reject themselves.

Q Is borderline personality disorder more common in men or women?

ANSWER: It occurs about twice as often in women.

14.15 Antisocial Personality Disorder Is Associated with a Lack of Empathy

In the 1800s, the term *psychopath* was coined to describe people who seem willing to take advantage of and to hurt others without any evidence of concern or of remorse (Koch, 1891). As discussed in Chapter 13, psychopathy can be considered a personality trait. This trait is part of the dark triad, in which people are callous toward others and willing to take advantage of people for personal gain. Psychopathy is a good example of the dimensional nature of personality disorders, in which people vary from having low levels of a particular trait to extreme and maladaptive levels.

In his classic book *The Mask of Sanity* (1941), the psychiatrist Hervey Cleckley described characteristics of psychopaths from his clinical experience. For example, such individuals could be superficially charming and rational; be insincere, unsocial, and incapable of love; lack insight; and be shameless. However, in 1980 the *DSM* dropped the label *psychopath*, which was seen as pejorative, and adopted the term **antisocial personality disorder (APD).** APD is the catchall diagnosis for individuals who behave in socially undesirable ways, such as breaking the law, being deceitful and irresponsible, and feeling a lack of remorse for their behavior. People with this disorder tend to be hedonistic, seeking immediate gratification of wants and needs.

antisocial personality disorder (APD)

A personality disorder in which people engage in socially undesirable behavior, are hedonistic and impulsive, and lack empathy.

APD AND EXTREME PSYCHOPATHY The *DSM*'s change in terminology has led to confusion because *psychopath* is still widely used to refer to a related but not identical type of personality disorder as defined by *DSM-5*. Those with APD who also are

FIGURE 14.29
Gary Gilmore After His Arrest
Under *DSM-5,* Gilmore would have been given a diagnosis of antisocial personality disorder. He also showed extreme psychopathic traits.

extremely uncaring and willing to hurt others for personal gain display more extreme behaviors than those with APD (Coid & Ullrich, 2010). These people are commonly referred to as psychopaths (or sometimes sociopaths). These individuals also tend to have other personality characteristics not found in those with APD, such as glibness, a grandiose sense of self-worth, shallow affect, and cunning/manipulativeness.

In other words, psychopaths would be classified as APD under *DSM-5,* but they are an extreme version of the disorder. They are also much more disturbed than those who display dark triad personality traits. True psychopaths are pathological in their degree of callousness and are particularly dangerous. For instance, one study of murderers found that those with psychopathic tendencies nearly always kill intentionally. They want to gain something, such as money, sex, or drugs. People without psychopathic tendencies are much more likely to commit murder impulsively, when provoked or angry (Woodworth & Porter, 2002). Psychopaths fit the stereotype of cold-blooded killers. Infamous examples include Dennis Rader—the BTK strangler, who bound, tortured, and killed 10 victims—and Gary Gilmore (**FIGURE 14.29**). In 1977, Gilmore was executed for the murder he describes here:

> I went in and told the guy to give me the money. I told him to lay on the floor and then I shot him. I then walked out and was carrying the cash drawer with me. I took the money and threw the cash drawer in a bush and I tried to push the gun in the bush, too. But as I was pushing it in the bush, it went off and that's how come I was shot in the arm. It seems like things have always gone bad for me. It seems like I've always done dumb things that just caused trouble for me. I remember when I was a boy I would feel like I had to do things like sit on a railroad track until just before the train came and then I would dash off. Or I would put my finger over the end of a BB gun and pull the trigger to see if a BB was really in it. Sometimes I would stick my finger in water and then put my finger in a light socket to see if it would really shock me. (Spitzer et al., 1983, pp. 66–68)

ASSESSMENT AND CONSEQUENCES It is estimated that 1–4 percent of the population have antisocial personality disorder (Compton, Conway, Stinson, Colliver, & Grant, 2005). People with this condition who also show more-extreme psychopathic traits are less common (Lenzenwegger et al., 2007). Both APD and psychopathy are much more common in men than in women (Goldstein et al., 2017).

Much of what psychologists know about the traits associated with antisocial personality disorder was discovered by the psychologist Robert Hare (1993). Hare also developed many of the assessment tools to identify people with psychopathic tendencies. He and colleagues have shown that the disorder—including its extreme version—is most apparent in late adolescence and early adulthood, and it generally improves around age 40 (Hare, McPherson, & Forth, 1988), at least for those without psychopathic traits. According to the *DSM-5* diagnostic criteria, APD cannot be diagnosed before age 18, but the person must have displayed antisocial conduct before age 15. This stipulation ensures that only those with a lifetime history of antisocial behaviors can be diagnosed with antisocial personality disorder. They also must meet other criteria, such as repeatedly performing illegal acts, repeatedly lying or using aliases, and showing reckless disregard for their own safety or the safety of others. Because many such individuals are quite bright and highly verbal, they can talk their way out of bad situations. In any event, punishment seems to have very little effect on them (Lykken, 1957, 1995), and they often repeat the problem behaviors a short time later.

THE ETIOLOGY OF ANTISOCIAL PERSONALITY DISORDER Various physiological abnormalities may play a role in antisocial personality disorder. In 1957,

David Lykken reported that true psychopaths do not become anxious when they are subjected to aversive stimuli. He and other investigators have continued this line of work, showing that such individuals do not seem to feel fear or anxiety (Lykken, 1995).

Electroencephalogram (EEG) examinations have demonstrated that criminals who meet the criteria for antisocial personality disorder have slower alpha-wave activity (Raine, 1989). This finding indicates a lower overall level of arousal. It is possible that low arousal prompts people with APD to engage in sensation-seeking behavior. In addition, because of low arousal, these individuals do not learn from punishment because they do not experience punishment as particularly aversive. This pattern of reduced psychophysiological response in the face of punishment also occurs in adolescents at risk for developing psychopathy (Fung et al., 2005).

Deficits in frontal lobe functioning have also been found and may account for the lack of forethought and the inability to consider the implications of actions, both characteristic of antisocial personality disorder (Decety, Chen, Harenski, & Kiehl, 2013). There is also evidence of amygdala abnormalities in those with antisocial tendencies, such as having a smaller amygdala and being less responsive to negative stimuli (Blair, 2003; Marsh et al., 2011). Adolescents with callous-unemotional traits (consisting of limited empathy, a lack of guilt, and superficial emotions) are at risk for developing APD. These at-risk individuals show reduced brain responses when viewing pictures of other people in pain (Marsh et al., 2013) and also show reduced activity in the amygdala when observing facial expressions of fear (Marsh et al., 2008; see "The Methods of Psychology: Amygdala Activity in Children at Risk for Antisocial Personality Disorder," on p. 602).

Although brain dysfunction may be at the root of antisocial behaviors and psychopathy, factors such as low socioeconomic status, dysfunctional families, and childhood abuse may also be important. Indeed, malnutrition at age 3 has been found to predict antisocial behavior at age 17 (Liu, Raine, Venables, & Mednick, 2004). An enrichment program for children that included a structured nutrition component was associated with less criminal and antisocial behavior 20 years later (Raine, Mellingen, Liu, Venables, & Mednick, 2003). This finding raises the possibility that malnutrition or other, similar environmental factors might contribute to the development of antisocial personality disorder. Moreover, it demonstrates that aspects of the environment might prove protective for children at risk of developing APD. One recent study found that the amount of positive reinforcement provided by adoptive mothers helped reduce callous/unemotional behaviors in children (Hyde et al., 2016).

ANSWER: Psychopaths are people with the *DSM-5* disorder APD who are also extremely uncaring and willing to injure others for their personal gain.

 Q How do people with antisocial personality disorder, as that condition is defined by *DSM-5*, differ from psychopaths?

Which Psychological Disorders Are Prominent in Childhood?

In his classic text on the classification of psychological disorders, published in 1883, Emil Kraepelin did not mention childhood disorders. The first edition of the *DSM*, published 70 years later, essentially considered children small versions of adults. Consequently, the manual did not consider childhood disorders separately from adulthood disorders. The current version of the manual includes a wide range

Learning Objectives

- Understand the childhood context of neurodevelopmental disorders.

- Identify the symptoms and possible causes of autism spectrum disorder.

- Identify the symptoms and possible causes of attention-deficit/hyperactivity disorder.

The Methods of Psychology
Amygdala Activity in Children at Risk for Antisocial Personality Disorder

HYPOTHESIS: Youths who show callous-unemotional traits that place them at risk for developing antisocial personality disorder will show abnormal amygdala activity when viewing faces displaying fear expressions.

RESEARCH METHOD:

1 Children and adolescents ages 10–17 were shown pictures of faces displaying emotional expressions while in the brain scanner. One group of children had been identified as possessing callous-unemotional traits (including limited empathy, a lack of guilt, and superficial emotions), another group had ADHD, and the final group was comparison children.

2 Brain activity was contrasted between when the participant was viewing emotional expressions (anger, fear) versus when the participant was viewing the neutral expression.

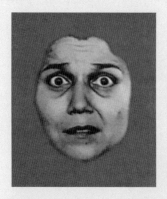 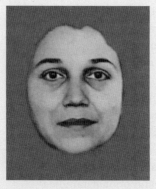 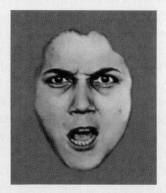

RESULT: Youths with callous-unemotional traits showed less activity in the amygdala in response to the fearful expressions (compared to the neutral expression) than did either those with ADHD or the healthy comparison youths. There were no differences in brain activity in response to the angry expressions (compared to the neutral expression).

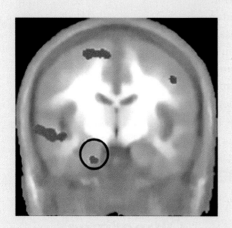 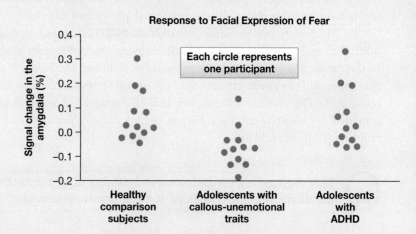

CONCLUSION: The results suggest that children at risk for developing antisocial personality disorder have reduced responses to distress-based social cues such as fear. In such children, the lack of amygdala response may produce impaired processing of social cues that indicate social distress. Therefore these at-risk youths may not avoid behaviors that distress others.

QUESTION: Did those who exhibited callous-unemotional traits show reduced amygdala activity to all emotional expressions?

ANSWER: No. They showed reduced amygdala activity only in response to fearful expressions.

Source: Marsh, A. A., Finger, E. C., Mitchell, D. G., Reid, M. E., Sims, C., et al. (2008). Reduced amygdala response to fearful expressions in children and adolescents with callous-unemotional traits and disruptive behavior disorders. *American Journal of Psychiatry, 165,* 712–720.

Table 14.10 *DSM-5* Neurodevelopmental Disorders

DISORDER	DESCRIPTION
Intellectual disabilities	Deficits in general mental abilities (e.g., reasoning, problem solving, planning, academic learning, learning from experience) and in adaptive functioning (e.g., independent living, working, social participation); begins during childhood or adolescence
Communication disorders	Deficits in language, speech, or communications, such as difficulty learning a language, stuttering, or failure to follow social rules for communication; begins in childhood
Autism spectrum disorder	Persistent impairment in social interaction; characterized by unresponsiveness; impaired language, social, and cognitive development; and restricted and repetitive behavior; begins during early childhood
Attention-deficit/hyperactivity disorder	A pattern of hyperactive, inattentive, and impulsive behavior that causes social or academic impairment; begins before age 12
Specific learning disorders	Difficulty learning and using academic skills; much lower performance in reading, mathematics, or written expression with regard to what is expected for age, amount of education, and intelligence; begins during school-age years
Motor disorders	Recurrent motor and vocal tics that cause marked distress or deficits in developing or being able to show coordinated motor skills; begins in childhood

Source: Based on American Psychiatric Association (2013).

of childhood disorders (**TABLE 14.10**). Some of these conditions—such as specific learning disorders—affect only limited and particular areas of a child's world. Other conditions—such as autism spectrum disorder, attention-deficit/hyperactivity disorder, and others listed in Table 14.8—affect every aspect of a child's life. Some of these disorders, such as autism spectrum disorder, usually do not get better over time. Others, such as attention-deficit/hyperactivity disorder, usually do improve over time.

All of the disorders in this category should be considered within the context of normal childhood development. Some symptoms of childhood psychological disorders are extreme manifestations of normal behavior or are actually normal behaviors for children at an earlier developmental stage. For example, bed-wetting is normal for 2-year-olds but not for 10-year-olds. Other behaviors, however, deviate significantly from normal development. Two disorders of childhood, autism spectrum disorder and attention-deficit/hyperactivity, are explored here as illustrations.

14.16 Autism Spectrum Disorder Involves Social Deficits and Restricted Interests

Prior to *DSM-5*, a number of similar disorders were considered variants of *autistic disorder*, commonly known as *autism*, which is characterized by deficits in social interaction, by impaired communication, and by restricted interests (Volkmar, Chawarska, & Klin, 2005). The disorder was first described in 1943, by the psychiatrist and physician Leo Kanner. Struck by the profound isolation of some children, Kanner coined the term *early infantile autism*. Researchers and clinicians recognized that autism varied considerably in severity, from mild social impairments to severe social and intellectual impairments. For example, those with high-functioning autism were considered to have *Asperger's syndrome,* named after the pediatrician who first described it. A child with Asperger's has normal intelligence but deficits in social interaction. These deficits reflect an underdeveloped theory of mind. As discussed in Chapter 9, theory of mind is both the understanding that other people have mental states and the ability to predict their behavior accordingly.

Based on the *DSM-IV* diagnosis of autistic disorder, approximately 3–6 children out of 1,000 showed signs of autism, and it is much more common in boys than girls (Muhle, Trentacoste, & Rapin, 2004). From 1991 to 1997, a dramatic escalation—of 556 percent—occurred in the number of children diagnosed with autism (Stokstad, 2001). This increase was likely due to a greater awareness of symptoms by parents and physicians and a willingness to apply the diagnosis to a wider spectrum of behaviors (Rutter, 2005). For example, a study of all children born between 1983 and 1999 in Western Australia found that the apparent growth in the diagnosis of autistic disorder was due to changes in how it was diagnosed as well as expanded funding for psychological services for children showing signs of autism (Nassar et al., 2009). In other words, the notion that autism was epidemic was somewhat misleading because what changed was how it was defined, not how many new cases developed (Gernsbacher, Dawson, & Goldsmith, 2005).

Autism spectrum disorder is a new *DSM-5* disorder that groups together all the variants in symptoms of autism, including Asperger's syndrome. Approximately 1–2 percent of children have a disorder along the autism spectrum, with boys about five times more likely to be diagnosed than girls (Blumberg et al., 2013; Christensen et al., 2015). This diagnosis classification is another excellent example of the dimensional approach to psychopathology, in that the disorder clearly varies along a continuum from mild to severe impairment. In *DSM-5,* the two essential features of autism spectrum disorder are impairments in social interactions along with restrictive or repetitive behaviors, interests, or activities. These symptoms are present in early childhood and limit or impair everyday functioning. The following sections use the terms *autism spectrum disorder* and *autism* interchangeably because most of the research to date has not used the *DSM-5* criteria for diagnosis. Most of this discussion focuses on the classic severe end of the autism spectrum, which definitely meets the *DSM-5* criteria.

CORE SYMPTOMS OF AUTISM SPECTRUM DISORDER Children on the more extreme end of the autism spectrum are seemingly unaware of others. As babies, they do not smile at their caregivers, do not respond to vocalizations, and may actively reject physical contact with others. Children with autism do not establish eye contact and do not use their gazes to gain or direct the attention of those around them (Moriuchi, Klin, & Jones, 2016). Although they show attention to the eyes before 2 months of age, they stop making eye contact by 6 months of age (Jones & Klin, 2013). One group of researchers had participants view video footage of the first birthdays of children with autistic disorder to see if characteristics of autism could be detected before the children were diagnosed (Osterling & Dawson, 1994). By considering only the number of times a child looked at another person's face, the participants correctly classified the children as having or not having autism 77 percent of the time (**FIGURE 14.30**).

Deficits in communication are the second major cluster of behaviors characteristic of autism spectrum disorders. Such deficits are evident by 14 months of age among children who are subsequently diagnosed with autism (Landa, Holman, & Garrett-Mayer, 2007). Children with autism show severe impairments in verbal and nonverbal communication. Even if they vocalize, it is often not with any intent to communicate. Children with autism who develop language usually exhibit odd speech patterns, such as echolalia (the mindless repeating of words or phrases that someone else has spoken, which is also observed in those with schizophrenia). The repeater may imitate

autism spectrum disorder
A developmental disorder characterized by deficits in social interaction, by impaired communication, and by restricted interests.

(a)

(b)

FIGURE 14.30
Scenes from Videotapes of Children's Birthday Parties
(a) This child focused more on objects than on people. The child was later diagnosed with autism. **(b)** This child focused appropriately on objects and on people. The child developed normally.

Viewer (2-year-old with autism).

Area focused on by a 2-year-old with autism.

D:088 H:443 V:327 23:13:37:51

FIGURE 14.31
Toddler Viewer with Autism
As shown in these combined video images from a 1994 study of autism, a 2-year-old with autism will focus on the unimportant details in the scene rather than on the social interaction.

the first speaker's intonation or may use a high-pitched monotone. Those who develop functional language also often interpret words literally, use language inappropriately, and lack verbal spontaneity.

A third category of deficits includes restricted activities and interests. Children with autism spectrum disorder appear oblivious to people around them, but they are acutely aware of their surroundings. Although most children automatically pay attention to the social aspects of a situation, those with autism may focus on seemingly inconsequential details (Klin, Jones, Schultz, & Volkmar, 2003; **FIGURE 14.31**).

Any changes in daily routine or in the placement of furniture or of toys are very upsetting for children with autism. Once they are upset, the children can become extremely agitated or throw tantrums. In addition, the play of children with autism tends to be repetitive and obsessive, with a focus on objects' sensory aspects. They may smell and taste objects, or they may spin and flick them for visual stimulation. Similarly, their own behavior tends to be repetitive, with strange hand movements, body rocking, and hand flapping. Self-injury is common, and some children must be forcibly restrained to keep them from hurting themselves.

BIOLOGICAL BASIS OF AUTISM SPECTRUM DISORDER Kanner, one of the first scientists to study autism, believed the disorder was innate in some children but exacerbated by cold and unresponsive mothers, whom he called "ice box mothers" or "refrigerator mothers." He described the parents of children with autism as insensitive, meticulous, introverted, and highly intellectual. This view is given little credence today, as it is now well established that autism spectrum disorder is the result of biological factors. For example, there is evidence for a genetic component to autism. A number of studies have found concordance rates to be as high as 70–90 percent for identical twins (Holmboe et al., 2013; Hyman, 2008; Ronald & Hoekstra, 2011).

In addition to autism being heritable, it also appears that gene mutations may play a role (Ronemus, Iossifov, Levy, & Wigler, 2014). An international study that compared 996 children with autism to 1,287 control children found a number of rare gene abnormalities (Pinto et al., 2010). These rare mutations involve cells having an abnormal number of copies of DNA segments. An independent study of over

1,000 individuals with autism spectrum disorder who had an unaffected sibling found that these mutations were much more common in the children with autism (Levy et al., 2011). The mutations may affect the way neural networks are formed during childhood development (Gilman et al., 2011). There is growing evidence that autism and schizophrenia share the same gene mutations (Fromer et al., 2014; McCarthy et al., 2014). There are also some similarities in the symptoms for the two disorders, including social impairment and avoiding eye contact. Recall the RDoC initiative, discussed earlier in the chapter, that integrates findings across multiple disorders rather than classifying by *DSM* diagnostic categories. The RDoC approach suggests that schizophrenia and ASD may be related disorders or involve similar deficits in core psychological domains.

Research into the causes of autism also points to prenatal and/or early childhood events that may result in brain dysfunction. The brains of children with autism grow unusually large during the first months of life, and then growth slows until age 5 (Courchesne et al., 2007; Courchesne, Redcay, & Kennedy, 2004). Rapid growth of the brain at 6–12 months of age predicts the likelihood of a diagnosis of autism spectrum disorder at age 2 in children with a genetic risk for the disorder (Hazlett et al., 2017). The brains of children with autism also do not develop normally during adolescence (Amaral, Schumann, & Nordahl, 2008). Researchers are investigating genetic factors, such as mutations, and nongenetic factors that might explain this overgrowth/undergrowth pattern.

Some recent work suggests that exposure to antibodies in the womb may affect brain development. Investigators found abnormal antibodies in the blood of the mothers of 11 percent of children with autism but not in a large sample of mothers with healthy children or mothers of children with other developmental disorders (Braunschweig et al., 2008). Following up on this study, researchers injected four pregnant rhesus monkeys with the antibodies from the mothers of children with autism. All the offspring of these monkeys demonstrated unusual behaviors characteristic of autism, such as repetitive movements and hyperactive limb movements (Martin et al., 2008). None of the offspring of monkeys injected with normal antibodies from mothers of healthy children showed this unusual behavior.

In addition, there is evidence that the brains of people with autism have faulty wiring in a large number of areas (Minshew & Williams, 2007). Some of those brain areas are associated with social thinking, and others might support attention to social aspects of the environment (Minshew & Keller, 2010).

One line of research examined the possibility that those with autism have impairments in the mirror neuron system. (Recall from Chapter 6 that mirror neurons are involved in observational learning and are activated when people watch others performing actions or perform those actions themselves.) This connection between mirror neurons and autism was suggested by an imaging study that found weaker activation in the mirror neuron system for those with autism than for those without (Dapretto et al., 2006). Other researchers, however, have not found impairments in mirror neuron activity for gestures and movements (Dinstein et al., 2010; Southgate & Hamilton, 2008). What might these apparently contradictory findings mean?

It is possible that impairments in the mirror neuron system prevent the person with autism from understanding the *why* of actions, not the *what* of actions (Rizzolatti & Fabbri-Destro, 2010). For example, suppose that the person with autism knows that another person is lifting a pair of scissors. The person with autism may have little insight into what the person intends to do with the scissors.

Q How does brain development in autism spectrum disorder differ from typical brain development?

ANSWER: The brains of those who develop autism spectrum disorder show unusually large growth beginning as early as 6 months of age.

14.17 Why Do People Believe Vaccinations Cause Autism?

What if you heard about a study in which researchers found that moving to Florida or Arizona is a leading cause of death? Or that wearing dentures is another leading cause of death, along with retiring, wearing bifocals, or moving to a nursing home? As a critical thinker, you probably noticed that these things are all associated with aging. It is getting older, rather than moving to Florida or buying bifocals, that is associated with dying. As you have been reminded throughout this book, correlation does not equal causation. We need to be especially vigilant for lurking third variables that might explain apparent correlations between unrelated variables.

Recognizing the third variable problem is especially important when trying to understand claims about causes of psychological disorders. In 1998, the British physician Andrew Wakefield published a study in the prestigious journal *Lancet* claiming to find a connection, in 12 children, between receiving vaccinations to prevent measles, mumps, and rubella (MMR) and developing autism (Wakefield et al., 1998). This finding was widely reported in the media even though most scientists were skeptical and urged people to be patient until the result could be replicated with larger samples. But many people panicked. In 2007, the celebrity Jenny McCarthy publicly blamed the MMR vaccine for her son's autism. She became a prominent spokesperson for the anti-vaccine movement, appearing on television shows such as *Oprah* to warn people about "the autism shot" (**FIGURE 14.32**). Deirdre Imus, the wife of the outspoken radio host Don Imus, joined the publicity war against vaccinations, claiming that the chemical thimerosal in the solutions used to administer vaccines is responsible for autism. Thimerosal is a preservative that contains small amounts of mercury and was widely used before 2000. Since then, it has been removed in all childhood vaccines except for one type of flu shot.

Unfortunately, the Wakefield study was fraudulent. Wakefield altered medical records and lied about several aspects of his study, including a financial conflict of interest (Godlee, Smith, & Marcovitch, 2011). His coauthors had earlier retracted the paper when they had developed doubts about the data and conclusions (Murch et al., 2004). Wakefield has subsequently been banished by the British medical community, and his license to practice medicine has been taken away.

The original *Lancet* report prompted several large international studies to examine the possibility of a link between autism spectrum disorder and the MMR vaccine. A thorough review of these studies by the Institute of Medicine found no evidence of any link between MMR vaccinations and autism (Immunization Safety Review Committee, 2004). Recent studies have continued to find no evidence of any link between childhood vaccinations and ASD (e.g., DeStefano, Price, & Weintraub, 2013; Jain et al., 2015). The results of dozens upon dozens of carefully designed studies have provided a firm conclusion: Vaccines do not cause ASD.

But the fear of ASD led many parents around the globe to forgo vaccinating their children. As one researcher noted, "Unfortunately, the media has given celebrities who comment on an autism-MMR link far more attention than they deserve, and the public, unfamiliar with the background science, has confused celebrity status with authority" (Poland, 2011, p. 870). Even today, with overwhelming scientific evidence that vaccines do not cause ASD, many parents refuse to vaccinate their children because of worries that it might do so (Opel et al., 2014).

As a consequence of the decline in childhood immunizations, there has been an increase in outbreaks of diseases that had become quite rare because of successful

FIGURE 14.32
Anti-Vaccination Statements
Jenny McCarthy speaks to the audience at a Green Our Vaccines press conference outside the U.S. Capitol in 2008.

vaccine programs. In 2011, France had 14,000 cases of measles, 6 of them fatal. In 2012, the Centers for Disease Control reported the largest number of cases of whooping cough in 60 years. In the first four months of 2013, rubella cases in Japan jumped from a few a year to more than 5,000. The reemergence of these diseases is occurring in many European nations (Eisenstein, 2014). Meanwhile, researchers at the CDC estimate that for children born between 1994 and 2013, vaccinations prevented an estimated 322 million illnesses, 21 million hospitalizations, and 732,000 deaths over their lifetimes (Whitney, Zhou, Singleton, & Schuchat, 2014).

Wakefield originally conducted his study because the parents of the 12 children with autism told him that they remembered the autism starting right after their children were immunized. Jenny McCarthy told Oprah that immediately after her son received the vaccine, "Boom—the soul's gone from his eyes" (September 18, 2007). Many have disputed her account, but the bottom line is that vaccines are given to children at about the same developmental period that symptoms of ASD become apparent. Think about the other characteristics that emerge at the same time in development. For example, lower molars emerge in children's mouths during early childhood. However, few people would suggest that being vaccinated causes molars to grow. Children start speaking at about this age, but no one thinks vaccines cause this ability. People see an apparent connection between vaccines and ASD, but the lurking third variable is age.

Since Wakefield's 1998 publication, cases of ASD have increased even though thimerosal is no longer used in vaccines and the number of children being immunized has dropped. These facts would indicate that vaccination and ASD are negatively correlated! As noted in the text, however, definitional changes in the diagnostic criteria are likely a better explanation for the increase in ASD. ∎

 Is there any evidence that vaccinating children is linked to the development of autism?

ANSWER: No. Dozens of carefully constructed studies have failed to find any evidence of a link.

14.18 Attention-Deficit/Hyperactivity Disorder Is a Disruptive Impulse Control Disorder

Suppose you are a child who exhibits hyperactivity. At home, you might have difficulty remembering not to trail your dirty hand along the clean wall as you run from the front door to the kitchen. While playing games with your peers, you might spontaneously change the rules. At school, you might ask what you are supposed to do immediately after the teacher has presented detailed instructions to the entire class. You might make warbling noises or other strange sounds that inadvertently disturb anyone nearby. You might seem to have more than your share of accidents—for example, knocking over the tower your classmates are erecting, spilling your juice, or tripping over the television cord while retrieving the family cat, thereby disconnecting the set in the middle of the Super Bowl (Whalen, 1989).

Symptoms such as these can seem humorous in the retelling, but the reality is a different story. Children with **attention-deficit/hyperactivity disorder (ADHD)** are restless, inattentive, and impulsive. They need to have directions repeated and rules explained over and over. Although these children are often friendly and talkative, they can have trouble making and keeping friends because they miss subtle social cues and make unintentional social mistakes. Many of these symptoms are exaggerations of typical toddler behavior, and thus the line between normal and abnormal behavior is hard to draw.

attention-deficit/hyperactivity disorder (ADHD)

A disorder characterized by restlessness, inattentiveness, and impulsivity.

The *DSM-5* requires at least six or more symptoms of inattention (e.g., careless mistakes, not listening, losing things, easily distracted) and six or more symptoms of hyperactivity or impulsiveness (e.g., fidgeting, running about when inappropriate, talking excessively, difficulty waiting) that last for at least six months and interfere with functioning or development. Several of these symptoms must be prior to age 12 and occur in multiple settings. Estimates of the prevalence of ADHD vary widely. The best available evidence for children in the United States is that 7 percent of children have the disorder, with it being more common in boys than girls (Thomas, Sanders, Doust, Beller, & Glasziou, 2015).

Although ADHD traditionally has been most common among white boys, recently girls and minorities have shown increases in the disorder (Collins & Cleary, 2016; Siegel, Laska, Wanderling, Hernandez, & Levenson, 2015). In addition, ADHD was once associated with being thin or normal weight, but children with ADHD are now more likely to be obese (Cortese et al., 2016). One possible explanation for these differences is that practitioners may be more willing to look beyond stereotypes of who has the disorder (**FIGURE 14.33**).

FIGURE 14.33
ADHD in Girls
The stereotype of ADHD is a thin and overactive white male. However, ADHD is increasingly diagnosed in girls and minorities, possibly because practitioners are looking beyond stereotypical characteristics in their assessment of disordered behaviors.

THE ETIOLOGY OF ADHD The causes of this disorder are unknown. One difficulty in pinpointing the etiology is that ADHD is most likely a heterogeneous disorder. In other words, the behavioral profiles of children with ADHD vary, so the causes of the disorder most likely vary as well. Children with ADHD may be more likely than other children to come from disturbed families. Factors such as poor parenting and social disadvantage may contribute to the onset of symptoms, as is true for all psychological disorders. Still, ADHD clearly has a genetic component: Concordance is about twice as high in identical twins than in dizygotic twins (Larsson, Chang, D'Onofrio, & Lichtenstein, 2014; Sherman, McGue, & Iacono, 1997).

In an early imaging study, Alan Zametkin and colleagues (1990) found that adults who had been diagnosed with ADHD in childhood had reduced metabolism in brain regions involved in the self-regulation of motor functions and of attentional systems. A general finding is that there is reduced volume in many regions of the brain for those with ADHD, particularly in regions involving attention, cognitive and motor control, emotional regulation, and motivation (Gallo & Posner, 2016). The pattern suggests delayed maturation of the brain among those with ADHD (Friedman & Rapoport, 2015; Shaw et al., 2012). Supporting the delayed maturation hypothesis is evidence that the reduced brain volumes observed in children mostly disappear by adulthood (Hoogman et al., 2017), along with many symptoms of the disorder (Rubia, Alegria, & Brinson, 2014).

The brain region most consistently shown to be involved in ADHD is the basal ganglia (see Figure 3.22). Researchers have also demonstrated volume reductions in the basal ganglia in the brains of those with ADHD (Hoogman et al., 2017). Because this structure is involved in regulating motor behavior and impulse control, dysfunction in the basal ganglia could contribute to the hyperactivity characteristic of ADHD.

ADHD ACROSS THE LIFE SPAN Children generally are not given diagnoses of ADHD until they enter structured settings in which they must conform to rules, get along with peers, and sit in their seats for long periods. In the past, these things happened when children entered school, between ages 5 and 7. Now, with the increasing prevalence of structured day care settings, the demands on children to conform are occurring much earlier. However, diagnoses for boys occur at younger ages than for girls, which may reflect a tendency for boys' behavior to be more readily identified as disordered (Davies, 2014).

FIGURE 14.34
Living with ADHD
Paula Luper, of North Carolina, was diagnosed with ADHD in elementary school. Here, as a senior in high school, she is taking a quiz in the teachers lounge to avoid distraction.

According to longitudinal studies, children do not outgrow ADHD by the time they enter adulthood (McGough & Barkley, 2004; Agnew-Blais et al., 2016). Adults with ADHD symptoms, about 4 percent of the population (Kessler et al., 2006), may struggle academically and vocationally. Studies conducted up to 30 years later show that they generally reach a lower-than-expected socioeconomic level, change jobs more often than other adults, have substance abuse problems, and are more likely to get divorced if married (Klein et al., 2012). At the same time, many adults with ADHD learn how to adapt to their condition, such as by reducing distractions while they work (**FIGURE 14.34**).

 How does the brain of a child with ADHD differ from that of a child without the disorder?

ANSWER: Delayed maturation of the brain leads it to be smaller in several areas relevant to the symptoms of ADHD.

Your Chapter Review

Chapter Summary

How Are Psychological Disorders Conceptualized and Classified?

14.1 Views on Psychopathology Have Changed over Time

Individuals with psychological disorders behave in ways that deviate from cultural norms and that are maladaptive. Psychological disorders are common in all societies.

14.2 Psychological Disorders Are Classified into Categories

The *Diagnostic and Statistical Manual of Mental Disorders* is a system for diagnosing psychological disorders. The current version is *DSM-5*. Psychological disorders are often comorbid—that is, they occur together. Assessment is the process of examining a person's mental functions and psychological condition to make a diagnosis. Assessment is accomplished through self-reports, psychological testing, observations, interviews, and neuropsychological testing.

14.3 Psychological Disorders Have Many Causes

According to the diathesis-stress model, mental health problems arise from a vulnerability coupled with stressful circumstances. Psychological disorders may arise from biological factors, situational factors, or cognitive-behavioral factors.

14.4 Psychological Disorders Vary by Sex and by Culture

Females are more likely than males to exhibit internalizing disorders (such as major depressive disorder and generalized anxiety disorder). Males are more likely than females to exhibit externalizing disorders (such as alcohol use disorder and conduct disorders). Most psychological disorders show some universal symptoms, but the *DSM* recognizes a number of cultural syndromes related to mental health problems.

Which Disorders Emphasize Emotional States?

14.5 Anxiety Disorders Make People Fearful and Tense

Specific phobias are exaggerated fears of specific stimuli. Social anxiety disorder is a fear of being negatively evaluated by others. Generalized anxiety disorder is diffuse and omnipresent. Panic disorder causes sudden overwhelming terror and may lead to agoraphobia. Cognitive, learning, and biological factors contribute to the onset of anxiety disorders.

14.6 Unwanted and Intrusive Thoughts Increase Anxiety

Obsessive-compulsive disorder involves frequent intrusive thoughts and compulsive actions. OCD may involve conditioning or be caused by genetic and environmental factors. Posttraumatic stress disorder involves frequent and recurring nightmares, intrusive thoughts, and flashbacks related to an earlier trauma. PTSD occurs in approximately 7 percent of the population and affects women more than men.

14.7 Depressive Disorders Consist of Sad, Empty, or Irritable Moods

Major depressive disorder is characterized by a number of symptoms, including depressed mood and a loss of interest in pleasurable activities. Persistent depressive disorder is less severe, with people being sad most of the day on more days than not for at least two years. Depressive disorders have biological components, including a genetic risk and possible dysfunction of the monoamine neurotransmitters norepinephrine and serotonin. Situational factors (such as poor relationships and stress) and cognitive factors (such as the cognitive triad and learned helplessness) also contribute to the occurrence of depression.

14.8 Bipolar Disorders Involve Depression and Mania

Bipolar disorder is characterized by manic episodes—that is, episodes of increased activity and euphoria—and depression. The impairment in bipolar I disorder is due to manic episodes, whereas the impairment in bipolar II disorder is due to depressive episodes. Genes may play a role in bipolar disorders.

14.9 Using Psychology in Your Life: You Think Your Friend Might Be Suicidal. What Should You Do?

Suicide is the second leading cause of death for young adults. According to Joiner's model, suicide risk involves a sense of lack of social belonging and feeling like a social burden coupled with an acquired capacity for self-harm. People should take suicide threats seriously and try to get the person professional help. Remind the suicidal person that you value the relationship.

Which Disorders Emphasize Thought Disturbances?

14.10 Dissociative Disorders Are Disruptions in Memory, Awareness, and Identity

Dissociative amnesia involves forgetting that an event happened or losing awareness of a substantial block of time. Dissociative fugue involves a loss of identity and travel to another location. Dissociative identity disorder involves the occurrence of two or more distinct identities in the same individual, along with memory gaps for everyday events. Dissociative identity disorder is believed to emerge as a consequence of severe abuse—through repeated dissociation, different identities develop to cope with different traumas. Dissociative identity disorder remains a controversial diagnosis.

14.11 Schizophrenia Involves a Disconnection from Reality

Schizophrenia is characterized by alterations in thought, in perceptions, or in consciousness. The positive symptoms associated with schizophrenia reflect excesses and include delusions, hallucinations, disorganized speech, and disorganized or catatonic behavior. The negative symptoms of schizophrenia reflect deficits and include apathy, lack of emotion, and slowed speech and movement.

14.12 The Cause of Schizophrenia Involves Biological and Environmental Factors

There is a strong genetic component to schizophrenia, and there is evidence that gene mutations may lead to abnormal brain development. Research suggests that schizophrenia is largely a brain disorder, with alteration in brain structure and brain chemistry evident in the disorder. Environmental factors also play a role in the development of schizophrenia, including dysfunctional family dynamics, urban stress, and exposure to pathogens.

What Are Personality Disorders?

14.13 Personality Disorders Are Maladaptive Ways of Relating to the World

The *DSM* identifies 10 personality disorders clustered into three groups. Paranoid, schizoid, and schizotypal make up the odd or eccentric cluster. Histrionic, narcissistic, borderline, and antisocial make up the dramatic, emotional, or erratic cluster. Avoidant, dependent, and obsessive-compulsive make up the anxious or fearful cluster.

14.14 Borderline Personality Disorder Is Associated with Poor Self-Control

Borderline personality disorder involves disturbances in identity, affect, and impulse control. Borderline personality disorder is associated with reduced frontal lobe capacity and a history of trauma and abuse.

14.15 Antisocial Personality Disorder Is Associated with a Lack of Empathy

Antisocial personality disorder is characterized by socially undesirable behavior, being deceitful and irresponsible, a lack of remorse, and hedonism. Antisocial personality disorder is associated with lower levels of arousal, deficits in frontal lobe functioning, and a smaller amygdala. Environment seems to contribute to the development of antisocial personality disorder.

Which Psychological Disorders Are Prominent in Childhood?

14.16 Autism Spectrum Disorder Involves Social Deficits and Restricted Interests

Autism spectrum disorder is marked by impaired social interaction, impaired communication, and restricted interests and emerges in infancy. Autism is heritable and may result from genetic mutations. Autism has been linked to abnormal brain growth, exposure to antibodies in the womb, faulty brain wiring, and mirror neuron impairment.

14.17 Think like a Psychologist: Why Do People Believe Vaccinations Cause Autism?

A fraudulent report led some people to believe that measles, mumps, and rubella vaccine causes autism. This conclusion is faulty thinking based on seeing relations that do not exist. The age at which children are vaccinated happens to be at about the same time symptoms of autism appear. Overwhelming research documents the lack of any true association between vaccines and the risk of developing autism.

14.18 Attention-Deficit/Hyperactivity Disorder Is a Disruptive Impulse Control Disorder

Children with ADHD are restless, inattentive, and impulsive. The causes of ADHD may include environmental factors such as poor parenting and social disadvantages; genetic factors; and brain abnormalities, particularly with regard to activation of the brain regions involving attention, cognitive and motor control, emotional regulation, and motivation. ADHD continues into adulthood, presenting challenges to academic work and to career pursuits.

Key Terms

agoraphobia, p. 576

antisocial personality disorder (APD), p. 599

anxiety disorders, p. 574

assessment, p. 567

attention-deficit/hyperactivity disorder (ADHD), p. 608

autism spectrum disorder, p. 604

bipolar I disorder, p. 583

bipolar II disorder, p. 583

borderline personality disorder, p. 597

cognitive-behavioral approach, p. 570

delusions, p. 590

diathesis-stress model, p. 568

disorganized behavior, p. 592

disorganized speech, p. 591

dissociative disorders, p. 586

dissociative identity disorder (DID), p. 587

etiology, p. 562

family systems model, p. 570

generalized anxiety disorder (GAD), p. 575

hallucinations, p. 591

learned helplessness, p. 582

major depressive disorder, p. 579

negative symptoms, p. 592

obsessive-compulsive disorder (OCD), p. 577

panic disorder, p. 576

persistent depressive disorder, p. 580

posttraumatic stress disorder (PTSD), p. 579

psychopathology, p. 562

Research Domain Criteria (RDoC), p. 566

schizophrenia, p. 589

sociocultural model, p. 570

What Are Forensic Psychologists?

On television crime dramas such as *Criminal Minds* and *CSI,* FBI investigators in the Behavioral Analysis Unit race to identify murderers. A case is typically solved when the show's forensic psychologist builds a specific psychological profile that leads to the suspect. Not surprisingly, the popularity of such shows has increased interest in forensic psychology as a career.

How accurate are these portrayals of forensic psychologists? The day-to-day job of forensic psychologists differs from that commonly depicted in the media. For example, forensic psychologists do not engage in "criminal profiling," which is conducted by law enforcement specialists. The American Psychological Association (APA) defines forensic psychology as "the application of clinical specialties to the legal arena" (Ward, 2013). As you have learned in this chapter, clinical psychologists study the causes, assessment, and behavioral implications of psychological disorders. Thus, forensic psychologists are clinical psychologists who apply their expertise in clinical assessment to legal questions and settings.

What do real-life forensic psychologists do? According to the APA, the job most often involves "psychological assessment of individuals who are involved, in one way or another, with the legal system." Forensic psychologists can work in medical examiners' offices, in law enforcement or social service agencies, in mental health centers, or as independent consultants. Their responsibilities may include evaluating child custody disputes, treating victims of crime, designing treatment programs for criminal offenders, and assessing the risk of a criminal's reoffending.

Forensic psychologists can be very influential in court cases. They may testify about the reliability of eyewitness testimony, or they may be called on to assess a defendant's state of mind, particularly in regard to an "insanity defense." Although an insanity plea is ultimately judged legally, not simply psychologically, forensic psychologists aid in the judgment by reconstructing the defendant's probable mental state at the time of the crime. A forensic psychologist might conclude that the accused is suffering from a psychological condition, such as schizophrenia, that prevents the person from distinguishing between right and wrong. Consider the case of Andrea Yates, a mother in Texas who drowned her five children. As a result of evaluations by forensic psychologists, Yates was found not guilty and sentenced to a psychiatric institution.

Becoming a certified forensic psychologist requires earning a doctoral degree (Ph.D. or Psy.D.) in clinical psychology. Clinical programs should include at least two years of supervised experience, such as internships or residency training.

The bottom line: An understanding of clinical assessments has important applications in legal settings and can lead to careers in forensic psychology. Working in offices or agencies or independently, forensic psychologists may provide expert testimony in court cases, evaluate the competency of defendants to stand trial, or design and implement prevention and treatment programs for criminal offenders. Forensic psychology requires a doctoral degree in clinical psychology, including a supervised internship or residency training.

Want to earn a better grade on your test?
Go to **INQUIZITIVE** to learn and review this chapter's content, with personalized feedback along the way.
Practice Tests and accompanying answer keys can be found at the back of the book on page PT-1.

Big Questions

- How Are Psychological Disorders Treated? 616

- What Are the Most Effective Treatments? 633

- Can Personality Disorders Be Treated? 650

- How Should Childhood Disorders and Adolescent Disorders Be Treated? 653

Treatment of Psychological Disorders

WELCOME TO THE FINAL CHAPTER OF THIS TEXTBOOK. If all has gone well, you have found your explorations of psychological science to be useful for understanding yourself and the people around you. But according to the research and statistics, some of you either have psychological disorders or have friends or family members who exhibit them. As noted in Chapter 14, psychological disorders are very common. This chapter has an important message for you. Psychological science has made great progress in identifying effective treatments for most psychological disorders. Ongoing research is refining those treatments and improving people's lives.

This chapter explores the basic principles of therapy and describes how those principles are adapted in the treatment of specific disorders. An important lesson in this coverage is that even though biological factors are present in most psychological disorders, such as autism, the most effective treatments usually involve changing behavior or cognition. For clinical psychologists, the big questions are: How are psychological disorders treated? What are the most effective treatments? Can personality disorders be treated? And how should childhood disorders and adolescent disorders be treated?

- Distinguish among the various
  forms of psychotherapy.

- Describe the major categories
  of psychotropic medications.

- Identify alternative biological
  treatments for psychological
  disorders.

- Understand the role
  of empirical studies in
  determining treatment
  effectiveness.

- Distinguish among the types
  of specialized providers of
  psychological treatment.

psychotherapy
The generic name given to formal
psychological treatment.

biological therapies
Treatment of psychological disorders
based on medical approaches to
disease (what is wrong with the body)
and to illness (what a person feels as
a result).

How Are Psychological Disorders Treated?

At this time, there are no instant cures for psychological disorders. Disorders need to be managed over time through treatment that helps alleviate symptoms so people can function in their daily lives until treatment is no longer necessary. Scientific research has produced tremendous advances in ways of treating many psychological disorders. The choice of treatment depends on the type and severity of symptoms, the diagnosis, and the motivational state of the person needing treatment. Most disorders can be treated in more than one way. However, some disorders are most successfully treated using a particular method or combination of methods.

15.1 Various Methods Have Been Used to Treat Psychopathology

Psychologists use two basic categories of techniques to treat psychological disorders: psychological and biological. Either type of treatment may be used alone, or they may be used in combination. The generic name given to formal psychological treatment is **psychotherapy.** The particular techniques used may depend on the practitioner's training, but all forms of psychotherapy involve interactions between practitioner and client. These interactions are aimed at helping the person understand her symptoms and problems and providing solutions for them. One limitation of any form of psychotherapy is that some psychological disorders are characterized by apathy or indifference and individuals may not be interested in being treated.

Biological therapies reflect medical approaches to disease (what is wrong with the body) and to illness (what a person feels as a result). In other words, these therapies are based on the notion that psychological disorders—often referred to as mental disorders in medical settings—result from abnormalities in neural and bodily processes. For example, the client—often referred to as the patient in medical settings—might be experiencing an imbalance in a specific neurotransmitter or a malfunction in a particular brain region.

Biological treatments range from drugs to electrical stimulation of brain regions to surgical intervention. *Psychopharmacology* is the use of medications that affect brain or body functions. These forms of treatment can be particularly effective for some disorders, at least on a short-term basis. One limitation of biological therapies, however, is that long-term success may require the person to continue treatment. Sometimes, treatment continues indefinitely. Moreover, nonbiological treatments may prove more effective for some disorders over the long term. For many disorders, the recent focus has been on combining biological therapies with other approaches to find the best treatment for each client.

RELATION OF THEORY TO TREATMENT As outlined in Chapter 14, psychologists have proposed a number of theories to account for psychopathology. Some of these theories are about general issues, such as the role of learning or cognition in all psychological disorders. Other theories are specific to a particular disorder, such as the theory that certain types of thought patterns underlie

depression. Each theory includes treatment strategies that are based on the theory's assumptions about the causes of psychological disorders.

Although researchers are continually gaining better understandings of the causes of particular disorders, these understandings do not always lead to further insights into how best to treat the disorders. For example, autism spectrum disorder is clearly caused by biological factors, but this knowledge has not led to any significant advances in therapies for the disorder. In fact, the best available treatment for autism spectrum disorder is based on behavioral, not biological, principles. Likewise, in a situation where the person's loss of a parent has led to clinical depression, drugs might be useful for treatment, at least in the short term. The therapist might favor this biological treatment for this particular person even though the depression was caused by the situation.

Regardless of the treatment provider's theoretical perspective, psychotherapy is generally aimed at changing patterns of thought, emotion, or behavior. The ways in which such changes are brought about can differ dramatically, however. It has been estimated that there are more than 400 approaches to treatment (Kazdin, 1994). Many therapists follow an *eclectic* approach, using various techniques that seem appropriate for a given client. The following discussion highlights the major components of the most common approaches, and it describes how therapists use these methods to treat specific psychological disorders.

 Suppose a particular disorder is clearly biological. Are biological treatments therefore the most appropriate for this disorder?

ANSWER: No. We cannot state that connection categorically. For example, even though autism is a biological disorder, the best available treatment is behavioral.

15.2 Psychodynamic Therapy Seeks to Reduce Unconscious Conflicts

One of the first people to develop psychological treatments for psychological disorders was Sigmund Freud. Freud believed that such disorders were caused by prior experiences, particularly early traumatic experiences. Along with Josef Breuer, he pioneered the method of psychoanalysis.

In early forms of psychoanalysis, the client would lie on a couch while the therapist sat out of view (FIGURE 15.1). This method was meant to reduce the client's inhibitions and allow freer access to unconscious thought processes. Treatment involved uncovering unconscious feelings and drives that Freud believed gave rise to maladaptive thoughts and behaviors. Techniques included *free association* and *dream analysis.* In free association, the client would say whatever came to mind and the therapist would look for signs of unconscious conflicts, especially where the client appeared resistant to discussing certain topics. In dream analysis, the therapist would interpret the hidden meaning of the client's dreams (see the discussion in Chapter 4, "Consciousness").

The general goal of psychoanalysis is to increase the client's awareness of his own unconscious psychological processes and how these processes affect daily functioning. By gaining **insight** of this kind, the client is freed from these unconscious influences. According to psychoanalysis, the client's symptoms diminish as a result of reducing unconscious conflicts. (Note that this use of the term *insight*—to mean an understanding of one's own psychological processes—is different from its use in Chapter 8. There, *insight* means the sudden solution of a problem.) Traditional psychoanalytic therapy is expensive and time consuming, sometimes continuing for many years. The evidence is weak, however, for its effectiveness in treating most psychological disorders. As mentioned throughout this textbook, minimal empirical evidence exists for much of Freudian theorizing, and therefore it is not surprising that treatments based on those theories are largely ineffective.

FIGURE 15.1
Psychoanalysis in Freud's Office
As part of the treatment process, Freud sat behind his desk (partly visible in the lower left corner). His clients reclined on the couch, facing away from him.

insight
The goal of psychoanalysis; a client's awareness of his own unconscious psychological processes and how these processes affect daily functioning.

psychodynamic therapy

A form of therapy based on Freudian theory; it aims to help clients examine needs, defenses, and motives as a way of understanding distress.

behavior therapy

Treatment based on the premise that behavior is learned and therefore can be unlearned through the use of classical and operant conditioning.

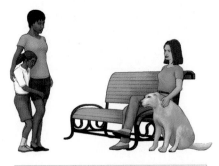

1 The little girl in the white shirt (on the left) has a phobia about dogs.

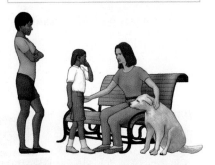

2 She is encouraged to approach a dog that scares her.

3 From this mild form of exposure she learns that the dog is not dangerous, and she overcomes her fear.

FIGURE 15.2
Exposure
Exposure is a common feature of many cognitive-behavioral therapies. In this sequence, a little girl gradually overcomes her fear of dogs by slowly increasing her level of exposure to a dog.

Psychotherapists later reformulated some of Freud's ideas, and these adaptations are known collectively as **psychodynamic therapy.** In using this approach, a therapist aims to help a client examine her needs, defenses, and motives as a way of understanding why the client is distressed. Most proponents of the psychodynamic perspective today continue to embrace Freud's "talking therapy." They have replaced the couch with a chair, however, and the talking tends to be more conversational.

Some features of contemporary psychodynamic therapy include exploring the client's avoidance of distressing thoughts, looking for recurring themes and patterns in thoughts and feelings, discussing early traumatic experiences, focusing on interpersonal relations and childhood attachments, emphasizing the relationship with the therapist, and exploring fantasies, dreams, and daydreams (Shedler, 2010). Some of these features, such as focusing on patterns in thoughts and feelings and addressing interpersonal relationships, are common to most forms of psychotherapy, and thus they do not distinguish psychodynamic therapy from other types of treatment (Tryon & Tryon, 2011).

During the past few decades, the use of psychodynamic therapy has become increasingly controversial. A new approach to psychodynamic therapy consists of offering fewer sessions and focusing more on current relationships than on early-childhood experiences. Therapists who use this approach do not necessarily accept all of Freud's ideas, but they do believe that people have underlying conflicts that need to be resolved, such as their relations with other people. Proponents argue that this short-term psychodynamic therapy has been shown in research as potentially useful for treating certain disorders, including depression, eating disorders, and substance abuse (Leichsenring, Rabung, & Leibing, 2004). Other brief forms of psychodynamic therapy, such as those focusing on emotional conflicts that result from defense mechanisms, have also been found to be more effective than no treatment at all (Lilliengren et al., 2016). However, it is not clear whether the psychodynamic aspects are superior to other brief forms of therapy, such as simply talking about personal problems to a caring therapist. The opportunity to talk about one's problems to someone who will listen plays a role in all therapeutic relationships.

Q What is the role of insight in psychodynamic therapy?

ANSWER: Insight makes people aware of their unconscious conflicts so that they can resolve them.

15.3 Behavioral and Cognitive Treatments Aim to Change Behavior, Emotion, or Thought Directly

Many of the most successful therapies involve trying to change people's behavior, emotion, or thought directly. These therapies are behavioral, cognitive, or a combination of the two. Whereas insight-based therapies consider maladaptive behavior the result of an underlying problem, behavioral and cognitive therapies treat the behavior, emotion, and thought as the problem. For example, the therapist will not be particularly interested in why a person has come to fear elevators, such as if childhood traumas produced the fear. Instead, the therapist is interested in helping the client overcome the fear.

BEHAVIOR THERAPY The premise of **behavior therapy** is that behavior is learned and therefore can be unlearned through the use of classical and operant conditioning.

As discussed in Chapter 6, behavior modification is based on operant conditioning. It is a method of helping people to learn desired behaviors and unlearn unwanted behaviors. Desired behaviors are rewarded (rewards might include small treats or praise). Unwanted behaviors are ignored or punished (punishments might include groundings, time-outs, or the administration of unpleasant tastes). Many treatment centers use token economies, in which people earn tokens for good behavior and can trade the tokens for rewards or privileges.

For a desired behavior to be rewarded, however, the client first must exhibit the behavior. A therapist can use *social skills training* to elicit desired behavior. When a client has particular interpersonal difficulties, such as with initiating a conversation, she learns appropriate ways to act in specific social situations. The first step is often *modeling,* in which the therapist acts out an appropriate behavior. Recall from Chapter 6 that people learn many behaviors by observing others perform them. In modeling, the client is encouraged to imitate the displayed behavior, rehearse it in therapy, and later apply the learned behavior to real-world situations. The successful use of newly acquired social skills is itself rewarding and encourages the continued use of those skills.

Many behavioral therapies for psychological disorders include an **exposure** component. Through this technique, the person is exposed repeatedly to the anxiety-producing stimulus or situation (**FIGURE 15.2**). The theory behind exposure is based on classical conditioning. By confronting feared stimuli in the absence of negative consequences, the person learns new, nonthreatening associations. Exposure therapy is the most effective treatment for any psychological disorder that involves anxiety or fear, including obsessive-compulsive disorder (OCD; Abramowitz, 2013; Foa & McLean, 2016). An intensive form of exposure therapy, called *prolonged exposure,* is effective for posttraumatic stress disorder (PTSD; Cusack et al., 2016; McLean & Foa, 2014). This treatment involves those with PTSD repeatedly revisiting and recounting their traumatic experience and gradually approaching situations that they have been avoiding because of reminders of their traumatic experience.

COGNITIVE THERAPY Cognitive therapy is based on the theory that distorted thoughts can produce maladaptive behaviors and emotions. Treatment strategies that modify these thought patterns should eliminate the maladaptive behaviors and emotions. A number of approaches to cognitive therapy have been proposed. For example, Aaron T. Beck (1964) has advocated **cognitive restructuring** (**FIGURE 15.3**). Through this approach, a clinician seeks to help a person recognize maladaptive thought patterns and replace them with ways of viewing the world that are more in tune with reality (**FIGURE 15.4**). Albert Ellis (1962), another major thinker in this area, introduced *rational-emotive therapy.* Through this approach, the therapist acts as a teacher, explaining the client's errors in thinking and demonstrating more-adaptive ways to think and behave.

In cognitive therapy and rational-emotive therapy, maladaptive behavior is assumed to result from individual belief systems and ways of thinking rather than from objective conditions. By contrast, *interpersonal therapy* focuses on circumstances—namely, relationships the client attempts to avoid. This approach integrates cognitive therapy with psychodynamic insight therapy (Markowitz & Weissman, 1995). Interpersonal therapy developed out of psychodynamic ideas on how people relate to one another, but it uses cognitive techniques that help people gain more-accurate insight into their social relationships. Because interpersonal

exposure
A behavioral therapy technique that involves repeated exposure to an anxiety-producing stimulus or situation.

cognitive therapy
Treatment based on the idea that distorted thoughts produce maladaptive behaviors and emotions; treatment strategies attempt to modify these thought patterns.

cognitive restructuring
A therapy that strives to help clients recognize maladaptive thought patterns and replace them with ways of viewing the world that are more in tune with reality.

FIGURE 15.3
Aaron T. Beck
Aaron T. Beck is one of the pioneers of cognitive therapy for psychological disorders, especially depression.

Maladaptive pattern:

"My boss yelled at me." → "I'm worthless." → Depression

After cognitive restructuring:

"My boss yelled at me." → "My boss was having a bad day." → No depression

FIGURE 15.4
Cognitive Restructuring
Through this technique, a therapist helps a client learn to replace maladaptive thought patterns with more-realistic, positive ones.

functioning is seen as critical to psychological adjustment, treatment focuses on helping clients explore their interpersonal experiences and express their emotions (Blagys & Hilsenroth, 2000).

To help prevent relapse of psychological disorders following treatment, John Teasdale and colleagues (2000) developed *mindfulness-based cognitive therapy*. The principle behind this method is that people who recover from depression continue to be vulnerable to faulty thinking when they experience negative moods. For instance, they may be prone to negative, ruminative thinking. Mindfulness-based cognitive theory is based on principles derived from mindfulness meditation, which originated from Eastern meditation and yoga practices. This therapy has two goals: to help clients become more aware of their negative thoughts and feelings at times when they are vulnerable and to help them learn to disengage from ruminative thinking through meditation. A recent review of studies using this method to prevent recurrence of major depression found that it is quite effective (Kuyken et al., 2016).

cognitive-behavioral therapy (CBT)

A therapy that incorporates techniques from cognitive therapy and behavior therapy to correct faulty thinking and change maladaptive behaviors.

Cognitive-behavioral therapy (CBT) incorporates techniques from cognitive therapy and behavior therapy. CBT tries to correct the client's faulty cognitions and to train the client to engage in new behaviors. Suppose the client has social anxiety disorder—a fear of being viewed negatively by others. The therapist will encourage the client to examine other people's reactions to the client. The aim is to help the client understand how his appraisals of other people's reactions might be inaccurate. At the same time, the therapist will teach the client social skills. CBT is perhaps the most widely used version of psychotherapy, and it is one of the most effective forms of psychotherapy for many types of psychological disorders, especially anxiety disorders and depressive disorders (Deacon & Abramowitz, 2004; Hollon, Thase, & Markowitz, 2002). Because anxiety disorders and depressive disorders are often comorbid, CBT that addresses symptoms of both disorders at the same time is especially effective (Newby, McKinnon, Gilbody, & Dalgleish, 2016).

ANSWER: It is most effective for anxiety disorders because the person learns to associate new, nonthreatening reactions with the feared stimulus.

 What kind of disorder is exposure therapy most effective for, and why?

15.4 The Context of Therapy Matters

Some people seek treatment because symptoms, possibly of a psychological disorder, are interfering with their lives. For example, a person would like to overcome feelings of social anxiety that keep the person trapped in lonely isolation. By contrast, some people are sent to treatment because they behave in ways that cause others significant distress, such as an addict whose behavior causes conflict for his family. The unique circumstances of people's lives affect their symptoms, psychological disorders, and treatments. Accordingly, treatments differ depending on family involvement, client resources, and the culture in which the person needing treatment lives.

One factor that affects the outcome of all therapy is the relationship between the therapist and the client. This connection is true partly because a good relationship can foster an expectation of receiving help (Miller, 2000; Talley, Strupp, & Morey, 1990). Most people in the mental health field use the curative power of client expectation to help their clients achieve success in therapy. This approach is not limited to psychological disorders, however. A good relationship with a service provider is important for any aspect of physical or mental health.

As noted in Chapter 13, the humanistic approach to personality emphasizes personal experience and the individual's belief systems. The goal of humanistic therapy is to treat the person as a whole, not as a collection of behaviors or a repository of repressed thoughts. One of the best-known humanistic therapies is **client-centered therapy.** Developed by the psychologist Carl Rogers (1951), this approach encourages people to fulfill their individual potentials for personal growth through greater self-understanding. A key ingredient of client-centered therapy is to create a safe and comforting setting for clients to access their true feelings (**FIGURE 15.5**). Therapists strive to be genuine and empathic, to take the client's perspective, and to accept the client through unconditional positive regard (see Chapter 13). Instead of directing the client's behavior or passing judgment on the client's actions or thoughts, the therapist helps the client focus on her subjective experience. Often, a client-centered therapist will use *reflective listening,* in which the therapist repeats the client's concerns to help the person clarify her feelings. Although relatively few practitioners follow the tenets of humanistic theory strictly, many techniques advocated by Rogers are used currently to establish a good therapeutic relationship between practitioner and client.

One modern form of humanistic treatment, motivational interviewing, uses a client-centered approach over a very short period (such as one or two interviews). This treatment addresses the client's ambivalence about problematic behaviors, as when a drug addict enjoys using drugs but recognizes the problems created by drug use. The treatment helps clients identify discrepancies between their current state and "where they would like to be" in their lives. By doing so, the therapist can spark the client's motivation for change. Motivational interviewing has proved a useful treatment for many seeking help with drug and alcohol abuse, as well as for increasing both healthy eating habits and exercise (Burke, Arkowitz, & Menchola, 2003). William Miller (2000), the psychologist who developed the technique, attributes the outstanding success of this brief form of empathic therapy to the warmth expressed by the therapist toward the client.

FAMILY THERAPY FOCUSES ON THE FAMILY CONTEXT The therapy a person receives is, of course, an important element in treating a psychological disorder. The person's family often plays an almost equally important role.

According to a *systems approach,* an individual is part of a larger context. Any change in individual behavior will affect the whole system. This effect is often clearest within the family. Each person in a family plays a particular role and interacts with the other members in specific ways. Over the course of therapy, the way the individual thinks, behaves, and interacts with others may change. Such changes can profoundly affect the family dynamics. For instance, an alcoholic who gives up drinking may start to criticize other members of the family when they drink. In turn, the family members might provide less support for the person's continuing abstinence. After all, if the family members do not have drinking problems, they might resent the comments. If they do have drinking problems, they might resist the comments because they do not want to give up drinking.

Family attitudes are often critical to long-term prognoses. For this reason, some therapists insist that family members be involved in therapy when practical, except when including them is impossible or would be counterproductive. All the family members involved in therapy are together considered the client. For instance, suppose a child's defiant behavior has led to conflict between the parents, who disagree about how to respond to the child (**FIGURE 15.6**). In this case, the treatment will involve not only working on the child's behavior but also helping the parents learn to resolve their parenting disagreements.

client-centered therapy
An empathic approach to therapy; it encourages people to fulfill their individual potentials for personal growth through greater self-understanding.

FIGURE 15.5
Humanistic Therapy
Carl Rogers founded the form of humanistic therapy called client-centered therapy. Here, Rogers **(far right, facing camera)** leads a group therapy session, demonstrating the importance of a safe and comforting environment in the pursuit of greater self-understanding.

FIGURE 15.6
Family Therapy
The actions, reactions, and interactions of family members can become important topics during therapy.

There is also evidence that helping families provide appropriate social support leads to better therapy outcomes and reduces relapses for individuals in treatment. The key is the type of family involvement. For instance, studies have documented the importance of attitudes expressed by family members toward people with schizophrenia. In this context, **expressed emotion** is a pattern of negative actions by a client's family members. The pattern includes making critical comments about the person, being hostile toward the person, and being emotionally overinvolved (e.g., being overprotective, pitying, or having an exaggerated response to the person's disorder). The level of expressed emotion from family members corresponds to the relapse rate for those with schizophrenia (Hooley, 2007; Hooley & Gotlib, 2000), and relapse rates are highest if the person has a great deal of contact with the family.

expressed emotion
A pattern of negative actions by a client's family members; the pattern includes critical comments, hostility directed toward the person by family members, and emotional overinvolvement.

CULTURAL BELIEFS AFFECT TREATMENT Societal definitions of both psychological health and psychological disorders are central to the treatments used in psychotherapy. Culture has multiple influences on the way psychological disorders are expressed, on which people with psychological disorders are likely to recover, and on people's willingness to seek help.

Psychotherapy is accepted to different extents in different countries. Some countries, such as China and India, have relatively few psychotherapists. Many of these countries are seeing a growing need, as the last two decades or so of economic expansion have brought increasingly stressful lifestyles and an awareness of the mental health problems that come with them. However, the people in some of these countries are resistant to even discussing psychological problems, much less treating them. Because of traditional cultural beliefs, many Chinese distrust emotional expression and avoid seeking help for depression, anger, or grief (Magnier, 2008). Likewise, in India, because of the stigma of psychological disorders, terms such as *mental illness, depression,* and *anxiety* are avoided; instead, terms such as *tension* and *strain* are used to communicate psychological health problems (Kohn, 2008). Thus, providers need to be sensitive both to the cultural meanings of disorders and to how psychological treatments are regarded within those cultures (**FIGURE 15.7**).

GROUP THERAPY BUILDS SOCIAL SUPPORT Group therapy rose in popularity after World War II. Because of the many stresses related to the war, more people needed therapy than there were therapists available to treat them. Therapists came to realize that in some instances group therapy offers advantages over individual therapy. The most obvious benefit is cost: Group therapy is often significantly less expensive than individual treatment. Especially when financial resources are limited, group therapy can be an effective way for people to experience the benefits of treatment. In addition, the group setting provides an opportunity for members to improve their social skills and learn from one another's experiences.

Group therapies vary widely in the types of people enrolled, the duration of treatment, the theoretical perspective of the therapist running the group, and the group size—although some practitioners believe around eight people is the ideal number. Many groups are organized around a particular type of problem (e.g., sexual abuse) or around a particular type of person (e.g., those who are transgender). Many groups continue over long periods, with some members leaving and others joining the group at various intervals. Depending on the approach favored by the therapist, the group may be highly structured, or

FIGURE 15.7
Cultural Effects on Therapy
A psychologist counsels a young victim of the massive earthquake in the Sichuan province of China, 2008.

it may be a more loosely organized forum for discussion. Behavioral and cognitive-behavioral groups are usually highly structured, with specific goals and techniques designed to modify the thought and behavior patterns of group members. This type of group has been effective for disorders such as bulimia and OCD.

In contrast, less structured groups usually focus on increasing insight and providing social support. In fact, the social support that group members can provide each other is one of the most beneficial aspects of this type of therapy. Those who are experiencing similar issues in their lives might more easily empathize with the experiences of other group members (Heck, 2016). As a result, group therapy is often used to augment individual psychotherapy.

 What is reflective listening?

ANSWER: a part of humanistic approaches to treatment, in which the therapist listens and then repeats the client's concerns to help the person clarify her feelings

15.5 Medication Is Effective for Certain Disorders

Drugs have proved effective for treating some psychological disorders. Their use is based on the assumption that psychological disorders result from deficits or excesses in specific neurotransmitters or because receptors for those neurotransmitters are not functioning properly. Although this assumption is not always supported by evidence, the use of drugs may provide relief from symptoms of psychological disorders. Drugs that affect mental processes are called **psychotropic medications.** They act by changing brain neurochemistry. For example, they inhibit action potentials, or they alter synaptic transmission to increase or decrease the action of particular neurotransmitters (see Chapter 3, "Biology and Behavior").

psychotropic medications
Drugs that affect mental processes.

Most psychotropic medications fall into three categories: anti-anxiety drugs, antidepressants, and antipsychotics. Note, however, that sometimes drugs from one category are used to treat a disorder from another category, such as using an anti-anxiety drug to treat depression. One reason for this is comorbidity. For example, as discussed in Chapter 14, a substantial number of people suffering from depression also meet diagnostic criteria for an anxiety disorder. Another reason is that in most cases there is insufficient evidence about why a particular drug is effective in reducing symptoms of a psychological disorder. That is, many questions remain about how brain chemistry is related to psychological disorders, and many drug treatments have been based on trial-and-error clinical studies in which different drugs have been used to see if they reduce symptoms.

Other drugs used to treat psychological disorders do not fall into traditional categories. Many of them are used as mood stabilizers. *Lithium* was long considered the most effective treatment for bipolar disorder, although the neural mechanisms of how it works are unknown. Drugs that prevent seizures, called *anticonvulsants,* can also stabilize moods in bipolar disorder. As discussed in Section 15.14, antipsychotic medications are also effective for treatment of bipolar disorder.

ANTI-ANXIETY DRUGS **Anti-anxiety drugs,** also called *anxiolytics,* are used for the short-term treatment of anxiety. One class of anti-anxiety drugs is the benzodiazepines (such as Xanax and Ativan). These drugs increase the activity of GABA, the most pervasive inhibitory neurotransmitter. Although benzodiazepines reduce anxiety and promote relaxation, they also induce drowsiness and are highly addictive. They should therefore be used sparingly. Sleeping pills (including Ambien and Lunesta) also produce their effects through GABA receptors, although they are not classic benzodiazepines. They bind mainly with receptors that induce sleep rather than relaxation.

anti-anxiety drugs
A class of psychotropic medications used for the treatment of anxiety.

antidepressants

A class of psychotropic medications used for the treatment of depression.

ANTIDEPRESSANTS The second class of psychotropic medications is the **antidepressants.** These drugs are primarily used to treat depression. However, they are often used for other disorders, particularly anxiety disorders. *Monoamine oxidase (MAO) inhibitors* were the first antidepressants to be discovered. Monoamine oxidase is an enzyme that breaks down serotonin, norepinephrine, and dopamine in the synapse. MAO inhibitors therefore stop this process and result in more of those neurotransmitters being available in the synapse. A second category of antidepressant medications is the *tricyclic antidepressants,* named after their core molecular structure of three rings. These drugs inhibit the reuptake of mainly serotonin and norepinephrine, resulting in more of each neurotransmitter being available in the synapse. More recently, *selective serotonin reuptake inhibitors (SSRIs)* have been introduced; the best-known is Prozac. These drugs inhibit the reuptake of serotonin, but they act on other neurotransmitters to a significantly lesser extent. (**FIGURE 15.8** depicts the way SSRIs work.)

Some critics have charged that SSRIs are too often used to treat people who are sad and have low self-esteem but who are not clinically depressed. Such widespread prescribing of SSRIs is a problem because, like all drugs, SSRIs have side effects. For example, SSRIs can lead to sexual dysfunction. At the same time, SSRIs have been valuable for various disorders. Therefore, when the use of SSRIs is being considered, the potential side effects should be weighed against the potential benefits.

antipsychotics

A class of psychotropic medications used for the treatment of schizophrenia and other disorders that involve psychosis.

ANTIPSYCHOTICS The third class of psychotropic medications is the **antipsychotics,** also known as *neuroleptics.* Antipsychotics are used to treat schizophrenia and other disorders that involve psychosis. These drugs reduce symptoms such as delusions and hallucinations. Traditional antipsychotics are dopamine antagonists that

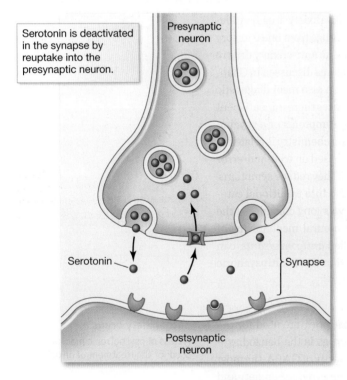

Serotonin is deactivated in the synapse by reuptake into the presynaptic neuron.

Presynaptic neuron

Serotonin

Synapse

Postsynaptic neuron

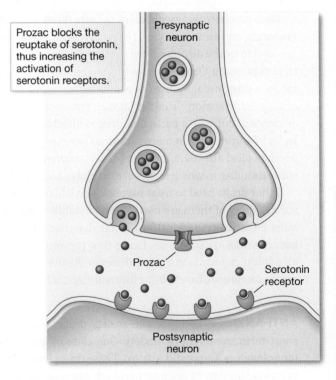

Prozac blocks the reuptake of serotonin, thus increasing the activation of serotonin receptors.

Presynaptic neuron

Prozac

Serotonin receptor

Postsynaptic neuron

FIGURE 15.8
Selective Serotonin Reuptake Inhibitors
SSRIs, such as Prozac, block reuptake of serotonin into the presynaptic neuron. In this way, they allow serotonin to remain in the synapse, where its effects on postsynaptic receptors are prolonged. The greater amount of serotonin in the synapse is presumed to alleviate depression.

bind to dopamine receptors, thus blocking the effects of dopamine. Antipsychotics are not always effective, however, and they have significant side effects that can be irreversible. One such side effect of long-term use is *tardive dyskinesia,* the involuntary twitching of muscles, especially in the neck and face. Moreover, these drugs are not useful for treating the negative symptoms of schizophrenia, such as apathy and social withdrawal (see Chapter 14, "Psychological Disorders").

USE OF PSYCHOTROPIC MEDICATIONS Psychotropic medications are very commonly prescribed in the United States. In 2013, about 1 in 6 U.S. adults reported filling one or more prescriptions for drugs to treat psychological disorders, including 12 percent for antidepressants, 8.3 percent for anti-anxiety drugs or sleeping pills, and 1.6 percent for antipsychotics (Moore & Mattison, 2017). Although the use of antipsychotics did not vary by any demographic group, women were about twice as likely as men to fill prescriptions for antidepressants and anti-anxiety drugs. White Americans were much more likely to have used these prescription psychotropic medications (**FIGURE 15.9**), although it is possible that bias in diagnosis and treatment may be involved.

The use of drugs to treat anxiety and depressive disorders has increased substantially over the past three decades. Some commentators have raised concerns that many people who are simply unhappy but otherwise well adjusted are diagnosed and treated medically for psychopathology (Dowrick & Francis, 2013). For another perspective on the increased use of biological treatments, however, consider the many white Americans who have turned to opioids or excessive alcohol intake to deal with their negative emotions. As noted in Chapter 11, white Americans without a college education have high rates of drug overdose and alcoholic-related diseases and increased mortality. Although the cause of this increase in premature deaths is not entirely clear (Case & Deaton, 2015), the use of prescribed biological treatments may serve an important role in relieving significant psychological distress—and therefore improving mortality rates—for this segment of the population.

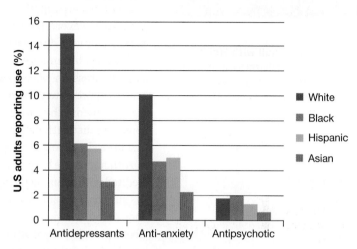

FIGURE 15.9

Racial Differences in Use of Psychotropic Medications

Overall, about 1 in 6 U.S. adults used some form of psychotropic medication. White Americans were much more likely to use antidepressants and anti-anxiety medications (including sleeping pills) than other groups. There are no differences in the use of antipsychotics.

 What is the primary neurotransmitter affected by anti-anxiety drugs?

ANSWER: Anti-anxiety drugs increase the activity of GABA, which is the primary neurotransmitter that inhibits brain activity.

15.6 Alternative Biological Treatments Are Used in Extreme Cases

Not all people are treated successfully with psychotherapy or medication or both combined. These people are called treatment resistant. To alleviate disorders, treatment providers may attempt alternative biological methods. Such alternatives include brain surgery, the use of magnetic fields, and electrical stimulation. All of these methods are used to alter brain function. These treatments are often used as last resorts because they are more likely to have serious side effects than psychotherapy or medication will. Many early efforts reflected crude attempts to control disruptive behavior. More-recent approaches reflect a growing understanding of the brain mechanisms that underlie various psychological disorders.

FIGURE 15.10
Prehistoric Skull with Holes
A skull at the Archaeological Museum in Cusco, Peru, bears the marks of a cranial surgical operation performed by the Incas.

electroconvulsive therapy (ECT)
A procedure that involves administering a strong electrical current to the person's brain to produce a seizure; it is effective for some cases of severe depression.

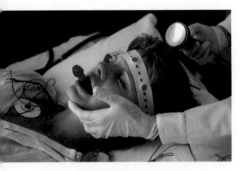

FIGURE 15.11
Electroconvulsive Therapy
A woman being prepared for ECT has a soft object placed between her teeth to prevent her from hurting her tongue. ECT is most commonly used to treat severe depression that has not been responsive to medication or psychotherapy.

As discussed in Chapter 1, for many centuries people have recognized that the brain is involved with the mind, including the mind's abnormalities. From locations as varied as France and Peru, scientists have found numerous prehistoric skulls in which holes were made (**FIGURE 15.10**). Many of the holes were healed over to some extent, indicating that the recipients survived for years after their procedures. Such surgery, called *trepanning,* may have been used to let out evil spirits believed to be causing unusual behavior. In parts of Africa and the Pacific, various groups still practice trepanning as a treatment for epilepsy, headaches, and symptoms of mental disturbance.

Early in the twentieth century, medical researchers went beyond cutting holes in the skull to manipulating the brain. One of the earliest formal procedures used on people with severe disorders was *psychosurgery,* in which areas of the frontal cortex were selectively damaged (see the discussion of lobotomy in Section 3.7). These prefrontal lobotomies were used to treat severe disorders, including schizophrenia, major depression, and anxiety disorders. To understand such drastic measures, we need to appreciate that treatment for psychological disorders had made almost no progress before the 1950s. Those with disorders were simply restrained and warehoused in institutions for their entire lives. In this climate of medical desperation, various risky procedures were explored.

Although some brain surgeries were performed as early as the 1880s, Egas Moniz is credited with bringing the practice to the attention of the medical world in the 1930s. His surgical procedure, later known as prefrontal lobotomy, involved severing nerve-fiber pathways in the prefrontal cortex (see Figure 3.28). After patients received lobotomies, they were often listless and had flat affect. Moreover, the procedure often impaired many important mental functions, such as abstract thought, planning, motivation, and social interaction. With the development of effective pharmacological treatments in the 1950s, the use of lobotomy was discontinued. Nowadays some brain surgery is used for disorders, but it involves small regions of the brain and is typically performed only as a last resort.

ELECTROCONVULSIVE THERAPY Electroconvulsive therapy (ECT) involves placing electrodes on a person's head and administering an electrical current strong enough to produce a seizure (**FIGURE 15.11**). This procedure was developed in Europe in the 1930s and tried on the first human in 1938. In the 1950s and 1960s, it was commonly used to treat some psychological disorders, including schizophrenia and depression.

The general public has a very negative view of ECT. Ken Kesey's 1962 novel *One Flew over the Cuckoo's Nest,* and the award-winning 1975 film version, did a great deal to expose the abuses in mental health care and graphically depicted ECT as well as the tragic effects of lobotomy. Although care for the disordered is still far from perfect, many reforms have been implemented. ECT now generally occurs under anesthesia, with powerful muscle relaxants to eliminate motor convulsions and confine the seizure to the brain. As you will learn in Section 15.12, ECT is particularly effective for some cases of severe depression, but there are some risks to its use.

TRANSCRANIAL MAGNETIC STIMULATION During transcranial magnetic stimulation (TMS), as discussed in Chapter 3, a powerful electrical current produces a magnetic field that is about 40,000 times Earth's magnetic field. When rapidly switched on and off, this magnetic field induces an electrical current in the brain region directly below the wire coil, thereby interrupting neural function in that region (**FIGURE 15.12**).

In *single-pulse TMS,* the disruption of brain activity occurs only during the brief period of stimulation. For instance, a pulse given over a motor region might interfere with a person's ability to reach smoothly toward a target object. A pulse given over the

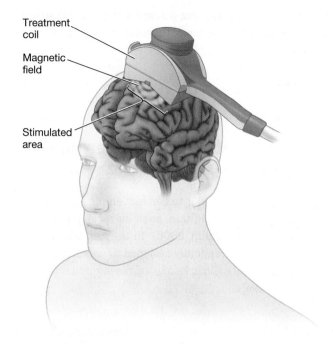

Treatment coil
Magnetic field
Stimulated area

FIGURE 15.12
Transcranial Magnetic Stimulation
In TMS, current flows through a wire coil placed over the scalp where a brain area is to be stimulated. The stimulation interrupts neural function in that region. TMS is used mainly to treat severe depression.

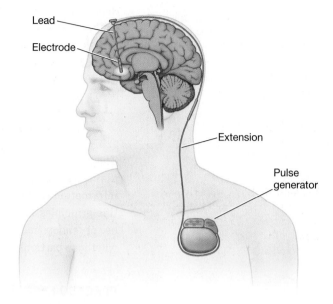

Lead
Electrode
Extension
Pulse generator

FIGURE 15.13
Deep Brain Stimulation
In DBS, an electrical generator placed just under the skin below the collarbone sends out continuous stimulation to the implanted electrodes. DBS is used for various medical conditions (such as Parkinson's disease), OCD, and major depression.

speech region may disrupt speaking momentarily. If multiple pulses of TMS occur over an extended time, the procedure is known as *repeated TMS*. Here, the disruption can last beyond the period of direct stimulation. Researchers are investigating the therapeutic potential of this procedure in treating various disorders; as noted in Section 15.12, TMS may be useful for treating depression (Brunoni et al., 2017; Padberg & George, 2009).

DEEP BRAIN STIMULATION One of the most dramatic new techniques for treating severe disorders is *deep brain stimulation (DBS)*. This technique involves surgically implanting electrodes deep within the brain. The location of the electrodes depends on which disorder is being treated. Mild electricity is then used to stimulate the brain at an optimal frequency and intensity, much the way a pacemaker stimulates the heart (**FIGURE 15.13**).

This procedure was first widely used to treat the symptoms of Parkinson's disease. As discussed in Chapter 3, Parkinson's is a disorder of the dopamine system and causes problems with movement. Electrodes implanted into motor regions of the brains of Parkinson's patients reverse many of the movement problems associated with the disease (DeLong & Wichmann, 2008). The success of DBS for Parkinson's is so great that it is now the treatment of choice for many patients. This is true, in part, because the drugs used to treat Parkinson's often cause undesirable side effects, such as increased involuntary movements. By contrast, DBS has few side effects and a low complication rate, as is typical of any minor surgical procedure. Given DBS's tremendous success in treating Parkinson's—with more than 75,000 people worldwide receiving this treatment (Shah et al., 2010)—DBS is being tested for treating other disorders, including psychological disorders. And as discussed in Section 15.12, DBS might be especially valuable for treating severe OCD and depression.

 What is the primary difference between ECT and TMS?

ANSWER: Although both forms of treatment disrupt brain activity, ECT uses electrical currents, whereas TMS uses a strong magnetic field.

15.7 Effectiveness of Treatment Is Determined by Empirical Evidence

The only way to know whether a treatment is valid is to conduct empirical research that compares the treatment with a control condition, such as receiving helpful information or having supportive listeners (Kazdin, 2008). In keeping with scientific principles, client-participants should be randomly assigned to conditions. The use of *randomized clinical trials* is one of the hallmarks of good research to establish whether a particular treatment is effective.

PLACEBO EFFECT A placebo is an inert substance. That is, it does not contain any active ingredients. Scientists often study a drug or treatment technique by comparing it with a control condition that consists of a placebo. As described in Chapter 2, research participants are typically assigned at random to either an experimental group or a control group. Randomization helps ensure that groups are comparable and also controls for many potential confounds. In studies of treatments for psychological disorders, the experimental group receives the drug or form of psychotherapy, and the control group receives a comparable placebo treatment. Ideally, everything about the two groups is as similar as possible. If the treatment consists of a large blue pill or weekly meetings with a therapist, the placebo group would take a large blue pill or meet weekly with a therapist. For the placebo group, however, the pill is inert (e.g., a "sugar pill"), or the therapist simply talks with rather than teaches the client specific cognitive or behavioral techniques being examined in the experimental condition. Any improvement in mental health, attributed to the inert drug or minimal contact, is called the **placebo effect.**

For a placebo to reduce symptoms of psychopathology, the participant must believe it will. The person who receives the placebo must not know that, for example, the pills are chemically inert. Indeed, placebos that also produce minor physical reactions that people associate with drug effects—such as having a dry mouth—produce the strongest placebo effects. The placebo effect is "all in the head," but the effect is real—all of our thoughts and feelings are in our heads. Brain imaging shows that when patients have positive expectations about a placebo, the neural processes involved in responding to it are similar to the ones activated in response to a biologically active treatment (Benedetti, Mayberg, Wager, Stohler, & Zubieta, 2005). Consider drugs that interfere with the body's natural method of reducing pain. These drugs also make pain relievers or placebos equally ineffective (Amanzio & Benedetti, 1999). This result indicates that the body has responded in the same way to the pain relievers and to the placebos. Thus, for studies to show that a particular treatment is effective, the results of those studies must illustrate that the treatment's effects are stronger than placebo effects.

The use of placebos for psychotherapy is more complicated than for drug research (Herbert & Gaudiano, 2005). Part of the complication is that a therapist likely knows if she is providing the treatment or the control procedure. Moreover, what if just meeting and talking to a therapist is sufficient to treat psychological disorders? One of the

placebo effect

An improvement in physical or mental health following treatment with a placebo—that is, with a drug or treatment that has no active component on the disorder being treated.

long-standing debates in clinical research is whether all therapies are pretty much equally effective because of *common factors* involved in all therapist-client interactions or whether *specific factors* make some treatments better than others (Baskin, Tierney, Minami, & Wampold, 2003; Bjornsson, 2011). Although the opportunity to talk about one's problems to someone who is caring and empathic is important in all therapies, compelling evidence indicates that particular treatments are most effective for specific disorders and are less effective for others (Barlow, Bullis, Comer, & Ametaj, 2013).

PSYCHOLOGICAL TREATMENTS David Barlow (2004), a leading researcher on anxiety disorders, points out that findings from medical studies often lead to dramatic changes in treatment practice. For example, within a year after evidence emerged that arthroscopic knee surgery did not produce better outcomes than sham surgery (in which there was no actual procedure), use of the knee surgery declined dramatically. Such developments reflect the increasing importance of *evidence-based treatments* in medicine. Barlow argues that psychological disorders should always be treated in ways that scientific research has shown to be effective. He prefers the term *psychological treatments* to distinguish evidence-based treatment from the more generic term *psychotherapy*, which refers to any form of therapy.

Three features characterize psychological treatments. First, treatments vary according to the particular psychological disorder and the person's specific psychological symptoms. Just as treatment for asthma differs from that for psoriasis, treatments for panic disorder are likely to differ from those for bulimia nervosa. Second, the techniques used in these treatments have been developed in the laboratory by psychologists, especially behavioral, cognitive, and social psychologists. Third, no overall grand theory guides treatment. Instead, treatment is based on evidence of its effectiveness.

There is some debate regarding the most appropriate methods and criteria used to assess clinical research (e.g., Benjamin, 2005; Westen, Novotny, & Thompson-Brenner, 2004). Jonathan Shedler (2015) has pointed out that evidence-based treatments can be statistically significant without providing any practical improvement in symptoms. That is, even though the treatment group may improve more than the nontreatment group on some measures, the treatment might not provide sufficient relief that people are able to function effectively in their daily lives.

DANGEROUS TREATMENTS Just as we need to use critical thinking to recognize and avoid flawed science, we also need to recognize and avoid therapies with no scientific basis to confirm their effectiveness. Unfortunately, many available therapies have no scientific basis. Such therapies include ones in which people reenact their own births, scream, or have their body parts manipulated (**FIGURE 15.14**).

Some treatments widely believed to be effective are actually counterproductive. These programs include encouraging people to describe their experiences following major trauma, such as an earthquake; scaring adolescents away from committing crimes by exposing them to prisoners or tough treatments; having police officers run drug education programs such as DARE; and using hypnosis to recover painful memories. These methods not only lack adequate evidence but also may produce results opposite to those intended (Hines, 2003; Lilienfeld, 2007). That is, people debriefed after natural disasters are slightly more likely to develop PTSD than those who are not debriefed, teens in "scared straight" programs show an increase in conduct problems, children in DARE programs are more likely to drink alcohol and smoke cigarettes than children who do not attend such programs, and hypnosis can produce false memories (as discussed in Chapter 7, "Memory").

FIGURE 15.14

John Lennon, Yoko Ono, and Primal Scream Therapy

The late Beatle John Lennon and his wife, the artist Yoko Ono, are probably the most famous people to have undergone scream therapy. They undertook this treatment for about four months in 1970. After ending the treatment early, Lennon said that he found it helpful but unnecessary— that he knew himself better than the therapist could. Lennon and Ono both used screams in their music. Regardless of possible artistic inspiration, there is no scientific evidence that scream therapy has any beneficial effect.

In addition, many self-help books make questionable claims. Consider *Make Anyone Fall in Love with You in 5 Minutes* or *Three Easy Steps for Having High Self-Esteem*. It is important to recognize the difference between evidence-based psychotherapies and "alternative," or "fringe," therapies because the latter can prevent people from getting effective treatment and may even be dangerous. In one tragic case, a 10-year-old girl died from suffocation after being wrapped in a blanket for 70 minutes during a supposed therapy session to simulate her own birth, an untested and unscientific method being used to correct the child's unruly behavior (Lowe, 2001). The people conducting the session were unlicensed. They had not passed the tests that certify knowledge about psychotherapy.

 Q Are placebo effects real?

ANSWER: Yes. Research shows that successful action of placebos results from brain activity similar to that produced by other treatments.

15.8 Various Providers Can Assist in Treatment for Psychological Disorders

As noted in Chapter 14, nearly half of all Americans meet *DSM* criteria for a psychological disorder at some point in their lives, with 25 percent of the population meeting criteria within any given year (Kessler & Wang, 2008). A dizzying array of providers offer treatment (**FIGURE 15.15**). The providers range from those with limited training (e.g., former addicts who provide peer counseling) to those with advanced degrees in psychopathology and its treatment (**TABLE 15.1**). In addition to mental health specialists, regular health care providers (e.g., internists, pediatricians), human-services workers (e.g., school counselors), and volunteers (e.g., self-help groups) also assist people with psychological disorders. No matter who administers the therapy, however, most of the techniques used have emerged from psychological laboratories.

One major difference between psychiatrists and clinical psychologists is the ability to prescribe medications. Clinical psychologists typically are not able to prescribe medications, although efforts are under way to give them such privileges. In New Mexico and Louisiana, clinical pyschologists with specialized training in psychoactive drugs can prescribe medications; similar legislation is being proposed

(a)

(b)

(c)

FIGURE 15.15
Providers of Psychological Treatment
Many types of professionals provide treatment for psychological disorders. **(a)** Psychiatrists work in hospitals and treatment centers and can prescribe drugs to treat people with psychological disorders. **(b)** Clinical psychologists either work with clients providing therapy or conduct research on the effectiveness of various treatments for psychological disorders. **(c)** Paraprofessionals often work in the community and provide outreach services to people with psychological disorders.

Table 15.1 Providers of Psychological Treatment

SPECIALTY	TRAINING	DEGREE	TYPICAL EMPLOYMENT
Clinical psychologists	5-7 years of graduate school conducting research on psychological disorders and treatment, including 1 year of clinical internship	Ph.D.	Academics, private practice, hospitals, schools, mental health centers, substance abuse programs
	4-6 years of graduate school developing clinical skills to treat people with psychological disorders, followed by 1 year of internship	Psy.D.	Private practice, medical settings, mental health centers, substance abuse programs
Psychiatrists	4 years of medical school with 3-5 years of additional specialization in residency programs to treat people with psychological disorders	M.D.	Hospitals, private practice, mental health centers, academics, substance abuse programs
Counseling psychologists	4-6 years of graduate school developing clinical skills to treat clients' adjustment and life stress problems (academic, relationship, work) but not psychological disorders	Ph.D., Ed.D.	University student health clinics, mental health centers, private practice, schools, wellness programs, rehabilitation facilities, business and organizational settings
Psychiatric social workers	2-3 years of graduate training on directing clients to appropriate social and community agency resources, plus specialized training in mental health care	M.S.W.	Mental health centers, private practice, hospitals, community and social service agencies, substance abuse programs
Psychiatric nurses	2 years for an associate's degree (A.S.N., R.N.), 4 years for a bachelor's degree (B.S.N.), or 2-3 additional years of graduate training (M.S.N.), but all focus on nursing plus special training in the care of clients with psychological disorders	A.S.N., R.N., B.S.N, M.S.N.	Hospitals, mental health centers, residential treatment programs
Paraprofessionals	Work under supervision to assist those with mental health problems in the challenges of daily living	Limited advanced training, no advanced degree	Community outreach programs, crisis centers, substance abuse centers, pastoral counseling, mental health hotlines

Note. Ph.D. = Doctor of Philosophy in Psychology; Psy.D. = Doctor of Psychology; M.D. = Doctor of Medicine; Ed.D. = Doctor of Education; M.S.W. = Master of Social Work; A.S.N. = Associate of Science in Nursing; R.N. = Registered Nurse; B.S.N. = Bachelor of Science in Nursing; M.S.N. = Master of Science in Nursing.

elsewhere in the United States (McGrath, 2010). However, in most places—including Canada, Australia, and the United Kingdom—only psychiatrists can legally prescribe medications.

TECHNOLOGY AND TREATMENT One of the central problems with treating psychological disorders is that there simply are not enough trained people available to provide traditional one-on-one psychotherapy to all who need it. After all, there is only around one mental health provider for every 529 Americans (Mental Health America, 2017). If one-quarter of the U.S. population has a disorder in a given year, then approximately 82 million people could benefit from treatment. Accordingly, a number of programs have been developed to broaden the reach of treatment (Kazdin & Blase, 2011). Through telephone hotlines, for instance, trained volunteers can help people in crisis deal with psychological issues.

Advances in technology have produced other methods for providing treatment to those who are not physically present. *Technology-based treatments* use minimal contact with therapists and rely on smartphones, computer programs, or the Internet to offer some form of psychological treatment. For instance, smartphone applications can enable people to keep track of their moods and mental states. The applications can then recommend specific exercises to help people deal with what they are feeling and thinking. These methods appear to be especially useful for treating problems with addiction, including drug abuse, pathological gambling, and smoking (Newman, Szkodny, Llera, & Przeworski, 2011). For example, the Web site ModeratedDrinking .com assists people who are dealing with alcohol problems. A study that randomly assigned problem drinkers to a control group or a Web-based treatment at ModeratedDrinking.com found that the program led to improved long-term outcomes in days abstaining from alcohol, although it was mainly effective for those who were not heavy drinkers (Hester, Delaney, & Campbell, 2011). Internet-based treatments are also successful for a wide range of psychological disorders (Andersson, 2016; Schmidt & Keough, 2011).

Q Can all providers prescribe psychotropic medications?

ANSWER: No. In most places, only psychiatrists can prescribe medications.

15.9 How Do You Find a Therapist Who Can Help You?

College students are sometimes apprehensive about seeking therapeutic support for dealing with life stressors or psychological problems. That apprehension is understandable. After all, stepping into a stranger's office and disclosing your personal thoughts and feelings is not easy (**FIGURE 15.16**). Nor is it easy to admit—to yourself or others—that you need extra support. If you decide the time has come, knowing how to find a therapist can quell some of the apprehension you might be feeling. The following questions and answers address issues commonly on the minds of therapy-seeking college students.

How do I know if I need therapy? Many times, family members, friends, professors, or physicians encourage college students to seek help for psychological problems. For example, if a student complains about feeling tired all the time, a doctor might ask if the student has been under stress or feeling sad. These conditions might indicate that the person is suffering from depression and could be helped by a therapist. Of course, sometimes a student knows he has a psychological problem and does not need encouragement to seek out a therapist. For example, a student who struggles night after night to fall asleep because of constant worry about academic performance might seek help for dealing with anxiety.

You do not have to be 100 percent certain that you need therapy before seeking it out. You can think of the first couple of sessions as a trial period to help you figure out if therapy might be a valuable tool in your situation.

What kinds of issues can therapists help with? Therapists can help students deal with various issues, ranging from acute stressors (e.g., preparing to move across the country for graduate school) to chronic concerns (e.g., managing generalized anxiety disorder). They can help students make lifestyle or behavior changes or provide treatments if the students have a psychological disorder.

How do I find a therapist who is a good fit with me and my needs? Most college campuses have counselors who can direct students to appropriate treatment providers. In addition, you can ask friends, teachers, and clergy members if they can

FIGURE 15.16
Meeting with a Therapist
The relationship between client and therapist is necessarily intimate. A person with some sort of problem meets with a professional who seeks to offer help. If the relationship succeeds, the trust that develops between the client and the therapist will be a major component of that success.

recommend someone in your area. And organizations such as the American Psychological Association host referral services, many of which are free and Web based.

But just because you have the name and phone number of a therapist does not mean she will be a good fit for you. To make that determination, you will want to do some information gathering up front. First, what are your preferences? Do you think you would be more comfortable working with someone who is the same gender as you? Or with someone from a similar cultural background? Second, it is a good idea to ask the therapist about her level of experience helping people with your particular problem (e.g., depression, procrastination, coming out to your parents). Third, pay attention to your comfort level as you interact with the therapist during the first session or two. It is critical that you find a therapist who is trustworthy and caring. The initial consultation should make you feel at ease and hopeful that your issue can be resolved.

If you do not feel a connection with one therapist, seek another. In other words, it might take more than one try for you to find someone you want to work with. This effort will be well spent. Ultimately, the rapport you feel with your therapist will be a key indicator of therapeutic success. Choosing the right therapist can be difficult, but it is extremely important for ensuring successful treatment.

Will my therapist prescribe medication? Typically, only psychiatrists (medical doctors with special training in treating psychological disorders; see Section 15.8) are legally permitted to prescribe medication, though the laws vary by state. That said, almost all therapists have arrangements with physicians who can prescribe medications, including psychotropic drugs, if necessary. The question of the ability to prescribe medication should play only a minor role in the choice of therapist. It is more important to find someone who strikes you as empathic and who is experienced in the effective treatments for your problem.

Remember, therapy involves a kind of relationship. Just as you would not expect every first date to be a love connection, do not expect every therapist to be a good fit for you. As in dating, you might have to shop around to find someone you connect with. ■

ANSWER: No. If you have a condition that is causing you distress or interfering with your ability to function, you should consider seeing if a therapist can help.

Q Do you have to be completely certain you have a psychological disorder to seek help?

What Are the Most Effective Treatments?

Research over the past three decades has shown that certain types of treatments are particularly effective for specific types of psychological disorders (Barlow et al., 2013). Other treatments do not have empirical support. Moreover, the scientific study of treatment indicates that although some psychological disorders are quite easily treated, others are not. For instance, highly effective treatments exist for anxiety disorders, mood disorders, and sexual dysfunction, but few treatments for alcoholism are superior to the natural course of recovery that many people undergo without psychological treatment (Seligman, Walker, & Rosenhan, 2001). People who experience depression following the death of a loved one usually feel better with the passage of time. That is, people often resolve personal problems on their own without psychological treatment. Because people tend to enter therapy when they experience crises, they often show improvements no matter what therapy they receive. The following sections examine the evidence used to find the treatments of choice for some of the most common psychological disorders.

Learning Objectives

- Understand why cognitive and behavioral treatments are preferred to drug treatments for anxiety disorders.

- Recognize when combined therapies or alternative therapies are used to treat depressive disorders.

- Understand why lithium and atypical antipsychotics are used to treat bipolar disorder.

- Describe the advantages of second-generation antipsychotics in the treatment of schizophrenia.

15.10 Treatments That Focus on Behavior and on Cognition Are Superior for Anxiety Disorders

According to the accumulated evidence, cognitive-behavioral therapy (CBT) works best to treat most adult anxiety disorders (Hofmann & Smits, 2008). A key ingredient, as mentioned in Section 15.3, is the use of exposure to the threatening stimuli (Foa & Maclean, 2016). Exposure to the feared object in a safe environment eventually produces extinction.

Anxiety-reducing drugs are also beneficial in some cases. With drugs, however, there are risks of side effects and, after drug treatment is terminated, the risk of relapse. For instance, anxiolytics work in the short term for generalized anxiety disorder, but they do little to alleviate the source of anxiety and are addictive. Therefore, they are not used much today. Antidepressant drugs that block the reuptake of both serotonin and norepinephrine have been effective for treating generalized anxiety disorder (Hartford et al., 2007; Nicolini et al., 2008). As with all drugs, the effects may be limited to the period during which the drug is taken. By contrast, the effects of CBT persist long after treatment (Hollon, Stewart, & Strunk, 2006).

One recent finding is that administering an antibiotic used to treat tuberculosis (d-cycloserine) may enhance the effects of exposure therapy on anxiety disorders (Mataix-Cols et al., 2017; McGuire et al., 2017). The use of this drug in treatment was based on animal studies, in which d-cycloserine facilitated the extinction of conditioned fear (Norberg, Krystal, & Tolin, 2008; Walker, Ressler, Lu, & Davis, 2002). Because exposure works by extinguishing fear responses, any drug that boosts extinction should help reduce fear. Unlike other drug treatments, d-cycloserine is used to boost the effects of the behavioral treatment rather than treat anxiety directly.

SPECIFIC PHOBIAS As discussed in Chapter 14, specific phobias are characterized by the fear and avoidance of particular stimuli, such as heights, blood, and spiders. Learning theory suggests these fears are acquired either through experiencing a trauma or by observing similar fear in others. Most phobias, however, apparently develop in the absence of any particular precipitating event. Although learning theory cannot completely explain the development of phobias, behavioral techniques are the treatment of choice.

One of the classic methods used to treat phobias is a form of exposure therapy known as *systematic desensitization*. The client first makes a *fear hierarchy:* a list of situations in which fear is aroused, in ascending order. The example in **TABLE 15.2** is from a client's therapy to conquer a fear of heights in order to go mountain climbing. The next step is *exposure*, in which the client is asked to imagine or enact scenarios that become progressively more upsetting. The theory behind this technique is that exposure to the threatening stimulus will extinguish as the client learns new, nonthreatening associations.

To expose clients without putting them in danger, practitioners may use *virtual environments,* sometimes called *virtual reality*. Computers can simulate the environments and the feared objects (**FIGURE 15.17**). There is substantial evidence that exposure to these virtual environments can reduce fear responses (Freeman et al., 2017).

Brain imaging data indicate that successful treatment with CBT alters the way the brain processes the fear stimulus. In one study, research participants suffering from severe spider phobia received brain scans while looking at pictures of

FIGURE 15.17
Using Virtual Environments to Conquer Fear
Computer-generated images can simulate feared environments or social interactions. For example, the client can virtually stand on the edge of a very tall building or virtually fly in an aircraft. The client can conquer the virtual environment before taking on the feared situation in real life.

Table 15.2 Anxiety Hierarchy

DEGREE OF FEAR	SITUATION
5	I'm standing on the balcony of the top floor of an apartment tower.
10	I'm standing on a stepladder in the kitchen to change a lightbulb.
15	I'm walking on a ridge. The edge is hidden by shrubs and treetops.
20	I'm sitting on the slope of a mountain, looking out over the horizon.
25	I'm crossing a bridge 6 feet above a creek. The bridge consists of an 18-inch-wide board with a handrail on one side.
30	I'm riding a ski lift 8 feet above the ground.
35	I'm crossing a shallow, wide creek on an 18-inch-wide board, 3 feet above water level.
40	I'm climbing a ladder outside the house to reach a second-story window.
45	I'm pulling myself up a 30-degree wet, slippery slope on a steel cable.
50	I'm scrambling up a rock, 8 feet high.
55	I'm walking 10 feet on a resilient, 18-inch-wide board, which spans an 8-foot-deep gulch.
60	I'm walking on a wide plateau, 2 feet from the edge of a cliff.
65	I'm skiing an intermediate hill. The snow is packed.
70	I'm walking over a railway trestle.
75	I'm walking on the side of an embankment. The path slopes to the outside.
80	I'm riding a chair lift 15 feet above the ground.
85	I'm walking up a long, steep slope.
90	I'm walking up (or down) a 15-degree slope on a 3-foot-wide trail. On one side of the trail the terrain drops down sharply; on the other side is a steep upward slope.
95	I'm walking on a 3-foot-wide ridge. The trail slopes on one side are more than 25 degrees steep.
100	I'm walking on a 2-foot-wide ridge. The trail slopes on either side are more than 25 degrees.

spiders (Paquette et al., 2003). The participants whose treatment had been successful showed decreased activation in a frontal brain region involved in the regulation of emotion. These findings suggest that psychotherapy effectively "rewires" the brain and, therefore, that both psychotherapy and medication affect the underlying biology of psychological disorders.

PANIC DISORDER Many people sometimes experience symptoms of a panic attack (**FIGURE 15.18**). They react to these symptoms in different ways. Some shrug off the symptoms. Others interpret heart palpitations as the beginnings of a heart attack or hyperventilation as a sign of suffocation. Panic disorder has multiple components, and each symptom may require a different treatment. This clinical observation is supported by the finding that imipramine, a tricyclic antidepressant, prevents panic attacks but does not reduce the anticipatory anxiety that occurs when people fear they might have an attack. To break

FIGURE 15.18
Panic Attacks
The stress of being in a crowd can bring on a panic attack, especially in someone who has an anxiety disorder.

the learned association between the physical symptoms and the feeling of impending doom, CBT can be effective.

An important psychotherapeutic method for treating panic disorder is based on cognitive therapy. When people feel anxious, they tend to overestimate the probability of danger. Thus, they potentially contribute to their rising feelings of panic. Cognitive restructuring addresses ways of reacting to the symptoms of a panic attack. First, the client identifies her specific fears, such as having a heart attack or fainting. The client then estimates how many panic attacks she has experienced. The therapist helps the client assign percentages to specific fears and then compare these numbers with the actual number of times the fears have been realized. For example, a client might estimate that she fears having a heart attack during 90 percent of her panic attacks and fainting during 85 percent of her attacks. The therapist can then point out that the actual rate of occurrence was zero. In fact, people do not faint during panic attacks. The physical symptoms of a panic attack, such as having a racing heart, are the opposite of fainting.

Even if people recognize the irrationality of their fears, they often still suffer panic attacks. From a cognitive-behavioral perspective, the attacks continue because of a conditioned response to the trigger (e.g., shortness of breath). The goal of therapy is to break the connection between the trigger symptom and the resulting panic. This break can be made by exposure treatment. For example, the therapist might induce feelings of panic—perhaps by having the client breathe in and out through a straw to bring about hyperventilation or by spinning the client rapidly in a chair. Whatever the method, it is done repeatedly to induce habituation and then extinction.

In the treatment of panic attacks, CBT appears to be as effective as or more effective than medication (Schmidt & Keough, 2011). For example, David Barlow and colleagues (2000) found that in the short term, CBT alone and an antidepressant alone were more effective than a placebo for treating panic disorder. Moreover, CBT and an antidepressant did not differ in results. Six months after treatment had ended, however, those who received CBT were less likely to relapse than those who had taken medication. These results support the conclusion that CBT is the treatment of choice for panic disorder, as it is for the other anxiety disorders.

 Q **Why is exposing people to objects they fear part of therapy for anxiety disorders?**

ANSWER: Exposure to a feared object in a safe environment helps extinguish the learned fear association for that object.

|15.11 Both Antidepressants and CBT Are Effective for Obsessive-Compulsive Disorder

As discussed in Chapter 14, obsessive-compulsive disorder (OCD) is a combination of recurrent intrusive thoughts (obsessions) and behaviors that an individual feels compelled to perform over and over (compulsions). Because these obsessions make people anxious, many practitioners believed that people with OCD would respond to drug treatment. Traditional anti-anxiety drugs are completely ineffective for OCD, however. This ineffectiveness is one of the reasons that *DSM-5* separates OCD from anxiety disorders.

When SSRIs were introduced to treat depression, they were particularly effective in reducing the obsessive components of some depressive disorders. For example, they helped reduce the constant feelings of worthlessness experienced by people when they suffer from depression. We do not know the reasons for these effects. As a result of the initial success, however, SSRIs were tried with people suffering from OCD and were found to be effective (Rapoport, 1989, 1991). The drug of choice for OCD is clomipramine, a potent serotonin reuptake inhibitor. It is not a true SSRI, since it blocks reuptake of other neurotransmitters as well, but its strong enhancement of the effects of serotonin appears to make it effective for OCD.

Cognitive-behavioral therapy (CBT) is also effective for OCD (Franklin & Foa, 2011). The two most important components of behavioral therapy for OCD are exposure and *response prevention* (Knopp, Knowles, Bee, Lovell, & Bower, 2013). The person is directly exposed to the stimuli that trigger compulsive behavior but is prevented from engaging in the behavior. This treatment derives from the theory that a particular stimulus triggers anxiety and that performing the compulsive behavior reduces the anxiety. For example, a person might compulsively wash her hands after touching a doorknob, using a public telephone, or shaking hands with someone. In exposure and response-prevention therapy, the person would be required to touch a doorknob and then would be instructed not to wash her hands afterward. The goal is to break the conditioned link between a particular stimulus and a compulsive behavior (**FIGURE 15.19**). Some cognitive therapies are also useful for OCD, such as helping the client recognize that most people occasionally experience unwanted thoughts and compulsions. In fact, unwanted thoughts and compulsions are a normal part of human experience.

How does drug treatment compare with CBT for OCD? In one study, the use of exposure and response prevention proved superior to the use of clomipramine, the drug of choice for OCD, although both were better than a placebo (Foa et al., 2005; **FIGURE 15.20**). CBT may thus be a more effective way of treating OCD than medication, especially over the long term (Foa et al., 2005). There is evidence that, at a minimum, adding CBT to SSRI treatment may improve outcomes (Simpson et al., 2008). Therefore, many practitioners recommend the combination of these treatments (Franklin & Foa, 2011).

DEEP BRAIN STIMULATION One exciting possibility is that deep brain stimulation (DBS) may be an effective treatment for those with OCD who have not found

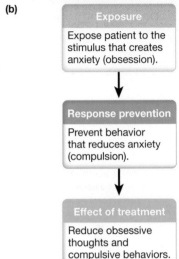

FIGURE 15.19

Using Exposure and Response Prevention to Treat Obsessive-Compulsive Disorder

(a) Someone who obsesses about germs might engage in a compulsive behavior, such as excessive handwashing. **(b)** In exposure and response therapy, the person would be asked to touch something dirty, then would be prevented from handwashing. The effect should be to break the link between the obsession and the compulsion, reducing both.

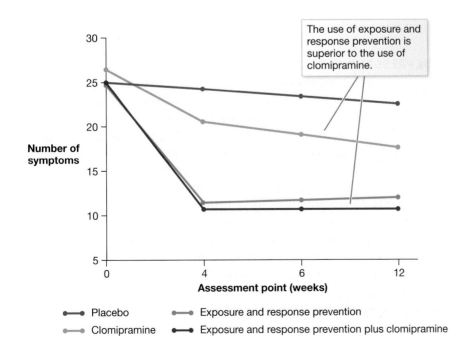

FIGURE 15.20

Treatments for Obsessive-Compulsive Disorder

Treatments for OCD include the drug clomipramine, exposure, and response prevention. This graph shows how, in the 2005 study by Foa and colleagues, the numbers of symptoms changed over a period of 12 weeks. With each type of treatment, rates of success are different.

relief from CBT or medications. Early studies used psychosurgery to remove brain regions thought to contribute to OCD. There were promising outcomes, and these surgical interventions involved much less damage than earlier methods, such as lobotomy. Still, brain surgery is inherently a risky therapy because it is irreversible. Deep brain stimulation offers new hope.

Consider the case of Mr. A., a 56-year-old man suffering from a severely debilitating case of OCD that had lasted for more than four decades. Mr. A. had a number of obsessions about body parts and about gastrointestinal functioning. His compulsions included repetitive movements and dietary restrictions. Researchers implanted DBS electrodes into the caudate, an area of the brain that is abnormal among people with OCD. DBS was very effective for Mr. A., who showed significant remission from symptoms after six months of treatment. After more than two years, Mr. A. continued to have stunning improvements in psychological functioning and the quality of his daily living (Aouizerate et al., 2004).

DBS leads to a clinically significant reduction of symptoms and increased daily functioning in about two-thirds of those receiving treatment (Greenberg et al., 2008). Although this method remains exploratory, it holds great promise for improving quality of life for those who have not benefited from other forms of treatment (Ooms et al., 2014; Raymaekers et al., 2017).

ANSWER: Compulsions. The goal of response prevention is to break the conditioned link between a particular stimulus and a compulsive behavior.

Q Is response prevention more relevant for treating obsessions or compulsions? Why so?

15.12 Many Effective Treatments Are Available for Depressive Disorders

As discussed in Chapter 14, depressive disorders are characterized by low mood or loss of interest in pleasurable activities. This condition is one of the most widespread psychological disorders, and it has become more common over the past few decades (Hollon et al., 2002). Fortunately, scientific research has validated a number of effective treatments. There is no "best" way to treat depressive disorders. Many approaches are available, and ongoing research is determining which type of therapy works best for which types of individuals.

ANTIDEPRESSANT TREATMENT In the 1950s, tuberculosis was a major health problem in the United States, particularly in urban areas. A common treatment was iproniazid. This drug reduced bacteria associated with tuberculosis in patients' saliva. It also stimulated patients' appetites, increased their energy levels, and gave them an overall sense of well-being. In 1957, researchers who had noted iproniazid's effect on mood reported preliminary success in using it to treat depression. In the following year, nearly half a million patients suffering from depression were given the drug.

Iproniazid is an MAO inhibitor. MAO inhibitors can be toxic because of their effects on various physiological systems. Patients taking these drugs must avoid ingesting any substances containing tyramine, an amino acid found in various foods, including red wine, cured meats, and aged cheeses. The interaction of an MAO inhibitor and tyramine can result in severe, sometimes lethal elevations in blood pressure. In addition, the interaction of an MAO inhibitor with particular prescription and over-the-counter medications can be fatal. As a result of these complications, MAO inhibitors are generally reserved for people who do not respond to other antidepressants.

Tricyclics, another type of antidepressant, were also identified in the 1950s. One of these—imipramine, developed as an antihistamine—was found effective in relieving clinical depression. This drug and others like it act on neurotransmitters as well as on the histamine system. Tricyclics are extremely effective antidepressants. Because of their broad-based action, however, they have a number of unpleasant side effects. For example, their use can result in drowsiness, weight gain, sweating, constipation, heart palpitations, dry mouth, or any combination of such problems.

The discovery of these early antidepressants was largely serendipitous. Subsequently, researchers began to search for antidepressants that did not affect multiple physiological and neurological systems and so would not have such troublesome side effects. In the 1980s, researchers developed Prozac. This SSRI does not affect histamine or acetylcholine. Therefore, it has none of the side effects associated with the tricyclic antidepressants, although it occasionally causes insomnia, headache, weight loss, and sexual dysfunction. Because they have fewer serious side effects than MAO inhibitors, Prozac and other SSRIs began to be prescribed more frequently. A number of other drug treatments for depressive disorders have also been validated. For example, bupropion (brand name Wellbutrin) affects many neurotransmitter systems, but it has fewer side effects for most people than other drugs. Unlike most antidepressants, bupropion does not cause sexual dysfunction. Unlike SSRIs, bupropion is not an effective treatment for panic disorder and OCD.

"Before Prozac, she loathed company."

Researchers have attempted to determine how particular types of people will respond to antidepressants. Still, physicians often must resort to a trial-and-error approach in treating people who are experiencing depression. No single drug stands out as being most effective. There is some evidence that tricyclics might be beneficial for the most serious depressive disorders, especially for hospitalized patients (Anderson, 2000). SSRIs and bupropion are generally considered first-line medications because they have the fewest serious side effects (Olfson et al., 2002). This is why they are often used for persistent depressive disorder, which—as noted in Chapter 14—is less severe than major depressive disorder (Craighead & Dunlop, 2014). Often the decision of which drug to use depends on the person's overall medical health and the possible side effects of each medication.

The use of antidepressants is based on the belief that depression (like other psychological disorders) is caused by deficits or excesses in neurotransmitters or problems with neural receptors. Recently, a number of critics have challenged this view, arguing that there is no evidence to suggest that people with depression had abnormal brain functioning before drug treatment (Angell, 2011). Indeed, faulty logical reasoning may be at play.

Yes, drugs such as SSRIs seem to help symptoms of depression. This success has been viewed as evidence that depression is caused by an abnormality in serotonin function. As a critical thinker, you probably recognize that this connection is not good proof. After all, when you have a cold, you might take a medication that treats your runny nose. Doing so does not prove that your cold was caused by your runny nose. Thus, antidepressants may help treat the symptoms of depression without having any influence on the underlying cause. Moreover, as discussed in Section 15.13, some of the success of SSRIs might be due to placebo effects.

COGNITIVE-BEHAVIORAL TREATMENT Not all depressed people benefit from antidepressant medications. In addition, some people cannot or will not tolerate the side effects. Fortunately, cognitive-behavioral therapy (CBT) is just as effective as antidepressants in treating depressive disorders (Hollon et al., 2002). From a cognitive perspective, people who become depressed do so because of automatic, irrational thoughts. According to the cognitive distortion model developed by Aaron Beck, depression is the result of a cognitive triad of negative thoughts about oneself, the situation, and the future (see Figure 14.20). The thought patterns of people with depressive disorders differ from the thought patterns of people with anxiety disorders. That is, people with anxiety disorders worry about the future. People with depressive disorders think about how they have failed in the past, how poorly they are dealing with the present situation, and how terrible the future will be.

The goal of the cognitive-behavioral treatment of depression is to help the person think more adaptively. This change is intended to improve mood and behavior. The specific treatment is adapted to the individual, but some general principles apply to this type of therapy. People may be asked to recognize and record their negative thoughts (**FIGURE 15.21**). Thinking about situations in a negative way can become automatic, and recognizing these thought patterns can be difficult. Once the patterns are identified and monitored, the clinician can help the client recognize other ways of viewing the same situation that are not so dysfunctional.

CBT can be effective on its own, but combining it with antidepressant medication can be more effective than either one of these approaches alone (Cuijpers et al., 2014). In addition, the response rates and remission rates of the combined-treatment approach are extremely good (Keller et al., 2000; Kocsis et al., 2003). The issue is not drugs versus psychotherapy. The issue is which treatment provides—or which treatments provide—relief for each individual. For instance, drug treatment may be the most effective option for those who are suicidal, in acute distress, or unable to commit to regular sessions with a therapist. For most people, especially those who have physical problems such as liver impairment or cardiac problems, psychotherapy may be the treatment of choice because it is long-lasting and does not have the side effects associated with medications (Hollon et al., 2006). Treatment selection also depends on the severity of the depressive disorder. In general, people who have chronic major depressive disorder receive the most benefit from combined drug treatments and psychotherapies (Craighead & Dunlop, 2014).

FIGURE 15.21

Recording Thoughts

Patients in CBT may be asked to keep a record of events and their reactions to those events, including their automatic thoughts. Such a log can help identify patterns in thought and behavior. This example comes from a person suffering from depression.

Date	Event	Emotion	Automatic thoughts
April 4	Boss seemed annoyed.	Sad, anxious, worried	Oh, what have I done now? If I keep making him angry, I'm going to get fired.
April 5	Husband didn't want to make love.	Sad	I'm so fat and ugly.
April 7	Boss yelled at another employee.	Anxious	I'm next.
April 9	Husband said he's taking a long business trip next month.	Sad, defeated	He's probably got a mistress somewhere. My marriage is falling apart.
April 10	Neighbor brought over some cookies.	A little happy, mostly sad	She probably thinks I can't cook. I look like such a mess all the time. And my house was a disaster when she came in!

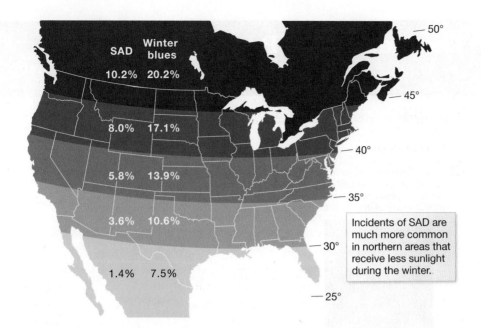

SAD   Winter blues

10.2% 20.2%

8.0%   17.1%

5.8%   13.9%

3.6%   10.6%

1.4%   7.5%

— 50°
— 45°
— 40°
— 35°
— 30°
— 25°

Incidents of SAD are much more common in northern areas that receive less sunlight during the winter.

FIGURE 15.22
Incidence of Seasonal Affective Disorder
As shown by this map, incidence of SAD varies by latitude.

As with other psychological disorders, treatment of depression with psychotherapy leads to changes in brain activation similar to those observed for drug treatments (Brody et al., 2001). One study found that although psychotherapy and drugs involved the same brain regions, activity in those regions was quite different during the two treatments (Goldapple et al., 2004). This finding suggests that psychotherapy and drugs operate through different mechanisms. Indeed, a meta-analysis of combined studies found that the effects of the drugs and psychotherapy are largely independent of one another, supporting other evidence that the combination of the two provides greater effectiveness than either one alone (Cuijpers et al., 2014).

ALTERNATIVE TREATMENTS In people with seasonal affective disorder (SAD), episodes of depression are most likely to occur during winter. A milder form of SAD has been called the winter blues. The rate of these disorders increases with latitude (**FIGURE 15.22**). Many people respond favorably to *phototherapy*, which involves exposure to a high-intensity light source for part of each day (**FIGURE 15.23**). However, a recent study of more than 34,000 Americans failed to find increased reports of symptoms of depression during the winter or in states that receive less sunshine (Traffanstedt, Mehta, & LoBello, 2016). Although the study did not include diagnostic assessment of SAD, it raises the issue of the extent of seasonal variation in depression. Research conducted with clients diagnosed with SAD find that phototherapy is effective (Meesters & Gordijn, 2016; Winkler et al., 2017).

For some people with depressive disorders, regular aerobic exercise can reduce the symptoms and prevent recurrence (Pollock, 2004). Aerobic exercise may reduce depression because it releases endorphins. As discussed in Chapter 4, the release of endorphins can cause an overall feeling of well-being (a feeling runners sometimes experience as "runner's high"). Aerobic exercise may also regularize bodily rhythms, improve self-esteem, and provide social support if people exercise with others. However, people with depression may have difficulty finding the energy and motivation to begin an exercise regimen.

Electroconvulsive therapy (ECT) is a very effective treatment for those who are severely depressed and do not respond to conventional treatments (Hollon et al., 2002). For a number of reasons, ECT might be preferable to other treatments for

FIGURE 15.23
Phototherapy
One treatment for SAD is phototherapy. In this method, the person sits in front of strong lighting for several hours each day to reduce symptoms.

The Methods of Psychology
Mayberg's Study of DBS and Depression

HYPOTHESIS: Deep brain stimulation of an area of the prefrontal cortex may alleviate depression.

RESEARCH METHOD:

1 A pair of small holes were drilled into the skulls of six participants. The participants had treatment-resistant depression for many years.

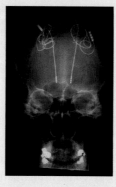

2 A pulse generator was attached under the collarbone, connecting to electrodes that passed through the holes in the skull to a specific area of the prefrontal cortex.

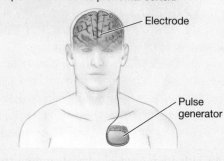

Electrode

Pulse generator

RESULTS: Some participants reported relief as soon as the electrodes were switched on, and ⅔ of the participants felt significantly better within months.

CONCLUSION: DBS may be an especially effective method for patients resistant to other treatments.

QUESTION: Is DBS used as an initial treatment for depression?

ANSWER: No. It is used only for those with treatment-resistant depression for whom other treatments do not produce relief.

Source: Mayberg, H. S., Lozano, A. M., Voon, V., McNeely, H. E., Seminowicz, D., Hamani, C., et al. (2005). Deep brain stimulation for treatment-resistant depression. *Neuron, 45,* 651–660.

depression. Antidepressants can take weeks to be effective, whereas ECT works quickly. For a suicidal person, waiting several weeks for relief can literally be deadly. In addition, ECT may be the treatment of choice for depression in pregnant women, since there is no evidence that the seizures harm the developing fetus. In contrast, many psychotropic medications can cause birth defects. Most important, ECT has proved effective in people for whom other treatments have failed.

ECT does, however, have some serious limitations, including a high relapse rate—often necessitating repeated treatments—and memory impairments (Fink, 2001). In most cases, memory loss is limited to the day of ECT treatment, but some people experience substantial permanent memory loss (Donahue, 2000). Some centers perform unilateral ECT over only the hemisphere not dominant for language, a treatment that seems to reduce memory disruption (Papadimitriou, Zervas, & Papakostas, 2001).

According to a series of studies, transcranial magnetic stimulation (TMS) over the left frontal regions results in a significant reduction in depression (Chistyakov et al., 2004; George, Lisanby, & Sackheim, 1999; George et al., 1995; Pascual-Leone, Catala, & Pascual-Leone, 1996). Because TMS does not involve anesthesia or have any major side effects (other than headache), it can be administered outside hospital settings. It is not likely, however, that TMS will ever completely replace ECT. The two methods may act via different mechanisms and may therefore be appropriate for different types of patients. The long-term value of TMS is that it is effective even for those who have not responded to treatment with antidepressants (Fitzgerald et al., 2003). In October 2008, TMS was approved by the FDA for the treatment of major depressive disorder in people who are not helped by traditional therapies.

DEEP BRAIN STIMULATION As with obsessive-compulsive disorder, DBS might be valuable for treating severe depressive disorders when all other treatments have failed. In 2003, Helen Mayberg and colleagues became the first to try out this novel treatment. Mayberg's earlier research had pointed to an area of the prefrontal cortex as abnormal in depression. Following the logic of using DBS for Parkinson's, neurosurgeons inserted electrodes into this brain region in six patients suffering from severe depression (Mayberg et al., 2005; McNeely, Mayberg, Lozano, & Kennedy, 2008). The results were stunning for four of the patients. In fact, some of them felt relief as soon as the switch was turned on. For all four, it was as if a horrible noise had stopped and a weight had been lifted, as if they had emerged into a more beautiful world (Dobbs, 2006; Ressler & Mayberg, 2007; see "The Methods of Psychology: Mayberg's Study of DBS and Depression").

Several studies have been conducted examining DBS for treatment-resistant depression, and each time at least half of the participants benefited from this treatment (Bewernick et al., 2010; Malone et al., 2009). One study followed 20 patients for three to six years and found that about two-thirds showed long-lasting benefits from DBS (Kennedy et al., 2011). These studies demonstrate that DBS is useful for helping people lead more productive lives. For instance, in the study just mentioned, only 10 percent of the people were able to work or engage in meaningful activities outside the house (e.g., volunteering) before DBS, whereas two-thirds were able to do so after DBS.

DBS differs from other treatments in that researchers can easily alter the electrical current without the person knowing, to demonstrate that the DBS is responsible for improvements in psychological functioning. Research using DBS to treat severe depressive disorders is now under way at a number of sites around the globe (Ryder & Holtzheimer, 2016).

GENDER ISSUES IN TREATING DEPRESSIVE DISORDERS As noted in Chapter 14, women are twice as likely to be diagnosed with depressive disorders as men are. Some portion of this difference relates to high rates of domestic and other violence against women, reduced economic resources, and inequities at work (American Psychological Association, 2007). Women are also the primary consumers of psychotherapy. The American Psychological Association therefore has published *Guidelines for Psychological Practice with Girls and Women* (2007). These guidelines remind therapists to be aware of gender-specific stressors, such as the way work and family interact to place additional burdens on women and the biological realities of reproduction and menopause. The guidelines also point out that women of color, lesbians, and women with disabilities are often stereotyped in ways that signal disregard for the challenges they face. All of these factors can interfere with the therapeutic process.

Problems also exist in the treatment of depression in men. Men's reluctance to admit to depression and even greater reluctance to seek appropriate therapy have been described as "a conspiracy of silence that has long surrounded depression in men" (Brody, 1997). Two prominent men—the late Mike Wallace, a journalist and television news anchor, and the late William Styron, a Pulitzer Prize–winning author—talked eloquently about their battles with depression (**FIGURE 15.24**). Wallace described it this way: "The sunshine means nothing to you at all. The seasons, friends, good food mean nothing. All you focus on is yourself and how bad you feel." Styron writes: "In

(a)

(b)

FIGURE 15.24

Men Who Have Broken the Conspiracy of Silence

Men are much less likely than women to admit that they have suffered from depression. Two famous men who were willing to break this conspiracy of silence are **(a)** Mike Wallace, a news correspondent best known for his work on the television show *60 Minutes*, whose depression began after accusations of libel and a related lawsuit; and **(b)** William Styron, best known as the author of the novels *The Confessions of Nat Turner* (1967) and *Sophie's Choice* (1979) and the memoir *Darkness Visible* (1990), which chronicled his bouts of depression.

severe depression, the entire body and spirit of a person is in a state of shipwreck, of desolate lostness. Nothing animates the body or spirit. It's a total wipeout" (both quoted in Brody, 1997).

Public statements from such well-respected men may help break the silence surrounding depression in men and increase the number of men who seek psychotherapy. One goal is to help men stop masking their depression with alcohol, isolation, and irritability. Any of these retreats from the social world may be a symptom of unacknowledged depression.

Q What is one problem with treating depression in men?

ANSWER: Men may be reluctant to admit they are depressed and therefore not seek treatment.

15.13 Should You Trust Studies Sponsored by Drug Companies?

The arrival of Prozac on the market, in 1987, led to a dramatic shift in the treatment of depression. Today, most people who experience depression are first treated by a medical doctor. The doctor is likely to prescribe an antidepressant rather than refer the person to a psychotherapist. An estimated 1 in 10 Americans over age 6 takes antidepressant medication (Angell, 2011; Moore & Mattison, 2017).

Concern is growing that the increased use of antidepressants (and other pharmacological treatments for psychological disorders) may be due in part to the marketing pressures of the drug industry. Critics charge that promotions by drug companies have given doctors an inflated sense of the evidence for the effectiveness of pharmacological treatment. Doctors may be relying on evidence funded by producers of the drugs.

Though the research may be sourced to scientists, it is paid for by the pharmaceutical industry. Such payments can represent a conflict of interest because the researcher may be motivated, even unconsciously, to obtain findings that please the company. After all, the researcher probably wants future funding from the company (**FIGURE 15.25**). Recall from Chapter 2 that experimenter bias can affect research outcomes. For this reason, many scientific journals require investigators to disclose any financial interests they have in the research.

There are also biases in the literature on the effectiveness of drug therapy (Turner, Matthews, Linardatos, Tell, & Rosenthal, 2008). In science, it is much easier to publish positive results—those that indicate treatment success—than negative results. Moreover, drug companies are much more likely to publicize studies that show their drugs are effective than those that do not. They might even attempt to suppress publication of research that questions their drugs' effectiveness. If they paid for the study, part of the agreement may give the drug company control over which aspects of the study can be published. How can researchers tell whether published studies present a different story than unpublished studies? The psychologist Irving Kirsch found a way to answer that question.

In approving a new drug, the U.S. Food and Drug Administration (FDA) requires drug companies to submit all clinical studies they have conducted regardless of whether those findings were ever published. Kirsch and colleagues (2008) used a Freedom of Information Act request to obtain all placebo-controlled studies of the most widely used antidepressants. Of the 42 studies they obtained, most had negative results. Overall, placebos were 80 percent as effective as antidepressants, and the change in self-reported depressive symptoms showed that improvement on drugs compared with

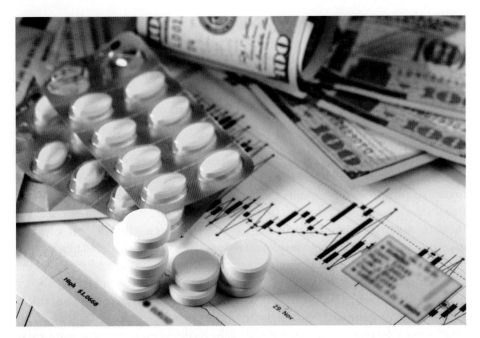

FIGURE 15.25

Antidepressants, Research, and Money

There are potential conflicts of interest in research on antidepressants that is funded by the pharmaceutical industry. The drug companies have an interest in receiving positive results for their products, and the researchers might consciously or unconsciously have an interest in pleasing those who underwrite their work. How can doctors and consumers determine the truth among the influences?

placebos was modest at best. To be clear: People felt less depressed after taking antidepressants, but they also felt better after taking placebos, and thus it is possible that placebo effects play a prominent role in the success of antidepressant drug treatments.

Thus, a look at all the data raises questions about whether drug companies' claims about the highly effective nature of drug treatments for depression are supported by empirical research. The drug companies focus on the studies that show their drugs work. This fact may lead those who prescribe or take the medications to overestimate how much the drugs will help alleviate psychological disorders, such as depression. Of course, it would be unethical to prescribe a placebo treatment, so that is not a treatment option. Moreover, taking antidepressants is helpful to many people. If you are on such a medication and have any concerns, you should discuss your situation with your physician. ∎

 Why is it a potential conflict of interest for a researcher to accept funding from a drug company?

ANSWER: because the researcher might be tempted to provide results that please the drug company in order to receive future funding

15.14 Lithium and Atypical Antipsychotics Are Most Effective for Bipolar Disorder

In *DSM-5*, the new category Bipolar and Related Disorders has been placed between disorders related to schizophrenia and those related to depression. In bipolar disorder, as discussed in Chapter 14, moods cycle between manic (or less intense hypomanic) episodes and depressive episodes. The manic phase includes alterations in thought that link it to the psychotic states found in schizophrenia. The negative moods associated with the depressive episodes link bipolar disorder to depression. This

FIGURE 15.26
Bipolar Disorders Can Be Successfully Treated
The actor Catherine Zeta-Jones has been diagnosed with bipolar II disorder. Zeta-Jones manages her symptoms through psychotropic medications and periodic residential treatment.

distinction will be useful as you learn about the treatment options for this disorder. It is one of the few psychological disorders for which there is a clear optimal treatment (**FIGURE 15.26**): psychotropic medications, especially the mood stabilizer lithium (Geddes, Burgess, Hawton, Jamison, & Goodwin, 2004; Geddes & Miklowitz, 2013).

As with the uses of other psychotropic drugs, the discovery of lithium for the treatment of bipolar disorder was serendipitous. In 1949, the researcher John Cade found that the urine of manic patients was toxic to guinea pigs. He believed that a toxin—specifically, uric acid—might be causing the symptoms of mania. If so, once the uric acid was removed from the body through the urine, the symptoms would diminish (a solution that would explain why the patients were not always manic). When he gave lithium urate, a salt in uric acid, to the guinea pigs, however, it proved nontoxic. To his surprise, it protected them against the toxic effects of the manic patients' urine and also sedated them. He next tried lithium salts on himself. When he was assured of their safety, he gave the salts to 10 hospitalized manic patients. All the patients recovered rapidly.

The mechanisms by which lithium stabilizes mood are not well understood, but the drug seems to modulate neurotransmitter levels, balancing excitatory and inhibitory activities (Jope, 1999). Lithium has unpleasant side effects, however, including thirst, hand tremors, excessive urination, and memory problems. The side effects often diminish after several weeks on the drug. Anticonvulsive medications, more commonly used to reduce seizures, can also stabilize mood and may be effective for intense bipolar episodes.

More recently, antipsychotic medications have been found to be effective in stabilizing moods and reducing episodes of mania. A class of drugs (commonly used in the treatment of schizophrenia) collectively called second-generation antipsychotics are also known as *atypical antipsychotics* because they differ from traditional antipsychotics in numerous ways. The drug quetiapine—better known as Seroquel—is an atypical antipsychotic that has grown in popularity and is now the most commonly prescribed drug for bipolar disorders (Hooshmand et al., 2014). Some evidence indicates that combining mood stabilizers, such as lithium, with atypical antipsychotics improves treatment outcomes (Buoli, Serati, & Altamura, 2014; Vieta, Suppes, Ekholm, Udd, & Gustafsson, 2012).

The important lesson here is that there is not a one-to-one mapping of drug treatment to psychological disorder. As discussed in Chapter 14, traditional *DSM* diagnoses might mask similarities between disorders. For instance, within families there is considerable overlap in susceptibility to bipolar disorder and schizophrenia (Craddock & Sklar, 2013). Family members of those with either of these disorders are at greater risk of developing either bipolar disorder or schizophrenia. Likewise, similar gene mutations are observed for both disorders (Malhotra et al., 2011). Recall that the Research Domain Criteria (RDoC) system classifies disorders according to similar genetic and neurophysiological findings. From the RDoC perspective, the use of drugs from one category to treat symptoms of another category may reflect similar underlying disturbances across diagnostic categories. That is, bipolar disorder and schizophrenia may be variants of the same disorder. Drugs treat symptoms, not disorders. Practically, the use of antipsychotics may be valuable for any disorder that involves impaired thought, regardless of *DSM* diagnosis.

Because lithium and atypical antipsychotics work better on mania than on depression, people are sometimes given an antidepressant as well. The risk of triggering a manic episode makes the use of antidepressants controversial, and they are generally not recommended (Pacchiarotti et al., 2013). When necessary, SSRIs are preferable to other antidepressants because they are less likely to trigger episodes of mania (Gijsman, Geddes, Rendell, Nolen, & Goodwin, 2004). However, the available evidence suggests that antidepressants may have limited usefulness in treatment of bipolar disorder (Nivoli et al., 2011).

As with all psychological disorders, compliance with drug therapy can be a problem for various reasons. For example, people may skip doses or stop taking the medications completely in an effort to reduce the side effects. In these situations, CBT can help increase compliance with medication regimens (Miller, Norman, & Keitner, 1989). Those with bipolar disorder also may stop taking their medications because they miss the "highs" of their hypomanic and manic phases. Psychotherapy can help these individuals accept their need for medication and understand the impact their disorder has on them and on those around them.

 Q A particular drug can be used to treat schizophrenia or bipolar disorder. What might this overlap in treatment indicate about these disorders?

ANSWER: Even though they have distinct diagnoses, the two disorders may be related or variants of the same disorder if they can be treated with the same drug.

15.15 Antipsychotics Are Superior for Schizophrenia

In the early 1900s, Freud's psychoanalytic theory and treatments based on it were widely touted as the answer to many psychological disorders. Freud, however, admitted that his techniques were effective only for what he termed "neuroses" and were unlikely to benefit patients with more-severe "psychotic" disorders, such as schizophrenia. Because psychotic patients were difficult to handle and even more difficult to treat, they were generally institutionalized in large mental hospitals. By 1934, according to estimates, the physician-to-patient ratio in such institutions in New York State was less than 1 to 200.

In this undesirable situation, the staff and administration of mental hospitals were willing to try any inexpensive treatment that had a chance of decreasing the patient population or that at least might make the inmates more manageable. Brain surgery, such as prefrontal lobotomy, was considered a viable option for patients with severe disorders. Egas Moniz initially reported that the operation was frequently successful (see Section 15.6). It soon became evident to him that patients suffering from anxiety or depression benefited most from the surgery. Patients with schizophrenia did not seem to improve following the operation. Fortunately, as noted earlier, the introduction of psychotropic medications in the 1950s eliminated the use of lobotomy.

PHARMACOLOGICAL TREATMENTS Since the sixteenth century, extracts from dogbane, a toxic herb, had been used to calm highly agitated people. The critical ingredient was isolated in the 1950s and named *reserpine*. When given to those with schizophrenia, reserpine not only had a sedative effect but also was effective in reducing the positive symptoms of schizophrenia, such as delusions and hallucinations. Shortly afterward, a synthetic version of reserpine was created that had fewer side effects. This drug, *chlorpromazine,* acts as a major tranquilizer. It reduces anxiety, sedates without inducing sleep, and decreases the severity and frequency of the positive symptoms of schizophrenia. Later, another antipsychotic, *haloperidol,* was developed that was chemically different and had less of a sedating effect than chlorpromazine.

Traditional antipsychotics such as haloperidol and chlorpromazine revolutionized the treatment of schizophrenia and became the most frequently used treatment for this disorder. People with schizophrenia who had been hospitalized for years were able to walk out of mental institutions and live independently. These antipsychotic drugs have drawbacks, however. For example, they have little or no impact on the negative symptoms of schizophrenia. In addition, they have significant side effects.

FIGURE 15.27
The Effectiveness of Clozapine
These graphs compare the effects, in representative cases, of using either clozapine or chlorpromazine to treat people with schizophrenia.

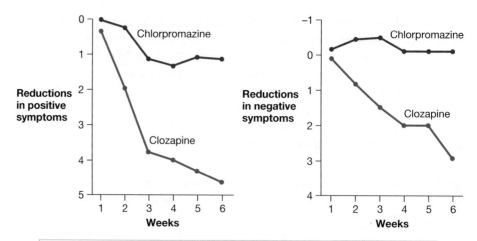

Many patients who had not responded to the previously available antipsychotics found that clozapine reduced the positive and negative symptoms of schizophrenia.

Chlorpromazine sedates people, can cause constipation and weight gain, and causes cardiovascular damage. Haloperidol does not cause these symptoms, but both drugs have significant motor side effects that resemble symptoms of Parkinson's disease: immobility of facial muscles, trembling of extremities, muscle spasms, uncontrollable salivation, and a shuffling walk. Tardive dyskinesia—as discussed in Section 15.5, involuntary movements of the lips, tongue, face, legs, or other parts of the body—is another devastating side effect of these medications and is irreversible once it appears. Despite these side effects, haloperidol and chlorpromazine were the only available options.

The late 1980s saw the introduction of atypical antipsychotics to treat schizophrenia. The initial drug of this type to be used in treatment, *clozapine*, has two important advantages over traditional antipsychotics. First, it is beneficial in treating the negative as well as the positive symptoms of schizophrenia (**FIGURE 15.27**). Many people with schizophrenia who had not responded to the previously available antipsychotics improved on clozapine. Second, no signs of Parkinson's symptoms or of tardive dyskinesia appeared in any of the people taking the drug. Clozapine has fewer side effects than chlorpromazine or haloperidol, but its side effects are serious: seizures, heart arrhythmias, and substantial weight gain. Of even greater concern is that clozapine can cause a fatal reduction in white blood cells. Although the risk of this problem is low, those taking the drug must have frequent blood tests. The cost of the blood tests, in addition to the high cost of the medication, has made this drug treatment prohibitively expensive for many who might benefit from it.

Other second-generation medications similar to clozapine in structure, pharmacology, and effectiveness have been introduced that do not reduce white blood cell counts. These are Risperdal and Zyprexa, which like clozapine are atypical antipsychotics. Like clozapine, they have about one-fifth the risk of producing tardive dyskinesia as first-generation drugs (Correll, Leucht, & Kane, 2004). These drugs are now the first line of defense in the treatment of schizophrenia (Walker, Kestler, Bollini, & Hochman, 2004), and clozapine is typically reserved for more-severe cases because of its more-serious side effects. However, other second-generation antipsychotics may not be as successful at treating negative symptoms as clozapine (Leucht et al., 2009).

PSYCHOSOCIAL TREATMENTS Medication is essential in the treatment of schizophrenia. Without it, people may deteriorate, experiencing more-frequent and more-severe psychotic episodes. When antipsychotic drugs became available, other types of therapies for schizophrenia were virtually dismissed. It became clear over time,

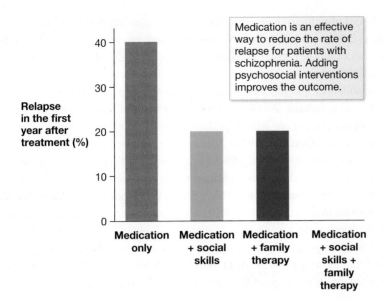

Medication is an effective way to reduce the rate of relapse for patients with schizophrenia. Adding psychosocial interventions improves the outcome.

however, that although medication effectively reduces delusions and hallucinations, it does not substantially affect the person's social functioning. Thus, antipsychotic drugs fall short of being a cure. The drugs must be combined with other treatments to help people lead productive lives.

For example, social skills training is an effective way to address some deficits in those with schizophrenia (**FIGURE 15.28**). These people can benefit from intensive training in regulating affect, recognizing social cues, and predicting the effects of their behavior in social situations. With intensive long-term training, people with schizophrenia can generalize the skills learned in therapy to other social environments. Also, when self-care skills are deficient, behavioral interventions can focus on areas such as grooming and bathing, management of medications, and financial planning. Training in specific cognitive skills, such as in modifying thinking patterns and in coping with auditory hallucinations, has been less effective.

PROGNOSIS IN SCHIZOPHRENIA Some people with schizophrenia have positive outcomes, eventually overcoming disruptive symptoms and able to function in daily life. However, estimating how frequently this happens is hard because of uncertainty in defining recovery. For instance, how long does a person have to go without symptoms before being considered recovered? One recent analysis looked at outcomes across 50 long-term studies. The researchers assessed the proportion of people who had good outcomes in terms of both reduction in symptoms and good social function for at least two years (Jääskeläinen et al., 2013). They found that only about 1 in 7 individuals achieved recovery by these standards.

One troubling aspect of this literature is the implication that in spite of major advances in diagnoses and treatment, the prognosis for those with schizophrenia has not improved in recent years (Jääskeläinen et al., 2013; Millan et al., 2016). The available studies have not examined prognosis based on treatments received, however, so it is not possible to know which treatments produce the best chances of recovery. What seems clear is that the longer a person with psychotic symptoms does not receive treatment, the worse the prognosis (Penttilä et al., 2014).

As noted, the cornerstone treatment for people diagnosed with schizophrenia is antipsychotic medications, such as clozapine. The evidence confirms that antipsychotic medications are extremely valuable in the short term for people experiencing psychotic symptoms (Goff et al., 2017; Harrow & Jobe, 2013). At issue is how long the person should remain on the medication. Some studies suggest that long-term use of these drugs may be associated with worse outcomes, possibly because of the effects of the drugs on dopamine receptors (Harrow, Jobe, & Faull, 2014). That is, long-term use changes dopamine receptors so that antipsychotic medication becomes less effective.

The prognosis for people with schizophrenia also depends on factors that include age of onset and culture. People diagnosed later in life tend to have a more favorable prognosis than people who experience their first symptoms during childhood or adolescence (McGlashan, 1988). This result could be because of delays in treatment or because schizophrenia affects brain development, much of which occurs during childhood and adolescence (Millan et al., 2016). Identifying those at risk and providing early treatment may possibly prevent progression of the disorder. Culture also plays a role in prognosis. In developing countries, schizophrenia often is not so severe as in developed countries (Leff, Sartorius, Jablensky, Korten, & Ernberg, 1992). Recovery also seems to be better in developing countries (Jääskeläinen et al., 2013). These differences may arise because more-extensive family networks in developing countries provide more support for patients with schizophrenia.

 Q **What were the two advantages of the second-generation antipsychotic clozapine over traditional antipsychotic medications?**

ANSWER: a reduction in negative and positive symptoms; no side effects of tardive dyskinesia

Learning Objective

- Discuss therapeutic approaches for borderline personality disorder and antisocial personality disorder.

FIGURE 15.29
Marsha Linehan
The psychologist Marsha Linehan pioneered the therapeutic technique DBT. Linehan experienced the kind of psychological disorder this technique is used to treat.

Can Personality Disorders Be Treated?

As discussed in Chapter 14, not much is known about the causes of personality disorders, such as borderline personality disorder and antisocial personality disorder. Likewise, little is known about how best to treat personality disorders. There is a growing literature of case studies that describe treatment approaches for these disorders, but few large, well-controlled studies have been undertaken.

The one thing about personality disorders that most therapists agree on is that they are notoriously difficult to treat. Individuals with personality disorders who are in therapy are usually also being treated for another disorder, such as OCD or depression. The other disorder is typically the problem for which the patient sought therapy in the first place. People rarely seek therapy for personality disorders, because one hallmark of these disorders is that patients see the environment rather than their own behavior as the cause of their problems. This outlook often makes individuals with personality disorders very difficult to engage in therapy.

15.16 Dialectical Behavior Therapy Is Most Successful for Borderline Personality Disorder

The impulsivity, emotional disturbances, and identity disturbances characteristic of borderline personality disorder make it very challenging to provide therapy for the people affected. Traditional psychotherapy approaches have been largely unsuccessful, so therapists have attempted to develop approaches specific to borderline personality disorder.

The most successful treatment approach to date for borderline personality disorder was developed by the psychologist Marsha Linehan in the 1980s (**FIGURE 15.29**).

Two decades earlier, as a young woman, Linehan had suffered from extreme social withdrawal, physical self-destructiveness, and recurrent suicidality (Carey, 2011). Institutionalized and diagnosed with schizophrenia, she was locked in a seclusion room, treated with various medications, given Freudian analysis, and treated with electroshock.

Eventually, after being released from the hospital with little hope of surviving, Linehan learned to accept herself rather than striving for some impossible ideal. This "radical acceptance," as she puts it, enabled her to function. She earned her Ph.D. in psychology with the goal of helping people who are chronically self-destructive or even suicidal. Linehan's **dialectical behavior therapy (DBT)** combines elements of the behavioral and cognitive treatments with a mindfulness approach based on Eastern meditative practices (Lieb, Zanarini, Schmahl, Linehan, & Bohus, 2004). All patients are seen in both group and individual sessions, and the responsibilities of the client and the therapist are made explicit.

Therapy proceeds in three stages (**FIGURE 15.30**). In the first stage, the therapist targets the person's most extreme and dysfunctional behaviors. Such behaviors often include self-cutting and threats of suicide or suicide attempts. The focus is on replacing these behaviors with more-appropriate ones. The person learns problem-solving techniques and more-effective ways of coping with his or her emotions. In this stage, the person is taught to control attention so that the person focuses on the present. Strategies for controlling attention are based on mindfulness meditation. In the second stage, the therapist helps the person explore past traumatic experiences that may be at the root of emotional problems. In the third stage, the therapist helps the person develop self-respect and independent problem solving. This stage is crucial because those with borderline personality disorder depend heavily on others for support and validation. These individuals must be able to generate the appropriate attitudes and necessary skills themselves, or they are likely to revert to their previous behavior patterns.

The symptoms experienced by individuals with borderline personality disorder can seem close to psychosis or resemble depression. As a result, researchers previously believed these patients would develop a disorder such as schizophrenia or depression. Studies that have followed individuals with borderline personality disorder over time, however, have demonstrated that their symptoms remain relatively unchanged (Plakun, Burkhardt, & Muller, 1985).

Therapeutic approaches targeted at borderline personality disorder, such as DBT, improve the prognosis for those with the disorder. Studies have demonstrated that people with borderline personality disorder undergoing DBT are more likely to remain in treatment and less likely to be suicidal than are those in other types of therapy (Linehan, Armstrong, Suarez, Allmon, & Heard, 1991; Linehan, Heard, & Armstrong, 1993). SSRIs are often prescribed along with DBT to treat feelings of depression.

 What role does mindfulness meditation play in dialectical behavior therapy?

ANSWER: It is used in the first stage of dialectical behavior therapy to help the person control attention to focus on the present.

15.17 Antisocial Personality Disorder Is Extremely Difficult to Treat

Treating people with borderline personality disorder can be very difficult. Treating those with antisocial personality disorder is often impossible. These individuals lie without thinking twice about it, care little for other people's feelings, and live for the

dialectical behavior therapy (DBT)

A form of therapy used to treat borderline personality disorder that combines elements of the behavioral and cognitive treatments with a mindfulness approach based on Eastern meditative practices.

(a)

(b)
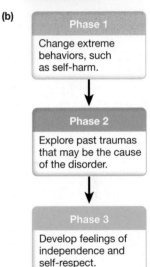

FIGURE 15.30
Dialectical Behavior Therapy Is Used to Treat Borderline Personality Disorder
(a) Suppose that a client with borderline personality disorder wants to hurt herself. **(b)** In phase 1 of DBT, she will learn to change extreme behaviors through problem solving, coping, and focusing on the present. In phase 2, the therapist helps her explore past traumas underlying her emotional problems. In phase 3, she works to increase her self-esteem and stop depending on others for validation.

present without consideration of the future. In addition, they are narcissistic and like themselves the way they are. All these factors make development of a therapeutic relationship and motivation for change remote possibilities at best. Individuals with this disorder are often more interested in manipulating their therapists than in changing their own behavior. Therapists working with these people must be constantly on guard.

THERAPEUTIC APPROACHES FOR ANTISOCIAL PERSONALITY DISORDER

Numerous treatment approaches have been tried for antisocial personality disorder (and the related but not identical disorder commonly called psychopathy; see Section 14.15). Because individuals with antisocial personality disorder apparently have diminished cortical arousal, stimulants have been prescribed to normalize arousal levels. There is evidence that these drugs are beneficial in the short term but not the long term. Anti-anxiety drugs may lower hostility levels somewhat, and lithium has shown promise in treating the aggressive, impulsive behavior of violent criminals who are psychopathic. Overall, however, psychotropic medications have not been effective in treating this disorder.

Similarly, traditional psychotherapeutic approaches seem of little use in treating antisocial personality disorder. Behavioral and cognitive approaches have had somewhat more success. Behavioral approaches reinforce appropriate behavior. They ignore inappropriate behavior in an attempt to replace maladaptive behavior patterns with behavior patterns that are more socially appropriate. This approach seems to work best when the therapist controls reinforcement, the person cannot leave treatment, and the person is part of a group. Individual therapy sessions rarely produce any change in antisocial behavior. Clearly, the behavioral approach cannot be implemented on an outpatient basis, since the person will receive reinforcement for his antisocial behavior outside of therapy and can leave treatment at any time. For these reasons, therapy for this disorder is most effective in a residential treatment center or a correctional facility.

Cognitive approaches have been tried for antisocial personality disorder. Therapists try to demonstrate that the person can meet his goals more easily by following the rules of society rather than by trying to get around them, as in the following example (Beck, Freeman, et al., 1990):

> Therapist: How well has the "beat-the-system" approach actually worked out for you over time?
> Brett: It works great . . . until someone catches on or starts to catch on. Then you have to scrap that plan and come up with a new one.
> Therapist: How difficult was it, you know, to cover up one scheme and come up with a new one?
> Brett: Sometimes it was really easy. There are some real pigeons out there.
> Therapist: Was it always easy?
> Brett: Well, no. Sometimes it was a real bitch. . . . Seems like I'm always needing a good plan to beat the system.
> Therapist: Do you think it's ever easier to go with the system instead of trying to beat it in some way?
> Brett: Well, after all that I have been through, I would have to say yes, there have been times that going with the system would have been easier in the long run. . . . But . . . it's such a challenge to beat the system. It feels exciting when I come up with a new plan and think I can make it work.

This dialogue illustrates both the cognitive approach and why such clients are so difficult to work with. Even if they know what they are doing is wrong, they do not care. They live for the thrill of getting away with something.

PROGNOSIS FOR ANTISOCIAL PERSONALITY DISORDER The prognosis that people with antisocial personality disorder will change their behaviors as a result of therapy is poor. This conclusion is especially true for those with psychopathic traits. Some of the more recently developed cognitive techniques show promise, but there is no good evidence that they produce long-lasting or even real changes. Fortunately for society, individuals with antisocial personality disorder but without psychopathy typically improve after age 40 (FIGURE 15.31).

The reasons for this improvement are unknown, but it may be due to a reduction in biological drives. Alternative theories suggest those with this disorder may gain insight into their self-defeating behaviors or may just get worn out and be unable to continue their manipulative ways. The improvement, however, is mainly in the realm of antisocial behavior. The underlying egocentricity, callousness, and manipulativeness can remain unchanged (Harpur & Hare, 1994), especially for those who are psychopathic. In fact, although criminal acts decrease among those with antisocial personality disorder after age 40, more than half of the individuals with psychopathic traits continue to be arrested after age 40 (Hare, McPherson, & Forth, 1988). Thus, although some aspects of their behavior mellow with age, psychopaths remain rather indifferent to traditional societal norms.

Because of the limited effectiveness of therapy for this disorder, time and effort may be better spent in prevention. *Conduct disorder* is a childhood condition known to be a precursor to antisocial personality disorder. It involves a persistent pattern of inappropriate behavior, such as bullying, cruelty to animals, theft, lying, and violating rules and social norms. Some of the environmental and developmental risk factors for conduct disorder have been identified. Focusing on these factors may reduce the likelihood that a child with conduct disorder will grow up to have antisocial personality disorder.

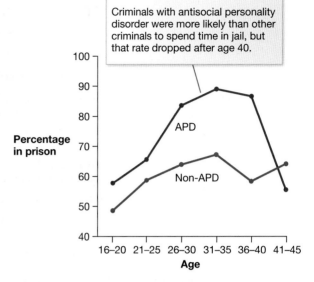

Criminals with antisocial personality disorder were more likely than other criminals to spend time in jail, but that rate dropped after age 40.

FIGURE 15.31
Antisocial Personality Disorder
For this longitudinal study, the percentage of participants in prison during each five-year period is shown.

ANSWER: Few therapies work for them, but most of those with antisocial personality disorder show a reduction in antisocial behavior after about age 40.

 What is the general prognosis for those with antisocial personality disorder?

How Should Childhood Disorders and Adolescent Disorders Be Treated?

It is estimated that in the United States at least 12–20 percent of children and adolescents suffer from psychological disorders (Leckman et al., 1995; Merikangas et al., 2010). Each person's experiences and development during early life are critically important to her mental health in adulthood. Problems not addressed during childhood or adolescence may persist into adulthood. Most theories of human development regard children and adolescents as more malleable than adults and therefore more amenable to treatment.

Medication is often used to treat emotional and behavioral problems in children. A recent study found that just over 7 percent of children (ages 6–17) were prescribed medications for psychological problems during the preceding six months in 2012

Learning Objectives

- Identify drugs and behavioral treatments for ADHD.

- Describe applied behavioral analysis.

- Discuss the use of oxytocin in the treatment of autism spectrum disorder.

- Discuss the current controversy regarding the use of drugs to treat depressive disorders among adolescents.

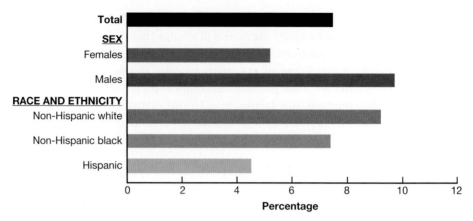

FIGURE 15.32
Children Given Medication
This chart shows the percentage of children in the United States aged 6–17 years prescribed medication over a six-month period for emotional or behavioral difficulties.

(Howie, Pastor, & Lukacs, 2014). Boys were more likely to receive medications than girls, and as was the case with adults discussed in Section 15.5, minorities were less likely to receive medications than non-Hispanic white children (**FIGURE 15.32**). To illustrate the issues involved in treating disorders of early life, this section considers treatment approaches for ADHD, autism, and adolescent depression.

15.18 Children with ADHD Can Benefit from Various Approaches

There is some dispute about whether attention-deficit/hyperactivity disorder (ADHD) is a psychological disorder or simply a troublesome behavior pattern that children eventually outgrow. Some people diagnosed with ADHD as children grow out of it. Many more, however, suffer from the disorder throughout adolescence and adulthood. These individuals are more likely to drop out of school and to reach a lower socioeconomic level than expected. They show continued patterns of inattention, of impulsivity, and of hyperactivity, and they are at increased risk for other psychiatric disorders (Wilens, Faraone, & Biederman, 2004). Because of this somewhat bleak long-term prognosis, effective treatment early in life may be of great importance.

PHARMACOLOGICAL TREATMENT OF ADHD The most common treatment for ADHD is a central nervous system stimulant, such as *methylphenidate*. This drug is most commonly known by the brand name Ritalin. (A time-release version of methylphenidate is called Concerta.) Ritalin's actions are not fully understood, but the drug may affect multiple neurotransmitters, particularly dopamine. Another drug used to treat ADHD is Adderall, which combines two other stimulants. The behavior of children with ADHD might suggest that their brains are overactive, and it may seem surprising that a stimulant would improve their symptoms. In fact, these drugs appear to selectively stimulate activity in frontal lobe regions that support both cognition and behavioral control (Spencer, Devilbiss, & Berridge, 2015). They act as cognitive enhancers by increasing attention and the ability to concentrate.

When children take these drugs as prescribed, they experience an increase in positive behaviors and a decrease in negative behaviors (**FIGURE 15.33**). They are able to

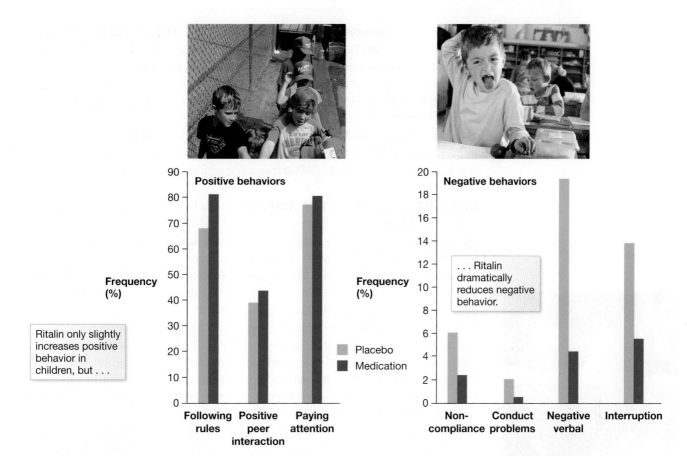

Ritalin only slightly increases positive behavior in children, but . . .

... Ritalin dramatically reduces negative behavior.

FIGURE 15.33
The Effects of Ritalin
These graphs compare the effects of Ritalin on the positive and negative symptoms of ADHD.

work more effectively on a task without interruption and are less impulsive. It is likely that these improvements in behavior have contributed to the large number of children who take this medication. Parents often feel pressured by school systems to medicate children who have ongoing behavior problems, and parents often pressure physicians to prescribe Ritalin because its effects can make home life much more manageable. Studies have shown that children taking Ritalin are happier, more adept socially, and somewhat more successful academically, although the effects on academic performance are modest (Chronis, Jones, & Raggi, 2006; Van der Oord, Prins, Oosterlaan, & Emmelkamp, 2008). These children also interact more positively with their parents, perhaps because they are more likely to comply with requests.

One classic study measured Ritalin's effects on the behavior of children playing baseball (Pelham et al., 1990). Children with ADHD who were taking the medication would assume the ready position in the outfield and could keep track of the game. Children with ADHD who were not taking the drug would often throw or kick their mitts even while the pitch was in progress.

The medication has its drawbacks, however. Side effects include sleep problems, reduced appetite, body twitches, and the temporary suppression of growth (Rapport & Moffitt, 2002; Schachter, Pham, King, Langford, & Moher, 2001). There is evidence that the short-term benefits of stimulants may not be maintained over the long term. In addition, because stimulants affect everyone who takes them, there is a very real risk of abuse, with numerous cases of children and adolescents buying and selling drugs such as Ritalin and Adderall. One study found that nearly 8 percent of college students had taken a nonprescribed stimulant in the past 30 days and that 60 percent reported knowing students who misused stimulants (Weyandt et al., 2009). Indeed, a controversial issue is whether using stimulants to treat children with ADHD may increase the risk that they will develop substance abuse problems as adults. Two recent studies have demonstrated that substance abuse problems are common among those who have had ADHD in childhood, but having taken Ritalin does not seem to have increased or decreased adult rates of substance abuse (Biederman et al., 2008; Mannuzza et al., 2008).

Perhaps most important, some children on medication may see their problems as beyond their control. They may not feel responsible for their behaviors and may not learn the coping strategies they will need if they discontinue their medication or if it ceases to be effective. Most therapists believe medication should be supplemented by psychological therapies, such as behavior modification. Some therapists even urge that medication be replaced by other treatment approaches when possible.

BEHAVIORAL TREATMENT OF ADHD Behavioral treatment of ADHD aims to reinforce positive behaviors and ignore or punish problem behaviors. The difficulties with this treatment approach are similar to those discussed in the following section, on autism. Treatment is very intensive and time consuming. A recent meta-analysis of 174 studies consisting of over 2,000 research participants found clear support for the effectiveness of behavioral therapy for ADHD (Fabiano et al., 2009). Many therapists advocate combining behavioral approaches with medication. The medication is used to gain control over the behaviors, and then behavioral modification techniques can be taught and the medication slowly phased out. Others argue that medication should be used only if behavioral techniques do not reduce inappropriate behaviors.

The National Institute of Mental Health, in collaboration with teams of investigators, began the Multimodal Treatment of Attention Deficit Hyperactivity Disorder (MTA) in 1992. The study involved 579 children, who were assigned randomly to a control group or to one of three treatment groups. The treatment groups lasted 14 months. One group received medical management (usually treatment with a stimulant such as Ritalin), the second group received intensive behavioral treatment, and the third group received a combination of the two. Follow-up studies a year later revealed that the children receiving medication and those receiving a combination of medication and behavioral therapy had greater improvement in their ADHD symptoms than did those in the behavioral treatment group (Jensen et al., 2001, 2005). Children who received medication and behavioral therapy showed a slight advantage in areas such as social skills, academics, and parent/child relations over those who received only medication.

After three years, however, the advantage of the medication therapy was no longer significant. The children who received behavioral therapy improved over the three years, whereas those who received medication improved quickly but then tended to regress over the three years (Jensen et al., 2007). These findings reinforce the key point here: Medications may be important in the short term, but psychological treatments may produce superior outcomes that last.

FIGURE 15.34
Applied Behavioral Analysis
This form of treatment involves intensive interaction between children with autism and their teachers and parents.

ANSWER: These drugs stimulate brain regions involved in behavioral control and paying attention.

 What is a possible reason that stimulants can help reduce ADHD?

15.19 Children with Autism Spectrum Disorder Benefit from Structured Behavioral Treatment

The treatment of children with autism spectrum disorder (ASD) presents unique challenges to mental health professionals. The core symptoms of ASD—impaired communication, restricted interests, and deficits in social interaction—make these children particularly difficult to work with. They often exhibit extreme behaviors as well as forms of self-stimulation, such as hand waving, rocking, humming, and jumping up and down. Although these behaviors must be reduced or eliminated before progress can occur in other areas, doing so is difficult because effective reinforcers are hard to find. Normal children respond positively to social praise and small prizes, but children with ASD are often oblivious to these rewards. In some cases, food is the only effective reinforcement in the initial stages of treatment.

Another characteristic of children with ASD is an overselectivity of attention. This tendency to focus on specific details while ignoring others interferes with generalizing learned behavior to other stimuli and situations. For example, a child who learns to set the table with plates may not know what to do when presented with bowls instead. Generalization of skills must be explicitly taught. For this reason, structured therapies are more effective for these children than are unstructured interventions, such as play therapy (in which the therapist tries to engage the child in conversation while the child plays with toys).

BEHAVIORAL TREATMENT FOR AUTISM SPECTRUM DISORDER As noted earlier, ASD clearly is caused by biological factors, but this knowledge has not led to any significant advances in therapies for the disorder. Indeed, one of the best-known and perhaps most effective treatments for children with autism was developed by Ivar Lovaas and his colleagues. The program, **applied behavioral analysis (ABA),** is based on principles of operant conditioning: Behaviors that are reinforced should increase in frequency. Behaviors that are not reinforced should diminish (**FIGURE 15.34**). There is evidence that this method can be used successfully to treat autism (Warren et al., 2011), particularly if treatment is started early in life (Vismara & Rogers, 2010).

This very intensive approach requires a minimum of 40 hours of treatment per week. In Lovaas's study, preschool-age children with autism were treated by teachers and by their parents, who received specific training. After more than two years of ABA treatment, the children had gained about 20 IQ points on average and most of them were able to enter a normal kindergarten program (Lovaas, 1987). In contrast, IQ did not change in a comparable control group of children who did not receive any treatment. A group of children who received 10 hours of treatment per week fared no better than the control group. Initiating treatment at a younger age also yielded better results, as did involving the parents and having at least a portion of the therapy take place in the home. Children with better language skills before entering treatment had better outcomes than those who were mute or echolalic (repeating whatever they heard).

Recent studies have shown that other tasks can improve ABA treatment. One study found that teaching children to engage in joint attention during ABA treatment, such as by having the parent or teacher imitate the child's actions and work to maintain eye contact, improved language skills significantly over ABA treatment alone (Kasari, Paparella, Freeman, & Jahromi, 2008). In another condition, children received instruction in symbolic play. Examples of symbolic play include imagining something, such as a doll driving a car, or pretending that one object represents another. Instruction in symbolic play also led to increased language use, greater parent/child play, and greater creativity in play (**FIGURE 15.35**).

applied behavioral analysis (ABA)

An intensive treatment for autism, based on operant conditioning.

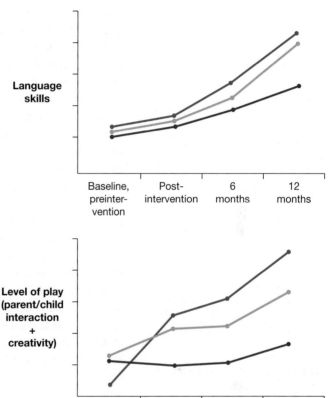

FIGURE 15.35

ABA Treatment, Joint Attention, and Symbolic Play

At the start of this study, the children were 3 or 4 years old. All the children received ABA treatment. Children receiving only ABA treatment were the control condition. In addition, some children received training in maintaining joint attention, and some children received training in symbolic play. Both of these combinations led to better language skills, greater parent/child play interaction, and greater creativity in play than did ABA alone.

Lovaas's ABA program has some drawbacks. The most obvious is the time commitment, because the therapy is very intensive and lasts for years. Parents essentially become full-time teachers for their child with ASD. The financial and emotional drains on the family can be substantial. If the family includes other children, they may feel neglected or jealous because of the amount of time and energy expended on the child with autism. Indeed, the other children might actually be neglected, as parents have only so much time and energy to devote to their children.

BIOLOGICAL TREATMENT FOR AUTISM SPECTRUM DISORDER There is good evidence that ASD is caused by brain dysfunction. Many attempts have been made to use this knowledge to treat the disorder. It is easy to find compelling case studies of children who have benefited from alternative treatment approaches. When the treatments are assessed in controlled studies, however, there is little or no evidence that most are effective.

One approach involves selective serotonin reuptake inhibitors. SSRIs have been tried as a treatment for ASD for two reasons. First, SSRIs such as Prozac reduce compulsions in patients with obsessive-compulsive disorder, and autism involves compulsive and repetitive behavior. Second, there is evidence that children with ASD have abnormal serotonin functioning. A review of pharmacological studies found that SSRIs are not helpful for treating the symptoms of ASD and actually may increase agitation (McPheeters et al., 2011). However, the review also found that antipsychotics, such as Risperdal, appear to reduce repetitive behaviors associated with self-stimulation. Unfortunately, antipsychotics have side effects, such as weight gain.

The important role of oxytocin in social behavior has been discussed throughout this textbook (see, for example, the discussion in Chapter 11, "Health and Well-Being," of the relationship between oxytocin and affiliation). Given oxytocin's role in social relations, some researchers have speculated that oxytocin plays a role in ASD. The first finding is that a deficit in oxytocin may be related to some of the behavioral manifestations of autism. Mice lacking oxytocin behave normally, except that they cannot recognize other mice or their mother's scent; a single dose of oxytocin reverses this effect until it wears off (Ferguson et al., 2000). In human studies, researchers have found that administering a nasal spray containing oxytocin leads people to make more eye contact, feel increased trust in others, and better infer emotions from other people's facial expressions (Ross & Young, 2009).

The question is whether oxytocin can improve social functioning in people with ASD. In one study, adults with ASD who received injections of oxytocin showed a dramatic improvement in their symptoms (Novotny et al., 2000). In another study, high-functioning adults with ASD were injected with oxytocin. Then they performed a social cognition task in which they listened to spoken sentences (e.g., "The boy went to the store") and had to identify the speaker's emotional tone. The participants who received oxytocin were better able to tell if the sentence was read in an angry, sad, happy, or indifferent tone than were the participants who received the placebo (Hollander et al., 2007). Oxytocin injections seem particularly useful for reducing repetitive behaviors (e.g., repeating the same phrase), questioning, inappropriate touching, and self-injury (Green & Hollander, 2010; Hollander et al., 2003). These findings are promising, but researchers need to do much more work before we can conclude that oxytocin is an empirically validated treatment for autism (Guastella & Hickie, 2016).

At this point, the neurobiology of ASD is not well understood. Attempts to use psychopharmacology to treat the disorder have led to some improvements in behavior, but much remains to be learned.

PROGNOSIS FOR CHILDREN WITH AUTISM SPECTRUM DISORDER Despite a few reports of remarkable recovery from ASD, the long-term prognosis remains poor. A follow-up study of men in their early 20s revealed that they continued to show the ritualistic self-stimulating behavior typical of ASD. In addition, nearly three-quarters had severe social difficulties and were unable to live and work independently (Howlin, Mawhood, & Rutter, 2000). Several factors affect the prognosis. Although therapists once believed the prognosis was particularly poor for children whose symptoms were apparent before age 2 (Hoshino et al., 1980), possibly only the most severe cases of ASD were diagnosed that early before public recognition of the disorder increased.

Early diagnosis clearly allows for more effective treatments (National Research Council, 2001). Still, severe cases—especially those involving notable cognitive deficiencies—are less likely to improve with treatment. Early language ability is associated with better outcome (Howlin et al., 2000), as is higher IQ. Children with ASD have difficulty generalizing from the therapeutic setting to the real world, and this limitation severely restricts their social functioning (Handleman, Gill, & Alessandri, 1988). A higher IQ may mean a better ability to generalize learning and therefore a better overall prognosis.

What is the most successful treatment for autism spectrum disorder, and what is the major drawback of that treatment?

ANSWER: Applied behavior analysis is the most successful treatment, especially when combined with symbolic play or joint attention, but it requires great commitment on the patient and family's part because it is very intensive and takes years.

15.20 The Use of Medication to Treat Adolescent Depressive Disorders Is Controversial

Adolescent depression is a serious problem. Recently, approximately 8 percent of the U.S. population aged 12–17 reported experiencing within the last year a major depressive episode that met *DSM* criteria (Substance Abuse and Mental Health Services Administration, 2011; **FIGURE 15.36**). Untreated adolescent depressive disorders are associated with drug abuse, dropping out of school, and suicide. In the United States, approximately 5,000 teenagers kill themselves each year, making suicide the third leading cause of death for that age group (Arias, MacDorman, Strobino, & Guyer, 2003). For many years, depression in children and adolescents was ignored or viewed as a typical part of growing up. Only about one-third of adolescents with psychological disorders receive any form of treatment (Merikangas et al., 2011). The percentage is even lower for adolescents from racial and ethnic minorities (Cummings & Druss, 2010). Understandably, then, many mental health professionals reacted favorably to the initial use of SSRIs, such as Prozac, to treat adolescent depressive disorders. Studies had found tricyclic antidepressants ineffective and the side effects potentially dangerous for adolescents, but the first studies using SSRIs found them effective and safe (e.g., Emslie et al., 1997).

Shortly after SSRIs were introduced as treatments for adolescent depression, some mental health researchers raised concerns that the drugs might cause some adolescents to become suicidal (Jureidini et al., 2004). These concerns arose partly from findings that SSRIs cause some adults to feel restless, impulsive, and suicidal. Following a report by one drug company of an increase in suicidal thoughts among adolescents taking its product, the FDA asked all drug companies to analyze their records for similar reports.

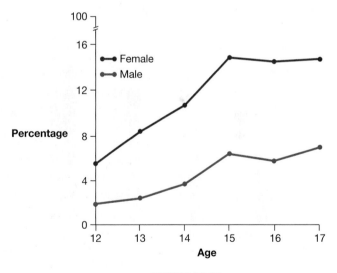

FIGURE 15.36
Rates of Depression in Teenagers
This graph shows results from the National Survey on Drug Use and Health undertaken by the Substance Abuse and Mental Health Services Administration (SAMHSA), a branch of the U.S. Department of Health and Human Services. The lines chart the rates of major depressive episodes and treatments among adolescents in 2009.

An analysis of reports on more than 4,400 children and adolescents found that about twice as many of those taking SSRIs reported having suicidal thoughts (4 percent) as those taking a placebo (2 percent). None of the children or adolescents committed suicide. Given evidence of increased thoughts of suicide, the FDA decided in 2004 to require manufacturers to add to their product labels a warning that antidepressants increase the risk of suicidal thinking and suicidal behavior in children and adolescents and that physicians prescribing these drugs to young people suffering from depression need to balance risk with clinical need. Physicians were also advised to watch their young patients closely, especially in the first few weeks of treatment. Suddenly many parents were wondering whether SSRIs were safe for their children.

Many questions about SSRIs and young people needed to be answered. First, were SSRIs effective for young people? If so, were they more effective than other treatments? Second, did these drugs cause suicidal feelings, or were young people with depressive disorders likely to feel suicidal whether or not they took medication? Finally, how many children and adolescents would be suicidal if their depression was left untreated?

TADS The Treatment for Adolescents with Depression Study (TADS Team, 2004) was an ambitious research program supported by the U.S. National Institutes of Health to answer these questions. TADS provided clear evidence that the SSRI Prozac is effective in treating adolescent depression.

The study examined 439 adolescents aged 12–17 who had suffered from depression for an average of 40 weeks before the study began. Participants were assigned randomly to a type of treatment and were followed for 12 weeks (**FIGURE 15.37**). The results indicated that 61 percent of participants taking Prozac showed improvement in symptoms, compared with 43 percent receiving cognitive-behavioral therapy (CBT) and 35 percent taking a placebo. The group receiving Prozac and CBT did best (71 percent improved). This latter finding is consistent with the findings of studies using adult participants. In short, combining drugs and psychotherapy often produces the strongest results for treating depression. At the end of 12 weeks, those in the placebo group were given treatment.

A 36-week follow-up study was conducted of the TADS treatment sample (March et al., 2007). The combined group had the best outcomes (86 percent improvement). Improvement with CBT alone (81 percent) was identical to that with Prozac alone (81 percent). The original placebo group was not included in the follow-up study, in part because those participants subsequently received treatment. A 3.5-year follow-up found that adolescents who received any of the treatments maintained positive outcomes (Peters et al., 2016). Measures of daily functioning did not indicate any major impairment.

In terms of suicidality, the results were more mixed. All treatment groups experienced a reduction in thoughts of suicide compared with the baseline. Participants in the Prozac group, however, were twice as likely to have serious suicidal thoughts or intentions compared with those undergoing other treatments. Of the seven adolescents who attempted suicide during the study, six were taking Prozac. The greater risk of suicidal thoughts or events continued through 36 weeks. Critics of adolescents receiving drugs point out that these findings are consistent with other studies showing a risk from SSRIs (Antonuccio & Burns, 2004).

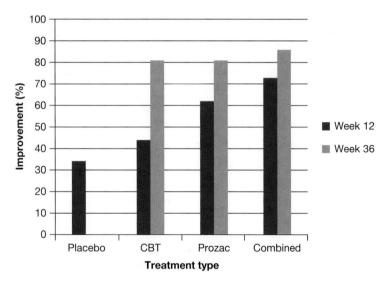

FIGURE 15.37

Treatment Outcomes in the TADS Study

Compared with placebo, treatment for adolescent depression with Prozac or Prozac combined with cognitive-behavioral therapy (CBT) was effective more quickly than CBT alone (i.e., at 12 weeks). However, by 36 weeks, CBT and Prozac were equally effective. Combining CBT with Prozac was slightly more effective at both times.

FURTHER THOUGHTS ON TREATMENT APPROACHES A few things should be kept in mind in analyzing the use of SSRIs for adolescent depressive disorders. In the TADS study, suicide attempts were quite uncommon (7 of 439 patients). This result is consistent with the FDA finding that about 4 percent of adolescents taking Prozac will become suicidal. Moreover, only a small number of the 5,000 adolescents who kill themselves each year are taking antidepressants of any kind. The question is whether the millions of children who take antidepressants experience more benefits than risks (Walkup, 2017).

According to some researchers, the relative success of psychotherapy for teenage depressive disorders makes it a better treatment choice (Mufson et al., 2004). But getting adolescents to comply with psychotherapy can be challenging. Young adolescents may lack the cognitive, emotional, or social skills necessary to benefit from treatment, thereby requiring individual tailoring of therapy to match the adolescent's current abilities (Garber, Frankel, & Herrington, 2016). Psychotherapy is also time consuming and expensive, and many health insurance companies provide only minimal support (Rifkin & Rifkin, 2004). In addition, it is unrealistic to expect there to be sufficient resources to provide psychotherapy to all adolescents who need it in the near future.

By contrast, it is relatively easy for pediatricians and family physicians to prescribe drugs. According to recent research, higher doses of SSRIs are especially likely to trigger suicidal attempts among adolescents (Miller, Swanson, Azrael, Pate, & Stürmer, 2014). The best advice to practitioners when using SSRIs to treat adolescents is *start low, go slow* (Brent & Gibbons, 2014).

 According to the initial and follow-up studies in TADS, were drugs or CBT most effective in treating adolescent depression?

ANSWER: Both were equally effective over the long term.

Your Chapter Review

Chapter Summary

How Are Psychological Disorders Treated?

15.1 Various Methods Have Been Used to Treat Psychopathology

Psychotherapy is the generic name for formal psychological treatment. Biological treatments range from drugs to electrical stimulation of brain regions to surgical intervention. Each theory of psychopathology includes treatment strategies that are based on the theory's assumptions about the causes of psychological disorders. Many therapists follow an eclectic approach.

15.2 Psychodynamic Therapy Seeks to Reduce Unconscious Conflicts

Originally developed by Sigmund Freud, psychodynamic therapy aims to identify and resolve unconscious conflicts and help the client develop insight into his problems. Contemporary approaches to psychodynamic therapy focus on interpersonal relations and emotional conflicts. Although there is some supportive evidence, it is unclear whether psychodynamic approaches offer any specific advantages over other forms of psychotherapy.

15.3 Behavioral and Cognitive Treatments Aim to Change Behavior, Emotion, or Thought Directly

Behavioral approaches focus on modifying maladaptive behaviors. The premise is that behavior is learned and therefore can be unlearned. Cognitive approaches restructure thinking. Cognitive-behavioral therapy (CBT) combines aspects of cognitive and behavioral therapies. It is the most widely used and perhaps most effective treatment for many psychological disorders.

15.4 The Context of Therapy Matters

As emphasized by the humanistic approach to therapy, an important factor is the relationship between the therapist and the client. Family therapy adopts a systems approach, seeing the individual as part of a larger context. Culture influences the expression of psychological disorders, recovery from psychological disorders, and willingness to seek psychotherapy. Group therapy is cost-effective, improves social skills, and provides social support.

15.5 Medication Is Effective for Certain Disorders

Psychotropic medications change neurochemistry. Anti-anxiety drugs increase GABA activity. Antidepressants affect serotonin availability or levels of norepinephrine and dopamine. Antipsychotics reduce symptoms such as delusions and hallucinations, blocking the effects of dopamine.

15.6 Alternative Biological Treatments Are Used in Extreme Cases

When traditional treatments are not successful, alternative treatments are used. These treatments include psychosurgery, electroconvulsive therapy, transcranial magnetic stimulation, and deep brain stimulation.

15.7 Effectiveness of Treatment Is Determined by Empirical Evidence

Randomized clinical trials should be used to assess the effectiveness of treatments for psychological disorders. Psychological treatments vary according to the particular disorder being addressed and the person's specific psychological symptoms; are based on techniques developed in the lab by psychologists; and are not guided by a single, overall grand theory. Some treatment approaches that have no scientific basis to support their use have proved detrimental, and they may prevent or delay a patient from receiving effective, evidence-based therapy.

15.8 Various Providers Can Assist in Treatment for Psychological Disorders

A variety of providers of psychological treatment exist. The providers differ in their training and work in diverse settings. These specialists include clinical psychologists, psychiatrists, counseling psychologists, psychiatric social workers, psychiatric nurses, and paraprofessionals.

15.9 Using Psychology in Your Life: How Do You Find a Therapist Who Can Help You?

Many college students experience life stressors or psychological problems. The good news is that there are many resources to assist students with psychological issues. Those seeking help should try to identify a therapist who is a good fit, which means someone with whom they feel at ease.

What Are the Most Effective Treatments?

15.10 Treatments That Focus on Behavior and on Cognition Are Superior for Anxiety Disorders

Behavioral techniques—in particular, systematic desensitization and exposure—alleviate specific phobias. Cognitive restructuring, coupled with exposure, is effective in treating panic disorder.

15.11 Both Antidepressants and CBT Are Effective for Obsessive-Compulsive Disorder

Obsessive-compulsive disorder (OCD) responds to medications that block serotonin reuptake and to CBT that includes exposure and response prevention. Deep brain stimulation holds promise for the treatment of severe cases of OCD.

15.12 Many Effective Treatments Are Available for Depressive Disorders

Pharmacological treatments include MAO inhibitors, tricyclics, and SSRIs. Cognitive-behavioral treatments target cognitive distortion—in particular, the cognitive triad. Alternative therapies include phototherapy, aerobic exercise, electroconvulsive therapy, transcranial magnetic stimulation, and deep brain stimulation. Gender issues in treating depressive disorders have resulted in the development of specific guidelines for treatment.

15.13 Think like a Psychologist: Should You Trust Studies Sponsored by Drug Companies?

There is concern that the increased use of antidepressants, such as Prozac, may be due to marketing pressures by drug companies. Research paid for by drug companies can produce conflicts of interest in experimenters. Studies often find that antidepressants are only modestly better than placebos in reducing depression. Drug companies' focus on only studies that work might lead to overestimation of the success of antidepressants.

15.14 Lithium and Atypical Antipsychotics Are Most Effective for Bipolar Disorder

Lithium has been found to be most effective in stabilizing mood among bipolar patients. This drug has considerable side effects, however. The drug quetiapine (better known as Seroquel) is an atypical antipsychotic that is currently the most commonly prescribed drug for bipolar disorders. Mood stabilizers such as lithium prescribed with atypical antipsychotics may improve treatment outcomes. Psychotherapy can help support compliance with drug treatment.

15.15 Antipsychotics Are Superior for Schizophrenia

First-generation antipsychotic medications are most effective for reducing the positive symptoms of schizophrenia. Tardive dyskinesia and other side effects are common with these older antipsychotic drugs. Clozapine reduces positive and negative symptoms, with fewer side effects. Drug therapy is most effective when combined with psychosocial treatment. The prognosis for patients depends on factors such as age of onset, gender, and culture.

Can Personality Disorders Be Treated?

15.16 Dialectical Behavior Therapy Is Most Successful for Borderline Personality Disorder

DBT combines elements of behavioral, cognitive, and a mindfulness approach. DBT proceeds in three stages. First, the most extreme and dysfunctional behaviors are targeted and replaced with more-appropriate behaviors. Next, the therapist helps the person explore past traumatic events. Finally, the therapist helps the patient develop self-respect and independent problem solving.

15.17 Antisocial Personality Disorder Is Extremely Difficult to Treat

Traditional psychotherapeutic approaches have not proved effective for treating antisocial personality disorder. Behavioral and cognitive approaches have been more effective, primarily in a controlled residential treatment environment. Generally, the prognosis is poor. Focusing on prevention by addressing conduct disorder in childhood may be the best strategy.

How Should Childhood Disorders and Adolescent Disorders Be Treated?

15.18 Children with ADHD Can Benefit from Various Approaches

Ritalin, despite its side effects, is an effective pharmacological treatment for ADHD. Research has provided support for the effectiveness of behavioral therapy in the treatment of ADHD, with behavioral therapy resulting in better long-term outcomes than medication therapy.

15.19 Children with Autism Spectrum Disorder Benefit from Structured Behavioral Treatment

Structured behavioral treatment has proved effective in improving the symptoms of autism. Applied behavioral analysis—an intensive treatment based on the principles of operant conditioning—has been used successfully in the treatment of autism. A biological treatment for autism has not been identified, but treatment with oxytocin holds promise.

15.20 The Use of Medication to Treat Adolescent Depressive Disorders Is Controversial

Many mental health professionals believe it is easier and more convenient to use Prozac and other SSRIs, rather than CBT, in the treatment of depressive disorders in adolescents. Although doses of SSRIs may lead to increased suicidal thoughts in adolescents, the available evidence indicates that such medications may have more benefits than costs. Cognitive-behavioral treatment is also effective in the treatment of depressive disorders, particularly when combined with drug treatment.

Key Terms

anti-anxiety drugs, p. 623
antidepressants, p. 624
antipsychotics, p. 624
applied behavioral analysis (ABA), p. 657
behavior therapy, p. 618
biological therapies, p. 616
client-centered therapy, p. 621

cognitive-behavioral therapy (CBT), p. 620
cognitive restructuring, p. 619
cognitive therapy, p. 619
dialectical behavior therapy (DBT), p. 651
electroconvulsive therapy (ECT), p. 626
exposure, p. 619
expressed emotion, p. 622

insight, p. 617
placebo effect, p. 628
psychodynamic therapy, p. 618
psychotherapy, p. 616
psychotropic medications, p. 623

Do You Want to Become a Clinical Psychologist?

Early in her career, the singer/songwriter Ellie Goulding experienced panic attacks that prevented her from leaving her house or going to the recording studio (McNamara, 2016). Cognitive behavioral therapy (CBT) helped Goulding manage her anxiety and function successfully in her private and public life. Goulding's experience with a psychological disorder and treatment for it is consistent with this chapter. As you have learned, the most effective treatments are related to the specific type of psychological disorder, with CBT proven to be the most effective treatment for anxiety and panic disorders.

As summarized in Table 15.1, a wide variety of mental health providers can administer therapy. They range from paraprofessionals, who may have little advanced training, to clinical psychologists, who have doctoral degrees. Although all types of providers can help people with mental health issues, it is typically clinical psychologists who use CBT to treat clients with serious psychological problems, such as anxiety or depressive disorders.

Perhaps after reading this chapter, or because of a personal or family experience with therapy, you are interested in becoming a clinical psychologist. Clinical psychology is the most popular doctoral degree in psychology, accounting for half of all psychology doctorates awarded annually (Norcross & Sayette, 2016). Admission to clinical psychology doctoral programs is very competitive, but you can take steps now to make you a stronger candidate for admission in the years to come.

According to one major study of psychology admission decisions, the most important factors for admission to doctoral programs are letters of recommendation, personal statements, undergraduate GPA, interview, research experience, GRE scores, and clinically related experience (Norcross & Sayette, 2016). Extracurricular experiences, such as participation or leadership in college organizations, or involvement in sorority or fraternity life, are given less weight in doctoral admissions.

How can you be sure to have strong letters of recommendation? Professors can write strong letters only if they believe you have the academic ability, experience, and research skills necessary to successfully complete a doctoral program in clinical psychology. Your professors know your exam scores and class participation efforts. However, strong letters of recommendation include more than just a summary of your academic performance. They also address who you are as a person. Therefore, in addition to giving your full effort to your academic performance, introduce yourself to your professors after class so they get to know you. Attend class regularly, read the assigned material carefully, and ask informed questions. Take advantage of office hours. Express interest in your professors' own research or other classes they teach.

Getting to know professors and doing well in their classes can also help you secure a position as a research assistant in a professor's research lab. Research experience is not only highly weighted in the admissions criteria, but can help you identify the area in which you would like to specialize. For example, if you think you might like to work with children, you can volunteer to work as an assistant in a lab that studies child development or child psychopathology. It is helpful to explore several areas so that you are exposed to a range of possible specialties. In addition, many colleges and universities grant course credit for research. Once you identify an area of particular interest, consider talking to a faculty member about conducting your own project, perhaps as an undergraduate honors thesis. Such a project will give you the opportunity to demonstrate your ability to design, implement, and analyze data. It may also provide an option to present your results at a local, state, or national conference.

Along with engaging in research, you can explore possible areas of interest, and gain experience, by working in a clinical setting. For example, you might volunteer at a crisis hotline, community mental health center, women's resource center, or drug and alcohol treatment program. These experiences can provide hands-on training in suicide prevention, sexual assault counseling, and substance rehabilitation treatments.

Identifying your area of interest through research and clinical experience is not only important in itself, but enables you to write a clear and articulate personal statement when you are ready to apply to doctoral programs. In most doctoral programs, graduate students work with an individual faculty mentor, and potential mentors typically make the final admission decision for a particular applicant. This means that your personal statement should describe your research interests, how they evolved, and why you applied to this particular program. The better you can explain why you are a good match for a particular advisor, and the more relevant experience you have, the better your chances of admission.

The bottom line: If a doctoral program in clinical psychology is your goal, keep admission criteria in mind to optimize your chances of acceptance. Strengthen your academic record by maintaining a high GPA and taking relevant classes. Gain research experience and explore your interests by volunteering in a lab. Because letters of recommendation will be vitally important, develop relationships with your professors. Your personal statement will matter as well, so think deeply about your interest in and commitment to the field of psychology and your chosen subfield.

Overview

Where Do Psychology Majors Work?

In each chapter of this book, the "Putting Psychology to Work" feature has shown you how the skills and knowledge you acquire as a psychology student can be directly applied in the workplace. Even at the introductory level—and whatever your major—psychology can help you develop many skills that employers value. These marketable attributes include strong analytical and statistical skills, such as the ability to use and interpret data. They also include "people skills," such as understanding human behavior and motivation and the ways in which people can influence and change the behavior of others.

In addition to benefiting introductory students, the field of psychology is extremely useful for psychology majors. With their unique and broad combination of skills, psychology majors can find employment in a wide range of sometimes unexpected settings. The figure below, from the U.S. Census Bureau (2014), looks at employment in relation to STEM majors (those in science, technology, engineering, and mathematics). The graphic first breaks down, by field, the ratios of STEM majors who go on to STEM occupations. The graphic then focuses on psychology graduates, differentiating between those who go on to STEM occupations and those who go on to non-STEM occupations.

As you can see, psychology graduates apply their analytical and statistical skills in science, technology, engineering, and other STEM occupations. As highlighted in previous "Putting Psychology to Work" features, specific jobs in this area include data scientists (Chapter 2); neuromarketers and neuroprosthetics specialists (Chapter 3); food scientists (Chapter 5); and video game engineers, Web developers, and software engineers (Chapter 6).

In addition, many psychology majors apply their understanding of human behavior and motivation in business, education, health care, and other non-STEM occupations. Specific examples include human resource managers (Chapter 2), teachers and school psychologists (Chapter 9), health psychologists (Chapter 11), and industrial/organizational psychologists (Chapter 13).

If introductory psychology has piqued your interest, consider taking more courses in the department or becoming a psychology major. Whether or not you continue to study psychology, however, it is a good idea to take a wide variety of courses in various disciplines, both to help you identify your interests and to make you a well-rounded person. Meanwhile, it is never too soon to start thinking about how to best prepare for future employment. Talk with your professors and academic and employment counselors about making the most of your education.

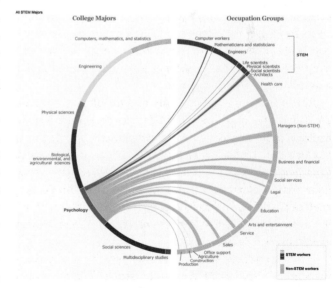

Want to earn a better grade on your test?
Go to **INQUIZITIVE** to learn and review this chapter's content, with personalized feedback along the way. Practice Tests and accompanying answer keys can be found at the back of the book on page PT-1.

Glossary

absentmindedness The inattentive or shallow encoding of events.

absolute threshold The minimum intensity of stimulation that must occur before you experience a sensation.

accommodation The process by which a new scheme is created or an existing scheme is drastically altered to include new information that otherwise would not fit into the scheme.

accuracy The degree to which an experimental measure is free from error.

acetylcholine (ACh) The neurotransmitter responsible for motor control at the junction between nerves and muscles; it is also involved in mental processes such as learning, memory, sleeping, and dreaming.

acquisition The gradual formation of an association between the conditioned and unconditioned stimuli.

action potential The electrical signal that passes along the axon and subsequently causes the release of chemicals from the terminal buttons.

activation-synthesis theory A theory of dreaming; this theory proposes that the brain tries to make sense of random brain activity that occurs during sleep by synthesizing the activity with stored memories.

actor/observer discrepancy People focus on situations to explain their own behavior while focusing on dispositions to explain other people's behavior.

adaptations In evolutionary theory, the physical characteristics, skills, or abilities that increase the chances of reproduction or survival and are therefore likely to be passed along to future generations.

addiction Drug use that remains compulsive despite its negative consequences.

affective forecasting The tendency for people to overestimate how events will make them feel in the future.

aggression Any behavior that involves the intention to harm another.

agoraphobia An anxiety disorder marked by fear of being in situations in which escape may be difficult or impossible.

all-or-none principle The principle that when a neuron fires, it fires with the same potency each time; a neuron either fires or not—it cannot partially fire, although the frequency of firing can vary.

altruism Providing help when it is needed, without any apparent reward for doing so.

amnesia A deficit in long-term memory—resulting from disease, brain injury, or psychological trauma—in which the individual loses the ability to retrieve vast quantities of information.

amygdala A brain structure that serves a vital role in learning to associate things with emotional responses and in processing emotional information.

analogical representations Mental representations that have some of the physical characteristics of objects; they are analogous to the objects.

anchoring The tendency, in making judgments, to rely on the first piece of information encountered or information that comes most quickly to mind.

anorexia nervosa An eating disorder characterized by excessive fear of becoming fat and therefore restricting energy intake to obtain a significantly low body weight.

anterograde amnesia A condition in which people lose the ability to form new memories.

anti-anxiety drugs A class of psychotropic medications used for the treatment of anxiety.

antidepressants A class of psychotropic medications used for the treatment of depression.

antipsychotics A class of psychotropic medications used for the treatment of schizophrenia and other disorders that involve psychosis.

antisocial personality disorder (APD) A personality disorder in which people engage in socially undesirable behavior, are hedonistic and impulsive, and lack empathy.

anxiety disorders Psychological disorders characterized by excessive fear and anxiety in the absence of true danger.

aphasia A language disorder that results in deficits in language comprehension and production.

applied behavioral analysis (ABA) An intensive treatment for autism, based on operant conditioning.

assessment In psychology, examination of a person's cognitive, behavioral, or emotional functioning to diagnose possible psychological disorders.

assimilation The process by which new information is placed into an existing scheme.

associative learning Linking two stimuli, or events, that occur together.

attachment A strong, intimate, emotional connection between people that persists over time and across circumstances.

attention-deficit/hyperactivity disorder (ADHD) A disorder characterized by restlessness, inattentiveness, and impulsivity.

attitudes People's evaluations of objects, of events, or of ideas.

attributions People's explanations for why events or actions occur.

audition Hearing; the sense of sound perception.

autism spectrum disorder A developmental disorder characterized by deficits in social interaction, by impaired communication, and by restricted interests.

autonomic nervous system (ANS) A component of the peripheral nervous system; it transmits sensory signals and motor signals between the central nervous system and the body's glands and internal organs.

availability heuristic Making a decision based on the answer that most easily comes to mind.

axon A long, narrow outgrowth of a neuron by which information is conducted from the cell body to the terminal buttons.

basal ganglia A system of subcortical structures that are important for the planning and production of movement.

behaviorism A psychological approach that emphasizes the role of environmental forces in producing observable behavior.

behavior modification The use of operant-conditioning techniques to eliminate unwanted behaviors and replace them with desirable ones.

behavioral approach system (BAS) The brain system involved in the pursuit of incentives or rewards.

behavioral inhibition system (BIS) The brain system that is sensitive to punishment and therefore inhibits behavior that might lead to danger or pain.

behavior therapy Treatment based on the premise that behavior is learned and therefore can be unlearned through the use of classical and operant conditioning.

binge-eating disorder An eating disorder characterized by binge eating that causes significant distress.

binocular depth cues Cues of depth perception that arise from the fact that people have two eyes.

binocular disparity A depth cue; because of the distance between the two eyes, each eye receives a slightly different retinal image.

biological therapies Treatment of psychological disorders based on medical approaches to disease (what is wrong with the body) and to illness (what a person feels as a result).

biopsychosocial model A model of health that integrates the effects of biological, behavioral, and social factors on health and illness.

bipolar I disorder A disorder characterized by extremely elevated moods during manic episodes and, frequently, depressive episodes as well.

bipolar II disorder A disorder characterized by alternating periods of extremely depressed and mildly elevated moods.

blocking The temporary inability to remember something.

body mass index (BMI) A ratio of body weight to height, used to measure obesity.

borderline personality disorder A personality disorder characterized by disturbances in identity, in affect, and in impulse control.

bottom-up processing Perception based on the physical features of the stimulus.

brain stem An extension of the spinal cord; it houses structures that control functions associated with survival, such as heart rate, breathing, swallowing, vomiting, urination, and orgasm.

Broca's area A small portion of the left frontal region of the brain, crucial for the production of language.

buffering hypothesis The idea that other people can provide direct emotional support in helping individuals cope with stressful events.

bulimia nervosa An eating disorder characterized by the alternation of dieting, binge eating, and purging (self-induced vomiting).

bystander intervention effect The failure to offer help by those who observe someone in need when other people are present.

Cannon-Bard theory of emotion Information about emotional stimuli is sent simultaneously to the cortex and the body and results in emotional experience and bodily reactions, respectively.

case study A descriptive research method that involves the intensive examination of an unusual person or organization.

cell body The site in the neuron where information from thousands of other neurons is collected and integrated.

central nervous system (CNS) The brain and the spinal cord.

central tendency A measure that represents the typical response or the behavior of a group as a whole.

cerebellum A large, convoluted protuberance at the back of the brain stem; it is essential for coordinated movement and balance.

cerebral cortex The outer layer of brain tissue, which forms the convoluted surface of the brain; the site of all thoughts, perceptions, and complex behaviors.

change blindness A failure to notice large changes in one's environment.

chromosomes Structures within the cell body that are made up of DNA, segments of which comprise individual genes.

chunking Organizing information into meaningful units to make it easier to remember.

circadian rhythms Biological patterns that occur at regular intervals as a function of time of day.

classical conditioning (Pavlovian conditioning) A type of associative learning in which a neutral stimulus comes to elicit a response when it is associated with a stimulus that already produces that response.

client-centered therapy An empathic approach to therapy; it encourages people to fulfill their individual potentials for personal growth through greater self-understanding.

cognition The mental activity that includes thinking and the understandings that result from thinking.

cognitive-behavioral approach A diagnostic model that views psychopathology as the result of learned, maladaptive thoughts and beliefs.

cognitive-behavioral therapy (CBT) A therapy that incorporates techniques from cognitive therapy and behavior therapy to correct faulty thinking and change maladaptive behaviors.

cognitive dissonance An uncomfortable mental state resulting from a contradiction between two attitudes or between an attitude and a behavior.

cognitive map A visual/spatial mental representation of an environment.

cognitive neuroscience The study of the neural mechanisms underlying thought, learning, perception, language, and memory.

cognitive restructuring A therapy that strives to help clients recognize maladaptive thought patterns and replace them with ways of viewing the world that are more in tune with reality.

cognitive therapy Treatment based on the idea that distorted thoughts produce maladaptive behaviors and emotions; treatment strategies attempt to modify these thought patterns.

companionate love A strong commitment based on friendship, trust, respect, and intimacy.

compliance The tendency to agree to do things requested by others.

concept A category, or class, of related items; it consists of mental representations of those items.

concrete operational stage The third stage in Piaget's theory of cognitive development; during this stage, children begin to think about and understand logical operations, and they are no longer fooled by appearances.

conditioned response (CR) A response to a conditioned stimulus; a response that has been learned.

conditioned stimulus (CS) A stimulus that elicits a response only after learning has taken place.

cones Retinal cells that respond to higher levels of light and result in color perception.

conformity The altering of one's behaviors and opinions to match those of other people or to match other people's expectations.

confound Anything that affects a dependent variable and that may unintentionally vary between the experimental conditions of a study.

consciousness One's subjective experience of the world, resulting from brain activity.

consolidation The neural process by which encoded information becomes stored in memory.

construct validity The extent to which variables measure what they are supposed to measure.

continuous reinforcement A type of learning in which behavior is reinforced each time it occurs.

control group The participants in an experiment who receive no intervention or who receive an intervention that is unrelated to the independent variable being investigated.

conventional level Middle stage of moral development; at this level, strict adherence to societal rules and the approval of others determine what is moral.

convergence A cue of binocular depth perception; when a person views a nearby object, the eye muscles turn the eyes inward.

coping response Any attempt made to avoid, escape from, or minimize a stressor.

corpus callosum A massive bridge of millions of axons that connects the hemispheres and allows information to flow between them.

correlation coefficient A descriptive statistic that indicates the strength and direction of the relationship between two variables.

correlational studies A research method that describes and predicts how variables are naturally related in the real world, without any attempt by the researcher to alter them or assign causation between them.

critical thinking Systematically questioning and evaluating information using well-supported evidence.

cryptomnesia A type of misattribution that occurs when a person thinks he has come up with a new idea, yet has only retrieved a stored idea and failed to attribute the idea to its proper source.

crystallized intelligence Intelligence that reflects both the knowledge acquired through experience and the ability to use that knowledge.

culturally sensitive research Studies that take into account the role that culture plays in determining thoughts, feelings, and actions.

culture The beliefs, values, rules, and customs that exist within a group of people who share a common language and environment.

data A collection of measurements gathered during the research process.

decision making Attempting to select the best alternative from among several options.

declarative memory The cognitive information retrieved from explicit memory; knowledge that can be declared.

deep structure In language, the implicit meanings of sentences.

defense mechanisms Unconscious mental strategies that the mind uses to protect itself from anxiety.

deindividuation A state of reduced individuality, reduced self-awareness, and reduced attention to personal standards; this phenomenon may occur when people are part of a group.

delusions False beliefs based on incorrect inferences about reality.

dendrites Branchlike extensions of the neuron that detect information from other neurons.

dependent variable The variable that gets measured in a research study.

descriptive research Research methods that involve observing behavior to describe that behavior objectively and systematically.

descriptive statistics Statistics that summarize the data collected in a study.

developmental psychology The study of changes, over the life span, in physiology, cognition, emotion, and social behavior.

dialectical behavior therapy (DBT) A form of therapy used to treat borderline personality disorder that combines elements of the behavioral and cognitive treatments with a mindfulness approach based on Eastern meditative practices.

diathesis-stress model A diagnostic model that proposes that a disorder may develop when an underlying vulnerability is coupled with a precipitating event.

difference threshold The minimum amount of change required for a person to detect a difference between two stimuli.

directionality problem A problem encountered in correlational studies; the researchers find a relationship between two variables, but they cannot determine which variable may have caused changes in the other variable.

discrimination The inappropriate and unjustified treatment of people as a result of prejudice.

disorganized behavior Acting in strange or unusual ways, including strange movement of limbs, bizarre speech, and inappropriate self-care, such as failing to dress properly or bathe.

disorganized speech Speaking in an incoherent fashion that involves frequently changing topics and saying strange or inappropriate things.

display rules Rules learned through socialization that dictate which emotions are suitable in given situations.

dissociative disorders Disorders that involve disruptions of identity, of memory, or of conscious awareness.

dissociative identity disorder (DID) The occurrence of two or more distinct identities in the same individual.

dizygotic twins Also called *fraternal twins*; twin siblings that result from two separately fertilized eggs and therefore are no more similar genetically than nontwin siblings.

dominant gene A gene that is expressed in the offspring whenever it is present.

dopamine A monoamine neurotransmitter involved in motivation, reward, and motor control over voluntary movement.

dreams Products of an altered state of consciousness in which images and fantasies are confused with reality.

drive A psychological state that, by creating arousal, motivates an organism to satisfy a need.

dynamic systems theory The view that development is a self-organizing process, in which new forms of behavior emerge through consistent interactions between a biological being and cultural and environmental contexts.

eardrum A thin membrane that marks the beginning of the middle ear; sound waves cause it to vibrate.

ego In psychodynamic theory, the component of personality that tries to satisfy the wishes of the id while being responsive to the dictates of the superego.

elaboration likelihood model The idea that persuasive messages lead to attitude changes in either of two ways: via the central route or via the peripheral route.

electroconvulsive therapy (ECT) A procedure that involves administering a strong electrical current to the person's brain to produce a seizure; it is effective for some cases of severe depression.

electroencephalograph (EEG) A device that measures electrical activity in the brain.

emotion An immediate, specific negative or positive response to environmental events or internal thoughts.

emotional intelligence (EI) A form of social intelligence that emphasizes the abilities to manage, recognize, and understand emotions and use emotions to guide appropriate thought and action.

emotion-focused coping A type of coping in which people try to prevent having an emotional response to a stressor.

encoding The processing of information so that it can be stored.

encoding specificity principle The idea that any stimulus that is encoded along with an experience can later trigger a memory of the experience.

endocrine system A communication system that uses hormones to influence thoughts, behaviors, and actions.

endorphins Neurotransmitters involved in natural pain reduction and reward.

episodic memory Memory for one's personal past experiences.

etiology Factors that contribute to the development of a disorder.

evolutionary theory A theory presented by the naturalist Charles Darwin; it views the history of a species in terms of the inherited, adaptive value of physical characteristics, of mental activity, and of behavior.

exemplar model A way of thinking about concepts: All members of a category are examples (exemplars); together they form the concept and determine category membership.

experiment A research method that tests causal hypotheses by manipulating and measuring variables.

experimental group The participants in an experiment who receive the treatment.

experimenter expectancy effect Actual change in the behavior of the people or nonhuman animals being observed that is due to the expectations of the observer.

explicit attitudes Attitudes that a person can report.

explicit memory The system underlying conscious memories.

exposure A behavioral therapy technique that involves repeated exposure to an anxiety-producing stimulus or situation.

expressed emotion A pattern of negative actions by a client's family members; the pattern includes critical comments, hostility directed toward the person by family members, and emotional overinvolvement.

external validity The degree to which the findings of a study can be generalized to other people, settings, or situations.

extinction A process in which the conditioned response is weakened when the conditioned stimulus is repeated without the unconditioned stimulus.

extrinsic motivation Motivation to perform an activity because of the external goals toward which that activity is directed.

family systems model A diagnostic model that considers problems within an individual as indicating problems within the family.

fear conditioning A type of classical conditioning that turns neutral stimuli into feared stimuli.

fight-or-flight response The physiological preparedness of animals to deal with danger by either fighting or fleeing.

five-factor theory The idea that personality can be described using five factors: openness to experience, conscientiousness, extraversion, agreeableness, and neuroticism.

flashbulb memories Vivid episodic memories for the circumstances in which people first learned of a surprising and consequential or emotionally arousing event.

fluid intelligence Intelligence that reflects the ability to process information, understand relationships, and think logically, particularly in novel or complex circumstances.

formal operational stage The final stage in Piaget's theory of cognitive development; in this stage, people can think abstractly, and they can formulate and test hypotheses through deductive logic.

fovea The center of the retina, where cones are densely packed.

framing In decision making, the tendency to emphasize the potential losses or potential gains from at least one alternative.

frontal lobes Regions of the cerebral cortex—at the front of the brain—important for movement and higher-level psychological processes associated with the prefrontal cortex.

functional fixedness In problem solving, having fixed ideas about the typical functions of objects.

functionalism An approach to psychology concerned with the adaptive purpose, or function, of mind and behavior.

functional magnetic resonance imaging (fMRI) An imaging technique used to examine changes in the activity of the working human brain by measuring changes in the blood's oxygen levels.

fundamental attribution error In explaining other people's behavior, the tendency to overemphasize personality traits and underestimate situational factors.

GABA Gamma-aminobutyric acid; the primary inhibitory transmitter in the nervous system.

general adaptation syndrome A consistent pattern of responses to stress that consists of three stages: alarm, resistance, and exhaustion.

gender identity One's sense of being male or female.

gender role A behavior that is typically associated with being male or female.

gene expression Whether a particular gene is turned on or off.

general intelligence (g) The idea that one general factor underlies intelligence.

generalized anxiety disorder (GAD) A diffuse state of constant anxiety not associated with any specific object or event.

genes The units of heredity that help determine the characteristics of an organism.

genotype The genetic constitution of an organism, determined at the moment of conception.

Gestalt theory A theory based on the idea that the whole of personal experience is different from the sum of its constituent elements.

glutamate The primary excitatory transmitter in the nervous system.

gonads The main endocrine glands involved in sexual behavior: in males, the testes; in females, the ovaries.

group polarization The process by which initial attitudes of groups become more extreme over time.

groupthink The tendency of a group to make a bad decision as a result of preserving the group and maintaining its cohesiveness; especially likely when the group is under intense pressure, is facing external threats, and is biased in a particular direction.

gustation The sense of taste.

habituation A decrease in behavioral response after repeated exposure to a stimulus.

hallucinations False sensory perceptions that are experienced without an external source.

haptic sense The sense of touch.

health psychology A field that integrates research on health and on psychology; it involves the application of psychological principles to promote health and well-being.

heredity Transmission of characteristics from parents to offspring through genes.

heritability A statistical estimate of the extent to which variation in a trait within a population is due to genetics.

heuristics Shortcuts (rules of thumb or informal guidelines) used to reduce the amount of thinking that is needed to make decisions.

hippocampus A brain structure that is associated with the formation of memories.

homeostasis The tendency for bodily functions to maintain equilibrium.

hormones Chemical substances, released from endocrine glands, that travel through the bloodstream to targeted tissues; the tissues are subsequently influenced by the hormones.

humanistic approaches Approaches to studying personality that emphasize how people seek to fulfill their potential through greater self-understanding.

humanistic psychology This approach focuses on the basic goodness of people and how they become happier and more fulfilled.

hypnosis A social interaction during which a person, responding to suggestions, experiences changes in memory, perception, and/or voluntary action.

hypothalamic-pituitary-adrenal (HPA) axis A body system involved in stress responses.

hypothalamus A brain structure that is involved in the regulation of bodily functions, including body temperature, body rhythms, blood pressure, and blood glucose levels; it also influences our basic motivated behaviors.

hypothesis A specific, testable prediction, narrower than the theory it is based on.

id In psychodynamic theory, the component of personality that is completely submerged in the unconscious and operates according to the pleasure principle.

idiographic approaches Person-centered approaches to assessing personality; they focus on individual lives and how various characteristics are integrated into unique persons.

immune system The body's mechanism for dealing with invading microorganisms, such as allergens, bacteria, and viruses.

implicit attitudes Attitudes that influence a person's feelings and behavior at an unconscious level.

implicit memory The system underlying unconscious memories.

incentives External objects or external goals, rather than internal drives, that motivate behaviors.

inclusive fitness An explanation for altruism that focuses on the adaptive benefit of transmitting genes, such as through kin selection, rather than focusing on individual survival.

independent variable The variable that gets manipulated in a research study.

infantile amnesia The inability to remember events from early childhood.

inferential statistics A set of procedures that enable researchers to decide whether differences between two or more groups are probably just chance variations or whether they reflect true differences in the populations being compared.

informational influence The tendency for people to conform when they assume that the behavior of others represents the correct way to respond.

ingroup favoritism The tendency for people to evaluate favorably and privilege members of the ingroup more than members of the outgroup.

insecure attachment The attachment style for a minority of infants; the infant may exhibit insecure attachment through various behaviors, such as avoiding contact with the caregiver, or by alternating between approach and avoidance behaviors.

insight (1) The sudden realization of a solution to a problem. (2) The goal of psychoanalysis; a client's awareness of his own unconscious psychological processes and how these processes affect daily functioning.

insomnia A disorder characterized by an inability to sleep that causes significant problems in daily living.

institutional review boards (IRBs) Groups of people responsible for reviewing proposed research to ensure that it meets the accepted standards of science and provides for the physical and emotional well-being of research participants.

intelligence The ability to use knowledge to reason, make decisions, make sense of events, solve problems, understand complex ideas, learn quickly, and adapt to environmental challenges.

intelligence quotient (IQ) An index of intelligence computed by dividing a child's estimated mental age by the child's chronological age, then multiplying this number by 100.

interactionism The theory that behavior is determined jointly by situations and underlying dispositions.

internal validity The degree to which the effects observed in an experiment are due to the independent variable and not to confounds.

intrinsic motivation Motivation to perform an activity because of the value or pleasure associated with that activity, rather than for an apparent external goal or purpose.

introspection A systematic examination of subjective mental experiences that requires people to inspect and report on the content of their thoughts.

James-Lange theory of emotion People perceive specific patterns of bodily responses, and as a result of that perception they feel emotion.

kinesthetic sense Perception of the positions in space and movements of our bodies and our limbs.

language A system of communication using sounds and symbols according to grammatical rules.

latent learning Learning that takes place in the absence of reinforcement.

law of effect Thorndike's general theory of learning: Any behavior that leads to a "satisfying state of affairs" is likely to occur again, and any behavior that leads to an "annoying state of affairs" is less likely to occur again.

learned helplessness A cognitive model of depression in which people feel unable to control events in their lives.

learning A relatively enduring change in behavior, resulting from experience.

linguistic relativity theory The claim that language determines thought.

locus of control Personal beliefs about how much control people have over outcomes in their lives.

long-term memory The relatively permanent storage of information.

long-term potentiation (LTP) Strengthening of a synaptic connection,

making the postsynaptic neurons more easily activated by presynaptic neurons.

lymphocytes Specialized white blood cells that make up the immune system; the three types are B cells, T cells, and natural killer cells.

magnetic resonance imaging (MRI) A method of brain imaging that uses a powerful magnetic field to produce high-quality images of the brain.

major depressive disorder A disorder characterized by severe negative moods or a lack of interest in normally pleasurable activities.

mean A measure of central tendency that is the arithmetic average of a set of numbers.

median A measure of central tendency that is the value in a set of numbers that falls exactly halfway between the lowest and highest values.

meditation A mental procedure that focuses attention on an external object or on a sense of awareness.

memory The nervous system's capacity to retain and retrieve skills and knowledge.

memory bias The changing of memories over time so that they become consistent with current beliefs or attitudes.

mental age An assessment of a child's intellectual standing compared with that of same-age peers; determined by comparing the child's test score with the average score for children of each chronological age.

mental sets Problem-solving strategies that have worked in the past.

mere exposure effect The idea that greater exposure to a stimulus leads to greater liking for it.

meta-analysis A "study of studies" that combines the findings of multiple studies to arrive at a conclusion.

mind/body problem A fundamental psychological issue: Are mind and body separate and distinct, or is the mind simply the physical brain's subjective experience?

mirror neurons Neurons in the brain that are activated when one observes another individual engage in an action and when one performs a similar action.

mnemonics Learning aids or strategies that improve recall through the use of retrieval cues.

mode A measure of central tendency that is the most frequent score or value in a set of numbers.

modeling The imitation of observed behavior.

modern racism Subtle forms of prejudice that coexist with the rejection of racist beliefs.

monocular depth cues Cues of depth perception that are available to each eye alone.

monozygotic twins Also called *identical twins*; twin siblings that result from one

zygote splitting in two and therefore share the same genes.

morphemes The smallest language units that have meaning, including suffixes and prefixes.

motivation A process that energizes, guides, and maintains behavior toward a goal.

myelin sheath A fatty material, made up of glial cells, that insulates some axons to allow for faster movement of electrical impulses along the axon.

narcolepsy A sleep disorder in which people experience excessive sleepiness during normal waking hours, sometimes going limp and collapsing.

natural selection In evolutionary theory, the idea that those who inherit characteristics that help them adapt to their particular environments have a selective advantage over those who do not.

naturalistic observation A type of descriptive study in which the researcher is a passive observer, separated from the situation and making no attempt to change or alter ongoing behavior.

nature/nurture debate The arguments concerning whether psychological characteristics are biologically innate or acquired through education, experience, and culture.

need A state of biological or social deficiency.

need hierarchy Maslow's arrangement of needs, in which basic survival needs must be met before people can satisfy higher needs.

need to belong theory The theory that the need for interpersonal attachments is a fundamental motive that has evolved for adaptive purposes.

negative correlation A relationship between two variables in which one variable increases when the other decreases.

negative punishment The removal of a stimulus to decrease the probability of a behavior's recurring.

negative reinforcement The removal of an unpleasant stimulus to increase the probability of a behavior's being repeated.

negative symptoms Symptoms of schizophrenia that are marked by deficits in functioning, such as apathy, lack of emotion, and slowed speech and movement.

neurons The basic units of the nervous system; cells that receive, integrate, and transmit information in the nervous system. They operate through electrical impulses, communicate with other neurons through chemical signals, and form neural networks.

neurotransmitters Chemical substances that transmit signals from one neuron to another.

nodes of Ranvier Small gaps of exposed axon, between the segments of myelin sheath, where action potentials take place.

nomothetic approaches Approaches to assessing personality that focus on how common characteristics vary from person to person.

nonassociative learning Responding after repeated exposure to a single stimulus, or event.

nonverbal behavior The facial expressions, gestures, mannerisms, and movements by which one communicates with others.

norepinephrine A monoamine neurotransmitter involved in states of arousal and attention.

normative influence The tendency for people to conform in order to fit in with the group.

obedience When a person follows the orders of a person of authority.

observational learning Acquiring or changing a behavior after exposure to another individual performing that behavior.

observer bias Systematic errors in observation that occur because of an observer's expectations.

object constancy Correctly perceiving objects as constant in their shape, size, color, and lightness, despite raw sensory data that could mislead perception.

object permanence The understanding that an object continues to exist even when it cannot be seen.

obsessive-compulsive disorder (OCD) A disorder characterized by frequent intrusive thoughts and compulsive actions.

obstructive sleep apnea A disorder in which a person, while asleep, stops breathing because his or her throat closes; the condition results in frequent awakenings during the night.

occipital lobes Regions of the cerebral cortex—at the back of the brain—important for vision.

olfaction The sense of smell.

olfactory bulb The brain center for smell, located below the frontal lobes.

olfactory epithelium A thin layer of tissue, within the nasal cavity, that contains the receptors for smell.

operant conditioning (instrumental conditioning) A learning process in which the consequences of an action determine the likelihood that it will be performed in the future.

operational definition A definition that *qualifies* (describes) and *quantifies* (measures) a variable so the variable can be understood objectively.

outgroup homogeneity effect The tendency to view outgroup members as less varied than ingroup members.

oxytocin A hormone that is important for mothers in bonding to newborns and may encourage affiliation during social stress.

panic disorder An anxiety disorder that consists of sudden, overwhelming attacks of terror.

parasympathetic division A division of the autonomic nervous system; it returns the body to its resting state.

parietal lobes Regions of the cerebral cortex—in front of the occipital lobes and behind the frontal lobes—important for the sense of touch and for attention to the environment.

partial reinforcement A type of learning in which behavior is reinforced intermittently.

partial-reinforcement extinction effect The greater persistence of behavior under partial reinforcement than under continuous reinforcement.

participant observation A type of descriptive study in which the researcher is involved in the situation.

passionate love A state of intense longing and desire.

perception The processing, organization, and interpretation of sensory signals.

peripheral nervous system (PNS) All nerve cells in the body that are not part of the central nervous system. The peripheral nervous system includes the somatic and autonomic nervous systems.

persistence The continual recurrence of unwanted memories.

persistent depressive disorder A form of depression that is not severe enough to be diagnosed as major depressive disorder.

personal attributions Explanations of people's behavior that refer to their internal characteristics, such as abilities, traits, moods, or efforts.

personality A person's characteristic thoughts, emotional responses, and behaviors.

personality trait A pattern of thought, emotion, and behavior that is relatively consistent over time and across situations.

persuasion The active and conscious effort to change an attitude through the transmission of a message.

phenotype Observable physical characteristics, which result from both genetic and environmental influences.

phobia An acquired fear that is out of proportion to the real threat of an object or of a situation.

phonemes The basic sounds of speech, the building blocks of language.

phonics A method of teaching reading in English that focuses on the association between letters and their phonemes.

pituitary gland A gland located at the base of the hypothalamus; it sends hormonal signals to other endocrine glands, controlling their release of hormones.

placebo effect An improvement in physical or mental health following treatment with a placebo—that is, with a drug or treatment that has no active component on the disorder being treated.

place coding A mechanism for encoding high-frequency auditory stimuli in which the frequency of the sound wave is encoded by the location of the hair cells along the basilar membrane.

plasticity A property of the brain that allows it to change as a result of experience or injury.

population Everyone in the group the experimenter is interested in.

positive correlation A relationship between two variables in which both variables either increase or decrease together.

positive punishment The administration of a stimulus to decrease the probability of a behavior's recurring.

positive reinforcement The administration of a stimulus to increase the probability of a behavior's being repeated.

positron emission tomography (PET) A method of brain imaging that assesses metabolic activity by using a radioactive substance injected into the bloodstream.

postconventional level Highest stage of moral development; at this level, decisions about morality depend on abstract principles and the value of all life.

posttraumatic stress disorder (PTSD) A disorder that involves frequent nightmares, intrusive thoughts, and flashbacks related to an earlier trauma.

preconventional level Earliest level of moral development; at this level, self-interest and event outcomes determine what is moral.

prefrontal cortex The frontmost portion of the frontal lobes, especially prominent in humans; important for attention, working memory, decision making, appropriate social behavior, and personality.

prejudice Negative feelings, opinions, and beliefs associated with a stereotype.

preoperational stage The second stage in Piaget's theory of cognitive development; during this stage, children think symbolically about objects, but they reason based on intuition and superficial appearance rather than logic.

primary appraisals Part of the coping process that involves making decisions about whether a stimulus is stressful, benign, or irrelevant.

primary emotions Emotions that are innate, evolutionarily adaptive, and universal (shared across cultures).

proactive interference Interference that occurs when prior information inhibits the ability to remember new information.

problem-focused coping A type of coping in which people take direct steps to confront or minimize a stressor.

problem solving Finding a way around an obstacle to reach a goal.

procedural memory A type of implicit memory that involves motor skills, habits, and other behaviors.

projective measures Personality tests that examine unconscious processes by having people interpret ambiguous stimuli.

prosocial behaviors Actions that tend to benefit others, such as doing favors or helping.

prospective memory Remembering to do something at some future time.

prototype model A way of thinking about concepts: Within each category, there is a best example—a prototype—for that category.

psychoanalysis A method developed by Sigmund Freud that attempts to bring the contents of the unconscious into conscious awareness so that conflicts can be revealed.

psychodynamic theory The Freudian theory that unconscious forces determine behavior.

psychodynamic therapy A form of therapy based on Freudian theory; it aims to help clients examine needs, defenses, and motives as a way of understanding distress.

psychological science The study, through research, of mind, brain, and behavior.

psychopathology Sickness or disorder of the mind; psychological disorder.

psychosexual stages According to Freud, developmental stages that correspond to distinct libidinal urges; progression through these stages profoundly affects personality.

psychotherapy The generic name given to formal psychological treatment.

psychotropic medications Drugs that affect mental processes.

puberty The beginning of adolescence, marked by the onset of sexual maturity and thus the ability to reproduce.

random assignment Placing research participants into the conditions of an experiment in such a way that each participant has an equal chance of being assigned to any level of the independent variable.

reactivity The phenomenon that occurs when knowledge that one is being observed alters the behavior being observed.

receptors In neurons, specialized protein molecules on the postsynaptic membrane; neurotransmitters bind to these molecules after passing across the synapse.

recessive gene A gene that is expressed only when it is matched with a similar gene from the other parent.

reciprocal determinism The theory that how personality is expressed can be explained by the interaction of environment, person factors, and behavior itself.

reconsolidation Neural processes involved when memories are recalled and then stored again for retrieval.

reinforcer A stimulus that follows a response and increases the likelihood that the response will be repeated.

reliability The degree to which a measure is stable and consistent over time.

REM sleep The stage of sleep marked by rapid eye movements, paralysis of motor systems, and dreaming.

replication Repetition of a research study to confirm or contradict the results.

representativeness heuristic Placing a person or an object in a category if that person or object is similar to one's prototype for that category.

Rescorla-Wagner model A cognitive model of classical conditioning; it holds that learning is determined by the extent to which a US is unexpected or surprising.

research A scientific process that involves the careful collection, analysis, and interpretation of data.

Research Domain Criteria (RDoC) A method that defines basic aspects of functioning and considers them across multiple levels of analysis, from genes to brain systems to behavior.

resting membrane potential The electrical charge of a neuron when it is not active.

restructuring A new way of thinking about a problem that aids its solution.

retina The thin inner surface of the back of the eyeball; it contains the sensory receptors that transduce light into neural signals.

retrieval The act of recalling or remembering stored information when it is needed.

retrieval cue Any stimulus that increases memory recall.

retroactive interference Interference that occurs when new information inhibits the ability to remember old information.

retrograde amnesia A condition in which people lose past memories, such as memories for events, facts, people, or even personal information.

reuptake The process whereby a neurotransmitter is taken back into the presynaptic terminal buttons, thereby stopping its activity.

rods Retinal cells that respond to low levels of light and result in black-and-white perception.

sample A subset of a population.

scatterplot A graphical depiction of the relationship between two variables.

schemas Cognitive structures in long-term memory that help us perceive, organize, process, and use information.

schizophrenia A psychological disorder characterized by alterations in thoughts, in perceptions, or in consciousness, resulting in psychosis.

scientific method A systematic and dynamic procedure of observing and measuring phenomena, used to achieve the goals of description, prediction, control, and explanation; it involves an interaction between research, theories, and hypotheses.

script A schema that directs behavior over time within a situation.

secondary appraisals Part of the coping process during which people evaluate their response options and choose coping behaviors.

secondary emotions Blends of primary emotions.

secure attachment The attachment style for a majority of infants; the infant is confident enough to play in an unfamiliar environment as long as the caregiver is present and is readily comforted by the caregiver during times of distress.

selection bias In an experiment, unintended differences between the participants in different groups; it could be caused by nonrandom assignment to groups.

self-actualization A state that is achieved when one's personal dreams and aspirations have been attained.

self-esteem The evaluative aspect of the self-concept in which people feel worthy or unworthy.

self-report methods Methods of data collection in which people are asked to provide information about themselves, such as in surveys or questionnaires.

self-serving bias The tendency for people to take personal credit for success but blame failure on external factors.

semantic memory Memory for knowledge of facts independent of personal experience.

sensation The detection of external stimuli and the transmission of this information to the brain.

sensitization An increase in behavioral response after exposure to a stimulus.

sensorimotor stage The first stage in Piaget's theory of cognitive development; during this stage, infants acquire information about the world through their senses and motor skills. Reflexive responses develop into more deliberate actions through the development and refinement of schemes.

sensory adaptation A decrease in sensitivity to a constant level of stimulation.

sensory memory A memory system that very briefly stores sensory information in close to its original sensory form.

serial position effect The idea that the ability to recall items from a list depends on the order of presentation, with items presented early or late in the list remembered better than those in the middle.

serotonin A monoamine neurotransmitter important for a wide range of psychological activity, including emotional states, impulse control, and dreaming.

sexual response cycle A four-stage pattern of physical and psychological responses during sexual activity.

sexual strategies theory A theory that maintains that women and men have evolved distinct mating strategies because they faced different adaptive problems over the course of human history. The strategies used by each sex maximize the probability of passing along their genes to future generations.

shaping A process of operant conditioning; it involves reinforcing behaviors that are increasingly similar to the desired behavior.

short-term memory A memory storage system that briefly holds a limited amount of information in awareness.

signal detection theory (SDT) A theory of perception based on the idea that the detection of a stimulus requires a judgment—it is not an all-or-nothing process.

situational attributions Explanations of people's behavior that refer to external events, such as the weather, luck, accidents, or other people's actions.

situationism The theory that behavior is determined more by situations than by personality traits.

social comparison The tendency for people to evaluate their own actions, abilities, and beliefs by contrasting them with other people's.

social facilitation The idea that the presence of others generally enhances performance.

social identity theory The idea that ingroups consist of individuals who perceive themselves to be members of the same social category and experience pride through their group membership.

social intuitionist model The idea that moral judgments reflect people's initial and automatic emotional responses.

social loafing The tendency for people to work less hard in a group than when working alone.

social norms Expected standards of conduct, which influence behavior.

sociocultural model A diagnostic model that views psychopathology as the result of the interaction between individuals and their cultures.

socioemotional selectivity theory As people grow older, they view time as limited and therefore shift their focus to meaningful events, experiences, and goals.

sociometer An internal monitor of social acceptance or rejection.

somatic markers Bodily reactions that arise from the emotional evaluation of an action's consequences.

somatic nervous system (SNS) A component of the peripheral nervous system; it transmits sensory signals and motor signals between the central nervous system and the skin, muscles, and joints.

sound wave A pattern of changes in air pressure during a period of time; it produces the percept of a sound.

source amnesia A type of misattribution that occurs when a person has a memory for an event but cannot remember where he or she encountered the information.

source misattribution Memory distortion that occurs when people misremember the time, place, person, or circumstances involved with a memory.

split brain A condition that occurs when the corpus callosum is surgically cut and the two hemispheres of the brain do not receive information directly from each other.

spontaneous recovery A process in which a previously extinguished conditioned

response reemerges after the presentation of the conditioned stimulus.

standard deviation A statistical measure of how far away each value is, on average, from the mean.

stereotypes Cognitive schemas that allow for easy, fast processing of information about people based on their membership in certain groups.

stereotype threat Apprehension about confirming negative stereotypes related to one's own group.

stimulus discrimination A differentiation between two similar stimuli when only one of them is consistently associated with the unconditioned stimulus.

stimulus generalization Learning that occurs when stimuli that are similar but not identical to the conditioned stimulus produce the conditioned response.

storage The retention of encoded representations.

stream of consciousness A phrase coined by William James to describe each person's continuous series of ever-changing thoughts.

stress A type of response that typically involves an unpleasant state, such as anxiety or tension.

stressor Something in the environment that is perceived as threatening or demanding and therefore produces stress.

structuralism An approach to psychology based on the idea that conscious experience can be broken down into its basic underlying components.

subliminal perception The processing of information by sensory systems without conscious awareness.

suggestibility The development of biased memories from misleading information.

superego In psychodynamic theory, the internalization of societal and parental standards of conduct.

surface structure In language, the sound and order of words.

symbolic representations Abstract mental representations that do not correspond to the physical features of objects or ideas.

sympathetic division A division of the autonomic nervous system; it prepares the body for action.

synapse The gap between the terminal buttons of a "sending" neuron and the dendrites of a "receiving" neuron; the site at which chemical communication occurs between neurons.

synaptic pruning The synaptic connections in the brain that are used are preserved, whereas those that are not used decay and disappear.

taste buds Sensory organs in the mouth that contain the receptors for taste.

telegraphic speech The tendency for toddlers to speak using rudimentary sentences that are missing words and grammatical markings but follow a logical syntax and convey a wealth of meaning.

temperaments Biologically based tendencies to feel or act in certain ways.

temporal coding A mechanism for encoding low-frequency auditory stimuli in which the firing rates of cochlear hair cells match the frequency of the sound wave.

temporal lobes Regions of the cerebral cortex—below the parietal lobes and in front of the occipital lobes—important for processing auditory information, for memory, and for object and face perception.

tend-and-befriend response Females' tendency to protect and care for their offspring and form social alliances rather than fight or flee in response to threat.

teratogens Agents that harm the embryo or fetus.

terminal buttons At the ends of axons, small nodules that release chemical signals from the neuron into the synapse.

thalamus The gateway to the brain; it receives almost all incoming sensory information before that information reaches the cortex.

theory A model of interconnected ideas or concepts that explains what is observed and makes predictions about future events. Theories are based on empirical evidence.

theory of mind The ability to understand that other people have mental states that influence their behavior.

thinking The mental manipulation of representations of knowledge about the world.

third variable problem A problem that occurs when the researcher cannot directly manipulate variables; as a result, the researcher cannot be confident that another, unmeasured variable is not the actual cause of differences in the variables of interest.

top-down processing How knowledge, expectations, or past experiences shape the interpretation of sensory information.

trait approach An approach to studying personality that focuses on how individuals differ in personality dispositions.

transcranial magnetic stimulation (TMS) The use of strong magnets to briefly interrupt normal brain activity as a way to study brain regions.

transduction The process by which sensory stimuli are converted to signals the brain can interpret.

traumatic brain injury (TBI) Impairments in mental functioning caused by a blow to or very sharp movement of the head.

two-factor theory of emotion A label applied to physiological arousal results in the experience of an emotion.

Type A behavior pattern A pattern of behavior characterized by competitiveness, achievement orientation, aggressiveness, hostility, restlessness, impatience with others, and inability to relax.

Type B behavior pattern A pattern of behavior characterized by noncompetitive, relaxed, easygoing, and accommodating behavior.

unconditioned response (UR) A response that does not have to be learned, such as a reflex.

unconditioned stimulus (US) A stimulus that elicits a response, such as a reflex, without any prior learning.

unconscious The place where mental processes operate below the level of conscious awareness.

variability In a set of numbers, how widely dispersed the values are from each other and from the mean.

variable Something in the world that can vary and that a researcher can manipulate (change), measure (evaluate), or both.

vestibular sense Perception of balance determined by receptors in the inner ear.

vicarious learning Learning the consequences of an action by watching others being rewarded or punished for performing the action.

well-being A positive state that includes striving for optimal health and life satisfaction.

Wernicke's area An area of the left hemisphere where the temporal and parietal lobes meet, involved in speech comprehension.

"what is beautiful is good" stereotype The belief that attractive people are superior in most ways.

whole language A method of teaching reading in English that emphasizes learning the meanings of words and understanding how words are connected in sentences.

working memory An active processing system that keeps different types of information available for current use.

Yerkes-Dodson law The psychological principle that performance on challenging tasks increases with arousal up to a moderate level. After that, additional arousal impairs performance.

zero correlation A relationship between two variables in which one variable is not predictably related to the other.

References

Abad-Merino, S., Newheiser, A. K., Dovidio, J. F., Tabernero, C., & González, I. (2013). The dynamics of intergroup helping: The case of subtle bias against Latinos. *Cultural Diversity and Ethnic Minority Psychology, 19,* 445–452.

Abizaid, A. (2009). Ghrelin and dopamine: New insights on the peripheral regulation of appetite. *Journal of Neuroendocrinology, 21,* 787–793.

Abram, S. V., & DeYoung, C. G. (2017). Using personality neuroscience to study personality disorder. *Personality Disorders: Theory, Research, and Treatment, 8,* 2–13.

Abramowitz, J. S. (2013). The practice of exposure therapy: Relevance of cognitive-behavioral theory and extinction theory. *Behavior Therapy, 44,* 548–558.

Abramson, L. Y., Metalsky, G., & Alloy, L. (1989). Hopelessness depression: A theory-based subtype of depression. *Psychological Review, 96,* 358–372.

Ackerman, P. L., Beier, M. E., & Boyle, M. O. (2005). Working memory and intelligence: The same or different constructs? *Psychological Bulletin, 131,* 30–60.

Adair, J., & Kagitcibasi, C. (1995). Development of psychology in developing countries: Factors facilitating and impeding its progress. *International Journal of Psychology, 30,* 633–641.

Adolphs, R., Gosselin, F., Buchanan, T. W., Tranel, D., Schyns, P., & Damasio, A. R. (2005). A mechanism for impaired fear recognition after amygdala damage. *Nature, 433,* 68–72.

Adolphs, R., Sears, L., & Piven, J. (2001). Abnormal processing of social information from faces in autism. *Journal of Cognitive Neuroscience, 13,* 232–240.

Adolphs, R., Tranel, D., & Damasio, A. R. (1998). The human amygdala in social judgment. *Nature, 393,* 470–474.

Agawu, K. (1995). *African rhythm: A northern ewe perspective.* Cambridge, England: Cambridge University Press.

Agnew-Blais, J. C., Polanczyk, G. V., Danese, A., Wertz, J., Moffitt, T. E., Arseneault, L., et al. (2016). Evaluation of the persistence, remission, and emergence of attention-deficit/hyperactivity disorder in young adulthood. *JAMA Psychiatry, 73,* 713–720.

Ahima, R. S., & Lazar, M. A. (2013). The health risk of obesity—better metrics imperative. *Science, 341,* 856–858.

Ainsworth, M. D. S., Blehar, M. C., Waters, E., & Wall, S. (1978). *Patterns of attachment: A psychological study of the strange situation.* Hillsdale, NJ: Erlbaum.

Aizpurua, A., & Koutstaal, W. (2015). A matter of focus: Detailed memory in the intentional autobiographical recall of older and younger adults. *Consciousness and Cognition, 33,* 145–155.

Al-Delaimy, W. K., Myers, M. G., Leas, E. C., Strong, D. R., & Hofstetter, C. R. (2015). E-cigarette use in the past and quitting behavior in the future: A population-based study. *American Journal of Public Health, 105,* 1213–1219.

Al-Khatib, T. (2013, October 30). Baseball superstitions not a game to players. *Discovery News.* Retrieved from http://news.discovery.com/human/baseball-superstitions-not-a-game-to-players-131030.htm

Alberini, C. M., & LeDoux, J. E. (2013). Memory reconsolidation. *Current Biology, 23,* R746–R750.

Alferink, L. A., & Farmer-Dougan, V. (2010). Brain-(not) based education: Dangers of misunderstanding and misapplication of neuroscience research. *Exceptionality, 18,* 42–52.

Algoe, S. B., & Fredrickson, B. L. (2011). Emotional fitness and the movement of affective science from lab to field. *American Psychologist, 66,* 35–42.

Ali, K., Ahmed, N., & Greenough, A. (2012). Sudden infant death syndrome (SIDS), substance misuse, and smoking in pregnancy. *Research and Reports in Neonatology, 2,* 95–101.

Alia-Klein, N., Wang, G. J., Preston-Campbell, R. N., Moeller, S. J., Parvaz, M. A., Zhu, W., et al. (2014). Reactions to media violence: It's in the brain of the beholder. *PLoS ONE, 9,* e107260.

Alicke, M. D., Klotz, M. L., Breitenbecher, D. L., Yurak, T. J., & Vredenburg, D. S. (1995). Personal contact, individuation, and the better-than-average effect. *Journal of Personality and Social Psychology, 68,* 804–825.

Allport, G. W. (1961). *Pattern and growth in personality.* New York, NY: Holt, Rinehart & Winston.

Allport, G. W., & Odbert, H. S. (1936). Trait-names: A psycho-lexical study. *Psychological Monographs, 47,* i–171.

Allred, K. D., & Smith, T. W. (1989). The hardy personality: Cognitive and physiological responses to evaluative threat. *Journal of Personality and Social Psychology, 56,* 257–266.

Almeida, D. M. (2005). Resilience and vulnerability to daily stressors assessed via diary methods. *Current Directions in Psychological Science, 14,* 64–68.

Alvarez, L. (1965). A pseudo experiment in parapsychology. *Science, 148,* 1541.

Alvergne, A., & Lummaa, V. (2010). Does the contraceptive pill alter mate choice in humans? *Trends in Ecology & Evolution, 25,* 171–179.

Amanzio, M., & Benedetti, F. (1999). Neuropharmacological dissection of placebo analgesia: Expectation-activated opioid systems versus conditioning-activated specific subsystems. *Journal of Neuroscience, 19,* 484–494.

Amaral, D. G., Schumann, C. M., & Nordahl, C. W. (2008). Neuroanatomy of autism. *Trends in Neurosciences, 3,* 137–145.

Amato, P. R., Johnson, D. R., Booth, A., & Rogers, S. J. (2003). Continuity and change in marital quality between 1980 and 2000. *Journal of Marriage and Family, 65,* 1–22.

Ambady, N., Hallahan, M., & Conner, B. (1999). Accuracy of judgments of sexual orientation from thin slices of behavior. *Journal of Personality and Social Psychology, 77,* 538–547.

Ambady, N., & Rosenthal, R. (1993). Half a minute: Predicting teacher evaluations from thin slices of nonverbal behavior and physical attractiveness. *Journal of Personality and Social Psychology, 64,* 431–441.

American Academy of Neurology. (2013). Recognizing sports concussions in athletes. Retrieved October 19, 2016, from https://www.aan.com/uploadedFiles/Website_Library_Assets/Documents/3Practice_Management/5Patient_Resources/1For_Your_Patient/6_Sports_Concussion_Toolkit/coaches.pdf

American College Health Association. (2014). Spring 2014 Reference Group Executive Summary. Hanover, MD: American College Health Association.

American Psychiatric Association. (2000b). Practice guidelines for the treatment of patients with eating disorders (revised). *American Journal of Psychiatry, 157,* 1–39.

American Psychiatric Association. (2013). *Diagnostic and statistical manual of mental disorders* (5th ed., text revision). Washington, DC: Author.

American Psychological Association. (2006). Answers to your questions about individuals with intersex conditions. Retrieved July 24, 2017, from http://www.apa.org/topics/lgbt/intersex.aspx

American Psychological Association. (2007, February). *Guidelines for psychological practice with girls and women.* Retrieved from http://www.apa.org/practice/guidelines/girls-and-women.pdf

American Psychological Association. (2008). Answers to your questions: For a better understanding of sexual orientation and homosexuality. Retrieved July 24, 2017, from http://www.apa.org/topics/lgbt/orientation.pdf

American Speech-Hearing-Language Association. (2017). Noise. Retrieved from http://www.asha.org/public/hearing/noise/

Amminger, G. P., Pape, S., Rock, D., Roberts, S. A., Ott, S. L., Squires-Wheeler, E., et al. (1999). Relationship between childhood behavioral disturbance and later schizophrenia in the New York high-risk project. *American Journal of Psychiatry, 156,* 525–530.

Anderson, A. K., Christoff, K., Stappen, I., Panitz, D., Ghahremani, D. G., Glover, G., et al. (2003). Dissociated neural representations of intensity and valence in human olfaction. *Nature Neuroscience, 6,* 196–202.

Anderson, A. K., & Phelps, E. A. (2000). Expression without recognition: Contributions of the human amygdala to emotional communication. *Psychological Science, 11,* 106–111.

Anderson, C. A. (1989). Temperature and aggression: Ubiquitous effects of heat on occurrence of human violence. *Psychological Bulletin, 106,* 74–96.

Anderson, C. A., & DeLisi, M. (2011). Implications of global climate change for violence in developed and developing countries. In J. Forgas, A. Kruglanski, & K. Williams (Eds.), *The psychology of social conflict and aggression* (pp. 249–265). New York, NY: Psychology Press.

Anderson, I. M. (2000). Selective serotonin reuptake inhibitors versus tricyclic antidepressants: A meta-analysis of efficacy and tolerability. *Journal of Affective Disorders, 58,* 19–36.

Anderson, N. H. (1968). Likableness ratings of 555 personality-trait words. *Journal of Personality and Social Psychology, 9,* 272–279.

Anderson, S. W., Bechara, A., Damasio, H., Tranel, D., & Damasio, A. R. (1999). Impairment of social and moral behavior related to early damage in human prefrontal cortex. *Nature Neuroscience, 2,* 1032–1037.

Andersson, G. (2016). Internet-delivered psychological treatments. *Annual Review of Clinical Psychology, 12,* 157–179.

Andrade, L. H., Alonso, J., Mneimneh, Z., Wells, J. E., Al-Hamzawi, A., Borges, G., et al. (2014). Barriers to mental health treatment: Results from the WHO World Mental Health surveys. *Psychological Medicine, 44,* 1303–1317.

Andreasen, N. C. (1984). *The broken brain: The biological revolution in psychiatry.* New York, NY: Harper & Row.

Angell, M. (2011, June 23). The epidemic of mental illness: Why? *The New York Review of Books.* Retrieved from http://www.nybooks.com

Ankiel, R., & Brown, T. (2017). *The phenomenon: Pressure, the yips, and the pitch that changed my life.* New York, NY: PublicAffairs.

Antonuccio, D., & Burns, D. (2004). Adolescents with depression [Letter to the editor]. *Journal of the American Medical Association, 292,* 2577.

Aouizerate, B., Cuny, E., Martin-Guehl, C., Guehl, D., Amieva, H., Benazzouz, A., et al. (2004). Deep brain stimulation of the ventral caudate nucleus in the treatment of obsessive-compulsive disorder and major depression: Case report. *Journal of Neurosurgery, 101,* 574–575.

Arem, H., Moore, S. C., Patel, A., Hartge, P., de Gonzalez, A. B., Visvanathan, K., et al. (2015). Leisure time physical activity and mortality: A detailed pooled analysis of the dose-response relationship. *JAMA Internal Medicine, 175,* 959–967.

Arias, E., MacDorman, M. F., Strobino, D. M., & Guyer, B. (2003). Annual summary of vital statistics: 2002. *Pediatrics, 112,* 1215–1230.

Ariely, D., & Berns, G. S. (2010). Neuromarketing: The hope and hype of neuroimaging in business. *Nature Reviews Neuroscience, 11,* 284–292.

Aron, A., Norman, C. C., Aron, E. N., McKenna, C., & Heyman, R. E. (2000). Couples' shared participation in novel and arousing activities and experienced relationship quality. *Journal of Personality and Social Psychology, 78,* 273–284.

Aronne, L. J., Wadden, T., Isoldi, K. K., & Woodworth, K. A. (2009). When prevention fails: Obesity treatment strategies. *American Journal of Medicine, 122,* S24–S32.

Aronson, E., & Mills, J. (1959). The effects of severity of initiation on liking for a group. *Journal of Abnormal and Social Psychology, 59,* 177–181.

Arrazola, R. A., Singh, T., Corey, C. G., Husten, C. G., Neff, L. J., Apelberg, B. J., et al. (2015). Tobacco use among middle and high school students—United States, 2011–2014. *Morbidity and Mortality Weekly Report, 64,* 381–385.

Asch, S. E. (1946). Forming impressions of personality. *Journal of Abnormal and Social Psychology, 41,* 258–290.

Asch, S. E. (1955). Opinions and social pressure. *Scientific American, 193,* 31–35.

Asch, S. E. (1956). Studies of independence and conformity: A minority of one against a unanimous majority. *Psychological Monographs, 70,* Whole No. 416.

Assad, L. K., Donnellan, M. B., & Conger, R. D. (2007). Optimism: An enduring resource for romantic relationships. *Journal of Personality and Social Psychology, 93,* 285–297.

Atkinson, R. C., & Shiffrin, R. M. (1968). Human memory: A proposed system and its control processes. *The Psychology of Learning and Motivation, 2,* 89–195.

Aune, D., Sen, A., Prasad, M., Norat, T., Janszky, I., Tonstad, S., et al. (2016). BMI and all cause mortality: Systematic review and non-linear dose-response meta-analysis of 230 cohort studies with 3.74 million deaths among 30.3 million participants. *BMJ;*353:i2156

Austin, E. J., Saklofske, D. H., & Mastoras, S. M. (2010). Emotional intelligence, coping and exam-related stress in Canadian undergraduate students. *Australian Journal of Psychology, 62,* 42–50.

Averill, J. R. (1980). A constructivist view of emotion. In R. Plutchik & H. Kellerman (Eds.), *Theories of emotion* (pp. 305–339). New York, NY: Academic Press.

Aviezer, H., Hassin, R. R., Ryan, J., Grady, C., Susskind, J., Anderson, A., et al. (2008). Angry, disgusted, or afraid? Studies on the malleability of emotion perception. *Psychological Science, 19,* 724–732.

Avinun, R., & Knafo, A. (2014). Parenting as a reaction evoked by children's genotype: A meta-analysis of children-as-twins studies. *Personality and Social Psychology Review, 18,* 87–102.

Avugos, S., Köppen, J., Czienskowski, U., Raab, M., & Bar-Eli, M. (2013). The "hot hand" reconsidered: A meta-analytic approach. *Psychology of Sport and Exercise, 14,* 21–27.

Baars, B. (1988). *A cognitive theory of consciousness.* Cambridge, England: Cambridge University Press.

Back, M. D., Stopfer, J. M., Vazire, S., Gaddis, S., Schmukle, S. C., Egloff, B., & Gosling, S. D. (2010). Facebook profiles reflect actual personality not self-idealization. *Psychological Science, 21,* 372–374.

Baddeley, A. D. (2002). Is working memory still working? *European Psychologist, 7,* 85–97.

Baddeley, A. D., & Hitch, G. (1974). Working memory. In G. H. Bower (Ed.), *The psychology of learning and motivation: Advances in research and theory* (Vol. 8, pp. 47–89). New York, NY: Academic Press.

Bagge, C. L., Littlefield, A. K., & Glenn, C. R. (2017). Trajectories of affective response as warning signs for suicide attempts: An examination of the 48 hours prior to a recent suicide attempt. *Clinical Psychological Science, 5,* 259–271.

Bailes, J. E., Petraglia, A. L., Omalu, B. I., Nauman, E., & Talavage, T. (2013). Role of subconcussion in repetitive mild traumatic brain injury: A review. *Journal of Neurosurgery, 119,* 1235–1245.

Bailey, J. M., Vasey, P. L., Diamond, L. M., Breedlove, S. M., Vilain, E., & Epprecht, M. (2016). Sexual orientation, controversy, and science. *Psychological Science in the Public Interest, 17,* 45–101.

Baillargeon, R. (1987). Object permanence in 3½- and 4½-month-old infants. *Developmental Psychology, 23,* 655–664.

Baillargeon, R. (1995). Physical reasoning in infancy. In M. S. Gazzaniga (Ed.), *The cognitive neurosciences* (pp. 181–204). Cambridge, MA: MIT Press.

Baillargeon, R., Li, J., Ng, W., & Yuan, S. (2009). A new account of infants' physical reasoning. In A. Woodward & A. Needham (Eds.), *Learning and the infant mind* (pp. 66–116). New York, NY: Oxford University Press.

Baillargeon, R., Scott, R. M., & Bian, L. (2016). Psychological reasoning in infancy. *Annual Review of Psychology, 67,* 159–186.

Baker, T. B., Brandon, T. H., & Chassin, L. (2004). Motivational influences on cigarette smoking. *Annual Review of Psychology, 55,* 463–491.

Baker, T. B., Mermelstein, R., Collins, L. M., Piper, M. E., Jorenby, D. E., Smith, S. S., et al. (2011). New methods for tobacco dependence treatment research. *Annals of Behavioral Medicine, 41,* 192–207.

Baldwin, D. A. (1991). Infants' contribution to the achievement of joint reference. *Child Development, 62,* 875–890.

Baldwin, D. A., & Baird, J. A. (2001). Discerning intentions in dynamic human action. *Trends in Cognitive Sciences, 5,* 171–178.

Baldwin, G. T., Breiding, M. J., & Sleet, D. (2016). Commentary—Using the public health model to address unintentional injuries and TBI: A perspective from the Centers for Disease Control and Prevention (CDC). *NeuroRehabilitation: An Interdisciplinary Journal, 39,* 1–4.

Baler, R. D., & Volkow, N. D. (2006). Drug addiction: The neurobiology of disrupted self-control. *Trends in Molecular Medicine, 12,* 559–566.

Balthazard, C. G., & Woody, E. Z. (1992). The spectral analysis of hypnotic performance with respect to "absorption." *International Journal of Clinical and Experimental Hypnosis, 40,* 21–43.

Baltimore, D. (2001). Our genome unveiled. *Nature, 409,* 814–816.

Banaji, M. R., & Greenwald, A. G. (1995). Implicit gender stereotyping in judgments of fame. *Journal of Personality and Social Psychology, 68,* 181–198.

Bandura, A. (1977a). Self-efficacy: Toward a unifying theory of behavioral change. *Psychological Review, 84,* 191–215.

Bandura, A. (1977b). *Social learning theory.* Englewood Cliffs, NJ: Prentice-Hall.

Bandura, A., Ross, D., & Ross, S. (1961). Transmission of aggression through imitation of aggressive models. *Journal of Abnormal and Social Psychology, 66,* 3–11.

Bandura, A., Ross, D., & Ross, S. (1963). Vicarious reinforcement and imitative learning. *Journal of Abnormal and Social Psychology, 67,* 601–607.

Bangerter, A., & Heath, C. (2004). The Mozart effect: Tracking the evolution of a scientific legend. *British Journal of Social Psychology, 43,* 605–623.

Bao, A. M., & Swaab, D. F. (2011). Sexual differentiation of the human brain: Relation to gender identity, sexual orientation and neuropsychiatric disorders. *Frontiers in Neuroendocrinology, 32,* 214–226.

Bao, W. N., Whitbeck, L. B., Hoyt, D. R., & Conger, R. D. (1999). Perceived parental acceptance as a moderator of religious transmission among adolescent boys and girls. *Journal of Marriage and Family, 61,* 362–374.

Barch, D. M., Sheline, Y. I., Csernansky, J. G., & Snyder, A. Z. (2003). Working memory and prefrontal cortex dysfunction: Specificity to schizophrenia compared with major depression. *Biological Psychiatry, 53,* 376–384.

Bard, P. (1934). On emotional expression after decortication with some remarks on certain theoretical views: Part I. *Psychological Review, 41,* 309–329.

Bargh, J. A. (2014). Our unconscious mind. *Scientific American, 310,* 30–37.

Barlow, D. H. (2002). *Anxiety and its disorders: The nature and treatment of anxiety and panic* (2nd ed.). New York, NY: Guilford Press.

Barlow, D. H. (2004). Psychological treatments. *American Psychologist, 59,* 869–878.

Barlow, D. H., Bullis, J. R., Comer, J. S., & Ametaj, A. A. (2013). Evidence-based psychological treatments: An update and a way forward. *Annual Review of Clinical Psychology, 9,* 1–27.

Barlow, D. H., Gorman, J. M., Shear, M. K., & Woods, S. W. (2000). Cognitive-behavioral therapy, imipramine, or their combination for panic disorder: A randomized controlled trial. *Journal of the American Medical Association, 283,* 2529–2536.

Barlow, D. H., Sauer-Zavala, S., Carl, J. R., Bullis, J. R., & Ellard, K. K. (2014). The nature, diagnosis, and treatment of neuroticism: Back to the future. *Clinical Psychological Science, 2,* 344–365.

Barnes, J., Dong, C. Y., McRobbie, H., Walker, N., Mehta, M., & Stead, L. F. (2010). Hypnotherapy for smoking cessation. *Cochrane Database of Systematic Reviews, 10,* CD001008.

Barnes, G. M., Welte, J. W., Hoffman, J. H., & Tidwell, M. C. O. (2010). Comparisons of gambling and alcohol use among college students and noncollege young people in the United States. *Journal of American College Health, 58,* 443–452.

Barnett, R. C., & Hyde, J. S. (2001). Women, men, work, and family: An expansionist theory. *American Psychologist, 56,* 781–796.

Baron-Cohen, S., Wheelwright, S., & Jolliffe, T. (1997). Is there a "language of the eyes"? Evidence from normal adults and adults with autism or Asperger syndrome. *Visual Cognition, 4,* 311–332.

Barrett, L. F., Mesquita, B., Ochsner, K. N., & Gross, J. J. (2007). The experience of emotion. *Annual Review of Psychology, 58,* 373–403.

Barretto, R. P., Gillis-Smith, S., Chandrashekar, J., Yarmolinsky, D. A., Schnitzer, M. J., Ryba, N. J., & Zuker, C. S. (2015). The neural representation of taste quality at the periphery. *Nature, 517,* 373–376.

Bartels, A., & Zeki, S. (2004). The neural correlates of maternal and romantic love. *Neuroimage, 21,* 1155–1166.

Bartels, J., Andreasen, D., Ehirim, P., Mao, H., Seibert, S., Wright, E. J., et al. (2008). Neurotrophic electrode: Method of assembly and implantation into human motor speech cortex. *Journal of Neuroscience Methods, 174,* 168–176.

Bartels, J. M. (2015). The Stanford prison experiment in introductory psychology textbooks: A content analysis. *Psychology Learning & Teaching, 14,* 36–50.

Bartels, J. M., Milovich, M. M., & Moussier, S. (2016). Coverage of the Stanford Prison Experiment in introductory psychology courses: A survey of introductory psychology Instructors. *Teaching of Psychology, 42,* 136–141.

Bartlett, F. C. (1932). *Remembering: An experimental and social study.* Cambridge, England: Cambridge University Press.

Barton, D. A., Esler, M. D., Dawood, T., Lambert, E. A., Haikerwal, D., Brenchley, C., et al. (2008). Elevated brain serotonin turnover in patients with depression: Effect of genotype and therapy. *Archives of General Psychiatry, 65,* 38–46.

Bartoshuk, L. M. (2000). Comparing sensory experiences across individuals: Recent psychophysical advances illuminate genetic variation in taste perception. *Chemical Senses, 25,* 447–460.

Bartoshuk, L. M., Duffy, V. B., & Miller, I. J. (1994). PTS/PROP tasting: Anatomy, psychophysics, and sex effects. *Physiology & Behavior, 56,* 1165–1171.

Baskin, T. W., Tierney, S. C., Minami, T., & Wampold, B. E. (2003). Establishing specificity in psychotherapy: A meta-analysis of structural equivalence of placebo controls. *Journal of Consulting and Clinical Psychology, 71,* 973–979.

Basten, U., Hilger, K., & Fiebach, C. J. (2015). Where smart brains are different: A quantitative meta-analysis of functional and structural brain imaging studies on intelligence. *Intelligence, 51,* 10–27.

Batson, C. D., Dyck, J. L., Brandt, J. R., Batson, J. G., Powell, A. L., McMaster, M. R., et al. (1988). Five studies testing two new egoistic alternatives to the empathy-altruism hypothesis. *Journal of Personality and Social Psychology, 55,* 52–77.

Batson, C. D., Turk, C. L., Shaw, L. L., & Klein, T. (1995). Information function of empathic emotion: Learning that we value the other's welfare. *Journal of Personality and Social Psychology, 68,* 300–313.

Baugh, C. M., Stamm, J. M., Riley, D. O., Gavett, B. E., Shenton, M. E., Lin, A., et al. (2012). Chronic traumatic encephalopathy: Neurodegeneration following repetitive concussive and subconcussive brain trauma. *Brain Imaging and Behavior, 6,* 244–254.

Baumeister, R. F. (1991). *Escaping the self: Alcoholism, spirituality, masochism, and other flights from the burden of selfhood.* New York, NY: Basic Books.

Baumeister, R. F. (2000). Gender differences in erotic plasticity: The female sex drive as socially flexible and responsive. *Psychological Bulletin, 126,* 347–374.

Baumeister, R. F., Bratslavsky, E., Finkenauer, C., & Vohs, K. D. (2001). Bad is stronger than good. *Review of General Psychology, 5,* 323–370.

Baumeister, R. F., Campbell, J. D., Krueger, J. I., & Vohs, K. D. (2003). Does high self-esteem cause better performance, interpersonal success, happiness, or healthier lifestyles? *Psychological Science in the Public Interest, 4,* 1–44.

Baumeister, R. F., Campbell, J. D., Krueger, J. I., & Vohs, K. D. (2005). Exploding the self-esteem myth. *Scientific American, 292,* 84–91.

Baumeister, R. F., Catanese, K. R., & Vohs, K. D. (2001). Is there a gender difference in strength of sex drive? Theoretical views, conceptual distinctions, and a review of the relevant literature. *Social Psychology Review, 5,* 242–273.

Baumeister, R. F., Dale, K., & Sommers, K. L. (1998). Freudian defense mechanisms and empirical findings in modern social psychology: Reaction formation, projection, displacement, undoing, isolation, sublimation, and denial. *Journal of Personality, 66,* 1081–1124.

Baumeister, R. F., Heatherton, T. F., & Tice, D. (1994). *Losing control: How and why people fail at self-regulation.* San Diego, CA: Academic Press.

Baumeister, R. F., & Leary, M. R. (1995). The need to belong: Desire for interpersonal attachments as a fundamental human motivation. *Psychological Bulletin, 117,* 497–529.

Baumeister, R. F., Smart, L., & Boden, J. M. (1996). Relation of threatened egotism to violence and aggression: The dark side of high self-esteem. *Psychological Review, 103,* 5–33.

Baumeister, R. F., Stillwell, A. M., & Heatherton, T. F. (1994). Guilt: An interpersonal approach. *Psychological Bulletin, 115,* 243–267.

Bäuml, K. T., & Samenieh, A. (2010). The two faces of memory retrieval. *Psychological Science, 21,* 793–795.

Baumrind, D. (1964). Some thoughts on ethics of research: After reading Milgram's "Behavioral Study of Obedience." *American Psychologist, 19,* 421.

Baxter, A. J., Charlson, F. J., Cheng, H. G., Shidhaye, R., Ferrari, A. J., & Whiteford, H. A. (2016). Prevalence of mental, neurological, and substance use disorders in China and India: A systematic analysis. *The Lancet Psychiatry, 3,* 832–841.

Baydala, L. T., Sewlal, B., Rasmussen, C., Alexis, K., Fletcher, F., Letendre, L., et al. (2009). A culturally adapted drug and alcohol abuse prevention program for aboriginal children and youth. *Progress in Community Health Partnerships, 3,* 37–46.

Bechara, A., Damasio, H., Tranel, D., & Damasio, A. R. (2005). The Iowa Gambling Task and the somatic marker hypothesis: Some questions and answers. *Trends in Cognitive Sciences, 9,* 159–162.

Bechtold, J., Hipwell, A., Lewis, D. A., Loeber, R., & Pardini, D. (2016). Concurrent and sustained cumulative effects of adolescent marijuana use on subclinical psychotic symptoms. *American Journal of Psychiatry, 173,* 781–789.

Beck, A. T. (1964). Thinking and depression: II. Theory and therapy. *Archives of General Psychiatry, 10,* 561–571.

Beck, A. T. (1967). *Depression: Clinical, experimental and theoretical aspects.* New York, NY: Harper & Row.

Beck, A. T. (1976). *Cognitive therapy and the emotional disorders.* New York, NY: International Universities Press.

Beck, A. T., Brown, G., Seer, R. A., Eidelson, J. L., & Riskind, J. H. (1987). Differentiating anxiety and depression: A test of the cognitive content-specificity hypothesis. *Journal of Abnormal Psychology, 96,* 179–183.

Beck, A. T., Freeman, A., & Associates. (1990). *Cognitive therapy of personality disorders.* New York, NY: Guilford Press.

Beck, A. T., Rush, A. J., Shaw, B., & Emery, G. (1979). *Cognitive therapy of depression.* New York, NY: Guilford Press.

Becker, D. V., Kenrick, D. T., Neuberg, S. L., Blackwell, K. C., & Smith, D. M. (2007). The confounded nature of angry men and happy women. *Journal of Personality and Social Psychology, 92,* 179–190.

Beggan, J. K. (1992). On the social nature of nonsocial perception: The mere ownership effect. *Journal of Personality and Social Psychology, 62,* 229–237.

Behne, T., Carpenter, M., Call, J., & Tomasello, M. (2005). Unwilling versus unable: Infants' understanding of intentional action. *Developmental Psychology, 41,* 328–337.

Békésy, G. von. (1957). The ear. *Scientific American, 197,* 66–79.

Belmaker, R. H., & Agam, G. (2008). Major depressive disorder. *New England Journal of Medicine, 358,* 55–68.

Belsky, J. (1990). Children and marriage. In F. D. Fincham & T. N. Bradbury (Eds.), *The psychology of marriage: Basic issues and applications* (pp. 172–200). New York, NY: Guilford Press.

Belsky, J., Houts, R. M., & Fearon, R. M. P. (2010). Infant attachment security and the timing of puberty: Testing an evolutionary hypothesis. *Psychological Science, 21,* 1195–1201.

Bem, D. J. (1967). Self-perception: An alternative explanation of cognitive dissonance phenomena. *Psychological Review, 74,* 183–200.

Bem, D. J. (2011). Feeling the future: Experimental evidence for anomalous retroactive influences on cognition and affect. *Journal of Personality and Social Psychology, 100,* 407–425.

Bem, D. J., & Honorton, C. (1994). Does psi exist? Replicable evidence for an anomalous process of information transfer. *Psychological Bulletin, 115,* 4–18.

Bem, D. J., Tressoldi, P., Rabeyron, T., & Duggan, M. (2015). Feeling the future: A meta-analysis of 90 experiments on the anomalous anticipation of random future events. *F1000Research, 4,* 1188. doi: 10.12688/f1000research.7177.2

Bem, S. L. (1981). Gender schema theory: A cognitive account of sex typing. *Psychological Review, 88,* 354–364.

Benedetti, F., Mayberg, H. S., Wager, T. D., Stohler, C. S., & Zubieta, J. K. (2005). Neurobiological mechanisms of the placebo effect. *Journal of Neuroscience, 25,* 10390–10402.

Benjamin, L. T. (2005). A history of clinical psychology as a profession in America (and a glimpse at its future). *Annual Review of Clinical Psychology, 1,* 1–30.

Ben-Shakhar, G., Bar-Hillel, M., & Kremnitzer, M. (2002). Trial by polygraph: Reconsidering the use of the guilty knowledge technique in court. *Law and Human Behavior, 26,* 527–541.

Bentler, P. M., & Newcomb, M. D. (1978). Longitudinal study of marital success and failure. *Journal of Consulting and Clinical Psychology, 46,* 1053–1070.

Berger, S. L., Kouzarides, T., Shiekhattar, R., & Shilatifard, A. (2009). An operational definition of epigenetics. *Genes & Development, 23,* 781–783.

Berkman, L. F., & Syme, S. L. (1979). Social networks, host resistance, and mortality: A nine-year follow-up study of Alameda County residents. *American Journal of Epidemiology, 109,* 186–204.

Berkowitz, L. (1990). On the formation and regulation of anger and aggression: A cognitive-neoassociationistic analysis. *American Psychologist, 45,* 494–503.

Berndt, A., Lee, S., Ramakrishnan, C., & Deisseroth, K. (2014). Structure-guided transformation of channelrhodopsin into a light-activated chloride channel. *Science, 344,* 420–424.

Bernhardt, P. C., Dabbs, J. M., Fielden, J. A., & Lutter, C. D. (1998). Testosterone changes during vicarious experiences of winning and losing among fans at sporting events. *Physiology & Behavior, 65,* 59–62.

Bernstein, C. A. (2011). Meta-structure in DSM-5 process. *Psychiatric News, 46,* 7.

Berridge, K. C. (2012). From prediction error to incentive salience: Meso-limbic computation of reward motivation. *European Journal of Neuroscience, 35,* 1124–1143.

Berridge, K. C., Ho, C. Y., Richard, J. M., & DiFeliceantonio, A. G. (2010). The tempted brain eats: Pleasure and desire circuits in obesity and eating disorders. *Brain Research, 1350,* 43–64.

Berridge, K. C., & Kringelbach, M. L. (2013). Neuroscience of affect: Brain mechanisms of pleasure and displeasure. *Current Opinion in Neurobiology, 23,* 294–303.

Berrington de Gonzalez, A., Hartge, P., Cerhan, J. R., Flint, A. J., Hannan, L., MacInnis, R. J., et al. (2010). Body-mass index and mortality among 1.46 million white adults. *New England Journal of Medicine, 363,* 2211–2219.

Berscheid, E., & Regan, P. (2005). *The psychology of interpersonal relationships.* New York, NY: Prentice-Hall.

Berscheid, E., & Walster, E. H. (1969). *Interpersonal attraction.* Reading, MA: Addison-Wesley.

Betancourt, H., & Lopez, S. R. (1993). The study of culture, ethnicity, and race in American psychology. *American Psychologist, 48,* 629–637.

Bewernick, B. H., Hurlemann, R., Matusch, A., Kayser, S., Grubert, C., Hadrysiewicz, B., et al. (2010). Nucleus accumbens deep brain stimulation decreases ratings of depression and anxiety in treatment-resistant depression. *Biological Psychiatry, 67,* 110–116.

Bian, L., Leslie, S. J., & Cimpian, A. (2017). Gender stereotypes about intellectual ability emerge early and influence children's interests. *Science, 355,* 389–391.

Bickerton, D. (1998). The creation and re-creation of language. In C. B. Crawford & D. L. Krebs (Eds.), *Handbook of evolutionary psychology: Ideas, issues, and applications* (pp. 613–634). Mahwah, NJ: Erlbaum.

Bidell, T. R., & Fischer, K. W. (1995). Between nature and nurture: The role of agency in the epigenesis of intelligence. In R. Sternberg & E. Grigorenko (Eds.), *Intelligence: Heredity and environment* (pp. 193–242). New York, NY: Cambridge University Press.

Biederman, J., Monuteaux, M. C., Spencer, T., Wilens, T. E., Macpherson, H. A., & Faraone, S. V. (2008). Stimulant therapy and risk for subsequent substance use disorders in male adults with ADHD: A naturalistic controlled 10-year follow-up study. *American Journal of Psychiatry, 165,* 597–603.

Biesanz, J., West, S. G., & Millevoi, A. (2007). What do you learn about someone over time? The relationship between length of acquaintance and consensus and self-other agreement in judgments of personality. *Journal of Personality and Social Psychology, 92,* 119–135.

Bjorklund, D. F. (2007). *Why youth is not wasted on the young: Immaturity in human development.* Malden, MA: Blackwell.

Bjornsson, A. S. (2011). Beyond the "psychological placebo": Specifying the nonspecific in psychotherapy. *Clinical Psychology: Science and Practice, 18,* 113–118.

Blackless, M., Charuvastra, A., Derryck, A., Fausto-Sterling, A., Lauzanne, K., & Lee, E. (2000). How sexually dimorphic are we? Review and synthesis. *American Journal of Human Biology, 12,* 151–166.

Blagys, M. D., & Hilsenroth, M. J. (2000). Distinctive feature of short-term psychodynamic-interpersonal psychotherapy: A review of the comparative psychotherapy process literature. *Clinical Psychology: Science and Practice, 7,* 167–188.

Blair, I. V. (2002). The malleability of automatic stereotypes and prejudice. *Personality and Social Psychology Review, 6,* 242–261.

Blair, R. J. (2003). Neurobiological basis of psychopathy. *British Journal of Psychiatry, 182,* 5–7.

Blakemore, C. (1983). *Mechanics of the mind.* Cambridge, England: Cambridge University Press.

Blakemore, S. J., & Choudhury, S. (2006). Development of the adolescent brain: Implications for executive function and social cognition. *Journal of Child Psychology and Psychiatry, 47,* 296–312.

Blakemore, S. J., Wolpert, D. M., & Frith, C. D. (1998). Central cancellation of self-produced tickle sensation. *Nature Neuroscience, 1,* 635–640.

Blanchard, R., & Ellis, L. (2001). Birth weight, sexual orientation, and the sex of preceding siblings. *Journal of Biosocial Science, 33,* 451–467.

Blasiman, R. N., Dunlosky, J., & Rawson, K. A. (2017). The what, how much, and when of study strategies: Comparing intended versus actual study behaviour. *Memory, 25,* 784–792.

Blass, T. (1991). Understanding behavior in the Milgram obedience experiment: The role of personality, situations, and their interactions. *Journal of Personality and Social Psychology, 60,* 398–413.

Bleidorn, W., Arslan, R. C., Denissen, J. J., Rentfrow, P. J., Gebauer, J. E., Potter, J., et al. (2016). Age and gender differences in self-esteem—A cross-cultural window. *Journal of Personality and Social Psychology, 111,* 396–410.

Bliss, T. V., & Lømo, T. (1973). Long-lasting potentiation of synaptic transmission in the dentate area of the anaesthetized rabbit following stimulation of the perforant path. *Journal of Physiology, 232,* 331–356.

Block, J., & Kremen, A. M. (1996). IQ and ego-resiliency: Conceptual and empirical connections and separateness. *Journal of Personality and Social Psychology, 70,* 349–361.

Bloom, P. (2002). Mindreading, communication and the learning of names for things. *Mind & Language, 17,* 37–54.

Blumberg, S. J., Bramlett, M. D., Kogan, M. D., Schieve, L. A., Jones, J. R., & Lu, M. C. (2013). Changes in prevalence of parent-reported autism spectrum disorder in school-aged US children: 2007 to 2011–2012. *National Health Statistics Reports, 65.* Hyattsville, MD: National Center for Health Statistics.

Bogaert, A. F. (2006). Biological versus nonbiological older brothers and men's sexual orientation. *Proceedings of the National Academy of Sciences, 103,* 10771–10774.

Bogen, J. E., & Gazzaniga, M. S. (1965). Cerebral commissurotomy in man: Minor hemisphere dominance for certain visuospatial functions. *Journal of Neurosurgery, 23,* 394–399.

Bohacek, J., Gapp, K., Saab, B. J., & Mansuy, I. M. (2013). Transgenerational epigenetic effects on brain functions. *Biological Psychiatry, 73,* 313–320.

Bohlin, G., Hagekull, B., & Rydell, A. M. (2000). Attachment and social functioning: A longitudinal study from infancy to middle childhood. *Social Development, 9,* 24–39.

Bolles, R. C. (1970). Species-specific defense reactions and avoidance learning. *Psychological Review, 77,* 32–48.

Bonanno, G. A. (2004). Loss, trauma, and human resilience: Have we underestimated the human capacity to thrive after extremely aversive events? *American Psychologist, 59,* 20–28.

Booth, A., Shelley, G., Mazur, A., Tharp, G., & Kittok, R. (1989). Testosterone, and winning and losing in human competition. *Hormones and Behavior, 23,* 556–571.

Bootzin, R. R., & Epstein, D. R. (2011). Understanding and treating insomnia. *Annual Review of Clinical Psychology, 7,* 435–458.

Bornstein, R. F. (1999). Criterion validity of objective and projective dependency tests: A meta-analytic assessment of behavioral prediction. *Psychological Assessment, 11,* 48–57.

Boroditsky, L., Fuhrman, O., & McCormick, K. (2011). Do English and Mandarin speakers think about time differently? *Cognition, 118,* 123–129.

Bosson, J. K., Lakey, C. E., Campbell, W. K., Zeigler-Hill, V., Jordan, C. H., & Kernis, M. H. (2008). Untangling the links between narcissism and self-esteem: A theoretical and empirical review. *Social and Personality Psychology Compass, 2,* 1415–1439.

Bouchard, C., & Pérusse, L. (1993). Genetics of obesity. *Annual Review of Nutrition, 13,* 337–354.

Bouchard, C., Tremblay, A., Despres, J. P., Nadeau, A., Lupien, J. P., Theriault, G., et al. (1990). The response to long-term overfeeding in identical twins. *New England Journal of Medicine, 322,* 1477–1482.

Bouchard, T. J., Jr. (2014). Genes, evolution and intelligence. *Behavior Genetics, 44,* 549–577.

Bouchard, T. J., Jr., Lykken, D. T., McGue, M., Segal, N. L., & Tellegen, A. (1990). Sources of human psychological differences: The Minnesota study of twins reared apart. *Science, 250,* 223–228.

Bouton, M. E. (1994). Context, ambiguity, and classical conditioning. *Current Directions in Psychological Science, 3,* 49–53.

Bouton, M. E., Trask, S., & Carranza-Jasso, R. (2016). Learning to inhibit the response during instrumental (operant) extinction. *Journal of Experimental Psychology: Animal Learning and Cognition, 42,* 246–258.

Bowlby, J. (1982). Attachment and loss: Retrospect and prospect. *American Journal of Orthopsychiatry, 52,* 664–678.

Boyden, E. S., Zhang, F., Bamberg, E., Nagel, G., & Deisseroth, K. (2005). Millisecond-timescale, genetically targeted optical control of neural activity. *Nature Neuroscience, 8,* 1263–1268.

Boysen, G. A., & VanBergen, A. (2014). Simulation of multiple personalities: A review of research comparing diagnosed and simulated dissociative identity disorder. *Clinical Psychology Review, 34,* 14–28.

Braadbaart, L., de Grauw, H., Perrett, D. I., Waiter, G. D., & Williams, J. H. G. (2014). The shared neural basis of empathy and facial imitation accuracy. *NeuroImage, 84,* 367–375.

Brackett, M. A., Rivers, S. E., & Salovey, P. (2011). Emotional intelligence: Implications for personal, social, academic, and workplace settings. *Social and Personality Psychology Compass, 5,* 88–103.

Bradbury, T. N., & Fincham, F. D. (1990). Attributions in marriage: Review and critique. *Psychological Bulletin, 107,* 3–33.

Bradlow, A. R., Pisoni, D. B., Akahane-Yamada, R., & Tohkura, Y. I. (1997). Training Japanese listeners to identify English/r/and/l: IV. Some effects of perceptual learning on speech production. *Journal of the Acoustical Society of America, 101,* 2299–2310.

Brakefield, P. M., & French, V. (1999). Butterfly wings: The evolution of development of colour patterns. *BioEssays, 21,* 391–401.

Brannigan, A., Nicholson, I., & Cherry, F. (2015). Introduction to the special issue: Unplugging the Milgram machine. *Theory & Psychology, 25,* 551–563.

Bransford, J. D., & Johnson, M. K. (1972). Contextual prerequisites for understanding: Some investigations of comprehension and recall. *Journal of Verbal Learning and Verbal Behavior, 11,* 717–726. (Reprinted and modified in *Human memory,* p. 305, by E. B. Zechmeister & S. E. Nyberg, Eds., 1982, Pacific Grove, CA: Brooks Cole.)

Braunschweig, D., Ashwood, P., Krakowiak, P., Hertz-Picciotto, I., Hansen, R., Croen, L. A., et al. (2008). Autism: Maternally derived antibodies specific for fetal brain proteins. *Neurotoxicology, 29,* 226–231.

Breedlove, S. M., Rosenzweig, M. R., & Watson, N. V. (2007). *Biological psychology* (5th ed.). Sunderland, MA: Sinauer Associates.

Breland, K., & Breland, M. (1961). The misbehavior of organisms. *American Psychologist, 16,* 681–684.

Brent, D. A., & Gibbons, R. (2014). Initial dose of antidepressant and suicidal behavior in youth: Start low, go slow. *JAMA Internal Medicine, 174,* 909–911.

Brewer, M. B., & Caporael, L. R. (1990). Selfish genes vs. selfish people: Sociobiology as origin myth. *Motivation and Emotion, 14,* 237–243.

Brickman, P., Coates, D., & Janoff-Bulman, R. (1978). Lottery winners and accident victims: Is happiness relative? *Journal of Personality and Social Psychology, 36,* 917–927.

Brigham, J. C., & Malpass, R. S. (1985). The role of experience and contact in the recognition of faces of own- and other-races persons. *Journal of Social Issues, 41,* 139–155.

Broadbent, D. E. (1958). *Perception and communication.* New York, NY: Oxford University Press.

Broadley, A. J., Korszun, A., Abdelaal, E., Moskvina, V., Jones, C. J., Nash, G. B., et al. (2005). Inhibition of cortisol production with metyrapone prevents mental stress-induced endothelial dysfunction and baroreflex impairment. *Journal of the American College of Cardiology, 46,* 344–350.

Brody, A. L., Saxena, S., Stoessel, P., Gillies, L. A., Fairbanks, L. A., Alborzian, S., et al. (2001). Regional brain metabolic changes in patients with major depression treated with either paroxetine or interpersonal therapy: Preliminary findings. *Archives of General Psychiatry, 58,* 631–640.

Brody, G. H., Gray, J. C., Yu, T., Barton, A. W., Beach, S. R., Galván, A., et al. (2017). Protective prevention effects on the association of poverty with brain development. *JAMA Pediatrics, 171,* 46–52.

Brody, J. E. (1997, December 30). Personal health: Despite the despair of depression, few men seek treatment. *New York Times.* Retrieved from http://www.nytimes.com

Brody, N. (1992). *Intelligence.* San Diego, CA: Academic Press.

Bromley, S. M., & Doty, R. L. (1995). Odor recognition memory is better under bilateral than unilateral test conditions. *Cortex, 31,* 25–40.

Broockman, D., & Kalla, J. (2016). Durably reducing transphobia: A field experiment on door-to-door canvassing. *Science, 352,* 220–224.

Brown, A. S. (1991). A review of the tip-of-the-tongue phenomenon. *Psychological Bulletin, 109,* 204–223.

Brown, A. S., & Derkits, E. J. (2009). Prenatal infection and schizophrenia: A review of epidemiologic and translational studies. *American Journal of Psychiatry, 167,* 261–280.

Brown, B. B., Mounts, N., Lamborn, S. D., & Steinberg, L. (1993). Parenting practices and peer group affiliations in adolescence. *Child Development, 64,* 467–482.

Brown, G. W., & Harris, T. O. (1978). *Social origins of depression: A study of psychiatric disorders in women.* New York, NY: Free Press.

Brown, J. D., & Kobayashi, C. (2002). Self-enhancement in Japan and America. *Asian Journal of Social Psychology, 5,* 145–168.

Brown, R. (1973). Development of the first language in the human species. *American Psychologist, 28,* 97–106.

Brown, R., & Hanlon, C. (1970). Derivational complexity and order of acquisition in child speech. In J. R. Hayes (Ed.), *Cognition and the development of language* (pp. 155–207). New York, NY: Wiley.

Brown, R., & Kulik, J. (1977). Flashbulb memories. *Cognition, 5,* 73–99.

Brown, R., & McNeill, D. (1966). The "tip-of-the-tongue" phenomenon. *Journal of Verbal Learning and Verbal Behavior, 5,* 325–337.

Brown, T. A., & Barlow, D. H. (2009). A proposal for a dimensional classification system based on the shared features of the DSM-IV anxiety and mood disorders: Implications for assessment and treatment. *Psychological Assessment, 21,* 256–271.

Brownell, C. A., & Brown, E. (1992). Peers and play in infants and toddlers. In V. Van Hasselt & M. Hersen (Eds.), *Handbook of social development: A lifespan perspective* (pp. 183–200). New York, NY: Plenum Press.

Brownell, K. D., Greenwood, M. R. C., Stellar, E., & Shrager, E. E. (1986). The effects of repeated cycles of weight loss and regain in rats. *Physiology & Behavior, 38,* 459–464.

Bruce, V., & Young, A. (1986). Understanding face recognition. *British Journal of Psychology, 77,* 305–327.

Bruder, C. E., Piotrowski, A., Gijsbers, A. A., Andersson, R., Erickson, S., de Ståhl, T. D., et al. (2008). Phenotypically concordant and discordant monozygotic twins display different DNA copy-number-variation profiles. *American Journal of Human Genetics, 82,* 763–771.

Bruneau, E. G., & Saxe, R. (2010). Attitudes towards the outgroup are predicted by activity in the precuneus in Arabs and Israelis. *Neuroimage, 52,* 1704–1711.

Bruneau, E. G., & Saxe, R. (2012). The power of being heard: The benefits of "perspective-giving" in the context of intergroup conflict. *Journal of Experimental Social Psychology, 48,* 855–866.

Bruni, F. (2000, September 13). The 2000 campaign: The Texas governor; Bush says rats reference in ad was unintentional. *New York Times,* p. A19.

Brunner, H. G., Nelen, M., Breakefield, X. O., Ropers, H. H., & Van Oost, B. A. (1993). Abnormal behavior associated with a point mutation in the structural gene for monoamine oxidase A. *Science, 262,* 578–580.

Brunoni, A. R., Chaimani, A., Moffa, A. H., Razza, L. B., Gattaz, W. F., Daskalakis, Z. J., et al. (2017). Repetitive transcranial magnetic stimulation for the acute treatment of major depressive episodes: A systematic review with network meta-analysis. *JAMA Psychiatry, 74,* 143–152.

Buckholtz, J. W., & Meyer-Lindenberg, A. (2008). MAOA and the neurogenetic architecture of human aggression. *Trends in Neurosciences, 31,* 120–129.

Buckholtz, J. W., & Meyer-Lindenberg, A. (2013). Genetic perspectives on the neurochemistry of human violence and aggression. In T. Canli (Ed.), *The Oxford handbook of molecular psychology.* New York, NY: Oxford University Press.

Bullen, C., Howe, C., Laugesen, M., McRobbie, H., Parag, V., Williman, J., et al. (2013). Electronic cigarettes for smoking cessation: A randomised controlled trial. *The Lancet, 382,* 1629–1637.

Bullough, V. (1990). The Kinsey scale in historical perspective. In D. P. Whirter, S. A. Sanders, & J. M. Reinisch (Eds.), *Homosexuality/heterosexuality: Concepts of sexual orientation* (pp. 3–14). New York, NY: Oxford University Press.

Buoli, M., Serati, M., & Altamura, A. (2014). Is the combination of a mood stabilizer plus an antipsychotic more effective than mono-therapies in long-term treatment of bipolar disorder? A systematic review. *Journal of Affective Disorders, 152,* 12–18.

Burger, J. M. (2009). Replicating Milgram: Would people still obey today? *American Psychologist, 64,* 1–11.

Burger, J. M., Girgis, Z. M., & Manning, C. C. (2011). In their own words: Explaining obedience to authority through an examination of participants' comments. *Social Psychological and Personality Science, 2,* 460–466.

Burke, B. L., Arkowitz, H., & Menchola, M. (2003). The efficacy of motivational interviewing: A meta-analysis of controlled clinical trials. *Journal of Consulting and Clinical Psychology, 71,* 843–861.

Bush, E. C., & Allman, J. M. (2004). The scaling of frontal cortex in primates and carnivores. *Proceedings of the National Academy of Sciences, 101,* 3962–3966.

Bushdid, C., Magnasco, M. O., Vosshall, L. B., & Keller, A. (2014). Humans can discriminate more than 1 trillion olfactory stimuli. *Science, 343,* 1370–1372.

Bushman, B. J., & Anderson, C. A. (2015). Understanding causality in the effects of media violence. *American Behavioral Scientist, 59,* 1807–1821.

Bushman, B. J., & Baumeister, R. F. (1998). Threatened egotism, narcissism, self-esteem, and direct and displaced aggression: Does self-love or self-hate lead to violence? *Journal of Personality and Social Psychology, 75,* 219–229.

Bushman, B. J., & Huesmann, L. R. (2001). Effects of televised violence on aggression. In D. G. Singer & J. L. Singer (Eds.), *Handbook of children and the media* (pp. 223–254). Thousand Oaks, CA: Sage.

Buss, A. H., & Plomin, R. (1984). *Temperament: Early developing personality traits.* Hillsdale, NJ: Erlbaum.

Buss, D. M. (1989). Sex differences in human mate preferences: Evolutionary hypotheses tested in 37 cultures. *Behavioral and Brain Sciences, 12,* 1–49.

Buss, D. M. (1995). Psychological sex differences: Origins through sexual selection. *American Psychologist, 50,* 164–168.

Buss, D. M. (2016). Human mating strategies. In R. J. Sterberg, S. T. Fiske, & D. J. Foss (Eds.), *Scientists making a difference* (pp. 383–388). New York, NY: Cambridge University Press.

Buss, D. M., & Kenrick, D. T. (1998). Evolutionary social psychology. In D. T. Gilbert, S. R. Fiske, & G. Lindzey (Eds.), *The handbook of social psychology* (4th ed., pp. 982–1026). New York, NY: McGraw-Hill.

Buss, D. M., & Schmitt, D. P. (1993). Sexual strategies theory: An evolutionary perspective on human mating. *Psychological Review, 100,* 204–232.

Buss, D. M., & Shackelford, T. K. (2008). Attractive women want it all: Good genes, investment, parenting indicators, and commitment. *Evolutionary Psychology, 6,* 134–146.

Buss, K. A., & McDoniel, M. E. (2016). Improving the prediction of risk for anxiety development in temperamentally fearful children. *Current Directions in Psychological Science, 25,* 14–20.

Butcher, J. N., Mineka, S., & Hooley, J. M. (2007). *Abnormal psychology* (13th ed.). Boston, MA: Allyn & Bacon.

Butcher, J. N., & Williams, C. L. (2009). Personality assessment with the MMPI-2: Historical roots, international adaptations, and current challenges. *Applied Psychology: Health and Well-Being, 1,* 105–135.

Butler, A. C., Chapman, J. E., Forman, E. M., & Beck, A. T. (2006). The empirical status of cognitive-behavioral therapy: A review of meta-analyses. *Clinical Psychology Review, 26,* 17–31.

Byers-Heinlein, K., Burns, T. C., & Werker, J. F. (2010). The roots of bilingualism in newborns. *Psychological Science, 21,* 343–348.

Cabanac, M. (1992). Pleasure: The common currency. *Journal of Theoretical Biology, 155,* 173–200.

Cabeza, R., & Dennis, N. A. (2012). Frontal lobes and aging. In D. T. Stuss & R. T. Knight (Eds.), *Principles of frontal lobes function* (pp. 628–652). New York, NY: Oxford University Press.

Cabeza, R., & Moscovitch, M. (2013). Memory systems, processing modes, and components functional neuroimaging evidence. *Perspectives on Psychological Science, 8,* 49–55.

Cacioppo, J. T., Hughes, M. E., Waite, L. J., Hawkley, L. C., & Thisted, R. A. (2006). Loneliness as a specific risk factor for depressive symptoms: Cross sectional and longitudinal analyses. *Psychology and Aging, 21,* 140–151.

Cahill, L., Prins, B., Weber, M., & McGaugh, J. L. (1994). Beta-adrenergic activation and memory for emotional events. *Nature, 371,* 702–704.

Cahn, B. R., & Polich, J. (2006). Meditation states and traits: EEG, ERP, and neuroimaging studies. *Psychological Bulletin, 132,* 180–211.

Cai, H., Wu, L., Shi, Y., Gu, R., & Sedikides, C. (2016). Self-enhancement among Westerners and Easterners: A cultural neuroscience approach. *Social Cognitive and Affective Neuroscience, 11,* 1569–1578.

Cain, M. A., Bornick, P., & Whiteman, V. (2013). The maternal, fetal, and neonatal effects of cocaine exposure in pregnancy. *Clinical Obstetrics and Gynecology, 56,* 124–132.

Cairns, R. B., & Cairns, B. D. (1994). *Lifelines and risks: Pathways of youth in our times.* Cambridge, England: Cambridge University Press.

Calder, A. J., Keane, J., Manes, F., Antoun, N., & Young, A. W. (2000). Impaired recognition and experience of disgust following brain injury. *Nature Neuroscience, 3,* 1077–1078.

Califf, R. M., Woodcock, J., & Ostroff, S. (2016). A proactive response to prescription opioid abuse. *New England Journal of Medicine, 374,* 1480–1485.

Campbell, W. K., Bush, C. P., Brunell, A. B., & Shelton, J. (2005). Understanding the social costs of narcissism: The case of tragedy of the commons. *Personality and Social Psychology, 31,* 1358–1368.

Campbell, W. K., & Sedikides, C. (1999). Self-threat magnifies the self-serving bias: A meta-analytic integration. *Review of General Psychology, 4,* 23–43.

Canetta, S., Sourander, A., Surcel, H. M., Hinkka-Yli-Salomäki, S., Leiviskä, J., Kellendonk, C., et al. (2014). Elevated maternal C-reactive protein and increased risk of schizophrenia in a national birth cohort. *American Journal of Psychiatry, 171,* 960–968.

Cannon, T. D., Cadenhead, K., Cornblatt, B., Woods, S. W., Addington, J., Walker, E., et al. (2008). Prediction of psychosis in youth at high clinical risk: A multisite longitudinal study in North America. *Archives of General Psychiatry, 65,* 28–37.

Cannon, W. B. (1927). The James-Lange theory of emotion: A critical examination and an alternative theory. *American Journal of Psychology, 39,* 106–124.

Cannon, W. B. (1932). *The wisdom of the body.* New York, NY: Norton.

Cantu, D., Walker, K., Andresen, L., Taylor-Weiner, A., Hampton, D., Tesco, G., & Dulla, C. G. (2015). Traumatic brain injury increases cortical glutamate network activity by compromising GABAergic control. *Cerebral Cortex, 25,* 2306–2320.

Caramaschi, D., de Boer, S. F., & Koolhaus, J. M. (2007). Differential role of the 5-HT receptor in aggressive and non-aggressive mice: An across-strain comparison. *Physiology & Behavior, 90,* 590–601.

Cardeña, E., & Carlson, E. (2011). Acute stress disorder revisited. *Annual Review of Clinical Psychology, 7,* 245–267.

Carew, T. J., Pinsker, H. M., & Kandel, E. R. (1972). Long-term habituation of a defensive withdrawal reflex in Aplysia. *Science, 219,* 397–400.

Carey, B. (2011, June 23). Expert on mental illness reveals her own fight. *New York Times.* Retrieved from http://newyorktimes.com

Carli, L. L., Ganley, R., & Pierce-Otay, A. (1991). Similarity and satisfaction in roommate relationships. *Personality and Social Psychology Bulletin, 17,* 419–426.

Carmichael, M. (2007, March 26). Stronger, faster, smarter. *Newsweek, 149.* Retrieved from http://www.newsweek.com

Carnagey, N. L., Anderson, C. A., & Bartholow, B. D. (2007). Media violence and social neuroscience: New questions and new opportunities. *Current Directions in Psychological Science, 16,* 178–182.

Carnagey, N. L., Anderson, C. A., & Bushman, B. J. (2007). The effect of video game violence on physiological desensitization to real-life violence. *Journal of Experimental Social Psychology, 43,* 489–496.

Carney, R. M., & Freedland, K. E. (2017). Depression and coronary heart disease. *Nature Reviews Cardiology, 14,* 145–155.

Carpenter, S. K. (2012). Testing enhances the transfer of learning. *Current Directions in Psychological Science, 21,* 279–283.

Carré, J. M., & Putnam, S. K. (2010). Watching a previous victory produces an increase in testosterone among elite hockey players. *Psychoneuroendocrinology, 35,* 475–479.

Carrère, S., Buehlman, K. T., Gottman, J. M., Coan, J. A., & Ruckstuhl, L. (2000). Predicting marital stability and divorce in newlywed couples. *Journal of Family Psychology, 14,* 42–58.

Carstensen, L. L. (1995). Evidence for a life-span theory of socioemotional selectivity. *Current Directions in Psychological Science, 4,* 151–156.

Carter, C. S. (2014). Oxytocin pathways and the evolution of human behavior. *Annual Review of Psychology, 65,* 17–39.

Carter, G. L., Campbell, A. C., & Muncer, S. (2014). The dark triad personality: Attractiveness to women. *Personality and Individual Differences, 56,* 57–61.

Caruso, S., Intelisano, G., Farina, M., Di Mari, L., & Agnello, C. (2003). The function of sildenafil on female sexual pathways: A double-blind, cross-over, placebo-controlled study. *European Journal of Obstetrics & Gynecology and Reproductive Biology, 110,* 201–206.

Carver, C. S., & Miller, C. J. (2006). Relations of serotonin function to personality: Current views and a key methodological issue. *Psychiatry Research, 144,* 1–15.

Case, A., & Deaton, A. (2015). Rising morbidity and mortality in midlife among white non-Hispanic Americans in the 21st century. *Proceedings of the National Academy of Sciences, 112,* 15078–15083.

Case, R. (1992). The role of the frontal lobes in development. *Brain and Cognition, 20,* 51–73.

Casey, B. J., Jones, R. M., & Somerville, L. H. (2011). Braking and accelerating of the adolescent brain. *Journal of Research in Adolescence, 21,* 21–33.

Casey, B. J., Somerville, L. H., Gotlib, I. H., Ayduk, O., Franklin, N. T., Askren, M. K., et al. (2011). Behavioral and neural correlates of delay of gratification 40 years later. *Proceedings of the National Academy of Sciences, 108,* 14998–15003.

Caspi, A. (2000). The child is father of the man: Personality continuities from childhood to adulthood. *Journal of Personality and Social Psychology, 78,* 158–172.

Caspi, A., & Herbener, E. S. (1990). Continuity and change: Assortative marriage and the consistency of personality in adulthood. *Journal of Personality and Social Psychology, 58,* 250–258.

Caspi, A., Houts, R. M., Belsky, D. W., Goldman-Mellor, S. J., Harrington, H., Israel, S., et al. (2014). The p factor: One general psychopathology factor in the structure of psychiatric disorders? *Clinical Psychological Science, 2,* 119–137.

Caspi, A., Houts, R. M., Belsky, D. W., Harrington, H., Hogan, S., Ramrakha, S., et al. (2016). Childhood forecasting of a small segment of the population with large economic burden. *Nature Human Behaviour, 1,* 0005.

Caspi, A., McClay, J., Moffitt, T. E., Mill, J., Martin, J., Craig, I. W., et al. (2002). Role of genotype in the cycle of violence in maltreated children. *Science, 29,* 851–854.

Caspi, A., Roberts, B. W., & Shiner, R. L. (2005). Personality development: Stability and change. *Annual Review of Psychology, 56,* 453–485.

Cattell, R. B. (1943). The description of personality: Basic traits resolved into clusters. *Journal of Abnormal and Social Psychology, 38,* 476–506.

Cattell, R. B. (1965). *The scientific analysis of personality.* London, England: Penguin.

Cattell, R. B. (1971). *Abilities: Their structure, growth, and action.* Boston, MA: Houghton Mifflin.

Cavanagh, J. O., Carson, A. J., Sharpe, M. M., & Lawrie, S. M. (2003). Psychological autopsy studies of suicide: A systematic review. *Psychological Medicine: A Journal of Research in Psychiatry and the Allied Sciences, 33,* 395–405.

Ceci, S. J. (1999). Schooling and intelligence. In S. J. Ceci & W. M. Williams (Eds.), *The nature-nurture debate: The essential readings* (pp. 168–175). Oxford, England: Blackwell.

Centers for Disease Control and Prevention. (2004, July). Fetal alcohol syndrome: Guidelines for referral and diagnosis. Retrieved July 24, 2017, from http://www.cdc.gov/ncbddd/fasd/documents/fas_guidelines_accessible.pdf

Centers for Disease Control and Prevention. (2010c). Tobacco use and United States students. Retrieved from http://www.cdc.gov/HealthyYouth/yrbs/pdf/us_tobacco_combo.pdf

Centers for Disease Control and Prevention. (2011a). Mental illness surveillance among adults in the United States. *Morbidity and Mortality Weekly Report, 60,* 1–32.

Centers for Disease Control and Prevention. (2011b). Sickle cell disease. Retrieved from http://www.cdc.gov/ncbddd/sicklecell/data.html

Centers for Disease Control and Prevention. (2011c). Nonfatal traumatic brain injuries related to sports and recreation activities among persons aged ≤19 years—United States, 2001–2009. *Morbidity and Mortality Weekly Report, 60,* 1337–1342.

Centers for Disease Control and Prevention. (2016a). [Table 15, Life expectancy at birth, at 65 years of age, and at 75 years of age, by race and sex: United States, selected years 1900–2014]. *Health, United States, 2015.* Retrieved from https://www.cdc.gov/nchs/data/hus/hus15.pdf

Centers for Disease Control and Prevention. (2016b). Ten leading causes of death by age group, United States—2014. Retrieved from https://www.cdc.gov/violenceprevention/suicide/statistics/

Chabas, D., Taheri, S., Renier, C., & Mignot, E. (2003). The genetics of narcolepsy. *Annual Review of Genomics & Human Genetics, 4,* 459–483.

Chabris, C. F. (1999). Prelude or requiem for the "Mozart effect"? *Nature, 400,* 826–827.

Chabris, C. F., Lee, J. J., Cesarini, D., Benjamin, D. J., & Laibson, D. I. (2015). The fourth law of behavior genetics. *Current Directions in Psychological Science, 24,* 304–312.

Chadwick, M. J., Anjum, R. S., Kumaran, D., Schacter, D. L., Spiers, H. J., & Hassabis, D. (2016). Semantic representations in the temporal pole predict false memories. *Proceedings of the National Academy of Sciences, 113,* 10180–10185.

Chambers, D. W. (1983). Stereotypic images of the scientist: The draw-a-scientist test. *Science Education, 67,* 255–265.

Chang, L. J., Yarkoni, T., Khaw, M. W., & Sanfey, A. G. (2013). Decoding the role of the insula in human cognition: Functional parcellation and large-scale reverse inference. *Cerebral Cortex, 23,* 739–749.

Chapman, H. A., Kim, D. A., Susskind, J. M., & Anderson, A. K. (2009). In bad taste: Evidence for the oral origins of moral disgust. *Science, 323,* 1222–1226.

Charles, S. T., Mogle, J., Urban, E. J., & Almeida, D. M. (2016). Daily events are important for age differences in mean and duration for negative affect but not positive affect. *Psychology and Aging, 31,* 661.

Chase, V. D. (2006). *Shattered nerves: How science is solving modern medicine's most perplexing problem.* Baltimore, MD: Johns Hopkins University Press.

Chase, W. G., & Simon, H. A. (1973). Perception in chess. *Cognitive Psychology, 4,* 55–81.

Chassin, L., Presson, C. C., & Sherman, S. J. (1990). Social psychological contributions to the understanding and prevention of adolescent cigarette smoking. *Personality and Social Psychology Bulletin, 16,* 133–151.

Chavez, R. S., Heatherton, T. F., & Wagner, D. D. (2017). Neural population decoding reveals the intrinsic positivity of the self. *Cerebral Cortex.* doi: 10.1093/cercor/bhw302.

Chen, Q., Yan, W., & Duan, E. (2016). Epigenetic inheritance of acquired traits through sperm RNAs and sperm RNA modifications. *Nature Reviews Genetics, 17,* 733–743.

Cherry, E. C. (1953). Some experiments on the recognition of speech, with one and two ears. *Journal of the Acoustical Society of America, 25,* 975–979.

Chess, S., & Thomas, A. (1984). *Origins and evolution of behavior disorders: From infancy to early adult life.* Cambridge, MA: Harvard University Press.

Chester, D. S., DeWall, C. N., Derefinko, K. J., Estus, S., Peters, J. R., Lynam, D. R., et al. (2015). Monoamine oxidase A (MAOA) genotype predicts greater aggression through impulsive reactivity to negative affect. *Behavioural Brain Research, 283,* 97–101.

Cheung, F. M., Cheung, S. F., & Leung, F. (2008). Clinical utility of the cross-cultural (Chinese) personality assessment inventory (CPAI-2) in the assessment of substance use disorders among Chinese men. *Psychological Assessment, 20,* 103–113.

Cheung, F. M., Leung, K., Zhang, J. X., Sun, H. F., Gan, Y. G., Song, W. Z., et al. (2001). Indigenous Chinese personality constructs: Is the five-factor model complete? *Journal of Cross-Cultural Psychology, 32,* 407–433.

Child Trends Databank. (2015). Attitudes toward spanking. Retrieved August 7, 2016, from http://www.childtrends.org/?indicators=attitudes-toward-spanking

Chistyakov, A. V., Kaplan, B., Rubichek, O., Kreinin, I., Koren, D., Feinsod, M., et al. (2004). Antidepressant effects of different schedules of repetitive transcranial magnetic stimulation vs. clomipramine in patients with major depression: Relationship to changes in cortical excitability. *International Journal of Neuropsychopharmacology, 8,* 223–233.

Choi, I., Dalal, R., Kim-Prieto, C., & Park, H. (2003). Culture and judgment of causal relevance. *Journal of Personality and Social Psychology, 84,* 46–59.

Choi, I., Nisbett, R. E., & Norenzayan, A. (1999). Causal attribution across cultures: Variation and universality. *Psychological Bulletin, 125,* 47–63.

Choleris, E., Gustafsson, J. A., Korach, K. S., Muglia, L. J., Pfaff, D. W., & Ogawa, S. (2003). An estrogen-dependent four-gene micronet regulating social recognition: A study with oxytocin and estrogen receptor-alpha and -beta knockout mice. *Proceedings of the National Academy of Sciences, 100,* 6192–6197.

Chomsky, N. (1959). A review of B. F. Skinner's *Verbal Behavior. Language, 35,* 26–58.

Christakis, N. A., & Fowler, J. H. (2007). The spread of obesity in a large social network over 32 years. *New England Journal of Medicine, 357,* 370–379.

Christensen, D. L., Baio, J., Braun, K. V., Bilder, D., Charles, J., & Constantino, J. N. (2015). Prevalence and characteristics of autism spectrum disorder among children aged 8 years—Autism and developmental disabilities monitoring network, 11 sites, United States, 2012. *Morbidity and Mortality Weekly Report. Surveillance Summaries, 65,* 1–23.

Christian, K. M., Song, H., & Ming, G. L. (2014). Functions and dysfunctions of adult hippocampal neurogenesis. *Annual Review of Neuroscience, 37,* 243–262.

Christianson, S. (1992). Emotional stress and eyewitness memory: A critical review. *Psychological Bulletin, 112,* 284–309.

Christopher, F. S., & Sprecher, S. (2000). Sexuality in marriage, dating, and other relationships: A decade review. *Journal of Marriage and Family, 62,* 999–1017.

Chronis, A. M., Jones, H. A., & Raggi, V. L. (2006). Evidence-based psychosocial treatments for children and adolescents with attention-deficit/hyperactivity disorder. *Clinical Psychology Review, 26,* 486–502.

Chronis-Tuscano, A., Degnan, K. A., Pine, D. S., Perez-Edgar, K., Henderson, H. A., Diaz, Y., et al. (2009). Stable early maternal report of behavioral inhibition predicts lifetime social anxiety disorder in adolescence. *Journal of the American Academy of Child & Adolescent Psychiatry, 48,* 928–935.

Cialdini, R. B. (2008). *Influence: Science and prejudice* (5th ed.). Boston, MA: Allyn & Bacon.

Cialdini, R. B., Shaller, M., Houlihan, D., Arps, K., Fultz, J., & Beaman, A. L. (1987). Empathy-based helping: Is it selflessly or selfishly motivated? *Journal of Personality and Social Psychology, 52,* 749–758.

Cialdini, R. B., Vincent, J. E., Lewis, S. K., Catalan, J., Wheeler, D., & Darby, B. L. (1975). Reciprocal concessions procedure for inducing compliance: The door-in-the-face technique. *Journal of Personality and Social Psychology, 31,* 206–215.

Cicchetti, D., Rogosh, F. A., & Toth, S. (1998). Maternal depressive disorder and contextual risk: Contributions to the development of attachment insecurity and behavior problems in toddlerhood. *Development and Psychopathology, 10,* 283–300.

Cikara, M., Botvinick, M. M., & Fiske, S. T. (2011). Us versus them: Social identity shapes neural responses to intergroup competition and harm. *Psychological Science, 22,* 306–313.

Cikara, M., & Van Bavel, J. J. (2014). The neuroscience of intergroup relations: An integrative review. *Perspectives on Psychological Science, 9,* 245–274.

Clark, A. S., Pfeifle, J. K., & Edwards, D. A. (1981). Ventromedial hypothalamic damage and sexual proceptivity in female rats. *Physiology & Behavior, 27,* 597–602.

Clark, L. A. (2007). Assessment and diagnosis of personality disorder: Perennial issues and an emerging reconceptualization. *Annual Review of Psychology, 58,* 227–257.

Clark, L. A., & Ro, E. (2014). Three-pronged assessment and diagnosis of personality disorder and its consequences: Personality functioning, pathological traits, and psychosocial disability. *Personality Disorders: Theory, Research, and Treatment, 5,* 55–69.

Clark, R. D., & Hatfield, E. (1989). Gender differences in receptivity to sexual offers. *Journal of Psychology and Human Sexuality, 2,* 39–55.

Clark, S. E., & Wells, G. L. (2008). On the diagnosticity of multiple-witness identifications. *Law and Human Behavior, 32,* 406–422.

Cleckley, H. M. (1941). *The mask of sanity: An attempt to reinterpret the so-called psychopathic personality.* St. Louis, MO: Mosby.

Cloninger, C., Adolfsson, R., & Svrakic, N. (1996). Mapping genes for human personality. *Nature and Genetics, 12,* 3–4.

Cloutier, J., Heatherton, T. F., Whalen, P. J., & Kelley, W. M. (2008). Are attractive people rewarding? Sex differences in the neural substrates of facial attractiveness. *Journal of Cognitive Neuroscience, 20,* 941–951.

Cockerham, W. C., Bauldry, S., Hamby, B. W., Shikany, J. M., & Bae, S. (2017). A comparison of black and white racial differences in health lifestyles and cardiovascular disease. *American Journal of Preventive Medicine, 52,* S56–S62.

Cogsdill, E. J., Todorov, A. T., Spelke, E. S., & Banaji, M. R. (2014). Inferring character from faces: A developmental study. *Psychological Science, 25,* 1132–1139.

Cohen, D., Nisbett, R. E., Bowdle, B. F., & Schwarz, N. (1996). Insult, aggression, and the Southern culture of honor: An "experimental ethnography." *Journal of Personality and Social Psychology, 70,* 945–960.

Cohen, G. L., Garcia, J., Apfel, N., & Master, A. (2006). Reducing the racial achievement gap: A social-psychological intervention. *Science, 313,* 1307–1310.

Cohen, S., Alper, C. M., Doyle, W. J., Treanor, J. J., & Turner, R. B. (2006). Positive emotional style predicts resistance to illness after experimental exposure to rhinovirus or influenza A virus. *Psychomatic Medicine, 68,* 809–815.

Cohen, S., Doyle, W. J., Skoner, D. P., Rabin, B. S., & Gwaltney, J. M. J. (1997). Social ties and susceptibility to the common cold. *Journal of the American Medical Association, 277,* 1940–1944.

Cohen, S., Janicki-Deverts, D., & Miller, G. E. (2007). Psychological stress and disease. *Journal of the American Medical Association, 298,* 1685–1687.

Cohen, S., Tyrrell, D. A. J., & Smith, A. P. (1991). Psychological stress and susceptibility to the common cold. *New England Journal of Medicine, 325,* 606–612.

Cohen, S., & Wills, T. A. (1985). Stress, social support, and the buffering hypothesis. *Psychological Bulletin, 98,* 310–357.

Cohn, J. F., & Tronick, E. Z. (1983). Three month old infants' reaction to simulated maternal depression. *Child Development, 54,* 185–193.

Coid, J., & Ullrich, S. (2010). Antisocial personality disorder is on a continuum with psychopathy. *Comprehensive Psychiatry, 51,* 426–433.

Colcombe, S. J., Erickson, K. I., Scalf, P., Kim, J., Prkash, R., McAuley, E., et al. (2006). Aerobic exercise training increases brain volume in aging humans. *Journal of Gerontology: Medical Sciences, 61A,* 1166–1170.

Collins, A. M., & Loftus, E. F. (1975). A spreading-activation theory of semantic processing. *Psychological Review, 82,* 407–428.

Collins, K. P., & Cleary, S. D. (2016). Racial and ethnic disparities in parent-reported diagnosis of ADHD: National Survey of Children's Health (2003, 2007, and 2011). *Journal of Clinical Psychiatry, 77,* 52–59.

Collins, T., Tillmann, B., Barrett, F. S., Delbé, C., & Janata, P. (2014). A combined model of sensory and cognitive representations underlying tonal expectations in music: From audio signals to behavior. *Psychological Review, 121,* 33–65.

Compton, W. M., Conway, K. P., Stinson, F. S., Colliver, J. D., & Grant, B. F. (2005). Prevalence, correlates, and comorbidity of DSM-IV antisocial personality syndromes and alcohol and specific drug use disorders in the United States: Results from the national epidemiologic survey on alcohol and related conditions. *Journal of Clinical Psychiatry, 66,* 677–685.

Compton, W. M., Han, B., Jones, C. M., Blanco, C., & Hughes, A. (2016). Marijuana use and use disorders in adults in the USA, 2002–14: Analysis of annual cross-sectional surveys. *The Lancet Psychiatry, 3,* 954–964.

Compton, W. M., Jones, C. M., & Baldwin, G. T. (2016). Relationship between nonmedical prescription-opioid use and heroin use. *New England Journal of Medicine, 374,* 154–163.

Comtesse, H., & Stemmler, G. (2016). Fear and disgust in women: Differentiation of cardiovascular regulation patterns. *Biological Psychology, 123,* 166–176.

Conn, C., Warden, R., Stuewig, R., Kim, E., Harty, L., Hastings, M., & Tangney, J. P. (2010). Borderline personality disorder among jail inmates: How common and how distinct? *Corrections Compendium, 35,* 6–13.

Connolly, A. C., Sha, L., Guntupalli, J. S., Oosterhof, N., Halchenko, Y. O., Nastase, S. A., et al. (2016). How the human brain represents perceived dangerousness or "predacity" of animals. *Journal of Neuroscience, 36,* 5373–5384.

Conway, A. R. A., Kane, M. J., Bunting, M. F., Hambrick, D. Z., Wilhelm, O., & Engle, R. W. (2005). Working memory span tasks: A methodological review and user's guide. *Psychonomic Bulletin & Review, 12,* 769–786.

Conway, A. R. A., Kane, M. J., & Engle, R. W. (2003). Working memory capacity and its relation to general intelligence. *Trends in Cognitive Sciences, 7,* 547–552.

Conway, M., & Ross, M. (1984). Getting what you want by revising what you had. *Journal of Personality and Social Psychology, 47,* 738–748.

Cook, G. I., Marsh, R. L., Clark-Foos, A., & Meeks, J. T. (2007). Learning is impaired by activated intentions. *Psychonomic Bulletin and Review, 14,* 101–106.

Cook, M., & Mineka, S. (1989). Observational conditioning of fear to fear-relevant versus fear-irrelevant stimuli in rhesus monkeys. *Journal of Abnormal Psychology, 98,* 448–459.

Cook, M., & Mineka, S. (1990). Selective associations in the observational conditioning of fear in rhesus monkeys. *Journal of Experimental Psychology: Animal Behavior Processes, 16,* 372.

Cooper, C. R., Denner, J., & Lopez, E. M. (1999). Cultural brokers: Helping Latino children on pathways toward success. *The Future of Children, 9,* 51–57.

Copeland, W. E., Wolke, D., Angold, A., & Costello, E. J. (2013). Adult psychiatric outcomes of bullying and being bullied by peers in childhood and adolescence. *Journal of the American Medical Association Psychiatry, 70,* 419–426.

Copen, C. E., Daniels, K., Vespa, J., & Mosher, W. D. (2012). First marriages in the United States: Data from the 2006–2010 National Survey of Family Growth. Washington, DC: Centers for Disease Control and Prevention, National Center for Health Statistics.

Coren, S. (1996). Daylight savings time and traffic accidents. *New England Journal of Medicine, 334,* 924.

Corr, P. J., DeYoung, C. G., & McNaughton, N. (2013). Motivation and personality: A neuropsychological perspective. *Social and Personality Psychology Compass, 7,* 158–175.

Correll, C. U., Leucht, S., & Kane, J. M. (2004). Lower risk for tardive dyskinesia associated with second-generation antipsychotics: A systematic review of 1-year studies. *American Journal of Psychiatry, 161,* 414–425.

Correll, J., Park, B., Judd, C. M., Wittenbrink, B., Sadler, M. S., & Keesee, T. (2007). Across the thin blue line: Police officers and racial bias in the decision to shoot. *Journal of Personality and Social Psychology, 92,* 1006–1023.

Cortese, S., Moreira-Maia, C. R., St. Fleur, D., Morcillo-Peñalver, C., Rohde, L. A., & Faraone, S. V. (2016). Association between ADHD and obesity: A systematic review and meta-analysis. *American Journal of Psychiatry, 173,* 34–43.

Cosmides, L., & Tooby, J. (1997). *Evolutionary psychology: A primer.* Retrieved from http://www.psych.ucsb.edu/research/cep/primer.html

Cosmides, L., & Tooby, J. (2000). The cognitive neuroscience of social reasoning. In M. S. Gazzaniga (Ed.), *The new cognitive neurosciences* (pp. 1259–1270). Cambridge, MA: MIT Press.

Costa, P. T., & McCrae, R. R. (1992). *Revised NEO Personality Inventory (NEO-PI-R) and NEO Five-Factor Inventory (NEO-FFI) professional manual.* Odessa, FL: Psychological Assessment Resources.

Costa, P. T., Terracciano, A., & McCrae, R. R. (2001). Gender differences in personality traits across cultures: Robust and surprising findings. *Journal of Personality and Social Psychology, 81,* 322–331.

Costanzi, M., Cannas, S., Saraulli, D., Rossi-Arnaud, C., & Cestari, V. (2011). Extinction after retrieval: Effects on the associative and nonassociative components of remote contextual fear memory. *Learning & Memory, 18,* 508–518.

Courchesne, E., Pierce, K., Schumann, C. M., Redcay, E., Buckwalter, J. A., Kennedy, D. P., et al. (2007). Mapping early brain development in autism. *Neuron, 56,* 399–413.

Courchesne, E., Redcay, E., & Kennedy, D. P. (2004). The autistic brain: Birth through adulthood. *Current Opinion in Neurology, 17,* 489–496.

Cowan, C. P., & Cowan, P. A. (1988). Who does what when partners become parents? Implications for men, women, and marriage. In R. Palkovitz & M. B. Sussman (Eds.), *Transitions to parenthood* (pp. 105–132). New York, NY: The Haworth Press.

Craddock, N., & Sklar, P. (2013). Genetics of bipolar disorder. *The Lancet, 381,* 1654–1662.

Craig, A. D. (2009). How do you feel—now? The anterior insula and human awareness. *Nature Reviews Neuroscience, 10,* 59–70.

Craighead, W. E., & Dunlop, B. W. (2014). Combination psychotherapy and antidepressant medication treatment for depression: For whom, when, and how. *Annual Review of Psychology, 65,* 267–300.

Craik, F. I. M., & Lockhart, R. S. (1972). Levels of processing: A framework for memory research. *Journal of Verbal Learning and Verbal Behavior, 11*, 671–684.

Craik, F. I. M., & Tulving, E. (1975). Depth of processing and the retention of words in episodic memory. *Journal of Experimental Psychology: General, 104*, 268–294.

Crawford, H. J., Corby, J. C., & Kopell, B. (1996). Auditory event-related potentials while ignoring tone stimuli: Attentional differences reflected in stimulus intensity and latency responses in low and highly hypnotizable persons. *International Journal of Neuroscience, 85*, 57–69.

Crocker, J., & Major, B. (1989). Social stigma and self-esteem: The self-protective properties of stigma. *Psychological Review, 96*, 608–630.

Cropley, V. L., Klauser, P., Lenroot, R. K., Bruggemann, J., Sundram, S., Bousman, C., et al. (2017). Accelerated gray and white matter deterioration with age in schizophrenia. *American Journal of Psychiatry, 174*, 286–295.

Crosnoe, R., & Elder, G. H., Jr. (2002). Successful adaptation in the later years: A life-course approach to aging. *Social Psychology Quarterly, 65*, 309–328.

Crowe, R. R. (2000). Molecular genetics of anxiety disorders. In D. S. Charney, E. J. Nestler, & B. S. Bunney (Eds.), *Neurobiology of mental illness* (pp. 451–462). New York, NY: Oxford University Press.

Crowley, S. J., & Eastman, C. I. (2015). Phase advancing human circadian rhythms with morning bright light, afternoon melatonin, and gradually shifted sleep: Can we reduce morning bright-light duration? *Sleep Medicine, 16*, 288–297.

Csikszentmihalyi, M. (1990). *Flow: The psychology of optimal experience.* New York, NY: Harper & Row.

Csikszentmihalyi, M. (1999). If we are so rich, why aren't we happy? *American Psychologist, 54*, 821–827.

Cuijpers, P., Sijbrandij, M., Koole, S. L., Andersson, G., Beekman, A. T., & Reynolds, C. F. (2014). Adding psychotherapy to antidepressant medication in depression and anxiety disorders: A meta-analysis. *World Psychiatry, 13*, 56–67.

Culler, E., Coakley, J. D., Lowy, K., & Gross, N. (1943). A revised frequency-map of the guinea-pig cochlea. *The American Journal of Psychology, 56*, 475–500.

Cummings, J. R., & Druss, B. G. (2010). Racial/ethnic differences in mental health service use among adolescents with major depression. *Journal of the American Academy of Child & Adolescent Psychiatry, 50*, 160–170.

Cunningham, M. R., Barbee, A. P., & Druen, P. B. (1996). Social allergens and the reactions they produce: Escalation of annoyance and disgust in love and work. In R. M. Kowalski (Ed.), *Aversive interpersonal behaviors* (pp. 189–214). New York, NY: Plenum Press.

Cunningham, M. R., Roberts, A. R., Barbee, A. P., Druen, P. B., & Wu, C. (1995). Their ideas of beauty are, on the whole, the same as ours: Consistency and variability in the cross-cultural perception of female physical attractiveness. *Journal of Personality and Social Psychology, 68*, 261–279.

Cunningham, W. A., Johnson, M. K., Raye, C. L., Gatenby, J. C., Gore, J. C., & Banaji, M. R. (2004). Separable neural components in the processing of black and white faces. *Psychological Science, 15*, 806–813.

Cupach, W. R., & Metts, S. (1990). Remedial processes in embarrassing predicaments. In J. Anderson (Ed.), *Communication yearbook* (pp. 323–352). Newbury Park, CA: Sage.

Cusack, K., Jonas, D. E., Forneris, C. A., Wines, C., Sonis, J., Middleton, J. C., et al. (2016). Psychological treatments for adults with posttraumatic stress disorder: A systematic review and meta-analysis. *Clinical Psychology Review, 43*, 128–141.

Cvetkovic-Lopes, V., Bayer, L., Dorsaz, S., Maret, S., Pradervand, S., Dauvilliers, Y., et al. (2010). Elevated tribbles homolog 2-specific antibody levels in narcolepsy patients. *Journal of Clinical Investigation, 120*, 713–719.

Dabbs, J. M., & Morris, R. (1990). Testosterone, social class, and antisocial behavior in a sample of 4462 men. *Psychological Science, 1*, 209–211.

Dalton, M. A., Bernhardt, A. M., Gibson, J. J., Sargent, J. D., Beach, M. L., Adachi-Mejia, A. M., et al. (2005). Use of cigarettes and alcohol by preschoolers while role-playing as adults: "Honey, have some smokes." *Archives of Pediatrics & Adolescent Medicine, 159*, 854–859.

Damasio, A. R. (1994). *Descartes' error.* New York, NY: Avon Books.

Damasio, H., Grabowski, T., Frank, R., Galaburda, A. M., & Damasio, A. R. (1994). The return of Phineas Gage: Clues about the brain from the skull of a famous patient. *Science, 264*, 1102–1105.

Dapretto, M., Davies, M. S., Pfeifer, J. H., Scott, A. A., Sigman, M., Bookheimer, S. Y., & Iacoboni, M. (2006). Understanding emotions in others: Mirror neuron dysfunction in children with autism spectrum disorders. *Nature Neuroscience, 9*, 28–30.

Darke, P. R., & Dahl, D. W. (2003). Fairness and discounts: The subjective value of a bargain. *Journal of Consumer Psychology, 13*, 328–338.

Darley, J. M., & Batson, C. D. (1973). "From Jerusalem to Jericho": A study of situational and dispositional variables in helping behavior. *Journal of Personality and Social Psychology, 27*, 100–108.

Darwin, C. (1859). *On the origin of species by means of natural selection, or the preservation of favoured races in the struggle for life.* London, England: John Murray.

Darwin, C. (1872). *The expression of the emotions in man and animals.* London, England: John Murray.

Darwin, C. (1892). *The autobiography of Charles Darwin and selected letters* (F. Darwin, Ed.). New York, NY: Dover.

Dasgupta, A. G., & Greenwald, A. G. (2001). Exposure to admired group members reduces automatic intergroup bias. *Journal of Personality and Social Psychology, 81*, 800–814.

Davies, G., Tenesa, A., Payton, A., Yang, J., Harris, S. E., Liewald, D., et al. (2011). Genome-wide association studies establish that human intelligence is highly heritable and polygenic. *Molecular Psychiatry, 16*, 996–1005.

Davies, W. (2014). Sex differences in attention deficit hyperactivity disorder: Candidate genetic and endocrine mechanisms. *Frontiers in Neuroendocrinology, 35*, 331–346.

Davis, J., Eyre, H., Jacka, F. N., Dodd, S., Dean, O., McEwen, S., et al. (2016). A review of vulnerability and risks for schizophrenia: Beyond the two hit hypothesis. *Neuroscience & Biobehavioral Reviews, 65*, 185–194.

Davis, S. R., Worsley, R., Miller, K. K., Parish, S. J., & Santoro, N. (2016). Androgens and female sexual function and dysfunction—findings from the Fourth International Consultation of Sexual Medicine. *Journal of Sexual Medicine, 13*, 168–178.

Daxinger, L., & Whitelaw, E. (2012). Understanding transgenerational epigenetic inheritance via the gametes in mammals. *Nature Reviews Genetics, 13*, 153–162.

Deacon, B. J., & Abramowitz, J. S. (2004). Cognitive and behavioral treatments for anxiety disorders: A review of meta-analytic findings. *Journal of Clinical Psychology, 60*, 429–441.

Deal, A. L., Erickson, K. J., Shiers, S. I., & Burman, M. A. (2016). Limbic system development underlies the emergence of classical fear conditioning during the third and fourth weeks of life in the rat. *Behavioral Neuroscience, 130*, 212–230.

DeAngelis, T. (2008). Psychology's growth careers. *Monitor on Psychology, 39*, 64.

Deary, I. J. (2000). *Looking down on human intelligence.* New York, NY: Oxford University Press.

Deary, I. J. (2001). *Intelligence: A very short introduction.* New York, NY: Oxford University Press.

Deary, I. J., Batty, G. D., Pattie, A., & Gale, C. R. (2008). More intelligent, more dependable children live longer: A 55-year longitudinal study of a representative sample of the Scottish nation. *Psychological Science, 19*, 874–880.

Deary, I. J., & Der, G. (2005). Reaction time explains IQ's association with death. *Psychological Science, 16*, 64–69.

Deaton, A., & Stone, A. A. (2014). Evaluative and hedonic well-being among those with and without children at home. *Proceedings of the National Academy of Science, 111*, 1328–1333.

DeCasper, A. J., & Spence, M. J. (1986). Prenatal maternal speech influences newborns' perception of speech sounds. *Infant Behavior and Development, 9,* 133–150.

Decety, J., Chen, C., Harenski, C., & Kiehl, K. A. (2013). An fMRI study of affective perspective taking in individuals with psychopathy: Imagining another in pain does not evoke empathy. *Frontiers in Human Neuroscience, 7,* 489. doi:10.3389/fnhum.2013.00489

Decety, J., & Howard, L. (2014). A neurodevelopmental perspective on morality. In M. Killen and J. Smetana (Eds.), *Handbook of moral development* (pp. 454–474). Mahwah, NJ: Erlbaum.

Decety, J., & Porges, E. C. (2011). Imagining being the agent of actions that carry different moral consequences: An fMRI study. *Neuropsychologia, 49,* 2994–3001.

deCharms, R. C., Maeda, F., Glover, G. H, Ludlow, D., Pauly, J. M., Soneji, D., et al. (2005). Control over brain activation and pain learned by using real-time functional MRI. *Proceedings of the National Academy of Sciences, 102,* 18626–18631.

Deci, E. L., & Ryan, R. M. (1987). The support of autonomy and the control of behavior. *Journal of Personality and Social Psychology, 53,* 1024–1037.

Dehaene, S., Changeux, J. P., Naccache, L., Sackur, J., & Sergent, C. (2006). Conscious, preconscious, and subliminal processing: A testable taxonomy. *Trends in Cognitive Sciences, 10,* 204–211.

de Hevia, M. D., Izard, V., Coubart, A., Spelke, E. S., & Streri, A. (2014). Representations of space, time, and number in neonates. *Proceedings of the National Academy of Sciences, 111,* 4809–4813.

DeJong, W., & Kleck, R. E. (1986). The social psychological effects of overweight. In C. P. Herman, M. P. Zanna, & E. T. Higgins (Eds.), *Physical appearance, stigma and social behavior: The Ontario Symposium* (pp. 65–87). Hillsdale, NJ: Erlbaum.

DeJong, W., Schneider, S. K., Towvim, L. G., Murphy, M. J., Doerr, E. E., Simonsen, N. R., et al. (2006). A multisite randomized trial of social norms marketing campaigns to reduce college student drinking. *Journal of Studies on Alcohol and Drugs, 67,* 868–879.

Dekker, S., Lee, N. C., Howard-Jones, P., & Jolles, J. (2012). Neuromyth in education: Prevalence and predictors of misconception among teachers. *Frontiers in Neuroscience, 3,* 1–8.

De Kloet, E. R., Joëls, M., & Holsboer, F. (2005). Stress and the brain: From adaptation to disease. *Nature Reviews Neuroscience, 6,* 463–475.

De Lisi, R., & Staudt, J. (1980). Individual differences in college students' performance on formal operations tasks. *Journal of Applied Developmental Psychology, 1,* 201–208.

DeLong, M. R., & Wichmann, T. (2008). *The expanding potential of deep brain stimulation: The 2008 progress report on brain research.* New York, NY: Dana Foundation.

DeLongis, A., Folkman, S., & Lazarus, R. S. (1988). The impact of daily stress on health and mood: Psychological and social resources as mediators. *Journal of Personality and Social Psychology, 54,* 486.

Demerouti, E. (2006). Job characteristics, flow, and performance: The moderating role of conscientiousness. *Journal of Occupational Health Psychology, 11,* 266–280.

Demir, E., & Dickson, B. J. (2005). Fruitless: Splicing specifies male courtship behavior in drosophila. *Cell, 121,* 785–794.

Demos, K. D., Kelley, W. M., & Heatherton, T. F. (2011). Dietary restraint violations influence reward responses in the nucleus accumbens and amygdala. *Journal of Cognitive Neuroscience, 23,* 1952–1963.

DeSantis, C., Naishadham, D., & Jemal, A. (2013). Cancer statistics for African Americans, 2013. *CA: A Cancer Journal for Clinicians, 63,* 151–166.

DeStefano, F., Price, C. S., & Weintraub, E. S. (2013). Increasing exposure to antibody-stimulating proteins and polysaccharides in vaccines is not associated with risk of autism. *Journal of Pediatrics, 163,* 561–567.

Detweiler, J. B., Bedell, B. T., Salovey, P., Pronin, E., & Rothman, A. J. (1999). Message framing and sunscreen use: Gain-framed messages motivate beach-goers. *Health Psychology, 18,* 189–196.

Devine, P. G. (1989). Stereotypes and prejudice: Their automatic and controlled components. *Journal of Personality and Social Psychology, 56,* 5–18.

de Wijk, R. A., Schab, F. R., & Cain, W. S. (1995). Odor identification. In F. R. Schab (Ed.), *Memory for odors* (pp. 21–37). Mahwah, NJ: Erlbaum.

DeYoung, C. G., & Gray, J. R. (2009). Personality neuroscience: Explaining individual differences in affect, behavior, and cognition. In P. J. Corr & G. Matthews (Eds.), *The Cambridge handbook of personality psychology* (pp. 323–346). New York, NY: Cambridge University Press.

DeYoung, C. G., Hirsh, J. B., Shane, M. S., Papademetris, X., Rajeevan, N., & Gray, J. R. (2010). Testing predictions from personality neuroscience: Brain structure and the Big Five. *Psychological Science, 21,* 820–828.

Diamond, L. M. (2016). Sexual fluidity in male and females. *Current Sexual Health Reports, 8,* 249–256.

Dickson, P. R., & Vaccarino, F. J. (1994). GRF-induced feeding: Evidence for protein selectivity and opiate involvement. *Peptides, 15,* 1343–1352.

Diener, E. (2000). Subjective well-being: The science of happiness and a proposal for a national index. *American Psychologist, 55,* 34–43.

Diener, E., Wolsic, B., & Fujita, F. (1995). Physical attractiveness and subjective well-being. *Journal of Personality and Social Psychology, 69,* 120–129.

Dijksterhuis, A., & Aarts, H. (2010). Goals, attention, and (un)consciousness. *Annual Review of Psychology, 61,* 467–490.

Dinstein, I., Thomas, C., Humphreys, K., Minshew, N., Behrmann, M., & Heeger, D. J. (2010). Normal movement selectivity in autism. *Neuron, 66,* 461–469.

Dion, K., Berscheid, E., & Walster, E. (1972). What is beautiful is good. *Journal of Personality and Social Psychology, 24,* 285–290.

Dittman, M. (2004). What you need to know to get licensed. Retrieved from http://www.apa.org/gradpsych/2004/01/get-licensed.aspx

Dobbs, D. (2006). Turning off depression. *Scientific American Mind,* 26–31.

Doblin, R., Greer, G., Holland, J., Jerome, L., Mithoefer, M. C., & Sessa, B. (2014). A reconsideration and response to Parrott AC (2013) "Human psychobiology of MDMA or 'Ecstasy': An overview of 25 years of empirical research." *Human Psychopharmacology: Clinical and Experimental, 29,* 105–108.

Docherty, N. M. (2005). Cognitive impairments and disordered speech in schizophrenia: Thought disorder, disorganization, and communication failure perspectives. *Journal of Abnormal Psychology, 114,* 269–278.

Dockray, A., & Steptoe, A. (2010). Positive affect and psychobiological process. *Neuroscience and Biobehavioral Reviews, 35,* 69–75.

Dohrenwend, B. P., Shrout, P. E., Link, B. G., Skodol, A. E., & Martin, J. L. (1986). Overview and initial results from a risk factor study of depression and schizophrenia. In J. E. Barrett (Ed.), *Mental disorders in the community: Progress and challenge* (pp. 184–215). New York, NY: Guilford Press.

Dolan, P., & Metcalfe, R. (2010). "Oops . . . I did it again": Repeated focusing effects in reports of happiness. *Journal of Economic Psychology, 31,* 732–737.

Dolan, R. J. (2000). Emotion processing in the human brain revealed through functional neuroimaging. In M. S. Gazzaniga (Ed.), *The new cognitive neurosciences* (pp. 115–131). Cambridge, MA: MIT Press.

Domhoff, G. W. (2003). *The scientific study of dreams: Neural networks, cognitive development, and content analysis.* Washington, DC: American Psychological Association.

Domjan, M. (2014). *Principles of learning and behavior* (7th ed.). Belmont, CA: Thomson/Wadsworth.

Donahue, A. B. (2000). Electroconvulsive therapy and memory loss: A personal journey. *Journal of ECT, 16,* 133–143.

Dondi, M., Simion, F., & Caltran, G. (1999). Can newborns discriminate between their own cry and the cry of another newborn infant? *Developmental Psychology, 35,* 418–426.

Dorfman, H. M., Meyer-Lindenberg, A., & Buckholtz, J. W. (2014). Neurobiological mechanisms for impulsive-aggression: The role of MAOA. *Current Topics in Behavioral Neuroscience.* doi: 10.1007/7854_2013_272

Dovidio, J. F., ten Vergert, M., Stewart, T. L., Gaertner, S. L., Johnson, J. D., Esses, V. M., et al. (2004). Perspective and prejudice: Antecedents and mediating mechanisms. *Personality and Social Psychology Bulletin, 30,* 1537–1549.

Dowrick, C., & Frances, A. (2013). Medicalising unhappiness: New classification of depression risks more patients being put on drug treatment from which they will not benefit. *BMJ, 347,* f7140.

Drescher, J., Schwartz, A., Casoy, F., McIntosh, C. A., Hurley, B., et al. (2016). The growing regulation of conversion therapy. *Journal of Medical Regulation, 102,* 7–12.

Duckworth, A. L., Peterson, C., Matthews, M. D., & Kelly, D. R. (2007). Grit: Perseverance and passion for long-term goals. *Journal of Personality and Social Psychology, 92,* 1087–1101.

Duckworth, A. L., & Quinn, P. D. (2009). Development and validation of the short grit scale (Grit-S). *Journal of Personality Assessment, 91,* 166–174.

Duckworth, A. L., Quinn, P. D., Lynam, D. R., Loeber, R., & Stouthamer-Loeber, M. (2011). Role of test motivation in intelligence testing. *Proceedings of the National Academy of Sciences, 108,* 7716–7720.

Duckworth, A. L., & Seligman, M. E. P. (2005). Self-discipline outdoes IQ in predicting academic performance of adolescents. *Psychological Science, 16,* 939–944.

Dugatkin, L. A. (2004). *Principles of animal behavior.* New York, NY: Norton.

Dunbar, R. I. M. (1998). The social brain hypothesis. *Brain, 9,* 178–190.

Dunbar, R. I. M. (2014). The social brain: Psychological underpinnings and implications for the structure of organizations. *Current Directions in Psychological Science, 23,* 109–114.

Duncan, J., Burgess, P., & Emslie, H. (1995). Fluid intelligence after frontal lobe lesions. *Neuropsychologia, 33,* 261–268.

Duncker, K. (1945). On problem solving. *Psychological Monographs, 58*(5, Whole No. 70).

Dunlap, K. (1927). *The role of eye-muscles and mouth-muscles in the expression of the emotions.* Worcester, MA: Clark University Press.

Dunning, D., Johnson, K., Ehrlinger, J., & Kruger, J. (2003). Why people fail to recognize their own incompetence. *Current Directions in Psychological Science, 12,* 83–87.

Durante, K. M., Li, N. P., & Haselton, M. G. (2008). Changes in women's choice of dress across the ovulatory cycle: Naturalistic and laboratory task-based evidence. *Personality and Social Psychology Bulletin, 34,* 1451–1460.

Dutton, D. G., & Aron, A. P. (1974). Some evidence for heightened sexual attraction under conditions of high anxiety. *Journal of Personality and Social Psychology, 30,* 510–517.

Dykman, B. M., Horowitz, L. M., Abramson, L. Y., & Usher, M. (1991). Schematic and situational determinants of depressed and nondepressed students' interpretation of feedback. *Journal of Abnormal Psychology, 100,* 45–55.

Eagly, A. H., Karau, S. J., & Makhijani, M. G. (1995). Gender and the effectiveness of leaders: A meta-analysis. *Psychological Bulletin, 117,* 125–145.

Eaker, E. D., Sullivan, L. M., Kelly-Hayes, M., D'Agostino, R. B., Sr., & Benjamin, E. J. (2004). Anger and hostility predict the development of atrial fibrillation in men in the Framingham Offspring Study. *Circulation, 109,* 1267–1271.

Ebbinghaus, H. (1964). *Memory* (H. A. Ruger & C. E. Bussenius, Trans.). New York, NY: Teachers College. (Original work published as *Das Gedächtnis,* 1885.)

Eberhardt, J. L., Goff, P. A., Purdie, V. J., & Davies, P. G. (2004). Seeing black: Race, crime, and visual processing. *Journal of Personality and Social Psychology, 87,* 876–893.

Egeland, J. A., Gerhard, D. S., Pauls, D. L., Sussex, J. N., Kidd, K. K., Allen, C. R., et al. (1987). Bipolar affective disorders linked to DNA markers on chromosome 11. *Nature, 325,* 783–787.

Eisenbarth, H., Chang, L. J., & Wager, T. D. (2016). Multivariate brain prediction of heart rate and skin conductance responses to social threat. *Journal of Neuroscience, 36,* 11987–11998.

Eisenberg, N. (2000). Emotion, regulation, and moral development. *Annual Review of Psychology, 51,* 665–697.

Eisenberg, N. (2002). Empathy-related emotional responses, altruism, and their socialization. In R. J. Davidson and A. Harrington (Eds.), *Visions of compassion: Western scientists and Tibetan Buddhists examine human nature* (pp. 131–164). New York, NY: Oxford University Press.

Eisenberg, N., & Valiente, C. (2002). Parenting and children's prosocial and moral development. In M. Bornstein (Ed.), *Handbook of parenting* (Vol. 5, pp. 111–142). Mahwah, NJ: Erlbaum.

Eisenberg, N., VanSchyndel, S. K., & Spinrad, T. L. (2016). Prosocial motivation: Inferences from an opaque body of work. *Child Development, 87,* 1668–1678.

Eisenberger, N. I., Lieberman, M. D., & Satpute, A. B. (2005). Personality from a controlled processing perspective: An fMRI study of neuroticism, extraversion, and self-consciousness. *Cognitive, Affective, & Behavioral Neuroscience, 5,* 169–181.

Eisenstein, M. (2014). Public health: An injection of trust. *Nature, 507,* S17–S19.

Ekelund, J., Lichtermann, D., Jaervelin, M., & Peltonen, L. (1999). Association between novelty seeking and type 4 dopamine receptor gene in a large Finnish cohort sample. *American Journal of Psychiatry, 156,* 1453–1455.

Ekman, P., & Friesen, W. V. (1971). Constants across cultures in the face and emotion. *Journal of Personality and Social Psychology, 17,* 124–129.

Ekman, P., Sorenson, E. R., & Friesen, W. V. (1969). Pancultural elements in facial displays of emotions. *Science, 164,* 86–88.

Elaad, E., Ginton, A., & Ben-Shakhar, G. (1994). The effects of prior expectations and outcome knowledge on polygraph examiners' decisions. *Journal of Behavioral Decision Making, 7,* 279–292.

Elfenbein, H. A., & Ambady, N. (2002). On the universality of cultural specificity of emotion recognition: A meta-analysis. *Psychological Bulletin, 128,* 203–235.

Ellis, A. (1962). Reason and emotion in psychotherapy. Secaucus, NY: Lyle Stuart.

Else-Quest, N., Hyde, J. S., Goldsmith, H. H., & Van Hulle, C. A. (2006). Gender differences in temperament: A meta-analysis. *Psychological Bulletin, 132,* 33–72.

Emery, C. F., Kiecolt-Glaser, J. K., Glaser, R., Malarkey, W. B., & Frid, D. J. (2005). Exercise accelerates wound healing among healthy older adults: A preliminary investigation. *Journals of Gerontology, 60A,* 1432–1436.

Emslie, G. J., Rush, A. J., Weinberg, W. A., Kowatch, R. A., Hughes, C. W., Carmody, T., et al. (1997). A double-blind, randomized, placebo-controlled trial of fluoxetine in children and adolescents with depression. *Archives of General Psychiatry, 54,* 1031–1037.

Endo, Y., & Meijer, Z. (2004). Autobiographical memory of success and failure experiences. In Y. Kashima, Y. Endo, E. S. Kashima, C. Leung, & J. McClure (Eds.), *Progress in Asian social psychology* (Vol. 4, pp. 67–84). Seoul, South Korea: Kyoyook-Kwahak-Sa Publishing.

Engle, R. W., & Kane, M. J. (2004). Executive attention, working memory capacity, and a two-factor theory of cognitive control. In B. Ross (Ed.), *The psychology of learning and motivation* (pp. 145–199). New York, NY: Elsevier.

Engle, R. W., Tuholski, S. W., Laughlin, J. E., & Conway, A. R. A. (1999). Working memory, short-term memory, and general fluid intelligence: A latent variable approach. *Journal of Experimental Psychology: General, 128,* 309–331.

Engwall, M., & Duppils, G. S. (2009). Music as a nursing intervention for postoperative pain: A systematic review. *Journal of Perianesthesia Nursing, 24,* 370–383.

Enns, J. (2005). *The thinking eye, the seeing brain.* New York, NY: Norton.

Epley, N., & Gilovich, T. (2001). Putting adjustment back in the anchoring and adjustment heuristic: Differential processing of self-generated and experimenter-provided anchors. *Psychological Science, 12,* 391–396.

Epstein, L. H., Robinson, J. L., Roemmich, J. N., Marusewski, A. L., & Roba, L. G. (2010). What constitutes food variety? Stimulus specificity of food. *Appetite, 54,* 23–29.

Era, P., Jokela, J., & Heikkinen, E. (1986). Reaction and movement times in men of different ages: A population study. *Perceptual and Motor Skills, 63,* 111–130.

Ericsson, K. A., Krampe, R. T., & Tesch-Römer, C. (1993). The role of deliberate practice in the acquisition of expert performance. *Psychology Review, 100,* 363–406.

Erikson, E. H. (1968). *Identity: Youth and crisis.* New York, NY: Norton.

Erikson, E. H. (1980). *Identity and the life cycle.* New York, NY: Norton.

Eriksson, P. S., Perfilieva, E., Bjork-Eriksson, T., Alborn, A. M., Nordborg, C., Peterson, D. A., et al. (1998). Neurogenesis in the adult human hippocampus. *Nature Medicine, 4,* 1313–1317.

Eron, L. D. (1987). The development of aggressive behavior from the perspective of a developing behaviorism. *American Psychologist, 42,* 435–442.

Eshel, N., Tian, J., & Uchida, N. (2013). Opening the black box: Dopamine, predictions, and learning. *Trends in Cognitive Sciences, 17,* 430–431.

Espie, C. A. (2002). Insomnia: Conceptual issues in the development, persistence, and treatment of sleep disorders in adults. *Annual Review of Psychology, 53,* 215–243.

Eysenck, H. J. (1967). *The biological basis of personality.* Springfield, IL: Thomas.

Eysenck, S. B., & Eysenck, H. J. (1967). Salivary response to lemon juice as a measure of introversion. *Perceptual and Motor Skills, 24,* 1047–1053.

Fabiano, G. A., Pelham, W. E., Coles, E. K., Gnagy, E. M., Chronis-Tuscano, A., & O'Connor, B. C. (2009). A meta-analysis of behavioral treatments for attention-deficit/hyperactivity disorder. *Clinical Psychology Review, 29,* 129–140.

Fagerström, K. O., & Schneider, N. G. (1989). Measuring nicotine dependence: A review of the Fagerström tolerance questionnaire. *Journal of Behavioral Medicine, 12,* 159–181.

Fallon, A. E., & Rozin, P. (1985). Sex differences in perceptions of desirable body shape. *Journal of Abnormal Psychology, 94,* 102–105.

Fantz, R. L. (1963). Pattern vision in newborn infants. *Science, 140,* 296–297.

Fantz, R. L. (1966). Pattern discrimination and selective attention as determinants of perceptual development from birth. In A. H. Kidd & L. J. Rivoire (Eds.), *Perceptual development in children* (pp. 143–173). New York, NY: International Universities Press.

Farah, M. J., Betancourt, L., Shera, D. M., Savage, J. H., Giannetta, J. M., Malmud, E. K., et al. (2008). Environmental stimulation, parental nurturance and cognitive development in humans. *Developmental Science, 11,* 793–801.

Farah, M. J., Hutchinson, J. B., Phelps, E. A., & Wagner, A. D. (2014). Functional MRI-based lie detection: Scientific and societal challenges. *Nature Reviews Neuroscience, 15,* 123–131.

Farb, N. A., Anderson, A. K., Mayberg, H., Bean, J., McKeon, D., & Segal, Z. V. (2010). Minding one's emotions: Mindfulness training alters the neural expression of sadness. *Emotion, 10,* 25–33.

Farooqi, I. S., Bullmore, E., Keogh, J., Gillard, J., O'Rahilly, S., & Fletcher, P. C. (2007). Leptin regulates striatal regions and human eating behavior. *Science, 317,* 1355.

Faul, M., Xu, L., Wald, M. M., & Coronado, V. G. (2010). Traumatic brain injury in the United States: Emergency department visits, hospitalizations, and deaths. Atlanta, GA: Centers for Disease Control and Prevention, National Center for Injury Prevention and Control.

Fawcett, J. (1992). Suicide risk factors in depressive disorders and in panic disorders. *Journal of Clinical Psychiatry, 53,* 9–13.

Fazio, R. H. (1995). Attitudes as object-evaluation associations: Determinants, consequences, and correlates of attitude accessibility. In R. E. Petty & J. A. Krosnick (Eds.), *Attitude strength: Antecedents and consequences* (pp. 247–282). Hillsdale, NJ: Erlbaum.

Fazio, R. H., Eisner, J. R., & Shook, N. J. (2004). Attitude formation through exploration: Valence asymmetries. *Journal of Personality and Social Psychology, 87,* 293–311.

Feingold, A. (1992). Good-looking people are not what we think. *Psychological Bulletin, 111,* 304–341.

Feingold, A. (1994). Gender differences in personality: A meta-analysis. *Psychological Bulletin, 116,* 429–456.

Feldman, R., Weller, A., Zagoory-Sharon, O., & Levine, A. (2007). Evidence for a neuroendocrinological foundation of human affiliation: Plasma oxytocin levels across pregnancy and the postpartum period predict mother-infant bonding. *Psychological Science, 18,* 965–970.

Feldman, S. S., & Rosenthal, D. A. (1991). Age expectations of behavioural autonomy in Hong Kong, Australian and American youth: The influence of family variables and adolescents' values. *International Journal of Psychology, 26,* 1–23.

Feldman Barrett, L., Lane, R. D., Sechrest, L., & Schwartz, G. E. (2000). Sex differences in emotional awareness. *Personality and Social Psychology Bulletin, 26,* 1027–1035.

Ferdinand, A. O., & Menachemi, N. (2014). Associations between driving performance and engaging in secondary tasks: A systematic review. *American Journal of Public Health, 104,* e39–e48.

Fergus, I., & McDowd, J. M. (1987). Age differences in recall and recognition. *Journal of Experimental Psychology: Learning, Memory, and Cognition, 13,* 474–479.

Ferguson, J. N., Young, L. J., Hearn, E. F., Matzuk, M. M., Insel, T. R., & Winslow, J. T. (2000). Social amnesia in mice lacking the oxytocin gene. *Nature Neuroscience, 25,* 284–288.

Fernald, A. (1989). Intonation and communicative intent in mothers' speech to infants: Is the melody the message? *Child Development, 60,* 1497–1510.

Fernández-Espejo, D., & Owen, A. M. (2013). Detecting awareness after severe brain injury. *Nature Reviews Neuroscience, 14,* 801–809.

Ferracioli-Oda, E., Qawasmi, A., & Bloch, M. H. (2013). Meta-analysis: Melatonin for the treatment of primary sleep disorders. *PLoS ONE, 8,* e63773.

Ferro, M. J., & Martins, H. F. (2016). Academic plagiarism: Yielding to temptation. *British Journal of Education, Society & Behavioural Science, 13,* 1–11.

Ferry, G. (Writer/Broadcaster). (2002, 12 & 19 November). Hearing colours, eating sounds. *BBC Radio 4, Science.* Retrieved from http://www.bbc.co.uk/radio4/science/hearingcolours.shtml

Festinger, L. (1954). A theory of social comparison processes. *Human Relations, 7,* 117–140.

Festinger, L. (1957). *A theory of cognitive dissonance.* Evanston, IL: Row, Peterson.

Festinger, L. (1987). A personal memory. In N. E. Grunberg, R. E. Nisbett, J. Rodin, & J. E. Singer (Eds.), *A distinctive approach to psychological research: The influence of Stanley Schachter* (pp. 1–9). New York, NY: Erlbaum.

Festinger, L., & Carlsmith, J. M. (1959). Cognitive consequences of forced compliance. *Journal of Abnormal and Social Psychology, 58,* 203–210.

Festinger, L., Schachter, S., & Back, K. W. (1950). *Social pressures in informal groups.* New York, NY: Harper.

Fibiger, H. C. (1993). Mesolimbic dopamine: An analysis of its role in motivated behavior. *Seminars in Neuroscience, 5,* 321–327.

Finger, S. (1994). *Origins of neuroscience.* Oxford, England: Oxford University Press.

Fink, M. (2001). Convulsive therapy: A review of the first 55 years. *Journal of Affective Disorders, 63,* 1–15.

Finsterwald, C., & Alberini, C. M. (2014). Stress and glucocorticoid receptor-dependent mechanisms in long-term memory: From adaptive responses to psychopathologies. *Neurobiology of Learning and Memory, 112,* 17–29.

Fiore, M. C., Schroeder, S. A., & Baker, T. B. (2014). Smoke, the chief killer—Strategies for targeting combustible tobacco use. *New England Journal of Medicine, 37,* 297–299.

Fischer, B., Kurdyak, P., Goldner, E., Tyndall, M., & Rehm, J. (2016). Treatment of prescription opioid disorders in Canada: Looking at the "other epidemic"? *Substance Abuse Treatment, Prevention, and Policy, 11,* 12.

Fischer, H., Nyberg, L., Karlsson, S., Karisson, P., Brehmer, Y., Rieckmann, A., et al. (2010). Simulating neurocognitive aging: Effects of dopaminergic antagonist on brain activity during working memory. *Biological Psychiatry, 67,* 575–580.

Fischer, K. (1980). A theory of cognitive development: The control and construction of hierarchies of skills. *Psychological Review, 87,* 477–531.

Fischer, P., Krueger, J. I., Greitemeyer, T., Vogrincic, C., Kastenmüller, A., Frey, D., et al. (2011). The bystander-effect: A meta-analytic review on bystander intervention in dangerous and non-dangerous emergencies. *Psychological Bulletin, 137,* 517–537.

Fisher, H. E., Aron, A., & Brown, L. L. (2006). Romantic love: A mammalian brain system for mate choice. *Philosophical Transactions of the Royal Society of London, 361B,* 2173–2186.

Fitch, W. T., de Boer, B., Mathur, N., & Ghazanfar, A. A. (2016). Monkey vocal tracts are speech-ready. *Science Advances, 2,* e1600723.

Fitzgerald, P. B., Brown, T. L., Marston, N. A., Daskalakis, Z. J., De Castella, A., & Kulkarni, J. (2003). Transcranial magnetic stimulation in the treatment of depression: A double-blind, placebo-controlled trial. *Archives of General Psychiatry, 60,* 1002–1008.

Fixx, J. F. (1978). *Solve it.* New York, NY: Doubleday.

Flegal, K. M., Kit, B. K., Orpana, H., & Graubard, B. I. (2013). Association of all-cause mortality with overweight and obesity using standard body mass index categories: A systematic review and meta-analysis. *Journal of the American Medical Association, 309,* 71–82.

Flegal, K. M., Kruszon-Moran, D., Carroll, M. D., Fryar, C. D., & Ogden, C. L. (2016). Trends in obesity among adults in the United States, 2005 to 2014. *Journal of the American Medical Association, 315,* 2284–2291.

Flentje, A., Heck, N. C., & Cochran, B. N. (2014). Experiences of ex-ex-gay individuals in sexual reorientation therapy: Reasons for seeking treatment, perceived helpfulness and harmfulness of treatment, and post-treatment identification. *Journal of homosexuality, 61,* 1242–1268.

Flynn, J. R. (1981). The mean IQ of Americans: Massive gains 1932 to 1978. *Psychological Bulletin, 95,* 29–51.

Flynn, J. R. (1987). Massive IQ gains in 14 nations: What IQ tests really measure. *Psychological Bulletin, 101,* 171–191.

Flynn, J. R. (2007, October/November). Solving the IQ puzzle. *Scientific American Mind,* 24–31.

Foa, E. B., Liebowitz, M. R., Kozak, M. J., Davies, S., Campeas, R., Franklin, M. E., et al. (2005). Randomized, placebo-controlled trial of exposure and ritual prevention, clomipramine, and their combination in the treatment of obsessive-compulsive disorder. *American Journal of Psychiatry, 162,* 151–161.

Foa, E. B., & McLean, C. P. (2016). The efficacy of exposure therapy for anxiety-related disorders and its underlying mechanisms: The case of OCD and PTSD. *Annual Review of Clinical Psychology, 12,* 1–28.

Foer, J. (2011, February 20). Secrets of a mind-gamer: How I trained my brain and became a world-class memory athlete. *New York Times Magazine.* Retrieved from http://www.nytimes.com

Foley, K. M. (1993). Opioids. *Neurologic Clinics, 11,* 503–522.

Folkman, S., & Lazarus, R. S. (1988). Coping as a mediator of emotion. *Journal of Personality and Social Psychology, 54,* 466–475.

Folkman, S., & Moskowitz, J. T. (2000). Positive affect and the other side of coping. *American Psychologist, 55,* 647–654.

Forbes, C. E., & Grafman, J. (2010). The role of the human prefrontal cortex in social cognition and moral judgment. *Annual Review of Neuroscience, 33,* 299–324.

Ford, E. S., Giles, W. H., & Dietz, W. H. (2002). Prevalence of the metabolic syndrome among U.S. adults: Findings from the third National Health and Nutrition Examination Survey. *Journal of the American Medical Association, 287,* 356–359.

Forgas, J. P. (1998). Asking nicely: Mood effects on responding to more or less polite requests. *Personality and Social Psychology Bulletin, 24,* 173–185.

Foterek, K., Buyken, A. E., Bolzenius, K., Hilbig, A., Nöthlings, U., & Alexy, U. (2016). Commercial complementary food consumption is prospectively associated with added sugar intake in childhood. *The British Journal of Nutrition, 115,* 2067–2074.

Fox, J. A., & DeLateur, M. J. (2014). Mass shootings in America moving beyond Newtown. *Homicide Studies, 18,* 125–145.

Fox, N. A., Henderson, H. A., Marshall, P. J., Nichols, K. E., & Ghera, M. M. (2005). Behavioral inhibition: Linking biology and behavior within a developmental framework. *Annual Review of Psychology, 56,* 235–262.

Fraley, R. C., & Shaver, P. R. (2000). Adult romantic attachment: Theoretical developments, emerging controversies, and unanswered questions. *Review of General Psychology, 4,* 132–154.

Frangou, S., Chitins, X., & Williams, S. C. (2004). Mapping IQ and gray matter density in healthy young people. *Neuroimage, 23,* 800–805.

Frank, C. K., & Temple, E. (2009). Cultural effects on the neural basis of theory of mind. *Progress in Brain Research, 178,* 213–223.

Franken, I. H. A., Muris, P., & Georgieva, I. (2006). Gray's model of personality and addiction. *Addictive Behaviors, 31,* 399–403.

Franken, R. E. (2007). *Human motivation* (6th ed.). Boston, MA: Cengage.

Franklin, M. E., & Foa, E. B. (2011). Treatment of obsessive compulsive disorder. *Annual Review of Clinical Psychology, 7,* 229–243.

Franklin, M. S., Baumgart, S. L., & Schooler, J. W. (2014). Future directions in precognition research: More research can bridge the gap between skeptics and proponents. *Frontiers in Psychology, 5,* 907. doi: 10.3389/fpsyg.2014.00907

Franklin, T. B., Linder, N., Russig, H., Thöny, B., & Mansuy, I. M. (2011). Influence of early stress on social abilities and serotonergic functions across generations in mice. *PLoS ONE, 6,* e21842.

Fratiglioni, L., Paillard-Borg, S., & Winblad, B. (2004). An active and socially integrated lifestyle in late life might protect against dementia. *Lancet Neurology, 3,* 343–353.

Fredrickson, B. L. (2001). The role of positive emotions in positive psychology: The broaden-and-build theory of positive emotions. *American Psychologist, 56,* 218–226.

Freedman, J. L. (1984). Effects of television violence on aggression. *Psychological Bulletin, 96,* 227–246.

Freedman, J. L., & Fraser, S. C. (1966). Compliance without pressure: The foot-in-the-door technique. *Journal of Personality and Social Psychology, 4,* 196–202.

Freeman, D., Reeve, S., Robinson, A., Ehlers, A., Clark, D., Spanlang, B., et al. (2017). Virtual reality in the assessment, understanding, and treatment of mental health disorders. *Psychological Medicine.* doi: https://doi.org/10.1017/S003329171700040X Published online March 22, 2017.

Freeman, J. B., & Johnson, K. L. (2016). More than meets the eye: Split-second social perception. *Trends in Cognitive Sciences, 20,* 362–374.

Freeman, J. B., Stolier, R. M., Ingbretsen, Z. A., & Hehman, E. A. (2014). Amygdala responsivity to high-level social information from unseen faces. *Journal of Neuroscience, 34,* 10573–10581.

Freud, A. (1936). *The ego and the mechanisms of defense.* New York, NY: International Universities Press.

Freud, S. (1900). *The interpretation of dreams. The standard edition of the complete psychological works of Sigmund Freud* (vols. 4 and 5). London: Hogarth Press.

Freud, S. (1923). *Das ich und das es,* Internationaler Psycho-analytischer Verlag, Leipzig, Vienna, and Zurich. Revised for *The standard edition of the complete psychological works of Sigmund Freud* (J. Strachey, Ed.). New York, NY: Norton.

Friedman, J. M., & Halaas, J. (1998). Leptin and the regulation of body weight in mammals. *Nature, 395,* 763–770.

Friedman, L. A., & Rapoport, J. L. (2015). Brain development in ADHD. *Current Opinion in Neurobiology, 30,* 106–111.

Frijda, N. H. (1994). Emotions are functional, most of the time. In P. Ekman & R. J. Davidson (Eds.), *The nature of emotion: Fundamental questions, Vol. 4. Series in affective science* (pp. 112–122). New York, NY: Oxford University Press.

Frisch, M., & Simonsen, J. (2013). Marriage, cohabitation and mortality in Denmark: National cohort study of 6.5 million persons followed for up to three decades (1982–2011). *International Journal of Epidemiology, 42,* 559–578.

Fromer, M., Pocklington, A. J., Kavanagh, D. H., Williams, H. J., Dwyer, S., Gormley, P., et al. (2014). De novo mutations in schizophrenia implicate synaptic networks. *Nature, 506,* 179–184.

Fryar, C. D., Carroll, M. D., & Ogden, C. L. (2016). Prevalence of overweight, obesity, and extreme obesity among adults aged 20 and over: United States, 1960–1962 through 2013–2014. National Center for Health Statistics. Division of Health and Nutrition Examination Surveys.

Funder, D. C. (1995). On the accuracy of personality judgment: A realistic approach. *Psychological Review, 102,* 652–670.

Funder, D. C. (2001). Personality. *Annual Review of Psychology, 52,* 197–221.

Funder, D. C. (2012). Accurate personality judgment. *Current Directions in Psychological Science, 21,* 177–182.

Fung, H. H., & Carstensen, L. L. (2004). Motivational changes in response to blocked goals and foreshortened time: Testing alternatives to socioemotional selectivity theory. *Psychology and Aging, 19,* 68–78.

Fung, M. T., Raine, A., Loeber, R., Lynam, D. R., Steinhauer, S. R., Venables, P. D., et al. (2005). Reduced electrodermal activity in psychopathy-prone adolescents. *Journal of Abnormal Psychology, 114,* 187–196.

Furnham, A., Richards, S. C., & Paulhus, D. L. (2013). The Dark Triad of personality: A 10 year review. *Social and Personality Psychology Compass, 7,* 199–216.

Fusar-Poli, P., Papanastasiou, E., Stahl, D., Rocchetti, M., Carpenter, W., Shergill, S., et al. (2015). Treatments of negative symptoms in schizophrenia: Meta-analysis of 168 randomized placebo-controlled trials. *Schizophrenia Bulletin, 41,* 892–899.

Gabrieli, J. D., Ghosh, S. S., & Whitfield-Gabrieli, S. (2015). Prediction as a humanitarian and pragmatic contribution from human cognitive neuroscience. *Neuron, 85,* 11–26.

Galef, B. G., Jr., & Whiskin, E. E. (2000). Social influences on the amount eaten by Norway rats. *Appetite, 34,* 327–332.

Galinsky, A. D., Wang, C. S., Whitson, J. A., Anicich, E. M., Hugenberg, K., & Bodenhausen, G. V. (2013). The reappropriation of stigmatizing labels: The reciprocal relationship between power and self-labeling. *Psychological Science, 24,* 2020–2029.

Gallagher, D. T., Hadjiefthyvoulou, F., Fisk, J. E., Montgomery, C., Robinson, S. J., & Judge, J. (2014). Prospective memory deficits in illicit polydrug users are associated with the average long-term typical dose of ecstasy typically consumed in a single session. *Neuropsychology, 28,* 43–54.

Gallese, V. (2013). Mirror neurons, embodied simulation and a second-person approach to mindreading. *Cortex, 49,* 2954–2956.

Gallo, E. F., & Posner, J. (2016). Moving towards causality in attention-deficit hyperactivity disorder: Overview of neural and genetic mechanisms. *The Lancet Psychiatry, 3,* 555–567.

Gallup. (2015). Trust in U.S. Government's terrorism protection at new low. Retrieved July 24, 2017, from http://www.gallup.com/poll/183557/trust-government-terrorism-protection-new-low.aspx?

Galton, F. (1879). Psychometric experiments. *Brain, 2,* 149–162.

Gandhi, A. V., Mosser, E. A., Oikonomou, G., & Prober, D. A. (2015). Melatonin is required for the circadian regulation of sleep. *Neuron, 85,* 1193–1199.

Gangestad, S. W., Simpson, J. A., Cousins, A. J., Garver-Apgar, C. E., & Christensen, P. N. (2004). Women's preferences for male behavioral displays change across the menstrual cycle. *Psychological Science, 15,* 203–207.

Garber, J., Frankel, S. A., & Herrington, C. G. (2016). Developmental demands of cognitive behavioral therapy for depression in children and adolescents: Cognitive, social, and emotional processes. *Annual Review of Clinical Psychology, 12,* 181–216.

Garcia, J., & Koelling, R. A. (1966). Relation of cue to consequence in avoidance learning. *Psychonomic Science, 4,* 123–124.

Gardner, H. (1983). *Frames of mind: The theory of multiple intelligences.* New York, NY: Basic Books.

Gardner, W. L., Pickett, C. L., Jefferis, V., & Knowles, M. (2005). On the outside looking in: Loneliness and social monitoring. *Personality and Social Psychology Bulletin, 31,* 1549–1560.

Garlick, D. (2002). Understanding the nature of the general factor of intelligence: The role of individual differences in neural plasticity as an explanatory mechanism. *Psychological Review, 109,* 116–136.

Garneau, N. L., Nuessle, T. M., Sloan, M. M., Santorico, S. A., Coughlin, B. C., & Hayes, J. E. (2014). Crowdsourcing taste research: Genetic and phenotypic predictors of bitter taste perception as a model. *Frontiers in Integrative Neuroscience, 8,* 33.

Garon, N., Bryson, S. E., & Smith, I. M. (2008). Executive function in preschoolers: A review using an integrative framework. *Psychological Bulletin, 134,* 31–60.

Garriga, M., Pacchiarotti, I., Kasper, S., Zeller, S. L., Allen, M. H., Vázquez, G., et al. (2016). Assessment and management of agitation in psychiatry: Expert consensus. *The World Journal of Biological Psychiatry, 17,* 86–128.

Garthe, A., Roeder, I., & Kempermann, G. (2016). Mice in an enriched environment learn more flexibly because of adult hippocampal neurogenesis. *Hippocampus, 26,* 261–271.

Gastil, J. (1990). Generic pronouns and sexist language: The oxymoronic character of masculine generics. *Sex Roles, 23,* 629–643.

Gatt, J. M., Burton, K. L., Williams, L. M., & Schofield, P. R. (2015). Specific and common genes implicated across major mental disorders: A review of meta-analysis studies. *Journal of Psychiatric Research, 60,* 1–13.

Gazzaniga, M. S. (2000). Cerebral specialization and interhemispheric communication: Does the corpus callosum enable the human condition? *Brain, 123,* 1293–1326.

Gazzaniga, M. S. (2015). *Tales from both sides of the brain: A life in neuroscience.* New York, NY: HarperCollins.

Gazzaniga, M. S., Ivry, R. B., & Mangun, G. R. (2014). *Cognitive neuroscience: The biology of the mind* (4th ed.). New York, NY: Norton.

Gazzaniga, M. S., & LeDoux, J. E. (1978). *The integrated mind.* New York, NY: Plenum Press.

Ge, X., Natsuaki, M. N., Neiderhiser, J. M., & Reiss, D. (2007). Genetic and environmental influences on pubertal timing: Results from two national sibling studies. *Journal of Research on Adolescence, 17,* 767–788.

Geddes, J. R., Burgess, S., Hawton, K., Jamison, K., & Goodwin, G. M. (2004). Long-term lithium therapy for bipolar disorder: Systematic review and meta-analysis of randomized controlled trials. *American Journal of Psychiatry, 161,* 217–222.

Geddes, J. R., & Miklowitz, D. J. (2013). Treatment of bipolar disorder. *The Lancet, 381,* 1672–1682.

Geen, R. G. (1984). Preferred stimulation levels in introverts and extraverts: Effects on arousal and performance. *Journal of Personality and Social Psychology, 46,* 1303–1312.

Gelman, R., & Gallistel, C. R. (2004). Language and the origin of numerical concepts. *Science, 306,* 441–443.

Gendron, M., Roberson, D., van der Vyver, J. M., & Barrett, L. F. (2014). Perceptions of emotion from facial expressions are not culturally universal: Evidence from a remote culture. *Emotion, 14,* 251.

Gentile, D. A., Li, D., Khoo, A., Prot, S., & Anderson, C. A. (2014). Mediators and moderators of long-term effects of violent video games on aggressive behavior: Practice, thinking, and action. *JAMA Pediatrics.* doi: 10.1001/jamapediatrics.2014.63

Gentile, D. A., Saleem, M., & Anderson, C. A. (2007). Public policy and the effects of media violence on children. *Social Issues and Policy Review, 1,* 15–51.

George, M. S., Lisanby, S. H., & Sackheim, H. A. (1999). Transcranial magnetic stimulation: Applications in neuropsychiatry. *Archives of General Psychiatry, 56,* 300–311.

George, M. S., Wassermann, E. M., Williams, W. A., Callahan, A., Ketter, T. A., Basser, P., et al. (1995). Daily repetitive transcranial magnetic stimulation (rTMS) improves mood in depression. *Neuroreport, 6,* 1853–1856.

Gergely, G., & Csibra, G. (2003). Teleological reasoning in infancy: The naive theory of rational action. *Trends in Cognitive Sciences, 7,* 287–292.

Gernsbacher, M. A., Dawson, M., & Goldsmith, H. H. (2005). Three reasons not to believe in an autism epidemic. *Current Directions in Psychological Science, 14,* 55–58.

Gershman, S. J., & Daw, N. D. (2017). Reinforcement learning and episodic memory in humans and animals: An integrative framework. *Annual Review of Psychology, 68,* 101–128.

Gershoff, E. T. (2002). Parental corporal punishment and associated child behaviors and experiences: A meta-analytic and theoretical review. *Psychological Bulletin, 128,* 539–579.

Gershoff, E. T., & Grogan-Kaylor, A. (2016). Spanking and child outcomes: Old controversies and new meta-analyses. *Journal of Family Psychology, 30,* 453–469.

Ghio, M., Vaghi, M. M. S., Perani, D., & Tettamanti, M. (2016). Decoding the neural representation of fine-grained conceptual categories. *NeuroImage, 132,* 93–103.

Gibson, S. (2013). Milgram's obedience experiments: A rhetorical analysis. *British Journal of Social Psychology, 52,* 290–309.

Gick, M. L., & Holyoak, K. J. (1983). Schema induction and analogical transfer. *Cognitive Psychology, 15,* 1–38.

Giedd, J. N., Castellanos, F. X., Rajapakse, J. C., Vaituzis, A. C., & Rapoport, J. L. (1997). Sexual dimorphism of the developing human brain. *Progress in Neuro-Psychopharmacology & Biological Psychiatry, 21,* 1185–1201.

Gigerenzer, G. (2004). Dread risk, September 11, and fatal traffic accidents. *Psychological Science, 15,* 286–287.

Gijsman, H. J., Geddes, J. R., Rendell, J. M., Nolen, W. A., & Goodwin, G. M. (2004). Antidepressants for bipolar depression: A systematic review of randomized, controlled trials. *American Journal of Psychiatry, 161,* 1537–1547.

Gilbert, D. T., Morewedge, C. K., Risen, J. L., & Wilson, T. D. (2004). Looking forward to looking backward: The misprediction of regret. *Psychological Science, 15,* 346–350.

Gilbert, D. T., Pinel, E. C., Wilson, T. D., Blumberg, S. J., & Wheatley, T. (1998). Immune neglect: A source of durability bias in affective forecasting. *Journal of Personality and Social Psychology, 75,* 617–638.

Gilbert, D. T., & Wilson, T. D. (2007). Prospection: Experiencing the future. *Science, 317,* 1351–1354.

Gilbert, D. T., King, G., Pettigrew, S., & Wilson, T. D. (2016). A response to the reply of our technical comment on 'Estimating the reproducibility of psychological science.' Retrieved July 24, 2017, from http://projects.iq.harvard.edu/files/psychology-replications/files/gkpw_response_to_osc_rebutal.pdf

Gildersleeve, K., Haselton, M. G., & Fales, M. R. (2014). Do women's mate preferences change across the ovulatory cycle? A meta-analytic review. *Psychological Bulletin, 140,* 1205–1259.

Gilligan, C. (1977). In a different voice: Women's conceptions of self and of morality. *Harvard Educational Review, 47,* 481–517.

Gillihan, S. J., & Farah, M. J. (2005). Is self special? A critical review of evidence from experimental psychology and cognitive neuroscience. *Psychological Bulletin, 131,* 76–97.

Gilman, S. R., Iossifov, I., Levy, D., Ronemus, M., Wigler, M., & Vitkup, D. (2011). Rare de novo variants associated with autism implicate a large functional network of genes involved in formation and function of synapses. *Neuron, 70,* 898–907.

Gilovich, T. (1991). *How we know what isn't so: The fallibility of human reason in everyday life.* New York, NY: Free Press.

Gilovich, T., Vallone, R., & Tversky, A. (1985). The hot hand in basketball: On the misperception of random sequences. *Cognitive psychology, 17,* 295–314.

Gingerich, A. C., & Lineweaver, T. T. (2014). OMG! Texting in class = U fail: Empirical evidence that text messaging during class disrupts comprehension. *Teaching of Psychology, 41,* 44–51.

Giynas Ayhan, M., Uguz, F., Askin, R., & Gonen, M. S. (2014). The prevalence of depression and anxiety disorders in patients with euthyroid Hashimoto's thyroiditis: A comparative study. *General Hospital Psychiatry, 36,* 95–98.

Gladden, R. M., Martinez, P., & Seth, P. (2016). Fentanyl law enforcement submissions and increases in synthetic opioid–involved overdose deaths—27 states, 2013–2014. *Morbidity and Mortality Weekly Report, 65,* 837–843.

Glaser, R., & Kiecolt-Glaser, J. K. (2005). Stress-induced immune dysfunction: Implications for health. *Nature Reviews, 5,* 243–251.

Glimcher, P. W. (2011). Understanding dopamine and reinforcement learning: The dopamine reward prediction error hypothesis. *Proceedings of the National Academy of Sciences, 108,* 15647–15654.

Glynn, T. J. (2014). E-cigarettes and the future of tobacco control. *Cancer Journal for Clinicians, 64,* 164–168.

Godden, D. R., & Baddeley, A. D. (1975). Context-dependent memory in two natural environments: On land and underwater. *British Journal of Psychology, 66,* 325–331.

Godlee, F., Smith, J., & Marcovitch, H. (2011). Wakefield's article linking MMR vaccine and autism was fraudulent. *British Medical Journal, 342,* c7452.

Goff, D. C., Falkai, P., Fleischhacker, W. W., Girgis, R. R., Kahn, R. M., Uchoda, H., et al. (2017). The long-term effects of antipsychotic medication on clinical course in schizophrenia. *American Journal of Psychiatry.* https://doi.org/10.1176/appi.ajp.2017.16091016

Goldapple, K., Segal, Z., Garson, C., Lau, M., Bieling, P., Kennedy, S., et al. (2004). Modulation of cortical-limbic pathways in major depression: Treatment-specific effects of cognitive behavior therapy. *Archives of General Psychiatry, 61,* 34–41.

Goldenberg, M. M. (2012). Multiple sclerosis review. *Pharmacy and Therapeutics, 37,* 175–184.

Goldin, C., & Rouse, C. (2000). Orchestrating impartiality: The impact of "blind" auditions on female musicians. *The American Economic Review, 90,* 715–741.

Goldstein, J. (2011, January 18). Life tenure for federal judges raises issues of senility, dementia. *ProPublica: Journalism in the Public Interest.* Retrieved from http://www.propublica.org/article/life-tenure-for-federal-judges-raises-issues-of-senility-dementia

Goldstein, R. B., Chou, S. P., Saha, T. D., Smith, S. M., Zhang, H., Pickering, R. P., et al. (2017). The epidemiology of antisocial behavioral syndromes in adulthood: Results from the National Epidemiologic Survey on Alcohol and Related Conditions-III. *Journal of Clinical Psychiatry, 78,* 90–98.

Goldstein, R. Z., Craig, A. D. B., Bechara, A., Garavan, H., Childress, A. R., Paulus, M. P., & Volkow, N. D. (2009). The neurocircuitry of impaired insight in drug addiction. *Trends in Cognitive Science, 13,* 372–380.

Gong, Q., Sluming, V., Mayes, A., Keller, S., Barrick, T., Cezayirli, E., et al. (2005). Voxel-based morphometry and stereology provide convergent evidence of the importance of medial prefrontal cortex for fluid intelligence in healthy adults. *Neuroimage, 25,* 1175–1186.

Gonzales, R., Mooney, L., & Rawson, R. A. (2010). The methamphetamine problem in the United States. *Annual Review of Public Health, 31,* 385–398.

Goodale, M. A., & Milner, A. D. (1992). Separate visual pathways for perception and action. *Trends in Neuroscience, 15,* 22–25.

Goodman, S. H., & Gotlib, I. H. (1999). Risk for psychopathology in the children of depressed mothers: A developmental model for understanding mechanisms of transmission. *Psychological Review, 106,* 458–490.

Goodman, S. N., Fanelli, D., & Ioannidis, J. P. (2016). What does research reproducibility mean? *Science Translational Medicine, 8,* 341ps12.

Goodwin, D. W., Powell, B., Bremer, D., Hoine, H., & Stern, J. (1969). Alcohol and recall: State-dependent effects in man. *Science, 163,* 1358.

Goodwin, R. D., Lieb, R., Hoefler, M., Pfister, H., Bittner, A., Beesdo, K., et al. (2004). Panic attack as a risk factor for severe psychopathology. *American Journal of Psychiatry, 161,* 2207–2214.

Gordon, P. (2004). Numerical cognition without words: Evidence from Amazonia. *Science, 306,* 496–499.

Gosling, S. D. (2008). *Snoop: What your stuff says about you.* New York, NY: Basic Books.

Gosling, S. D., Ko, S. J., Mannarelli, T., & Morris, M. E. (2002). A room with a cue: Judgments of personality based on offices and bedrooms. *Journal of Personality and Social Psychology, 82,* 379–398.

Gosselin, P., & Larocque, C. (2000). Facial morphology and children's categorization of facial expressions and emotions: A comparison between Asian and Caucasian faces. *Journal of Genetic Psychology, 161,* 346–358.

Gottesman, I. I. (1991). *Schizophrenia genesis: The origins of madness.* New York, NY: Freeman.

Gottfredson, L. S. (2003). Dissecting practical intelligence theory: Its claims and evidence. *Intelligence, 31,* 343–397.

Gottfredson, L. S. (2004a). Intelligence: Is it the epidemiologists' elusive "fundamental cause" of social class inequalities in health? *Journal of Personality and Social Psychology, 86,* 174–199.

Gottfredson, L. S. (2004b, Summer). Schools and the g factor. *The Wilson Quarterly, 28,* 35–45.

Gottfredson, L. S., & Deary, I. J. (2004). Intelligence predicts health and longevity: But why? *Current Directions in Psychological Science, 13,* 1–4.

Gottman, J. (1995). *Why marriages succeed or fail . . . and how you can make yours last.* New York, NY: Simon & Schuster.

Gottman, J. (1998). Psychology and the study of marital processes. *Annual Review of Psychology, 49,* 169–197.

Gould, E., & Tanapat, P. (1999). Stress and hippocampal neurogenesis. *Biological Psychiatry, 46,* 1472–1479.

Graf, P., & Schacter, D. L. (1985). Implicit and explicit memory for new associations in normal and amnesic subjects. *Journal of Experimental Psychology: Learning, Memory and Cognition, 13,* 45–53.

Graf, P., & Uttl, B. (2001). Prospective memory: A new focus for research. *Consciousness and Cognition, 10,* 437–450.

Graff, H., & Stellar, E. (1962). Hyperphagia, obesity, and finickiness. *Journal of Comparative and Physiological Psychology, 55,* 418–424.

Gräff, J., Joseph, N. F., Horn, M. E., Samiei, A., Meng, J., et al. (2014). Epigenetic priming of memory updating during reconsolidation to attenuate remote fear memories. *Cell, 156,* 261–276.

Gräff, J., & Tsai, L. H. (2013). The potential of HDAC inhibitors as cognitive enhancers. *Annual Review of Pharmacology and Toxicology, 53,* 311–330.

Granot, D., & Mayseless, O. (2001). Attachment security and adjustment to school in middle childhood. *International Journal of Behavioral Development, 25,* 530–541.

Gray, J. A. (1982). On mapping anxiety. *Behavioral and Brain Sciences, 5,* 506–534.

Gray, J. A., & McNaughton, N. (2000). *The neuropsychology of anxiety: An enquiry into the functions of the septo-hippocampal system.* New York, NY: Oxford University Press.

Gray, J. R., & Thompson, P. M. (2004). Neurobiology of intelligence: Science and ethics. *Nature Reviews Neuroscience, 5,* 471–482.

Gray, K., Rand, D. G., Ert, E., Lewis, K., Hershman, S., & Norton, M. I. (2014). The emergence of "us and them" in 80 lines of code: Modeling group genesis in homogeneous populations. *Psychological Science, 25,* 982–990.

Green, B. S., & Zwiebel, J. (2017). The hot-hand fallacy: Cognitive mistakes or equilibrium adjustments? Evidence from major league baseball. *Management Science.* Retrieved from http://dx.doi.org/10.2139/ssrn.2358747

Green, D. M., & Swets, J. A. (1966). *Signal detection theory and psychophysics.* New York, NY: Wiley.

Green, E. D., Watson, J. D., & Collins, F. S. (2015). Twenty-five years of big biology. *Nature, 526,* 29–31.

Green, J. J., & Hollander, E. (2010). Autism and oxytocin: New developments in translational approaches to therapeutics. *Neurotherapeutics, 7,* 250–257.

Greenberg, B. D., Gabriels, L. A., Malone, D. A., Jr., Rezai, A. R., Friehs, G. M., Okun, M. S., et al. (2008). Deep brain stimulation of the ventral internal capsule/ventral striatum for obsessive-compulsive disorder: Worldwide experience. *Molecular Psychiatry, 15,* 64–79.

Greene, J. A. (1939). Clinical study of the etiology of obesity. *Annals of Internal Medicine, 12,* 1797–1803.

Greene, J. D., Sommerville, R. B., Nystrom, L. E., Darley, J. M., & Cohen, J. D. (2001). An fMRI investigation of emotional engagement in moral judgment. *Science, 293,* 2105–2108.

Greenwald, A. G. (1968). Cognitive learning, cognitive response to persuasion, and attitude change. In A. G. Greenwald, T. C. Brock, & T. M. Ostrom (Eds.), *Psychological foundations of attitudes* (pp. 147–170). New York, NY: Academic Press.

Greenwald, A. G. (1992). New look 3: Reclaiming unconscious cognition. *American Psychologist, 47,* 766–779.

Greenwald, A. G., & Banaji, M. R. (1995). Implicit social cognition: Attitudes, self-esteem, and stereotypes. *Psychological Review, 102,* 4–27.

Greenwald, A. G., McGhee, D., & Schwartz, J. (1998). Measuring individual differences in implicit cognition: The implicit association test. *Journal of Personality and Social Psychology, 74,* 1464–1480.

Greenwald, A. G., Oakes, M. A., & Hoffman, H. (2003). Targets of discrimination: Effects of race on responses to weapons holders. *Journal of Experimental Social Psychology, 39,* 399–405.

Greenwald, A. G., Poehlman, T. A., Uhlmann, E., & Banaji, M. R. (2009). Understanding and using the Implicit Association Test: III. Meta-analysis of predictive validity. *Journal of Personality and Social Psychology, 97,* 17–41.

Greitemeyer, T. (2009). Effects of songs with prosocial lyrics on prosocial behavior: Further evidence and a mediating mechanism. *Personality and Social Psychology Bulletin, 35,* 1500–1511.

Griebel, U., Pepperberg, I. M., & Oller, D. K. (2016). Developmental plasticity and language: A comparative perspective. *Topics in Cognitive Science, 8,* 435–445.

Griggs, R. A. (2017). Milgram's obedience study: A contentious classic reinterpreted. *Teaching of Psychology, 44,* 32–37.

Grill-Spector, K., Knouf, N., & Kanwisher, N. (2004). The fusiform face area subserves face perception, not generic within-category identification. *Nature Neuroscience, 7,* 555–562.

Gross, J. J. (1999). Emotion and emotion regulation. In L. A. Pervin & O. P. John (Eds.), *Handbook of personality: Theory and research* (2nd ed., pp. 525–552). New York, NY: Guilford Press.

Gross, J. J. (2013). Emotion regulation: Taking stock and moving forward. *Emotion, 13,* 359–365.

Grossman, M., & Wood, W. (1993). Sex differences in intensity of emotional experience: A social role interpretation. *Journal of Personality and Social Psychology, 65,* 1010–1022.

Grossniklaus, U., Kelly, W. G., Ferguson-Smith, A. C., Pembrey, M., & Lindquist, S. (2013). Transgenerational epigenetic inheritance: How important is it? *Nature Reviews Genetics, 14,* 228–235.

Gruzelier, J. H. (2000). Redefining hypnosis: Theory, methods, and integration. *Contemporary Hypnosis, 17,* 51–70.

Guassi Moreira, J. F., Van Bavel, J. J., & Telzer, E. H. (2017). The neural development of "Us and Them." *Social Cognitive and Affective Neuroscience, 12,* 184–196.

Guastella, A. J., & Hickie, I. B. (2016). Oxytocin treatment, circuitry, and autism: A critical review of the literature placing oxytocin into the autism context. *Biological Psychiatry, 79,* 234–242.

Guenther, F. H., Brumberg, J. S., Wright, E. J., Nieto-Castanon, A., Tourville, J. A., et al. (2009). A wireless brain-machine interface for real-time speech synthesis. *PLoS ONE, 4,* e82128.

Guerin, B. (1994). What do people think about the risks of driving? Implications for traffic safety interventions. *Journal of Applied Social Psychology, 24,* 994–1021.

Guimond, S. (2008). Psychological similarities and differences between women and men across cultures. *Social and Personality Psychology Compass, 2,* 494–510.

Guimond, S., Branscombe, N. R., Brunot, S., Buunk, A. P., Chatard, A., Desert, M., et al. (2007). Culture, gender, and the self: Variations and impact of social comparison processes. *Journal of Personality and Social Psychology, 92,* 1118–1134.

Gunderson, J. G. (1984). *Borderline personality disorder.* Washington, DC: American Psychiatric Press.

Gunter, B. (2016). *Does playing video games make players more violent?* London, England: Macmillan.

Hackel, L. M., Looser, C. E., & Van Bavel, J. J. (2014). Group membership alters the threshold for mind perception: The role of social identity, collective identification, and intergroup threat. *Journal of Experimental Social Psychology, 52,* 15–23.

Hagerty, B. (2010, July 1). Can your genes make you murder? Retrieved from http://www.npr.org/templates/story/story.php?storyId=128043329

Haggarty, P., Hoad, G., Harris, S. E., Starr, J. M., Fox, H. C., Deary, I. J., & Whalley, L. J. (2010). Human intelligence and polymorphisms in the DNA methyltransferase genes involved in epigenetic marking. *PLoS ONE, 5,* e11329.

Hagger-Johnson, G., Deary, I. J., Davies, C. A., Weiss, A., & Batty, G. D. (2014). Reaction time and mortality from the major causes of death: The NHANES-III study. *PLoS ONE, 9,* e82959.

Hahn, A., Kranz, G. S., Küblböck, M., Kaufmann, U., Ganger, S., Hummer, A., et al. (2015). Structural connectivity networks of transgender people. *Cerebral Cortex, 25,* 3527–3534.

Haidt, J. (2001). The emotional dog and its rational tail: A social intuitionist approach to moral judgment. *Psychological Review, 108,* 814–834.

Haidt, J. (2003). The moral emotions. In R. J. Davidson, K. R. Scherer, & H. H. Goldsmith (Eds.), *Handbook of affective sciences* (pp. 852–870). Oxford, England: Oxford University Press.

Haidt, J. (2007). The new synthesis in moral psychology. *Science, 316,* 998–1002.

Haier, R. J., Jung, R. E., Yeo, R. A., Head, K., & Alkire, M. T. (2005). The neuroanatomy of general intelligence: Sex matters. *Neuroimage, 25,* 320–327.

Hair, N. L., Hanson, J. L., Wolfe, B. L., & Pollak, S. D. (2015). Association of child poverty, brain development, and academic achievement. *JAMA Pediatrics, 169,* 822–829.

Halász, P. (2016). The K-complex as a special reactive sleep slow wave—A theoretical update. *Sleep medicine reviews, 29,* 34–40.

Hallan, S., Cross, I., & Thaut, M. (2016). *Oxford handbook of music psychology* (2nd ed.). Oxford, England: Oxford University Press.

Halldorsdottir, T., & Binder, E. B. (2017). Gene× environment interactions: From molecular mechanisms to behavior. *Annual Review of Psychology, 68,* 215–241.

Halligan, P. W., & Marshall, J. C. (1998). Neglect of awareness. *Consciousness and Cognition, 7,* 356–380.

Halpern, C. T., Udry, J. R., & Suchindran, C. (1997). Testosterone predicts initiation of coitus in adolescent females. *Psychosomatic Medicine, 59,* 161–171.

Halpern, D. F., Benbow, C., Geary, D., Gur, D., Hyde, J., & Gernsbacher, M. A. (2007). The science of sex differences in science and mathematics. *Psychological Science in the Public Interest, 8,* 1–51.

Halpin, L. E., Collins, S. A., & Yamamoto, B. K. (2014). Neurotoxicity of methamphetamine and 3, 4-methylenedioxymethamphetamine. *Life Sciences, 97,* 37–44.

Hambrecht, M., Maurer, K., Hafner, H., & Sartorius, N. (1992). Transnational stability of gender differences in schizophrenia: Recent findings on social skills training and family psychoeducation. *Clinical Psychology Review, 11,* 23–44.

Hamer, D. H., Hu, S., Magnuson, V. L., Hu, N., & Pattatucci, A. M. (1993). A linkage between DNA markers on the X chromosome and male sexual orientation. *Science, 261,* 321–327.

Hamilton, J. P., Farmer, M., Fogelman, P., & Gotlib, I. H. (2015). Depressive rumination, the default-mode network, and the dark matter of clinical neuroscience. *Biological Psychiatry, 78,* 224–230.

Hamilton, W. D. (1964). The genetical evolution of social behaviour. I. *Journal of Theoretical Biology, 7,* 1–16.

Hammen, C. (2005). Stress and depression. *Annual Review of Clinical Psychology, 1,* 293–319.

Handleman, J. S., Gill, M. J., & Alessandri, M. (1988). Generalization by severely developmentally disabled children: Issues, advances, and future directions. *Behavior Therapist, 11,* 221–223.

Hanewinkel, R., & Sargent, J. D. (2008). Exposure to smoking in internationally distributed American movies and youth smoking in Germany: A cross-cultural cohort study. *Pediatrics, 121,* 108–117.

Haney, C., Banks, C., & Zimbardo, P. (1973). Interpersonal dynamics in a simulated prison. *International Journal of Criminology and Penology, 1,* 69–97.

Hansen, C. J., Stevens, L. C., & Coast, J. R. (2001). Exercise duration and mood state: How much is enough to feel better? *Health Psychology, 20,* 267–275.

Hansen, T. (2012). Parenthood and happiness: A review of folk theories versus empirical evidence. *Social Indicators Research, 108,* 29–64.

Hansen, W. B., Graham, J. W., Sobel, J. L., Shelton, D. R., Flay, B. R., & Johnson, C. A. (1987). The consistency of peer and parental influences on tobacco, alcohol, and marijuana use among young adolescents. *Journal of Behavioral Medicine, 10,* 559–579.

Harari, G. M., Lane, N. D., Wang, R., Crosier, B. S., Campbell, A. T., & Gosling, S. D. (2016). Using smartphones to collect behavioral data in psychological science: Opportunities, practical considerations, and challenges. *Perspectives on Psychological Science, 11,* 838–854.

Harburger, L. L., Nzerem, C. K., & Frick, K. M. (2007). Single enrichment variables differentially reduce age-related memory decline in female mice. *Behavioral Neuroscience, 121,* 679–688.

Harding, C. M., Zubin, J., & Strauss, J. S. (1987). Chronicity in schizophrenia: Fact, partial fact, or artifact? *Hospital and Community Psychiatry, 38,* 477–486.

Hare, R. D. (1993). *Without conscience: The disturbing world of the psychopaths among us.* New York, NY: Pocket Books.

Hare, R. D., McPherson, L. M., & Forth, A. E. (1988). Male psychopaths and their criminal careers. *Journal of Consulting and Clinical Psychology, 56,* 710–714.

Harlow, H. F., & Harlow, M. K (1966). Learning to love. *American Scientist, 54,* 244–272.

Harlow, H. F., Harlow, M. K., & Meyer, D. R. (1950). Learning motivated by a manipulation drive. *Journal of Experimental Psychology, 40,* 228–234.

Harlow, J. M. (1868). Recovery from the passage of an iron bar through the head. *Publications of the Massachusetts Medical Society, 2,* 327–347.

Harmon, K. G., Drezner, J. A., Gammons, M., Guskiewicz, K. M., Halstead, M., Herring, S. A., et al. (2013). American Medical Society for Sports Medicine position statement: Concussion in sport. *British Journal of Sports Medicine, 47*, 15–26.

Harpur, T. J., & Hare, R. D. (1994). Assessment of psychopathy as a function of age. *Journal of Abnormal Psychology, 103*, 604–609.

Harris, J. R. (1995). Where is the child's environment? A group socialization theory of development. *Psychological Review, 102*, 458–489.

Harris, J. R. (2011). *The nurture assumption: Why children turn out the way they do.* New York, NY: Simon & Schuster.

Harris, L. T., & Fiske, S. T. (2006). Dehumanizing the lowest of the low neuroimaging responses to extreme out-groups. *Psychological Science, 17*, 847–853.

Harris, L. T., & Fiske, S. T. (2011). Dehumanized perception: A psychological means to facilitate atrocities, torture, and genocide? *Zeitschrift für Psychologie/Journal of Psychology, 219*, 175–181.

Harris, M. A., Brett, C. E., Johnson, W., & Deary, I. J. (2016). Personality stability from age 14 to age 77 years. *Psychology and Aging, 31*, 862–874.

Harrison, M. A. (2011). College students' prevalence and perceptions of text messaging while driving. *Accident Analysis & Prevention, 43*, 1516–1520.

Harrow, M., & Jobe, T. H. (2013). Does long-term treatment of schizophrenia with antipsychotic medications facilitate recovery? *Schizophrenia Bulletin, 39*, 962–965.

Harrow, M., Jobe, T. H., & Faull, R. N. (2014). Does treatment of schizophrenia with antipsychotic medications eliminate or reduce psychosis? A 20-year multi-follow-up study. *Psychological Medicine, 44*, 3007–3016.

Hart, A. J. (1995). Naturally occurring expectation effects. *Journal of Personality and Social Psychology, 68*, 109–115.

Hartford, J., Kornstein, S., Liebowitz, M., Pigott, T., Russell, J., Detke, M., et al. (2007). Duloxetine as an SNRI treatment for generalized anxiety disorder: Results from a placebo and active-controlled trial. *International Clinical Psychopharmacology, 22*, 167–174.

Haslam, N., & Loughnan, S. (2014). Dehumanization and Infrahumanization. *Annual Review of Psychology, 65*, 399–423.

Haslam, S. A., Reicher, S. D., & Birney, M. E. (2016). Questioning authority: New perspectives on Milgram's "obedience" research and its implications for intergroup relations. *Current Opinion in Psychology, 11*, 6–9.

Haslam, S. A., Reicher, S. D., Millard, K., & McDonald, R. (2015). "Happy to have been of service": The Yale archive as a window into the engaged followership of participants in Milgram's "obedience" experiments. *British Journal of Social Psychology, 54*, 55–83.

Hawkley, L., & Cacioppo, J. T. (2010). Loneliness matters: A theoretical and empirical review of consequences and mechanisms. *Annals of Behavioral Medicine, 40*, 218–227.

Haxby, J. V., Connolly, A. C., & Guntupalli, J. S. (2014). Decoding neural representational spaces using multivariate pattern analysis. *Annual Review of Neuroscience, 37*, 435–456.

Haxby, J. V., Hoffman, E. A., & Gobbini, M. I. (2000). The distributed human neural system for face perception. *Trends in Cognitive Sciences, 4*, 223–233.

Hayakawa, S., Kawai, N., & Masataka, N. (2011). The influence of color on snake detection in visual search in human children. *Scientific Reports, 1*, 1–4.

Hayatbakhsh, M. R., Flenady, V. J., Gibbons, K. S., Kingsbury, A. M., Hurrion, E., Mamun, A. A., & Najman, J. M. (2011). Birth outcomes associated with cannabis use before and during pregnancy. *Pediatric Research, 71*, 215–219.

Hayne, H. (2004). Infant memory development: Implications for childhood amnesia. *Developmental Review, 24*, 33–73.

Hayne, H., Imuta, K., & Scarf, D. (2015). Memory development during infancy and early childhood across cultures. In J. D. Wright (Ed.), *International encyclopedia of the social & behavioral sciences* (2nd ed., Vol. 15, pp. 147–154). Oxford, England: Elsevier.

Hayward, W. G., Crookes, K., Chu, M. H., Favelle, S. K., & Rhodes, G. (2016). Holistic processing of face configurations and components. *Journal of Experimental Psychology: Human Perception and Performance, 42*, 1482–1489.

Hazan, C., & Shaver, P. R. (1987). Romantic love conceptualized as an attachment process. *Journal of Personality and Social Psychology, 52*, 511–524.

Hazlett, E. A. (2016). Neural substrates of emotion-processing abnormalities in borderline personality disorder. *Biological Psychiatry, 7*, 74–75.

Hazlett, H. C., Gu, H., Munsell, B. C., Kim, S. H., Styner, M., Wolff, J. J., et al. (2017). Early brain development in infants at high risk for autism spectrum disorder. *Nature, 542*, 348–351.

Heatherton, T. F. (2011). Neuroscience of self and self-regulation. *Annual Review of Psychology, 62*, 363–390.

Heatherton, T. F., Herman, C. P., & Polivy, J. (1991). Effects of physical threat and ego threat on eating behavior. *Journal of Personality and Social Psychology, 60*, 138–143.

Heatherton, T. F., & Vohs, K. D. (2000). Interpersonal evaluations following threats to self: Role of self-esteem. *Journal of Personality and Social Psychology, 78*, 725–736.

Heatherton, T. F., & Wagner, D. D. (2011). Cognitive neuroscience of self-regulation failure. *Trends in Cognitive Sciences, 15*, 132–139.

Heatherton, T. F., & Weinberger, J. L. (1994). *Can personality change?* Washington, DC: American Psychological Association.

Hebb, D. O. (1949). *The organization of behavior: A neuropsychological approach.* New York, NY: Wiley.

Hebl, M. R., & Heatherton, T. F. (1998). The stigma of obesity in women: The difference is black and white. *Personality and Social Psychology Bulletin, 24*, 417–426.

Heck, N. C. (2016). Group psychotherapy with transgender and gender nonconforming adults: Evidence-based practice applications. *Psychiatric Clinics of North America, 40*, 157–175.

Hedegaard, H., Warner, M., & Miniño, A. (2017). Drug overdose deaths in the United States, 1999–2015. NCHS data brief, no. 273. Hyattsville, MD: National Center for Health Statistics.

Heider, F. (1944). Social perception and phenomenal causality. *Psychological Review, 51*, 358–374.

Heim, C., Newport, D. J., Mletzko, T., Miller, A. H., & Nemeroff, C. B. (2008). The link between childhood trauma and depression: Insights from HPA axis studies in humans. *Psychoneuroendocrinology, 33*, 693–710.

Heine, S. J. (2003). An exploration of cultural variation in self-enhancing and self-improving motivations. In V. Murphy-Berman & J. J. Berman (Eds.), *Nebraska symposium on motivation: Vol. 49. Cross-cultural differences in perspectives on the self* (pp. 101–128). Lincoln: University of Nebraska Press.

Heine, S. J. (2005). Where is the evidence for pancultural self-enhancement? A reply to Sedikides, Gaertner, & Toguchi. *Journal of Personality and Social Psychology, 89*, 531–538.

Heine, S. J. (2015). *Cultural psychology.* (3rd ed.). New York, NY: Norton.

Heine, S. J., Buchtel, E., & Norenzayan, A. (2008). What do cross-national comparisons of self-reported personality traits tell us? The case of conscientiousness. *Psychological Science, 19*, 309–313.

Heine, S. J., Kitayama, S., & Hamamura, T. (2007). The inclusion of additional studies yields different conclusions: A reply to Sedikides, Gaertner, & Vevea (2005), Journal of Personality and Social Psychology. *Asian Journal of Social Psychology, 10*, 49–58.

Heine, S. J., & Lehman, D. R. (1999). Culture, self-discrepancies, and self-satisfaction. *Personality and Social Psychology Bulletin, 25*, 915–925.

Heine, S. J., Lehman, D. R., Markus, H. R., & Kitayama, S. (1999). Is there a universal need for positive self-regard? *Psychological Review, 106*, 766–794.

Heller, D., Watson, D., & Ilies, R. (2004). The role of person versus situation in life satisfaction: A critical examination. *Psychological Bulletin, 130*, 574–600.

Helmreich, R., Aronson, E., & LeFan, J. (1970). To err is humanizing sometimes: Effects of self-esteem, competence, and a pratfall on interpersonal attraction. *Journal of Personality and Social Psychology, 16,* 259–264.

Henrich, J., Heine, S. J., & Norenzayan, A. (2010). The weirdest people in the world? *Behavioral and Brain Sciences, 33,* 61–83, 111–135.

Henry, P. J., & Sears, D. O. (2002). The Symbolic Racism (2000) Scale. *Political Psychology, 23,* 253–283.

Herbert, J. D., & Gaudiano, B. A. (2005). Introduction to the special issue on the placebo concept in psychotherapy. *Journal of Clinical Psychology, 61,* 787–790.

Herbert, T. B., & Cohen, S. (1993). Stress and immunity in humans: A meta-analytic review. *Psychosomatic Medicine, 55,* 364–379.

Herdener, M., Esposito, F., di Salle, F., Boller, C., Hilti, C. C., et al. (2010). Musical training induces functional plasticity in human hippocampus. *Journal of Neuroscience, 30,* 1377–1384.

Hering, E. (1964). *Outlines of a theory of the light sense* (L. M. Hurvich & D. Jameson, Trans.). Cambridge, MA: Harvard University Press. (Original work published 1878.)

Heron, M. (2016). Deaths: Leading causes for 2014. *National vital statistics reports, 65* (Report No. 5).

Herring, B. E., & Nicoll, R. A. (2016). Long-term potentiation: From CaMKII to AMPA receptor trafficking. *Annual Review of Physiology, 78,* 351–365.

Hester, R. K., Delaney, H. D., & Campbell, W. (2011). ModerateDrinking .com and moderation management: Outcomes of a randomized clinical trial with non-dependent problem drinkers. *Journal of Consulting and Clinical Psychology, 79,* 215–234.

Hickok, G. (2009). Eight problems for the mirror neuron theory of action understanding in monkeys and humans. *Journal of Cognitive Neuroscience, 21,* 1229–1243.

Higgins, E. T. (1997). Beyond pleasure and pain. *American Psychologist, 52,* 1280–1300.

Higgins, L. T., & Zheng, M. (2002). An introduction to Chinese psychology—its historical roots until the present day. *Journal of Psychology, 136,* 225–239.

Higgins, S. C., Gueorguiev, M., & Korbonits, M. (2007). Ghrelin, the peripheral hunger hormone. *Annals of Medicine, 39,* 116–136.

Hilgard, E. R. (1973). A neodissociation interpretation of pain reduction in hypnosis. *Psychological Review, 80,* 396–411.

Hilgard, E. R., & Hilgard, J. R. (1975). *Hypnosis in the relief of pain.* Los Altos, CA: Kaufmann.

Hill, S. E., & Durante, K. M. (2009). Do women feel worse to look their best? Testing the relationship between self-esteem and fertility status across the menstrual cycle. *Personality and Social Psychology Bulletin, 35,* 1592–1601.

Hines, T. (1987). Left brain/right brain mythology and implications for management and training. *Academy of Management Review, 12,* 600–606.

Hines, T. (2003). *Pseudoscience and the paranormal.* Amherst, NY: Prometheus.

Hingson, R. W., Zha, W., & Weitzman, E. R. (2009). Magnitude of and trends in alcohol-related mortality and morbidity among U.S. college students ages 18–24, 1998–2005. *Journal of Studies on Alcohol and Drugs, 16,* 12–20.

Hirst, W., & Phelps, E. A. (2016). Flashbulb memories. *Current Directions in Psychological Science, 25,* 36–41.

Hirst, W., Phelps, E. A., Buckner, R. L., Budson, A. E., Cuc, A., Gabrieli, J. D. E., et al. (2009). Long-term memory for the terrorist attack of September 11: Flashbulb memories, event memories, and the factors that influence their retention. *Journal of Experimental Psychology: General, 138,* 161–176.

Hirst, W., Phelps, E. A., Meksin, R., Vaidya, C. J., Johnson, M. K., Mitchell, K., et al. (2015). A ten-year follow-up of a study of memory for the attack of September 11, 2001: Flashbulb memories and memories for

flashbulb events. *Journal of Experimental Psychology: General, 144,* 604–623.

Ho, B. C., Andreasen, N. C., Nopoulos, P., Arndt, S., Magnotta, V., & Flaum, M. (2003). Progressive structural brain abnormalities and their relationship to clinical outcome: A longitudinal magnetic resonance imaging study early in schizophrenia. *Archives of General Psychiatry, 60,* 585–594.

Hobson, J. A. (1999). *Dreaming as delirium: How the brain goes out of its mind.* Cambridge, MA: MIT Press.

Hobson, J. A. (2009). REM sleep and dreaming: Towards a theory of protoconsciousness. *Nature Reviews Neuroscience, 10,* 803–814.

Hobson, J. A., & McCarley, R. (1977). The brain as a dream state generator: An activation-synthesis hypothesis of the dream process. *American Journal of Psychiatry, 134,* 1335–1348.

Hobson, J. A., Pace-Schott, E. F., & Stickgold, R. (2000). Consciousness: Its vicissitudes in waking and sleep. In M. S. Gazzaniga (Ed.), *The new cognitive neurosciences* (pp. 1341–1354). Cambridge, MA: MIT Press.

Hockley, W. E. (2008). The effect of environmental context on recognition memory and claims of remembering. *Journal of Experimental Psychology: Learning, Memory, and Cognition, 34,* 1412–1429.

Hoerger, M., Chapman, B. P., Prigerson, H. G., Fagerlin, A., Mohile, S. G., Epstein, R. M., et al. (2014). Personality change pre- to post-loss in spousal caregivers of patients with terminal lung cancer. *Social Psychological and Personality Science, 5,* 722–729.

Hoffman, E., Myerberg, N. R., & Morawski, J. G. (2015). Acting otherwise: Resistance, agency, and subjectivities in Milgram's studies of obedience. *Theory & Psychology, 25,* 670–689.

Hofmann, S. G., & Smits, J. A. J. (2008). Cognitive-behavioral therapy for adult anxiety disorders: A meta-analysis of randomized placebo-controlled trials. *Journal of Clinical Psychiatry, 69,* 621–632.

Hogan, M. J., Parker, J. D., Wiener, J., Watters, C., Wood, L. M., & Oke, A. (2010). Academic success in adolescence: Relationships among verbal IQ, social support and emotional intelligence. *Australian Journal of Psychology, 62,* 30–41.

Hogarty, G. E., Anderson, C. M., Reiss, D. J., Kornblith, S. J., Greenwald, D. P., et al. (1986). Family psychoeducation, social skills training, and maintenance chemotherapy in the aftercare treatment of schizophrenia: I. One-year effects of a controlled study on relapse and expressed emotion. *Archives of General Psychiatry, 43,* 633–642.

Hogg, M. A. (2012). *Social identity and the psychology of groups.* In M. R. Leary & J. P. Tangney (Eds.), *Handbook of self and identity* (pp. 502–519). New York, NY: Guilford Press.

Hogg, M. A. (2016). Social identity theory. In S. McKeown, R. Haji, & N. Ferguson (Eds.), *Understanding peace and conflict through social identity theory* (pp. 3–17). Switzerland: Springer International Publishing.

Holland, P. C. (1977). Conditioned stimulus as a determinant of the form of the Pavlovian conditioned response. *Journal of Experimental Psychology: Animal Behavior Processes, 3,* 77–104.

Hollander, E., Bartz, J., Chaplin, W., Phillips, A., Sumner, J., Soorya, L., et al. (2007). Oxytocin increases retention of social cognition in autism. *Biological Psychiatry, 61,* 498–503.

Hollander, E., Novotny, S., Hanratty, M., Yaffe, R., DeCaria, C. M., Aronowitz, B. R., et al. (2003). Oxytocin infusion reduces repetitive behaviors in adults with autistic and Asperger's disorders. *Neuropsychopharmacology, 28,* 193–198.

Holliday, R. (1987). The inheritance of epigenetic defects. *Science, 238,* 163–170.

Hollon, S. D., Stewart, M. O., & Strunk, D. (2006). Enduring effects for cognitive behavior therapy in the treatment of depression and anxiety. *Annual Review of Psychology, 57,* 285–315.

Hollon, S. D., Thase, M. E., & Markowitz, J. C. (2002). Treatment and prevention of depression. *Psychological Science in the Public Interest, 3,* 39–77.

Holmbeck, G. N. (1996). A model of family relational transformations during the transition to adolescence: Parent-adolescent conflict and adaptation. In J. A. Graber, J. Brooks-Gunn, & A. C. Petersen (Eds.), *Transitions through adolescence* (pp. 67–200). Mahwah, NJ: Erlbaum.

Holmboe, K., Rijsdijk, F. V., Hallett, V., Happé, F., Plomin, R., & Ronald, A. (2013). Strong genetic influences on the stability of autistic traits in childhood. *Journal of the American Academy of Child & Adolescent Psychiatry, 53,* 221–230.

Holmes, T. H., & Rahe, R. H. (1967). The Social Readjustment Rating Scale. *Journal of Psychosomatic Research, 11,* 213–218.

Holstein, S. B., & Premack, D. (1965). On the different effects of random reinforcement and presolution reversal on human concept-identification. *Journal of Experimental Psychology, 70,* 335–337.

Holt-Lunstad, J., Smith, T. B., Baker, M., Harris, T., & Stephenson, D. (2015). Loneliness and social isolation as risk factors for mortality: A meta-analytic review. *Perspectives on Psychological Science, 10,* 227–237.

Honein, M. A., Dawson, A. L., Petersen, E. E., Jones, A. M., Lee, E. H., Yazdy, M. M., et al. (2017). Birth defects among fetuses and infants of US women with evidence of possible Zika virus infection during pregnancy. *Journal of the American Medical Association, 317,* 59–68.

Honts, C. R., Raskin, D. C., & Kircher, J. C. (1994). Mental and physical countermeasures reduce the accuracy of polygraph tests. *Journal of Applied Psychology, 79,* 252.

Hoogman, M., Bralten, J., Hibar, D. P., Mennes, M., Zwiers, M. P., Schweren, L. S., et al. (2017). Subcortical brain volume differences in participants with attention deficit hyperactivity disorder in children and adults: A cross-sectional mega-analysis. *The Lancet Psychiatry, 4,* 310–319. http://dx.doi.org/10.1016/S2215-0366(17)30049-4

Hooley, J. (2007). Expressed emotion and relapse of psychopathology. *Annual Review of Clinical Psychology, 3,* 329–352.

Hooley, J. M., & Gotlib, I. H. (2000). A diathesis-stress conceptualization of expressed emotion and clinical outcome. *Applied and Preventive Psychology, 9,* 135–152.

Hooshmand, F., Miller, S., Dore, J., Wang, P. W., Hill, S. J., Portillo, N., & Ketter, T. A. (2014). Trends in pharmacotherapy in patients referred to a bipolar specialty clinic, 2000–2011. *Journal of Affective Disorders, 155,* 283–287.

Horikawa, T., Tamaki, M., Miyawaki, Y., & Kamitani, Y. (2013). Neural decoding of visual imagery during sleep. *Science, 340,* 639–642.

Horn, J. L. (1968). Organization of abilities and the development of intelligence. *Psychological Review, 75,* 242–259.

Horn, J. L., & Hofer, S. M. (1992). Major abilities and development in the adult period. In R. J. Sternberg & C. A. Berg (Eds.), *Intellectual development* (pp. 44–99). New York, NY: Cambridge University Press.

Horn, J. L., & McArdle, J. J. (2007). Understanding human intelligence since Spearman. In R. Cudeck & R. C. MacCallum (Eds.), *Factor analysis at 100: Historical developments and future directions* (pp. 205–247). Mahwah, NJ: Erlbaum.

Hoshino, Y., Kumashiro, H., Yashima, Y., Tachibana, R., Watanabe, M., & Furukawa, H. (1980). Early symptoms of autism in children and their diagnostic significance. *Japanese Journal of Child and Adolescent Psychiatry, 21,* 284–299.

House, J. S., Landis, K. R., & Umberson, D. (1988). Social relationships and health. *Science, 241,* 540–545.

Hovland, C. I., Janis, I. L., & Kelley, H. H. (1953). *Communication and persuasion: Psychological studies of opinion change.* New Haven, CT: Yale University Press.

Howie, L. D., Pastor, P. N., & Lukacs, S. L. (2014). Use of medication prescribed for emotional or behavioral difficulties among children aged 6–17 years in the United States, 2011–2012. NCHS data brief, no. 148. Hyattsville, MD: National Center for Health Statistics.

Howlin, P., Mawhood, L., & Rutter, M. (2000). Autism and developmental receptive language disorder—A follow-up comparison in early adult life. II: Social, behavioural, and psychiatric outcomes. *Journal of Child Psychology and Psychiatry and Allied Disciplines, 41,* 561–578.

Hoyert, D. L., & Xu, J. (2012). Deaths: Preliminary data for 2011. *National vital statistics reports, 61 (Report No. 6),* 1–51.

Hoyme, H. E., Kalberg, W. O., Elliott, A. J., Blankenship, J., Buckley, D., Marais, M. S., et al. (2016). Updated clinical guidelines for diagnosing fetal alcohol spectrum disorders. *Pediatrics, 138,* e20154256.

Hoyt, C. L., Burnette, J. L., & Auster-Gussman, L. (2014). "Obesity is a disease": Examining the self-regulatory impact of this public health message. *Psychological Science, 25,* 997–1002.

Huesmann, L. R. (1998). The role of social information processing and cognitive schemas in the acquisition and maintenance of habitual aggressive behavior. In R. G. Geen & E. Donnerstein (Eds.), *Human aggression: Theories, research, and implications for policy* (pp. 73–109). New York, NY: Academic Press.

Hughes, M. E., & Waite, L. J. (2009). Marital biography and health at midlife. *Journal of Health and Social Behavior, 50,* 344–358.

Hughes, V. (2013). The big fat truth. *Nature, 497,* 428–430.

Hull, C. L. (1943). *Principles of behavior: An introduction to behavior theory.* New York, NY: Appleton-Century.

Hull, J. G., & Bond, C. F. (1986). Social and behavioral consequences of alcohol consumption and expectancy: A meta-analysis. *Psychological Bulletin, 99,* 347–360.

Hull, J. G., Brunelle, T. J., Prescott, A., & Sargent, J. D. (2014). A longitudinal study of risk-glorifying video games and behavioral deviance. *Journal of Personality and Social Psychology, 107,* 300–325.

Hull, J. G., Draghici, A. M., & Sargent, J. D. (2012). A longitudinal study of risk-glorifying video games and reckless driving. *Psychology of Popular Media Culture, 1,* 244–253.

Hunsley, J., & Mash, E. J. (2007). Evidence-based assessment. *Annual Review of Clinical Psychology, 3,* 29–51.

Hunt, E., & Agnoli, F. (1991). The Whorfian hypothesis: A cognitive psychology perspective. *Psychological Review, 98,* 377–389.

Hurley, S. W., & Johnson, A. K. (2015). The biopsychology of salt hunger and sodium deficiency. *Pflügers Archiv-European Journal of Physiology, 467,* 445–456.

Hyatt, C. J., Assaf, M., Muska, C. E., Rosen, R. I., Thomas, A. D., Johnson, M. R., et al. (2012). Reward-related dorsal striatal activity differences between former and current cocaine dependent individuals during an interactive competitive game. *PLoS ONE, 7,* e34917.

Hyde, J. S. (2005). The gender similarities hypothesis. *American Psychologist, 60,* 581–592.

Hyde, L. W., Waller, R., Trentacosta, C. J., Shaw, D. S., Neiderhiser, J. M., Ganiban, J. M., et al. (2016). Heritable and nonheritable pathways to early callous-unemotional behaviors. *American Journal of Psychiatry, 173,* 903–910.

Hyman, S. E. (2008). A glimmer of light for neuropsychiatric disorders. *Nature, 455,* 890–893.

Hyman, I. E., Boss, S. M., Wise, B. M., McKenzie, K. E., & Caggiano, J. M. (2010). Did you see the unicycling clown? Inattentional blindness while walking and talking on a cell phone. *Applied Cognitive Psychology, 24,* 597–607.

Hymel, S., Rocke-Henderson, N., & Bonanno, R. A. (2005). Moral disengagement: A framework for understanding bullying among adolescents. *Journal of Social Sciences, 8,* 1–11.

Iacoboni, M. (2009). Imitation, empathy, and mirror neurons. *Annual Review of Psychology, 60,* 653–670.

Ibrahim, A. K., Kelly, S. J., Adams, C. E., & Glazebrook, C. (2013). A systematic review of studies of depression prevalence in university students. *Journal of Psychiatric Research, 47,* 391–400.

Ilan, A. B., Smith, M. E., & Gevins, A. (2004). Effects of marijuana on neurophysiological signals of working and episodic memory. *Psychopharmacology, 176,* 214–222.

Immunization Safety Review Committee. (2004). *Immunization safety review: Vaccines and autism.* Washington, DC: National Academies Press.

Imuta, K., Henry, J. D., Slaughter, V., Selcuk, B., & Ruffman, T. (2016). Theory of mind and prosocial behavior in childhood: A meta-analytic review. *Developmental Psychology, 52,* 1192–1205.

Inbar, Y., Pizarro, D. A., & Bloom, P. (2012). Disgusting smells cause decreased liking of gay men. *Emotion, 12,* 23–27.

Insel, T. R. (2014). The NIMH Research Domain Criteria (RDoC) Project: Precision medicine for psychiatry. *American Journal of Psychiatry, 171,* 395–397.

Insel, T. R., & Charney, D. S. (2003). Research on major depression. *Journal of the American Medical Association, 289,* 3167–3168.

Insel, T. R., Cuthbert, B., Garvey, M., Heinssen, R., Pine, D. S., Quinn, K., et al. (2010). Research domain criteria (RDoC): Toward a new classification framework for research on mental disorders. *American Journal of Psychiatry, 167,* 748–751.

Insel, T. R., & Young, L. J. (2001). The neurobiology of attachment. *Nature Reviews Neuroscience, 2,* 129–136.

Institute of Medicine (IOM) and National Research Council (NRC). (2015). *Transforming the workplace for children birth through age 8: A unifying foundation.* Washington, DC: National Academies Press.

Intersex Society of North America. (2008). How common is intersex? Retrieved July 24, 2017, from http://www.isna.org/faq/frequency

Ioannidis, J. P. (2014). How to make more published research true. *PLoS Medicine, 11,* e1001747.

Isen, A. M. (1993). Positive affect and decision making. In M. Lewis & J. M. Haviland (Eds.), *Handbook of emotions* (pp. 261–277). New York, NY: Guilford Press.

Ishigami, Y., & Klein, R. M. (2009). Is a handsfree phone safer than a handheld phone? *Journal of Safety Research, 40,* 157–164.

Ivanovic, D. M., Leiva, B. P., Perez, H. T., Olivares, M. G., Diaz, N. S., Urrutia, M. S., et al. (2004). Head size and intelligence, learning, nutritional status and brain development: Head, IQ, learning, nutrition and brain. *Neuropsychologia, 42,* 1118–1131.

Iyengar, S. S., & Lepper, M. R. (2000). When choice is demotivating: Can one desire too much of a good thing? *Journal of Personality and Social Psychology, 79,* 995–1006.

Iyengar, S. S., Wells, R. E., & Schwartz, B. (2006). Doing better but feeling worse: Looking for the best job undermines satisfaction. *Psychological Science, 17,* 143–150.

Jääskeläinen, E., Juola, P., Hirvonen, N., McGrath, J. J., Saha, S., Isohanni, M., et al. (2013). A systematic review and meta-analysis of recovery in schizophrenia. *Schizophrenia Bulletin, 39,* 1296–1306.

Jablensky, A. (1989). Epidemiology and cross-cultural aspects of schizophrenia. *Psychiatric Annals, 19,* 516–524.

Jackson, B., Kubzansky, L. D., Cohen, S., Jacobs, D. R., Jr., & Wright, R. J. (2007). Does harboring hostility hurt? Associations between hostility and pulmonary function in the coronary artery risk development in (young) adults (CARDIA) study. *Health Psychology, 26,* 333–340.

Jackson, J. J., Hill, P. L., Payne, B. R., Roberts, B. W., & Stine-Morrow, E. A. L. (2012). Can an old dog learn (and want to experience) new tricks? Cognitive training increases openness to experience in older adults. *Psychology and Aging, 27,* 286–292.

Jackson, S. A., Thomas, P. R., Marsh, H. W., & Smethurst, C. J. (2001). Relationships between flow, self-concept, psychological skills, and performance. *Journal of Applied Sport Psychology, 13,* 129–153.

Jacoby, L. L., Kelley, C., Brown, J., & Jasechko, J. (1989). Becoming famous overnight: Limits on the ability to avoid unconscious influences of the past. *Journal of Personality and Social Psychology, 56,* 326–338.

Jacoby, L. L., & Witherspoon, D. (1982). Remembering without awareness. *Canadian Journal of Psychology, 32,* 300–324.

Jacowitz, K. E., & Kahneman, D. (1995). Measures of anchoring in estimation tasks. *Personality and Social Psychology Bulletin, 21,* 1161–1167.

Jain, A., Marshall, J., Buikema, A., Bancroft, T., Kelly, J. P., & Newschaffer, C. (2015). Autism occurrence by MMR vaccine status among US children with older siblings with and without autism. *Journal of the American Medical Association, 313,* 1534–1540.

Jakubovski, E., Varigonda, A. L., Freemantle, N., Taylor, M. J., & Bloch, M. H. (2016). Systematic review and meta-analysis: Dose-response relationship of selective serotonin reuptake inhibitors in major depressive disorder. *American Journal of Psychiatry, 173,* 174–183.

James, W. (1884). What is an emotion? *Mind, 9,* 188–205.

James, W. (1890). *The principles of psychology.* New York, NY: Henry Holt.

James, W. H. (1983). Decline in coital rates with spouses' ages and duration of marriage. *Journal of Biosocial Science, 15,* 83–87.

Jamieson, G. A. (2007). *Hypnosis and conscious states: The cognitive neuroscience perspective.* New York, NY: Oxford University Press.

Janata, P. (2009). The neural architecture of music-evoked autobiographical memories. *Cerebral Cortex, 19,* 2579–2594.

Jang, K. L., Hu, S., Livesley, W. J., Angleitner, A., Riemann, R., Ando, J., et al. (2001). Covariance structure of neuroticism and agreeableness: A twin and molecular genetic analysis of the role of the serotonin transporter gene. *Journal of Personality and Social Psychology, 81,* 295–304.

Janis, I. L. (1972). *Victims of groupthink: A psychological study of foreign-policy decisions and fiascoes.* Boston, MA: Houghton Mifflin.

Jencks, C. (1979). *Who gets ahead? The determinants of economic success in America.* New York, NY: Basic Books.

Jensen, A. R. (1998). *The g factor: The science of mental ability.* Westport, CT: Praeger.

Jensen, P. S., Arnold, L. E., Swanson, J. M., Vitiello, B., Abikoff, H. B., Greenhill, L. L., et al. (2007). 3-year follow-up of the NIMH MTA study. *Journal of the American Academy of Child and Adolescent Psychiatry, 46,* 989–1002.

Jensen, P. S., Garcia, J. A., Glied, S., Crowe, M., Foster, M., Schlander, M., et al. (2005). Cost-effectiveness of ADHD treatments: Findings from the multimodal treatment study of children with ADHD. *American Journal of Psychiatry, 162,* 1628–1636.

Jensen, P. S., Hinshaw, S. P., Swanson, J. M., Greenhill, L. L., Conners, C. K., Arnold, L. E., et al. (2001). Findings from the NIMH multimodal treatment study of ADHD (MTA): Implications and applications for primary care providers. *Journal of Developmental and Behavioral Pediatrics, 22,* 60–73.

Jetten, J., & Mols, F. (2014). 50:50 hindsight: Appreciating anew the contributions of Milgram's obedience experiments. *Journal of Social Issues, 70,* 587–602.

Jha, P., Ramasundarahettige, C., Landsman, V., Rostron, B., Thun, M., Anderson, R. N., et al. (2013). 21st-century hazards of smoking and benefits of cessation in the United States. *New England Journal of Medicine, 368,* 341–350.

Jiang, Y., Sheikh, K., & Bullock, C. (2006). Is there a sex or race difference in stroke mortality? *Journal of Stroke and Cerebrovascular Disease, 15,* 179–186.

Joel, D., Berman, Z., Tavor, I., Wexler, N., Gaber, O., Stein, Y., et al. (2015). Sex beyond the genitalia: The human brain mosaic. *Proceedings of the National Academy of Sciences, 112,* 15468–15473.

John, O. P., & Srivastava, S. (1999). The Big Five trait taxonomy: History, measurement, and theoretical perspectives. In L. A. Pervin & O. P. John (Eds.), *Handbook of personality: Theory and research* (2nd ed., pp. 102–138). New York, NY: Guilford Press.

Johns, F., Schmader, T., & Martens, A. (2005). Knowing is half the battle—Teaching stereotype threat as a means of improving women's math performance. *Psychological Science, 16,* 175–179.

Johnson, W., Jung, R. E., Colom, R., & Haier, R. J. (2008). Cognitive abilities independent of IQ correlate with regional brain structure. *Intelligence, 36,* 18–28.

Johnston, L. D., O'Malley, P. M., Bachman, J. G., & Schulenberg, J. E. (2011). *Monitoring the future national results on adolescent drug use: Overview of key findings, 2010.* Ann Arbor: Institute for Social Research, University of Michigan.

Joiner, T. E. (2005). *Why people die by suicide.* Cambridge, MA: Harvard University Press.

Joiner, T. E., Coyne, J. C., & Blalock, J. (1999). On the interpersonal nature of depression: Overview and synthesis. In T. E. Joiner & J. C. Coyne

(Eds.), *The interactional nature of depression: Advances in interpersonal approaches* (pp. 3–19). Washington, DC: American Psychological Association.

Joiner, T. E., Walker, R. L., Pettit, J. W., Perez, M., & Cukrowicz, K. C. (2005). Evidence-based assessment of depression in adults. *Psychological Assessment, 17,* 267–277.

Jokela, M., Elovainio, M., Kivimaki, M., & Keltikangas-Jarvinen, L. (2008). Temperament and migration patterns in Finland. *Psychological Science, 19,* 831–837.

Jones, E. E., & Davis, K. E. (1965). From acts to dispositions: The attribution process in person perception. *Advances in Experimental Social Psychology, 2,* 219–266.

Jones, M. C. (1924). A laboratory study of fear: The case of Peter. *The Pedagogical Seminary, 31,* 308–315.

Jones, W., & Klin, A. (2013). Attention to eyes is present but in decline in 2–6-month-old infants later diagnosed with autism. *Nature, 504,* 427–431.

Jope, R. S. (1999). Anti-bipolar therapy: Mechanism of action of lithium. *Molecular Psychiatry, 4,* 117–128.

Jorm, A. F. (2000). Does old age reduce the risk of anxiety and depression?: A review of epidemiological studies across the adult life span. *Psychological Medicine, 30,* 3011–3022.

Junco, R., & Cotten, S. R. (2012). No A 4 U: The relationship between multitasking and academic performance. *Computers & Education, 59,* 505–514.

Jureidini, J. N., Doecke, C. J., Mansfield, P. R., Haby, M., Menkes, D. B., & Tonkin, A. L. (2004). Efficacy and safety of antidepressants for children and adolescents. *British Medical Journal, 328,* 879–883.

Kagan, J. (2011). Three lessons learned. *Perspectives in Psychological Science, 6,* 107–113.

Kagan, J., & Snidman, N. (1991). Infant predictors of inhibited and uninhibited profiles. *Psychological Science, 2,* 40–44.

Kahneman, D. (2007, July 20–22). *A short course in thinking about thinking: A master class by Danny Kahneman.* [Online video.] Retrieved from *Edge, The Third Culture,* at http://www.edge.org/3rd_culture/kahneman07/kahneman07_index.html/

Kahneman, D. (2011). *Thinking, fast and slow.* London, England: Macmillan.

Kahneman, D., & Tversky, A. (1979). Prospect theory: An analysis of decision under risk. *Econometrica: Journal of the Econometric Society, 47,* 263–291.

Kalkhoran, S., & Glantz, S. A. (2016). E-cigarettes and smoking cessation in real-world and clinical settings: A systematic review and meta-analysis. *The Lancet Respiratory Medicine, 4,* 116–128.

Kallio, S., & Revonsuo, A. (2003). Hypnotic phenomena and altered states of consciousness: A multi-level framework of description and explanation. *Contemporary Hypnosis, 20,* 111–164.

Kamara, S., Colom, R., Johnson, W., Deary, I., Haier, R., Waber, D., et al., and the Brain Development Cooperative Groups. (2011). Cortical thickness correlates of specific cognitive performance accounted for by the general factor of intelligence in healthy children aged 6 to 18. *Neuroimage, 55,* 1443–1453.

Kandel, E. R. (2001). The molecular biology of memory storage: A dialogue between genes and synapses. *Science, 294,* 1030–1038.

Kandel, E. R., Dudai, Y., & Mayford, M. R. (2014). The molecular and systems biology of memory. *Cell, 157,* 163–186.

Kane, M. J., Hambrick, D. Z., & Conway, A. R. (2005). Working memory capacity and fluid intelligence are strongly related constructs: Comment on Ackerman, Beier, and Boyle (2005). *Psychological Bulletin, 131,* 66–71.

Kang, D. H., Coe, C. L., McCarthy, D. O., & Ershler, W. B. (1997). Immune responses to final exams in healthy and asthmatic adolescents. *Nursing Research, 46,* 12–19.

Kanno, T., Iijima, K., Abe, Y., Koike, T., Shimada, N., Hoshi, T., et al. (2013). Hemorrhagic ulcers after Great East Japan earthquake and tsunami: Features of post-disaster hemorrhagic ulcers. *Digestion, 87,* 40–46.

Kanwisher, N., Tong, F., & Nakayama, K. (1998). The effect of face inversion on the human fusiform face area. *Cognition, 68,* 1–11.

Kaplan, R. M. (2007). Should Medicare reimburse providers for weight loss interventions? *American Psychologist, 62,* 217–219.

Kapur, S. E., Craik, F. I. M., Tulving, E., Wilson, A. A., Houle, S., & Brown, G. R. (1994). Neuroanatomical correlates of encoding in episodic memory: Levels of processing effects. *Proceedings of the National Academy of Sciences, 91,* 2008–2011.

Karpicke, J. D., & Blunt, J. R. (2011). Retrieval practice produces more learning than elaborative studying with concept mapping. *Science, 331,* 772–775.

Kasari, C., Paparella, T., Freeman, S., & Jahromi, L. B. (2008). Language outcomes in autism: Randomized comparison of joint attention and play interventions. *Journal of Counseling and Clinical Psychology, 76,* 125–137.

Kassin, S. M., Dror, I. E., & Kukucka, J. (2013). The forensic confirmation bias: Problems, perspectives, and proposed solutions. *Journal of Applied Research in Memory and Cognition, 2,* 42–52.

Kawachi, I., Kennedy, B., & Glass, R. (1999). Social capital and self-rated health: A contextual analysis. *American Journal of Public Health, 89,* 1187–1193.

Kawakami, K., Dovidio, J. F., Moll, J., Hermsen, S., & Russin, A. (2000). Just say no (to stereotyping): Effects of training in the negation of stereotypic associations on stereotype activation. *Journal of Personality and Social Psychology, 78,* 871–888.

Kawakami, K., Dovidio, J. F., & van Kamp, S. (2005). Kicking the habit: Effects of nonstereotypic association training and correction processes on hiring decisions. *Journal of Experimental Social Psychology, 41,* 68–75.

Kawas, C., Gray, S., Brookmeyer, R., Fozard, J., & Zonderman, A. (2000). Age-specific incidence rates of Alzheimer's disease: The Baltimore longitudinal study of aging. *Neurology, 54,* 2072–2077.

Kazak, A., Simms, S., & Rourke, M. (2002). Family systems practice in pediatric psychology. *Journal of Pediatric Psychology, 27,* 133–143.

Kazdin, A. E. (1994). Methodology, design, and evaluation in psychotherapy research. In A. E. Bergin & S. L. Garfield (Eds.), *International handbook of behavior modification and behavior change* (4th ed., pp. 19–71). New York, NY: Wiley.

Kazdin, A. E. (2008). Evidence-based treatment and practice: New opportunities to bridge clinical research and practice, enhance the knowledge base, and improve patient care. *American Psychologist, 63,* 146–159.

Kazdin, A. E., & Benjet, C. (2003). Spanking children: Evidence and issues. *Current Directions in Psychological Science, 12,* 99–103.

Kazdin, A. E., & Blase, S. L. (2011). Rebooting psychotherapy research and practice to reduce the burden of mental illness. *Perspectives in Psychological Science, 6,* 21–37.

Keel, P. K., Baxter, M. G., Heatherton, T. F., & Joiner, T. E. (2007). A 20-year longitudinal study of body weight, dieting, and eating disorder symptoms. *Journal of Abnormal Psychology, 116,* 422–432.

Keel, P. K., & Mitchell, J. E. (1997). Outcome in bulimia nervosa. *American Journal of Psychiatry, 154,* 313–321.

Keil, F. C. (2011). Science starts early. *Science, 331,* 1022–1023.

Keller, J., & Bless, H. (2008). Flow and regulatory compatibility: An experimental approach to the flow model of intrinsic motivation. *Personality and Social Psychology Bulletin, 34,* 196–209.

Keller, M. B., McCullough, J. P., Klein, D. N., Arnow, B., Dunner, D. L., Gelenberg, A. J., et al. (2000). A comparison of nefazodone, a cognitive behavioral analysis system of psychotherapy, and their combination for the treatment of chronic depression. *New England Journal of Medicine, 342,* 1462–1470.

Kelley, W. M., Wagner, D. D., & Heatherton, T. F. (2015). In search of a human self-regulation system. *Annual Review of Neuroscience, 38,* 389–411.

Kelley, W. M., Macrae, C. N., Wyland, C., Caglar, S., Inati, S., & Heatherton, T. F. (2002). Finding the self? An event-related fMRI study. *Journal of Cognitive Neuroscience, 14,* 785–794.

Kellman, P. J., Spelke, E. S., & Short, K. R. (1986). Infant perception of object unity from translatory motion in depth and vertical translation. *Child Development, 57,* 72–86.

Kelly, G. A. (1955). *The psychology of personal constructs.* New York, NY: Norton.

Keltner, D., & Anderson, C. (2000). Saving face for Darwin: The functions and uses of embarrassment. *Current Directions in Psychological Science, 9,* 187–192.

Keltner, D., & Bonanno, G. A. (1997). A study of laughter and dissociation: Distinct correlates of laughter and smiling during bereavement. *Journal of Personality and Social Psychology, 73,* 687–702.

Keltner, D., Young, R. C., Heerey, E. A., Oemig, C., & Monarch, N. D. (1998). Teasing in hierarchical and intimate relations. *Journal of Personality and Social Psychology, 75,* 1231–1247.

Kendler, K. S., Prescott, C. A., Myers, J., & Neale, M. C. (2003). The structure of genetic and environmental risk factors for common psychiatric and substance use disorders in men and women. *Archives of General Psychiatry, 60,* 929–937.

Kennedy, D. P., & Adolphs, R. (2010). Impaired fixation to eyes following amygdala damage arises from abnormal bottom-up attention. *Neuropsychologia, 48,* 3392–3398.

Kennedy, Q., Mather, M., & Carstensen, L. L. (2004). The role of motivation in the age-related positivity effect in autobiographical memory. *Psychological Science, 15,* 208–214.

Kennedy, S. H., Giacobbe, P., Rizvi, S., Placenza, F. M., Nishikawa, Y., Mayberg, H. S., & Lozano, A. M. (2011). Deep brain stimulation for treatment-resistant depression: Follow-up after 3 to 6 years. *American Journal of Psychiatry, 168,* 502–510.

Kenrick, D. T., & Funder, D. C. (1991). The person-situation debate: Do personality traits really exist? In V. J. Derlega, B. A. Winstead, & W. H. Jones (Eds.), *Personality: Contemporary theory and research* (pp. 149–174). Chicago, IL: Nelson Hall.

Kessler, R. C., Adler, L., Barkley, R., Biederman, J., Conners, C. K., Demler, O., et al. (2006). The prevalence and correlates of adult ADHD in the United States: Results from the national comorbidity survey replication. *American Journal of Psychiatry, 163,* 716–723.

Kessler, R. C., Berglund, P., Demler, O., Jin, R., Koretz, D., Merikangas, K., et al. (2003). The epidemiology of major depressive disorder: Results from the national comorbidity survey replication (NCS-R). *Journal of the American Medical Association, 289,* 3095–3105.

Kessler, R. C., Chiu, W. T., Demler, O., & Walters, E. E. (2005a). Prevalence, severity, and comorbidity of twelve-month DSM-IV disorders in the national comorbidity survey replication (NCS-R). *Archives of General Psychiatry, 62,* 617–627.

Kessler, R. C., Demler, O., Frank, R. G., Olfson, M., Pincus, M. A., Walters, E. E., et al. (2005b). Prevalence and treatment of mental disorders, 1990 to 2003. *New England Journal of Medicine, 352,* 2515–2523.

Kessler, R. C., McGonagle, K. A., Zhao, S., Nelson, C. B., Hugh, M., Eshleman, S., et al. (1994). Lifetime and 12-month prevalence of DSM-III-R psychiatric disorders in the United States: Results from the national comorbidity study. *Archives of General Psychiatry, 51,* 8–19.

Kessler, R. C., & Wang, P. S. (2008). The descriptive epidemiology of commonly occurring mental disorders in the United States. *Annual Review of Public Health, 29,* 115–129.

Keyes, D. (1981). *The minds of Billy Milligan.* New York, NY: Random House.

Keyes, K. M., Cerdá, M., Brady, J. E., Havens, J. R., & Galea, S. (2014). Understanding the rural–urban differences in nonmedical prescription opioid use and abuse in the United States. *American Journal of Public Health, 104,* e52–e59.

Keys, A., Brozek, J., Henschel, A. L., Mickelsen, O., & Taylor, H. L. (1950). *The biology of human starvation.* Minneapolis: University of Minnesota Press.

Kida, T. E. (2006). *Don't believe everything you think: The 6 basic mistakes we make in thinking.* Amherst, NY: Prometheus Books.

Kiecolt-Glaser, J. K., & Glaser, R. I. (1991). Stress and immune function in humans. In R. Ader, D. Felten, and N. Cohen (Eds.), *Psychoneuroimmunology II* (pp. 849–867). San Diego, CA: Academic Press.

Kiecolt-Glaser, J. K., Page, G. G., Marucha, P. T., MacCullum, R. C., & Glaser, R. (1998). Psychological influences on surgical recovery: Perspectives from psychoneuroimmunology. *American Psychologist, 53,* 1209–1218.

Kihlstrom, J. F. (2005). Dissociative disorder. *Annual Review of Clinical Psychology, 1,* 227–253.

Kihlstrom, J. F. (2016a). Unconscious mental life. In H. S. Friedman (Ed.), *Encyclopedia of mental health* (2nd ed., pp. 345–349). Waltham, MA: Academic Press.

Kihlstrom, J. F. (2016b). Hypnosis. In H. S. Friedman (Ed.), *Encyclopedia of mental health* (2nd ed., Vol. 2, pp. 361–365).Waltham, MA: Academic Press.

Kihlstrom, J. F., & Eich, E. (1994). Altering states of consciousness. In D. Druckman & R. A. Bjork (Eds.), *Learning, remembering, and believing: Enhancing performance* (pp. 207–248). Washington, DC: National Academy Press.

Kilbride, J. E., Robbins, M. C., & Kilbride, P. L. (1970). The comparative motor development of Bagandan, American white, and American black infants. *American Anthropologist, 72,* 1422–1428.

Kim, M. J., Solomon, K. M., Neta, M., Davis, F. C., Oler, J. A., Mazzulla, E. C., & Whalen, P. J. (2016). A face versus non-face context influences amygdala responses to masked fearful eye whites. *Social Cognitive and Affective Neuroscience, 11,* 1933–1941.

Kim, S. J., Lyoo, I. K., Hwang, J., Chung, A., Hoon Sung, Y., Kim, J., et al. (2006). Prefrontal grey-matter changes in short-term and long-term abstinent methamphetamine abusers. *International Journal of Neuropsychopharmacology, 9,* 221–228.

Kimura, D. (1999). *Sex and cognition.* Cambridge, MA: MIT Press.

Kirsch, I., Deacon, B. J., Huedo-Medina, T. B., Scoboria, A., Moore, T. J., & Johnson, B. T. (2008). Initial severity and antidepressant benefits: A metaanalysis of data submitted to the Food and Drug Administration. *PLoS Medicine, 5,* e45.

Kirsch, I., & Lynn, S. J. (1995). The altered state of hypnosis: Changes in the theoretical landscape. *American Psychologist, 10,* 846–858.

Klatsky, A. (2009). Alcohol and cardiovascular health. *Physiology and Behavior, 100,* 76–81.

Klauer, S. G., Guo, F., Simons-Morton, B. G., Ouimet, M. C., Lee, S. E., & Dingus, T. A. (2014). Distracted driving and risk of road crashes among novice and experienced drivers. *New England Journal of Medicine, 370,* 54–59.

Klein, A. M., van Niekerk, R., ten Brink, G., Rapee, R. M., Hudson, J. L., Bögels, S. M., et al. (2017). Biases in attention, interpretation, memory, and associations in children with varying levels of spider fear: Interrelations and prediction of behavior. *Journal of Behavior Therapy and Experimental Psychiatry, 54,* 285–291.

Klein, R. A., Ratliff, M., Vianello, R. B., Adams Jr., B., Bernstein, M. J., et al. (2014). Investigating variation in replicability: A "many labs" replication project. *Social Psychology, 45,* 142–152.

Klein, R. G., Mannuzza, S., Olazagasti, M. A. R., Roizen, E., Hutchison, J. A., Lashua, E. C., et al. (2012). Clinical and functional outcome of childhood attention-deficit/hyperactivity disorder 33 years later. *Archives of General Psychiatry, 69,* 1295–1303.

Klin, A., Jones, W., Schultz, R., & Volkmar, F. (2003). The enactive mind, or from actions to cognition: Lessons from autism. *Philosophical Transactions of the Royal Society of London, 358B,* 345–360.

Klingberg, T. (2010). Training and plasticity of working memory. *Trends in Cognitive Sciences, 14,* 317–324.

Klonoff, E. A. (2014). Introduction to the special section on discrimination. *Health Psychology, 33,* 1–2.

Klonsky, E. D., May, A. M., & Saffer, B. Y. (2016). Suicide, suicide attempts, and suicidal ideation. *Annual Review of Clinical Psychology, 12,* 307–330.

Klump, K. L., Culbert, K. M., & Sisk, C. L. (2017). Sex differences in binge eating: Gonadal hormone effects across development. *Annual Review of Clinical Psychology, 13,* 183–207.

Klump, K. L., & Culbert, K. M. (2007). Molecular genetic studies of eating disorders: Current status and future directions. *Current Directions in Psychological Science, 16,* 37–41.

Knight, R. (1953). Borderline states. *Bulletin of the Menninger Clinic, 17,* 1–12.

Knopp, J., Knowles, S., Bee, P., Lovell, K., & Bower, P. (2013). A systematic review of predictors and moderators of response to psychological therapies in OCD: Do we have enough empirical evidence to target treatment? *Clinical Psychology Review, 33,* 1067–1081.

Knowles, T. P., Vendruscolo, M., & Dobson, C. M. (2014). The amyloid state and its association with protein misfolding diseases. *Nature Reviews Molecular Cell Biology, 15,* 384–396.

Knox, S. S., Weidner, G., Adelman, A., Stoney, C. M., & Ellison, R. C. (2004). Hostility and physiological risk in the National Heart, Lung, and Blood Institute Family Heart Study. *Archives of Internal Medicine, 164,* 2442–2447.

Knutson, B., Fong, G. W., Adams, C. M., Varner, J. L., & Hommer, D. (2001). Dissociation of reward anticipation and outcome with event-related fMRI. *NeuroReport, 12,* 3683–3687.

Kobasa, S. C. (1979). Personality and resistance to illness. *American Journal of Community Psychology, 7,* 413–423.

Koch, J. L. (1891). *Die psychopathischen Minderwertigkeiten.* Ravensburg, Germany: Maier.

Kochanek, K. D., Arias, E., & Bastian, B. A. (2016). The effect of changes in selected age-specific causes of death on non-Hispanic white life expectancy between 2000 and 2014. NCHS data brief, no. 250, 1–8. Hyattsville, MD: National Center for Health Statistics.

Kochanek, K. D., Murphy, S. L., Xu, J., & Tejada-Vera, B. (2016). Deaths: Final data for 2014. *National vital statistics reports, 65* (Report No. 4), 1.

Kocsis, J. H., Rush, A. J., Markowitz, J. C., Borian, F. E., Dunner, D. L., Koran, L. M., et al. (2003). Continuation treatment of chronic depression: A comparison of nefazodone, cognitive behavioral analysis system of psychotherapy, and their combination. *Psychopharmacology Bulletin, 37,* 73–87.

Koelsch, S., Offermanns, K., & Franzke, P. (2010). Music in the treatment of affective disorders: A new method for music-therapeutic research. *Music Perception, 27,* 307–316.

Koh, K., Joiner, W. J., Wu, M. N., Yue, Z., Smith, C. J., & Sehgal, A. (2008). Identification of SLEEPLESS, a sleep-promoting factor. *Science, 321,* 372–376.

Kohlberg, L. (1984). *Essays on moral development: Vol. 2. The psychology of moral development.* San Francisco, CA: Harper & Row.

Köhler, W. (1925). *The mentality of apes.* New York, NY: Harcourt Brace.

Kohn, D. (2008, March 11). Cases without borders: Psychotherapy for all. *New York Times.* Retrieved from http://www.nytimes.com

Kolar, D. W., Funder, D. C., & Colvin, C. R. (1996). Comparing the accuracy of personality judgments by the self and knowledgeable others. *Journal of Personality, 64,* 311–337.

Kontsevich, L. L., & Tyler, C. W. (2004). What makes Mona Lisa smile? *Vision Research, 44,* 1493–1498.

Koob, G. F., & Le Moal, M. (2005). Plasticity of reward neurocircuitry and the "dark side" of drug addiction. *Nature Neuroscience, 8,* 1442–1444.

Koob, G. F., & Mason, B. J. (2016). Existing and future drugs for the treatment of the dark side of addiction. *Annual Review of Pharmacology and Toxicology, 56,* 299–322.

Koob, G. F., & Volkow, N. D. (2010). *Neurocircuitry of addiction. Neuropharmacology, 35,* 217–238.

Koole, S. L., Dijksterhuis, A., & van Knippenberg, A. (2001). What's in a name: Implicit self-esteem and the automatic self. *Journal of Personality and Social Psychology, 80,* 669–685.

Korn, M. L., Kotler, M., Molcho, A., Botsis, A. J., Grosz, D., Chen, C., et al. (1992). Suicide and violence associated with panic attacks. *Biological Psychiatry, 31,* 607–612.

Kosslyn, S. M., Thompson, W. L., Constantine-Ferrando, M. F., Alpert, N. M., & Spiegel, D. (2000). Hypnotic visual illusion alters color processing in the brain. *American Journal of Psychiatry, 157,* 1279–1284.

Kowalski, P., & Taylor, A. K. (2004). Ability and critical thinking as predictors of change in students' psychological misconceptions. *Journal of Instructional Psychology, 31,* 297.

Kozorovitskiy, Y., & Gould, E. (2004). Dominance hierarchy influences adult neurogenesis in the dentate gyrus. *Journal of Neuroscience, 24,* 6755–6759.

Kragel, P. A., Knodt, A. R., Hariri, A. R., & LaBar, K. S. (2016). Decoding spontaneous emotional states in the human brain. *PLoS Biology, 14,* e2000106.

Kragel, P. A., & LaBar, K. S. (2016). Decoding the nature of emotion in the brain. *Trends in Cognitive Sciences, 20,* 444–455.

Krakauer, N. Y., & Krakauer, J. C. (2012). A new body shape index predicts mortality hazard independently of body mass index. *PLoS ONE, 7,* e39504.

Krakauer, N. Y., & Krakauer, J. C. (2014). Dynamic association of mortality hazard with body shape. *PLoS ONE, 9,* e88793.

Kramer, M. S., Aboud, F., Mironova, E., Vanilovich, I., Platt, R. W., & Matush, L., et al. (2008). Breastfeeding and child cognitive development: New evidence from a large randomized trial. *Archives of General Psychiatry, 65,* 578–584.

Krantz, D. S., & McCeney, M. K. (2002). Effects of psychological and social factors on organic disease: A critical assessment of research on coronary heart disease. *Annual Review of Psychology, 53,* 341–369.

Krendl, A. C., Richeson, J. A., Kelley, W. M., & Heatherton, T. F. (2008). The negative consequences of threat: An fMRI investigation of the neural mechanisms underlying women's underperformance in math. *Psychological Science, 19,* 168–175.

Kringelbach, M. L., & Berridge, K. C. (2009). Toward a functional neuroanatomy of pleasure and happiness. *Trends in Cognitive Sciences, 13,* 479–487.

Kroes, M. C., Schiller, D., LeDoux, J. E., & Phelps, E. A. (2016). Translational approaches targeting reconsolidation. *Current Topics in Behavioral Neurosciences, 28,* 197–230.

Krueger, R. F. (1999). The structure of common mental disorders. *Archives of General Psychiatry, 56,* 921–926.

Krueger, R. F., & Markon, K. E. (2006). Understanding psychopathology: Melding behavior genetics, personality, and quantitative psychology to develop an empirically based model. *Current Directions in Psychological Science, 15,* 113–117.

Kruger, J., & Dunning, D. (1999). Unskilled and unaware of it: How difficulties in recognizing one's own incompetence lead to inflated self-assessments. *Journal of Personality and Social Psychology, 77,* 1121.

Kuchibhotla, K. V., Goldman, S. T., Lattarulo, C. R., Wu, H. Y., Hyman, B. T., & Bacskai, B. J. (2008). Aß plaques lead to aberrant regulation of calcium homeostasis in vivo resulting in structural and functional disruption of neuronal networks. *Neuron, 59,* 214–225.

Kuhl, P. K. (2000). A new view of language acquisition. *Proceedings of the National Academy of Sciences, 97,* 11850–11857.

Kuhl, P. K. (2004). Early language acquisition: Cracking the speech code. *Nature Reviews Neuroscience, 5,* 831–843.

Kuhl, P. K. (2006). Is speech learning "gated" by the social brain? *Developmental Science, 10,* 110–120.

Kuhl, P. K., Stevens, E., Hayashi, A., Deguchi, T., Kiritani, S., & Iverson, P. (2006). Infants show a facilitation effect for native language phonetic perception between 6 and 12 months. *Developmental Science, 9,* F13–F21.

Kuhl, P. K., Tsao, F. M., & Liu, H. M. (2003). Foreign-language experience in infancy: Effects of short-term exposure and social interaction on phonetic learning. *Proceedings of the National Academy of Sciences, 100,* 9096–9101.

Kuhn, C., Swartzwelder, S., & Wilson, W. (2003). *Buzzed: The straight facts about the most used and abused drugs from alcohol to ecstasy* (2nd ed.). New York, NY: Norton.

Kühn, S., & Gallinat, J. (2012). Quantitative meta-analysis on state and trait aspects of auditory verbal hallucinations in schizophrenia. *Schizophrenia Bulletin, 38,* 779–786.

Kulhara, P., & Chakrabarti, S. (2001). Culture and schizophrenia and other psychotic disorders. *Psychiatric Clinics of North America, 24,* 449–464.

Kuncel, N. R., Hezlett, S. A., & Ones, D. S. (2004). Academic performance, career potential, creativity, and job performance: Can one construct predict them all? *Journal of Personality and Social Psychology, 86,* 148–161.

Kunda, Z., & Spencer, S. J. (2003). When do stereotypes come to mind and when do they color judgment? A goal-based theoretical framework for stereotype activation and application. *Psychological Bulletin, 129,* 522–544.

Kuppens, P., Tuerlinckx, F., Russell, J. A., & Barrett, L. F. (2013). The relation between valence and arousal in subjective experience. *Psychological Bulletin, 139,* 917.

Kuyken, W., Warren, F. C., Taylor, R. S., Whalley, B., Crane, C., Bondolfi, G., et al. (2016). Efficacy of mindfulness-based cognitive therapy in prevention of depressive relapse: An individual patient data meta-analysis from randomized trials. *JAMA Psychiatry, 73,* 565–574.

Kyllonen, P. C., & Christal, R. E. (1990). Reasoning ability is (little more than) working-memory capacity?! *Intelligence, 14,* 389–433.

LaBar, K. S., & Cabeza, R. (2006). Cognitive neuroscience of emotional memory. *Nature Reviews Neuroscience, 7,* 54–64.

Ladenvall, P., Persson, C. U., Mandalenakis, Z., Wilhelmsen, L., Grimby, G., Svärdsudd, K., & Hansson, P. O. (2016). Low aerobic capacity in middle-aged men associated with increased mortality rates during 45 years of follow-up. *European Journal of Preventive Cardiology, 23,* 1557–1564.

LaFrance, M. L., & Banaji, M. (1992). Toward a reconsideration of the gender-emotion relationship. In M. Clarke (Ed.), *Review of personality and social psychology* (pp. 178–201). Beverly Hills, CA: Sage.

Lager, A., Bremberg, S., & Vågerö, D. (2009). The association of early IQ and education with mortality: 65 year longitudinal study in Malmö, Sweden. *British Medical Journal, 339,* b5282.

Lambert, T. J., Fernandez, S. M., & Frick, K. M. (2005). Different types of environmental enrichment have discrepant effects on spatial memory and synaptophysin levels in female mice. *Neurobiology of Learning and Memory, 83,* 206–216.

Lameira, A. R., Hardus, M. E., Mielke, A., Wich, S. A., & Shumaker, R. W. (2016). Vocal fold control beyond the species-specific repertoire in an orang-utan. *Scientific Reports, 6,* 30315.

Lamm, C., Decety, J., & Singer, T. (2011). Meta-analytic evidence for common and distinct neural networks associated with directly experienced pain and empathy for pain. *Neuroimage, 54,* 2492–2502.

Landa, R., Holman, K., & Garrett-Mayer, E. (2007). Social and communication development in toddlers with early and later diagnosis of autism spectrum disorders. *Archives of General Psychiatry, 64,* 853–864.

Langleben, D. D., & Moriarty, J. C. (2013). Using brain imaging for lie detection: Where science, law, and policy collide. *Psychology, Public Policy, and Law, 19,* 222.

Langlois, J. H., Kalakanis, L., Rubenstein, A. J., Larson, A., Hallam, M., & Smoot, M. (2000). Maxims or myths of beauty? A meta-analytic and theoretical review. *Psychological Bulletin, 126,* 390–423.

Langlois, J. H., & Roggman, L. A. (1990). Attractive faces are only average. *Psychological Science, 1,* 115–121.

Larrick, R. P., Timmerman, T. A., Carton, A. M., & Abrevaya, J. (2011). Temper, temperature, and temptation: Heat-related retaliation in baseball. *Psychological Science, 22,* 423–428.

Larsen, J. T., McGraw, A. P., & Cacioppo, J. T. (2001). Can people feel happy and sad at the same time? *Journal of Personality and Social Psychology, 81,* 684–696.

Larson, E. B., Wang, L., Bowen, J. D., McCormick, W. C., Teri, L., Crane, P., & Kukull, W. (2006). Exercise is associated with reduced risk for incident dementia among persons 65 years of age and older. *Annals of Internal Medicine, 144,* 73–81.

Larsson, H., Chang, Z., D'Onofrio, B. M., & Lichtenstein, P. (2014). The heritability of clinically diagnosed attention deficit hyperactivity disorder across the lifespan. *Psychological Medicine, 44,* 2223–2229.

Lashley, K. S. (1950). In search of the engram. *Symposia of the Society for Experimental Biology, 4,* 454–482.

Latané, B., & Darley, J. M. (1968). Group inhibition of bystander intervention in emergencies. *Journal of Personality and Social Psychology, 10,* 215–221.

Latané, B., Williams, K., & Harkins, S. G. (1979). Many hands make light the work: The causes and consequences of social loafing. *Journal of Personality and Social Psychology, 37,* 822–832.

Laureys, S., Celesia, G. G., Cohadon, F., Lavrijsen, J., León-Carrión, J., Sannita, W. G., et al. (2010). Unresponsive wakefulness syndrome: A new name for the vegetative state or apallic syndrome. *BMC Medicine, 8,* 68.

Lautenschlager, N. T., Cox, K. L., Flicker, L., Foster, J. K., van Bockxmeer, F. M., Xiao, J., et al. (2008). Effect of physical exercise on cognitive function in older adults at risk for Alzheimer disease. *Journal of the American Medical Association, 300,* 1027–1037.

Lavie, C. J., Arena, R., Swift, D. L., Johannsen, N. M., Sui, X., Lee, D. C., et al. (2015). Exercise and the cardiovascular system. *Circulation Research, 117,* 207–219.

Lawrence, E. M., Rogers, R. G., & Wadsworth, T. (2015). Happiness and longevity in the United States. *Social Science & Medicine, 145,* 115–119.

Lawson, G. M., Duda, J. T., Avants, B. B., Wu, J., & Farah, M. J. (2013). Associations between children's socioeconomic status and prefrontal cortical thickness. *Developmental Science, 16,* 641–652.

Layton, M. (1995, May/June). Emerging from the shadows. *Family Therapy Networker,* 35–41.

Lazarus, R. S. (1993). From psychological stress to the emotions: A history of changing outlooks. *Annual Review of Psychology, 44,* 1–21.

Lazerus, T., Ingbretsen, Z., Stolier, R. M., Freeman, J. B., & Cikara, M. (2017). Positivity bias in judging in-group members' emotional expressions. *Emotion, 16,* 1117–1125.

Le, K., Donnellan, M. B., & Conger, R. (2014). Personality development at work: Workplace conditions, personality changes, and the corresponsive principle. *Journal of Personality, 82,* 44–56.

Leach, J., & Patall, E. A. (2013). Maximizing and counterfactual thinking in academic major decision making. *Journal of Career Assessment, 21,* 414–429.

Leary, M. R. (2004). The function of self-esteem in terror management theory and sociometer theory: Comment on Pyszczynski et al. *Psychological Bulletin, 130,* 478–482.

Leary, M. R., & MacDonald, G. (2003). Individual differences in self-esteem: A review and theoretical integration. In M. R. Leary & J. P. Tangney (Eds.), *Handbook of self and identity* (pp. 401–418). New York, NY: Guilford Press.

Leary, M. R., Tambor, E. S., Terdal, S. K., & Downs, D. L. (1995). Self-esteem as an interpersonal monitor: The sociometer hypothesis. *Journal of Personality and Social Psychology, 68,* 518–530.

Leckman, J. F., Elliott, G. R., Bromet, E. J., Campbell, M., Cicchetti, D., Cohen, D. J., et al. (1995). Report card on the national plan for research on child and adolescent mental disorders: The midway point. *Archives of General Psychiatry, 34,* 715–723.

LeDoux, J. E. (2000). Emotion circuits in the brain. *Annual Review of Neuroscience, 23,* 155–184.

LeDoux, J. E. (2002). *Synaptic self.* New York, NY: Viking.

LeDoux, J. E. (2007). The amygdala. *Current Biology, 17,* R868–R874.

LeDoux, J. E. (2014). Coming to terms with fear. *Proceedings of the National Academy of Sciences, 111,* 2871–2878.

LeDoux, J. E. (2015a). *Anxious: Using the brain to understand and treat fear and anxiety.* New York, NY: Penguin.

LeDoux, J. E. (2015b). Feelings: What are they & how does the brain make them? *Daedalus, 144,* 96–111.

LeDoux, J. E., & Pine, D. S. (2016). Using neuroscience to help understand fear and anxiety: A two-system framework. *American Journal of Psychiatry, 173,* 1083–1093.

Lee, P. A. (1980). Normal ages of pubertal events among American males and females. *Journal of Adolescent Health Care, 1,* 26–29.

Lefevre, C. E., Lewis, G. J., Perrett, D. I., & Penke, L. (2013). Telling facial metrics: Facial width is associated with testosterone levels in men. *Evolution and Human Behavior, 34,* 273–279.

Leff, J., Sartorius, N., Jablensky, A., Korten, A., & Ernberg, G. (1992). The international pilot study of schizophrenia: Five-year follow-up findings. *Psychological Medicine, 22,* 131–145.

Lehnart, J., Neyer, F. J., & Eccles, J. (2010). Long-term effects of social investment: The case of partnering in young adulthood. *Journal of Personality, 78,* 639–670.

Leichsenring, F., Rabung, S., & Leibing, E. (2004). The efficacy of short-term psychodynamic psychotherapy in specific psychiatric disorders: A meta-analysis. *Archives of General Psychiatry, 61,* 1208–1216.

Leigh, B. C., & Schafer, J. C. (1993). Heavy drinking occasions and the occurrence of sexual activity. *Psychology of Addictive Behaviors, 7,* 197–200.

Leigh, B. C., & Stacy, A. W. (2004). Alcohol expectancies and drinking in different age groups. *Addiction, 99,* 215–217.

Lench, H. C., Flores, S. A., & Bench, S. W. (2011). Discrete emotions predict changes in cognition, judgment, experience, behavior, and physiology: A meta-analysis of experimental emotion elicitations. *Psychological Bulletin, 137,* 834–855.

Lenzenweger, M. F., Lane, M. C., Loranger, A. W., & Kessler, R. C. (2007). DSM-IV personality disorders in the national comorbidity survey replication. *Biological Psychiatry, 62,* 553–564.

Lepper, M. R., Greene, D., & Nisbett, R. E. (1973). Undermining children's intrinsic interest with extrinsic reward: A test of the "overjustification" hypothesis. *Journal of Personality and Social Psychology, 28,* 129–137.

Lerner, J. S., Li, Y., Valdesolo, P., & Kassam, K. S. (2015). Emotion and decision making. *Annual Review of Psychology, 66,* 799–823.

Leucht, S., Corves, C., Arbter, D., Engel, R. R., Li, C., & Davis, J. M. (2009). Second-generation versus first-generation antipsychotic drugs for schizophrenia: A meta-analysis. *The Lancet, 373,* 31–41.

LeVay, S. (1991). A difference in hypothalamic structure between heterosexual and homosexual men. *Science, 253,* 1034–1037.

Levenson, R. W. (2003). Blood, sweat, and fears. *Annals of the New York Academy of Sciences, 1000,* 348–366.

Levenson, R. W. (2014). The autonomic nervous system and emotion. *Emotion Review, 6,* 100–112.

Levenstein, S., Ackerman, S., Kiecolt-Glaser, J. K., & Dubois, A. (1999). Stress and peptic ulcer disease. *Journal of the American Medical Association, 281,* 10–11.

Leventhal, H., & Cleary, P. D. (1980). The smoking problem: A review of research and theory in behavioral risk modification. *Psychological Bulletin, 88,* 370–405.

Levey, S., Levey, T., & Fligor, B. J. (2011). Noise exposure estimates of urban MP3 player users. *Journal of Speech, Language, and Hearing Research, 54,* 263–277.

Levinson, D. F. (2006). The genetics of depression: A review. *Biological Psychiatry, 60,* 84–92.

Levinson, S. C. (2003). *Space in language and cognition: Explorations in cognitive diversity.* Cambridge, MA: Cambridge University Press.

Levitin, D. J. (2006). *This is your brain on music: The science of a human obsession.* New York, NY: Dutton/Penguin.

Levitin, D. J., & Menon, V. (2003). Musical structure in "language" areas of the brain: A possible role for Brodmann Area 47 in temporal coherence. *NeuroImage, 20,* 2142–2152.

Levy, D., Ronemus, M., Yamrom, B., Lee, Y., Leotta, A., Kendall, J., et al. (2011). Rare de novo and transmitted copy-number variation in autistic spectrum disorders. *Neuron, 70,* 886–897.

Lewinsohn, P. M., Allen, N. B., Seeley, J. R., & Gotlib, I. H. (1999). First onset versus recurrence of depression: Differential processes of psychosocial risk. *Journal of Abnormal Psychology, 108,* 483–489.

Lewinsohn, P. M., Rodhe, P. D., Seeley, J. R., & Hops, H. (1991). Comorbidity of unipolar depression: I. Major depression with dysthymia. *Journal of Abnormal Psychology, 98,* 107–116.

Lewontin, R. C. (1976). Race and intelligence. In N. J. Block & G. Dworkin (Eds.), *The IQ controversy.* New York, NY: Pantheon Books.

Li, N. P., Bailey, J. M., Kenrick, D. T., & Linsenmeier, J. A. W. (2002). The necessities and luxuries of mate preferences: Testing the tradeoffs. *Journal of Personality and Social Psychology, 82,* 947–955.

Lichtenstein, S., Slovic, P., Fischhoff, B., Layman, M., & Combs, B. (1978). Judged frequency of lethal events. *Journal of Experimental Psychology: Human Learning and Memory, 4,* 551.

Lick, D. J., Cortland, C. I., & Johnson, K. L. (2016). The pupils are the windows to sexuality: Pupil dilation as a visual cue to others' sexual interest. *Evolution and Human Behavior, 37,* 117–124.

Lieb, K., Zanarini, M. C., Schmahl, C., Linehan, M. M., & Bohus, M. (2004). Borderline personality disorder. *Lancet, 364,* 453–461.

Lieberman, M. D. (2000). Intuition: A social cognitive neuroscience approach. *Psychological Bulletin, 126,* 109–137.

Lieberman, M. D., Ochsner, K. N., Gilbert, D. T., & Schacter, D. L. (2001). Do amnesiacs exhibit cognitive dissonance reduction? The role of explicit memory and attention in attitude change. *Psychological Science, 121,* 135–140.

Lilienfeld, S. O. (2007). Psychological treatments that cause harm. *Perspectives on Psychological Science, 2,* 53–67.

Lilienfeld, S. O., & Treadway, M. T. (2016). Clashing diagnostic approaches: DSM-ICD versus RDoC. *Annual Review of Clinical Psychology, 12,* 435–463.

Lilliengren, P., Johansson, R., Lindqvist, K., Mechler, J., & Andersson, G. (2016). Efficacy of experiential dynamic therapy for psychiatric conditions: A meta-analysis of randomized controlled trials. *Psychotherapy, 53,* 90–104.

Lin, J. Y., Arthurs, J., & Reilly, S. (2017). Conditioned taste aversions: From poisons to pain to drugs of abuse. *Psychonomic Bulletin & Review, 24,* 335–351.

Lindell, A. K. (2006). In your right mind: Right hemisphere contributions to language processing and production. *Neuropsychology Review, 16,* 131–148.

Lindemann, B. (2001). Receptors and transduction in taste. *Nature, 413,* 219–225.

Linehan, M. M. (1987). Dialectical behavior therapy for borderline personality disorder: Theory and method. *Bulletin of the Menninger Clinic, 51,* 261–276.

Linehan, M. M., Armstrong, H. E., Suarez, A., Allmon, D., & Heard, H. (1991). Cognitive behavioral treatment of chronically parasuicidal borderline patients. *Archives of General Psychiatry, 48,* 1060–1064.

Linehan, M. M., Heard, H., & Armstrong, H. E. (1993). Naturalistic follow-up of a behavioral treatment for chronically parasuicidal borderline patients. *Archives of General Psychiatry, 50,* 971–974.

Lissek, S., Kaczkurkin, A. N., Rabin, S., Geraci, M., Pine, D. S., & Grillon, C. (2014). Generalized anxiety disorder is associated with overgeneralization of classically conditioned fear. *Biological Psychiatry, 75,* 909–915.

Liu, B., Floud, S., Pirie, K., Green, J., Peto, R., Beral, V., et al. (2016). Does happiness itself directly affect mortality? The prospective UK Million Women Study. *The Lancet, 387,* 874–881.

Liu, H., & Reczek, C. (2012). Cohabitation and U.S. adult mortality: An examination by gender and race. *Journal of Marriage and Family, 74,* 794–811.

Liu, J., Raine, A., Venables, P. H., & Mednick, S. A. (2004). Malnutrition at age 3 years and externalizing behavior problems at ages 8, 11, and 17 years. *American Journal of Psychiatry, 161,* 2005–2013.

Lledo, P. M., Gheusi, G., & Vincent, J. D. (2005). Information processing in the mammalian olfactory system. *Physiological Review, 85,* 281–317.

Lloyd-Fox, S., Blasi, A., Everdell, N., Elwell, C. E., & Johnson, M. H. (2011). Selective cortical mapping of biological motion processing in young infants. *Journal of Cognitive Neuroscience, 23,* 2521–2532.

Locke, E. A., & Latham, G. P. (1990). *A theory of goal setting and task performance.* Englewood Cliffs, NJ: Prentice-Hall.

Loehlin, J. C., & Nichols, R. C. (1976). *Heredity, environment, and personality: A study of 850 sets of twins.* Austin: University of Texas Press.

Loewenstein, G. F., Weber, E. U., Hsee, C. K., & Welch, N. (2001). Risk as feelings. *Psychological Bulletin, 127,* 267–286.

Loftus, E. F. (1993). The reality of repressed memories. *American Psychologist, 48,* 518–537.

Loftus, E. F., Miller, D. G., & Burns, H. J. (1978). Semantic integration of verbal information into a visual memory. *Journal of Experimental Psychology: Human Learning and Memory, 4,* 19–31.

Loftus, E. F., & Palmer, J. C. (1974). Reconstruction of automobile destruction: An example of the interaction between language and memory. *Journal of Learning and Verbal Behavior, 13,* 585–589.

Logan, J. M., Sanders, A. L., Snyder, A. Z., Morris, J. C., & Buckner, R. L. (2002). Under-recruitment and nonselective recruitment: Dissociable neural mechanisms associated with aging. *Neuron, 33,* 1–20.

Loggia, M. L., Mogil, J. S., & Bushnell, M. C. (2008). Experimentally induced mood changes preferentially affect pain unpleasantness. *Journal of Pain, 9,* 784–791.

Lombardo, M. V., Ashwin, E., Auyeung, B., Chakrabarti, B., Taylor, K., Hackett, G., Bullmore, E. T., & Baron-Cohen, S. (2012). Fetal testosterone influences sexually dimorphic gray matter in the human brain. *Journal of Neuroscience, 32,* 674–680.

Loprinzi, P. D., Branscum, A., Hanks, J., & Smit, E. (2016). Healthy lifestyle characteristics and their joint association with cardiovascular disease biomarkers in US adults. *Mayo Clinic Proceedings, 91,* 432–442.

Lorenz, K. (1935). Der kumpan in der umwelt des vogels. *Journal of Ornithology, 83,* 289–413.

Lovaas, O. I. (1987). Behavioral treatment and normal educational and intellectual functioning in young autistic children. *Journal of Consulting and Clinical Psychology, 55,* 3–9.

Lovett, I. (2013, June 20). After 37 years of trying to change people's sexual orientation, group is to disband. *New York Times,* p. A12.

Lowe, P. (2001, October 12). No prison for Candace's adoptive mom. *Denver Rocky Mountain News,* p. 26A.

Luchins, A. S. (1942). Mechanization in problem solving. *Psychological Monographs, 54,* Whole No. 248.

Luria, A. R. (1968). *The mind of a mnemonist.* New York, NY: Avon.

Lykken, D. T. (1957). A study of anxiety in the sociopathic personality. *Journal of Abnormal Social Psychology, 55,* 6–10.

Lykken, D. T. (1995). *The antisocial personalities.* Hillsdale, NJ: Erlbaum.

Lykken, D. T., McGue, M., Tellegen, A., & Bouchard, T. J., Jr. (1992). Emergenesis: Genetic traits that may not run in families. *American Psychologist, 47,* 1565–1577.

Lynn, R., & Eysenck, H. J. (1961). Tolerance for pain, extraversion and neuroticism. *Perceptual and Motor Skills, 12,* 161–162.

Lyubomirsky, S., King, L., & Diener, E. (2005). The benefits of frequent positive affect: Does happiness lead to success? *Psychological Bulletin, 131,* 803–855.

Lyubomirsky, S., & Nolen-Hoeksema, S. (1995). Effects of self-focused rumination on negative thinking and interpersonal problem solving. *Journal of Personality and Social Psychology, 69,* 176–190.

Maccoby, E. E., & Jacklin, C. N. (1974). *The psychology of sex differences.* Stanford, CA: Stanford University Press.

MacCormack, J. K., & Lindquist, K. A. (2017). Bodily contributions to emotion: Schachter's legacy for a psychological constructionist view on emotion. *Emotion Review, 9,* 36–45.

MacDonald, G., & Leary, M. R. (2005). Why does social exclusion hurt? The relationship between social and physical pain. *Psychological Bulletin, 131,* 202–223.

MacKay, D. G. (1973). Aspects of a theory of comprehension, memory and attention. *Quarterly Journal of Experimental Psychology, 25,* 22–40.

MacLean, P. D. (1952). Some psychiatric implications of physiological studies on frontotemporal portion of limbic system (visceral brain). *Electroencephalography and Clinical Neurophysiology, 4,* 407–418.

MacLeod, C., & Mathews, A. (2012). Cognitive bias modification approaches to anxiety. *Annual Review of Clinical Psychology, 8,* 189–217.

Macrae, C. N., Bodenhausen, G. V., & Calvini, G. (1999). Contexts of cryptomnesia: May the source be with you. *Social Cognition, 17,* 273–297.

Macrae, C. N., Milne, A. B., & Bodenhausen, G. V. (1994). Stereotypes as energy-saving devices: A peek inside the cognitive toolbox. *Journal of Personality and Social Psychology, 66,* 37–47.

Macrae, C. N., Moran, J. M., Heatherton, T. F., Banfield, J. F., & Kelley, W. M. (2004). Medial prefrontal activity predicts memory for self. *Cerebral Cortex, 14,* 647–654.

Maddi, S. (2013). *Hardiness: Turning stressful circumstances into resilient growth.* Dordrecht: Springer Netherlands.

Madsen, H. B., & Kim, J. H. (2016). Ontogeny of memory: An update on 40 years of work on infantile amnesia. *Behavioural Brain Research, 298,* 4–14.

Maes, M., Van Gastel, A., Delmeire, L., Kenis, G., Bosmans, E., & Song, C. (2002). Platelet alpha2-adrenoceptor density in humans: Relationships to stress-induced anxiety, psychasthenic constitution, gender and stress-induced changes in the inflammatory response system. *Psychological Medicine, 32,* 919–928.

Magnier, M. (2008, May 26). China quake survivors show signs of posttraumatic stress. *Los Angeles Times,* p. 1.

Maguire, E. A., Spiers, H. J., Good, C. D., Hartley, T., Frackowiak, R. S. J., & Burgess, N. (2003). Navigation expertise and the human hippocampus: A structural brain imaging analysis. *Hippocampus, 13,* 250–259.

Maher, B. A., & Maher, W. R. (1994). Personality and psychopathology: A historical perspective. *Journal of Abnormal Psychology, 103,* 72–77.

Mahlios, J., De la Herrán-Arita, A. K., & Mignot, E. (2013). The autoimmune basis of narcolepsy. *Current Opinion in Neurobiology, 23,* 767–773.

Maier, N. R. F. (1931). Reasoning in humans, II: The solution of a problem and its appearance in consciousness. *Journal of Comparative Psychology, 12,* 181–194.

Malhotra, D., McCarthy, S., Michaelson, J. J., Vacic, V., Burdick, K. E., Yoon, S., et al. (2011). High frequencies of de novo CNVs in bipolar disorder and schizophrenia. *Neuron, 72,* 951–963.

Malle, B. F. (2006). The actor-observer asymmetry in causal attribution: A (surprising) meta-analysis. *Psychological Bulletin, 132,* 895–919.

Malone, D. A., Jr., Dougherty, D. D., Rezai, A. R., Carpenter, L. L., Friehs, G. M., Eskandar, E. N., et al. (2009). Deep brain stimulation of the ventral capsule/ventral striatum for treatment-resistant depression. *Biological Psychiatry, 65,* 267–275.

Mandel, H. (2009). *Here's the deal: Don't touch me.* New York, NY: Bantam.

Maner, J. K., Luce, C. L., Neuberg, S. L., Cialdini, R. B., Brown, S., & Sagarin, B. J. (2002). The effects of perspective taking on motivations for helping: Still no evidence for altruism. *Personality and Social Psychology Bulletin, 28,* 1601–1610.

Manning, R., Levine, M., & Collins, A. (2007). The Kitty Genovese murder and the social psychology of helping: The parable of the 38 witnesses. *American Psychologist, 62,* 555–562.

Manns, J. R., & Bass, D. I. (2016). The amygdala and prioritization of declarative memories. *Current Directions in Psychological Science, 25,* 261–265.

Mannuzza, S., Klein, R. G., Truong, N. L., Moulton, J. L., III, Roizen, E. R., Howell, K. H., et al. (2008). Age of methylphenidate treatment initiation in children with ADHD and later substance abuse: Prospective follow-up into adulthood. *American Journal of Psychiatry, 165,* 604–609.

Manrique-Garcia, E., Zammit, S., Dalman, C., Hemmingsson, T., Andreasson, S., & Allebeck, P. (2012). Cannabis, schizophrenia and other non-affective psychoses: 35 years of follow-up of a population-based cohort. *Psychological Medicine, 42,* 1321–1328.

Mar, R. A. (2011). The neural bases of social cognition and story comprehension. *Annual Review of Psychology, 62,* 103–134.

March, J. S., Silva, S., Petrycki, S., Curry, J., Wells, K., Fairbank, J., et al. (2007). The Treatment for Adolescents with Depression Study (TADS): Long-term effectiveness and safety outcomes. *Archives of General Psychiatry, 64,* 1132–1143.

Marcus, G. F. (1996). Why do children say "breaked"? *Current Directions in Psychological Science, 5,* 81–85.

Marcus, G. F. (2004). *The birth of the mind: How a tiny number of genes creates the complexities of human thought.* New York, NY: Basic Books.

Marder, S. R. (2014). Perspective: Retreat from the radical. *Nature, 508,* S18.

Marin, M. M., Rapisardi, G., & Tani, F. (2015). Two-day-old newborn infants recognise their mother by her axillary odour. *Acta Paediatrica, 104,* 237–240.

Marin, M. F., Song, H., VanElzakker, M. B., Staples-Bradley, L. K., Linnman, C., Pace-Schott, E. F., et al. (2016). Association of resting metabolism in the fear neural network with extinction recall activations and clinical measures in trauma-exposed individuals. *American Journal of Psychiatry, 173,* 930–938.

Markon, J. (2001, October 8). Elderly judges handle 20 percent of U. S. caseload. *The Wall Street Journal,* p. A15.

Markowitz, J. C., & Weissman, M. M. (1995). Interpersonal psychotherapy. In E. E. Beckham & W. R. Leber (Eds.), *Handbook of depression* (2nd ed., pp. 376–390). New York, NY: Guilford Press.

Markus, H. R. (1977). Self-schemata and processing information about the self. *Journal of Personality and Social Psychology, 35,* 63–78.

Markus, H. R., & Kitayama, S. (1991). Culture and the self: Implications for cognition, emotion, and motivation. *Psychological Review, 98,* 224–253.

Marlatt, G. A. (1999). Alcohol, the magic elixir? In S. Peele & M. Grant (Eds.), *Alcohol and pleasure: A health perspective* (pp. 233–248). Philadelphia, PA: Brunner/Mazel.

Marsella, A. J., & Yamada, A. M. (2007). Culture and psychopathology: Foundations, issues, directions. In S. Kitayama & D. Cohen (Eds.), *Handbook of cultural psychology* (pp. 797–819). New York, NY: Guilford Press.

Marsh, A. A., Finger, E. C., Fowler, K. A., Adalio, C. J., Jurkowitz, I. T., Schechter, J. C., et al. (2013). Empathic responsiveness in amygdala and anterior cingulate cortex in youths with psychopathic traits. *Journal of Child Psychology and Psychiatry, 54,* 900–910.

Marsh, A. A., Finger, E. C., Mitchell, D. G., Reid, M. E., Sims, C., Kosson, D. S., et al. (2008). Reduced amygdala response to fearful expressions in children and adolescents with callous-unemotional traits and disruptive behavior disorders. *American Journal of Psychiatry, 165,* 712–720.

Marsh, A. A., Finger, E. C., Schechter, J. C., Jurkowitz, I. T. N., Reid, M. E., & Blair, R. J. R. (2011). Adolescents with psychopathic traits report reductions in physiological responses to fear. *Journal of Child Psychology & Psychiatry, 52,* 834–841.

Marshall, B., & Warren, J. R. (1984). Unidentified curved bacilli in the stomach of patients with gastritis and peptic ulceration. *The Lancet, 323,* 1311–1315.

Marshall, G. D. J., Agarwal, S. K., Lloyd, C., Cohen, L., Henninger, E. M., & Morris, G. J. (1998). Cytokine dysregulation associated with exam stress in healthy medical students. *Brain, Behavior, and Immunity, 12,* 297–307.

Marsland, A. L., Pressman, S., & Cohen, S. (2007). Positive affect and immune function. *Psychoneuroimmunology, 2,* 761–779.

Martin, A. (2007). The representation of object concepts in the brain. *Annual Review of Psychology, 58,* 25–45.

Martin, A., Wiggs, C. L., Ungerleider, L. G., & Haxby, J. V. (1996). Neural correlates of category-specific knowledge. *Nature, 379,* 649–652.

Martin, G. B., & Clark, R. D. (1982). Distress crying in neonates: Species and peer specificity. *Developmental Psychology, 18,* 3–9.

Martin, L. A., Ashwood, P., Braunschweig, D., Cabanlit, M., Van de Water, J., & Amaral, D. G. (2008). Stereotypes and hyperactivity in rhesus monkeys exposed to IgG from mothers of children with autism. *Brain, Behavior, and Immunity, 22,* 804–805.

Maruta, T., Colligan, R. C., Malinchoc, M., & Offord, K. P. (2002). Optimism-pessimism assessed in the 1960s and self-reported health status 30 years later. *Mayo Clinic Proceedings, 77,* 748–753.

Maslow, A. (1968). *Toward a psychology of being.* New York, NY: Van Nostrand.

Masters, W. H., & Johnson, V. E. (1966). *Human sexual response.* Boston, MA: Little, Brown.

Mataix-Cols, D., de la Cruz, L. F., Monzani, B., Rosenfield, D., Andersson, E., Pérez-Vigil, A., et al. (2017). D-Cycloserine augmentation of exposure-based cognitive behavior therapy for anxiety, obsessive-compulsive, and posttraumatic stress disorders: A systematic review and meta-analysis of individual participant data. *JAMA Psychiatry, 74,* 501–510.

Matarazzo, J. D., Carmody, T. P., & Jacobs, L. D. (1980). Test-retest reliability and stability of the WAIS: A literature review with implications for clinical practice. *Journal of Clinical and Experimental Neuropsychology, 2,* 89–105.

Mather, M., & Carstensen, L. L. (2003). Aging and attentional biases for emotional faces. *Psychological Science, 14,* 409–415.

Mathews, A. (2012). Effects of modifying the interpretation of emotional ambiguity. *Journal of Cognitive Psychology, 24,* 92–105.

Matsui, M., Tanaka, C., Niu, L., Noguchi, K., Bilker, W. B., Wierzbicki, M., et al. (2016). Age-related volumetric changes of prefrontal gray and white matter from healthy infancy to adulthood. *International Journal of Clinical and Experimental Neurology, 4,* 1–8.

Mattern, J. L., & Neighbors, C. (2004). Social norms campaigns: Examining the relationship between changes in perceived norms and changes in drinking levels. *Journal of Studies on Alcohol and Drugs, 65,* 489–493.

May, A. (2011). Experience-dependent structural plasticity in the adult human brain. *Trends in Cognitive Sciences, 15,* 475–482.

May, P. A., Baete, A., Russo, J., Elliott, A. J., Blankenship, J., Kalberg, W. O., et al. (2014). Prevalence and characteristics of fetal alcohol spectrum disorders. *Pediatrics, 134,* 855–866.

Mayberg, H. S., Lozano, A. M., Voon, V., McNeely, H. E., Seminowicz, D., Hamani, C., et al. (2005). Deep brain stimulation for treatment-resistant depression. *Neuron, 45,* 651–660.

Mayer, J. (1953). Glucostatic mechanism of regulation of food intake. *New England Journal of Medicine, 249,* 13–16.

Mazur, A., & Booth, A. (1998). Testosterone and dominance in men. *Behavioral and Brain Science, 21,* 353–397.

Mazza, S., Gerbier, E., Gustin, M. P., Kasikci, Z., Koenig, O., Toppino, T. C., & Magnin, M. (2016). Relearn faster and retain longer along with practice, sleep makes perfect. *Psychological Science, 27,* 1321–1330.

McAdams, D. P. (1999). Personal narratives and the life story. In L. A. Pervin & O. P. John (Eds.), *Handbook of personality: Theory and research* (2nd ed., pp. 478–500). New York, NY: Guilford Press.

McAdams, D. P. (2001). The psychology of life stories. *Review of General Psychology, 5,* 100–122.

McCabe, D. P., Roediger, H. L., McDaniel, M. A., Balota, D. A., & Hambrick, D. Z. (2010). The relationship between working memory capacity and executive functioning: Evidence for a common executive attention construct. *Neuropsychology, 24,* 222–243.

McCabe, K. O., & Fleeson, W. (2016). Are traits useful? Explaining trait manifestations as tools in the pursuit of goals. *Journal of Personality and Social Psychology, 110,* 287–301.

McCabe, S. E., West, B. T., Teter, C. J., & Boyd, C. J. (2014). Trends in medical use, diversion, and nonmedical use of prescription medications among college students from 2003 to 2013: Connecting the dots. *Addictive Behaviors, 7,* 1176–1182.

McCann, F. F., & Marek, E. A. (2016). Achieving diversity in STEM: The role of drawing-based instruments. *Creative Education, 7*, 2293.

McCarthy, G., Puce, A., Gore, J. C., & Allison, T. (1997). Face-specific processing in the human fusiform gyrus. *Journal of Cognitive Neuroscience, 9*, 605–610.

McCarthy, S. E., Gillis, J., Kramer, M., Lihm, J., Yoon, S., Berstein, Y., et al. (2014). De novo mutations in schizophrenia implicate chromatin remodeling and support a genetic overlap with autism and intellectual disability. *Molecular Psychiatry, 19*, 652–658.

McClelland, D. C. (1987). *Human motivation.* New York, NY: Cambridge University Press.

McClelland, D. C., Koestner, R., & Weinberger, J. (1989). How do self-attributed and implicit motives differ? *Psychological Review, 96*, 690–702.

McConahay, J. B. (1986). Modern racism, ambivalence, and the Modern Racism Scale. In J. F. Dovidio & S. L. Gaertner (Eds.), *Prejudice, discrimination, and racism* (pp. 91–125). San Diego, CA: Academic Press.

McCrae, R. R., & Costa, P. T., Jr. (1990). *Personality in adulthood.* New York, NY: Guilford Press.

McCrae, R. R., & Costa, P. T., Jr. (1999). A five-factor theory of personality. In L. A. Pervin & O. P. John (Eds.), *Handbook of personality: Theory and research* (2nd ed., pp. 139–153). New York, NY: Guilford Press.

McCrae, R. R., Costa, P. T., Jr., Ostendorf, F., Angleitner, A., Hrebickova, M., Avia, M. D., et al. (2000). Nature over nurture: Temperament, personality, and life span development. *Journal of Personality and Social Psychology, 78*, 173–186.

McEwen, B. S. (2008). Central effects of stress hormones in health and disease: Understanding the protective and damaging effects of stress and stress mediators. *European Journal of Pharmacology, 583*, 174–185.

McEwen, B. S. (2016). Stress-induced remodeling of hippocampal CA3 pyramidal neurons. *Brain Research, 1645*, 50–54.

McEwen, B. S., & Gianaros, P. J. (2011). Stress- and allostatis-induced brain plasticity. *Annual Review of Medicine, 62*, 431–435.

McGaugh, J. L. (2015). Consolidating memories. *Annual Review of Psychology, 66*, 1–24.

McGlashan, T. H. (1988). A selective review of recent North American long-term follow-up studies of schizophrenia. *Schizophrenia Bulletin, 14*, 515–542.

McGough, J. J., & Barkley, R. A. (2004). Diagnostic controversies in adult attention deficit hyperactivity disorder. *American Journal of Psychiatry, 161*, 1948–1956.

McGrath, R. W. (2010). Prescriptive authority for psychologists. *Annual Review of Clinical Psychology, 6*, 21–47.

McGregor, H. R., Cashaback, J. G., & Gribble, P. L. (2016). Functional plasticity in somatosensory cortex supports motor learning by observing. *Current Biology, 26*, 921–927.

McGue, M., Bacon, S., & Lykken, D. T. (1993). Personality stability and change in early adulthood: A behavioral genetic analysis. *Developmental Psychology, 29*, 96–109.

McGuire, J. F., Wu, M. S., Piacentini, J., McCracken, J. T., & Storch, E. A. (2017). A meta-analysis of d-cycloserine in exposure-based treatment: Moderators of treatment efficacy, response, and diagnostic remission. *Journal of Clinical Psychiatry, 78*, 196–206.

McKinnon, M. C., Palombo, D. J., Nazarov, A., Kumar, N., Khuu, W., & Levine, B. (2015). Threat of death and autobiographical memory: A study of passengers from flight AT236. *Clinical Psychological Science, 3*, 487–502.

McLean, C. P., & Foa, E. B. (2014). The use of prolonged exposure therapy to help patients with post-traumatic stress disorder. *Clinical Practice, 11*, 233–241.

McNamara, B. (2016, May 24). How Ellie Goulding learned to cope with her debilitating panic attacks. *Teen Vogue.* Retrieved from http://www.teenvogue.com/story/ellie-goulding-panic-attacks-anxiety

McNeely, H. E., Mayberg, H. S., Lozano, A. M., & Kennedy, S. H. (2008). Neuropsychological impact of Cg25 deep brain stimulation for treatment-resistant depression: Preliminary results over 12 months. *Journal of Nervous and Mental Disease, 196*, 405–410.

McNeil, D. G., Jr. (2006, November 23). For rare few, taste is in the ear of the beholder. *New York Times.* Retrieved from http://www.nytimes.com

McPheeters, M. L., Warren, Z., Sathe, N., Bruzek, J., Krishnaswami, S., et al. (2011). A systematic review of medical treatments for children with autism spectrum disorders. *Pediatrics, 127*, e1312–e1321.

McQuown, S. C., & Wood, M. A. (2011). HDAC3 and the molecular brake pad hypothesis. *Neurobiology of Learning and Memory, 96*, 27–34.

Meddis, R. (1977). *The sleep instinct.* London, England: Routledge & Kegan Paul.

Medin, D. L., & Schaffer, M. M. (1978). Context theory of classification learning. *Psychological Review, 85*, 207–238.

Mednick, S. A., Huttunen, M. O., & Machon, R. A. (1994). Prenatal influenza infections and adult schizophrenia. *Schizophrenia Bulletin, 20*, 263–267.

Meesters, Y., & Gordijn, M. C. (2016). Seasonal affective disorder, winter type: Current insights and treatment options. *Psychology Research and Behavior Management, 9*, 317.

Mehl, M. R., Gosling, S. D., & Pennebaker, J. W. (2006). Personality in its natural habitat: Manifestations and implicit folk theories of personality in daily life. *Journal of Personality and Social Psychology, 90*, 862–877.

Mehl, M. R., Pennebaker, J. W., Crow, M. D., Dabbs, J., & Price, J. H. (2001). The electronically activated recorder (EAR): A device for sampling naturalistic daily activities and conversations. *Behavior Research Methods, Instruments, and Computers, 33*, 517–523.

Mehler, J., & Bever, T. G. (1967). Cognitive capacity of very young children. *Science, 158*, 141–142.

Mehta, P. H., & Beer, J. (2010). Neural mechanisms of the testosterone-aggression relation: The role of orbitofrontal cortex. *Journal of Cognitive Neuroscience, 22*, 2357–2368.

Mehta, P. H., Jones, A. C., & Josephs, R. A. (2008). The social endocrinology of dominance: Basal testosterone predicts cortisol changes and behavior following victory and defeat. *Journal of Personality and Social Psychology, 94*, 1078–1093.

Meier, M. H., Caspi, A., Ambler, A., Harrington, H., Houts, R., Keefe, R. S., McDonald, K., Poulton, R., & Moffitt, T. E. (2012). Persistent cannabis users show neuropsychological decline from childhood to midlife. *Proceedings of the National Academy of Sciences, 109*, E2657–E2664.

Melby-Lervåg, M., Lyster, S. A. H., & Hulme, C. (2012). Phonological skills and their role in learning to read: A meta-analytic review. *Psychological Bulletin, 138*, 322.

Meltzoff, A. N., & Moore, M. K. (1977). Imitation of facial and manual gestures by human neonates. *Science, 198*, 75–78.

Melzack, R., & Wall, P. D. (1965). Pain mechanisms: A new theory. *Science, 150*, 971–979.

Melzack, R., & Wall, P. D. (1982). *The challenge of pain.* New York, NY: Basic Books.

Mendrek, A., & Mancini-Marïe, A. (2016). Sex/gender differences in the brain and cognition in schizophrenia. *Neuroscience & Biobehavioral Reviews, 67*, 57–78.

Mennella, J. A., Bobowski, N. K., & Reed, D. R. (2016). The development of sweet taste: From biology to hedonics. *Reviews in Endocrine and Metabolic Disorders, 17*, 171–178.

Mennella, J. A., Jagnow, C. P., & Beauchamp, G. K. (2001). Prenatal and postnatal flavor learning by human infants. *Pediatrics, 107*, e88.

Menon, M., Tobin, D. D., Corby, B. C., Menon, M., Hodges, & Perry, D. G. (2007). The developmental costs of high self-esteem for antisocial children. *Child Development, 78*, 1627–1639.

Mental Health America. (2016). The state of mental health in America 2017. Retrieved from http://www.mentalhealthamerica.net/issues/state-mental-health-america

Mercer, K. B., Orcutt, H. K., Quinn, J. F., Fitzgerald, C. A., Conneely, K. N., Barfield, R. T., et al. (2011). Acute and posttraumatic stress symptoms in a prospective gene x environment study of a university campus shooting. *Archives of General Psychiatry, 69,* 89–97.

Merikangas, K. R., Burstein, M., Swanson, S. A., Avenevoli, S., Cui, L., Benjet, C., et al. (2010). Lifetime prevalence of mental disorders in U.S. adolescents: Results from the National Comorbidity Survey Replication—Adolescent Supplement (NCS-A). *Journal of the American Academy of Child and Adolescent Psychiatry, 49,* 980–989.

Merikangas, K., He, J., Burstein, M., Swendsen, J., Avenevoli, S., Case, B., et al. (2011). Service utilization for lifetime mental disorders in U.S. adolescents: Results of the National Comorbidity Survey—Adolescent Supplement (NCS-A). *Journal of the American Academy of Child and Adolescent Psychiatry, 50,* 32–45.

Meston, C. M., & Frohlich, P. F. (2000). The neurobiology of sexual function. *Archives of General Psychiatry, 57,* 1012–1030.

Mesulam, M. (2013). Cholinergic circuitry of the human nucleus basalis and its fate in Alzheimer's disease. *Journal of Comparative Neurology, 521,* 4124–4144.

Metcalfe, J., & Mischel, W. (1999). A hot/cool-system analysis of delay of gratification: Dynamics of willpower. *Psychological Review, 106,* 3–19.

Mez, J., Daneshvar, D. H., Kiernan, P. T., Abdolmohammadi, B., Alvarez, V. E., Huber, B. R., et al. (2017). Clinicopathological evaluation of chronic traumatic encephalopathy in players of American football. *Journal of the American Medical Association, 318,* 360–370.

Mezulis, A. H., Abramson, L. Y., Hyde, J. S., & Hankin, B. L. (2004). Is there a universal positivity bias in attributions? A meta-analytic review of individual, developmental, and culture differences in the self-serving attributional bias. *Psychological Bulletin, 130,* 711–747.

Michalski, D., Kohout, J., Wicherski, M., & Hart, B. (2011). 2009 Doctorate employment survey (Table 3). Retrieved July 24, 2017, from the APA website, http://www. apa.org/workforce/publications/09-doc-empl/table-3.pdf

Mickelson, K. D., Kessler, R. C., & Shaver, P. R. (1997). Adult attachment in a nationally representative sample. *Journal of Personality and Social Psychology, 73,* 1092–1106.

Miles, E., & Crisp, R. J. (2014). A meta-analytic test of the imagined contact hypothesis. *Group Processes & Intergroup Relations, 17,* 3–26.

Milgram, S. (1963). Behavioral study of obedience. *Journal of Abnormal and Social Psychology, 67,* 371–378.

Milgram, S. (1974). *Obedience to authority: An experimental view.* New York, NY: Harper & Row.

Mill, J. S. (1843). *A system of logic, ratiocinative and inductive: Being a connected view of the principles of evidence and the methods of scientific investigation.* London, England: John W. Parker.

Millan, M. J., Andrieux, A., Bartzokis, G., Cadenhead, K., Dazzan, P., et al. (2016). Altering the course of schizophrenia: Progress and perspectives. *Nature Reviews Drug Discovery, 15,* 485–515.

Miller, D. I., & Halpern, D. F. (2014). The new science of cognitive sex differences. *Trends in Cognitive Sciences, 18,* 37–45.

Miller, D. T., & Prentice, D. A. (2016). Changing norms to change behavior. *Annual Review of Psychology, 67,* 339–361.

Miller, G. A. (1956). The magical number seven, plus or minus two: Some limits on our capacity for processing information. *Psychological Review, 63,* 81–97.

Miller, G. A. (2005). How are memories stored and retrieved? *Science, 309,* 92–93.

Miller, I. W., Norman, W. H., & Keitner, G. I. (1989). Cognitive-behavioral treatment of depressed inpatients: Six- and twelve-month follow-up. *American Journal of Psychiatry, 146,* 1274–1279.

Miller, J. B., & Sanjurjo, A. (2016). A primer and frequently asked questions for "surprised by the gamblers and hot hand fallacies? A truth in the law of small numbers" (February 7, 2016). Retrieved from http://dx.doi.org/10.2139/ssrn.2728151

Miller, L. C., & Fishkin, S. A. (1997). On the dynamics of human bonding and reproductive success: Seeking windows on the adapted-for human-environmental interface. In J. Simpson & D. T. Kenrick (Eds.), *Evolutionary social psychology* (pp. 197–236). Mahwah, NJ: Erlbaum.

Miller, M., Swanson, S. A., Azrael, D., Pate, V., & Stürmer, T. (2014). Antidepressant dose, age, and the risk of deliberate self-harm. *JAMA Internal Medicine, 174,* 899–909.

Miller, R. S. (1996). *Embarrassment: Poise and peril in everyday life.* New York, NY: Guilford Press.

Miller, W. T. (2000). Rediscovering fire: Small interventions, large effects. *Psychology of Addictive Behaviors, 14,* 6–18.

Mills, K. L., Lalonde, F., Clasen, L. S., Giedd, J. N., & Blakemore, S. J. (2014). Developmental changes in the structure of the social brain in late childhood and adolescence. *Social Cognitive and Affective Neuroscience, 9,* 123–131.

Milner, B. (1962). Les troubles de la memoire accompagnant des lesions hippocampiques bilaterales. *Physiologie de l'hippocampe, 207,* 257–272.

Milner, B., Corkin, S., & Teuber, H. L. (1968). Further analysis of the hippocampal amnesic syndrome: 14-year follow-up study of HM. *Neuropsychologia, 6,* 215–234.

Milojev, P., & Sibley, C. G. (2016). Normative personality trait development in adulthood: A 6-year cohort-sequential growth model. *Journal of Personality and Social Psychology, 112,* 510–526.

Milton, J., & Wiseman, R. (2001). Does psi exist? Reply to Storm and Ertel (2001). *Psychological Bulletin, 127,* 434–438.

Minnes, S., Lang, A., & Singer, L. (2011). Prenatal tobacco, marijuana, stimulant, and opiate exposure: Outcomes and practice implications. *Addiction Science & Clinical Practice, 6,* 57–70.

Minshew, N. J., & Keller, T. A. (2010). The nature of brain dysfunction in autism: Functional brain imaging studies. *Current Opinions in Neurology, 23,* 124–130.

Minshew, N. J., & Williams, D. L. (2007). The new neurobiology of autism: Cortex, connectivity, and neuronal organization. *Archives of Neurology, 64,* 945–950.

Miranda, D., & Claes, M. (2004). Rap music genres and deviant behaviors in French-Canadian adolescents. *Journal of Youth and Adolescence, 34,* 113–122.

Mischel, W. (1961). Delay of gratification, need for achievement, and acquiescence in another culture. *Journal of Abnormal and Social Psychology, 62,* 543–552.

Mischel, W., & Shoda, Y. (1995). A cognitive-affective system theory of personality: Reconceptualizing situations, dispositions, dynamics, and invariance in personality structure. *Psychological Review, 102,* 246–268.

Mischel, W., Shoda, Y., & Rodriguez, M. L. (1989). Delay of gratification in children. *Science, 244,* 933–938.

Mitchell, J. P., Heatherton, T. F., & Macrae, C. N. (2002). Distinct neural systems subserve person and object knowledge. *Proceedings of the National Academy of Sciences, 99,* 15238–15243.

Mitelman, S. A., Shihabuddin, L., Brickman, A. M., Hazlett, E. A., & Buchsbaum, M. S. (2005). Volume of the cingulate and outcome in schizophrenia. *Schizophrenia Research, 72,* 91–108.

Mithoefer, M. C., Grob, C. S., & Brewerton, T. D. (2016). Novel psychopharmacological therapies for psychiatric disorders: Psilocybin and MDMA. *The Lancet Psychiatry, 3,* 481–488.

Mithoefer, M. C., Wagner, M. T., Mithoefer, A. T., Jerome, L., Martin, S. F., Yazar-Klosinski, B., & Doblin, R. (2013). Durability of improvement in post-traumatic stress disorder symptoms and absence of harmful effects or drug dependency after 3, 4-methylenedioxymethamphetamine-assisted psychotherapy: A prospective long-term follow-up study. *Journal of Psychopharmacology, 27,* 28–39.

Mittal, V. A., Neumann, C., Saczawa, M., & Walker, E. F. (2008). Longitudinal progression of movement abnormalities in relation to psychotic symptoms in adolescents at high risk of schizophrenia. *Archives of General Psychiatry, 65,* 165–171.

Miyake, K. (1993). Temperament, mother-child interaction, and early development. *Japanese Journal of Research on Emotions, 1,* 48–55.

Miyamoto, Y., & Kitayama, S. (2002). Cultural variation in correspondence bias: The critical role of attitude diagnosticity of socially constrained behavior. *Journal of Personality and Social Psychology, 83,* 1239–1248.

Mobbs, D., Greicius, M. D., Abdel-Azim, E., Menon, V., & Reiss, A. L. (2003). Humor modulates the mesolimbic reward centers. *Neuron, 40,* 1041–1048.

Moffitt, T. E., Arseneault, L., Belsky, D., Dickson, N., Hancox, R. J., Harrington, H., et al. (2011). A gradient of childhood self-control predicts health, wealth, and public safety. *Proceedings of the National Academy of Sciences, 108,* 2693–2698.

Mogg, K., & Bradley, B. P. (2016). Anxiety and attention to threat: Cognitive mechanisms and treatment with attention bias modification. *Behaviour Research and Therapy, 87,* 76–108.

Moll, J., & de Oliveira-Souza, R. (2007). Moral judgments, emotions and the utilitarian brain. *Trends in Cognitive Sciences, 11,* 319–321.

Moll, J., de Oliveira-Souza, R., Eslinger, P. J., Bramati, I. E., Mourão-Miranda, J., Andreiuolo, P. A., & Pessoa, L. (2002). The neural correlates of moral sensitivity: A functional magnetic resonance imaging investigation of basic and moral emotions. *Journal of Neuroscience, 22,* 2730–2736.

Monaghan, P., Sio, U. N., Lau, S. W., Woo, H. K., Linkenauger, S. A., & Ormerod, T. C. (2015). Sleep promotes analogical transfer in problem solving. *Cognition, 143,* 25–30.

Monteith, M. J., Ashburn-Nardo, L., Voils, C. I., & Czopp, A. M. (2002). Putting the brakes on prejudice: On the development and operation of cues for control. *Journal of Personality and Social Psychology, 83,* 1029–1050.

Montgomery, G. H., DuHamel, K. N., & Redd, W. H. (2000). A meta-analysis of hypnotically induced analgesia: How effective is hypnosis? *International Journal of Clinical and Experimental Hypnosis, 48,* 138–153.

Monti, M. M., Vanhaudenhuyse, A., Coleman, M. R., Boly, M., Pickard, J. D., Tshibanda, L., et al. (2010). Willful modulation of brain activity in disorders of consciousness. *New England Journal of Medicine, 362,* 579–589.

Moore, S. C., Lee, I. M., Weiderpass, E., Campbell, P. T., Sampson, J. N., Kitahara, C. M., et al. (2016). Association of leisure-time physical activity with risk of 26 types of cancer in 1.44 million adults. *JAMA Internal Medicine, 176,* 816–825.

Moore, T. J., & Mattison, D. R. (2017). Adult utilization of psychiatric drugs and differences by sex, age, and race. *JAMA Internal Medicine, 177,* 274–275.

Mørch-Johnsen, L., Nesvåg, R., Jørgensen, K. N., Lange, E. H., Hartberg, C. B., Haukvik, K. V., et al. (2017). Auditory cortex characteristics in schizophrenia: Associations with auditory hallucinations. *Schizophrenia Bulletin, 43,* 75–83.

Morefield, K. M., Keane, M., Felgate, P., White, J. M., & Irvine, R. J. (2011). Pill content, dose and resulting plasma concentrations of 3, 4-methylendioxymethamphetamine (MDMA) in recreational "ecstasy" users. *Addiction, 106,* 1293–1300.

Morin, C. M., Vallières, A., Guay, B., Ivers, H., Savard, J., Mérette, C., et al. (2009). Cognitive behavioral therapy, singly and combined with medication, for persistent insomnia: A randomized controlled trial. *Journal of the American Medical Association, 301,* 2005–2015.

Moriuchi, J. M., Klin, A., & Jones, W. (2016). Mechanisms of diminished attention to eyes in autism. *American Journal of Psychiatry, 174,* 26–35.

Morman, M. T., & Floyd, K. (1998). "I love you, man": Overt expressions of affection in male-male interaction. *Sex Roles, 38,* 871–881.

Morrison, A. B., & Chein, J. M. (2011). Does working memory training work? The promise and challenges of enhancing cognition by training working memory. *Psychonomic Bulletin Review, 18,* 46–60.

Mortensen, E. L., & Hogh, P. (2001). A gender difference in the association between APOE genotype and age-related cognitive decline. *Neurology, 57,* 89–95.

Mortensen, E. L., Michaelsen, K. F., Sanders, S. A., & Reinisch, J. M. (2002). The association between duration of breastfeeding and adult intelligence. *Journal of the American Medical Association, 287,* 2365–2371.

Morton, J., & Johnson, M. H. (1991). CONSPEC and CONLERN: A two-process theory of infant face recognition. *Psychological Review, 98,* 164–181.

Moskowitz, A. K. (2004). "Scared stiff": Catatonia as an evolutionary-based fear response. *Psychological Bulletin, 111,* 984–1002.

Moss, M. (2014). *Salt, sugar, fat: How the food giants hooked us.* New York, NY: Random House.

Moulton, S. T., & Kosslyn, S. M. (2008). Using neuroimaging to resolve the psi debate. *Journal of Cognitive Neuroscience, 20,* 182–192.

Mowery, P. D., Brick, P. D., & Farrelly, M. (2000). Pathways to established smoking: Results from the 1999 national youth tobacco survey (Legacy First Look Report No. 3). Washington, DC: American Legacy Foundation.

Mroczek, D. K., & Kolarz, C. M. (1998). The effect of age on positive and negative affect: A developmental perspective on happiness. *Journal of Personality and Social Psychology, 75,* 1333–1349.

Mucci, A., Merlotti, E., Üçok, A., Aleman, A., & Galderisi, S. (2017). Primary and persistent negative symptoms: Concepts, assessments and neurobiological bases. *Schizophrenia Research, 186,* 19–28. http://dx.doi.org.dartmouth.idm.oclc.org/10.1016/j.schres.2016.05.014

Mueller, P. A., & Oppenheimer, D. M. (2014). The pen is mightier than the keyboard: Advantages of longhand over laptop note taking. *Psychological Science, 25,* 1159–1168.

Muenks, K., Wigfield, A., Yang, J. S., & O'Neal, C. R. (2017). How true is grit? Assessing its relations to high school and college students' personality characteristics, self-regulation, engagement, and achievement. *Journal of Educational Psychology, 109,* 599–620. Retrieved from http://dx.doi.org/10.1037/edu0000153

Mufson, L. Dorta, K. P., Wikramaratne, P., Nomura, Y., Olfson, M., & Weissman, M. M. (2004). A randomized effectiveness trial of interpersonal psychotherapy for depressed adolescents. *Archives of General Psychiatry, 61,* 577–584.

Muhle, R., Trentacoste, S. V., & Rapin, I. (2004). The genetics of autism. *Pediatrics, 113,* 472–486.

Mukherjee, R. A. S., Hollins, S., Abou-Saleh, M. T., & Turk, J. (2005). Low levels of alcohol consumption and the fetus. *British Medical Journal, 330,* 375–385.

Munafò, M. R. (2012). The serotonin transporter gene and depression. *Depression and Anxiety, 29,* 915–917.

Munafò, M. R., & Flint, J. (2011). Dissecting the genetic architecture of human personality. *Trends in Cognitive Sciences, 15,* 395–400.

Munson, J. A., McMahon, R. J., & Spieker, S. J. (2001). Structure and variability in the developmental trajectory of children's externalizing problems: Impact of infant attachment, maternal depressive symptomatology, and child sex. *Development and Psychopathology, 12,* 277–296.

Murch, S. H., Anthony, A., Casson, D. H., Malik, M., Berelowitz, M., Dhillon, A. P., et al. (2004). Retraction of an interpretation. *Lancet, 363,* 750.

Murray, H. A. (1943). *Analysis of the personality of Adolf Hitler: With predictions of his future behavior and suggestions for dealing with him now and after Germany's surrender.* Washington, DC: OSS Archives.

Murray, S. L., Holmes, J. G., & Griffin, D. W. (1996). The benefits of positive illusions: Idealization and the construction of satisfaction in close relationships. *Journal of Personality and Social Psychology, 70,* 79–98.

Mustanski, B. S., Chivers, M. L., & Bailey, J. M. (2002). A critical review of recent biological research on human sexual orientation. *Annual Review of Sex Research, 13,* 89–140.

Mustroph, M. L., Chen, S., Desai, S. C., Cay, E. B., DeYoung, E. K., & Rhodes, J. S. (2012). Aerobic exercise is the critical variable in an enriched environment that increases hippocampal neurogenesis and water maze learning in male C57BL/6J mice. *Neuroscience, 219,* 62–71.

Myers, D. G. (2000). The funds, friends, and faith of happy people. *American Psychologist, 55*, 56–67.

Myers, D. G., & Lamm, H. (1976). The group polarization phenomenon. *Psychological Bulletin, 83*, 602–627.

Naci, H., & Ioannidis, J. P. (2013). Comparative effectiveness of exercise and drug interventions on mortality outcomes: Metaepidemiological study. *BMJ: British Medical Journal, 347*: f5577.

Nadel, L., Hoscheidt, S., & Ryan, L. R. (2013). Spatial cognition and the hippocampus: The anterior-posterior axis. *Journal of Cognitive Neuroscience, 25*, 22–28.

Nader, K., & Einarsson, E. O. (2010). Memory reconsolidation: An update. *Annals of the New York Academy of Sciences, 1191*, 27–41.

Nader, K., Schafe, G. E., & LeDoux, J. E. (2000). Fear memories require protein synthesis in the amygdala for reconsolidation after retrieval. *Nature, 406*, 722–726.

Nakano, K., & Kitamura, T. (2001). The relation of the anger subcomponent of type A behavior to psychological symptoms in Japanese and foreign students. *Japanese Psychological Research, 43*, 50–54.

Naqvi, N. H., Rudrauf, D., Damasio, H., & Bechara, A. (2007). Damage to the insula disrupts addiction to cigarette smoking. *Science, 315*, 531–534.

Nash, M., & Barnier, A. (2008). *The Oxford handbook of hypnosis.* New York, NY: Oxford University Press.

Nassar, N., Dixon, G., Bourke, J., Bower, C., Glasson, E., de Klerk, N., et al. (2009). Autism spectrum disorders in young children: Effect of changes in diagnostic practices. *International Journal of Epidemiology, 38*, 1245–1254.

National Association of Colleges and Employers. (2016, April 6). Economics projected as top-paid class of 2016 social sciences major. Retrieved from http://www.naceweb.org/s04062016/top-paid-social-sciences-major-economics.aspx

National Center for Learning Disabilities. (2009). *LD at a glance.* Retrieved from http://www.ncld.org/ld-basics/ld-explained/basic-facts/learning-disabilities-at-a-glance

National Highway Traffic Safety Administration. (2012b). Traffic safety facts: 2010 data. Washington, DC: National Center for Statistics and Analysis.

National Highway Traffic Safety Administration. (2013). 2012 motor vehicle crashes: Overview. U.S. Department of Transportation. DOT HS 811 856. Retrieved from http://www-nrd.nhtsa.dot.gov/Pubs/811856.pdf

National Institute of Drug Abuse. (2010). *MDMA (Ecstasy)* [Fact sheet]. Retrieved from http://teens.drugabuse.gov/facts/facts_xtc1.php

National Institute of Drug Abuse. (2014). National survey of drug use and health. Retrieved from http://www.drugabuse.gov/national-survey-drug-use-health

National Institute of Mental Health. (2011). NIMH Research Domain Criteria (RDoC). Draft 3.1. Retrieved from http://www.nimh.nih.gov/research-priorities/rdoc/nimh-research-domain-criteria-rdoc.shtml

National Institutes of Health. (2017). Noise-induced hearing loss. Retrieved from http://www.nidcd.nih.gov/health/hearing/pages/noise.aspx

National Research Council, Committee on Educational Interventions for Children with Autism. (2001). *Educating young children with autism.* Washington, DC: National Academy Press.

Nawata, H., Ogomori, K., Tanaka, M., Nishimura, R., Urashima, H., Yano, R., et al. (2010). Regional cerebral blood flow changes in female to male gender identity disorder. *Psychiatry and Clinical Neurosciences, 64*, 157–161.

Neimeyer, R. A., & Mitchell, K. A. (1988). Similarity and attraction: A longitudinal study. *Journal of Social and Personal Relationships, 5*, 131–148.

Neisser, U. (1967). *Cognitive psychology.* New York, NY: Appleton-Century-Crofts.

Neisser, U., Boodoo, G., Bouchard, T. J., Jr., Boykin, A. W., Brody, N., Ceci, S. J., et al. (1996). Intelligence: Knowns and unknowns. *American Psychologist, 51*, 77–101.

Nellis, A. M., & Savage, J. (2012). Does watching the news affect fear of terrorism? The importance of media exposure on terrorism fear. *Crime & Delinquency, 58*, 748–768.

Nelson, S. K., Kushlev, K., English, T., Dunn, E. W., & Lyubomirsky, S. (2013). In defense of parenthood: Children are associated with more joy than misery. *Psychological Science, 24*, 3–10.

Nestler, E. J., Peña, C. J., Kundakovic, M., Mitchell, A., & Akbarian, S. (2016). Epigenetic basis of mental illness. *The Neuroscientist, 22*, 447–463.

Newby, J. M., McKinnon, A., Kuyken, W., Gilbody, S., & Dalgleish, T. (2015). Systematic review and meta-analysis of transdiagnostic psychological treatments for anxiety and depressive disorders in adulthood. *Clinical Psychology Review, 40*, 91–110.

Newman, G., Keil, F., Kuhlmeier, V., & Wynn, K. (2010). Preverbal infants appreciate that only agents can create order. *Proceedings of the National Academy of Sciences, 107*, 17140–17145.

Newman, M. G., Llera, S. J., Erickson, T. M., Przeworski, A., & Castonguay, L. G. (2013). Worry and generalized anxiety disorder: A review and theoretical synthesis of evidence on nature, etiology, mechanisms, and treatment. *Annual Review of Clinical Psychology, 9*, 275–297.

Newman, M. G., Szkodny, L., Llera, S. J., & Przeworski, A. (2011). A review of technology assisted self-help and minimal contact therapies for drug and alcohol abuse and smoking addiction: Is human contact necessary for therapeutic efficacy? *Clinical Psychology Review, 31*, 178–186.

Ng, M., Fleming, T., Robinson, M., Thomson, B., Graetz, N., Margono, C., et al. (2014). Global, regional, and national prevalence of overweight and obesity in children and adults during 1980–2013: A systematic analysis for the Global Burden of Disease Study 2013. *The Lancet, 384*, 766–781.

Nicholson, I. (2011). "Torture at Yale": Experimental subjects, laboratory torment and the "rehabilitation" of Milgram's "Obedience to Authority." *Theory & Psychology, 21*, 737–761.

Nickel, T., Sonntag, A., Schill, J., Zobel, A. W., Ackl, N., et al. (2003). Clinical and neurobiological effects of tianeptine and paroxetine in major depression. *Journal of Clinical Psychopharmacology, 23*, 153–168.

Nicolini, H., Bakish, D., Duenas, H., Spann, M., Erickson, J., Hallberg, C., et al. (2008). Improvement of psychic and somatic symptoms in adult patients with generalized anxiety disorder: Examination from a duloxetine, venlafaxine extended-release and placebo-controlled trial. *Psychological Medicine, 19*, 1–10.

Nielsen, J. A., Zielinski, B. A., Ferguson, M. A., Lainhart, J. E., & Anderson, J. S. (2013). An evaluation of the left-brain vs. right-brain hypothesis with resting state functional connectivity magnetic resonance imaging. *PLoS ONE 8*, e71275.

Nilsson, H. (2014). A four-dimensional model of mindfulness and its implications for health. *Psychology of Religion and Spirituality, 6*, 162–174.

Nir, Y., & Tononi, G. (2010). Dreaming and the brain: From phenomenology to neurophysiology. *Trends in Cognitive Sciences, 14*, 88–100.

Nisbett, R. E. (2009). *Intelligence and how to get it: Why schools and cultures count.* New York, NY: Norton.

Nisbett, R. E., Peng, K., Choi, I., & Norenzayan, A. (2001). Culture and systems of thought: Holistic versus analytic cognition. *Psychological Review, 108*, 291–310.

Nishino, S. (2007). Narcolepsy: Pathophysiology and pharmacology. *Journal of Clinical Psychiatry, 68*, 9–15.

Nivoli, A., Colom, F., Murru, A., Pacchiarotti, I., Castro-Loli, P., González-Pinto, A., et al. (2011). New treatment guidelines for acute bipolar depression: A systematic review. *Journal of Affective Disorders, 129*, 14–26.

Noble, K. G., Korgaonkar, M. S., Grieve, S. M., & Brickman, A. M. (2013). Higher education is an age-independent predictor of white matter integrity and cognitive control in late adolescence. *Developmental Science, 16*, 653–664.

Noftle, E. E., & Robins, R. W. (2007). Personality predictors of academic outcomes: Big Five correlates of GPA and SAT scores. *Journal of Personality and Social Psychology, 93*, 116–130.

Nokia, M. S., Lensu, S., Ahtiainen, J. P., Johansson, P. P., Koch, L. G., Britton, S. L., et al. (2016). Physical exercise increases adult hippocampal neurogenesis in male rats provided it is aerobic and sustained. *Journal of Physiology, 594,* 1855–1873.

Norberg, M. M., Krystal, J. H., & Tolin, D. F. (2008). A meta-analysis of D-cycloserine and the facilitation of fear extinction and exposure therapy. *Biological Psychiatry, 63,* 1118–1126.

Norcross, J. C., & Sayette, M. A. (2016). *Insider's guide to graduate programs in clinical and counseling psychology* (2016–2017 ed.). New York, NY: Guilford Press.

Norman, K. A., Polyn, S. M., Detre, G. J., & Haxby, J. V. (2006). Beyond mind-reading: Multi-voxel pattern analysis of fMRI data. *Trends in Cognitive Sciences, 10,* 424–423.

Norris, A. L., Marcus, D. K., & Green, B. A. (2015). Homosexuality as a discrete class. *Psychological Science, 26,* 1843–1853.

Norton, M. I., Frost, J. A., & Ariely, D. (2007). Less is more: The lure of ambiguity, or why familiarity breeds contempt. *Journal of Personality and Social Psychology, 92,* 97–106.

Nosek, B. A., Hawkins, C. B., & Frazier, R. S. (2011). Implicit social cognition: From measures to mechanisms. *Trends in Cognitive Sciences, 15,* 152–159.

Novotny, S. L., Hollander, E., Allen, A., Aronowitz, B. R., DeCaria, C., Cartwright, C., et al. (2000). Behavioral response to oxytocin challenge in adult autistic disorders. *Biological Psychiatry, 47,* 52.

Noyes, R. (1991). Suicide and panic disorder: A review. *Journal of Affective Disorders, 22,* 1–11.

Null, J. (2016). Heatstroke deaths of children in vehicles. Retrieved from http://noheatstroke.org

Nummenmaa, L., Glerean, E., Hari, R., & Hietanen, J. K. (2014). Bodily maps of emotions. *Proceedings of the National Academy of Sciences, 111,* 646–651.

Nurnberger, J. J., Goldin, L. R., & Gershon, E. S. (1994). Genetics of psychiatric disorders. In G. Winokur & P. M. Clayton (Eds.), *The medical basis of psychiatry* (pp. 459–492). Philadelphia, PA: Saunders.

Oberauer, K., Schulze, R., Wilhelm, O., & Süß, H. M. (2005). Working memory and intelligence—Their correlation and their relation: Comment on Ackerman, Beier, and Boyle (2005). *Psychological Bulletin, 131,* 61–65.

O'Brien, L. T., Hitti, A., Shaffer, E., Van Camp, A. R., Henry, D., & Gilbert, P. N. (2017). Improving girls' sense of fit in science increasing the impact of role models. *Social Psychological and Personality Science, 8,* 301–309.

Ochsner, K. N., Bunge, S. A., Gross, J. J., & Gabrieli, J. D. E. (2002). Rethinking feelings: An fMRI study of the cognitive regulation of emotion. *Journal of Cognitive Neuroscience, 14,* 1215–1299.

Ochsner, K. N., Silvers, J. A., & Buhle, J. T. (2012). Functional imaging studies of emotion regulation: A synthetic review and evolving model of the cognitive control of emotion. *Annals of the New York Academy of Sciences, 1251,* E1–E24.

O'Donovan, G., Lee, I. M., Hamer, M., & Stamatakis, E. (2017). Association of "weekend warrior" and other leisure-time physical activity patterns with risks for all-cause, cardiovascular disease, and cancer mortality. *JAMA Internal Medicine, 177,* 335–342.

Oei, N. Y. L., Everaerd, W. T. A. M., Elzinga, B. M., Van Well, S., & Bermond, B. (2006). Psychosocial stress impairs working memory at high loads: An association with cortisol levels and memory retrieval. *Stress, 9,* 133–141.

Ogbu, J. U. (1994). From cultural differences to differences in cultural frames of reference. In P. M. Greenfield & R. R. Cocking (Eds.), *Cross-cultural roots of minority child development* (pp. 365–392). Hillsdale, NJ: Erlbaum.

Ogden, C. L., Carroll, M. D., Lawman, H. G., Fryar, C. D., Kruszon-Moran, D., Kit, B. K., et al. (2016). Trends in obesity prevalence among children and adolescents in the United States, 1988–1994 through 2013–2014. *Journal of the American Medical Association, 315,* 2292–2299.

Ogletree, S. M., Turner, G., Vieira, A., & Brunotte, J. (2005). College living: Issues related to housecleaning attitudes. *College Student Journal, 39,* 729–733.

Ohla, K., & Lundström, J. N. (2013). Sex differences in chemosensation: Sensory or emotional? *Frontiers in Human Neuroscience, 7,* 607.

Ohloff, G. (1994). *Scent and fragrances: The fascination of odors and their chemical perspectives.* Berlin, Germany: Springer-Verlag.

O'Kane, G. O., Kensinger, E. A., & Corkin, S. (2004). Evidence for semantic learning in profound amnesia: An investigation with the patient H. M. *Hippocampus, 14,* 417–425.

Olfson, M., Marcus, S. C., Druss, B., Elinson, L., Tanielian, T., & Pincus, H. A. (2002). National trends in the outpatient treatment of depression. *Journal of the American Medical Association, 287,* 203–209.

Oliveira-Pinto, A. V., Santos, R. M., Coutinho, R. A., Oliveira, L. M., Santos, G. B., Alho, A. T., et al. (2014). Sexual dimorphism in the human olfactory bulb: Females have more neurons and glial cells than males. *PLoS ONE, 9,* e111733.

Olsen, E. O. M., Shults, R. A., & Eaton, D. K. (2013). Texting while driving and other risky motor vehicle behaviors among U.S. high school students. *Pediatrics, 131,* e1708–e1715.

Olshansky, S. J., Passaro, D. J., Hershow, R. C., Layden, J. C., Bruce, A., Brody, J., & Ludwig, D. S. (2005). A potential decline in life expectancy in the United States in the 21st century. *Journal of Obstetrical & Gynecological Survey, 60,* 450–452.

Olson, J. M., Vernon, P. A., Harris, J. A., & Jang, K. L. (2001). The heritability of attitudes: A study of twins. *Journal of Personality and Social Psychology, 80,* 845–860.

Olson, K. R., Key, A. C., & Eaton, N. R. (2015). Gender cognition in transgender children. *Psychological Science, 26,* 467–474.

Olson, R., Hogan, L., & Santos, L. (2006). Illuminating the history of psychology: Tips for teaching students about the Hawthorne studies. *Psychology Learning and Teaching, 5,* 110–118.

Olson, R. K. (2011). Genetic and environmental influences on phonological abilities and reading achievement. In S. Brady, D. Braze, & C. Fowler (Eds.), *Explaining individual differences in reading: Theory and evidence* (pp. 197–216). New York, NY: Psychology Press/Taylor-Francis.

Olsson, A., Ebert, J. P., Banaji, M. R., & Phelps, E. A. (2005). The role of social groups in the persistence of learned fear. *Science, 309,* 785–787.

Olsson, A., Nearing, K. I., & Phelps, E. A. (2007). Learning fears by observing others: The neural systems of social fear transmission. *Social Cognitive and Affective Neuroscience Advance Access, 2,* 3–11.

Olsson, A., & Phelps, E. A. (2007). Social learning of fear. *Nature Neuroscience, 10,* 1095–1102.

Omalu, B. I., DeKosky, S. T., Minster, R. L., Kamboh, M. I., Hamilton, R. L., & Wecht, C. H. (2005). Chronic traumatic encephalopathy in a National Football League player. *Neurosurgery, 57,* 128–134.

O'Neal, J. M. (1984). First person account: Finding myself and loving it. *Schizophrenia Bulletin, 10,* 109–110.

O'Neil, S. (1999). Flow theory and the development of musical performance skills. *Bulletin of the Council for Research in Music Education, 141,* 129–134.

Ooms, P., Mantione, M., Figee, M., Schuurman, P. R., van den Munckhof, P., & Denys, D. (2014). Deep brain stimulation for obsessive-compulsive disorders: Long-term analysis of quality of life. *Journal of Neurology, Neurosurgery & Psychiatry, 85,* 153–158.

Opel, D. J., Feemster, K. A., Omer, S. B., Orenstein, W. A., Richter, M., & Lantos, J. D. (2014). A 6-month-old with vaccine-hesitant parents. *Pediatrics, 133,* 526–530.

Opendak, M., Briones, B. A., & Gould, E. (2016). Social behavior, hormones and adult neurogenesis. *Frontiers in Neuroendocrinology, 41,* 71–86.

Open Science Collaboration. (2015). Estimating the reproducibility of psychological science. *Science, 349,* 943 (aac4716).

Ortigue, S., Bianchi-Demicheli, F., Hamilton, C., & Grafton, S. T. (2007). The neural basis of love as a subliminal prime: An event-related functional magnetic resonance imaging study. *Journal of Cognitive Neuroscience, 19,* 1218–1230.

Oskamp, S. (Ed.). (2013). *Reducing prejudice and discrimination.* Philadelphia, PA: Psychology Press.

Osterling, J., & Dawson, G. (1994). Early recognition of children with autism: A study of first birthday home videotapes. *Journal of Autism and Developmental Disorders, 24,* 247–257.

Oswald, F. L., Mitchell, G., Blanton, H., Jaccard, J., & Tetlock, P. E. (2013). Predicting ethnic and racial discrimination: A meta-analysis of IAT criterion studies. *Journal of Personality and Social Psychology, 105,* 171–192.

O'Toole, A. J., Natu, V., An, X., Rice, A., Ryland, J., & Phillips, P. J. (2014). The neural representation of faces and bodies in motion and at rest. *NeuroImage, 84,* 698–711.

Otte, C., Gold, S. M., Penninx, B. W., Pariante, C. M., Etkin, A., Fava, M., et al. (2016). Major depressive disorder. *Nature Reviews. Disease Primers, 2,* 16065. doi: 10.1038/nrdp.2016.65

Ottieger, A. E., Tressell, P. A., Inciardi, J. A., & Rosales, T. A. (1992). Cocaine use patterns and overdose. *Journal of Psychoactive Drugs, 24,* 399–410.

Otto, A. R., Raio, C. M., Chiang, A., Phelps, E. A., & Daw, N. D. (2013). Working-memory capacity protects model-based learning from stress. *Proceedings of the National Academy of Sciences, 110,* 20941–20946.

Oudiette, D., & Paller, K. A. (2013). Upgrading the sleeping brain with targeted memory reactivation. *Trends in Cognitive Sciences, 17,* 142–149.

Owen, A. M., Coleman, M. R., Boly, M., Davis, M. H., Laureys, S., & Pickard, J. D. (2006). Detecting awareness in the vegetative state. *Science, 313,* 1402.

Pacchiarotti, I., Bond, D. J., Baldessarini, R. J., Nolen, W. A., Grunze, H., Licht, R. W., et al. (2013). The International Society for Bipolar Disorders (ISBD) Task Force Report on antidepressant use in bipolar disorders. *American Journal of Psychiatry, 170,* 1249–1262.

Pack, A. I., & Pien, G. W. (2011). Update on sleep and its disorders. *Annual Review of Medicine, 62,* 447–460.

Padberg, F., & George, M. S. (2009). Repetitive transcranial magnetic stimulation of the prefrontal cortex in depression. *Experimental Neurology, 219,* 2–13.

Padwal, R., Leslie, W. D., Lix, L. M., & Majumdar, S. R. (2016). Relationship among body fat percentage, body mass index, and all-cause mortality: A cohort study. *Annals of Internal Medicine, 164,* 532–541.

Pagnoni, G., & Cekic, M. (2007). Age effects on gray matter volume and attentional performance in Zen meditation. *Neurobiology of Aging, 28,* 1623–1627.

Palombo, D. J., McKinnon, M. C., McIntosh, A. R., Anderson, A. K., Todd, R. M., & Levine, B. (2016). The neural correlates of memory for a life-threatening event: An fMRI study of passengers from flight AT236. *Clinical Psychological Science, 4,* 312–319.

Panksepp, J. (1992). Oxytocin effects on emotional processes: Separation distress, social bonding, and relationships to psychiatric disorders. *Annals of the New York Academy of Sciences, 652,* 243–252.

Papadimitriou, G. N., Zervas, I. M., & Papakostas, Y. G. (2001). Unilateral ECT for prophylaxis in affective illness. *Journal of ECT, 17,* 229–231.

Papez, J. W. (1937). A proposed mechanism of emotion. *Archives of Neurology & Psychiatry, 38,* 725–743.

Paquette, V., Levesque, J., Mensour, B., Leroux, J. M., Beaudoin, G., Bourgouin, P., et al. (2003). "Change the mind and you change the brain": Effects of cognitive-behavioral therapy on the neural correlates of spider phobia. *Neuroimage, 18,* 401–409.

Parashar, U., Steele, D., Neuzil, K., Quadros, C. D., Tharmaphornpilas, P., Serhan, F., et al. (2013). Progress with rotavirus vaccines: Summary of the Tenth International Rotavirus Symposium. *Expert Reviews in Vaccines, 12,* 113–117.

Paredes, M. F., James, D., Gil-Perotin, S., Kim, H., Cotter, J. A., Ng, C., et al. (2016). Extensive migration of young neurons into the infant human frontal lobe. *Science, 354,* aaf7073.

Parkinson, C., Sinnott-Armstrong, W., Koralus, P., Mendelovici, A., McGeer, V., & Wheatley, T. (2011). Is morality unified? Evidence that distinct neural systems underlie judgments of harm, dishonesty, and disgust. *Journal of Cognitive Neuroscience, 23,* 3162–3180.

Parnas, J. (2014). The RDoC program: Psychiatry without psyche? *World Psychiatry, 13,* 46–47.

Parrott, A. C. (2013). MDMA, serotonergic neurotoxicity, and the diverse functional deficits of recreational "ecstasy" users. *Neuroscience & Biobehavioral Reviews, 37,* 1466–1484.

Pascual-Leone, A., Catala, M. D., & Pascual-Leone, P. A. (1996). Lateralized effect of rapid-rate transcranial magnetic stimulation of the prefrontal cortex on mood. *Neurology, 46,* 499–502.

Pasquinelli, E. (2012). Neuromyths: Why do they exist and persist? *Mind, Brain, and Education, 6,* 89–96.

Pasupathi, M., & Carstensen, L. L. (2003). Age and emotional experience during mutual reminiscing. *Psychology and Aging, 18,* 430–442.

Patel, V., Chisholm, D., Parikh, R., Charlson, F. J., Degenhardt, L., Dua, T., et al. (2016). Addressing the burden of mental, neurological, and substance use disorders: Key messages from Disease Control Priorities. *The Lancet, 387,* 1672–1685.

Patel, V., Xiao, S., Chen, H., Hanna, F., Jotheeswaran, A. T., Luo, D., et al. (2017). The magnitude of and health system responses to the mental health treatment gap in adults in India and China. *The Lancet, 388,* 3074–3084.

Patrick, M. E., & Schulenberg, J. E. (2014). Prevalence and predictors of adolescent alcohol use and binge drinking in the United States. *Alcohol Research: Current Reviews, 35,* 193–200.

Patrick, M. E., Schulenberg, J. E., Martz, M. E., Maggs, J. L., O'Malley, P. M., & Johnston, L. D. (2013). Extreme binge drinking among 12th-grade students in the United States: Prevalence and predictors. *JAMA Pediatrics, 167,* 1019–1025.

Patterson, C. M., & Newman, J. P. (1993). Reflectivity and learning from aversive events: Toward a psychological mechanism for the syndromes of disinhibition. *Psychological Review, 100,* 716–736.

Patterson, D., & Jensen, M. (2003). Hypnosis and clinical pain. *Psychological Bulletin, 129,* 495–521.

Paulhus, D. L. (2014). Toward a taxonomy of dark personalities. *Current Directions in Psychological Science, 23,* 421–426.

Paulhus, D. L., & Williams, K. M. (2002). The dark triad of personality: Narcissism, Machiavellianism, and psychopathy. *Journal of Research in Personality, 36,* 556–563.

Paul-Labrador, M., Polk, D., Dwyer, J. H., Velasquez, I., Nidich, S., Rainforth, M., et al. (2006). Effects of a randomized controlled trial of transcendental meditation on components of the metabolic syndrome in subjects with coronary heart disease. *Archives of Internal Medicine, 166,* 1218–1224.

Pauls, D. L. (2008). The genetics of obsessive compulsive disorder: A review of the evidence. *American Journal of Medical Genetics, 148C,* 133–139.

Paulson, S., Chalmers, D., Kahneman, D., Santos, L., & Schiff, N. (2013). The thinking ape: The enigma of human consciousness. *Annals of the New York Academy of Sciences, 1303,* 4–24.

Paunonen, S. V., & Ashton, M. C. (2001). Big Five factors and facets and the prediction of behavior. *Journal of Personality and Social Psychology, 81,* 524–539.

Paykel, E. S. (2003). Life events and affective disorders. *Acta Psychiatrica Scandinavica, 108,* 61–66.

Payne, B. K. (2001). Prejudice and perception: The role of automatic and controlled processes in misperceiving a weapon. *Journal of Personality and Social Psychology, 81,* 181–192.

Paz-Elizur, T., Krupsky, M., Blumenstein, S., Elinger, D., Schechtman, E., & Livneh, Z. (2003). DNA repair activity for oxidative damage and risk of lung cancer. *Journal of the National Cancer Institute, 95,* 1312–1331.

Pedersen, P. M., Stig Jørgensen, H., Nakayama, H., Raaschou, H. O., & Olsen, T. S. (1995). Aphasia in acute stroke: Incidence, determinants, and recovery. *Annals of Neurology, 38,* 659–666.

Pelham, W. E., McBurnett, K., Harper, G. W., Milich, R., Murphy, D. A., Clinton, J., et al. (1990). Methylphenidate and baseball playing in ADHD children: Who's on first? *Journal of Consulting and Clinical Psychology, 58,* 130–133.

Pembrey, M. E., Bygren, L. O., Kaati, G., Edvinsson, S., Northstone, K., Sjöström, M., & Golding, J. (2006). Sex-specific, male-line transgenerational responses in humans. *European Journal of Human Genetics, 14,* 159–166.

Penton-Voak, I. S., Perrett, D. I., Castles, D., Burt, M., Koyabashi, T., & Murray, L. K. (1999). Female preference for male faces changes cyclically. *Nature, 399,* 741–742.

Penttilä, M., Jääskeläinen, E., Hirvonen, N., Isohanni, M., & Miettunen, J. (2014). Duration of untreated psychosis as predictor of long-term outcome in schizophrenia: Systematic review and meta-analysis. *British Journal of Psychiatry, 205,* 88–94.

Pepperberg, I. M. (2010). Vocal learning in Grey parrots: A brief review of perception, production, and cross-species comparisons. *Brain & Language, 115,* 81–91.

Pepperberg, I. M., & Nakayama, K. (2016). Robust representation of shape in a Grey parrot (Psittacus erithacus). *Cognition, 153,* 146–160.

Peretz, I., & Zatorre, R. J. (2005). Brain organization for music processing. *Annual Review of Psychology, 56,* 89–114.

Perkins, W. J. (2007). How does anesthesia work? *Scientific American Mind, 18,* 84.

Perrett, D. I., Burt, D. M., Penton-Voak, I. S., Lee, K. J., Rowland, D. A., & Edwards, R. (1999). Symmetry and human facial attractiveness. *Evolution and Human Behavior, 20,* 295–307.

Perrett, D. I., May, K. A., & Yoshikawa, S. (1994). Facial shape and judgments of female attractiveness. *Nature, 368,* 239–242.

Perry, B. D. (2002). Childhood experience and the expression of genetic potential: What childhood neglect tells us about nature and nurture. *Brain and Mind, 3,* 79–100.

Perry, G. (2013). *Behind the shock machine: The untold story of the notorious Milgram psychology experiments.* New York, NY: The New Press.

Pert, C. B., & Snyder, S. H. (1973). Opiate receptor: Demonstration in nervous tissue. *Science, 179,* 1011–1014.

Pessiglione, M., Schmidt, L., Draganski, B., Kalisch, R., Lau, H., Dolan, R. J., et al. (2007, May 11). How the brain translates money into force: A neuroimaging study of subliminal motivation. *Science, 316,* 904–906.

Peters, A. T., Jacobs, R. H., Feldhaus, C., Henry, D. B., Albano, A. M., Langenecker, S. A., et al. (2016). Trajectories of functioning into emerging adulthood following treatment for adolescent depression. *Journal of Adolescent Health, 58,* 253–259.

Peterson, C. B., Becker, C. B., Treasure, J., Shafran, R., & Bryant-Waugh, R. (2016). The three-legged stool of evidence-based practice in eating disorder treatment: Research, clinical, and patient perspectives. *BMC Medicine, 14,* 69.

Petitto, L. A. (2000). On the biological foundations of human language. In H. Lane & K. Emmorey (Eds.), *The signs of language revisited* (pp. 447–471). Mahwah, NJ: Erlbaum.

Petitto, L. A., & Seidenberg, M. S. (1979). On the evidence for linguistic abilities in signing apes. *Brain and Language, 8,* 162–183.

Petronis, A., & Kennedy, J. L. (1995). Unstable genes—Unstable mind? *American Journal of Psychiatry, 152,* 164–172.

Petty, R. E., & Cacioppo, J. T. (1986). *Communication and persuasion: Central and peripheral routes to attitude change.* New York, NY: Springer-Verlag.

Petty, R. E., & Wegener, D. T. (1998). Attitude change: Multiple roles for persuasion variables. In D. T. Gilbert, S. T. Fiske, & G. Lindzey (Eds.), *The handbook of social psychology* (4th ed., pp. 323–390). Boston, MA: McGraw-Hill.

Pezdek, K., & Hodge, D. (1999). Planting false childhood memories in children: The role of event plausibility. *Child Development, 70,* 887–895.

Pfaus, J. G. (2009). Pathways of sexual desire. *Journal of Sex Medicine, 6,* 1506–1533.

Phelan, J. (2006). Foreword. In A. Ziv (Ed.), *Breeding between the lines: Why inter-racial people are healthier and more attractive.* Lanham, MD: National Book Network.

Phelps, E. A. (2004). Human emotion and memory: Interactions of the amygdala and hippocampal complex. *Current Opinion in Neurobiology, 14,* 198–202.

Phelps, E. A. (2006). Emotion and cognition: Insights from studies of the human amygdala. *Annual Review of Psychology, 57,* 27–53.

Phelps, E. A., Lempert, K. M., & Sokol-Hessner, P. (2014). Emotion and decision making: Multiple modulatory neural circuits. *Annual Review of Neuroscience, 37,* 263–287.

Phelps, E. A., Ling, S., & Carrasco, M. (2006). Emotion facilitates perception and potentiates the perceptual benefits of attention. *Psychological Science, 17,* 292–299.

Phillips, M. D., Lowe, M. J., Lurito, J. T., Dzemidzic, M., & Mathews, V. P. (2001). Temporal lobe activation demonstrates sex-based differences during passive listening. *Radiology, 220,* 202–207.

Phillips, M. L., & Kupfer, D. J. (2013). Bipolar disorder diagnosis: Challenges and future directions. *The Lancet, 381,* 1663–1671.

Phinney, J. S. (1990). Ethnic identity in adolescents and adults: Review of research. *Psychological Bulletin, 108,* 499–514.

Piaget, J. (1924). *Judgment and reasoning in the child.* London, England: Routledge.

Pietschnig, J., Voracek, M., & Formann, A. K. (2010). Mozart effect–Shmozart effect: A meta-analysis. *Intelligence, 38,* 314–323.

Pillow, D. R., Zautra, A. J., & Sandler, I. (1996). Major life events and minor stressors: Identifying mediational links in the stress process. *Journal of Personality and Social Psychology, 70,* 381.

Pinker, S. (1984). *Language learnability and language development.* Cambridge, MA: Harvard University Press.

Pinker, S. (1994). *The language instinct.* New York, NY: Morrow.

Pinker, S. (2011). *The better angels of our nature: The decline of violence in history and its causes.* London, England: Penguin UK.

Pinker, S., & Bloom, P. (1990). Natural language and natural selection. *Behavioral and Brain Sciences, 13,* 707–727.

Pinto, D., Pagnamenta, A. T., Klei, L., Anney, R., Merico, D., Regan, R., et al. (2010). Functional impact of global rare copy number variation in autism spectrum disorders. *Nature, 466,* 368–372.

Pitman, R., Sanders, K., Zusman, R., Healy, A., Cheema, F., Lasko, N., et al. (2002). Pilot study of secondary prevention of posttraumatic stress disorder with propranolol. *Biological Psychiatry, 51,* 189–192.

Pizarro, D., Inbar, Y., & Helion, C. (2011). On disgust and moral judgment. *Emotion Review, 3,* 267–268.

Plakun, E. M., Burkhardt, P. E., & Muller, A. P. (1985). Fourteen-year follow-up of borderline and schizotypal personality disorders. *Comprehensive Psychiatry, 26,* 448–455.

Plant, E. A., Hyde, J. S., Keltner, D., & Devine, P. G. (2000). The gender stereotyping of emotions. *Psychology of Women Quarterly, 24,* 81–92.

Plant, E. A., & Peruche, M. (2005). The consequences of race for police officers' responses to criminal suspects. *Psychological Science, 16,* 180–183.

Plassmann, H., & Wager, T. D. (2014). How expectancies shape consumption experiences. In S. D. Preston, M. L. Kringelbach, & B. Knutson (Eds.), *The Interdisciplinary science of consumption* (pp. 219–240). Cambridge, MA: MIT Press.

Plomin, R., & Caspi, A. (1999). Behavioral genetics and personality. In L. A. Pervin & O. P. John (Eds.), *Handbook of personality: Theory and research* (2nd ed., pp. 251–276). New York, NY: Guilford Press.

Plomin, R., & Daniels, D. (1987). Why are children in the same family so different from one another? *Behavioral and Brain Sciences, 10,* 1–16.

Plomin, R., & Daniels, D. (2011). Why are children in the same family so different from one another? *International Journal of Epidemiology, 40,* 563–582.

Plomin, R., DeFries, J. C., Knopik, V. S., & Neiderhiser, J. M. (2016). Top 10 replicated findings from behavioral genetics. *Perspectives on Psychological Science, 11,* 3–23.

Plomin, R., & Spinath, F. M. (2004). Intelligence: Genetics, genes, and genomics. *Journal of Personality and Social Psychology, 86,* 112–129.

Poland, G. A. (2011). MMR vaccine and autism: Vaccine nihilism and postmodern science. *Mayo Clinic Proceedings, 86,* 869 – 871.

Polivy, J., & Herman, C. P. (1985). Dieting and bingeing: A causal analysis. *American Psychologist, 40,* 193–201.

Polivy, J., & Herman, C. P. (2002). Causes of eating disorders. *Annual Review of Psychology, 53,* 187–213.

Pollock, K. M. (2004). Exercise in treating depression: Broadening the psychotherapist's role. *Journal of Clinical Psychology, 57,* 1289–1300.

Poo, M. M., Pignatelli, M., Ryan, T. J., Tonegawa, S., Bonhoeffer, T., Martin, K. C., et al. (2016). What is memory? The present state of the engram. *BMC Biology, 14,* 40.

Post, R. M., Leverich, G. S., Kupka, R., Keck, P., McElroy, S., Altshuler, L., et al. (2013). Increased parental history of bipolar disorder in the United States: Association with early age of onset. *Acta Psychiatrica Scandinavica, 129,* 375–382.

Poulton, R., Moffitt, T. E., & Silva, P. A. (2015). The Dunedin Multidisciplinary Health and Development Study: Overview of the first 40 years, with an eye to the future. *Social Psychiatry and Psychiatric Epidemiology, 50,* 679–693.

Powell, R. A., Digdon, N., Harris, B., & Smithson, C. (2014). Correcting the record on Watson, Rayner, and Little Albert: Albert Barger as "psychology's lost boy." *American Psychologist, 69,* 600–611.

Pratkanis, A. R., Eskenazi, J., & Greenwald, A. G. (1994). What you expect is what you believe (but not necessarily what you get): A test of the effectiveness of subliminal self-help audiotapes. *Basic and Applied Social Psychology, 15,* 251–276.

Pratt, L. A., & Brody, D. J. (2014). Depression in the US household population, 2009–2012. NCHS data brief, no. 172. Hyattsville, MD: National Center for Health Statistics.

Pratt, L. A., Druss, B. G., Manderscheid, R. W., & Walker, E. R. (2016). Excess mortality due to depression and anxiety in the United States: Results from a nationally representative survey. *General Hospital Psychiatry, 39,* 39–45.

Premack, D. (1959). Toward empirical behavior laws: 1. Positive reinforcement. *Psychological Review, 66,* 219–233.

Premack, D. (1970). Mechanisms of self-control. In W. A. Hunt (Ed.), *Learning mechanisms in smoking* (pp. 107–123). Chicago: Aldine.

Premack, D., & Woodruff, G. (1978). Does the chimpanzee have a theory of mind? *Behavioral and Brain Sciences, 1,* 515–526.

Prentiss, D., Power, R., Balmas, G., Tzuang, G., & Israelski, D. (2004). Patterns of marijuana use among patients with HIV/AIDS followed in a public health care setting. *Journal of Acquired Immune Deficiency Syndromes, 35,* 38–45.

Prescott, J., Gavrilescu, M., Cunnington, R., O'Boyle, M. W., & Egan, G. F. (2010). Enhanced brain connectivity in math-gifted adolescents: An fMRI study using mental rotation. *Cognitive Neuroscience, 1,* 277–288.

Price, D. D., Harkins, S. W., & Baker, C. (1987). Sensory-affective relationships among different types of clinical and experimental pain. *Pain, 28,* 297–307.

Primack, B. A., Soneji, S., Stoolmiller, M., Fine, M. J., & Sargent, J. D. (2015). Progression to traditional cigarette smoking after electronic cigarette use among US adolescents and young adults. *JAMA Pediatrics, 169,* 1018–1023.

Probst, F., Meng-Hentschel, J., Golle, J., Stucki, S., Akyildiz-Kunz, C., & Lobmaier, J. S. (2017). Do women tend while men fight or flee? Differential emotive reactions of stressed men and women while viewing newborn infants. *Psychoneuroendocrinology, 75,* 213–221.

Provencher, V., Polivy, J., & Herman, C. P. (2009). Perceived healthiness of food: If it's healthy, you can eat more! *Appetite 2009, 52,* 340–344.

Public Health England. (2106). Modern life responsible for "worrying" health in middle aged. Department of Health. Retrieved rom https://www.gov.uk/government/news/modern-life-responsible-for-worrying-health-in-middle-aged

Purcell, S. M., Moran, J. L., Fromer, M., Ruderfer, D., Solovieff, N., Roussos, P., et al. (2014). A polygenic burden of rare disruptive mutations in schizophrenia. *Nature, 506,* 185–190.

Putnam, A. L., Sungkhasettee, V. W., & Roediger, H. L. (2016). Optimizing learning in college: Tips from cognitive psychology. *Perspectives on Psychological Science, 11,* 652–660.

Raab, M., Gula, B., & Gigerenzer, G. (2012). The hot hand exists in volleyball and is used for allocation decisions. *Journal of Experimental Psychology: Applied, 18,* 81.

Radcliffe, N. M., & Klein, W. M. (2002). Dispositional, unrealistic, and comparative optimism: Differential relations with the knowledge and processing of risk information and beliefs about personal risk. *Personality and Social Psychology Bulletin, 28,* 836–846.

Raevuori, A., Keski-Rahkonen, A., & Hoek, H. W. (2014). A review of eating disorders in males. *Current Opinion in Psychiatry, 27,* 426–430.

Raine, A. (1989). Evoked potentials and psychopathy. *International Journal of Psychopathology, 8,* 1–16.

Raine, A., Mellingen, K., Liu, J., Venables, P., & Mednick, S. A. (2003). Effects of environmental enrichment at ages 3–5 years on schizotypal personality and antisocial behavior at ages 17 and 23 years. *American Journal of Psychiatry, 160,* 1627–1635.

Rainville, P., Duncan, G. H., Price, D. D., Carrier, B., & Bushnell, M. C. (1997). Pain affect encoded in human anterior cingulate but not somatosensory cortex. *Science, 277,* 968–971.

Rainville, P., Hofbauer, R. K., Bushnell, M. C., Duncan, G. H., & Price, D. D. (2002). Hypnosis modulates activity in brain structures involved in the regulation of consciousness. *Journal of Cognitive Neuroscience, 14,* 887–901.

Ram, S., Seirawan, H., Kumar, S. K., & Clark, G. T. (2010). Prevalence and impact of sleep disorders and sleep habits in the United States. *Sleep Breath, 14,* 63–70.

Ramachandran, V. S., & Hirstein, W. (1998). The perception of phantom limbs: The D. O. Hebb lecture. *Brain, 121,* 1603–1630.

Ramachandran, V. S., & Hubbard, E. M. (2001). Psychophysical investigations into the neural basis of synaesthesia. *Proceedings of the Royal Society of London, 268B,* 979–983.

Rampon, C., Jiang, C. H., Dong, H., Tang, Y., Lockhart, D. J., Schultz, P. G., et al. (2000). Effects of environmental enrichment on gene expression in the brain. *Proceedings of the National Academy of Sciences, 97,* 12880–12884.

Rapoport, J. L. (1989). The biology of obsessions and compulsions. *Scientific American, 260,* 83–89.

Rapoport, J. L. (1990). *The boy who couldn't stop washing: The experience and treatment of obsessive-compulsive disorder.* New York, NY: Penguin.

Rapoport, J. L. (1991). Recent advances in obsessive-compulsive disorder. *Neuropsychopharmacology, 5,* 1–10.

Rapport, M. D., & Moffitt, C. (2002). Attention-deficit/hyperactivity disorder and methylphenidate: A review of the height/weight, cardiovascular, and somatic complaint side effects. *Clinical Psychology Review, 22,* 1107–1131.

Rapuano, K. M., Zieselman, A. L., Kelley, W. M., Sargent, J. D., Heatherton, T. F., & Gilbert-Diamond, D. (2017). Genetic risk for obesity predicts nucleus accumbens size and responsivity to real-world food cues. *Proceedings of the National Academy of Sciences, 114,* 160–165.

Rasmussen, S. A., Jamieson, D. J., Honein, M. A., & Petersen, L. R. (2016). Zika virus and birth defects—reviewing the evidence for causality. *New England Journal of Medicine, 374,* 1981–1987.

Rauscher, F. H., Shaw, G. L., & Ky, K. N. (1993). Music and spatial task performance. *Nature, 365,* 611.

Raymaekers, S., Vansteelandt, K., Luyten, L., Bervoets, C., Demyttenaere, K., Gabriëls, L., & Nuttin, B. (2017). Long-term electrical stimulation of bed nucleus of stria terminalis for obsessive-compulsive disorder. *Molecular Psychiatry, 22,* 931–934.

Rayner, K., Foorman, B. R., Perfetti, C. A., Pesetsky, D., & Seidenberg, M. S. (2001). How psychological science informs the teaching of reading. *Psychological Science in the Public Interest, 2,* 31–74.

Rayner, K., Pollatsek, A., Ashby, J., & Clifton Jr., C. (2012). *Psychology of reading.* New York, NY: Psychology Press.

Rayner, K., Schotter, E. R., Masson, M. E., Potter, M. C., & Treiman, R. (2016). So much to read, so little time: How do we read, and can speed reading help? *Psychological Science in the Public Interest, 17*, 4–34.

Raynor, H. A., & Epstein, L. H. (2001). Dietary variety, energy regulation, and obesity. *Psychological Bulletin, 127*, 325–341.

Read, J. P., & Brown, R. A. (2003). The role of exercise in alcoholism treatment and recovery. *Professional Psychology: Research and Practice, 34*, 49–56.

Reber, P. J. (2013). The neural basis of implicit learning and memory: A review of neuropsychological and neuroimaging research. *Neuropsychologia, 51*, 2026-2042.

Redick, T. S., Shipstead, Z., Harrison, T. L., Hicks, K. L., Fried, D. E., Hambrick, D. Z., et al. (2013). No evidence of intelligence improvement after working memory training: A randomized, placebo-controlled study. *Journal of Experimental Psychology: General, 142*, 359–379.

Reeck, C., Ames, D. R., & Ochsner, K. N. (2016). The social regulation of emotion: An integrative, cross-disciplinary model. *Trends in Cognitive Sciences, 20*, 47–63.

Reeves, L. M., & Weisberg, R. W. (1994). The role of content and abstract information in analogical transfer. *Psychological Bulletin, 115*, 381–400.

Regard, M., & Landis, T. (1997). "Gourmand syndrome": Eating passion associated with right anterior lesions. *Neurology, 48*, 1185–1190.

Reifman, A. S., Larrick, R. P., & Fein, S. (1991). Temper and temperature on the diamond: The heat-aggression relationship in major league baseball. *Personality and Social Psychology Bulletin, 17*, 580–585.

Reilly, D., Neumann, D. L., & Andrews, G. (2015). Sex differences in mathematics and science achievement: A meta-analysis of National Assessment of Educational Progress assessments. *Journal of Educational Psychology, 107*, 645–662.

Reinders, A. A., Nijenhuis, E. R., Paans, A. M., Korf, J., Willemsen, A. T., & den Boer, J. A. (2003). One brain, two selves. *Neuroimage, 20*, 2119–2125.

Reis, D. L., Brackett, M. A., Shamosh, N. A., Kiehl, K. A., Salovey, P., & Gray, J. R. (2007). Emotional intelligence predicts individual differences in social exchange reasoning. *Neuroimage, 35*, 1385–1391.

Reis, H. X., Wheeler, L., Spiegel, N., Kernis, M. H., Nezlek, J., & Perri, M. (1982). Physical attractiveness in social interaction: II. Why does appearance affect social experience? *Journal of Personality and Social Psychology, 43*, 979–996.

Renfrow, P. J., & Gosling, S. D. (2003). The do re mi's of everyday life: The structure and personality correlates of music preferences. *Journal of Personality and Social Psychology, 84*, 1236–1256.

Rescorla, R. A. (1966). Predictability and number of pairings in Pavlovian fear conditioning. *Psychonomic Science, 4*, 383–384.

Rescorla, R. A., & Wagner, A. R. (1972). A theory of Pavlovian conditioning: Variations in the effectiveness of reinforcement and non-reinforcement. In A. H. Black & W. F. Prokosy (Eds.), *Classical conditioning II: Current research and theory* (pp. 64–99). New York, NY: Appleton-Century-Crofts.

Ressler, K. J., & Mayberg, H. S. (2007). Targeting abnormal neural circuits in mood and anxiety disorders: From the laboratory to the clinic. *Nature Neuroscience, 10*, 1116–1124.

Reyna, C., Brandt, M., & Viki, G. T. (2009). Blame it on hip-hop: Anti-rap attitudes as a proxy for prejudice. *Group Process and Intergroup Relations, 12*, 361–380.

Rhodewalt, F., & Morf, C. C. (1998). On self-aggrandizement and anger: A temporal analysis of narcissism and affective reactions to success and failure. *Journal of Personality and Social Psychology, 74*, 672–685.

Riboni, F. V., & Belzung, C. (2017). Stress and psychiatric disorders: From categorical to dimensional approaches. *Current Opinion in Behavioral Sciences, 14*, 72–77.

Richman, L. S., Kubzansky, L., Maselko, J., Kawachi, I., Choo, P., & Bauer, M. (2005). Positive emotion and health: Going beyond the negative. *Health Psychology, 24*, 422–429.

Rideout, V. J., Foehr, U. G., & Roberts, D. F. (2010). *Generation M2: Media in the lives of 80- to 18-year-olds.* Menlo Park, CA: Henry J. Kaiser Foundation.

Ridley, M. (2003). *Nature versus nurture: Genes, experience, and what makes us human.* New York, NY: HarperCollins.

Ridout, B., & Campbell, A. (2014). Using Facebook to deliver a social norm intervention to reduce problem drinking at university. *Drug and Alcohol Review.* doi: 10.1111/dar.12141

Rifkin, A., & Rifkin, W. (2004). Adolescents with depression. *Journal of the American Medical Association, 292*, 2577–2579.

Rivera, M. T., Soderstrom, S. B., & Uzzi, B. (2010). Dynamics of dyads in social networks: Assortative, relational, and proximity mechanisms. *Annual Review of Sociology, 36*, 91–115.

Rizzolatti, G., & Fabbri-Destro, M. (2010). Mirror neurons: From discovery to autism. *Experimental Brain Research, 200*, 223–237.

Roberts, B. W. (2009). Back to the future: Personality and assessment and personality development. *Journal of Research in Personality, 43*, 137–114.

Roberts, B. W., Donnellan, M. B., & Hill, P. L. (2012). Personality trait development in adulthood: Findings and implications. In H. Tennen & J. Suls (Eds.), *Handbook of psychology* (2nd ed., pp. 183–196). New York, NY: Wiley.

Roberts, B. W., & Friend-DelVecchio, W. (2000). The rank-order consistency of personality traits from childhood to old age: A quantitative review of longitudinal studies. *Psychological Bulletin, 126*, 3–25.

Roberts, B. W., & Mroczek, D. (2008). Personality trait change in adulthood. *Current Directions in Psychological Science, 17*, 31–35.

Roberts, B. W., Walton, K. E., & Viechtbauer, W. (2006). Patterns of mean-level change in personality traits across the life course: A meta-analysis of longitudinal studies. *Psychological Bulletin, 132*, 3–21.

Roberts, B. W., & Wood, D. (2006). Personality development in the context of the neo-socioanalytic model of personality. In D. Mroczek & T. Little (Eds.), *Handbook of personality development* (pp. 11–39). Mahwah, NJ: Erlbaum.

Roberts, B. W., Wood, D., & Caspi, A. (2008). Personality development. In O. P. John, R. W. Robins, & L. A. Pervin (Eds.), *Handbook of personality: Theory and research* (3rd ed.). New York, NY: Guilford.

Robins, L. N., Helzer, J. E., & Davis, D. H. (1975). Narcotic use in Southeast Asia and afterward: An interview study of 898 Vietnam-returnees. *Archives of General Psychiatry, 32*, 955–961.

Robins, L. N., & Regier, D. A. (1991). *Psychiatric disorders in America: The epidemiological catchment areas study.* New York, NY: Free Press.

Robinson, T. E., & Berridge, K. C. (1993). The neural basis of drug craving: An incentive-sensitization theory of addiction. *Brain Research Reviews, 18*, 247–291.

Robles, T. F., & Kiecolt-Glaser, J. K. (2003). The physiology of marriage: Pathways to health. *Physiology & Behavior, 79*, 409–416.

Rock, I. (1984). *Perception.* New York, NY: Scientific American Books.

Roediger, H. L., III, & Karpicke, J. D. (2006). The power of testing memory: Basic research and implications for educational practice. *Psychological Science, 1*, 181–210.

Roediger, H. L., III, & McDermott, K. B. (1995). Creating false memories: Remembering words not presented in lists. *Journal of Experimental Psychology: Learning, Memory, and Cognition, 21*, 803–814.

Roethlisberger, F. J., & Dickson, W. J. (1939). *Management and the worker: An account of a research program conducted by the Western Electric Company, Hawthorne Works, Chicago.* Cambridge, MA: Harvard University Press.

Rogeberg, O. (2013). Correlations between cannabis use and IQ change in the Dunedin cohort are consistent with confounding from socioeconomic status. *Proceedings of the National Academy of Sciences, 110*, 4251–4254.

Rogers, C. R. (1951). *Client-centered therapy: Its current practice, implications and theory.* Boston, MA: Houghton Mifflin.

Rogers, P. J., & Brunstrom, J. M. (2016). Appetite and energy balancing. *Physiology & Behavior, 164*, 465–471.

Rogers, T. B., Kuiper, N. A., & Kirker, W. S. (1977). Self-reference and the encoding of personal information. *Journal of Personality and Social Psychology, 35,* 677–688.

Rolls, B. J., Roe, L. S., & Meengs, J. S. (2007). The effect of large portion sizes on energy intake is sustained for 11 days. *Obesity Research, 15,* 1535–1543.

Rolls, E. T. (2007). Sensory processing in the brain related to the control of food intake. *Proceedings of the Nutritional Society, 66,* 96–112.

Rolls, E. T., Burton, M. J., & Mora, F. (1980). Neurophysiological analysis of brain-stimulation reward in the monkey. *Brain Research, 194,* 339–357.

Ronald, A., & Hoekstra, R. A. (2011). Autism spectrum disorders and autistic traits: A decade of new twin studies. *American Journal of Medical Genetics Part B: Neuropsychiatric Genetics, 156,* 255–274.

Ronemus, M., Iossifov, I., Levy, D., & Wigler, M. (2014). The role of de novo mutations in the genetics of autism spectrum disorders. *Nature Reviews Genetics, 15,* 133–141.

Rosch, E. (1975). Cognitive representations of semantic categories. *Journal of Experimental Psychology: General, 104,* 192–233.

Rosenman, R. H., Brand, R. J., Jenkins, C. D., Friedman, M., Straus, R., & Wurm, M. (1975). Coronary heart disease in the Western Collaborative Group Study: Final follow-up experience of 8½ years. *Journal of the American Medical Association, 233,* 872–877.

Rosenman, R. H., Friedman, M., Straus, R., Wurm, M., Kositchek, R., Hahn, W., et al. (1964). A predictive study of heart disease. *Journal of the American Medical Association, 189,* 15–22.

Rosenthal, R., & Fode, K. L. (1963). The effect of experimenter bias on the performance of the albino rat. *Behavioral Science, 8,* 183–189.

Rosenzweig, M. R., Bennett, E. L., & Diamond, M. C. (1972). Brain changes in response to experience. *Scientific American, 226,* 22–29.

Ross, C. E., Mirowsky, J., & Goldsteen, K. (1990). The impact of the family on health: The decade in review. *Journal of Marriage and the Family, 52,* 1059–1078.

Ross, H. E., & Young, L. J. (2009). Oxytocin and the neural mechanisms regulating social cognition and affiliative behavior. *Frontiers in Neuroendocrinology, 30,* 534–547.

Ross, L. (1977). The intuitive psychologist and his shortcomings: Distortions in the attribution process. *Advances in Experimental Social Psychology, 10,* 173–220.

Rothbart, M. K. (2011). *Becoming who we are: Temperament and personality in development.* New York, NY: Guilford Press.

Rothman, K. J. (2008). BMI-related errors in the measurement of obesity. *International Journal of Obesity, 32,* S56–S59.

Rotter, J. B. (1954). *Social learning and clinical psychology.* New York, NY: Prentice-Hall.

Rovee-Collier, C. (1999). The development of infant memory. *Current Directions in Psychological Science, 8,* 80–85.

Rowe, D. C., Chassin, L., Presson, C., & Sherman, S. J. (1996). Parental smoking and the "epidemic" spread of cigarette smoking. *Journal of Applied Social Psychology, 26,* 437–445.

Rowe, D. C., Woulbroun, E. J., & Gulley, B. L. (2013). Peers and friends as nonshared environmental influences. In E. Hetherington, D. Reiss, & R. Plomin (Eds.), *Separate social worlds of siblings: The impact of nonshared environment on development* (pp. 159–174). Hillsdale, NJ: Erlbaum.

Roy, A. (1992). Are there genetic factors in suicide? *International Review of Psychiatry, 4,* 169–175.

Rozin, P. (1996). Sociocultural influences on human food selection. In E. D. Capaldi (Ed.), *Why we eat what we eat: The psychology of eating* (pp. 233–263). Washington, DC: American Psychological Association.

Rubia, K., Alegria, A., & Brinson, H. (2014). Imaging the ADHD brain: Disorder-specificity, medication effects and clinical translation. *Expert Review of Neurotherapeutics, 14,* 519–538.

Rudd, R. A., Aleshire, N., Zibbell, J. E., & Gladden, R. M. (2016). Increases in drug and opioid overdose deaths—United States, 2000–2014. *Morbidity and Mortality Weekly Report, 64,* 1378–1382.

Rudman, L. A., & Goodwin, S. A. (2004). Gender differences in automatic in-group bias: Why do women like women more than men like men? *Journal of Personality and Social Psychology, 87,* 494–509.

Rule, N. O., & Alaei, R. (2016). "Gaydar": The perception of sexual orientation from subtle cues. *Current Directions in Psychological Science, 25,* 444–448.

Rupp, H. A., James, T. W., Ketterson, E. D., Sengelaub, D. R., Janssen, E., & Heiman, J. R. (2009). Neural activation in the orbitofrontal cortex in response to male faces increases during the follicular phase. *Hormones and Behavior, 56,* 66–72.

Rusbult, C. E., & Buunk, B. D. (1993). Commitment processes in close relationships: An interdependence analysis. *Journal of Social and Personal Relationships, 10,* 175–204.

Rusbult, C. E., & Van Lange, P. A. M. (1996). Interdependence processes. In E. T. Higgins & A. Kruglanski (Eds.), *Social psychology: Handbook of basic principles* (pp. 564–596). New York, NY: Guilford Press.

Ruscio, A. M., Brown, T. A., Chiu, W. T., Sareen, J., Stein, M. B., & Kessler, R. C. (2008). Social fears and social phobia in the USA: Results from the national comorbidity survey replication. *Psychological Medicine, 35,* 15–28.

Russell, C. A., Clapp, J. D., & Dejong, W. (2005). Done 4: Analysis of a failed social norms marketing campaign. *Health Communication, 17,* 57–65.

Russell, C. J., & Keel, P. K. (2002). Homosexuality as a specific risk factor for eating disorders in men. *International Journal of Eating Disorders, 31,* 300–306.

Russell, J. A. (1994). Is there universal recognition of emotion from facial expressions? A review of the cross-cultural studies. *Psychological Bulletin, 115,* 102–141.

Russell, J. A. (2003). Core affect and the psychological construction of emotion. *Psychological Review, 110,* 145–172.

Russell, M. A. H. (1990). The nicotine trap: A 40-year sentence for four cigarettes. *British Journal of Addiction, 85,* 293–300.

Rutgers, A. H., Bakermans-Kranenburg, M. J., van Ijzendoorn, M. H., & van Berckelaer-Onnes, I. A. (2004). Autism and attachment: A meta-analytic review. *Journal of Child Psychology and Psychiatry, 45,* 1123–1134.

Rutter, M. (2005). Incidence of autism disorders: Changes over time and their meaning. *Acta Paediatrica, 94,* 2–15.

Ryan, S. A., Ammerman, S. D., & AAP Committee on Substance Use and Prevention (2017). Counseling parents and teens about marijuana use in the era of legalization of marijuana. *Pediatrics, 139,* e20164069.

Ryder, J. G., & Holtzheimer, P. E. (2016). Deep brain stimulation for depression: An update. *Current Behavioral Neuroscience Reports, 3,* 102–108.

Saarimäki, H., Gotsopoulos, A., Jääskeläinen, I. P., Lampinen, J., Vuilleumier, P., Hari, R., et al. (2016). Discrete neural signatures of basic emotions. *Cerebral Cortex, 26,* 2563–2573.

Sabol, S. Z., Nelson, M. L., Fisher, C., Gunzerath, L., Brody, C. L., Hu, S., et al. (1999). A genetic association for cigarette smoking behavior. *Health Psychology, 18,* 7–13.

Sacks, J. J., Roeber, J., Bouchery, E. E., Gonzales, K., Chaloupka, F. J., & Brewer, R. D. (2013). State costs of excessive alcohol consumption, 2006. *American Journal of Preventive Medicine, 45,* 474–485.

Sacks, O. (1995). *An anthropologist on Mars: Seven paradoxical tales.* New York, NY: Knopf.

Saha, S., Chant, D. C., Welham, J. L., & McGrath, J. J. (2006). The incidence and prevalence of schizophrenia varies with latitude. *Acta Psychiatrica Scandinavica, 114,* 36–39.

Sahakyan, K. R., Somers, V., Rodriguez-Escudero, J. P., Hodge, D. O., Carter, R. E., Sochor, O., et al. (2015). Normal-weight central obesity: Implications for total and cardiovascular mortality. *Annals of Internal Medicine, 163,* 827–835.

Sala Frigerio, C., & De Strooper, B. (2016). Alzheimer's disease mechanisms and emerging roads to novel therapeutics. *Annual Review of Neuroscience, 39,* 57–79.

Salimpoor, V. N., Benovoy, M., Larcher, K., Dagher, A., & Zatorre, R. J. (2011). Anatomically distinct dopamine release during anticipation and experience of peak emotion to music. *Nature Neuroscience, 14,* 257–262.

Salovey, P., & Grewel, D. (2005). The science of emotional intelligence. *Current Directions in Psychological Science, 14,* 281–286.

Salovey, P., & Mayer, J. D. (1990). Emotional intelligence. *Imagination, Cognition, and Personality, 9,* 185–211.

Salthouse, T. (1992). The information-processing perspective on cognitive aging. In R. Sternberg & C. Berg (Eds.), *Intellectual development* (pp. 261–277). Cambridge, England: Cambridge University Press.

Salthouse, T. A., & Madden, D. J. (2013). Information processing speed and aging. In J. DeLuca & J. H. Kalmar (Eds.), *Information processing speed in clinical populations* (pp. 221–241). New York, NY: Taylor & Francis.

Salum, G. A., Polanczyk, G. V., Miguel, E. C., & Rohde, L. A. (2010). Effects of childhood development on late-life mental disorders. *Current Opinion in Psychiatry, 23,* 498–503.

Salvador, R., Vega, D., Pascual, J. C., Marco, J., Canales-Rodríguez, E. J., Aguilar, S., et al. (2016). Converging medial frontal resting state and diffusion-based abnormalities in borderline personality disorder. *Biological Psychiatry, 79,* 107–116.

Samson, A. C., & Gross, J. J. (2012). Humour as emotion regulation: The differential consequences of negative versus positive humour. *Cognition & Emotion, 26,* 375–384.

Sana, F., Weston, T., & Cepeda, N. J. (2013). Laptop multitasking hinders classroom learning for both users and nearby peers. *Computers & Education, 62,* 24–31.

Sanford, A. J., Fay, N., Stewart, A., & Moxey, L. (2002). Perspective in statements of quantity, with implications for consumer psychology. *Psychological Science, 13,* 130–134.

Santiago, C. D., Wadsworth, M. E., & Stump, J. (2011). Socioeconomic status, neighborhood disadvantage, and poverty-related stress: Prospective effects on psychological syndromes among diverse low-income families. *Journal of Economic Psychology, 32,* 218–230.

Sapolsky, R. M. (1994). *Why zebras don't get ulcers.* New York, NY: Freeman.

Sargent, J. D., Beach, M. L., Adachi-Mejia, A. M., Gibson, J. J., Titus-Ernstoff, L. T., Carusi, C. P., et al. (2005). Exposure to movie smoking: Its relation to smoking initiation among US adolescents. *Pediatrics, 116,* 1183–1191.

Sargent, J. D., & Heatherton, T. F. (2009). Comparison of trends for adolescent smoking and smoking in movies, 1990–2007. *Journal of the American Medical Association, 301,* 2211–2213.

Sargent, J. D., Morgenstern, M., Isensee, B., & Hanewinkel, R. (2009). Movie smoking and urge to smoke among adult smokers. *Nicotine & Tobacco Research, 11,* 1042–1046.

Sassenrath, C., Hodges, S. D., & Pfattheicher, S. (2016). It's all about the self: When perspective taking backfires. *Current Directions in Psychological Science, 25,* 405–410.

Satpute, A. B., Nook, E. C., Narayanan, S., Shu, J., Weber, J., & Ochsner, K. N. (2016). Emotions in "black and white" or shades of gray? How we think about emotion shapes our perception and neural representation of emotion. *Psychological Science, 27,* 1428–1442.

Savage-Rumbaugh, S., Shanker, S. G., & Taylor, T. J. (1998). *Apes, language, and the human mind.* New York, NY: Oxford University Press.

Savic, I., Berglund, H., & Lindström, P. (2005). Brain responses to putative pheromones in homosexual men. *Proceedings of the National Academy of Sciences, 102,* 7356–7361.

Savin-Williams, R. C. (2016). Sexual orientation: Categories or continuum? Commentary on Bailey et al. (2016) *Psychological Science in the Public Interest, 17,* 37–44.

Savin-Williams, R. C., Cash, B. M., McCormack, M., & Rieger, G. (2017). Gay, mostly gay, or bisexual leaning gay? An exploratory study distinguishing gay sexual orientations among young men. *Archives of Sexual Behavior, 46,* 265–272. doi: 10.1007/s10508-016-0848-6

Savin-Williams, R. C., & Vrangalova, Z. (2013). Mostly heterosexual as a distinct sexual orientation group: A systematic review of the empirical evidence. *Developmental Review, 33,* 58–88.

Sayette, M. A. (1993). An appraisal-disruption model of alcohol's effects on stress responses in social drinkers. *Psychological Bulletin, 114,* 459–476.

Schachter, H. M., Pham, B., King, J., Langford, S., & Moher, D. (2001). How efficacious and safe is short-acting methylphenidate for the treatment of attention-deficit hyperactivity disorder in children and adolescents? A meta-analysis. *Canadian Medical Association Journal, 165,* 1475–1488.

Schachter, S. (1951). Deviation, rejection, and communication. *Journal of Abnormal Psychology, 46,* 190–207.

Schachter, S. (1959). *The psychology of affiliation.* Stanford, CA: Stanford University Press.

Schachter, S., & Singer, J. (1962). Cognitive, social, and physiological determinants of emotional state. *Psychological Review, 69,* 379–399.

Schacter, D. L. (1996). *Searching for memory: The brain, the mind, and the past.* New York, NY: Basic Books.

Schacter, D. L., & Tulving, E. (1994). What are the memory systems of 1994? In D. L. Schacter & E. Tulving (Eds.), *Memory systems 1994* (pp. 1–38). Cambridge, MA: MIT Press.

Schagdarsurengin, U., & Steger, K. (2016). Epigenetics in male reproduction: Effect of paternal diet on sperm quality and offspring health. *Nature Reviews Urology, 13,* 584–595.

Schaie, K. W. (1990). Intellectual development in adulthood. In J. E. Birren & K. W. Schaie (Eds.), *Handbook of the psychology of aging* (3rd ed., pp. 291–319). New York, NY: Van Nostrand Reinhold.

Schank, R. C., & Abelson, R. P. (1977). *Scripts, plans, goals, and understanding.* Hillsdale, NJ: Erlbaum.

Scheerer, M. (1963). Problem-solving. *Scientific American, 208,* 118–128.

Schellenberg, E. G. (2012). Cognitive performance after listening to music: A review of the Mozart effect. In R. A. Macdonald, G. Kreutz, & L. Mitchell (Eds.), *Music, health, and well-being* (pp. 324–338). New York, NY: Oxford University Press.

Schiffman, J., Walker, E., Ekstrom, M., Schulsinger, F., Sorensen, H., & Mednick, S. (2004). Childhood videotaped social and neuro-motor precursors of schizophrenia: A prospective investigation. *American Journal of Psychiatry, 161,* 2021–2027.

Schiller, D., Monfils, M., Raio, C., Johnson, D., LeDoux, J. E., & Phelps, E. A. (2010). Preventing the return of fear in humans using reconsolidation update mechanisms. *Nature, 463,* 49–54.

Schizophrenia Working Group of the Psychiatric Genomics Consortium. (2014). Biological insights from 108 schizophrenia-associated genetic loci. *Nature, 511,* 421–427.

Schlam, T. R., & Baker, T. B. (2013). Interventions for tobacco smoking. *Annual Review of Clinical Psychology, 9,* 675–702.

Schmader, T. (2010). Stereotype threat deconstructed. *Current Directions in Psychological Science, 19,* 14–18.

Schmader, T., Johns, M., & Forbes, C. (2008). An integrated process model of stereotype threat effects on performance. *Psychological Review, 115,* 336–356.

Schmidt, F. L., & Hunter, J. (2004). General mental ability in the world of work: Occupational attainment and job performance. *Journal of Personality and Social Psychology, 96,* 162–173.

Schmidt, N. B., & Keough, M. E. (2011). Treatment of panic. *Annual Review of Clinical Psychology, 6,* 241–256.

Schmitt, D. P., Alcalay, L., Allik, J., Angleitner, A., Ault, L., Austers, I., et al. (2003). Universal sex differences in the desire for sexual variety: Tests from 52 nations, 6 continents, and 13 islands. *Journal of Personality and Social Psychology, 85,* 85–104.

Schmitt, D. P., Allik, J., McCrae, R. R., & Benet-Martinez, V. (2007). The geographic distribution of Big Five personality traits: Patterns and profiles of human self-description across 56 nations. *Journal of Cross-Cultural Psychology, 38,* 173–212.

Schmitt, D. P., Realo, A., Voracek, M., & Allik, J. (2008). Why can't a man be more like a woman? *Journal of Personality and Social Psychology, 94,* 168–182.

Schmitz, T. W., De Rosa, E., & Anderson, A. K. (2009). Opposing influences of affective state valence in visual cortical encoding. *Journal of Neuroscience, 29,* 7199–7207.

Schoch, H., & Abel, T. (2014). Transcriptional co-repressors and memory storage. *Neuropharmacology, 80,* 53–60.

Schoenbaum, G., Esber, G. R., & Iordanova, M. D. (2013). Dopamine signals mimic reward prediction errors. *Nature Neuroscience, 16,* 777–779.

Schoenemann, P. T., Sheehan, M. J., & Glotzer, L. D. (2005). Prefrontal white matter volume is disproportionately larger in humans than in other primates. *Nature Neuroscience, 8,* 242–252.

Schuch, F. B., Vancampfort, D., Richards, J., Rosenbaum, S., Ward, P., & Stubbs, B. (2016a). Exercise as a treatment for depression: A meta-analysis adjusting for publication bias. *Journal of Psychiatric Research, 77,* 42–51.

Schuch, F. B., Vancampfort, D., Sui, X., Rosenbaum, S., Firth, J., Richards, J., et al. (2016b). Are lower levels of cardiorespiratory fitness associated with incident depression? A systematic review of prospective cohort studies. *Preventive Medicine, 93,* 159–165.

Schultz, P. W., Nolan, J. M., Cialdini, R. B., Goldstein, N. J., & Griskevicius, V. (2007). The constructive, destructive, and reconstructive power of social norms. *Psychological Science, 18,* 429–434.

Schultz, W. (2016). Dopamine reward prediction-error signalling: A two-component response. *Nature Reviews Neuroscience, 17,* 183–185.

Schultz, W., Dayan, P., & Montague, P. R. (1997). A neural substrate of prediction and reward. *Science, 275,* 1593–1599.

Schulz, K. M., & Sisk, C. L. (2016). The organizing actions of adolescent gonadal steroid hormones on brain and behavioral development. *Neuroscience & Biobehavioral Reviews, 70,* 148–158.

Schurz, M., Radua, J., Aichhorn, M., Richlan, F., & Perner, J. (2014). Fractionating theory of mind: A meta-analysis of functional brain imaging studies. *Neuroscience & Biobehavioral Reviews, 42,* 9–34.

Schwartz, B. (2004). *The paradox of choice: Why more is less.* New York, NY: Ecco.

Schwartz, B., Ward, A., Monterosso, J., Lyubomirsky, S., White, K., & Lehman, D. R. (2002). Maximizing versus satisficing: Happiness is a matter of choice. *Journal of Personality and Social Psychology, 83,* 1178–1197.

Schwartz, C. E., Wright, C. I., Shin, L. M., Kagan, J., & Rauch, S. L. (2003). Inhibited and uninhibited infants "grown up": Adult amygdalar response to novelty. *Science, 300,* 1952–1953.

Schwartz, S., & Maquet, P. (2002). Sleep imaging and the neuropsychological assessment of dreams. *Trends in Cognitive Sciences, 6,* 23–30.

Schwarz, N., & Clore, G. L. (1983). Mood, misattribution, and judgments of well-being: Informative and directive functions of affective states. *Journal of Personality and Social Psychology, 45,* 513–523.

Schwarzkopf, D. S. (2014). We should have seen this coming. *Frontiers in Human Neuroscience, 8,* 332. doi: 10.3389/fnhum.2014.00332

Schwebel, D. C., Stavrinos, D., Byington, K. W., Davis, T., O'Neal, E. E., & de Jong, D. (2012). Distraction and pedestrian safety: How talking on the phone, texting, and listening to music impact crossing the street. *Accident Analysis & Prevention, 45,* 266–271.

Sclafani, A., & Springer, D. (1976). Dietary obesity in adult rats: Similarities to hypothalamic and human obesity syndromes. *Physiology and Behavior, 17,* 461–471.

Sedikides, C., Gaertner, L., & Toguchi, Y. (2003). Pancultural self-enhancement. *Journal of Personality and Social Psychology, 84,* 60–79.

Sedikides, C., & Gregg, A. (2008). Self-enhancement: Food for thought. *Perspectives on Psychological Science, 3,* 102–116.

Seegmiller, J. K., Watson, J. M., & Strayer, D. L. (2011). Individual differences in susceptibility to inattentional blindness. *Journal of Experimental Psychology: Learning, Memory, and Cognition, 37,* 785–791.

Segerstrom, S. C., & Miller, G. E. (2004). Psychological stress and the human immune system: A meta-analytic study of 30 years of inquiry. *Psychological Bulletin, 130,* 601–630.

Seligman, M. E. P. (1970). On the generality of the laws of learning. *Psychological Review, 77,* 406–418.

Seligman, M. E. P. (1974). Depression and learned helplessness. In R. J. Friedman & M. M. Katz (Eds.), *The psychology of depression: Contemporary theory and research* (pp. 83–113). Washington, DC: V. H. Winston.

Seligman, M. E. P. (1975). *Helplessness: On depression, development, and death.* San Francisco, CA: Freeman.

Seligman, M. E. P. (2011). *Flourish.* New York, NY: Simon & Schuster.

Seligman, M. E. P., & Csikszentmihalyi, M. (2000). Positive psychology: An introduction. *American Psychologist, 55,* 5–14.

Seligman, M. E. P., Steen, T. A., Park, N., & Peterson, C. (2005). Positive psychology progress: Empirical validation of interventions. *American Psychologist, 60,* 410–421.

Seligman, M. E. P., Walker, E. F., & Rosenhan, D. L. (2001). *Abnormal psychology* (4th ed.). New York, NY: Norton.

Selkie, E. M., Fales, J. L., & Moreno, M. A. (2016). Cyberbullying prevalence among US middle and high school–aged adolescents: A systematic review and quality assessment. *Journal of Adolescent Health, 58,* 125–133.

Selye, H. (1936). A syndrome produced by diverse nocuous agents. *Nature, 138,* 32.

Shah, R. S., Chang, S., Min, H., Cho, Z., Blaha, C., & Lee, K. H. (2010). Deep brain stimulation: Technology at the cutting edge. *Journal of Clinical Neurology, 6,* 167–182.

Shallice, T., & Warrington, E. (1969). Independent functioning of verbal memory stores. *Quarterly Journal of Experimental Psychology, 22,* 261–273.

Shapiro, A. F., Gottman, J. M., & Carrère, S. (2000). The baby and the marriage: Identifying factors that buffer against decline in marital satisfaction after the first baby arrives. *Journal of Family Psychology, 14,* 59–70.

Shaw, P., Malek, M., Watson, B., Sharp, W., Evans, A., & Greenstein, D. (2012). Development of cortical surface area and gyrification in attention-deficit/hyperactivity disorder. *Biological Psychiatry, 72,* 191–197.

Shedler, J. (2010). The efficacy of psychodynamic psychotherapy. *American Psychologist, 65,* 98–109.

Shedler, J. (2015). Where is the evidence for "evidence-based" therapy? *Journal of Psychological Therapies in Primary Care, 4,* 47–59.

Shedler, J., & Block, J. (1990). Adolescent drug use and psychological health: A longitudinal inquiry. *American Psychologist, 45,* 612–630.

Shenhav, A., & Greene, J. D. (2014). Integrative moral judgment: Dissociating the roles of the amygdala and prefrontal cortex. *Journal of Neuroscience, 34,* 4741–4749.

Shenkin, S. D., Starr, J. M., & Deary, I. J. (2004). Birth weight and cognitive ability in childhood: A systematic review. *Psychological Bulletin, 130,* 989–1013.

Shephard, R. J. (1997). *Aging, physical activity, and health.* Champaign, IL: Human Kinetics Publishers.

Sher, L. (2000). Sociopolitical events and technical innovations may affect the content of delusions and the course of psychotic disorders. *Medical Hypotheses, 55,* 507–509.

Sherif, M. (1936). *The psychology of social norms.* Oxford, England: Harper.

Sherif, M., Harvey, O. J., White, B. J., Hood, W. R., & Sherif, C. W. (1961). *Intergroup cooperation and competition: The Robbers Cave experiment.* Norman, OK: University Book Exchange.

Sherman, D. K., McGue, M. K., & Iacono, W. G. (1997). Twin concordance for attention deficit hyperactivity disorder: A comparison of teacher's and mother's reports. *American Journal of Psychiatry, 154,* 532–535.

Sherman, R. A., Nave, C. S., & Funder, D. C. (2010). Situational similarity and personality predict behavioral consistency. *Journal of Personality and Social Psychology, 99,* 330–343.

Sherman, S. J., Presson, C., Chassin, L., Corty, E., & Olshavsky, R. (1983). The false consensus effect in estimates of smoking prevalence: Underlying mechanisms. *Personality and Social Psychology Bulletin, 9,* 197–207.

Sherwin, B. B. (1988). A comparative analysis of the role of androgen in human male and female sexual behavior: Behavioral specificity, critical thresholds, and sensitivity. *Psychobiology, 16,* 416–425.

Sherwin, B. B. (1994). Sex hormones and psychological functioning in postmenopausal women. *Experimental Gerontology, 29,* 423–430.

Sherwin, B. B. (2008). Hormones, the brain, and me. *Canadian Psychology, 49,* 42–48.

Shetty, A. K., & Upadhya, D. (2016). GABA-ergic cell therapy for epilepsy: Advances, limitations and challenges. *Neuroscience & Biobehavioral Reviews, 62,* 35–47.

Shih, M., Pittinsky, T. L., & Ambady, N. (1999). Stereotype susceptibility: Identity salience and shifts in quantitative performance. *Psychological Science, 10,* 80–83.

Shin, L. M., Rauch, S. L., & Pitman, R. K. (2006). Amygdala, medial prefrontal cortex, and hippocampal function in PTSD. *Annals of the New York Academy of Sciences, 1071,* 67–79.

Shiner, R. L., Allen, T. A., & Masten, A. S. (2017). Adversity in adolescence predicts personality trait change from childhood to adulthood. *Journal of Research in Personality, 67,* 171–182. Retrieved from http://dx.doi.org/10.1016/j.jrp.2016.10.002

Shipstead, Z., Redick, T. S., & Engle, R. W. (2012). Is working memory training effective? *Psychological Bulletin, 138,* 628–654.

Siegel, C. E., Laska, E. M., Wanderling, J. A., Hernandez, J. C., & Levenson, R. B. (2015). Prevalence and diagnosis rates of childhood ADHD among racial-ethnic groups in a public mental health system. *Psychiatric Services, 67,* 199–205.

Siegel, J. M. (2008). Do all animals sleep? *Trends in Neuroscience, 31,* 208–213.

Siegel, S. (1984). Pavlovian conditioning and heroin overdose: Reports by overdose victims. *Bulletin of the Psychonomic Society, 22,* 428–430.

Siegel, S. (2005). Drug tolerance, drug addiction, and drug anticipation. *Current Directions in Psychological Science, 14,* 296–300.

Siegel, S. (2016). The heroin overdose mystery. *Current Directions in Psychological Science, 25,* 375–379.

Siegel, S., Baptista, M. A. S., Kim, J. A., McDonald, R. V., & Weise-Kelly, L. (2000). Pavlovian psychopharmacology: The associative basis of tolerance. *Experimental and Clinical Psychopharmacology, 8,* 276–293.

Siegel, S., Hinson, R. E., Krank, M. D., & McCully, J. (1982). Heroin "overdose" death: Contribution of drug-associated environmental cues. *Science, 216,* 436–437.

Siegler, I. C., Costa, P. T., Brummett, B. H., Helms, M. J., Barefoot, J. C., Williams, R., et al. (2003). Patterns of change in hostility from college to midlife in the UNC alumni heart study predict high-risk status. *Psychosomatic Medicine, 65,* 738–745.

Sievers, B., Polansky, L., Casey, M., & Wheatley, T. (2013). Music and movement share a dynamic structure that supports universal expressions of emotion. *Proceedings of the National Academy of Sciences, 110,* 70–75.

Siklenka, K., Erkek, S., Godmann, M., Lambrot, R., McGraw, S., Lafleur, C., et al. (2015). Disruption of histone methylation in developing sperm impairs offspring health transgenerationally. *Science, 350,* 651.

Silbersweig, D., Clarkin, J. F., Goldstein, M., Kernberg, O. F., Tuescher, O., Levy, K. N., et al. (2007). Failure of frontolimbic inhibitory function in the context of negative emotion in borderline personality disorder. *American Journal of Psychiatry, 64,* 1832–1841.

Silva, C. E., & Kirsch, I. (1992). Interpretive sets, expectancy, fantasy proneness, and dissociation as predictors of hypnotic response. *Journal of Personality and Social Psychology, 63,* 847–856.

Silvers, J. A., Insel, C., Powers, A., Franz, P., Helion, C., Martin, R., et al. (2017). The transition from childhood to adolescence is marked by a general decrease in amygdala reactivity and an affect-specific ventral-to-dorsal shift in medial prefrontal recruitment. *Developmental Cognitive Neuroscience, 25,* 128–137.

Simeone, J. C., Ward, A. J., Rotella, P., Collins, J., & Windisch, R. (2015). An evaluation of variation in published estimates of schizophrenia prevalence from 1990–2013: A systematic literature review. *BMC Psychiatry, 15,* 193.

Simner, J., Mulvenna, C., Sagiv, N., Tsakanikos, E., Witherby, S. A., Fraser, C., et al. (2006). Synaesthesia: The prevalence of atypical cross-modal experiences. *Perception, 35,* 1024–1033.

Simons, D. J., Boot, W. R., Charness, N., Gathercole, S. E., Chabris, C. F., Hambrick, D. Z., & Stine-Morrow, E. A. (2016). Do "brain-training" programs work? *Psychological Science in the Public Interest, 17,* 103–186.

Simons, D. J., & Levin, D. T. (1998). Failure to detect changes to people during a real-world interaction. *Psychonomic Bulletin and Review, 5,* 644–649.

Simpson, H. B., Foa, E. B., Liebowitz, M. R., Ledley, D. R., Huppert, J. D., Cahill, S., et al. (2008). A randomized, controlled trial of cognitive-behavioral therapy for augmenting pharmacotherapy in obsessive-compulsive disorder. *American Journal of Psychiatry, 165,* 621–630.

Simpson, J., & Kelly, J. P. (2011). The impact of environmental enrichment in laboratory rats—behavioural and neurochemical aspects. *Behavioural Brain Research, 222,* 246–264.

Sims, H. E. A., Goldman, R. F., Gluck, C. M., Horton, E., Kelleher, P., & Rowe, D. (1968). Experimental obesity in man. *Transactions of the Association of American Physicians, 81,* 153–170.

Sims, T., Hogan, C. L., & Carstensen, L. L. (2015). Selectivity as an emotion regulation strategy: Lessons from older adults. *Current Opinion in Psychology, 3,* 80–84.

Sirois, B. C., & Burg, M. M. (2003). Negative emotion and coronary heart disease: A review. *Behavior Modification, 27,* 83–102.

Six most feared but least likely causes of death. (2005, July 13). *Be Safe, Live Long & Prosper* [E-newsletter]. Retrieved from http://www.sixwise.com/newsletters/05/07/13/the_six_most_feared_but_least_likely_causes_of_death.htm

Skinner, B. F. (1948a). "Superstition" in the pigeon. *Journal of Experimental Psychology, 38,* 168.

Skinner, B. F. (1948b). *Walden two.* Indianapolis, IN: Hackett.

Skinner, B. F. (1957). *Verbal behavior.* New York, NY: Appleton-Century-Crofts.

Skinner, B. F. (1971). *Beyond freedom and dignity.* New York, NY: Wiley.

Slovic, P., Finucane, M., Peters, E., & MacGregor, D. (2002). The affect heuristic. In T. Gilovich, D. Griffin, & D. Kahneman (Eds.), *Heuristics and biases: The psychology of intuitive judgment* (pp. 397–420). New York, NY: Cambridge University Press.

Slovic, P., Fischhoff, B., Lichtenstein, S., & Roe, F. J. C. (1981). Perceived risk: Psychological factors and social implications [and discussion]. *Proceedings of the Royal Society of London. A. Mathematical and Physical Sciences, 376,* 17–34.

Slutske, W. S., Moffitt, T. E., Poulton, R., & Caspi, A. (2012). Undercontrolled temperament at age 3 predicts disordered gambling at age 32: A longitudinal study of a complete birth cohort. *Psychological Science, 23,* 510–516.

Small, G. W., Kepe, V., Siddarth, P., Ercoli, L. M., Merrill, D. A., Donoghue, N., et al. (2013). PET scanning of brain tau in retired National Football League players: Preliminary findings. *American Journal of Geriatric Psychiatry, 21,* 138–144.

Smith, A., Floerke, V., & Thomas, A. (2016). Retrieval practice protects memory against acute stress. *Science, 354,* 1046–1048.

Smith, A. L., & Chapman, S. (2014). Quitting smoking unassisted: The 50-year research neglect of a major public health phenomenon. *Journal of the American Medical Association, 311,* 137–138.

Smith, C., & Lapp, L. (1991). Increases in number of REMs and REM density in humans following an intensive learning period. *Sleep, 14,* 325–330.

Smith, D. M., Langa, K. M., Kabeto, M. U., & Ubel, P. A. (2005). Health, wealth, and happiness: Financial resources buffer subjective well-being after the onset of a disability. *Psychological Science, 16,* 663–664.

Smith, K. S., Berridge, K. C., & Aldridge, J. W. (2011). Disentangling pleasure from incentive salience and learning signals in brain reward circuitry. *Proceedings of the National Academy of Sciences, 108,* E255–E264.

Smith, L. B., & Thelen, E. (2003). Development as a dynamic system. *Trends in Cognitive Sciences, 7,* 343–348.

Smith, S. M., Glenberg, A. M., & Bjork, R. A. (1978). Environmental context and human memory. *Memory and Cognition, 6,* 342–353.

Smith, T. W., Orleans, C. T., & Jenkins, C. D. (2004). Prevention and health promotion: Decades of progress, new challenges, and an emerging agenda. *Health Psychology, 23,* 126–131.

Snarey, J. R. (1985). Cross-cultural universality of social-moral development: A critical review of Kohlbergian research. *Psychological Bulletin, 97,* 202–232.

Snider, L. A., & Swedo, S. E. (2004). PANDAS: Current status and directions for research. *Molecular Psychiatry, 9,* 900–907.

Snowling, M. J., & Melby-Lervåg, M. (2016). Oral language deficits in familial dyslexia: A meta-analysis and review. *Psychological Bulletin, 142,* 498–545.

Snyder, E. E., Walts, B. M., Pérusse, L., Chagnon, Y. C., Weisnagel, S. J., Rankinen, T., et al. (2004). The human obesity gene map: The 2003 update. *Obesity Research, 12,* 369–438.

Snyder, H. R., Young, J. F., & Hankin, B. L. (2016). Strong homotypic continuity in common psychopathology-, internalizing-, and externalizing-specific factors over time in adolescents. *Clinical Psychological Science, 5,* 98–110.

Snyder, M., & Cantor, N. (1998). Understanding personality and personal behavior: A functionalist strategy. In D. T. Gilbert, S. T. Fiske, & G. Lindzey (Eds.), *Handbook of social psychology* (pp. 635–679). New York, NY: McGraw-Hill.

Solms, M. (2000). Dreaming and REM sleep are controlled by different brain mechanisms. *Behavioral and Brain Sciences, 23,* 793.

Somerville, L. H., Hare, T. A., & Casey, B. J. (2011). Frontostriatal maturation predicts cognitive control failure to appetitive cues in adolescents. *Journal of Cognitive Neuroscience, 23,* 2123–2134.

Somerville, L. H., Kim, H., Johnstone, T., Alexander, A. L., & Whalen, P. J. (2004). Human amygdala responses during presentation of happy and neutral faces: Correlations with state anxiety. *Biological Psychiatry, 55,* 897–903.

Sommerville, J. A., & Woodward, A. L. (2005). Pulling out the intentional structure of action: The relation between action processing and action production in infancy. *Cognition, 95,* 1–30.

Son Hing, L. S., Chung-Yan, G. A., Hamilton, L. K., & Zanna, M. P. (2008). A two-dimensional model that employs explicit and implicit attitudes to characterize prejudice. *Journal of Personality and Social Psychology, 94,* 971–987.

Sorensen, T., Holst, C., Stunkard, A. J., & Skovgaard, L. T. (1992). Correlations of body mass index of adult adoptees and their biological and adoptive relatives. *International Journal of Obesity and Related Metabolic Disorders, 16,* 227–236.

Southgate, V., & Hamilton, A. F. (2008). Unbroken mirrors: Challenging a theory of autism. *Trends in Cognitive Science, 12,* 225–229.

Spain, S. M., Harms, P., & LeBreton, J. M. (2013). The dark side of personality at work. *Journal of Organizational Behavior, 35,* 41–60.

Spanos, N. P., & Coe, W. C. (1992). A social-psychological approach to hypnosis. In E. Fromm & M. Nash (Eds.), *Contemporary hypnosis research* (pp. 102–130). New York, NY: Guilford Press.

Spearman, C. (1904). "General intelligence," objectively determined and measured. *American Journal of Psychology, 15,* 201–293.

Spector, N. (2017, January 1). 2017 New Year's resolutions: The most popular and how to stick to them. *NBC News.* Retrieved from http://www.nbcnews.com/business/consumer/2017-new-year-s-resolutions-most-popular-how-stick-them-n701891

Spelke, E. S. (2016). Cognitive abilities of infants. In R. J. Sternberg, S. T. Fiske, & D. J. Foss (Eds.), *Scientists making a difference: One hundred eminent behavioral and brain scientists talk about their most important contributions* (pp. 22–234). Cambridge, England: Cambridge University Press.

Spencer, M. B., Fegley, S. G., & Harpalani, V. (2003). A theoretical and empirical examination of identity as coping: Linking coping resources to the self processes of African American youth. *Applied Developmental Science, 7,* 181–188.

Spencer, R. C., Devilbiss, D. M., & Berridge, C. W. (2015). The cognition-enhancing effects of psychostimulants involve direct action in the prefrontal cortex. *Biological Psychiatry, 77,* 940–950.

Spencer, S. J., Logel, C., & Davies, P. G. (2016). Stereotype threat. *Annual Review of Psychology, 67,* 415–437.

Spencer, S. J., Steele, C. M., & Quinn, D. M. (1999). Stereotype threat and women's math performance. *Journal of Experimental Social Psychology, 35,* 4–28.

Sperling, G. (1960). The information available in brief visual presentations. *Psychological Monographs, 74,* 1–29.

Spiegel, D., Lewis-Fernández, R., Lanius, R., Vermetten, E., Simeon, D., & Friedman, M. (2013). Dissociative disorders in DSM-5. *Annual Review of Clinical Psychology, 9,* 299–326.

Spieker, L. E., Hürlimann, D., Ruschitzka, F., Corti, R., Enseleit, F., Shaw, S., & Noll, G. (2002). Mental stress induces prolonged endothelial dysfunction via endothelin-A receptors. *Circulation, 105,* 2817–2820.

Spitzer, R. L., Skodol, A. E., Gibbon, M., & Williams, J. B. W. (1983). *Psychopathology: A case book.* New York, NY: McGraw-Hill.

Spreng, R. N., & Turner, G. R. (2013). Structural covariance of the default network in healthy and pathological aging. *Journal of Neuroscience, 33,* 15226–15234.

Spurk, D., Keller, A. C., & Hirschi, A. (2016). Do bad guys get ahead or fall behind? Relationships of the dark triad of personality with objective and subjective career success. *Social Psychological and Personality Science, 7,* 113–121.

Spurr, K. F., Graven, M. A., & Gilbert, R. W. (2008). Prevalence of unspecified sleep apnea and the use of continuous positive airway pressure in hospitalized patients, 2004 national hospital discharge survey. *Sleep and Breathing, 12,* 229–234.

Squire, L. R. (1987). *Memory and brain.* Oxford, England: Oxford University Press.

Squire, L. R., Amaral, D. G., Zola-Morgan, S., Kritchevsky, M., & Press, G. (1989). Description of brain injury in the amnesic patient NA based on magnetic resonance imaging. *Experimental neurology, 105,* 23–35.

Squire, L. R., Stark, C. E. L., & Clark, R. E. (2004). The medial temporal lobe. *Annual Review of Neuroscience, 27,* 279–306.

Srivastava, S., John, O. P., Gosling, S. D., & Potter, J. (2003). Development of personality in early and middle adulthood: Set like plaster or persistent change? *Journal of Personality and Social Psychology, 84,* 1041–1053.

Srivastava, S., McGonigal, K. M., Richards, J. M., Butler, E. A., & Gross, J. J. (2006). Optimism in close relationships: How seeing things in a positive light makes them so. *Personality Processes and Individual Differences, 91,* 143–153.

Stanovich, K. E. (2013). *How to think straight about psychology* (10th ed.). Upper Saddle River, NJ: Pearson.

Stark, S. (2000, December 22). "Cast Away" lets Hanks fend for himself. *Detroit News.* Retrieved from http://www.detnews.com

Stavrinos, D., Byington, K. W., & Schwebel, D. C. (2011). Distracted walking: Cell phones increase injury risk for college pedestrians. *Journal of Safety Research, 42,* 101–107.

Steele, C. M., & Aronson, J. (1995). Stereotype threat and the intellectual test performance of African-Americans. *Journal of Personality and Social Psychology, 69,* 797–811.

Steeves, J. K., Culham, J. C., Duchaine, B. C., Pratesi, C. C., Valyear, K. F., Schindler, I., et al. (2006). The fusiform face area is not sufficient for face recognition: Evidence from a patient with dense prosopagnosia and no occipital face area. *Neuropsychologia, 4,* 594–609.

Stefanik, M. T., Moussawi, K., Kupchik, Y. M., Smith, K. C., Miller, R. L., Huff, M. L., et al. (2013). Optogenetic inhibition of cocaine seeking in rats. *Addiction Biology, 18,* 50–53.

Stein, M. B., & Stein, D. J. (2008). Social anxiety disorder. *Lancet, 371,* 1115–1125.

Steinberg, L. (2001). We know some things: Parent-adolescent relationships in retrospect and prospect. *Journal of Research on Adolescence, 11,* 1–19.

Steinberg, L., & Sheffield, A. M. (2001). Adolescent development. *Journal of Cognitive Education and Psychology, 2,* 55–87.

Steiner, J. E. (1977). Facial expressions of the neonate infant indicating the hedonics of food-related chemical stimuli. In J. M. Weiffenbach (Ed.), *Taste and development* (pp. 173–189). Bethesda, MD: National Institutes of Health.

Stender, J., Mortensen, K. N., Thibaut, A., Darkner, S., Laureys, S., Gjedde, A., & Kupers, R. (2016). The minimal energetic requirement of sustained awareness after brain injury. *Current Biology, 26,* 1494–1499.

Sternberg, R. J. (1986). A triangular theory of love. *Psychological Review, 93,* 119–135.

Sternberg, R. J. (1999). The theory of successful intelligence. *Review of General Psychology, 3,* 292–316.

Stewart, P. A. (2008). Subliminals in the 2000 presidential election: Policy implications of applied neuroscience. *Public Integrity, 10,* 215–232.

Stice, E. (2002). Risk and maintenance factors for eating pathology: A meta-analytic review. *Psychological Bulletin, 128,* 825–848.

Stickgold, R., Whidbee, D., Schirmer, B., Patel, V., & Hobson, J. A. (2000). Visual discrimination task improvement: A multi-step process occurring during sleep. *Journal of Cognitive Neuroscience, 12,* 246–254.

Stockwell, T., Zhao, J., Panwar, S., Roemer, A., Naimi, T., & Chikritzhs, T. (2016). Do "moderate" drinkers have reduced mortality risk? A systematic review and meta-analysis of alcohol consumption and all-cause mortality. *Journal of Studies on Alcohol and Drugs, 77,* 185–198.

Stokstad, E. (2001). New hints into the biological basis of autism. *Science, 294,* 34–37.

Stone, A. A., Neale, J. M., Cox, D. S., Napoli, A., Valdimardottir, H., & Kennedy-Moore, E. (1994). Daily events are associated with a secretory immune response to an oral antigen in men. *Health Psychology, 13,* 440–446.

Stone, V. E., Baron-Cohen, S., & Knight, R. T. (1998). Frontal lobe contributions to theory of mind. *Journal of Cognitive Neuroscience, 10,* 640–656.

Stoner, J. A. (1968). Risky and cautious shifts in group decisions: The influence of widely held values. *Journal of Experimental Social Psychology, 4,* 442–459.

Strack, F. (2016). Reflection on the smiling registered replication report. *Perspectives on Psychological Science, 11,* 929–930.

Strack, F., Martin, L. L., & Stepper, S. (1988). Inhibiting and facilitating conditions of the human smile: A nonobtrusive test of the facial feedback hypothesis. *Journal of Personality and Social Psychology, 54,* 768–777.

Strahan, E. J., Spencer, S. J., & Zanna, M. P. (2002). Subliminal priming and persuasion: Striking while the iron is hot. *Journal of Experimental Social Psychology, 38,* 556–568.

Strayhorn, T. L. (2014). What role does grit play in the academic success of black male collegians at predominantly white institutions? *Journal of African American Studies, 18,* 1–10.

Striegel-Moore, R. H., & Franko, D. L. (2008). Should binge eating disorder be included in the DSM-V? A critical review of the state of the evidence. *Annual Review of Clinical Psychology, 4,* 305–324.

Stroebe, W., & Strack, F. (2014). The alleged crisis and the illusion of exact replication. *Perspectives on Psychological Science, 9,* 59–71.

Stunkard, A. J. (1996). Current views on obesity. *American Journal of Medicine, 100,* 230–236.

Süß, H. M., Oberauer, K., Wittman, W. W., Wilhelm, O., & Schulze, R. (2002). Working-memory capacity explains reasoning ability—and a little bit more. *Intelligence, 30,* 261–288.

Substance Abuse and Mental Health Services Administration. (2011). Major depressive episode and treatment among adolescents: 2009. *National Survey on Drug Use and Health.* Retrieved from http://www .oas.samhsa.gov/2k11/009/AdolescentDepression.htm

Substance Abuse and Mental Health Services Administration. (2014). *Results from the 2013 National Survey on Drug Use and Health: Summary of national findings.* NSDUH Series H-48, HHS Publication No. (SMA) 14-4863. Rockville, MD: Substance Abuse and Mental Health Services Administration.

Sulin, R. A., & Dooling, D. J. (1974). Intrusion of a thematic idea in retention of prose. *Journal of Experimental Psychology, 103,* 255–262.

Sullivan, M. J. L., Thorn, B., Haythornthwaite, J. A., Keefe, F., Martin, M., Bradley, L. A., et al. (2001). Theoretical perspectives on the relation between catastrophizing and pain. *Clinical Journal of Pain, 17,* 52–64.

Suls, J., Lemos, K., & Stewart, H. L. (2002). Self-esteem, construal, and comparisons with the self, friends, and peers. *Journal of Personality and Social Psychology, 82,* 252–261.

Super, C. M. (1976). Environmental effects on motor development: The case of African precocity. *Developmental Medicine and Child Neurology, 18,* 561–567.

Susilo, T., & Duchaine, B. (2013). Advances in developmental prosopagnosia research. *Current Opinion in Neurobiology, 23,* 423–429.

Sutter, M. E., Gerona, R., Davis, M. T., Roche, B. M., Colby, D. K., Chenoweth, J. A., et al. (2017). Fatal fentanyl: One pill can kill. *Academic Emergency Medicine, 24,* 106–113. doi: 10.1111/acem.13034

Svenson, O. (1981). Are we all less risky and more skillful than our fellow drivers? *Acta Psychologica, 47,* 143–148.

Swaab, D. F. (2004). Sexual differentiation of the human brain: Relevance for gender identity, transsexualism and sexual orientation. *Gynecological Endocrinology, 19,* 301–312.

Swann, W. B., Jr., Buhrmester, M. D., Gómez, A., Jetten, J., Bastian, B., Vázquez, A., et al. (2014). What makes a group worth dying for? Identity fusion fosters perception of familial ties, promoting self-sacrifice. *Journal of Personality and Social Psychology, 106,* 912–926.

Swanson, S. A., Crow, S. J., Le Grange, D., Swendsen, J., & Merikangas, K. R. (2011). Prevalence and correlates of eating disorders in adolescents: Results from the national comorbidity survey replication adolescent supplement. *Archives of General Psychiatry, 68,* 714–723.

Swartz, M. S., Blazer, D., George, L., & Winfield, I. (1990). Estimating the prevalence of borderline personality disorder in the community. *Journal of Personality Disorders, 4,* 257–272.

Swendsen, J., Burstein, M., Case, B., Conway, K. P., Dierker, L., He, J., & Merikangas, K. R. (2012). Use and abuse of alcohol and illicit drugs in U.S. adolescents: Results of the National Comorbidity Survey—Adolescent supplement. *Archives of General Psychiatry, 69,* 390–398.

Tajfel, H. (1982). Social psychology of intergroup relations. *Annual Review of Psychology, 33,* 1–39.

Tajfel, H., & Turner, J. C. (1979). An integrative theory of intergroup conflict. In W. G. Austin & S. Worchel (Eds.), *The social psychology of intergroup relations* (pp. 33–47). Monterey, CA: Brooks/Cole.

Talarico, J. M., & Rubin, D. C. (2003). Confidence, not consistency, characterizes flashbulb memories. *Psychological Science, 14,* 455–461.

Talley, P. R., Strupp, H. H., & Morey, L. C. (1990). Matchmaking in psychotherapy: Patient-therapist dimensions and their impact on outcome. *Journal of Consulting and Clinical Psychology, 58,* 182–188.

Talmi, D. (2013). Enhanced emotional memory: Cognitive and neural mechanisms. *Current Directions in Psychological Science, 22,* 430–436.

Tang, C. S. K. (2007). Trajectory of traumatic stress symptoms in the aftermath of extreme natural disaster: A study of adult Thai survivors of the 2004 Southeast Asian earthquake and tsunami. *Journal of Nervous and Mental Disease, 195,* 54–59.

Tang, Y. P., Wang, H., Feng, R., Kyin, M., Tsien, J. Z. (2001). Differential effects of enrichment on learning and memory function in NR2B transgenic mice. *Neuropharmacology, 41,* 779–790.

Tang, Y. Y., Ma, Y. H., Wang, J. H., Fan, Y. X., Feng, S. G., Lu, Q. L., et al. (2007). Short-term meditation training improves attention and self-regulation. *Proceedings of the National Academy of Sciences, 104,* 17152–17156.

Tangney, J. P., Stuewig, J., & Mashek, D. J. (2007). Moral emotions and moral behavior. *Annual Review of Psychology, 58,* 345–372.

Tateyama, M., Asai, M., Kamisada, M., Hashimoto, M., Bartels, M., & Heimann, H. (1993). Comparison of schizophrenic delusions between Japan and Germany. *Psychopathology, 26,* 151–158.

Taylor, A. K., & Kowalski, P. (2012). Students' misconceptions in psychology: How you ask matters... sometimes. *Journal of the Scholarship of Teaching and Learning, 12,* 62–77.

Taylor, S. E. (2006). Tend and befriend: Biobehavioral bases of affiliation under stress. *Current Directions in Psychological Science, 15,* 273–277.

Taylor, S. E., & Brown, J. D. (1988). Illusion and well-being: A social psychological perspective on mental health. *Psychological Bulletin, 103,* 193–210.

Taylor, S. E., Lewis, B. P., Gruenewald, T. L., Gurung, R. A. R., Updegraff, J. A., & Klein, L. C. (2002). Sex differences in biobehavioral responses to threat: Reply to Geary and Flinn. *Psychological Review, 109,* 751–753.

Taylor, S. E., Saphire-Bernstein, S., & Seeman, T. E. (2010). Are plasma oxytocin in women and plasma vasopressin in men biomarkers of distressed pair-bond relationships? *Psychological Science, 21,* 3–7.

Teasdale, J. D., Segal, Z. V., Williams, J. M. G., Ridgeway, V. A., Soulsby, J. M., & Lau, M. A. (2000). Prevention of relapse/recurrence in major depression by mindfulness-based cognitive therapy. *Journal of Consulting and Clinical Psychology, 68,* 615–623.

Teller, D. Y., Morse, R., Borton, R., & Regal, C. (1974). Visual acuity for vertical and diagonal gratings in human infants. *Vision Research, 14,* 1433–1439.

Temple, E., Poldrack, R. A., Salidis, J., Deutsch, G. K., Tallal, P., Merzenich, M. M., & Gabrieli, J. D. (2001). Disrupted neural responses to phonological and orthographic processing in dyslexic children: An fMRI study. *Neuroreport, 12,* 299–307.

Terracciano, A., Abdel-Khalek, A. M., Ádám, N., Adamovová, L., Ahn, C. K., Ahn, H. N., et al. (2005). National character does not reflect mean personality trait levels in 49 cultures. *Science, 310,* 96–100.

Tesser, A. (1993). The importance of heritability: The case of attitudes. *Psychological Review, 100,* 129–142.

Tessler, L. G. (1997). *How college students with learning disabilities can advocate for themselves.* Retrieved from http://www.ldanatl.org /aboutld/adults/post_secondary/print_college.asp

Thoits, P. A. (2010) Stress and health: Major findings and policy implications. *Journal of Health and Social Behavior, 51,* 41–53.

Thomas, R., Sanders, S., Doust, J., Beller, E., & Glasziou, P. (2015). Prevalence of attention-deficit/hyperactivity disorder: A systematic review and meta-analysis. *Pediatrics, 135,* 994–1001.

Thompson, K. M., & Huynh, C. (2017). Alone and at risk: A statistical profile of alcohol-related college student deaths. *Journal of Substance Use.* http://dx.doi.org/10.1080/14659891.2016.1271032.

Thompson, P. (1980). Margaret Thatcher: A new illusion. *Perception, 9,* 483–484.

Thompson, P. M., Hayashi, K. M., Simon, S. L., Geaga, J. A., Hong, M. S., Sui, Y., et al. (2004). Structural abnormalities in the brains of human subjects who use methamphetamine. *Journal of Neuroscience, 24,* 6028–6036.

Thompson, W. F., Schellenberg, E. G., & Husain, G. (2001). Arousal, mood, and the Mozart effect. *Psychological Science, 12,* 248–251.

Thorgeirsson, T. E., Geller, F., Sulem, P., Rafnar, T., Wiste, A., Magnusson, K. P., et al. (2008). A variant associated with nicotine dependence, lung cancer and peripheral arterial disease. *Nature, 452,* 638–642.

Thorndike, E. L. (1927). The law of effect. *American Journal of Psychology, 39,* 212–222.

Thornhill, R., & Gangestad, S. W. (2006). Facial sexual dimorphism, developmental stability, and susceptibility to disease in men and women. *Evolution and Human Behavior, 27,* 131–144.

Thornicroft, G., Mehta, N., Clement, S., Evans-Lacko, S., Doherty, M., Rose, D., et al. (2016). Evidence for effective interventions to reduce mental-health-related stigma and discrimination. *The Lancet, 387,* 1123–1132.

Tickle, J. J., Sargent, J. D., Dalton, M. A., Beach, M. L., & Heatherton, T. F. (2001). Favorite movie stars, their tobacco use in contemporary movies and its association with adolescent smoking. *Tobacco Control, 10,* 16–22.

Tienari, P., Lahti, I., Sorri, A., Naarala, M., Moring, J., Kaleva, M., et al. (1990). Adopted-away offspring of schizophrenics and controls: The Finnish adoptive family study of schizophrenia. In L. Robins & M. Rutter (Eds.), *Straight and devious pathways from childhood to adulthood* (pp. 365–379). New York, NY: Cambridge University Press.

Tienari, P., Wynne, L. C., Moring, J., Lahti, I., Naarala, M., Sorri, A., et al. (1994). The Finnish adoptive family study of schizophrenia: Implications for family research. *British Journal of Psychiatry, 23,* 20–26.

Tienari, P., Wynne, L. C., Sorri, A., Lahti, I., Laksy, K., Moring, J., et al. (2004). Genotype-environment interaction in schizophrenia spectrum disorder. *British Journal of Psychiatry, 184,* 216–222.

Tipper, C. M., Handy, T. C., Giesbrecht, B., & Kingstone, A. F. (2008). Brain responses to biological relevance. *Journal of Cognitive Neuroscience, 20,* 879–891.

Todd, A. R., Bodenhausen, G. V., Richeson, J. A., & Galinsky, A. D. (2011). Perspective taking combats automatic expressions of racial bias. *Journal of Personality and Social Psychology, 100,* 1027–1042.

Todorov, A., Mandisodza, A. N., Goren, A., & Hall, C. C. (2005). Inferences of competence from faces predict election outcomes. *Science, 308,* 1623–1626.

Todorov, A., Mende-Siedlecki, P., & Dotsch, R. (2013). Social judgments from faces. *Current Opinion in Neurobiology, 23,* 373–380.

Tolman, E. C., & Honzik, C. H. (1930). Introduction and removal of reward, and maze performance in rats. *University of California Publications in Psychology, 4,* 257–275.

Tomasello, M. (1999). *The cultural origins of human cognition.* Cambridge, MA: Harvard University Press.

Tomkins, S. S. (1963). *Affect imagery consciousness: Vol. 2. The negative affects.* New York, NY: Tavistock/Routledge.

Tonegawa, S., Liu, X., Ramirez, S., & Redondo, R. (2015). Memory engram cells have come of age. *Neuron, 87,* 918–931.

Tong, F., Nakayama, K., Vaughan, J. T., & Kanwisher, N. (1998). Binocular rivalry and visual awareness in human extrastriate cortex. *Neuron, 21,* 753–759.

Torgersen, S., Kringlen, E., & Cramer, V. (2001). The prevalence of personality disorders in a community sample. *Archives of General Psychiatry, 58,* 590–596.

Torrey, E. F. (1999). Epidemiological comparison of schizophrenia and bipolar disorder. *Schizophrenia Research, 39,* 101–106.

Torrey, E. F., Torrey, B. B., & Peterson, M. R. (1977). Seasonality of schizophrenic births in the United States. *Archives of General Psychiatry, 34,* 1065–1070.

Tovote, P., Esposito, M. S., Botta, P., Chaudun, F., Fadok, J. P., Markovic, M., et al. Midbrain circuits for defensive behaviour. *Nature, 534,* 206–212.

Tracy, J. L., & Matsumoto, D. (2008). The spontaneous display of pride and shame: Evidence for biologically innate nonverbal displays. *Proceedings of the National Academy of Sciences, 105,* 11655–11660.

Tracy, J. L., & Robins, R. W. (2008). The nonverbal expression of pride: Evidence for cross-cultural recognition. *Journal of Personality and Social Psychology, 94,* 516–530.

Traffanstedt, M. K., Mehta, S., & LoBello, S. G. (2016). Major depression with seasonal variation: Is it a valid construct? *Clinical Psychological Science, 4,* 825–834.

Treanor, M., Brown, L. A., Rissman, J., & Craske, M. G. (2017). Can memories of traumatic experiences or addiction be erased or modified? A critical review of research on the disruption of memory reconsolidation and its applications. *Perspectives on Psychological Science, 12,* 290–305.

Treatment for Adolescents with Depression Study (TADS) Team. (2004). Fluoxetine, cognitive-behavioral therapy, and their combination for adolescents with depression: Treatment for Adolescents with Depression Study (TADS) randomized controlled trial. *Journal of the American Medical Association, 292,* 807–820.

Treffert, D. A., & Christensen, D. D. (2006, June/July). Inside the mind of a savant. *Scientific American Mind,* 50–55.

Triandis, H. C. (1989). The self and social behavior in differing cultural contexts. *Psychological Review, 96,* 506–520.

Trivers, R. L. (1971). The evolution of reciprocal altruism. *Quarterly Review of Biology, 46,* 35–57.

Tryon, W. W., & Tryon, G. S. (2011). No ownership of common factors. *American Psychologist, 66,* 151–152.

Trzesniewski, K. H., Donnellan, M. B., & Roberts, R. W. (2008). Is "generation me" really more narcissistic than previous generations? *Journal of Personality, 76,* 903–918.

Tsien, J. Z. (2000). Building a brainier mouse. *Scientific American, 282,* 62–68.

Tugade, M. M., & Fredrickson, B. L. (2004). Resilient individuals use positive emotions to bounce back from negative emotional experiences. *Journal of Personality and Social Psychology, 86,* 320–333.

Tulving, E. 1972. Episodic and semantic memory. In E. Tulving & W. Donaldson (Eds.), *Organization of memory* (pp. 381–403). New York, NY: Academic Press.

Tulving, E., & Thomson, D. M. (1973). Encoding specificity and retrieval processes in episodic memory. *Psychological Review, 80,* 352–373.

Turecki, G., & Meaney, M. J. (2016). Effects of the social environment and stress on glucocorticoid receptor gene methylation: A systematic review. *Biological Psychiatry, 79,* 87–96.

Turkheimer, E., Pettersson, E., & Horn, E. E. (2014). A phenotypic null hypothesis for the genetics of personality. *Annual Review of Psychology, 65,* 515–540.

Turner, E. H., Matthews, A. M., Linardatos, B. S., Tell, R. A., & Rosenthal, R. (2008). Selective publication of antidepressant trials and its influence on apparent efficacy. *New England Journal of Medicine, 358,* 252–260.

Twenge, J. M., & Campbell, W. K. (2003). "Isn't it fun to get the respect that we're going to deserve?" Narcissism, social rejection, and aggression. *Personality and Social Psychology Bulletin, 29,* 261–272.

Twenge, J. M., Konrath, S., Foster, J. D., Campbell, K. W., & Bushman, B. J. (2008). Egos inflating over time: A cross-temporal meta-analysis of the narcissistic personality inventory. *Journal of Personality, 76,* 875–902.

Twenge, J. M., Sherman, R. A., & Wells, B. E. (2016). Changes in American adults' reported same-sex sexual experiences and attitudes, 1973–2014. *Archives of Sexual Behavior, 45,* 1713–1730.

Tye, K. M., Prakash, R., Kim, S. Y., Fenno, L. E., Grosenick, L., Zarabi, H., et al. (2011). Amygdala circuitry mediating reversible and bidirectional control of anxiety. *Nature, 471,* 358–362.

Üçok, A., & Ergül, C. (2014). Persistent negative symptoms after first episode schizophrenia: A 2-year follow-up study. *Schizophrenia Research, 158,* 241–246.

Umberson, D. (1992). Gender, marital status and the social control of health behavior. *Social Science & Medicine, 34,* 907–917.

Unger, R. H., & Scherer, P. E. (2010). Gluttony, sloth and the metabolic syndrome: A roadmap to lipotoxicity. *Trends in Endocrinology & Metabolism, 21,* 345–352.

Ungerleider, L. G., & Mishkin, M. (1982). Two cortical visual systems. In D. J. Ingle, R. J. W. Mansfield, & M. S. Goodale (Eds.), *The analysis of visual behavior* (pp. 549–586). Cambridge, MA: MIT Press.

United Nations Office on Drugs and Crime (UNODC). (2013a). *Global study on homicide 2013: Trends, contexts, data.* Vienna, Austria: Author.

United Nations Office on Drugs and Crime. (2013b). *World drug report 2013.* United Nations publication, Sales No. E.13.XI.6.

Urberg, K. A., Degirmencioglue, S. M., Tolson, J. M., & Halliday-Scher, K. (1995). The structure of adolescent peer networks. *Developmental Psychology, 31,* 540–547.

U.S. Bureau of Labor Statistics, U.S. Department of Labor. (2015). *Occupational outlook handbook, 2014–2015 edition.* Retrieved from https://www.bls.gov/ooh

U.S. Bureau of Labor Statistics, U.S. Department of Labor. (2016, May). Occupational employment statistics. Occupational employment and wages. Industrial organizational psychologists. Retrieved from https://www.bls.gov/oes/current/oes193032.htm

U.S. Bureau of Labor Statistics, U.S. Department of Labor. (2017). *Occupational outlook handbook, 2016–2017 edition.* Retrieved from https://www.bls.gov/ooh

U.S. Census Bureau. (2014, July 10). Where do college graduates work? A special focus on science, technology, engineering and math. Retrieved from http://www.census.gov/dataviz/visualizations/stem/stem-html/

U.S. Department of Health and Human Services. (2004, May 27). *The health consequences of smoking: A report of the Surgeon General.* Retrieved from http://www.surgeongeneral.gov/library/smokingconsequences

U.S. Department of Health and Human Services. (2008). 2008 physical activity guidelines for Americans. Retrieved August 7, 2016, from https://health.gov/paguidelines/pdf/paguide.pdf

U.S. Department of Health and Human Services. (2014). *The health consequences of smoking—50 years of progress: A report of the Surgeon General.* Atlanta, GA: U.S. Government Printing Office.

U.S. Department of State. (2012). Terrorism deaths, injuries, kidnappings of private U.S. citizens, 2011. Retrieved from http://www.state.gov/j/ct/rls/crt/2011/195556.htm

Uvnas-Moberg, K. (1998). Oxytocin may mediate the benefits of positive social interaction and emotions. *Psychoneuroendocrinology, 23,* 819–835.

Valentine, K. A., Li, N. P., Penke, L., & Perrett, D. I. (2014). Judging a man by the width of his face: The role of facial ratios and dominance in mate choice at speed-dating events. *Psychological Science, 25,* 806–811.

Vallabha, G. K., McClelland, J. L., Pons, F., Werker, J. F., & Amano, S. (2007). Unsupervised learning of vowel categories from infant-directed speech. *Proceedings of the National Academy of Sciences, 104,* 13273–13278.

Van Bavel, J. J., Mende-Siedlecki, P., Brady, W. J., & Reinero, D. A. (2016). Contextual sensitivity in scientific reproducibility. *Proceedings of the National Academy of Sciences, 113,* 6454–6459.

Van der Oord, S., Prins, P. J. M., Oosterlaan, J., & Emmelkamp, P. M. G. (2008). Efficacy of methylphenidate, psychosocial treatments and their combination in school-aged children with ADHD: A meta-analysis. *Clinical Psychology Review, 28,* 783–800.

Van Haren, N. E., Schnack, H. G., Cahn, W., van den Heuvel, M. P., Lepage, C., Collins, L., et al. (2011). Changes in cortical thickness during the course of illness in schizophrenia. *Archives of General Psychiatry, 68,* 871–880.

Van Lange, P. A., Rinderu, M. I., & Bushman, B. J. (2017). Aggression and violence around the world: A model of Climate, Aggression, and Self-control in Humans (CLASH). *Behavioral and Brain Sciences, 40,* e75. https://doi.org/10.1017/S0140525X16000406

Vargas-Reighley, R. V. (2005). *Bicultural competence and academic resilience among immigrants*. El Paso, TX: LFB Scholarly Publishing.

Vargha-Khadem, F., Gadian, D. G., Watkins, K. E., Connelly, A., Van Paesschen, W., & Mishkin, M. (1997). Differential effects of early hippocampal pathology on episodic and semantic memory. *Science, 277,* 376–380.

Vazire, S. (2010). Who knows what about a person? The self-other knowledge asymmetry (SOKA) model. *Journal of Personality and Social Psychology, 98,* 281–300.

Vazire, S., & Carlson, E. N. (2011). Others sometimes know us better than we know ourselves. *Current Directions in Psychological Science, 20,* 104–108.

Vazire, S., & Gosling, S. D. (2004). e-perceptions: Personality impressions based on personal websites. *Journal of Personality and Social Psychology, 87,* 123–132.

Vazire, S., & Mehl, M. R. (2008). Knowing me, knowing you: The accuracy and unique predictive validity of self and other ratings of daily behavior. *Journal of Personality and Social Psychology, 95,* 1202–1216.

Vecsey, C. G., Hawk, J. D., Lattal, K. M., Stein, J. M., Fabian, S. A., Attner, M. A., et al. (2007). Histone deacetylase inhibitors enhance memory and synaptic plasticity via CREB: CBP-dependent transcriptional activation. *Journal of Neuroscience, 27,* 6128–6140.

Venkatraman, V., Dimoka, A., Pavlou, P. A., Vo, K., Hampton, W., Bollinger, B., et al. (2015). Predicting advertising success beyond traditional measures: New insights from neurophysiological measures and market response modeling. *Journal of Marketing Research, 52,* 436–452.

Vernon, P. A., Wickett, J. C., Bazana, P. G., Stelmack, R. M., & Sternberg, R. J. (2000). The neuropsychology and psychophysiology of human intelligence. In R. J. Sternberg (Ed.), *Handbook of intelligence* (pp. 245–264). Cambridge, England: Cambridge University Press.

Veronese, N., Li, Y., Manson, J. E., Willett, W. C., Fontana, L., & Hu, F. B. (2016). Combined associations of body weight and lifestyle factors with all cause and cause specific mortality in men and women: Prospective cohort study. *British Medical Journal, 355,* i5855.

Victora, C. G., Horta, B. L., de Mola, C. L., Quevedo, L., Pinheiro, R. T., Gigante, D. P., et al. (2015). Association between breastfeeding and intelligence, educational attainment, and income at 30 years of age: A prospective birth cohort study from Brazil. *The Lancet Global Health, 3,* e199–e205.

Vieta, E., Suppes, T., Ekholm, B., Udd, M., & Gustafsson, U. (2012). Long-term efficacy of quetiapine in combination with lithium or divalproex on mixed symptoms in bipolar I disorder. *Journal of Affective Disorders, 142,* 36–44.

Villemagne, V. L., Burnham, S., Bourgeat, P., Brown, B., Ellis, K. A., Salvado, O., et al. (2013). Amyloid β deposition, neurodegeneration, and cognitive decline in sporadic Alzheimer's disease: A prospective cohort study. *The Lancet Neurology, 12,* 357–367.

Vismara, L., & Rogers, S. (2010). Behavioral treatments in autism spectrum disorders: What do we know? *Annual Review of Clinical Psychology, 6,* 447–468.

Vohs, K. D., & Heatherton, T. F. (2004). Ego threat elicits different social comparison processes among high and low self-esteem people: Implications for interpersonal perceptions. *Social Cognition, 22,* 168–190.

Volkmar, F., Chawarska, K., & Klin, A. (2005). Autism in infancy and early childhood. *Annual Review of Psychology, 56,* 1–21.

Volkow, N. D. (2007). This is your brain on food. Interview by Kristin Leutwyler-Ozelli. *Scientific American, 297,* 84–85.

Volkow, N. D. (2016). Opioids in pregnancy. *British Medical Journal, 352,* i19.

Volkow, N. D., Koob, G. F., & McLellan, A. T. (2016). Neurobiologic advances from the brain disease model of addiction. *New England Journal of Medicine, 374,* 363–371.

Volkow, N. D., & Muenke, M. (2012). The genetics of addiction. *Human Genetics, 131,* 773–777.

Volkow, N. D., Wang, G. J., & Baler, R. D. (2011). Reward, dopamine, and the control of food intake: Implications for obesity. *Trends in Cognitive Science, 15,* 37–46.

Volz, K. G., Kessler, T., & von Cramon, D. Y. (2009). In-group as part of the self: In-group favoritism is mediated by medial prefrontal cortex activation. *Social Neuroscience, 4,* 244–260.

Vygotsky, L. S. (1978). *Mind in society.* Cambridge, MA: Harvard University Press.

Vytal, K., & Hamann, S. (2010). Neuroimaging support for discrete neural correlates of basic emotions: A voxel-based meta-analysis. *Journal of Cognitive Neuroscience, 22,* 2864–2885.

Wadden, T. A., & Anderton, C. H. (1982). The clinical use of hypnosis. *Psychological Bulletin, 91,* 215–243.

Wagenmakers, E. J., Beek, T., Dijkhoff, L., Gronau, Q. F., Acosta, A., Adams Jr., R. B., et al. (2016). Registered replication report: Strack, Martin, & Stepper (1988). *Perspectives on Psychological Science, 11,* 917–928.

Wagner, C., & Wheeler, L. (1969). Model, need, and cost effects in helping behavior. *Journal of Personality and Social Psychology, 12,* 111–116.

Wagner, D. D., Dal Cin, S., Sargent, J. D., Kelley, W. M., & Heatherton, T. F. (2011). Spontaneous action representation in smokers when watching movie characters smoke. *Journal of Neuroscience, 31,* 894–898.

Waite, L. J. (1995). Does marriage matter? *Demography, 32,* 483–507.

Wakefield, A. J., Murch, S. H., Anthony, A., Linnell, J., Casson, D. M., Malik, M., et al. (1998). RETRACTED: Ileal-lymphoid-nodular hyperplasia, non-specific colitis, and pervasive developmental disorder in children. *The Lancet, 351,* 637–641.

Wakefield, J. C. (2016). Diagnostic issues and controversies in DSM-5: Return of the false positives problem. *Annual Review of Clinical Psychology, 12,* 105–132.

Walder, D. J., Faraone, S. V., Glatt, S. J., Tsuang, M. T., & Seidman, L. J. (2014). Genetic liability, prenatal health, stress and family environment: Risk factors in the Harvard Adolescent Family High Risk for Schizophrenia Study. *Schizophrenia Research, 157,* 142–148.

Walker, D. L., Ressler, K. J., Lu, K. T., & Davis, M. (2002). Facilitation of conditioned fear extinction by systemic administration or intra-amygdala infusions of D-cycloserine as assessed with fear-potentiated startle in rats. *Journal of Neuroscience, 22,* 2343–2351.

Walker, E., Kestler, L., Bollini, A., & Hochman, K. M. (2004). Schizophrenia: Etiology and course. *Annual Review of Psychology, 55,* 401–430.

Walkup, J. T. (2017). Antidepressant efficacy for depression in children and adolescents: Industry- and NIMH-funded studies. *American Journal of Psychiatry, 174,* 430–437.

Walsh, T., McClellan, J. M., McCarthy, S. E., Addington, A. M., Pierce, S. B., Cooper, G. M., et al. (2008). Rare structural variants disrupt multiple genes in neurodevelopmental pathways in schizophrenia. *Science, 320,* 539–543.

Walton, G. M., & Spencer, S. J. (2009). Latent ability: Grades and test scores systematically underestimate the intellectual ability of negatively stereotyped students. *Psychological Science, 20,* 1132–1139.

Waltrip, R. W., Buchanan, R. W., Carpenter, W. T., Kirkpatrick, B., Summerfelt, A., Breier, A., et al. (1997). Borna disease virus antibodies and the deficit syndrome of schizophrenia. *Schizophrenia Research, 23,* 253–257.

Wamsley, E. J., Tucker, M., Payne, J. D., Benavides, J. A., & Stickgold, R. (2010). Dreaming of a learning task is associated with enhanced sleep-dependent memory consolidation. *Current Biology, 20,* 850–855.

Wang, C. S., Ku, G., Tai, K., & Galinsky, A. D. (2014). Stupid doctors and smart construction workers: Perspective-taking reduces stereotyping of both negative and positive targets. *Social Psychological and Personality Science, 5,* 430–436.

Wang, C. S., Whitson, J. A., Anicich, E. M., Kray, L. J., & Galinsky, A. D. (2017). Challenge your stigma: How to reframe and revalue negative stereotypes and slurs. *Current Directions in Psychological Science, 26,* 75–80.

Ward, J. T. (2013, September). What is forensic psychology? *Psychology Student Network.* Retrieved from http://www.apa.org/ed/precollege/psn/2013/09/forensic-psychology.aspx

Wardenaar, K. J., Lim, C. C. W., Al-Hamzawi, A. O., Alonso, J., Andrade, L. H., Benjet, C., et al. (2017). The cross-national epidemiology of specific phobia in the World Mental Health Surveys. *Psychological Medicine, 47,* 1744–1760. doi: 10.1017/S0033291717000174

Wardle, J., Carnell, S., Haworth, C. M., & Plomin, R. (2008). Evidence for a strong genetic influence on childhood adiposity despite the force of the obesogenic environment. *American Journal of Clinical Nutrition, 87,* 398–404.

Warneken, F. (2015). Precocious prosociality: Why do young children help? *Child Development Perspectives, 9,* 1–6.

Warren, Z., McPheeters, M. L., Sathe, N., Foss-Feig, J. H., Glasser, A., & Veenstra-VanderWeele, J. (2011). A systematic review of early intensive intervention for autism spectrum disorders. *Pediatrics, 127,* e1303–e1311.

Watson, D., & Clark, L. A. (1997). Extraversion and its positive emotional core. In R. Hogan, J. Johnson, & S. Briggs (Eds.), *Handbook of personality psychology* (pp. 767–793). San Diego, CA: Academic Press.

Watson, D., Wiese, D., Vaidya, J., & Tellegen, A. (1999). The two general activation systems of affect: Structural findings, evolutionary considerations, and psychobiological evidence. *Journal of Personality and Social Psychology, 76,* 820–838.

Watson, J. B. (1924). *Behaviorism.* New York, NY: Norton.

Watson, J. B., & Rayner, R. (1920). Conditioned emotional reactions. *Journal of Experimental Psychology, 3,* 1–14.

Waugh, C. E., Wager, T. D., Fredrickson, B. L., Noll, D. N., & Taylor, S. F. (2008). The neural correlates of trait resilience when anticipating and recovering from threat. *Social Cognitive and Affective Neuroscience, 3,* 322–332.

Waxler, N. E. (1979). Is outcome for schizophrenia better in nonindustrial societies? The case of Sri Lanka. *Journal of Nervous and Mental Disease, 167,* 144–158.

Webb, T. L., Miles, E., & Sheeran, P. (2012). Dealing with feeling: A meta-analysis of the effectiveness of strategies derived from the process model of emotion regulation. *Psychological Bulletin, 138,* 775–808.

Wechsler, H., Nelson, T. F., Lee, J. E., Seibring, M., Lewis, C., & Keeling, R. P. (2003). Perception and reality: A national evaluation of social norms marketing interventions to reduce college students' heavy alcohol use. *Journal of Studies on Alcohol and Drugs, 64,* 484–494.

Wegner, D., Shortt, J., Blake, A., & Page, M. (1990). The suppression of exciting thoughts. *Journal of Personality and Social Psychology, 58,* 409–418.

Weiner, B. (1974). *Achievement motivation and attribution theory.* Morristown, NJ: General Learning Press.

Weissman, M. M., Bland, R. C., Canino, G. J., Greenwald, S., Hwu, H. G., Lee, C. K., et al. (1994). The cross national epidemiology of obsessive compulsive disorder: The cross national collaborative group. *Journal of Clinical Psychiatry, 55,* 5–10.

Wells, G. L. (2008). Field experiments on eyewitness identification: Towards a better understanding of pitfalls and prospects. *Law and Human Behavior, 32,* 6–10.

Wells, G. L., & Seelau, E. P. (1995). Eyewitness identification: Psychological research and legal policy on lineups. *Psychology, Public Policy, and Law, 1,* 765–791.

Wells, G. L., Small, M., Penrod, S., Malpass, R. S., Fulero, S. M., & Brimacombe, C. A. E. (1998). Eyewitness identification procedures: Recommendations for lineups and photospreads. *Law and Human Behavior, 22,* 603–647.

Werker, J. F., Gilbert, J. H., Humphrey, K., & Tees, R. C. (1981). Developmental aspects of cross-language speech perception. *Child Development, 52,* 349–355.

Wertz, A. E., & Wynn, K. (2014). Selective social learning of plant edibility in 6- and 18-month-old infants. *Psychological Science, 25,* 874–882.

Westen, D. (1998). The scientific legacy of Sigmund Freud: Toward a psychodynamically informed psychological science. *Psychological Bulletin, 124,* 333–371.

Westen, D., Novotny, C. M., & Thompson-Brenner, H. (2004). The empirical status of empirically supported psychotherapies: Assumptions, findings, and reporting in controlled clinical trials. *Psychological Bulletin, 130,* 631–663.

Weyandt, L. L., Janusis, G., Wilson, K., Verdi, G., Paquin, G., Lopes, J., Varejao, M., & Dussault, C. (2009). Nonmedical prescription stimulant use among a sample of college students: Relationships with psychological variables. *Journal of Attention Disorders, 13,* 284–296.

Weyandt, L. L., Marraccini, M. E., Gudmundsdottir, B. G., Zavras, B. M., Turcotte, K. D., Munro, B. A., & Amoroso, A. J. (2013). Misuse of prescription stimulants among college students: A review of the literature and implications for morphological and cognitive effects on brain functioning. *Experimental and clinical psychopharmacology, 21,* 385–407.

Whalen, C. K. (1989). Attention deficit and hyperactivity disorders. In T. H. Ollendick & M. Herson (Eds.), *Handbook of child psychopathology* (2nd ed., pp. 131–169). New York, NY: Plenum Press.

Whalen, P. J., Kagan, J., Cook, R. G., Davis, F. C., Kim, H., Polis, S., et al. (2004). Human amygdala responsivity to masked fearful eye whites. *Science, 306,* 2061–2061.

Whalen, P. J., & Phelps, E. A. (2009). *The human amygdala.* New York, NY: Guilford Press.

Whalen, P. J., Raila, H., Bennett, R., Mattek, A., Brown, A., Taylor, J., et al. (2013). Neuroscience and facial expressions of emotion: The role of amygdala–prefrontal interactions. *Emotion Review, 5,* 78–83.

Whalen, P. J., Rauch, S. L., Etcoff, N. L., McInerney, N. L., Lee, M. B., & Jenike, M. A. (1998). Masked presentations of emotional facial expressions modulate amygdala activity without explicit knowledge. *Journal of Neuroscience, 18,* 411–418.

Whalen, P. J., Shin, L. M., McInerney, S. C. L., Fischer, H., Wright, C. I., & Rauch, S. L. (2001). A functional MRI study of human amygdala responses to facial expressions of fear versus anger. *Emotion, 1,* 70–83.

Wheatley, T., & Haidt, J. (2005). Hypnotic disgust makes moral judgments more severe. *Psychological Science, 16,* 780–784.

White, A., & Hingson, R. (2014). The burden of alcohol use: Excessive alcohol consumption and related consequences among college students. *Alcohol Research: Current Reviews, 35,* 201.

White, C. M. (2014). 3, 4-Methylenedioxymethamphetamine's (MDMA's) impact on posttraumatic stress disorder. *Annals of Pharmacotherapy, 48,* 908–915.

Whitney, C. G., Zhou, F., Singleton, J., & Schuchat, A. (2014). Benefits from immunization during the Vaccines for Children program era—United States, 1994–2013. *Morbidity and Mortality Weekly Report, 63,* 352–355.

Whorf, B. L. (1956). *Language, thought, and reality.* Cambridge, MA: MIT Press.

Wicker, B., Keysers, C., Plailly, J., Royet, J. P., Gallese, V., & Rizzolatti, G. (2003). Both of us disgusted in *my* insula: The common neural basis of seeing and feeling disgust. *Neuron, 40,* 655–664.

Widiger, T. A. (2011). Personality and psychopathology. *World Psychiatry, 10,* 103–106.

Wierson, M., Long, P. J., & Forehand, R. L. (1993). Toward a new understanding of early menarche: The role of environmental stress in pubertal timing. *Adolescence, 28,* 913–924.

Wiesel, T. N., & Hubel, D. H. (1963). Single-cell responses in striate cortex of kittens deprived of vision in one eye. *Journal of Neurophysiology, 26,* 1003–1017.

Wight, R. G., LeBlanc, A. J., & Lee Badgett, M. V. (2013). Same-sex legal marriage and psychological well-being: Findings from the California Health Interview Survey. *American Journal of Public Health, 103,* 339–346.

Wilens, T. E., Faraone, S. V., & Biederman, J. (2004). Attention-deficit/hyperactivity disorder in adults. *Journal of the American Medical Association, 292,* 619–623.

Wilfley, D. E., Bishop, M., Wilson, G. T., & Agras, W. S. (2007). Classification of eating disorders: Toward DSM-V. *International Journal of Eating Disorders, 40,* S123–S129.

Wilke, M., Sohn, J. H., Byars, A. W., & Holland, S. K. (2003). Bright spots: Correlations of gray matter volume with IQ in a normal pediatric population. *Neuroimage, 20,* 202–215.

Williams, K., Harkins, S. G., & Latané, B. (1981). Identifiability as a deterrent to social loafing: Two cheering experiments. *Journal of Personality and Social Psychology, 40,* 303–311.

Williams, M. E., & Fredriksen-Goldsen, K. I. (2014). Same-sex partnerships and the health of older adults. *Journal of Community Psychology, 42,* 558–570.

Williams, S. C., & Deisseroth, K. (2013). Optogenetics. *Proceedings of the National Academy of Sciences, 110,* 16287.

Wills, T. A., DuHamel, K., & Vaccaro, D. (1995). Activity and mood temperament as predictors of adolescent substance use: Test of a self-regulation mediational model. *Journal of Personality and Social Psychology, 68,* 901–916.

Wills, T. A., Knight, R., Sargent, J. D., Gibbons, F. X., Pagano, I., & Williams, R. J. (2017). Longitudinal study of e-cigarette use and onset of cigarette smoking among high school students in Hawaii. *Tobacco Control, 26,* 34–39.

Wilson, A. E., & Ross, M. (2001). From chump to champ: People's appraisals of their earlier and present selves. *Journal of Personality and Social Psychology, 80,* 572–584.

Wilson, M. A., & McNaughton, B. L. (1994). Reactivation of hippocampal ensemble memories during sleep. *Science, 265,* 676–679.

Wilson, T. D., & Gilbert, D. T. (2003). Affective forecasting. In M. Zanna (Ed.), *Advances in experimental social psychology* (Vol. 35, pp. 345–411). New York, NY: Elsevier.

Wilson-Mendenhall, C. D., Barrett, L. F., & Barsalou, L. W. (2013). Neural evidence that human emotions share core affective properties. *Psychological Science, 24,* 947–956.

Winberg, J., & Porter, R. H. (1998). Olfaction and human neonatal behaviour: Clinical implications. *Acta Paediatrica, 87,* 6–10.

Winkler, D., Pjrek, E., Spies, M., Willeit, M., Dorffner, G., Lanzenberger, R., & Kasper, S. (2017). Has the existence of seasonal affective disorder been disproven? *Journal of Affective Disorders, 208,* 54–55.

Winter, J. E., MacInnis, R. J., Wattanapenpaiboon, N., & Nowson, C. A. (2014). BMI and all-cause mortality in older adults: A meta-analysis. *American Journal of Clinical Nutrition.* doi:10.3945/ajcn.113.068122

Wolf, E., Kuhn, M., Norman, C., Mainberger, F., Maier, J. G., Maywald, S., et al. (2016). Synaptic plasticity model of therapeutic sleep deprivation in major depression. *Sleep Medicine Reviews, 30,* 53–62.

Wolters, C. A., & Hussain, M. (2015). Investigating grit and its relations with college students' self-regulated learning and academic achievement. *Metacognition and Learning, 10,* 293–311.

Wood, D. M., Stribley, V., Dargan, P. I., Davies, S., Holt, D. W., & Ramsey, J. (2011). Variability in the 3, 4-methylenedioxymethamphetamine content of "ecstasy" tablets in the UK. *Emergency Medicine Journal, 28,* 764–765.

Wood, J. M., Garb, H. N., Lilienfeld, S. O., & Nezworski, M. T. (2002). Clinical assessment. *Annual Review of Psychology, 53,* 519–543.

Wood, W., & Carden, L. (2014). Elusiveness of menstrual cycle effects on mate preferences: Comment on Gildersleeve, Haselton, and Fales (2014). *Psychological Bulletin, 140,* 1265–1271.

Woodworth, M., & Porter, S. (2002). In cold blood: Characteristics of criminal homicides as a function of psychopathy. *Journal of Abnormal Psychology, 111,* 436–445.

World Health Organization. (2008). *WHO report on the global tobacco epidemic.* Retrieved from http://www.who.int/tobacco/mpower/en/

World Health Organization. (2011). *The top ten causes of death* [Fact sheet]. Retrieved from http://www.who.int/mediacentre/factsheets/fs310/en/index.html

World Health Organization. (2014). *Malaria* [Fact sheet]. Retrieved from http://www.who.int/mediacentre/factsheets/fs094/en/

World Health Organization. (2016). *Obesity and overweight* [Fact sheet]. Retrieved from http://www.who.int/mediacentre/factsheets/fs311/en/

World Health Organization. (2017a). *Depression and other common mental disorders: Global health estimates.* Geneva: World Health Organization.

World Health Organization. (2017b). *Depression* [Fact sheet]. Retrieved from http://www.who.int/mediacentre/factsheets/fs369/en/

Wray, N. R., Byrne, E. M., Stringer, S., & Mowry, B. J. (2014). Future directions in genetics of psychiatric disorders. In S. H. Rhee & A. Ronald (Eds.), *Behavior genetics of psychopathology* (pp. 311–337). New York, NY: Springer.

Wray, N. R., & Gottesman, I. I. (2012). Using summary data from the Danish national registers to estimate heritabilities for schizophrenia, bipolar disorder, and major depressive disorder. *Frontiers in Genetics, 3,* 118.

Wright, S. C., & Tropp, L. R. (2005). Language and intergroup contact: Investigating the impact of bilingual instruction on children's intergroup attitudes. *Group Processes and Intergroup Relations, 8,* 309–328.

Wu, H., Luo, Y., & Feng, C. (2016). Neural signatures of social conformity: A coordinate-based activation likelihood estimation meta-analysis of functional brain imaging studies. *Neuroscience & Biobehavioral Reviews, 71,* 101–111.

Wu, P., Wilson, K., Dimoulas, P., & Mills, E. J. (2006). Effectiveness of smoking cessation therapies: A systematic review and meta-analysis. *BMC Public Health, 6,* 300.

Xie, L., Kang, H., Xu, Q., Chen, M. J., Liao, Y., Thiyagarajan, M., et al. (2013). Sleep drives metabolite clearance from the adult brain. *Science, 342,* 373–377.

Xu, J., Murphy, S. L., Kochanek, K. D., & Arias, E. (2016). *Mortality in the United States, 2015.* (NCHS Data Brief No. 267). Hyattsville, MD: National Center for Health Statistics.

Xu, J., & Roberts, R. E. (2010). The power of positive emotions: It's a matter of life or death—subjective well-being and longevity in a general population. *Health Psychology, 29,* 9–19.

Xu, X., Zuo, X., Wang, X., & Han, S. (2009). Do you feel my pain? Racial group membership modulates empathic neural responses. *Journal of Neuroscience, 29,* 8525–8529.

Yamagata, S., Suzuki, A., Ando, J., Ono, Y., Kijima, N., Yoshimura, K., et al. (2006). Is the genetic structure of human personality universal? A cross-cultural twin study from North America, Europe, and Asia. *Journal of Personality and Social Psychology, 90,* 987–998.

Yamaguchi, S., Greenwald, A. G., Banaji, M. R., Murakami, F., Chen, D., Shiomura, K., et al. (2007). Apparent universality of positive implicit self-esteem. *Psychological Science, 18,* 498–500.

Yang, J. (2014). The role of the right hemisphere in metaphor comprehension: A meta-analysis of functional magnetic resonance imaging studies. *Human Brain Mapping, 35,* 107–122.

Yates, D. (2014). Learning and memory: Unlearning fear. *Nature Reviews Neuroscience, 15,* 134–135.

Yazdy, M. M., Desai, R. J., & Brogly, S. B. (2015). Prescription opioids in pregnancy and birth outcomes: A review of the literature. *Journal of Pediatric Genetics, 4,* 56–70.

Yerkes, R. M., & Dodson, J. D. (1908). The relation of strength of stimulus to rapidity of habit formation. *Journal of Comparative Neurology & Psychology, 18,* 459–482.

Yeshurun, Y., & Sobel, N. (2010). An odor is not worth a thousand words: From multidimensional odors to unidimensional odor objects. *Annual Review of Psychology, 61,* 219–41.

Yoo, S. S., Hu, P. T., Gujar, N., Jolesz, F. A., & Walker, M. P. (2007). A deficit in the ability to form new human memories without sleep. *Nature Neuroscience, 10,* 385–392.

Yoon, P. W., et al. (2014, May 2). Potentially preventable deaths from the five leading causes of death—United States, 2008–2010. *Morbidity and Mortality Weekly Report, 63,* 368–374.

Youyou, W., Schwartz, H. A., Stillwell, D., & Kosinski, M. (2017). Birds of a feather do flock together: Behavior-based personality-assessment method reveals personality similarity among couples and friends. *Psychological Science, 28,* 276–284. doi:10.1177/0956797616678187

Yucel, M., Solowij, N., Respondek, C., Whittle, S., Fornito, A., Pantelis, C., & Lubman, D. I. (2008). Regional brain abnormalities associated with long-term heavy cannabis use. *Archives of General Psychiatry, 65,* 694.

Yuille, J. C., & Cutshall, J. L. (1986). A case study of eyewitness memory of a crime. *Journal of Applied Psychology, 71,* 291–301.

Zabetian, A., Sanchez, I. M., Narayan, K. M., Hwang, C. K., & Ali, M. K. (2014). Global rural diabetes prevalence: A systematic review and meta-analysis covering 1990–2012. *Diabetes Research and Clinical Practice, 104,* 206–213.

Zahn-Waxler, C., & Radke-Yarrow, M. (1990). The origins of empathic concern. *Motivation and Emotion, 14,* 107–130.

Zahn-Waxler, C., & Robinson, J. (1995). Empathy and guilt: Early origins of feelings of responsibility. In J. P. Tangney & K. W. Fischer (Eds.), *Self-conscious emotions: The psychology of shame, guilt, embarrassment, and pride* (pp. 143–173). New York, NY: Guilford Press.

Zaidan, H., Leshem, M., & Gaisler-Salomon, I. (2013). Prereproductive stress to female rats alters corticotropin releasing factor type 1 expression in ova and behavior and brain corticotropin releasing factor type 1 expression in offspring. *Biological Psychiatry, 74,* 680–687.

Zajonc, R. B. (1965). Social facilitation. *Science, 149,* 269–274.

Zajonc, R. B. (1968). Attitudinal effects of mere exposure. *Journal of Personality and Social Psychology Monographs, 9,* 1–27.

Zajonc, R. B. (2001). Mere exposure: A gateway to the subliminal. *Current Directions in Psychological Science, 10,* 224–228.

Zak, P. J., Kurzban, R., & Matzner, W. T. (2005). Oxytocin is associated with human trustworthiness. *Hormones and Behavior, 48,* 522–527.

Zaki, J., Davis, J. I., & Ochsner, K. N. (2012). Overlapping activity in anterior insula during interoception and emotional experience. *Neuroimage, 62,* 493–499.

Zametkin, A. J., Nordahl, T. E., Gross, M., King, A. C., Stemple, W. E., Rumsey, J., et al. (1990). Cerebral glucose metabolism in adults with hyperactivity of childhood onset. *New England Journal of Medicine, 323,* 1361–1366.

Zebian, S., Alamuddin, R., Mallouf, M., & Chatila, Y. (2007). Developing an appropriate psychology through culturally sensitive research practices in the Arab-speaking world: A content analysis of psychological research published between 1950 and 2004. *Journal of Cross-Cultural Psychology, 38,* 91–122.

Zetterberg, H., Smith, D. H., & Blennow, K. (2013). Biomarkers of mild traumatic brain injury in cerebrospinal fluid and blood. *Nature Reviews Neurology, 9,* 201–210.

Zhang, T. Y., & Meaney, M. J. (2010). Epigenetics and the environmental regulation of the genome and its function. *Annual Review of Psychology, 61,* 439–466.

Zihl, J., von Cramon, D., & Mai, N. (1983). Selective disturbance of movement vision after bilateral brain damage. *Brain, 106,* 313–340.

Zimmermann, J., & Neyer, F. J. (2013). Do we become a different person when hitting the road? Personality development of sojourners. *Journal of Personality and Social Psychology, 105,* 515–530.

Ziv, N., & Goshen, M. (2006). The effect of "sad"and "happy" background music on the interpretation of a story in 5- to 6-year-old children. *British Journal of Music Education, 23,* 303–314.

Zorrilla, E. P., Iwasaki, S., Moss, J. A., Chang, J., Otsuji, J., Inoue, K., et al. (2006). Vaccination against weight gain. *Proceedings of the National Academy of Sciences, 103,* 13226–13231.

Zuberbühler, K. (2015). Linguistic capacity of non-human animals. *Wiley Interdisciplinary Reviews: Cognitive Science, 6,* 313–321.

Zucchi, F. C., Yao, Y., Ward, I. D., Ilnytskyy, Y., Olson, D. M., Benzies, K., et al. (2013). Maternal stress induces epigenetic signatures of psychiatric and neurological diseases in the offspring. *PLoS ONE, 8,* e56967.

Zuckerman, M., Li, C., & Hall, J. A. (2016). When men and women differ in self-esteem and when they don't: A meta-analysis. *Journal of Research in Personality, 64,* 34–51.

Practice Tests

Chapter 1

1. When you mention to your family that you enrolled in a psychology course, your family members share their understanding of the field. Which comment best reflects psychological science?
   a. "You're going to learn how to get in touch with your feelings."
   b. "The concept of 'psychological science' is such an oxymoron. It is impossible to measure and study what goes on in people's heads."
   c. "I think you'll be surprised by the range of questions psychologists ask about the mind, the brain, and behavior, not to mention the scientific methods they use to answer these questions."
   d. "By the end of the class, you'll be able to tell me why I am the way I am."

2. Match each definition with one or more of the following ideas from evolutionary theory: adaptations, natural selection, survival of the fittest.
   a. the physical characteristics, skills, and abilities that increase an organism's chances of survival and of reproduction, and that are likely to be passed on to offspring
   b. Individuals better adapted to their environment will leave more offspring.
   c. the process by which changes that are adaptive are passed along, and changes that hinder both survival and reproduction are not

3. Titles of recent research articles appear below. Indicate which of the four levels of analysis—cultural, social, individual, or biological—each article likely addresses.
   a. "Pals, Problems, and Personality: The Moderating Role of Personality in the Longitudinal Association Between Adolescents' and Best Friends' Delinquency" (Yu, Branje, Keijsers, Koot, & Meeus, 2013)
   b. "The Role of Dynamic Microglial Alterations in Stress-Induced Depression and Suppressed Neurogenesis" (Kreisel et al., 2013)
   c. "Culture, Gender, and School Leadership: School Leaders' Self-Perceptions in China" (Law, 2013)
   d. "Anchoring Bullying and Victimization in Children Within a Five-Factor Model-Based Person-Centered Framework" (De Bolle & Tackett, 2013)

4. Several schools of thought in psychology are listed below. Match each of the following psychologists with the school he is most identified with: William James, Wolfgang Köhler, Kurt Lewin, George Miller, Ulrich Neisser, B.F. Skinner, Edward Titchener, John B. Watson, Max Wertheimer, Wilhelm Wundt.
   a. structuralism
   b. functionalism
   c. Gestalt psychology
   d. behaviorism
   e. cognitive psychology
   f. social psychology

5. Match each description with one of the following theoretical ideas: dualism, introspection, localization, stream of consciousness.
   a. a systematic examination of subjective mental experience that requires people to inspect and report on the contents of their thoughts
   b. the notion that the mind and the body are separate and distinct
   c. the idea that some psychological processes are located in specific parts of the brain
   d. a continuous series of ever-changing thoughts

6. Imagine you have decided to seek mental health counseling. You mention this to a few of your friends. Each friend shares an opinion with you. Based on your understanding of psychological science, which friend offers the strongest advice?
   a. "I wouldn't bother if I were you. All therapy is a bunch of psychobabble."
   b. "I know a therapist who uses this really cool method that can fix any problem. Seriously, she knows the secret!"
   c. "That's great! Psychologists do research to figure out which interventions are most helpful for people with different concerns."
   d. "Well, I guess if you like relaxing on couches and talking, you might get a lot out of therapy."

7. Which of the following practices are hallmarks of critical thinking? Check all that apply.
   a. asking questions
   b. considering alternative explanations
   c. considering the possibility that biases are coloring the evidence

d. keeping an open mind

e. looking for holes in evidence

f. skepticism

g. reasoning logically to see whether information makes sense

h. accepting statements from an authority

8. Psychologists work in a wide variety of research-related subfields. Match each sample research question with one of the following subfields: industrial/organizational psychology, cognitive psychology, personality psychology, developmental psychology.

a. How do people make decisions and solve problems?

b. Do people who are outgoing report being happier?

c. When do children start to form mental representations of the world?

d. How does office design influence worker productivity?

9. You attend your friend's audition for an opening for a pianist in a student musical and you notice that he frequently misses notes and is off tempo. He doesn't get the spot. According to the Dunning-Krueger effect, which of the following statements is he likely to make?

a. "I'm not surprised, since I didn't play well."

b. "I played as well as the person who got the spot, and so I should have gotten it."

c. "I thought I was good, but now see that others may have been better."

d. "I played poorly because I was nervous."

10. Your brother reads that research shows eating ice cream makes people more intelligent. He starts downing a pint of ice cream every day to increase his intelligence. To help your brother better understand this claim (and avoid obesity), which of the following questions would help you evaluate whether to believe the study? Check all that apply.

a. "Does the article mention how much ice cream people had to eat to become more intelligent?"

b. "Does the article say how the researchers measured intelligence?"

c. "Does the article mention whether the person who conducted the research is a famous scholar?"

d. "I wonder how the researchers designed the study. Were they doing good science?"

e. "I'd want to know who sponsored the study. Would you believe these results if the study was paid for and conducted by researchers at the world's largest ice cream company?"

Answer Key for Chapter 1

1. c. "I think you'll be surprised by the range of questions psychologists ask about the mind, the brain, and behavior, not to mention the scientific methods they use to answer these questions."

2. a. adaptations; b. survival of the fittest; c. natural selection

3. a. social; b. biological; c. cultural; d. individual

4. a. Titchener, Wundt; b. James; c. Köhler, Wertheimer; d. Skinner, Watson; e. Miller, Neisser; f. Lewin

5. a. introspection; b. dualism; c. localization; d. stream of consciousness

6. c. "That's great! Psychologists do research to figure out which interventions are most helpful for people with different concerns."

7. All except h are correct.

8. a. cognitive; b. personality; c. developmental; d. industrial/organizational

9. b

10. b. "Does the article say how the researchers measured intelligence?"; d. "I wonder how the researchers designed the study. Were they doing good science?"; e. "I'd want to know who sponsored the study. Would you believe these results if the study was paid for and conducted by researchers at the world's largest ice cream company?"

Chapter 2

1. Which of the following is a technique that increases scientists' confidence in the findings from a given research study?

a. meta-analysis

b. operationalization of variables

c. replication

d. serendipity

For the following four questions, imagine you are designing a study to investigate whether deep breathing causes students to feel less stressed. Because you are investigating a causal question, you will need to employ experimental research. For each step in the design process, indicate the most scientifically sound decision.

2. Which hypothesis is stronger? Why?

a. Stress levels will differ between students who engage in deep breathing and those who do not.

b. Students who engage in deep breathing will report less stress than those who do not engage in deep breathing.

3. Which sampling method is strongest? Why?

a. Obtain an alphabetical list of all students enrolled at the college. Invite every fifth person on the list to participate in the study.

b. Post a note to your Facebook page letting friends know you would like their help with the study. Ask your friends to let their friends know about the study, too.

   c. Post fliers around local gyms and yoga studios inviting people to participate in your study.

4. Which set of conditions should be included in the study? Why?

   a. All participants should be given written directions for a deep-breathing exercise.

   b. Some participants should be given written directions for a deep-breathing exercise. Other participants should be given a DVD with demonstrations of deep-breathing exercises.

   c. Some participants should be given written directions for a deep-breathing exercise. Other participants should be given no instructions regarding their breathing.

5. How should participants be chosen for each condition? Why?

   a. Once people agree to participate in the study, flip a coin to decide if each will be in the experimental condition or the control condition.

   b. Let participants select which condition they would like to be in.

6. Which operational definition of the dependent variable, stress, is stronger? Why?

   a. Stress is a pattern of behavioral and physiological responses that match or exceed a person's abilities to respond in a healthy way.

   b. Stress will be measured using five questions asking the participant to rate his or her stress level on a scale from 1 to 10, where 1 equals "not at all stressed" and 10 equals "as stressed as I've ever been."

For the following three questions, imagine you want to know whether students at your college talk about politics in their day-to-day lives. To investigate this issue, you would like to conduct an observational study and need to make three design decisions. For each decision, recommend the most appropriate choice.

7. Should you conduct the study in a lab or in a natural setting (e.g., in the campus dining hall)? Why?

8. Should you use written descriptions of what is heard or a running tally of prespecified categories of behavior? Why?

9. Should participants know you are observing them? Why?

10. Indicate which quality of good data is violated by each description. Response options are "accuracy," "reliability," and "internal validity."

   a. A booth at the local carnival announces the discovery of a new way to assess intelligence. The assessment method involves interpreting the pattern of creases on one's left palm.

   b. At the end of a long night of grading, a professor reads what he believes to be the last essay in the pile. He assigns it a grade of 80%. When he goes to write the grade on the back of the paper, he realizes he has already graded this paper earlier in the evening—and gave it only a 70% the first time around.

   c. A five-year-old counts the jelly beans in a jar, often skipping over numbers ending in 8 (e.g., 8, 18, 28).

Answer Key for Chapter 2

1. c. replication.

2. b, because it offers a specific prediction.

3. a, because it is random.

4. c, because it includes experimental and control groups.

5. a, because it uses random assignment.

6. b, because it describes how the variable will be measured.

7. natural setting, because you want to know what people do in their daily lives.

8. prespecified categories of behavior, because you want to know whether a specific behavior, discussing politics, occurs; a simple tally of "yes" or "no" would answer this question.

9. No, because doing so will create reactivity.

10. a. internal validity; b. reliability; c. accuracy

Chapter 3

1. Which label accurately describes neurons that detect information from the physical world and pass that information along to the brain?

   a. motor neuron

   b. sensory neuron

   c. interneuron

   d. glia

2. Parkinson's disease is associated with the loss of neurons that produce which of the following neurotransmitters?

   a. acetylcholine

   b. norepinephrine

   c. dopamine

   d. serotonin

3. Drugs can produce the following actions on neurotransmitter activity. Label each example as either an agonist or antagonist effect.

   a. mimic the neurotransmitter and activate the postsynaptic receptor

   b. block the reuptake of neurotransmitter

   c. decrease neurotransmitter release

   d. clear neurotransmitter from the synapse

4. Which of the following statements about behavioral genetics is false?

   a. Heritability refers to traits passed from parent to offspring.

   b. Similarities among nonbiological adopted siblings are inferred to reflect environmental influences.

c. Identical twins raised apart are often more similar than identical twins raised together.

   d. Greater similarities between monozygotic twins compared with dizygotic twins are inferred to reflect genetic influences.

5. In what order are incoming signals processed by a neuron? Place a 1, 2, 3, or 4 in front of each of the following parts of a neuron.

_____ soma

_____ terminal buttons

_____ dendrites

_____ axon

6. Which of the following techniques can provide information about whether a particular brain region is necessary for a task?

   a. electroencephalograph (EEG)

   b. functional magnetic resonance imaging (fMRI)

   c. positron emission tomography (PET)

   d. transcranial magnetic stimulation (TMS)

7. Which statement about split-brain patients is true?

   a. They have had surgery to therapeutically remove one hemisphere of the brain.

   b. The left hemisphere can perceive stimuli, but the right hemisphere cannot.

   c. The left hemisphere can verbally report its perception. The right hemisphere cannot articulate what it saw but can act on its perception.

   d. The left hemisphere is analytical, and the right hemisphere is creative.

8. You witness a major car accident on your way to school. You pull over and rush to help one of the victims, who has severe cuts across his forehead and legs. When you ask if he is in any pain, he says no. Which neurochemical is likely keeping the man pain free despite his obvious injuries?

   a. dopamine

   b. GABA

   c. glutamate

   d. endorphins

   e. substance P

9. Someone suffers a stroke that causes damage to the left motor cortex. Which of the following impairments will the person most likely exhibit?

   a. an inability to comprehend spoken language

   b. an inability to recognize faces

   c. paralysis of the left side of the body

   d. paralysis of the right side of the body

10. The adage *You can't teach an old dog new tricks* is consistent with which phenomenon?

   a. plasticity

   b. critical periods

   c. cortical reorganization

   d. synesthesia

Answer Key for Chapter 3

1. b. sensory neuron

2. c. dopamine

3. a. agonist; b. agonist; c. antagonist; d. antagonist

4. a. Heritability refers to traits passed from parent to offspring.

5. soma, 2; terminal buttons, 4; dendrites, 1; axon, 3

6. d. transcranial magnetic stimulation (TMS)

7. c. The left hemisphere can verbally report its perception. The right hemisphere cannot articulate what it saw but can act on its perception.

8. d. endorphins

9. d. paralysis of the right side of the body

10. b. critical periods

Chapter 4

1. What is a key distinction between a person in an unresponsive wakefulness state and a person in a minimally conscious state?

   a. The person in the minimally conscious state is less responsive to her or his surroundings.

   b. The person in the unresponsive wakefulness state is more likely to regain full consciousness at some point in the future.

   c. The person in the minimally conscious state shows some degree of brain activity, whereas the person in the unresponsive wakefulness state shows no brain activity.

   d. The person in the minimally conscious state is dreaming, whereas the person in the unresponsive wakefulness state is in a coma.

2. A researcher subliminally flashes the words *outgoing, talkative,* and *smile* to subjects in Condition A. In Condition B, the flashed words are *standoffish, silent,* and *frown.* After participants complete the word game, they meet and interact with a stranger. What do you predict participants' behavior during that interaction will reveal?

   a. Participants in Conditions A and B will behave nearly identically.

   b. Participants in Condition A will be more friendly toward the stranger than will participants in Condition B.

   c. Participants in Condition B will be more friendly toward the stranger than will participants in Condition A.

3. Match each definition with one of the following attention terms: change blindness, automatic processing, controlled processing, shadowing.
   a. well-practiced tasks that can be done quickly, with little conscious effort
   b. ability to extract meaning from stimuli that are not processed consciously
   c. failure to notice large changes in one's environment
   d. difficult or challenging tasks that require conscious effort

4. For each description below, name the sleep disorder: insomnia, apnea, narcolepsy, somnambulism.
   a. Despite feeling well-rested, Marcus falls asleep suddenly while practicing piano.
   b. Emma walks through the living room in the middle of the night, seemingly oblivious to those around her.
   c. Sophia spends most of the night trying to fall asleep.
   d. Ivan's roommate regularly complains that Ivan's snoring wakes him multiple times throughout the night.

5. Which of the following pieces of evidence does not support the idea that sleep is an adaptive behavior?
   a. Sleep allows the body and brain to restore themselves.
   b. Some animals, such as frogs, don't sleep.
   c. Humans sleep at night because our ancestors were more at risk in the dark.
   d. Students who study more tend to have more REM sleep.

6. Which of the following instruction sets would a yoga teacher trained in concentrative meditation be most likely to give?
   a. "Close your eyes while sitting in a comfortable position. Let your thoughts move freely through your mind, like clouds passing through the sky. Acknowledge them, but do not react to them."
   b. "Lying on your back, rest your hands gently on your abdomen. As you breathe in and out, focus attention on your breath. Notice the rhythmic rise and fall of your abdomen and the slow, deep movement of your chest."
   c. "Standing in place, bend one knee and lift that leg. Grasp the foot and bring it back as far as possible. Focus all your attention on this action. Then lower the foot and repeat this action with the other knee, leg, and foot."

7. Which of the following drugs is classified as a stimulant?
   a. marijuana
   b. cocaine
   c. heroin
   d. alcohol
   e. LSD

8. Label each of the following statements as true or false.
   _____ a. Long-term use of opiates (narcotics) always leads to addiction.
   _____ b. Nicotine and caffeine are stimulants.
   _____ c. Methamphetamine and MDMA (ecstasy) decrease dopamine levels.
   _____ d. Alcohol is a depressant.
   _____ e. People can become physically addicted but not psychologically addicted to prescription medications.
   _____ f. The gender gap in alcohol consumption is increasing.

9. Match each of the following drugs with the appropriate description of a user's typical response: alcohol, marijuana, MDMA, opiates, stimulants.
   _____ a. increased heart rate, elevated mood, restlessness
   _____ b. relaxation, contentment, vivid perceptual experiences
   _____ c. impaired motor skills, decreased sexual performance
   _____ d. energy, slight hallucinations
   _____ e. lack of pain, euphoria, intense pleasure

10. Which of the following phenomena are best described as symptoms of physical dependence?
   a. symptoms of withdrawal when the substance is stopped
   b. elevated tolerance for the substance
   c. habitually reaching for the substance when in certain environments (e.g., lighting a cigarette each time you get into your car)
   d. using the substance as prescribed by a physician

Answer Key for Chapter 4

1. c. The person in the minimally conscious state shows some degree of brain activity, whereas the person in the unresponsive wakefulness state shows no brain activity.

2. b. Participants in Condition A will be more friendly toward the stranger than will participants in Condition B.

3. a. automatic processing; b. shadowing; c. change blindness; d. controlled processing

4. a. narcolepsy; b. somnambulism; c. insomnia; d. apnea

5. b. Some animals, such as frogs, don't sleep.

6. b. "Lying on your back, rest your hands gently on your abdomen. As you breathe in and out, focus attention on your breath. Notice the rhythmic rise and fall of your abdomen and the slow, deep movement of your chest."

7. b. cocaine

8. a. false; b. true; c. false; d. true; e. false; f. false

9. a. stimulants; b. marijuana; c. alcohol; d. MDMA; e. opiates

10. a. symptoms of withdrawal when the substance is stopped; b. elevated tolerance for the substance

Chapter 5

1. Which answer accurately lists the order in which these structures participate in sensation and perception (except for smell)?
   a. thalamus, specialized receptors, cortex
   b. specialized receptors, cortex, thalamus
   c. cortex, specialized receptors, thalamus
   d. specialized receptors, thalamus, cortex

2. Match the definition to each stage of sensory processing: sensation, perception, bottom-up processing, top-down processing
   a. interpretation of sensory information that is influenced by prior knowledge or expectation
   b. detection of sensory signals by receptors
   c. processing and interpretation of sensory signals
   d. perception based on physical features of sensory stimuli

3. Which sense organ is largest in humans?
   a. eyes, due to the large number of cones densely packed in the fovea
   b. ears, due to the curvature of the cochlea, which increases surface area of the basilar membrane to house an infinite number of hair cells
   c. nose, due to the dense array of cells packed within the olfactory epithelium
   d. tongue, due to the large number of taste buds that can be housed within each papilla
   e. skin, due to the large surface area

4. In audition, detecting the _____ of the sound wavelength results in the perception of loudness. Detecting the _____ of the wavelength results in the perception of the pitch.
   a. frequency, amplitude
   b. amplitude, frequency
   c. frequency, hertz
   d. hertz, frequency

5. Identify each of the following visual perceptions as an example of size constancy, shape constancy, color constancy, or lightness constancy.
   a. recognizing a dinner plate as circular, even when viewing it at an angle makes it appear elliptical
   b. labeling grass as green, even in the dark
   c. correctly identifying a building as a skyscraper, even though it appears smaller than other objects in your field of vision
   d. recognizing a door as a door, even when it is fully open so that you see only the edge
   e. noticing the color of your friend's T-shirt looks lighter when he stands next to a brick wall than when he stands against a white wall

6. Imagine you have a dull, chronic pain across your lower back. No matter how you position yourself, you cannot make the pain go away. Select the answer choices most relevant to this type of pain. More than one choice may be correct.

   a. activated by chemical changes in tissue
   b. activated by strong physical pressure of temperature extremes
   c. fast fibers
   d. myelinated axons
   e. nonmyelinated axons
   f. slow fibers

7. After hours of waiting, a bird watcher hears the call of a rare bird species. The bird watcher instinctively turns his head about 45 degrees to the left and sees the bird. Which of the following statements best describes how the bird watcher knew where to turn his head?
   a. The call reached the bird watcher's left ear before it reached his right ear; the call was less intense in the bird watcher's right ear than in his left ear.
   b. The call reached the bird watcher's left ear before it reached his right ear; the call was less intense in the bird watcher's left ear than in his right ear.
   c. The call reached the bird watcher's right ear before it reached his left ear; the call was less intense in the bird watcher's right ear than in his left ear.
   d. The call reached the bird watcher's right ear before it reached his left ear; the call was less intense in the bird watcher's left ear than in his right ear.

8. In which lobe of the brain (frontal, occipital, parietal, temporal) does each of the following sensory cortices reside?
   a. primary auditory cortex
   b. primary somatosensory cortex
   c. primary visual cortex

9. Which of the following statements about the gustatory system are true?
   a. Taste is a mixture of five basic kinds of gustatory receptors.
   b. Different regions of the tongue are more sensitive to different tastes.
   c. The texture of a food can affect how it tastes.
   d. People lose half of their taste buds by age 20.
   e. Supertasters tend to be overweight and are more likely to be male.

10. Imagine you are preparing to conduct a brain imaging study of visual processing. Which pathway—dorsal or ventral—do you hypothesize will be activated by each of the following experimental tasks?
    a. deciding which of two objects is farther away
    b. describing an object's color
    c. describing a silhouette's shape
    d. naming an object
    e. selecting which two of three objects are closest together

Answer Key for Chapter 5

1. d. specialized receptors, thalamus, cortex

2. a. top-down processing; b. sensation; c. perception; d. bottom-up processing

3. e. skin, due to the large surface area

4. b. amplitude, frequency

5. a. shape constancy; b. color constancy; c. size constancy; d. shape constancy; e. lightness constancy

6. Choices a, e, and f are correct.

7. a. The call reached the bird watcher's left ear before it reached his right ear; the call was less intense in the bird watcher's right ear than in his left ear.

8. a. temporal; b. parietal; c. occipital

9. Choices a, c, and d are true.

10. dorsal ("where") pathway activated by a and e; ventral ("what") pathway activated by b, c, d

Chapter 6

1. On the first day of summer school, the air conditioner in Matt's history classroom broke down. All the other rooms were unaffected. After several weeks of attending class in the sweltering room, Matt started sweating every time he approached the history room. In this example of classical conditioning, what are the US, UR, CS, and CR?

2. At a psychology lecture, each student receives 10 lemon wedges. The professor instructs the students to bite into a lemon wedge whenever a large blue dot appears within her slide presentation. Nearly every time the students bite into lemons, their mouths pucker. The 11th time a blue dot appears on the screen, many students' mouths pucker visibly. In this case, what are the US, UR, CS, and CR?

3. A few minutes later in that same psychology lecture, the professor projects the image of a turquoise dot. How will the students likely respond to this image?
   a. The students will not experience puckering responses, because the conditioned association has been extinguished.
   b. The students will not experience puckering responses, because they are able to discriminate between the two dot colors.
   c. The students will experience puckering responses, because of stimulus generalization.

4. Jason just moved his dog's food to the cupboard, which creaks noisily when it is opened. In which situation is Jason's dog likely to learn an association between the sound of the cupboard opening and the food?
   a. The door reliably opens shortly after the food is delivered.
   b. The door reliably opens shortly before the food is delivered.
   c. The door reliably opens just as the food is delivered.
   d. The door reliably opens along with the sound of a can opener, which has previously signaled food delivery.

5. Identify each statement as an example of negative punishment, positive punishment, negative reinforcement, or positive reinforcement.
   a. Whenever a puppy barks, it gets its belly rubbed, so it barks more.
   b. A professor directs all questions to the student who arrives late to class.
   c. A person with a clean driving record receives a reduced insurance premium.
   d. Your date arrives an hour late, and you refuse to speak for the rest of the evening.

6. Match each scenario with one of the following reinforcement schedules: fixed ratio, variable ratio, fixed interval, variable interval.
   a. You check your mailbox for mail at the same time every day.
   b. Every once in a while, you receive exciting mail.
   c. Every seventh newspaper you receive is loaded with coupons you want to use.
   d. Every week, a boy buys packets of baseball cards. Sometimes none of the packets include a valuable card, but sometimes multiple packets hold valuable cards.

7. Match each example with the type of learning it describes: non-associative, associative, observational.
   a. Maya finds that she is speaking up more in class after her professor compliments Maya on the questions she asks.
   b. Donae no longer responds to a persistent beep from a broken appliance in his apartment.
   c. After watching a YouTube video, Rohan was able to change the air filter in his heater.

8. Which of the following statements are true?
   a. Any behavior can be shaped through reinforcement.
   b. Psychologists believe that punishment is more effective than positive reinforcement for shaping behavior.
   c. Animals can be conditioned to fear flowers as easily as they can be to fear snakes.
   d. A conditioned taste aversion can be learned in a single trial.

9. Why is it important that treatment for addiction include exposing addicts to drug cues?

10. Which statement correctly describes the relationship between dopamine and reinforcement?
    a. Dopamine is especially important for the "wanting" aspect of reward.
    b. Dopamine activity in the brain is increased when a behavior leads to an unexpected reward.
    c. Only primary reinforcers are linked with dopamine activity.

Answer Key for Chapter 6

1. The US is heat, the UR is sweating, the CS is the history room, and the CR is sweating.

2. The US is lemon, the UR is a pucker, the CS is a blue dot, and the CR is a pucker at the sight of the blue dot.

3. c. The students will experience puckering responses, because of stimulus generalization.

4. b. The door reliably opens shortly before the food is delivered.

5. a. positive reinforcement; b. positive punishment; c. negative reinforcement; d. negative punishment (removal of affection)

6. a. fixed interval; b. variable interval; c. fixed ratio; d. variable ratio

7. a. associative; b. nonassociative; c. observational

8. Only d. It is true that a conditioned taste aversion can be learned in a single trial.

9. Exposure helps extinguish conditioned responses to the cues, preventing those cues from triggering conditioned craving.

10. b. Dopamine activity in the brain is increased when a behavior leads to an unexpected reward.

Chapter 7

1. Identify each of the following terms as either a memory phase or a memory system.
   a. encoding
   b. explicit memory
   c. implicit memory
   d. storage
   e. procedural memory
   f. retrieval
   g. episodic memory
   h. semantic memory

2. Which of the following phenomena can lead to forgetting? Check all that are correct.
   a. shallow encoding
   b. elaborative encoding
   c. blocking
   d. proactive interference
   e. retroactive interference
   f. persistence
   g. suggestibility

3. True or false: Flashbulb memories are always more accurate than normal memories.

4. Which of the following facts suggests that working memory and long-term memory are distinct memory processes?
   a. Patient H.M. retained working memory without being able to form new long-term memories.
   b. The primacy effect requires long-term memory, whereas the recency effect requires working memory.
   c. The primacy effect requires working memory, whereas the recency effect requires long-term memory.
   d. choices a and b
   e. choices a and c

5. How can capacity of working memory be increased?
   a. blocking
   b. maintenance rehearsal
   c. chunking
   d. reconsolidation

6. Imagine you are a manager seeking to hire a new employee. Before leaving work Monday afternoon, you look through a stack of 30 resumes organized alphabetically by last name. When you return to work Tuesday morning, which job applicant are you most likely to remember?
   a. Alvarado
   b. Martonosi
   c. Russo

7. You are asked to memorize a list of words. Which encoding strategy will likely result in the best recall performance?
   a. As you read each word, repeat it five times.
   b. As you read each word, count the number of letters in it.
   c. As you read each word, think of a word that rhymes with it.
   d. As you read each word, think of a synonym for it.

8. You ask a friend to memorize the following list: bed, rest, night, tired, blanket, pillow, relaxed. Later, you ask your friend to tell you as many words from the list as he or she can remember. In addition to remembering some of the words, your friend lists the word *sleep*, which did not appear on the original list. Which of the following phenomena is most related to your friend's error in recall?
   a. context-dependent encoding
   b. culturally relevant schemas
   c. networks of associations
   d. state-dependent encoding

9. Which memory flaw is demonstrated in each of the following examples?
   a. A friend introduces you to her brother; five minutes later, you find you cannot remember the brother's name.
   b. A friend introduces you to her brother. Later, you ask your friend, "How's your brother ... ah, what's his name? Jake? John? Oh, James! How is James?"

10. Fill in the blanks. People experiencing _____ amnesia are unable to recall memories from the past, whereas people experiencing _____ amnesia are unable to form new memories.

Answer Key for Chapter 7

1. a. memory phase; b. memory system; c. memory system; d. memory phase; e. memory system; f. memory phase; g. memory system; h. memory system

2. Choices a, c, d, and e can all lead to forgetting.

3. false

4. d. choices a and b

5. c. chunking

6. a. Alvarado

7. d. As you read each word, think of a synonym for it.

8. c. networks of associations

9. a. absentmindedness; b. blocking

10. retrograde; anterograde

Chapter 8

1. Which of the following examples represent an analogical representation, a symbolic representation, or both?
   a. the word *cat*
   b. a picture of a cat
   c. a mental map of the United States
   d. the word *America*

2. Insight can often be achieved when people overcome _____.
   a. stereotype threat
   b. functional fixedness
   c. prototypical models
   d. the use of exemplars

3. The _____ model of teaching reading is better for poor readers and inexperienced ones.
   a. syntax
   b. whole language
   c. phonics
   d. exemplar

4. Which theory of language development suggests that people are born with an innate ability for language, called the language acquisition device?
   a. Whorf's language relativity theory
   b. Sternberg's triarchic theory
   c. Skinner's theory of behaviorism
   d. Chomsky's universal grammar theory

5. Which of the following statements about brain regions and language processing is correct?
   a. Broca's area controls speech production.
   b. Wernicke's area controls speech comprehension.
   c. The amygdala controls the acquisition of vocabulary.
   d. both a and b

6. Match each example with the correct heuristic: anchoring, framing, availability heuristic, representativeness heuristic.
   a. Magda believes that she is very likely to contract the Zika virus because she frequently sees news reports about it.
   b. Jacob decides to keep his textbook because he is more concerned with how much he would lose if he sold it back to the bookstore than with any potential gain from doing so.
   c. His doctor doesn't consider Steven's symptoms of chest pain to be serious because Steven is thin and young, which doesn't fit the classic profile of a patient having a heart attack.
   d. Because oranges are being sold "10 for $10," Sylvia decides to buy 10.

7. A 3-year-old reports that her "foots" are itchy. Which stage of language acquisition does this statement represent?
   a. telegraph speech
   b. overgeneralization
   c. babbling
   d. joint attention

8. Casey is very empathic. It is as if he can read the minds of the people around him, knowing instantly if someone is uncomfortable with a topic of conversation, interested in garnering someone's affections, stressed out, and so on. We would expect Casey to score well on which indicator of intelligence?
   a. crystallized intelligence
   b. EQ
   c. fluid intelligence
   d. g

9. Which of the following characteristics is *not* typically correlated with high scores on intelligence tests?
   a. faster reaction times, particularly in a choice reaction time test
   b. decreased likelihood of premature death
   c. increased working memory performance
   d. missing corpus callosum

10. Which one of the following comments most accurately reflects the facts about the roles of nature and of nurture in intelligence?
    a. "There's overwhelming evidence that genes are the most important predictor of intelligence."
    b. "Give any child a stimulating environment, early schooling, and good health care, and he or she can evidence genius."
    c. "About 50 percent of intelligence is a function of what you're born with, and 50 percent is a function of the environment in which you're raised."
    d. "Group differences in intelligence cannot be attributed to genetic differences if there are environmental differences between the groups."

Answer Key for Chapter 8

1. a. symbolic; b. analogical; c. both; d. symbolic

2. b. functional fixedness

3. c. phonics

4. d. Chomsky's universal grammar theory

5. d. both a and b

6. a. availability heuristic; b. framing; c. representativeness heuristic; d. anchoring

7. b. overgeneralization

8. b. EQ

9. d. missing corpus callosum

10. d. "Group differences in intelligence cannot be attributed to genetic differences if there are environmental differences between the groups."

Chapter 9

1. A 1-week-old infant normally can _____. Choose all that apply.
   a. differentiate between sweet and nonsweet tastes
   b. display social smiles
   c. grasp a caregiver's finger
   d. make eye contact
   e. orient toward loud sounds
   f. recognize her name
   g. roll over from stomach to back
   h. see a caregiver across the room
   i. turn his head toward the smell of the mother's breast milk
   j. turn toward a nipple near her mouth

2. Piaget's theories of development have been very influential, but recent findings present challenges to some of his ideas. Which of the following statements is NOT a challenge to Piaget's theories?
   a. Children can move back and forth between stages when working on tasks.
   b. Babies can demonstrate object permanence in the first few months of life.
   c. Children younger than 3 can understand the concepts of "more than" and "less than" when using M&M's.
   d. All of the above are challenges to Piaget's theories.

3. A 9-month-old child watches as three cubes are covered by a panel, then as three more cubes appear to move behind the panel. Once the panel is lifted, only three cubes appear. Which of the following statements describes the infant's likely reaction?
   a. The infant quickly will lose interest in the screen.
   b. The infant will try to grab the three remaining cubes.
   c. The infant will stare at the researcher's face.
   d. The infant will stare at the three remaining cubes for a relatively long time.

4. Imagine reading a young child a story. In the story, Schuyler calls Emma a mean name. Emma retaliates by biting Schuyler. You ask the child what she thinks about the fact that Emma bit Schuyler. Three possible responses appear below. Label each as typical of one of the levels of moral reasoning described by Kohlberg: preconventional, conventional, postconventional.

a. "Emma better not bite again if she doesn't want to get bitten back!"
b. "Even if someone hurts us, it's never okay to hurt them back."
c. "It is wrong to bite people. Emma is going to get a time out."

5. Which of the following conclusions about the relationship between parenting style and child well-being is supported by empirical research? Optimal social development occurs when _____.
   a. parents attempt to grant a child's every wish
   b. parents determine the child's needs without input from the child
   c. the parenting style fits the child's temperament

6. In the strange-situation paradigm, the child is not distressed when the caregiver leaves and ignores the caregiver when he returns. Which attachment style is exhibited?
   a. secure
   b. insecure/ambivalent
   c. insecure/avoidant

7. Which statement most accurately describes the research on gender identity?
   a. Gender identity begins in adolescence, when puberty occurs.
   b. Biology has a strong influence on whether someone identifies as male, female, or transgender.
   c. Biological sex is always consistent with gender identity.

8. Igor is 83 years old. Which of his behaviors and cognitions are consistent with the socioemotional selectively theory?
   a. Anticipating he will die within the next few years, he sells his house and invests his money in a start-up company.
   b. He gets together with his closest friends and family to reminisce about the good old days.
   c. He spends his days sitting on the porch feeling sorry for himself.
   d. He travels for a few months in Bolivia, a country he has always wanted to learn more about.
   e. He volunteers his time mentoring boys in a residential home for troubled youth.

9. Which of the following statements are true regarding marriage and children?
   a. Married people are happier and healthier than single people.
   b. Having children generally increases marital satisfaction.
   c. Marriage decreases immune functioning in men.
   d. When spouses are supportive of each other's needs, having children can bring them closer together.

10. Which of the following characteristics describe most older adults? Select all that apply.
   a. happy
   b. mentally healthy
   c. greedy
   d. feeling more positive emotions than negative ones

Answer Key for Chapter 9

1. a. differentiate between sweet and nonsweet tastes; c. grasp a caregiver's finger; e. orient toward loud sounds; i. turn his head toward the smell of the mother's breast milk; j. turn toward a nipple near her mouth

2. c. Children younger than 3 can understand the concepts of "more than" and "less than" when using M&M's.

3. d. The infant will stare at the three remaining cubes for a relatively long time.

4. a—preconventional; b—postconventional; c—conventional

5. c. The parenting style fits the child's temperament.

6. c. insecure/avoidant

7. b. Biology has a strong influence on whether someone identifies as male, female, or transgender.

8. b. He gets together with his closest friends and family to reminisce about the good old days.

9. a. Married people are happier and healthier than single people.

10. a. happy; b. mentally healthy; d. feeling more positive emotions than negative ones

Chapter 10

1. Students enrolled in a difficult class are preparing to give end-of-term presentations, which will count 50 percent toward final grades. Which student below is likely to perform the best?
   a. Ahn is not at all stressed about the presentation. He has done well all semester and is confident he will do just fine this time around, too. He puts together his slides a week before the due date and then reviews the talk a few hours before giving the presentation.
   b. Sonya is somewhat anxious about this presentation. She knows her stuff but recognizes how much is riding on the quality of this presentation. This anxious energy motivates her to polish her slides and practice her talk.
   c. Marcus is very stressed about this presentation. A bad evaluation on the presentation will ruin his grade for the class, which in turn will ruin his strong GPA. He decides to spend every waking moment preparing the talk, working late into the night and sometimes dreaming about the presentation.

2. Which neurotransmitter is *not* implicated in the sexual response?
   a. dopamine
   b. GABA
   c. nitric oxide
   d. serotonin

3. Identify each of the following emotions as primary or secondary.
   a. fear
   b. happiness
   c. jealousy
   d. guilt
   e. disgust
   f. romantic love
   g. anger
   h. remorse

4. True or false: Research suggests that some emotions and emotional expressions are culturally universal.

5. Identify each of the following phenomena as a need or a drive.
   a. food
   b. hunger
   c. thirst
   d. water
   e. oxygen
   f. money

6. According to the research, which of the following people will be most likely to set challenging but attainable goals for themselves?
   a. a person low in self-efficacy but high in achievement motivation
   b. a person high in self-efficacy but low in achievement motivation
   c. a person low in self-efficacy and low in achievement motivation
   d. a person high in self-efficacy and high in achievement motivation

7. The hormone _____ motivates eating behavior. The hormone _____ is involved in long-term body fat regulation.

    a. leptin; ghrelin

    b. ghrelin; leptin

    c. ghrelin; oxytocin

    d. oxytocin; ghrelin

8. A classmate tells you he is having a hard time remembering which eating outcomes are associated with damage to different parts of the hypothalamus. Which of the following verbal mnemonics would be most helpful to your classmate? Select all that apply.

    a. Organisms with damage to the **hyp**othalamus have **hyp**erphagia.

    b. Organisms with damage to the lateral area of the hypothalamus (**L**H) eat **l**ittle.

    c. Organisms with damage to the preoptic area of the hypothalamus (**P**H) **p**ut on the **p**ounds.

    d. Organisms with damage to the ventromedial region of the hypothalamus (**VM**H) eat **v**ery **m**uch.

9. Which statement below is backed by empirical findings?

    a. Parental treatment of a child gives rise to the child's sexual orientation.

    b. High levels of androgens in women cause them to become lesbian, and high levels of estrogens in men cause them to become gay.

    c. Prenatal exposure to hormones is associated with sexual orientation.

    d. People are attracted to what is different: "The exotic becomes erotic."

10. Which of these statements are true regarding involvement of the amygdala in emotion?

    a. Information reaches the amygdala along two separate pathways.

    b. Increased activity in the amygdala during an emotional event is associated with improved long-term memory for that event.

    c. The amygdala helps process the emotional content of facial expressions.

Answer Key for Chapter 10

1. b. Sonya is somewhat anxious about this presentation. She knows her stuff but recognizes how much is riding on the quality of this presentation. This anxious energy motivates her to polish her slides and practice her talk.

2. b. GABA

3. a. primary; b. primary; c. secondary; d. secondary; e. primary; f. secondary; g. primary; h. secondary

4. true

5. a. need; b. drive; c. drive; d. need; e. need; f. need

6. d. a person high in self-efficacy and high in achievement motivation

7. b. ghrelin; leptin

8. b. Organisms with damage to the lateral area of the hypothalamus (**L**H) eat **l**ittle.; d. Organisms with damage to the ventromedial region of the hypothalamus (**VM**H) eat **v**ery **m**uch.

9. c. Prenatal exposure to hormones is associated with sexual orientation.

10. All three choices are true.

Chapter 11

1. Which of the following comments most accurately represents health psychologists' current understanding of illness?

    a. Illness is totally under our own control. We can stay healthy simply by making healthy decisions.

    b. Illness is a matter of luck. If our bodies are destined to become ill, we're out of luck.

    c. When a person has a family history of heart disease, breast cancer, or diabetes, the person's genetic predisposition guarantees that she will develop the illness.

    d. Genetic predispositions to some diseases exist. But living healthily can help reduce the chance of developing a disease.

2. The correct answer to the previous question is consistent with the _____ model of health and illness.

    a. biomedical

    b. biopsychosocial

    c. moral

    d. self-efficacy

3. Which of the following statements are true?

    a. Our bodies have natural defenses against weight loss that limit dieting's effectiveness.

    b. Body weight seems to be determined mostly by a set-point.

    c. Dieters who lose and regain weight repeatedly tend to become lighter over time.

    d. Body weight seems to be socially contagious.

4. According to research, _____ is as effective as medication for preventing diabetes or heart disease and for promoting recovery from heart attacks.

    a. remaining underweight for body size

    b. having children

    c. drinking red wine

    d. exercise

5. True or false: Mothers' highly stressful experiences can affect their offspring's behavior across generations, even if the stress occurs before pregnancy.

6. Label each of the following statements as applying to anorexia nervosa (AN), bulimia nervosa (BN), or both.

   a. This disorder can result in death if not treated.

   b. A person with this disorder exhibits eating that is out of control and excessive.

   c. The person will be at least 15 percent to 25 percent underweight.

   d. The person refuses to eat.

   e. The person will tend to be average weight or slightly overweight.

   f. This disorder results in a loss of bone density.

   g. This disorder typically develops in early adolescence.

   h. This disorder typically develops in late adolescence.

   i. Typically other people do not realize the person is suffering from this disorder.

   j. The person worries excessively about body weight issues.

7. Imagine your grandfather is preparing to move to a retirement community. Which of the following might you say if you wanted to help him promote physical and mental health? Choose all that apply.

   a. "Keep in mind there are a lot of shady characters out there looking to take advantage of people. Be suspicious of new people until you have a reason to trust them."

   b. "Know that I care about you and am here for you if there's anything I can do to help with the transition to your new home."

   c. "Make a point of meeting a lot of other residents."

   d. "Make sure to stay in touch with your close friends."

   e. "Your cable service offers over 100 channels; you won't run out of interesting programs to watch!"

8. Match each statement with one of the following coping mechanisms: emotion-focused coping, problem-focused coping, positive reappraisal, downward comparison.

   a. "I wish my family wasn't moving, but I'll get a chance to explore a new region of the country."

   b. "My hours at work may have been cut, but at least I didn't lose my job like other people did."

   c. "I'm not getting along with my roommate, so I'll avoid being home much."

   d. "I'd better schedule an appointment with the professor to improve my grades."

9. Chronic stress can have which of the following physiological consequences?

   a. damage to neurons in the hippocampus, leading to memory problems

   b. decreased numbers of lymphocytes, or white blood cells, leading to immune system problems

   c. increased blood pressure and constriction of blood vessels in the heart

   d. all of the above

10. Which of the following statements are true regarding oxytocin?

   a. Oxytocin is critical in the fight-or-flight response to stress.

   b. Oxytocin is released when people feel empathy.

   c. Oxytocin is secreted when males engage in aggressive behaviors.

   d. Participants dosed with oxytocin behave more trustingly than control participants do.

   e. Oxytocin is involved in mother/child attachments.

Answer Key for Chapter 11

1. d. Genetic predispositions to some diseases exist. But living healthily can help reduce the chance of developing a disease.

2. b. biopsychosocial

3. Choices a and d are true.

4. d. exercise

5. True. When female rats were exposed to stress two weeks before pregnancy, their offspring exhibited abnormalities in fear learning and heightened physiological response to stress as adults.

6. a. AN and BN (though BN is seldom fatal); b. BN; c. AN; d. AN; e. BN; f. AN; g. AN; h. BN; i. BN; j. AN and BN

7. b. "Know that I care about you and am here for you if there's anything I can do to help with the transition to your new home."; c. "Make a point of meeting a lot of other residents."; d. "Make sure to stay in touch with your close friends."

8. a. positive reappraisal; b. downward comparison; c. emotion-focused coping; d. problem-focused coping

9. d. all of the above

10. b. Oxytocin is released when people feel empathy.; d. Participants dosed with oxytocin behave more trustingly than control participants do.; e. Oxytocin is involved in mother/child attachments.

Chapter 12

1. Dorm A and Dorm B have a long-standing rivalry. Recently, the rivalry has intensified, resulting in destructive acts to property and harassment of outgroup members. A couple of students from each dorm encourage their fellow students to get together to brainstorm possible strategies for easing the tension. According to the ideas presented in this chapter, which suggestion would be most effective?

   a. "Let's hold a series of dorm dinners. Dorm A can invite people from Dorm B over one week, and Dorm B can invite people from Dorm A over the following week."

b. "Since people in Dorm A are such strong math students, we could have Dorm A offer math tutoring to students from Dorm B."

c. "The administration should hold a meeting with the dorm presidents to let them know that funding for dorm activities will be cut unless the interdorm tension subsides."

d. "We can hold an all-campus competition, where teams of dorms would compete for prizes. Dorm A and Dorm B could be on one team; Dorm C and Dorm D could be on the other team."

2. Why do people form groups?
   a. enhanced capacity to obtain food and other resources
   b. fundamental need to belong
   c. to create a social identity
   d. only a and b
   e. All of the above may be reasons why people form groups.

3. Which of the following statements is a likely explanation for ingroup favoritism?
   a. Typically, people become assigned to outgroups because there is something wrong with them that cannot be corrected, and so assisting outgroup members would be unproductive.
   b. Outgroup members could be "foes," and so supporting them could be to the detriment of the ingroup.
   c. Only ingroups that have members with high levels of bias, discrimination, and aggression show ingroup favoritism.
   d. All of the above are explanations.

4. Which of the following phenomena explain the bystander intervention effect? Choose all that apply.
   a. groupthink
   b. perceived risk as greater than perceived benefit
   c. discrimination against those in need
   d. diffusion of responsibility
   e. apathy
   f. unclear situation and unsureness of the correct response
   g. anonymity
   h. ingroup favoritism
   i. selfishness

5. Tanya is establishing a fundraiser so her organization can provide children in need with clothing and school supplies. While everyone in the organization supports her cause, Tanya has been having trouble getting people to volunteer to make phone calls for one hour a night to request donations. Research demonstrates that which of the following strategies might help Tanya get people to sign up for the one-hour time slots?
   a. Ask people to sign up for six-hour time slots. If they say no, ask if they could volunteer for just one hour of their time.
   b. Ask people to bring in cookies for a bake sale to support the cause. If they say yes, ask if they could also volunteer for one hour of their time to make phone calls.
   c. Ask people to make calls for 15 minutes. If they say yes, ask if they could stay for additional time.
   d. All of the above strategies should be effective.
   e. None of the above strategies would be effective.

6. Which of the following scenarios illustrates postdecisional dissonance?
   a. Josh has always wanted to attend College A. During his senior year of high school, he applies to College A and College B. Although he receives acceptance letters from both institutions, he decides to attend College A. When asked to explain why he wants to attend College A, he says, "I like that I can live on campus. There's a great community vibe here. Plus I can major in international business. None of these things are true of the other school."
   b. Adrianna wants to go on a community service trip during her spring break. After struggling for weeks to decide between two options, she opts to build houses in rural Mexico instead of doing hurricane cleanup in Louisiana. When asked to explain why she made this decision, she says, "The Mexico trip will give me a chance to travel outside the United States, which I've always wanted to do. Plus, the Louisiana trip sounded pretty stale."

7. Which of the following examples of social norms marketing is likely to be the most effective?
   a. "Eighty percent of the residents in your neighborhood recycle."
   b. "Eighty percent of the residents in your neighborhood recycle. Keep up the great work!"
   c. "Recycle!"
   d. "Recycle! It's the right thing to do!"

8. Match each definition below with the appropriate term: altruism, inclusive fitness, kin selection, reciprocal helping.
   a. a process in which individuals behave helpfully toward those with whom they share genes
   b. providing help without any apparent reward for doing so
   c. the tendency for one animal to help another because the other can return the favor in the future
   d. the adaptive benefits of transmitting genes rather than focusing on individual survival

9. Which statement below about Shelly, who is very attractive, is most consistent with the "what is beautiful is good" stereotype?
   a. "Shelly is a total ditz!"
   b. "Shelly is easily the happiest person I know!"
   c. "Shelly sure knows how to manipulate other people with her looks!"
   d. "Shelly's parents are really attractive, too."

10. Which of the following examples most accurately describes the relationship between relationship length and frequency of sex?
   a. After an initial period of frequent sex, there is a negative correlation between relationship length and frequency of sex.
   b. There is a near-zero correlation between relationship length and frequency of sex.
   c. There is a negative correlation between relationship length and frequency of sex.
   d. There is a positive correlation between relationship length and frequency of sex.

Answer Key for Chapter 12

1. d. "We can hold an all-campus competition, where teams of dorms would compete for prizes. Dorm A and Dorm B could be on one team; Dorm C and Dorm D could be on the other team."

2. e. All of the above may be reasons why people form groups.

3. b. Outgroup members could be "foes," and so supporting them could be to the detriment of the ingroup.

4. Choices b, d, f, and g are all reasons for the bystander intervention effect.

5. d. All of the above strategies should be effective.

6. b. Adrianna wants to go on a community service trip during her spring break. . . . When asked to explain why she made this deci-

sion, she says, "The Mexico trip will give me a chance to travel outside the United States, which I've always wanted to do. Plus, the Louisiana trip sounded pretty stale."

7. b. "Eighty percent of the residents in your neighborhood recycle. Keep up the great work!"

8. a. kin selection; b. altruism; c. reciprocal helping; d. inclusive fitness

9. b. "Shelly is easily the happiest person I know!"

10. a. After an initial period of frequent sex, there is a negative correlation between relationship length and frequency of sex.

Chapter 13

1. Your psychology instructor asks the students in your class to form groups of five and then take turns answering the question *What do we need to know about you to truly know you?* The people in your group give the following answers; label each as representative of psychodynamic approaches, humanistic theory, type and trait perspectives, or learning and cognition perspectives.
   a. "To know me, you would have to ask me questions about myself. I took a survey once that said I am an extremely intuitive introvert."
   b. "To know me, you would have to know how I've responded in the past and what I think about the world."
   c. "To know me, you would have to figure out a way to peer into my unconscious. There's so much I can't even know about myself; I'm not sure you could ever really know me."
   d. "To know me, you would have to know about my hopes and aspirations. I seek to become the best person I can be."

2. June asks people to watch a five-minute recording of a play in which two characters find themselves in a dangerous situation. Then she asks her research participants to write an ending to the story, which she codes to reveal features of each participant's personality. This proposed measure of personality can best be described as _____ and _____.
   a. idiographic; projective
   b. nomothetic; projective
   c. idiographic; objective
   d. nomothetic; objective

3. Which of the following statements might explain why our close acquaintances sometimes are better able to predict our behaviors than we are? Select all that apply.
   a. Our ego defense mechanisms prevent us from knowing our true personalities and thus undermine our abilities to accurately predict our own behaviors.

   b. Predictions of our own behaviors may be biased in favor of our subjective perceptions (how we *think* we act) rather than our objective behaviors (how we *do* act).
   c. We tend to pay more attention to others than to ourselves and thus fail to notice our own behavior; others notice how we behave and are better able to predict our future behaviors.

4. Which of the following statements is suggested by research on the genetic basis of personality?
   a. Specific genes control specific personality traits.
   b. Only some traits, such as temperament, have a genetic basis.
   c. Probably thousands of genes are involved in personality, and epigenetic mechanisms can cause environmental events to affect the expression of these genes.
   d. Personality has no genetic basis.

5. Which of the following statements most accurately summarizes the research on how sex and culture influence personality?
   a. The Big Five personality traits are valid only in Western cultures.
   b. Men tend to report and be rated as more assertive, while women tend to report and be rated higher on agreeableness and neuroticism.
   c. Sex differences in personality are smallest in Western countries.

6. According to sociometer theory, self-esteem is _____. Select all that are true.
   a. based on the perceived belief that one is living up to the standards of one's culture
   b. highest when perceived risk of social exclusion is low
   c. based on the perceived probability of social rejection

7. True or false: Psychological research shows that high self-esteem is critical to life success and has no negative side effects.

8. Which of the following phenomena are associated with the behavioral approach system (BAS), and which are associated with the behavioral inhibition system (BIS)?
   a. "go" system
   b. avoiding punishments
   c. pursuit of rewards
   d. "stop" system

9. Which of the following statements best describes the distinctions among traits, temperaments, and characteristic adaptations?
   a. Temperaments, which are broader than traits, influence personality throughout development. Situational demands can lead to characteristic adaptations, which, although they do not reflect changes in the underlying dispositions, can reflect changes in how these dispositions are expressed.
   b. Temperaments, which are broader than traits, influence personality throughout development. After childhood, situational demands lead to characteristic adaptations, which reflect changes in underlying dispositions.
   c. Temperaments, which are narrower than traits, influence personality only during childhood. After childhood, situational demands lead to characteristic adaptations, which reflect changes in underlying dispositions.
   d. Temperaments, which are narrower than traits, influence personality only during childhood. Situational demands can lead to characteristic adaptations, which, although they do not reflect changes in the underlying dispositions, can reflect changes in how these dispositions are expressed.

10. A professional athlete makes the following statements during an interview with a sports reporter. Which statements are most likely to reflect a positive illusion?
   a. "I had a better-than-average game today."
   b. "I'm sure that wearing my lucky socks helped."
   c. "But it also helped that I've been taking care of my injury—lots of ice and physical therapy."
   d. "I'm done with injuries. From here on out, I'll have a clean bill of health."

Answer Key for Chapter 13

1. a. type and trait; b. learning and cognition; c. psychodynamic; d. humanistic

2. a. idiographic; projective

3. b. Predictions of our own behaviors may be biased in favor of our subjective perceptions (how we *think* we act) rather than our objective behaviors (how we *do* act).; c. We tend to pay more attention to others than to ourselves and thus fail to notice our own behavior; others notice how we behave and are better able to predict our future behaviors.

4. c. Probably thousands of genes are involved in personality, and epigenetic mechanisms can cause environmental events to affect the expression of these genes.

5. b. Men tend to report and be rated as more assertive, while women tend to report and be rated higher on agreeableness and neuroticism.

6. b. highest when perceived risk of social exclusion is low; and c. based on the perceived probability of social rejection

7. False. Research shows there is little relationship between self-esteem and objective measurement of success. Violent criminals, bullies, and narcissists all have high self-esteem, with very negative effects.

8. BAS—a, c; BIS—b, d

9. a. Temperaments, which are broader than traits, influence personality throughout development. Situational demands can lead to characteristic adaptations, which, although they do not reflect changes in the underlying dispositions, can reflect changes in how these dispositions are expressed.

10. b. "I'm sure that wearing my lucky socks helped."; d. "I'm done with injuries. From here on out, I'll have a clean bill of health."

Chapter 14

1. Which of the following questions would a clinician consider in order to determine whether a behavior represents psychopathology? Select all that apply.
   a. Does the behavior deviate from cultural norms?
   b. Is the behavior causing the individual personal distress?
   c. Is the behavior maladaptive?
   d. Is the behavior unusual?

2. Two students visit the campus health center. Student A describes feeling constantly fearful and anxious. Student B describes feeling persistently agitated and often exhibiting violent outbursts.

Student A's symptoms are consistent with an _____ disorder, which is more common in ____; student B's symptoms are consistent with an _____ disorder, which is more common in _____.
   a. externalizing, females; internalizing, males
   b. externalizing, males; internalizing, females
   c. internalizing, females; externalizing, males
   d. internalizing, males; externalizing, females

3. True or false: The *DSM-5* is proven to offer definitive and accurate diagnoses coupled with the best recommended treatment options for all accepted psychological disorders.

4. What of the following are examples of neuropsychological assessments?
   a. the patient's self-report of symptoms
   b. reports from interviews with people who know the patient well
   c. blood tests
   d. card-sorting tasks
   e. having the person copy a picture by hand
   f. having the person place books on a mat while blindfolded
   g. having the person draw designs from memory

5. Indicate whether each of the following constellations of symptoms is best described as phobic disorder, generalized anxiety disorder, panic disorder, or obsessive-compulsive disorder.
   a. Harlow is hypervigilant, constantly on the lookout for problems. He often has trouble sleeping and experiences constant fatigue.
   b. While hiking a looped path, Susan comes across a snake sunning itself. She walks a considerable distance off the path just to avoid the snake.
   c. Juan frequently has recurrent thoughts that harm might come to him or others and can find relief only by repeating certain behaviors.

6. Indicate whether each of the following constellations of symptoms is best described as major depression, dysthymia, or bipolar disorder.
   a. Claudia has felt a sense of sadness for the past couple of years. She seems to function well enough in her daily life, but she always feels glum.
   b. Lorenzo's mother died about a year ago. Since then, he has not found any satisfaction in his hobbies, spends most nights lying awake in bed, and has lost nearly 10 pounds.

7. Match each of the following statements with the correct label for that symptom of schizophrenia: delusion of grandeur, delusion of persecution, flat affect, hallucination, loosening of associations, social withdrawal. Not all labels will be used.
   a. "I sat on the rock dock clock clock clock."
   b. "People from the Central Intelligence Agency are following me; they are out to get me. You and I will need to talk in the elevator so they can't listen in on our conversation."
   c. "The bugs keep crawling on my skin; I wipe them off, but they keep coming."

8. Which of the following statements describe key objections to categorizing personality disorders as true mental disorders? Check all that apply.
   a. If environmental factors contribute to the expression of personality disorders, it makes more sense to label the environment as disordered rather than the person.
   b. Overlap in the characteristics of different disorders suggests that the categories may not be conceptually clear cut.
   c. Some features of personality disorders are not as stable as researchers once thought.
   d. The features of personality disorders are merely extreme versions of normal personality traits.

9. Royce takes swimming lessons at the community pool. He often arrives without all the things he needs for practice, such as his towel, a change of clothes, and goggles. As the teacher instructs the class, Royce often blows bubbles at the water's surface. And although he listens to what the teacher tells him about how to modify his swim strokes, he has difficulty using the suggestions. Based on this description, which of the following disorders does Royce most likely have?
   a. agoraphobia
   b. attention-deficit/hyperactivity disorder
   c. autism
   d. obsessive-compulsive disorder

10. Are females or males more likely to be diagnosed with each of the following disorders?
    a. antisocial personality disorder
    b. attention-deficit/hyperactivity disorder
    c. autism
    d. borderline personality disorder
    e. depression
    f. generalized anxiety disorder
    g. obsessive-compulsive disorder
    h. panic disorder

Answer Key for Chapter 14

1. Choices a, b, and c apply.

2. c. internalizing, females; externalizing, males

3. false

4. All but choice c apply.

5. a. generalized anxiety disorder; b. phobic disorder; c. obsessive-compulsive disorder

6. a. dysthymia; b. major depression

7. a. loosening of associations; b. delusion of persecution; c. hallucination

8. b. Overlap in the characteristics of different disorders suggests that the categories may not be conceptually clear cut.; c. Some features of personality disorders are not as stable as researchers once thought.; d. The features of personality disorders are merely extreme versions of normal personality traits.

9. b. attention-deficit/hyperactivity disorder

10. Females are more likely to be diagnosed with d. borderline personality disorder, e. depression, f. generalized anxiety disorder, g. obsessive-compulsive disorder, h. panic disorder; males are more likely to be diagnosed with a. antisocial personality disorder, b. attention-deficit/hyperactivity disorder, c. autism.

Chapter 15

1. Which of the following statements are true regarding how culture can affect the therapeutic process?
   a. Culture can influence people's willingness to seek help.
   b. Culture can influence the expression of psychological disorders.
   c. Definitions of mental health are consistent across cultures.
   d. Psychotherapy is accepted to similar degrees across cultures.
   e. The extent to which mental disorders is stigmatized varies by culture.

2. Barlow advocates distinguishing between psychological treatments and general talk therapy. Which of the following attributes characterize psychological treatments?
   a. Treatments should be based on evidence of their effectiveness.
   b. Treatments should be appropriate for the particular disorders.
   c. Specific techniques for treatment should be developed in the laboratory by psychologists.
   d. Treatments should be guided by grand theories.

3. Dialectical behavior therapy takes place in three stages. Place the descriptions of the three stages below in the correct order.
   a. The therapist helps the client explore past traumatic experiences that may be at the root of emotional problems.
   b. The therapist helps the patient develop self-respect and independent problem solving.
   c. The therapist works with the client to replace the most dysfunctional behaviors with more-appropriate behaviors.

4. During his early adult years, Joshua was diagnosed with anti-social personality disorder. Joshua is now 40. Over the coming years, his friends and family will likely see a decrease in which of the following behaviors? Select all that apply.
   a. Joshua's lack of remorse for hurting others' feelings
   b. Joshua's tendency to feel entitled to special treatment
   c. Joshua's tendency to get into fistfights

5. Three-year-old Marley recently received a diagnosis of autism. Which of the following are true about her likely treatment?
   a. Many individuals will need to be involved in Marley's treatment, including parents, teachers, and mental health practitioners.
   b. Marley's treatment is likely to strain family dynamics and family finances.
   c. Marley's treatment will focus largely on using social praise and small gifts to reinforce desired behavior.
   d. Marley's treatment will need to be highly structured.
   e. Marley's treatment will require a minimum of 20 hours per week and will likely last for two to three months.

6. Selective serotonin reuptake inhibitors (SSRIs) are useful in the treatments of which of the two following psychological disorders?
   a. depression and bipolar disorder
   b. depression and borderline personality disorder

   c. obsessive-compulsive disorder (OCD) and schizophrenia
   d. depression and schizophrenia
   e. obsessive-compulsive disorder (OCD) and depression

7. Which controversial therapy has been found to be quite effective in the treatment of depression in patients who fail to respond to other treatments?
   a. tricyclics
   b. phototherapy
   c. electroconvulsive therapy (ECT)
   d. lobotomy

8. Label each point below as an argument either for or against the practice of prescribing Ritalin (methylphenidate) to children with ADHD.
   a. Children taking Ritalin are happier, more socially adept, and more academically successful than those who do not receive treatment.
   b. Children taking Ritalin can experience disordered sleep, reduced appetite, bodily twitches, and temporary growth suppression.
   c. Children taking Ritalin may come to see their ADHD as a problem beyond their control and may not learn coping strategies they will need later if they discontinue their medication or if it ceases to be effective.
   d. Children taking Ritalin show a decrease in negative behaviors and an increase in positive behaviors.
   e. The benefits of Ritalin are not maintained over the long run.

9. Which of the following treatments is the most effective treatment for the disorders listed below: dialectical behavioral therapy (DBT), cognitive-behavioral therapy, pharmacological therapy.
   a. bipolar disorder
   b. anxiety disorders
   c. borderline personality disorder

10. Imagine you are asked to evaluate the quality of the following two methodologies for an empirical evaluation of a new treatment for ADHD. Label each of the methodologies as strong or weak. If a methodology is strong, briefly explain why. If a methodology is weak, provide a brief recommendation for strengthening it.
    a. Parents will be asked whether they would like their child to receive medication or the new psychotherapy. Each child will be assigned to a condition based on the parents' preference.
    b. The study will include four conditions: a nontreatment control group, a group receiving medication only, a group receiving the new psychotherapy only, and a group receiving both medication and the new psychotherapy.

Answer Key for Chapter 15

1. Choices a, b, and e are true.

2. a. Treatments should be based on evidence of their effectiveness.; b. Treatments should be appropriate for the particular disorders.; c. Specific techniques for treatment should be developed in the laboratory by psychologists.

3. The correct order is c, a, b.

4. c. Joshua's tendency to get into fistfights

5. Choices a, b, and d are likely true.

6. e. obsessive-compulsive disorder (OCD) and depression

7. c. electroconvulsive therapy (ECT)

8. Choices a and d support the use of Ritalin in treating ADHD. Choices b, c, and e argue against the use of Ritalin in this population.

9. a. pharmacological therapy; b. cognitive-behavioral therapy; c. dialectical behavioral therapy (DBT)

10. a. weak, would be improved if random assignment to condition were used; b. strong because of the use of treatment and control groups

Permissions Acknowledgments

Table of Contents

Chapter 1 Blend Images/Alamy Stock Photo
Chapter 2 Shutterstock **Chapter 3** Granger
Wootz/Blend Images/Gallery Stock **Chapter 4**
Fancy/Veer/Corbis **Chapter 5** Joel Sartore/
National Geographic Creative **Chapter 6**
Shutterstock **Chapter 7** Alberto Coto/The
Image Bank/Getty Images **Chapter 8** Roberto
Westbrook/Blend Images **Chapter 9** Gallery
Stock **Chapter 10** Guenther Philipp/Gallery
Stock **Chapter 11** Aflo Co., Ltd./Alamy Stock
Photo **Chapter 12** Sarah Lawrence/Getty
Images **Chapter 13** Gallery Stock **Chapter 14**
Ronald van Erkel/Getty Images **Chapter 15**
Steve Coleman/Getty Images

Author Photos

Michael S. Gazzaniga George Foulsham, UCSB
Office of Public Affairs and Communications

Todd F. Heatherton Office of Communications,
Dartmouth College

Chapter 1

p. 2 Blend Images/Alamy Stock Photo
4 © The New Yorker Collection 1998 Sam Gross
from cartoonbank.com. All Rights Reserved.
5 top http://www.dailymail.co.uk/news/article
-3301204/The-quiz-makes-60s-better-cooks
-Computer-brain-games-stave-mental-decline
.html#ixzz4XSTceYl0 **5 bottom** Courtesy
Dr. Elliot T. Berkman **6 top** Ramin Talaie/Getty
Images **6 bottom** Rick Baldwin/CartoonStock
7 bottom Balkis Press/Sipa USA/Newscom
8 top John Lamparski/WireImage/Getty
Images **9** Rischgitz/Getty Images **10** Sarin
Images/Granger, NYC. All rights reserved.
11 top Imagno/Getty Images **11 bottom**
Bettmann/Getty Images **12 both** The Drs.
Nicholas and Dorothy Cummings Center for the
History of Psychology, The University of Akron
13 Bettmann/Getty Images **14** Library of
Congress/Corbis/VCG via Getty Images
15 top The Drs. Nicholas and Dorothy
Cummings Center for the History of Psychology,
The University of Akron **15 bottom** American
Journal of Psychology © 1974 by the Board of
Trustees of the University of Illinois. Used with
permission of the University of Illinois Press.
16 top From *Mind Sights* by Roger N. Shepard ©
1960 by Roger N. Shepard. Henry Holt and com-
pany, LLC **16 bottom** Courtesy of Carl Rogers
Memorial Library **17 top** Courtesy of George
Miller, Princeton University © 2001, Pryde
Brown Photographs, Princeton, NJ **17 bottom**
Science Daily/Wake Forest Baptist Medical

Center **19 top** © The New Yorker Collection
2011 Zachary Kanin from cartoonbank.com.
All Rights Reserved. **19 bottom** Photo
Illustration: Cary Wolinsky & Jen Christensen.
Cover reproduced with permission ©
Scientific American, Inc. **20 top** Rick Gomez/
Getty Images **20 bottom** © Luke Duggleby
21 top Petr Janata/UC Davis Image **21 center
top** Stockbyte/Alamy **21 center bottom**
Somos Images LLC/Alamy **21 bottom** Bruno
De Hogues/Getty Images **22** Levitin and
Menon, V. (2003). Musical structure is processed
in 'language' areas of the brain. *NeuroImage,
20,* 2142–2152. 2003 © Elsevier Inc., All rights
reserved. **23** Pie chart, "Where Psychologists
Work," from American Psychological Associa-
tion, *Careers in Psychology.* Copyright © 2011
by the American Psychological Association.
Adapted with permission. **25 top** Brad Wilson/
Getty Images **25 center** Neustockimages/Getty
Images **25 bottom** Wavebreak Media Ltd/
Alamy **27** Mike Cardew/Akron Beacon Journal/
TNS via Getty Images

Chapter 2

p. 28 Shutterstock **29** Photo provided by the
Raffaele Family **32 top left** Christina Kennedy/
Getty Images **32 top center** Leren Lu/Getty
Images **32 top right** Sapsiwai/Shutterstock
32 bottom right Strayer, D. L., & Drews, F. A.
(2004). Profiles in driver distraction: Effects of
cell phone conversations on younger and older
drivers. *Human Factors, 46,* 640–649, Copyright
© 2004, Sage Publications **32 bottom center**
© 2014 Department of Psychology, Clemson
University. All Rights Reserved **32 bottom left**
Christy Varonfakis Johnson/Alamy **33** © David
Donar/Cartoonstock **34 top** Courtesy of Kristen
Frosio **34 bottom** Olivia Drake/Wesleyan University **35 top** © Sidney Harris, science-
cartoonsplus.com **35 bottom** © 2016 Gallup, Inc.
All rights reserved. http://www.gallup.com/poll
/169640/sex-marriage-support-reaches-new
-high.aspx **38** *Journal of Cognitive Neuroscience,
22:*6 (June 2010), Cover Image. © 2010 by the
Massachusetts Institute of Technology. **39 top**
Spencer Grant/Science Source **39 bottom**
Squire et al. (1989) Description of Brain Injury
in the Amnesic Patient N.S. Based on Magnetic
Resonance Imaging. *Experimental Neurology
105,* 23–35 (July 1989). © 1989 Elsevier **40 top**
Lawrence S. Sugiyama/University of Oregon
40 bottom Karl Ammann/Getty Images
41 Janine Wiedel Photolibrary/Alamy **42 both**
© Hawthorne Studies Collection, Baker Library,
Harvard Business School. All rights reserved.
43 Blend Images/Alamy Stock Photo **46 top**
Michael J. LeBrecht II/Sports Illustrated/Getty
Images **49 top left** Corbis/SuperStock **49 inset**

Corbis/SuperStock **50 top** Yuriko Nakao/
Bloomberg via Getty Images **50 bottom** Joan
Bardaletti/Pano Pictures **52 top** AP Photo/
Doug Mills **53** © Sidney Harris, sciencecartoons-
plus.com **54 top** Lovette/Reynolds/Nikitin/
Sipa **61** © The New Yorker Collection Sidney
Harris from cartoonbank.com. All Rights
Reserved. **63** Reuters/Mike Segar/Newscom
67 Daviles/Getty Images

Chapter 3

p. 68 Granger Wootz/Blend Images/Gallery
Stock **71** James Cavallini/Science Source
79 top Thinkstock **79 bottom** Cartoonstock.
com **80 top** AP Photo/Morry Gash **80 bottom**
The Asahi Shimbun via Getty Images
81 ImageZoo/Alamy **82 top** Rorden 2004
Using human brain lesions to infer function.
*Nature Reviews Neuroscience 5.*812.819. ©
2004, Rights Managed by Nature Publishing
Group **82 center left** Mark Burnett/Alamy
82 center right Richard T. Nowitz /Science
Source **82 bottom left** AJ Photo/Science
Source **82 bottom right** James Cavallini/
Science Source **83 top left** Michael Ventura/
Alamy **83 top right** WDCN/Univ. College
London/Science Source **83 center left** Charles
Thatcher/Getty Images **83 bottom left** Mark
Harmel/Alamy **83 bottom right** Courtesy of
Psych Central **84 left** Marcello Massimini/
University of Wisconsin-Madison **84 right**
Dr K Singh, Liverpool University/Dr S Hamdy &
Dr Q Aziz, Manchester University **89 both**
From Penfield, Wilder (1958), The excitable
cortex in conscious man. Liverpool University
Press **90** Ramachandran, V. S., and Blakeslee, S.,
Fig. 6.1, Drawing made by a neglect patient,
from *Phantoms in the brain.* Copyright © 1998
by V. S. Ramachandran and Sandra Blakeslee.
Reprinted by permission of HarperCollins
Publishers Inc. **91 top left** Collection of Jack
and Beverly Wilgus/Wikimedia Commons
Attribution License **91 top center** Center for
the History of Medicine, Countway Library,
Harvard Medical School **91 top right** Dama-
sio et al. (1994) The Return of Phineas Gage.
Science. Copyright © 1994, AAAS. **91 bottom**
Bettmann/Getty Images **96** The Photo Works
100 Stringer/Photoshot/Newscom **101** © The
New Yorker Collection 1999 William Haefeli
from cartoonbank.com. All Rights Reserved
102 both Provided by The Mack Family
103 both Indiana University School of Medicine
105 AP Photo **106 left** Shutterstock **106 center**
Dennis Kunkel Microscopy, Inc. **106 right**
CNRI/Science Source **107 both** Courtesy Fred
Nijhout **108 top** AP Photo/Ron Edmonds
108 center Dave J. Williams/Alamy
108 bottom James Jenkins/Natural History

Chapter 12

Chapter 13

Chapter 14

Chapter 15

Name Index

Page numbers in *italics* refer to figures and illustrations.

Aarts, H., 131
Abad-Merino, S., 501
Abdelaal, E., 456
Abdel-Azim, E., 237
Abdel-Khalek, A. M., 539
Abe, Y., 447
Abel, T., 253
Abelson, R., 295
Abikoff, H. B., 656
Abizaid, A., 414
Aboud, F., 329
Abou-Saleh, M. T., 340
Abram, S. V., 529
Abramowitz, J. S., 619, 620
Abramson, L. Y., 554, 556, 582
Abrevaya, J., 483
Ackerman, P. L., 325
Ackerman, S., 453
Ackl, N., 581
Adachi-Mejia, A. M., 256, 295, *296*
Adair, J., 50
Adám, N., 539
Adamovová, L., 539
Adams, C. E., 573
Adams, C. M., 238
Addington, A. M., 593
Addington, J., 594
Adelman, A., 455
Adolfsson, R., 518
Adolphs, R., 87, 388
Agam, G., 581
Agarwal, S. K., 453
Agawu, K., 22
Agnello, C., 417
Agnew-Blais, J. C., 610
Agnoli, F., 313
Agras, W. S., 440
Aguilar, S., 599
Ahima, R. S., 434
Ahmed, N., 340
Ahn, C. K., 539
Ahn, H. N., 539
Ahtiainen, J. P., 444
Aichhorn, M., 360
Ainsworth, M. D. S., 350
Aizpurua, A., 377
Akahane-Yamada, R., 314
Akbarian, S., 569
Akyildir-Kuntz, C., 451
Alaei, R., 497
Alamuddin, R., 50
Albano, A. M., 660
Alberini, C. M., 250, 449
Alborn, A. M., 102
Alcalay, L., 419
Al-Delaimy, W. K., 442
Aldridge, J. D., 221
Aldridge, J. W., 149

Alegrio, A., 609
Aleman, A., 592
Alemeida, D. M., 376
Aleshire, N., 152
Alessandri, M., 659
Alexander, A. L., 388
Alexis, K., 332
Alexy, U., 414
Alferink, L. A., 96
Algoe, S. B., 459
Al-Hamzawi, A. O., 575, 581
Alho, A. T., 198
Ali, K., 340
Ali, M. K., 432
Alia-Klein, N., 242
Alicke, M. D., 552
Al-Khatib, T., *46*
Alkire, M. T., 323, 326
Allebeck, P., 594
Allen, A., 658
Allen, C. R., 583
Allen, M. H., 583
Allen, N. B., 580
Allik, J., 538, 540
Allison, T., 181
Allman, J. M., 90
Allmon, D., 651
Alloy, L., 582
Allport, G., 516, *516*, 528
Allred, K. D., 460
Almeida, D. M., 448
Almond, P., 534
Alonso, J., 575, 581
Alper, C. M., 461
Altamura, A., 646
Altshuler, L., 583
Alvarez, L., 171
Alvergne, A., 101
Amano, S., 348
Amanzio, M., 628
Amaral, D. G., 39, 606
Amato, P. R., 373
Ambady, N., 331, 398, 496
Ambler, A., 152
American Academy of Neurology, 124
American Psychiatric Association, 135, 439–40,
    516, *565*, *572*, *589*, *590*, *603*
American Psychological Association, 287, 367,
    422, 633, 643
American Speech-Hearing-Language
    Association, 193
Ames, A., 184
Ametaj, A. A., 629, 633
Amieva, H., 638
Amminger, G. P., 594
Amoroso, A. J., 150
An, X., 122
Anderson, A. K., 87, 146, 198, 277, 387, 639
Anderson, C., 402
Anderson, C. A., 241, 242, 483

Anderson, C. M., *649*
Anderson, J. S., 96
Anderson, N., 504, *505*
Anderson, S. W., 362–63
Andersson, E., 634
Andersson, G., 618, 632, 640–41
Andersson, R., 111
Anderton, C. H., 143
Ando, J., 517, 518
Andrade, L. H., 575, 581
Andreasen, D., 127
Andreasen, N. C., 580, 591, 593
Andreasson, S., 594
Andreiuolo, P. A., 363
Andresen, L., 80
Andrews, G., 330
Andrieux, A., 649
Angell, M., 639, 644
Angleitner, A., 518, 535–36
Angold, A., 370
Anicich, E. M., 502
Anjum, R. S., 282
Ankiel, R., 287
Anney, R., 605
Anrep, G. V., *213*
Anthony, A., 607–8
Antonuccio, D., 660
Antoun, N., 387
Aouizerate, B., 638
Apelberg, B. J., 442
Apfel, N., 332
Arem, H., 443
Arena, R., 444
Arias, E., 372, 431, 659
Ariely, D., 119, 504
Aristotle, 562
Arkowitz, H., 621
Armstrong, H. E., 651
Arndt, S., 593
Aron, A. P., 393, 507, 510
Aron, E. N., 510
Aronne, L. J., 437
Aronowitz, B. R., 658
Aronson, E., 494, 505
Aronson, J., 331
Arrazola, R. A., 442
Arseneault, L., 409, 610
Arslan, R. C., 549
Arthurs, J., 217
Asai, M., 590
Asch, S. E., 298, 476–77, *477*
Ashburn-Nardo, L., 502
Ashby, J., 319
Ashton, M. C., 529
Ashwin, E., 103
Ashwood, P., 606
Askin, R., 568
Assad, L. K., 508
Assaf, M., 157
Atkinson, R., 256
Ault, L., 419

Austers, I., 419
Austin, E. J., 324
Auyeung, B., 103
Avants, B. B., 329, 339
Avenevoli, S., 653, 659
Averill, J. R., 400
Avia, M. D., 535–36
Aviezer, H., 397
Avinun, R., 518
Avugos, S., 69
Azrael, D., 661

Baars, B., 123
Bachman, J. G., 154, 441
Back, K., 504
Back, M. D., 543
Bacon, S., 536
Bacskai, B. J., 149
Baddeley, A. D., 258
Badgett, M. V., 373
Bae, S., 432
Baete, A., 340
Bagge, C. L., 585
Bailes, J. E., 124
Bailey, J. M., 421–23
Baillargeon, R., 357, 360
Baio, J., 604
Baird, J. A., 360
Baker, C., 145
Baker, M., 461
Baker, T. B., 441, 442–43
Bakersman-Kranenburg, M. J., 352
Bakish, D., 634
Baldessarini, R. J., 646
Baldwin, D. A., 313, 360
Baldwin, G. T., 124, 151
Baler, R. D., 148, 156
Balmas, G., 153
Balota, D. A., 259
Balthazard, C. G., 144
Baltimore D., 107
Bamberg, E., 116
Banaji, M. R., 217, 399, 491–92, 496, 499, 502, 556
Bancroft, T., 607
Bandura, A., 239, *239*, 240, 408, 525, *526*
Banfield, J. F., 547
Bangerter, A., 347
Banks, C., 473
Bao, A. M., 367
Bao, W. N., 371
Baptista, M. A. S., 224
Barbee, A. P., 420, 505
Barch, D. M., 593
Bard, Philip, 391, *392*
Barefoot, J. C., 455
Bar-Eli, M., 69
Barfield, R. T., 578
Bargh, J. A., 131
Bar-Hillel, M., 389
Barkley, R. A., 610
Barlow, D. H., 566, 574, 576, 629, 633, 636
Barnes, G. M., 143, 154
Barnett, R. C., 580
Barnier, A., 144
Baron-Cohen, S., 103, 360, 397
Barrett, F. S., 22
Barrett, L. F., 384, 385, 398
Barretto, R. P., 195
Barrick, T., 326
Barsalou, L. W., 385
Bartels, A., 416
Bartels, J., 127
Bartels, J. M., 474
Bartels, M., 590
Bartholow, B. D., 241

Bartlett, F., 264
Barton, A. W., 339
Barton, D. A., 581
Bartoshuk, L. M., 195, *195*
Bartz, J., 658
Bartzokis, G., 649
Baskin, T. W., 629
Bass, D. I., 388
Basser, P., 642
Basten, U., 326
Bastian, B., 470
Bastian, B. A., 432
Batson, C. D., 485, 487
Batson, J. G., 485
Batty, G. D., 323, 325
Bauer, M., 460
Baugh, C. M., 124
Bauldry, S., 432
Baumeister, R. F., 147, 401, 410, 419, 452, 490, 523, 550–51
Baumgart, S. L., 172
Bäuml, K. T., 266
Baumrind, D., 481
Baxter, A. J., 581
Baxter, M. G., 440
Baydala, L. T., 332
Bazana, P. G., 326
Beach, M. L., 240, 295, *296*
Beach, S. R., 339
Bean, J., 146
Beauchamp, G. K., 196, *197*
Beaudoin, G., 635
Bechara, A., 156, 301, 363
Bechtold, J., 153
Beck, A. T., 570, 582, 619, *619*, 640, 652
Becker, C. B., 441
Becker, D. V., 182
Bedell, B. T., 302
Bee, P., 637
Beekman, A. T., 640–41
Beer, J., 483
Beesdo, K., 576
Beggan, J. K., 551
Behne, T., 360
Behrmann, M., 606
Beier, M. E., 325
Beller, E., 609
Belmaker, R. H., 581
Belsky, D. W., 339, 409, 566
Belsky, J., 364, 374
Belzung, C., 568
Bem, D., 171, 172, 406
Bem, S. L., 367
Benavides, J. A., 138
Benazzouz, A., 638
Benbow, C. P., 330
Bench, S. W., 385
Benedetti, F., 628
Benet-Martinez, V., 538
Benjamin, D. J., 518
Benjamin, E. J., 455
Benjamin, L. T., 629
Benjet, C., 233, 575, 653
Bennett, E. L., 102
Bennett, R., 87
Benovoy, M., 238
Ben-Shakhar, G., 389, 390
Bentler, P. M., 504
Beral, V., 460
Berelowitz, M., 607
Berglund, H., 424
Berkman, L. F., 461
Berkowitz, L., 483
Berman, Z., 104
Bermond, B., 449

Berndt, A., 116
Bernhardt, A. M., 295, *296*
Bernhardt, P. C., 484
Berns, G. S., 119
Bernstein, C. A., 565
Berridge, C. W., 654
Berridge, K. C., 148–49, 161, 221, 238
Berrington de Gonzalez, A., 432
Berscheid, E., 419, 503, 506, 507, 508
Berstein, Y., 606
Bervoets, C., 638
Betancourt, H., 51
Betancourt, L., 339
Bever, T., 317, 358, *359*
Bewernick, B. H., 643
Bian, L., 294, 360
Bianchi-Demicheli, F., 507
Bickerton, D., 317
Bidell, T. R., 357
Biederman, J., 610, 654, 656
Bieling, P., 641
Biesanz, J., 544
Bilder, D., 604
Bilker, W. B., 339
Binder, E. B., 569
Binet, A., 320, 322
Birney, M. E., 481
Bishop, M., 440
Bittner, A., 576
Bjork, R. A., 266
Bjork-Eriksson, T., 102
Bjorklund, D. F., 354, 355
Bjornsson, A. S., 629
Blackless, M., 367
Blackwell, K. C., 182
Blagys, M. D., 619
Blaha, C., 627
Blair, I. V., 502
Blair, R. J. R., 601
Blakemore, C., 11
Blakemore, S. J., 200, 364
Blalock, J., 582
Blanchard, R., 423
Blanco, C., 153
Bland, R. C., 577
Blankenship, J., 340
Blanton, H., 492
Blase, S. I., 631
Blasi, A., 344
Blasiman, R. N., 268
Blass, T., 481
Blazer, D., 598
Blehar, M. C., 350
Bleidorn, W., 549
Blennow, K., 124
Bless, H., 147
Bliss, T. V., 252
Bloch, H. M., 133
Bloch, M. H., 79
Block, J., 156, 458
Bloom, D. A., 362
Bloom, P., 313, 315
Blumberg, S. J., 301, 604
Blumenstein, S., 45
Blunt, J. R., 261
Bobowski, N. K., 414
Boden, J. M., 550
Bodenhausen, G. V., 280, 499, 502, 503
Bogaert, A. F., 423
Bogen, J. E., 93
Bohacek, J., 449
Bohlin, G., 352
Bohus, M., 599, 651
Boller, C. C., 22
Bolles, R., 236

Bollini, A., 593, 594, 648
Boly, M., 125
Bolzenius, K., 414
Bonanno, G. A., 396, 458
Bonanno, R. A., 369
Bond, Charles, 155
Bond, D. J., 646
Bondolfi, G., 620
Bonhoeffer, T., 254
Boodoo, G., 322, 327, 329, 331
Bookheimer, S. Y., 606
Booth, A., 373, 483–84
Bootzin, R. R., 135
Borges, G., 581
Borian, F. E., 640
Bornick, P., 340
Bornstein, R. F., 542
Boroditsky, L., 313
Borton, R., 345
Bosmans, E., 453
Boss, S. M., 129
Bosson, J. K., 551
Botsis, A. J., 576
Botta, P., 221
Botvinick, M. M., 472
Bouchard, C., 436
Bouchard, T. J., Jr., 112, *112*, 322, 327, 329, 331
Bouchery, E. E., 154
Bourgeat, P., 376
Bourgouin, P., 635
Bourke, J., 604
Bousman, C., 593
Bouton, M. E., 216
Bowdle, B. F., 485
Bowen, J. D., 376
Bower, C., 604
Bower, P., 637
Bowlby, J., 346, 348
Boyd, C. J., 150
Boyden, E. S., 116
Boykin, A. W., 327, 329, 331
Boyle, M. O., 325
Braadbaart, L., 244
Brackett, M. A., 324
Bradbury, T. N., 509
Bradley, B. P., 576
Bradley, L. A., 202
Bradlow, A. R., 314
Brady, W. J., 36
Brakefield, P. M., 107
Bramati, I. E., 363
Bramlett, M. D., 604
Brandon, T. H., 442
Brandt, J. R., 485
Brandt, M., 22
Brannigan, A., 481
Branscombe, N. R., 540
Branscum, A., 431
Bransford, J. K., 264
Bratslavsky, E., 490
Bratten, J., 609
Braun, K. V., 604
Braunschweig, D., 606
Breakefield, X. O., 483
Breedlove, S. M., 101, 421–23
Brehmer, Y., 378
Breiding, M. J., 124
Breitenbecher, D. L., 552
Breland, K., 235
Breland, M., 235
Bremberg, S., 323
Bremer, D., 267
Brenchley, C., 581
Brent, D. A., 661
Brett, C. E., 535

Brewer, M. B., 410
Brewer, R. D., 154
Brewerton, T. D., 153
Brick, P. D., 442
Brickman, A. M., 329, 593
Brickman, P., 302
Brigham, J. C., 181
Brinson, H., 609
Briones, B. A., 103
Britton, S. L., 444
Broadbent, D., 128
Broadley, A. J., 456
Broca, P., 312, *312*
Brody, C. L., 442
Brody, D. J., 580, 581
Brody, G. H., 339
Brody, J., 372
Brody, J. E., 643–44
Brody, N., 322, 327, 329, 330, 331
Brogly, S. B., 340
Bromet, E. J., 653
Bromley, S. M., 198
Broockman, D., 503
Brookmeyer, R., 376
Brown, A., 87
Brown, A. M., 574
Brown, A. S., 275, 595
Brown, B., 376
Brown, B. B., 370
Brown, E., 369
Brown, G. W., 581, 582
Brown, J., 273, 552
Brown, J. D., 554, 556
Brown, L. L., 507
Brown, R., 275, 279, 315
Brown, R. A., 444
Brown, S., 486
Brown, T. L., 643
Brownell, C. A., 369
Brownell, K. D., 438
Brozek, J., 437
Bruce, A., 372
Bruce, V. V., 180
Bruder, C. E., 111
Bruggemann, J., 593
Brumberg, J. S., 127
Brummett, B. H., 455
Bruneau, E. G., 503
Brunell, A. B., 551
Brunelle, T. J., 242
Brunner, H. G., 483
Brunoni, A. R., 627
Brunot, S., 540
Brunotte, J., 545
Bruzek, J., 658
Bryant-Waugh, R., 441
Bryson, S. E., 259
Buchanan, R. W., 595
Buchsbaum, M. S., 593
Buchtel, E., 539
Buckholtz, J. W., 483
Buckley, D., 340
Buckner, R. L., 279
Budson, A. E., 279
Buehlman, K. T., 373
Buhle, J. T., 396
Buhrmester, M. D., 470
Buikema, A., 607
Bullen, C., 442
Bullis, J. R., 566, 629, 633
Bullmore, E. T., 103, 414
Bullock, C., 103
Bullough, V., 421
Bunge, S. A., 396
Bunting, M. F., 259

Buoli, M., 646
Burdick, K. E., 646
Burg, M. M., 455
Burger, J. M., 481, 482
Burgess, N., 86
Burgess, P., 326
Burgess, S., 646
Burke, B. L., 621
Burman, M. A., 221
Burnham, S., 376
Burns, D., 660
Burns, H. J., 281, *281*
Burns, T. C., 313
Burstein, M., 155, 653, 659
Burt, D. M., 506
Burton, K. L., 569
Burton, M. J., 237
Bush, E. C., 90, 551
Bushdid, C., 198
Bushman, B. J., 241, 242, 483, 551
Bushnell, M. C., 144, 145, 202
Buss, A. H., 519
Buss, D. M., 13, 366, 420, 421, 470, 520
Buss, K. A., 577
Butcher, J. N., 542, 587
Butler, A. C., 570
Butler, E. A., 508
Buunk, A. P., 540
Buunk, B. D., 510
Buyken, A. E., 414
Byars, A. W., 326
Byers-Heinlein, K., 313
Bygren, L. O., 114
Byington, K. W., 40
Byrne, E. M., 583

Cabanac, M., 407
Cabanlit, M., 606
Cabeza, R., 375, 388
Cacioppo, J. T., 385, 410, 461
Cade, J., 646
Cadenhead, K., 594, 649
Caggiano, J. M., 129
Caglar, S., 547, *547*
Cahill, L., 278
Cahill, S., 637
Cahn, B. R., 145
Cahn, W., 593
Cai, H., 8
Cain, M. A., 340
Cain, W. S., 198
Cairns, B., 370
Cairns, R., 370
Calder, A. J., 386
Califf, R. M., 152
Call, J., 360
Callahan, A., 642
Caltran, G., 344
Calvini, G., 280
Campbell, A., 479
Campbell, A. T., 543
Campbell, J. D., 550, 551
Campbell, M., 653
Campbell, P. T., 443
Campbell, W., 632
Campbell, W. B., 554
Campbell, W. K., 550
Campeas, R., 637
Canales-Rodríguez, E. J., 599
Canetta, S., 595
Canino, G. I., 577
Cannas, S., 278
Cannon, T. D., 594
Cannon, W. B., 391, *392*, 403, 450–51
Cantu, D., 80

Caporael, L. R., 410
Caramasch, D., 483
Carden, L., 418
Cardeña, E., 586
Carew, T. J., 210
Carey, B., 651
Carl, J. R., 566
Carli, L. L., 545
Carlsmith, M., 493
Carlson, E., 586
Carlson, E. N., 544
Carmichael, M., 444
Carmody, T., 659
Carmody, T. P., 321
Carnagey, N. L., 241
Carnell, S., 436
Carney, R. M., 455
Carpenter, L. L., 643
Carpenter, M., 360
Carpenter, S. K., 261
Carpenter, W. T., Jr., 592, 595
Carranza-Jasso, R., 216
Carrasco, M., 128
Carré, J. M., 484
Carrère, S., 373, 374
Carrier, B., 145
Carroll, M., 435
Carson, A. J., 585
Carstensen, L., 376, 377
Carter, C. S., 416
Cartese, S., 609
Carton, A. M., 483
Cartwright, C., 658
Caruso, S., 417
Carver, C. S., 483
Case, A., 432, 625
Case, B., 155, 659
Case, R., 357
Casey, B., 500
Casey, B. J., 364, 409
Casey, M., 399
Cash, B. M., 422
Cashaback, J. G., 244
Caspi, A., 113, *115*, 152, 339, 483, 504, 517, 520,
        535, 566
Casson, D. H., 607
Castellanos, F. X., 103
Castonguay, L. G., 575
Castro-Loli, P., 646
Catala, M. D., 642
Catalan, J., 479
Catanese, K. R., 419
Cattell, R., 322–23, 528
Cavanagh, J. O., 585
Cay, E. B., 103
Ceci, S. J., 322, 327, 329, 331
Cekic, M., 146
Celesia, G. G., 126
Centers for Disease Control and Prevention
        (CDC), 110, 124, 340, 432, 441, 442, 445,
        564, 584, 608
Cepeda, N. J., 130
Cerhan, J. R., 432
Cesarini, D., 518
Cestari, V., 278
Cezayirli, E., 326
Chabas, D., 136
Chabris, C. F., 347, 518
Chadwick, M. J., 282
Chagnon, Y. C., 436
Chaimani, A., 627
Chakrabarti, B., 103
Chakrabarti, S., 589
Chalmers, D., 313
Chaloupka, F. J., 154

Chambers, D. W., 294
Chandrashekar, J., 195
Chang, L., 414
Chang, L. J., 385, 387
Chang, S., 627
Chang, Z., 609
Changeux, J. P., 123
Chant, D. C., 589
Chaplin, W., 658
Chapman, B. P., 537
Chapman, H. A., 362
Chapman, J. E., 570
Chapman, S., 443
Charles, J., 604
Charles, S. T., 376
Charlson, F. J., 563, 581
Charney, D. S., 580
Charuvastra, A., 367
Chase, V. D., 191
Chase, W. G., 259
Chassin, L., 157, 441, 442
Chatard, A., 540
Chatila, Y., 50
Chaudun, F., 221
Chavez, R. S., 122
Chawarska, K., 603
Cheema, F., 278
Chein, J. M., 259
Chen, C., 576, 601
Chen, D., 556
Chen, M. J., 137
Chen, Q., 341
Chen, S., 102
Cheng, H. G., 581
Chenowith, J. A., 151
Cherry, E. C., 128
Cherry, F., 481
Chess, S., 370
Chester, D. S., 483
Cheung, F. M., 529
Cheung, S. F., 529
Chiang, A., 449
Chikritzhs, T., 154
Childress, A. R., 156
Child Trends Database, 233
Chisholm, D., 563
Chistyakov, A. V., 642
Chitins, X., 326
Chiu, W. T., 564, 575
Chivers, M. L., 423
Cho, Z., 627
Choi, I., 20, 189, 498
Choleris, E., 116
Chomsky, N., 316, 317
Choo, P., 460
Chou, S. P., 600
Choudhury, S., 364
Christakis, N. A., 435
Christal, R. E., 325
Christensen, D. D., 326
Christensen, P. N., 101, 417
Christian, K. M., 102
Christianson, S., 280
Christiensen, D. L., 604
Christoff, K., 198
Christopher, F. S., 373
Chronis, A. M., 655
Chronis-Tuscano, A., 577, 656
Chu, M. H., 181
Chung, A., 150
Chung-Yan, G. A., 501
Cialdini, R. B., 303, 478, 479, 480, 486
Cicchetti, D., 352, 653
Cikara, M., 471, 472
Cimpian, A., 294

Claes, M., 22
Clapp, J. D., 480
Clark, A. C., 530
Clark, A. S., 416
Clark, D., 634
Clark, G. T., 136
Clark, L. A., 597
Clark, R. D., 344, 420
Clark, R. E., 256
Clark, S. E., 284
Clark-Foos, A., 267
Clarkin, J. F., 599
Clasen, L. S., 364
Cleary, P. D., 441
Cleary, S. D., 609
Cleckley, H., 599
Clement, S., 581
Clifton, C., Jr., 319
Cloninger, C., 518
Clore, G. L., 300
Cloutier, J., 505
Coakley, J. D., 192
Coan, J. A., 373
Coast, J. R., 444
Coates, D., 302
Cochran, B. N., 424
Coe, C. L., 453
Coe, W. C., 144
Cogsdill, E. J., 496
Cohadon, F., 126
Cohen, D., 485
Cohen, D. J., 653
Cohen, G. L., 332
Cohen, J. D., 363
Cohen, L., 453
Cohen, S., 452, 453, *454*, 456, 461
Cohn, J. F., 348
Coid, J., 600
Cokerham, W. C., 432
Colby, D. K., 151
Colcombe, S. J., 444
Coleman, M. R., 125
Coles, E. K., 656
Colligan, R. C., 455
Collins, A., 265, 487
Collins, F. S., 107
Collins, K. P., 609
Collins, L., 593
Collins, L. M., 442–43
Collins, S. A., 153
Collins, T., 22
Colliver, J. D., 600
Colom, F., 646
Colom, R., 326
Colvin, C. R., 544
Combs, B., 445
Comer, J. S., 629, 633
Compton, W. M., 151, 153, 600
Comtesse, H., 385
Conger, R. D., 371, 508, 536
Conn, C., 599
Conneely, K. N., 578
Connelly, A., 272
Conners, C. K., 610, 656
Connolly, A. C., 122, 292, 293
Constantino, J. N., 604
Conway, A. R. A., 259, 323, 325
Conway, K. P., 155, 600
Conway, M., 279
Cook, G. I., 267
Cook, M., 217, 243
Cook, R. G., 397
Cooper, C. R., 368
Cooper, G. M., 593
Copeland, W. E., 370

Copen, C. E., 508
Corby, B. C., 370
Corby, J. C., 144
Coren, S., 138
Corey, C. G., 442
Corkin, S., 255, 276
Cornblatt, B., 594
Coronado, V. G., 124
Corr, P. J., 531
Correll, C. U., 648
Corti, R., 456
Cortland, C. I., 173
Corty, E., 441
Cosmides, L., 19
Costa, P. T., Jr., 455, 528, 534, 535–36, 540, 542
Costanzi, M., 278
Costello, E. J., 370
Cotten, S. R., 130
Cotter, J. A., 339
Coubart, A., 359
Coughlin, B. C., 195
Courchesne, E., 606
Cousins, A. J., 101, 417
Coutinho, R. A., 198
Cowan, C. P., 374
Cowan, P. A., 374
Cox, D. S., 453
Cox, K. L., 444
Coyne, J. C., 582
Craddock, N., 583, 646
Craig, A. D. B., 156, 386
Craig, I. W., 113, *115*, 483
Craighead, W. E., 639, 640
Craik, F., 263
Cramer, V., 598
Crane, C., 620
Crane, P., 376
Crawford, H. J., 144
Crisp, R. J., 502
Crocker, J., 553
Croen, L. A., 606
Crookes, K., 181
Cropley, V. L., 593
Crosier, B. S., 543
Crosnoe, R., 376
Cross, I., 21
Crouch, D. J., *37*
Crow, M. D., 543
Crowe, M., 656
Crowe, R. R., 578
Crowley, S. J., 133
Csernansky, J. G., 593
Csibra, G., 360
Csikszentmihalyi, M., 16, 146–47, 459
Cuc, A., 279
Cui, L., 653
Cuijpers, P., 640–41
Cukrowicz, K. C., 568
Culbert, K. M., 435, 440
Culham, J. C., 190
Culler, E., 192
Cummings, J. R., 659
Cunningham, M. R., 420
Cunningham, W. A., 502, 505
Cunnington, R., 96
Cuny, E., 638
Cupach, W. R., 401
Curry, J., 660
Cuthbert, B., 566–67
Cutshall, J. L., 282
Czienskowski, U., 69
Czopp, A. M., 502

Dabbs, J. M., 483–84, 543
Dagher, A., 238

D'Agostino, R. B. Sr., 455
Dahl, D. W., 302
Dalal, R., 498
Dal Cin, S., 131, 405
Dale, K., 523
Dalgleish, T., 620
Dalman, C., 594
Dalton, M. A., 240, 295, *296*
Damasio, A. R., 91, 301, 363, 388
Damasio, H., 91, 156, 301, 363
Danese, A., 610
Daniels, D., 518, 537
Daniels, K., 508
Dapretto, M., 606
Darby, B. L., 479
Dargan, P. I., 153
Dark, P. R., 302
Darkner, S., 126
Darley, J. M., 363, 487, *487*
Darwin, C. D., 13, *13*, 212, 225, 397, 401, 537
Dasgupta, A. G., 502
Daskalakis, Z. J., 627, 643
Davies, C. A., 325
Davies, G., 327
Davies, M. S., 606
Davies, P. G., 331, 500
Davies, S., 153, 637
Davies, W., 609
Davis, D. H., 158
Davis, F. C., 87, 397
Davis, J., 594
Davis, J. I., 386
Davis, K. E., 497
Davis, M., 634
Davis, M. H., 125
Davis, M. T., 151
Davis, S. R., 101
Daw, N. D., 237, 449
Dawood, T., 581
Dawson, A. L., 340
Dawson, M., 604
Dayan, P., 220
Dazzan, P., 649
Deacon, B. J., 620, 644
Deal, A. L., 221
Dean, O., 594
DeAnglis, T., 24
Deary, I. J., 323, 325, 326, 328, 329, 535
Deaton, A., 374, 432, 625
de Boer, B., 317
de Boer, S. F., 483
DeCaria, C. M., 658
DeCasper, A. J., 344
De Castella, A., 643
Decety, J., 361–62, 601
deCharms, R. C., 203
Deci, E., 406
DeFries, J. C., 516
Degenhardt, L., 563
Degirmencioglue, S. M., 369
Degnan, K. A., 577
de Gonzalez, A. B., 443
de Grauw, H., 244
Dehaene, S., 123
de Hevia, M. D., 359
Deisseroth, K., 116
DeJong, W., 436, 473–80
Dekker, S., 96
de Klerk, N., 604
De Kloet, E. R., 449
DeKosky, S. T., 124
de la Cruz, L. F., 634
Delaney, H. D., 632
DeLateur, M. J., 483
Delbé, C., 22

DeLisi, M., 483
De Lisi, R., 357
Delmeire, L., 453
DeLong, M. R., 627
DeLongis, A., 448
Demerouti, E., 147
Demir, E., 423
Demler, O., 277, 564, 578, 610
de Mola, C. L., 329
Demos, K. D., 438
Demytttengere, K., 638
den Boer, J. A., 588
Denissen, J. J., 549
Denner, J., 368
Dennis, N. A., 375
Denys, D., 638
de Oliveria-Souza, R., 362, 363
Der, G., 325
Derefinko, K. J., 483
Derkits, E. J., 595
De Rosa, E., 87
Derryck, A., 367
Desai, R. J., 340
Desai, S. C., 102
DeSantis, C., 432
Descartes, R., 122
Desert, M., 540
de Ståhl, T. D., 111
DeStefano, F., 607
De Strooper, B., 376
Detke, M., 634
Detre, G. J., 122
Detweiler, J. B., 302
Deutsch, G. K., 319
Devilbliss, D. M., 654
Devine, P. G., 399, 498
DeWall, C. N., 483
de Wijk, R. A., 198
DeYoung, C. G., 529–30, 531–32
DeYoung, E. K., 102
Dhillon, A. P., 607
Diamond, L. M., 421–23
Diamond, M. C., 102
Diaz, N. S., 326
Diaz, Y., 577
Dickson, B. J., 423
Dickson, N., 409
Dickson, P. R., 100
Dickson, W. J., 41, *42*
Diener, E., 460, 464, 507
Dierker, L., 155
Dietz, W. H., 434
DiFeliceantonio, A. G., 238
Digdon, N., 223
Dijksterhuis, A., 131, 552
Di Mari, L., 417
Dimoulas, P., 443
Dingus, T. A., 33
Dinstein, I., 606
Dion, K., 506
di Salle, F., 22
Dix, D., 562
Dixon, G., 604
Dobbs, D., 643
Doblin, R., 153
Dobson, C. M., 376
Docherty, N. M., 591
Dockray, A., 461
Dodd, S., 594
Doecke, C. J., 659
Doerr, E. E., 473–80
Doffner, G., 641
Doherty, M., 581
Dohrenwend, B. P., 581
Dolan, P., 301

Dolan, R. J., 132, 388, 405
Domhoff, G. W., 141
Donahue, A. B., 642
Dondi, M., 344
Dong, H., 329
Donnellan, M. B., 508, 536, 551
D'Onofrio, B. M., 609
Donoghue, N., 124
Dooling, D. J., 263
Dore, J., 646
Dorfman, H. M., 483
Dorta, K. P., 661
Dotsch, R., 388
Doty, R. L., 198
Doust, J., 609
Dovidio, J. F., 489, 501–2
Dowrick, C., 625
Doyle, W. J., 461
Draganski, B., 132, 405
Draghici, A. M., 242
Drews, F. A., 37
Drezner, J. A., 124
Dror, I. E., 390
Druen, P. B., 420, 505
Druss, B. G., 573, 659
Dua, T., 563
Duan, E., 341
Dubois, A., 453
Duchaine, B. C., 181
Duckworth, A. L., 322, 331, 409–10
Duda, J. T., 329, 339
Dudai, Y., 210
Duenas, H., 634
Duffy, V. B., 195
Dugatkin, L. A., 486
DuHamel, K. N., 144, 157
Dulia, C. G., 80
Dunbar, R. I. M., 470
Duncan, G. H., 144, 145
Duncan, J., 326
Duncker, K., 305, 305, 306
Dunlap, K., 397
Dunlop, B. W., 639, 640
Dunlosky, J., 268
Dunn, E. W., 374
Dunner, D. L., 640
Dunning, D., 9
Duppils, G. S., 203
Durante, K. M., 101
Dussault, C., 655
Dutton, D. G., 393
Dwyer, J. H., 145
Dwyer, S., 593, 606
Dyck, J. L., 485
Dykman, B. M., 582
Dzemidzic, M., 111

Eagly, A. H., 62
Eaker, E. D., 455
Eastman, C. I., 133
Eaton, D. K., 33, 45
Eaton, N. R., 368
Ebbinghaus, H., 273
Eberhardt, J. L., 500
Ebert, J. P., 217
Eccles, J., 536
Edvinsson, S., 114
Edwards, D. A., 416
Edwards, R., 506
Egan, G. F., 96
Egas Moniz, A., 91–92
Egeland, J. A., 583
Egloff, B., 543
Ehirim, P., 127
Ehlers, A., 634

Ehrlinger, J., 9
Eich, E., 143
Eidelson, J. L., 582
Einarsson, E. O., 250
Eisenbarth, H., 385
Eisenberg, N., 361, 371
Eisenberger, N. I., 530
Eisenstein, M., 608
Eisner, J. R., 490
Ekelund, J., 518
Ekholm, B., 646
Ekman, P., 397, 398, 398
Elaad, E., 390
Elder, G. H., 376
Elfenbein, H. A., 398
Elinger, D., 45
Ellard, K. K., 566
Elliott, A. J., 340
Elliott, G. R., 653
Ellis, A., 619
Ellis, K. A., 376
Ellis, L., 423
Ellison, R. C., 455
Elovainio, M., 519
Else-Quest, N., 519
Elwell, C. E., 344
Elzinga, B. M., 449
Emery, C. F., 444
Emery, G., 582
Emmelkamp, P. M. G., 655
Emslie, G. J., 659
Emslie, H., 326
Endo, Y., 555
Engle, R. W., 259, 323, 325, 326
English, T., 374
Engwall, M., 203
Enns, J., 172
Enseleit, F., 456
Epley, N., 298
Epprecht, M., 421–23
Epstein, D. R., 135
Epstein, L. H., 435
Epstein, R. M., 537
Era, P., 377
Ercoli, L. M., 124
Ergül, C., 592
Erickson, J., 634
Erickson, K. I., 444
Erickson, K. J., 221
Erickson, S., 111
Erickson, T. M., 575
Ericsson, K. A., 322
Erikson, E. H., 365, 366, 459
Eriksson, P. S., 102
Ernberg, G., 650
Eron, L., 241
Ershler, W. B., 453
Ert, E., 471
Esber, G. R., 218
Escoffier, J., 195
Eshel, N., 221
Eskandar, E. N., 643
Eskenazi, J., 132
Esler, M. D., 581
Eslinger, P. J., 363
Espie, C. A., 136
Esposito, F., 22
Esposito, M. S., 221
Esses, V. M., 489
Estus, S., 483
Etcoff, N. L., 388
Etkin, A., 580
Evans, A., 609
Evans-Lacko, S., 581
Everaerd, W. T. A. M., 449

Everdell, N., 344
Eyre, H., 594
Eysenck, H. J., 530–31
Eysenck, S. B., 531

Fabbri-Destro, M., 606
Fabiano, G. A., 656
Fadok, J. P., 221
Fagerlin, A., 537
Fagerström, K. O., 442
Fairbank, J., 660
Fales, M. R., 418
Falkai, P., 649
Fallon, A. E., 436
False, J. L., 370
Fan, Y. X., 145
Fanelli, D., 35
Fantz, R. L., 345, 358
Farah, M. J., 329, 339, 390, 547
Faraone, S. V., 568, 594, 609, 654, 656
Farb, N. A., 146
Farina, M., 417
Farmer, M., 18
Farmer-Dougan, V., 96
Farooqi, I. S., 414
Farrelly, M., 442
Faul, M., 124
Fausto-Sterling, A., 367
Fava, M., 580
Favelle, S. K., 181
Fawcett, J., 576
Fay, N., 302
Fazio, R. H., 490, 491
Fearon, R. M. P., 364
Fechner, G., 167
Feemster, K. A., 607
Fegley, S. G., 368
Fein, S., 483
Feingold, A., 506, 540
Feinsod, M., 642
Feldhaus, C., 660
Feldman, R., 352
Feldman, S. S., 371
Feldman Barrett, L., 400
Felgate, P., 153
Feng, C., 478
Feng, R., 329
Feng, S. G., 145
Fenno, L. E., 116
Ferdinand, A. O., 61
Fergus, I., 377
Ferguson, J. N., 658
Ferguson, M. A., 96
Ferguson-Smith, A. C., 114
Fernald, A., 348
Fernandez, S. M., 329
Fernández-Espejo, D., 125
Ferracioli-Oda, E., 133
Ferrari, A., 581
Ferro, M. J., 280
Ferry, G., 170
Festinger, L., 279, 411, 493, 504
Fibiger, H. C., 148
Fiebach, C. J., 326
Fielden, J. A., 484
Figee, M., 638
Fincham, F. D., 509
Fine, M. J., 442
Finger, E. C., 601, 602
Finger, S., 81
Fink, M., 642
Finkenauer, C., 490
Finsterwald, C., 449
Finucane, M., 300
Fiore, M. C., 441

Firth, J., 444
Fischer, B., 152
Fischer, H., 378, 388
Fischer, K., 357
Fischer, P., 487
Fischhoff, B., 445
Fisher, C., 442
Fisher, H. E., 507
Fishkin, S. A., 419
Fisk, J. E., 153
Fiske, S. T., 472
Fitch, W. T., 317
Fitzgerald, C. A., 578
Fitzgerald, P. B., 643
Fixx, J. F., 306
Flaum, M., 593
Flay, B. R., 441
Fleeson, W., 529
Flegal, K. M., 433
Fleischhacker, W. W., 649
Fleming, T., 434, 436
Flenady, V. J., 340
Fletcher, F., 332
Fletcher, P. C., 414
Fletje, A., 424
Flicker, L., 444
Fligor, B. J., 193
Flint, A. J., 432
Flint, J., 518–19
Floerke, V., 269
Flores, S. A., 385
Floud, S., 460
Floyd, K., 472
Flynn, J. R., 327, 329–30
Foa, E. B., 619, 634, 637
Fode, K. L., 42
Foehr, U. G., 241
Foer, J., 267
Fogelman, P., 18
Foley, K. M., 80
Folkman, S., 448, 457, 458
Fong, G. W., 238
Foorman, B. R., 319
Forbes, C., 331
Forbes, C. E., 363
Ford, E. S., 434
Forehand, R. L., 364
Forgas, J., 478
Forman, E. M., 570
Formann, A. K., 347
Fornito, A., 152
Forterek, K., 414
Forth, A. E., 600, 653
Foster, J. D., 551
Foster, J. K., 444
Foster, M., 656
Fowler, J. H., 435
Fox, H. C., 328
Fox, J. A., 483
Fox, N. A., 577
Fozard, J., 376
Frackowiak, R. S. J., 86
Fraley, R. C., 507
Francis, A., 625
Frangou, S., 326
Frank, C. K., 360
Frank, R., 91
Frank, R. G., 277, 564, 578
Frankel, S. A., 661
Franken, I. H. A., 532
Franken, R. E., 406
Franklin, E., 283
Franklin, G., 283
Franklin, M. E., 637
Franklin, M. S., 172

Franklin, T. B., 449
Franko, D. L., 440
Franz, P., 18
Franzke, P., 22
Fraser, C., 170
Fraser, S., 478
Fratiglioni, L., 376
Frazier, R. S., 491
Fredrickson, B. L., 459
Fredriksen-Goklsen, K. I., 373
Freedland, K. E., 455
Freedman, J., 241, 478
Freeman, A., 652
Freeman, D., 634
Freeman, J. B., 18, 388, 471
Freeman, S., 657
Freemantle, N., 79
French, V., 107
Freud, A., 523, 523
Freud, S., 31, 208, 562, 617
Frey, D., 487
Frick, K. M., 329, 444
Frid, D. J., 444
Fried, D. E., 259
Friedman, J. M., 414
Friedman, L. A., 609
Friedman, M., 455, 586
Friehs, G. M., 638, 643
Friend-DelVecchio, W., 534
Friesen, W. V., 397, 398, 398
Frijda, N. H., 396
Frisch, M., 372
Frith, C. D., 200
Frohlich, P. F., 416
Fromer, M., 593, 606
Frost, J. A., 504
Fryar, C. D., 435
Fuhrman, O., 313
Fujita, F., 507
Funder, D. C., 516, 528, 533, 543, 544
Fung, H. H., 376
Fung, M. T., 601
Furukawa, H., 659
Fusar-Poli, P., 592

Gaber, O., 104
Gabrieli, J. D., 569
Gabrieli, J. D. E., 279, 319, 396
Gabriels, L. A., 638
Gaddis, S., 543
Gadian, D. G., 272
Gaertner, L., 556
Gaisler-Salomon, I., 449
Galaburda, A. M., 91
Galderisi, S., 592
Gale, C. R., 323
Galef, B. G., Jr., 415
Galinsky, A. D., 502, 503
Gallagher, D. T., 153
Gallese, V., 244, 386
Gallinat, J., 591
Gallistel, C. R., 313
Gallo, E. F., 609
Galton, F., 131, 322, 324
Galvin, A., 339
Gammons, M., 124
Gan, Y. G., 529
Gandhi, A. V., 133
Ganger, S., 367
Gangestad, S. W., 101, 418, 506
Ganiban, J. M., 601
Ganley, R., 545
Gapp, K., 449
Garavan, H., 156
Garb, H N., 541

Garber, J., 661
Garcia, J., 217, 332
Garcia, J. A., 656
Gardner, H., 323
Gardner, W. L., 410
Garlick, D., 323
Garneau, N. L., 195
Garon, N., 259
Garrett-Mayer, E., 604
Garriga, M., 583
Garson, C., 641
Garthe, A., 339
Gartner, S. L., 489
Garver-Apgar, C. E., 101, 418
Garvey, M., 566–67
Gastil, J., 313
Gatenby, J. C., 502
Gatt, J. M., 569
Gattaz, W. F., 627
Gaudiano, B. A., 628
Gavett, B. E., 124
Gavrilescu, M., 96
Gazzaniga, M. S., 92, 93, 94–95, 96, 311–12
Ge, X., 363
Geaga, J. A., 150
Geary, D., 330
Gebauer, J. E., 549
Geddes, J. R., 646
Geen, R. G., 531
Geller, F., 45
Gendron, M., 398
Gentile, D. A., 241, 242
George, L., 598
George, M. S., 627, 642
Georgieva, I., 532
Geraci, M., 576
Gerbier, E., 138
Gergely, G., 360
Gerhard, D. S., 583
Gernsbacher, M. A., 330, 604
Gerona, R., 151
Gershman, S. J., 237
Gershoff, E. T., 233
Gershon, E. S., 583
Gevins, A., 152
Ghahremani, D. G., 198
Ghazanfar, A. A., 317
Ghera, M. M., 577
Gheusi, G., 198
Ghio, M., 292
Ghosh, S. S., 569
Giacobbe, P., 643
Gianaros, P., 452
Giannetta, J. M., 339
Gibbon, M., 576, 600
Gibbons, F. X., 442
Gibbons, K. S., 340
Gibbons, R., 661
Gibson, J. J., 295, 296
Gick, M. L., 306
Giedd, J. N., 103, 364
Giesbrecht, B., 128
Gigante, D. P., 329
Gigerenzer, G., 445
Gigerenzer, Z., 69
Gijsbers, A. A., 111
Gijsman, H. J., 646
Gilbert, D. T., 35, 301–2, 493
Gilbert, J. H., 313
Gilbert, R. N., 294
Gilbert, R. W., 136
Gilbert-Diamond, D., 412, 435
Gilbody, S., 620
Gildersleave, K., 418
Gile, W. H., 434

Gill, M. J., 659
Gillard, J., 414
Gilligan, C., 362
Gillihan, S. J., 547
Gillis, J., 606
Gillis-Smith, S., 195
Gilman, S. R., 606
Gilovich, T., 6, 63, 298, 552
Gil-Perotin, S., 339
Gingerich, A. C., 130
Ginton, A., 390
Girgis, R. R., 649
Girgis, Z. M., 481
Girob, C. S., 153
Giynas Ayhan, M., 568
Gjedde, A., 126
Gladden, R. M., 152
Glantz, S. A., 442
Glaser, R. I., 444, 453
Glass, R., 462
Glasson, E., 604
Glasziou, P., 609
Glatt, S. J., 568, 594
Glazebrook, C., 573
Gleman, R., 313
Glenberg, A. M., 266
Glenn, C. R., 585
Glerean, E., 385
Glied, S., 656
Glimcher, P. W., 221
Glotzer, L. D., 90
Glover, G. H., 198, 203, 209
Gluck, C. M., 437
Glynn, T. J., 442
Gnagy, E. M., 656
Gobbini, M. I., 181
Godlee, F., 607
Goff, D. C., 649
Goff, P. A., 500
Gold, S. M., 580
Goldapple, K., 641
Goldenberg, M. M., 74
Goldin, C., 295
Goldin, L. R., 583
Golding, J., 114
Goldman, R. F., 437
Goldman, S. T., 138
Goldman-Mellor, S. J., 566
Goldner, E., 152
Goldsmith, H. H., 519, 604
Goldsteen, K., 372
Goldstein, J., 375
Goldstein, M., 599
Goldstein, N. J., 480
Goldstein, R. B., 600
Goldstein, R. Z., 156
Golle, J., 451
Gómez, A., 470
Gonen, M. S., 568
Gong, Q., 326
González, I., 501
Gonzales, K., 154
Gonzales, R., 150
González-Pinto, A., 646
Good, C. D., 86
Goodale, M. A., 175
Goodman, S. H., 570
Goodman, S. N., 35
Goodwin, D. W., 267
Goodwin, G. M., 646
Goodwin, R. D., 576
Goodwin, S. A., 472
Gordijn, M. C., 641
Gordon, P., 313
Gore, J. C., 181, 502
Goren, A., 496

Gormley, P., 593, 606
Goshen, M., 22
Gosling, S. D., 535, 543, 549
Gosselin, P., 181
Gotlib, I. H., 570, 580, 622
Gotlib, J. H., 18
Gotsopoulos, A., 385
Gottesman, I. I., 593
Gottfredson, L. S., 321, 323, 324
Gottman, J. M., 373, 374, 508, 509–10
Gould, E., 103–4
Goulding, E., 664
Grabowski, T., 91
Graetz, N., 434, 436
Graf, P., 267, 270
Graff, H., 412
Gräff, J., 254, 278
Grafman, J., 363
Grafton, S. T., 507
Graham, J. W., 441
Granot, D., 352
Grant, B. F., 600
Graubard, B. I., 433
Graven, M. A., 136
Gray, J. A., 531–32
Gray, J. C., 339
Gray, J. R., 323, 324, 325, 529–30, 531–32
Gray, K., 470, 471
Gray, S., 376
Green, B. A., 422
Green, D. M., 168, 658
Green, E. D., 107
Green, J., 460
Greenberg, B. D., 638
Greene, D., 406
Greene, J. A., 412
Greene, J. D., 363
Greenhill, L. L., 656
Greenough, A., 340
Greenstein, D., 609
Greenwald, A. G., 132, 491–92, 494, 499, 501, 502, 556
Greenwald, D. P., 649
Greenwald, S., 577
Greenwood, M. R. C., 438
Gregg, A., 554
Greicius, M. D., 237
Greitemeyer, T., 22, 487
Grewel, D., 324
Gribble, P. L., 244
Griebel, U., 317
Grieve, S. M., 329
Griffin, D. W., 509
Griggs, R. A., 221, 481
Grillon, C., 576
Grill-Spector, K., 181
Grimby, G., 443
Griskevicius, V., 480
Grogan-Kaylor, A., 233
Grosenick, L., 116
Gross, J. J., 385, 395, 396, 508
Gross, N., 192
Grossman, M., 400
Grossniklaus, U., 114
Grosz, D., 576
Grubert, C., 643
Gruenewald, T. L., 451
Grunze, H., 646
Gruzelier, J. H., 144
Gu, H., 606
Gu, R., 8
Guassi Moreira, J. F., 470
Guastella, A. J., 658
Guay, B., 136
Gudmundsdottir, B. G., 150
Guehl, D., 638

Guenther, F. H., 127
Gueorguiev, M., 414
Guerin, B., 552
Guimond, S., 540
Gujar, N., 139
Gula, B., 69
Gulley, B. L., 518
Gunderson, J. G., 598
Gunter, B., 242
Guntupalli, J. S., 122, 292, 293
Gunzerath, L., 442
Guo, F., 33
Gur, D., 330
Gurung, R. A. R., 451
Guskiewicz, K. M., 124
Gustafson, J. A., 116
Gustafsson, U., 646
Gustin, M. P., 138
Guyer, B., 659
Gwaltney, J. M. J., 461

Haby, M., 659
Hackel, L. M., 472
Hackett, G., 103
Hadjiefthyvoulou, F., 153
Hadrysiewicz, 643
Hagekull, B., 352
Hagerty, B., 483
Haggarty, P., 328
Hagger-Johnson, G., 325
Hahn, A., 367
Hahn, W., 455
Haidt, J., 143, 361–62
Haier, R. J., 323, 326
Haikerwal, D., 581
Hair, N. L., 339
Halaas, J., 414
Halász, P., 134
Halbrook, D., 283
Halchenko, Y. O., 293
Hall, C. C., 496
Hall, J. A., 549
Hallam, M., 506
Hallan, S., 21
Hallberg, C., 634
Halldorsdottir, T., 569
Hallet, V., 605
Halliday-Scher, K., 369
Halligan, P. W., 123
Halpern, C. T., 416
Halpern, D. F., 103, 330
Halpin, L. E., 153
Halstead, M., 124
Hamamura, T., 556
Hamani, C., 642, 643
Hamann, S., 391
Hambrick, D. Z., 259, 325
Hamby, B. W., 432
Hamer, D. H., 423
Hamer, M., 444
Hamilton, A. F., 606
Hamilton, C., 507
Hamilton, J. P., 18
Hamilton, L. K., 501
Hamilton, R. L., 124
Hamilton, W., 486
Hammen, C., 581
Hampton, D., 80
Han, B., 153
Han, S., 472
Hancox, R. J., 409
Handleman, J. S., 659
Handy, T. C., 128
Hanewinkel, R., 131, 442
Haney, C., 473
Hankin, B. L., 554, 556, 566

Hanks, J., 431
Hanlon, C., 315
Hanna, F., 581
Hannan, L., 432
Hanratty, M., 658
Hansen, C. J., 444
Hansen, R., 606
Hansen, T., 374
Hansen, W. B., 441
Hanson, J. L., 339
Hansson, P. O., 443
Happé, F., 605
Harari, G. M., 543
Harberg, C. B., 591
Harburger, L. L., 444
Hardus, M. E., 317
Hare, R. D., 600, 653
Hare, T. A., 364
Harenski, C., 601
Hari, R., 385
Hariri, A. R., 391
Harkins, S. G., 475
Harkins, S. W., 145
Harlow, H. F., 349, *350*, 406
Harlow, J. M., 91
Harlow, M. K., 349, *350*, 406
Harmon, K. G., 124
Harpalani, V., 368
Harpur, T. J., 653
Harrington, H., 152, 339, 409, 566
Harris, B., 223
Harris, J. A., 517
Harris, J. R., 518
Harris, L. T., 472
Harris, M. A., 535
Harris, S. E., 327, 328
Harris, T., 461
Harris, T. O., 581
Harrison, M. A., 29
Harrison, T. L., 259
Harrow, M., 649
Hart, A. J., 497
Hart, B., 23
Hartford, J., 634
Hartge, P., 432, 443
Hartley, T., 86
Harty, L., 599
Harvey, O. J., 488
Hasboer, F., 449
Haselton, M. G., 101, 418
Hashimoto, M., 590
Haslam, N., 472
Haslam, S. A., 481
Hassabias, D., 282
Hastings, M., 599
Hatfield, E., 420, 507
Haukvik, K. V., 591
Hawkins, C. B., 491
Hawkley, L. C., 410, 461
Haworth, C. M., 436
Hawton, K., 646
Haxby, J. V., 122, 181, 292, 293
Hayashi, K. M., 150
Hayatbakhsh, M. R., 340
Hayes, J. E., 195
Hayne, H., 346
Haythornthwaite, J. A., 202
Hayward, W. G., 181
Hazan, C., 507
Hazlett, E. A., 593, 598
Hazlett, H. C., 606
He, J., 155, 659
Head, K., 323, 326
Healy, A., 278
Heard, H., 651
Hearn, E. F., 658

Heath, C., 347
Heatherton, T. F., 122, 131, 223, 240, 295, *296*, 331, 405, 412, 435, 436, 438, 440, 452, 470, 472, 483, 505, 534, 547–48, *547*, 550
Hebb, D., 252
Hebl, M. R., 436
Heck, N. C., 322, 623
Hedegaard, H., 152
Heeger, D. J., 606
Heerey, E. A., 508
Hehman, E. A., 388
Heider, F., 497
Heikkinen, E., 377
Heim, C., 449
Heiman, J. R., 101
Heimann, H., 590
Heine, S. J., 20, 50, 539, 554–56
Heinssen, R., 566–67
Helion, C., 18, 362
Heller, D., 529
Helmreich, R., 505
Helms, M. J., 455
Helzer, J. E., 158
Hemmingsson, T., 594
Henderson, H. A., 577
Henninger, E. M., 453
Henrich, J., 50
Henry, C., 221
Henry, D., 294
Henry, D. B., 660
Henry, J. D., 361
Henry, P. J., 501
Henschel, A. L., 437
Herbener, E. S., 504
Herbert, J. D., 628
Herbert, T. B., 453
Herdener, M., 22
Hering, E., 177
Herman, C. P., 438, 439
Hermsen, S., 502
Hernandez, J. C., 609
Heron, M., 431
Herring, B. E., 253
Herring, S. A., 124
Herrington, C. G., 661
Hershman, S., 470, 471
Hershow, R. C., 372
Hertz-Picciotto, I., 606
Hester, R. K., 632
Heyman, R. E., 510
Hezlett, S. A., 321
Hibar, D. P., 609
Hickie, I. B., 658
Hickok, G., 244
Hicks, K. L., 259
Hietanen, J. K., 385
Higgins, E. T., 407
Higgins, L. T., 9
Higgins, S. C., 414
Hilbig, A., 414
Hilgar, K., 326
Hilgard, E. R., 144
Hilgard, J. R., 144
Hill, P. L., 536, 538
Hill, S. E., 101
Hill, S. J., 646
Hilsenroth, M. J., 619
Hines, T., 6, 96, 525, 629
Hingson, R. W., 155
Hinshaw, S. P., 656
Hinson, R. E., 224
Hippocrates, 562
Hipwell, A., 153
Hirsh, J. B., 529–30
Hirshkowitz, M., 146
Hirst, W., 279

Hirstein, W., 104
Hirvonen, N., 589, 649
Hitch, G., 258
Hitti, A., 294
Ho, B. C., 593
Ho, C. Y., 238
Hoad, G., 328
Hobson, J. A., 137, 139, 140
Hochman, K. M., 593, 594, 648
Hockley, W. E., 266
Hodge, D., 283
Hodges, S. D., 503
Hoefler, M., 576
Hoekstra, R. A., 605
Hoerger, M., 537
Hofbauer, R. K., 144
Hofer, S. M., 378
Hoffman, E., 481
Hoffman, E. A., 181
Hoffman, H., 501
Hoffman, J. H., 143
Hoffman, J. J., 154
Hofmann, S. G., 634
Hofstetter, C. R., 442
Hogan, C. L., 376
Hogan, L., 41
Hogan, M. J., 324
Hogan, S., 339
Hogarty, G. E., *649*
Hogg, M. A., 471
Hogh, P., 378
Hoine, H., 267
Hold, D. W., 153
Holland, P. C., 217
Holland, S. K., 326
Hollander, E., 658
Hollins, S., 340
Hollon, S. D., 620, 634, 638, 640, 641
Holman, K., 604
Holmbeck, G. N., 371
Holmboe, K., 605
Holmes, J. G., 509
Holmes, T. H., 447, *448*
Holst, C., 436
Holstein, S. B., 229
Holt-Lunstad, J., 461
Holtzheimer, P. E., 643
Holyoak, K. J., 306
Hommer, D., 238
Honein, M. A., 340
Hong, M. S., 150
Honorton, C., 171
Honts, C. R., 390
Honzik, C. H., 236
Hood, W. R., 488
Hoogman, P., 609
Hooley, J. M., 587, 622
Hoon Sung, Y., 150
Hooshmand, F., 646
Hops, H., 580
Horikawa, T., 141
Hork, H. W., 439
Horn, E. E., 516–17, 518
Horn, J. L., 322, 378
Horowitz, L. M., 582
Horta, B. L., 329
Horton, E., 437
Hoscheidt, S., 95
Hoshi, T., 447
Hoshino, Y., 659
House, J. S., 372, 461
Houts, R. M., 152, 339, 364, 566
Hovland, C. I., 494
Howard, L., 361
Howard-Jones, P., 96
Howe, C., 442

Howell, K. H., 656
Howie, L. D., 654
Howlin, P., 659
Hoyert, D. L., 445
Hoyme, H. E., 340
Hoyt, D. R., 371
Hrebickova, M., 535–36
Hsee, C. K., 300
Hu, K. L., 518
Hu, N., 423
Hu, P. T., 139
Hu, S., 423, 442
Hubbard, E. M., 170, 174
Hubel, D., 102
Huedo-Medina, T. B., 644
Huesmann, L. R., 242
Huff, M. L., 116
Hugenberg, K., 502
Hughes, A., 153
Hughes, C. W., 659
Hughes, M. E., 372, 410
Hughes, V., 434
Hull, C., 404, 473
Hull, J. G., 155, 242
Hulme, C., 319
Hummer, A., 367
Humphrey, K., 313
Humphreys, K., 606
Hunsley, J., 568
Hunt, E., 313
Hunter, J., 321
Huppert, J. D., 637
Hurlemann, R., 643
Hurley, S. W., 413
Hürlimann, D., 456
Hurrion, E., 340
Husain, G., 347
Hussain, M., 410
Husten, C. G., 442
Hutchinson, J. B., 390
Huttunen, M. O., 595
Huynh, C., 155
Hwang, C. K., 432
Hwang, J., 150
Hwu, H. G., 577
Hyatt, C. J., 157
Hyde, J. S., 330, 366–67, 399, 519, 554, 556, 580
Hyde, L. W., 601
Hyman, B. T., 138
Hyman, I. W., 129
Hyman, S. E., 605
Hymel, S., 369

Iacoboni, M. I., 244, 606
Iacono, W. G., 609
Ibrahim, A. K., 573
Iijima, K., 447
Ikeda, Kikunae, 195
Ilan, A. B., 152
Ilies, R., 529
Immunization Safety Review Committee, 607
Imuta, K., 346, 361
Inati, S., 547, 547
Inbar, Y., 362
Inciardi, J. A., 150
Ingbretsen, Z. A., 388, 471
Inoue, K., 414
Insel, C., 18
Insel, T. R., 116, 566–67, 580, 658
Intelisano, G., 417
Intersex Society of North America, 367
Ioannides, J. P., 35, 444
Iordanova, M. D., 218
Iossifov, I., 605, 606
Irvine, R. J., 153

Isen, A. M., 300
Isensee, B., 131
Ishigami, Y., 128
Isohanni, M., 589, 649
Isoldi, K. K., 437
Israel, S., 566
Israelski, D., 153
Ivanovic, D. M., 326
Ivers, H., 136
Ivry, R. B., 311–12
Iwasaki, E., 414
Iyengar, S. S., 308, 308
Izard, V., 359

Jääkeläinen, I. P., 385
Jääskeläinen, E., 589, 649
Jablensky, A., 650
Jaccard, J., 492
Jacka, F. N., 594
Jacklin, C. N., 540
Jackson, B., 456
Jackson, J. J., 538
Jackson, S. A., 147
Jackson, W., 284
Jacobs, D. R., 456
Jacobs, L. D., 321
Jacobs, R. H., 660
Jacoby, L., 272, 273
Jacowitz, K. E., 298
Jaervelin, M., 518
Jagnow, C. P., 196, 197
Jahromi, L. B., 657
Jain, A., 607
Jakubouski, E., 79
James, D., 339
James, T. W., 101
James, W., 12, 12, 225, 391, 391
James, W. H., 508
Jamieson, G. A., 143
Jamison, D. J., 340
Jamison, K. R., 646
Janata, P., 22, 22
Jang, K. L., 517, 518
Janicki-Deverts, D., 452
Janis, I. L., 475, 494
Janoff-Bulman, R., 302
Janssen, E., 101
Janusis, G., 655
Jasechko, J., 273
Jefferis, V., 410
Jemal, A., 432
Jencks, C., 321
Jenike, M. A., 388
Jenkins, C. D., 431
Jennings, J., 272
Jensen, A., 325, 330
Jensen, M., 144
Jensen, P. S., 656
Jerome, L., 153
Jetten, J., 470, 481
Jha, P., 441
Jiang, C. H., 329
Jiang, Y., 103
Jobe, T. H., 649
Joel, D., 104
Joëls, M., 449
Johannsen, N. M., 444
Johanssen, P. P., 444
Johansson, R., 618
John, O. P., 529, 535
Johns, M., 331, 332
Johnson, A. K., 413
Johnson, B. T., 644
Johnson, C. A., 441
Johnson, D., 278, 373

Johnson, J. D., 489
Johnson, K. L., 9, 18, 173
Johnson, M. H., 344, 496
Johnson, M. K., 264, 502
Johnson, M. R., 157
Johnson, V., 418
Johnson, W., 326, 535
Johnson, D., 257
Johnston, L. D., 154, 441
Johnston, W., 154
Johnstone, T., 388
Joiner, T. E., Jr., 440, 568, 582, 584, 585
Jokela, J., 377
Jokela, M., 519
Jolesz, F. A., 139
Jolles, J., 96
Jolliffe, T., 397 .
Jones, A. C., 484
Jones, A. M., 340
Jones, C. J., 456
Jones, C. M., 151, 153
Jones, E. E., 497
Jones, H. A., 655
Jones, J. R., 604
Jones, M. C., 223
Jones, R. M., 364, 409
Jones, W., 604–5
Jope, R. S., 646
Jordan, C. H., 550
Jorenby, D. E., 442–43
Jorgensen, K. N., 591
Jorm, A. F., 376
Josephs, R. A., 484
Jotheeswaran, A. T., 581
Judge, J., 153
Junco, R., 130
Jung, R. E., 323, 326
Juola, P., 589, 649
Jureidini, J. N., 659
Jurkowitz, I. T. N., 601

Kaati, G., 114
Kabeto, M. U., 461
Kaczkurkin, A. N., 576
Kagan, J., 397, 520, 521
Kagan, M. D., 604
Kagitcibasi, C., 50
Kahn, R. M., 649
Kahneman, D., 8, 127, 297, 297, 298–99, 302, 313, 335
Kalakanis, L., 506
Kalberg, W. O., 340
Kaleva, M., 594
Kalisch, R., 132, 405
Kalkhoran, S., 442
Kalla, J., 503
Kallio, S., 143
Kamara, S., 326
Kamboh, M. I., 124
Kamisada, M., 590
Kamitani, Y., 141
Kandel, E. R., 210, 252
Kane, J. M., 648
Kane, M. J., 259, 323, 325, 326
Kang, D. H., 453
Kang, H., 137
Kanno, T., 447
Kanwisher, N., 122, 181
Kaplan, B., 642
Kaplan, R. M., 437
Kapur, S. E., 263
Karau, S. J., 62
Karisson, P., 378
Karlsson, S., 378
Karpicke, J. D., 261

Kasari, C., 657
Kasikci, Z., 138
Kasper, S., 583, 641
Kassam, K. S., 300
Kassin, S. M., 390
Kastenmüller, A., 487
Kaufmann, U., 367
Kavanagh, D. H., 593, 606
Kawachi, I., 460, 462
Kawakami, D., 502
Kawas, C., 376
Kayser, S., 643
Kazak, A., 570
Kazdin, A. E., 233, 617, 628, 631
Keane, J., 386
Keane, M., 153, 306
Keck, P., 583
Keefe, F., 202
Keefe, R. S., 152
Keel, P. K., 439–40
Keeling, R. P., 480
Keil, F. C., 313
Keitner, G. I., 647
Kelleher, P., 437
Kellendonk, C., 595
Keller, A., 198
Keller, J., 147
Keller, M. B., 640
Keller, S., 326
Keller, T. A., 606
Kelley, C., 273
Kelley, H. H., 494, 497
Kelley, W. M., 131, 223, 331, 412, 435, 438, 505, 547, 547
Kellman, P., 358
Kelly, D. R., 409
Kelly, G., 525
Kelly, J. P., 102, 607
Kelly, S. J., 573
Kelly, W. G., 114
Kelly, W. M., 405
Kelly-Hayes, M., 455
Keltikangas-Jarvinen, L., 519
Keltner, D., 396, 399, 401, 402, 508
Kempermann, G., 339
Kendall, J., 606
Kendler, K. S., 569
Kenis, G., 453
Kennedy, B., 462
Kennedy, D. P., 87, 606
Kennedy, J. L., 583
Kennedy, Q., 377
Kennedy, S. H., 641, 643
Kennedy-Moore, E., 453
Kenrick, D. T., 182, 421, 470, 533
Kensinger, E. A., 276
Keogh, J., 414
Keough, M. E., 632, 636
Kepe, V., 124
Kernberg, O. F., 599
Kernis, M. H., 507, 550
Keski-Rahkonen, A., 439
Kessler, R. C., 277, 507, 564, 574, 575, 576, 577, 578, 580–81, 583, 596, 598, 601, 610, 630
Kessler, T., 472
Kestler, L., 593, 594, 648
Ketter, T. A., 642, 646
Ketterson, E. D., 101
Key, A. C., 368
Keyes, D., 587
Keys, A., 437
Keysers, C., 386
Khaw, M. W., 387
Khoo, A., 242
Kida, T. E., 6

Kidd, K. K., 583
Kiecolt-Glaser, J. K., 373, 444, 453
Kiehl, K. A., 324, 601
Kihlstrom, J. F., 132, 143, 588
Kijima, N., 517
Kilbride, J. E., 342
Kilbride, P. L., 342
Kim, D. A., 362
Kim, E., 599
Kim, H., 339, 388, 397
Kim, J., 150, 444
Kim, J. A., 224
Kim, J. H., 346
Kim, M. J., 87
Kim, S. H., 606
Kim, S. J., 150, 150
Kim, S. Y., 116
Kim-Prieto, C., 498
Kimura, D., 103
King, J., 655
King, L., 464
Kingsbury, A. M., 340
Kingstone, A. F., 128
Kircher, J. C., 390
Kirker, W. S., 547
Kirkpatrick, B., 595
Kirsch, I., 144, 644
Kit, B. K., 433
Kitahara, C. M., 443
Kitamura, T., 455
Kitayama, S., 498, 555, 556
Kittok, R., 484
Kivimaki, M., 519
Klatsky, A., 463
Klauer, S. G., 33
Klauser, P., 593
Kleck, R. E., 436
Klei, L., 605
Klein, L. C., 451
Klein, R. G., 610, 656
Klein, R. M., 128
Klein, T., 485
Klein, W. M., 445
Klin, A., 603, 604–5
Klingberg, T., 259
Klonoff, E. A., 432
Klonsky, E. D., 584
Klotz, M. L., 552
Klump, K. L., 435, 440
Knafo, A., 518
Knight, R., 442, 598
Knight, R. T., 360
Knodt, A. R., 391
Knopik, V. S., 516
Knopp, J., 637
Knouf, N., 181
Knowles, M., 410
Knowles, S., 637
Knowles, T. P., 376
Knox, S. S., 455
Knutson, B., 238
Ko, S. J., 543
Kobasa, S., 458
Kobayashi, C., 556
Koch, J. L., 599
Koch, L. G., 444
Kochanek, K. D., 372, 431, 432
Kocsis, J. H., 640
Koelling, R. A., 217
Koelsch, S., 22
Koenig, O., 138
Koestner, R., 542
Koh, K., 133
Kohlberg, L., 361
Kohler, W., 307, 307

Kohn, D., 622
Kohout, J., 23
Koike, T., 447
Kolar, D. W., 544
Kolarz, C. M., 376
Konrath, S., 551
Kontsevich, L. L., 397
Koob, G. F., 156–57
Koole, S. L., 552, 640–41
Koolhaus, J. M., 483
Koppell, B., 144
Köppen, J., 69
Korach, K. S., 116
Koralus, P., 363
Koran, L. M., 640
Korbonits, M., 414
Koren, D., 642
Korf, J., 588
Korgaonkar, M. S., 329
Korn, M. L., 576
Kornblith, S. J., 649
Kornstein, S., 634
Korszun, A., 456
Korten, A., 650
Kosinski, M., 504
Kositchek, R., 455
Kosslyn, S., 171, 171, 172
Kotler, M., 576
Koutstaal, W., 377
Kowalski, P., 6, 132
Kowatch, R. A., 659
Kozak, M. J., 637
Kozorovitskiy, Y., 104
Kraepelin, E., 601
Kragel, P. A., 385, 391
Krakauer, J. C., 433
Krakauer, N. Y., 433
Krakowiak, P., 606
Kramer, M., 606
Kramer, M. S., 329
Krampe, R. T., 322
Krank, M. D., 224
Krantz, D. S., 455
Kranz, G. S., 367
Kray, L. J., 502
Kreinin, I., 642
Kremen, A. M., 458
Kremnitzer, M., 389
Krendl, A. C., 331
Kringelbach, M. L., 148–49, 161, 238
Kringlen, E., 598
Krishnaswami, S., 658
Kritchevsky, M., 39
Kroes, M. C., 252
Krogel, P. A., 122
Krueger, J. I., 487, 550–51
Krueger, R. F., 569, 571, 571
Kruger, J., 9
Krupsky, M., 45
Krystal, J. H., 634
Ku, G., 503
Kublböck, M., 367
Kubzansky, L. D., 456, 460
Kuchibhotla, K. V., 138
Kuhl, P. K., 313–14, 316
Kuhlmeier, V., 313
Kuhn, C., 151
Kuhn, M., 138
Kühn, S., 591
Kuiper, N. A., 547
Kukucka, J., 390
Kukull, W., 376
Kulhara, P., 589
Kulik, J., 279
Kulkarni, J., 643

Kumar, S. K., 136
Kumaran, D., 282
Kumashiro, H., 659
Kuncel, N. R., 321
Kunda, Z., 499
Kundakovic, M., 569
Kupchik, Y. M., 116
Kupers, R., 126
Kupfer, D. J., 583
Kupka, R., 583
Kuppens, P., 384
Kurdyak, P., 152
Kurzban, R., 462
Kushlev, K., 374
Kushner, H., 463
Kuyken, W., 620
Ky, K. N., 347
Kyin, M., 329
Kyllonen, P. C., 325

LaBar, K. S., 122, 385, 388, 391
Ladenwall, P., 443
LaFrance, M., 399
Lager, A., 323
Lahti, I., 594
Laibson, D. I., 518
Lainhart, J. E., 96
Lakey, C. E., 550
Lalonde, F., 364
Lambert, E. A., 581
Lambert, T. J., 329
Lameira, A. R., 317
Lamm, C., 361
Lamm, H., 474
Lampinen, J., 385
Landa, R., 604
Landis, K. R., 372, 461
Landis, T., 412
Lane, M. C., 596, 598, 600
Lane, N. D., 543
Lane, R. D., 400
Lang, A., 340
Langa, K. M., 461
Lange, C., 391, 391
Lange, E. H., 591
Langenecker, S. A., 660
Langford, S., 655
Langleben, D. D., 390
Langlois, J. H., 506
Lanius, R., 586
Lantos, J. D., 607
Lanzenberger, R., 641
Lapp, L., 138
Larcher, K., 238
Larocque, C., 181
Larrick, R. P., 483
Larsen, J. T., 385
Larson, A., 506
Larson, E. B., 376
Larson, H., 609
Lashley, K., 254
Laska, E. M., 609
Lasko, N., 278
Latané, B., 475, 487, 487
Latham, G., 408
Lattarulo, C. R., 138
Lau, H., 132, 405
Lau, M., 641
Lau, S., 133
Laugesen, M., 442
Laughlin, J. E., 325
Laureys, S., 125, 126
Lautenschlager, N. T., 444
Lauzanne, K., 367
Lavie, C. J., 444
Lavrijsen, J., 126

Lawrence, E. M., 461
Lawrie, S. M., 585
Lawson, G. M., 329, 339
Layden, J. C., 372
Layman, M., 445
Layton, M., 598–99
Lazar, M. A., 434
Lazarus, R. S., 448, 457
Lazerus, T., 471
Le, K., 536
Leach, J. D., 308
Leary, M. R., 146, 410, 483, 550
Leas, E. C., 442
LeBlanc, A. J., 373
Leckman, J. F., 653
Ledley, D. R., 637
LeDoux, J. E., 94, 221, 250, 278, 387, 388, 392, 402
Lee, C. K., 577
Lee, D. C., 444
Lee, E., 367
Lee, E. H., 340
Lee, I. M., 443, 444
Lee, J. E., 480
Lee, J. J., 518
Lee, K. H., 627
Lee, K. J., 506
Lee, M. B., 388
Lee, N. C., 96
Lee, P. A., 364
Lee, S., 116
Lee, S. E., 33
Lee, Y., 606
LeFan, J., 505
Lefevre, C. E., 506
Leff, J., 650
Lehman, D. R., 308–10, 554–56
Lehnart, J., 536
Lehrner, J. P., 209
Leibing, E., 618
Leichsenring, F., 618
Leigh, B. C., 155
Leiva, B. P., 326
Leiviskä, J., 595
Le Moal, M., 157
Lemos, K., 552
Lempert, K. M., 300
Lench, H. C., 385
Lenroot, R. K., 593
Lensu, S., 444
Lenzenweger, M. F., 596, 598, 600
Leonardo da Vinci, 183
León-Carrión, J., 126
Leotta, A., 606
Lepage, C., 593
Lepper, M., 308, 308, 406
Lerner, J. S., 300
Leroux, J. M., 635
Leshem, M., 449
Leslie, S. J., 294
Leslie, W. D., 434
Letendre, L., 332
Leucht, S., 648
Leung, K., 529
LeVay, S., 423
Levenson, R. B., 609
Levenson, R. W., 385, 391
Levenstein, S., 453
Leventhal, H., 441
Leverich, G. S., 583
Levesque, J., 635
Levey, S., 193
Levey, T., 193
Levin, D. T., 129, 130
Levine, A., 352
Levine, B., 277

Levine, M., 487
Levinson, S. C., 313
Levitin, D. J., 22, 188
Levy, D., 605, 606
Levy, K. N., 599
Lewinsohn, P. M., 580
Lewis, B. P., 451
Lewis, C., 480
Lewis, D. A., 153
Lewis, G. J., 506
Lewis, K., 470, 471
Lewis, S. K., 479
Lewis-Fernández, R., 586
Lewontin, R., 327
Li, C., 549
Li, D., 242
Li, J., 360
Li, N. P., 101, 421, 506
Liao, Y., 137
Lichenstein, P., 609
Licht, R. W., 646
Lichtenstein, S., 445
Lichtermann, D., 518
Lick, D. J., 173
Lieb, K., 599, 651
Lieb, R., 576
Lieberman, M. D., 492, 493, 530
Liebowitz, M. R., 634, 637
Liewald, D., 327
Lihm, J., 606
Lilienfeld, S. O., 541, 567, 629
Lim, C. C. W., 575
Lin, A., 124
Lin, J. Y., 217
Linardatos, B. S., 644
Lindell, A. K., 313
Lindeman, B., 194
Linder, N., 449
Lindquist, K. A., 393
Lindquist, S., 114
Lindqvist, K., 618
Lindström, P., 424
Linehan, M. M., 599, 650–51, 650, 651
Lineweaver, T. T., 130
Ling, S., 128
Link, B. G., 581
Linkenauger, S. A., 133
Linnell, J., 607–8
Linnman, C., 579
Linsenmeier, J. A. W., 421
Lisanby, S. H., 642
Lissek, S., 576
Littlefield, A. K., 585
Liu, B., 460
Liu, H. M., 314
Liu, J., 373, 600
Liu, X., 252
Livesley, W. J., 518
Livneh, Z., 45
Lix, L. M., 434
Lledo, P. M., 198
Llera, S. J., 575, 632
Lloyd, C., 453
Lloyd-Fox, S., 344
Lo Bello, S. G., 641
Lobmaier, J. S., 451
Locke, E., 408
Locke, J., 208
Lockhart, D. J., 329
Lockhart, R., 263
Loeber, R., 153, 331, 601
Loehlin, J., 516
Loewenstein, G. F., 300
Loftus, E. F., 265, 281, 281, 282–83
Logan, J. M., 377
Logel, C., 331

Loggia, M. L., 202
Lombardo, M. V., 103
Lomo, T., 252
Long, P. J., 364
Looser, C. E., 472
Lopes, J., 655
Lopez, E. M., 368
Lopez, S. R., 51
Loprinzi, P. D., 431
Loranger, A. W., 596, 598, 601
Lorenz, K., 349, *349*
Loughnan, S., 472
Lovaas, I., 657–58
Lovell, L., 637
Lovett, I., 424
Lowe, M. J., 103
Lowe, P., 630
Lowy, K., 192
Lozano, A. M., *642*, 643
Lu, K. T., 634
Lu, M. C., 604
Lu, Q. L., 145
Lubman, D. I., 152
Luce, C. L., 486
Luchins, A., 304, *305*
Ludlow, D., 203
Ludwig, S. D., 372
Lukacs, S. L., 654
Lummaa, V., 101
Lundström, J. N., 198
Luo, D., 581
Luo, Y., 478
Luria, A. R., 273
Lurito, J. T., 103
Lutter, C. D., 484
Luus, C. A., 284
Luyten, L., 638
Lykken, D. T., 112, 518, 536, 600–1
Lynam, D. R., 331, 483, 601
Lynn, R., 531
Lynn, S. J., 144
Lyoo, I. K., 150
Lyster, S. A. H., 319
Lyubomirsky, S., 308–10, 374, 395, 464

Ma, Y. H., 145
McAdams, D., 543
McArdle, J. J., 322
McAuley, E., 444
McCabe, D. P., 259
McCabe, K. O., 529
McCabe, S. E., 150
McCann, F. F., 294
McCarthy, D. O., 453
McCarthy, G., 181
McCarthy, S. E., 593, 606, 646
McCeney, M. K., 455
McClay, J., 113, *115*
McClellan, J. M., 593
McClelland, D. C., 409, 542
McClelland, J. L., 348
Maccoby, E. E., 540
McCollough, C., *179*
McConahay, J. B., 501
MacCormack, J. K., 393
McCormack, M., 422
McCormick, K., 313
McCormick, W. C., 376
McCracken, J. T., 634
McCrae, R. R., 528, 534, 535–36, 538, 540, 542
MacCullum, R. C., 453
McCully, J., 224
McCurley, R., 140
McDaniel, M. A., 259
McDaniel, M. E., 577
McDermott, K. B., 282

MacDonald, G., 410, 482, 550
McDonald, K., 152
McDonald, R., 481
McDonald, R. V., 224
MacDorman, M. F., 659
McDowd, J. M., 377
McElroy, S., 583
McEwen, B. S., 449, 452, 574
McEwen, S., 594
McGaugh, J. L., 277
McGeer, V., 363
McGhee, D., 492
McGlashan, T. H., 650
McGonigal, K. M., 508
McGough, J. J., 610
McGrath, J. J., 589, 649
McGrath, R. W., 631
McGraw, A. P., 385
MacGregor, D., 300
McGregor, H. R., 244
McGue, M. K., 112, 536, 609
McGuire, J. F., 634
Machon, R. A., 595
McInerney, S. C., 388
MacInnis, R. J., 432, 434
McIntosh, A. R., 277
MacKay, D., G., 128
McKenna, C., 510
McKenzie, K. E., 129
McKeon, D., 146
McKinnon, A., 620
McKinnon, M. C., 277
McLean, C. P., 619, 634
MacLean, P., 386
MacLeod, C., 576
McMahon, R. J., 352
McMaster, M. R., 485
McNaughton, B. L., 138
McNaughton, N., 531
McNeely, H. E., *642*, 643
McNeil, D. G., 170
MacNeill, D., 275
McPheeters, M. L., 657, 658
Macpherson, H. A., 656
McPherson, L. M., 600, 653
McQuown, S. C., 254
Macrae, C. N., 280, 472, 499, 547, *547*
McRobbie, H., 442
Madden, D. J., 377
Maddi, S., 458
Madsen, H. B., 346
Maeda, F., 203
Maes, M., 453
Maggs, J. L., 155
Magnasco, M. O., 198
Magnier, M., 622
Magnin, M., 138
Magnotta, V., 593
Magnuson, V. L., 423
Magnusson, K. P., 45
Maguire, E. A., 86
Maher, B. A., 562
Maher, W. R., 562
Mai, N., 186
Maier, J. G., 138
Maier, N., 307, *307*
Mainberger, F., 138
Major, B., 553
Majumbdar, S. R., 434
Makhijani, M. G., 62
Malarkey, W. B., 444
Malek, M., 609
Malhotra, D., 646
Malik, M., 607–8
Malinchoc, M., 455
Malle, B. F., 498

Mallouf, M., 50
Malmud, E. K., 339
Malone, D. A., 638, 643
Malpass, R. S., 181
Mamun, A. A., 340
Mancini-Marïe, A., 592
Mandalenakis, Z., 443
Manderscheid, R. W., 573
Mandisodza, A. N., 496
Maner, J. K., 486
Manes, F., 386
Mangun, G. R., 311–12
Mannarelli, T., 543
Manning, C. C., 481
Manning, R., 487
Manns, J. R., 388
Mannuzza, S., 610, 656
Manrique-Garcia, E., 594
Mansfield, P. R., 659
Mansuy, I. M., 449
Mantione, M., 638
Mao, H., 127
Maquet, P., 140
Mar, R. A., 360
Marais, M. S., 340
March, S. J., 660
Marco, J., 599
Marcovitch, H., 607
Marcus, D. K., 422
Marcus, G. F., 106, 116, 315
Marder, S. R., 567
Marek, E. A., 294
Margono, C., 434, 436
Marin, M. F., 579
Markon, J., 375
Markon, K. E., 571, *571*
Markovic, M., 221
Markowitz, J. C., 619, 620, 638, 640, 641
Markus, H., 547, 555
Marlatt, A., 155
Marraccini, M. E., 150
Marsella, A. J., 573
Marsh, A. A., 601, *602*
Marsh, H. W., 147
Marsh, R. L., 267
Marshall, B., 452
Marshall, G. D. J., 453
Marshall, J., 607
Marshall, J. C., 123
Marshall, P. J., 577
Marsland, A. L., 461
Marston, N. A., 643
Martens, A., 332
Martin, A., 292–93
Martin, G. B., 344
Martin, J., 113, *115*, 483
Martin, J. L., 581
Martin, K. C., 254
Martin, L. A., 606
Martin, L. L., 391
Martin, R., 18
Martin, S. F., 153
Martinez, P., 152
Martin-Guehl, C., 638
Martins, H. F., 280
Martz, M. E., 155
Marucha, P. T., 453
Marusewski, A. L., 435
Maruta, T., 455
Maselko, J., 460
Mash, E. J., 568
Mashek, D. J., 362
Maslow, A., 402–3, *403*, 459–60
Mason, B. J., 157
Masson, M. E., 268
Master, A., 332

Masters, W., 418
Mastoras, S. M., 324
Mataix-Cols, D., 634
Matarazzo, J. D., 321
Mather, M., 377
Mathews, V. P., 103
Mathur, N., 317
Matsui, M., 339
Matsumoto, D., 399
Mattek, A., 87
Mattern, J. L., 479
Matthews, A., 576
Matthews, A. M., 644
Matthews, M. D., 409
Mattison, D. R., 625, 644
Matusch, A., 643
Matush, L., 329
Matzner, W. T., 462
Matzuk, M. M., 658
Mawhood, L., 659
May, A., 329
May, A. M., 584
May, K. A., 506
May, P. A., 340
Mayberg, H. S., 146, 628, *642*, 643
Mayer, J., 324
Mayes, A., 326
Mayford, M. R., 210
Mayseless, O., 352
Maywald, S., 138
Mazur, A., 483–84
Mazza, S., 138
Mazzulla, B. C., 87
Meaney, M. J., 449, 519
Mechler, J., 618
Meddis, R., 133
Medin, D. L., 292
Mednick, S. A., 595, 600
Meeks, J. T., 267
Meengs, J. S., 435
Meesters, Y., 641
Mehl, M. R., 543, 544
Mehler, J., 358, *359*
Mehta, N., 581
Mehta, P. H., 483–84
Mehta, S., 641
Meier, M. H., 152
Meijer, Z., 555
Melby–Lervag, M., 319
Mellingen, K., 601
Meltzoff, A. N., *344*
Melzack, R., 202
Menachemi, N., 61
Menchola, M., 621
Mendelovici, A., 363
Mende-Siedlecki, P., 36, 388
Meng-Hentschel, J., 451
Menkes, D. B., 659
Mennella, J. A., 196, *197*, 414
Mennes, M., 609
Menon, M., 370
Menon, V., 22, 237
Mensour, B., 635
Mental Health America, 631
Mercer, K. B., 578
Mérette, C., 136
Merico, D., 605
Merikangas, K. R., 155, 653, 659
Meriotti, E., 592
Mermelstein, R., 442–43
Merrill, D. A., 124
Merzenich, M. M., 319
Mesquita, B., 385
Meston, C. M., 416
Mesulam, M., 79

Metalsky, G., 582
Metcalfe, J., 409
Metcalfe, R., 301
Metts, S., 401
Meyer, D. R., 406
Meyer-Lindenberg, A., 483
Mezulis, A. H., 554, 556
Michaelsen, K. F., 328
Michaelson, J. J., 646
Michalski, D., *23*
Mickelsen, O., 437
Mickelson, K. D., 507
Mielke, A., 317
Miettunen, J., 649
Mignot, E., 136
Miguel, E. C., 568
Miklowitz, D. J., 646
Miles, E., 396, 502
Milgram, S., 480, *480*, 482
Mill, J., 113, *115*, 483
Mill, J. S., 11
Millan, M. J., 649
Millard, K., 481
Miller, A. H., 449
Miller, C. J., 483
Miller, D., 103
Miller, D. G., 281, *281*
Miller, D. T., 479
Miller, G. A., 250, 259
Miller, G. E., 452, 453, 454
Miller, I. J., 195
Miller, I. W., 647
Miller, J. B., 63
Miller, K. K., 101
Miller, L. C., 419
Miller, M., 661
Miller, R. L., 116
Miller, S., 646, 647
Miller, W. T., 620, 621
Millevoi, A., 544
Mills, E. J., 443
Mills, J., 494
Mills, K. L., 364
Milne, A. B., 499
Milner, A. D., 175
Milner, B., 255
Milojev, P., 535
Milovich, M. M., 474
Milton, J., 171
Min, H., 627
Minami, T., 629
Mineka, S., 217, 243, 587
Ming, G. L., 102
Miniño, A., 152
Minnes, S., 340
Minshew, N. J., 606
Minster, R. L., 124
Miranda, D., 22
Mironova, E., 329
Mirowsky, J., 372
Mischel, W., 409
Mishkin, M., 175, 272
Mitchell, A., 569
Mitchell, D. G., *602*
Mitchell, G., 492
Mitchell, J. E., 440
Mitchell, J. P., 472
Mitchell, K. A., 504
Mitelman, S. A., 593
Mithoefer, A. T., 153
Mithoefer, M. C., 153
Mittal, V. A., 594
Miyake, K., 51
Miyamoto, Y., 498
Miyawaki, K., 141

Mletzko, T., 449
Mneimneh, Z., 581
Mobbs, D., 237
Moffa, A. H., 627
Moffit, T. E., 520
Moffitt, C., 655
Moffitt, T. E., 113–14, *115*, 152, 409, 483, 610
Mogg, K., 576
Mogil, J. S., 202
Mogle, J., 376
Moher, D., 655
Mohile, S. G., 537
Molcho, A., 576
Moll, J., 362, 363, 502
Mols, F., 481
Monaghan, P., 133
Monarch, N. D., 508
Monfils, M., 252, 278
Moniz, E., 626
Montague, P. R., 220
Monteith, M. J., 502
Monterosso, J., 308–10
Montgomery, C., 153
Montgomery, G. H., 144
Monti, M. M., 125
Monuteaux, M. C., 656
Monzani, B., 634
Mooney, L., 150
Moore, M. K., *344*
Moore, S. C., 443
Moore, T. J., 625, 644
Mora, F., 237
Moran, J. L., 593
Moran, J. M., 547
Morawski, J. G., 481
Morch-Johnsen, L., 591
Morcillo-Peñalver, C., 609
Morefield, K. M., 153
Moreira-Maia, C. R., 609
Moreno, M. A., 370
Morewedge, C. K., 302
Morey, L. C., 620
Morf, C. C., 551
Morgan, C., 541, *541*
Morgenstern, M., 131
Moriarty, J. C., 390
Morin, C. M., 136
Moring, J., 594
Moriuchi, J. M., 604
Morman, M. T., 472
Morris, G. J., 453
Morris, M. E., 543
Morris, R., 483
Morrison, A. B., 259
Morse, R., 345
Mortensen, E. L., 328, 378
Mortensen, K. N., 126
Morton, J., 496
Mosher, W. D., 508
Moskowitz, A. K., 591
Moskowitz, J. T., 458
Moskvina, V., 456
Moss, J. A., 414
Moss, M., 205
Mosser, E. A., 133
Moulton, J. L., III, 656
Moulton, S., 171, *171*, 172
Mourao-Miranda, J., 363
Moussawi, K., 116
Moussier, S., 474
Mowery, P. D., 442
Mowry, B. J., 583
Moxey, L., 302
Mroczek, D. K., 376, 535, 536
Mucci, A., 592

Mueller, P. A., 130
Muenke, M., 157
Muenks, K., 410
Mufson, L., 661
Muglia, L. J., 116
Muhle, R., 604
Mukherjee, R. A. S., 340
Mulvenna, C., 170
Munafò, M. R., 518–19
Munro, B. A., 150
Munsell, B. C., 606
Munson, J. A., 352
Murakami, F., 556
Murch, S. H., 607–8
Muris, P., 532
Murphy, M. J., 473–80
Murphy, S. L., 372, 431, 432
Murray, H., 408, 541, *541*
Murray, S. L., 509
Murru, A., 646
Muska, C. E., 157
Mustanski, B. S., 423
Mustroph, M. L., 102
Myerberg, N. R., 481
Myers, D. G., 462, 463, 474
Myers, J., 569
Myers, M. G., 442

Naarala, M., 594
Naccache, L., 123
Naci, H., 444
Nadel, L., 86
Nader, K., 250
Nagel, G., 116
Naimi, T., 154
Naishadham, D., 432
Najman, J. M., 340
Nakano, K., 455
Nakayama, H., 312
Nakayama, K., 122, 181, 317
Napoli, A., 453
Naqvi, N. H., 156
Narayan, K. M., 432
Narayanam, S., 393
Nash, G. B., 456
Nash, M., 144
Nassar, N., 604
Nastase, S. A., 293
National Association of Colleges and
    Employers, 27
National Center for Learning Disabilities, 105
National Highway Traffic Safety Administration
    (NHTSA), 40, 154
National Institute of Drug Abuse, 153
National Institute of Mental Health, 566,
    567, 578
National Institutes of Health (NIH), 193, 660
National Research Council, 659
National Sleep Foundation, 142
Natsuaki, M. N., 363
Natu, V., 122
Nauman, E., 124
Nave, C. S., 533
Nawata, H., 367
Neale, J. M., 453
Neale, M. C., 569
Nearing, K. I., 243
Neff, L. G., 442
Neiderhiser, J. M., 363, 516, 601
Neighbors, C., 479
Neimeyer, R. A., 504
Neisser, U., 319, 322, 327, 329, 331
Neisser, V., 16
Nelen, M., 483
Nellis, A. M., 445

Nelson, M. L., 442
Nelson, S. K., 374
Nelson, T. F., 480
Nemeroff, C. B., 449
Nestler, E. J., 569
Nesvag, R., 591
Neta, M., 87
Neuberg, S. L., 182, 486
Neumann, C., 594
Neumann, D. L., 330
Neuzil, K., 432
Newby, J. M., 620
Newcomb, M. D., 504
Newheiser, A. K., 501
Newman, G., 313
Newman, J. P., 532
Newman, M. G., 575, 632
Newport, C., 449
Newschaffer, C., 607
Neyer, F. J., 536, 537
Nezlek, J., 507
Nezworski, M. T., 541
Ng, C., 339
Ng, M., 434, 436
Ng, W., 360
Nichols, K. E., 577
Nichols, R., 516
Nicholson, I., 481, 482
Nickel, T., 581
Nicolini, H., 634
Nicoll, R. A., 253
Nidich, S., 145
Nielsen, J. A., 96
Nieto-Castanon, A., 127
Nijenhuis, E. R., 588
Nilsson, H., 463
Nir, Y., 141
Nisbett, R. E., 20, 180, 329, 406, 485, 498
Nishikawa, Y., 643
Nishimura, R., 367
Nishino, S., 136
Niu, L., 339
Nivoli, A., 646
Noble, K. G., 329
Noftle, E. E., 529
Noguchi, K., 339
Nokia, M. S., 444
Nolan, J. M., 480
Nolen, W. A., 646
Nolen-Hoeksema, S., 395
Noll, D. N., 459
Noll, G., 456
Nomura, Y., 661
Nook, E. C., 393
Nopoulos, P., 593
Norberg, M. M., 634
Norcross, J. C., 664
Nordahl, C. W., 606
Nordborg, C., 102
Norenzayan, A., 20, 50, 189, 498, 539
Norman, C., 138
Norman, C. C., 510
Norman, K. A., 122
Norman, W. H., 647
Norris, A. L., 422
Northstone, S., 114
Norton, M. I., 470, 471, 504
Nosek, B. A., 491
Nöthlings, U., 414
Novotny, C. M., 629
Novotny, S. L., 658
Nowson, C. A., 434
Noyes, R., 576
Nuessle, T. M., 195
Null, J., 275

Nummenmaa, L., 385
Nurnberger, J. J., 583
Nutton, B., 638
Nyberg, L., 378
Nystrom, L E., 363
Nzerem, C. K., 444

Oakes, M. A., 501
Oasson, D. M., 607–8
Oberauer, K., 325
O'Boyle, M. W., 96
O'Brien, L. T., 294
Ochsner, K. N., 385, 386, 393, 396, 493
O'Connor, B. C., 656
Odbert, H., 528
O'Donovan, G., 444
O'Donovan, M. C., 593
Oei, N, Y. L., 449
Oemig, C., 508
Offermanns, K., 22
Offord, K. P., 455
Ogawa, S., 116
Ogbu, J., 331
Ogden, C. L., 435
Ogletree, S. M., 545, *546*
Ogomori, K., 367
Ohla, K., 198
Ohloff, G., 198
Oikonomou, G., 133
O'Kane, G. O., 276
Oke, A., 324
Okun, M. S., 638
Oler, J. A., 87
Olfson, M., 277, 564, 578, 639, 661
Olivares, M. G., 326
Oliveira, L. M., 198
Oliveira-Pinto, A. V., 198
Oller, D. K., 317
Olsen, E. O. M., 33, 45
Olsen, T. S., 312
Olshansky, S. J., 372
Olshavsky, R., 441
Olson, J. M., 517
Olson, K. R., 368
Olson, R., 41
Olson, R. K., 319
Olsson, A., 217, 243
O'Malley, P. M., 155, 165, 441
Omalu, B. I, *124*
Omer, S. B., 607
O'Neal, C. R., 410
O'Neal, J. M., 591
O'Neil, S., 147
Onen, H., 581
Ones, D. S., 321
Ooms, P., 638
Oosterhof, N., 293
Oosterlaan, J., 655
Opel, D. J., 607
Opendak, M., 103
Oppenheimer, D. M., 130
O'Rahilly, S., 414
Orcutt, H. K., 578
Orenstein, W. A., 607
Orleans, C. T., 431
Ormerod, T. C., 133
Orpana, H., 433
Ortigue, S., 507
Oskamp, S., 503
Ostendorf, F., 535–36
Osterling, J., 604
Ostroff, J., 152
Oswald, F. L., 492
O'Toole, A. J., 122
Otsuji, J., 414

Ott, S. L., 594
Otte, C., 580
Ottieger, A. E., 150
Otto, A. R., 449
Ouchi, H., *179*
Ouimet, M. C., 33
Owen, A. M., 125

Paans, A. M., 588
Pacchiarotti, I., 646
Pace-Schott, E. E., 579
Pack, A. I., 136
Padberg, F., 627
Padwal, R., 434
Paechiarotti, I., 583
Pagano, I., 442
Page, G. G., 453
Pagnamenta, A. T., 605
Pagnoni, G., 146
Paillard-Borg, S., 376
Palmer, J., 281
Palombo, D. J., 277
Panitz, D., 198
Panksepp, J., 463
Pantelis, C., 152
Panwar, S., 154
Papademetris, X., 529–30
Papadimitriou, G. N., 642
Papakostas, Y. G., 642
Paparella, T., 657
Pape, S., 594
Papez, J., 386
Pappanastasiou, E., 592
Paquette, V., 635
Paquin, G., 655
Parag, V., 442
Parashar, U., 432
Pardini, D., 153
Paredes, M. F., 339
Pariante, C. M., 580
Parikh, R., 563
Parish, S. J., 101
Park, H., 498
Park, N., 459
Parker, J. D., 324
Parkinson, C., 363
Parnas, J., 567
Parrott, A. C., 153
Parsons, Jim, 323
Pascual, J. C., 599
Pascual-Leone, A., 642
Pascual-Leone, P. A., 642
Pasqualucci, C. A., 198
Pasquinelli, E., 347
Passaro, D. J., 372
Pastor, P. N., 654
Pasupathi, M., 376
Patall, E. A., 308
Pate, V., 661
Patel, A., 443
Patel, V., 563, 581
Patrick, M. E., 155, 157
Pattatucci, A. M., 423
Patterson, C. M., 532
Patterson, D., 144
Pattie, A., 323
Paul-Labrador, M., 145
Pauls, D. L., 578, 583
Paulson, S., 313
Paulus, M. P., 156
Pauly, J. M., 203
Paunonen, S. V., 529
Pavlov, I. P., 211, *211, 213,* 226
Paykel, E. S., 581
Payne, B. K., 500
Payne, B. R., 538

Payne, J. D., 138
Payton, A., 327
Paz-Elizur, T., 45
Pederson, P. M., 312
Pelhamm, W. E., 656
Peltonen, L., 518
Pembrey, M. W., 114
Peña, C. J., 569
Peng, K., 20
Penke, L., 506
Pennebaker, J. W., 543
Penninx, B. W., 580
Penton-Voak, I. S., 418, 506
Penttilä, M., 649
Pepperberg, I., 316–17
Perani, D., 292
Peretz, I., 22
Perez, H. T., 326
Perez, M., 568
Perez-Edgar, K., 577
Pérez-Vigil, A., 634
Perfetti, C. A., 319
Perfilieva, E., 102
Perkins, W. J., 203
Perner, J., 360
Perrett, D. I., 244, 506
Perri, M., 507
Perry, B. D., 339
Perry, D. G., 370
Perry, G., 482
Persson, C. U., 443
Pert, C., 80
Peruche, M., 501
Pérusse, L., 436
Pesetsky, D., 319
Pessiglione, M., 132, 405
Pessoa, L., 363
Peters, A. T., 660
Peters, E., 300
Peters, J. R., 483
Petersen, E. E., 340
Peterson, C., 409, 459
Peterson, C. B., 441
Peterson, D. A., 102
Peterson, L. R., 340
Peterson, M. R., 595
Petitto, L. A., 316–17
Peto, R., 460
Petraglia, A. L., 124
Petronis, A., 583
Petrycki, S., 660
Pettersson, E., 516–17, 518
Pettit, J. W., 568
Petty, R., 494
Pezdek, K., 283
Pfaff, D. W., 116
Pfattheicher, S., 503
Pfaus, J. G., 417
Pfeifer, J. H., 606
Pfeifle, J. K., 416
Pfister, H., 576
Pham, B., 655
Phelan, J., 506
Phelps, E. A., 128, 217, 243, 252, 278, 279, 300,
    387, 388, 390, 449
Phillips, A., 658
Phillips, M. D., 103
Phillips, M. L., 583
Phillips, P. J., 138
Phinney, J. S., 368
Piacentini, J., 634
Piaget, J., 31, 353
Pickard, J. D., 125
Pickering, R. P., 600
Pickett, C. L., 410
Pien, G. W., 136

Pierce, S. B., 593
Pierce-Otay, A., 545
Pietschnig, J., 347
Pignatelli, M., 254
Pigott, T., 634
Pillow, D. R., 447
Pincus, M. A., 277, 564, 578
Pine, D. S., 392, 566–67, 576, 577
Pinel, E. C., 301
Pinel, P., 562
Pinheiro, R. T., 329
Pinker, S., 314, 315, 400
Pinsker, H. M., 210
Pinto, D., 605
Piotrowski, A., 111
Piper, M. E., 442–43
Pirie, K., 460
Pisoni, D. B., 314
Pitman, R. K., 278, 579
Pittinsky, T. L., 331
Piven, J., 388
Pizarro, D., 362
Pjrek, E., 641
Placenza, F. M., 643
Plailly, J., 386
Plakun, E. M., 651
Plant, E. A., 399, 501
Plassmann, H., 223
Platt, R. W., 329
Plomin, R., 327, 436, 516, 518, 519, 537, 605
Pocklington, A. J., 593, 606
Poehlman, T. A., 492
Polanczyk, G. V., 568, 610
Poland, G. A., 607
Polansky, L., 399
Poldrack, R. A., 319
Polich, J., 145
Polis, S., 397
Polivy, J., 438, 439
Polk, D., 158
Pollak, S. D., 339
Pollatsek, A., 319
Pollock, K. M., 641
Polyn, S. M., 122
Pons, F., 348
Ponzo, M., 184
Poo, M. M., 254
Porges, E. C., 363
Porter, R. H., 344
Porter, S., 600
Portillo, N., 646
Posner, J., 609
Post, R. M., 583
Potter, J., 535, 549
Potter, M. C., 268
Poulton, R., 114, 152, 520
Powell, B., 267
Powell, R. A., 223
Power, R., 153
Powers, A., 18
Prakash, R., 116
Pratesi, C. C., 181
Pratkanis, A. R., 132
Pratt, L. A., 573, 580, 581
Premack, D., 229, 360, 443
Prentice, D. A., 479
Prentiss, D., 153
Prescott, A., 242
Prescott, C. A., 569
Prescott, J., 96
Press, G., 39
Pressman, S., 461
Presson, C. C., 157, 441
Price, C. S., 607
Price, D. D., 144, 145
Price, J. H., 543

Prigerson, H. G., 537
Primack, B. A., 442
Prins, B., 278
Prins, P. J. M., 655
Prkash, R., 444
Prober, D. P., 133
Probst, F., 451
Pronin, E., 302
Prot, S., 242
Provencher, V., 438
Przeworski, A., 575, 632
Public Health England, 372
Puce, A., 181
Purcell, S. M., 593
Purdie, V. J., 500
Pussin, J., 562
Putnam, A. L., 261, 268
Putnam, S. K., 484

Qawasmi, A., 133
Quadros, C. D., 432
Quevedo, L., 329
Quinn, D. M., 331
Quinn, J. F., 578
Quinn, K., 566–67
Quinn, P. D., 331, 410

Raab, M., 69
Rabin, B. S., 461
Rabin, S., 576
Rabung, S., 618
Radcliffe, N. M., 445
Radke-Yarrow, M., 361, 486
Radua, J., 360
Raevaori, A., 439
Rafnar, T., 45
Raggi, V. L., 655
Rahe, R. H., 447, *448*
Raila, H., 87
Raine, A., 600, 601
Rainforth, M., 145
Rainville, P., 144, 145
Raio, C. M., 252, 278, 449
Rajapakse, J. C., 103
Rajeevan, N., 529–30
Ram, S., 136
Ramachandran, V. S., 104, 170
Ramakrishnan, C., 116
Ramirez, S., 252
Rampon, C., 329
Ramrakha, S., 339
Ramsey, J., 153
Rand, D. G., 470, 471
Rapin, I., 604
Rapoport, J. L., 103, 577, 609, 637
Rapport, M. D., 655
Rapuano, K. M., 412, 435
Raskin, D. C., 390
Rasmussen, C., 332
Rasmussen, S. A., 340
Rasschou, H. O., 312
Rauch, S. L., 388, 520, *521*, 579
Rauscher, F. H., 347
Rawson, K. P., 268
Rawson, R. A., 150
Raye, C. L., 502
Raymaekers, S., 638
Rayner, K., 268, 318–19
Rayner, R., 221
Raynor, H. A., 435
Razza, L. B., 627
Read, J. P., 444
Realo, A., 540
Reber, P. J., 237
Reczek, C., 373
Redcay, E., 606

Redd, W. H., 144
Redick, T. S., 259
Redondo, R., 252
Reed, D. R., 414
Reeve, S., 634
Reeves, L. M., 306
Regal, C., 345
Regan, P., 419, 503, 508
Regan, R., 605
Regard, M., 412
Regier, D. A., 577
Rehm, J., 152
Reicher, S. D., 481
Reid, M. E., 601, *602*
Reifman, A., 63
Reifman, A. S., 483
Reilly, D., 330
Reilly, S., 217
Reinders, A. A., 588
Reinero, D. A., 36
Reinisch, J. M., 328
Reis, D. L., 324
Reis, H. X., 507
Reiss, A. L., 237
Reiss, D., 363
Reiss, D. J., *649*
Rendell, J. M., 646
Renier, C., 136
Rentfrow, P. J., 549
Rescorla, R. A., 218
Respondek, C., 152
Ressler, K. J., 634, 643
Revonsuo, A., 143
Reyna, C., 22
Reynolds, C. F., 640–41
Rezai, A. R., 638, 643
Rhodes, G., 181
Rhodes, J. S., 102
Rhodewalt, F., 551
Riboni, F. V., 568
Rice, A., 122
Richard, J. M., 238
Richards, J., 444
Richards, J. M., 508
Richeson, J. A., 331, 503
Richlan, F., 360
Richman, L. S., 460
Richter, M., 607
Rideout, V. J., 241
Ridley, M., 116
Ridout, B., 479
Rieckmann, A., 378
Rieger, G., 422
Riemann, R., 518
Rifkin, A., 661
Rifkin, W., 661
Rijsdijk, F. V., 605
Riley, D. D., 124
Rinderu, M. I., 483
Risen, J. L., 302
Riskind, J. H., 582
Rivera, M. T., 504
Rivers, S. E., 324
Rizvi, S., 643
Rizzolatti, G., 386, 606
Ro, E., 597
Roba, L. G., 435
Robbins, M. C., 342
Roberson, D., 398
Roberts, A. R., 505
Roberts, B. W., 534, 535–36, 538
Roberts, D. F., 241
Roberts, R. E., 461
Roberts, R. W., 551
Roberts, S. A., 594
Roberts, W. O., 124

Robins, L. N., 158, 577
Robins, R. W., 399, 529, 549
Robinson, A., 634
Robinson, J., 401
Robinson, J. L., 435
Robinson, M., 434, 436
Robinson, R., *184*
Robinson, S. J., 153
Robinson, T. E., 238
Robles, T. F., 373
Rocchetti, M., 592
Roche, B. M., 151
Rock, D., 594
Rock, I., 184
Rocke-Henderson, N., 369
Rockstuhl, L., 373
Rodhe, P. D., 580
Rodriguez, M. L., 409
Roe, F. J. C., 445
Roe, L. S., 435
Roeber, J., 154
Roeder, I., 339
Roediger, H. L., III, 261, 268, 282
Roemer, A., 154
Roemmich, J. N., 435
Roethlisberger, F. J., 41, *42*
Rogeberg, R., 152
Rogers, C., 459, 621
Rogers, R. G., 461
Rogers, S., 657
Rogers, S. J., 373
Rogers, T. B., 547
Roggman, L. A., 506
Rogosh, F. A., 352
Rohde, L. A., 568, 609
Roizen, E. R., 656
Rolls, B. J., 435
Rolls, E. T., 237, 412
Ronald, A., 605
Ronemus, M., 605, 606
Ropers, H. H., 483
Rosales, T. A., 150
Rosch, E., 291
Rose, D., 581
Rosen, R. I., 157
Rosenbaum, S., 444
Rosenfield, D., 634
Rosenhan, D. L., 633
Rosenman, R. H., 455
Rosenthal, D. A., 371
Rosenthal, R., 42, 496, 644
Rosenzweig, M. R., 101, 102
Ross, C. E., 372
Ross, D., 239, *239*, 240
Ross, H. E., 658
Ross, L., 497
Ross, M., 279, 553, *553*
Ross, S., 239, *239*, 240
Rossi-Arnaud, C., 278
Rotella, B., 287
Rothbart, M. K., 519
Rothman, A. J., 302
Rothman, K. J., 433
Rotter, J., 525, *525*
Rourke, M., 570
Rouse, C., 295
Roussos, P., 593
Rovee-Collier, C., 345
Rowe, D., 437
Rowe, D. C., 157, 518
Rowland, D. A., 506
Roy, A., 585
Royet, J. P., 386
Rozin, P., 415, 436
Rubenstein, A. J., 506
Rubia, K., 609

Rubichek, O., 642
Rubin, D. C., 280
Rudd, R. A., 152
Ruderfer, D., 593
Rudman, L. A., 472
Rudrauf, D., 156
Ruffman, T., 361
Rule, N. O., 497
Rupp, H. A., 101
Rusbult, C. E., 509, 510
Ruschitzka, F., 456
Ruscio, A. M., 575
Rush, A. J., 582, 640, 659
Russell, C. A., 480
Russell, C. J., 439
Russell, J., 384, 442, 634
Russell, M. A. H., 398
Russig, H., 449
Russin, A., 502
Russo, J., 340
Rutgers, A. H., 352
Rutter, M., 604, 659
Ryan, L. R., 86
Ryan, R., 406
Ryan, S. A., 153
Ryan, T. J., 254
Ryba, N. J., 195
Rydell, A. M., 352
Ryder, J. G., 643
Ryland, J., 122

Saab, B. J., 449
Saarimäki, H., 385
Sabol, S. Z., 442
Sackheim, H. A., 642
Sacks, J. J., 154
Sacks, O., 327
Sackur, J., 123
Saczawa, M., 594
Saffer, B. Y., 584
Sagarin, B. J., 486
Sagiv, N., 170
Saha, S., 589, 649
Saha, T. D., 600
St. Fleur, D., 609
Saklofske, D. H., 324
Sala Frigerio, C., 376
Saleem, M., 241
Salidis, J., 319
Salimpoor, V. N., 238
Salovey, P., 302, 324
Salthouse, T., 377
Salum, G. A., 568
Salvado, O., 376
Salvador, R., 599
Samenieh, A., 266
Sampson, J. N., 443
Samson, A. C., 396
Sana, F., 130
Sanchez, I. M., 432
Sanders, K., 278
Sanders, S., 609
Sanders, S. A., 328
Sanderson, W. C., 575
Sandler, I., 447
Sanfey, A. G., 387
Sanford, A. J., 302
Sanjurjo, A., 63
Sannita, W. G., 126
Santiago, C. D., 448
Santorico, S. A., 195
Santoro, N., 101
Santos, G. B., 198
Santos, L., 41, 313
Santos, R. M., 198

Saphire-Bernstein, S., 452
Sapolsky, R., 449
Saraulli, D., 277
Sareen, J., 575
Sargent, J. D., 131, 240, 242, 295, *296*, 405, 412, 435, 442
Sartorius, N., 650
Sassenrath, C., 503
Sathe, N., 657, 658
Satpute, A. B., 393, 530
Sauer-Zavala, S., 566
Savage, J., 445
Savage, J. H., 339
Savage-Rumbaugh, S., 317
Savard, J., 136
Savic, I., 424
Savin-Williams, R. C., 421
Saxe, R., 503
Sayette, M. A., 155, 664
Scalf, P., 444
Scarf, D., 346
Schab, F. R., 198
Schachler, D. L., 282
Schachter, H. M., 655
Schachter, S., 392, *392*, *394*, 411, 478, 504
Schacter, D., 270, 283, 493
Schafe, G. E., 251
Schaffer, M. M., 292
Schagdarsurengin, U., 340
Schaie, K. W., 378
Schank, R., 295
Schechter, J. C., 601
Schechtman, E., 45
Scheerer, M., 304, *304*
Schellenberg, E. G., 347
Scherer, P. E., 434
Schieve, L. A., 604
Schiff, N., 313
Schill, J., 581
Schiller, D., 252, 278
Schindler, I., 181
Schizophrenia Working Group of the Psychiatric Genomics Consortium, 593
Schlam, T. R., 443
Schlander, M., 656
Schmader, T., 331, 332
Schmahl, C., 599, 651
Schmidt, F. L., 321
Schmidt, L., 132, 405
Schmidt, N. B., 632, 636
Schmitt, D. P., 419, 420, 538, 540
Schmitz, T. W., 87
Schmukle, S. C., 543
Schnack, H. G., 593
Schneider, N. G., 442
Schneider, S. K., 473–80
Schnitzer, M. J., 195
Schoch, H., 253
Schoenbaum, G., 218
Schoenemann, P. T., 90
Schofield, P. R., 569
Schooler, J. W., 172
Schotter, E. R., 268
Schroeder, S. A., 441
Schuch, F. B., 444
Schuchat, A., 608
Schulenberg, J. E., 154, 155, 157, 441
Schultz, P. G., 329
Schultz, P. W., 480
Schultz, R., 605
Schultz, W., 220, 237
Schulz, K. M., 416
Schulze, R., 325
Schumann, C. M., 606
Schurz, M., 360

Schuurman, P. R., 638
Schwartz, B., 308–10
Schwartz, C. E., 520, *521*
Schwartz, G. E., 400
Schwartz, H. A., 504
Schwartz, J., 492
Schwartz, S., 140
Schwarz, N., 300, 485
Schwarzkopf, D. S., 172
Schwebel, D. C., 40
Schwerer, L. S., 609
Sclafani, A., 435
Scoboria, A., 644
Scott, A. A., 606
Scott, R. M., 360
Sears, D. O., 501
Sears, L., 388
Sechrest, L., 400
Sedikides, C., 8, 554–56
Seegmiller, J. K., 129
Seeley, J. R., 580
Seeman, T. E., 452
Seer, R. A., 582
Segal, N. L., 112
Segal, Z. V., 146, 641
Segerstrom, S. C., 453, 454
Sehgal, A., 133
Seibert, S., 127
Seibring, M., 480
Seidenberg, M. S., 317, 319
Seidman, L. J., 568, 594
Seirawan, H., 136
Selcuk, B., 361
Seligman, M. E. P., 16, 322, 459–60, 582, 633
Selkie, E. M., 370
Selye, H., 450
Seminowicz, D., *642*, 643
Sengelaub, D. R., 101
Serati, M., 646
Sergent, C., 123
Serhan, F., 432
Seth, P., 152
Sewlal, B., 332
Sha, L., 293
Shackelford, T. K., 421
Shaffer, E., 294
Shafran, R., 441
Shah, R. S., 627
Shallice, T., 261
Shamosh, N. A., 324
Shane, M. S., 529–30
Shanker, S. G., 317
Shapiro, A. F., 374
Sharp, W., 609
Sharpe, M. M., 585
Shaver, P. R., 507
Shaw, B., 582
Shaw, D. S., 601
Shaw, G. L., 347
Shaw, L. L., 485
Shaw, P., 609
Shaw, S., 456
Shedler, J., 618
Sheehan, M. J., 90
Sheeran, P., 396
Sheffield, A. M., 365
Sheidler, J., 156
Sheikh, K., 103
Sheline, Y. I., 593
Shelley, G., 484
Shelton, D. R., 441
Shelton, J., 551
Shenhav, A., 363
Shenkin, S. D., 329
Shenton, M. E., 124

Shepard, R., *187*
Shephard, R. J., 372
Sher, L., 591
Shera, D. M., 339
Shergill, S., 592
Sherif, C. W., 488
Sherif, M., 476, 488, *488–89*
Sherman, D. K., 609
Sherman, R. A., 424, 533
Sherman, S. J., 157, 441
Sherwin, B. B., 100, 416
Shetty, A. K., 80
Shi, Y., 8
Shidhaye, R., 581
Shiers, S. I., 221
Shiffrin, R., 256, 273
Shih, M., 331
Shihabuddin, L., 593
Shikany, J. M., 432
Shimada, N., 447
Shin, L. M., 388, 520, *521*, 579
Shiner, R. L., 535
Shiomura, K., 556
Shipstead, Z., 259
Shoda, Y., 409
Shook, N. J., 490
Short, K. R., 358
Shrager, E. E., 438
Shrout, P. E., 581
Shu, J., 393
Shults, R. A., 33, 45
Shumaker, R. W., 317
Sibley, C. G., 535
Siddarth, P., 124
Siegel, C. E., 609
Siegel, J. M., 137
Siegel, S., 223
Siegler, I. C., 455
Sievers, B., 399
Sigman, M., 606
Sijbrandij, M., 640–41
Siklenka, K., 340
Silber, M., 134
Silbersweig, D., 599
Silva, C. E., 144
Silva, P. A., 114, 520
Silva, S., 660
Silvers, J. A., 18, 396
Simeon, D., 586
Simion, F., 344
Simms, S., 570
Simner, J., 170
Simon, H. A., 259
Simon, S. L., 150
Simon, T., 320
Simoniswa, 267
Simons, D. J., 129, *130*
Simonsen, J., 372
Simonsen, N. R., 473–80
Simons-Morton, B. G., 40
Simpson, H. B., 637
Simpson, J., 102
Simpson, J. A., 101, 418
Sims, C., *602*
Sims, H. E. A., 437
Sims, T., 376
Singer, J., 392, *392*, *394*
Singer, L., 340
Singer, T., 361
Singh, T., 442
Singleton, J. B., 608
Sinnott-Armstrong, W., 363
Sio, U. N., 133
Sirois, B. C., 455
Sisk, C. L., 416, 440

Sjöström, M., 114
Skinner, B. F., 15, 224, *224*, 226, *226*, 227,
    232–233, 315, 525
Sklar, P., 583, 646
Skodol, A. E., 576, 581, 600
Skoner, D. P., 461
Skovgaard, L. T., 436
Slaughter, V., 361
Sleet, D., 124
Sloan, M. M., 195
Slovic, P., 300, 445
Sluming, V., 326
Slutske, W. S., 520
Small, G. W., 124
Smart, L., 550
Smethurst, C. J., 147
Smit, E., 431
Smith, A., 269
Smith, A. L., 443
Smith, A. P., *454*
Smith, C. J., 133, 138
Smith, D. H., 124
Smith, D. M., 182, 461
Smith, I. M., 259
Smith, J., 607
Smith, K. C., 116
Smith, K. S., 149, 221
Smith, L. B., 343
Smith, M. E., 152
Smith, S. M., 266, 431, 600
Smith, T. W., 458
Smithson, C., 223
Smits, J. A. J., 634
Smoot, M., 506
Snarey, J. R., 362
Snider, L. A., 578
Snidman, N., 520
Snowling, M. J., 319
Snyder, A. Z., 593
Snyder, E. E., 436
Snyder, H. R., 566
Snyder, S., 80
Sobel, J. L., 441
Sobel, N., 198
Soderstrom, S. B., 504
Sohn, J. H., 326
Sokol-Hessner, P., 300
Solms, M., 135, 140
Solomon, K. M., 87
Solovieff, N., 593
Solowij, N., 152
Somerville, L. H., 364, 388, 409
Sommers, K. L., 523
Sommerville, J. A., 360
Sommerville, R. B., 363
Soneji, D., 203
Soneji, S., 442
Song, C., 453
Song, H., 102, 579
Song, W. Z., 529
Son Hing, L. S., 501
Sonntag, A., 581
Soorya, L., 658
Sorensen, T., 436
Sorri, A., 594
Sourander, A., 595
Southgate, V., 606
Spanlang, B., 634
Spann, M., 634
Spanos, N. P., 144
Spearman, C., 322
Spelke, E. S., 357–58, 359, 496
Spence, M. J., 344
Spencer, M. B., 368
Spencer, R. C., 654

Spencer, S. J., 132, 331–32, 499
Spencer, T., 656
Sperling, G., *257*, 258
Sperry, R., 92, 96
Spiegel, D., 586
Spiegel, N., 507
Spieker, L. E., 456
Spieker, S. J., 352
Spiers, H. J., 86, 282
Spies, M., 641
Spinath, F. M., 327
Spinrad, T. L., 361
Spitzer, R. L., 576, 600
Sprecher, S., 373
Spreng, R. N., 376
Springer, D., 435
Spurr, K. F., 136
Squire, L. R., 39, 256
Squires-Wheeler, E., 594
Srivastava, S., 508, 529, 535
Stacy, A. W., 155
Stahl, D., 592
Stamatakis, E., 444
Stamm, J. M., 124
Stanovich, K. E., 6
Staples-Bradley, L. K., 579
Stappen, I., 198
Stark, C. E. L., 256
Stark, S., 411
Starr, J. M., 328, 329
Staudt, J., 357
Stavrinos, D., 40
Steele, C. M., 331
Steele, D., 432
Steen, T. A., 459
Steeves, J. K., 181
Stefanik, M. T., 116
Steger, K., 340
Stein, D. J., 575
Stein, M. B., 575
Stein, Y., 104
Steinberg, L., 365, 371
Steiner, J. E., 407
Steinhauer, S. R., 601
Stellar, E., 412, 438
Stelmack, R. M., 326
Stemmler, G., 385
Stender, J., 126
Stephenson, D., 461
Stepper, S., 391
Steptoe, A., 461
Stern, J., 267
Stern, W., 321
Sternberg, R. J., 323, 326, 507
Stevens, L. C., 444
Stewart, A., 302
Stewart, H. L., 552
Stewart, M. O., 634, 640
Stewart, T. L., 489
Stice, E., 436
Stickgold, R., 138
Stig Jorgensen, H., 312
Stillwell, D., 504
Stine-Morrow, E. A. L., 538
Stinson, F. S., 600
Stockwell, T., 154
Stohler, C. S., 628
Stokstad, E., 604
Stolier, R. M., 388, 471
Stone, A. A., 374, 453
Stone, V. E., 360
Stoner, J., 474
Stoney, C. M., 455
Stoolmiller, M., 442
Stopfer, J. M., 543

Storch, E. A., 634
Stouthamer-Loeber, M., 331
Strack, F., 131, 391
Strahan, E. J., 132
Straus, R., 455
Strayer, D. L., *37*, 129
Strayhom, T. L., 410
Streri, A., 359
Stribley, V., 153
Striegel-Moore, R. H., 440
Stringer, S., 583
Strobino, D. M., 659
Stroebe, W., 131
Strong, D. R., 442
Strunk, D., 634, 640
Strupp, H. H., 620
Stubbs, B., 444
Stucki, S., 451
Stuewig, J., 362
Stuewig, R., 599
Stump, J., 448–49
Stunkard, A. J., 436
Stürmer, T., 661
Styner, M., 606
Suarez, A., 651
Süß, H. M., 325
Substance Abuse and Mental Health Services
    Administration (SAMHSA), 659, *659*
Suchindran, C., 416
Sui, X., 444
Sui, Y., 150
Sulem, P., 45
Sulin, R. A., 263
Sullivan, L. M., 455
Sullivan, M. J. L., 202
Suls, J., 552
Summerfelt, A., 595
Sumner, J., 658
Sun, H. F., 529
Sundram, S., 593
Sungkhasettee, V. W., 261, 268
Super, C. M., 342
Suppes, T., 646
Surcet, H. M., 595
Susilo, T., 181
Sussex, J. N., 583
Susskind, J. M., 362
Sutter, M. E., 151
Suzuki, A., 517
Svärdsudd, K., 443
Svenson, O., 552
Svrakic, N., 518
Swaab, D. F., 367
Swann, W. B., Jr., 470
Swanson, J. M., 656
Swanson, S. A., 653, 661
Swartz, M. S., 598
Swartzwelder, S., 151
Swedo, S., 578
Swendsen, J., 155, 659
Swets, J. A., 168
Swift, D. L., 444
Syme, S. L., 461
Szkodny, L., 632

Tabernero, C., 501
Tachibana, R., 659
TADS Team, 660
Taheri, S., 136
Tai, K., 503
Tajfel, H., 471
Talarico, J. M., 280
Talavage, T., 124
Tallal, P., 319
Talley, P. R., 620
Talmi, D., 388

Tamaki, M., 141
Tanaka, C., 339
Tanaka, M., 367
Tanapat, P., 103
Tang, C. S. K., 447
Tang, Y., 329
Tang, Y. Y., 145
Tangney, J. P., 362, 599
Tateyama, M., 590
Tavor, I., 104
Taylor, A. K., 6, 132
Taylor, H. L., 437
Taylor, J., 87
Taylor, K., 103
Taylor, M. J., 79
Taylor, R. S., 620
Taylor, S. E., 451, 452, 552, 554
Taylor, S. F., 459
Taylor, T. J., 317
Taylor-Weiner, A., 80
Teasdale, J. D., 619
Tees, R. C., 313
Tejada-Vera, B., 432
Tell, R. A., 644
Tellegen, A., 112, 385, 407
Teller, D. Y., 345
Telzer, E. H., 470
Temple, E., 319, 360
Tenesa, A., 327
ten Vergert, M., 489
Teri, L., 376
Terman, L., 320
Terracciano, A., 539, 540
Terrace, H., 317
Tesch-Romer, C., 322
Tesco, G., 80
Tesser, A., 518
Tessler, L., 105
Teter, C. J., 150
Tetlock, P. E., 492
Tettamanti, M., 292
Teuber, H. L., 255
Tharmaphornpilas, P., 432
Tharp, G., 484
Thase, M. E., 620, 638, 640, 641
Thelen, E., 343
Thibaut, A., 126
Thisted, R. A., 410
Thiyagarajan, M., 137
Thomas, A., 269, 370
Thomas, A. D., 157
Thomas, C., 606
Thomas, P. R., 147
Thomas, R., 609
Thompson, K. M., 155
Thompson, L., 133
Thompson, P., 181
Thompson, P. M., 150, 323, 325
Thompson-Brenner, H., 629
Thomson, B., 434, 436
Thomson, D. M., 266
Thöny, B., 449
Thorgeirsson, T. E., 45
Thorn, B., 202
Thorndike, E., 225, *225*
Thornhill, R., 506
Thornicroft, G., 581
Thout, M., 21
Tian, J., 221
Tice, D., 452
Tickle, J. J., 240
Tienari, P., 594
Tierney, S. C., 629
Tillmann, B., 22
Timmerman, T. A., 483

Tipper, C. M., 128
Titus-Ernstoff, L. T., 295, *296*
Tobin, D. D., 370
Todd, A. R., 503
Todd, R. M., 277
Todorov, A. T., 388, 496
Toguchi, Y., 556
Tohkura, Y. I., 314
Tolin, D. F., 634
Tolman, E. C., 236, *236*
Tolson, J. M., 369
Tomasello, M., 313, 360
Tomkins, S., 391
Tonegawa, S., 252, 254
Tong, F., 122, 181
Tonkin, A. L., 659
Tononi, G., 141
Tooby, J., 19
Toppino, T. C., 138
Torgerson, S., 598
Torrey, B. B., 595
Torrey, E. F., 594–95
Toth, S., 352
Tourville, J. A., 127
Tovote, P., 221
Towvim, L. G., 473–80
Tracy, J. L., 399, 549
Traffanstedt, M. K., 641
Tranel, D., 301, 363, 388
Trask, S., 216
Treadway, M. T., 567
Treanor, J. J., 461
Treasure, J., 441
Treffert, D. A., 326
Treiman, R., 268
Tremblay, A., 436
Trentacosta, C. J., 601
Trentacoste, S. V., 604
Tressel, P. A., 150
Triandis, H., 555
Triplett, N., 473
Trivers, R. L., 486
Tronick, E. Z., 348
Tropp, L. R., 502
Trudeau, J., *490*
Truong, N. L., 656
Tryon, G. S., 618
Tryon, W. W., 618
Trzesniewski, K. H., 549
Tsai, L. H., 278
Tsakanikos, E., 170
Tsao, F. M., 314
Tshibanda, L., 125
Tsien, J. Z., 253–54, 329
Tsuang, M. T., 568, 594
Tucker, M., 138
Tuerlinckx, F., 384
Tuescher, O., 599
Tugade, M. M., 459
Tuholski, S. W., 325
Tulving, E., 263, 266, 270, 272
Turcotte, K. D., 150
Turecki, G., 449
Turk, C. L., 485
Turk, J., 340
Turkheimer, E., 516–17, 518
Turner, E. H., 644
Turner, G., 545
Turner, G. R., 376
Turner, J., 471
Turner, R. B., 461
Tversky, A., 297, *297*, 302, 335
Twenge, J. M., 424, 551
Tye, K. M., 116
Tyler, C. W., 397
Tyndall, M., 152

Tyrrell, D. A., *454*
Tzuang, G., 153

Ubel, P. A., 461
Uchida, N., 221
Uçok, A., 592
Udd, M., 646
Udry, J. R., 416
Uguz, F., 568
Uhlmann, E., 492
Ullrich, S., 600
Umberson, D., 372, 461
Unger, R. H., 434
Ungerleider, L. G., 175, 293
United Nations Office on Drugs and Crime, 147, 484, *484*
Upadhya, D., 80
Updegraff, J. A., 451
Urashima, H., 367
Urban, E. J., 376
Urberg, K. A., 369
Urrutia, M. S., 326
U.S. Bureau of Labor Statistics, 25, 205
U.S. Department of Health and Human Services, 234
U.S. Department of Transporation, *37*
U.S. Fish and Wildlife Service, 207
U.S. Food and Drug Administration, 191, 644
U.S. Health and Human Services Department, 441, 442, 443, *659*
U.S. State Department, 445
Usher, M., 582
Uttl, B., 267
Uvnas-Moberg, K., 462
Uzzi, B., 504

Vaccarino, F. J., 100
Vaccaro, D., 168
Vacic, V., 646
Vågerö, D., 323
Vaghi, M. M. S., 292
Vaidya, J., 385, 407
Vaituzis, A. C., 103
Valdesolo, P., 300
Valdimaradottir, H., 453
Valentine, K. A., 506
Valiente, C., 371
Vallabha, G. K., 348
Vallières, A., 136
Valyear, K. F., 181
Van Bavel, J. J., 36, 470, 472
van Berckelaer-Onnes, I. A., 352
Van Bockxmeer, F. M., 444
Van Camp, A. R., 294
Vancampfort, D., 444
van den Heuvel, M. P., 593
van den Munckhof, P., 638
Van der Oord, S., 655
van der Vyver, J. M., 398
Van de Water, J., 606
VanElzakker, M. B., 579
Van Gastel, A., 453
Van Haren, N. E., 593
Vanhaudenhuyse, A., 125
Van Hulle, C. A., 519–20
van Ijzendoorn, M. H., 352
Vanilovich, I., 329
van Kamp, S., 502
van Knippenberg, A., 552
Van Lange, P. A. M., 483, 509
Van Oost, B. A., 483
Van Paesschen, W., 272
VanSchyndel, S. K., 361
Vansteelandt, K., 638
Van Well, S., 449
Vardenaar, K. J., 575

Varejao, M., 655
Vargas-Reighley, R. V., 368
Vargha-Khadem, F., 272
Varigonda, A. L., 79
Varner, J. L., 238
Vasey, P. L., 421–23
Vaughan, J. T., 122
Vazire, S., 543, 544, *544*
Vázquez, A., 470
Vázquez, G., 583
Vchoda, H., 649
Vega, D., 599
Velasquez, I., 145
Venables, P., 600, 601
Vendruscolo, M., 376
Venkatraman, V., 119
Verdi, G., 655
Vermetten, E., 586
Vernon, P. A., 326, 517
Vespa, J., 508
Victora, C. G., 329
Viechtbauer, W., 536
Vieira, A., 545
Vieta, E., 646
Viki, G. T., 22
Vilain, E., 421–23
Villemagne, V. L., 376
Vincent, J. D., 198
Vincent, J. E., 479
Vismara, L., 657
Vitkup, D., 606
Vivanathan, K., 443
Vogrincic, C., 487
Vohs, K. D., 419, 490, 550
Voils, C. I., 502
Volkmar, F., 603, 605
Volkow, N. D., 148, 156, 340, 412
Volkow, N. E., 168
Volz, K. G., 472
von Békésy, G., 192
von Cramon, D. Y., 186, 472
von Helholtz, H., 192
Voon, V., *642*, 643
Voracek, M., 347, 540
Vosshall, L. B., 198
Vrangalova, Z., 422
Vredenburg, D. S., 552
Vuilleumier, P., 385
Vygotsky, L., 356
Vytal, K., 391

Waber, D., 326
Wadden, T., 437
Wadden, T. A., 143
Wadsworth, M. E., 448–49
Wadsworth, T., 461
Wager, T. D., 223, 385, 459, 628
Wagner, A. D., 390
Wagner, A. R., 218
Wagner, C., 486
Wagner, D. D., 122, 131, 223, 405, 483
Wagner, M. T., 153
Waite, L. J., 372, 410
Waiter, G. D., 244
Wakefield, A. J., 607–8
Wakefield, J. C., 565
Wald, M. M., 124
Walder, D. J., 568, 594
Walker, D. L., 634
Walker, E. F., 593, 594, 633, 648
Walker, E. R., 573
Walker, K., 80
Walker, M. P., 139
Walker, R. L., 568
Walkup, J. T., 661
Wall, P. D., 202

Wall, S., 350
Waller, R., 601
Walsh, T., 593
Walster, E. H., 506, 507
Walters, E. E., 277, 564, 578
Walton, G. M., 332
Walton, K. E., 536
Waltrip, R. W., 595
Walts, B. M., 436
Wampold, B. E., 629
Wamsley, E. J., 138
Wanderling, J. A., 609
Wang, C. S., 502, 503
Wang, G. J., 148
Wang, H., 329
Wang, J. H., 145
Wang, L., 376
Wang, P. S., 564, 574, 576, 577, 580, 583, 630
Wang, P. W., 646
Wang, R., 543
Wang, X., 472
Ward, A., 308–10
Ward, P., 444
Warden, R., 599
Wardle, J., 436
Warneken, F., 361
Warner, M., 152
Warren, F. C., 620
Warren, J. R., 452
Warren, Z., 657, 658
Warrington, E., 261
Warsley, R., 101
Wassermann, E. M., 642
Watanabe, M., 659
Waters, E., 350
Watkins, K. E., 272
Watson, B., 609
Watson, D., 385, 407, 529, 530
Watson, J. B., 208, 211, 221, 226, 570
Watson, J. D., 107
Watson, J. M., 129
Watson, N. V., 101
Wattanapenpaiboon, N., 434
Watters, C., 324
Waugh, C. E., 459
Waxler, N. E., 589
Webb, T. L., 396
Weber, E., 167
Weber, E. U., 300
Weber, J., 393
Weber, M., 278
Wechsler, D., 320, *320*
Wechsler, H., 480
Wecht, C. H., 124
Wegener, D. T., 494
Wegner, D., 395
Weiderpass, E., 443
Weidner, G., 455
Weinberg, W. A., 659
Weinberger, J. L., 534, 542
Weiner, B., 497
Weintraub, E. S., 607
Weisberg, R. W., 306
Weise-Kelly, L., 224
Weisnagel, S. J., 436
Weiss, A., 325
Weissman, M. M., 577, 619, 661
Weitzman, E. R., 155
Welch, N., 300
Welham, J. L., 589
Weller, A., 352
Wells, B. E., 424
Wells, G. L., 284
Wells, H. G., 226
Wells, J. E., 581
Wells, K., 660

Wells, R. E., 308
Welte, J. W., 143, 154
Werker, J. F., 313, 348
Wernicke, C., 312, *312*
Wertz, A. E., 239
Wertz, J., 610
West, B. T., 150
West, S. G., 544
Westen, D., 525, 629
Weston, T., 130
Wexler, N., 104
Weyandt, L. L., 150, 655
Whalen, C. K., 608
Whalen, P. J., 87, 387, 388, 397, 505
Whalley, B., 620
Whalley, L. J., 328
Wheatley, T., 143, 301, 363, 399
Wheeler, D., 479
Wheeler, L., 486, 507
Wheelwright, S., 397
Whiskin, E. E., 415
Whitbeck, L. B., 371
White, A., 155
White, B. J., 488
White, C. M., 153
White, J. M., 153
White, K., 308–10
Whiteford, H. A., 581
Whiteman, V., 340
Whitfield-Gabrieli, S., 569
Whitney, C. G., 608
Whitson, J. A., 502
Whittle, S., 152
Whorf, B., 313, *313*
Wich, S. A., 317
Wicherski, M., *23*
Wichmann, T., 627
Wicker, B., 386
Wickett, J. C., 326
Widiger, T. A., 597
Wiener, J., 324
Wierson, M., 364
Wierzbicki, M., 339
Wiese, D., 385, 407
Wiesel, T. N., 102
Wigfield, A., 410
Wiggs, C. L., 293
Wight, R. G., 373
Wigler, M., 605, 606
Wikramaratne, P., 661
Wilens, T. E., 654, 656
Wilfley, D. E., 440
Wilhelm, O., 259, 325
Wilhelmsen, L., 443
Wilke, M., 326
Willeit, M., 641
Willemsen, A. T., 588
Williams, C. L., 542
Williams, H. J., 593, 606
Williams, J. B. W., 576, 600
Williams, J. H. G., 244
Williams, K., 475
Williams, L. M., 569
Williams, M. E., 373
Williams, R., 455
Williams, R. J., 442
Williams, S. C., 116, 326
Williams, W. A., 642
Williman, J., 442
Wills, T. A., 168, 442, 461
Wilson, A. E., 553, *553*
Wilson, G. T., 440
Wilson, K., 443, 655
Wilson, M. A., 138
Wilson, T. D., 301–2

Wilson, W., 151
Wilson-Mendenhall, C. D., 385
Wiltshire, S., *326*, 327
Winberg, J., 344
Winblad, B., 376
Winfield, I., 598
Winkler, D., 641
Winslow, J. T., 658
Winter, J. E., 434
Wise, B. M., 129
Wiseman, R., 171
Wiste, A., 45
Witherby, S. A., 170
Witherspoon, D., 272
Wittmann, W. W., 325
Wolf, E., 138
Wolfe, B. L., 339
Wolff, J. J., 606
Wolke, D., 370
Wolpert, D. M., 200
Wolsic, B., 507
Wolters, C. A., 410
Woo, H. K., 133
Wood, D., 535, 536, 538
Wood, D. M., 153
Wood, J. M., 541
Wood, L. M., 324
Wood, M. A., 254
Wood, W., 400, 418
Woodcock, J., 152
Woodruff, G., 360
Woods, S. W., 594
Woodward, A. L., 360
Woodworth, K. A., 437
Woodworth, M., 600
Woody, E. Z., 144
World Health Organization, 432, 434, 441, 454,
    564, 580
Woulbroun, E. J., 518
Wray, N. R., 583, 593
Wright, C. I., 388, 520, *521*
Wright, E. J., 127
Wright, R. J., 456
Wright, S. C., 502
Wu, C., 505
Wu, H., 478
Wu, H. Y., 138
Wu, J., 329, 339
Wu, L., 8
Wu, M. N., 133
Wu, M. S., 634
Wu, P., 443
Wurm, M., 455
Wyland, C. L., 547, *547*
Wynn, K., 239, 313
Wynne, L. C., 594

Xiao, J., 444
Xiao, S., 581
Xie, L., 137
Xu, J., 372, 431, 432, 445, 461
Xu, L., 124
Xu, Q., 137
Xu, X., 472

Yaffe, R., 658
Yamada, A. M., 573
Yamagata, S., 517
Yamaguchi, S., 556
Yamamoto, B. K., 153
Yamrom, B., 606
Yan, W., 341
Yang, J., 313, 327
Yang, J. S., 410
Yano, R., 367

Yardy, M. M., 340
Yarkoni, T., 387
Yarmolusky, D. A., 195
Yashima, Y., 659
Yates, D., 278
Yazar-Klosinski, B., 153
Yazdy, M. M., 340
Yeo, R. A., 323, 326
Yeshurun, Y., 198
Yoo, S. S., 139
Yoon, P. W., 445
Yoon, S., 606, 646
Yoshikawa, S., 506
Yoshimura, K., 517
Young, A. W., 180, 387
Young, J. F., 566
Young, L. J., 116, 658
Young, R. C., 508
Youyou, W., 504
Yu, T., 339
Yuan, S., 360
Yucel, M., 152
Yue, Z., 133
Yuille, J. C., 282
Yurak, T. J., 552

Zabetian, A., 432
Zagoory-Sharon, O., 352
Zahn-Waxler, C., 361, 401, 486
Zaidan, H., 449
Zajonc, R., 473, 490, 504
Zak, P. J., 462
Zaki, J., 386
Zametkin, A. J., 609
Zammit, T., 594
Zanarini, M. C., 599, 651
Zanna, M. P., 132, 501
Zarabi, H., 116
Zatorre, R. J., 22, 238
Zautra, A. J., 447
Zavras, B. M., 150
Zebian, S., 50
Zeigler Hill, V., 550
Zeki, S., 416
Zeller, S. L., 583
Zervas, I. M., 642
Zetterberg, H., 124
Zha, W., 155
Zhang, F., 116
Zhang, H., 600
Zhang, J. X., 529
Zhang, T. Y., 519
Zhao, J., 154
Zheng, M., 9
Zhou, F., 608
Zibbell, J. E., 152
Zielinski, B. A., 96
Zieselman, A. L., 412, 435
Zihl, J., 186
Zimbardo, P., 473
Zimmermann, J., 537
Ziv, N., 22
Zobel, A. W., 581
Zola-Morgan, S., 39
Zonderman, A., 376
Zorrilla, E. P., 414
Zuberbühler, K., 317
Zubieta, J. K., 628
Zuckerman, M., 549
Zuker, C. S., 195
Zuo, X., 472
Zusman, R., 278
Zwiers, M. P., 609

Subject Index

Page numbers in *italics* refer to illustrations.

Abelson, Robert, 295
absentmindedness, 275–76, *275*
Abu Ghraib prison (Iraq), 474, *474*
abuse:
    and memory, 283
    and psychological disorders, 587, 599
    self-, 598, 651
    substance, 621
    see also addiction; *specific substance*
acceptance, unconditional, 527, 621
accidental death, 445–46
accommodation, in relationships, 509
accommodation, in schemes, 354
accommodation, visual, 173, 509
accuracy, and research methodology, 57
acetaminophen, 203
acetylcholine (ACh), 78–79, *78, 79*, 639
    and Alzheimer's, 376
achievement motivation, 408
Acquired Immune Deficiency Syndrome
    (AIDS), 153, 155, 453
acquisition, and learning, 236–37
action potential:
    and nervous system, 72–75, *74*
    and psychological disorders, 623
activation, and self-knowledge, 547–48, *547*
    see also spreading activation models
activation-synthesis theory, 140–41
activity level, and temperament, 519–21
actor-observer discrepancy, 498
adaptation:
    and attachment, 347–48, 349, *349*
    and brain, 18–19, 339
    characteristic, 535
    and culture, 20–21
    and development, 339
    and emotions, 396–402
    and genes, 13, 110
    and harming and helping others, 486
    and learning, 217
    of mind, 19
    and motivation, 406, 421
    and personality, 535
    and psychological disorders, 574
    and reproduction, 13, 18–19
    and scientific foundations of psychology, 13
    and self-knowledge, 552
    and sensation, 169, *169*
    and sexual behavior, 421
    and sleep as adaptive behavior, 137–39
    and survival, 13, 20
    and themes of psychological science, 13
    see also brain, plasticity of
adaption, and learning, 212
Adderall, 150, 654, 655
addiction:
    to alcohol, 155–56
    and behaviors affecting health,
        442, 443

biology of, 156–58
    to drugs, 156–58, 223–24
    and genetics, 442
    and learning, 221
adenosine, and sleep, 142
adjustment disorder, 579
Adler, Alfred, 524
adolescence:
    and biology, *364*
    changes during, 363–71, *364*
    depression in, *660*
    and identity, 365–68
    and psychological disorders, 600, 606, 609,
        653–61, *660*
    and risk taking, 364
    and stress, 364
    see also puberty
adolescent growth spurt, 363
adoption studies:
    and genetic basis of psychological science,
        111–13
    and obesity, 436
    and personality, 517–18
    and psychological disorders, 569,
        594, 601
adrenal glands, 449, 450
adrenaline, 79, 393
adulthood, meaning in, 371–78
affect, *see* emotions
affect-as-information theory, 300
affective disorders, 600
    see also moods; psychological disorders
affective forecasting, 301, *301*
affective heuristic, 301–2
affiliation, 451, 504–7
aftereffects, 186
afterimage, 177, *177*
after-the-fact explanations, 7, 94–95, *95*
age, aging, 375–76, *375*, 650
    and low BMI, 434
    and personality, 535–36
    and psychological disorders, 650, 653
age regression, 283
aggression:
    biological factors in, 483–84
    definition of, 482
    factors influencing, 482–85
    and learning, 239, *239*, 241–43
    and personality, 530
    and psychological disorders, 652
    and situation factors, 473–74
    social and cultural aspects of, 484–85, *484,
        485*
    see also violence
agonists, 77, *78*
agoraphobia, 576
agreeableness, 528, 538–39
AIDS, 153, 155, 453
Ainsworth, Mary D. Salter, 349–50
air pressure, and audition, 188–91
Albert B. (case study), 221, *222*, 571

alcohol:
    abuse of, 148–49, 155–56, 372, 452, 564, 571,
        571, 621, 632
    addiction to, 155–56
    and aging, 375
    and behaviors affecting health, 463
    and binge drinking, 154–55, *154*
    and children, 155, *296*
    and consciousness, 156–58
    and development, 340
    and driving, 155
    effects of, 37
    and epigenetic tags, 114
    and GABA, 155
    and gender, 155, *155*
    and influence of neurotransmission, 80
    and memory, 267
    and sleep, 142
    treatment of problems with, 621
alcoholism, *see* alcohol, abuse of
alertness, 531, *531*
Alex (parrot), 317–18
algorithm, 305
all-or-none principle, 75
Allport, Gordon, 516, *516*, 528
Almond, Paul, 534
alpha waves, 134, *134*
alternative treatments, 625–28, 641–43, 658
    see also biological therapies
altruism, 482, 486
Alvarez, Luis, 171
Alzheimer's disease, 79, 375, 376, *376*
Amazon, 67
Ambady, Nalini, 496
ambivalent attachment, 351–52, 507
American Honey (film), *507*
American Psychiatric Association, 440, 564
American Psycho (film), 551
American Psychological Association,
    633, 643
American Sign Language, 316
American Speech-Hearing-Language
    Association, 193
America's Got Talent (TV show), 8
Ames, Albert, 184
Ames boxes, 184, *185*
amiable skepticism, 5–6, 27
Amish community study, 583–84
amnesia, 79, 276–77, 586
    childhood, 280
    retrograde, 587
    source, 280
amphetamines, 148, 150, 153
amplitude, of sound waves, *188*, 189
amputation, 104, *104*, 201
amygdala, 579
    and aggression, 483
    and basic structure and functions of brain,
        86–87, *86*
    and emotions, 386–88, *386, 387*, 388
    and judging trustworthiness, 496

amygdala (*continued*)
    and memory, 277
    and morality, 363
    and motivation, 409
    and personality, 520
    and psychological disorders, 601, *602*
    and sensation, *199*
    and sleep, 139, *140*
    and stereotypes, 502
analogical representations, 290, *290*, 291
analogies, finding appropriate, 306
anal-retentive personalities, 525
anal stage, 524
analysis, *see* data, analysis and evaluation of;
        levels of analysis
analytical intelligence, 323
analytical skills, 67
anchoring, 298, *298*, *302*
    versus framing, 302–3
Anderson, Norman, 504
androgens, 100, 367, 416, 423
anger, 460, 598, 622
    see also hostility
animals:
    communication of, 317–18, *317*
    olfactory capabilities of, 199
    research on, 53–54, *54*, 101–2, 114, *114*, 116,
        449, 606, 658
Ankiel, Rick, 287
anonymity, 52, *52*
    and bystander apathy, 487
anorexia nervosa, *438*, 439, *439*, 570, *571*
antagonists, 77, *78*
anterograde amnesia, 276, *276*
anti-anxiety medications, 623, 634, 636, 652
antibodies, and autism spectrum disorder, 606
anticipatory coping, 457
anticonvulsive medications, 623, 646
antidepressant medications, 624, 638–39, 640, 646
    and placebo effect, 644
antipsychotic medications, 592, 624–25, 647–50,
        649
antisocial personality disorders (APD), *571*, 596,
        599–601, *600*, 650, 652–53, *653*
anxiety, 566, 640
    and addiction, 155
    and behaviors affecting health, 436, 437, 442,
        460
    and conformity, 478
    and culture, 622
    and health, 460
    and immune system, 453
    and influence of neurotransmission, 80
    and inhibition, *602*
    and insomnia, 136
    and interpersonal relations, 401
    and learning, 221, 232
    and motivation, 410–11
    and psychological disorders, 564, 566, 573–76,
        598, *602*
    and self-knowledge, 550
    separation, 349–50
    social, 550
    treatment for, 619, 626, 634–36
anxiolytics, 623
anxious attachment, 351
anxious/resistant attachment, 351
aphagia, 412
aphasia, 312–13
aplysia, 209, *210*
applied behavioral analysis (ABA), *656*, 657–58,
        657
appraisals:
    and coping, 457
    reflected, 549

approach motivations, 407
Apted, Michael, 534
aptitude, 320
argument, 494–95
Aristotle, 10, 562
Armstrong, Lance, 100, *100*
Aronson, Eliot, 494
arousal:
    of emotions, 384, *384*, 391–95
    and influence of neurotransmission, 79
    and motivation, 403, 404, 417
    and personality traits, 531, *531*
    and psychological disorders, 574, 600, 652
    and sleep, 135
    and themes of psychological science, 17
Asch, Solomon, 476–77, *477*
asexuality, 422
Asperger's syndrome, 604
assessment:
    and clinical interview, 567
    definition of, 567
    evidence-based, 568
    of personality, 540–46
    of psychological disorders, 564–68, *565*,
        567–68, *567*
    see also specific tests
assimilation, 354
association:
    of events, 218
    loosening of, 591
association networks, 265–68, *265*
Ativan, 623
Atkinson, Richard, 256, *257*
attachment, 347–52, *348*, 507
    definition of, 347
attention:
    and conscious awareness, 127–31
    and intelligence, 326
    joint, 313, *314*
    overselectivity of, 657
    and psychological disorders, 564, 651, 657,
        657
    selective, 128–29
    and technology in the classroom, 120–31, *130*
    see also focusing
attention-deficit/hyperactivity disorder
        (ADHD), *571*, 603, *603*, 608–9, *609*, 654–56,
        655
attention span, 574
attitudes:
    accessibility of, 491
    and behavior, 490–95
    change in, 493
    definition of, 490
    and emotions, 460
    formation of, 490–95
    and health, 459–65
    and social psychology, 490–95
attributional dimensions, 497
attributions, 497–98, 509, 582
atypical antipsychotic medications, 648
audition, 188
    see also hearing
auditory cortex, 189
auditory hallucinations, 591, 649
auditory information, *see* hearing
auditory localization, *192*
auditory nerve, 189
auditory processing, and levels of analysis, 22
authority, 480–82, *481*
autism spectrum disorder (ASD), 326, 327, 352,
        603–6, *603*, *604*, *605*, 617, 654, 656–59, *656*
    and antibodies, 606
    and brain, 606
    and IQ, 657, 659

and mirror neurons, 606
and schizophrenia, 606
and vaccinations, 607–8, *607*
autokinetic effect, 476
automatic processing, 127–28, *128*
autonomic arousal, and polygraph tests, 389–90,
        389–90
autonomic nervous system (ANS), 70, 98–99,
        574
    and emotions, 385, 391
autoreception, 77
autoshaping, 243
availability heuristic, 299, *299*
averaging, 50
avoidance motivations, 407
avoidant attachment, *351*, 507
avoidant personality disorder, 597
awareness:
    and psychological disorders, 586–89
    self-, 474, 547
    and stereotypes, 501
    and study of consciousness, *123*
    see also autism spectrum disorder;
        consciousness
axons:
    and basic structure and functions of brain, 87
    definition of, 71
    and development of brain, 101
    and nervous system, 71–72, *72*, 74
    and sensation, 174, 201
Azelea, Iggy, *499*

babbling, 314
Back, Kurt, 504
Baillargeon, Renée, 357
balance, 189–90
Bale, Christian, 551
Banaji, Mahzarin, 491
Bandura, Albert, 239, *239*, 408, 525, *526*
Bard, Philip, 391
Barger, Albert, 222
Bargh, John, 131
Barlow, David, 629, 636
Barnum, P. T., 91
Bartlett, Frederic, 264
Bartoshuk, Linda, 195, *196*
basal ganglia, *86*, 87, 609
base rate, 299
basic tendencies, 535
basilar membrane, 189
Batson, Daniel, 485
Baumeister, Roy, 147, 401, 410, 419, 550
Bayer Aspirin Company, 150–51, *151*
B cells, 453
Beautiful Mind, A (film), *589*
Beck, Aaron T., 582, 619, *619*, 640
Beckham, David, 240, *240*
bedwetting, 603
behavior:
    affecting physical health, 430–32
    and attitudes, 490–95
    and biology, 69–119
    crowd, 475
    and culture, 20–21
    and death, 445–46
    definition of, 4
    deviant, 473–74
    disorganized and inappropriate, 592
    and genetics/genes, 18, 111–13, 436, 442
    groups' influence on individual, 473–75
    influence of neurotransmission on, 76–80
    interpreting of, 94–95, *95*
    as learned, 619
    and motivation, 402–27
    and operant conditioning, 224–38

and personality, 543, *543*
and psychological disorders, 574, 589, 592, 594, 604
purpose of, 13
and scripts, 295
and study of consciousness, 131
and themes of psychological science, 4, 18–19, *20*
thin slices of, 497
and thought/thinking, 16
unconscious processing as influence on, 131
see also behavioral approach system; behavioral genetics; behavioral inhibition system; behavioral therapy; behaviorism; behavior modification; cognitive-behavioral therapy; dialectical behavior therapy; emotions; learning; motivation; rewards; social psychology; *specific psychological disorders; types of behavior*
behavioral approach system (BAS), 531, *531*
behavioral economics, 335
behavioral genetics, 111–13, 116, 422–24
behavioral inhibition system (BIS), 531, *531*
behavioral therapy:
  and choosing a practitioner, 630–33, *632*
  and treatment of psychological disorders, 618–19, 637, 651, 652, 656, 657
  see also cognitive-behavioral therapy
behaviorism:
  definition of, 15
  and development, 348
  founding of, 208
  influence of, 208
  and learning, 235–37
  and personality, 525, 526
  and psychological disorders, 570, 617
  and scientific foundations of psychology, 15
Behaviorism (Watson), 226
behavior modification, 230–35, *234*, 617, 619, 656
  definition of, 233
  and exercise, 232–33, *234*
  and scientific foundations of psychology, 15
Békésy, Georg von, 192
beliefs:
  and development, 366, 368
  and identity, 366, 368
  and memory, 273, 278–79
  and personality, 526
  and treatment of psychological disorders, 619
Bem, Daryl, 171–72
benzodiazepines, 80, 149, 623
Berscheid, Ellen, 507
beta waves, 134, *134*
better-than-average effect, 552
Bever, Tom, 317, 358, *359*
Beyoncé, *504*
Beyond Freedom and Dignity (Skinner), 15
bias:
  attributional, 497–98
  confirmation, 284, *284*
  correspondence, 497
  and critical thinking, 5
  in decision making, 298
  heuristic, 7–8
  ingroup-outgroup, 500
  and memory, 278, 280
  observer, 42
  optimism, 446
  and psychological reasoning, 6–8
  and research methodology, 42, 644
  response, 169, *169*
  selection, 50
  self-serving, 7, 553–54
  and sensation, 169, *169*
biases, 335

Bickerton, Derek, 317
bicultural identity, 368
Bieber, Justin, 516, *516*
Big Bang Theory (TV show), 323, *323*
Big Five, 528–29, *529*, 534, 538, 541, 542, 543, 597
Bill and Melinda Gates Foundation, 23–24, 432
Binet, Alfred, 320, *320*, 322
Binet-Simon Intelligence Scale, 320
binge drinking, 154–55, *155*
  and social norms marketing, 479–80
binge eating, *439*, 440
binocular convergence, 183, *183*
binocular depth cues, 182, *184*
binocular disparity, 182, *183*
biological needs, 228, 403, 407, 412
biological preparedness, 217–18, *218*
biological psychology, 24
biological revolution, 17–18, *17*
biological therapies:
  and brain stimulation, 626–28, 637–38, *642*, 643
  limitation of, 616
  and magnetic fields, 626–27
  and pseudotherapies, 629–30
  and psychosurgery, 626, 638, 647
  and treatment of psychological disorders, 616, 625–28, 658
  see also alternative treatments
biological trait theory, 529–32, *530*
biology:
  of addiction, 156–58
  and adolescence, *364*
  and aggression, 483–84
  and behavior, 69–119
  constraints of, 235–36, *236*
  and culture, 365–68
  and development, 363–71
  and gender, 367–68
  and identity, 365–68
  and learning, 235–38
  and motivation, 423–24
  and operant conditioning, 235–36
  of personality, 516
  and psychological disorders, 79, 568–69, *569*, 574, 577, 581–82, 605–6
  and psychopathology, 563
  and schizophrenia, 592–95
  and sexual behavior, 416–18, *417*, 423–24
  and stress, 449–50
  see also brain; genetics/genes; *specific parts of brain*
biopsychosocial approach, 430, *430*
bipolar disorder, 561–62, 570, *571*, 582–84, 623, 645–47
  and genetics, 583–84, 646
bipolar I disorder, 583, *583*
bipolar II disorder, 583, *583*
bisexuality, 422
blank slate, mind as, 208
blind spots, 174, *174*
Block, Jack, 156, 458
blocking, 237, 274–75
blocking effect, 237
blushing, 401
Bobo doll study, 239, *239*, 240–41
body, *see* mind-body problem
body language, 496–97, *496*
body maps of emotion, *386*
body mass index (BMI), 432–33, *433*
  as predictor of health, 433–34
body shape index, 433
body weight, as socially contagious, 435, *436*
Boggs, Wade, 243
Bolles, Robert, 236
Bonanno, George, 396

bonobo ape, Kanzi, 317
borderline personality disorder, 596, 597–99, *598*, 650–51, *651*
Boston Marathon bombings, 279, *279*, 445
Botox, 79, *79*
bottom-up processing, 164, 182
botulism, 79
Bouchard, Claude, 436
Bowlby, John, 348, 349
brain:
  adaptation of, 18–19, 339
  and aging, 375, 376
  and autism spectrum disorder, 606
  basic structure and functions of, 81–97, *91*, *93*, 326
  bilateral structure of, 103
  computer analogy of, 16
  critical periods for, 101
  and deep brain stimulation, 88–89
  development of, 101–5, 339–40, 360
  division of, 92–95, *93*
  and eating, 339, 412
  and emotions, 360–61, 384, 385–88
  and environment, 87
  evolution of, 18–19
  and exercise, 444
  and finding patterns, 6
  and gender, 103–4, *103*, 366–67
  and group membership, 470, *471*, 472
  hemisphere specialization in, 96
  information-processing theories about, 16
  injuries to, 22, 39, 90–92, 103, 104, 124–27, 139, 254–55, 272
  and intelligence, 324–27
  and language, 93, 103, *103*, 312–13, *312*, 314, 316
  and learning, 87, 102, 221, 237–38, 360
  and learning disabilities, 105
  and levels of analysis, *21*, 22
  localization of function in, 17–18
  and malnutrition, 339
  and meditation, 145–46, *146*
  and memory, 252–54, 255, 263, *268*, 272–73, 277, 376
  and mind, 4, 9, 16
  and motivation, 412, 416, 421, 423–24
  neonatal, 595
  and neuron integration into communication systems, 97–101
  and perception, *165*, 181, 194–95
  and personality, 90–91, *91*, 520
  plasticity of, 101–3, *102*, 104, 339
  and psychological disorders, 569, 574, 593–94, 601, *602*, 606, 623, 625–26, 634–35, 638, 639, 641, 643, 647, 658
  and psychophysiological assessment, 82–84
  and research methodology, 39, 81–85
  and restrained eaters, 438
  and scientific foundations of psychology, 16
  and self-knowledge, 547–48, *547*
  and sensation, *165*, *166*, 188, *194–95*, *200–1*
  and sexual behavior, 423–24
  size of, 326, 606
  and sleep, 133–42, *134*
  and smell, *198–99*
  specialization in, 81
  and speech production, *82*
  speed of mental processing in, 324–25
  and spinal cord, *81*
  stimulation of, 627–28, *627*, 637–38, *642*, 643
  and stress, 449
  and study of consciousness, 122–24, *123*
  and teen years, 364
  and treatment of psychological disorders, 623, 625–26, 634–35, 638, 639, 641, 643, 647, 654, 658

brain (*continued*)
    and visual receptors, 172–76
    see also neurons; neurotransmission; *specific
        parts and functions of brain*
brain activity, patterns of, 292–93, *293*
brain connectivity, 18
brain death, 126, *126*
Braingatez, 119
brain imaging:
    and basic structure and functions of brain,
        83–84
    and brain death, 126, *126*
    and brain injury, 125–26, *126*
    and brain size, 326
    and coma, 124–26, *125*
    and development, 360
    and hallucinations, 591
    and hypnosis, 144
    and learning, 223
    and locked-in syndrome, 127
    and memory, 263
    and morality, 362–63
    and OCD, 578
    and pain, 203
    and passionate love, 507
    and personality traits, 530
    and physical attractiveness, 505
    and placebo effect, 628–29
    and psychological disorders, 569, 578, *602,*
        634–35, 638
    and research methodology, 83–84,
        83
    and schizophrenia, 593
    and self-knowledge, 547–48, *547*
    and sensory deprivation neglect, *339*
    and sleep, 141
    and social conformity, 478
    and stress, 459
    and synesthesia, 170
    see also functional magnetic resonance
        imaging
brain stem, 84–85, *85,* 87, 135, *140*
Brand, Russell, 561
Breaking Bad (TV show), 150
breast-feeding, and intelligence, 328
Breland, Keller, 235
Breland, Marian, 235
Broadbent, Donald, 128–29
broaden-and-build theory, 459
Broca, Paul, *82,* 91
Broca's area, 81–82, *82,* 312, *312*
Brown, B. Bradford, 370
Brown, Jonathan, 552
Brown, Roger, 275, 279, 315
buffering hypothesis, 461
bulimia nervosa, *439,* 440, 623
bullying, 369–70, *370,* 550
Bund, Charles, 155
bupropion (Wellbutrin), 639
Bush, George W., 132, 475
Bush, Jeb, 27
Buss, Arnold, 519
Buss, David, 420
bystander apathy, 486–87, *486*
bystander intervention effect, *486,* 487

Cade, John, 646
caffeine, 148, 223, *223*
    and sleep, 142
Cairns, Beverly, 370
Cairns, Robert, 370
California Q-sort, 542, *542*
Calkins, Mary Whiton, 12, *12*
cancer, 153, 446, 564
candle problem, 305, *305, 306*

Cannon, Walter B., 391, 403, 450–51
Cannon-Bard theory of emotion, 390–92, *392*
Capecci, Mario, 116
car accident study, 281–82, *281*
careers, 23–24, *24*
caregivers, caregiving:
    and infant development, 347–48, *348*
    and personality, 537
    and psychological disorders, 599
    see also attachment; parent-child
        relationship; parenting, style of; parents
Carrey, Jim, *278*
Carstensen, Laura, 376
case studies:
    and memory, 255, 261
    and research methodology, 39–40, *39*
Casey, Brian, 500
Caspi, Avshalom, 113–14, *115,* 566
Cast Away (film), 410, *411*
castration, 100
catatonic behavior, and schizophrenia, 592
categorical approach, 565
categorization:
    definition of, 291, *292*
    of psychological disorders, 564–68, *565*
    and stereotypes, 498–501
    and thought/thinking, 291
Cattell, Raymond, 322, 323, 528
caudate, 578, 638
causal connection, establishing of, 48
causality:
    establishing of, 48
    and research methodology, 44, *46,* 48
Ceci, Stephen, 329
cell bodies, 71, *72*
cell phone use:
    while driving, 29, *29,* 36–38
    versus intoxication, while driving, 37
cells:
    and genetic basis of psychological science,
        106–7, *106*
    see also type of cells
Centers for Disease Control and Prevention
        (CDC), 441, 446, 608
central nervous system (CNS), 70, *70,* 97, 200,
        569, 654
central tendency, 58
central traits, 541
cerebellum, 84–85, *85*
cerebral cortex, 87
    and basic structure and functions of brain,
        84–85, *85, 86,* 87–92, *88*
    see also left hemisphere; right hemisphere
"change blindness" phenomenon, 129, *130*
characteristic adaptations, 535
cheating, 19, 401
Cherry, E. C., 128
Chess, Stella, 370
Chiffons, the, 280
childhood amnesia, 280
children, 337–52
    and cigarettes and alcohol, *296*
    decision to have, 374, *374*
    and life transitions, 374
    and psychological disorders, 577, 578, 594,
        601–10, *602, 603,* 653–61
    see also adolescence; development, human;
        parent-child relationship; parenting, style
        of
chimpanzee, Nim Chimpsky, 317
chlorpromazine, 647–48
choice, and multiple options, 308, *308*
Chomsky, Noam, 316, 317
chromosomes, 106–7, *106,* 109, *110*
chronic pulmonary disease, 455

chunking, 251, 259, *259*
Cialdini, Robert, 303, 478, 486
cigarettes, *see* smoking
cigarettes, electronic, 442, *443*
circadian rhythms, 133, *133,* 139
circumplex model, 384, *384*
clang associations, 591
classical conditioning, 210, *211, 271*
    and attitudes, 490
    definition of, *211,* 212
    and emotions, 387
    and learning, 210–12, 221–24, *222,*
        224–27
    and memory, 272
    and motivation, 158
    operant conditioning as different than,
        224–27
    and psychological disorders, 570, 618
cleanliness, and roommates (college),545–546,
    546
Cleckley, Hervey, 599
client-centered therapy, 621
client-practitioner relationship, 652
clinical interview, 567
clinical psychologists, 630–31, *631*
clinical psychology, 23–24, 664–65
Clinton, Bill, *52,* 475
Clinton, Hillary, 298
cliques, 369, *369*
clomipramine, 637, *637*
Clooney, George, 490
Clore, Gerald, 300
closure, 180, *180*
    in visual perception, 180
clozapine, 648, *648*
clustering of visual elements, 180
Coca-Cola, and cocaine, 150, *150*
cocaine, 148, 149–50, 223
    and Coca-Cola, 150, *150*
cochlea, 189, *190*
cochlear implants, 191, *191*
cocktail party phenomenon, 128, 547
codeine, 149
coding, *see* encoding
cognition:
    and adulthood, 372
    and aging, 377–78
    definition of, 290
    and development, 315–18, 337–52, 353–59
    and emotions, 300, 384
    and exercise, 444
    information-processing theories of,
        16–17
    innate, 358
    and intelligence, 324–27
    and language, 313, 315–18
    and learning, 218–21, 236–37
    and moral values, 361–62
    and operant conditioning, 235–38
    and personality, 522, 525–26
    Piaget's stages of development for, 353–56,
        353
    and psychological disorders, 574, 576, *576,*
        582, *582,* 589
    and sleep, 137
    and social and cultural context, 356–57
    and social psychology, 493–94
    and treatment of psychological disorders,
        649, 659
    see also cognitive-behavioral therapy;
        cognitive dissonance; cognitive
        restructuring; cognitive therapy; decision
        making; problem solving; representations,
        mental; schemas; thought/thinking
cognitions, hot/cold, 409

cognitive-behavioral therapy (CBT):
    and sleep, 136
    and treatment of psychological disorders, 570, 620, 634–38, 640–41, *640*, 647, 649, 660–61
cognitive dissonance, 493–94, *493*
cognitive maps, 236
cognitive neuroscience, 17
cognitive perspective, 218
cognitive psychology, 24
    and scientific foundations of psychology, 16–17
Cognitive Psychology (Neisser), 16
cognitive restructuring, 619, *619*
cognitive-social theories, of personality, 525
cognitive therapy, and treatment of psychological disorders, 619–20, 634–36, 651, 652
    see also cognitive-behavioral therapy
cognitive triad, 582, *582*
Cohen, Sheldon, 453
collective self, *554–55*, 555
College Board Examination Survey, 552
Collins, Allan, 265
color, 175, 176–78, *176*, *178*
color blindness, 176, *177*
color constancy, 187
coma, 124–26, *125*
common factors, 629
common sense, *10*, 11
communication:
    and adaptation, 20
    of animals, 317–18
    and autism spectrum disorder, 604
    and basic structure and functions of brain, 87
    and nervous system, 71–72
    neuron integration into systems of, 97–101
    and psychological disorders, 603, *603*, 656, 657
    and specialization of neurons, 71–72
    and themes of psychological science, 20
    see also language; speech
comorbidity, 566, *566*, 568, 575, *575*, 623
companionate love, 507, *507*
competition, cooperation versus, *488*
compliance, 478, 480–82
compulsions, 577–78
    see also obsessive-compulsive disorder
computers:
    brain as analogous to, 16
    and memory, 250, *251*, 260
    and scientific foundations of psychology, 16
concepts:
    in the brain, 292–93
    definition of, 291
    as symbolic representations, 291–93
Concerta, 654
concordance rates, 581, 605, 609
concrete operational stage, *353*, 355–56
concussions, 124, *124*
conditioned response (CR), 212, *213*, 214, *214*, *220*, 636
conditioned stimulus (CS), 212–21, *213*, *214*, 218, *220*, 223, 228
conditioned taste aversion, 217, *217*
conditioning, 212, *213*
    and attitudes, 490–91
    and choosing a practitioner, *632*
    and emotions, 387
    and psychological disorders, 570, 578, *578*
    second-order, 214–15
    see also classical conditioning; operant conditioning
conditioning trials, 212
conduct disorder, 653

cones, 173, *174*, 176, 345
confidentiality, 52, 55
confirmation bias, 7, 284, *284*, 298, 389–90, *389*
conflict, 508
    and romantic relationships, *508*, 510
    and scientific foundations of psychology, 14
conformity, 475–79, *476*, *477*, 480–82
confounds, 48
Confucius, 9, *9*
conscience, 523
conscientiousness, 528, 529, 530, 538–39
consciousness, 124–32
    and alcohol, 156–58
    altered, 143–47
    and attention, 127–31
    and brain activity, 122–24, 125
    definitions of, 122
    and drugs, 147–58
    and escapism, 147, *147*
    and flow, 146–47
    and hypnosis, 143–45, *143*
    and immersion in action/activities, 146–47
    levels of, *536*
    and meditation, 145–46, *145*
    and memory, 271
    and neural responses in the brain, 122, *123*
    and personality, 522, *522*
    and psychological disorders, 570, 589
    and scientific foundations of psychology, 12, 14
    sleep as altered state of, 133–35
    and split brain, 92–95, *94*, *95*
    study of, 121–58, *122*, *125*
conscious strategies, in problem solving, 305–6
consolidation, and memory, 250
constraint, 530
construct validity, 56, *56*
contact comfort, 349
context-dependent memory, 266, *266*
contexts, and emotions, 397, *397*
contiguity, and learning, 214, 216
continuation, good, 180, *180*
continuity, in visual perception, 180
continuous reinforcement, 230
control, 30, 406, 656
    in establishing causality, 48
    and research methodology, 47
    see also locus of control; self-regulation
control group, 47
controlled processing, 127–28, *128*
convenience sampling, 49, *49*
conventional morals, 362
convergence, binocular, 183, *183*
conversion theory, 424
cooperation, 488–89, *488*, *489*
    competition versus, *489*
coping:
    and appraisals, 457
    and behaviors affecting health, 463–65
    and individual differences, 458–59
    as process, 457–59
    and psychological disorders, 568, 651, 656
    with stress, 447–52, 463–65
    types of, 457–58
coping response, 447
cornea, 173, *174*
corpus callosum, 87, *88*, 92–93, *92*
correlation, direction of, 43–44, *44*
correlational studies:
    and ethics, 45
    and prediction, 46
    and research methodology, 43–46, *43*, 60–61, *60*
    and trauma, 45
correlation coefficient, 60, *60*
correspondence bias, 497

cortex:
    and basic structure and functions of brain, 87
    and development of brain, 104
    reorganization of, 104, *104*
    specialization of, 91
    see also specific cortexes
cortical maps, *104*
cortisol, 449, 450, 456
Costa, Paul, 535
counseling psychologists, 23, 630
counter conditioning, 223
Craik, Fergus, 263
cramming, and memory, 268–70
creation of positive events, 458
creative intelligence, 323
creativity:
    definition of, 406
    and motivation, 406
creole, 316–17, *335*
criminals:
    and psychological disorders, 588, 599, 601, 652, 653
    self-esteem of, 550
critical periods, 101, 338
critical thinking, *see* thought/thinking, critical
Crocker, Jennifer, 553
cross-cultural studies, *50*
cross-sensory experience, *see* synesthesia
crowd behavior, 475
Crowe, Russell, *589*
cryptomnesia, 280, *280*
crystallized intelligence, 322–23, 326, 327, 378
Csikszentmihalyi, Mihaly, 146–47
Cuban, Mark, 501
cultural psychology, 24
cultural syndromes, 572–73, *572*
culture:
    and adaptation, 20–21
    and aging, 375
    and anxiety, 622
    and behavior, 20–21, *20*
    and biology, 365–68
    and cognitive strategies, 356–57, *356*
    and depressive disorders, 580–81, 622
    and development, 313–14, 316–17, 337, 342–43, *343*, 362, 365–68
    East-West, 20, *20*, 180
    and eating, 415–16, *415*
    and emotions, 397–98, *398*, 622
    and euphemisms, 622
    evolution of, 20–21
    and gender, 367
    and harming and helping others, 484–85, *484*
    and identity, 365–68
    and impressions, 498
    and intelligence, *331*
    and language, 316–17
    and levels of analysis, 21–24
    and memory, 264, *264*
    and motivation, 415–16, 419–21
    and nature/nurture debate, 10
    and obesity, 436–37, *437*
    and perception, 180
    and personality, 529, 536, *536*, 538–40, *539*
    and psychological disorders, 563, 570, *570*, 572–73, 590, 622, *622*, 650
    and psychotherapy, 622, *622*
    and research methodology, 42, 50–51, *50*
    and scripts, 295
    and self-knowledge, 554–56, *554–55*
    and self-serving bias, 554–56, *554–55*
    and sexual behavior, 419–21
    and stress, 622
    and themes of psychological science, 20–21, *20*
    and women working, 20

culture of honor, 484
curiosity, 406
cyberbullying, 370, *370*

"daily hassles" stress, 448
Damasio, Antonio, 301
Damon, Matt, 249, *250*
dark triad, 566, 599–600
Darley, John, 487
Darwin, Charles, 13, *13*, 212, 225, 397, 401, 537
Darwin, Erasmus, 13
Darwinism, 13
    see also evolution
data, 30
    analysis and evaluation of, 55–64
    analyzing of, *32*, 34
    and research methodology, 34, 55–64
    see also romantic relationships
data science skills, 67
deafness, 191, *191*
Deary, Ian, 325
death:
    and accidents, 445–46
    and behavior, 445–46
    and lifestyle, 446
    and psychological disorders, 580, 633
    and smoking, 441
    see also suicide
debriefing, 53, 55
deception, 53, 55
decision making:
    bias in, 298
    and emotions, 300–2, 362
    group, 474–75
    and heuristics, 297–300
    and intelligence, 325
    and levels of analysis, 22
    and life transitions, 374
    and moods, 300
    overview about, 296–97
    and problem solving, 296–10, *297*
    psychology of, 335
    and scientific foundations of psychology, 16
decision science, 335
declarative memory, 271
deep brain stimulation (DBS), 88–89, 627–28, *627*, 637–38, *642*, 643
deep structure, 316
defense mechanisms, 523, *523*
dehumanizing, of outgroups, 472
deindividuation, 473–74, *475*
delayed gratification, 409, *409*
delta waves, 134, *134*
delusions, 589, 590, *590*, 647, 649
    of grandeur, 590
    of harassment, 590
dementia, 375–76
dementia praecox, 564
demonic possession, 562, *562*
demonstration, teaching through, 240
dendrites, 71, *72*, 73
dependence, 156–58, 597, 598, 599
dependent personality disorder, 597
dependent variables (DV), 47
depolarization, 73
depressants, 148–49, *148*
depression, 566
    and adolescence, 659–61, *659*
    and aging, 376
    and behaviors affecting health, 436, 437, 444
    causes of, 581–82, *582*
    and culture, 622
    definition of, 638
    and gender, 643–44
    and heart disease, 455

major, 579
and mood, *384*
and nervous system, 79
as psychological disorder, 564, 566, 575, 579–82, 598
and race/ethnicity, 643, 659
and reproduction, 643
and sexual behavior, 639
and sleep, 138
and stereotypes, 643
treatment for, 617, 619, 624, 626, 627, 638–44, 659–61
and violence, 643
    see also bipolar disorder; moods
depressive disorders, 579–80, *580*
    and culture, 580–81
    and gender, 580–81
    persistent, 580
    and situations, 581
    see also depression
depth perception, 182–84, *185*
Descartes, René, 11, *11*, 122
Descartes' Error (Damasio), 301
description, 30
descriptive statistics, 58–60, *59*
descriptive studies, and research methodology, 39–43, *39*
desensitization, systematic, 634
development, human, 337–81
    and adaptation, 339
    and attachment, 347–52, *348*
    and biology, 363–71
    and brain, 316, 339–40, 360
    and cognition, 315–18, 337, 353–59
    and culture, 313–14, 316–17, 337, 342–43, *343*, 362, 365–68
    and dynamic systems theory, 343, *343*
    and environment, 316–17, 337, 339, 341–43, *343*
    Erikson's eight stages of, 365–66, *365*
    and gender, 363–64
    and genetics, 337, 339–40
    and how children learn about world, 352–63
    and identity, 365–68
    and learning, 352–63
    and meaning in adulthood, 371–78
    and memory, 345–46
    overview about, 337–38
    parents' role in, 351–52, 361, 370–71
    and perception, 344–45, 358–59
    and personality, 520–21, 523–24
    Piaget's stages of, 353–56
    prenatal, 339–41
    and psychological disorders, 601–10, *603*, 653
    and scientific foundations of psychology, 16
    and sensitive periods, 339–41
    and sensory information, 344–45, 354–55
    see also children; psychosexual stages; *type of development*
developmental psychology, 24
    definition of, 338
Devine, Patricia, 502
D.F. (case study), 175–78, 181
diabetes, 144, 414, 432, 444, 458, 460
Diagnostic and Statistical Manual of Mental Disorders (DSM), 439, *439*, 564, *565*, 566–67, 569, 573, 575, 577, 579, 589, *590*, 596, 597, 598, 599, 600, *600*, 601, 603, *603*, 609, 630, 636, 645
dialectical behavior therapy (DBT), 650–651, *650–51*
diathesis, 568, *569*
diathesis-stress model, 568, 569, *569*
Diener, Ed, 460

diet, restrictive, 437–41
difference threshold, 168
dimensional approach, 565
Dion, Karen, 506
directionality problem, 44
direction of correlation, 43–44, *44*
discrimination, 215, 489, 500, 553
    in learning, 228
disease:
    and emotions, 460
    and exercise, 443
    and genetics/genes, 110
disgust, 361–62
dishabituation, 209
disordered eating, 438–41, *438*
disorganized behavior, 592, *592*
disorganized speech, 589, 591–92
display rules, 399–400
dissociative amnesia, 586
dissociative disorders, 586–89
dissociative fugue, 587
dissociative identity disorder (DID), 586–589, *588*
    see also multiple personality disorder
dissonance:
    and attitudes, 493–94, *500*
    postdecisional, 493
    see also cognitive dissonance
distortion, of memory, 250, 278–84
distraction, 409, *409*
    in control of emotions, 396
    and pain, 202–3
distress (duress), 447
distrust, *see* trust
divorce, 508
Dix, Dorothea, 562
DNA (deoxyribonucleic acid), 54, 106–7, *106*, 110, 114, 518, 593, 605
Doctors Without Borders, 482, *483*
dogbane, 647
domains of functioning, 566
dominance, and emotions, 399
Doogie mice, 253, *253*
door-in-the-face effect, 479
dopamine, 223, 650
    and addiction, 148, 150, 156
    and basic structure and functions of brain, 79
    definition of, 79–80
    and emotions, 385
    functions of, *78*, 79–80
    and influence of neurotransmission, 79–80
    and learning, 237–38
    and motivation, 417
    and personality, 518
    and prediction error, 220–21, *220*
    and psychological disorders, 593
    and rewards, 237–38, *238*
    and sexual behavior, 417
    and smoking, 442
    and treatment of psychological disorders, 624–25, 654
Dorr, Richard, *424*
dorsal stream, *166*, 175
double standard, 419
downward comparisons, 458
dreams:
    and behavioral study of learning, 208
    content of, 140
    definition of, 139
    and influence of neurotransmission, 79
    and latent content, 140
    and manifest content, 140
    meaning of, 140
    and motor cortex, *140*
    and prefrontal cortex, *140*
    and psychological disorders, 617, 618

remembering, 139, 141
and scientific foundations of psychology, 14
and sleep, 134, 139–41
drive reduction, and homeostasis, 403–4, *403*
drives, 402–5, *403*, 617, 653
see also specific drives
driving:
cell phone use during, 29, *29*
cell phone use versus alcohol use and, 37
drug companies, studies sponsored by, 644–45, *645*
drug overdoses, 151–52, *152*
drugs:
abuse of, 564, *571*, 594, 618, 632
addiction to, 156–58, 223–24
and children, 157
as consciousness-altering, 147–58
and development, 338, 340
and influence of neurotransmission, 77, *78*, 79–80
and memory, 255, 277–78
and pharmaceutical industry research, 644
prescribing, 630–31, 633
"recreational," 148–49
and sexual behavior, 417
and suicide, 585
see also medications; pharmacology; *specific drugs*
DSM, *see Diagnostic and Statistical Manual of Mental Disorders*
dualism, 11, 122–23
Duncker, Karl, 305
Dunlap, Knight, 397
duress (distress), 447
dynamic systems theory, 343, *343*
dyslexia, 105, *105*, 319
dysthymia, 580, *580*

EAR (electronically activated record), 543
eardrums, 189, *190*
early infantile autism, 603
ears, *190*
eating:
and behaviors affecting health, 432–39, 463
and brain, 339
and influence of neurotransmission, 79
and internal sensations, 413
and learning, 414–15
and motivation, 412–16, *414*
and portion size, 435
and psychological disorders, 621
restrained, 438
and variety of food, 435, *435*
see also obesity; taste
eating disorders, treatments for, 440–41
Ebbinghaus, Hermann, 274
eccentricity, 570
echoic memory, 257
echolalia, 592, 604, 657
ecstasy, 153, *153*
education, and learning disabilities, 105
Egas Moniz, António, 92, 626, 647
ego, 523
egocentrism, in child development, 355, *355*
ejaculation, 364
Ekman, Paul, 397, *398*
elaboration likelihood model, 495, *495*
elaborative rehearsal, 263
electrical stimulation, 626
electroconvulsive therapy (ECT), 626, *626*, 641–42
electroencephalogram (EEG), 82, *82*, 134, *134*
and psychological disorders, 601
electronically activated record (EAR), 543
electronic cigarettes, 442, *443*

electronic devices, and sleep, 142
electrophysiology, 82
electroshock therapy, 651
Elgort, Ansel, *507*
Ellis, Albert, 619
embarrassment, 361, 400, 401–2, *401*, 494
embryo, 338, *338*, 340
emotion, body maps of, *386*
emotional anxiety disorder, 634
emotional artificial intelligence, 427
emotional expression, as nonverbal communication, 400, *400*
emotional intelligence (EI), 324
emotionality, 519
emotional stability, 530
emotion-focused coping, 457, *457*
emotions:
activation of, 384
and adaptation, 396–402
and aging, 376
and amygdala, *86*, 87
arousal of, 384, *384*, 391–95
and attitudes, 460
and brain, 85, *86*, 360–61, 384, 385–88
and cognition, 300, 384
components of, 384–96
and contexts, 397, *397*
controlling of, 395–96, *395*
and culture, 622
and decision making, 300–2, 362
definition of, 384
and development, 347–48
and disease, 460
and environment, 393
and gender, 399–400
and health, 395–96, 460
how people experience, 384–96
influence of neurotransmission on, 76–80
and interpersonal relations, 400–2
and learning, 232
and levels of analysis, 22
and limbic system, 386–88
and memory, 277, 280, 282, 388
misattribution of source of, 392–95
and moods, 300, 384–85, 400
and moral values, 362
and motivation, 383–27
negative, 362, 460, 571
negative, and aggression, 483
overview about, 383–84
and perception, 386
and personality, 530
positive, 460
and pride expressions, 399, *399*
and psychological disorders, 571, 573–86, 594, 598, 600–1, 619–20, 622, 634, 651
and sensory system, 198, 386
and sleep, 140, 141
strategies for controlling of, 395–96
and survival, 396, 400, 401
types of, 384, *384*
valence of, 384, *384*
see also moods; stress; *specific emotions*
empathic therapy, 621
empathy, 90, 244, *244*, 361, 486, 539, 621
lack of, 600–1
empiricism, 30
encoding:
and descriptive research, 40
frequency, 192–93
in observational studies, 40
encoding specificity principle, 266
endocrine system, 97, 98–100, *100*
endorphins, *78*, 80, *80*, 146, 641
engrams, 254

Enns, James, 172–73
environment:
and brain, 87
and brain development, 339
and brain plasticity, 103
and development, 316–17, 337, 339, 341–43, *343*
and emotions, 393, 401
enriched, 339, 601
and genetics/genes, 106–7, *107*, 109, 111–13, 114, *115*, 328
and group differences, 330–32
and hormones, 364
and identity, 368
and intelligence, 323, 327–30
and language, 316–17
and learning, 208, 209
and motivation, 422
and nature/nurture debate, 10
and obesity, 435, 436
and perception, *165*
and personality, 536–40
and psychological disorders, 568–70, 578, 594–95, *595*, 599, 601, 608
and psychopathology, 563
and representations, 293–95
schemas as means of organizing information about, 293–95
and scientific foundations of psychology, 15
and sensation, 169
and sexual behavior, 422
and themes of psychological science, 18
and treatment of psychological disorders, 630
virtual, 634
see also experience
environmental cues, 223
enzyme deactivation, 77
epigenetics, 114, 327–28, 329–30
of memory, 253–54
epilepsy, 88, 91, 254–55
epinephrine, 79, 450
functions of, 79
episodic memory, *271*, 272
equilibrium, 403
equipotentiality, 254
Erikson, Erik, 365–66, *365*, 459
erogenous zones, 524
erotic plasticity, 419
errors, and research methodology, 58
escapism, 147, *147*
Escoffier, Auguste, 195
ESP (extrasensory perception), 171–72, *171*
estrogens, 100, 367, 416
estrus, 100
Eternal Sunshine of the Spotless Mind (film), *278*
ethics:
and altering memory, 278
and cochlear implants, 191
and correlational studies, 45
in psychological research, 54
and research methodology, 51–55
ethnicity, *see* race/ethnicity
ethnomusicology, 22
ethyl alcohol, 80
etiology, 562, 564, 578, 592, 600–1, 609
euphemisms, for psychological disorders, 622
eustress, 447
evaluating, and scientific method, 36–38
Evans, Martin, 116
event-related potential (ERP), 82–83
evidence-based assessment, 568
evidence-based treatments, 629

evolution:
  and attitudes, 490
  of brain, 18–19
  of culture, 20–21
  and harming and helping others, 486
  and impressions, 496
  and ingroup-outgroup bias, 500
  and learning, 216–18, 228
  and mate selection, 505
  and memory, 262
  and menstrual cycle, 364
  and motivation, 420
  and scientific foundations of psychology, 13
  and sexual behavior, 420
  and stereotypes, 500
  and stress, 451
  and themes of psychological science, 13, *13*, 18–19
evolutionary psychology, 18–19
  definition of, 19
examinations, studying for, 268–70
excitation, and nervous system, 73, 75, 76, 80
excitation phase, 418
excitation transfer, 395
exemplars, 292, *292*
exercise:
  and behavior modification, 233–35, *234*
  and consciousness, 146
  and endorphin production, *80*
  and health, 443–44, *444*, 463–64
  and sleep, 142
  and stress, 463–64
  as therapy, 641
expectations, and personality, 525–26, *525*
experience:
  and attitudes, 490–93
  and development, 337
  and development of brain, 101–2
  and learning, 208–9, 212
  and memory, 250, 262, 272
  and nature/nurture debate, 10
  openness to new, 528, 529
  and personality, 526
  and psychological disorders, 617, 618
  and scientific foundations of psychology, 14
  see also environment; *type of experience*
experimental groups, 47, 50
experimental method, in psychological research, 46–48, *50*
experimental psychology, 11–13
experimental studies:
  and research methodology, 46–48
  and scientific foundations of psychology, 11–13
experimenter expectancy, effects, 42–43
experiments, and scientific method, 33
explanation, 30
explicit attitudes, 491
explicit memory, 271, *271*, *272*
exposure, 619, *619*, 634, 636, 637, *637*
exposure and response prevention, 619
expressed emotion, 622
Expression of Emotion in Man and Animals
  (Darwin), 397
expressive aphasia, 312
externalizing disorders, 571, *571*
external validity, 56
extinction, 212–16, *214*, 222, 231, 636
extrasensory perception (ESP), 171–72, *171*
extraversion, 528, 532, 538–39
  and BAS, 532
extraverts, 528, 530–31, *530*, *531*, 533, 543
Extreme Memory Tournament, *268*
extrinsic motivation, 405, *406*
eye contact, in infants, 341, 348
eyes, 102, 172–74

eyewitnesses, 284, *284*
Eysenck, Hans, 530–31

face, *see* facial attractiveness; facial expressions;
  facial recognition; fusiform face area
Facebook, 130, *479*, 543, 551
facial attractiveness, 506, *506*
facial expressions:
  across cultures, *398*
  and basic structure and functions of brain, 87
  and development, 348, *348*
  and emotions, 388, *388*, 397–400, *397*, *401*
  and impression formation, 497
facial feedback hypothesis, 391, *391*
facial gestures, and disgust, 362, *362*
facial recognition:
  and basic structure and functions of brain, 90
  and perception, 181, *181*
  and psychological disorders, *602*
facial symmetry, and attractiveness, 506
factor analysis, 322
fairness, in animal research, 53
faking bad, 542
faking good, 542
false-consensus effect, 441
false fame effect, 273, 280, 499
false memories, *250*, 282–83
falsifiable hypotheses, 31
familiarity, and relationships, 504
family systems model, 570
family therapy, 621–22, *621*
Fantz, Robert, 345, *345*
Fault in Our Stars, The (film), *507*
favoritism, 551–52, *552*
Fazio, Russell, 491
fear, 445–46, 619
  as adaptive, 574–75
  and brain, 87, 388
  and health, 445–46
  hierarchy of, 634, *635*
  and learning, 217–18, 221, 232, 243, 570, 634
  and psychological disorders, 576–77, 601
  and relationships, 504
  and social influence, 478
  of terrorism, *445*
  see also phobias
fear conditioning, 221
Fechner, Gustave, 167
feelings, *see* emotions
Festinger, Leon, 278, 411, 493, *493*, 504
fetal alcohol syndrome (FAS), 340, *340*
fetus, 338, *338*, 340
fight-or-flight response, 450–51, *451*
figure and ground, 180
Fish and Wildlife Service, U. S., 207
five-factor theory, 528–29, *529*, 541, 542, 543
  see also Big Five
fixation, 524
fixed interval schedule (FI), 230, *230*
fixed ratio schedule (FR), 230–31, *231*
fixed schedules, 230, *230–31*
flashbacks, 579
flashbulb memories, 279–80, *279*
Flourish (Seligman), 460
flow, 146–47
fluid intelligence, 322–23, 326, 327, 378
fluoxetine hydrochloride, *see* Prozac
Flynn effect, 329
Flynn, James R., 329
focusing, 326
Foer, Joshua, 267
Folkman, Susan, 457, 458
Food and Drug Administration (FDA), U.S., 643,
  644, 659, 660–61
foot-in-the-door effect, 478

forebrain, 85, *86*
forecasting, affective, 301, *301*
forensic psychologists, 23
Forgas, Joseph, 478
forgetting, 255, 274–77, 376
formal operation stage, *353*, 356
fovea, 173, *174*
Fox, Michael J., 80, *80*
framing, 299, *302*, 335
  definition of, 299
  versus anchoring, 302–3
Franklin, Eileen, *283*
Franklin, George, *283*
Fraser, Scott, 478
fraternal twins, *see* twins, dizygotic
Fredrickson, Barbara, 459
free association, 14–15, 208, 617
Freedman, Jonathan, 478
Freedom of Information Act, 644
Freeman, Walter, *91*
freezing response, 221
Fremdschämen, 8–9
frequency, of sound waves, 189, *198*
Freud, Anna, 523, *523*
Freud, Sigmund, 14, *14*, 31, 140, 208, 349, 407,
  522–23, *522*, 562, 569, 617, *617*, 647
Freudianism, 208, 221, 400, 522–23, *522*, 526,
  569, 617–18, 651
  and scientific foundations of psychology,
  14–15, *14*
Freudian slips, 131, 522
friendships:
  and development, 369–70, *369*
  and identity, 369–70, *369*
  making and keeping, 410–11, *410*
  and psychological disorders, 608
  and quality of relationships, 504–7
frontal lobes, *166*, 194
  and aging, 375, 377, 378
  and basic structure and functions of brain,
  88, 90, *123*
  and development, 360
  and emotions, 301
  and intelligence, 326
  and learning, 360
  and memory, 377
  and morality, 362–63
  and motivation, 421
  and psychological disorders, 593, 599, 601,
  626, 635, 642
  and self-knowledge, 547–48, *547*
  and sensation, 199
  and sexual behavior, 421
  and sleep, 140
  and stereotypes, 502
  and teenagers, 364
  see also prefrontal cortex
fugue, dissociative, 587
Fukushi, Kayoko, 80
fully functioning person, 527
functional fixedness, 305, *305*
functionalism, 12–13, 18
functional magnetic resonance imaging (fMRI),
  83, *83*, *103*, 593
functioning, domains of, 566
fundamental attribution error, 497–98, *498*
Funder, David, 543
fusiform face area, 90, *123*
fusiform gyrus, 181

g, *see* general intelligence
GABA (gamma-aminobutyric acid), *78*, 80, 155,
  623
Gage, Phineas, 90–91, *91*
Gall, Franz, 81

Galton, Francis, 14, 131, 322, 324
gambling, 632
ganglion cells, 174, *174*, 177
Garcia, John, 217
Gardner, Howard, 323
gate-control theory, 202–3, *202*
"gaydar," 497
gay/gayness, *see* homosexuality
Gazzaniga, Michael, 92, 96
gender:
  and ADHD, 609, *609*
  and alcohol, 155, *155*
  and biology, 367–68
  and brain, 103–4, *103*, 366–67
  and culture, 367
  and depression, 643–44
  and depressive disorders, 580–81
  and development, 363–64
  and emotions, 399–400
  and hormones, 100–1
  and identity, 366–68
  and impressions, 499
  and intelligence, 330
  and motivation, 419–20
  and personality, 539–40
  and psychological disorders, 570–73, *571*, 576,
    580–81, 598, 604
  and psychotherapy, 643–44
  roles, *294*, 366, 367
  and schizophrenia, 570, *570*
  and scripts, 295
  and sex characteristics, 363–64, 367
  and sexual behavior, 100–1, 419–20,
    420
  and smell, 198
  and social identity theory, 472
  and socialization, 367
  and social psychology, 499
  and stereotypes, *294*
  and stress, 451–52
  and temperament, 519–20
gene expression, 106–7, *107*
  and environment, 114
  and personality, 516–17
general adaptation syndrome, 450, *450*
general intelligence (g), 322–24, *322*,
    325–26
  and gender, 330
generalization, and learning, 215, 228
generalized anxiety disorder (GAD),575–576
generalized learned behavior, 657, 659
genetics/genes:
  and adaptation, 13, 110
  and addictions, 442
  and aggression, 483
  and aging, 376
  and autism spectrum disorder, 606
  as basis of psychological science, 106–16
  and behavior, 18, 111–13, 116, 436, 442
  and bipolar disorders, 583–84
  and development, 337, 339–40
  dominant, 108, 110
  and environment, 106–7, 109, 111–13, *115*,
    328
  and harming and helping others, 486
  and heart disease, 454
  and heredity, 108–10, *110*
  and intelligence, 327–30, *328*
  modification of, 113–16, *116*
  and motivation, 423–24
  and mutations, 110
  natural selection at level of, 486
  and nature/nurture debate, 10
  and obesity, 436, 437
  and personality, 516–19, 536

and psychological disorders, 106–7, 568–69,
    578, 581, 592, *593*, 594, 605, 609, 646
  and RDoC, 566
  recessive, 108, 110
  and scientific foundations of psychology, 13
  and sensation, 195
  and sexual behavior, 423–24
  and smoking, 442
  and suicide, 585
  and themes of psychological science, 18
  see also DNA; gene expression; genotypes;
    Human Genome Project; phenotypes
genetic variation, 110
Genie (case study), *357*
genital stage, 524
genome, 106–7
genotypes, 108–9, *109*
Genovese, Kitty, 486–87, *486*
Gestalt psychology:
  definition of, 15
  and learning, 15
  and perception, 179–80, *180*
  and scientific foundations of psychology, 15
ghrelin, *413*, 414
Giffords, Gabrielle, 124–25, *125*
Gilmore, Gary (case study), 600, *600*
Gilovich, Thomas, 6, 63
glial cells, *72*, 74
global aphasia, 312
globalization, 20
global workspace model, 123–24
glucose, 413–14
glucostatic theory, 413–14
glutamate, *78*, 80
  and OCD, 578
goals:
  achievement of personal, 408–10
  and aging, 376
  and emotions, 396
  and motivation, 408–10
  and organization of subgoals, 303–4
  and problem solving, 303–8
goal setting, 234
gonads, 100, 416
Goodall, Jane, *40*
good continuation, 180, *180*
Google, 67
Google Scholar, 31
Gore, Al, *52*, 131, *132*
Gosling, Sam, 543
Gottfredson, Linda, 323
Gottman, John, 508, 509–10
Gould, Elizabeth, 103
gourmand syndrome, 412
Graf, Peter, 271
grasping reflex, 341, *341*
gratification, delayed, 409, *409*
gratitude, 361
Gray, Jeffrey, 531
gray matter, 84, 86, 104
Green Our Vaccines, *607*
Greenwald, Anthony, 491
Grey's Anatomy (TV show), 235
grief, 622
grit, 409–10
Gross, James, 395
ground, figure and, 180
groups:
  decision making by, 474–75
  and environment, 330–32
  experimental, 47, 50
  and genes, 330–32
  and harming and helping others, 486
  influence on individual behavior of, 473–75
  and intelligence, 330–32

polarization in, 474
  see also ingroup-outgroup bias
group therapy, 622–23, 652
groupthink, 475
growth hormone (GH), 99–100, 137
*Guidelines for Psychological Practice with Girls
    and Women* (American Psychological
    Association), 643
guilt, 361, 400–1, 580
Guimond, Serge, 540
gustation, *see* taste
gut feelings, 301

habits, 273, 404
habituation, 209, *209*, 358, 636
Haidt, Jonathan, 143, 362
hair cells, 189
Halbrook, Diana, 283
hallucinations, 589, *590*, 591, 597, 647, 649
  and mania, 583
hallucinogens, 149
haloperidol, 647–48
Hamer, Dean, 423
Hamilton, Alexander, 262
Hamilton, William, 486
handwriting, 588, *588*
Haney, Chris, 473
Hanks, Tom, 410, *411*
happiness, 459, 464–65
  and well-being, 459–65, *460*
haptic experiences, 200
haptic receptors, 200
haptic sense, 199, 200, *200–1*
  see also touch
hardiness, 458
Hare, Robert, 600
Harlow, Harry, 349, *350*, 351, 406
harming others, 482–90
Harrison, George, 280
Hatfield, Elaine (Walster), 507
Hawthorne effect, 41, *42*
Hawthorne Works, 41
Hayek, Salma, 499
Hazan, Cindy, 507
hazing study, 493–94, *494*
HDAC (histone deacetylases), 253
HDAC inhibitors, 278
head, size of, 326
headaches, 574
health:
  and anger/hostility, 460
  and anxiety, 460
  and attitudes, 459–65
  behaviors affecting, 430–32
  and cognition, 430
  and emotions, 395–96, 460
  and fear, 445–46
  and general intelligence, 323
  and happiness, 459–65, *460*, 464–65
  and loneliness, 461
  and oxytocin, 462
  and personality, 454–55, *455*
  and positive psychology, 459–65
  and psychosocial factors, 430–32
  racial disparity in, 431–32
  and resilience, 458–59
  and social integration, 461–62
  and social support, 461–62
  and spirituality, 463
  strategies for improving, 463–65
  and stress, 452–59, *454*, 464
  and trust, 462, *462*
  and well-being, 428–67
Health and Human Services Department
    (USDHHS), U.S., 441, *659*

health psychology, 23, 430
hearing:
    and aging, 377
    as basic sensory process, 188–93, *190*
    and basic structure and functions of brain, 90
    and development, 344
    and language, 314
    and memory, 257
    and perception, *166*
hearing loss, noise-induced, 193
heart disease, 99, 431, 432, 441, 443, 444, 446,
    451, 454–57, *455*, 456, 458, 463, 564
heat, and aggression, 483
Heatherton, James, *184*
Heatherton, Sarah, *184*
Hebb, Donald, 252
hedonism, 407, 599
Heider, Fritz, 497
Heine, Steven, 539, 555
Helmoltz, Hermann von, 192
helping others, 482–90
hemineglect, 89, *90*, 123
Hemingway, Ernest, 562
heredity, 108–10, *110*, 113
Here's the Deal: Don't Touch Me (Mandel),
    577
heritability, *110*, 113, 516–19
Herman, Peter, 438
heroin, 77, 80, 149–51, *152*, *157*, 158, 223
hertz, 189
"He's So Fine" (song), 280
heterosexuality, 421–22
heuristic biases, 7–8
heuristics, 297–300, 306, 335
    definition of, 297
hierarchy, of fears, 634, *635*
hindsight bias, 298
hippocampus, 152
    atrophy of, 574
    and basic structure and functions of brain,
        86, *86*
    and development of brain, 102
    and emotions, 388
    and exercise, 444
    and memory, 53, 255, 386, 388
    and psychological disorders, 574
    size of, 86
    and sleep, 137
Hippocrates, 562
histamine, 639
histrionic personality, 596
Hitler, Adolf, 542, *542*
HIV, 432, 453
H.M. (case study), 254–56, *255*, 261, 271, 276
hoarding disorder, 577
Hobson, John Alan, 140–41
Hoffman, Dustin, 326
homeostasis, 403, *404*, 413
    and drive reduction, 403–4, *404*
homicidal death, 600
homosexuality, 422, *424*, 643
    and modern prejudice, *501*
homunculus, 104
honor, culture of, 484
Honorton, Charles, 171
hormones:
    and aggression, 483
    definition of, 99–100
    and development, 352
    and environment, 364
    and gender, 100–1, 367
    and motivation, 413–14, 416
    and neuron integration into communication
        systems, 99–100
    and puberty, 363

and sexual behavior, 100–1, 416–24, *417*, 423
and stress, 449
and trust, 462
see also specific hormones
Horney, Karen, 524
hostility, 455–56, *455*, 457, 489
    see also anger
"hot hand" hypothesis, 63, *63*
Hovland, Carl, 494
*How Opal Mehta Got Kissed, Got Wild, and Got a
    Life* (Viswanathan), 280
*How We Know What Isn't So: The Fallibility of
    Human Reason in Everyday Life* (Gilovich), 6
HPA (hypothalamic-pituitary-adrenal) axis,
    449, *449*, 451
hue, 177
Hull, Clark, 404, 473
Hull, Jay, 155
Human Connectome Project, 18
human development, *see* development,
    human
human genome, and themes of psychological
    science, 18
Human Genome Project, 107, 108
    see also genetics/genes
humanistic approach:
    to personality, 526–27, *527*, 541
    and treatment of psychological disorders,
        620–21, *621*
humanistic psychology, 16, *16*
humor, 396
    in control of emotions, 396
Huntington's disease, 87
hyperactivity disorders, 564
hyperphagia, 412, *412*
hyperpolarization, 73
hypertension, 574
hypnosis:
    and brain imaging, 144
    and consciousness, 143–45
    dissociation theory of, 144, 145
    and memory, 283
    and pain, 144
    self-, 144, *144*
    sociocognitive theory of, 144
    theories of, 144
hypnotic analgesia, 144
hypomanic episodes, 583
hypothalamus:
    and basic structure and functions of brain,
        86, *86*
    and body temperature, 404
    and eating, 412–13, *413*, 414
    functions of, 99
    and motivation, 386, 412, 416, 417, *417*, 418,
        423–24
    and neuron integration into communication
        systems, 99
    and sexual behavior, 416, 417, *417*, 418,
        423–24
    and sleep, 133, *133*
    and stress, 449, 452
    suprachiasmatic nucleus of, 133, *133*
hypotheses:
    definition of, 31
    forming of, *32*, 33
    and scientific method, 32–34

ibuprofen, 203
iconic memory, 257
id, 522
identical twins, *see* twins, monozygotic
identity:
    adolescent, 365–68
    bicultural, 368

and biology, 365–68
and culture, 365–68
and development, 365–68
and environment, 368
and friendships, 369–70, *369*
gender, 366–68
multiple, 587–89
and norms, 367
and psychological disorders, 586–89, 597
race/ethnicity, 368
and socialization, 367, 368
idiographic approach, 541
Ikeda, Kikunae, 195
illusions, *179*, *181*, 187, *187*
illusory contours, 180, *181*
    in visual perception, 180
illusory correlations, 499
images, *see* representations, mental
imagination, and mind/body problem, 11
imipramine, 635, 639
imitation, 240, *240*
    in infants, 344, *344*
immediate memory, *see* short-term memory
immersion in action/activities, 146–47
immune system, 137, 450, 578
    and positivity, 461
    and stress, 452–54, *454*
Implicit Association Test (IAT), 492, *492*
implicit attitudes, 491
implicit memory, 271–73, *271*, *273*, 491
impressions:
    first, 496–98
    formation of, 496–502
imprinting, 348–49, *349*
impulsivity:
    and basic structure and functions of brain,
        90–91, 609
    and influence of neurotransmission, 79
    and personality, 530
    and psychological disorders, 578, 597, 599,
        600, 608–9, 652
Imus, Deirdre, 607
incentives, 405–8
inclusive fitness, 486
independent self-construals, *554–55*, 555
independent variables, 46
individual differences, *see* uniqueness,
    individual
industrial melanism, 110, *110*
industrial psychologists, 24
infancy, factors shaping, 338–52
infant attachment behaviors, 348, *348*
infantile amnesia, 346
infant reflexes, *341*
infectious diseases, 432
inferential statistics, 61–62, *62*
inferiority complex, 524
influence:
    and conformity, 475–79
    informational, 476
    normative, 476
    social, 469–513
information processing, *see* neurotransmission
information processing model, and memory,
    250, *251*
information-processing theories, and scientific
    foundations of psychology, 16
informed consent, 52–53, *52*, 54
Ingram, Jeff, 587, *587*
ingroup favoritism, 471, 489, 500
ingroup-outgroup bias, 500
ingroups, 20, 470–71, *471*
inhibiting stereotypes, 502
inhibition:
    and learning, 531

and nervous system, 73, 75, 76
   and personality, 520, *521*, 531
   and social anxiety, *602*
injury, self-, 605
innate knowledge, 358
inner ear, 189, *190*
insecure attachment, 351–52, 507
insight, and problem solving, 306–7, *307*
insight, in psychotherapy, 617, 653
insight learning, 237
insomnia, 135
   cognitive-behavioral therapy and, 136
inspection time tasks, 325, *325*
Institute of Medicine, 607
Institutional Animal Care and Use Committee
   (IACUC), 53
institutional review boards (IRBs), 52
instrumental behavior, 224
instrumental conditioning, *see* operant
   conditioning
insula, 156, *156*
   and emotions, 386–87, *386*
   and morality, 363
insulin, 413–14, *413*
intellectual disabilities, *603*
intelligence, 319–32
   and aging, 378
   and birth weight, 329, *329*
   and brain, 324–27
   and breast-feeding, 328
   cognitive approach to, 324–27
   and culture, *331*
   and decision making, 325
   definition of, 319
   and environment, 323, 327–30
   gender and, 330
   and genes, 327–30, *328*
   and group differences, 330–32
   and language, 289–32
   measurement of, 319–32, *320*
   and memory, 255, 272
   and Mozart Effect, 346–47, *346*
   multiple, 323–24
   overview about, 319
   and problem solving, 325
   and psychological disorders, 657, 659
   psychometric approach to, 320–22, *320*
   and race, 330–31
   and scientific foundations of psychology, 16
   and speed of mental processing, 324–25,
      378
   testing of, 320–22, 378
   and working memory, 325–26
   see also specific types of intelligence
intelligence quotient, *see* IQ
intentionality, 360
interactionist approach, to personality, 533–34
interdependent self-construals, *554–55*, 555
interference, and memory, 274
internalizing disorders, 570–71, *571*
internal validity, 56, *56–57*
international travel, and personality, 537–38
Internet, 5, 130
   and globalization, 20
interpersonal psychotherapy, 619–20
interpersonal relations, *see* relationships;
   support, social
interpersonal skills, *25*
Interpretation of Dreams, The (Freud), 31
interpreter, brain, 94–95, *95*
intersexuality, 367, *367*
interval schedules, 230–31, *230*
interviews:
   clinical, 567
   motivational, 621

intrinsic motivation, 405, *406*
introspection, 12, 208
introverts, 528, 530, *530*, 531, *531*, 533
intrusive thoughts, 577–79
intuition, 5–6
ion channels, 72, 73
ions, 72
   see also types of ions
iproniazid, 638
IQ (intelligence quotient):
   and aging, 378
   and autism spectrum disorder, 657, 659
   and birth weight, 329, *329*
   definition of, 321
   and measurement of intelligence, *320*, 321,
      321
   and memory, 255, 272
   and psychological disorders, 657, 659
   and working memory, 259
Iraq War, 474
iris, 173
isolation, 592, 603
Iyengar, Sheena, 308, *308*

Jackson, William, *284*
Jacoby, Larry, 273
James, LeBron, 63, *63*
James, William, 12–13, *12*, 18, 225, 391
James-Lange theory of emotion, 390–91, *391*
Janis, Irving, 475
Jaws (film), 212, *212*, 214
Jay-Z, *504*
Jennings, Ken, *272*
Jensen, Arthur, 330
Jeopardy! (TV show), *272*, 497, *498*
job, *see* careers
Johnson, Virginia, 418
Joiner, Thomas, 584–85
joint attention, 313, *314*
Jones, Edward, 497
Jones, Mary Cover, 223
Jordan, Michael, 227
Joudrie, Dorothy, 586
Jung, Carl, 524
justifying effort, 493–95, *494*

Kagan, Jerome, 520
Kahneman, Daniel, 127, 297–98, *297*
Kandel, Eric, 210, 252
Kanner, Leo, 603, 605
Kanzi (bonobo ape), 317
k-complexes, 134, *134*
Keenan, Sara, 367
Keller, Helen, 264
Kelley, Harold, 497
Kelly, George, 525
Keltner, Dacher, 396, *401*
Kennedy, John F., 277, 279
Kesey, Ken, 626
Keyes, Daniel, 587
Kim Jae-beom, 147
Kim Yun-jeong, 147
kinesthetic sense, 199
kin selection, 486
Kirsch, Irving, 644
Kitaoka, Akiyoshi, *186*
Kitayama, Shinobu, 555
knock-out/knock-in studies, 114, 116
knowledge, innate, 358
Kobasa, Suzanne, 458
Kohlberg, Lawrence, 361–62, 363
Köhler, Wolfgang, 15, 307, *307*
Kosslyn, Stephen, 171–72, *171*

Kowalski, Patricia, 6
Kraepelin, Emil, 564, *564*, 601
Kuhl, Patricia, 314
Kujawski Taylor, Annette, 6
Kulik, James, 279
Kunis, Mila, *181*
Kushner, Harold, 463

LaBeouf, Shia, *507*
Lancet (journal), 607
Lane, Sasha, *507*
Lange, Carl, 391
language, 310–19
   acquisition of, 315–18, *316*
   and aging, 376
   and brain, 93, 94, 103, *103*, 312–13, *312*, 314,
      316
   and cognition, 313, 315–18
   and culture, 316–17
   development of, 313–15, 340
   and environment, 316–17
   errors in, 315
   and hearing, 314
   hierarchical structure of, 310
   and intelligence and thinking, 289–32
   learning of, 313–15
   and operant reinforcement, 315, *315*
   and overgeneralization, 315
   and psychological disorders, 604
   and reading, 318–19
   and scientific foundations of psychology, 16
   sign, 316, *316*
   and social and cultural context, 356–57
   surface versus deep structure of, 316
   as system of communication, 310–13
   teaching of, *315*
   units of, *311*
   and universal grammar, 316
language acquisition device, 316
Lashey, Karl, 254
Latané, Bibb, 487
latency stage, 524
latent content, 140
latent learning, *236*, 237
Latham, Gary, 408
laughter, 396
law of conservation, *354*
law of parsimony, 32
laws of nature, understanding the, 357–59
Layton, Molly, 598
Lazarus, Richard, 457
L-DOPA, 80
Leach, Jennifer Kay, 308
learned helplessness model, 582
learning:
   and anxiety disorder, 576
   associative, *208*, 209
   and biology, 235–38
   and brain, 87, 102, 221, 237–38, 360
   and cognition, 218–21, 236–37
   demonstration, 240
   and development, 352–63
   and environment, 208, 209
   and evolution, 216–18, 228
   and expectation, 218–21
   facilitation of, 138–39
   and fear, 217–18, 221–24, 232, 243, *243*, 570,
      634
   generalized, 657, 659
   and imitation, 240
   importance of, 208
   and influence of neurotransmission, 79, 80
   latent, *236*, 237
   and levels of analysis, 22

learning (*continued*)
  and nature/nurture debate, 10
  nonassociative, 208, *208*, 209, *209*
  observational, 209, 238–44, *525*
  and operant conditioning, 224–38, *225*
  and personality, 525–26, 531
  and prediction, 218–21
  and punishment, 232, *232*
  and reinforcement, 226–27, 237–38
  and rewards, 237–38
  and scientific foundations of psychology, 15, 16
  simple models of, 209–10
  and sleep, 138–39
  and specific disorders, *603*
  vicarious, 240–41
  see also conditioning; language; *type of learning*
learning disabilities, 105
  and brain, 105
  and succeeding in college, 105
learning theory, 208
Leary, Mark, 410, 550
LeDoux, Joseph, 250, 387, 392
left hemisphere, 94–95, *95*, 96, *96*
  and language, 312, *312*
  and memory, 377
Lennon, John, *629*
lens, 173
Leonardo da Vinci, *10*, 11, 183
Lepper, Mark, 308, *308*, 406
leptin, *413*, 414
lesbians/lesbiansim, 643
  see also homosexuality
LeVay, Simon, 423
levels of analysis, and themes of psychological science, 21–24, *21*
levels of processing model, and memory, 263
Levey, Gerald, *112*
Levitin, Daniel, 188
Lewinsky, Monica, 475
Lewontin, Richard, 328
libido, 522–23, 524
lie-detector tests, 82, *82*, 389–90, *389–90*
life, using psychology in, 24–25, *25*
life expectancies, 378, 431–32, *431–32*
life experience, and personality, 536–38, *537*
life history data, 542–43
life span, 372, 378, 609
lifestyle, and death, 446
life transitions, 371–73
light, color of, 176–78, *176*, *178*
lightness, 177, *178*
limbic system:
  definition of, 86, 386
  and eating, 412
  and emotions, 386–88, *386*, 392
  and learning, 223
  and motivation, 417
  and sexual behavior, 417
Lincoln, Abraham, *262*
Linehan, Marsha, 650–51, *650*
linguistic relativity theory, 313
lipostatic theory, 414
listening, 503, *503*
literature review, *32*, 33
lithium, 623, 645, 646, 652
Little Albert, 222, *222*, 570
lobotomies, 91, *91*, 626, 647
localization of function, and brain, 17–18
Locke, Edwin, 408
Locke, John, 208
locked-in syndrome, 119, 126–27, *127*
Lockhart, Robert, 263
locus of control, 525

Loehlin, James, 516
Loftus, Elizabeth, 265, 281, *281*, 282
Logan, Jessica, 377
London taxi drivers, study of, 86
loneliness, and health, 461
longitudinal studies, and psychological disorders, 610
long-term memory, 449
  and aging, 377
  different systems of, 270–73, *271*
  and forgetting, 276–77
  number of systems of, 270
  organization of information in, 262–70, 499
  retrieval from, 250, 266–67
  short-term working distinguished from, 260–61, *260*
  as stage of memory, 256, *257*, 260–62
  storage in, 261–62, 499
long-term potentiation (LTP), 252–53, *253*
loosening of associations, 591
Lopez, Jennifer, 499
Lorenz, Konrad, 348–49, *349*
loss aversion, 299, *299*
Lovaas, Ivar, 657–58
Lovato, Demi, 561, 562
love, 507–11, *507*
low-balling strategy, 479
LSD (lysergic acid diethylamide), 149
Luchins, Abraham, 304, *305*
Luper, Paula, *610*
Lykken, David, 518, 601
lymphocytes, 450, 453

Ma, Yo-Yo, *275*
Mace, John, *424*
Machiavelli, Niccolò, 551
Machiavellianism, 551, 566
Mack, Michelle, 102, *102*, 104
MacLean, Paul, 386
MacNeill, David, 275
Madonna (performer), 375, *375*
magnetic field treatment, 626–27
magnetic resonance imaging (MRI), 83, *83*, 567, 569
Maier, Norman, 307, *307*
maintenance rehearsal, 263
Major, Brenda, 553
major depression, 579, *580*, 645
major life stressors, 447
maladaptiveness, in psychological disorders, 563
malaria, 110, 432
malnutrition, 339, 601
Mandel, Howie, *577*
M&M's study, 358, *359*
mania, 562, 645–47
manic depression, 561, 582–84
  see also bipolar disorder
manic episodes, 583
manifest content, 140
manipulating variables, in experimental method, 47–48
mantra, 145
MAOA gene, and aggression, 483
marble test, Piaget's, 358, *359*
marijuana, 149, 152–53, 158
  and chemotherapy, 153
  medicinal use of, 153, *153*
  and memory, 152
  and mental health problems, 152
  recreational use of, 152
Markus, Hazel, 547, 555
Marlatt, Alan, 155

marriage, 372–73, *373*, 508
  success rates for, *508*
Martian, The (film), 249
Mask of Sanity, The (Cleckley), 599
Maslow, Abraham, 16, 402–3, *403*, 459, 460, 527
Masters, William, 418
masturbation, 419
matching principle, 504
Mateen, Omar, 7, *7*
mates, selection of, 20, 372–73, 420–21
mathematics, understanding, 358–59
mating selection, 20
Matsumoto, David, 399
maximization scale, *309*
Mayberg, Helen, *642*, 643
McAdams, Dan, 543
McCarley, Robert, 140–41
McCarthy, Jenny, 607–8, *607*
McCollough, Celeste, *179*
McCollough effect, *179*
McCrae, Robert, 535
McKinnon, Margaret, 277
McMath, Jahi, 126, *126*
MDMA, 153, *153*
  medicinal uses of, 153
mean, 58, *59*
media, 5, *5*
  and imitation, 240
  misrepresentation of scientific findings by, 96, *96*
  and scientific reporting, 35
  and violence, 241–43, *242*
medial prefrontal cortex:
  and group membership, 472
  and social influence, 478
medial temporal lobes, and memory, 255–56
median, 59, *59*
media use, and youth, *241*
Medical College Admission Test (MCAT), 25
medications:
  and children with psychological disorders, 653, *654*
  and choosing a practitioner, 630–31
  and treatment of psychological disorders, 581, 592, 623–25, 634, 636, 638–39, 647–48, 652, 656
  see also drugs; psychopharmacology; *specific medications*
medicine, placebos as, 462
meditation, 145–46, 464
  and brain function, 145–46, *146*
  concentrative form of, 145, *145*
  and consciousness, 145–46
  mindfulness form of, 145, *145*, 620, 651
  and sleep, 142
medulla oblongata, 84, *85*
Mehl, Matthias, 543
Mehler, Jacques, 358, *359*
melancholia, 562
melatonin, 133
Melzack, Ronald, 202
memory, 249–84
  and addiction, 150
  and age regression, 283
  and aging, 376, 377–78
  altering of, 277, *278*
  and attitudes, 491
  and brain, 85, 86, 91, 102–3, 252–54, 255, 272–73, 277, 376
  and childhood, 280
  competitions, 267, *268*
  computer analogy of, 250, *251*, 260
  and conscious awareness, 586
  and consolidation, 250

context-dependent, 266, *266*
and cramming, 268–70
as crucial to our lives, 249
and culture, 264, *264*
definition of, 250
and development, 345–46
distortion of, 250, 278–84
and drugs, 255, 277–78
and emotions, 277, 280, 282, 388
encoding of, 250, *251*, 258, 263, *263*, 377
epigenetics of, 253–54
and evolution, 262
and exercise, 444
and experience, 250, 262, 263, 272
false, 282–83
and forgetting, 255, 274–77, 376
and hippocampus, 53
and hypnosis, 283
and influence of neurotransmission, 79, 80
information process model of, 250, *251*
and intelligence, 255, 272
and levels of analysis, 22
and levels of processing model, 263
long-term, 260–62, 381, 499
and marijuana, 152
and MDMA, 153
meaningful, 263
and medial temporal lobes, 255–56
and mind/body problem, 11
and misattributions, 280
network models of, 265–68, *265*
organization of information in, 259, 262–70
overview of, 250–56
and persistence, 277–78
physical location of, *254*, 255–56
and psychological disorders, 642
repressed, 283–84, *283*
retrieval of, 250, 266–67
and scientific foundations of psychology, 16
and sensation, 198, 256–58
sensory, *257*
and sleep, 133, 135, 138, 139, 141
span of, 259, 325, *325*
storage of, 250, *251*, 256–62
strategies for improving, 267
and stress, 449
and synaptic connections, 253
and themes of psychological science, 17, 18
and unconsciousness, 272–73, *273*
see also type or system of memory
memory bias, 278
memory formation and retrieval, 287
memory palace, 267
memory-retention test, *345*
Mendel, Gregor, 108, *108*, *109*
menopause, *see* menstrual cycle
menstrual cycle, 364, 417–18, 451, 643
and evolution, 364
mental age, 321
mental disorders, *see* psychological disorders
mental health continuum, 565, *565*
mental health practitioner, choosing a, 630–33, *632*
mental maps, 290, *291*
mental representation, 263
mental sets, 304–5, *305*
mere exposure effect, 490, *490*, 494, 504, 506
Merritte, Douglas (Albert B.), 221
message content, and persuasion, 494
meta-analysis, 62
metabolic syndrome, 434
metabolism, 414, 438, 609
Metcalfe, Janet, 409
methamphetamine, 148, 150, *150*, *151*, 153
method of loci, 267

methods of savings, 274
methylphenidate, 654
Miami Heat, 63
Michael J. Fox Foundation, *80*
microsleep, 138
midbrain, 84, *85*
middle ear, 189, *190*
Milgram, Stanley, 480–82, *480*, *481*
Mill, John Stuart, 11
Miller, George A., 16, *17*, 259
Miller's Analogy Test, 321
Milligan, Billy (case study), 587
Mills, Judson, 494
Milner, Brenda, 255
mind:
    adaptivity of, 19
    as blank slate, 208
    and brain, 4, 9, 16, 90
    functions of, 12–13
    and influence of neurotransmission, 79–80
    rational, 11
    representations of, 290–96
    and scientific foundations of psychology, 12–13, 16
    and study of consciousness, 121–58, *122*
    see also mind-body problem; psychological disorders; theory of mind
mind-body problem, 10–11
mindfulness-based cognitive therapy, 620
mindfulness meditation, 620, 651
Minds of Billy Milligan, The (Keyes), 587
minimal group paradigm, 471, *472*
minimally conscious state, 125
Minnesota Multiphasic Personality Inventory (MMPI), 542
Minnesota Twin Project, 112
mirror neurons, 244
    and autism spectrum disorder, 606
misattributions:
    of arousal, 392–95, *393*
    and memory, 280
    source, 280
Mischel, Walter, 409, 532
Miss M. (case study), 133
mnemonics, 267–68
mode, 59, *59*
modeling, 619
    and imitation, 240
ModeratedDrinking.com, 632
modern prejudice, 501, *501*
modern racism, 501
Molaison, Henry, *see* H.M.
Molly (MDMA), 153, *153*
monoamine oxidase (MAO), and aggression, 483
monoamine oxidase (MAO) inhibitors, 114, 624, 638
monoamines, 79, 483, 581
    see also specific monoamine
monocular depth perception, 182
moods:
    and emotions, 300, 384–85, 400
    and exercise, 444
    and influence of neurotransmission, 79
    and levels of analysis, 22
    and life satisfaction, *300*
    and memory, 267
    and psychological disorders, 573–86, 597, 598, 623, 645
    and sleep, 138
    see also emotions; *specific disorder*
moral dilemmas, 361–62
moral treatment, 562
moral values, 361–63

and development, 361–63
and emotion, 362
Morgan, Christiana, 541
morphemes, 310, *311*, 312
morphine, 80, 149–51, 158
mortality, *see* death
mortality, causes of, 431
Moskowitz, Judith, 458
Moss, Michael, 205
mothers:
    and psychological disorders, 605
    surrogate, 350, *350*
motion:
    aftereffects of, 186
    and perception, 185–86
motivation:
    and adaptive behavior, 406, 421
    and behavior, 402–27
    and behaviors for their own sake, 405
    and biology, 423–24
    and brain, 412, 416, 423–24
    and culture, 419–21
    and drives, 402–5
    and eating, 412–16, *414*
    and emotion, 383–27
    and environment, 422
    and genes, 423–24
    and goals, 408–10
    and incentives, 405–8
    and intelligence, 323
    and needs, 402–5
    overview of, 383–84
    and personality, 526, 531, 541
    pleasure as, *406*, *407*, *407*
    and self-determination, 406
    and self-perception, 406–7
    and self-regulation, 408
    and sexual behavior, 416–24
    and social influence, 473–74
    and social needs, 410–11
    and social psychology, 473–74
    and stereotypes, 500
    and treatment of psychological disorders, 621, 652
    see also incentives; rewards; *types of motivation*
motivational interviewing, 621
motor disorders, *603*
motor functions:
    and brain, 84, *85*, 87, *88*, *89*, 90, 609
    and development, 341–43
    and memory, 255, 272, *273*
    and nervous system, 75, 79
    and psychological disorders, 574, 589, 594, 609, 648
motor memory, *see* procedural memory
motor neurons, 71
motor skills, and memory, 271
Moulton, Samuel, 171–72, *171*
Mozart, Wolfgang Amadeus, 346–47
Mozart effect, 346–47, *346*
M.P. (case study), 186
Multimodal Treatment of Attention-Deficit Hyperactivity Disorder (MTA), 656
multiple personality disorder, 587–89
    see also dissociative identity disorder
multiple sclerosis (MS), 74–75
murder, *see* homicidal death
Murray, Henry, 408, 541, 542, *542*
music, 21–23, *22*, 346–47
    and negative behaviors, 22
mutations, 110, 605–6
mutilation, self-, 598
    see also self-abuse
myelination, 201, 339, 364

myelin sheath, *72*, 74
Myers, David, 463
MySpace, 551
"My Sweet Lord" (song), 280

N.A. (case study), 39, *39*
naloxone, 152
narcissism, 550–51, 554
narcissistic personality, 550–51, 596
narcolepsy, 136
Nash, John Forbes, *589*
National Center for Learning Disabilities, 105
National Institute of Drug Abuse, 153
National Institute of Mental Health
      (NIMH), U.S., 566, 578, 656
National Institutes of Health (NIH), 193, 660
National Suicide Prevention Lifeline, 585
National Survey of Drug Use and Health, 150,
      659
naturalistic observation, 33, 40, *40*
natural killer cells, 453
natural selection:
   at gene level, 486
   and harming and helping others, 486
   and themes of psychological science, 13
nature/nurture debate, 10, 111, 114, 327, 337, 367,
      568, *569*
Nazis, 472, 542
needs:
   hierarchy of, 402, *403*
   and motivation, 402–5, *403*, 410–11
   see also specific needs
need to belong, 410–11, *410*, 478
negative activation, 384, *384*
negative correlation, 44
negative feedback model, 404, *404*
negative punishment, 231–32, *232*
negative reinforcement, 229, *229*, 232
negative symptoms, of schizophrenia, 589, 592,
      647, 648
Neisser, Ulrich, 16
neocortex, and social groups, *471*
neo-Freudians, 524
NEO Personality Inventory, 542
neophobia, 504
nervous system:
   and biological basis of psychological science,
      70–80
   divisions of, *70*
   and endocrine system, 99–100, *100*
   and influence of neurotransmission on
      emotion, thought, and behavior, 75–80
   major divisions of, 97–99, *98*
   operation of, 70–80
   see also central nervous system; memory;
      peripheral nervous system
network models, of memory, 265–68
neural networks, 70
neurochemistry:
   and memory, 250, 256
   and psychological disorders, 569, 578
   and themes of psychological science, 17
   and treatment of psychological disorders,
      623, 639
neurodevelopmental disorders, *603*
neurogenesis, 102
neuroleptics, 624–25
neuromarketing, 119
neuronal firing, *see* action potential
neurons:
   and basic structure and functions of brain, 84
   as basic units of nervous system, 70, *71*
   definition of, 70
   and development of brain, 102
   and eating, 413

and hearing, 193
integration into communication systems of,
      97–101
   mirror, 244
   and motivation, 413
   and operation of nervous system, 70–72
   and sensation, 165, *166*, 170
   and sleep, 138, 140
   structure of, 71–72, *72*
neuroprosthetics, 119
neuropsychological testing, 567, *567*, *568*
neuroscience, 17–18
   clinical and consumer applications of, 119
   and RDoC, 566
neuroscience/biological psychology, 23
neuroses, 647
neuroticism, 520, 528, 530, 532, 539, 540, 566
   and BIs, 532
   and job satisfaction, 536
neurotransmission, 237
   and categories of transmitters, 76–80, *78*
   definition of, 75
   drugs and, 148
   and exercise, 444
   influence on emotion, thought, and behavior
      of, 76–80
   and learning, 210, 253
   and motivation, 417
   and nervous system, 75–80
   and psychological disorders, 569, 578, 581,
      593, 623, 636, 654
   relationship of receptors and, 76, *76*
   and sexual behavior, 417
   see also category of transmitter
neutral stimulus, 211–12, *213*
New Guinea study, 397, *398*
Newman, Mark, *112*
New York Longitudinal Study, 370
New Zealand study, 113–14, 483
Nichols, Robert, 516
nicotine, 148, 442
nicotine replacement therapy, 442–43, *443*
nightmares, 579
Nim Chimpsky (chimpanzee), 317, *317*
nine-dot problem, 304, *304*, *306*
Nisbett, Richard, 180, 329
nitric oxide, 417
NMDA receptors, 253
nodes, 265
nodes of Ranvier, *72*, *73*, 74
nomothetic approach, 541
nonspecific stress response, 450
nonverbal behavior, 496–97, *496*
norepinephrine, *78*
   definition of, 79
   and emotions, 385
   functions of, 79
   and influence of neurotransmission, 79
   and memory, 277
   and psychological disorders, 581, 624, 634
normal distribution, 321, *321*
norms:
   and adaptation, 20
   and binge drinking, 479–80, *479*
   conformity to, 475–79, *476*, *477*
   and eating, 415
   and identity, 367
   and motivation, 415
   and research methodology, 42
   and social influence, 475–79
   and themes of psychological science, 20
Northern Illinois University, shooting at, 579
Novocain, 203
nucleus accumbens, 87
nutrition, and brain, 339

Obama, Barack, 298, 335
obedience, 480–82, *480*, 481–82, *481*
obesity, 23, 79, 412, *412*, 414, 432–37, *434*
   and ADHD, 609
   global rates of, 434–35
   and life spans, 372
   and sleep apnea, 136
   stigma of, 436–37
object agnosia, 175
object constancy, 186–87, *187*
objective method, for personality assessment,
      543
object perception, 179–82
object permanence, 354–55
object relations theory, 524–25
observation:
   and actor-observer discrepancy, 498
   and learning, 209, 238–44, *239*, 525
   naturalistic, 40, *40*
   participant, 40, *40*
   and personality, 540, 543–44
   and research methodology, 40
   and scientific foundations of psychology, 11,
      16
   see also eyewitnesses
observational studies, *see* descriptive studies
observer bias, 42
obsessive-compulsive disorder (OCD), 79,
      577–78, *577*, *578*, 597, 619, 623, *627*, 628,
      636–38, *637*, 650, 658
obstructive sleep apnea, 136, *136*
Occam's Razor, 31–32
occipital cortex, and sleep, 135
occipital lobe:
   and basic structure and functions of brain,
      88, *123*
   and perception, *166*
occlusion, 183
Odbert, Henry, 528
odorants, 197–98, *198*
Oedipus complex, 524
Ogbu, John, 331
olfaction, *see* smell
olfactory bulb, 198, *198*
olfactory epithelium, 197, *198*
olfactory hallucinations, 591
Oliver, Jamie, *105*
Olympics, Rio, 2016, *80*
Omalu, Behnet, 124, *124*
One Flew over the Cuckoo's Nest (Kesey), 626
Ono, Yoko, *629*
On the Origin of Species (Darwin), 212
openness to new experience, 528, 529
operant chamber, 226, *226*
operant conditioning, 210, *211*, 224, 657
   and attitudes, 491
   and behavior modification, 230–35
   biology's influence on, 235–36
   classical conditioning as different than,
      224–27
   cognition's influence on, 235–38
   and learning, 224–38, *225*
   and psychological disorders, 570, 578, *578*,
      618
   and schedules of reinforcement, 230–35
operant reinforcement, and learning language,
      315, *315*
operational definitions, 47
opiate abuse, 80
opiod abuse, 151
opiod epidemic, 340
opiods, 149–51
opium, 158
opponent-process theory, 177
optical illusions, 179, 184–85, *185*

optic chiasm, 174, *175*
optic nerves, 174, *174*, *175*, 177
optimism bias, 446
optogenetics, 116, *118*
oral personalities, 524
oral stage, 524
organizational psychologists, 24
orgasm, 416
orgasm phase, 418
orienting reflex, 358
Orlando, Florida shootings, 7
ossicles, 189, *190*
Oswald, Lee Harvey, 277
Ouchi, Hajime, *179*
outer ears, 189, *190*
outgroup homogeneity effect, 471, 489
outgroups, 20, 470–71, *471*
oval window, 189
oxycodone, 150
oxytocin, 352, 416, 452, 462, 658

pain:
    and attitudes, 494
    and basic sensory processes, *202*
    controlling of, 202–3
    gate-control theory of, 202–3, *202*
    and humor, 396
    and hypnosis, 144
    and influence of neurotransmission, 80, *80*
    as motivation, 407
    and personality, 531
    phantom, 201
    types of, 201–2
Palmer, John, 281
panic attacks, *635*
panic disorder, 576, 635–36
Papez, James, 386
paradoxical sleep, *see* REM sleep
Paradox of Choice, The (Schwartz), 309–10
paralysis, 126
paranoid personality, 596
paraprofessionals, 631
parasympathetic division, 98–99, *98*
parent-child relationship:
    and development, 351–52, 361, 370–71
    and identity, 370–71
    and personality, 517–18, 523–24, 527
    see also attachment
parenting:
    and life transitions, 374
    style of, 361, *361*, 517–18
parents:
    development role of, 351–52, 361, 370–71
    and identity, 370–71
    and psychological disorders, 605, 609, 655
    and punishment, 232–33
    and sense of self, 370–71
    see also parent-child relationship;
        parenting
parietal lobes, 88–89, *88*, *123*, *166*
    and touch, 200
Paris mass shootings, 445
Parkinson's disease, 80, *80*, 87, 627, 643, 648
Parsons, Jim, 323
partial-reinforcement, 230
partial-reinforcement extinction effect, 231
participant observation, 40, *40*
passionate love, 507–8, *507*
Patall, Erika A., 308
Paterno, Joe, 475
patterns, and brain, 6
Pavlov, Ivan, 15, 211, *211*, *213*, 214, 215, 216, 217, 226
    experiments of, 211–12, *211*, *213*

Pavlovian conditioning, *see* classical
        conditioning
Peek, Kim, 326
peer review, 34, 35, *38*
peers, and sense of self, 369–70, *369*
    see also friendships
Pemberton, John, 150
"pendulum" experiment, 307, *307*
Penfield, Wilder, 88–89, *89*
Pennebaker, James, 543
Pepperberg, Irene, 318
perception, *175*
    and basic sensory processing systems, 171–72
    and brain, 164, *165*, 181, 194–95
    and color, 176–78, *176*, *177*, 187
    constancies in, 186–87, *187*
    and culture, 180
    depth, 182–84, *185*
    and development, 344–45, 358–59, *358*
    and emotions, 386
    and environment, *165*
    and figure and ground, 180
    Gestalt principles of, 179–80, *180*
    and hearing, *166*
    how we sense the world, *165*
    and illusions, 187, *187*
    and location of objects, 182–87
    and motion, 185–86
    object, 179–82
    and proximity and similarity, 180, *180*
    and psychological disorders, 589
    and scientific foundations of psychology,
        15–16, *15*
    and sensation, 164–72
    and shape, 187, *187*
    and sixth sense, 171–72
    size, 184–85, *187*
    and smell, *166*
    and spatial relationships, 182–87
    and stereotypes, 500–1, *500*
    and study of consciousness, *122*
    and survival, 180–81
    and taste, *166*
    and touch, *166*
    and vision, *166*
    and what versus where, 181
performance:
    and motivation, 404
    self-assessment of, 8–9, *8*
performance psychologists, 287
peripheral nervous system (PNS), 70, *70*, 97–99
persistence, and memory, 277–78
persistent depressive disorder, 580, *580*
persistent vegetative state, *see* coma
personal attributions, 497, 498
personal constructs, 525
personality, 515–59
    and adaptation, 535
    and age, 535–36
    assessment of, 540–46
    and behavior, 543, *543*
    and behaviorism, 525, 526
    biological basis of, 516, *535*
    and brain, 90–91, *91*
    changes in, 536–40, *538*
    and cognition, 522, 525–26
    and committed relationships, 536
    and consciousness, 522
    on a continuum, 528, *528*
    and culture, 529, 536, *536*, 538–40, *539*
    definition of, 516
    and development, 520–21, 523–24
    disorders of, 595–601, *596*
    and emotions, 530
    and environment, 536–38

and experience, 526, 528, 529
    and gender, 539–40
    and genetics, 516–19, 536
    and health, 454–55, *455*
    humanistic approach to, 526–27, *527*, 541
    and identity, 370
    and inconsistency, 532–34
    interactionist approach to, 533–34
    and learning, 525–26, 531
    and life experience, *537*
    and motivation, 526, 531, 541
    and neo-Freudians, 524
    parents' role in development of, 370
    and prediction, 541–42
    psychodynamic theories of, 522–25
    and psychological disorders, 582, 587–89,
        595–601, *596*, 650–53
    psychologists, 24
    and relationships, 504–5, *504*, *505*
    and self-construals, *554–55*, 555
    and situations, 525, 532–34, 536–38, 543–44
    socio-cognitive approach to, 525
    stability of, 532–40, *535*
    and stereotypes, 539
    structural model of, 522–23
    and temperament, *518*, 519–21
    theories of, 521–32
    traits, *see* traits, personality
    and unconsciousness, 522–25, *522*, 541
    and values, 525, *525*
personal myths, 543
person-centered approach, and personality, 527,
    527
person/situation debate, 533
perspective giving, 503
perspective taking, 503
persuasion, 494–95
Petitto, Laura Ann, 316, 317, *317*
p factor, 566
phallic stage, 524
phantom limbs, 104, *104*
phantom pain, 201
pharmaceutical industry, and drug research,
    644–45
pharmacology, and treatment of psychological
    disorders, 638–39, 647–48, 654–56, 658
Phenomenon, The (Ankiel), 287
phenotypes, 108–9, *109*, 110
pheromones, 199, 424
philosophy, 9
phobias, 221–24, *222*, 574–75, *575*, 619, 634–35
    see also specific phobias
phonemes, 311–12, *311*, 313–14
phonics, 318, *318*
photopigments, 173
phototherapy, 641, *641*
phrases, *311*
phrenitis, 562
phrenology, 81, *81*
physical activity, and sleep, 137
physical appearance, and first impressions,
    496–98
physical attractiveness, 505–7, *506*
    in mate selection, 505–7
physical condition, and aging, 372, 375
physical dependence, 156–58
physical development, 337–52, *342*
physical exercise, and brain development, 102
physical fitness, and behavior modification,
    233–35, *234*
physics, understanding of, 357–58
physiology, 12, 385–88, 569
    and eating, 412–14
Piaget, Jean, 353–59, *353*, *359*
    and cognitive development, 37

pidgin, 317
Pine, Daniel, 392
pineal gland, 133, *133*
Pinel, Philippe, 562
Pinker, Steven, 400
pitch, 192–93
pituitary gland, 99, 449
placebo/placebo effect, 462, 628–29, 636, 639,
    658
    and antidepressants, 644–45, 660
place coding, 192, *192*, 193
planning, 79, 326
    and basal ganglia, 87
plaque, and heart disease, 456
plasticity, of brain, 101–4, *102*, 104, 339
plateau phase, 418
Plato, 10
play, 406, 657, *657*
pleasure:
    as motivation, *406*, 407
    and personality, 522
pleasure principle, 407, 522
Plomin, Robert, 519
polarization:
    group, 474
    and nervous system, 73
political psychologists, 513
politics, and social psychology, 513
Polivy, Janet, 438
polygenic effects, 109
polygraphs, *see* lie-detector tests
polypeptides, 107
pons, 84, *85*
Ponzo, Mario, 184
Ponzo illusion, 184, *185*
population, research, *48*, 49
portable listening devices, 193, *193*
positive activation, *384*, 385
positive correlation, 43
positive illusions, 552
positive psychology, 459–65, *460*
positive punishment, 231, *232*
positive reappraisal, 458
positive reinforcement, 229, *229*, 232, 234–35
positive symptoms, of schizophrenia, 589, 647,
    648
positron emission tomography (PET), 83, *83*,
    567, 569
    see also brain imaging
postconventional morals, 362
postdecisional dissonance, 493
poster sessions, 34, *34*
posthypnotic suggestion, 143
postsynaptic neurons, 75
posttraumatic stress disorder (PTSD), 277, 566,
    571, 578–79, 586, 589, 619
potassium, and nervous system, 73
potentiation, long-term, 252–53, *253*
poverty, and development, 339–40
practical intelligence, 324
practice, and memory, 261
practitioners, *see* therapists
"pratfall effect," 505
prayer, 146
Preacher (TV show), *442*
preconscious, 522
preconventional morals, 362
prediction, 30, 46
    and correlational studies, 46
    and development, 360
    and learning, 218–21
    and personality, *520*, 541–42
    and research methodology, 30
prediction error, 219
    and dopamine, 220–21, *220*

predispositions, and psychological disorders,
    568
preferential-looking technique, 345, *345*
prefontal lobotomy, *see* lobotomies
prefrontal cortex:
    and basic sensory processes, 198, *199*
    and basic structure and functions of brain,
        90–92, *123*
    and eating, 412
    and emotions, 362–63
    and learning, 223
    and motivation, 412
    and psychological disorders, 643, 647
pregnancy:
    and alcohol and drug use, 340
    and psychological disorders, 595, 606, 642
    and stress, 340, 451
prejudice, 500–3
    definition of, 500
    modern, 501
Premack, David, 229, 360, 443
Premack principle, 229
prematurity, 338, *338*
prenatal period, 338
    see also pregnancy
preoperational stage, *353*, *354*, 355
prescribing drugs, 630–31, 633
presynaptic neurons, 75
pride, 361
    expressions of, 399, *399*
primacy effect, 260, *260*
primary appraisals, 457
primary auditory cortex, 90, 189
primary emotions, 384
primary motor cortex, 90
primary reinforcers, 228
primary sensory areas, *see* cerebral cortex
primary somatosensory cortex, 88, *88*, *89*
    and touch, 200
primary visual cortex, *see* visual cortex
Prince (musician), 161
privacy, 52, 55
proactive interference, 274, *275*
problem-focused coping, 457, *457*
problem solving:
    and brain structure and function, 326
    and choices, 308, *308*
    and decision making, 296–10, *297*
    and goals, 303–8
    and insight, 306–7, *307*
    and intelligence, 325
    and learning, 237
    overview about, 296–97
    and Piaget's cognitive development stages,
        356
    and psychological disorders, 574, 651
    and representations, 304–5
    and structural model of personality, 523
    and themes of psychological science, 19
procedural memory, *271*, 272–73
processing, automatic versus controlled, 127–28,
    128
product optimization, 205
progesterone, 416
prognosis, and psychological disorders, 568
projective methods, for personality assessment,
    541, *541*, 568
prolonged exposure, 619
propanolol, 278
prosocial behavior, 361, 485
prosopagnosia, 181
prospective memory, 267, *267*
protein, and genetics/genes, 107
prototypes, 291, *292*
proximity:

and relationships, 504
and similarity, 180, *180*
Prozac, 79, 581, 624, 639, 644, 658, 659, 660–61
pseudoinsomnia, 136
pseudotherapies, 629–30, *629*
psilocybin mushrooms, 149
psychiatrists, 630–31, *630*
psychoactive drugs, 148–49, *148*
psychoanalysis:
    definition of, 14
    and scientific foundations of psychology,
        14–15, *14*
    and treatment of psychological disorders, 617,
        617, 647
psychobiography, 543
psychodynamic theories:
    of personality, 522–25
    and treatment of psychological disorders,
        616–17
psychodynamic therapy, definition of, 618
psychological disorders, 560–13
    and adolescence, 600, 653–61, *660*
    and age, 650, 653
    and anxiety as root of different disorders,
        573–76
    assessment/diagnosis of, 564–68, *568*
    and behavior, 574, 578, 589, 592, 604
    and behaviorism, 570
    and biology, 79, 568–69, *569*, 574, 577, 581,
        605–6
    and brain, 569, 574, 593–94, 601, *602*, 606, 623,
        625–26, 634–35, 638, 639, 643, 647, 658
    and brain stimulation, 627–28, 637–38, 643
    categories of, 564–68, *565*
    causes of, 562, *562*, 568–70, *569*, 617
    and children, 594, 601–10, 653–61
    and cognition, 574, 576, *576*, 582, *582*, 589,
        649, 659
    and comorbidity, *566*, 568
    conceptualization and classification of,
        562–73, *583*
    and conditioning, 570, 578, *578*
    and consciousness, 570, 589
    and continuous dimensions, 565, *566*
    and culture, 563, 570, *570*, 572–73, 590, 622,
        622, 650
    and death/grieving, 633
    and development, 601–10, *603*, 653
    dimensional approach to, 565
    and emotions, 571, 574, 594, 598, 600–1,
        619–20
    and environment, 568–70, 578, 594–95, *595*,
        599, 601, 608, 630
    and etiology, 564, *565*
    and experience, 617, 618
    externalizing, 571, *571*
    and gender, 570–73, *571*, 576, 580–81, 598
    and genetics/genes, 106–7, 568–69, 578, 581,
        592, *593*, 594, 605, 609
    historical view of, 562, *562*
    and intelligence, 657, 659
    internalizing, 571, *571*
    and magnetic field treatment, 626–27
    as maladaptive, 563
    and medications, 581, 592
    and mood, 579–82, *580*, 597, 598, 645
    and parents, 605, 609, 655
    and personality, 582, 587–89, 595–601, 650–53
    and pregnancy, 595, 606, 642
    and pseudotherapies, 629–30, *629*
    and psychosurgery, 626, 628, 638, 647
    and sexual behavior, 583, 599
    and situations, 581, 640
    and social functioning, 575, *575*, 592, 603, *604*,
        658, 659

and suicide, 584
and testing, 567, *568*, 601
and thought disturbances, 586–95
treatment of, 615–65
treatment resistant, 625
and unconscious, 569
and violence, 599
see also specific disorder or type of treatment
psychological reasoning:
and critical thinking, 6–8
definition of, 6
psychological research, participation in, 54–55, *54*
psychological science:
and biological revolution, 17–18
and biology and behavior, 69–119
definition of, 4–9
genetic foundations of, 106–16
interdisciplinary aspects of, 23
and levels of analysis, 21–24, *21*
methods of, 4
psychological testing, 567, *568*, 601
psychological treatments, 629
psychotherapy versus, 633
psychology:
application of, 664–65
definitions of, 11
developments in, 17–25
and RDoC, 566
schools of thought and, 13–17, *14*
scientific foundations of, 9–17
study of, and wide ranging careers, 24–25, *24*
subfields of, 23–24
psychology of decision making, 335
psychometric approach, to intelligence, 320–22, *320*
psychoneuroimmunology studies, 453
psychopathology, 562, 566
psychopathy, 551, *551*, 599, 600, 652, 653
psychopharmacology, 616
psychophysics, 167
psychophysiological assessment, 82–84
psychosexual stages, 523–24
psychosis, 586, 594, 624–25, 651
definition of, 589
psychosocial factors, and health, 430–32
psychosocial motives, 408–10
psychosocial therapy, 648–49
psychosurgery, 626, 627, 638, 647
psychotherapy, 616–32, 643, 661
psychological treatments versus, 633
see also specific technique or method
psychotic disorder, 647
definition of, 588
see also specific disorder
psychotic episodes, 648, 649
psychoticism, 530
psychotropic medications, 623–25, 646, *646*, 647, 652
PsycINFO, 31
puberty, 363–65, 416
see also adolescence
Public Health Service, U.S., *52*
PubMed, 31
punishment:
and behavior, 231–35
definition of, 231
and learning, 232, *232*
and parents, 232–33
and personality, 531–32
physical, 233
as positive or negative, 231–32, *232*
and psychological disorders, 600
and treatment of psychological disorders, 619
pupil, 173, *174*

Pussin, Jean-Baptiste, 562
"Putting Psychology to Work," 27, 67, 119, 161, 205, 247, 287, 335, 381, 427, 467, 513, 559, 613, 665

qualitative information, and sensation, 166, *167*
quantitative information, and sensation, 166, *167*
questioning, and scientific method, 36–38
quetiapine, 646

race/ethnicity:
and depression, 643, 659
and identity, 368
and impressions, 500, *500*, 501
and intelligence, 330–31
and perception, 181
and stereotypes, 500, 501
racism, modern, 501
Rader, Dennis, 600
radical acceptance, 651
Raffaele, Kelsey, 29, *29*
Rain Man (movie), 326
Ramachandran, V. S., 170
Ramsey, Eddie, *127*
Ramsey, Erik, 126–27, *127*
random assignment, 49–50, *49*
random errors, 58, *58*
randomized clinical trials, 628
random sampling, 49
range, *59*, 60
rapid eye movements, *see* REM sleep
rational-emotive therapy, 619
rationalizing, 523
ratio schedule, 230–31
Raven Progressive Matrices Test, 331, *331*
raw values, 58
Rayner, Rosalie, 221
reaction time, 11
reaction times, 324–25
reactivity, 41
and descriptive research, 41
in observational studies, 41
reactivity effect, 41
reading, learning of, 318–19
reality:
and delusions, 590
virtual, 634
reality principle, 523
reappraising, 395–96
reasoning:
abstract, 356
and brain structure and function, 326
definition of, 6
moral, 362
and Piaget's cognitive development stages, 356
psychological, 6–8
see also thought/thinking
rebound effect, 395
receivers, and persuasion, 494
recency effect, 260, *260*
receptive aphasia, 312
receptors:
definition of, 76
and nervous system, 76
and sensation, 165, *166*, *190*, *194–95*, 197–98, *200*
and smell, *198*
see also sensation; *type of receptors*
reciprocal determinism, 525–26, *526*
reciprocal helping, 486
reciprocity, 470
recognition, and aging, 377
see also facial recognition
reconsolidation process, 282

and memory, 250–52, *251*
"recreational drugs," 148–49
reflected appraisal, 549
reflective listening, 621
reflexes, 71, 84, 341, 354
reframing, 502
reinforcement:
absence of, 237
as conditioning, 228–29
and definition of reinforcer, 226
and learning, 226–27
and personality, 525–26, 531
as positive or negative, 229, *244*
and potency of reinforcers, 229
and rewards, 237–38
schedules of, 230–35, *230–31*
successive approximations in, 227
and treatment of psychological disorders, 652, 657
vicarious, 240–41
see also rewards
reinforcement schedule, 234–35
rejection, and aggression, 482
relationships:
client-practitioner, 652
and development, 337, 369–71
and emotions, 400–2
healthy, 459
and learning, 232
and life transitions, 371–73
and psychological disorders, 582, 596, 599, 608, 618, 619
quality of, 503–11
romantic, 507–9, *507*, *509*, *510*
of roommates (college), 545–46
seeing nonexistent, 7
see also attachment; friendships; parent-child relationship; social interaction
relative comparisons, 298–99
relaxation techniques, *see* meditation
releasing factor, 99
reliability, 56–57
religion, 463
religious ecstasy, 146, *147*
REM behavior disorder, 137
REM dreams, 139
REM sleep, 134–35, 136, 138, *140*
repeated TMS, 627
replication, of studies, 35–36, *35*
representations:
analogical, 290, 291, *291*
and memory, 263
mental, 290–96
and Piaget's cognitive development stages, 353–56
and problem solving, 304–5
restructuring, 304, 305
symbolic, 291–93, *291*
representativeness heuristic, 299–300
repressed memories, 283–84, *283*
Reproducibility Project, 35–36
reproduction:
and adaptation, 13, 18–19
and depression, 643
and genetic basis of psychological science, 109–10
and heredity, 108–10, *110*
and life transitions, 374
and motivation, 407, 410, 420
and sexual behavior, 420
and themes of psychological science, 13
Rescorla, Robert, 218
Rescorla-Wagner model, 218, *219*
Research Domain Criteria (RDoC), 566–567, 646

research methodology, 29–67
  and animals, 53–54
  and averaging, 50
  and bias, 42, 644, *645*
  and case studies, 39, *39*
  and causality, 44, *46*, 48
  and correlational studies, 43–46, *43*, 60–61,
    60
  and cross-cultural studies, 50–51, *50*
  and data, 34
  and descriptive studies, 39–43, *39*
  and ethics, 51–55
  and experimental studies, 46–48, *50*
  and hypotheses, 32–34
  and meta-analysis, 62
  and observation, 40
  and prediction, 30
  and psychological science, 4
  and scientific method, 30–38, *32*
  and self-reporting, 40, *41*
  and statistical procedures, 55–64
  and theories, 31–32
  and types of studies, 38–51, *41*
  and unexpected findings, 36
  and variables, 46–48
reserpine, 647
resilience, and health, 458–59
resiliency, 458–59
resolution phase, 418
response:
  bias, 169, *169*
  and scientific foundations of psychology, 16
  and sensation, 167–69, *167*
response-prevention therapy, 637, *637*
responsibility:
  diffusion of, 487
  and psychological disorders, 656
rest, and sleep, 137
resting membrane potential, 72–73, *73*
restrained eating, 438
restrictive dieting, 437–41
restructuring:
  cognitive, 619, *619*
  of representations, 304, 305
results, reporting of, *32*, 34
reticular activating system (RAS), 531
reticular formation, 84, *85*
retina, 173, *174*, *175*, 176, 182, *183*, 184, 345
retrieval, of memory, 250, *251*, 259, 266–67, 275
  aging and, 377
retrieval cues, 266–67
retroactive interference, 274, *275*
retrograde amnesia, 276, *276*, 587
reuptake, 77, 79, 637
rewards, 228
  and attitudes, 493
  biological basis of, 237–38
  and learning, 237–38
  and motivation, 405, *406*
  and personality, 531–32
  and psychological disorders, 619
  and scientific foundations of psychology, 16
  wanting vs. liking, 238, *238*
  see also incentives
right hemisphere, 94–95, *95*, 96, *96*, 181
  and aging, 377
  and language, 312–13
risk, and BIs, 532
risk aversion, 335
risk-benefit ratio, 52
risk judgments, and emotions, 301
risky-shift effect, 474
Risperdal, 648, 658
Ritalin, 654–56, *655*, 656
Robins, Lee, 158

Rocco, Johnny, 478
rods, 173, *174*
Rogan, Seth, 249
Rogers, Carl, 16, *16*, 459, 527, *527*, 621, *621*
Rogers, Tim, 547
role models, 157
Rolling Stones, the, 375, *375*
romantic relationships, 507–9, *507*
  and conflict, *508*, 510
  principles of, 509, *510*
roommates, college, and cleanliness, 545–46,
  546
rooting reflex, 341, *341*
Rorschach inkblot test, 541, *541*
Rosch, Eleanor, 291
Rosenthal, Robert, 42, 496
Ross, M., *553*
rotavirus, 432
Rotella, Bob, 287
Rotter, Julian, 525, *525*
round window, 189
Rozin, Paul, 415
rumination, 395
runner's high, 146, 641
Russian newspaper reporter, memory of, 274

Sacks, Oliver, 327
sadism, 473–74
Salem witch trials, 149
salivary reflex, 211, *214*
Salt, Sugar, Fat (Moss), 205
same-sex marriage, 373
sampling, *48*, 49, *49*
Sanders, Bernie, 298
Sandusky, Jerry, 475
SAT (Scholastic Aptitude Test), 409
satiety, 412
saturation, 177
savants, 326–27
savings, and memory, 274
scatterplots, 43, 60, *60*
Schachter, Stanley, 392, 411, 478, 504
Schachter-Singer Two-Factor theory of
  emotion, 390–95, *392*, *394*
Schacter, Daniel, 271, 283–84
Schank, Roger, 295
schemas:
  cognitive, 498
  definition of, 263
  and memory, 263–65
  and scripts, 295
  self-, 547–548, *547*
  and stereotypes, 294, *294*
  and thinking/thought, 293–95
  see also stereotypes
schemes, and Piaget's cognitive development
  stages, 353, 354–56
Schiavo, Terri, 126, *126*
schizoid personality, 596
schizophrenia, 566, 595
  and autism spectrum disorder, 606
  and biology, 592–95
  and conceptualization and classification of
    psychological disorders, *569*, 570, 589–92,
    589, 593
  definition of, 589
  and dementia praecox, 564
  diagnostic criteria for, 589–92, *590*
  and gender, 570, *571*
  and genetics, 646
  treatment for, 622, 624–25, 626, 646, 647–50
  virus hypothesis of, 594
schizotypal personality, 596
schizovirus hypothesis, 594
schooling, and IQ, 329

school psychologists, 23
Schultz, Wolfram, 220
Schwartz, Barry, 309–10
Schwarz, Norbert, 300
science, four primary goals of, 30–32
scientific conferences, 34
scientific method, 9, 30, *31*, *32*
  and critical thinking, 30–38
scientific thinking, 34, 37, *37*, *38*, 42, *42*, 44, *115*,
  122–23, *123*, 130, *130*, 196, *197*, 213, 222, *222*,
  236, *239*, 257, *266*, *281*, 296, 345, *350*, 394,
  398, *454*, *477*, *481*, 488–89, *500*, 642, 660
scripts, 295
  and schemas, *295*
  sexual, 419, *419*
seasonal affective disorder (SAD), 641, *641*
Seattle Longitudinal Study, 378
secondary appraisals, 457
secondary emotions, 384
secondary reinforcement, 228, 234
secondary traits, 541
second-generation antipsychotics, 648
second-order conditioning, 214–15
secure attachment, 350–51, 507
seizures, 625, 626, 642, 648
selection bias, 50
  see also bias, and research methodology
selective attention, 128–29
selective breeding, 108, *108*
selective permeability, 73
selective serotonin reuptake inhibitors (SSRIs),
  79, 581, 624, *624*, 636–37, 639, 658, 659–61
self:
  collective, *554–55*, 555
  independent, *554–55*, 555
  interdependent, *554–55*, 555
  and memory, 255
  mental strategies to main views of, 551–54
  and psychological disorders, 598
  sense of, 255, 369–71, 599
self-abuse, 598
self-actualization, 403, 527
self-awareness, 474, 547
  of one's own inadequacies, 8–9, *8*
self-care, 649
self-concept, 547–49
self-construals, *554–55*, 555
self-control, *see* self-regulation
self-destructiveness, 651
self-determination theory, 406
self-efficacy, 408
self-enhancement, 546–56
self-esteem:
  across the life span, *549*
  and obesity, 436
  and personality, 527
  and prejudice/discrimination, 489, 500
  and psychological research, 54–55
  and relationships, 507
  and social regard, 549–51, *550*
  and treatment of psychological disorders,
    624, 641
self-help, 630
self-hypnosis, 144, *144*
self-injury, 651
  and autism spectrum disorder, 605, 658
  and suicide, 585
self-judgment, and performance, 8–9
self-knowledge, 543, 547–56
self-labeling, 502
self-monitoring, 533
self-mutilation, 598, 651
  see also self-abuse
self-perception theory, 406–7
self-ratings, social comparisons and, *553*

self-regulation, and motivation, 408
self-reporting, 538–39, 542, 543, *544*
    in research methodology, 40, *41*
self-respect, 651
self-schema, 547–48, *547*
self-serving biases, 7, 553–56, *554–55*
Seligman, Martin, 16, 217, 459, 582
Selye, Hans, 99, 450, 452
semantic memory, *271*, 272
semantics, 311
semi-starvation study, 437–38, *437*
sensation, 164–72
    and adaptation, 169, *169*
    and aging, 377
    basic processes of, *190*, *198–99*, *200–1*
    and brain, *165*, *166*, *190*, *194–95*, *198–99*,
        200–1
    definition of, 164
    and development, *339*, 344–45, 354–55
    and emotions, 386
    and environment, 169
    and genetics, 195
    and learning, *208*
    and memory, 198, 256–58
    and sensory thresholds, 167–68, *167–68*
    and sixth sense, 171–72
    see also specific senses
sensation-seeking, 601
sensitive periods, 338–41, 348
sensitization, 209–10, *211*
sensorimotor stage, *353*, 354–55
sensory coding, 165, *167*
sensory memory, 256–58, *257*, *258*
sensory neurons, 71
sensory receptors, 165
sensory science, employment opportunities in,
    205
sensory-specific satiety, 415
sensory thresholds, 167–68, *167–68*
sentences, *311*
separation anxiety, 349–50
September 11, 2001, terrorist attacks, 279, *279*,
    445
serial position effect, 260, *260*
Seroquel, 646
serotonin:
    and aggression, 483
    definition of, 79
    functions of, *78*, 79
    and influence of neurotransmission, 79
    and motivation, 417
    and personality, 518
    and psychological disorders, 581, 624, 634,
        637, 639, 658
    and sexual behavior, 417
    and sleep, 138
set-points, 404, 413, 437
setting goals, 234
sex, *see* gender
sex characteristics, primary and secondary,
    363–64, 367
sexual anxiety, 520, *521*
sexual behavior:
    and adaptive behavior, 421
    and alcohol, 155
    and behaviors affecting health, 464
    and biology, 416–18, *417*, 423–24
    and brain, 86, 423–24
    and depression, 639
    and endocrine system, 100
    and environment, 422
    and frequency of sex, 508
    and gender, 100, 419–20, *420*
    and hormones, 100–1, 416–24, *417*
    and love, 508

    and mania, 583
    and mating strategies, 420–21
    and motivation, 407, 416–24
    and nervous system, 100
    and psychological disorders, 599
    and relationships, 508
    and safe sex, 464
    and scientific foundations of psychology, 14
    and sexual orientation, 421–24
sexual dysfunction, 624, 639
sexual orientation, 421–24, *424*
sexual reproduction, *see* reproduction
sexual response cycle, 418, *418*
sexual strategies theory, 420
shadowing, 128, *129*
shame, 361
shape constancy, 187
shape perception, 187, *187*
shaping, 227, *227*, 316–17
Shapiro, Alexis, *412*
Shaver, Phillip, 507
Shaw, Herman, *52*
Shedler, Jonathan, 156
Shepard, Roger, *16*, *187*
Sherif, Muzafer, 476, 488
Shiffrin, Richard, 256, *257*, 273
Shiva Fellowship Church Earth Faire, *157*
shock experiments, 480–82, *481*
short-term memory, 256, *257*, 258
    see also working memory
"shotgun interventions," 465
shyness, 520, 532–33
sickle-cell disease, 110, *110*
Siegel, Shepard, 223–24
signal-detection theory, 168–69, *168–69*
sign language, 316, *316*
similarity, proximity and, 180
Simon, Théodore, 320
Simonides, 267
Singer, Jerome, 392
single-pulse TMS, 626
situational attributions, 497
situationism, 532–34, *532*, 543–44
situations:
    and aggression, 483
    and depressive disorders, 581
    and genetics and behavior, 18
    and harming and helping others, 485–88
    and impressions, 497–98
    influence on behavior of, 473–74
    and personality, 525, 532–34, 536–38
    and psychological disorders, 581
    and relationships, 504–7
    and research methodology, 41
    and social influence, 480–82
    and social psychology, 473–74, 480–82,
        485–88, 497–98
    strong, 533, *533*
    and treatment of psychological disorders, 640
    weak, 533, *533*
sixth senses, 171–72
size constancy, 186–87
size perception, 184–85, *184*, *187*
skepticism, 5
skills, 322
skin, and sensory receptors, 200
Skinner, B. F., 15, 224, *225*, 226–27, *226*, 232–33,
    235, 237, 315, 525, 526
Skinner box, 226, *226*
sleep, 133–42
    as adaptive behavior, 137–39
    and adenosine, 142
    and alcohol, 142
    as altered state of consciousness, 133–35
    amount of, 133

    and basic structure and functions of brain,
        84, *85*
    and brain, 133–42, *134*
    and caffeine, 142
    and cognitive behavioral therapy, 136
    deprivation of, *see* sleep deprivation
    disorders, 135–37, *136*
    and electronic devices, 142
    and exercise, 142
    and meditation, 142
    and moods, 138
    and narcolepsy, 136
    and nervous system, 79
    and obstructive sleep apnea, 136, *136*
    and psychological disorders, 574, 575, 580, 598
    purpose of, 137–39
    and restoration, 137
    and sleep-wake cycles, 100
    stages of, 134, *135*
    strategies for, 141–42, *142*
    see also dreams; REM sleep
sleep apnea, 136, *136*
sleep deprivation, 137–38, *142*
    and adenosine, 142
    and caffeine, 142
    and exercise, 142
    and meditation, 142
    and napping, 142
sleeper effect, 280
sleep spindles, 134
sleepwalking, 137
slow-wave sleep, 134, 138
smell, 86, 196–99, *198*, 344
    and perception, *166*
Smith, Will, 124, *124*
Smithies, Oliver, 116
smoking, 44–45, 51, *51*, 156, 157, 441–43, *441*,
    442, 455, 463, 464, 632
    and children, 157
    and epigenetic tags, 114
    and imitation, 240, *240*
    quitting of, 442–43
Snoop (Gosling), 543
sociability, 519
social anxiety disorder, 575, *575*, 577, 634
    see also social phobia
social blunders, and bystander apathy, 487
social brain hypothesis, 470, *471*
social comparisons, 411, 552–53, *553*
social development, 337, 347–52
social exclusion, 478
social facilitation, 473, *473*
social factors:
    and emotions, 400–1
    and genetic basis of psychological science,
        113–14
    and psychological disorders, 575, 592–95,
        604, 658, 659
    see also relationships
social identity theory, 471
social influence, 469–13
social integration, 461–62
social interaction:
    and psychological disorders, 592, 603, *604*
    and treatment of psychological disorders,
        649, 656, 658, 659
    see also relationships
social intuitionist model, and morality, 362
socialization:
    and attitudes, 490–93, *490*
    and development, 337
    and emotions, 399, 401
    and gender, 367
    and identity, 367, 368
    and morality, 362

social learning, 239
social loafing, 475
social multiplier, 327
social needs, and motivation, 410–11
social neuroscience, 17
social norms, 476
    see also norms
social norms marketing, and binge drinking, 479–80
social phobia, 575, *575*, 620
social psychology, 23–24
    and adaptation, 486, 552
    and attitudes, 490–95
    and attributions, 496–98, 509
    and cognition, 493–94
    and evolution, 486, 500
    and gender, 499
    and harming and helping others, 482–90
    and impressions, 496–502
    and motivation, 473–74
    and politics, 513
    and relationships, 503–11
    and self-knowledge, 547–56
    and situations, 473–74, 480–82, 485–88, 497–98
social regard, 549–51
social-skills training, 619, 620, 649, *649*
social support, *see* support, social
socio-cognitive theories, of personality, 525
sociocultural model, and psychological disorders, *569*, 570
socioeconomic status (SES), and intelligence, 329
socioemotional development, 340
socioemotional selectivity theory, 376, 377
sociometer theory, 550, *550*
sodium, and nervous system, 73
somatic markers, 301
somatic marker theory, 301
somatic nervous system, *70*, 97–99
somatosensory hallucinations, 591
somatosensory homunculus, 88, *89*
somatosensory nerves, 71
somatosensory signals, 97–98
somnambulism, 137
sound localization, 189
sound waves, 188, *188*, *190*
    definition of, 188
source amnesia, 280
source attribution, 494
source credibility, 96, *96*, 346–47, *346*, 644–45, *645*
    judging of, 5–7, 38
source misattributions, *see* misattributions, source
spanking, 233, *233*
spatial relationships, 88, 175, 182–87
Spearman, Charles, 322, *322*
Spears, Britney, 561–62
species, attachment across, 348–49, *349*
specific factors, 629
specific learning disorders, *603*
speech, *94*, 591, 604
    disorganized, 591–92
speech production, 314
speech waveform, *312*
Spelke, Elizabeth, 357
Sperling, George, *257*, 258
Sperry, Roger, 92, 96
spinal cord:
    and basic structure and functions of brain, 84
    and brain, *81*
    and sensation, *202*
spirituality, *462*, 463–64
    and well-being, *462*, 463–64

split brain, 92–95, *92*, 94–95, *94*, *95*, 96
spontaneous recovery, and learning, *214*, 215–16
sports concussions, 124, *124*
sports psychologists, 23, 287
spreading activation models, 265
Spurzheim, Johann, 81
SSRIs, *see* selective serotonin reuptake inhibitors
standard deviation, 60, *321*
Stanford-Binet test, 320
Stanford prison study, 473–74, *474*
Stanford Revision of the Binet-Simon Scale, 320
Stark, Susan, 411
startle response, 574
State Department, U.S., 445
state-dependent memory, 267
statistical procedures, 55–64
statistical significance, 62
statistics, misunderstanding, 63, 171–72
status, in mate selection, 505
STEM occupations, 665
stereoscopic vision, 183
stereotypes:
    automatic categorization as basis of, 498–501, *499*
    and depression, 643
    and emotions, 399
    and gender, *294*
    and impressions, 498–503
    and ingroup-outgroup bias, 500
    inhibiting, 502
    and perception, 500–1, *500*
    and personality, 539
    and prejudice, 489, 500–3
    and race, 500–1
    and schemas, *294*, *294*
stereotype threat, 331, *331*, *332*
Stern, Wilhelm, 321
Sternberg, Robert, 323
Steve Jobs (film), 249
Stickgold, Robert, 138
stigma:
    of obesity, 436–37
    and psychological disorders, 581, *581*
stigma, and psychotherapy, 622
stimulants, and addiction, 148, *148*, 150
stimulus, and detection, 165
    see also sensation
stimulus discrimination, 215, *215–16*
stimulus generalization, 215, *215–16*, 221, *222*
Stohr, Oskar, 112
Stoner, James, 474
storage, of memory, 250, *251*, 256–62, 270
Strange Situation Test, 349–50, *351*
stream of consciousness, 12–13
streptococcal infections, 578
stress, 579
    and adolescence, 364
    and biology, 449–50
    and brain, 449, 459
    chronic, 452, 453
    coping with, 447–50, *450*, 464
    and culture, 622
    in daily life, 447–48
    definition of, 447
    and development, 338, 340
    and dissociative disorders, 586
    as distress (duress), 447
    as eustress, 447
    and evolution, 451
    and exercise, 463–64
    and gender, 451–52
    and health, 452–59, *454*, 463
    and heart disease, 454–57, *455*
    and hostility, 455–56, *455*

and immune system, 452–54, *454*
    and interpersonal relations, 448
    and pregnancy, 340
    and psychological disorders, 568, *569*, 574, 582, 643
    and restrained eaters, 438
    stages of, 450
    types of, 447–48
    and working memory, 449
stressors, 447
    short term, and immune system, 450
stress resistance, 458
stress scale, 447, *448*
stroboscopic motion perception, 186, *196*
stroke, 80, 89, 102, 103, 136, 156, 375, 412, 431
structuralism, 12
structural model of personality, 522–23
studies:
    conducting of, *32*, 34
    designing of, *32*, 33–34
    replication of, 35–36
    sponsored by drug companies, 644–45, *645*
studying, strategies for, 268–70, *270*
study-skills course study, 278
Stunkard, Albert, 436
Styron, William, 643–44, *643*
subcortical structures:
    and basic structure and functions of brain, 85–87, *86*
    and emotions, 392
    and memory, 256, *256*
    see also specific structures
subjectivity, 12
    and study of consciousness, 122, *122*
subliminal perception, 131–32, *132*
substance abuse, 564, 575, 655–56
    see also alcohol, abuse of; drugs, abuse of
Substance Abuse and Mental Health Services Administration (SAMHSA), 659, *659*
substance abuse prevention and treatment, 161
subtyping, 499
successive approximations, 227
sucking reflex, 341, *341*, 354
suggestibility, 281–84, *281*
    see also hypnosis
Sugiyama, Lawrence, *40*
suicide, 580, 581, 584–86, *585*, 599, 640, 642, 651, 659–60, *660*
    factors in, 584–85, *585*
    and genetics, 585
    and panic attacks, 576
    and psychological disorders, 584
    and self-injury, 585
suicide attempts, 584
suicide ideation, 584
superego, 523
superordinate goals, 489
superstitions, 227–28, *227*
supertasters, 195–96, *196*
support, social:
    and health, 461–62
    and stress, 461
    and treatment of psychological disorders, 619, 622, 641
suppression, thought, 395
suprachiasmatic nucleus, 133, *133*
surface structure, 316
surgery, and psychological disorders, 626, 627, 638, 647
surrogate mothers, 350, *350*
surveys, 33
survival:
    and adaptation, 13, 18–19, 20
    and basic structure and functions of brain, 84
    and development, 347–52

and emotions, 396, 400, 401
and harming and helping others, 486
and ingroup-outgroup bias, 500
and memory, 262
and motivation, 402, 407, 410
and perception, 182
and stress, 451
and themes of psychological science, 13, 18–19, 20
survival of the fittest, 13
Swedo, Susan, 578
symbolic representations, 290, *290*
concepts as, 291–93
sympathetic division, 98–99, *98*
sympathetic nervous system, 456
and stress, 449
sympathy, 361
synapse/synapses, 339
definition of, 72–73
and development, 339, *339*
and intelligence, 329
and learning, 210
and nervous system, 72–73, *72*, 75–76, 80
and psychological disorders, 623
synaptic pruning, 339
synesthesia, 170, *170*
syntax, 311, 315, 317
systematic desensitization, 619, 634
systematic errors, 58, *58*
systems approach, 621

taboos, 416
tabula rasa, 208
tactile stimulation, 200
Tajfel, Henri, 471
Tajin Kyufusho, 572
"talk" psychotherapy, 618
see also psychoanalysis; psychodynamic theories
tardive dyskinesia, 625, 648
taste, 194–96, *194, 197*, 344, 412, 414
cultural influences on, 196
five basic sensations of, 194–96
and mother's diet, 196, *197*
and perception, *166*
taste buds, 194, *194, 195*
Taylor, Amillia Sonja, *338*
Taylor, Shelley, 451, 552
T cells, 453
Teasdale, John, 620
technology, 4
in the classroom, 130–31, *130*
technology-based treatments, 631–32
technology companies, 67
teenage brain, 364
teenagers:
and frontal cortex, 364
and limbic system, 364
telegraphic speech, 315
temperament:
definition of, 519
and development, 370
and gender, 519–20
and personality, *518,* 519–21
temperature, and sensation, 200
temporal coding, 192, 193
temporal lobes:
and basic structure and functions of brain, *88,* 90, *123*
and memory, 255–56, *255*
and perception, *166*
and psychological disorders, 593
tend-and-befriend response, 451, *451*
teratogens, 340–41
Terman, Lewis, 320

terminal buttons, 71, 72, *72,* 77
Terrace, Herbert, 317
terrorism, 24, 279, 482
Tessler, Linda, 105
testable hypotheses, 31
testing:
aptitude, 320
intelligence, 324, 329, 331–32
as measurement of intelligence, 320–22
neuropsychological, 567, *567*
psychological, 567, 601
and psychological disorders, 567, *568,* 601
validity of, 321–22
see also specific tests
testosterone, 100, 416
and aggression, 483–84
and facial width, *506*
test trials, 212
texting, see cell phone use
texture gradient, 183
thalamus, *175*
and basic structure and functions of brain, 86, *86*
and emotions, 387, *387*
and perception, *166,* 179
and sensation, 165, 174, *195,* 198, 200, *201*
and taste, 194
and touch, 200
Thatcher, Margaret, *181*
Thatcher illusion, 181, *181*
THC (tetrahydrocannabinol), 152
Thematic Apperception Test (TAT), 541, *541*
theories:
good, 31
and research methodology, 31–32
theory, definition of, 31
theory of mind, 359–60, *360,* 361, 604
therapists:
choosing of, 630–33, *631, 632*
client relationship with, 652
theta waves, 134, *134*
thimerosal, in vaccines, 607–8
Thinking Eye, the Seeing Brain, The (Enns), 172–73
Thinking Fast and Slow (Kahneman), 127
"Think like a Psychologist," 63, 96, 171–72, 227–28, 284, *284,* 302–3, 346–47, 389, 445–46, *445,* 479, 554–56
thin slices of behavior, 497
third-variable problem, 45
This Is Your Brain on Music (Levitin), 188
Thomas, Alexander, 370
Thorndike, Edward, 225–26, *225*
Thorndike's puzzle box, 225, *225*
thought suppression, 395
thought/thinking:
abstract, 356
and application of psychological science, 4, 5
and behavior, 16
biased, and anxiety disorder, 576, *576*
and categorization, 291
critical, 4–6, 36–38, 171–72, 227–28, 356
definition of, 290
influence of neurotransmission on, 76–80
and language, 289–32
and Piaget's cognitive development stages, 353
and psychological disorders, 570
rational, 523
and representations, 290–91
and scientific foundations of psychology, 13–17
and structural model of personality, 522–21

unwanted, and anxiety disorders, 577–79
see also cognition; decision making; mind; problem solving; reasoning; representations
threats, 576
thresholds, 167–68, *167–68*
tickling, 200
time, and eating, 414
tip-of-the-tongue phenomenon, 275
Titchener, Edward, 12, 15
tobacco, and children, *296*
Todd, Amanda, 370, *370*
token economies, 234
tolerance, 156, 224
Tolman, Edward, 236, *236*
Tomasello, Michael, 313
Tomkins, Silvan, 391
Tong, Frank, 122
top-down processing, 164, 182
touch, 199–203, *200–1,* 344
and parietal lobes, 88
and perception, *166*
sensory receptors for, 200
"Tower of Hanoi" problem, 303–4, *304*
toxins, and influence of neurotransmission, 77, 79
Tracy, Jessica, 399
traits, personality:
as approach for studying personality, 522, 528–29
assessment of, 540–43, 541–42, *544*
as behavioral dispositions, 528–29
central, 541
consistency of, 516
on a continuum, 528, *528*
definition of, 516
and life events, 536–38
and person-situation debate, 533
secondary, 541
stability of, 534–38
tranquilizers, 623, 647
transcendental meditation, 145
transcranial magnetic stimulation (TMS), 84, *84,* 626–27, *627,* 642
repeated, 627
single-pulse, 626
transduction, and sensation, 165, 172
transgender, 367–68, *368*
transgenic mice, 54, *54*
transitions, life, 371–73
transitivity, 470
trauma, 277, *277,* 568, 570, 579, 586, 599, 617, 618, 619, 629, 634, 651
and correlational studies, 45
traumatic brain injuries (TBIs), 124, *125*
Treatment of Adolescents with Depression Study (TADS), 660–661, *660*
treatment resistant disorders, 625
Trebek, Alex, 497, *498*
trepanning, 626, *626*
Triandis, Harry, 555
trichromatic theory, *176*
tricyclic antidepressants, 624, 638, 639
Triplett, Norman, 473
Trivers, Robert, 486
Trudeau, Justin, *490*
Trump, Donald, 298
trust, 462–63, *462*
Tsien, Joseph, 253
Tugade, Michele, 459
Tulving, Endel, 266, 272
Turner, John, 471
Tuskegee Institute, 52
Tversky, Amos, 297–98, *297*
Twain, Mark, 401

twins:
  dizygotic, 111–13, *112*
  and emotions, 401
  and genetic basis of psychological science,
    111–13
  and intelligence, 327
  monozygotic, 111–13, *112*
  and motivation, 423
  and obesity, 436
  and OCD, 578
  and personality, 516–17, *517*, 536
  and psychological disorders, 569, *569*, 581,
    583, 593, *593*, 605, 609
  and sexual behavior, 423
twin studies, 111–13, *112*, 423
two-factor theory, 392–95, *392*, *394*
Type A behavior pattern, 455, *455*
Type B behavior pattern, 455, *455*
tyramine, 638

unattended information processing, 128
unconditional positive regard, 527, 621
unconditioned response (UR), 212, *213*
unconditioned stimulus (US), 212, *213*, 214, *214*,
  218–19, *220*, 223, 228
unconscious:
  definition of, 14
  as influencing behavior, 131
  and memory, 272–73, *273*
  and personality, 521–25, 541
  and psychological disorders, 569
  and scientific foundations of psychology, 14
  and study of consciousness, 131
  and treatment of psychological disorders,
    617–18
unexpected findings, 36
unihemispheric sleep, 137
uniqueness, individual, and personality, 541
United Nations Office on Drugs and Crime, 147
universal grammar, 316
unresponsive wakefulness syndrome, 126, *126*
Up documentary series, 534, *534*
U.S.A. Memory Championships, 267
"use it or lose it" policy, 339
"Using Psychology in Your Life," 24–25, 54–55,
  60, 105, *105*, 141–42, *142*, 193, 233–35,
  268–70, *270*, 308–9, *309*, 374, *374*, 395–96,
  395, 463–65, 509–10, *510*, 545–46, *546*,
  584–85, *585*, 632–33, *632*

vaccinations, and autism spectrum disorder,
  607–8, *607*
valence, of emotions, 384, *384*
validation, 651
validity:
  construct, 56, *56*
  external, 56
  internal, 56, *56–57*
  and research methodology, 55–56, *56–57*
  of tests, 321–22
Valium, 80
values, and personality, 525, *525*
variability, 60
variable interval schedule (VI), 230, *230*
variable ratio schedule (VR), 231, *231*
variables:
  dependent, 47
  manipulating, in experimental method,
    47–48

and research methodology, 38, 46–48, *46*,
  60–61
variable schedules, 230–31, *230*, *231*
variation, 113
variety, and eating, 414–15, *414*
Vazire, Simine, 544
Ventner, J. Craig, *108*
ventral stream, *166*, 175
vestibular senses, 189–90
vicarious learning, 240–41
Vicki (case study),598–599
Vietnam War, 157–58, *157*
violence:
  and alcohol, 155
  and depression, 643
  and genetic basis of psychological science,
    113–14
  and ingroup-outgroup bias, 488–89
  and learning, 233, *239*, 241–43, *242*
  and media, 241–43, *242*
  and psychological disorders, 599
  see also aggression
virtual environments, 634, *634*
virus hypothesis, 594
vision, 345
  as basic sensory processing system, 172–73
  and basic structure and functions of brain,
    88, *88*, *93*
  and development, 345, *345*
  as important source of knowledge, 172
  and learning, 217
  and perception, 165, *165*, *166*
  and psychological disorders, 605
  and sleep, 138, 140, *140*
  see also visual cortex
visual acuity, *344*, 345
visual cortex, 173, 345
  and basic sensory processes, 174, *175*
  and basic structure and functions of brain,
    88, *88*
  and development, 345
  and development of brain, 102
  and emotion, *387*
  and perception, *166*, 186
visual hallucinations, 591
visual information, and memory, 257
vocal cords, 311, *311*
vocal tract, human, *311*
von Restorff effect, 280
Vygotsky, Lev, 356

Wagner, Allan, 218
Wahlberg, Mark, 249, *250*
Wakefield, Andrew, 607–8
Walker, Elaine, 594
Wall, Patrick, 202
Wallace, Mike, *643*
Washington, Denzel, 502
waterfall effect, 186
"water lily" problem, 306
Watney, Mark, 249
Watson, John B., 15, *15*, 208, 211, 221, *222*, 226,
  570
Weber's law, 168
Webster, Mike, 124
Wechsler, David, 320
Wechsler Adult Intelligence Scale (WAIS), 320
Wegner, Daniel, 395
weight, *see* eating; obesity

Weiner, Bernard, 497
well-being:
  definition of, 430
  and happiness, 460, *460*
  and health, 428–67
  and spirituality, *462*, 463–64
Wells, Gary, 284
Wells, H. G., 226
Werker, Janet, 313
Wernicke's area, 312, *312*
Wertheimer, Max, 15
Western Collaborative Group, 455
Wharf, Benjamin, 313, *313*
"what is beautiful is good" stereotype, 506
Wheatley, Thalia, 143
white matter, 84
whole language approach, in learning to read,
  318
*Why Marriages Succeed or Fail... and How You
  Can Make Yours Last* (Gottman), 509
Why People Die by Suicide (Joiner), 584
Williams, Robin, 580, *580*
Wilson, A. E., *553*
Wiltshire, Stephen, *326*, 327
Winfrey, Oprah, 100, *100*, 607–8
withdrawal, 156, 223, 592
women:
  and ingroup bias, 472, *472*
  working, 20
Wonder, Stevie, 375, *375*
Woodley, Shailene, *507*
Woodruff, Guy, 360
word salad, 591
working backward, 306
working memory, 258
  and aging, 377
  and basic stages of memory, 258–59
  and brain structure and functions, 325–26
  definition of, 325
  and intelligence, 325–26
  long-term memory distinguished from,
    260–61, *260*
  and organization of information, 266
  and stress, 449
  see also short-term memory
working self-concept, 548–49, *548*
World Health Organization (WHO), 434, 441,
  454
Wundt, Wilhelm, 11, *11*

Xanax, 80, 623

Yerkes-Dodson law, 404, *404*
yoga, 145, 620
youth, *see* adolescence; children
youth, and media use, *241*
yo-yo dieting, 438
Yufe, Jack, 112

Zajonc, Robert, 473, *473*, 490
Zametkin, Alan, 609
Zen meditation, 145
zero correlations, 44
Zeta-Jones, Catherine, 561, *646*
Zika virus, and birth defects, 340, *340*
Zilstein study, 411
Zimbardo, Philip, 473
zygotes, 110, 338, *338*
Zyprexa, 648